D1518041

SPECIAL EDITION

USING

Microsoft®

Office
2007

Ed Bott

Woody Leonhard

800 East 96th Street

Indianapolis, Indiana 46240

CONTENTS AT A GLANCE

Introduction

I Common Tasks and Features

1 Getting Started with Office 2007 9
2 Using and Customizing the Office 2007 Interface .. 27
3 Managing Office Files and Formats 53
4 Creating, Editing, and Formatting Documents 75
5 Creating, Editing, and Using Pictures
    and Graphics 103
6 Sharing and Reviewing Office Files 135
7 Office Security and Privacy 159

II Using Outlook

8 Outlook Essentials 177
9 Reading, Writing, and Organizing Email 219
10 Keeping Your Contacts List Under Control 259
11 Working with Calendars and Tasks 277
12 Outlook Security and Privacy 307

III Using Word

13 Building a Better Word Document 329
14 Using Themes, Styles, and Templates 387
15 Advanced Document Formatting 415
16 Professional Document Tools and Advanced
    Document Sharing 455
17 Letters, Envelopes, and Data-Driven
    Documents 477

IV Using Excel

18 Building a Better Workbook 507
19 Advanced Worksheet Formatting 553
20 Using Formulas and Functions 593
21 Organizing Data with Tables and PivotTables 627
22 Creating and Editing Charts 665

V Using PowerPoint

23 Building a Perfect Presentation 703
24 Advanced Presentation Formatting 737
25 Adding Graphics, Multimedia, and
    Special Effects 759
26 Planning and Delivering a Presentation 779

VI Other Office Applications

27 Publisher Essentials 797
28 Access Essentials 835
29 Using OneNote 879
30 Using Office 2007 on a Corporate Network 907

VII Appendixes

A Advanced Setup Options 929
B Macros and Add-Ins 943
C Using Office on a Tablet PC 961
    Index 969

Special Edition Using Microsoft Office 2007

International Standard Book Number: 0-7897-3517-2

Library of Congress Cataloging-in-Publication data is on file

Printed in the United States of America

First Printing: December 2006

09 08 07 06   4 3 2 1

Trademarks

All terms mentioned in this book that are known to be trademarks or service marks have been appropriately capitalized. Que Publishing cannot attest to the accuracy of this information. Use of a term in this book should not be regarded as affecting the validity of any trademark or service mark.

Warning and Disclaimer

Every effort has been made to make this book as complete and as accurate as possible, but no warranty or fitness is implied. The information provided is on an "as is" basis. The authors and the publisher shall have neither liability nor responsibility to any person or entity with respect to any loss or damages arising from the information contained in this book.

Bulk Sales

Que Publishing offers excellent discounts on this book when ordered in quantity for bulk purchases or special sales. For more information, please contact

> **U.S. Corporate and Government Sales**
> **1-800-382-3419**
> **corpsales@pearsontechgroup.com**

For sales outside of the U.S., please contact

> **International Sales**
> **international@pearsoned.com**

This Book Is Safari Enabled

 The Safari® Enabled icon on the cover of your favorite technology book means the book is available through Safari Bookshelf. When you buy this book, you get free access to the online edition for 45 days.

Safari Bookshelf is an electronic reference library that lets you easily search thousands of technical books, find code samples, download chapters, and access technical information whenever and wherever you need it.

To gain 45-day Safari Enabled access to this book:

- Go to http://www.quepublishing.com/safarienabled
- Complete the brief registration form
- Enter the coupon code KFHH-A2QI-CZB7-ZJIZ-3AZN

If you have difficulty registering on Safari Bookshelf or accessing the online edition, please e-mail customer-service@safaribooksonline.com.

Associate Publisher
Greg Wiegand

Acquisitions Editor
Loretta Yates

Executive Editor
Rick Kughen

Development Editors
Kevin Howard
Mark Reddin
Rick Kughen

Managing Editor
Gina Kanouse

Project Editor
Andy Beaster

Copy Editor
Barbara Hacha

Indexer
Erika Millen

Proofreader
Sarah Kearns

Technical Editors
Helen Bradley
Steve Kovsky

Team Coordinator
Cindy Teeters

Interior Designer
Anne Jones

Cover Designer
Anne Jones

Compositor
Gloria Schurick

CONTENTS

Introduction 1

Who Should Buy This Book 2

How This Book Is Organized 3

Conventions Used in This Book 4

I   Common Tasks and Features

1   Getting Started with Office 2007 9

What's New in Office 2007 10
   A Quick Look at the New Office Interface 11
   File Formats and Other Compatibility Questions 11
   How Windows and Office Work Together 12

An Overview of Office 2007 Applications 13
   Outlook 2007 15
   Word 2007 15
   Excel 2007 16
   PowerPoint 2007 17
   Access 2007 18
   Publisher 2007 19
   OneNote 2007 19
   Other Office Programs 20

Installation, Activation, and Validation 21
   Activation and Validation 21
   Finding Service Packs and Other Updates 22

Online Help and Other Support Options 23

Diagnosing Problems 25

2   Using and Customizing the Office 2007 Interface ... 27

The New Office Interface 28
   Applications That Have the New UI 28
   Terminology for Working with the New UI 29

Customizing Your Interface 32
   Adding Frequently Used Commands to the Quick Access Toolbar ... 33
   Customizing Toolbars and Menus in Outlook and Publisher 34

Getting Quick Results with Keyboard Shortcuts 38

Setting Options for Office and Individual Applications ... 40
   Configuring Shared Office Features 40
   Setting Up Spell-Checking Options 41
   Configuring the Research Task Pane 44
   Configuring Individual Applications 45

Troubleshooting 48

Secrets of the Office Masters: Creating the Ultimate Office Working Environment ... 50

3 **Managing Office Files and Formats** 53

The New File Formats in Office 2007 54

Understanding and Choosing File Formats 54
Office 2007 File Formats at a Glance 55
Saving Files in Alternate Formats 56
Publishing Documents as PDF and XPS Files 57
Using Office Files with Older Office Versions 57
Converting and Importing Files Between Office Programs 59
Using Office Programs to Create and Edit Web Pages 59

Setting Up Office File Storage Locations 60
Manage Files Locally 60

Managing Files and Folders Remotely 62
Storing Files on the Web or an Intranet 62
Save Documents to a SharePoint Server 63

Creating New Files 63

Using and Customizing Common Dialog Boxes 65

Storing Document Details 67

Searching for Office Files 69
Windows Desktop Search and Instant Search 69

Working with Multiple Files 70

Setting Up Automatic Backup and Recovery Options 70

Troubleshooting 72

Secrets of the Office Masters: Folder Options That Make Your Life Easier 73

4 **Creating, Editing, and Formatting Documents** 75

Working With Documents in Office 2007 76

Entering Text 76
Inserting Symbols and Special Characters 76
Entering Accented and International Characters 78
Entering Text Through Speech Recognition 79
Entering Text in Another Language 79

Selecting Text 80

Finding and Replacing Text 82

Converting Scanned Documents to Text 84

Using AutoCorrect to Speed Up Text Entry 86
How AutoCorrect Works 86
Setting AutoCorrect Options 88
Customizing the AutoCorrect Lists 89
AutoCorrect Do's and Don'ts 91

Using the Office Clipboard 92
Managing the Office Clipboard Pane 92
Converting Clipboard Data into Alternate Formats 93
Dragging and Dropping Data 94

Using and Managing Fonts 94
    Common Formatting Options 95
    Changing Character Attributes 95
    Using Bullets and Numbers to Set Off Lists 97

Working with Hyperlinks 98

Undoing and Repeating Changes 99

Troubleshooting 100

Secrets of the Office Masters: Working with Speech Recognition in Windows Vista 100

5 Creating, Editing, and Using Pictures and Graphics **103**

Graphical Improvements in Office 2007 104

Using Office Drawing Tools 104
    Working with the Drawing Layer 105
    Working with a Drawing Canvas 106
    Working with Shapes 107
    Complex Shapes 109
    Changing Background Colors and Line Formats 112
    Adding Shadows, Rotation, and 3D Effects 113
    Adding Text to a Drawing 114
    Aligning and Grouping Graphic Elements 115
    Wrapping, Layout, and Stacking Options 117

Creating and Using SmartArt Graphics 119
    Choosing a SmartArt Layout 119
    Entering and Editing Text 120
    Adding Graphics and Pictures 121
    Changing a Layout 121
    Changing Colors and Styles 122
    Arranging and Formatting Text 123

Creating and Editing Charts 123

Viewing, Editing, and Managing Pictures 124
    Adding Pictures to Office Documents 125
    Resizing and Cropping Pictures 126
    Editing Image Files 127
    Working with Scanned Images 128

Using Clip Art 129

Turning Text into Graphics 131
    Using Text Boxes to Create Pull Quotes 132
    Using WordArt for Logos 132

Troubleshooting 133

Secrets of the Office Masters: Compressing Graphics in Your Presentations
    for Email, Internet Websites, Blogs, or Presentations 134

6   Sharing and Reviewing Office Files 135

   Sharing and Reviewing Features in Office 2007 136

   Keeping Shared Documents Secure 136
      Protecting Office Documents with Passwords 136
      Creating a Backup Copy Automatically 138
      How Office Locks Documents to Prevent Conflicts 139
      Opening Documents in Read-Only Mode 139
      Mark Document as Final 140
      Controlling File Access with Windows Permissions 141
      Protecting Private Data in Office Documents 141
      Securing Documents with Information Rights Management (IRM) 142
      Securing Documents with Digital Signatures 143
      Adding Signature Lines to a Document 143

   Routing, Reviewing, and Revising Documents 145
      Sending an Office File as Email 145
      Sending a File as an Email Attachment 146
      Adding Comments and Tracking Changes 147
      Adding Comments to Documents 147
      Restricting Edits to Comments Only 147
      Tracking Revisions 149
      Comparing, Reviewing, and Merging Changes 150

   Printing Office Documents 150

   Publishing Office Documents to a Website 150

   Combining Two or More Data Types in One Document 151
      Embedding Versus Linking 152

   Overview of File Sharing on an Office Network 153

   Troubleshooting 155

   Secrets of the Office Masters: Setting Up and Using Information Rights Management ...155

7   Office Security and Privacy 159

   What Is the Office Trust Center? 160

   Using the Office Trust Center 160
      Defining Trusted Publishers 160
      Defining Trusted Locations 161
      Controlling Add-Ins and ActiveX Controls 162
      Controlling Macros and VBA Projects 166
      Setting Message Bar and Privacy Options 167

   Installing and Managing Add-Ins 169

   Backup and Recovery Options 170

   Protecting Personal Information 170
      What's the Risk of Sending Out Personal Information? 171
      Inspecting Office Documents 171
      Scrubbing Personal Details from a Document 172

Troubleshooting 172

Secrets of the Office Masters: Backup and Recovery Basics 173

II Using Outlook 175

8 Outlook Essentials 177

What's New in Outlook 2007 178

Using and Customizing the Outlook Interface 179

Customizing the Navigation Pane 180

Customizing the To-Do Bar 183

Customizing the Reading Pane 183

Managing Outlook Data Files 184

How Outlook Stores Data 184

Managing Your Personal Folders File 185

Choosing a Data File Type 186

Cleaning Up and Archiving Personal Information 187

Repairing a Damaged Personal Folders File 191

Creating, Editing, and Managing Outlook Items 191

Moving, Copying, and Deleting Items 192

Entering Dates and Times Automatically 193

Assigning Items to Categories 194

Flagging Items for Follow-Up 196

Finding Outlook Items 199

Using Custom Views to Display Information 204

Using Views to Display, Sort, and Filter Items 204

Arranging Items in a View 205

Customizing an Existing View 206

Creating Custom Views to Sort, Filter, and Group Items 212

Managing Custom Views 213

Importing, Exporting, and Synchronizing Outlook Items 214

Importing Data from External Programs 214

Exporting Outlook Data 216

Troubleshooting 217

Secrets of the Office Masters: Synchronizing Outlook Items with a Handheld
PC or Smartphone 218

9 Reading, Writing, and Organizing Email 219

Setting Up Email Accounts 220

Configuring Internet Standard Email Accounts 221

Connecting to an Exchange Server 224

Using Hotmail, MSN, and Other HTTP Accounts 226

Managing Multiple Email Accounts 227

Setting Up Alternative Profiles 227

Configuring Your SMTP Server to Send Mail 228

Sending and Receiving Email 230
   Setting Up Send/Receive Groups 230
   Choosing Which Messages to Download 231
   Checking for New Messages 232
   Setting Notifications 233
   Speed-Reading New Messages with the Reading Pane 233

Using the Outlook Address Book 235
   Configuring Address Book Options 236
   Addressing an Email Message 238
   Using Personal Distribution Lists 239

Composing a New Email Message 240
   Choosing a Message Format 240
   Using a Specific Account to Send a Message 242
   Managing Email Signatures 242
   Advanced Message Formatting 244
   Setting Custom Message Options 244
   Setting Reply and Forward Options 246

Organizing Your Email 247
   Creating and Using Search Folders 248
   Using Email Rules to Sort and Process Mail 249
   Creating a New Rule 249
   Managing Email Rules and Alerts 254

Troubleshooting 255

Secrets of the Office Masters: Using Outlook with AOL Accounts 257

10 Keeping Your Contacts List Under Control **259**

Viewing and Organizing the Contacts Folder 260

Entering and Editing Contact Information 261
   Entering and Editing Names 263
   Working with Addresses 264
   Entering Job and Company Details 264
   Managing Phone, Fax, and Other Numbers 265
   Entering and Editing Email and Web Addresses 265
   Entering Extra Information About a Contact 266

Working Smarter with Contact Items 266
   Changing How a Contact Item Is Filed 266
   Entering Several New Contact Items at Once 267
   Sharing Contact Information 268
   Merging Duplicate Contact Items 269

Communicating with Contacts 270

Printing Phone Lists and Address Books 271

Troubleshooting 273

Secrets of the Office Masters: Creating a Memorable Business Card 274

11 Working with Calendars and Tasks 277

   Managing Your Personal Calendar 278
      Switching Between Day, Week, and Month Views 279
      Customizing the Calendar 280
      Taming Time Zones 282

   Creating a New Appointment or Event 284
      Entering Recurring Appointments 288
      Rescheduling an Appointment or Event 289

   Managing Meeting Requests 289
      Creating a New Meeting Request 290
      Responding to Meeting Requests 293
      Checking the Status of a Meeting You've Arranged 294
      Rescheduling or Canceling a Meeting 294

   Maintaining Your Personal Task List 295
      Entering Tasks 295
      Entering Recurring Tasks 296
      Sorting and Filtering the Task List 297

   Sharing Your Schedule with Other People 298
      Sharing a Calendar on an Exchange Server 299
      Publishing a Calendar Using Office Online 300
      Sending a Calendar via Email 301
      Viewing Shared or Published Calendars 302
      Using Group Schedules 303

   Troubleshooting 304

   Secrets of the Office Masters: Publishing a Calendar as a Web Page ... 305

12 Outlook Security and Privacy 307

   What You Need to Know About Email Security 308

   Blocking Malware 309
      Controlling Execution of Scripts 309
      Restricting Access to the Outlook Address Book 310
      Configuring Attachment Options 311

   Stopping Spam and Other Unwanted Email 313
      Fine-Tuning Outlook's Junk Mail Filter 314
      Using Email Rules to Block Junk Email 319
      Using Third-Party Spam-Blocking Tools 319

   Protecting Your Privacy 319

   Disabling HTML-Based Email 322

   Troubleshooting 324

   Secrets of the Office Masters: Tracking Down the Source of Spam 324

III Using Word

13 Building a Better Word Document **329**

What's New in Word 2007? 330

Choosing the Right Document View 332
    Using Built-in Views 332
    Navigating with Thumbnails and the Document Map 338
    Zoom Options 339
    Splitting a Document Window 340
    Viewing Documents Side by Side 341

Navigating Through a Word Document 342
    Using the Keyboard to Move Through a Document 342
    Using the Mouse to Move Through a Document 343
    Navigating with the Document Map 344
    Navigating Through Documents with the Select Browse Object Menu 344

Understanding Your Formatting Options 346
    Direct Formatting Versus Styles and Themes 347
    Character Formats 348
    Paragraph Formats 351
    Revealing Formatting Within a Document 351
    Copying Formats 352
    Removing Text Formatting 353
    Locking a Document's Formatting 353
    Page/Section Setup Options 354

Changing Text Formatting 356
    Using Drop Caps for Emphasis 358

Changing Paragraph Formatting 358
    Adjusting Paragraph Alignment 359
    Indenting Paragraphs for Emphasis 360
    Adjusting Line and Paragraph Spacing 361
    Controlling Page Breaks 362
    Positioning Text with Tabs 363

Entering Text Automatically 365
    AutoText and AutoCorrect Usage in Word 2007 365
    Building a Document with Quick Parts 366

Using Bullets, Numbering, and Multilevel Lists 367

Finding and Replacing Text and Formatting 369

Checking Spelling, Contextual Spelling, and Grammar 374

Printing Word Documents 376
    Previewing Printed Pages 376
    Choosing What to Print 377
    Advanced Printing Techniques 378

Customizing the Word Interface 379

Troubleshooting 384

Secrets of the Office Masters: Using Word as a Blog Editor 385

14 Using Themes, Styles, and Templates **387**

How Themes, Styles, and Templates Work Together 388

Using Themes to Format an Entire Document 389

Formatting a Document with Styles 391
Paragraph Versus Character Styles 391
List and Table Styles 394
Applying Styles Manually 395
Saving Formats as Named Styles 396
Managing Styles 399

Creating, Using, and Managing Templates 404
Customizing the Normal Document Template 405
Using Word's Built-in Templates 406
Building a Template from Scratch 407
Copying Styles and Settings Between Templates 408

Troubleshooting 409

Secrets of the Office Masters: Working with the Building Block Organizer 410

15 Advanced Document Formatting **415**

Using Tables to Organize Information 416
Adding a Table to a Document 417
Entering and Editing Data 419
Formatting, Aligning, and Rotating Text 420
Changing a Table's Layout 426
Converting Text and Data to Tables 428
Converting Data to a Table 429
Sorting Data Within Tables 431
Positioning Tables on the Page 432
Formatting a Table 433

Adding and Organizing Figures and Graphics 436
Inserting Pictures 436
Inserting Clip Art 438
Inserting Shapes 438
Inserting SmartArt 439
Inserting a Chart 440
One More Thing…Word Art 441

Using Headers and Footers 441
What You Can and Can't Do with Headers and Footers 442
Setting Header and Footer Options 443
Numbering Pages 444
Adding Dates and Document Details 444

Adding Lines, Borders, Shading, and Backgrounds 444
    Quick Ways to Create Lines 445
    Borders and Boxes 446
    Shading Characters, Paragraphs, and Pages 447

Formatting Documents by Section 448
    Inserting and Deleting Section Breaks 449
    Copying Formatting Between Sections 450

Formatting a Document with Columns 451

Troubleshooting 452

Secrets of the Office Masters: Saving Files as PDF or XPS 453

16 Professional Document Tools and Advanced Document Sharing 455

Keeping Long Documents Under Control 456
    One File or Many? 456
    Using Bookmarks 457
    Inserting Cross-References 458
    Creating Indexes 460
    Creating a Table of Contents 462

Tools for Academic and Professional Documents 464
    Footnotes and Endnotes 464
    Citations and Bibliographies 464
    Specialized Tools for Legal Documents 465
    Summarizing a Document Automatically 466

Document Properties 467

Sharing Documents 468
    Tracking Revisions 469
    Adding Comments to Documents 473
    Restricting Changes to a Shared Document 473

Troubleshooting 474

Secrets of the Office Masters: Preparing Your Documents for Distribution 474

17 Letters, Envelopes, and Data-Driven Documents 477

Creating and Editing Letters 478
    Using Letter Templates 478
    Customizing Letter Templates 479

Creating Envelopes and Labels 480
    Creating and Printing Envelopes 480
    Creating and Printing Labels 481

Using Mail Merge to Personalize Letters and Envelopes 483
    Using the Mail Merge Wizard 484
    Creating the Form Letter 486
    Connecting to a Data Source 486
    Placing Data Fields Within a Document 487
    Previewing Mail-Merge Results 488

Advanced Mail-Merge Techniques 490
Merge Labels 493

Using Fields to Add Intelligence to a Document 496
Showing and Hiding Field Codes 497
Field Code Syntax 498
Inserting a Field into a Document 498
Formatting Field Results 500
General * Format Switches 501

Troubleshooting 502

Secrets of the Office Masters: Creating a Fill-in-the-Blanks Form with Fields 503

IV Using Excel

18 Building a Better Workbook 507

What's New in Excel 2007 508

Working with Worksheets and Workbooks 508
Working with Multiple Worksheets 509
Moving, Copying, Inserting, and Deleting Worksheets 510
Renaming and Labeling a Worksheet 512
Using Ranges to Enter and Select Data 512
Navigating in a Workbook 514
Using Cell References and Range Names to Navigate in a Workbook 515
Selecting Ranges of Data with the Go To Dialog Box 516

Controlling Data Entry with AutoComplete Options 518

Automatically Filling In a Series of Data 519
Using AutoFill 521
Creating Custom AutoFill Lists to Fit Your Projects 522

Finding, Replacing, and Transforming Data 523
Finding and Replacing the Contents of a Cell or Range 524
Dragging and Dropping to Convert Data 524
Transforming Data with Paste Options 525

Customizing the Worksheet Window 528
Hiding Rows and Columns 528
Using the Zoom Controls 529
Locking Row and Column Labels for Onscreen Viewing 529
Splitting the Worksheet Window 530

Using Links to Automatically Update or Consolidate Worksheet Data 531

Restricting and Validating Data Entry for a Cell or Range 532
Defining Data-Validation Rules 532
Displaying Helpful Input Messages 534
Alerting the User to Errors 535
Deleting, Moving, or Copying Data-Validation Rules 536
Circling Data Errors 536

Printing Worksheets 537
    Defining a Print Area 538
    Inserting Page Breaks 539
    Extra Items You Can Print 540
    Labeling Printed Pages with Headers and Footers 541
    Using Repeating Titles for Multiple Page Printouts 542
    Forcing a Worksheet to Fit on a Specified Number of Pages 542

Publishing a Worksheet to the Web 543

Customizing Excel 545
    Changing Default Formatting for New Workbooks and Worksheets 548
    Excel Startup Switches 549

Troubleshooting 550

Secrets of the Office Masters: Installing and Managing Excel Add-Ins 551

19 Advanced Worksheet Formatting **553**

Entering Data in an Excel Worksheet 554
    Using the General Number Format 554
    Controlling Automatic Number Formats 555
    Avoiding Rounding Errors 556
    The Limits of Precision 558
    Working with Numbers in Scientific Notation 559
    Entering Numbers as Text 559

Changing Formatting for a Cell or Range 560
    Setting Number Formats 560
    Setting Date and Time Formats 565
    Excel and Year 2000 Issues 567
    Creating Custom Cell Formats 568

Designing and Formatting a Worksheet for Maximum Readability 573
    Changing Fonts and Character Attributes 573
    Using Cell Styles 574
    Working with Formats, Styles, and Alignment 576
    Aligning, Wrapping, and Rotating Text and Numbers 576
    Using Borders, Boxes, and Colors 579
    Merging Cells 581
    Changing Row Height and Column Width 581

Using Conditional Formatting to Identify Key Values 583
    Using Top/Bottom Rules 585
    Using Colored Data Bars 585
    Using Color Scales 586
    Using Icon Sets 586

Copying Formats with the Format Painter 587

Troubleshooting 588

Secrets of the Office Masters: Storing Multiple Scenarios in a Single Workbook ..588

20 Using Formulas and Functions 593

Entering and Editing Formulas 594

Using Cell References 594

Absolute Versus Relative Cell References 595

Using 3D References to Cells on Other Worksheets 596

Using the Range Finder to Locate Parts of a Formula 597

Controlling the Order and Timing of Calculations 597

Preventing Formulas from Displaying in the Formula Bar 599

Using Array Formulas 600

Using Range Names and Labels in Formulas 601

Using Named Ranges in Formulas 601

Managing Range Names 603

Manipulating Data with Worksheet Functions 604

Entering Error-Free Formulas 605

Using Functions Within Functions 607

Finding the Right Function 608

AutoSum Functions 609

Financial Calculations 610

Logical Tests 610

Text Manipulation Functions 611

Date and Time Functions 613

Lookup and Reference Functions 614

Mathematical Calculations 616

Performing Statistical Analyses 617

Database Functions 618

Testing and Debugging Formulas 618

How Formula AutoCorrect Works 618

Resolving Common Error Messages 619

Checking for Errors in a Worksheet 621

Using the Watch Window to Monitor Calculations 623

Troubleshooting 624

Secrets of the Office Masters: Using Goal Seek to Find Answers 625

21 Organizing Data with Tables and PivotTables 627

Defining a Range as a Table 628

Sorting and Filtering Data in a Table 631

Performing Simple Sorts 631

Sorting by Multiple Columns 632

Sorting by Dates or Custom Series 633

Using Filters to Find Sets of Data 634

Using Comparison Criteria to Create Custom Filters 638

Filtering with Advanced Criteria 639

Importing and Exporting Data 643

Connecting a Worksheet to External Databases 645
  Using the Query Wizard 646
  Integrating External Data into a Worksheet 648

Creating and Using Web Queries 649

Analyzing Information with PivotTables 651

When Should You Use a PivotTable? 655

Creating a PivotTable 655

Editing and Updating a PivotTable 657
  Changing a PivotTable's Appearance 659
  Adding and Removing Subtotals 660
  Removing Blank Cells and Error Messages 661
  Changing or Refreshing PivotTable Data 661

Troubleshooting 661

Secrets of the Office Masters: Combining Data from Several Web Sources
  in a Custom Page 662

22 Creating and Editing Charts **665**

A Revamped Charting Engine 666

Building an Excel Chart 666
  Selecting Data to Plot 667
  Selecting a Chart Type 669
  Choosing a Standard Chart Type 669
  Using Combination Charts 677
  Creating and Saving Custom Chart Types 678
  Creating a Default Chart 679
  Selecting a Layout and Style 680
  Moving Charts 681

Labeling a Chart's Elements 682
  Adding or Editing a Title 683
  Adding Labels to Axes 685
  Adding or Editing a Legend 685
  Displaying Data Labels 686
  Adding a Data Table 687

Customizing Axes 688
  Displaying Vertical Axis in Thousands, and So On 688
  Using a Time Series Along a Horizontal Axis 689
  Showing Numbers of Different Scale Using a Logarithmic Axis 690
  Plotting One Series on a Secondary Axis 691
  Not Starting the Axis at Zero 692
  Showing or Hiding Gridlines 694
  Adding Trendlines, Droplines, and Error Bars 694

Customizing a Chart's Appearance 695
  Changing Fill and Outline Colors 695
  Adding Visual Effects 695

Working with PivotTable Charts 696

Creating Other Chart Types 697

Troubleshooting 698

Secrets of the Excel Masters: Leave the Top-Left Cell Blank 699

V   Using PowerPoint

23 Building a Perfect Presentation **703**

What's New in PowerPoint 2007 704

Anatomy of a PowerPoint Presentation 704

Creating a Presentation 706

    Creating a Blank Presentation 707

    Starting PowerPoint with a Template or Theme 708

    Copying the Design of an Existing Presentation 709

    Building a Presentation from a Word Outline 710

Editing the Presentation Outline 710

    Editing Slides in Outline View 710

    Reordering Slides 711

Changing a Slide Layout 712

Editing Slides 713

    Adding and Editing Text 713

    Working with Bulleted and Numbered Lists 715

    Working with Tables 717

    Adding Pictures, SmartArt, and Clip Art 719

    Inserting an Excel Chart or Range 720

Viewing a Presentation 722

    Using Slide Sorter View to Rearrange a Presentation 723

    Previewing Your Presentation in Slide Show View 724

    Adding Notes 724

    Viewing Presentations in a Web Browser 725

Managing Slide Shows 726

Navigating Through a Presentation 729

    Mouse and Keyboard Shortcuts 729

    Using Hyperlinks 730

    Advanced Navigation with Action Settings 730

    Navigation Shorthand with Action Buttons 731

Troubleshooting 732

Secrets of the Office Masters: PowerPoint File Types 733

24 Advanced Presentation Formatting **737**

Organizing Formats with Master Slides 738

    Using the Slide Master 738

    Using the Layout Masters 741

Changing the Background of Every Slide 741
Working with Headers and Footers 742
Removing Slide Master Elements from a Single Slide 744
Creating Speaker Notes and Audience Handouts 745

Applying and Modifying Themes 746
Choosing the Best Theme for Your Presentation 747
Modifying Theme Colors 748
Choosing New Theme Colors 749
Changing Colors on Selected Slides 750
Using Theme Fonts 750
Using Theme Effects 752
Choosing the Best Background 752
Saving a Custom Theme 755

Changing Paragraph and Text Formatting 756
Using Paragraph Formatting 756
Using Fonts 756
Replacing Fonts Throughout a Presentation 757

Troubleshooting 757

Secrets of the Office Masters: Creating Top-Notch Notes and Handouts 758

25 Adding Graphics, Multimedia, and Special Effects 759

Using Transitions to Control Pacing 760
Applying a Transition to One Slide 760
Applying a Transition to a Group of Slides 761
Controlling Slide Transition Speed 762

Animating Text and Objects on a Slide 762
Animating Bullet Points 763
Creating a Custom Animation 764
Animating the Drawing Layer 768
Hiding and Uncovering Slide Contents 769
Animating Chart Components 770

Adding Music, Sounds, and Video to Your Presentation 771
Adding Music, Sounds, and Video Clips 771
Controlling a Video or Sound Clip 773

Combining Transition Effects 775

Troubleshooting 776

Secrets of the Office Masters: Animating Charts to Emphasize Data 776

26 Planning and Delivering a Presentation 779

Planning Your Presentation 780
The Importance of Preparation 780
Organizing Your Remarks with Speaker Notes 780
Using PowerPoint's Timer to Rehearse a Presentation 781

Running a Slideshow 783

Creating Presentations for the Web 783

Setting Up a Slideshow 785
    Tuning Your Presentation for Your Hardware 785
    Using Two Monitors 786

Using Hidden Slides to Anticipate Questions 787

Packaging a Presentation for Use on Other Computers 788
    Saving a Presentation on a CD 788
    Using the PowerPoint Viewer 790

Printing Your Presentation 790
    Choosing Which Elements to Print 790
    Preparing a Color Presentation for a Black-and-White Printer 791
    Turning a Presentation into 35mm Slides 791

Troubleshooting 792

Secrets of the Office Masters: Anticipating Questions with Hidden Slides 792

27 Publisher Essentials 797

What's New in Publisher 2007 798

What Can You Do with Publisher? 798

Creating and Customizing a New Publication 799
    Starting with a Publisher Template 799
    Creating a Publication from Scratch 803
    Creating a Custom Template 805
    Creating Simple Web Pages and Sites 806
    Using Publisher and Word Together 809

Managing Your Publication's Layout 810
    Zooming and Moving Around Your Publication 810
    Grouping, Selecting, and Moving Objects 811
    Using Other View Options 812
    Setting Up and Using Guides 812

Working with Text 815
    Laying Out Text 815
    Widows and Orphans 818
    Kerning and Tracking 818
    Drop Caps 818

Inserting Images 819

Using Tables as a Page Layout Tool 820
    Creating a Table 820
    Importing a Table 822

Customizing Publisher Options 823
    Customizing Business Information 823
    Creating Custom Color Schemes 824

Using the Design Gallery 825

Using the Content Library 826

Using Master Pages 827
    Adding Elements to a Master Page 828

Printing a Publication 830
    Using the Design Checker to Polish Your Publication 830
    Printing Your Publication 831

Troubleshooting 833

Secrets of the Office Masters: Good Design Principles 833

28 Access Essentials **835**

Planning an Access Database 836
    Tables 837
    Queries 837
    Forms 838
    Reports 838
    Macros and Modules 838

Working with Database Objects 839
    Creating New Objects 839
    Managing Database Objects 840
    Modifying Object Properties 841
    Using Expressions in Database Objects 841

Exporting and Importing Data 843

Creating and Customizing Tables 844
    Choosing a Field's Data Type 846
    Setting a Primary Key 847
    Speeding Up Sorts and Queries with Indexes 848

Defining Relationships Among Tables 848
    Defining a One-to-Many Relationship 850
    Working with One-to-Many Relationships 851

Building Forms and Reports 852
    Working with Controls 853
    Making Forms Easier to Use 857
    Making Reports Easier to Understand 859
    Grouping and Sorting Records in a Report 860

Using Queries to Extract Data from a Database 861
    Choosing the Right Query Type 862
    Inserting, Deleting, and Rearranging Fields 869
    Defining a Calculated Column 870
    Defining Criteria 870
    Defining Query Properties 871

Creating and Applying Filters 872

Troubleshooting 873

Secrets of the Office Masters: Restricting Data Entry 874
Defining Validation Rules.....................................874
Using an Input Mask to Define Data Formats 876
Setting a Default Value 877
Requiring a Value 877

29 Using OneNote 879

What's New in OneNote 2007 880

Using Notebooks 881
Creating a New Notebook 882
Organizing Information with Sections 883
Color Coding Notebooks and Sections 886
Sharing a Notebook.....................................886

Working with Pages 887
Adding a New Page 887
Creating and Using Page Templates 888
Managing Pages 890
Entering Text 893
Inserting Graphics.....................................894
Working with Data on a Page 895
Creating Links to Notebooks, Sections, Pages, and Notes 897

Finding Information in OneNote 898

Adding Audio and Video to a Notebook 899

Keeping Track of Tasks and To-Do Lists 901
Using Note Tags to Set Up a OneNote To-Do List 901
Linking OneNote to Outlook Tasks.....................................903

Troubleshooting 904

Secrets of the Office Masters: Sending Information to OneNote 904

30 Using Office 2007 on a Corporate Network 907

Office Collaboration and SharePoint 908

Collaborating on Data with SharePoint Lists.....................................908
Exporting an Excel Table to a SharePoint List 909
Importing Excel Data from a SharePoint List 910
More Excel-Related SharePoint List Commands 911
Exporting Access Data to a SharePoint List 911
Importing Access Data from a SharePoint List 912
Creating a New Access Database Linked to a SharePoint Site 913
Moving a Database to SharePoint 914

Sharing Outlook Data with SharePoint 914
Publishing an Outlook Calendar to a SharePoint Site 914
Synchronizing a SharePoint Calendar with Outlook 915
Synchronizing SharePoint Tasks with Outlook 915

Document Collaboration with SharePoint 916
    Publishing a Document to a SharePoint Library 916
    Opening a Document from a SharePoint Library 917

Creating a Document Workspace 917

Publishing an InfoPath Form to a SharePoint Site 919

Creating a Meeting Workspace 920

Using Outlook with Microsoft Exchange 921
    Sending a Sharing Invitation 921
    Using Permissions to Share a Folder 922
    Accessing Another User's Shared Folder 923

Troubleshooting 924

Secrets of the Office Masters: Assigning a Delegate to Your Outlook Folders 925

VII Appendixes

A   **Advanced Setup Options** 929

Before You Begin... 930

Using the Office Installer 930

Customizing Your Office Installation 933

Installing Office 2007 Alongside an Older Office Version 935

Updating or Repairing an Office Installation 937
    Adding and Removing Office Features 937
    Repairing an Office Installation 938
    Uninstalling Office 2007 938

Saving a Set of Custom Installation Options 939

Troubleshooting 940

B   **Macros and Add-ins** 943

What's New in Office 2007 944

How Macros Work 945
    Using Object Models 945
    How Office Applications Store Macros 946

Recording Simple Macros 947
    How the Macro Recorder Captures Actions 948
    Recording a Macro 949
    Testing the Macro 950

Troubleshooting Recorded Macros 951
    Stepping Through and Editing Recorded Macros 951
    Common Recorded Macro Mistakes 952
    Testing and Bullet-Proofing Macros 953

Running Macros 954

Using Auto Macros 955
    Using Auto Macros in Word 955
    Using Auto Macros in Excel 956
    Using Auto Macros in PowerPoint 958
Digitally Signing Macros You Create 958

C Using Office on a Tablet PC **961**

Office 2007 and the Tablet PC 962

All About Ink 962

Editing Text on a Tablet PC 966

Viewing and Printing Annotations and Comments 967

Troubleshooting 967

Index **969**

ABOUT THE AUTHORS

Ed Bott is a best-selling author of more than 25 computer books and an award-winning computer journalist with two decades of experience in the personal computer industry. For nearly 10 years, he was responsible for *PC Computing* magazine's extensive coverage of every conceivable flavor of Microsoft Windows and Microsoft Office. He is a three-time winner of the Computer Press Award, and he and Woody Leonhard won the prestigious Jesse H. Neal Award, sometimes referred to as "the Pulitzer Prize of the business press," in back-to-back years for their work on *PC Computing*'s "Windows SuperGuide." He lives in an extremely civilized corner of the American Southwest with his wife, Judy, and a growing menagerie of affectionate pets who are sometimes smarter than he is. You can read more of Ed's writing at http://www.edbott.com/weblog and at http://blogs.zdnet.com/bott.

Curmudgeon, critic, and perennial "Office Victim," **Woody Leonhard** runs a fiercely independent Web site with up-to-the-nanosecond news, observations, tips, and help for both Office and Windows. AskWoody.com has become the premier source of unbiased information for people who need to really use Windows and Office, and for people concerned about juggling the never-ending stream of Microsoft patches. In the past 15 years, Woody has written more than three dozen books, drawing an unprecedented six Computer Press Association awards and two American Business Press awards. Woody was one of the first Microsoft Consulting Partners and is a charter member of the Microsoft Solutions Provider organization.

Woody moved to Phuket, Thailand, in 2000. He lives in Patong with his wife, Duangkhae Tongthueng (better known as "Add"), his father George, his son Justin, and his all-American beagle, Chronos.

DEDICATION

To Judy, who has kept me healthy and sane throughout the many sleepless nights and frantic days that a book like this demands.

—Ed

To Add, for filling my life with happiness. And to Justin, for keeping me on my toes.

—Woody

ACKNOWLEDGMENTS

We'd like to thank the good folks at Microsoft, who have built a pretty amazing piece of software called Office and have continued to improve it through the years. But we'd also like to ask them what on earth they were thinking when they decided to release Office 2007 and Windows Vista at the same time. That decision made our lives miserable as we juggled multiple deadlines for multiple books. Fortunately, we were able to call on some capable helpers for this project. Our sincere thanks to Peter Bruzzese, who pitched in on the sections covering the Office interface and Word; Greg Perry and Bill Jelen, who updated the Excel section; and wordsmith extraordinaire Paul McFedries, who assisted with the chapters on PowerPoint, Publisher, Access, and OneNote.

Thanks also to Loretta Yates and Andy Beaster, who kept the trains running on time, and to development editors Kevin Howard, Mark Reddin, and Rick Kughen, and technical editor Todd Meister, for their invaluable input on the manuscript itself. And we owe a big, big shout-out to the community of fellow beta testers and Microsoft techies who helped us decode, decipher, unravel, and ultimately explain the mysteries of Office 2007. Last but definitely not least: Our heartfelt thanks to Rick Kughen, whose indispensable advice, support, and editorial experience have contributed immeasurably to every edition of this book.

WE WANT TO HEAR FROM YOU!

As the reader of this book, *you* are our most important critic and commentator. We value your opinion and want to know what we're doing right, what we could do better, what areas you'd like to see us publish in, and any other words of wisdom you're willing to pass our way.

As an associate publisher, I welcome your comments. You can email or write me directly to let me know what you did or didn't like about this book—as well as what we can do to make our books better.

Please note that I cannot help you with technical problems related to the topic of this book. We do have a User Services group, however, where I will forward specific technical questions related to the book.

When you write, please be sure to include this book's title and author as well as your name, email address, and phone number. I will carefully review your comments and share them with the author and editors who worked on the book.

Email: feedback@quepublishing.com

Mail: Greg Wiegand
          Associate Publisher
          Que Publishing
          800 East 96th Street
          Indianapolis, IN 46240 USA

For more information about this book or another Que Publishing title, visit our website at **www.quepublishing.com**. Type the ISBN (excluding hyphens) or the title of a book into the Search field to find the page you're looking for.

INTRODUCTION

In this Introduction

Who Should Buy This Book   2

How This Book Is Organized   3

Conventions Used in This Book   4

Over the past dozen years, Microsoft Office has gone through a half-dozen upgrades. And every time, pundits and reviewers trot out the same complaint: there's nothing new.

No one's saying that about Office 2007.

It's taken Microsoft nearly four years to deliver this upgrade, which is roughly twice as long as the average gap between each of the five previous versions. What were they doing in all that time? Oh, just replacing the core interface that has defined desktop software since the earliest days of Windows. Adding a new graphics engine. Tightening security. You know, little stuff.

In its early years, Office was little more than a bundle of programs built by teams that sometimes worked at cross purposes with one another, and the whole package was held together with the digital equivalent of baling wire and chewing gum. In this massive update, however, Microsoft has delivered something genuinely new and surprisingly well integrated.

The new Office interface, with its Ribbon, tabs, and groups of commands, is a shock at first. The more you know about the old interface, the more you'll have to unlearn to become productive again. And the old interface with its menus and toolbars isn't gone completely. It still has odd inconsistencies, as well as bugs, features that don't work as advertised, and some limitations guaranteed to drive expert users crazy. But for the fourth edition of this book, we were pleasantly surprised to see how many of the new features actually work as advertised.

As befits the name, Office 2007 has a decidedly corporate bias. In fact, some of the collaborative features that are at its core are available only if you enlist an army of IT professionals to run a room full of servers. To help show you how to make Office programs work with SharePoint and other network-based services, we had to build our own corporate network. (In the process, we developed a deep empathy for the challenges that network administrators have to deal with every day.) But we didn't lose sight of the fact that most of our readers still think of Office as *personal* productivity software.

Some of what you see in *Special Edition Using Microsoft Office 2007* will be familiar to you if you've worked with an earlier edition of this book. We didn't take the easy way out and simply reprint some of those old chapters on the theory that the programs didn't change much. Instead, we went through every chapter, sentence by sentence, testing, verifying, updating, and adding a wealth of new information to ensure that this book is accurate and absolutely up-to-date.

WHO SHOULD BUY THIS BOOK

If you need an Office reference book you can rely on—one that won't bore you with the obvious, pull punches when Office comes up short, or turn mealy-mouthed when you hit the really hard parts—you have the right book in your hands.

As with other titles in Que's best-selling *Special Edition Using* series, this book focuses on the unique needs of business professionals and business users. We assume you're experienced with Windows, the Web, and, for the most part, previous versions of Microsoft Office. We know that Office is an absolutely essential part of your everyday working life. We're also certain you've experienced your fair share of Office bugs and annoyances firsthand. Because we're confident you've already figured out the basics, we've spent our time figuring out how these programs *really* work. Trust us—Office still has bugs and poorly designed features, and Microsoft doesn't always make it easy to see how you can combine features or customize applications to increase productivity.

What you'll find documented here is the raw Office, in all its glory, seen through the eyes of experts who have been pushing Office to the limit for years and years. We don't gloss over the rough spots. We show you what works and what doesn't—giving real-world examples and advice for the former and, whenever possible, workarounds for the latter.

We figure you're smart enough to experiment with basic features and to read the online help when you want to know how an Office program is *supposed* to work. That's why you won't find beginner-level instructions in this book. Instead, you'll find what isn't in the official documentation—key details, insight, and real-world advice you can't find anywhere else. And it's all arranged so that you can get in, find the answer you need, apply it to your work at hand, and get out. This book may weigh a ton, but if you need the straight scoop on anything related to Office, this is where you should look first.

We're proud to present *Special Edition Using Microsoft Office 2007*.

How This Book Is Organized

Special Edition Using Microsoft Office 2007 is organized into seven parts. Naturally, each of the major applications in the Office suite gets its own section. Before diving into specific features of Outlook, Word, Excel, and the rest, however, we recommend that you read through the sections that cover the techniques common to all applications.

Part I, "Common Tasks and Features," covers the essentials of Office, most notably the new, radically revamped Office interface. We show you how to customize the one and only user-configurable element of the new interface, the Quick Access Toolbar. This section also covers Office 2007's exceptional new graphics tools, especially the slick SmartArt engine.

Office 2007 has a variety of new tools intended to enhance your privacy and your online security. Turn to Chapter 7, "Office Security and Privacy," for an overview of these new features and detailed instructions on how you can make sure your personal information stays private.

In Part II, "Using Outlook," we'll help you tame the flood of email, banish spam forever with Outlook's surprisingly effective junk-mail filter, keep your address book up-to-date, and set up reminders so that you never miss another appointment. We'll also explain how you can use its hybrid interface (old-style menus and toolbars in the main window, ribbons and tabs in message editing windows, and a new To-Do pane) to tie together contacts, calendars, tasks, and email for maximum productivity.

Part III, "Using Word," covers the oldest and most polished productivity application in Office. We'll walk you through every customization option (including a few you probably never even knew you needed). We'll show you how to supercharge your text-editing and formatting skills, how to manage long documents, and how to automate everyday documents so that they practically write themselves.

Part IV, "Using Excel," shows you tricks you never realized you could perform with this incredibly versatile tool. Check out the examples in our formatting chapters to see how you can turn drab rows and columns into eye-catching data graphics. We'll explain how to master any of Excel's 300+ functions, as well as which ones are worth memorizing. We'll unravel the secrets of making drop-dead gorgeous charts, and we'll show you how to use the effective new list-editing tools that turn Excel 2007 into one of the best flat-file database programs around.

Of all the Office applications, PowerPoint is probably the least appreciated. In Part V, "Using PowerPoint," we explain how this program really works, and we'll help you create compelling presentations that you can deliver in front of a large audience or a small one—or completely unattended over the Web.

In Part VI, "Other Office Applications," we focus on three programs found in selected Office versions. Access is Microsoft's industrial-strength database-management program. We explain how to build tables, forms, and reports, as well as simple (and not-so-simple) queries to find and filter data. We'll also clue you in on techniques you can use to automate everyday business tasks without having to become a programmer.

This section also covers Publisher, which takes up where Word leaves off to perform advanced page-layout tasks. And we look at OneNote, an offbeat but incredibly useful freeform note-taking application. And finally, we offer a broad overview of what you'll get with Office 2007 when you combine it with a growing family of server-based components.

If you need to install Office on one PC or several hundred, we'll run through all your options in Appendix A, "Advanced Setup Options," one of three appendixes at the back of the book. In Appendix B, "Macros and Add-Ins," we provide a whirlwind tour of how the tools to create, edit, and run macros have changed in Office 2007. And in Appendix C, "Using Office on a Tablet PC," we explain what's new when you install Office 2007 on a Tablet PC.

CONVENTIONS USED IN THIS BOOK

Special conventions are used to help you get the most from this book and from Office 2007.

TEXT CONVENTIONS

Various typefaces in this book identify terms and other special objects. These special typefaces include the following:

Type	Meaning
Italic	New terms or phrases when initially defined. An italic term followed by a page number indicates the page where that term is first defined.
Monospace	Information that you type or onscreen messages.
UPPERCASE	Typically used to indicate Excel objects, such as functions and cell references.
Initial Caps	Menus, dialog box names, dialog box elements, and commands are capitalized.

Key combinations are represented with a plus sign. For example, if the text calls for you to enter Ctrl+S, you would press the Ctrl key and the S key at the same time.

SECRETS OF THE OFFICE MASTERS

While using Office, you'll find many features that work well together or others that simply don't work well at all without some poking and prodding. We've used this chapter-ending element to point out some key areas in which you can combine features or find startlingly productive new uses for everyday features.

SPECIAL ELEMENTS

Throughout this book, you'll find Tips, Notes, Cautions, Sidebars, Cross-References, and Troubleshooting Tips. These elements provide a variety of information, ranging from warnings you shouldn't miss to ancillary information that will enrich your Office experience, but isn't required reading.

ED AND WOODY'S "SIGNATURE" TIPS

TIP FROM

Ed & Woody

> Tips are designed to point out features, annoyances, and tricks of the trade that you might otherwise miss. These aren't wimpy, run-of-the-mill tips that you learned the first week you used Office—ones that you don't need us to tell you. Watch for our signatures on the tips to indicate some industrial-strength—and in many cases, never-before-documented—information.

NOTES

NOTE

> Notes point out items that you should be aware of, although you can skip these if you're in a hurry. Generally, we've added notes as a way to give you some extra information on a topic without weighing you down.

CAUTIONS

CAUTION

> Pay attention to Cautions! These could save you precious hours in lost work. Don't say we didn't warn you.

TROUBLESHOOTING NOTES

We designed these elements to call attention to common pitfalls that you're likely to encounter. When you see a Troubleshooting note, you can flip to the "Troubleshooting" section at the end of the chapter to learn how to solve or avoid a problem.

CROSS-REFERENCES

Cross-references are designed to point you to other locations in this book (or other books in the Que family) that will provide supplemental or supporting information. Cross-references appear as follows:

→ For a full discussion of the wonders of PivotTables, **see** "Organizing Data with Tables and PivotTables," **p. 627**.

SIDEBARS

Want to Know More?
Sidebars are designed to provide information that is ancillary to the topic being discussed. Read these if you want to learn more about an application or task.

COMMON TASKS AND FEATURES

1 Getting Started with Office 2007   9

2 Using and Customizing the Office 2007 Interface   27

3 Managing Office Files and Formats   53

4 Creating, Editing, and Formatting Documents   75

5 Creating, Editing, and Using Pictures and Graphics   103

6 Sharing and Reviewing Office Files   135

7 Office Security and Privacy   159

CHAPTER 1

GETTING STARTED WITH OFFICE 2007

In this chapter

What's New in Office 2007   10

An Overview of Office 2007 Applications   13

Installation, Activation, and Validation   21

Online Help and Other Support Options   23

Diagnosing Problems   25

WHAT'S NEW IN OFFICE 2007

Microsoft Office has been in existence for more than a decade. Some of the individual programs that are part of the Office family date back to the 1980s. So it's tempting to think of Office as a doddering old relic, frozen in time.

You'll change your thinking the first time you start up Office 2007.

You don't need to dig deep into dialog boxes to discover what's new in this massive upgrade. If you've used any previous Office version, many of the changes are immediately obvious, and the more you work with Office 2007, the more new features—and new ways of working with old, familiar features—you'll see. Here's the short list of changes you need to know about before you can consider yourself an Office 2007 expert:

- **A brand-new interface**—Menus? Gone. Toolbars? Gone. For the core programs in the Office family, you now interact with the program using the Ribbon—an oversize strip of icons and commands, organized into multiple tabs, that takes over the top of each program's interface. If your muscles have memorized Office menus, you'll have to unlearn a lot of old habits for this version.

- **New file formats**—The native file formats in all Office 2007 programs are based on XML, unlike the binary formats from Office 2003 and earlier. If you routinely share files with users of previous Office versions, be sure to read our instructions in Chapter 3, "Managing Office Files and Formats," for shifting between the old and new formats.

- **Integrated search**—If you use Windows Vista, you can search for any document, worksheet, presentation, or email—directly from the Start menu, from Windows Explorer, or from within Outlook and OneNote. In Windows XP, a limited subset of search features are available when you install the Windows Desktop Search add-in.

- **Snappy visuals**—Anyone who works with Excel charts will notice the slick new charting options immediately. In addition, you can create sharp-looking process diagrams, flowcharts, and other business-related diagrams for any Office document using the new SmartArt tools.

- **Corporate network features**—The Office 2007 family includes an assortment of server products designed to enhance the capability of Office client programs. The newest SharePoint servers, for example, enable a range of collaboration options for groups of people working within a corporate network.

- **Security and privacy features**—Office documents can contain information that might be embarrassing or damaging if revealed to an outsider. In addition, Office documents can contain program code that could introduce viruses and other unwanted software on your computer or network. New features in Office 2007 significantly tighten restrictions on potentially dangerous code and give you new tools to inspect and remove personal or confidential information from files.

- **Internet support**—As in previous versions, you can save just about any Office document in a format that can be viewed within a web browser. Office 2007 includes built-in tools for some new web-based features as well—most notable is the capability to use Word to create posts for a weblog.

A QUICK LOOK AT THE NEW OFFICE INTERFACE

As we noted in the previous section, the core Office programs—Word, Excel, and PowerPoint—sport a completely new interface, as does the Office database management program, Access. Outlook's main window uses the old-style menus and toolbars, but switches to the new Ribbon-based interface when you compose or read an email message or work with individual items in the Contacts or Calendar folder. The Office 2007 versions of all other programs in the Office family, including OneNote and Publisher, have new features but still use the old interface.

Figure 1.1 shows most of the new interface elements.

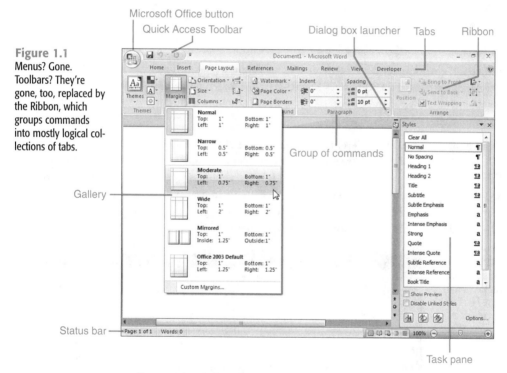

Figure 1.1
Menus? Gone. Toolbars? They're gone, too, replaced by the Ribbon, which groups commands into mostly logical collections of tabs.

→ For a detailed discussion of all the elements in the new Office interface, **see** "The New Office Interface," **p. 28**.

→ To learn how the Outlook interface mixes old and new elements, **see** "Using and Customizing the Outlook Interface," **p. 179**.

FILE FORMATS AND OTHER COMPATIBILITY QUESTIONS

Making the switch to Office 2007 means switching to new file formats for all applications. In Office 2003 and earlier versions, the default file formats are the familiar .doc (Word document), .xls (Excel workbook), and .ppt (PowerPoint presentation).

By contrast, the default file formats in Office 2007 are based on Extensible Markup Language (XML). To denote the change in format, the filename extensions associated with each format have changed, adding an x at the end of each one—Word's new default format is .docx instead of .doc, for example.

Office 2007 programs can still open and save files using the older formats, although some features new to Office 2007 will be lost in the conversion. If you regularly share files with people who use older Office versions, you have two options—save your files in the older format or convince your co-workers to install a conversion utility that allows them to open (but not save) files created using the new formats.

→ For a more complete discussion of the new Office file formats, **see** "Understanding and Choosing File Formats," **p. 54**.

HOW WINDOWS AND OFFICE WORK TOGETHER

Office 2007 works only on recent versions of Windows—specifically, Windows XP (with Service Pack 2 or later), Windows Server 2003 (or later), or Windows Vista. If you try to install any member of the Office 2007 family on an older version of Windows, you'll see an error message.

You might notice subtle differences in some Office 2007 visual elements, depending on your Windows version and the Office theme you've selected. Under Windows XP or Windows Server 2003, for instance, the default color scheme is blue, whereas in Windows Vista you'll see title bars, backgrounds, and other visual elements in gray. Other differences depend on features in the operating system itself. When you save a file, for instance, Windows XP displays the familiar Save As dialog box shown in Figure 1.2.

Figure 1.2
This dialog box should be familiar to anyone who has used an earlier version of Office under Windows XP.

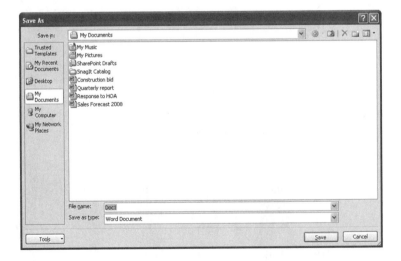

Now look at the same dialog box in Windows Vista, as illustrated in Figure 1.3. The look is dramatically different, and so is the functionality available to you. See the Search box in the top-right corner? That takes advantage of integrated search capabilities built in to Windows Vista. You'll also notice a Tags area, where you can quickly enter keywords that help you find a file later.

Figure 1.3
Common Office dialog boxes in Windows Vista look different and offer new features, such as integrated search and the capability to "tag" files with keywords.

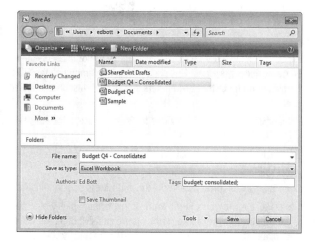

Throughout this book, we assume you're using Office 2007 with Windows Vista. If a feature behaves differently under Windows XP, we point out the differences in a note.

AN OVERVIEW OF OFFICE 2007 APPLICATIONS

Microsoft packages the individual programs that make up Office 2007 into eight separate editions, which in turn are sold through a variety of channels. Every version includes Word and Excel, as well as a handful of smaller programs, such as the Clip Organizer and Picture Manager utilities. All editions except Office Basic Edition (which is available as an option on new PCs and is not sold in a retail version) include PowerPoint. An additional group of programs and feature sets are included with some, but not all, Office editions. In large corporations that purchase and deploy Office Enterprise Edition (not available through normal retail channels), for example, you'll find support for Electronic Forms, digital rights management, and Office Communicator, a program that adds instant messaging capabilities into Office programs, with an emphasis on ways people in a corporation can communicate and collaborate.

Confused? We were too. That's why we put together a field guide to the different Office editions, followed by individual sections that describe the functions and features available in each of the major Office programs.

The Office Packages at a Glance

Microsoft gathers various programs from the Office family (officially, these programs belong to what the company prefers to call the Microsoft Office System, but we digress...) into eight separate suites. To help make sense of the collection, we've divided them according to the sales channel in which you'll find each one.

Sold with new PCs only

Office Basic 2007 is a low-cost option for budget-conscious PC buyers. It offers the most limited selection of all the Office suites, with only Word, Excel, and Outlook included.

Sold in retail outlets

Office Home and Student 2007 is a low-cost package available only to home users–the terms of its license expressly prohibit its use for business purposes. This edition is unique among all the Office suites in that it can be legally installed and activated on up to three computers in a single household. It includes Word, Excel, PowerPoint, and OneNote.

Office Standard 2007 is the basic retail package intended for business use. It includes Word, Excel, PowerPoint, and Outlook.

Office Small Business 2007 includes all the programs in the Standard edition, plus Publisher and the Business Contact Manager add-in for Outlook.

Office Professional 2007 includes all the programs in the Small Business edition, plus Access.

Office Ultimate 2007 includes all the programs in the Professional edition, plus OneNote and all enterprise networking features except Communicator. This package, the most expensive of all the Office editions, is virtually identical to the Enterprise edition. It's intended for business users who need to be able to connect to a corporate network but are not interested in or eligible to purchase Office through a volume licensing program.

Sold through volume licensing only

All but one of the Office editions available as retail packages are also available through volume licensing programs (the exception is, of course, the Home and Student edition). With volume licenses, a corporation, governmental agency, educational institution, or nonprofit organization can purchase the right to use Office in multiple units, usually saving money over the cost of purchasing individual retail packages.

(For more information about licensing options, visit http://www.microsoft.com/licensing.)

Two Office 2007 suites are available only through volume licensing programs. Both include a set of enterprise networking programs and features that we describe in more detail in Chapter 30, "Using Office 2007 on a Corporate Network."

Office Professional Plus 2007 is functionally equivalent to the retail Professional suite, minus the Business Contact Manager program and with the addition of all the enterprise networking features described in Chapter 30.

Office Enterprise 2007 is functionally equivalent to the retail Ultimate suite. It contains everything in the Professional Plus suite and adds OneNote and the Office Groove collaboration client.

This book covers most of the applications found in the Ultimate Edition of Office 2007 sold in retail outlets and bundled with new computers. If you've purchased a different Office edition, the program code for individual applications is the same and our advice applies just as well. We do not include coverage of programs that are official members of the Office family but are not included with any version of Office sold at retail or with new computers. This group includes SharePoint Designer (formerly FrontPage), Project, and Visio.

The sections that follow describe the functions and features available in each of these applications.

OUTLOOK 2007

With every new Office version, Outlook seems to get more changes than any other program. That's certainly true in Office 2007. Previously, you could choose whether to use Microsoft Word or Outlook's built-in editor to compose email messages. In this version, Word is locked in as the one and only editor. But the most noteworthy—and welcome—improvement is a new tool to help you keep on top of the details of a busy life. As Figure 1.4 shows, the new To-Do Bar sits on the right side of Outlook's main window, where it keeps track of tasks, appointments, email messages, and anything else you've flagged for follow up.

Figure 1.4
The To-Do Bar on Outlook's main page offers instant access to anything you flag as needing a follow-up reminder.

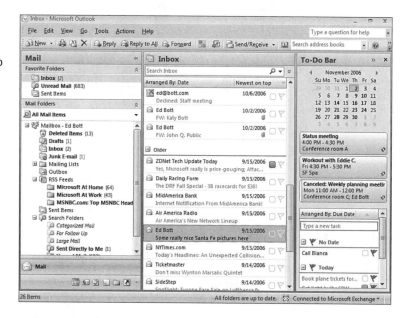

→ For details on how to work with the To-Do Bar, **see** "Using and Customizing the Outlook Interface," **p. 179**.

Other changes in Outlook might not be as immediately obvious, but it won't take much poking around to discover them. Most are focused on making common tasks easier. Outlook automates most of the process of adding a new email account, for instance; after you enter your email address, a setup wizard communicates directly with the server at your chosen domain, trying most common settings and usually making a successful connection. Finding email messages, even in a crowded Inbox, is easier, too. Type a word or name into the Instant Search box and any message that contains the text you entered appears instantly in the list beneath the search box.

WORD 2007

The oldest and most mature of the Office programs, Word is also the most popular. It's an extremely versatile tool—ideal for creating short documents, such as letters and memos, with enough layout and graphics-handling capabilities to also make it suitable for sophisticated publishing chores. In this version, it even adds the capability to create and publish posts on weblogs.

Perhaps more than any other Office program, Word benefits from the addition of the Ribbon interface. The Home tab now offers a visual selection of the styles you're most likely to use, rather than the sparse drop-down Styles list from previous versions. When you make a selection, a floating mini toolbar containing quick links to common editing options fades into view just above the selection. If you move the mouse pointer in the direction of the toolbar, you can use any of those buttons. Move the mouse pointer away, and the toolbar disappears. As Figure 1.5 shows, it also appears along with the context menus if you right-click within a Word document.

Figure 1.5
Word's mini toolbar (shown below the context menu) offers instant access to common editing options and tasks.

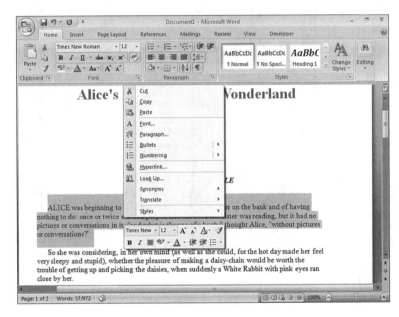

→ For more details on the changes in Word's editing capabilities, **see** "What's New in Word 2007," **p. 330**.

EXCEL 2007

As an all-purpose number-crunching tool, Excel is incredibly useful for tasks as simple as balancing a checkbook or as complex as modeling a hostile takeover of a Fortune 500 corporation. The list of changes in Excel 2007 is long and sweeping. Sure, the basics of building formulas and entering text into cells are pretty much the same, but the way you present that information is radically changed.

The process of building charts, for instance, is much simpler, and the charts you end up with are better looking, thanks to the new graphics engine that all Office programs share. Excel 2007 is also smarter with tables—in earlier versions they were called *lists*. When you designate a range as a list—er, table—you can automatically add totals to it, easily insert new columns and rows, and change the table's formatting by choosing from a gallery of ready-made formats like the ones shown in Figure 1.6. (For an extensive discussion of these tools, read Chapter 21, "Organizing Data with Tables and PivotTables.")

Figure 1.6
Choosing a table for-mat from Excel's gallery makes even complex lists easier to understand.

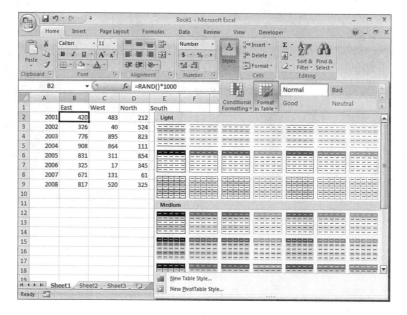

POWERPOINT 2007

PowerPoint has always been an effective way to create PC-based slideshows for presenta-tions to large audiences. Recent versions add the capability to create effective web-based presentations as well. You can't truly appreciate the effectiveness of web-based presentations until you create one. PowerPoint can turn slide titles into a table of contents in the left pane of a frame, and then display each slide on the right, with the viewer pointing and clicking to drive the show.

→ For step-by-step instructions that will help you get a PowerPoint presentation into web format in record time, **see** "Creating Presentations for the Web," **p. 783**.

For novices and experts alike, PowerPoint has earned a reputation as the most user friendly. That's good news, because many PowerPoint users dust off the program only every few months, unlike Word and Excel. The new Office interface makes it much easier to perform complex tasks that used to require diving into dialog boxes. In particular, the new galleries for themes (see Figure 1.7) make changing slide designs a simple point-and-click process.

Unlike the documentation—or other Office books—we also show you exactly how to use each of PowerPoint's many file formats.

Figure 1.7
Aiming the mouse pointer at a slide design in the Themes gallery gives you a live preview. Click to keep the new design or move the pointer to return to the current design.

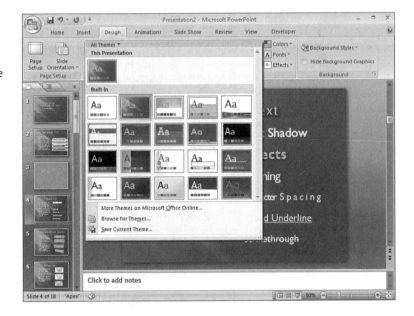

ACCESS 2007

Of all the Office applications, Access is by far the most challenging. As the name implies, Access lets you tap into data from a variety of sources. For example, you can use it as a front end to industrial-strength corporate databases such as SQL Server. Or you can run the data storage components directly on a client machine and save data locally. Access 2007 integrates tightly with SharePoint servers, allowing you to share databases in smaller workgroups.

Experienced developers will still be able to work with the raw code that lurks behind Access database objects. If you're a casual user who found previous Access versions daunting and unfriendly, take a fresh look at Access 2007. It includes a wide range of ready-made applications for keeping track of all sorts of data, including the Assets database shown in Figure 1.8.

Figure 1.8
The ready-made Access applications can get you working right out of the box, with slick features such as data entry via email forms.

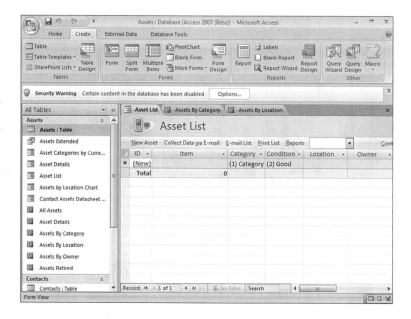

PUBLISHER 2007

Publisher has always been a bit of a misfit in the Office box, and in Office 2007 it's still out of step, with an outdated interface and a distinctly nonstandard way of accomplishing many common tasks. With its extensive hand-holding and a sometimes inflexible interface, Publisher isn't for everyone. If you're an experienced Office user, in fact, you'll find yourself scratching your head over the large and small inconsistencies in the way this program works. But for home users and small businesses, it's an ideal way to create simple newsletters, brochures, postcards, websites, and even HTML-based email messages.

ONENOTE 2007

The newest member of the Office family, OneNote, is also the most interesting, which makes us wonder why it's only in the Enterprise, Ultimate, and Home and Student editions. OneNote is an ideal program for anyone who prefers to keep random thoughts, lists, snippets from web pages, meeting notes, and screen clippings, and just about anything else that can be typed or pasted into a loosely structured digital notebook. OneNote's basic organization is the notebook, which in turn contains tabbed sections, which in turn contain pages like the one shown in Figure 1.9. The whole thing is searchable, sortable, synchronizable, and exportable in a thoroughly elegant way. You can learn enough to become productive by reading our coverage in Chapter 29, "Using OneNote."

Figure 1.9
OneNote's metaphor of a notebook organized into sections and pages is instantly understandable.

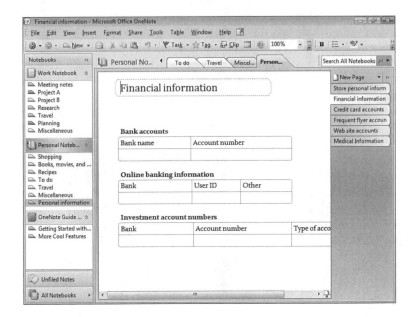

OTHER OFFICE PROGRAMS

In addition to the major programs, every edition of Office 2007 includes an assortment of utilities and add-ins. In this version, thankfully, Microsoft has finally jettisoned a few ancient and mostly useless tools left over from a decade ago; the clunky old Org Chart tool, for example, has been admirably replaced by the new SmartArt graphics capabilities. Those that remain are mostly useful and usable, including the Microsoft Clip Organizer, which helps you find and use clip art, and the Document Imaging and Document Scanning tools, which allow you to view and edit scanned documents and faxes.

The star of these helper programs, though, is the Microsoft Office Picture Manager (found in the Microsoft Office Tools group on the All Programs menu). It lets you organize collections of image files from local hard disks, shared network folders, and SharePoint websites. You can compress and resize images and perform basic image-editing tasks, such as removing "red eye" from portraits (see Figure 1.10). You can also convert images to alternative formats (from the space-hogging Bitmap format to the more efficient JPEG or GIF format, for instance), a trick that comes in especially handy when creating web pages.

Figure 1.10
Use Picture Manager to perform basic image-editing tasks.

INSTALLATION, ACTIVATION, AND VALIDATION

For most people, installing Office 2007 is ridiculously simple. If you purchase a new PC that includes an OEM version of Office, you don't have to do a thing; just find the shortcuts on the Start menu and get to work. To install a retail copy, pop the installation media into the CD/DVD drive, enter a valid product key, choose the default installation options, and let the setup program go about its business. No rebooting is required, and in the case of an upgrade, the installation process picks up all your existing settings without any manual intervention.

→ You can choose to make setup more complicated if you want, as we explain in Appendix A, "Advanced Setup Options," **p. 929**.

Three aspects of setup deserve special mention here. One is Office Product Activation, a controversial antipiracy technology designed to prevent casual copying; a second is Office Genuine Advantage, a supplemental antipiracy program that periodically checks your installed copy of Office to verify that you didn't somehow slip a bootleg copy past the Activation process. Finally, you should know about Microsoft's online services that automatically keep Office up-to-date.

ACTIVATION AND VALIDATION

After you complete the setup process from a retail or OEM version of Office 2007, you can begin using Office programs immediately. However, you may be required to complete one final step before you can continue using Office past an initial trial period. For these copies, you must *activate* the product by contacting Microsoft over the Internet or by phone. This antipiracy system uses two values:

■ The unique 25-character product key associated with your copy of Office.

- A hardware identifier derived from an inventory of the hardware in your system (no personally identifiable information is included).

If you choose the option to activate over the Internet (the simpler option by far), these two values are sent to Microsoft's activation server, which checks to see that the product ID hasn't been used more often than the license terms allow. A copy of Office Home and Student Edition can legally be installed on up to three computers in one home; a retail copy of Office Professional can be installed on one desktop and one portable computer for use by the same person.

For most users with an Internet connection, product activation happens automatically and takes only a few seconds. If you reinstall the software on the same system (after reformatting the hard drive, for instance), reactivation should be automatic. If you try to install the software on another computer, however, you may have to call Microsoft to get a new activation code.

Adding a new hard drive or video card will not trigger a demand for reactivation, but substantially upgrading a PC (by swapping the motherboard and switching hard drives and replacing the network card) probably will. In any case, you can reinstall Office 2007 an unlimited number of times on the same hardware.

A product activation reminder pops up each time you start a new Office program. If you don't have ready access to the Internet, you can delay activation, but don't wait too long. Without activating the product, you can use individual Office programs a maximum of 50 times (each time you launch a different program counts as a single use, even if you are forced to restart after a crash); after you use your 50 free starts, a process that can take less than a week, Office switches into a limited mode that allows you to open files but not edit or save them.

What happens if the activation server decides you've installed Office on more machines than the license allows? In that case, you'll have no choice but to phone the toll-free activation number, speak to a representative, explain that your Office installation is indeed legal, and enter the lengthy activation code he or she provides to you.

So, after you've jumped through all those hoops, you're in the clear, right? Sorry, no. A separate antipiracy program called Office Genuine Advantage (a spinoff from the Windows Genuine Advantage program) kicks in periodically to *validate* your copy of Office. The idea is to identify pirated copies of Office that snuck through the activation process using stolen product IDs or hacked program files. At the time we wrote this, the Office Genuine Advantage program was still in a pilot stage and was voluntary, required only if you want to download updates or add-on features for Office.

Finding Service Packs and Other Updates

After installing Office on a new computer or upgrading an existing one, it's always a smart idea to check for Office updates. Also known as *patches*, these are executable programs, usually small in size, intended to fix specific bugs or to plug security holes in Office programs.

Microsoft typically releases security updates on the second Tuesday of each month, a day that Microsoft watchers affectionately call "Patch Tuesday." Less frequently, Microsoft releases comprehensive updates to Office called *service packs*.

To check for updates interactively rather than automatically, use Internet Explorer to visit the Office Update website (http://officeupdate.microsoft.com). There you can download a tool that scans your system and identifies any updates you need based on the Office version you have installed.

We don't recommend that you rely on manual checks for updates. Because updates often plug security holes that can place your computer and your network at risk, it's better to automate the process. That way, you can be assured that updates will be delivered and installed as soon as they're available. When you first install Office, the setup program asks if you want to replace the Windows Update tool with Microsoft Update. If you say yes, you're done. If you turn down the initial offer, you can change your mind later by visiting http://update.microsoft.com.

ONLINE HELP AND OTHER SUPPORT OPTIONS

As in previous versions, each Office 2007 program includes detailed help content for Office users at any level, regardless of technical sophistication or experience.

The Help interface for programs in the Office 2007 family is completely rewritten. For programs that use the Ribbon interface, you ask for help by clicking the Help icon at the far right of the Tab bar—look for the white question mark in a blue circle. (For programs that still use old-style menus, click the Help menu and look for that same icon at the top of the list of commands.)

TIP FROM

Ed & Woody

> Or use the keyboard. As in every version of Office since the beginning of time, F1 still summons Help for the current program.

Think of the new Help windows (shown in Figure 1.11) as a small, stripped-down web browser, with five buttons at the left of its toolbar that mirror functions in a web browser. The active topic always appears in the main window. You can show or hide the Table of Contents for the current program by clicking a button on the toolbar. Click the button with the pushpin icon to set the Help window so it's always on top.

Table of Contents   Show/hide Table of Contents   Keep On Top

Figure 1.11
The Table of Contents pane (left) allows you to browse Help topics. The selected topic appears in the viewer pane on the right.

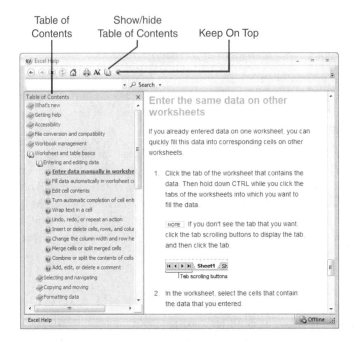

You can enter any text into the Search box to find topics containing that term. Use the drop-down Search list to change the scope of the search. By default, your search request looks for up-to-date content using Microsoft's Office Online servers. You can restrict your search to specific types of content, as in Figure 1.12; or, if you're working offline or have a slow Internet connection, specify that you want to use only locally stored content. To view only topics from the locally stored Help files, click the Show Me Offline Results from My Computer link in the contents pane, or choose any of the options from the Content from This Computer heading on the Search list.

Figure 1.12
The drop-down search list lets you specify the scope of a search. The left side of the status bar shows the current search scope.

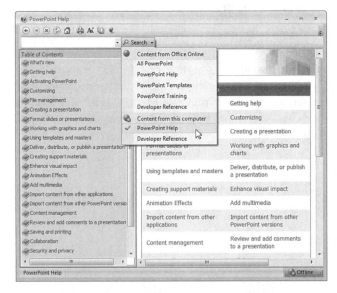

You can open multiple Help windows, one for each Office program in use. Some Help settings are shared among programs. For example, if you use the Change Font Size button to make text in the Help window larger or smaller, your choice applies to the current window and to any Help windows you open in the future, even in another Office program; it doesn't affect any other currently open windows.

DIAGNOSING PROBLEMS

If you're experiencing problems with one or more Office programs, including crashes or unexplained hangs, run the Microsoft Office Diagnostics utility. This tool, new in Office 2007, replaces the Detect and Repair feature in earlier Office versions and adds the capability to automatically check for hardware errors in memory and hard disks.

To run this utility, click the Microsoft Office Diagnostics shortcut in the Microsoft Office Tools group on the All Programs menu. As Figure 1.13 shows, it's an all-or-nothing proposition; you can't select individual tests to run.

Figure 1.13
The Microsoft Office Diagnostics tool checks for solutions to common problems with hardware and software.

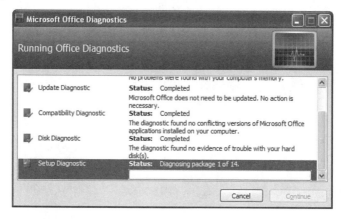

After the Diagnostic utility runs, you get a chance to review its results and make any necessary changes. It does not make any changes without your consent.

CHAPTER 2

USING AND CUSTOMIZING THE OFFICE 2007 INTERFACE

In this chapter

The New Office Interface   28

Customizing Your Interface   32

Getting Quick Results with Keyboard Shortcuts   38

Setting Options for Office and Individual Applications   40

Troubleshooting   48

Secrets of the Office Masters: Creating the Ultimate Office Working Environment   50

THE NEW OFFICE INTERFACE

To say things look a little different in Office 2007 would be a tremendous understatement. Microsoft has gone to great lengths to alter the appearance of the Office Suite, not only to present us with a new way of doing our work, but to provide a streamlined approach. In addition, changes in the Office 2007 interface provide a uniform look and feel so that Office users can slide from one application to another more easily.

The first step on the road to becoming an Office expert is to understand the new Office user interface (UI). Learning how to weave between each ribbon and between each application and find the shortcut keys that work for you—these are the skills of an expert.

Some have asked, "Why the change in the interface; it worked just fine for years." That's true, but our abilities, and the capabilities of Office, have changed over the years. The first release of Word 1.0, for example, had about 100 commands, but Word 2007 has about 1,500 commands, so a better way to display all these tools had to be discovered. Microsoft is convinced that after you try the new interface and get comfortable with it, you won't want to go back. From our honest perspective, that sounded too good to be true, but after trying it, we have come to love the new interface.

For years, Office programs have had access to spell-checking tools, grammatical tools, and a thesaurus. Office 2007 supplements these basic tools with a customizable Research task pane that offers access to online services, including an online encyclopedia, translation tools, business reference books, and news archives, among others.

Each Office application includes hundreds of customization options. We cover features and techniques specific to a particular program in the chapters devoted exclusively to that program. Because Office uses shared program code to display ribbons, the techniques for customizing these elements are absolutely consistent from one application to another, and we try to cover them fully in this chapter.

APPLICATIONS THAT HAVE THE NEW UI

Chapter 1 discussed the various applications that are now included in the various offers of the Office Suites. Not all of these applications received the overhaul. Here are the ones that have the new look:

- Office Access 2007
- Office Excel 2007
- PowerPoint 2007 (shown in Figure 2.1)
- Office Word 2007
- Parts of Outlook 2007 (for example, email message authority, shown in Figure 2.2)

Figure 2.1
The PowerPoint 2007 user interface with the new ribbon format.

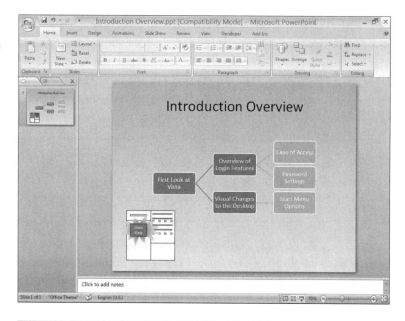

Figure 2.2
The Outlook interface will have the new look for email messages, in creating tasks and contacts, or setting up meetings.

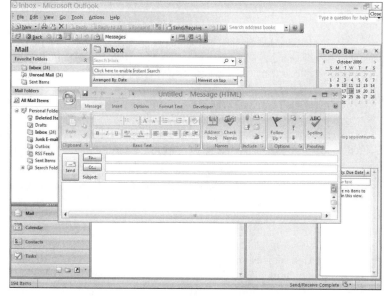

TERMINOLOGY FOR WORKING WITH THE NEW UI

You are going to hear a lot of confusion regarding the different terms for the new interface. Words such as Ribbons and Galleries and Tabs will be used left and right, and it will make your brain hurt at first. So, let's get a clearer understanding of the new interface terminology.

THE OFFICE BUTTON

This is a sleek circular launching pad for multiple options for your documents. You can select the Office button to begin new documents, save existing ones, prepare your documents for deployment, and so on, and you can access special application options from your Office button.

THE RIBBON

In previous versions of Office, there were menus and toolbars. Some of these have survived into the Office 2007 world, but the talk around the water cooler is all about the new ribbon. The ribbon is the toolbar and menu successor. Each ribbon has a set of tools specific to that ribbon's functionality that you cannot change.

For example, the Home ribbon in Word 2007 has all your formatting options. You cannot take these tools and hide them or push them off to another ribbon if you want.

Each application has ribbons that relate to the work for that particular application. For example, the Excel 2007 set of ribbons will contain Formulas and Data ribbons, whereas PowerPoint 2007 will have ribbons that relate to Animations and Slide Show. The purpose of the ribbon is to organize the different command options in a way that makes it easier for people to work because all the commands for a particular subject are together.

NOTE

> The ribbons each have a tab. The tab is just the little part of the ribbon where the name is located. So, although you might be directed to select the Home tab in Word 2007, this would, in reality, take you to the Home ribbon, not the Home tab. The tab is just the selection point. Got that? It's only confusing at first.

The commands are organized into groups or groupings. So, for example, you might be asked to select the References tab to go to the References ribbon. And from here you would be directed to look for the Cross-reference option from the Captions group (or grouping).

NOTE

> You can minimize the ribbons so that they no longer appear, but the ribbon tab would still remain visible. Again, this might help you to keep the two concepts separate in your mind.

In the bottom-right corner of some of the groups (groupings) on the ribbons are little arrow-pointing widgets. These have been given many names—Selection Arrows, Dialog Locators, Option Clicks, and so on. Widgets are the coolest so far, but establish a terminology that works for you and stick with it. These widgets open the dialog boxes that give you more control over certain groupings.

CONTEXTUAL TABS

With such a huge command set to place before a user, it was virtually impossible to have all your ribbons available at the same time. To compensate for that, certain ribbons are contextual in the sense that they appear only when obviously needed. For example, although you can create a table from the Insert ribbon, you cannot format that table until it exists.

The actual ribbons (Design and Layout), shown in Figure 2.3, aren't even available until you have the table created and are in the table.

Figure 2.3
Design and Layout ribbons are contextual in that they appear only after the table has been created and you are working with it.

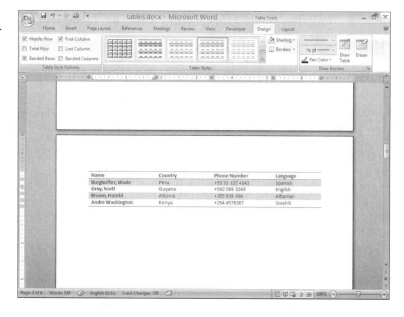

GALLERIES

When you go into an ice-cream place, isn't it the best thing in the world to try a few flavors before picking the one you want? Not only do you feel good about getting a couple of different tastes for free, but when you make that final decision, it's with no regrets. That's the Gallery concept in Office 2007 (one example of which is shown in Figure 2.4).

Figure 2.4
One of the Galleries in PowerPoint that makes your life easier.

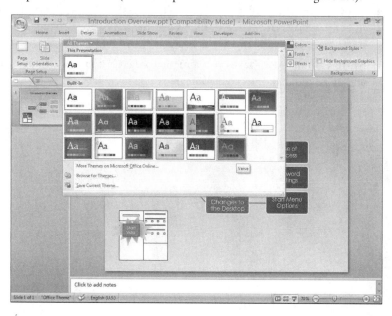

Galleries provide users with different choices by presenting visually appealing results, as opposed to complicated choices from old-fashioned grayish dialog boxes. That's not to say our dialog boxes are gone—they aren't yet. When you need to retain greater control, you can use the dialog box options to make changes to your document's features. But the Gallery approach will save you time and make your documents immediately professional looking.

LIVE PREVIEWS

This feature works hand-in-hand with the gallery options because, although a gallery might show you what MIGHT be, the Live Preview shows you what WILL be. As you move your cursor over the gallery options, the actual text, or formatting, etc., will update immediately to show you the results, if you choose that selection.

CUSTOMIZING YOUR INTERFACE

Although you can't alter the appearance of your ribbons, there are a few customization options that you can call on to help personalize your Office experience. For example, you are given one toolbar to work with and customize however you like. It's called the Quick Access Toolbar, and you can add or remove all the commands you like to it so that you have all the functionality you want, right at your fingertips.

You can also make some layout decisions about your ribbons and the Quick Access Toolbar. For example, you can use the Customize Quick Access Toolbar options, shown in Figure 2.5, located in each of the Office applications (with the new format) to perform the following:

- **Minimize the Ribbon**—This allows you keep your ribbon tabs visible while allowing you a little more room at the top of your screen. The ribbons will reappear if you select the ribbon tab.

- **Show Below the Ribbon**—The Quick Access toolbar will grow as you add buttons to it, but you may not want it all the way at the top of your document. You can give it a bit more space to expand if you put it below the ribbon.

- **More Commands**—Takes you directly to the Customize settings that will allow you to add more commands to your toolbar. We discuss that next.

Figure 2.5
The Customize Quick Access Toolbar options in Word 2007.

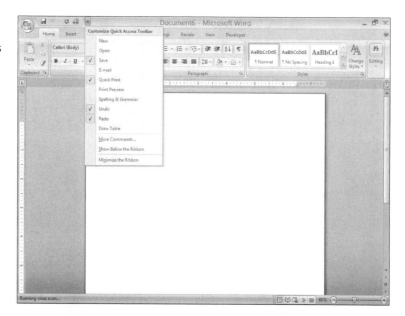

ADDING FREQUENTLY USED COMMANDS TO THE QUICK ACCESS TOOLBAR

You are going to want to customize your Quick Access Toolbar eventually, after you get comfortable with the interface. You can do this from any of the updated applications through the Customize Quick Access Toolbar settings and choosing More Commands. In addition, each application has a set of special options located off the Office button. For example, in Word 2007 when you select the Office button, you'll see an option called Word Options. And, by extension, an Excel Options and a PowerPoint Options selection are in those applications. From these options, you can choose Customize and this will show you the commands you can add to your Quick Access Toolbar. You could also right-click your Office button and choose Customize Quick Access Toolbar, and the Customization page shown in Figure 2.6 is displayed.

1. Use the Choose Commands From drop-down list to select the category of commands you want to choose from.

2. Use the Customize Quick Access Toolbar drop-down list to determine whether your changes will apply for all documents (databases) or for only the specific document that you are working with.

3. Select a command from the list box on the left side of the dialog box and click Add to add it to the list box on the right side of the dialog box. Sometimes you really have to search for the command you are looking for.

Figure 2.6
Customizing Quick Access settings by adding Command buttons.

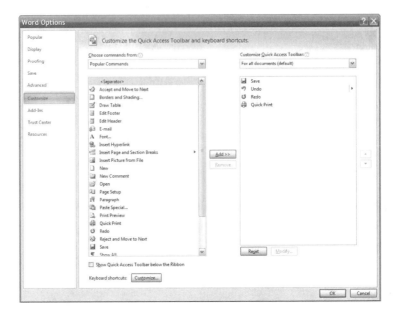

TIP FROM

EQ & Woody

The normal inclination for people is to get settled in with their applications and leave them as they are. This would be a mistake with Office 2007. You must take advantage of the capability to customize your Quick Access Toolbar. In some ways, it's the only freedom you have to give you the working environment you need. Adjusting the toolbar is like adjusting your chair before you start working. You need a comfortable and functional position before you begin.

4. Use the up and down arrows on the right side of the dialog box to move the command up or down within the list of existing commands.

5. After adding all the desired commands, click OK to complete the process. The Quick Access Toolbar now appears with the icons associated with the commands that you added to the toolbar.

TIP FROM

EQ & Woody

If you want to reset the Quick Access Toolbar back to its default state, click the Reset button on the Customization page.

CUSTOMIZING TOOLBARS AND MENUS IN OUTLOOK AND PUBLISHER

Because Outlook and Publisher (and some of the other applications you might encounter in the Office Suite) are still using toolbars and menus, we thought it was a good idea to review the way to make changes to these options as well.

Instead of using personalized menus and toolbars, most expert users prefer to customize built-in toolbars, adding and grouping buttons they use most often. Click the Toolbar Options arrow (the slim, downward-pointing arrow at the right side of every toolbar), select

Add or Remove Buttons, and choose the name of the toolbar to display the list of available buttons, as shown in Figure 2.7 (if you add a button, it appears on this list as well). A check mark next to any item on the list means that the button is currently visible. Click to toggle this check mark and display or hide the button.

Figure 2.7
Changing toolbar buttons in Outlook.

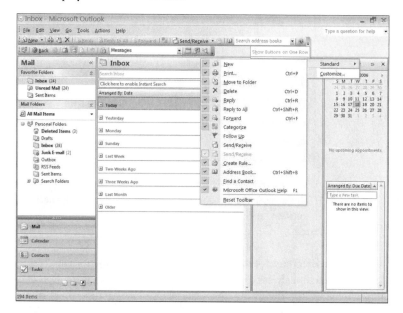

When customizing the selection of buttons on a toolbar, you're not limited to choices on the Add or Remove Buttons menu. You can add any command, macro, or existing menu to a toolbar. To add a new toolbar or add commands to a visible menu or toolbar, follow these steps:

1. Select Tools, Customize (or right-click any toolbar or menu and choose Customize from the bottom of the shortcut menu). The Customize dialog box opens.

2. If the toolbar you want to customize is not visible, click the Toolbars tab and check the box for that toolbar. Or choose New and make your own toolbar for your command buttons.

3. Click the Commands tab, select an entry from the Categories list on the left, and then select the command you want to add from the Commands list on the right, as shown in Figure 2.8.

4. Drag the command from the Customize dialog box to the toolbar where you want to add the button. When you see a thick black I-beam in the correct position, drop the button to add it.

5. Repeat steps 3 and 4 to add more buttons to any toolbar.

6. When you've finished working with the toolbar, click Close to put away the Customize dialog box.

Figure 2.8
Drag items from the list on the right side of this dialog box to create new toolbar buttons.

NOTE

The items in the Categories list typically correspond to top-level menu choices, built-in toolbars, and some collections of tools.

If you never use certain toolbar buttons, clear them away to make room for the buttons you do use. It's ridiculously easy to remove a button from a toolbar: Point to the button you want to remove, and then hold down the Alt key as you drag it off the toolbar. When the pointer displays a tool icon with an X, release the mouse button to delete the item. If the Customize dialog box is open, you can remove any button or menu item by dragging it off the menu bar.

TIP FROM

Ed & Woody

Use these same drag-and-drop techniques to move buttons and menu items, either on the same toolbar or between toolbars. From any editing window, hold down the Alt key and drag a button to move it to a different place on the same toolbar or to a different toolbar altogether. With the Customize dialog box visible, hold down the Ctrl key and drag any button to create a copy. And here's an undocumented shortcut we guarantee you haven't read anywhere else: Hold down the Alt key as you drag a button, and then (while continuing to hold down the Alt key) press the Ctrl key and release the button. This shortcut creates a copy, either on the same toolbar or on another toolbar, without opening the Customize dialog box. This technique is especially effective if you want to create slightly different versions of the same toolbar for different tasks: Base one toolbar on an existing toolbar, and then modify the new copy and use macros to switch between them for different tasks.

Office 2007 offers an alternative way to customize toolbars and menus, even when those interface elements are currently hidden. From any Office program, choose Tools, Customize, click the Commands tab, and then click the Rearrange Commands button. In the Rearrange Commands dialog box (see Figure 2.9), choose any menu, submenu, or toolbar. The Controls list shows all items currently available on the menu or toolbar you selected. The five buttons to the right allow you to add, delete, move, or edit a toolbar button.

Figure 2.9
Using the Rearrange Commands dialog box is less convenient than drag-and-drop techniques, but is valuable for editing menus and toolbars that are not currently visible.

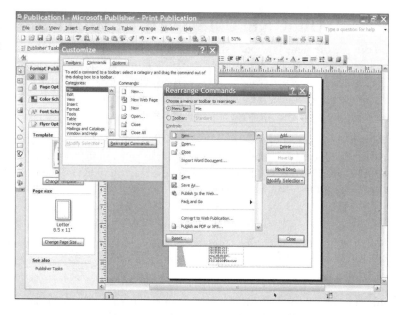

NOTE

> Outlook allows you to create custom toolbars, and the program stores all customizations as part of the program options rather than associating them with data files. There's no need to copy these toolbars to a different location.

TIP FROM

> To perform similar toolbar customizations for InfoPath, OneNote, SharePoint Designer, Publisher, or Visio, go to the Tools menu and select Customize.

ADDING MENUS

In applications that are not using the new ribbon interface, to add a new menu to any toolbar (including the default menu bar), be sure the toolbar you want to customize is visible, and then select Tools, Customize. Click the Commands tab and select New Menu from the bottom of the Categories list. Drag the New Menu item from the Commands list and drop it in the correct position on the toolbar.

Right-click to rename the new menu. Then add buttons and menu items by dragging and dropping commands, macros, and other objects from the Customize dialog box or from other toolbars. When you drag an item over a pull-down menu, the menu drops down so you can drop the item (whether a command or macro) in the correct location.

GETTING QUICK RESULTS WITH KEYBOARD SHORTCUTS

You can use the same keyboard shortcuts with Microsoft Office 2007 as you could with previous versions of Office. This means that, if you prefer, you can perform many of the commonly used features (such as Save) using the keyboard shortcuts that you are familiar with. When you hover your mouse pointer over the ribbon on a button that is associated with a keyboard shortcut, the shortcut appears as a tool.

Another way that you can identify keyboard shortcuts is to tap your Alt key while on a particular tab. All of the Alt key shortcuts appear as small indicators (see Figure 2.10). For example, when you press Alt with the Home tab active, you can see that Alt+F will access the Microsoft Office Access button.

Figure 2.10
A cool way to view your shortcuts off the ribbons.

Office includes an overwhelming number of keyboard shortcuts for nearly every task. Some mnemonic shortcuts, such as Ctrl+B (Bold), Ctrl+U (Underline), and Ctrl+I (Italic), are common to every Office application. Others follow Windows standards, such as the universal Ctrl+X (Cut), Ctrl+C (Copy), and Ctrl+V (Paste) shortcuts. Still others give you access to commands that are nearly impossible to access any other way. For example, there's no menu choice in Word to convert field codes to their results; you have to know the shortcuts: Ctrl+6 (from the numeric keypad, not the row of numbers above the QWERTY keys) or Ctrl+Shift+F9.

Office applications are remarkably consistent in their use of keyboard shortcuts, with one notable exception: Outlook is the black sheep, with many, many nonstandard keyboard shortcuts. Throughout every other Office application, for example, you use Ctrl+F to display the Find and Replace dialog boxes; in Outlook, however, that key combination forwards an item via email. To find text in Outlook, press F4, which works as the Repeat key everywhere else in Office.

Only a savant could memorize every Office keyboard shortcut, but learning a select few can dramatically increase your productivity, especially for commands and functions you use regularly.

TIP FROM

Ed & Woody

To make discovering keyboard shortcuts for a particular Office program easier, turn on the option that displays keyboard shortcuts along with ScreenTips. In the ribbon-oriented applications select your Office button, then go into the Options for the application, and within the Advanced settings under the Display heading, choose Show Shortcut Keys in ScreenTips. For nonribbon-oriented applications (such as Outlook), select Tools, Customize, click the Options tab, and select the Show Shortcut Keys in ScreenTips check box.

Of all the Officewide keyboard shortcuts, one stands out as by far the most useful. F4 is the Repeat key, which repeats the previous action; it comes in handy in a variety of situations. For example, you can use F4 to apply a new style to a series of paragraphs scattered throughout a Word document. Click in the first paragraph and select the style from the drop-down list. Click in the next paragraph and press F4 instead of going back to the Style menu; F4 will continue to apply that style until you perform another action, such as typing or formatting. Add or delete a row in an Excel worksheet, and then move the insertion point and press F4 to add or delete another row, again without using menus.

Printing out an exhaustive list of shortcut keys for each Office application would take hundreds of pages. To see a generally complete list organized by category, search in each application's online help for a topic called "Keyboard Shortcuts."

Of all Office programs, only Word enables you to easily customize keyboard shortcuts. Under your Quick Access Customization settings, you can select the Keyboard Settings: Customize button. Select a command, a macro, an AutoText entry, a font, a style, or a common symbol. The Customize Keyboard dialog box displays the current key combination assigned to each item you select (see Figure 2.11).

Figure 2.11
Only Word enables you to easily customize keyboard shortcuts.

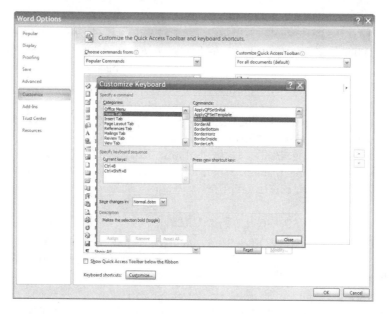

To add or change a key combination, first select the item you want to assign; then click in the Press New Shortcut Key box and press the key combination. Check the text just below this box to see whether the key combination you've selected is already assigned to another function; if the option is available, click Assign. Look in the Current Keys box to see whether a key combination is already assigned to that function; to remove that definition, select the item and click Remove.

For details on how to restore default keyboard shortcuts if you inadvertently reassign the wrong key, see "Restoring Default Shortcut Keys" in the "Troubleshooting" section at the end of this chapter.

SETTING OPTIONS FOR OFFICE AND INDIVIDUAL APPLICATIONS

In every Office application, you'll find most customization settings off the Office button, under the Options for that particular application. Under those options, you can find common settings that you can find in the same location for other applications.

You can typically customize the following:

- Control the number of files on the recently used file list. The default is 17, and the maximum is 50 for most Office applications. If the list doesn't fit on the screen, you will see fewer documents.
- Set spelling preferences, as explained in the following section.
- Enter user information, including your name and initials, for use with comments.
- Control whether you see and hear animation and sound effects when you use menus and other interface elements. If sound effects annoy you, turn them off here.
- Set AutoRecover options (Word, Excel, and PowerPoint) to automatically save snapshots of files in memory at regular intervals so that the program can recover them in the event of a system crash. (This is not a substitute for saving your work regularly!)
- Hide or show status bars at the bottom of each program window. These typically display information about the current document, worksheet, presentation, or other data file.
- Hide or show rulers, scrollbars, and other interface elements.

Some of these options can be changed in one application and it carries over to others. For example, if you open up Microsoft Word and change your color scheme from Blue to Silver, it makes this change in all your applications. That's nice for a consistent appearance to your working environment, and it's a nice feature that you have to change this only once. Let's discuss a few other configuration features.

CONFIGURING SHARED OFFICE FEATURES

Some of the options in Office can be configured from one application and will stretch to cover the configuration for the other applications (for example, custom dictionaries). Let's discuss a few.

NOTE Although certain configuration settings within your advanced options may look like they are the same between applications, it doesn't mean that they are. For example, on the Popular settings dialog box, you will see an option for using Live Previews. Each application has the same option. But if you change it in one application, it has absolutely no effect on the others.

PERSONALIZE YOUR COPY OF OFFICE

You can go into your Options for any of the applications by going to your Office button and selecting the Options. On the first group of settings, called Popular, are several settings that will span your applications. You can put in a username, a set of initials, and establish the languages for your applications. If you make changes to these in any one application, it will span the others.

SETTING UP SPELL-CHECKING OPTIONS

All Office applications use a common spell-checking module, based on the same dictionaries. When you add words to your custom dictionary, regardless of which Office application you use, your changes are stored in a single text file, which you can easily open and edit.

To adjust spelling options for each application, use the following techniques:

- For Word, select the Office button, select Word Options, and go to the Proofing settings. Use the dialog box shown in Figure 2.12 to adjust options.

Figure 2.12
Word's spelling options are by far the richest of any Office program.

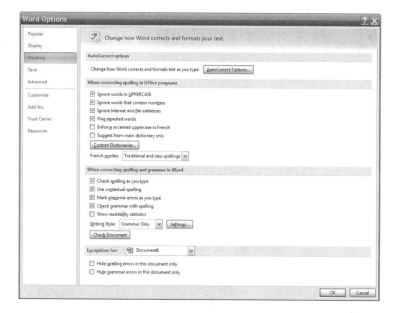

Word has the most extensive set of spelling options, including the capability to add supplemental dictionaries for specialized vocabularies, such as those used in a medical or legal practice.

To tame some of Word's aggressive spell-checking tendencies, see "Word Changes Text Mysteriously" in the "Troubleshooting" section at the end of this chapter.

→ For more details on how Word automatically uses suggestions from the spelling checker, **see** "Checking Spelling, Contextual Spelling, and Grammar," **p. 374**.

- Excel and Access offer identical Spelling options (see Figure 2.13). In both programs, you can specify the language you want to use, as well as which dictionary file you want to use when adding words.

Figure 2.13
Excel users might want to create separate custom dictionaries to recognize specialized financial terms in worksheets.

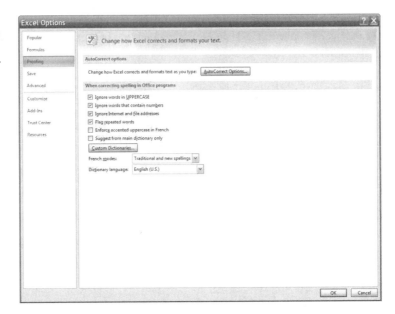

■ PowerPoint's spelling options are far less comprehensive. Go into the PowerPoint Options from the Office button and look into the Proofing settings in the dialog box shown in Figure 2.14.

Figure 2.14
PowerPoint's spelling options are far less extensive than those in other Office programs.

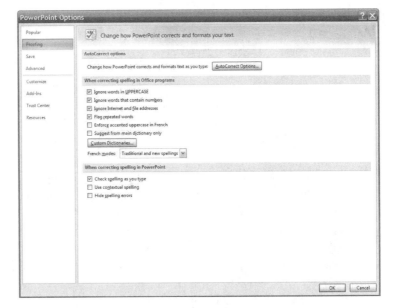

- To hide the red squiggly line under spelling errors for a given presentation, check the Hide All Spelling Errors box. To turn off automatic spell-checking completely, clear the check mark next to the Check Spelling as You Type box. To turn on contextual spelling, select the Use Contextual Spelling options.

TIP FROM

Ed & Woody

> Contextual spelling involves a new feature in Office 2007 that allows your applications to check for errors with words that aren't necessarily misspelled, but are in the wrong context. For example, suppose you write "We don't want to loose the game." The word "loose" is spelled correctly, but it's the wrong word in the context of the sentence. This isn't a perfect tool and doesn't catch every last problem, but it really does help out. When you have a word out of context, the word will be underlined with a blue squiggly line, in contrast to the red squiggly for normal spelling errors or the green squiggly for grammatical errors.

In Outlook, you can select Tools, Options, and click the Spelling tab to set spelling options. Outlook lets you check spelling on any message you compose, including replies. The options you notice are limited on the Spelling tab, but you can alter these by selecting the Spelling and Auto-Correction button. This will actually take you into the Proofing tab for your Outlook options. These options look just like the other applications, even though Outlook doesn't have the full ribbon-oriented shell.

All Office spelling tools share the following dictionary files:

- A main dictionary, as determined by your language settings. On a system configured for U.S. English, for example, this file is `MSSP3EN.LEX`.
- A custom dictionary, which stores words you add while spell checking. The default name for this file is `Custom.dic`.

Where will you find these dictionary files? The exact location depends on how you installed Office and how you've configured Windows. In most cases, the main dictionary file will be in `%programfiles%\Common Files\Microsoft Shared\Proof`.

The custom dictionary file, on the other hand, should appear in a personal data folder, such as `%userprofile%\Application Data\Microsoft\Proof`. Because the custom dictionary file is a simple text file, shared by all applications, you can use any text editor to edit it. Office makes this task easy—click the Custom Dictionaries button from the Proofing settings in your application options to open the custom dictionary tool. Microsoft has added a much simpler interface than what existed in previous versions, which is accessible from all the applications through the Proofing settings. Select the correct file from the list, if necessary, and click Modify. This opens up a neat dialog box where you can add a word at a time, as in Figure 2.15.

Figure 2.15
To edit the Officewide Custom dictionary, click the Modify button and add one word at a time.

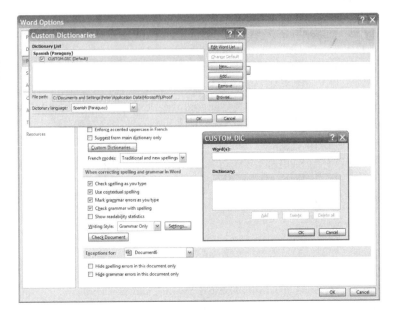

CONFIGURING THE RESEARCH TASK PANE

In Office 2007, the Review ribbon includes an extensive collection of reference books and online research services, all available throughout Office. To quickly look up the definition of a word or phrase, select the text, right-click, and choose Look Up from the shortcut menu. The Research task pane opens, with the Encarta dictionary definition of the word you selected in place, as shown in Figure 2.16. Scroll down through the list to find synonyms, translate the word or phrase into another language, or search in additional reference books.

Figure 2.16
Definitions, drawn from the Encarta online dictionary, appear in the Reference task pane.

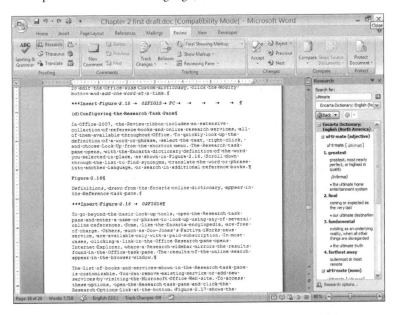

To go beyond the basic look-up tools, open the Research task pane and enter a name or phrase to look up using any of several online references. Some, like the Encarta encyclopedia, are free of charge. Others, such as the Dow Jones Factiva iWorks news service, are available only with a paid subscription. In most cases, clicking a link in the Office Research pane opens Internet Explorer, where a Research sidebar mirrors the results found in the Office task pane. The results of the online search appear in the browser window.

The list of books and services shown in the Research task pane is customizable. You can remove existing services or add new services by visiting the Microsoft Office website. To access these options, open the Research task pane and click the Research Options link at the bottom. Figure 2.17 shows the complete list.

Figure 2.17
Select or clear these check boxes to add services to the Research task pane.

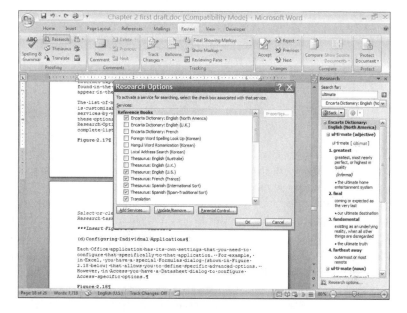

CONFIGURING INDIVIDUAL APPLICATIONS

Each Office application has its own settings that you need to configure that apply specifically to that application, which is logical because the different tools do different things. Word handles document creation; Excel handles spreadsheet and charting information. Each application is bound to have a different set of tools. For example, in Excel, you have a special Formulas dialog box (shown in Figure 2.18) that allows you to define specific advanced options. However, in Access you have a Datasheet dialog box to configure Access-specific options.

Figure 2.18
The Formulas dialog box allows you to make Excel-specific configuration settings.

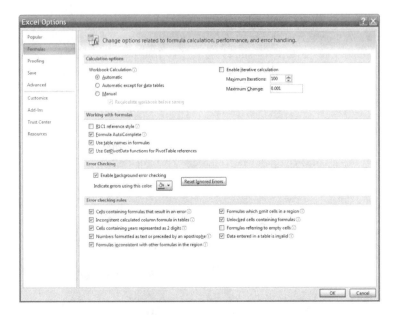

To review a few application settings, and this list is by no means conclusive, let's consider one of the dialog boxes that spans the applications, the Popular dialog box. These settings include ones that are supposedly "popular" for needing to change. To access these settings, select your Office button, and then, for whatever application you are working in, you go to the Options for that application (for Word, it's called Word Options, for PowerPoint, PowerPoint Options, and so on). If you are working in another application, such as Outlook, you will find Advanced Options under the Tools menu by selecting Options, selecting the Other tab, and then selecting Advanced Options.

TIP FROM

Again, keep in mind that although these options look the same between your applications, they do not affect each other. Making a change to one doesn't have any effect on the others. We already discussed some of the settings that do have widespread effect, such as the color scheme, the spelling and dictionary settings, and the like.

SHOW MINITOOLBAR ON SELECTION

This is a setting that allows you to select text, and when you move your cursor over that selection, a minitoolbar shows up automatically.

TIP FROM

You may want to turn this off immediately. If you are already an avid Office user, one thing you might do often is quickly select text, right-click, click Copy or Cut, and go to move your text. The problem with the minitoolbar showing up right away is that you select the text, move your cursor over, and this rude toolbar gets in the way of your right-click, copy/cut routine. The best thing is to make sure it never happens by turning this setting off.

ENABLE LIVE PREVIEW

We discussed this earlier as a feature that allows you to put your cursor in a table or paragraph and then to hover your mouse pointer over the various galleries and to see an immediate change of your document to show you what will happen if you select that particular option.

SHOW DEVELOPER TAB IN THE RIBBON

The average user will never need the Developer tab, and it's not included in your ribbon tabs by default. But if you want to create advanced forms or work with an XML schema, make macros, and so on, you need to turn this ribbon tab on.

NOTE

> Showing the Developer tab can be done in any application, but if you turn it on in one, it turns on in all the others. Technically this is an Office-wide change, but generally you'll use it with only one application or another at any given time.

→ For more details on how you can create an advanced form using the Developer tab, **see** "Secrets of the Office Masters: Creating a Fill-in-the-Blanks Form with Fields," **p. 503**.

NOTE

> One of the other Popular dialog box settings is Always Use Clear-Type. Although nothing indicates that this is an Office-wide setting, if you deselect this box (which is on by default), you will receive a message saying that you need to close all your Office applications for this to take effect.

CONFIGURING SMART TAGS

Smart Tags were introduced in Office XP; these tiny button/menu combinations appear automatically after certain types of actions. They are similar to contextual ribbons in that they aren't always available or viewable, but in the event they are needed, they appear. For instance, Smart Tags appear whenever you use the AutoCorrect or Paste function in any Office program. If the results aren't what you expect, you can use options on the Smart Tag menu to change the way the data appears. Smart Tags assist in error checking in Excel worksheets and are used for layout functions in PowerPoint. They can also automatically identify words or phrases that meet certain criteria. For instance, you can configure Word to automatically recognize the names of persons, or ask Excel to recognize stock ticker symbols.

Subtle indicators mark the positions of each Smart Tag in an Office document. In a Word document, a faint purple line under a name means a Smart Tag is buried there. In Excel, triangular indicators in the corner of a cell mark the presence of a Smart Tag. Hover the mouse pointer over the Smart Tag to display an Action button; click the button to see a list of actions you can take in response to the tag.

A wide array of options is available for customizing Smart Tags. To adjust these options for any Office program, select your Office button, choose your applications Options, on the

Proofing tab go to the AutoCorrect Options, and then click the Smart Tags tab. Figure 2.19, for instance, shows the full range of options available in Word. Using this dialog box, you can specify which types of data will be recognized, or you can turn off Smart Tags completely.

Figure 2.19
If you find Smart Tags more annoying than helpful, clear this check box to turn them off for good.

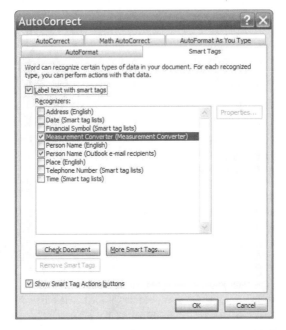

If an Office program insists on incorrectly recognizing a word, phrase, or name and assigning a Smart Tag to it, use the actions menu to clean up the clutter. You can remove a single Smart Tag, stop recognizing a certain word or phrase in a particular type of Smart Tag, or tell Office to completely ignore a particular word or phrase when checking for Smart Tags.

TROUBLESHOOTING

BACK TO SQUARE ONE

I've configured a Quick Access Toolbar that is overly cluttered. I just want to go back to the beginning and redesign the whole thing.

This isn't so difficult. Go back into the Customization settings using any one of several methods (the easiest is to select the down-arrow off the Quick Access Toolbar and choose More Commands) and then choose the Reset button to restore the toolbar to its original setting. You will see a confirmation dialog box to ensure that you really want to do this. After you have things back to the beginning, you can go through the process of selecting new command options.

In Outlook or Publisher, I've customized menus and toolbars a bit too much, and now I can't find several key commands.

You can restore any toolbar, including the main menu bar, to its default settings. Select Tools, Customize, and click the Toolbars tab. Choose the toolbar whose customized settings you want to remove (select Menu Bar for the main menus) and click Reset. Word users can specify whether the change applies to the current document only or to the template in use.

RESTORING DEFAULT SHORTCUT KEYS

I inadvertently replaced a useful system shortcut and want to reset the default shortcut.

When you assign a keyboard shortcut to a specific function, it removes that shortcut for any other function that uses that combination. To restore the shortcut, select the original function and assign the proper key combination. To restore every default Word key combination, go into your Customization settings, click the Customize button next to Keyboard shortcuts, and click the Reset All button in the Customize Keyboard dialog box.

WORD CHANGES TEXT MYSTERIOUSLY

As I created a document, I discovered that Word is consistently changing some words or abbreviations as I type. I've checked thoroughly, and I know the text that triggers the change is not in the AutoCorrect list. What's up?

Word is aggressively changing text, using a well-hidden spell-checking option. To stop this behavior, go into your Word Options, and under the Proofing selection, choose AutoCorrect Options, click the AutoCorrect tab, and clear the check mark from the Automatically Use Suggestions from the Spelling Checker box.

WHERE IS THE OFFICE ASSISTANT?

I love coming in and seeing that little paper clip or my Einstein assistant pop-up wiggle around. How do I turn him back on?

Seriously? The Office Assistant has gone the way of the pet rock. It's not really a pet, it really is a rock. The Office Assistant was not very assistive, it was more of an annoying distraction than anything else, and Microsoft has opted for a better Help structure that you can use without being accosted by a cartoon vaudeville act. But if you really must have it, we recommend that you take a paper clip and tape it to your screen in the lower-right corner.

RIBBON COMMANDS

It was here a minute ago! I changed my screen resolution, went back into Word, and I cannot find some of my commands! Where are they?

The Ribbon is optimized for a 1024 × 768 resolution (if maximized on the screen). If your resolution makes for too small a space or you don't have your application opened to maximize, the icons shrink down and rearrange. This can make it very difficult for you to find the options that were once right before your eyes.

The solution is either to maximize the application again or change your resolution. But if neither of these options is possible, you are going to have to get used to seeing the options as they are. You can hover your mouse over an option to see what it is with a ScreenTip.

2

SECRETS OF THE OFFICE MASTERS: CREATING THE ULTIMATE OFFICE WORKING ENVIRONMENT

Throughout this chapter, we have discussed a variety of options and tips on how to work with Office 2007. But to truly be a master in the Office world, you first have to establish your environment, your "way," as it were. Just like some people have a routine they go through before they begin a job (for example, chefs make sure they have all their cooking tools for the meal at hand, and artists have their brushes), you need to prepare your environment.

Here is how we would start:

Begin with one application—Word, for example—and start there. To begin with, pick a color scheme for your Office environment. You have three to choose from: Blue, Silver, and Black. To do this, go to your Word Options off the Office button. On the Popular tab, you can determine the Color scheme. Remember, this scheme carries with you into all the other applications.

Next, take a look at your ribbons and make sure you have a clear view of all your commands. If you can adjust your screen resolution to make sure your applications give you the full view of command options, this would be the most productive structure.

Move your Quick Access Toolbar below your ribbon. To do this, select the down-arrow next to your toolbar and choose Show Below the Ribbon. This is just an opinion, of course, and you don't have to move it, but keep in mind that this will bring your commands that much closer to you and will give you the enlarged toolbar to keep adding commands, without cluttering up the heading itself.

Customize your Quick Access Toolbar. Microsoft starts you off with a standard set of options. Choose the options you know you'll need, and then go hunting for those that are either missing from the ribbons, or that you know you will need more often, even if they already have a place on the ribbon.

NOTE

You may not see immediately what the big deal is with setting up this toolbar, but consider the following: It's your only act of liberty in setting up your environment. Office 2007 is not like other Office versions that allowed you to change toolbars and menus, even changing the appearance of buttons or making your own buttons. Microsoft has decided to take a stand on how they want the applications to look, and the Quick Access Toolbar is the only liberty you have. Where it benefits you to use it involves commands that you know you need. For example, suppose you love using the Format Painter tool. You use it all the time. Well, it's on the Home tab. So, every time you want to use it, no matter what tab you are working off of, you have to go back to the Home tab (or select it from your right-click toolbar). By putting it on the Quick Access Toolbar, it become easily accessible, regardless of the ribbon you are on. Other good examples are the Print Preview options that are buried under the Office button, under the Print settings. You can bring it right to the top.

Keep in mind that each application will have its own Quick Access Toolbar, so you will need to configure the toolbar in each one. In addition, in applications such as Outlook and Publisher that do not use the ribbon interface, you will need to use previous toolbar/menu configuration methods.

Now, turn off the Allow Mini-Toolbar on Selection option. You can do this from your Word Options—Popular settings. Remember, we mentioned earlier that this can get in the way of selecting text and immediately working with it, because this phantom toolbar just shows up without being invited.

You will find additional settings to configure for your work environment over time. But for now, you are ready to get started.

2

CHAPTER **3**

Managing Office Files and Formats

In this chapter

The New File Formats in Office 2007   54

Understanding and Choosing File Formats   54

Setting Up Office File Storage Locations   60

Managing Files and Folders Remotely   62

Creating New Files   63

Using and Customizing Common Dialog Boxes   65

Storing Document Details   67

Searching for Office Files   69

Working with Multiple Files   70

Setting Up Automatic Backup and Recovery Options   70

Troubleshooting   72

Secrets of the Office Masters: Folder Options That Make Your Life Easier   73

THE NEW FILE FORMATS IN OFFICE 2007

If you want to become an Office master, you need to become an expert in file management. Without a sensible file-naming strategy and a clear understanding of where and how Office stores files, you'll quickly be overwhelmed by the sheer number of files that Office programs generate.

Fortunately, Office 2007 integrates well with Windows Explorer, the essential file management tool used throughout the operating system. The common Open and Save As dialog boxes used throughout Office act like mini-Explorer windows, and unlike previous Office versions, the Places bar at the left of these dialog boxes is identical to the one found in other Windows programs.

 What is absolutely new in Office 2007 is the use of an XML-based file format. It's officially called "Microsoft Office XML Format" and applies to all documents created in Word, Excel, and PowerPoint. In the next section, we discuss what the advantages are of this new file format and then later on we talk about how to interoperate with older documents.

UNDERSTANDING AND CHOOSING FILE FORMATS

Before we go over the different files themselves, let's discuss what the benefits are to the new file formats. Here are some of the ones that Microsoft documents:

- **Compact files**—Your files are compressed automatically and can, at times, be between 50 and 75 percent smaller. Basically, a zip format automatically zips the document when you save it and unzips it when you open it again. So, when you send files over email, they are automatically smaller in the new Office XML format without any new utilities needed. Smaller files mean less disk space used on your hard drives, and it also means less bandwidth utilized when files are accessed over the Internet or within your internal network.

- **Damage recovery improvements**—Files are saved in a component-oriented structure. Components are tables, charts, images, or document metadata, for example. So if your table or chart becomes corrupted, this won't affect your ability to open the entire document.

- **Safer Office XML files**—Files saved with the default "x" ending (such as .docx or .pptx) cannot include VBA macros or ActiveX controls. There is another file type, as you can see in the next section, that can contain these macros, but they have an "m" ending (such as .docm or .pptm). This means that you have a sense of safety from these types of macro and ActiveX problems that creep into your network. And antivirus software can easily identify which documents might be problems by the extension alone.

- **Metadata removal**—All the little document properties and comments, for example, that might be personal information or company-only information can now be removed from your documents. You can use a tool called the Document Inspector, which you can configure to search for and remove metadata before sharing that document with another department or others outside your company.

- **Integration**—Saving documents in an open XML format allows other applications to utilize that data. To open an Office file, all you need is a Zip tool and an XML editor.

After all these years, you may be wondering why Microsoft would make this change to an entirely new format—especially one that will absolutely make your newer documents inaccessible from earlier versions of Office. Several years ago, Microsoft made a commitment to the XML industry standard. Office 2003 showed that commitment by including the capability to save files as XML. This is the next step in that move toward an open format and toward handling customer requests for the capability that XML will afford their documents.

You may be wondering what the difference is between the XML in 2007 and the one provided in 2003; the 2007 version includes the zip capability we mention earlier and the modular structure for components of the document.

OFFICE 2007 FILE FORMATS AT A GLANCE

The following tables give a list of all the different file extensions for Word 2007, Excel 2007, and PowerPoint 2007. You can find this list within Microsoft help files, either online or within the integrated online help from any of the Office applications. This chart, however, includes the file formats for the backward-compatible side to Office 2007, which we discuss in a future section. Notice that the new extensions have four letters.

WORD 2007

Type of File	Extension
Document	.docx
Macro-enabled document	.docm
Template	.dotx
Macro-enabled template	.dotm

In addition to these new formats, Word will support opening and saving .doc and .dot files for backward compatibility, along with other options such as .htm files.

EXCEL 2007

Type of File	Extension
Workbook	.xlsx
Macro-enabled workbook	.xlsm
Template	.xltx
Macro-enabled template	.xltm
Non-XML binary workbook	.xlsb
Macro-enabled add-in	.xlam

In addition to these new formats, Excel will support opening and saving .xls and .xlt files for backward compatibility, along with other options such as .htm files.

POWERPOINT 2007

Type of File	Extension
Presentation	.pptx
Macro-enabled presentation	.pptm
Template	.potx
Macro-enabled template	.potm
Macro-enabled add-in	.ppam
Show	.ppsx
Macro-enabled show	.ppsm
Slide	.sldx
Macro-enabled slide	.sldm
Office theme	.thmx

In addition to these new formats, PowerPoint will support opening and saving .ppt and .pot files for backward compatibility, along with other options such as .htm files.

ACCESS 2007 FILE FORMATS

Access 2007 comes with a new file format as well. Now files will have the .accdb file extension. This is more than a simple extension change, but it comes with a variety of enhancements. Keep in mind, though, that if you save your databases in the .accdb format they will not be compatible with earlier versions of Access. Access 2007 does provide the capability to Open and Save databases in the older .mdb format if necessary. You may be asked if you want to save these databases in the new .accdb format, which is encouraged so you can take advantage of the new features. However, if you need these databases to be available to older versions of Access, do not convert them.

SAVING FILES IN ALTERNATE FORMATS

You have the flexibility in Office to open up one kind of file and save it as something else. For example, you can open up an .htm file in Word and save it as a .docx file if you would like. Or you can open a Word file and save it as a text file (.txt).

To do this in applications with the updated ribbon format, open the document you want to save and then select the Office button, move your mouse over Save As, and then choose the option you need. If you want to save your document in one of the more obscure formats, you can choose Other Formats from Word, Excel, or PowerPower.

With Access, you can save documents in older formats, as mentioned earlier, but you cannot save an Access database as a .jpg the way you can with a PowerPoint slide.

From applications that didn't get the updated look, you can save your files in different formats by going to the File menu selection and choosing Save As.

PUBLISHING DOCUMENTS AS PDF AND XPS FILES

One of the latest and greatest features of Office 2007 is the capability for many of the applications to save (or publish) a document as a PDF or XPS file. For anyone who has needed to do this in the past, you already know how frustrating it used to be. But with the free add-in, which you have to download first, you can publish within seconds.

For those of you who may not know what PDF or XPS is, here is a quick review. PDF is a file format that is very common because it takes your document and preserves it for sharing. So you don't have to worry that someone will work on it or make changes; it's already set, all formatting included, for others to read. To read PDF files, you need a reader program, and the most popular is Acrobat Reader, which is free from Adobe. XPS is the XML Paper Specification, which is also a format for sharing documents.

In either case, if you want to save a file in PDF or XPS format, you have to download and install an add-in from Microsoft. It's free, though. Go to Microsoft.com and do a search (or go to the Downloads center and look for) "2007 Microsoft Office Add-in: Microsoft Save as PDF or XPS." It's only a 696KB file. Keep in mind that this add-in is going to enable not only Word, but Access, Excel, PowerPoint, Publisher, and Visio to save documents in the PDF or XPS file format.

For applications that have the updated interface, you select your Office button, choose Save As, and then select PDF or XPS. You could also choose it as an option when you are saving a document normally. For applications such as Publisher or Visio, which haven't received the ribbon overhaul, you go to the File menu and choose Publish as PDF or XPS.

After you make configuration choices for your PDF or XPS file, you can choose Publish to complete the conversion.

→ For a deeper look at converting to PDF in Word 2007, **see** "Secrets of the Office Masters: Saving Files as PDF or XPS " **p. 453**.

USING OFFICE FILES WITH OLDER OFFICE VERSIONS

When you create a new document in Office 2007, you have to consider a few things. Is the document for you only? If you are going to send it to others, what versions of Office are they running? If you have any doubt that they are using Office 2007, you should save your documents in a backward-compatible file format.

If you open a document that has been created in an earlier version of Word (or if you create a new document and save it in a backward-compatible format), the document will be in Compatibility Mode, and you will see this in the title bar of the document, as shown in Figure 3.1.

If you have a document that you have created in the newer file format and you know that to share it with others, you have to convert it to an older version, you may be concerned that you will lose some functionality in the document. This is very possible, especially if you have used special features like the new SmartArt tools. To check what functionality you might lose, go to your Office button, and then to the Prepare options. From here you run the Compatibility Checker.

Figure 3.1
Compatibility Mode ensures that 2007 enhanced features are unavailable.

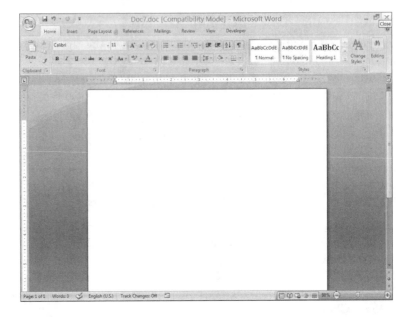

You'll notice in Figure 3.2 that a list of issues will be reported to you so that you can prepare mentally for the lack of functionality, make modifications before saving the document, or choose to avoid the change.

Figure 3.2
The Compatibility Checker gives you a summary of issues with saving files in an older format.

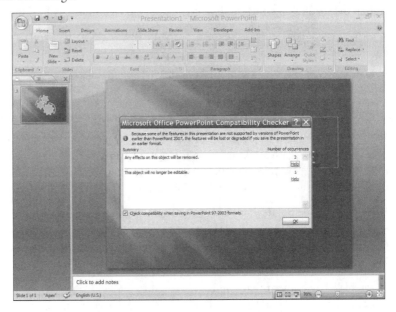

If you would like to work with the newer features, you have to convert your document to the new file format. That will be addressed in the next section.

3

TIP FROM

We keep saying that you cannot open an Office 2007 document in an older version of Office. This is accurate, by default. However, you can download and install Office Compatibility Packs (http://www.microsoft.com/office/preview/beta/converter.mspx) that will allow you to open the XML file formats in Office 2000/XP or 2003 applications. If you download this Compatibility Pack and then open the document, you won't have complete functionality. But you will be able to at least open it, edit a few items (not all, depending on how complicated the document is), and save those files. After they are saved, if you open them again in Office 2007, all the functionality will return.

CONVERTING AND IMPORTING FILES BETWEEN OFFICE PROGRAMS

There is an actual Convert button that will help you to move your files into Office 2007. If you have a document that is in Compatibility Mode and you want to convert it, select your Office button and choose Convert. The dialog box shown in Figure 3.3 appears and gives you instructions on moving forward. You select OK, and the document is converted to the new format.

Figure 3.3
The conversion process is simple and the benefits are broad.

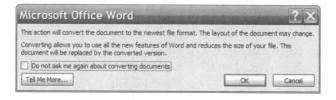

TIP FROM

Initially, after converting your document, you might not notice anything different. Even the `.doc` extension for your document might be left in the document bar. But if you close the document and open it again, you will see that the document is now in the `.docx` format.

Now, you might not want to convert the document, but save it as another file altogether (this way, you have a copy of the original format). To do this, choose Save As and select the new file format up at the top.

USING OFFICE PROGRAMS TO CREATE AND EDIT WEB PAGES

Saving your documents as web pages is a very easy task in Office applications. You can select the Office button and hover your mouse over Save As. Then choose Other Formats, find the `.htm/.html` formats, and save the document. You can see the results if you open the web page in your web browser.

TIP FROM

Word 2007 now has a Blog feature that can help you to post your blog thoughts to the Web. To learn more about this, go to Chapter 13 under the section, "Secrets of the Office Masters: Using Word as a Blog Editor."

SETTING UP OFFICE FILE STORAGE LOCATIONS

Office 2007 works especially well in the typical well-connected office, making it easy to store and retrieve Office files in a variety of locations. You might keep some files on your local hard disk, others on a network file server, and still others on a web server with Microsoft Windows SharePoint Services installed. In an environment this complex, having a well-thought-out storage system is the only way to stay organized.

MANAGE FILES LOCALLY

Microsoft introduced the My Documents folder in Windows 95. The idea was simple: to create a default location for personal data files, making it easier for users to find and back up files they create. In practice, however, the first implementations of this idea were poorly thought out, and most expert Office users ignored the My Documents icon on the desktop—or quickly figured out how to delete it.

Since its first appearance in 1995, the My Documents folder has evolved into a standard feature of Windows. In Windows 2000 and Windows XP, the My Documents icon—located near the top of the Windows Explorer hierarchy, just below the desktop—isn't actually a folder at all; instead, it is a system shortcut that points to a standard location in your personal profile. By default, the Open and Save As dialog boxes used throughout Office applications start out in the My Documents folder, and this system shortcut is also hard-wired to one of the large icons on the Places bar in those dialog boxes.

NOTE

In Windows Vista, the My Documents folder has been renamed Documents. My Computer has also been renamed Computer. In this chapter, we will continue to refer to My Documents, but keep in mind that if you are working on a Vista system, some of these names have changed, but the underlying functionality remains the same.

The My Documents icon on the desktop, in Windows Explorer windows and on the Windows XP Start menu, is actually a *shell extension*—a virtual folder like the My Computer and Network Neighborhood or My Network Places icons, not an actual physical location. Opening this shortcut opens the folder that's registered as the current user's My Documents location. The exact physical location of the My Documents folder varies, depending on which Windows version you have installed and whether it was a clean installation or an upgrade. On most computers running Windows 2000 and XP, the My Documents folder appears in your user profile, normally `C:\Documents and Settings\<username>\My Documents`. On computers running Vista, it resides under `C:\Users\<username>\Documents`.

Advanced Office users might cringe at the name of the My Documents folder, but if you currently store data files in other locations and you're willing to reorganize your storage system, you can substantially increase the odds that you'll find files you're looking for when you need them. Doing so also makes it easier to back up data files.

You can change the default location that individual Office programs use for data files; it's also possible to point the My Documents shortcut to another location. (If the name bugs you, just change it, or you could update to Vista and you might just find that you miss the "My" part. Now you might think, "Well, if they aren't my documents and this isn't "My Computer," then whose is it?)

To move the My Documents folder to a new location, right-click My Documents (or Documents in Vista), go into Properties, and on the target tab (or the Location tab, shown in Figure 3.4), click Move, and then click OK or Apply. If you want to leave all your documents in their current location and point the My Documents folder to a new location, enter the full path to that folder in the Target box and click OK. To rename the My Documents folder, open Windows Explorer, right-click the My Documents icon, and choose Rename from the shortcut menu. Renaming the shortcut doesn't change the actual name of the folder that it points to.

Figure 3.4
Moving the location of the My Documents (Documents) folder.

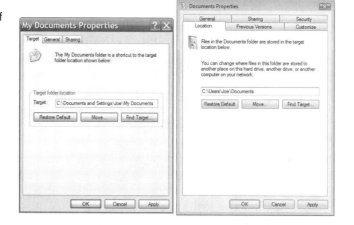

Finally, you can change the default working folder for any individual Office application, although the exact procedure is slightly different, depending on the program you're working with. Why would you want to reset the default working folder? If you're working on an extended project that requires constant access to files on a shared network folder, for example, you might want to define that location as the default working folder; whenever you choose File, Open or File, Save As, the dialog box will display the contents of this folder. Follow these steps, for example, to adjust the default document folder in Word: go into the Word Options from the Office button. On the Save settings dialog box, notice the Default file location setting. You can choose Browse and find a new location.

Follow the same basic procedure for Excel, PowerPoint, Publisher, and Access, with the following exceptions: Excel and PowerPoint don't have Browse buttons to find the location you want. Access does have the Browse button, but the settings are not on the Save settings dialog box (which doesn't exist in Access) but on the Popular settings dialog box.

The default file location setting for each application is independent. If you set Word's default Documents folder to a location on your network, for example, Excel and PowerPoint continue to open to the default location—typically the local My Documents folder.

Logically, you can save your files wherever you like. The default settings may make life easier, but essentially, when you go to save, you are asked where you want to put that document. At that time, you can determine the location. However, especially for larger projects or projects that require collaboration with others, you will want to put these files up on a server and maybe use a special set of services to assist in collaboration.

MANAGING FILES AND FOLDERS REMOTELY

Office 2007 lets you work with files over a network or on the Web in much the same way that you access files and folders on a standalone PC. If you are connected to a network, contact your network administrator to find locations on the network where you're permitted to read or write files. You should get a network share address for the location, using *UNC syntax* (*Server_name**Share_Name*\). Unless the network administrator has restricted your rights, you can create and manage your own subfolders in this location.

Although you can type UNC-style network addresses directly from within Open or Save As dialog boxes, doing so is usually more trouble than it's worth. For easier access, browse to the My Network Places (in Vista, just Network) folder and navigate to the correct server, share, and folder.

Aside from the additional navigation steps, there is no difference between using network shares and using local drives, assuming that you have proper authorization from your network administrator.

Using the UNC path that you are given, if you know how to, you can map a drive letter that's available on your system to a network folder. The concept is this: You have a C: drive, a D: drive, and so on. You can tell the computer that your G: drive (or whatever letter you have available, usually starting from Z backward to make sure it really is available) is now going to be such-and-such server and such-and-such folder (essentially the UNC path of \\servername\share). You do this by right-clicking the My Network Places (or Network in Vista), selecting Map Network Drive, and then putting in the information. You can choose to have this connection occur every time you reconnect.

STORING FILES ON THE WEB OR AN INTRANET

Storing files on the Web—whether to a web server or to an FTP server—is almost as simple as working with files on a local network. You can usually open a web-based file by copying the URL from your web browser's Address box and pasting it into the File Name box on the Office program's Open dialog box. On servers that support the Web-based Distributed Authoring and Versioning (WebDAV) standard, you need only the URL for the location (for example, `http://www.example.com/someplace` or `ftp://example.com/incoming`) and logon credentials (a username and password) to save files to that location. In Windows Explorer, collections of documents on a WebDAV-compatible server appear as folder icons in the My Network Places folder. (In previous Windows and Office versions, this feature was known as *Web folders*.)

To save a file to a web server or an FTP site on the Internet or an intranet, choose File, Save As, and click the My Network Places icon in the Places bar. If the list of available network places includes the location you want to use, double-click it and then enter a filename. If the location does not have an icon in the My Network Places folder, enter the full URL for the location and then fill in your logon credentials when prompted.

NOTE

> From a technical standpoint, there are almost no differences between publishing to an intranet web server and publishing to one on the Internet. The format of the URL that you use likely will be different—intranet servers are typically identified with a one-word name (such as `http://marketing`) rather than a fully qualified domain name (such as `http://www.example.com`). You'll likely encounter different security issues, including password-protected logons and possibly disk quotas (which limit the amount of disk space a user can fill with web content) on both types of server.

SAVE DOCUMENTS TO A SHAREPOINT SERVER

Some editions of Office XP included an add-on called SharePoint Team Services. An updated version of this software, Windows SharePoint Services, is included with Microsoft Windows 2003 Server. Microsoft sells a more powerful version of this collaboration platform, called SharePoint Portal Server, for use on large networks. With a SharePoint server available (usually on an intranet), co-workers can share and discuss files on a web server, using an attractive web-based front end.

Office 2007 integrates exceptionally well with SharePoint servers. Depending on how the SharePoint administrator has configured the network, you can access SharePoint document libraries directly from Office common dialog boxes. Storing an Office document on a SharePoint server also allows Office 2007 users to take advantage of a number of collaborative functions.

→ For more details on how to use SharePoint services with Office 2007, **see**, "Office Collaboration and SharePoint," **p. 908**.

To save documents to a SharePoint site, you use the Publish options located off the Office button and then choose Document Management Server.

CREATING NEW FILES

When you choose the Office button and then select New in an Office 2007 program, the New Document, New Workbook, New Presentation, New Publication, or New File task pane opens (the exact name varies, depending on the Office program in use). As Figure 3.5 illustrates, these task panes are simpler and less cluttered than their predecessors. Choose an option from the Templates block at the top of the task pane to create a blank document (or blog post) or to create a new workbook, database, or presentation from an existing file. There are standard templates, and those that have been used recently show up. Or select from the templates available from Microsoft Office Online, where you can look for custom templates that match the needs of your current project.

Figure 3.5
Every Office program offers a variation of this task pane, which gives you options for creating a new blank file or one based on existing content.

Templates are stored in different locations depending on the template, as noted below:

- The default collection of Office templates is stored in a subfolder that corresponds to the system's current language settings; on a default U.S. English installation, this is %programfiles%\Microsoft Office\Templates\1033. All users of the current system see these templates.

- Each user's custom templates are stored in the location specified for User Templates. By default, this is %appdata%\Microsoft\Templates. The actual location can be changed in Word's File Locations dialog box. You go into the Word Options, to the Advanced settings dialog box, and then to the File Locations button. Choose to Modify the location for these files.

- If you've used Word's File Locations dialog box to specify a Workgroup Templates folder, Office displays templates from this location in the New dialog box as well. If a template in the Workgroup Templates location and one in the User Templates location have the same name, the Office program displays and uses only the one from the User Templates location.

> **NOTE**
>
> The default Office installation does not install all available templates; instead, you'll find shortcuts to some templates in the task pane and the New dialog box. The first time you use one of these templates, Office attempts to install the supporting files.

 If you're having trouble finding templates that you've saved, see "Putting Templates in Their Place" in the "Troubleshooting" section at the end of this chapter.

→ For more details on how to install templates and other Office components, **see** "Adding and Removing Office Features," **p. 937**.

Although you can manage the contents of template folders in an Explorer window, the easiest and safest way to make new templates available to an Office program is to save the file in Template format.

USING AND CUSTOMIZING COMMON DIALOG BOXES

The Open and Save As dialog boxes used throughout Office have a series of shortcut icons on the left side, called the Places bar (see Figure 3.6), designed to speed navigation through common file locations. As we noted earlier in this chapter, the Office version of the Places bar looks identical to the one available in the common Open and Save As dialog boxes found in other Windows programs. However, with a small amount of effort, you can easily customize the Office version. The default icons are as follows:

Figure 3.6
Customize the Places bar by adding shortcuts to commonly used data folders. To see more choices, use the Small Icons option.

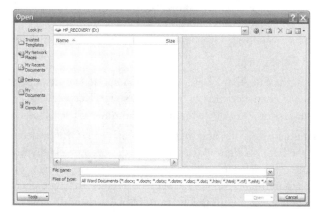

3

- My Recent Documents—Opens the Recent folder, which contains shortcuts to files and folders that you've worked with. When you click this icon from within an Office program, Office displays only shortcuts appropriate to the application you're using.

NOTE

Don't confuse the Office Recent folder with the Windows system folder of the same name. Office manages a separate Recent folder for each user profile on a system. To manage the Office shortcuts from an Explorer window, enter `%appdata%\Microsoft\Office\Recent` in the Run dialog box or in the Address bar of an Explorer window.

TIP FROM

Ed & Woody

The Tweak UI utility allows you to turn off tracking of recently used files throughout Windows; its settings affect all Office programs. For more information on Tweak UI and to download the utility, go to http://www.microsoft.com/windowsxp/downloads/powertoys/xppowertoys.mspx.

To clear the Most Recently Used Files (MRU) list for all Office programs, fire up Registry Editor (Regedit.exe) and navigate to HKEY_CURRENT_USER\Software\Microsoft\Office\12.0\Common\Open Find. Delete the entire Open Find subkey to remove all MRU lists for all Office programs. Office will begin building a new set of MRU lists the next time you use an Office program. This procedure is documented in detail in Knowledge Base article 826208, http://support.microsoft.com/kb/826208. Although the article itself discusses previous versions of Office (XP and 2003), the same registry key exists for 2007.

- **Desktop**—Opens or saves files on the Windows desktop. Use the desktop as a holding area when you want to create a file and move it elsewhere using Windows Explorer. Using the desktop as a permanent storage area is generally a bad idea because most Office applications have a tendency to create temporary files in the same location as the file you're working with. Those temporary files disappear when you close down the original file.

- **My Documents**—Opens the personal data folder for the user currently logged on. As noted earlier in this chapter, Windows allows you to change the target folder that Office opens when you click this icon.

- **My Computer**—Displays icons for local drives and document folders.

- **My Network Places**—Lets you manage files stored in shared folders on your network, an FTP server, or on WebDAV-compatible servers.

In Open and Save dialog boxes, Office includes two features that make it easier to find a file by name:

- As you type in the File Name box, the AutoComplete feature suggests the first name that matches the characters that you've typed so far. Keep typing, or press Enter to accept the suggestion. Note that the list of files does not scroll as you type.

- If you click in the list of files and then type a character, Office selects the first file that begins with the letter or number that you typed. If you quickly type several characters in rapid succession, the selection moves to the first file that begins with those characters. If you pause for more than a second between characters, this type-ahead feature resets. Note that as you select files in this fashion, Office does not fill in the File Name box.

To adjust the display of files in the Open and Save As dialog boxes, use the Views button. The drop-down arrow lets you choose from a list of views, or you can click the button to cycle through the following icon arrangements:

- Thumbnails, Tiles, Icons, and List views mirror their counterparts in Windows Explorer.

- Details view displays size, file type, and other information. Click any heading to sort the list by that category.

- Properties displays summary information about the selected document in the right half of the dialog box.

- Preview displays a thumbnail version of the document in the right half of the dialog box as you move from file to file in the list. In general, you should avoid this option because of the performance penalty you pay: As you scroll through a dialog box, the program that you're working with has to open each file. Find an import filter, if necessary, and generate the preview. Switch to this view when you want to quickly verify that the file you're about to open is the correct one, and then switch back to List or Details view after peeking at the file.

- WebView uses an HTML template to display files stored in a SharePoint document library.

Some files, especially certain Excel worksheets, can't be seen in the Preview pane. For suggestions on the possible reasons, see "No Preview in Common Dialog Boxes," in the "Troubleshooting" section at the end of this chapter.

TIP FROM

ExDe Woody

To manage files in Open and Save As dialog boxes, select the filename and right-click. Shortcut menus here work the same as they do in an Explorer window. You can move, copy, delete, or rename a file, for example, as long as the file you select is not currently open.

The Places bar can be customized to make it easier and faster to get to frequently used folders. To add your own folders to the Places bar, select the icon for the folder that you want to add, and then right-click in the Places bar and choose to Add or Remove it from the Places bar. (You can't rename or delete the five default locations on the Places bar.) Keep in mind that you select the folder and then right-click in the Places bar in a grey part of the bar.

TIP FROM

ExDe Woody

If you add more icons than can be displayed in the Places bar, small scroll arrows appear at the top and bottom of the list. You can see more icons in the Places bar if you right-click it and choose Small Icons. Put no more than 15 locations in the Places bar; with any more, you'll spend too much time scrolling.

To rearrange folders in the Places bar, right-click an icon that you want to move, and choose Move Up or Move Down.

NOTE

Changes you make to the Places bar apply to all Office programs.

STORING DOCUMENT DETAILS

The Windows file system keeps track of details about each file: its size, when it was created, and when you last modified it, for example. Windows enables you to store extra details about Office file types; these *properties* include the author's name, a title and a subject for the file, and comments or keywords that you can use to search for documents later. A Custom properties sheet lets you track more than two dozen built-in categories or add your own.

Maintaining file properties takes a fair amount of up-front work, but it can have a profound payoff, especially in a networked office where many users share documents.

To view and edit the properties of a file currently open in an Office program, go to your Office button, select Prepare and choose Properties. Initially you will see a subset of properties, but you can select the down arrow and choose Advanced Properties to add more detail (as shown in Figure 3.7).

Figure 3.7
The Properties dialog box displays summary information about Office file types.

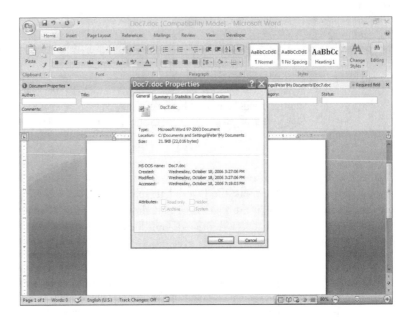

The Properties dialog box for an Office file includes the five tabs described in Table 3.1.

TABLE 3.1   OFFICE FILE PROPERTIES

Properties	Description
General	Basic information from the Windows file system: name, location, size, and so on.
Summary	Information about the current file and its author, including fields for company name, category, and keywords. The Comments field is particularly useful when you use Outlook's file management capabilities because the text appears beneath each filename when you turn on AutoPreview.
Statistics	Details about the size and structure of the file, such as the number of words in a document or the number of slides in a presentation; also displays revision statistics and total editing time. This tab is not visible when inspecting file properties from within Windows Explorer; instead, the information is displayed on the Summary tab. This information is frequently incorrect, especially when you inspect it from within an Explorer window. Professional writers and students who rely on these statistics should always inspect them from within the document itself to guarantee that the information is up-to-date.
Contents	The parts of the file: the outline of a Word document, based on heading styles; worksheet titles in an Excel workbook; or slide titles in a PowerPoint presentation. This tab is not visible when inspecting file properties from within Windows Explorer.

Properties	Description
Custom	Twenty-seven built-in fields that you can choose from, including Client, Document Number, and Date Completed. Alternatively, you can add a field of your own. Custom fields can contain text, dates, numbers, or Yes/No information; they can also be linked to Word bookmarks, named Excel ranges, or PowerPoint text selections

NOTE

You can inspect most Office file properties by right-clicking a filename in Windows Explorer and choosing Properties from the shortcut menu. Information in this dialog box is arranged differently from what you see within an Office program, and many properties are not available when the file is open for editing. For data files located on a disk formatted with the NTFS file system, you'll see an additional tab that contains security settings.

For simple projects, you might choose to ignore file properties; in these cases, a descriptive filename can tell you everything you need to know about the file. For more complicated documents, however, adding file details—including keywords and categories—can help you or a co-worker quickly find a group of related data files, even months or years after you last worked with them. Use the Comments box to add freeform notes about a given file.

To enter additional details about an Office file, you must open the Properties dialog box before you save the file. If you use this feature regularly, you can configure Word, Excel, and PowerPoint to display the File Properties dialog box every time you save a file.

SEARCHING FOR OFFICE FILES

The Open dialog box displays a list of all files and subfolders in a single folder. Searching for a specific file can be tedious if the folder is full of files with similar names or if it's organized into many subfolders. To make this task easier, you are going to have to use the operating system integrated search options.

NOTE

In Office 2003, you had the option of using a task pane Search tool. But, in case you are wondering where it is–it has been removed. The reason given was that this feature just wasn't used and the new search features in Outlook 2007 are better, at least for searching email.

WINDOWS DESKTOP SEARCH AND INSTANT SEARCH

A new search tool has been included in Windows Vista (and can be downloaded from Microsoft for Windows XP) called Windows Desktop Search (WDS). This tool provides the following features to enhance your searching capabilities:

- **Fast search capability**—You can now find what you need through your documents and your email in seconds.

- **Multiple file type support**—You can search through various Office documents, images, video, pdf, and so on.

- **Indexing**—The file index is done when the system has idle time so that performance isn't affected.

This search component allows a new feature in Outlook 2007, called Instant Search, to function. This pane is available in Mail, Calendar, Contacts, Tasks, Notes, Folder List, and Journal.

Working with Instant Search will be discussed in the Outlook section of this book.

WORKING WITH MULTIPLE FILES

Word, Excel, PowerPoint, and Publisher allow you to open more than one file at a time. Access does not, and you can't open multiple files directly by using the New File task pane. To open multiple files using the common dialog boxes, follow these steps:

1. Choose the Office button, Open (or press Ctrl+O) to display the Open dialog box.
2. Hold down the Ctrl key and click to select multiple filenames.
3. Click the Open button or press Enter to open all selected files.

To open multiple files from an Explorer window, hold down the Ctrl key and click each icon; then right-click and choose Open.

You can also open any file by dragging its icon from an Explorer window into an Office program window. When you drag an Excel or PowerPoint icon from an Explorer window into an open program window, Office opens the new file in its own window. On the other hand, if you drop a Word icon into an open document window, Word assumes that you want to insert the file at the point where you dropped it. To open the document in a new window instead, drop the icon onto the title bar of the Word program window.

In Office 2007 (as in previous Office versions), each new data file gets its own button on the Windows taskbar, and you can switch between document windows the same way you switch between programs.

SETTING UP AUTOMATIC BACKUP AND RECOVERY OPTIONS

Like its predecessor, Office 2007 comes with "air bags"—a sophisticated set of programs that are designed to make crashes less frequent, to make crashes less devastating when they do occur, and to increase your chances of recovering a document when Office does crash. Following are the important points to keep in mind:

AutoRecover is an option found in most Office programs, whereas AutoSave is in Outlook. These can help you avoid losing your data. The process is quite simple. First, your data is saved automatically if you enable these options. That can really help you out if, for example, you are working for a while and forget to save your document and then the power goes out or your little brother comes alone and spitefully turns over the powerstrip (or, although this should never happen, if your Office crashes).

Along with the data itself, the program state is saved. For example, you might have Excel workbooks open and you are working with multiple windows in a specific layout. When Excel opens up again, the windows should be restored in the same working state. Or course, these are ideal restore possibilities and they may not always work exactly as promised.

In some cases, the recovery procedure will actually repair damage to a file when reopening it. In this case, you can use the drop-down menu to open a dialog box that shows you which repairs were made.

To configure these options depends on the application you are working in. If you are setting them for Word, Excel, or PowerPoint, go to Options and to the Save tab, shown in Figure 3.8. There you can configure the number of minutes between saved documents and the location of the AutoRecover files.

Figure 3.8
Configuring
AutoRecover in Word,
Excel, or PowerPoint
2007.

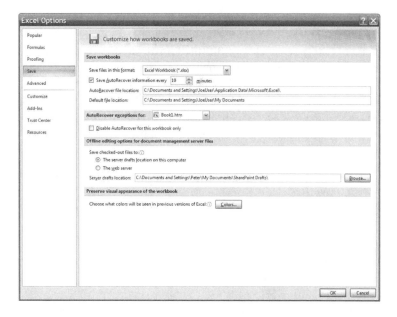

To do the same thing in Outlook, go to the Tools menu, to Options. From there, go to the Preferences tab, select E-mail Options, and then select Advanced E-mail Options. Select the Auto Save Items Every __ Minutes check box and specify the number of minutes you want.

The fewer the number of minutes you choose, the more frequently the recovery file is saved.

TROUBLESHOOTING

PUTTING TEMPLATES IN THEIR PLACE

I created a group of templates and saved them along with the standard Office templates in the %programfiles%\Microsoft Office\Templates\1033 folder. But when I choose File, New, none of my custom templates are visible.

Microsoft designed the folder that stores system templates so that users cannot add templates to it. Instead, you should save your templates to the default User Templates location. The safest way to save templates to this location is one at a time. If you choose Template from the Files of Type list in the Save As dialog box, all Office programs will save your work to the correct location. If you want to add a large number of files to this location, open Word, and under your Word Options on the Advanced settings dialog box, go down to the bottom and select the File Locations button and verify the location of your User Templates to make sure they will be put in the right location.

COMPATIBILITY ISSUES

I just created a PowerPoint presentation, saved it, and emailed it to a friend. My friend says the presentation will not open. What can I do?

Remember that the new Office 2007 file formats do not, by default, allow for backward compatibility. There are a couple of ways you can make it so that your friend can open the document. You could save the document in the 97–2003 file format and re-send it. You could encourage your friend to download the Office Compatibility Pack, which will open documents in the new format. Or your friend could just install Office 2007. It is the future, albeit that's probably the most expensive solution.

NO PREVIEW IN COMMON DIALOG BOXES

I selected Preview from the drop-down menu of views in an Office common dialog box, but when I click a file in the pane on the left, Windows displays the words `Preview not available` instead of showing my file.

The Preview pane shows a static snapshot of the document as it existed the last time you saved it. By default, this option is not selected because it tends to add roughly 60KB to every file that you create. To make this preview picture available, you must go into your Advanced Document Properties. Select the Office button, go to Prepare, and select the Properties option. Then you select the down arrow to get into Advanced Properties. On the Summary tab, select the Save Preview Picture box. You can do this at any time with a Word document or PowerPoint presentation. However, this option is effective with Excel workbooks only if you use it when you first create the file. Checking this box on an Excel workbook after you've saved it with this option off has no effect at all. To enable the preview, select the Save Preview Picture check box and save the file under a new name. Then close the file and use Windows Explorer to delete the old version and rename the new one with the old name.

SECRETS OF THE OFFICE MASTERS: FOLDER OPTIONS THAT MAKE YOUR LIFE EASIER

In common dialog boxes, trying to use information in the Type column is an exercise in frustration. Making all file extensions visible is a crude solution to this problem, but Explorer windows don't allow you to sort by this information anyway.

So here's a better idea: Regain control of the file types that you use most often, removing the useless Microsoft tag at the beginning of each one and making extensions visible for selected file types, such as HTML documents, where you might want to edit that change on demand.

Open any Windows Explorer window (the My Documents or My Computer folder is a good choice), choose Tools, Folder Options, and then click the File Types tab. Scroll through the list of registered file types until you reach the Microsoft block, and begin editing each file type. Select a file type (Microsoft Office Excel Worksheet, for example) and click the Advanced button. In the Edit File Type dialog box, remove the unnecessary "Microsoft" from the file type name. Click the Always Show Extension box to ensure that .xlsx extensions are always visible (and editable) in Explorer windows.

Repeat this process for other file types, such as Microsoft Word Document and Microsoft Office Document Imaging File. Now, when you use Details view, you'll really see the details that matter.

3

CHAPTER 4

CREATING, EDITING, AND FORMATTING DOCUMENTS

In this chapter

Working With Documents in Office 2007   76

Entering Text   76

Selecting Text   80

Finding and Replacing Text   82

Converting Scanned Documents to Text   84

Using AutoCorrect to Speed Up Text Entry   86

Using the Office Clipboard   92

Using and Managing Fonts   94

Working with Hyperlinks   98

Undoing and Repeating Changes   99

Troubleshooting   100

Secrets of the Office Masters: Working with Speech Recognition in Windows Vista   100

WORKING WITH DOCUMENTS IN OFFICE 2007

In Office 2007, the basic collection of tools and techniques for entering and formatting text are essentially unchanged from previous versions. In this chapter, we explain how to enter characters you won't find on the keyboard, how to select text quickly and accurately, and the best ways to find and replace text in every Office program. We also dig into the sometimes confusing minutiae of the AutoCorrect feature.

ENTERING TEXT

Most Office users don't think about entering text until they encounter a character that's not part of their daily repertoire: a currency symbol such as ¥, perhaps, or a Greek character such as π.

In fact, Office 2007 contains full support for the *Unicode standard*, a universally recognized character set containing tens of thousands of letters, ideographs, and other symbols, which spans the majority of all written languages. If the operating system you are using supports the characters used in a specific language, those characters are available in Office.

INSERTING SYMBOLS AND SPECIAL CHARACTERS

Office supports three relatively easy methods to place a single symbol or other special character in an Office document:

- Your first stop should be the Symbol dialog box. Choose the Insert tab, and select Symbol, and then choose a symbol in the gallery or select More Symbols, where you will see the symbols dialog box to scroll through a comprehensive and easy-to-use list of every character available in normal or decorative fonts (see Figure 4.1).

Figure 4.1
The Symbols dialog box makes it easy to insert a symbol or a special character.

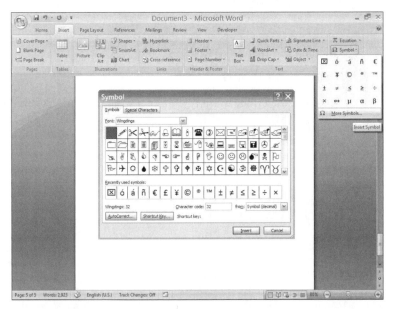

TIP FROM

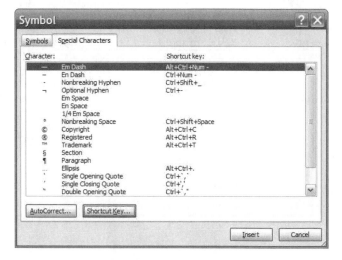

When you click a symbol, a short description of the character, as well as its character code, appears at the bottom of the Symbol dialog box. Most characters include a keyboard shortcut, typically triggered by holding down the Alt key while entering a four-digit numeric ANSI code from the numeric keypad (the numbers on the top row of the keyboard do not work for these shortcuts). Although these shortcuts are usable in any Windows program, the shortcut hint is visible only when you open the Symbol dialog box in Word.

NOTE

After you insert a character, the Symbol dialog box remains open so that you can insert additional characters, if necessary. To dismiss this dialog box, press Esc or click Close (X) or Cancel.

- The Special Characters tab in the Symbol dialog box (see Figure 4.2) gives you quick access to the most common punctuation characters (also known as *special characters*). The tab is available only in Word, Outlook, and Excel. If you are tired of scrolling through the Symbol dialog box's detailed lists, this is the place to turn. The shortcut-key reminders are visible in Word only.

Figure 4.2
The Special Characters tab includes only a small subset of the characters listed on the Symbols tab, but the ones that are there are easier to find.

Character:		Shortcut key:
—	Em Dash	Alt+Ctrl+Num -
–	En Dash	Ctrl+Num -
-	Nonbreaking Hyphen	Ctrl+Shift+_
¬	Optional Hyphen	Ctrl+-
	Em Space	
	En Space	
	1/4 Em Space	
°	Nonbreaking Space	Ctrl+Shift+Space
©	Copyright	Alt+Ctrl+C
®	Registered	Alt+Ctrl+R
™	Trademark	Alt+Ctrl+T
§	Section	
¶	Paragraph	
…	Ellipsis	Alt+Ctrl+.
'	Single Opening Quote	Ctrl+`,`
'	Single Closing Quote	Ctrl+','
"	Double Opening Quote	Ctrl+`,`"

AutoCorrect...   Shortcut Key...

Insert   Cancel

- If you know that you're going to be using a specific symbol or special character repeatedly, set up an AutoCorrect entry for it by clicking the AutoCorrect button on the Symbol dialog box in Word, or by going into your advanced Options off the Office button menu, then to the Proofing settings and choosing AutoCorrect Options. For example, if you use the ¥ (Japanese Yen) symbol frequently, tell Office to AutoCorrect the two characters Y= to ¥. The entry will work in Outlook, Word, Excel, Publisher, or PowerPoint.

→ To learn more about saving and reusing text, **see** "Using AutoCorrect to Speed Up Text Entry," **p. 86**.

NOTE

To find various dashes, "curly" quotes, daggers, ellipses, and many more common marks quickly, open the Symbol dialog box and choose General Punctuation from the Subset list on the Symbols tab. Keep in mind that, depending on the font you have selected, you may not see a subset tab. So you may have to change the font option.

When it comes to inserting symbols into your documents, you have many more choices. For example, you can use the Windows Character Map applet (Charmap.exe), or you can click the buttons on the Word version of the Symbol dialog to create AutoCorrect entries or shortcut keys. You can write a macro in any Office application that inserts a specific character. You can also choose from an endless assortment of management utilities designed for general-purpose use with Windows

Entering Accented and International Characters

If you use the U.S. English version of Office 2007 and you have only occasional need for an accented, inflected, or otherwise altered character common in European languages, Word and Outlook recognize the shortcuts in Table 4.1.

TABLE 4.1 Word and Outlook's Accented Character Shortcuts

To Type Any of These Accented Characters	First, Press This Key Command	Then Type the Desired Letter
ÀàÈèÌìÒòÙù	Ctrl+`	AaEeIiOoUu
Áá´D´dÉéÍíÓóÚúÝý	Ctrl+'	AaDdEeIiOoUuYy
Ââ êÎîÔôÛû	Ctrl+Shift+^	AaEeIiOoUu
ÄäËëÏïÖöÜüŸÿ	Ctrl+Shift+:	AaEeIiOoUuYy
ÃãÑñÕõ	Ctrl+Shift+~	AaNnOo
ÆæŒœß	Ctrl+Shift+&	AaOos
Çç	Ctrl+,	Cc
Åå	Ctrl+Shift+@	Aa
Øø	Ctrl+/	Oo

To enter an inverted question mark or exclamation point (¿, ¡) for use with Spanish text, press Alt+Ctrl+Shift+? or Alt+Ctrl+Shift+!.

NOTE

When entering text in Spanish, if you have configured Word to use Spanish as the background language, the inverted question mark will come up automatically if you put a regular question mark symbol at the beginning of a sentence.

Entering Text Through Speech Recognition

With each passing year, speech recognition technology improves. This exciting capability is still in its infancy, however, and Office's implementation (in previous versions) only underscores that fact. Speech recognition can be a godsend to those who are physically challenged; however, text input using dictation rates as little more than a novelty to serious Office users.

In previous versions of Office, Microsoft had speech recognition technology included. However, starting with Office 2007, we rely on the Operating System to provide us with that capability. Both XP and Vista have speech recognition capabilities built in.

Entering Text in Another Language

Office interprets the keys on your keyboard according to the conventions established inside Windows. To change the mapping of keys to characters in XP, use the Control Panel's Regional and Language applet: Click Start, Settings, Control Panel, select the Regional and Language applet, and then click the Languages tab. Select the Details button and then, from the "Text Services and Input Languages" dialog, you can choose to Add alternative keyboard layouts.

Note: To do the same thing in Vista, go into Control Panel, under Clock, Language and Region, and select Change Keyboards or other input methods (unless you are in Classic view for your Control Panel). Then you select Regional Language Options and select the Keyboards and Languages tab (see Figure 4.3).

Figure 4.3
In Vista, depending on the view you have selected for Control Panel, you can change your keyboard settings to input other languages.

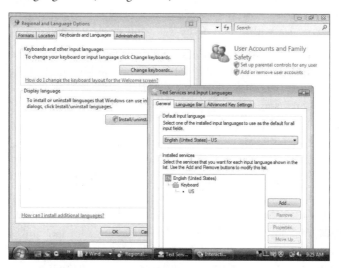

When you switch keyboards, Word automatically switches fonts to those that are designed for the language, and it sets the proofing language for spell checking and grammar checking. This is the way recommended by Microsoft to manage enabled languages. However, you can also consider looking into the 2007 Microsoft Office Tools for the Language Setting options.

TIP FROM

Ed & Woody

If you want your Office ribbons to display text and option information in another language, you have to install a Language Pack for that particular language for your Office applications. You can purchase a Language Pack from Microsoft Office Online. You can also download a free Language Interface Pack (LIP) to get an interface in another language. However, a Language Pack isn't necessary to type or enter text in another language.

Some languages require additional tools. Arabic, Hebrew, and Farsi, for example, need *bidirectional support*, because they are input and read from right to left. Ideographic languages need the Microsoft Input Method Editor to make it possible to type "text" (ideograms) at all. (*Ideograms*, the cornerstone of several written Asian languages, are symbols more related to ideas or things than to a spoken sound. Ideographic languages are notoriously difficult to input into a computer because they typically contain thousands of "characters.") For more details, consult the online Help topic "About Multilingual Features in Office."

SELECTING TEXT

Text selection is one of the most fundamental of Office activities, but the specific techniques used in each program vary widely. In fact, mastering the different shortcuts each Office application uses to handle text selection is a key step on the road to becoming an Office master.

When you select text with a mouse, the following shortcuts apply:

- Double-clicking a word selects the word in all Office applications. In the text-centered Office programs—Outlook, Word, PowerPoint, and Publisher—double-clicking also selects the word's trailing space(s), if any; in Excel and Access, it does not. That can be somewhat confusing when switching between applications.

- Triple-clicking selects an entire paragraph in Outlook, Word, PowerPoint, and Publisher. Triple-clicking in Excel does not select an entire cell.

- In Word, moving the mouse pointer to the left margin changes it from an I-beam insertion point to an arrow that points up and to the right. When you see this pointer, you can click once to select the current line; twice to select the paragraph; or three times to select the entire document. The Outlook email editor has a similar capability.

- In Word, Outlook, Publisher, and PowerPoint, the selection automatically extends to include entire words when you click and drag over more than one word. In all four applications, you can turn this off. In Word and PowerPoint, go into the Options, Advanced settings, and under the Editing section, clear the box marked When Selecting, Automatically Select Entire Word. For Publisher and Outlook, you do this from the Tools, Options dialog box on the Editing tab.

- When working with text boxes in the drawing layer, Office takes on the clicking conventions of the underlying application: Triple-clicking in a paragraph in an Excel text box does nothing; the same action in Word or PowerPoint selects the entire paragraph.

Many advanced Word users—especially proficient typists—prefer to use the keyboard to select characters and words. By memorizing a few simple commands and avoiding the round trip to the mouse, they can plow through text much faster. Keyboard-selection techniques stay fairly uniform throughout Office (see Table 4.2).

TABLE 4.2 KEYBOARD SELECTIONS VALID IN ALL OFFICE PROGRAMS

To Select	Press
Next character to right	Shift+Right Arrow
Next character to left	Shift+Left Arrow
To end of word	Ctrl+Shift+Right Arrow
To beginning of word	Ctrl+Shift+Left Arrow
To end of line	Shift+End
To beginning of line	Shift+Home
Entire document	Ctrl+A

In addition, Outlook and Word have two important shortcuts that experienced users will want to memorize (see Table 4.3). These shortcuts come in handy when you're trying to select blocks of text in large documents, "from this point to the beginning" or "from this point to the end." No menu or toolbar button equivalents exist for either.

TABLE 4.3 KEYBOARD SELECTIONS VALID ONLY IN OUTLOOK AND WORD

To Select	Press
To end of document	Ctrl+Shift+End
To beginning of document	Ctrl+Shift+Home

In Word and Outlook, you can select noncontiguous characters—that is, characters that are not next to each other—by holding down the Ctrl and Shift keys simultaneously as you make your selections. (If you hold down Ctrl when you click, your initial selection extends to a complete sentence.) In Excel, you can select noncontiguous cells the same way. In PowerPoint, you're allowed to select noncontiguous slides. But you can't select noncontiguous text in Excel, PowerPoint, or Publisher.

4

FINDING AND REPLACING TEXT

When you want to find or replace a piece of text in an Office document, the method varies depending on which application you use. To find a particular text string, do the following:

1. On the Home ribbon is an Editing grouping. Choose the Find option. Type the text you want to locate in the Find What box. Word's Find and Replace dialog box is shown in Figure 4.4.

Figure 4.4
Word has the most comprehensive Find and Replace options.

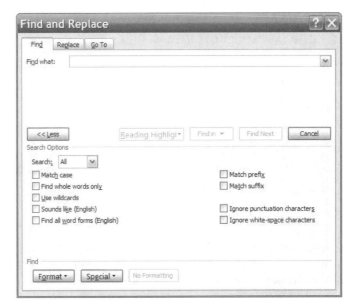

2. Set up the parameters, known as *criteria*, for your search. Depending on which Office application you are using, the process of setting up your search criteria will vary.

3. With the find criteria established the way you want, click Find Next, and the application selects the next occurrence of the text.

Here are some criteria considerations:

■ In Outlook, Word, and Access, you can choose whether you want to search Up (toward the beginning of the document) or Down (toward the end). (To reach this option in Word, click the More button.) In Excel (see Figure 4.5) or PowerPoint, you have no choice as to direction—the first Find uncovers the first occurrence of the string; subsequent Find Next selections move to later occurrences. In Word and Access, you can choose the Search All option, which finds the first occurrence of your search text in the current document or database object, the same as an Excel or PowerPoint Find.

Figure 4.5
Excel's Find and
Replace is remarkably
different from Word's.

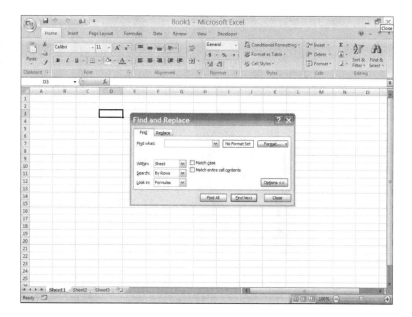

- Excel enables you to choose whether you want to search row-major (Search by Rows going across the current row before dropping down to the next one) or column-major (Search By Columns going down the current column before looking at the next one to the right). Make your choice in the Search box. Excel also enables you to look at formulas or values (that is, formula results). If you have a cell that contains the formula =SUM(A1:B3), for example, searching the formulas for B3 results in a hit, whereas searching the values doesn't.

NOTE

Excel allows you to easily search for text in comments. This feature can come in handy if you're scanning for comments from a specific individual or those that apply to a given topic. To do so, select Comments in the Look In box.

- All the Office applications allow you to specify that you want to Match Case (as in the PowerPoint dialog box shown in Figure 4.6). With this check box selected, the capitalization shown in the Find What text box must match the capitalization of the text in the document precisely to get a "hit."

- Using the Find dialog box in Outlook, Word, and PowerPoint, you can select a check box that restricts the search to Find Whole Words Only. When this option is enabled, the text in the Find What field must appear in the document preceded and followed by a space or punctuation mark: beast, for example, will match beast but not beasts. Excel has a comparable check box that limits hits to cells where the entire cell contents matches the text in the Find What box. Similarly, Access can limit hits to those that match the entire field.

Figure 4.6
PowerPoint's Spartan Find dialog box is limited.

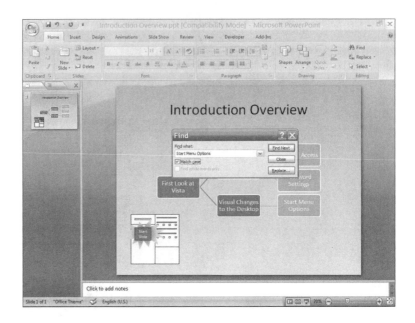

Outlook, Word, Excel, and Access accept wildcards:

- * matches one or more letters. For example, s*ap will turn up hits on snap or strap, but not on sap.

- ? matches one single letter. For example, b?t will match bit or bat, but not boot.

- In Excel only, the tilde character (~) followed by a ~, ?, or * matches ~, ?, or *. So hop~* matches hop*, but not hop? or hope, and tr~?p matches tr?p but not tr*p or tr~p or trip.

Word has an enormous number of additional search features; the other Office applications pale in comparison.

CONVERTING SCANNED DOCUMENTS TO TEXT

Office 2007 includes a surprisingly good optical character recognition (OCR) system that can convert a paper document into a Word file with relative ease. You can scan the document and dump its text directly into Word in a single operation. Or start with a scanned document, perform OCR, and then select some or all of the recognized text to use in any Office program.

NOTE

Windows Fax and Scan is a new feature included in Windows Vista that now embeds these features into the Operating System. You will still want to use third-party tools for their higher level of functionality, but at least you know you have options.

If you have a scanner connected to your PC, use the Microsoft Office Document Scanning utility to scan the document and perform OCR on the resulting TIFF file in one operation. You'll find the Document Scanning program in the Microsoft Office Tools group. If you have trouble locating these, first check your All Programs and then look in your Microsoft Office programs. Sometimes, because there are so many applications, you might miss the extra set of tools. The Scan New Document dialog box (see Figure 4.7) is fairly easy to use: Click the Scanner button to check and, if necessary, adjust the settings of your scanner, and then click the Scan button.

Figure 4.7
When scanning a multi-page paper document, be sure to select the option to prompt for additional pages.

The resulting document includes two components: a graphic representation of the scanned page, in TIFF format, and a version that includes OCR information. The results appear in the Microsoft Office Document Imaging utility. If you have a saved TIFF file, you can open it directly in this program (you'll find its shortcut in the Microsoft Office Tools group as well).

TIP FROM

Options available for the Document Scanning utility depend on your hardware. Some drivers support automatic page feeders; others include the option to "restitch" documents that are printed on both sides of the paper. You scan one side and then the other, and the software puts the two halves together, in sequence. It's a very handy feature.

The Document Imaging utility includes an enormous number of options—too many to describe here. The speed of the OCR engine depends on your system resources, but the results can be exceptional. After performing OCR, you can select a portion of the recognized text, right-click, and copy the selection to the Clipboard as an image or as text. Click the Send Text to Word icon to export just that portion to a new Word document.

We found these tools to be more than adequate to handle almost all your scanned-text needs. But again, your scanner probably came with its own software that offers a few more bells and whistles, if that's what you need. If not, this is a reliable way to move text from a scanned document into Word.

USING AUTOCORRECT TO SPEED UP TEXT ENTRY

No doubt you've seen the result of AutoCorrect when you type a word like *teh* and it comes up *the*. Don't take AutoCorrect's name too literally. Yes, it's true that AutoCorrect watches over you, correcting typos in Outlook or Word—for example, type **isn;t** and AutoCorrect converts it to isn't. But it does much more:

- AutoCorrect also works in Outlook, Excel, PowerPoint, Publisher, and Access. Entries in one application work in all the others (with one exception discussed later in this section); if you tell Access to change mouses into mice, the correction applies in all other Office applications.

- You can create your own AutoCorrect entries to supercharge your typing—for example, changing your shorthand tpfp into the Party of the First Part or otoh into on the other hand.

- If you commonly work with boilerplate text, AutoCorrect can handle it for you. Do you have an addendum that you add to the end of most contracts? Set up a code you can remember—such as addend1—so it expands into paragraphs, even pages, of text, footnotes, and the like.

TIP FROM

> Even though you can use AutoCorrect for boilerplate text, we would recommend that you instead work with the new Quick Parts feature, which allows you to make your boilerplate text into a building block that can be added easily later. The same is true for using AutoCorrect for graphics. Although this was recommended in the past, the new way to include common graphics is through Quick Part building blocks.

- AutoCorrect can even help you with odd capitalization. For example, if one of your company's major customers is called ZapItInc, you might have trouble getting the caps right when you type the company name. Set up an AutoCorrect entry for zapitinc (all lowercase) and have it corrected to ZapItInc. Then every time you type zapitinc—or Zapitinc, ZapItinc, ZapitInc, or even zApitiNc—AutoCorrect automatically changes the word to ZapItInc.

TIP FROM

> In all Office applications except Excel, a Smart Tag appears whenever AutoCorrect changes something you've typed. Hover your mouse over the changed text and click the Smart Tag (look for the lightning bolt icon) for easy access to all AutoCorrect options—including the capability to undo, or even permanently turn off, whatever correction was made.

HOW AUTOCORRECT WORKS

The AutoCorrect engine watches as you type. Whenever you press the spacebar, type a punctuation mark, or press Enter, this Office component looks to see whether the preceding characters match an entry in your AutoCorrect list. If it finds a match, it replaces the old text with the contents of the AutoCorrect entry.

In a default installation, the AutoCorrect list includes a large collection of commonly mis-spelled words and phrases. Figure 4.8 shows an AutoCorrect entry that changes accomodate to accommodate. Because of this entry, if you ever type accomodate followed by a space, punctua-tion mark, or paragraph mark, the misspelling will be automatically changed to accommodate.

Figure 4.8
The AutoCorrect dia-log box includes a ready-made list of commonly mistyped words and phrases.

The entry must match precisely. Using the default AutoCorrect entry shown in Figure 4.8, Word would not change accomodated to its correct spelling—unless, of course, you add a custom AutoCorrect entry to handle that word.

If AutoCorrect changes a word and you want the original back, click to position the inser-tion point within the changed word. Then let the mouse pointer hover over the underline beneath the changed word, click the lightning bolt icon to reveal the action menu (shown in Figure 4.9), and choose Undo Automatic Corrections. Alternatively—and much more quickly—you can immediately press Ctrl+Z, or you can choose Edit, Undo AutoCorrect, or click the Undo button. Any of these actions will reverse the change made by AutoCorrect and restore what you typed to its original state. The same action menu lets you quickly remove an entry from the AutoCorrect Options list or stop AutoCorrect from performing a certain type of correction.

Figure 4.9
The action menu for AutoCorrect options.

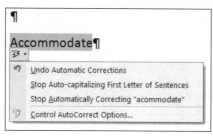

SETTING AUTOCORRECT OPTIONS

The actual AutoCorrect settings, which were shown in Figure 4.8, is located off the Office button, under <Program Name> Options, on the Proofing settings dialog box. Select the AutoCorrect Options button.

In addition to replacing one string of text with another, Office has four additional AutoCorrect settings:

- When you check the Correct TWo INitial CApitals box, AutoCorrect examines each word you type in an Office program; if it detects a word that starts with two consecutive capitals and that word appears in the dictionary, Word changes the second letter to lowercase. For example, if you miscapitalize AHead, Word changes it to Ahead; but if you type JScript, CDnow, or XYwrite, Word leaves it alone. You might want to override AutoCorrect on certain two-capital combinations such as GOpher. To do so, click the Exceptions button.

  You can bypass this dialog box and automatically add words that begin with two capital letters to the Exceptions list by immediately undoing the change. If you type GOpher, for example, and Word, Publisher, or PowerPoint "corrects" the entry to Gopher, click the AutoCorrect Smart Tag for the changed text and choose Stop Automatically Correcting GOpher from the action menu. (You can also press Ctrl+Z in any application to undo the change.) Office restores the second capital letter and adds the word to the Exceptions list in one operation. To disable this feature, click the Exceptions button on the AutoCorrect dialog box and clear the Automatically Add Words to List check box.

- The Capitalize First Letter of Sentence box presupposes that Office can recognize when you're starting a new sentence. That's not an easy task. If this setting causes Office to make capitalization mistakes more frequently than you like, turn it off. Office generally assumes that you're about to start a new sentence when it detects the presence of a period followed by a space, but tempers that judgment by a lengthy list of exceptions, including approx. and corp., which rarely signal the end of a sentence.

- The Capitalize Names of Days check box works as you would expect.

- The Correct Accidental Usage of cAPS LOCK Key check box, however, comes into play only when you type one lowercase letter, followed by pushing the Caps Lock key, and then continue typing. With this box checked, Office turns the first character into a capital, makes the other characters lowercase, and turns off the Caps Lock function.

Word offers two more AutoCorrect check boxes, which are also available in Outlook. The first, Capitalize First Letter of Table Cells, works much like the Capitalize First Letter of Sentences setting. The second option, Automatically Use Suggestions from the Spelling Checker, configures Word to consult the spelling checker if the usual AutoCorrect lookup doesn't find the word in question in the AutoCorrect list. If the spelling checker comes back with one—and only one—suggested correct spelling, the word you typed is replaced with the one offered by the spell checker.

CAUTION

> You could have an embarrassing mistake if Word substitutes the absolute wrong word for a misspelled one. However, Word's automatic substitution routines don't seem to generate vulgar expressions. In addition, AutoCorrect will not change proper nouns and other capitalized words (so, for example, if you type `Mr. Turkye`, it will remain `Turkye`, and not be AutoCorrected to `Turkey`).

→ To learn more about Word's spelling checker, **see** "Checking Spelling, Contextual Spelling, and Grammar," **p. 374**.

If you type `tiime`, and there's no entry for `tiime` in the AutoCorrect list, Word consults the spelling checker. The spelling checker offers only one correct spelling—time—so, with this box checked, `tiime` is replaced by `time`.

CUSTOMIZING THE AUTOCORRECT LISTS

Office maintains two AutoCorrect lists. The first one includes all unformatted Word AutoCorrect entries, plus all entries for the other Office applications. The second AutoCorrect list exclusively handles formatted entries available in Word and Outlook.

Use a formatted AutoCorrect entry whenever it's important that formatting be applied in the replaced text. For example, if you always want the term "Congressional Record" to appear in underlined, italic text, you might set up a formatted AutoCorrect entry called `cr` that always produces *Congressional Record*.

Adding your own formatted entries to the AutoCorrect list is easy:

1. Select the text you want AutoCorrect to produce. Apply whatever formatting you want.
2. Go into your AutoCorrect Options. The text you've selected appears in the With box. Click the Formatted text radio button.
3. Type the text you want to trigger an AutoCorrect replacement in the Replace box. In Figure 4.10, we instructed Office to replace `cr` with *Congressional Record*.
4. Click Add.

Formatted AutoCorrect entries apply only to Word and Outlook. If you add the formatted `cr` entry shown in Figure 4.10 and then type **cr** in Excel, PowerPoint, or Access, nothing happens. The text *cr* is AutoCorrected only in Word and Outlook.

CAUTION

When Word searches for AutoCorrect entries, it looks for formatted entries first. Building on the previous example, if you create a formatted entry for *cr* in Word and then create an unformatted (plain text) entry for *cr* in another program, typing *cr* in Word will bring up the formatted entry, but typing *cr* in Excel or PowerPoint will bring up the unformatted (plain text) entry. To make things even more confusing, only the unformatted entry will show in the Word AutoCorrect list, although the formatted entry will still be used. If you can't make sense of a specific AutoCorrect entry, your best bet is to first remove the unformatted entry from Excel or PowerPoint, then remove the entry from Word, and start over.

Figure 4.10
Configuring formatted AutoCorrect entries for both Word and Outlook.

You can also add AutoCorrect entries while performing a spell check. Right-click a word with a red squiggly underline, choose AutoCorrect, and select the correct spelling. Office corrects the misspelling and adds a matching AutoCorrect entry automatically.

Deleting AutoCorrect entries is as easy as adding them. Open the AutoCorrect dialog box, select the entry you want to remove, and click Delete.

If you type the name of the entry you want to delete into the Replace box, Office jumps immediately to that part of the list.

Word fields can appear in AutoCorrect entries, but only as Formatted Text. If you switch to Plain Text when creating an AutoCorrect entry that contains a field, Word converts the field to its field result before storing the entry.

Unformatted AutoCorrect entries are stored in a file that includes the extension `.acl` in the `%appdata%\Microsoft\Office` folder. In a default U.S. English installation, this file is called

`MS01033.acl`. The file can be moved from one computer to another along with other Office personal information. Formatted AutoCorrect entries are stored in Word's global template.

Also consider adding words you commonly type that have odd punctuation—Yahoo! comes to mind—so the capitalizing routine will operate properly. You might have other abbreviations that appear frequently in your writing: tb. or exec., for example. To add these exceptions, go into your AutoCorrect Options, and then click the Exceptions button. Type `Yahoo!` and click Add. Type `tb.` and click Add again; type `exec.`, and click Add one last time.

The AutoCorrect list is filled with hundreds of entries—not all of which might be to your liking. Consider removing the ones you find obtrusive. For example:

- Several combinations of colons, semicolons, dashes, lines, and parentheses are automatically turned into smiley faces. If you don't want smiley faces to appear in your documents and email messages, delete those entries from the AutoCorrect list. They're all near the beginning of the list.

- If you commonly create numbered lists by hand, and use (a), (b), (c), and so on within the numbers, you'll quickly discover that (c) is automatically turned into a copyright symbol. To override that behavior, use the lightning bolt icon that appears when you hover over the copyright symbol and choose Stop Automatically Correcting "(c)".

- Another AutoCorrect entry turns a standalone lowercase i into an uppercase I. That, too, can be problematic if you create numbered lists by hand. To get around it, click the AutoCorrect Smart Tag (the lightning-bolt icon) and use the action menu.

- One AutoCorrect entry changes three consecutive periods (...) into an ellipsis. The ellipsis is a single character that looks like three periods, squished close together (…). As long as your documents are destined to be used only by other Office programs, the ellipses pose no problem. But when you copy the text into an email message, for example, or post the document on the Web, the ellipsis character can turn into something totally inscrutable. To keep Office from changing three periods to an ellipsis, use the AutoCorrect action menu.

AutoCorrect Do's and Don'ts

The most common problem with AutoCorrect entries arises when you create an entry that has unexpected side effects. For example, while working on technical documentation, you might create an entry called *prn* that AutoCorrects to *insert the paper in the printer*. Then, weeks or months later, you might type a line like this:

```
...create a file called Output.prn and...
```

and the AutoCorrect entry kicks in:

```
...create a file called Output.insert the paper in the printer...
```

 If you find it difficult to locate some AutoCorrect entries, see "Finding Obscure AutoCorrect Entries" in the "Troubleshooting" section at the end of this chapter.

To minimize the chances for side effects like these, many Office experts use punctuation marks in their AutoCorrect entries. You might be tempted to set up an AutoCorrect entry called usr, for example, to "correct" into United Steel & Resources, Inc. Unfortunately, every time your finger slips on the keyboard and you misspell use as usr, AutoCorrect kicks in and you get gibberish. If you define the entry as usr., on the other hand—note the trailing period—you can type the entry almost as quickly as usr, and the chance for accidental side effects are greatly reduced. Or, you might just want to turn off the AutoCorrect features altogether. To do this, you click the Office Button, the Word Options, on the Proofing tab and choose AutoCorrect Options and deselect the "Replace text as you type" option.

TIP FROM

> You have the ability to move AutoCorrect lists, but you should avoid swapping around AutoCorrect lists unless it's absolutely necessary. Instead, use AutoText entries attached to the appropriate template. Although you lose a few of AutoCorrect's niftier features, you'll find it far easier to keep track of the entries if you store and move them with their appropriate template(s).

USING THE OFFICE CLIPBOARD

The Clipboard (shown in Figure 4.11) lets you copy multiple text and graphical elements from other Office documents, the same Office document or application, or even other applications. For example, you can copy text from a Word document and paste it easily into a PowerPoint presentation. Using the Clipboard task pane, you can organize these copied items and determine when and where you want to paste them.

MANAGING THE OFFICE CLIPBOARD PANE

To view your Clipboard pane, go to the Home ribbon and select the arrow widget next to the Clipboard grouping (or in Publisher or SharePoint Designer you select Edit/Office Clipboard). The clipboard will show you the different items you have copies and pasted and will not eliminate these items until you close all Office programs (see Figure 4.11). As long as one Office application is open, the Clipboard stays at the ready.

If you want to remove items from the Clipboard, you can select the item from the list and choose Delete.

At the bottom of the Clipboard are a set of options for display (as shown in Figure 4.12).

If you have Show Office Clipboard Automatically on, the Clipboard will appear whenever you are copying things. You can make it so that the Clipboard appears if you press Ctrl+C two times. You can have items copied without having the Clipboard displayed by using the Collect Without Showing Office Clipboard. You also have the Show Office Clipboard Icon on the Taskbar. This is on by default and will show a little Office icon when the Clipboard is on. Finally, "Show Status Near Taskbar When Copying" displays the collected item message and is turned on by default.

Figure 4.11
The Clipboard keeps a collection of your copy/paste items until you exit all Office applications.

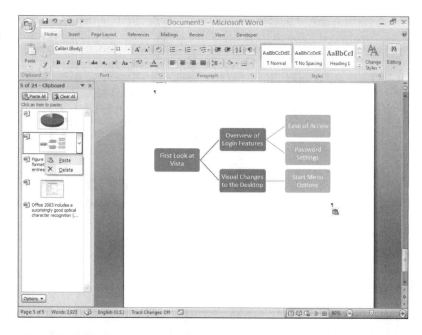

Figure 4.12
Clipboard display options.

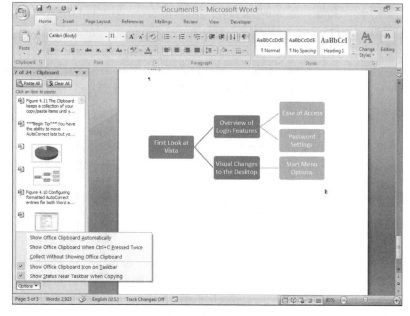

CONVERTING CLIPBOARD DATA INTO ALTERNATE FORMATS

The only way your Office Clipboard can insert items from the Clipboard is by a standard Paste command. You cannot use Paste Special options. So, it's important to remember that when you want to convert Clipboard data into something else (unformatted text, or a picture, for example), you need to use Paste Special, which actually works with the System Clipboard, not the Office Clipboard. Basically, the last item you copied on the Office

Clipboard is also in the System Clipboard, and it's this item that can be converted into another format through Paste Special.

> **NOTE**
>
> In addition to the Office Clipboard is a System Clipboard. They work together in many ways; for example, if you copy items to the Office Clipboard, the last one you copy is copied to the System Clipboard. If you clear the Office Clipboard, the system one is cleared, too. Anytime you use the Paste options, you are not pasting from the Office Clipboard, but from the System Clipboard. Does that clear it all up?

Another option is to paste your item, recut or recopy it, and then use Paste Special to put the item into the new formatting. The recut or recopy makes it the last item to be put into the System Clipboard.

DRAGGING AND DROPPING DATA

You can move selections of text, images, or tables, and so on in a faster manner by using the drag-and-drop method.

To do this, you select the text (image, table) you want to move. Place your pointer in the middle of the selection and then hold down your left mouse button. Then move your mouse and you will see an insertion point that is moving instead of the typical mouse pointer. Move that where you want to put the item and then release.

> **NOTE**
>
> If you hold down the Ctrl key when you move this, you will make a copy of the selection. But if you let go of the key before you release your mouse button, the copy isn't made. The items are moved instead.

You can turn the drag-and-drop features off by going into your options; for Word 2007 and PowerPoint 2007, under Advanced settings and under Editing, you find Allow Text to Be Dragged and Dropped. For Excel 2007, it's Enable Fill Handle and Cell Drag-and-Drop. For Outlook, Publisher, and Project, it takes some searching through the Tools menu/Options dialog box. Look for the Edit tab and find the drag-and-drop check box.

USING AND MANAGING FONTS

The first law of typography: Don't use more than three different fonts (typefaces) in any single document—one for the body text, one for headings, and at most one more for the masthead or main titles. Using these guidelines, you might settle on Garamond for body text, Arial for headings, and Verdana for the title page.

The second law of typography: Nobody follows the first law.

Unless you have a compelling reason to flout convention, most business letters and memos use at most two fonts: one font for the logo, return address, or any other fixed text at the top and bottom of the first sheet; and a second font for all the rest. In the United States, it's customary to use a serif font as the main font (for body text), and sans serif fonts are commonly used for heading text. In Europe, sans serif is almost as common as a body font, with serif fonts frequently used in headings.

TIP FROM

Ed & Woody

A *serif* font, such as Times New Roman, has curlicues on the ends of the letters, sometimes referred to as feet; a *sans serif* font, such as Arial, has straight ends.

You can mix and match as you like, of course, but be aware that each font you add to a document increases the likelihood that typography will obscure, not enhance, your message. The sure sign of an amateur document designer is a wild mixture of fonts, of varying sizes, with *lots* of italic and **even more** bold italic.

When you include the fonts that come with Windows and the fonts included with different Office applications, you have more than 150 fonts at your disposal. Third-party programs add still more fonts, sometimes by the hundreds. That's enough to overwhelm all but the most dedicated font aficionado.

If you find that your collection becomes unmanageable (and it surely will by the time you hit 300–400 fonts), invest in a third-party font-management program. These programs enable you to load and store groups of fonts, bringing them up when they're needed.

At this writing, the gold standard for font management software is Bitstream's Font Reserve for Windows (previously Font Navigator). See http://www.bitstream.com/fonts/index.html for details. If its price tag is too high, try the more reasonably priced Printer's Apprentice, from Lose Your Mind Development (http://www.loseyourmind.com).

NOTE

The new default font is Calibri 11 point. This replaces the veteran Times New Roman 12 point that lasted for many years. Not everyone is completely happy with the change, which was made because it's one of the newer true-type fonts, and it's supposedly a lot more pleasant on the eyes. Some claim that certain words have too much spacing between them, making words look odd.

Common Formatting Options

Although each Office application enables you to modify font formatting, and those with paragraphs (Outlook, Word, and PowerPoint) enable you to change paragraph formats, only Word and Outlook use the same dialog boxes to do so, and each application has its own quirks.

Changing Character Attributes

To change character formatting, follow these steps:

1. In all Office applications, select the characters you want to change. In Word, Publisher, or PowerPoint, if you don't make a selection, your changes apply to the entire word in which the insertion point is located.

2. In Word, Excel, and PowerPoint, you look on the Home ribbon to see your font and paragraph (no paragraph formatting for Excel) groupings. From here you can make many changes, but if you need to go deeper in your formatting, you can select the widget that opens the dialog boxes with further options. In Outlook, when creating an email, you have formatting options on your Message ribbon, as shown in Figure 14.13.

Figure 4.13
Outlook offers a ribbon-oriented setting for creating emails. On the Message ribbon, you have the ability to format your text.

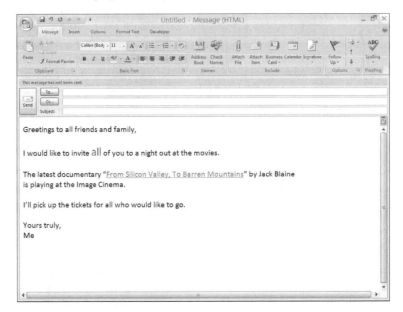

3. Set the characteristics. All Office applications enable you to change the font (that is, the typeface), the size (in fractional increments), the style (regular/roman, bold, italic, or bold italic), the color, and the single-line underline. Excel has several kinds of underlines, strikethrough, superscript, and subscript. PowerPoint enables you to specify the super/subscript distance, shadow, and emboss. Publisher includes a long list of exotic underlining options.

TIP FROM

In theory, the Automatic color tells Office to choose a color that contrasts with the color of the background. If you choose Automatic for the text color, for example, and then change the background to black, the text color changes to white and you can still read it. Unfortunately, thanks to a wide-ranging bug in Office, this feature works only in Word documents and tables. If you specify the Automatic color in a PowerPoint text placeholder, an Excel worksheet cell, or a text box in any application, Office ignores your request and formats the text as black. If you then change the background to black, your text disappears from sight.

4. Click OK to change the selected text.

→ To learn more about adding different formatting to your text, **see** "Changing Text Formatting," **p. 356**.

Three Office applications—Word, Excel, and PowerPoint—include check boxes that refer to the Default or Normal font. Each of these boxes works in different ways; only Word's actually changes the default font for new documents:

- In Word, the Default button sets the properties you want to use for the default font in all documents created in the future, from the current template. When you click the Default button, Word asks whether you want to use the font settings for all new documents based on the current template. Click Yes. That sets the character formatting for the Normal style in the current template.

→ To see how you can put templates, styles, and themes to work in your Word document, **see** "Using Themes, Styles, and Templates," **p. 387**.

- In Excel, by contrast, whenever you check the Normal Font box, Excel sets the font, style, and size of the current selection to match the characteristics of the current workbook's Normal style. To change the standard font used in Excel—in other words, to set the font for the Normal style in new workbooks you create—choose Tools, Options, and modify the Standard font entry on the General tab.

- In PowerPoint, you can set the font, style, size, and so on, and then click the box marked Default for New Objects. That merely sets the default font for newly created items in the drawing layer—basically, the size of the font in new Text Boxes and Auto Shapes in the current presentation.

USING BULLETS AND NUMBERS TO SET OFF LISTS

Bulleted and numbered lists come in handy both to emphasize and to organize. In general, you'll use bulleted lists to draw attention to important members of collections, and you'll want to use numbered lists when there's some sort of internal hierarchy (for example, a top-ten list), or when the sequence of points is important (for example, when describing each step in a complex procedure).

Word, PowerPoint, and Outlook all offer a Bullets and Numbering option on the Home ribbon. Publisher has its options under the Format menu. In each case, you choose the paragraphs you want to bullet or number, and then choose the Bullets or Numberings buttons. If you don't make a selection, the formatting applies to the current paragraph and any succeeding paragraphs until you either turn off the formatting or press Enter twice.

Using the Bullets and Numbering menu allows you to choose a picture or any character as a bullet. You can control whether the numbering continues from the previous number or starts fresh. You can also start AutoNumbering by typing a number followed by a period and space or tab. The primary differences are the following:

- Word allows outline numbering, where you construct numbering schemes such as 1.A.3, 1.A.4, and so on. Word also applies bullet formatting automatically if you type a *, >, ·, or a similar character, followed by a space or tab.

→ To learn more about constructing customized numbering schemes, **see** "Using Bullets, Numbering, and Multilevel Lists," **p. 367**.

- PowerPoint enables you to easily scale the size of the bullet so you can select the best size for your presentation.

WORKING WITH HYPERLINKS

Hyperlinks allow you to jump from your current location within a document to a possible other location within the same document, to a website, to a blank email message, and so on. They are designed to assist us in moving quickly to other locations.

To quickly create a hyperlink to a website, type in the name of the site and press Enter, and it will automatically be transformed into a hyperlink with blue text and a bright blue line underneath to indicate its purpose.

TIP FROM

EQ & Woody

> This change from typed Internet or network paths into a hyperlink is part of the AutoCorrect options we discussed earlier. If you don't like this feature, you can go to your Office Button, Word Options under your Proofing settings, select the AutoCorrect Options button, and on the AutoCorrect tab, clear the Internet and Network Paths with Hyperlinks check box.

To insert a hyperlink, you go to the Insert ribbon and under the Links grouping, you choose Hyperlink. From within the hyperlink dialog box (shown in Figure 4.14), you can do one of the following: select Existing File or Web Page to link to the address you type in the Address box (if you aren't sure of the address, you can select the Look In arrow and navigate to where it is). Or you can link to a new file by selecting Create New Document.

You'll notice that there is a ScreenTip setting, and this allows you to type in some information for the link. If it's left blank, the address itself is put in there.

Figure 4.14
The hyperlink dialog box allows you to determine the type of hyperlink you are adding to your document.

You can also select the Email Address option to make the hyperlink connect to an email address (and you can even set the subject line). This is good for documents that you eventually convert over to web pages. These links will be functional.

You can work with bookmarks to create hyperlinks that take you to certain bookmarks that you have already established. For example, you might have a book in a document and you want to make the Table of Contents a hyperlinking experience. Set bookmarks to the various heading and then use the hyperlinks dialog box to create links to each of those bookmarks. These same bookmarks can be used in other documents, so you can have hyperlinks that take you from your location to a specified point in another document, or another office application altogether. Basically, you can have a link in your Word document take you over to a pie chart in an Excel spreadsheet and another link that takes you to a PowerPoint slideshow.

To learn more about hyperlinks, search for further information within the Office help files.

UNDOING AND REPEATING CHANGES

All Office applications include Undo features. If you make a mistake, click the Undo icon, which is conveniently located in the upper-left corner on your Quick Access Toolbar (or, if you are using a non-ribbon-oriented application, it's under the Edit menu), or press Ctrl+Z. Every Office application supports at least one level of Undo, and some enable you to undo a number of successive changes. If you discover you made a mistake five minutes ago, you might be able to recover by clicking the Undo button repeatedly. If you close your file, however, all bets are off—all Office applications clear the Undo history when you close the document.

Word and Outlook include a virtually unlimited number of Undo levels. As long as you don't close the document, you can undo anything you've done. (There are some physical limitations to the size of the Undo file, but in practice they aren't significant.)

Word's tremendously powerful Undo capability enables you to bring back material that you might have thought was lost. For example, if you're working on a speech and you decide the opening paragraph you started with is better than the one you ended with, you can easily restore it. First, save your current document! If anything goes wrong while using Undo in this way, you can exit without saving and reopen your document to start over.

TIP FROM

> Click the drop-down Undo list off the Quick Access Toolbar and scroll all the way to the bottom, selecting every action on the list. When you release the mouse button, Word undoes everything you've done in the current session, restoring your document to the state it was in when you first opened it. Next, select the text you want to restore and copy it to the Clipboard (do not, under any circumstances, use the Cut command). Now scroll to the bottom of the drop-down Redo list and click to redo every action you just undid. Your document is now back to the state it was in before you performed the multiple-level undo, and you're free to paste in the paragraph from the Clipboard.

If you've lost the ability to redo changes in Word, see the tip "Cutting Text Clears the Redo List" in the "Troubleshooting" section near the end of this chapter.

Excel used to limit you to 16 levels of Undo. This relatively severe limitation has been part of Excel for years, since the Undo feature was first introduced. But in Excel 2007, you can undo up to 100 levels.

PowerPoint enables you to select the number of levels of Undo you want to support. The default value is 20, but you can increase this to a maximum of 150 by clicking the Office Button, then choosing Options, Advanced.

One odd thing about the Undo feature in your email message box in Outlook is that you cannot select from a drop-down arrow to choose more than one at a time. You have to keep clicking the button to undo a bunch of changes.

TROUBLESHOOTING

FINDING OBSCURE AUTOCORRECT ENTRIES

A rogue AutoCorrect entry is causing unwanted text to appear in my documents, but I can't find the offending entry in the AutoCorrect list.

Most of the time, it's fairly easy to figure out which entry is causing the problem. Unfortunately, AutoCorrect isn't always so simple. In particular, note that AutoCorrect entries can have embedded spaces so, for example, an entry for *any where* might correct to *anywhere*. That behavior can be puzzling until you realize that you might be the victim of an AutoCorrect entry that begins with *any*.

CUTTING TEXT CLEARS THE REDO LIST

I used Word's multiple-level Undo capability to roll back a large number of changes, and then I cut a block of text. But when I wanted to restore my document to its previous state, the Redo button was grayed out.

Did you save your changes before you performed the Undo operation? If so, exit the document without saving, and restore your saved copy. If not, you're out of luck. When you use Word's multilevel Undo, you can *copy* anything you want to the Clipboard; if you use the Cut command, however, you wipe out the Redo list, and nothing will bring it back.

PASTE ALL AND THE OFFICE CLIPBOARD

Why is the Paste All button on the Office Clipboard grayed out?

When you click the Paste All button, the effect is the same as if you were to paste each item individually, pressing Enter (if necessary) between items. In some cases, the data types are incompatible with the current location of the insertion point. For example, if you've clicked in a cell within an Excel worksheet, you cannot paste a collection that contains a mix of text and graphics items. In that case, Office disables the Paste All button. Delete the incompatible data types from the Clipboard task pane, or paste the items one at a time.

BROKEN LINKS TO IMAGE FILES

There are placeholder icons in my document instead of the pictures that should be visible there.

Those placeholder icons represent broken links to image files. Ask the network administrator to check the permission on the shared drive or folder. If it's necessary to move the linked files, you might need to recreate the links.

SECRETS OF THE OFFICE MASTERS: WORKING WITH SPEECH RECOGNITION IN WINDOWS VISTA

Some may say that a serious Office user doesn't need to use speech recognition, but that would exclude so many persons who cannot use the keyboard for any number of reasons from being part of our "Office Master" club. Instead, let's appreciate that the technology exists for more to take advantage of the tools we have at our fingertips (or, our voices).

NOTE

If you are working with XP and want speech recognition, you have to install it. There is no default Speech Recognition Engine (SRE) in XP. However, there are several ways to obtain this. One is by installing it with an older version of Office (2002/2003) that will include the Engine. You could purchase the Plus! Pack from Microsoft, too.

A Speech Recognition Engine (SRE) is included by default in Windows Vista. You can configure it for accepting commands (so you can work with the operating system itself) and dictation (for creating documents). To manage your speech setting, go into your Control Panel and open your Ease of Access settings and then choose Speech Recognition Options. You see a group of settings to choose from, shown in Figure 4.15.

Figure 4.15
The Control Panel selections under Ease of Access, Speech Recognition Settings.

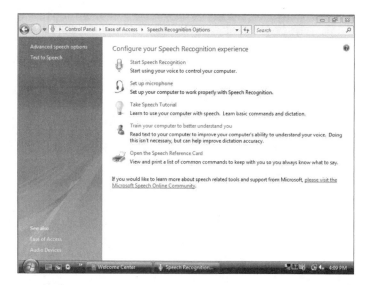

From here you can configure your Microphone settings, turn on the speech capabilities, take a tutorial, and so on. The engine isn't perfect yet. It does make mistakes, but with a little practice you will be creating incredible documents without even lifting a finger.

To find out more information about speech recognition in Windows Vista, you can visit the Online Community at www.microsoft.com/windowsvista/features/foreveryone/speech.mspx.

CREATING, EDITING, AND USING PICTURES AND GRAPHICS

In this chapter

Graphical Improvements in Office 2007   104

Using Office Drawing Tools   104

Creating and Using SmartArt Graphics   119

Creating and Editing Charts   123

Viewing, Editing, and Managing Pictures   124

Using Clip Art   129

Turning Text into Graphics   131

Troubleshooting   133

Secrets of the Office Masters: Compressing Graphics in Your Presentations for Email, Internet Websites, Blogs, or Presentations   134

GRAPHICAL IMPROVEMENTS IN OFFICE 2007

Office experts do not live by words alone. Photographs, charts, diagrams, and even whimsical illustrations do wonders to make printed documents more readable, web pages more accessible, workbooks more lively, and presentations more engaging. Office 2007 includes all the drawing tools you've used in previous versions, plus a few newcomers (like the Microsoft Office Picture Manager) expressly aimed at making digital photos easier to use. New charting and diagramming features include three-dimensional shapes, transparency, drop shadows, and other effects.

In this chapter, you'll find a thorough explanation of the often-confusing Drawing tools used throughout Office. If you're not sure of the difference between an AutoShape and a Clip Art object, or if you can't tell the difference between a drawing canvas and a drawing object, you should read this chapter closely.

In this version of Office, Microsoft has also greatly improved the tools and techniques for working with clip art, including some impressive integration with the Office Online website. For this edition, we've expanded our explanation of how to use these cool (and often underrated) tools.

So, let's get started.

USING OFFICE DRAWING TOOLS

Every version of Office 2007 includes an assortment of applications designed to help you create, insert, edit, and manage graphics (for example, the Microsoft Office Picture Manager comes as a separate tool with your Office applications). But some surprisingly powerful graphics tools are built directly into Office, and you can access them directly in Word, Outlook, Excel, Publisher, and PowerPoint. With a few clicks, you can insert a prebuilt diagram, chosen from seven main categories, each with many options. With the help of the Insert ribbon with its Illustrations grouping and Text grouping (the Objects toolbar in Publisher), you can add geometric shapes, lines, arrows, and text boxes to a document, worksheet, or presentation, and then add colors, shadows, and backgrounds to create images with impact. These aren't simple one-dimensional shapes, either—you can stretch, layer, and combine Office Shapes to create complex flowcharts and diagrams.

If you're a graphics professional, you'll quickly outgrow the basic capabilities of the Office Drawing tools. But for most business purposes, they're a welcome way to avoid the typical dull gray report or presentation.

NOTE
One important note to keep in mind is that the graphical features (such as SmartArt) have limited capabilities when working in Compatibility Mode. You may recall that this mode allows you to work with documents that are from earlier versions of Office or that will be used by earlier versions. You lose some of the functionality by not using Office 2007's default file format.

Working with the Drawing Layer

Before you can even hope to harness the power of Office's Drawing tools, you need to come to terms with a fundamental concept: Word, Excel, and PowerPoint documents, as well as formatted (HTML) Outlook email messages, are *layered*.

NOTE

> When we use the term *document* in this chapter, we're referring to any Office data file that includes a drawing layer, including formatted (HTML) Outlook email messages, Word documents, Excel worksheets, and PowerPoint presentations. Access also has drawing tools, but they are integrated into its object creation mechanism in a different way. We don't cover Access drawing tools in this chapter.

It's tempting but misleading to think of an Office document as two-dimensional and directly analogous to a piece of paper or a computer screen. Actually, that finished product is only a snapshot of the real document, which consists of multiple layered drawings in addition to the main layer of the document itself. By changing the order, grouping, and arrangement of these drawings and the main layer, you can dramatically change a document's appearance.

The main layer is called the *text layer*. The graphic material is in a *drawing layer*, which exists independently of—but can interact with—material in the text layer. Technically, just one drawing layer is present; however, because you can position each object within the drawing layer independently, from front to back—and the text layer can be set at any depth—it's more useful to think of each object as a layer unto itself.

Think of the layered transparencies that you probably saw in your high school biology book. As you peel back each layer, a dissected frog appears, with each layer revealing some additional aspect of the frog's anatomy. The drawing layer works like that: Objects in the drawing layer are arranged from top to bottom (called the *Z order*), as if each drawing were on its own sheet, and each drawing can be moved independently toward the top or sent toward the back.

When you begin working with the drawing layer, it helps to visualize a complex document as consisting of many transparencies, each with its own data and properties:

- Because each layer, including the text layer, is transparent, you can see the contents of any one layer through all other layers.
- Although the text layer is normally at the bottom of the stack, with individual drawing objects in front of it, you can also position a drawing object behind the text layer.
- The contents of the text layer can be wrapped around a drawing layer.
- You can reorder and reposition virtually every object in the drawing layer; you can also group drawing items together and treat them as a single object, and then ungroup them to work on each individually.

The various capabilities for manipulating data in Office—everything from search-and-replace to master formatting functions—apply only to the text layer. The information in drawing layers will not appear in your table of contents, nor will the appearance of the drawing layers change if you alter the formatting of your document.

5

You generally work with the Drawing layer through the Drawing tools contextual Format ribbon, which appears only *after* you have a graphical element to work with (either a picture or shape). To see an example of this ribbon in action, consider Figure 5.1, which appeared after we inserted a Shape from the Illustrations grouping on the Insert ribbon.

Figure 5.1
The starting point for the Office Drawing objects contextual ribbon called Format.

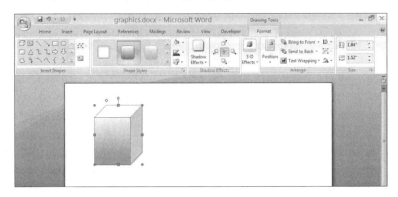

WORKING WITH A DRAWING CANVAS

Frequently you want to treat several drawings as a group so they can be moved or resized together, or so you can be sure that they will always appear on the same page together. That's the reason for the *drawing canvas*, which acts as a frame that forms a boundary between drawing objects and helps hold them together. The drawing canvas appears explicitly only in Word, although you'll see vestiges of its design when you use drawing objects throughout the other Office applications.

By default, the drawing canvas is turned off, but you can insert a drawing canvas by doing one of two things:

- You can enable this behavior by going into your Options, and on the Advanced settings dialog, under the Edit settings, select the box that says "Automatically Create Drawing Canvas When Inserting AutoShapes".

- Or you can select Shapes off the Illustrations grouping from the Insert ribbon and select the New Drawing Canvas option.

Continuing the analogy we used in the preceding section, you can think of the drawing canvas as a transparent sheet that can be cut to almost any size (as long as it is rectangular). You can then position any number of drawing objects on this canvas. You can move and resize individual objects, but when you select the drawing canvas, it handles all the objects as a single unit. (You can have more than one drawing canvas in a Word document.)

TIP FROM

EQ & Woody

What exactly is the purpose of the drawing canvas? Office Masters have worked for hundreds of years (well, let's say 20 years and fewer) and never needed this canvas. Why do we need it now? The basic answer is: you don't. Usually. However, if you are going to make your own organization chart and have situations that require multiple shapes working with each other and you want a nice way to establish a working layer within the document—then the drawing canvas is a huge help.

The corners and edges of a drawing canvas are characterized by a distinctive outline (see Figure 5.2). When you click and drag any edge or corner of a drawing canvas, you change the size of the canvas, but the size and position of each drawing on that canvas remains unchanged. When the document is printed, all the drawings in the canvas appear on one page.

Figure 5.2
The short, bold corner and edge lines distinguish a drawing canvas.

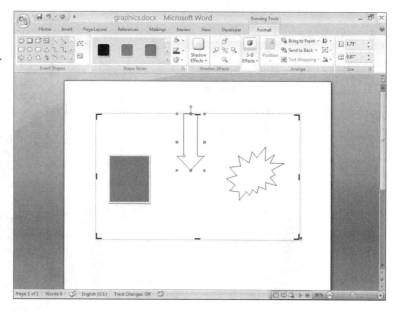

After a drawing canvas is selected, if you insert a drawing object (a picture or AutoShape, for example) into your document, the drawing is placed inside the canvas, where you can move and resize it along with the other objects on that canvas. To remove the drawing from the canvas, click it and drag it to any spot outside the borders of the canvas.

In times past, the drawing canvas received its own toolbar when you selected it. But now, the canvas is treated as if it is a picture, and so all the same tools exist for having text move around it or scaling the canvas, placing the canvas somewhere specific on the page. It's all part of the same Format ribbon that appears when you select either a specific shape or the canvas itself.

To apply formatting to the drawing canvas (outline, background color, and so on), right-click the border of the canvas and choose Format Drawing Canvas. The dialog options that appear help you to add fills, outlines, decide text placement, and so on.

WORKING WITH SHAPES

On the Insert ribbon, under the Illustrations grouping, is a button called Shapes. When you select this option, you see all the different preconfigured shapes you can call up immediately to insert into your documents. For simple shapes, there are sections called Lines, Basic Shapes, and Block Arrows (as you can see in Figure 5.3). Use the Line, Arrow, Rectangle, and Oval buttons from the Shapes tool to draw simple geometric shapes.

Shapes come in really handy in your documentation, especially when you want certain material to stand out. You can use arrows in your documents to indicate special focus points. In PowerPoint presentations, you can use these shapes to point out information for viewers. In addition, you can combine these simple shapes to form more complex shapes or organization charts to illustrate your thoughts more dynamically.

Figure 5.3
In PowerPoint, the Shapes tool can make graphical elements appear quickly in your presentations.

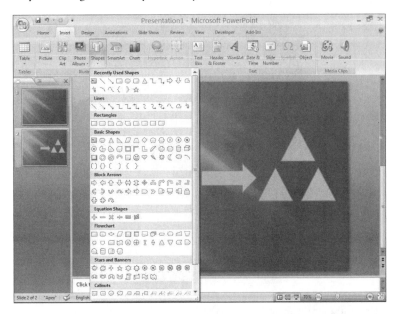

TIP FROM

EQ & Woody

For many shapes, holding down the Shift key while you drag makes the shape symmetrical. For example, Shift+drag with the rectangle shape to produce a square; use the same technique with the oval shape to draw a perfect circle.

If you routinely create complex shapes that aren't represented on the Shapes selection drop-down list, you can save these shapes as a Quick Part. To save your complex shape, first create it just the way you want it to be. Then select the shapes (or canvas), and then from the Insert ribbon, choose Quick Parts from the Text grouping. Then choose Save Selection to a Quick Parts Gallery and fill out the options shown in Figure 5.4.

One of the easiest ways to add professional-quality graphics to a document is through the use of *AutoShapes*, geometric shapes that form the basis for graphics and charts routinely used in business reports.

Figure 5.4
Saving shapes as a
Quick Part makes it
easy to insert again.

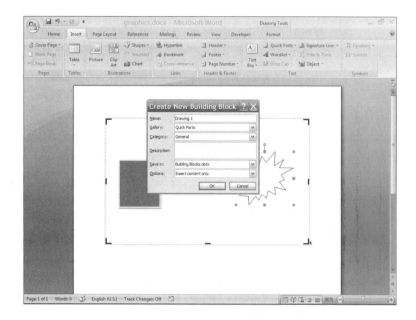

NOTE

Quick Parts will be discussed at a later time in Chapter 13, "Building a Better Word
Document," along with the Building Blocks Organizer in Chapter 14, "Using Themes,
Styles, and Templates."

COMPLEX SHAPES

In addition to rectangles, ovals, and other basic shapes, the library of AutoShapes covers
most of the important bases in diagramming: flowchart symbols, generic geometric shapes,
and display arrows. You can also add *callouts*, balloon-shaped drawing objects typically used
to provide information on specific items in a document; for example, you might add a callout to a sales table or chart to show the spike in sales when a new product was introduced.
PowerPoint goes even further, providing Action Buttons—not unlike controls on a form—
that can be set to execute commands or macros when clicked.

TIP FROM

EQ & Woody

As we mentioned earlier, if you have a set of related shapes that work together, such as
an organization chart, place them into a single drawing canvas so that you can move or
resize all of them simultaneously.

If you're creating a diagram that includes several instances of the same shape, a useful
approach is to create one example of the graphic item you need, and then copy that
AutoShape to the Clipboard and paste it in position as needed.

TIP FROM

Ed & Woody

> Instead of having to eyeball a shape, you can set specific dimensions for it. The best approach is to start by drawing in the rough dimensions of your shape with the mouse, right-click the shape, choose Format AutoShape, and click the Size tab. Options in this dialog box enable you to specify a precise size for the shape.

USING LINES AND ARROWS

After you have your basic shapes down, you'll frequently want lines, dashed lines, and arrows to connect them all and illustrate the relationships in your charts.

Excel and PowerPoint provide true charting *connectors*—lines that stay connected to preset positions on shapes—for every shape in a document. As you move the shapes, the connectors move with them without requiring you to manually redraw them. Word and Outlook have connectors, too, as long as all the connected shapes sit in the same drawing canvas.

To create a connector, do the following:

1. Draw the shapes you want to connect. In Word or Outlook, make sure all the shapes are in the same drawing canvas.
2. From the Shapes options, look in the Lines section for a Connector. To know if one of the options is a connector, hover your mouse over a selection and it will tell you if it is an arrow or a connector. Pick the type of connector you want to use—straight, elbow, or curved, with or without arrows.
3. Move the mouse pointer over one of the shapes you want to connect. The pointer turns into a square with four radiating lines and the predefined connection points for the shape appear as colored dots on the perimeter of the shape. Click the starting point for your connector.
4. Repeat the previous step at the desired connector point on the shape where you want the connector to end.

To change a connection point, click the connector, and then click and drag one of the red connection boxes at the beginning or end of the connector. Move it over the shape until you see the colored dots that indicate automatic connection points, and then pick one of those points to snap the connector into position.

TIP FROM

Ed & Woody

> If you've moved an AutoShape so that its connectors are on the incorrect side of the shape, let Office make a more logical connection for you; right-click the connector and choose Reroute Connector. (This option is available only when Office determines that your connections are incorrect.)

In addition to the connector capability, Excel and PowerPoint also include *snap* and *grid* settings—crucial tools for placing lines and other shapes. Word offers similar capabilities, although they are implemented differently.

When you use the drawing layer, you can take advantage of a hidden layout grid. By default, drawing objects align to this grid. Although it's usually a helpful shortcut, this *Snap to Grid* feature can be a problem when you're drawing a line manually. Because the edges of shapes are tied to grid positions, they might not line up visually with other shapes that are arranged in slightly different positions on the grid. The fix is to *snap objects to other objects* (in Excel, it's called S*nap to Shape*) so, for example, the end point of a line connecting two shapes ends up at a reasonable point on each shape.

Word, Excel, and PowerPoint all have some form of the Snap options, with Excel's being the easiest to configure. And all three applications have these settings on the Format ribbon. If you look for the Alignment down arrow under the Arrange grouping, you will see different options for different applications (shown in Figure 5.5).

Figure 5.5
This is one super complicated figure. The top left is your grid dialog for PowerPoint. Below that is your Word grid dialog settings. Then on your right are your Excel settings, which you can see are just three little buttons.

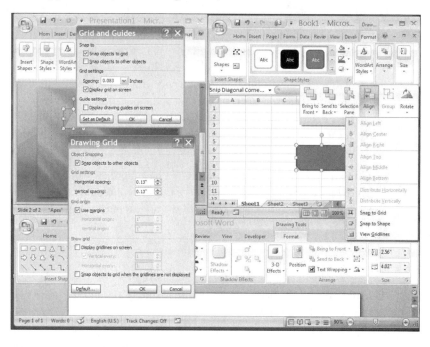

Notice that in Excel, you have only two options, Snap to Shape and Snap to Grid, which you can toggle by selecting the option.

PowerPoint and Word have more options for working with the grid and making the objects line up.

NOTE

> Don't be confused by the terminology. In this case, a "shape" in Excel is identical to an "object" in Word and PowerPoint.

It's possible to move one or more objects in very fine increments without completely disabling the grid. Hold down the Alt key as you drag the object, and it moves freely rather than following the grid. You can also use the keyboard to move objects. Normally, when you select one or more objects and press any arrow key, the selection moves to the next point on the grid. If you make a selection and then hold down the Ctrl key while pressing any arrow, the selection moves in much finer increments.

5

NOTE

> If the grid isn't enabled, you can turn it on by clicking the View Ribbon, then selecting the Show/Hide grouping.

CHANGING BACKGROUND COLORS AND LINE FORMATS

Using the Office Drawing tools, you can draw shapes and lines galore, but they won't look right unless you can make them blend in with your document.

AutoShape backgrounds can have their own colors. (A background color is called a "fill" color.) By default, the fill color is white—rarely a good choice because it obscures everything underneath the AutoShape.

Color backgrounds can come in handy if you're working with a color medium—color printer, onscreen documents, or web pages. But the same technology that makes background color inviting can also jump up and bite you. Unless you choose high-contrast color combinations to differentiate text from background, your message can be lost completely. Remember that PC monitors in particular are notorious for not reproducing colors accurately. A carefully crafted color scheme on one monitor can morph into an illegible splotch on another.

In addition to the fill color, all AutoShapes have borders around the outer edge. You can adjust the border width, style (dashed lines, for example), color, and size. In many cases, the border is superfluous and detracts from the appearance of your document; don't hesitate to get rid of it.

To edit an AutoShape or line, follow these steps:

1. Select one or more of the shapes or lines in the drawing layer.

2. Right-click and choose Format AutoShape. In the Format AutoShape dialog box, click the Colors and Lines tab (see Figure 5.6).

3. Adjust the fill color, lines, and arrows per the dialog box. If you want to be able to see through the shape, make sure you change the Color setting to No Fill, or adjust the Transparency slider to a value greater than 0%. The higher the value set here, the clearer the object underneath it will appear. At 70% Transparency, for example, black text beneath a drawing will appear as fuzzy gray but quite readable.

Another way to make quick formatting changes to your Shapes is by using the Format ribbon while working with your shape. From the Shape Style grouping, you can choose from a gallery of options for your shape. You can quickly change fill colors and border colors and types.

Figure 5.6
Use the Format
AutoShape dialog box
to add colors and
change the appearance
of lines and borders.

TIP FROM

After you adjust formatting settings—fill color, line size, arrow types, and so on—you can configure Office to use those settings for all new shapes in the current document. Right-click the object and choose Set AutoShape Defaults.

ADDING SHADOWS, ROTATION, AND 3D EFFECTS

3D effects rarely add to, and frequently detract from, the effectiveness of a document. Before you consider using a 3D effect, ask yourself—repeatedly—whether the inherently 2D medium you're working with will be able to properly convey that third dimension. The answer is usually no. However, in PowerPoint, you might like to add 3D effects to make certain items stand out.

Shadows, on the other hand, if applied consistently and with attention to detail, can add depth to a document without detracting from the main story.

To apply Shadow or 3D effects, follow these steps:

1. Click once on the shape you want to modify, or Ctrl+click to select several.

2. On the Format ribbon, you can use the Shadow Effects grouping to work on shadows and the 3D Effects grouping for 3D options.

3. A drop-down menu of effects opens up. Click the effect you want, and Office transforms the selected shapes.

In addition to the choice of effects, each menu also includes a Settings button for fine-tuning the effects. For example, you can change the depth and "lighting" of a 3D object, or the extent and placement of the shadow. One of the greatest features of Office 2007 is your ability to see these changes in Live Previews so that all you have to do is hover your mouse over the preview and it automatically shows what will happen to your shape if you choose that particular one.

TIP FROM

A few effects go a long way. A business chart is not abstract art; if you use a red 3D rectangle for one particular item, then similar items also should be red 3D rectangles.

Rotating your shapes is something you can do manually, by selecting the green circle usually located beyond the top of your shape if you select it, and then moving your mouse so that the shape rotates visually (as shown in Figure 5.7). Or you can right-click your shape and choose Format AutoShape. On the Size tab in the Format AutoShape dialog box, you can choose the degree of rotation you want for your shape.

Figure 5.7
Rotating your shapes couldn't be easier with the manual technique, but if you need precision, use the Format AutoShape options.

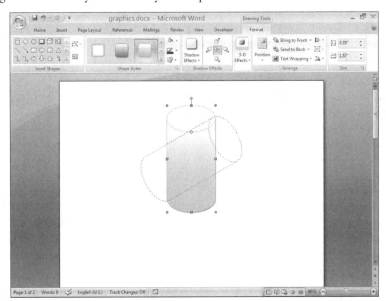

ADDING TEXT TO A DRAWING

In some drawings, you will want to put text inside your AutoShapes—to identify the steps in a flowchart, for example, or the decision points in a decision matrix. All the AutoShapes (except lines) can be converted to text boxes, if you know the trick.

To add text to a shape, right-click the shape and choose Add Text. You could also add a text box that is separate from your drawing. You do this from the Insert ribbon; under the Text grouping, select Text box and the Draw Text Box. The text you enter can be formatted just like any text in your document.

One particularly effective way to draw your attention to specific locations in a picture is to use callouts. (In this book, for example, we sometimes use callouts to identify screen elements in figures.) In Office parlance, a callout is a text box with a line attached to it. You can move, resize, and format the text box, line, and connector independently. Several of the built-in Office callouts look like dialog balloons, similar to those you see in a comic strip. Here's how to use them:

1. On the Insert ribbon, you can select the Shapes option from the Illustrations grouping. You will see the Callout options toward the bottom of your choices. Choose the callout type you want. For illustrative purposes, let's choose the Cloud Callout choice.

2. Click in the drawing layer where you want the callout to originate from, and then drag to form the rest of the callout.

3. Immediately begin typing; the text you type appears in the callout.

4. Right-click the callout and set its formatting. In the example in Figure 5.8, we set the balloon to have a light yellow fill, retained the border line, and then adjusted the size of the balloon.

Figure 5.8
AutoShape callouts come in many forms. This one looks like a thought balloon from a comic strip.

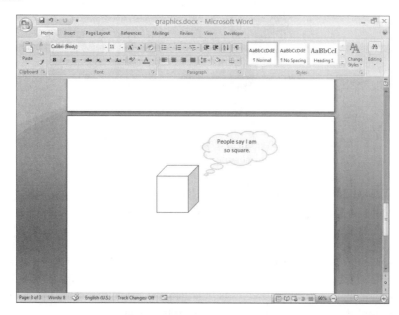

TIP FROM

Don't worry about getting the text or formatting in a callout perfect the first time. To change text in a callout, click once in the callout text, and then add, delete, or edit the text. To change formatting in a callout, select the text, right-click, and choose an option from the shortcut menu.

ALIGNING AND GROUPING GRAPHIC ELEMENTS

Depending on the naked eye to center shapes in a drawing isn't always reliable. Office has built-in drawing tools with the capability to bring symmetry out of chaos. When *aligning* objects, the key is to do it one step at a time, carefully planning out what you need to do to redistribute or align them, and in which order.

If you have four objects on the drawing layer above an Excel worksheet and you want to organize them as shown in Figure 5.9, follow these steps:

Figure 5.9
Use the Format ribbon's alignment tools to make your graphics line up.

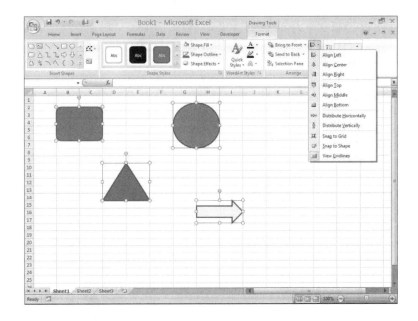

1. Select all the shapes by holding down the Shift key as you click each one.

2. To evenly space the shapes, from the Format ribbon select the Align options, also shown in Figure 5.9. You can choose the Distribute Horizontally options to establish even spacing.

3. To line up the shapes, from the Align tools you can choose from a number of different options, aligning your shapes to the top or middle, and so on, whichever seems best for your particular circumstance.

After you have properly formatted, connected, aligned, and distributed all your AutoShapes, you can take one more step to *group* them all into a single graphical object. This step is crucial; it enables you to preserve the relationships between objects and it helps prevent the chance that you'll accidentally move or resize a shape.

Select all the elements you want to group, and then choose the Group option off the Format ribbon, under the Arrange grouping. Keep in mind that with Word or Outlook shapes, you won't need to group them if they are already in a drawing canvas together. But Excel and PowerPoint do not have drawing canvases.

TIP FROM

EQ & Woody

> When you're creating complex drawings that consist of several AutoShapes, it's easy to leave one out accidentally. After selecting multiple items for grouping, it's always a good practice to drag the collection left and right just a little; you can see whether any odd pieces are hiding behind other shapes. If you missed one, press Ctrl+Z to undo the move, and regroup.

The individual elements in a group can be edited independently. If you find you need to make a revision, you can select your group and then select your shapes directly and make changes. Or you might decide to ungroup, make your edits, and then regroup. To ungroup a composite graphic, select the graphic, and then go back to the grouping options on the Format ribbon and choose Ungroup.

> **NOTE**
>
> We have been discussing all these options with the idea that you'll be using the ribbon to group your shapes. But if you right-click your selected shape (or shapes), you can group or ungroup from here. You can also determine the stacking options, which we discuss next.

WRAPPING, LAYOUT, AND STACKING OPTIONS

Graphics don't always appear where you want them—at least not without a bit of persuading. When you insert a complex graphic into a Word document, for instance, the graphic shoves the text in your report out of the way. In this case, you may prefer to *wrap* the text around a drawing object.

The solution? Use layout options (which are available only in Word) to adjust the placement of graphics relative to the text layer. Right-click the graphic object (or the drawing canvas, if all your drawing objects are enclosed in a drawing canvas) and choose the Format option (Format AutoShape or Format Drawing Canvas, for instance). In the Format dialog box, choose the Layout tab.

- To lay out your graphic so that it appears as a background to the document, choose Behind Text or In Front of Text. When using this option, use only very light-colored graphic objects; otherwise, the graphic will overwhelm the text on the page and make it unreadable.

- Use the standard Square method to wrap text around the rectangular borders of the graphic. This option is most appropriate when the graphic has a defined border.

- Use Tight wrapping if the graphic object or drawing layer does not have a border. With this option selected, Word ignores the empty spaces of the graphic and wraps the text snugly up to the drawing elements themselves.

> **NOTE**
>
> In addition to using the right-click Format properties, you can use the Text Wrapping selection from the Arrange grouping on the Format ribbon to accomplish the same thing. In addition, there is a Position option, shown in Figure 5.10, that allows you to determine where you want your image or shape, and you can establish advanced settings by selecting this option and choosing More Layout Options.

5

Figure 5.10
Use the Format ribbon's alignment tools to make your graphics line up.

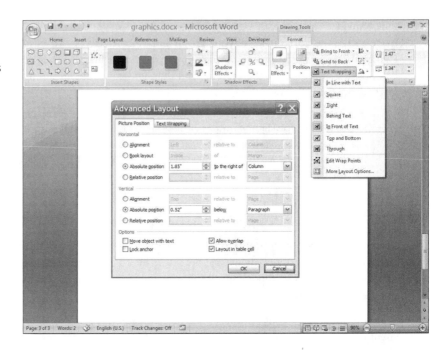

In Word, Excel, and PowerPoint, you can also change the order of objects so that one is in front of another. By default, when you create or position a graphic object so that it overlaps another graphic object (including a drawing canvas), the new element appears on top of the old one. To change the front-to-back ordering, right-click the graphic element or drawing canvas you want to move, and choose Order. At that point, you can

- Float the graphic all the way to the top (Word calls it Bring to Front) or sink it all the way to the bottom (Send to Back).

- Bring the graphic up one level (Bring Forward) or push it down one level (Send Backward).

- Move the graphic so it's on top of the text layer (Bring in Front of Text), or place it behind the text layer (Send Behind Text). These options are not available in Excel or PowerPoint.

When should you use each wrapping option? The simplest rule is this: If you want to turn a single graphic into a background or an overlay for a Word document, use the Layout tab. If you have multiple graphic elements or drawing canvases you want to arrange in the document, go with the Order tools.

TIP FROM

Ed & Woody

Adjusting the order also enables you to create sophisticated effects interweaving the text and graphics. For example, you can use Word's Bring in Front of Text layout option to place a group graphic on top of the text, and then ungroup and move some elements of it under the text.

CREATING AND USING SMARTART GRAPHICS

First off, what is SmartArt? What is so smart about it? Well, the feature is not named after any intuitive ability hidden within, it's named after the fact that SmartArt options are on the higher scale of shape usage. You use SmartArt to create diagrams, organization charts, flow charts, and other things of this nature.

There are two versions of SmartArt choices in Office 2007. One set is for Compatibility Mode documents. In Compatibility Mode, Office shows the older SmartArt possibilities, rather than the new, sleek design for 2007. However, if you want to see what SmartArt can do, you will insert it in a document using the new file format.

SmartArt really enhances your presentations. With the formatting possibilities combined with the variety of colors, shadows, bevels, glows, and so on, you can literally spend days playing around with all your SmartArt Options.

CHOOSING A SMARTART LAYOUT

On the Insert ribbon, under the Illustrations grouping, select the SmartArt option. You will be presented with the Choose a SmartArt Graphic dialog box. From here you have seven types of layouts to choose from, with a host of options within those layouts (as shown in Figure 5.11).

Figure 5.11
SmartArt choices can be confusing at times. Notice the helpful description on the right side of the dialog box to make sure you choose the SmartArt that's right for your presentation.

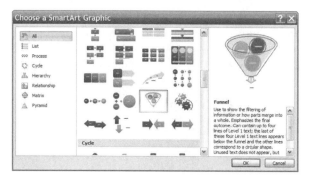

After you have inserted the SmartArt choice, you will receive a new contextual ribbon under SmartArt tools called Design, shown in Figure 5.12.

The Design tools allow you to manipulate your SmartArt in many ways, including changing the layout, the colors, and the dimensional look of the SmartArt diagram. The features are numerous.

Figure 5.12
The contextual Design ribbon appears when you insert or are working on your SmartArt diagram.

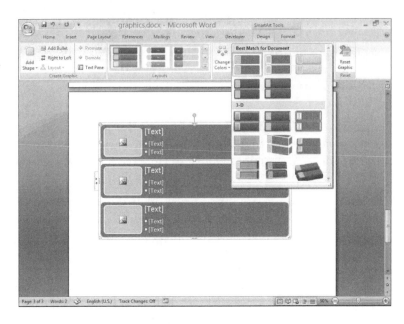

ENTERING AND EDITING TEXT

Text can be entered in different ways. The simplest way is to click directly into your SmartArt and begin typing. However, you can also select the Text pane option (shown in Figure 5.13) off the Create Graphic grouping for the Design ribbon and this will offer you a separate box for adding your text. This is especially helpful for bulleted list diagrams.

Figure 5.13
Entering text from the Text pane tool.

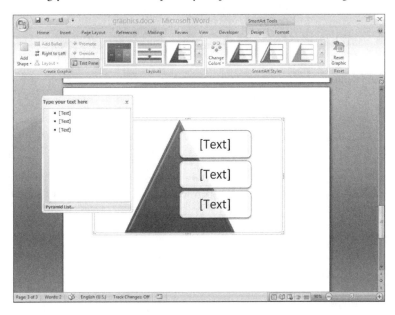

ADDING GRAPHICS AND PICTURES

SmartArt is designed to allow for more than shapes with cool formatting applied to make informational points. An image is worth a thousand words sometimes, so images play a large role in some of your SmartArt choices.

Some SmartArt options are predesigned to accommodate inserted shapes and pictures. If you choose to edit these objects, you can go into the Format properties for any shape and then change the Fill settings, as shown in Figure 5.14.

Figure 5.14
SmartArt makes provisions for adding graphics and pictures directly into the diagram and preselected locations.

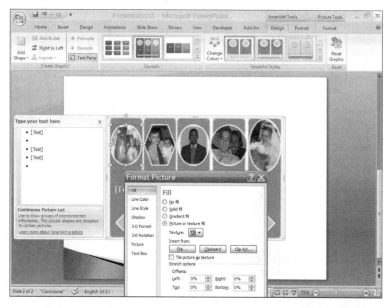

NOTE

SmartArt is contained within its own canvas. If you add a graphic or picture outside the structure of that canvas, although it will show up in your documents or presentations, keep in mind that it is not considered part of the SmartArt diagram itself. If you choose to save the diagram as a picture (by right-clicking and choosing the Save As Picture option), your graphic outside the canvas will not be included.

CHANGING A LAYOUT

You can alter the layout of your SmartArt anytime. Maybe you want to try a different type of the same diagram, or perhaps you want to go for something completely new.

To accomplish this, you can right-click the diagram and choose Change Layout from the menu options. Or you can select the Design tab, and from the Layouts grouping, you can select one from the gallery provided or choose More Layouts and go back to the original dialog box that presents all the options for you to choose from.

Keep in mind that when you change a layout, your text may carry over, but it may not be where you think it should be. You will have to readjust it to your liking. And graphics that you purposely added to your SmartArt won't survive the move to a new format.

CHANGING COLORS AND STYLES

Office 2007 makes these changes easily within your SmartArt. If you want to change the color scheme or the style of your diagram, you can do this from the Design tab. You have many options to choose from, starting with galleries of choices that you can view in Live Preview style by hovering your mouse over the selections. Notice these capabilities in Figure 5.15.

Figure 5.15
Changing SmartArt colors and styles couldn't be easier with the Design ribbon to provide a host of gallery options to choose from.

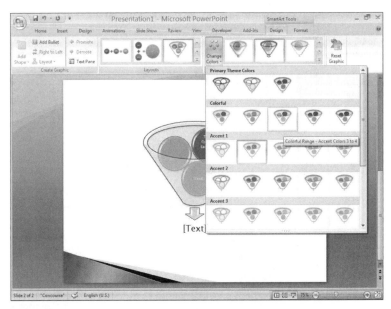

In addition to the gallery options, you can literally control the appearance of each and every shape within your SmartArt canvas, and the canvas itself. If you right-click and choose the Format options, you will be given the opportunity to alter the following: Fill, Line Color, Line Style, Shadow, 3D Format, 3D Rotation, Picture, and Text Box. Each one of these settings comes with a variety of options to choose from and configure.

NOTE

Keep in mind that having the capability to do something in SmartArt doesn't mean you should. The goal of these tools is to make your documents more impressive, not more cluttered. One of the other great things about SmartArt is the capability to use SmartArt graphics from one Office application to another. With the use of Themes, SmartArt that is pulled into your document from, for instance, a PowerPoint presentation, will automatically inherit the Theme you have applied to your Word document (if you have one applied).

ARRANGING AND FORMATTING TEXT

You can format text from within the Text pane. Although it will not show any of the formatting within the pane, you will be able to see the results within the SmartArt graphic. You can also select the graphic directly and arrange and format your text any way you would like, just as if it were text in a text box.

TIP FROM

Ed & Woody

> Sometimes you may like the visual effect of SmartArt so much that you would like to export that graphic and use it in other things. In the past you might have thought to do a screenshot of your image and then crop away what you don't need to get your image. That works, but you might want to try a different approach. You can save your document as a web page (*.html or *.htm format) and Word will save your image as a GIF file in a specific folder for your web page that can now be used in other documents.

CREATING AND EDITING CHARTS

Everyone knows that a good number of the charts that we create in Excel end up in a Word document or PowerPoint presentation. We copy and use the Paste Special as a picture to get that chart into our documents. If we are really hard pressed, we use the Microsoft Graph tools that are provided. Well, not anymore. The new idea is "true" interoperability among your Office applications, and Chart options are included.

Again, your functionality will be limited in Compatibility Mode. You will only be able to insert Charts that are backward compatible with older versions of Office because you will using Microsoft Graph tools. But if you insert a Chart in Word 2007 compatible documents, you should have more options. We say "should have" because it depends on whether you have Excel installed. Without Excel, you will still have to use Microsoft Graph tools.

Here is the way it works. Now when you insert a Chart (in Full Functionality Mode), Excel and Word (or Excel and PowerPoint) tile side by side with each other. The chart is in your Word document and your data is in your Excel spreadsheet.

Anytime you need to edit your data, you can do this by going to your Design ribbon (that comes up contextually because of the chart you've inserted) to the Data grouping and choose Edit Data, as shown in Figure 5.16.

After you have your chart data the way you like, it's time to format it. There are three contextual ribbons that show up: Design, Layout, and Format. These ribbons will help you to completely control the look of your chart so that it will fit perfectly within the style of your document. However, if you've chosen a document theme, your chart should automatically adapt to the theme you've chosen.

5

Figure 5.16
Insert a chart in PowerPoint and watch Excel come to life (in Full Functionality Mode).

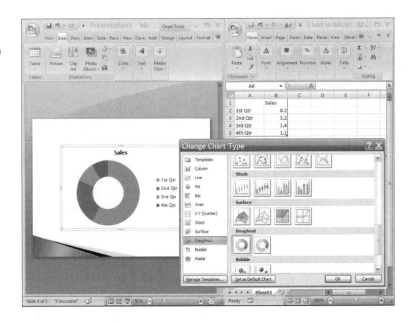

VIEWING, EDITING, AND MANAGING PICTURES

Clip art has its place, especially in presentations and informal documents. But professional-quality corporate reports typically require graphics such as photographs or image files produced by professional graphic artists.

Office can read any graphics file format for which it has "filters," the software that converts the graphic format into data usable inside the Office application. Windows 2000 and Windows XP include support for the Windows Bitmap (*.bmp), Windows Metafile (*.wmf), and Tagged Image File Format (*.tif, *.tiff) formats. A default installation of Office 2007 adds filters for the following widely used formats:

- Encapsulated PostScript (*.eps)
- WordPerfect Graphics (*.wpg)
- Portable Network Graphics (*.png)
- Macintosh Graphics (*.pict)
- Graphics Interchange Format (*.gif)
- Joint Photographics Expert Group (*.jpg, *.jpeg)
- Computer Graphics Metafile (*.cgm)
- CorelDRAW (*.cdr)
- Kodak PhotoCD (*.pcd)

Filters for the last three formats in the preceding list are available for use by Office programs but are not actually installed until first use.

To add graphic files to Office documents, go to your Insert ribbon and choose Picture from the Illustrations grouping. Browse to the folder that contains the picture, select the file-name, and click Insert.

TIP FROM

Ed & Woody

By default, Office programs insert a copy of the selected picture directly into the docu-ment as an inline object. You can change this default setting so that pictures are auto-matically inserted as floating objects. To do so, go into your Option settings and choose the Advanced settings. Look for the Cut, Copy, and Paste options for a setting that says Insert/Paste Pictures As and then change it from Inline with Text to some other setting from the selection list.

ADDING PICTURES TO OFFICE DOCUMENTS

To insert the image is simple to start with. You use the Insert ribbon, select Picture from the Illustrations grouping, and choose the picture you want to insert. When you go to insert the picture, however, you'll see an arrow next to your Insert button. If you select the arrow, you receive the following options to choose from:

- **Insert**—This choice *embeds* the picture, physically placing it in the document. If you aren't overly worried about file sizes, if you don't need any history telling you where the picture came from, and if you don't care whether the picture gets updated, this is your best choice.

- **Link to File**—This choice puts a pointer to the picture in the document. The picture itself is not stored in the document. Instead, it's brought in as needed to display on the screen or print on the printer. If there's a chance the picture will be changed, and your document *must* reflect those changes, this is your only option.

- **Insert and Link**— It puts a copy of the picture in the document, but maintains a link as well. When the picture is needed, Office first looks for the linked file. If the picture file is unavailable, it reverts to the copy stored in the document. This option is especially useful for documents stored on portable computers, because it ensures that graphics will be available when you are away from the office and your network, while still allowing the option to update the image when you reconnect to the network.

Office frequently uses fully qualified filenames as the links, which can cause problems if you move either the picture file or the document. If you link the picture `%userprofile%\My Documents\My Pictures\Corplogo.jpg` in a document and then send the document to a co-worker as an attachment, the picture must be located in the same folder hierarchy or Office won't be able to find it and will substitute a meaningless placeholder.

When should you embed graphics and when should you link? Follow these guidelines:

- If you repeatedly use the same graphic—for example, a letterhead logo—link to it and make sure it doesn't move. Otherwise, your document archive will explode in size.

- In a networked environment, linking works if the graphic is in a *shared network folder* that's accessible to all persons who use the document. If you don't have ready access to the shared folder, insert the graphic.

5

- If you plan to distribute documents externally, you must insert the graphics, unless all the files reside in the same folder as the document, or the recipients are savvy enough to replicate the folder structure on the machine where the document was first created.

 If you discover broken image links in your document, see "Fixing Broken Image Links" in the "Troubleshooting" section at the end of this chapter.

RESIZING AND CROPPING PICTURES

When you insert a picture into a document, it appears full size. If the picture file is six inches wide, that's what you'll see in your document. More often than not, you'll need to make some adjustments to fit the picture to the document. You can *crop* the picture—that is, cut away portions of the image to show only the parts you want to see in your document. Or you can *resize* the picture, leaving the image intact but changing its height and width (and thus the number of pixels it occupies). You can also combine the two operations, cropping to the correct proportions and resizing to fit the page. (Although you can expand a small image to fit a larger space, the more typical task in Office documents is to shrink large digital images to a manageable file size.)

You have two choices:

- Make a copy of your original picture and then crop or resize it using the Microsoft Office Picture Manager, which comes with Office 2007 and is installed in your Office Tools. If you use the photo editor to adjust the image to the exact size and shape you need, you can import it into your document without requiring any additional work.

- If you want your original picture to remain the same, or if you're still designing your document and you think you may want to do additional cropping or resizing, use the built-in Office tools.

To crop an image within an Office document, first select the image, then choose Crop from the Format ribbon off the Size grouping. The mouse pointer changes to match the icon on the Crop button. To begin cutting away portions of the picture, point to any of the eight cropping points, one on each corner of the image and one in the center of each side; then click and drag toward the center of the image. Hold down the Ctrl key and drag the handles in the center of any side to crop identical amounts from the top and bottom or left and right. To maintain the same *aspect ratio* and crop equal amounts from all sizes, hold down the Ctrl key and drag any of the corner handles in.

TIP FROM

Ed & Woody

In Word, you can avoid some sizing hassles by drawing a text box where you want to place the graphic and then inserting the graphic into the text box. The graphic is resized automatically. If the picture is already in the document, click it once, and then click the Text Box button on the Drawing toolbar to surround the image with a box.

If you make a mistake while cropping, click the Reset Picture button from the Size dialog box that appears when you select the widget next to Size on the Format ribbon.

Buttons on the Format ribbon, under the Adjust grouping, also allow you to make a few adjustments in picture quality: contrast, brightness, color, and the like. Again, any changes you make here affect only the picture in the document, not the original source file.

EDITING IMAGE FILES

If you want to start a raging debate, gather a bunch of graphics professionals in one place and ask them to name their favorite image-editing program. Then duck. Web designers and desktop publishers are typically passionate about their editing tools, and you'll probably get an earful.

The Office Picture Manager utility can't compete with professional-strength editing packages. In fact, its collection of features matches those found in many freeware and shareware image-management programs. If you're already experienced with one of these tools, you should at least look at Picture Manager and decide whether you want to make the switch.

To use Picture Manager's editing tools, while you are in Picture Manager, first select one or more images, and then click the Edit Pictures button to open the task pane shown in Figure 5.17.

Figure 5.17
Click any of the editing options shown here to open a new task pane with specialized tools for that task.

The AutoCorrect button adjusts brightness, contrast, and color automatically. For images that appear washed out or dull, you should always try this option first (if the results are unsatisfactory, press Ctrl+Z to undo the changes and start over). Use any of the following editing tools to alter specific parts of an image:

- **Brightness and Contrast**—Use this feature to correct pictures that appear too light or too dark. Try the Auto Brightness button first; then adjust manually.

- **Color**—Click to adjust the hue and saturation of the image. This option is useful for "punching up" dull pictures or fixing images where poor lighting caused unnatural tints.

- **Crop**—Remove extraneous portions of an image. You can crop out unnecessary elements or choose from the drop-down Aspect Ratio list to select a specific size—3×5, for instance. This option is not available when multiple images are selected.

- **Rotate and Flip**—Change an image from landscape to portrait orientation, and vice versa, or use the By Degree control to fix a scanned image that's slightly crooked.

- **Red Eye Removal**—This feature allows you to remove ghostly red dots caused by your camera's flash. This option is available only when a single image is selected.

- **Resize**—Change the dimensions of a picture without cropping out any information, by choosing a predefined or custom height and width or selecting a percentage of the original size. This feature is most useful for reducing file size for images you plan to use in email messages or on Web pages.

As you edit images, Picture Manager keeps track of the changes you make. Click the Unsaved Edits icon in the Picture Shortcuts page to see any changes you have not yet saved.

TIP FROM

EQ & Woody

> If you close Picture Manager, you'll be given the chance to save your changes, discard the changes, or cancel. Be careful! Choosing Save Changes will overwrite the original images. If you don't have backup copies, those originals will be gone for good.

When in doubt, open the Unsaved Edits folder and review your changes.

TIP FROM

EQ & Woody

> Picture Library offers one especially elegant way to add a consistent naming strategy to a disorganized folder made up of image files gathered from many sources. Add the folder to the Picture Shortcuts pane and press Ctrl+A to select all images in the folder. Then click the Rename Pictures link in the Getting Started task pane. Choose from the impressive array of options for using names and numbers to bring order out of chaos. This option is also available when you click Rename Pictures in the Export task pane.

WORKING WITH SCANNED IMAGES

Two helpful tools in Microsoft Office Tools are the Document Imaging and Document Scanning tools. Usually you would use the software that came with your scanner to scan in any images or documents. But it's nice to know that you do have these tools and can scan your images in and then pull them into your Office applications as needed.

TIP FROM

EQ & Woody

The scanning capability, in combination with Office's graphics layer, provides a solution to a relatively new problem: How do you type up a printed form when you don't have a typewriter anymore? The answer: Scan the form into a Word document, and then insert it as a picture in the document header. Crop and resize the image as needed, and format the picture layout as Behind Text. Exit from the header, and you can type over the form.

Alternatively, scan the form and place the image in the main text layer. Crop and resize as needed, and then format the graphic object by using the Behind Text option. Add a text box on top of each field in the form; use the ordering options to place this layer in front of the form and make the box semitransparent.

→ For instructions on how to translate scanned documents into editable Word documents, **see** "Converting Scanned Documents to Text," **p. 84**.

Using Clip Art

Clip art—reusable drawings, photos, and the like—derives its name from the not-so-distant past, when designers actually clipped images from books and pasted them onto layout boards to produce master images for printed documents. The electronic versions of these tools are easier to use, but the effect is the same: to enliven an informal document. Much depends on the audience you want to reach and the effect you want to achieve.

A dynamite piece of clip art can tell a story worth a thousand words. A really poor piece of clip art hinders communication, leaving people scratching their heads and wondering "What's *that* all about?"

Gratuitous clip art—that is, clip art that doesn't relate to the topic at hand or otherwise impedes the flow of your documents—distracts your audience and often detracts from the point you're trying to make.

Through the years, Office has steadily improved its tools for managing and using clip art. In Office 2007, the Clip Art collection is accessible through its own task pane. The built-in clip art collection includes more than 1,600 graphic images, bullets, lines, and a few media files. The Clip Art task pane is tightly connected to the Office Online Clip Art and Media page, where you can download thousands of additional images, sounds, video clips, animated graphics, and the like. The result is organized in a fully indexed and searchable graphics database, sorted into collections, categorized by keywords, and eminently customizable.

At its simplest, you can search for relevant images by category or keyword. From any Office program, from the Insert ribbon, choose Clip Art from the Illustrations grouping to open the Insert Clip Art task pane (shown in Figure 5.18).

5

Figure 5.18
The Clip Art pane is easy to use, and if you don't see what you want, you can always look online.

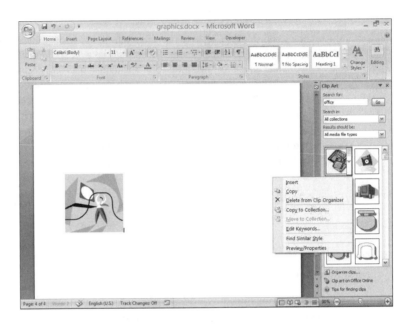

After the task pane is available, you can do the following:

1. Click the drop-down arrow to the right of the Search In box to display the list of available collections.

2. Select or clear check boxes to choose the collections you want to search. This list includes three main groups:

   - **My Collections**—This group consists of clips you've added to your personal collection. In a default Office installation, it is empty.

   - **Office Collections**—These are the files installed on your hard disk with the initial Office setup, plus any files you've added from the Office Online site.

   - **Web Collections**—This group consists of content available from Microsoft's Office Online website.

   Click a top-level collection to clear all existing check marks and then select only the specific categories you want.

3. In the Results Should Be box, choose the media type you're looking for. Click the + buttons to narrow your search to very specific types of media (for example, photographs in JPEG format and clip art in Windows Metafile format).

4. Type keywords into the Search For box, and click Go.

The results of your search appear in the scrolling pane at the bottom of the Clip Art task pane. If one of the images meets your needs, click to insert it in the current document, worksheet, or presentation. To see additional choices, click the drop-down arrow at the right side of every clip. You can copy an item to the Clipboard for use in another program, for example, or make it available offline in one of your personal collections. You can also preview the clip in a larger window that shows additional properties.

The keywords and other saved details for clips that are part of Office clip art collections, whether they're stored locally or pulled from the Web, are not available for editing. In clips that are stored in your personal collections, however, you're free to customize the built-in keywords and captions. To set your own keywords for a particular clip, follow these steps:

1. Right-click the clip and choose Edit Keywords. The Keywords dialog box opens.

2. In the Caption box, type a descriptive name for the clip. The caption can be virtually any length and may include punctuation marks and other special symbols. The caption text will appear as a ScreenTip when you hover the mouse pointer over the clip in the task pane.

3. In the Keywords for Current Clip box, add or remove keywords for the particular clip.

CAUTION

> Office helps you maintain consistency in your keywords by use of the drop-down list. If you're careful to use uniform keywords, your efforts will pay off later with more effective searches.

You can also add photographs and graphic images from files on an individual computer or on the company network to your personal collection, with the option to move or copy a graphic onto your computer or link the item in the collection to the original file location. If you regularly produce graphics-intensive documents using a library of images you've drawn from many sources, you may find it useful to make those images available in the Clip Art pane.

To open the Clip Organizer, click Organize Clips at the bottom of the Insert Clip Art task pane. You can also open the Clip Organizer on its own, without having to go through the Clip Art task pane—its shortcut is in the Microsoft Office Tools. Then choose File, Add Clips to Organizer. You can have the Clip Organizer automatically scan your disk for compatible files, or click the On My Own option to specify a location from which you want to import graphics files.

The Clip Organizer is also the ideal way to add files from the Office Online collections. Click the Clips Online button to visit the website and select clips you want to download. The Office Online site installs an ActiveX control that makes it easy to import new clips, which show up in the Downloaded Clips category.

Images you download from Office Online go into the Microsoft Clip Organizer subfolder in your My Pictures (or Pictures folder in Vista). The index to your personal collection is stored in a Media Catalog file (with the extension `*.mcg`) in the `%appdata%\Microsoft\Clip Organizer`.

Turning Text into Graphics

In addition to pure graphics, Office programs also include features you can use to turn text into graphics. The result can add personality and visual interest to documents without requiring more than a modicum of artistic talent on your part.

USING TEXT BOXES TO CREATE PULL QUOTES

One well-known technique for livening up text is to throw in a *pull quote*—a usually provocative excerpt from the text that is enclosed in a box and formatted with large type. Newspaper editors and magazine designers use pull quotes as visual cues to "draw in" readers who are casually flipping through the pages looking at headlines and pictures without reading the body text. Word has an exceptionally cool technique to create pull quotes:

1. Select the text excerpt you want to use. Press Ctrl+C to copy it, and then paste a copy in the general location where you want to create the pull quote.

2. Select the copied text and click the Text Box button on the Insert ribbon under the Text grouping. Word immediately creates a text box containing the selected text.

3. Select the text within the text box and adjust its font, alignment, and other formatting.

4. Format the text box, resize, and move it to your desired location.

Text boxes can be used to put freestanding text of any kind into your document. The device works for a short sidebar; for example, to highlight a point, you can use the method described in the preceding section to combine a text box with an AutoShape.

The term *text box* is a bit misleading, at least in Word. More accurately, this drawing object is a subdocument that appears in the drawing layer over (or under) the text layer of the document. In Word, you can insert a picture into a document, select the picture, and then insert a text box, which has the practical effect of enclosing the picture completely within the text box. You can then add text or other graphics to the "text box." In Excel, PowerPoint, and Publisher, however, a text box can contain only text (although you can group text boxes with other shapes).

TIP FROM

Ed & Woody

> If you want to make it easy to move and position a picture on a Word document slide, insert the picture into a text box. Move the text box, and the picture goes along for the ride.

USING WORDART FOR LOGOS

WordArt is an Office application used to manipulate TrueType fonts and save the result as a graphic image. The resulting picture can be dropped into the drawing layer of documents, charts, or slides. Don't let the name fool you into thinking this utility is just for Word—the WordArt application is available in Excel, PowerPoint, and Publisher as well.

For the small business without a graphic arts department, WordArt can form the basis of a simple logo. You can take advantage of WordArt's capabilities to lay text out vertically, curve it, and add 3D effects. In Word 2007, the WordArt options off the Insert ribbon appear the same as they did from when they were first invented for Word 97. But the tool has received an upgrade. To see the upgrade in Word, you have to see the Format ribbon from your SmartArt graphics, and you will see a WordArt set of grouping styles. But to see the new WordArt options in PowerPoint, you select WordArt from the Text grouping on the Insert ribbon, as shown in Figure 5.19.

Figure 5.19
WordArt has received an upgrade in Office 2007, as seen here in PowerPoint

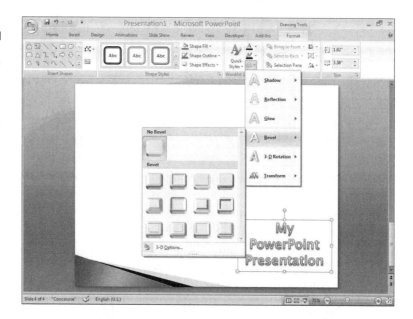

You can see from the figure that WordArt allows you to really customize your text. You can bevel it, shadow it, make it glow—really enhance your text—which is perfect for your PowerPoint presentations.

TROUBLESHOOTING

FIXING BROKEN IMAGE LINKS

I created a link to an image stored on a networked computer and everything worked fine. When I opened the document later, however, the image link was broken.

If links get messed up, you have one tool at your disposal, short of directly editing Word field codes to fix the broken links. Go to your Office button, choose Prepare, and click Edit Links to Files (which you will see only if there are links in your document). Select the link and then make the necessary changes.

PICTURES CHANGING BETWEEN MODES

I was working on a photo and using all the tools available to me. I saved the document and when I opened it up, the photo isn't the same and tools are all different.

Most likely what happened is you were working with the photo under the new file extension and then saved it in Compatibility Mode. When that happens the photo remains, but it becomes a still image that remains fixed the way it was formatted. The tools are different because the Compatibility Mode is for backward compatibility.

Secrets of the Office Masters: Compressing Graphics in Your Presentations for Email, Internet Websites, Blogs, or Presentations

In our modern times, it seems like bandwidth (network or Internet) allows for files of any size. But you might be surprised to know that in many parts of the world, the bandwidth range is still around 56Kbps. Hard to believe, we know, but it's true. So, the size of your files does matter.

A document with multiple inserted images can become quite huge. And you could go through the effort of using a third-party tool to reduce your images before putting them in your documents or emails. You could also save your document as a PDF file, which will reduce the size somewhat. But there is an adjuster included in Office to help you with this.

When you insert a picture, the Format ribbon appears, and there is an option on the ribbon called Compress Pictures on the Adjust grouping. Depending on which mode you are, in you will see a different version of this dialog box. Both dialog boxes are shown to you in Figure 5.20.

Figure 5.20
Depending on the mode, you will receive different dialog boxes for compressing your pictures within your documents. Both do pretty much the same thing, however.

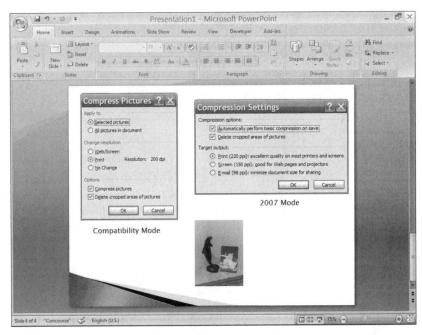

You can choose your options depending on which setting you need. Keep in mind that this doesn't affect the photo itself, just the way it is displayed in your document (and the size).

SHARING AND REVIEWING OFFICE FILES

In this chapter

Sharing and Reviewing Features in Office 2007   136

Keeping Shared Documents Secure   136

Routing, Reviewing, and Revising Documents   145

Printing Office Documents   150

Publishing Office Documents to a Website   150

Combining Two or More Data Types in One Document   151

Overview of File Sharing on an Office Network   153

Troubleshooting   155

Secrets of the Office Masters: Setting Up and Using Information Rights Management   155

SHARING AND REVIEWING FEATURES IN OFFICE 2007

When you're working on an Office document, sometimes you need comments or contributions from other people to make it complete. You don't have to print, collate, staple, and route paper copies of the work in progress. Instead, you can use a variety of electronic tools to pass documents around.

Many of the features we discuss in this chapter are similar to those already available in previous Office versions. The most noteworthy additions are available when you pair Office 2007 with a network that includes at least one computer running SharePoint services. In that configuration, which we discuss in more detail in a later chapter, members of a workgroup can share documents, conduct threaded discussions, maintain shared calendars and contact lists, and even create custom sites devoted exclusively to a single document, meeting, or project.

Office 2007 supports Information Rights Management, an emerging technology that allows you to secure documents from unauthorized users and allow them to "expire" after a predetermined amount of time.

If you simply want to route documents via email, you can do so by attaching an electronic routing slip to each document and then using Outlook to send it to one or several co-workers. Office does an excellent job of managing the process and ensuring that each reviewer's changes remain available.

KEEPING SHARED DOCUMENTS SECURE

Before you share an Office document with anyone else—via email, on a corporate intranet, or on the Internet at an FTP or website—you should first consider how you're going to protect the document, both from prying eyes and from unwanted changes.

To that end, let's discuss password security, security through backups, document locking, and read-only mode. In addition, we will cover in this section Information Rights Management and marking your documents as Final, along with using standard Windows permissions to keep your shared documents secured on your network. Finally, we will cover digital signatures and how they are implemented directly into 2007 documents.

PROTECTING OFFICE DOCUMENTS WITH PASSWORDS

Your first line of defense is to protect the document file itself with a password. That simple precaution will usually keep out casual snoops, and with a little extra attention, you can scramble a document so effectively that only a determined cryptologist could unlock it without knowing the password.

Password protection works by *encrypting* a file—scrambling its data so it can't be read without being unlocked. The encryption options in Office 2007 (as well as Office XP and 2003) are significantly improved over the password-protection options in earlier Office versions.

If you want to quickly encrypt a document and put a password on it before you send it out, all you have to do is finish your document and save it. While the document is still open, click your Office button, and then select Prepare and then Encrypt Document. You will see a simple box that asks for a password (shown in Figure 6.1).

Figure 6.1
Encrypting a document is as easy as inserting a password.

By default, Office documents are protected with at least 40-bit RC4 encryption, which is difficult, but not impossible, to crack on a typical PC. If the password is at least six characters long, random (that is, it doesn't appear in a typical cracking dictionary), and contains a mix of numbers, letters, and symbols, a well-written password-cracking routine running on a fast PC can still crack it, but it will take more time.

That's the good news if you're concerned about security (or the bad news, if you've forgotten your document's password). Password protection used elsewhere in Office is much, much simpler.

6

The forms of password protection vary slightly from application to application:

- Word, Excel, and PowerPoint allow you to protect an entire document, workbook, or presentation, respectively, using the new CryptoAPI support. A file using this level of password protection cannot be opened using versions in Office 2000 or earlier.

- On the Protect Document dialog box, Word allows you to password protect documents to track changes, allow comments only, or for forms (choose the Review ribbon tab and select Protect Document). All those passwords are trivial to break.

- Excel allows you to protect individual worksheets (contents, formats, objects, and scenarios), workbooks (structure, windows), and the logs that track changes to a shared workbook, all by choosing Tools, Protection. These passwords are also easy to crack with any commercial password cracker.

- Outlook offers password protection for individual *.pst files. These passwords are also easy to break.

- Access security differs from the other Office applications. You can set a database password that locks out anyone who doesn't have that key. You can also encrypt a database using the Tools, Security, Encrypt/Decrypt Database menu commands, but you can't select encryption levels. If user-level security definitions are in the database, being able to open the database won't accomplish much. Database passwords are easy to crack, but the internal security definitions are much more difficult.

- Publisher offers no document password security, period.

- Visual Basic for Applications modules can be password protected (VBA calls it "locked for viewing"). VBA passwords can be cracked easily.

NOTE

Although macro software developers sometimes criticize the weak password protection in VBA, there's a hitch: Some macro viruses are designed to encrypt VBA modules. If the VBA password protection were stronger, antivirus products would have a much harder time rooting out viruses.

 If you've forgotten your password, see "Forgotten Passwords" in the "Troubleshooting" section at the end of this chapter.

I think we have made it pretty clear that password protection on documents can only deter individuals. Anyone can purchase or download the right cracker and get at your document. But there are other options that we will consider in this chapter, too. One of those is the new Information Rights Management tools.

CREATING A BACKUP COPY AUTOMATICALLY

Each time you open or save a Word document or Excel workbook, you can protect the original file. To do this, go to your advanced Options; under Advanced, look for the Save settings and select the check box Always Create Backup Copy.

This option saves a backup copy of the original version every time you open or save a file, using the previously saved version of the file.

CAUTION

> This protective measure is of limited value. It's designed to protect you from incredibly obvious mistakes, and it's useful only if you discover your mistake immediately. Suppose you open a Word document, make some changes, and save the changed document under the same name. If you then discover to your horror that you've altered the master copy of a crucial document, you can open the backup copy and recover the original. However, if you make some more changes and save your work a second time, Word creates a backup of the first set of changes you made, replacing the backup it created when you opened the file. You can still use Undo to "roll back" your changes, but as soon as you close Word, your original document is history, and you better hope you have an alternative backup copy to restore.

HOW OFFICE LOCKS DOCUMENTS TO PREVENT CONFLICTS

Office keeps track of which documents are open on the network. If you try to open a document that's already in use by someone else, you'll receive a warning message.

This kind of protection is necessary to keep unsynchronized changes from compromising the document's integrity. If you and your partner are simultaneously working on copies of your business plan in Word, what happens when she changes a paragraph that you're working on? For collaborating on documents in this fashion, you're better off using Word's revision-tracking features.

 If you get `File in Use` *messages when you're the only user attempting to use a document, see "Hidden Applications Lock Files" in the "Troubleshooting" section at the end of this chapter.*

Excel allows more than one person to work on a workbook simultaneously, but you have to set up the sharing before others on the network start opening the workbook.

OPENING DOCUMENTS IN READ-ONLY MODE

You can help (or force) yourself and your co-workers to open particular Office files in read-only mode. As the name implies, applying the read-only attribute allows anyone who opens the file to view its contents. To make changes, you must save a copy of the file under a new name and then make changes to the copy.

You have the following read-only options in Office 2007:

- When saving a file, you can discourage users (including yourself) from making changes to a Word document. To do this, select your Office button and choose Save As. From the Tools menu, click the arrow button and choose General Options. You will see the dialog box shown in Figure 6.2. Select the check box that says Read-Only Recommended. This technique is particularly useful when you frequently use the same document or worksheet as the base for new files, and you occasionally forget to use the From Existing Document option in the New *<file type>* task pane. When you try to open a file saved with this option, you'll see the dialog box shown in Figure 6.3. Click yes to prevent accidental changes to your original file.

6

Figure 6.2
The General Options you can set for a document, including the ability to recommend a file for Read-Only.

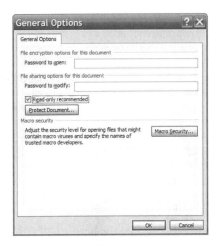

Figure 6.3
When you try to open a file saved with the Recommend Read-Only attribute, this dialog box appears.

TIP FROM

If your goal is to prevent other users from damaging an important file (especially users who might not be sophisticated enough to understand the consequences of this option), use a Modify password instead.

- When you open a document in Word, Excel, or PowerPoint, you can choose to open it as a read-only file. Click the Open icon, or choose File, Open. From the Open dialog box, click the arrow to the right of the Open button and choose Open Read-Only from the drop-down list.

- For most Office documents, you can assign separate passwords for read-only access and full read-write access, using the Password to Open and Password to Modify boxes, respectively. If you add a password in the Password to Modify box and leave the Password to Open box blank, your correspondents will be able to open the file and read its contents, but they will need to enter the password to make changes to the file.

MARK DOCUMENT AS FINAL

For your applications that generally get shared (for instance, Word, Excel, and PowerPoint), you can use a feature called Mark as Final, which is more of a preventative than a cure. This will make the document read-only and thereby prevent anyone from altering the document. In this situation, typing, editing, proofing, and so on is disabled.

To set a document to the Mark as Final setting, select the Office button, Prepare, and then Mark as Final in Word, Excel, or PowerPoint.

NOTE

> Keep in mind that documents marked as final can still be edited. All a person has to do is remove that option. However, it will deter persons from inadvertently making changes to the document and from editing it if they don't know how to take off the Mark as Final options (which is done simply by going back to your Prepare settings and deselecting that button). You also should note that this document will not be read-only if persons are using older versions of Office.

CONTROLLING FILE ACCESS WITH WINDOWS PERMISSIONS

You can also use Windows to restrict access to Office files or the folders in which they're stored. Local and network file and folder restrictions depend on your Windows version and the format of the disk on which the file is stored:

- Windows 2000, XP, or Vista running the NT File System (NTFS) provide the only secure Windows environment for controlling access to files. Using advanced NTFS options, you can restrict access to files or folders by individuals or groups; you can also encrypt files and entire folders for maximum security. Using the Encrypting File System on an NTFS volume provides absolutely ironclad protection. In addition, in Windows Vista, a new encryption exists, called Bitlocker, for your drives and data. It's pretty advanced encryption and supposedly has no backdoor method of entry, so your data is truly secure.

- Windows XP Home Edition allows you to make folders (but not individual files) private. Private folders are inaccessible over a network and cannot be accessed by other users on a shared computer. The only way for someone to open a file in a private folder is to log on using your username and password.

- On any disk formatted using the FAT16 or FAT32 file system, you can restrict access over the network, but any user who can log on to the computer locally can open and change the file.

PROTECTING PRIVATE DATA IN OFFICE DOCUMENTS

Every Office document includes information about the document, its creator, and anyone who has edited it. This information, which is known as *metadata*, is stored within the document and can be viewed and edited by selecting the Office button, choosing Prepare, and then Properties. For advanced properties, you can select a down arrow and choose Advanced Properties, which will bring you a multitabbed dialog box. Used properly, metadata is a convenient tool for tracking changes, organizing files, and searching for data. Unfortunately, it also offers a way for anyone to poke around within a document to see who worked on it, and even see material that should have been deleted. In sensitive situations, that can cause acute embarrassment. In early 2003, for instance, reporters poking around in a Word document released by the British government discovered the names of four individuals who had worked on earlier versions of the document. We've received press releases, also in Word format, where revisions and comments from reviewers were still embedded in the file—to the chagrin of the managers who distributed the document.

6

By using the Document Inspector in Word, PowerPoint, and Excel, you can remove potentially sensitive data before you save the document. For more information on erasing sensitive document data, read Chapter 7, "Office Security and Privacy."

CAUTION

> You cannot set this option on a global basis. It must be set on each individual document file before saving it.

In Word, you can also choose an option that warns you before saving, printing, or emailing a file that contains any kind of metadata, including tracked changes and comments. (This option is buried pretty deep, but if you go to the document's Options through the Office button, then go to the Trust Center settings and choose Privacy Options, you can see under the Document-specific settings the option to `Warn before printing, saving, or sending a file that contains tracked changes or comments`.) If you see this warning, cancel the operation, remove the unwanted data from the document, and try again.

Using the Document Inspector can help to keep that information out of the hands of others. But using multiple methods described within this chapter can really make your security solid. Another possible consideration for security documents is to trust another source through IRM.

SECURING DOCUMENTS WITH INFORMATION RIGHTS MANAGEMENT (IRM)

Although this technology was introduced in Office 2003, it was something that many have never heard of, so we again discuss IRM here and its advantages. Office 2007 includes support for an emerging technology called Information Rights Management. Using IRM, you can set permissions that define who can open, edit, print, forward, or copy documents or email messages.

CAUTION

> Microsoft's IRM is a new and controversial technology. It made its debut in Office 2003 and has not been widely accepted. As with all Office innovations, you can expect it to undergo changes in the next few years. If you intend to use it for mission-critical applications, we strongly recommend that you test it thoroughly first. And don't rely on it to do more than stop casual snoops. Even Microsoft admits that a determined data thief can circumvent many IRM restrictions using high- and low-tech approaches.

To use this technology, you must first install the latest Windows Rights Management client. In addition, you must have access to one of the following authentication systems:

- Windows Server 2003 with Windows Rights Management Services. This software uses the server's Active Directory as the authentication mechanism.

- A .NET Passport registered with Microsoft's Information Rights Management Service. Currently, this is available as a free trial. You can sign up when you install the client software.

To see a step-by-step walk through of configuring and using IRM through the free service that Microsoft provides, see "Secrets of the Office Masters: Setting Up and Using Information Rights Management" at the end of this chapter.

IRM works by installing a digital certificate that allows you to encrypt the document. You assign permissions based on email addresses, which represent a unique way to identify individuals. If the recipient of an IRM-encrypted message does not have access to a Windows Rights Management Server, he can register with Microsoft's free service using a .NET Passport and receive a full certificate or a temporary one.

SECURING DOCUMENTS WITH DIGITAL SIGNATURES

When you sign a document and date it, it is a loose form of identifying that you are, indeed, agreeing to the document, or agreeing that the document came from you. Unless a signature expert verifies that you signed it, it remains a loose guarantee that you do, in fact, agree with the contents and stand behind them. However, in many cases, you can go one step further and have a document notarized by a third party or have several witnesses to your signing of a document (for example, a marriage certificate). Digitally, this is what you are doing when you work with a digital signature.

Digital information can be authenticated through cryptography. This helps to ensure that the signature itself is valid and coming from the person who is claiming to have signed the document digitally, that the content of the document is still intact and hasn't been tampered with since the time it has been digitally signed, and that the signer cannot refute that it came from that person, and only that person. That is quite a bit to guarantee without having any physical witnesses present to ensure it. But there are digital witnesses available:

A signature must be registered by a certificate authority (CA), a third-party agency who will assign a valid signature to the requesting party. The certificate that is given is a way of proving identity (like a driver's license) and can expire. So, basically, when you send a digitally signed document, your computer adds these credentials to it. The recipient can check your signature certificate against the CA database to make sure you truly are the sender and the document hasn't been tampered with.

Office 2007 allows you to either add a visible signature line to a document or add a hidden digital signature to the document. Let's consider the difference between the two.

ADDING SIGNATURE LINES TO A DOCUMENT

Only into Word documents and Excel workbooks can you add a visible signature line (which is logical because you don't need this feature for your PowerPoint presentations of Publisher documents).

A signature line shows the added visible line to a document. To the untrained eye, this looks just like a graphic to make the document look "chic" to the receiver, but it is more than a graphical element.

When you first go to insert a digital signature line, you have to answer some questions, as shown in Figure 6.4. You can put in the name, the title, and even an email address. You can add some direction to the person who has to add his signature.

6

Figure 6.4
Configuration options for your digital signature line.

When the recipient gets the document, he or she is notified that a signature is requested. The person can type a signature, select an image of his or her signature, or write one with Tablet PC. The recipient has a choice of either using a real digital signature (which is added to the document as well so that it proves that the visible signature is truly from the one who adds it, logically preventing someone else from signing and returning the document) or the recipient can add a made-up digital signature, which cannot really validate that the user is truly who the user claims to be (see Figure 6.5).

Figure 6.5
Using a digital signature line allows the receiver to know that they need to agree to the document with a digital signature that proves they are the signer.

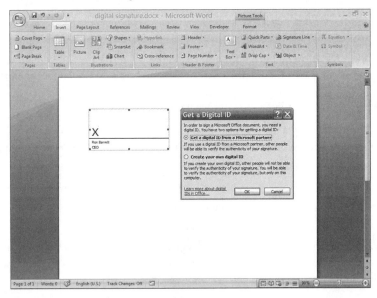

After a document is signed, it becomes read-only so that it cannot be tampered with from that point forward.

Adding a signature line is easy. You go to the Insert ribbon and from the Text grouping, select Signature Line. Then you need to add information about the recipient in the Signature Setup dialog box, including adding the sign date (which is standard in most documents).

To literally sign the document, the recipient needs to double-click the line where the signature is requested. At this point, the recipient gets to either add in a typed name, choose the image of his or her signature, or write it with a Tablet PC handwritten tool through the inking feature. When you are done, click the Sign button.

ADDING HIDDEN DIGITAL SIGNATURES TO A DOCUMENT

On other occasions, you may not need a literal line for a visible signature to be added to your document. You may just want to guarantee that the document is authentic and that its integrity is intact and from you. You can add an invisible signature to your Word, Excel, and PowerPoint documents.

You won't be able to see the signature, but a little icon indicates that the document has been signed. To ensure that it hasn't been tampered with since the signing of the document, it becomes read-only, too.

To add only an invisible signature to a document, select the Office button, choose the Prepare option, and select Add a Digital Signature. From here you follow options similar to the previous ones, and you can even indicate why you are signing the particular document.

ROUTING, REVIEWING, AND REVISING DOCUMENTS

Sometimes server-based collaboration doesn't have the urgency of email: You can tell people over and over that they need to connect to the server and make their comments, and some never will. But if they receive the document by email, the immediacy can help spur them to action. Add a routing slip that details how long an individual has been procrastinating, and you might have enough incentive to move mountains.

Office includes several tools that help you mail, route, and control your documents.

SENDING AN OFFICE FILE AS EMAIL

Sometimes you may want to send the body of your document by email, rather than sending an attachment, as discussed later. The simplest way to send a document to an individual or group is by sending it as an email message, in HTML format.

Keep in mind that you can send attachments of any of your office files; however, the method of sending text directly within the body of your document can be done only with Word and Excel.

To do this, you have to first add the command to your Quick Access Toolbar. You open the Customization settings and search All Commands for one called Send To Mail Recipient.

From the Quick Access Toolbar, you can now select this and, as you can see in Figure 6.6, you will be able to send that information directly within the body of your email message.

Figure 6.6
An Excel workbook, with multiple sheets embedded within your email message.

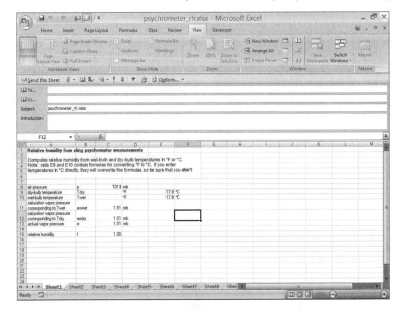

When the document is sent as an HTML message, each recipient can modify the document directly, as long as the recipient's email reader can handle Office's particular version of HTML (this includes most modern mail clients, including Outlook 98 or later, Netscape Mail 4.5 or later, and Eudora 5 or later; Outlook 97, AOL, and many older mail programs cannot). The recipient can then send the message back, and you have the challenge of assembling the HTML messages, converting them to native Office file formats, and comparing the results.

If you decide that you don't want to send a copy as a mail message after all, click the Email button again to make the message header disappear.

SENDING A FILE AS AN EMAIL ATTACHMENT

If all your correspondents are using Office 97 or later versions, and you want them to be able to edit the document properly, you'll no doubt find it much more reliable to send the document as an attachment to an email message.

You can do that from any of the Office applications, although keep in mind that Access forces you to choose a different format for your email. We will go through the steps in Word, but the same basic format would be used for Excel or PowerPoint, too. Follow these steps:

1. Open (or create) the document.

2. From the Office button, select Send, and then choose from a number of options. You can choose to send it as an Email, or a Fax (through an Internet fax service). In addition, if you have installed the PDF/XPS add-in that allows you to convert your documents, you would be able to send your document in one of these formats, too.

NOTE

> For sending an email in OneNote, Project, or Visio, click Send To from the File menu and then select Mail Recipient (as Attachment). From Publisher, click Send Email from the File menu and select Send Publication as Attachment.

ADDING COMMENTS AND TRACKING CHANGES

Although the Office Suite comes with multiple applications, not all of them need to be collaborated on. For example, your saved OneNote thoughts don't need collaboration, but your Excel spreadsheet just might. How do you see who has altered the document and what they have altered? Later in the book, we discuss ways to track changes in each application. At this point, we will give a quick overview for this feature, but we will highlight your ability to use Protection to allow only certain capabilities (for example, comments only when editing, but no changes).

ADDING COMMENTS TO DOCUMENTS

When you're collaborating on a document with other people, it's helpful to leave comments along the way, explaining the reasons for certain changes or suggesting places where additional changes may be necessary.

To enter a comment, highlight the text that pertains to the comment and choose New Comment from the Comments grouping on the Review ribbon. (If you don't make a selection, Word attaches the comment to the word immediately preceding the insertion point.) Type your comment into the comment box.

To cycle through all the comments in a document, use the Next button on the Review ribbon.

You can print all the comments attached to a document by choosing the Office button, Print, and selecting Document Showing Markup in the Print What drop-down box.

RESTRICTING EDITS TO COMMENTS ONLY

In Word, you have the ability to restrict editing of your documents to comments only. To do this, go to the Review ribbon and select Protect Document. You will see the Restrict Formatting and Editing dialog box shown in Figure 6.7.

6

Figure 6.7
From the Restrict Formatting and Editing dialog box, you can establish editing restrictions that allow for comments only.

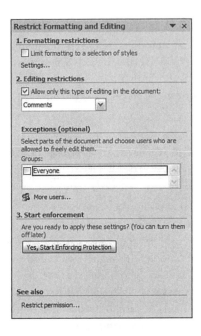

You can allow for exceptions to the document or to specific parts of the document. You can also change the settings to allow for tracked changes or filling in forms. When you start the enforcement of the restrictions, you can determine a password method of protection or an encryption method.

For going to the next level of document protection, however, note the section at the end of the chapter, "Secrets of the Office Masters: Setting Up and Using Information Rights Management."

NOTE

We've mentioned the Comments ability of Word because Word generally has the most extensive set of tools for comments and tracking changes. However, you can go to the Review tab in Excel and insert comments, too, as well as in PowerPoint, as you can see in Figure 6.8.

You can see from Figure 6.8 that PowerPoint allows you to add comments that can be turned on and off. Even though they are in the background, you won't see them unless you go to the Review ribbon, under the Comments grouping, and select Show Markup. You can toggle this option to turn comments on or off.

6

Figure 6.8
Word isn't the only application that allows for comments. Excel and PowerPoint also give you that capability.

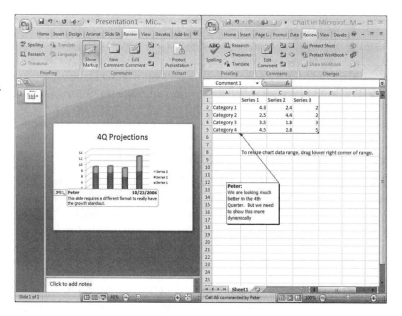

TRACKING REVISIONS

The surest way to maintain the integrity of a document is to ensure that changes—if they're allowed at all—are clearly identified so that anyone reviewing the edited document can trace specific changes back to their originator. When Word tracks changes made to a document, text that is added, deleted, or modified is marked to emphasize the changes made. You can subsequently go through those changes, one at a time, and accept or reject them. Word 2007 offers a tri-pane review panel to make it easier for you to work with revisions made within documents.

→ For a complete discussion of tracking changes in Word 2007, **see** "Sharing Documents," **p. 468**.

Excel also allows you to track changes within your documents. In fact, in one click you can add password protection and set tracking.

To do this, in your Excel workbook, select the Review ribbon and choose the Protect and Share workbook option under the Changes grouping. The dialog box opens and from here you can choose to set a password (see Figure 6.9).

Figure 6.9
Sharing an Excel workbook allows for password protection and tracked changes.

6

COMPARING, REVIEWING, AND MERGING CHANGES

When multiple Office users work on the same document, workbook, or presentation, you can compare the contents of each version and merge the changes into a single document. Word and Excel allow you to review each change individually or merge all changes at one time. PowerPoint does only a full comparison and merge between two presentations.

→ For details on how to track changes in Word documents, **see** "Sharing Documents," **p. 468**.

PRINTING OFFICE DOCUMENTS

These days, many people think we should move away from printing altogether. With the quality of online reading improving, and the ability to make documents that can be read on your computer, there is less need to print those documents. Nevertheless, nothing beats an in-hand document. Printing in Office 2007 is pretty much the same as it was in previous versions of Office. The exception is that Word, Excel, PowerPoint, and Access have a new interface, so you may need some direction on how to Print.

In Word, Excel, PowerPoint or Access, elect the Microsoft Office button and choose Print (or press Ctrl+P). You'll notice that you also have the options to Print Preview (which gives you a preview of your documents and how they will look when printed) and to Quick Print, which helps you avoid the Print dialog box. Quick Print is useful only if you are comfortable with the default Print settings and don't need to make any changes.

In OneNote, Outlook, Project, Publisher, or Visio, the Print option is found under the File menu (or you can press Ctrl+P).

PUBLISHING OFFICE DOCUMENTS TO A WEBSITE

You can publish your documents to websites in multiple ways. You can save documents as HTML format and use an FTP application to upload them. If the website is your local Intranet site or your company website, you can add your pages directly to those servers off your network (see your network administrator for permission and instruction on how to do this).

In addition, you can select the Publish option off the Microsoft Office button and choose from several topics depending on the application. In Word, you have the ability to blog now.

→ For details on how to use Word 2007 as a Blog editor, **see** "Secrets of the Office Masters: Using Word as a Blog Editor," **p. 385**.

In all other applications, you have the ability to publish your documents to a Document Management Server or to Create a Document Workspace. Let's consider the differences:

- **Document Management Server**—When you publish a document with this option, you are saving a copy of your file to a network server. You need to know the name of the server so that you can find it within your network to put the document up on it.

- **Create Document Workspace**—A Document Workspace site is a SharePoint site that allows collaboration with people on a team, or in the same group. The site will help keep the files updated and will alert others about the status of those files. When you create a Document Workspace site, your file is saved within a document library so that others can access those files and work on them if they have permission to so do. File versions are kept track of so that a history can be maintained to ensure that all involved within a project are aware of the progression. For more information on how to create a Document Workspace, see "Create a Document Workspace" from within the Word help files.

COMBINING TWO OR MORE DATA TYPES IN ONE DOCUMENT

After you get beyond simple letter writing and number crunching, you get to the really interesting aspects of Office as a unified system. For maximum effect, you can build *compound documents* by combining data created in a variety of sources—starting with a Word document and integrating an Excel worksheet into it, for instance, or incorporating an Excel chart into a PowerPoint presentation.

The most common example is a corporate report, in which financial data from Excel (or tabular material from Access) is blended into a Word document. Or you might use Word to generate explanatory text for an Excel worksheet. You can store résumés from job candidates as Word documents in a field in an Access database. PowerPoint presentations almost routinely are compound documents with slides containing charts and tables from Excel.

By creating compound documents, you can use links between data so that each element is available for updating. When you click in a résumé stored in Word format in an Access table, for example, Office automatically opens Word for you to read and modify the document. You can continuously revise those Excel data ranges in the annual report, even as co-workers edit the text around them.

This all works because Office has an *object design*: Each Office document is essentially a container into which several kinds of information can be poured.

You'll see references to *OLE objects*, *COM objects*, and *ActiveX objects* in the online documentation and elsewhere. For everyday use, these terms all refer to the same thing. For simplicity's sake, we call them "objects" in this book.

6

NOTE

> You'll also see *OLE container*, *ActiveX container*, and *COM container* in the Help files and Knowledge Base articles. Don't be confused. These terms refer to Office files—documents, workbooks, and presentations.

EMBEDDING VERSUS LINKING

Office offers two very different methods for putting objects (such as text, charts, pictures, or a worksheet range) into a Word document, Excel worksheet, Access database, Outlook item, or PowerPoint presentation. The two methods are called *embedding* and *linking*:

- Embedding stores the data as an object inside the document, including an indication of which application made the object. So, if you embed an Excel chart in a Word document, all the data for the chart resides inside the Word document and Word "knows" it can be edited with Excel. All the data for the chart is inside Word and is not available in an external file; thus, you can't start Excel and edit the chart directly. Instead, you must start with Word and edit from there. The real benefit here is that you don't need to worry about another file location that is connected to your document. If you know the data isn't going to change and the chart is final, then embedding is the best way to go.

- Linking, on the other hand, inserts a pointer to data stored in an external file. When you create a link, the document that contains the link might include a snapshot of the data, but the container document attempts to update the link whenever necessary. Thus, if you insert a named range from an Excel worksheet stored in the file \\Corporate\ Payroll\Salaries.xls into a Word document, the document stores a code that instructs Word to retrieve that range from its location on the network whenever you open or print the document. Because the data exists in an external file, you can use Excel to update Salaries.xls at any time, and your changes will be reflected the next time anyone opens or prints the Word document that contains the link. One of the negative sides to linking is that you have to worry about your files locations. If they change, then the link no longer will work. However, the positive side to linking is that your data remains as up to date as the linked document itself. It ensures you have the latest changes the moment you open the document.

> **NOTE**
>
> Pictures frequently appear in documents as, simply, pictures—they're neither embedded nor linked.

Embedded objects are edited in place: If you double-click an Excel worksheet embedded in your Word document, for example, Excel's menus and toolbars replace the Word equivalents—even though you're still working in the Word window.

On the other hand, if you double-click a linked object, the originating application opens and loads the data from the linked external file. If you double-click an Excel chart linked in a PowerPoint presentation, Excel starts with the chart ready for work.

When you consider whether to link, embed, or place objects in documents, you must juggle three competing considerations:

- **File Size**—Will the objects bloat the document? An embedded Office object (an Excel chart, for instance) can take up twice as much room as a picture of that same object. In a large file, the difference can be dramatic.

- **Update Capability**—Will the object change? If so, you need to keep your options open. Yes, you can paste an Excel range into a Word document as a table, and then convert it back to an Excel range for updates. But if you plan to update the data frequently, it's easier to embed or link the data.

- **Portability**—Will the document and objects stay on a single computer or in easily accessible network locations? Or do you plan to move them to a portable PC, or distribute them to one or more people who are not connected to the same network?

With those three considerations in mind, here's how to select the best method for putting an object into a document:

- If you're not particularly worried about file size, and you won't need to update the object or change its formatting, forget about linking or embedding. Insert the data—picture, table, chart, whatever—into the document.

- If file size is the overriding concern, use links to external data such as pictures and charts. You might encounter problems when moving documents, but if you duplicate the folder structure for document and objects on all the computers, linking will work.

- If portability is the main concern, and it's possible you'll need to update the object or move the file that contains the source data, use embedding. That way, you'll always have the object at hand—the object and its data travel with the document.

- In a workgroup, linking is the best way to handle items on which you plan to collaborate: One person or group can be working on the document while another person or group works on, for example, the linked chart. When both groups are ready, update the document to bring in the latest version of all linked objects. This process is particularly easy when a SharePoint server is available for use as a central storage location.

TIP FROM

EQ & Woody

> You can quickly tell whether an object in Word is embedded or linked. By going into your Word Options, under the Advanced settings, Show Document Content, select the Show field codes instead of their value option (or you can simply hit Alt+F9 to toggle field codes). An embedded object appears with an {Embed} field code; a linked object appears as a {Link} field code. Pictures that are part of the file won't have any field code, and you can see the picture.

→ To learn more about putting field codes to work in your Word documents, **see** "Using Fields to Add Intelligence to a Document," **p. 496**.

6

OVERVIEW OF FILE SHARING ON AN OFFICE NETWORK

In an office, one of the most common barriers to sharing information is figuring out where to put it. If you store documents on your own hard drive, you have to figure out how to give other people secure access. On a network server, you have to deal with filenames, permissions, and the logistics of figuring out how to get people working cooperatively.

Several years ago, Microsoft introduced SharePoint Team Services and SharePoint Portal Server—two versions of a web-based server package designed to make it easy for members of a workgroup to communicate, collaborate, and share information with one another, preferably while using Office XP (and now Office 2007). As befits a Microsoft "version 1.0" product, the two members of the SharePoint family were loaded with promise but also plagued by design limitations and some usability snafus.

With the release of Office 2003, Microsoft updated its SharePoint servers as well. The two products were considerably more usable and useful than their predecessors, and they integrate tightly with Office 2003. Moving forward with Office 2007, that integration has continued to allow for a stronger collaboration capability with your documents.

In some respects, SharePoint defies a quick explanation, but we'll try anyway. SharePoint services expand the capabilities of a web server to allow members of a team to store documents, carry on discussions in a threaded bulletin-board format, create lists, and share tasks, contacts, and calendars. The server administrator defines permissions for team members, giving some full administrative rights over the team websites and allowing others rights to upload files, change documents, or create new special-purpose sites.

SharePoint sites come in two varieties:

- **Windows SharePoint Services**—An add-on to Windows Server 2003, it replaces the previous FrontPage Server Extensions and SharePoint Team Services. Its primary purpose is to create a customizable website for a single team.

- **SharePoint Portal Server 2003/2007**—An enterprise-strength version of the same software that adds the capability to integrate business applications, create separate sites for different business units, and take advantage of sophisticated document workflow systems. In SharePoint 2007, there are feature enhancements to look forward to, as well as brand new features—for example, task coordination capabilities, email integration (similar to Public Folder capabilities found in Exchange), blog posting abilities, support for Wiki sites, and a Social Networking Web part to allow for collaboration between workers with the same social interests. It's a lot to consider all at once, but SharePoint Portal Server allows you to take Office 2007 to the next level, to the level where we no longer simply create documents, we collaborate the production of documentation.

NOTE

For more information about these two server products, visit Microsoft's SharePoint website at http://www.microsoft.com/sharepoint.

TROUBLESHOOTING

FORGOTTEN PASSWORDS

I saved a document with a password months ago. I tried to open the document, but I forgot the password. What can I do?

If you forgot the password for a Word document, Excel workbook, Access database, or PowerPoint presentation, brace yourself: It's going to take a long time to recover the password, if it can be recovered at all. Start by ordering one of the commercial password-cracking programs at http://www.accessdata.com or http://www.lostpassword.com. If you need to crack only one document, ask the manufacturer for a money-back guarantee that its product will be successful.

On the other hand, if you lost a different kind of password, such as those used to protect formatting in a Word document, your task is much simpler. You can check with either of the previously mentioned companies, or search on the Web for many other "crackers."

HIDDEN APPLICATIONS LOCK FILES

When I try to open a Word document or an Excel workbook, the File in Use dialog box appears. I know no one else has the file open. Sometimes, the dialog box even accuses me of being the one using the file. The program only allows me to open the file as Read Only.

If you know that nobody else on your network has the file open and you get the File in Use dialog box, a hidden instance of one of the Office apps might be holding on to the file. Or, if the program that had the file open crashes, it might not correctly remove the file that tracks the lock.

When this happens, use the Windows Task Manager (Ctrl+Alt+Del) to find any hidden instances of the program in question and end them. If the dialog box appears after Word crashed on your system, look for an owner file in the same directory as the file that refuses to open. This temporary file has a .doc extension; the filename itself is the same as the original file, except the first two letters are replaced with a tilde (~) followed by a dollar sign. This temporary file holds the logon name of the person opening the file. Delete it to remove the lock.

SECRETS OF THE OFFICE MASTERS: SETTING UP AND USING INFORMATION RIGHTS MANAGEMENT

We started this discussion a little earlier in the chapter, but let's go through a step-by-step of the process to make you feel more comfortable with these tools that Microsoft provides.

To start with, you should have already downloaded the client (as we mentioned earlier). So now when you go to your Review ribbon and select Protect Document (or when you go to your Office button, select Prepare, and then choose Restrict Permission), if you select the Restrict Permission option, you will see the first set of dialog (shown in Figure 6.10).

Figure 6.10
You are asked if you want to sign up for the trial service. If you say no, you cannot select Next, so it's really not a choice if you want to move forward.

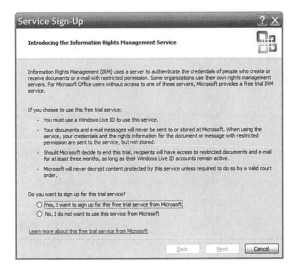

Next, you will be asked if you have a .NET Passport (shown in Figure 6.11). If not, you will have to create one.

Figure 6.11
Microsoft wants to verify that you have the proper credentials.

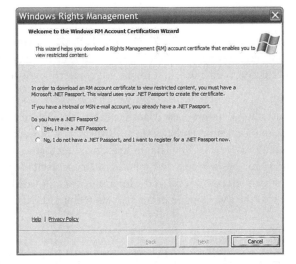

In Figure 6.12, you see you are asked to confirm your email.

Figure 6.12
Confirming your email is important because your passport email may not be the one you want to use for your IRM.

In Figure 6.13, you are asked whether you want a standard or temporary certificate. For testing, you might choose temporary, but if you decide you want to continue using this feature in the future, you might want to select Standard.

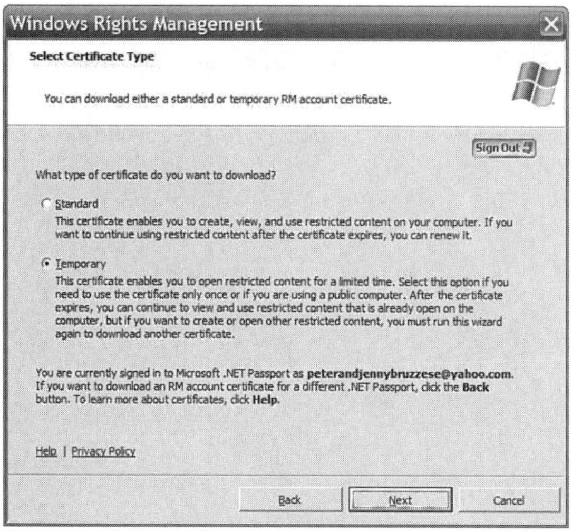

Figure 6.13
Standard or Temporary Certificate—that's your decision; test it out and see what you think.

6

Finally, you'll get a screen that says you have completed the setup. Then you can see the different settings you can configure for your documents (see Figure 6.14).

Figure 6.14
You add email addresses to ensure that these documents are confirmed against their email.

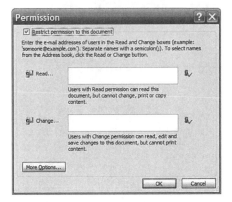

As the author of a document, you have full control over it. To set access rights for other people, go to your Review ribbon and select Protect Document for your options. Choose one of the following three options:

- **Unrestricted Access**—This option means anyone can perform any action with the file, subject to any other restrictions (such as password protection) that you've set.

- **Do Not Distribute**—This option prevents anyone from attaching the document to an email message.

- **Restrict Permission As**—This option allows you to set further options, including control over whether the document can be printed or copied. You can also set an expiration date, after which the document no longer opens for anyone except its author.

CHAPTER 7

OFFICE SECURITY AND PRIVACY

In this chapter

What Is the Office Trust Center?   160

Using the Office Trust Center   160

Installing and Managing Add-Ins   169

Backup and Recovery Options   170

Protecting Personal Information   170

Troubleshooting   172

Secrets of the Office Masters: Backup and Recovery Basics   173

What Is the Office Trust Center?

Office 2007 has a Trust Center to assist you in modifying your security and privacy settings. From the past, you might recall security settings such as Very High, High, and so on, but now the entire security system has received a badly needed makeover. It's time we take security seriously.

To open the Trust Center (in Word, Excel, PowerPoint, and Access), you select the Office button, the Options (for whichever program you are in), and then select Trust Center, and Trust Center Settings.

To open the Trust Center in other Office 2007 applications (Visio, Outlook, Publisher, and InfoPath), go to Tools and choose Trust Center.

Using the Office Trust Center

When you first open the Trust Center settings, you are going to be initially unimpressed. As is often the case, those items that protect us the most don't necessarily come with pretty wrapping. The Trust Center is not like a cool designed application. There is no eye candy to wow us. But it has functionality on its side—no doubt Microsoft will add to it and dress it up a bit in future Office versions...after we have established security.

Each setting is different, so we will start at the top and work our way down to cover each one.

Defining Trusted Publishers

If this setting had been renamed "Defining Trusted Developers," you would instinctively know what it was. Using the word "publishers" confuses us. But a publisher, in this sense, is a developer who has created a macro, an ActiveX control, an add-in, or some other application. To protect us from running code that isn't safe, that code needs to meet certain specifications, such as a valid and current digital signature combined with a Certificate Authority that validates the signature.

What happens if you try to run code that doesn't have all this? You get a security warning that lets you know that settings have been disabled, as you see in Figure 7.1.

When you get a security warning like the one shown in Figure 7.1, you have options that allow you to keep the macro disabled, enable the macro, or trust the publisher explicitly. Enable the macro if you trust it, but trust the publisher only if you are sure that you can trust explicitly for other macros in the future.

If you don't see the option to trust, that's possibly because there is no certificate involved. You either trust the content or not, but the developer doesn't have an established relationship with a CA to vouch for them. In cases where you aren't sure, or you receive warning that the signature isn't valid or out of date, you should not enable the content.

7

Figure 7.1
The Trust Center is more like the No-Trust Center. When something comes up that it doesn't like, it disables the application from working and gives you a warning and some options to choose from. You are still driving here, but now there are helpful traffic signals.

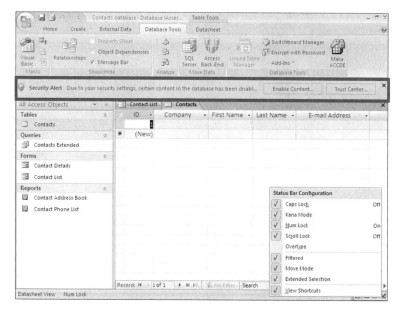

If you do choose to trust the publisher, that information will show up in your Trust Center under Trusted Publisher. If you want to remove the publisher at some time in the future, select it and choose Remove.

To view the certificate connected to the publisher, go into your trust center, choose Trusted Publishers, and then select the publisher you want to view and choose View.

DEFINING TRUSTED LOCATIONS

Let's face it, the heading here sounds a bit 007-ish. "I'll meet you at the trusted location for the drop off." Well, sorry to bring us back to reality, but these locations are generally folders on our disks or on the network that we trust. Essentially, this means we can open files from that location without the Trust Center getting involved.

You may be wondering why you would want to open a file without the Trust Center protecting you. Perhaps you have files that you know are running macros that are not from a trusted source. You want to open them without the interference, and you don't want to alter your security settings for these documents. So, you put them in a folder and trust that folder location.

Some locations are trusted by default. For example, the location of your Microsoft Office\Templates and your Microsoft Office\Office12\Startup files are both pretrusted folders (as you can see in Figure 7.2).

7

Figure 7.2
Predefined trusted locations are helpful. And you can add more if you like.

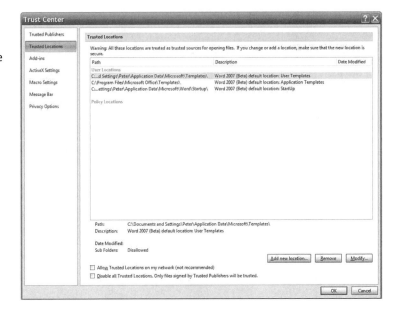

With trusted locations, it's logically safer if the folder is located on your personal system, if you have password protection on your system. The reason it's stronger than a network location is because the first rule of protection is access. A network share is accessible by outsiders, but your personal system is not (hopefully). The key is to have your security settings configured, your firewall on, no backdoor applications running—and a strong password.

TIP FROM

Microsoft recommends in its Help files that we not designate the entire My Documents (or just Documents in Vista) folder as trusted, because this could leave a hole open for attack. Better to make a subfolder trusted.

To add a trusted location, go to those settings within the Trust Center and click Add New Location. Type the path or browse for it. You can select to allow subfolders as well and add a Description if you choose.

You can remove that location or change it in the same location that you created it.

CONTROLLING ADD-INS AND ACTIVEX CONTROLS

When you initially look at the settings here, there isn't much to be overly concerned about. Some shy away from securing their systems out of fear of the tools themselves. But notice in these settings how little is required of you. With a little bit of knowledge, you can make wise choices to secure yourself.

7

TRUST CENTER—ADD-INS

First off, what are add-ins? Basically, they "add" into your current applications. You can install an add-in to an Office application that will give you greater capability. For example, by default you cannot convert your documents to PDF, but you can download and install an add-in that will give you that added functionality. To start off, you might want to see what add-ins you currently have. To do this, go to your Options and choose Add-Ins (shown in Figure 7.3).

Figure 7.3
Add-ins provide increased functionality, but they can also be dangerous if from the wrong source.

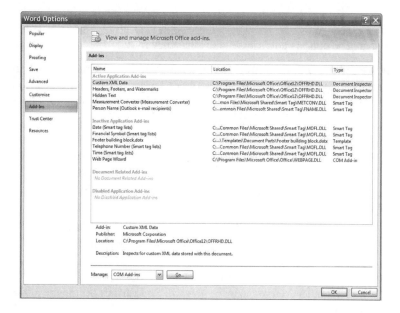

You will note several types of add-ins:

- **Active Application**—Shows the extensions that are running currently in your Office application.

- **Inactive Application**—Shows add-ins that you have on your system but that aren't running at the moment.

- **Document Related**—Shows template files that currently opened documents have referenced.

- **Disabled Application**—This area would show any add-ins that had to be disabled because they were causing problems in Office.

Where does the Trust Center help us? If you go to your Trust Center and select the Add-Ins settings, you'll notice only a few options.

The basic problem with add-ins is that they can contain harmful content and you wouldn't know it until after it was already installed. The Trust Center will challenge add-ins that aren't from a trusted source (if you want it to). None of these settings will change until after you close the application and reopen it.

7

Figure 7.4
Add-in settings in the
Trust Center.

Here are the options you can set and what they mean:

- **Require Application Add-ins to Be Signed by Trusted Publisher**—We discussed the benefits of this earlier. If the Trust Center looks for a trusted digital signature from a trusted Certificate Authority, the add-in will install with no problems. This ensures that the add-in came from a trusted source and that the add-in was not tampered with in any way between the developer and your system.

- **Disable Notification for Unsigned Add-ins (Code Will Remain Disabled)**—This option is grayed out by default, unless you select the option above it. Sometimes, some portions of the add-in are signed, but the .dll files called on by the add-ins are not. These will be disabled.

- **Disable All Application Add-ins (May Impair Functionality)**—This option is self-explanatory. If you need to stop all trust of add-ins, this will do it.

Outlook has similar features, but to access them you have to go to the Trust Center from the Tools menu. Under Macro Security, you will find various options to allow/disallow macros. These can be applied to Add-ins.

TRUST CENTER—ACTIVEX CONTROLS

Back to the normal first question—what is an ActiveX control? Don't feel ashamed to have to ask. Many, many computer experts use terminology all the time without knowing what the terms really mean. Let's fix that for you now.

An ActiveX control can be a text box, a toolbar, a dialog box, or a website application or…have we cleared this up yet? Basically, ActiveX controls piggyback off other application functionality. They don't work with every application, but with Internet Explorer (not Firefox) and Office, these controls are created by developers, using Microsoft proprietary tools, to run with Microsoft applications. Why are they dangerous? Because they are, as "they" say, COM objects, which mean that they have unrestricted access to your computer. Now why would anyone, especially Microsoft, create such a dangerous concept? Well, sometimes to be the best, you want your tools to perform the best. Tools that can reach down and grab the most amount of power will shine—and will leave a dangerously gapping hole in your security. For this reason (and others), Firefox and other alternative Internet browsers pulled many away from Microsoft's Internet Explorer. Internet Explorer 7.0 has some increased functionality to protect against ActiveX components by disabling them from running.

So, how do we protect ourselves from these powerful, yet dangerous, applications?

If you look into your Trust Center and choose ActiveX Settings, as shown in Figure 7.5, you can see four option buttons. Several things are needed to achieve a safe environment for ActiveX controls. Your system needs to look for the "kill-bit" for the control. This is a Registry entry that alerts your system to ActiveX controls that are noted to exploit situations, and then that control will not be installed or run. The next part in your ActiveX settings that is needed relates to the control being marked as Safe for Initializations. The developer establishes this setting and the Trust Center will check to see whether it is safe or unsafe.

Figure 7.5
ActiveX Settings for all Office applications.

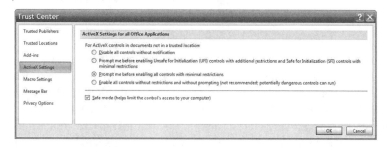

Let's review all the settings in Figure 7.5:

- **Disable All Controls Without Notification**—Obviously, the safest way to stop all ActiveX controls is to completely turn off their ability to function. If you try to open one, you will see a red x or a picture in its place.

- **Prompt Me Before Enabling Unsafe for Initialization (UFI) Controls with Additional Restrictions and Safe for Initialization (SFI) Controls with Minimal Restrictions**—The way this option will react depends on whether the document with the ActiveX control has a VBA project. The whole thing gets complicated at this point, but the basic thing to remember is that you will be prompted with the Message bar and will be asked how to proceed.

- **Prompt Me Before Enabling All Controls with Minimal Restrictions**—This is the default setting and has differing behavior depending on whether the ActiveX control has a VBA project. "Minimal Restrictions" means that if any persisted values exist, the restrictions will apply.

- **Enable All Controls Without Restrictions and Without Prompting (Not Recommended; Potentially Dangerous Controls Can Run)**—The reasons why this is dangerous are obvious if you read any of the preceding information about how powerful ActiveX controls can be. However, if you do decide to enable this setting, you won't see the Message bar with any security messages regarding ActiveX controls.

You'll notice beneath your option button selections that there is a check box called Safe Mode (Helps Limit the Control's Access to Your Computer). This enables only SFI controls in safe mode, meaning the developer has marked the control safe.

7

The Kill Bit

We mentioned earlier that ActiveX is powerful and yet very dangerous because of the ability for evil developers to use it to create spyware and other harmful programs that can attack our systems. You can disable ActiveX controls from running completely, but that may not be what you want. Another option is for certain ActiveX controls, called *kill bits*, that are registered in the Registry, to be disabled. The kill bit is a flag in the Class Identifier (CLSID) for the control. These CLSIDs are designed to be globally unique, meaning that after you block a control using the kill bit in the Registry, it's blocked forever (or until someone re-creates the control with a new CLSID). There are sites on the Internet that are updated often with ActiveX controls that are known to be spyware. You can use this information to set the kill bit in your Registry so that those controls are never used.

CONTROLLING MACROS AND VBA PROJECTS

What exactly is a macro? Macros are ways to automate frequent tasks. For example, if the first thing you do each day is open Word, change some settings, type the same text, format that text—you could create a template to help you do all that. Or you could create a simple recorded macro to keep track of everything you do and then save it in Visual Basic code so that it can repeat it very quickly anytime you run that macro. You can make more advanced macros by using VBA code. Hackers can also use macros to do certain things. For example, one day we had a macro in our department that deleted all the letter e's when you opened a document. Doesn't sound too serious, but in 100+ page documents, it could take a long time to find all those e's. (We restored from a backup for most of it.)

But VBA macros are much more powerful than that little example. They can spread from document to document and cost your company time and money.

We have already discussed ways to work with the Security dialog box that comes up in the Message bar asking if you want to continue when an item, in this case a macro, is found to be without a digital signature or someone to vouch for it. At that point, it's your choice whether to allow it to run.

Figure 7.6
Macro Settings within the Trust Center.

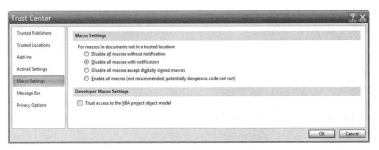

From the Trust Center, under the Macro Settings, there are options to enhance (or relax) your macro security, as shown in Figure 7.6. Let's consider these:

- **Disable All Macros Without Notification**—If this option is selected, no macros will be trusted to run. All macros are disabled. The only exceptions are documents placed in the trusted locations folders.

- **Disable All Macros with Notification**—Macros are disabled by default. But you will be notified each time, and you have the option of saying yes or no to a specific macro-oriented document.

- **Disable All Macros Except Digitally Signed Macros**—This allows those macros that are signed to pass through without the Message bar coming up to warn us. However, if there is a macro that is not digitally signed, the security Message bar will come up and ask us what we would like to do.

- **Enable All Macros (Not Recommended, Potentially Dangerous Code Can Run)**—With this setting, you are pretty much asking for trouble from any harmful macro virus that comes your way.

You'll notice that there is a section called Developer Macro Settings with a check box Trust Access to the VBA Project Object Model. This option should only concern you if you are a developer working with VBA objects. You can turn the permissions on or off through this checkbox.

SETTING MESSAGE BAR AND PRIVACY OPTIONS

The last two settings are less about security and more about personal choice in regard to what we want to have displayed or shared with others.

The Message bar is your friend. It displays the security alerts that come up when you have a problem. The Message bar (shown in Figure 7.7) can also be turned off if you don't want to see these alerts.

Figure 7.7
Message Bar settings within the Trust Center.

The final settings within your Trust Center relate to Privacy Options shown in Figure 7.8.

7

Figure 7.8
Privacy Option settings
within the Trust Center.

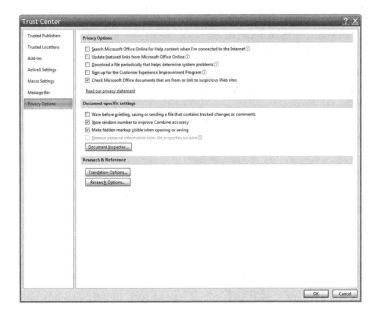

The Privacy Options offer a wide range of options to choose from. Let's consider what they are:

- **Search Microsoft Office Online for Help Content When I Am Connected to the Internet**—This selection ensures that you get the latest help information from Microsoft when you make a request.

- **Update Featured Links from Microsoft Office Online**—This gives you the most up-to-date headlines and featured templates from the Internet.

- **Download a File Periodically That Helps Determine System Problems**—This allows your system to download a file that will work with your diagnostics programs to determine the cause of crashes and errors that you may be experiencing.

- **Sign Up for the Customer Experience Improvement Program**—This requires no work on your part, just your permission. If you allow this, Microsoft can collect information from your computer to help determine what errors you are facing and why. The information is collected anonymously, so you don't have to worry about it being a sales gimmick.

- **Check Microsoft Office Documents That Are From or Link to Suspicious Web Sites**—For links within your document, with this setting the application now has the permission to check for you to see if these links are dangerous to keep.

- **Warn Before Printing, Saving, or Sending a File That Contains Tracked Changes or Comments**—You may want to eliminate these things from your documents before you send them to others. You can use the Document Inspector to accomplish this.

- **Store Random Number to Improve Combine Accuracy**—Allows for greater possibility of good results when merging documents that have tracked changes from different reviewers.

- **Make Hidden Markup Visible When Opening or Saving**—This is an option that relates to tracked changes to allow you to see if any tracked changes are still left in a document so that you can remove them.

- **Remove Personal Information from File Properties on Save (Disabled)**—Allows for greater possibility of good results when merging documents that have tracked changes from different reviewers.

In addition to these options, within the Privacy options you have a Research & Reference section. There are only two buttons present: one for Translation Options (which allows you to select languages available for your bilingual dictionary and for your document translation tools) and the other for Research Options (which allows you to select which reference books will be available to you in your research tools.

You may not see each of these options in every application, but in Word you can see the most options available.

INSTALLING AND MANAGING ADD-INS

We discussed protecting ourselves from add-ins, but let's discuss how to install these. It's not difficult, just a little obscure. To find the location of the installation point, select your Office button, click Word Options, and then select Add-ins. From here, you choose Word Add-ins from the Manage list and click Go.

A dialog box will open up (shown in Figure 7.9). From the Templates tab, under Global Templates and Add-ins, select the check box next to the template you want loaded. If you don't see it, then click Add, switch to the folder that has what you want, and click OK.

From within this same location, you remove add-ins from your documents.

Figure 7.9
Installing templates and add-ins.

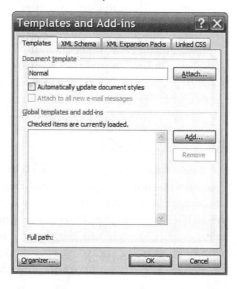

7

BACKUP AND RECOVERY OPTIONS

You should always make it a point to back up your documents. It's a good idea to make regular copies to either disk or an alternative hard drive. If your data is extra sensitive, you should consider saving backup copies in another location in case of a local disaster.

There are a few things you can do to assist you in working with files so that you do not lose your data. One is to have files that are on a remote server stored locally while you are working on it. The benefit of this is that in the event you lose your network connection, the document isn't lost. To do this, open your Word Options, choose Advanced, and in the Save section choose the Copy Remotely Stored Files onto Your Computer and Update the Remote File When Sharing box.

You can tell Word to save a backup copy of the same document you are working on each time you save your document. The backup of the document actually has the same name as the original but it says backup of <original name>. You set this in the same Advanced settings as mentioned previously. Select Always Create Backup Copy. Every time you save the document, it will save over the previous backup copy.

Sometimes you have files that have been damaged and you want to recover the document. You can open a document using the Open and Repair option. You find this option when you go to open a document, select the document you want to open (but do not double-click it to force it to open), then select the arrow button next to the Open button, and choose Open and Repair.

One tool that helps in recovering documents that are saved for the 97–2003 file format is the Recover Text from Any File option. The document may be damaged, but you can recover your text at least. To do this, you need to make sure the setting Confirm File Format Conversion on Open is on. You find this under the General section of the Advanced settings in your Word Options. You also need to make sure that the Recover Text Converter is installed from your Add/Remove features for this to work correctly.

Finally, we've already discussed the Office capability to make automatic backup copies at preestablished time intervals. This means that if your Office application crashes, or your system crashes, your documents will be brought back to you from recovery. You will be shown a Recovery task pane that allows you to choose the document and specify whether you want to save the recovered one or go back to the original.

PROTECTING PERSONAL INFORMATION

Don't you wish sometimes that you could take back what you said? Well, as the southern scholar Scott Grey once said, "You cannot un-ring a bell." Once it's out there, it's out. Now that may be true with our words, but it shouldn't be the case with our written words. We send out only what we have prepared and altered, reread, edited, spell checked, sent through an editing committee, and so on; our documents should be the ultimate completion. And yet many times we send out work that contains personal information, tracked changes, hidden parts—not only to our embarrassment, but sometimes to the embarrassment of our entire firm.

We must protect our personal information and the personal information of the company.

WHAT'S THE RISK OF SENDING OUT PERSONAL INFORMATION?

Let's just consider tracked changes. These allow a person to vent a little. They can perhaps add some comments, speak openly, and so on; it's liberating. Unfortunately, if you don't remove all of these comments and changes, they go with the document when it gets emailed offsite.

In addition, your document might contain your name, your computer's name, comments you made regarding the document in the document properties, names of others who have worked on the documents, and so on.

On the surface, none of that information should be too damaging. But if you gave some of that information to Kevin Mitnick (the guru of social engineering, or the king of the con-men, whichever you prefer), he would tell you that you are just begging to have your identity stolen or some other form of identity manipulation problem. That's because with some of that very basic knowledge, such as your name and computer, a social engineer can accomplish a world of trouble.

INSPECTING OFFICE DOCUMENTS

The solution is simple: the Document Inspector. It first examines the document to determine whether you have hidden data that you might want removed, and then it presents you with the option of removing that data.

If you go to the Office button and select Prepare and then Inspect Document, you might see a message that tells you to save your document first. Select Yes if this message appears, and then you will see your options, shown in Figure 7.10.

Figure 7.10
Document Inspector will check through your document for metadata, revision marks, headers and footers, watermarks, and so on, unless you specify otherwise.

Select the Inspect button to get the process started; it should take no time at all for Document Inspector to return with the results.

7

SCRUBBING PERSONAL DETAILS FROM A DOCUMENT

The results from a document sweep are shown in Figure 7.11.

Figure 7.11
The inspection results allow you to determine to what extent you would like to remove hidden and personal data from the document.

As you consider the results, you can select Remove All for different parts of the document. Or you can choose to reinspect the document itself.

After you have removed all the hidden data, the document is ready to be sent out without fear of that information being shared with others.

TROUBLESHOOTING

THE MESSAGE BAR IS NOT YOUR ENEMY

That security error kept popping up and I finally had someone turn it off. Now I cannot seem to get certain features to work in my Access database, and I cannot tell it to use the macros. What do I do?

Most likely your Message Bar settings from within your Trust Center have been set to not show you messages. So, even if there is a problem, you are unaware. Try going back into your Trust Center and turning your message settings back on.

DOCUMENT INSPECTOR—JUMPING THE GUN

We are in the middle of multiple revisions on this incredibly important document. I send it to Bill and when he sends it back, it's missing everything! All the comments, revisions. How do I get it back?

First off, ask Bill if he has been playing with the Document Inspector. If you put it to work before you are done, it will prepare the document for being sent out. Your next option is to check your sent items and find the document you sent. It should be available to you within moments. If that's been deleted somehow, in this case go find your latest backup. In the future, make sure your staff knows not to use the Document Inspector before it's time. Best practice is to save a copy of your document and remove the metadata and personal side from the copied document.

SECRETS OF THE OFFICE MASTERS: BACKUP AND RECOVERY BASICS

In a small to large organization, usually the network administrator will worry about backing up your data. It's his responsibility to ensure you have everything covered in case of emergency. The data is backed up and a plan is in place to restore it quickly if necessary.

But what if you don't have a network admin taking care of this for you? You might work from home, working with many important files. Consider one woman named Donna who works from home, editing videos from weddings and parties into a final product that she sells to the family. These are large files that need to be backed up, not only in case of drive failure, but in case of disaster striking (fire, earthquake, and so on). Data is money, so it's important to have a plan in mind for backing up and recovering your data.

To start with, you need to decide if you want to do a full backup each night. This is called a Normal backup (or Full backup). You basically get a copy of all your data to some backup medium, which could be an external drive, a DVD, or even a tape drive if you have one.

If you are working with really large files and your backup window isn't big enough, you don't have to do full backups each night. You could take one full one each week and then do incremental backups each day during the week. (Note: your backup window is the time you have from when work stops one night to when it begins again the next night.) An incremental backup only backs up data that has changed that day, so it's shorter than a full backup. Each day, however, it increments so that it backs up all the data since the last full backup. This means that if you do a full backup on Friday and then an incremental one on Monday, Tuesday, and Wednesday, and then the system crashes Thursday morning, you just have to restore the full backup from Friday and the last incremental backup. To perform a real backup (as opposed to a copy backup, where you just copy all your documents), you need backup software. Depending on the version of XP or Vista, you may have it automatically. But it's necessary to perform true backups. You could also search online for a variety of backup solutions for your home office.

In addition to backups, you should consider the tips given in this chapter to help you to recover your Office files from any kind of crash. Backups keep you "up to the last backup" prepared for trouble. Some of the options in Office keep you prepared "up to the last automatic recovery save" of your data. So, keep that in mind when you are working.

In the end, nothing is better than remembering to click that Save button every chance you get.

7

PART II

USING OUTLOOK

8 Outlook Essentials   177

9 Reading, Writing, and Organizing Email   219

10 Keeping Your Contacts List Under Control   259

11 Working with Calendars and Tasks   277

12 Outlook Security and Privacy   307

OUTLOOK ESSENTIALS

In this chapter

What's New in Outlook 2007   178

Using and Customizing the Outlook Interface   179

Managing Outlook Data Files   184

Creating, Editing, and Managing Outlook Items   191

Finding Outlook Items   199

Using Custom Views to Display Information   204

Importing, Exporting, and Synchronizing Outlook Items   214

Troubleshooting   217

Secrets of the Office Masters: Synchronizing Outlook Items with a Handheld PC or Smartphone   218

8

WHAT'S NEW IN OUTLOOK 2007

Believe it or not, Outlook is now more than a decade old. The first version of Outlook was released in 1997, and 10 years later only the bare bones of that debut release are recognizable. With each revision since its introduction in Office 97, Outlook has undergone wholesale changes. But despite those changes, it has retained a rich collection of shortcomings and idiosyncrasies that have made it difficult to set up and that have been a source of endless frustration for support professionals and (ahem) computer book authors.

Today, Outlook still has inconsistencies and annoyances, but its core features work exceptionally well, and for many it's the centerpiece of Office. Outlook does email, of course, and much, much more: Its capability to integrate and synchronize calendars, contacts, tasks, and email on individual computers, handheld devices, and corporate networks makes it an indispensable tool for anyone who wants to get organized and stay that way.

If you skipped over a revision or two on your way to Office 2007, you'll see a lot of the changes that were new in Outlook 2003, including the customizable Navigation pane (replacing the old Outlook Bar), search folders that automatically find messages based on criteria you define, and built-in junk mail filters. What's new in Outlook 2007? Here's a partial list of the features, security improvements, and usability enhancements you'll find:

- The new **To-Do List**, which appears along the right side of the main Outlook window when you view email, contacts, or tasks, displays an integrated list of everything you need to do today, tomorrow, or anytime in the future, including tasks, appointments, flagged messages, and notes.

- The window for composing and reading email messages uses the new **Ribbon interface**, making it much easier to find common tasks that were previously buried in obscure menus.

- Procedures for **connecting to an email account** are dramatically simpler. In many cases, you don't need to know a single detail about server names or ports—Outlook does the configuration automatically when you supply your email address and password.

- An **Instant Search box** at the top of every window allows you to find messages, contacts, and appointments in moments. You can also create complex searches and save them as search folders.

- Color-coded **categories and task flags** replace the Follow-up flags introduced in Outlook 2003. You can customize the list of categories, apply them to any type of item, assign dates and time for follow-up reminders, and see the results in the To-Do List or in custom views.

- When you receive one or more file attachments in an email message, you can now **preview them directly** in the Reading pane, without having to open a separate window.

- **Junk email filters** are greatly improved, and a new phishing filter protects you from scammers trying to deceive you into entering passwords and credit card numbers at counterfeit websites.

- You can use Outlook to automatically gather information from websites and blogs that use **web feeds** in RSS format.

- The design of the **main Outlook window** is overhauled. You can collapse the Navigation bar and To-Do Bar into thin strips along either side of the screen, leaving the majority of the screen available for the items you're working with.

NOTE

> A few things are missing in Outlook 2007. We'll point out some of them as we go along, but the most noteworthy change is that you can no longer remove Word as the editor for Outlook email messages. In previous versions, you could choose a lightweight Outlook message editor in place of Word. No more.

If you're new to Outlook, we recommend that you read the five chapters in this section from start to finish to help you master the complex and sometimes confusing Outlook interface. If you consider yourself an Outlook expert, we recommend that you skim this section and pay special attention to our instructions for customizing the new Outlook interface. You may find that some of the annoyances and pet peeves that plagued you in earlier Outlook versions have been fixed, and our in-depth explanations should help you uncover valuable features you might otherwise overlook.

In this chapter, we introduce the Outlook interface, with a special emphasis on features that are new in Outlook 2007, and we explain how to use features that are common throughout Outlook. In Chapter 9, "Reading, Writing, and Organizing Email," you'll find our advice on the smartest ways to work with email—including step-by-step instructions for setting up new accounts and customizing rules and desktop alerts. Chapter 12, "Outlook Security and Privacy," contains extensive information about blocking spam, preventing attacks from hostile file attachments, and protecting your privacy; it's a must-read for anyone who uses Outlook.

USING AND CUSTOMIZING THE OUTLOOK INTERFACE

Outlook stores all information in a *flat-file* database—a simple list. In Outlook parlance, each record is an *item*, and the type of item—email message, contact, appointment, and so on— defines which fields are available for entering and displaying information. Each of Outlook's default folders displays items of a single type, and you can create new folders as well.

 In early versions of Outlook, the left side of the program window was reserved for a pane that you could toggle between the Outlook Bar (a list of folder icons) or an Explorer-style folder list. In Outlook 2003 and 2007, the left side of the screen is occupied by a customizable *Navigation pane*, the contents of which change dynamically based on which of seven navigation buttons you've selected from the bottom of the pane. In Outlook 2007, each of these regions can be individually resized or collapsed using the double arrows at the right of each section heading. Figure 8.1 shows all these interface elements.

Drag this handle to expand
or shrink the button list

Expand or collapse section

Figure 8.1
Click the Minimize button to shrink the Navigation pane to a thin strip on the left, leaving more room to work with Outlook items.

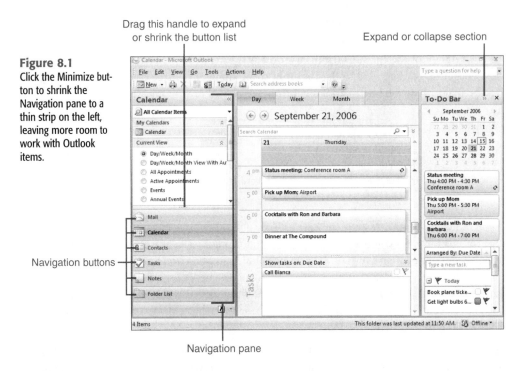

Navigation buttons

Navigation pane

CUSTOMIZING THE NAVIGATION PANE

As we noted earlier, the contents of the Navigation pane change, depending on which button you've clicked from the list at the bottom of the pane. Click the Mail button, and you'll see all mail folders plus a short list of user-definable Favorite folders. Click the Calendar button, and the top of the Navigation pane displays a month calendar for the currently selected date, with clickable links below it to add shared calendars from other users on a corporate network or on Microsoft's Office Online service.

At most screen resolutions, you can leave the Navigation bar visible with no ill effects. If you find it distracting, however, or if it keeps you from seeing enough items in a particular view, click the double arrow to the right of the heading for the current section. This collapses the Navigation bar into a thin strip on the left. Click the bar to display a pop-out navigation aid that you can use to move to a different email folder (as in Figure 8.2) or choose a different date in the Calendar folder.

8

Figure 8.2
In Minimized view, the Navigation pane takes up fewer than 40 pixels on the left edge of the screen. Click to see this navigation helper.

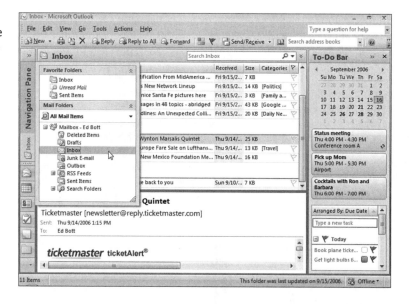

TIP FROM

Ed & Woody

Want to hide the Navigation pane completely, so that not even the slim Minimized view shows? You can use the pull-down menus—View, Navigation Pane, Off—to make the pane go away completely. Use the same menus to bring it back, or learn the keyboard shortcut, Alt+F1, which cycles among the three views: Normal, Minimized, Off.

By default, the buttons on the Navigation pane use a disproportionate amount of space, potentially cutting into space you might prefer to use for viewing and switching between folders. Although you can't make these buttons disappear completely, you can tweak the button list so that it takes up only a single row. You can also change the order of buttons and hide buttons for views you never use. Use any or all of the following techniques to tweak the Navigation pane:

- To expand or shrink the list, click and drag the handle just above the topmost button. As you shrink the list, buttons that previously had their own row appear in a button bar across the bottom of the Navigation pane.

- To add or remove buttons from the list, right-click any visible button (or click the double-up arrow at the right side of the list) and choose Navigation Pane Options. Select or clear the check boxes to the left of each item to show or hide that button.

- In the same dialog box, select any item and click Move Up or Move Down to change the order of buttons.

- To display a list of currently available views for the selected folder on the Navigation pane, choose View, Navigation Pane, and click the Current View Pane option. This setting is separate for each folder, so you can have views on for Contacts but off for the Calendar folder.

- Click and drag the thick black separator bar to the right of the Navigation pane to make the pane larger or smaller.

8

Figure 8.3 shows the Navigation pane after shrinking the button bar to a single row. The large, bold labels for each button are gone, although clicking the icon for each button in the list still switches to that folder. This view is especially useful if you have a large number of mail folders and you want to avoid constantly having to scroll through the folder list.

Figure 8.3

Shrink the buttons at the bottom of the Navigation pane to a single row to reclaim space for use at the top of the pane.

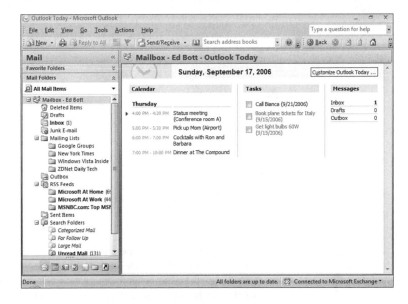

Five of the buttons at the bottom of the Navigation pane correspond to different types of data: Mail, Calendar, Contacts, Tasks, and Notes (the Journal button is disabled by default). The Folder List button displays all available folders, regardless of their data type; select this view if you prefer to navigate between folders using a no-frills, Explorer-style interface. The Shortcuts button is unlike any other, as we explain in the next section.

If the full list of folders provides too much detail and you prefer to build a pane filled with only those folders that you use the most, click the Shortcuts button. In this view, you can build a custom list of shortcuts and arrange them in any order. You can add shortcuts to any or all of the following items:

- **Outlook folders**—Click the Add New Shortcut link to choose an existing folder containing any type of item. Use this same technique to select a search folder, such as Unread Mail.

→ For more information about Search Folders, **see** "Creating and Using Search Folders," **p. 248**.

- **Web pages**—As with previous Outlook versions, you can drag any Internet shortcut and drop its icon on the Shortcuts group heading (not the large Shortcuts section heading at the top of the pane) or onto the heading for any additional groups you've created. Clicking a web shortcut opens the web page in the contents pane of the Outlook program window. This option is especially useful with SharePoint sites.

- **Programs**—Drag any program shortcut onto the Shortcuts list to give you one-click access to that program. The program opens in its own window, just as if you had clicked a shortcut on the Start menu or the desktop. Enhanced security settings in Windows Vista will cause one or more error messages to appear each time you try to open a program this way.

- **Files or folders**—Drag a file or folder shortcut from Windows Explorer and drop it onto a group heading. Clicking a file shortcut opens the file in the program with which it's associated (with one or more security warnings in Windows Vista); clicking a folder shortcut opens Windows Explorer in its own window (not in the Outlook program window) and displays the contents of the folder.

At any time, you can click the Add New Group link. Give the group a name, and then drag existing shortcuts into the group to reorganize the list. Figure 8.4 shows a customized Shortcuts pane.

Figure 8.4
A customized Shortcuts pane can include Outlook folders, shortcuts to programs, files, and folders, and even web pages (which appear in the Contents pane as shown here).

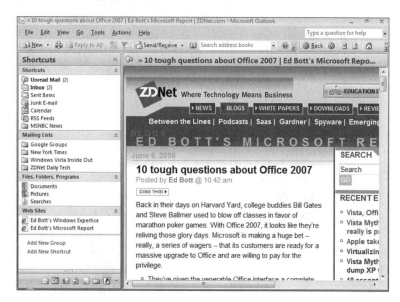

CUSTOMIZING THE TO-DO BAR

By default, the To-Do Bar is hidden when you first start Office 2007. To make it visible, choose View, To-Do Bar, Normal (or use the keyboard shortcut Alt+F2). Like its counterpart on the other side of the screen, the To-Do Bar has three modes—Normal, Minimized, and Off—which work the same as with the Navigation pane.

CUSTOMIZING THE READING PANE

The Reading pane displays the contents of the currently selected item. Choose View, Reading Pane to see the limited options—you can position the pane on the right or bottom, or choose Off to hide it. The Reading pane is available in every Outlook folder and can be configured separately for each folder.

8

For most configurations, having the Reading pane on the right is most conducive to productivity. With the message list to the left of the Reading pane, you can use the arrow keys to scroll quickly through a list of unread messages and in many cases read their full content in the Reading pane. Placing this pane on the bottom makes sense if you are working with a limited screen resolution (1024×768 or less) and you want both the Navigation pane and the To-Do Bar visible at all times.

MANAGING OUTLOOK DATA FILES

As we mentioned earlier in this chapter, Outlook is, at its core, a flat-file database. When new mail arrives, or when you create and save a new item in one of Outlook's default folders (Contacts, for example), Outlook adds the new item to the location specified as the default data file (in previous Outlook versions, this was sometimes called the *primary store*). That location might be a local file, or it could be a set of folders on a Microsoft Exchange Server. The exact location depends on how you (and, in some cases, your network administrator) have configured Outlook. In most of the examples in this book, we assume that your default data file is a Personal Folders file (with a .pst extension) stored on your local PC.

Outlook 2007 incorporates several key changes to data file formats that were introduced in Office 2003, as we explain in this section.

HOW OUTLOOK STORES DATA

A Personal Folders file is the basic storage format for a single user's data. These files use the extension .pst. When you configure Outlook for use with one or more Internet-standard or HTTP email accounts (no Exchange servers), Outlook creates a single Personal Folders file called Outlook.pst and stores it in your user profile, along with a handful of other files that contain settings and preferences. This file holds all Outlook data—messages, attachments, the Contacts and Calendar folder—the works.

TIP FROM

Where are your Outlook data files and settings stored? For a remarkably complete listing of these locations, open the Help system and search for the topic "Where does Outlook save my information and configurations?." Unless you change the default settings, your Personal Folders file is located in a hidden folder within your user profile. You can open this folder directly by entering %appdata%\Microsoft\Outlook (be sure to include the percent signs) in the Run box, in the Address bar of Windows Explorer, or in the Search box in Windows Vista.

If Outlook is running, you can open this folder directly: Choose File, Data File Management, and then click the Open Folder button. If Outlook is installed but not running, open Control Panel, double-click the Mail icon (in Category view, you'll find this option under User Accounts), and click Data Files.

In this configuration, the Personal Folders file is the primary store: New messages are delivered to the Inbox in that file, and all other default Outlook folders are stored there as well. If you connect to an Exchange Server, a Personal Folders file is optional. Regardless of your email configuration, however, the file format is identical.

TIP FROM

Ed & Woody

> Even if your main mail account is on an Exchange server, we highly recommend that you create a Personal Folders file and save it on your computer. You can move email messages and other items off your server, where the network administrator typically imposes limits on the amount of space you can use, and guarantee that you have quick, easy access to email archives. Of course, doing so means you won't be able to access those items remotely using Outlook Web Access, and it might violate your company's email retention policies. So check with your administrator before you try this.

If you connect to a Microsoft Exchange Server, Outlook creates one (and only one) Offline Store file and stores it on your computer. This file type, which uses the extension `.ost`, closely resembles a Personal Folders file.

Items in an Offline Store file can be synchronized with your primary store on a Microsoft Exchange Server. When you're connected to the server in Cached Exchange Mode (the default setting for modern versions of the Exchange Server software), Outlook automatically compares the items on the server with those in your Offline Store file and adds, updates, or deletes items in both places so that they always contain the same information. This enables you to read and compose email or other items when the server is unavailable—for example, when you're sitting in an airplane seat reading mail on a notebook computer. When you connect to the server via remote access, or when you return to the office and reconnect your notebook computer to the network, Outlook automatically transfers changes in both directions.

NOTE

> In highly managed corporations where administrators are concerned about security and/or local storage space on users' computers, Outlook can be configured to connect to a Microsoft Exchange Server without an Offline Store folder. In this setup, you access mail and create calendar and contact items by connecting directly to your Mailbox folders on the server. If you lose the network connection, you lose all access to your data. We do not cover this rarely used option in this book.

MANAGING YOUR PERSONAL FOLDERS FILE

The Personal Folders file that serves as the default destination for incoming email messages must be stored on your local hard drive. You can also create additional Personal Folders files, store them on a local drive or on a shared network drive, and access data in these files along with the data in your primary store. In this configuration, the additional Personal Folders files are defined as *secondary data files*. Outlook does not save new items directly in these files, but you can move items into a secondary store by dragging and dropping them from your primary store, or you can define rules that automatically move incoming messages into the secondary store based on their content.

8

TIP FROM

To back up your most important Outlook data, all you have to do is copy your default Personal Folders file. The best way to accomplish this task is with a backup program that is aware of how and where Outlook stores data. In Windows XP, you can easily back up everything in your user profile using the Ntbackup program. In Windows Vista, you'll find one or more excellent backup tools in the Backup and Restore Center, under the System and Maintenance category in Control Panel. If you have a backup program from a third-party software developer, check the documentation to see if it can save and restore Outlook data files.

CHOOSING A DATA FILE TYPE

Beginning with Outlook 2003, Microsoft created a new format for Personal Folders files, while preserving the capability to create new files and use existing ones in the original Outlook 97-2002 format. When you choose File, New, Outlook Data File, you see the dialog box shown in Figure 8.5. What's the difference?

Figure 8.5
The Office Outlook Personal Folders File format has a much larger storage capacity then the Outlook 97-2002 format. Choose the latter only if you absolutely must.

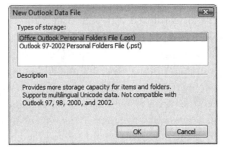

- The newer Office Outlook Personal Folders File (.pst) format stores text in Unicode format, which means it supports multilanguage input. It also allows file sizes to exceed 20GB, with an essentially unlimited number of items and folders.

- The older Outlook 97-2002 Personal Folder File (.pst) format supports only ANSI text and allows a maximum file size of 2GB with up to 65,535 items and 65,535 folders per file.

So, which one should you choose? If you are absolutely certain that you will never need to share a Personal Folders file with Outlook 2002 or earlier, choose the newer Unicode format. The 2GB limit on file size may sound large, but in practice it's all too easy to hit that ceiling, especially with archive files that contain many large file attachments. Select the older Outlook 97-2002 format only if you need to open the data file in Outlook 2002 or earlier.

To create a new Personal Folders file, choose File, New, Outlook Data File. Choose a file format from the dialog box. Give the file a name, choose a location, and click OK. You'll see the dialog box shown in Figure 8.6, which allows you to define the top-level name that appears in Outlook's Folders List and set compression and encryption options.

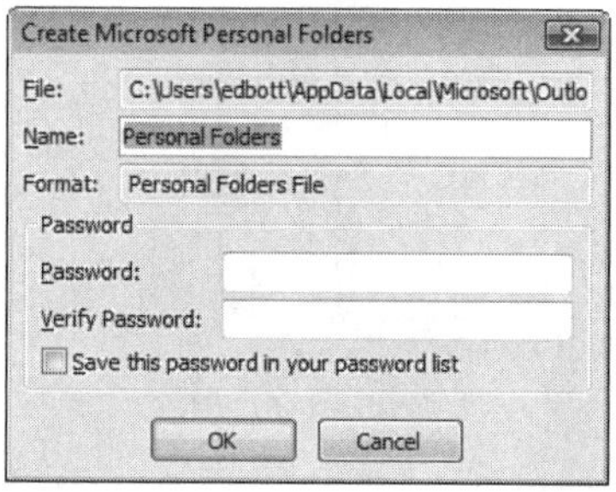

Figure 8.6
Outlook uses the name you enter here to identify the top-level folder for a Personal Folders file.

TIP FROM

There's no relationship at all between the filename of the Personal Folders data file and the text label that appears in the Folders List. If you create a second Personal Folders file that you intend to use for messages from mailing lists, for example, you might choose to use a filename such as `Lists.pst`, and then change the top-level folder name to My Mailing Lists.

After creating the additional Personal Folders file, Outlook automatically opens it. To close the file, right-click its icon in the Navigation pane (you may need to click the Folder List button to see its icon). You can also use this shortcut menu to adjust the properties of any Personal Folders file.

CLEANING UP AND ARCHIVING PERSONAL INFORMATION

Left unchecked, an Outlook data file can grow to mammoth proportions quickly. If your data file gets too large, you'll encounter trouble trying to back it up, and if you're using the old-style PST format, you run the risk of losing data completely if it hits 2GB. In this section, we explain how to keep your mailbox slim and trim. We also list tools and techniques you can use to prevent and recover from Outlook errors.

The Mailbox Cleanup dialog box, shown in Figure 8.7, is a useful starting point for some basic housekeeping tasks. Virtually all the options contained here are available from other menus, scattered throughout the Outlook interface. The advantage of this collection of shortcuts and buttons is the simplicity of finding them consolidated in one location. To open it, choose Tools, Mailbox Cleanup.

Figure 8.7
Use these Mailbox Cleanup options for basic housekeeping in an Outlook data file.

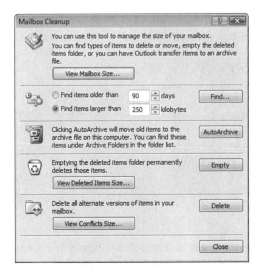

Most of the options listed here are self-explanatory. View Mailbox Size, for instance, shows how much disk space is occupied by each folder in an Outlook data file; if you're connected to an Exchange Server, the Server Data tab displays the same information for your Mailbox. The last option is visible only if you're connected to an Exchange Server; it allows you to see and reconcile conflicts between locally stored items and those in the matching folder on the server.

By default, Outlook automatically moves items out of your Personal Folders file after a specified amount of time has passed. Using this AutoArchive feature, Outlook checks every item in your Personal Folders file at regular intervals. When it finds appointments, tasks, and email messages that exceed the age limits you specify, it automatically moves them to an archive file. By default, Outlook runs an AutoArchive check every 14 days and looks for any items that are more than 6 months old. Unless you change the name or location, the archive file is called Archive.pst, and it's located in the default folder for Outlook data files. You can also force Outlook to archive items instead of waiting for its next scheduled archive operation.

TIP FROM

Ed & Woody

Cleaning up and archiving mail folders is easier if junk mail and other nonessential messages never get there in the first place. Use the Junk E-mail folder and custom rules to delete unwanted messages and move others directly into folders as they arrive. The folder you specify as the destination in each rule can be in a different Personal Folders file; if you use rules to move messages into different folders in your primary Outlook data file, you can specify custom AutoArchive options for those folders.

Configuring AutoArchive options in Outlook is a fairly straightforward process. From the AutoArchive dialog box, you tell Outlook how often you want it to scan your Personal Folders file (or files) and perform AutoArchive options. Then, optionally, you can adjust archiving options for individual folders.

To adjust the default AutoArchive options, choose Tools, Options, click the Other tab, and click the AutoArchive button. This action displays the dialog box shown in Figure 8.8.

Figure 8.8
By default, Outlook scans all Personal Folders files every 14 days. Click Apply These Settings to All Folders Now to change settings for all folders.

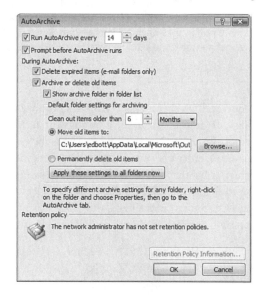

Use any or all of these AutoArchive settings:

- To enable the AutoArchive option, make sure a check mark appears in the Run AutoArchive Every *nn* Days box. Clear this box if you want AutoArchive to run only when you specifically choose to do so.

- To adjust the AutoArchive interval from its default of 14 days, pick a new number between 1 and 60 here. Choose a smaller number if you want Outlook to aggressively manage your data.

- If you want the AutoArchive operation to occur automatically without your explicit approval, clear the Prompt Before AutoArchive Runs check box.

- Specify a filename and location in the Move Old Items To box. Unless you change this setting, Outlook creates a new Personal Folders file called `Archive.pst` and stores it in the default Outlook data files location, along with your main Outlook data file.

TIP FROM

By definition, the archive file includes data you don't need every day, so it doesn't make sense to keep this file open. Clear the Show Archive in Folder List option to keep Outlook from adding it to your Folder List when AutoArchive runs. If you want to search for an item in this file, choose File, Open, Outlook Data File (`.pst`), and select the `Archive.pst` file. Then switch to the Folder List to display the contents of individual folders in the archive file.

8

CAUTION

Unless you're absolutely positive that you don't want any archives at all, do *not* select the Permanently Delete Old Items check box. If you set this option as the default, any message that is older than the specified interval will be permanently and irretrievably deleted from your email archives when AutoArchive runs. Reserve this option for folders that contain types of messages you know you won't want to keep, such as time-sensitive newsletters.

Each time Outlook runs its AutoArchive check, it performs operations on each folder separately, using the default settings. To adjust AutoArchive options for an individual folder, click the Folder List button at the bottom of the Navigation bar, right-click the folder's icon, and then choose Properties. The AutoArchive tab of the Properties dialog box (see Figure 8.9) lets you enable or disable archiving for that folder. (With AutoArchiving disabled, old items hang around until you choose to delete them.) This dialog box also lets you specify an alternative location where you want Outlook to move items (the default is the file you specified in the global AutoArchive options), or you can choose to delete all items that are older than the specified time.

Figure 8.9
Use this dialog box to set alternative AutoArchive options for each folder.

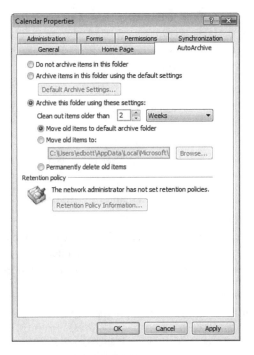

NOTE

Because items in the Contacts folder do not have a date associated with them, there is no AutoArchive tab in this folder's Properties dialog box, and AutoArchive operations do not affect this folder.

In our opinion, the default AutoArchive settings make little sense because they assume that every item should be archived in the same way. Some judicious adjustments to the default settings can pay off handsomely in helping you save what you really need and toss the nonessential items. For example, if you never refer to your Calendar folder to look up old meetings and appointments, you can safely specify that you want to delete these items when AutoArchiving. On the other hand, if you live and die by email, you might want to keep a year's worth of messages in your Personal Folders file so you can search for information easily. In that case, right-click the Inbox folder, choose Properties, click the AutoArchive tab, select Archive This Folder Using These Settings, and adjust the Clean Out Items Older Than *nn* Months option to 12; then do the same for the Sent Items folder.

TIP FROM

Ed & Woody

> Deleting items from your Outlook data files doesn't immediately recover the space the deleted items used. Outlook automatically compacts data files in the background, reducing the total file size, during times when Outlook is idle. After performing extensive pruning, you might want to hasten this process by manually compacting the file. Empty the Deleted Items folder, switch to the Folder List, right-click the icon at the top of the folder tree, and choose Properties. On the General tab, click Advanced, and then click Compact Now.

REPAIRING A DAMAGED PERSONAL FOLDERS FILE

If you begin encountering error messages or suspect that a Personal Folders file is damaged, a well-hidden Outlook tool called the Microsoft Personal Folders Scan/Repair Utility can help you set things right in short order. Search your hard drive for a file called `Scanpst.exe` (in Office 2007, it's normally located in `%ProgramFiles%\Microsoft Office\Office12`). Double-click the file, use the Browse button to select the Personal Folders file you want to scan, and click Start. If the utility finds any damage, it asks your permission and creates a backup before attempting to repair the errors. Note that this process might take several hours on a large PST file, so be prepared to wait. (Another utility, `Scanost.exe`, works with Offline Folder files.)

CAUTION

> Personal Folders files are remarkably resilient, but they're not indestructible. If you keep irreplaceable information, such as important email messages or contact details, in one of these files, back it up regularly—preferably to removable media (an external hard drive or writable CD or DVD, for instance) or on a server stored in a different physical location. You must shut down Outlook before you can copy a Personal Folders file.

CREATING, EDITING, AND MANAGING OUTLOOK ITEMS

When you create, view, and edit items, Outlook uses a variety of standard and custom forms to control which fields are visible. When you double-click any item, it opens using the default form for its type. The basic techniques for managing items are the same, regardless of the item type.

8

MOVING, COPYING, AND DELETING ITEMS

To move or copy items between Outlook folders, you can use many of the same techniques you use to manage files in an Explorer window. After switching to the Folder List view in the Navigation pane, you can move an item by dragging it out of the Contents pane and dropping it on the icon for another folder; hold down the Ctrl key while dragging to make a copy. Or use shortcut keys to cut (Ctrl+X), copy (Ctrl+C), and then paste (Ctrl+V) the item into the destination folder. Curiously, although Outlook's pull-down Edit menu includes all three choices, the shortcut menus available when you right-click on any item (such as a mail message) don't allow you to cut, copy, or paste.

 If you try to move an item into a folder and it opens a new item instead, see "Dragging Doesn't Always Move an Item" in the "Troubleshooting" section at the end of this chapter.

Although it's possible to create multiple folders for any type of Outlook items, you'll most commonly use subfolders to manage email messages. To do major message management, click the Mail or Folder List button at the bottom of the Navigation pane and then drag messages out of the message list and drop them onto destination folders as you would in Windows Explorer.

To move one or more selected messages into folders without using the Folder List, click the Move to Folder button on the Standard toolbar. This displays a menu showing the folders you've used most recently. If the folder you want isn't listed, choose Move to Folder from the bottom of the menu. (This option is also available if you right-click one or more items to display the shortcut menu.) Click the New button to create a new folder in any open Personal Folders file.

TIP FROM

Ed & Woody

> You can drag any item onto the Windows desktop or into a folder to create a copy of that item. This is a convenient way to keep a contact's personal information at hand or to keep a copy of a mail message available for ready reference. When you create a copy using this technique, you create a new file containing only that item. Be careful when using such a copy, however: Because there is no link between the item you create on the desktop and the one that remains in Outlook, any changes you make in either place are not reflected in the other.

To delete items in any Outlook folder, first make a selection, and then click the Delete button on the Standard toolbar; use the keyboard shortcut Ctrl+D, press the Delete key, or drag the item and drop it onto the Deleted Items icon in the Folder List.

By default, Outlook saves the contents of the Deleted Items folder until the next time you archive. To empty this folder manually, right-click its shortcut in the Navigation pane and choose Empty "Deleted Items" Folder. If you prefer to empty this folder automatically every time you close Outlook, choose Tools, Options, click the Other tab, and click the Empty the Deleted Items Folder Upon Exiting check box.

To create a new folder at any time, choose File, New, Folder. In the Create New Folder dialog box (see Figure 8.10), enter the name of the new folder, specify the type of items you want to store in the folder, select the folder in which you want to store the new subfolder, and then click OK.

Figure 8.10
When creating a new folder, be sure you specify the correct type of item you want to store in the folder.

To move, copy, delete, or rename a folder, click the Folder List button at the bottom of the Navigation pane and use the right-click shortcut menus.

ENTERING DATES AND TIMES AUTOMATICALLY

One of Outlook's most impressive time-saving features is its capability to interpret dates using almost any text you enter. To enter a date in any date field in any type of Outlook item, use any of the following techniques:

TIP FROM

Ed & Woody

These techniques are useful throughout Outlook, not just in appointments or meetings. For example, you can use AutoDate shortcuts to define the dates for follow-up flags on email messages or to specify the due date for an upcoming task.

- Type the date in a format that Outlook recognizes, such as 9-29-07, 9/29, 9.29, or Sep 29. If you omit the year, Outlook automatically fills in this year's date if that date is in the future; if appending the current year to the date results in a date that has already passed, Outlook uses next year's date instead.

- To pick dates from a calendar, click the drop-down arrow to the right of the date field and use the control showing the current month (see Figure 8.11). Use the arrows to scroll backward or forward, and click to insert any date in the current field. Clicking the Today button quickly returns you to the current date.

8

■ When you enter dates and times for appointments, you can also use words and phrases and let Outlook use its AutoDate feature to interpret your meaning.

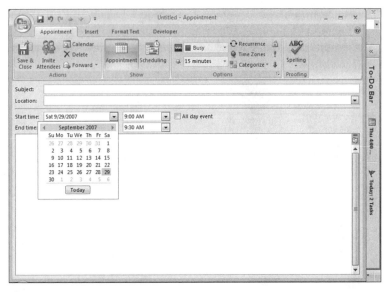

Figure 8.11

Outlook can recognize text such as `this Thursday`, `next Thursday`, `one week from today`, or `tomorrow`, substituting the correct date for you. To schedule a staff meeting for next Wednesday at 2:00 p.m., for example, click in the Start Time box, enter **next wed**, and then press Tab and type **2** (Outlook assumes that times you enter are during the default workday unless you specify otherwise).

AutoDate understands dates and times that you spell out or abbreviate, such as `6a` (for 6:00 a.m.), or `first of jan`. If you type `30 days` in the Start Time box, Outlook converts it to the date 30 days from today; if you enter that same text as the end time, Outlook adds 30 days to the start date you specified. AutoDate recognizes holidays that fall on the same day every year, such as Halloween, New Year's Eve, and Christmas. It can also correctly interpret dozens of words you might use to define a date or an interval of time, including `now`, `yesterday`, `today`, `tomorrow`, `next`, `following`, `through`, and `until`.

CAUTION

> You can't use AutoDate to define a recurring appointment. If you enter `every Wednesday` in the Start Time box, for example, Outlook will refuse to accept your entry. To create a recurring appointment, you have to use the Appointment Recurrence dialog box, as explained later in this section.

ASSIGNING ITEMS TO CATEGORIES

You can assign most Outlook items, including email messages, contacts, appointments, meetings, and tasks, to *categories*. In earlier versions of Outlook, you started with a predefined Master Category List containing 20 text labels you could apply to any item and then (optionally) added your own categories to this list. Outlook 2007 simplifies the process by offering a default selection of six color-coded categories. Using categories can be a powerful way to organize tasks and other items on the To-Do Bar. They also allow you to extract groups of information from a list of contacts or to categorize email messages and appointments by client or by project.

TIP FROM

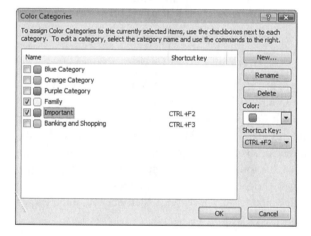

Categories work exceptionally well in conjunction with Word's mail-merge feature. Assign a group of contacts to a category, such as Sales Prospects or Holiday Cards, and you can use that category to extract address information from your Outlook Contacts folder to print address labels or personalized letters.

By default, Outlook 2007 includes a half-dozen colors, using the generic labels Red Category, Blue Category, and so on. To see all available categories, click the Categorize button on the Standard toolbar (or choose Actions, Categorize) and then click All Categories. As you can see in Figure 8.12, the list is customizable, and you can assign categories to items individually or in groups by clicking the check boxes to the left of individual categories.

Figure 8.12
Select the check boxes to the left of a category to apply it to all currently selected items.

You can customize the All Categories list in at least five ways:

- Click Rename to change the name assigned to the selected category. (You'll be prompted to rename any category using one of the default names the first time you try to apply it to an Outlook item.) A category name can contain up to 255 characters, including spaces, but in practice you should keep category names much shorter.

- Click New to add a category to the list. You can have as many as 255 categories, but for practical purposes you'll want to keep the number much lower. Only 15 entries show up on the Categorize menu, and managing additional categories is a hassle.

- Click Delete to delete the selected category.

- Choose an entry from the Shortcut Key list to assign one of 11 custom key combinations (Ctrl plus F2 through F12) to the selected category.

8

■ From the main Outlook window, click the Categorize button on the Standard toolbar (or choose Actions, Categorize) and then click Set Quick Click to choose the default category. Whichever category you select will be automatically applied to email items in the message list or items in the To-Do Bar when you click the Categories column.

In the case of email messages, you can assign categories automatically, by defining rules.

→ For more details on how to create rules for handling incoming mail, **see** "Using Email Rules to Sort and Process Mail," **p. 249**.

TIP FROM

Ed & Woody

> You can assign multiple categories to a single item. This flexibility lets you work with the same item in multiple contexts—for example, you might define the Red Category as VIP and the green category as Holiday Cards, and then assign both categories to your key contacts to make sure that you get the proper subset of names each time you assemble a mailing list based on either of these categories. When you assign a single category to an item, the color code for that category appears at the top of the detail view of that item and alongside its entry in list views. Outlook splits the color box in the message list and in the To-Do Bar to show up to three color codes.

FLAGGING ITEMS FOR FOLLOW-UP

Outlook allows you to attach follow-up flags to email messages, contact items, and tasks. For flagged items, you can also define pop-up reminders similar to those available with appointments and meetings. In Outlook 2003, follow-up flags could be customized to use a wide range of colors; in Outlook 2007, bright colors are now associated with categories and follow-up flags use different shades of red to indicate the follow-up date you've assigned: bright red for items that are due today or that have no date, and increasingly lighter shades of pink based on how far away the follow-up date is. In table-based views, you can add a follow-up flag with a single click, and a built-in search folder lets you quickly see all messages that are flagged for follow up.

NOTE

> In older versions of Outlook, pop-up reminders and follow-up flags worked only in specific folders. In Outlook 2007, you can set a flag and an optional reminder on any item in any folder. Flagged items show up in the To-Do Bar regardless of their location, and follow-up reminders continue to work even when you move a flagged message out of the Inbox and into a subfolder.

Follow-up flags help you keep track of unfinished business. Reminders help you avoid the embarrassment of missing a meeting or a phone call because you forgot to check your calendar. By default, Outlook adds a reminder to all meetings and appointments, set for 15 minutes before the scheduled time. To change this setting, choose Tools, Options; on the Preferences tab, set the preferred interval by using the pull-down list (or typing an entry) in the Default Reminder box. Clear the Default Reminder check box if the only reminders you want to see are those you expressly add to an item in the Calendar folder.

You can enter or edit the reminder for an appointment or meeting by opening the item and selecting or entering a time from the drop-down Reminder list in the Options group on the Appointment tab. This time is always relative to the start time of the appointment or meeting; you can request a reminder by entering any number of minutes, hours, days, weeks, months, or years in this box. For example, if you enter 1 week, Outlook dutifully pops up a reminder exactly one week before the meeting is scheduled to start. You cannot, however, enter a specific date or time when you want to receive a meeting or appointment reminder.

Outlook does not automatically include reminders for tasks unless you specifically enable this option. To manually set a reminder for a task, open the item and click the Reminder check box; by default, the reminder uses the date you enter in the Due Date field and a default time of 8:00 a.m. (If you specify no due date, the default reminder uses today's date.) If your workday begins earlier or you want a reminder to appear at the end of the day, you can change this default setting: Choose Tools, Options, click the Preferences tab, and select a new time from the drop-down list in the Tasks section.

TIP FROM

Ed & Woody

To specify that you want Outlook to automatically set a reminder on every new task, choose Tools, Options, and then click the Task Options button on the Preferences tab. Click to select the Set Reminders on Tasks with Due Dates check box. Close all open dialog boxes to return to Outlook with your new preferences in place.

To flag an email message, task, or contact for follow up, use one of the following techniques:

- To flag an item in any table view, including the email message list, click the flag icon in the far right column. This applies the default red flag, with the generic "Follow up" message, a Start Date and Due Date of today's date, and no reminder. Right-click this icon to choose from the same list of options available on the Follow Up menu.

TIP FROM

Ed & Woody

If you prefer to enter details for every follow-up instead of applying a generic flag, here's a customization option that should work. Select any item in the Mail or Contacts folder, right-click the Follow Up icon (the red flag) on the Standard toolbar, and choose Customize. In the Customize dialog box, the Commands tab opens automatically; select Actions from the Categories list and scroll through the Commands list until you find the Custom menu choice with an identical red flag icon. Drag the Custom command from that list up to the toolbar and drop it alongside the original Follow Up button; then drag the original button down and off the toolbar. Click Close to close the Customize dialog box. From now on, when you click this button, you'll open a dialog box that lets you set every option for a follow-up flag.

- To flag any item in any view, including an open email message or contact, click the Follow Up button on the Standard toolbar (the bright red flag) and choose one of the options on its menu of predefined flags. The This Week and Next Week options assign a Start Date and Due Date that correspond with the end of the respective work week—normally Friday.

■ To change the status of a follow-up flag to Completed, click the Follow Up button on the Standard toolbar and choose Mark Complete. In table views, click the flag icon to toggle between the active default flag and the Completed flag, which is indicated by a check mark.

■ To remove a follow-up flag, click the Follow Up button (or right-click the flag icon in any table view) and choose Clear Flag.

If you choose the Custom option from the Follow Up menu, you'll see the dialog box shown in Figure 8.13.

Figure 8.13
To flag a message or contact, choose one of the canned messages in the Flag To list, or enter a text message of your own.

The default text in a flag is Follow Up. You can choose from other alternatives, including Call, Read, or Review. If none of the canned alternatives is suitable, you can enter your own text. For example, if you're expecting a shipment of catalogs from the printer next Monday and you want to make sure your best customers get a copy ASAP, you can flag a group of contacts with the text Send Catalog and set a reminder for next Monday.

To set a reminder for an email message or a contact, you must first assign a follow-up flag for that item. When you add a flag to either of these types of items, Outlook creates a matching task and displays it in the To-Do List (in the Tasks folder) and the To-Do Bar. The title of the task is the text you enter in the Flag To box; the pop-up reminder notice always displays the subject of the original item.

If a co-worker sends you a status report via email, for example, you might attach a follow-up flag to the message and set a reminder follow-up on unfinished items next week. Similarly, if you want to call a handful of key customers next Monday after your company makes an important announcement, you can select the corresponding items in the Contacts folder, one at a time, and flag each one for a phone call. (The Custom option is not available if you choose multiple contact items.)

The reminder date and time are optional parts of a follow-up flag. Enter a value here if you want a reminder to pop up at a specified date or time. By default, if you enter a date, Outlook sets the time to one hour before the end of your normal workday, or 4:00 p.m. unless you redefine the settings on the Calendar Options dialog box. You can enter a specific reminder time for any follow-up flag by using the exact date and time or any text that Outlook's AutoDate feature recognizes. If you received an email from a key customer and you need to follow up first thing next week, for example, enter **next mon** in the date portion of the Due By box and **9am** in the time box. Outlook translates the date and time for you.

8

In table views, flagged items include a flag icon; overdue items appear in red text. The follow-up message text and date appear in the information header at the top of a flagged message or contact item, whether you open it in its own window or use the Preview pane.

Regardless of how you set a reminder, when the specified time rolls around, Outlook plays a sound (if you selected that option) and pops up a reminder message. All current reminders are consolidated in a single window, as shown in Figure 8.14.

Figure 8.14
This Reminder dialog box can stay open while you work with items in Outlook folders. Click each item to see its details at the top of the dialog box.

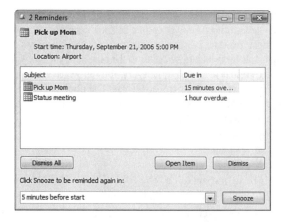

Whe you see a reminder, you can dismiss it so you don't see it again, or open it so you can view the item itself. This option is especially useful when you want to review notes for an upcoming appointment or look up the phone number of a contact you plan to call.

Use the Snooze button to hide the reminder for a while. The default setting is five minutes, but you can use the drop-down list to select a new reminder time as much as one week later.

 If reminders don't appear when you expect them to, see "Alarms Fail to Go Off" in the "Troubleshooting" section at the end of this chapter.

TIP FROM

> To see all flagged email messages from all folders, display the Inbox and then choose the For Follow Up search folder. To see all flagged contacts, open the Contacts folder and switch to the built-in By Follow-up Flag view. This table view shows all items that include flags at the top of the list.

FINDING OUTLOOK ITEMS

If you use Outlook regularly, your collection of personal data will eventually become so large that you won't be able to find information simply by browsing through items. Outlook offers two tools to help you track down items based on their content. The Instant Search box, accessible via a text box at the top of every Outlook folder view, is fast, simple, and practically magic. It's new in Outlook 2007 and it works via an index that includes not just Outlook items but files, digital photographs, and music tracks. You can quickly locate items by typing a word or two into the Instant Search box, or you can use the Query Builder to narrow down your search in a more structured fashion.

Outlook also includes the old-style Advanced Find dialog box, which allows you to build queries by filling in a form that searches through fields in Outlook items. It requires much more work than Instant Search and the results appear in a separate window; its primary use in Outlook 2007 is to construct Search Folders.

→ For more details on how to work with Search Folders, **see** "Creating and Using Search Folders," **p. 248**.

TIP FROM

Ed & Woody

> For some tasks, using built-in or custom Outlook views and arrangements is a perfect complement to Instant Search. For example, if you use categories in the Contacts, Calendar, and Tasks folders, switching to the built-in By Category view lets you see all your search results organized by category. You can switch views before or after performing a search. If you start with a Search Folder that displays only items that already belong in a specific category and then perform a search, you can narrow down the results more quickly than if you were to add the criterion for that category after performing the initial search.

To use the Instant Search box, first switch to the folder in which you want to search (and, if necessary, switch to a different view). Then click in the Instant Search box and begin typing your search text. You don't need to click a button to actually perform the search; Outlook filters the results on-the-fly as you type. Because the search is indexed, the results display with lightning speed. Figure 8.15 shows the results of a simple search in the Inbox folder.

Figure 8.15
The text you enter as an Instant Search term appears highlighted in the search results.

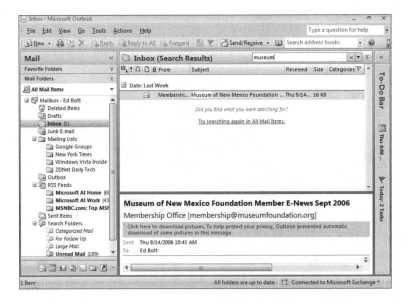

When you kick off a search from the Instant Search box, it looks for matching items only in the current folder, filtered by the current view. If your search is unsuccessful but you know the item you're looking for is there somewhere, click the Try Searching Again link at the bottom of the search results; this expands the search to include all items of the type in the folder you looked in.

To clear the search results and restore the normal display of items in the current folder and view, click the Clear Search button—the small X at the right of the Instant Search box.

Instant Search is fine when you have a pretty good idea of what you're looking for and the search term you're using will narrow the list down quickly. But what if you're trying to find a specific message from a specific sender containing a specific word or phrase, sent in a specific period of time? For complex searches like those, click the double down arrow at the right of the Instant Search box to display the Query Builder. As Figure 8.16 shows, this form allows you to build a query by filling in forms that correspond to different fields in the selected item type.

Figure 8.16
Using the Query Builder lets you find matching items based on a list of criteria instead of just a snippet of text.

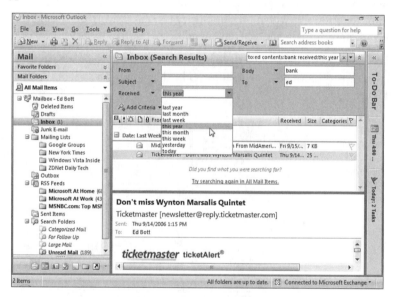

As with the Instant Search box, the Query Builder results appear as you type—you don't need to click a button to execute the search.

The default criteria in the Query Builder vary depending on the type of item you're searching for. Click the Add Criteria button at the bottom of the Query Builder form to choose fields that aren't on the default form.

> **NOTE**
>
> Any changes you make in the Query Builder are persistent. If you add the Received field to the Query Builder form for the Mail folder, that field appears the next time you open Query Builder in a folder containing the same type of items. These changes persist even if you close and reopen Outlook in the meantime.

Outlook searches for the exact text you enter in the Instant Search box. If you enter two or more words separated by a space or punctuation, all the words you entered must appear in

8

the item, in any order. To search for an exact phrase, enclose the search string in quotes. If you enter a search term in the Query Builder pane, Outlook restricts its search for that term to that field only. The search results replace the contents below the Find pane. To reuse a search you ran previously, with or without the Query Builder, click the arrow just to the right of the Instant Search box and choose an entry from the Recent Searches list. To expand your search so that it includes files as well, enter your search term, open this same menu, and click Search Desktop.

Although Instant Search is fast, easy, and customizable, Outlook allows you to use the more complex Advanced Find dialog box. This option allows you to find items that contain specific types of information; you can also use it to search for virtually unlimited combinations of criteria. The biggest advantage of this search tool is in folders that contain email messages, where you can save and reuse your search as a search folder. For instance, you might want to create a view that includes messages sent in the past seven days from addresses in your company's domain, where your address is in the To: field.

To open the Advanced Find dialog box, choose Tools, Instant Search, Advanced Find, or use its keyboard shortcut—Ctrl+Shift+F. The dialog box consists of three tabs, as shown in Figure 8.17.

Figure 8.17
Use this dialog box to search for Outlook items using a combination of criteria.

Follow these steps to use the Advanced Find dialog box:

1. Use the drop-down Look For list to specify the type of items you want to search for— messages or appointments, for example. By default, this value is set to the type of item stored in the current folder. For the widest possible search, choose Any Type of Outlook Item—this option is useful if you want to search for all messages, contacts, appointments, and tasks related to a specific company, for example.

2. By default, your search covers only the current folder. To change that folder or select more than one folder, click the Browse button and select or clear check boxes as needed.

NOTE

> You can search multiple folders only within a single Personal Folders file. Thus, to search for related messages in current and archived folders, you'll need to perform two searches. Open a second copy of the Advanced Find dialog box if you want to see all search results simultaneously.

3. Fill in your search criteria using one or more of the three tabs in the Advanced Find dialog box.

- The most common options appear on the first tab; the name of this tab and the exact choices available vary slightly, depending on the type of item you're looking for. For example, when searching through mail messages, you can look for text in the subject field only, in the subject field and message body, or in frequently used text fields.

- Click the More Choices tab to see additional options that are specific to the type of item you're looking for. When searching for Outlook items, this tab always lets you select from the Categories field or find items based on their size.

- Use the Advanced tab (see Figure 8.18) to define criteria based on any Outlook field. Click the Field button to select a field, and then enter a Condition and (if necessary) a Value. Click the Add to List button to insert the criteria in the box above the button. Repeat this step to use multiple criteria.

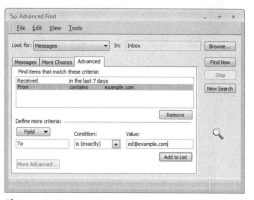

Figure 8.18

4. Click the Find Now button to begin the search, using the criteria you entered. The results of the search appear in a simple list below the Advanced Find dialog box. Click the Stop button to interrupt the search at any point.

Double-click to open any item in the search results list. You can move, copy, delete, or edit items in this folder as well, using right-click shortcut menus (or click and drag to folders in the Outlook window). You can't choose a view other than the Table view; however, you can customize the fields that appear in the search results, change the sort order, and apply grouping. Right-click any column heading in the search results and use the Field Chooser to add or remove columns; you can also group messages in this display. When you save the search, these settings are saved as well.

TIP FROM

The settings in the Advanced Find dialog box are identical to those in the Filter dialog box that you use to define a custom view. Unfortunately, you can't transfer settings between these two dialog boxes. When you use the Advanced Find dialog box, you can view the results only as a simple list; if you want to see the search results in a different view, such as Address Cards, define a new view and create a filter for it. For searches that start in folders containing email items, you can also choose File, Save Search as Search Folder, and change the view or arrangement in the search folder.

Click the New Search button to clear all previously defined criteria and start from scratch.

USING CUSTOM VIEWS TO DISPLAY INFORMATION

Outlook uses forms to display the data in individual items. To see groups of items within a folder, you use views. By default, every Outlook folder includes a selection of built-in views available to all folders containing that item type. If none of the ready-made views matches the way you work, create custom views to sort, filter, and group items as required.

You don't have to use menus to switch views; you can select any available view for the current folder by clicking an option button in the Navigation pane. The View menu also includes an Arrange By option; for folders based on Table views, such as those that contain email messages or tasks, you can quickly choose from more than a dozen predefined arrangements that instantly sort and group the items in the current view—by date, size, or importance, for instance.

USING VIEWS TO DISPLAY, SORT, AND FILTER ITEMS

Every folder starts with a default view. For example, when you first open the Calendar folder, you see today's appointments, with a clickable calendar at the top of the Navigation pane; you can switch to Recurring Appointments view to see a list of all recurring items, grouped according to whether they repeat Daily, Weekly, Monthly, or Yearly. Likewise, items in the Contacts folder appear by default as address cards with minimal details, but you can choose to see more detailed cards or a simple Phone List view with one contact per row instead, as we've done in Figure 8.19.

To switch between views, select an entry from the list of defined views in the Navigation pane or in the drop-down list on the Advanced toolbar; if neither of these interface elements is visible, choose View, Current View. Outlook remembers the view you used most recently and reapplies that view whenever you return to that folder.

Figure 8.19
Click any view in the Navigation pane to instantly switch to that view.

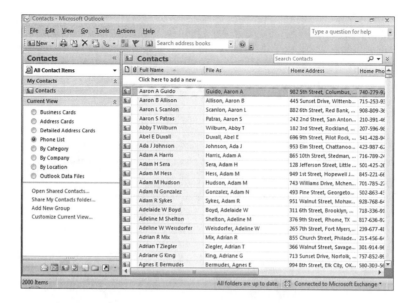

TIP FROM

If you can't see the list of available views on the Navigation pane for a particular folder, choose View, Navigation Pane, and click Current View Pane.

ARRANGING ITEMS IN A VIEW

When you're working with folders that contain mail or task items, Outlook 2007 allows you to apply one of 13 predefined arrangements of grouping and sorting options. These choices appear at the top of the View, Arrange By menu. You can group email messages by date, for instance, to see today's messages in one group, yesterday's messages in another group, and so on.

The groupings are logical and in many cases contain preset groupings. For example, when you view the contents of your Inbox and choose Size from the Arrange By menu, the contents are grouped into distinct "buckets" (see Figure 8.20)—Enormous (>5MB), Huge (1–5MB), Very Large (500KB–1MB), Large (100–500KB), Medium (25–100KB), Small (10–25KB), and Tiny (<10KB).

Using any of these Arrange By options has the same effect as if you had customized the current view, using the techniques described in the next section.

If your email messages no longer appear in the grouping you select, see "Restoring Groups to an Arrangement" in the "Troubleshooting" section at the end of this chapter.

Figure 8.20
Choices on the Arrange By menu automatically group items by the categories you select.

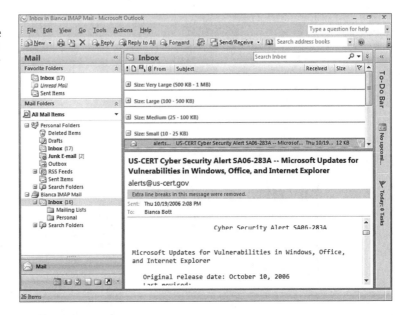

TIP FROM

In table-based views, you can click any column heading to quickly sort by that column. Click again to sort in reverse order. If the Show in Groups option on the View menu is selected, clicking a column heading changes the grouping, just as if you had clicked the corresponding choice on the Arrange By menu.

CUSTOMIZING AN EXISTING VIEW

If none of the built-in views offers the arrangement of data you're looking for, you can customize the current view. As you'll learn shortly, you can change some aspects of a view directly, without using dialog boxes. To see all your customization options, click Customize Current View in the Navigation pane (if this option isn't visible, choose View, Current View, Customize Current View). The Customize View dialog box appears, as shown in Figure 8.21.

Figure 8.21
Use this dialog box to customize all available options for the current view. Depending on the view type, some options may be unavailable.

Customize View: Phone List	
Description	
Fields...	Icon, Attachment, Full Name, File As, Home Address, Home ...
Group By...	None
Sort...	Full Name (ascending)
Filter...	Off
Other Settings...	Fonts and other Table View settings
Automatic Formatting...	User defined fonts on each message
Format Columns...	Specify the display formats for each field
Reset Current View	OK Cancel

The sections that follow explain how to modify each characteristic of the selected view. Note that some of these options will not be available for specific view types. For example, you can group items or adjust column formats only in a table-based view; these options are grayed out if you attempt to modify a card-based view, such as the Address Cards or Detailed Address Cards options in the Contacts folder. In table-based views, you can also apply changes to the current view interactively.

 If you've customized a built-in view and you need to undo your settings, see "Resetting the Standard Views" in the "Troubleshooting" section at the end of this chapter.

If you skipped Outlook 2003 and are upgrading from Outlook 2002 or earlier, you'll notice two additions to the Customize View dialog box in Outlook 2003: The Format Columns button gives you control over the display of nontext data types, such as icons and dates. The Reset Current View button offers the capability to instantly roll back to the default settings for a predefined view.

TIP FROM

The most effective way to create a custom view is to start with a built-in view and then modify it. If you prefer the modified view to the built-in one, leave your changes in place. If you want to switch between your custom view and the original built-in view, save the changes under a new name, as we explain later in this chapter.

CUSTOMIZING FIELDS

You can add fields to or remove fields from the current view. If most of your contacts are business related, for example, you might want to include the Company field in the Address Cards view of the Contacts folder and remove the Home Phone and Home Fax fields.

Using the Customize View dialog box, click the Fields button to display the Show Fields dialog box (see Figure 8.22). Select fields from the list on the left and click the Add button to add them to the current view. Select fields from the list on the right and click Remove to eliminate them from the view. (Hold down Ctrl as you click to select multiple fields from either list.)

Figure 8.22
Use this dialog box to control exactly which fields appear in a custom view.

8

If you're customizing a table-based view, such as the Messages view of the Inbox or the Phone List view of the Contacts folder, you can drag and drop to add or remove fields. Click the Field Chooser button on the Advanced toolbar or right-click the field headings and click Field Chooser to display a list of available fields. Drag fields onto the headings in the current view to add them to the view; to remove fields, drag column headings down onto the list itself, and release when you see the large X. Drag headings from side to side to change their left-to-right order in the list.

TIP FROM

EQ & Woody

When you add fields to a view using either the Customize View dialog box or the Field Chooser, Outlook displays only its limited selection of frequently used fields. To see a broader list of available fields, use the drop-down list in either dialog box. For example, if a folder contains Contact items, you can see all Name fields, all Phone Number fields, or an enormous list of all Contact fields.

GROUPING ITEMS

Outlook's grouping options allow you to arrange the contents of a folder in outline style, with each item in the outline corresponding to a field you select. Some folders include ready-made views with grouping already enabled—the Contacts folder, for instance, includes a By Company view that sorts your list by the contents of the Company field and then groups individual items according to Company. The resulting list allows you to collapse or expand each grouping.

Whenever possible, you should use the options on the Arrange By menu to do grouping. But the Group By box can come in handy for specialized tasks, such as grouping by multiple fields or by fields that are not represented in the predefined arrangements. To add grouping to a view, click the Group By button in the Customize View dialog box. This displays the Group By dialog box shown in Figure 8.23.

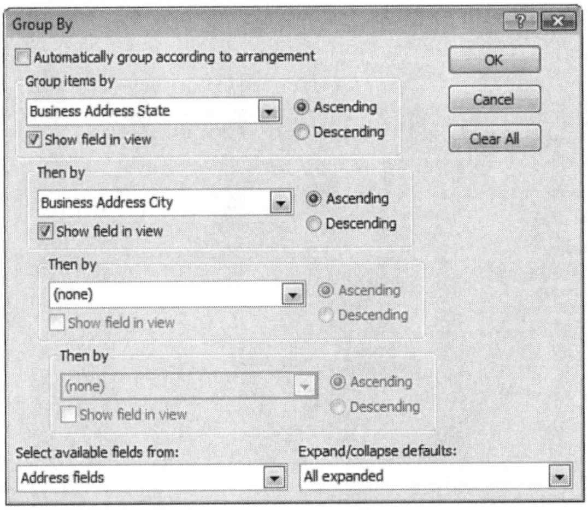

Figure 8.23
Use this dialog box to define grouping levels; note that you can choose whether the view starts with all items expanded or collapsed.

You can group by multiple fields; for example, if you're planning a business trip you might want to group by State and then by Category to see all the contacts in a particular area organized according to categories you've defined.

In any table-based view, you can change grouping on-the-fly. To group by any field that's visible, right-click its column heading and choose Group By This Field. You can also drag headings into or out of the Group By box, which appears just above the column headings. Click the Group By Box button or right-click the column heading and choose Group By Box from the shortcut menus to show or hide this area. To move an item between groups in this type of view, drag it out of its old group and drop it under the new group heading.

SORTING ITEMS

In any view, you can sort your data in a specific order—tasks by Due Date, contacts by Last Name, email messages by Subject, for example. In the Customize View dialog box, click the Sort button to choose up to four fields for sorting.

TIP FROM

Ed & Woody

> The Unread Mail search folder shows all unread messages grouped by folder and sorted by the date and time each message was received. When items are grouped this way, you can use the keyboard to jump to a specific group. Type the first letter of the folder name you want to go to, as it is displayed in this list. Outlook jumps immediately to the first message in the first folder beginning with that letter. If this view contains multiple folders that begin with the same letter, quickly type the first few letters of the folder name to jump to that folder.

FILTERING ITEMS

Filters show a subset of the items in any folder, based on criteria you define. The Overdue Tasks view in the Tasks folder, for example, displays only those tasks that you should have completed by now. If you inspect this view, you'll see that it uses a filter consisting of two items: Complete Equals No and Due Date on or Before Yesterday. Likewise, the Annual Events view of the Calendar folder shows all the birthdays and anniversaries you've defined, using a custom filter that shows only all-day events that recur yearly.

In combination with custom views, filters are a powerful way to manage information. In the Contacts folder, for example, you can define filters that show you only people who work for a specific company or who belong to a category you define. If you have a large family, you can create a filtered view of your Contacts folder that includes only people who share your last name or who belong to the Family category.

→ When working with email folders, Search Folders are often more useful than filtered views, as we explain in "Creating and Using Search Folders," **p. 248**.

To define a filter for any view, open the Customize View Summary dialog box, click the Filter button, and select the criteria you want to use in your filter. This dialog box is identical to the one used in the Advanced Find dialog box.

→ For more information about how to define filters and searches, **see** "Finding Outlook Items," **p. 199**.

FORMATTING

Two formatting options allow you to control the display of fields used in a specific view. For table-based views, click the Format Columns button to open the dialog box shown in Figure 8.24. As this example shows, you can adjust the display format of columns that contain date/time information. You can also change the label used in column headings and change the width and alignment of data in selected columns.

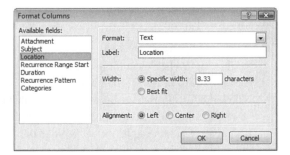

Figure 8.24

You can also tell Outlook to automatically apply a specific color or font to an item based on conditions you define. In the Calendar folder, you can automatically apply color-coded labels to appointments that meet specified conditions. Some formatting options are preset; unread messages and group headers in email folders, for instance, appear in bold. You can also add your own conditions, such as one that applies bold italic font formatting in red to any message from your boss, or one that applies the Important label to any appointment that includes your boss in the list of attendees.

To define automatic formatting, follow these steps:

1. In the Customize View dialog box, click the Automatic Formatting button. The Automatic Formatting dialog box (see Figure 8.25) shows all existing rules.

2. Click the Add button to create a new rule. Outlook gives it the default name Untitled. Replace this text with a descriptive name.

3. Click the Font button and select the formatting you want to use for items that match the condition. In the case of Calendar items, choose a color and matching text label from the Label list.

4. Click the Condition button and define the criteria that an item must match to be subject to automatic formatting. This dialog box works the same as the Advanced Find dialog box.

Figure 8.25

5. Click OK to save the rule and apply it instantly to the contents of the current folder.

Note that rules are applied according to their order in the Automatic Formatting dialog box. Rules that are higher on the list prevail over those beneath them. Note, too, that manual formatting always overrides automatic formatting. Finally, be aware that automatic formatting is applied only in the current view. If you switch to a different view, you need to create a new set of automatic formatting conditions.

OTHER VIEW SETTINGS

You can define custom display formats for many items in many views. In general, these options are available from shortcut menus. For example, in a table view, you can right-click any column heading to set its alignment (left, right, or center), change its column size to automatically fit the widest entry in the view, or change the column heading. Font changes apply to all fields in a section (card body or a row in a table); you can't pick out one field and format it separately.

From the Customize View dialog box, you can also set a variety of other options. Click the Other Settings button to see a dialog box like the one in Figure 8.26. The specific options vary by the type of view selected; in table views, as shown here, you can control whether it's permitted to edit in rows and whether gridlines appear.

Figure 8.26
Use this dialog box to set overall formatting options for a table or other type of view.

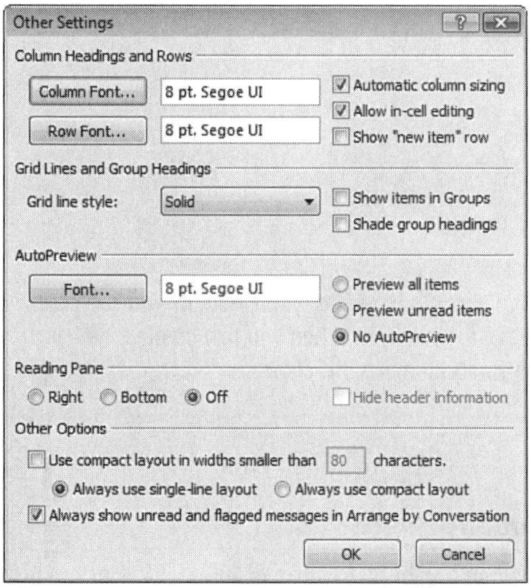

The AutoPreview option is a useful way to see additional information about items that contain details. In your Inbox folder, it shows the first three lines of each message so you can tell at a glance what's inside without having to open and read each message. In other folders, you can use it to see details—notes about each person in your Contacts folder, for example, or the beginning of an appointment's description.

To add the AutoPreview option to a view's settings, use the Other Settings tabs of the Customize View dialog box, or click the AutoPreview button on the Advanced toolbar to hide and show this information on-the-fly.

NOTE

Don't confuse AutoPreview with the Reading pane. When the Reading pane is visible, you can view the contents of any Outlook item—an entire email message, a contact item, or an appointment—in a window just below or to the right of the Contents pane; by contrast, enabling the AutoPreview feature shows only the first three lines of an item, and in the case of email messages, the preview disappears after you've opened and read the message. If you use AutoPreview in other folder types, the text remains visible at all times.

CREATING CUSTOM VIEWS TO SORT, FILTER, AND GROUP ITEMS

Sometimes the fastest and surest way to create the view you're looking for is to start from scratch. To begin defining a new custom view, switch to the folder that contains the items you want to view, and then choose View, Current View, Define Views. Click the New button to display the dialog box shown in Figure 8.27.

Figure 8.27
When defining a new view, you must start by defining a view type.

> **NOTE**
>
> You can't change a view's type after you create it—you can't convert a Card-style view to a Table-style view, for example. When you first create a new view, you have one, and only one, opportunity to make this choice.

All views start with one of the following arrangements.

Type of View	Description
Table	Default view for Tasks folder and Inbox, although you can use it with any folder. Displays data in worksheet style, with each item in its own row, each field in its own column, and headings for each column. Useful for displaying simple lists.
Timeline	A bar along the top displays days or hours; tiny icons underneath show all the items in the folder according to when they were created, received, or started. Especially useful with Tasks folder.
Card	Displays item title in bold, with selected details underneath. Most useful in Contacts folder, which includes two built-in Card views.
Business Card	New in Outlook 2007. Displays item title in bold in a resizable box that resembles a business card. Most useful in Contacts folder, where each contact's business card also appears in their item view.
Day/Week/Month	Available for all folders, but appropriate only for the Calendar folder. Options determine how many days you can see at once; more days mean less detail for each entry.

Type of View	Description
Icon	Displays each item as a large or small icon with title text underneath, as in an Explorer window. You can't add fields or group by different fields. Default view for Notes folder is inappropriate for other item types.

After you select a view type, choose where you want to use the view from the set of three options at the bottom of the dialog box. Choose This Folder, Visible to Everyone or This Folder, Visible Only to Me if you do not want the view to be available from the list of named views in other folders that contain the same type of data.

NOTE

> This Folder, Visible to Everyone is applicable if you're creating a view for a public folder on an Exchange Server or if you've chosen to share a particular personal folder with other Exchange users. This option has no effect if you're not connected to an Exchange Server.

If you want the custom view type to be available for all folders containing the same type of items as the current folder, choose All *<Item Type>* Folders. In general, this is your best choice; make an exception when you've defined a view that is relevant only to a specific folder.

After completing this step, the process of creating a new view is identical to the procedure for customizing an existing view. Add fields, set grouping and filter options if necessary, and save the view under a new name.

Managing Custom Views

Outlook gives you a complete set of tools for managing custom views you create. Choose View, Current View, Define Views to display a dialog box listing all views available for the current folder. Select any entry in this list and use the following buttons to work with that view:

- Click Copy to make a copy of the selected view. Give the view a new name to add it to the list. This technique lets you experiment with view options without worrying that you'll mess up a view you've carefully constructed.

- Click Modify to edit any available view setting for the selected view. Note that you cannot change the view type, and some settings are unavailable for certain views.

- Click Rename to give a view a different name; the name you enter is the one that appears in the drop-down list on the Advanced toolbar.

- Click Delete to remove a custom view completely. Note that you cannot remove or rename Outlook's built-in views, although you can edit their settings.

- Click Reset to remove all customizations from a built-in Outlook view. This option is not available for custom views.

8

IMPORTING, EXPORTING, AND SYNCHRONIZING OUTLOOK ITEMS

The simplest way to transfer data between Outlook and other programs is with the help of the Import and Export Wizard. You can import and export names and addresses, appointments, and RSS feed information, among others. The Import list includes a selection (mostly outdated) of third-party programs. The Export list includes only Excel 97-2003 and Access 97-2003 as named options. If the Import and Export Wizard doesn't include the specific name and version number of the program you plan to use as the source or destination, you need to use a delimited text file or a database file as an intermediate format.

NOTE

Many portable devices, including Apple's iPod, have the ability to sync your Outlook Contacts and Calendar. Consult the documentation that came with your portable device to learn how to use these nifty features.

TIP FROM

EQ & Woody

If you use multiple Personal Folders files to maintain your mail, use the Import and Export Wizard to effortlessly move items from one file to another. Choose File, Import and Export, and then select Export to a File or Import from Another Program or File. In either case, you'll find a Personal Folder File (.pst) option. Follow the wizard's prompts to select the folder or folders you want to move—defining a filter if necessary, so you move only items that match criteria you specify—and choose the name of the destination file.

IMPORTING DATA FROM EXTERNAL PROGRAMS

Outlook makes it relatively easy to import personal information, including contacts and appointments, from other software. Using the Import and Export Wizard, choose Import from Another Program or File, and then select one of the supported file formats.

If Outlook can't work directly with the native format of the program that contains the data you want to import, you'll have to first export the data to a supported format. Comma Separated Values and Tab Separated Values are the most common. Using Excel as an import format requires that you create a named range for the date to import before you begin the wizard.

NOTE

Both delimited text formats (Comma Separated Values and Tab Separated Values) offer DOS and Windows alternatives. The DOS version uses the ASCII character set, whereas the Windows versions incorporate the ANSI character set, which includes international and publishing characters. When in doubt, always choose the Windows option.

To import data, follow these steps:

1. Choose File, Import and Export.

2. In the Import and Export Wizard, choose Import from Another Program or File; then follow the wizard's prompts to select the specific data format and the file that contains the data.

3. In the Import a File dialog box (see Figure 8.28), specify how you want Outlook to handle items that duplicate those in the current folder. You can replace the existing item with the imported one, ignore the duplicate item, or allow Outlook to create duplicates. When in doubt, allow Outlook to create duplicate items and manually resolve the differences later.

Figure 8.28
Specify whether you want to create duplicate items (based on the title) when importing information. Regardless of your choice, Outlook does not warn you whether it created or rejected any duplicates.

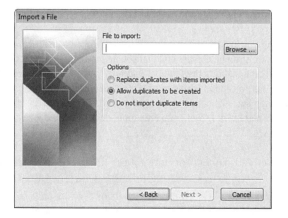

TIP FROM

> When you import data, Outlook doesn't give you any feedback as to how many new items it created, or whether it dealt with any duplicate items. If you want to know how many new items were created, open the destination folder before importing and check the status bar (just below the Navigation pane) to see how many items the folder contains. After completing the import, check the new count to see how many items were added.

→ Under some circumstances, Outlook can help you merge duplicate items that creep into your Contacts list so that you don't inadvertently keep outdated information; **see** "Merging Duplicate Contact Items," **p. 269**.

4. Select the destination folder into which you want to import the data, and then click Next.

5. In the last step of the Import and Export Wizard, click the Map Custom Fields button if you want to verify that Outlook plans to stuff information from the source file into the correct folder. The Map Custom Fields dialog box (shown in Figure 8.29) reads the field names from the source file and makes its best guess at matching them in the destination file.

Figure 8.29
The pane on the left shows the field names from the source file; drag names into the pane on the right to match them with Outlook field names.

TIP FROM

Whenever you import any amount of data, large or small, into your primary Outlook data file, we strongly recommend that you first create a new temporary folder. Give the folder a name that describes the data, such as "Imported Addresses," and then start the import. This precaution lets you inspect the imported items for errors and correct any information that was damaged during the import. When you're satisfied that the new items are correct, drag them into the proper destination folder.

6. Outlook displays the field names from the source file in the left pane. Scroll through the list of mappings on the right to see how Outlook has matched the field names in the source file to Outlook fields. Drag field names from the left pane and drop them onto the corresponding fields in the right pane to create a mapping. For example, if your source file includes a field called Full Name, drop it onto the Name field in the right pane.

7. Click Finish to import the data.

TIP FROM

You don't need to map all the fields from your source file to Outlook. If your original database includes hundreds of fields for each record, but all you want to import is the name and business address so that you can prepare a mailing, click the Clear Map button to eliminate all mappings. Then drag just the handful of fields you want to use into the destination pane.

EXPORTING OUTLOOK DATA

When you need to export data, Outlook offers fewer options than on the corresponding import side. In most cases, you'll need to export the data from one or more folders into a file using one of the standard data-interchange formats described in this section.

Outlook enables you to export to an Excel worksheet or a Microsoft Access database; choose the Excel option if you want to manipulate the data using Excel's list-management features.

→ To learn more about working with Excel's list-management features, **see** Chapter 21, "Organizing Data with Tables and PivotTables," **p. 627**.

If you plan to export the data into a non-Office program, choose one of the comma- or tab-delimited text formats. To export data to a file, choose File, Import and Export. In the Import and Export Wizard, choose Export to a File, and then follow the prompts to select the folder you want to export from, the file format you want to create, and the name and location of the resulting output file. As with the import version of this wizard, you can map custom fields. This is an excellent way to quickly export selected information from your Contacts folder into a format that other programs (including Word and Excel) can readily use.

 If your exported data contains stray characters that cause problems when you try to open the file in another program, see "Removing Multiline Addresses from Your Contacts Folder" in the "Troubleshooting" section at the end of this chapter.

TROUBLESHOOTING

DRAGGING DOESN'T ALWAYS MOVE AN ITEM

I tried to move an item from one folder to another, but Outlook opened the form for a new item instead.

You can move items only to folders capable of storing that type of item. If you try to move one type of item (such as an email message) to a folder intended for a different item (such as the Contacts folder), Outlook assumes you want to create a new item, just as if you had dropped the original icon on the folder's shortcut in the Navigation pane. Choose a different destination folder.

ALARMS FAIL TO GO OFF

I set a reminder on an Outlook item, but I never received a pop-up reminder.

It sounds obvious, but Outlook must be running if you expect to receive reminders. Outlook displays past-due reminders the next time you start the program, but these reminders don't do you much good if you've already missed an important meeting or appointment. To ensure that Outlook runs every time you start your computer, place a shortcut to the program in your Startup group. And if you use reminders, avoid shutting down Outlook except when you plan to turn off your PC.

RESTORING GROUPS TO AN ARRANGEMENT

In my Inbox, I chose the Size option from the View, Arrange By menu, but I got one long list instead of the logical groupings I usually see. What happened?

You must have inadvertently cleared the Automatically Group According to Arrangement option on the Group By dialog box for the current view. This can easily happen if you tinker with view settings. To restore the groups, choose View, Arrange By, and click Show in Groups.

RESETTING THE STANDARD VIEWS

When I view information using a built-in Outlook view, some fields are missing, or the sorting and grouping options aren't what I want.

Outlook makes it too easy to customize the built-in views, which is usually the cause when fields disappear from standard views. Fortunately, it's also easy to return a built-in Outlook view to its original settings. If you've messed up the Messages view of the Inbox or the Address Cards view of the Contacts folder, for example, just choose View, Current View, Define Views, and then select the view name and click Reset. This option is not available for custom views.

REMOVING MULTILINE ADDRESSES FROM YOUR CONTACTS FOLDER

When I open the Outlook data I exported to another program, the file contains stray characters that I didn't put there. What's happening?

Your exported data contains stray characters that cause problems when you try to open the file in another program. The culprit might be multiline addresses from your Contacts folder. In some export formats, Outlook includes carriage return characters with each line of the address, and the program you're using to import the data interprets these as end-of-record markers. Try exporting your data again, this time using the Comma Separated Text format, which adds carriage returns only at the end of a line.

SECRETS OF THE OFFICE MASTERS: SYNCHRONIZING OUTLOOK ITEMS WITH A HANDHELD PC OR SMARTPHONE

If you own a handheld computer such as a Smartphone, a Pocket PC, or a portable media player, you can synchronize data between your Outlook Personal Folders file and the handheld device. Don't use Outlook's Import and Export Wizard, however; instead, use the synchronization software included with the computer. In most cases, this software can exchange data directly with Outlook data files.

To set up and synchronize with a device running Windows Mobile software (formerly Windows CE), use the software that's compatible with your operating system. For Windows XP, this is the ActiveSync utility, available for download from `http://www.microsoft.com/windowsmobile`. For Windows Vista, use the Windows Mobile Device Center, available via Windows Update. In either operating system, you can synchronize your calendar and contacts list, download a limited selection of email messages, and move files between your handheld device and a desktop or portable PC; you can also configure space-saving options, such as restricting the size of messages on the handheld device and ignoring attachments.

CHAPTER **9**

READING, WRITING, AND ORGANIZING EMAIL

In this chapter

Setting Up Email Accounts   220

Configuring Your SMTP Server to Send Mail   228

Sending and Receiving Email   230

Using the Outlook Address Book   235

Composing a New Email Message   240

Organizing Your Email   247

Troubleshooting   255

Secrets of the Office Masters: Using Outlook with AOL Accounts   257

SETTING UP EMAIL ACCOUNTS

In Outlook 2007, you can connect to any combination of accounts from any supported mail server, including Internet-standard (SMTP/POP3/IMAP) accounts, Exchange Server mailboxes, Hotmail and MSN accounts, and older third-party servers with MAPI transports. Your account settings are saved in a *user profile*.

→ Most users need only a single Outlook user profile; to learn when multiple profiles may be necessary and how to create them, see "Setting Up Alternative Profiles," **p. 227**.

NOTE

> Beginning with Outlook 2002, Microsoft's developers eliminated the frustrating split personality that plagued Outlook 98 and Outlook 2000. Configuring those earlier versions required that you make a choice between two modes when setting up a profile—Corporate/Workgroup (CW) and Internet Mail Only (IMO)—with different menus, feature sets, and options for each one. If you're upgrading from Outlook 2000 or earlier, you can safely forget all the mumbo-jumbo you had to memorize about multiple modes.

The first time you run Outlook 2007, it scans your system for compatible email client software. If it finds a previously configured version of Outlook (any edition), Outlook Express, or any of several mostly older third-party programs, it offers to import your account settings (server information, username, and so on) and any existing mail messages. If you accept this option, you're done—Outlook creates a default profile, sets up mail accounts, and copies all your messages to your Inbox. You may be asked to reenter passwords the first time you connect to a mail server, but otherwise you shouldn't have to jump through any extra hoops to complete your configuration.

If Outlook can't find a compatible email program to upgrade, you'll need to create a profile with at least one email account. This process is almost completely automatic for many common account types. How to set up a new account depends on what you've previously done with Outlook:

- If this is the first time you've run Outlook under this user account, you jump straight to a wizard that offers to set up an email account. If you click Yes, you reach the Auto Account Setup dialog box, which is described in the next section.

- If you've previously set up Outlook, click the Mail icon in Windows' Control Panel, which opens the dialog box shown in Figure 9.1, and then click E-Mail Accounts. On the E-mail tab, click New. In the Choose E-mail Service page, select the Microsoft Exchange, POP3, IMAP, or HTTP option, and click Next to open the Auto Account Setup dialog box.

- If Outlook is already running, choose Tools, Account Settings. On the E-mail tab, click New. In the Choose E-mail Service page, select the Microsoft Exchange, POP3, IMAP, or HTTP option and click Next to open the Auto Account Setup dialog box.

All of these roads lead to the same place: the Auto Account Setup dialog box shown in Figure 9.2.

Figure 9.1
To configure Outlook accounts, data files, or profiles, you can use the Mail icon in Control Panel, which opens this dialog box.

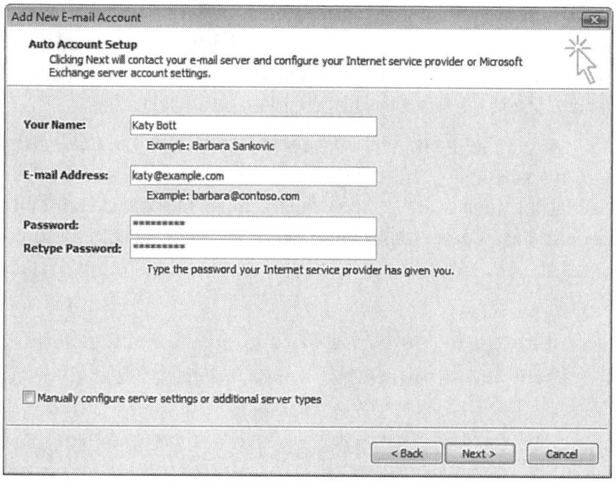

Figure 9.2
When you enter the most basic information about your email account, Outlook tries to automatically configure settings that allow you to send and retrieve messages.

After you enter your name, your email address, and your password (twice), click Next. Outlook tries to deduce your correct server settings and automatically establish a connection. You're most likely to succeed if your account uses plain-vanilla settings, or if it's provided by a well-known Internet service provider or hosted service.

Outlook first tries to make a secure connection; if that fails, it prompts you to try again, this time using an unencrypted connection. If neither option succeeds, Outlook tries some basic troubleshooting logic, giving you the option to reenter your email address and password. If auto setup fails, click the Manually Configure Server Settings Or Additional Server Types check box and then click Next.

In the remainder of this section, we'll explain how to manually configure the different types of email accounts and how to manage multiple accounts.

CONFIGURING INTERNET STANDARD EMAIL ACCOUNTS

Outside of the corporate world, the most popular email configuration by far is an Internet-standard SMTP server that supports POP3 connections. To successfully retrieve messages from this type of server, you have to configure Outlook to communicate with incoming and outgoing mail servers (which may be located on the same physical machine with the same address).

NOTE

> SMTP stands for *Simple Mail Transfer Protocol*, which is the most widely used method for transferring outgoing mail to its ultimate destination. Typically, you connect to an SMTP server at your Internet service provider, which accepts the message on your behalf and makes contact with the SMTP server that handles mail for the recipient. The recipient's SMTP server stores the message in a *mailbox*.
>
> To retrieve messages from a mailbox at most Internet service providers, you use a mail client that supports *Post Office Protocol 3* (POP or POP3, for short). When you set up Outlook for use as a POP3 client, it downloads headers, message bodies, and attachments to your Personal Folders file.
>
> A much less popular option for retrieving mail is *Internet Message Access Protocol 4* (IMAP). With IMAP, messages are stored on the server itself rather than in your Personal Folders file. If you set up an IMAP account, you will see an additional tab (IMAP) on the *<Account>* Properties dialog box, and the account name will appear in your folder list as a new icon at the same level as your Personal Folders file.
>
> You can only set up IMAP if your server supports it. The IMAP protocol offers options that are especially useful over slow connections, but it also creates some configuration headaches when using Outlook. For example, in some circumstances you won't receive notifications of new mail, even if you've set up Outlook to do so.

If the automatic setup fails (or if you bypass it to choose a manual setup), you see the dialog box shown in Figure 9.3. Choose Internet E-mail and click Next to continue.

Figure 9.3
When automatic setup fails, choose one of these options to begin setting up your account manually.

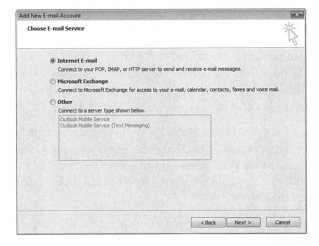

To begin manual setup, enter information on the Internet E-mail Settings dialog box shown in Figure 9.4. All information here is required. For technical details such as the names of mail servers and the username and password you use to log on, fill in the information exactly as it's provided to you by your Internet service provider or mail system administrator. In the User Information section, enter your name and email address exactly as you want mail recipients to see these details in the From line on messages you send.

Figure 9.4
To set up an Internet email account manually, enter this required information and click Test Account Settings.

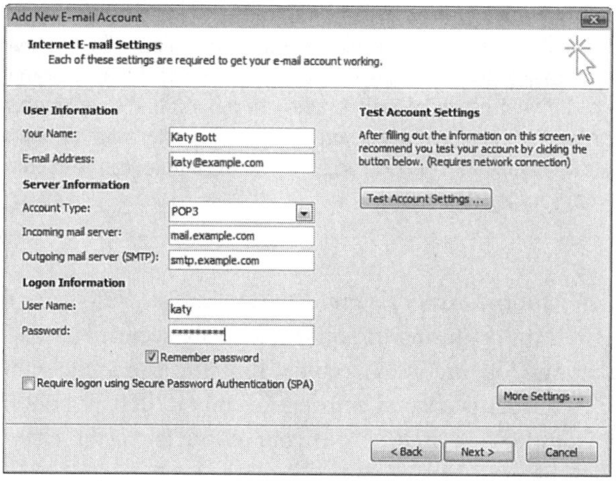

When filling out this dialog box, the input fields are identical regardless of whether you choose POP3 or IMAP as the account type. After filling in the required details, click Test Account Settings to verify that the information you entered works properly. As part of the test, Outlook connects to your incoming and outgoing mail servers and sends a test message to your account. If you receive an error message, check your username, password, and server names carefully. If the test succeeds, you can adjust advanced settings, as we explain here, or click the Next button to add the newly created account to your profile.

TIP FROM

Ed & Woody

> If you use more than one mail account, enter slightly different information in the Name field so that you can clearly differentiate which is which. For example, in the account you use to send and receive mail through a corporate server, add your company name in parentheses after your username. When you receive replies to messages you sent through that account, you'll usually be able to spot them quickly just by looking at the name in the To field.

In the Server Information section, you must specify fully qualified domain names for both incoming and outgoing mail servers. At some Internet service providers, both names are identical, usually in the form `mail.example.com`. Other common configurations use `smtp`, `pop`, or `pop3` as part of the full server name, with separate server names for incoming and outgoing mail servers. Most ISPs provide this information when you establish an account, and those that care about their customers also make it easily available on the Web. (Browse to your ISP's home page and look for a support or setup link.)

Pay special attention to the User Name box in the Logon Information section. Some servers require your full email address, including domain name, whereas others use only the portion that occurs before the @ sign. If you want Outlook to supply your password automatically each time you connect to the server, enter it in the Password field and select the Remember Password check box.

NOTE

> Leave the Password box blank if you want to minimize the risk that another user can send mail from your computer using this account; in that configuration, Outlook prompts you for your password the first time you connect to the server after starting Outlook. This precaution isn't foolproof; if you start Outlook, enter your password, and then walk away, anyone with physical access to your computer can read email and send messages from your account.

What should you do with the *Secure Password Authentication (SPA)* box? In general, you should leave it blank. This confusing option is a separate security package that prompts the user for credentials when logging in to a server. Today, it is extremely rare at ISPs; older versions of MSN (POP3 accounts created before November 2000 and never converted to web-based format) and CompuServe used SPA. If your ISP tells you to select this check box, do so; otherwise, leave it blank.

After you use this dialog box to create a new account, click the More Settings button and adjust the information on the General tab (see Figure 9.5). In particular, give the account a friendly name (the default is the name of the incoming mail server or your email address); you can choose to fill in the optional Organization and Reply E-mail fields here as well.

Figure 9.5
If you have multiple email accounts, be sure to change this default account name to something more descriptive.

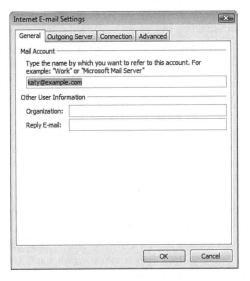

 If your outgoing mail keeps getting rejected, see "Solving SMTP Snags" in the "Troubleshooting" section at the end of this chapter.

CONNECTING TO AN EXCHANGE SERVER

If you have an account on an Exchange Server, your setup options are dramatically different from those on a POP3 server. You must be online and able to connect to the Exchange server to perform this setup. Make sure you have the server name, your username and password, and any other required information before starting.

CAUTION

> On corporate networks that use Exchange Server, administrators handle the work of set-
> ting up user accounts, and they typically have a low tolerance for users who screw up
> their mail settings. Before you change any of the details in your Exchange Server account
> settings, we recommend you contact your mail administrator.

To add an Exchange account to your profile manually, you must close Outlook first. Then follow these steps:

1. Open Control Panel, double-click the Mail icon, and click E-mail Accounts.
2. With the E-Mail tab of the Account Settings dialog box active, click New.
3. Select the Microsoft Exchange, POP3, IMAP, or HTTP option in the Choose E-mail Service dialog box and click Next.
4. Click the Manually Configure Server Settings or Additional Server Types option in the Auto Account Setup dialog box and click Next.
5. In the Choose E-mail Service dialog box, click Microsoft Exchange and click Next.
6. Outlook presents the dialog box shown in Figure 9.6. Enter the name of the Exchange Server and your username, and then click the Check Name button. After making the connection to the server, Outlook changes the User Name display to include the correct form of your mailbox name and underlines it.

Figure 9.6
Click the Check Name button to verify your settings. After connecting with the Exchange Server, Outlook displays the User Name with an underline.

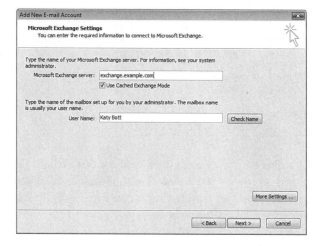

By default, your new connection uses Cached Exchange Mode, in which Outlook stores a copy of your mailbox locally, synchronizing the local copy with the server while you're connected. If you clear the Use Cached Exchange Mode check box, you'll have to periodically synchronize the contents of your mailbox when you're online.

Click the More Settings dialog box to adjust any or all of the following settings:

- **General**—Give your account a descriptive name and specify how you want to control the connection.

9

- **Advanced**—Use these settings to specify that you want to open additional mailboxes or public folders. You can also control Cached Exchange Mode settings here.

- **Security**—These options set up an encrypted connection between Outlook and your Exchange Server, preventing anyone who intercepts your data stream from reading your mail or "sniffing" passwords. The server administrator will tell you which options are supported for your configuration.

- **Connection**—Options on this tab resemble those used for Internet Explorer. You can specify whether you want to use your local area network or a dial-up connection. The most interesting option available here is Outlook Anywhere (shown in Figure 9.7), which allows you to connect to your Exchange Server using the standard HTTP protocol; this option allows you to bypass many proxy servers and firewalls that might otherwise block the ports used by Exchange Server. You'll need to confirm with your server administrator that this connection mode is supported before enabling it.

Figure 9.7
The Outlook Anywhere check box allows you to connect to your Exchange Server using the standard HTTP protocol, bypassing restrictions on many firewalls.

- **Remote Mail**—This tab allows you to define filters that exclude messages from being downloaded based on criteria you define. This option is useful if you are on a slow or expensive connection and you want to prevent messages with large attachments or those in specific folders from being downloaded.

USING HOTMAIL, MSN, AND OTHER HTTP ACCOUNTS

If you have a free Hotmail or MSN account that you normally access via the Web, you can read and send messages from within Outlook. For many web-based mail providers, including Hotmail, MSN, and Google Mail, the automatic account setup option is easy and foolproof. You can also use the manual options described in the previous section. In the Internet E-mail Settings dialog box, select the HTTP option from the Account Type list, and select Hotmail or MSN.

Microsoft disingenuously offers an "Other" option that allows you to enter the URL of an HTTP server from a non-Microsoft provider. As of this writing, no other web-based email providers are compatible with this option. To access Google Mail via Outlook, you use its POP3 settings (which are recognized and configured automatically when you enter a gmail.com address). Yahoo! Mail also uses POP3 settings and requires a premium account.

As with a POP3 account, you need to specify your username and password for an HTTP account. However, the server details are filled in automatically for you and you have limited connection options.

You can set up multiple HTTP-based Hotmail and MSN accounts in a single Outlook profile. If you have more than one Hotmail account, use the technique described in the previous section to give each account a descriptive name so you can identify it easily.

Hotmail accounts work differently from POP3 accounts. For more details, see the following section.

MANAGING MULTIPLE EMAIL ACCOUNTS

How many email addresses do you use? Between work, home, and web-based accounts, it's not unusual for even a casual email user to have three or more accounts to check. If you're an email addict, you could easily have more than 10 email addresses to keep track of.

Outlook includes a variety of tools and features that you can use to manage multiple email accounts effectively:

- Outlook 2007 offers full support for Microsoft's web-based mail accounts, Hotmail and MSN, and supports other web-based services via POP3 settings.
- You can define multiple Send/Receive groups with separate connection settings for each mail account. This allows you to check your favorite mail accounts regularly while downloading from infrequently used mail accounts only when you want to do so.
- You can define rules to process incoming and outgoing mail automatically—moving it to folders, color coding it, or assigning a message priority, for example.

Later in this chapter, we'll explain how to use each of these options most effectively.

 If you experience problems sending mail through multiple accounts from a single connection, see "Working Around Antispam Filters" in the "Troubleshooting" section at the end of this chapter.

SETTING UP ALTERNATIVE PROFILES

Outlook *profiles* allow you to manage groups of accounts. In Outlook 2007, your main profile is configured automatically during the initial setup process; you can set up additional profiles later, although this is rarely required. For most people, a single profile containing all accounts is the correct configuration.

When you set up a new profile, you associate email accounts and data files with that profile. This option allows you to use one profile to access mail directly from an Exchange server, with another profile set up for remote access synchronized to an Offline Folders file. You might want to set up separate profiles if you have highly confidential work email and you want to avoid any possibility of mixing messages and accounts between your work connection and your personal files.

To set up an Outlook profile, double-click the Mail icon in Control Panel and click the Show Profiles button. This option displays the dialog box shown in Figure 9.8.

Figure 9.8
Use the options at the bottom of this dialog box to select a profile when you start Outlook.

Click the Add button to create a new profile. A series of dialog boxes will prompt you to add email accounts and specify a data file. Click the Remove button to eliminate an existing profile. To work with a profile without opening Outlook, choose the profile and click the Properties button.

Normally, Outlook creates a single profile and uses it automatically each time you start. Choose the Prompt for a Profile to Be Used option if you want to select from a list of available profiles every time you start Outlook.

CONFIGURING YOUR SMTP SERVER TO SEND MAIL

In the never-ending battle against junk mail, Internet service providers are increasingly installing locks on their outgoing mail servers to keep them from being taken over by spammers intent on illicitly relaying bulk messages to an unwilling audience. In the good old days, you could simply enter the name or IP address of your SMTP server and start sending mail. Today, some ISPs allow access to SMTP servers only when you can prove your identity. Others allow access only when your IP address is on their network.

If your network administrator or email host has enabled extra security precautions on your SMTP server, you may need to go through additional configuration steps to prove that you're an authorized user before you can successfully send messages to the outside world.

To set up custom authentication options for an account, click the More Settings button on the Internet E-mail Settings dialog box and click the Outgoing Server tab. You'll see the dialog box shown in Figure 9.9. Select the My Outgoing Server (SMTP) Requires Authentication check box and then use one of the following options:

Figure 9.9
For networks that restrict access to SMTP servers, use this dialog box to adjust authentication options.

- In the simplest scenario, the server requires you to log in with the same credentials as you use for your incoming POP3 server. Select the Use Same Settings as My Incoming Mail Server option.

- In some cases, you may have to log on with a specific username and password that is different from the one specified for the incoming server. This might be true if you're receiving mail from a remote server on one network while sending messages out through your ISP's SMTP server. Click the Log On Using option and then fill in the User Name and Password boxes.

- Some SMTP servers require that you log on to your incoming POP3 server (authenticating yourself with your username and password) before you're allowed to send mail. Choose the final option, Log On to Incoming Mail Server Before Sending Mail.

An increasing number of ISPs block all traffic outside their own network on port 25 (the default port used by SMTP servers). This prevents spammers from using the ISP's network to relay junk mail through a server on another network. If this is how your Internet service provider has chosen to configure your network, you have two options:

- Use the ISP's SMTP server for all outgoing mail and customize the Outgoing Server options as noted previously in the second option.

- Configure your outgoing server on the "foreign" network so that it uses a port other than port 25. This option is available only if you directly control the configuration of the SMTP server or if the server administrator provides an alternative configuration designed to address this issue.

9

SENDING AND RECEIVING EMAIL

Some experts recommend that you check email only twice a day—any more often, they say, and you won't be able to concentrate on what's really important. At companies that live and die by email (including many in the computer and Internet industries), following that advice would be a classic career-limiting move.

Still, the general point is valid: Figure out how often you need to check email, and use Outlook to do as much of the work as possible. You have a variety of manual and automatic choices that control how you check messages.

SETTING UP SEND/RECEIVE GROUPS

By default, Outlook assigns the same mail-checking options to all your email accounts. Messages you create are sent out as soon as you click the Send button. When you press F9 or click the Send/Receive button, Outlook sends any messages in the Outbox and then checks each account for new messages, going through the accounts in the order in which they appear in the E-mail Accounts dialog box. To adjust the settings for this All Accounts group, or to create additional groups, choose Tools, Options; click the Mail Setup tab; and click the Send/Receive button. This opens the Send/Receive Groups dialog box (see Figure 9.10).

Figure 9.10
Using offline settings is especially helpful for notebook users; in this configuration, for instance, Outlook checks for new mail every three hours when online and never when offline.

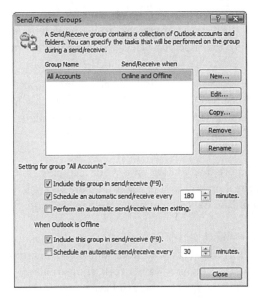

Most of the options here are fairly self-explanatory. You can create a new group; edit, copy, or rename a group; or remove a group from the list. Note that you can also define separate online and offline settings, which are controlled by the Work Offline choice on Outlook's File menu. New in Outlook 2007 is the capability to separately allow or suppress checking of RSS web feeds. These options are especially useful if you have a dial-up connection; users with always-on broadband connections can safely ignore offline settings.

To add a Send/Receive group, click the New button. Give the group a name and click OK to display the dialog box shown in Figure 9.11. (Note that the options vary depending on the type of account you've selected.)

Figure 9.11
Adjust settings for each mail account (and RSS web feeds) in a Send/Receive group.

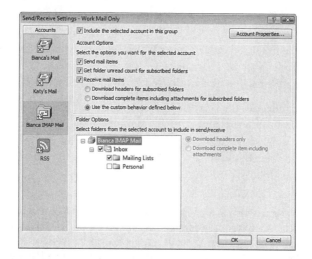

In each Send/Receive Group, you can define whether to send or receive mail items and whether you want to download headers only or retrieve complete items. In the case of web-based mail accounts or IMAP accounts, you can specify which folders to download.

Each Send/Receive Group you create appears on the Tools menu, under the cascading Send/Receive list. Using this menu, you can select all accounts, choose a group you've defined, or check messages for a single account.

CHOOSING WHICH MESSAGES TO DOWNLOAD

With any Internet email account (including Hotmail and MSN accounts), you can specify that you want Outlook to download only the headers of messages, rather than the full message bodies. This option is a lifesaver when you have a slow connection, especially when you're paying by the minute. It's also a useful way to keep spam and unwanted attachments from clogging up your mailbox.

To tell Outlook you want to work with message headers from a specified account, open the Send/Receive Settings dialog box as described in the previous section, click the icon in the Accounts pane at left, and select Download Headers Only. (For an IMAP account, you can specify this option on a folder-by-folder basis or choose the Download Headers for Subscribed Folders option to specify that you want to retrieve headers for all folders.) For POP3 accounts only, you can specify that you want to receive messages below a certain size threshold (typically regular text messages) but leave larger messages on the server while you decide what to do with them; select the Download Only Headers for Items Larger Than *nn* KB box.

9

When you connect to an email account that is configured to download headers only, Outlook downloads the envelope information (subject, sender, size, and so on) to your Inbox. An icon to the left of the item indicates that it hasn't yet been downloaded. Select one or more items and right-click to see a shortcut menu that lets you choose whether to download or delete each message.

If you double-click the message header, Outlook displays a dialog box offering the same choices that are available from the shortcut menu. Or you can use the keyboard shortcuts: Ctrl+Alt+M to mark a message to be downloaded, Ctrl+Alt+U to unmark the selected headers.

The next time you connect to the server, Outlook processes the marked headers. To manually connect and download or delete the messages immediately, click Tools, Send/Receive, and choose Process All Marked Headers or Process Marked Headers in This Folder. If you mark a message to be deleted, Outlook tells the server to delete it immediately, without ever downloading it to your Inbox.

NOTE

> When you work with message headers, Outlook's Junk Mail filters don't have a chance to kick in until you actually download the message. If you have an account that receives a lot of spam, you'll have to decide whether to mark the messages to be deleted without downloading, or to download the messages and let the Junk Mail filters do their work.

CHECKING FOR NEW MESSAGES

By default, Outlook checks messages at startup, or when you press F9, or when you click the Send/Receive button. If you have a permanent Internet connection, you can configure Outlook to check for new messages automatically by choosing options on the Send/Receive Groups dialog box.

Under several circumstances, you might prefer to check your email manually rather than setting an automatic option:

- If you're on a business trip and using Outlook on a notebook computer, you can't predict when you'll have an Internet connection. Configure Outlook's Send/Receive Groups to skip automatic mail checking when you work offline.

- For secondary mail accounts that you use only sporadically, you might choose to check your mail once every few days or even less frequently. When setting up a mail account in this configuration, clear the Include the Selected Account in This Group check box.

- If you're expecting an important message and your next scheduled automatic connection is hours away, make a manual connection.

- If your Internet connection is via the single phone line that serves your home or office, you probably want to check for mail only when you're certain other family members aren't on the phone.

When you click the Send/Receive button on the Standard toolbar, Outlook uses the settings from the All Accounts group. To check a single account, choose Tools, Send/Receive; then select the correct account or group from the cascading menu.

SETTING NOTIFICATIONS

Outlook offers to notify you in several ways when you've received new mail. To change notification settings, choose Tools, Options; click the E-mail Options button on the Preferences tab; and click the Advanced E-mail Options button. As Figure 9.12 shows, all of the following options are enabled by default, but can be disabled by clearing a check box.

- The two most subtle options play a sound and briefly change the mouse pointer when you receive new mail. To adjust either setting, you need to burrow several dialog boxes into the Outlook interface. If you're not at your computer, you'll completely miss both these cues.

- A more persistent but still subtle reminder is the icon that appears in the notification area to the right of the Windows taskbar (this area is also sometimes called the tray). An envelope icon here means you've received new mail; double-click the icon to open the Inbox and read the messages.

Figure 9.12

- The final notification option, introduced in Outlook 2003, is the *desktop alert*, a small window that fades up from the lower right corner of the screen to show you the subject and sender when a new message arrives in your Inbox, and then fades out after a few seconds. Click the Desktop Alert Settings button in the Advanced E-mail Options dialog box to adjust its behavior. (See Figure 9.13.) To make the alert window more or less visible, drag the Transparency control to the right or left; to control how long alerts stay on screen, use the Duration slider.

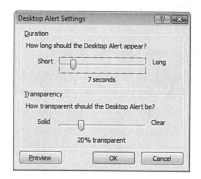

Figure 9.13

 If some of your messages are mysteriously missing from desktop alert windows, see "Forcing Outlook to Show Desktop Alerts" in the "Troubleshooting" section at the end of this chapter.

SPEED-READING NEW MESSAGES WITH THE READING PANE

How many email messages do you get every day? If your business revolves around email, you may get hundreds of messages a day, and dealing with them effectively means you have to make decisions about each one in just a few seconds. When time is of the essence, the

9

Reading pane can be a tremendous time-saver. The Reading pane previews the formatted text of messages and allows you to preview attachments in compatible formats. As you can see in Figure 9.14, turning on the Reading pane shrinks the message list to a still-readable display that shows the sender, date, and subject of each message. As you select items in the list, the contents appear in the pane to the right.

Figure 9.14
When the Reading pane is visible, the message list shrinks in width, and individual entries spread out to two lines each.

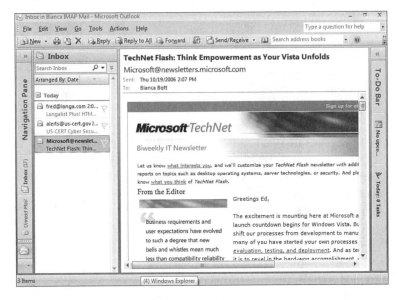

TIP FROM

Ed & Woody

If you prefer, you can arrange the screen so the Reading pane appears below the message list. Choose View, Reading Pane, Bottom to select this configuration.

Here's how to use the Reading pane to blast through messages at lightning speed:

1. Click the Mail or Folder List button on the Navigation pane and click the Unread Messages search folder. (If this search folder doesn't exist, you'll have to create it using the techniques described in "Creating and Using Search Folders," later in this chapter.)

2. If you can't see the contents of a message when you click its entry in the message list, click the Reading Pane button. Using this pane lets you quickly scan any message without having to open it.

3. Choose Tools, Options; click the Other tab; and click the Reading Pane button to display the Reading Pane dialog box shown in Figure 9.15. Select the middle check box (Mark Item as Read When Selection Changes) to mark mail as read when you view it in the Preview pane; if you want to be able to skip over some messages and leave them marked as unread,

Figure 9.15

select only the check box at top (Mark Items as Read When Viewed in the Reading Pane) instead, and leave the wait time at least 5 seconds.

 If you're unable to view some messages in the Reading pane, see "When Active Means Invisible" in the "Troubleshooting" section at the end of this chapter.

4. Begin reading your mail. Use the spacebar to move through the contents of each message, one screen at a time. (Don't use the arrow keys.) As you finish with each message, press Ctrl+R to compose a reply, Ctrl+Shift+R to reply to all. Press the Delete key to send the current message to the Deleted Items folder and move to the next one in the list, or press the spacebar to mark the previous message as read and jump to the next unread message.

USING THE OUTLOOK ADDRESS BOOK

In terms of complexity, Outlook's address-book structure historically has fallen somewhere between baseball's infield-fly rule and the U.S. tax code. What looks simple on the surface quickly becomes baffling, thanks to the many locations in which Outlook can store email addresses and other contact information, and two completely different interfaces for viewing and editing that information. Outlook 2007 is slightly simpler than its predecessors because it no longer supports the Office 97-style Personal Address Book file format. On Windows Vista, you can eliminate the old Windows Address Book format as well.

Where are your email addresses stored? Depending on your configuration, Outlook might use any of the locations listed in Table 9.1.

TABLE 9.1   OUTLOOK ADDRESS BOOK OPTIONS

Location	Description
Global Address List	This is the master address book on a network running Microsoft Exchange Server.
Offline Address Book	Available only on networks running Exchange Server; by default, it includes all addresses from your site, typically a subset of the Global Address List. To create an Offline Address Book, you must be connected to an Exchange Server; choose Tools, Send/Receive, Download Address Book. As Figure 9.16 shows, you can reduce the size of the download by choosing the No Details option.

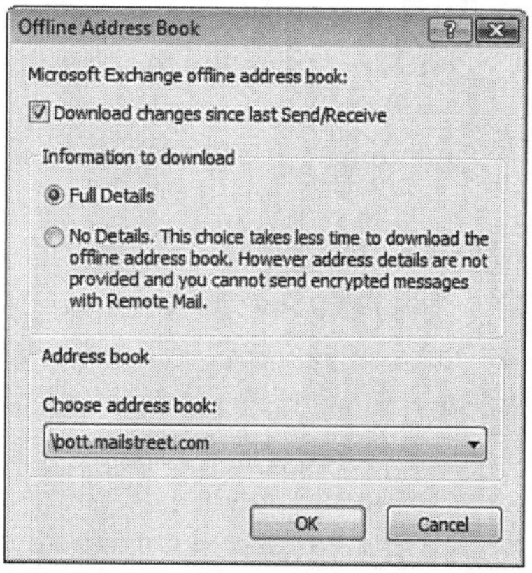

Figure 9.16

continues

TABLE 9.1 CONTINUED

Location	Description
Contacts Folder	The default location for addresses in your primary store; you can create additional folders containing Contact items and make them available for use with email messages as well.
Windows Address Book (*.wab)	This application, included with Outlook Express in Windows XP, stores addresses in its own file format (using the .wab extension). This format is not used in Windows Vista, which stores each contact item as a separate file in its Address Book in the Contacts folder (the one in your user profile, not Outlook's version).
Other MAPI-based address books	Third-party software developers can hook into Outlook as services, using their own file formats to store address information.

Did you notice that we didn't mention the Outlook Address Book? In Outlook 2007, the Address Book does not point to a physical location for storing addresses. Instead, it represents an important alternative method for viewing the contents of the Contacts folder and any other folders that contain Contact items. As you'll see shortly, this is a crucial concept in understanding how to configure Outlook addresses.

TIP FROM

EQ & Woody

> When you install other programs, they might take over functions you expect Outlook to handle, including email and address-book management. To specify that you want to use Outlook as your default email, calendar, and contact manager, choose Tools, Options; select the Other tab; and select the Make Outlook the Default Program for E-mail, Contacts, and Calendar check box.

Outlook includes the Contacts folder as a default store for contact information, but you might find it useful to create additional contact folders. For example, at work you might want to segregate information about friends and family in one folder and reserve your main Contacts folder for business contacts. If you're a frequent traveler, put listings for hotels, airlines, restaurants, and other on-the-road resources in a Travel folder. If your collection of contacts is particularly large, you can subdivide it even further, into separate folders for Customers and Suppliers, for example, all stored as subfolders under the Contacts folder.

CONFIGURING ADDRESS BOOK OPTIONS

Savvy Outlook users do most address management from the Contacts folder. Its default data-entry form is the most flexible way to enter new items, and its support for custom views and filters makes it the best choice for quickly viewing information. But Outlook also offers another view of the Contacts folder; click the Address Book button on the Standard toolbar to display a window on your Contacts like the one shown in Figure 9.17. To narrow the list, enter all or part of a name in the Search box and click Go. Unlike folders that contain Contact items, this view shows only items that have an email address or a fax number.

Figure 9.17
To filter the Address Book view, enter some text in the Search box and click Go.

→ For full details on how to use the Contacts folder, **see** "Keeping Your Contacts List Under Control," **p. 259**.

If you set up Outlook on a new computer with Internet-standard email accounts, you'll end up with a single location for storing addresses—the Contacts folder. If you connect to an Exchange Server, you'll have the Global Address List in your Address Book list, and possibly a local copy of that list (the Offline Address Book). And you might choose to create additional Contacts folders for the sake of organization.

If you have more than one address book, we recommend that you double-check your Outlook setup to make sure you've eliminated the possibility of creating duplicate addresses and that your Address Book is correctly configured. To verify your current settings, you'll need to look in three places:

- Right-click the Contacts folder icon in the Navigation pane and choose Properties. On the Outlook Address Book tab, be sure the Show This Folder As an E-mail Address Book check box is selected. Click OK to close the dialog box. Repeat this step for any other folders that contain contact items with email addresses.

- Choose Tools, Account Settings, and click the Address Books tab. Select the Outlook Address Book entry in the list and click Change. Verify that this entry points to the correct folder. If it's incorrect, click Remove Address Book. Adjust the way names display if necessary in the Show Names By section of the dialog box.

- If the Outlook Address Book is not listed in your profile, click the New button on the Address Books tab if the Account Settings dialog box, choose Additional Address Books, and click Next. Choose Outlook Address Book and follow the prompts. Close and restart Outlook if prompted.

TIP FROM

Ed & Woody

You don't have to designate all contact folders as address books. Reserve this honor for folders filled with items that have email addresses or fax numbers. If you create a folder with contact items that identify restaurants, hotels, airlines, and other travel-related institutions that you typically contact over the phone rather than through email, don't designate this folder as an address book.

NOTE

> If you receive email through an Exchange Server, your profile might also include an Offline Address Book. Do not remove this entry from your profile.

Close all dialog boxes and choose Tools, Address Book. Click the drop-down Address Book list Show Names to verify that the folders you specified are available in the Address Book.

ADDRESSING AN EMAIL MESSAGE

When addressing an email message, you have several options:

- The most reliable way to make sure you address each message correctly is to reply to an email message you've received. In this situation, you can almost always be certain that the address is accurate. (If it turns out to be wrong, you can blame the original sender.)

 If you reply to a message and get a delivery failure, see "When Your Email Bounces" in the "Troubleshooting" section at the end of this chapter.

TIP FROM

EQ & Woody

> Although it's not immediately obvious, all address information in the header of a message you receive is "live." Right-click any address to display a shortcut menu. Choose Add to Contacts to create a new item in your Contacts folder using the name and email address displayed in the header, or choose Look Up Contact to search your Contacts folder for an item that contains a matching email address. You can also use the shortcut menu to copy the address and paste it in the To or CC box in another message.

- For addresses you don't plan to reuse (such as a request for information from a merchant), enter the full email address in the To, Cc, or Bcc box.
- Open the Address Book, select one or more names, and click the New Message button.
- Open the Contacts folder, select one or more names, and choose Actions, New Message to Contact.
- Start a new message and click the To, Cc, or Bcc buttons to display the Select Names dialog box, which shows the Address Book with boxes below the list where you can enter addresses. Select one or more names and then click the To, Cc, or Bcc button to add addresses to that field. This is the easiest way to add a large number of addresses to a message quickly and accurately. Click OK to return to the message window.
- For people you send mail to most frequently, enter any portion of the recipient's name in any envelope field (To, Cc, or Bcc) and let Outlook's AutoComplete feature resolve the address for you. (To enter multiple names this way, separate each name with a comma or semicolon.)

AutoComplete is a power user's dream. It searches in your Contacts folder and other Address Book locations; it also remembers addresses you've recently entered manually or by replying to a message. If Outlook finds one and only one matching item, it completes the name automatically, using the default email address. If Outlook finds multiple matching names, it shows a drop-down list of matching names so you can select one.

CAUTION

> AutoComplete can also cause nightmares if you're unaware of how it really works. Because the list of AutoComplete possibilities includes addresses you've entered manually, Outlook may "remember" a name and suggest it to you. The name looks all right in the To field, so you accept it; unfortunately, you don't realize that the message is going to a rarely used email account for that contact, rather than the address she checks 10 times a day. To avoid this possibility, double-click the name in the To field to display a dialog box that shows the Display Name and E-mail Address fields.

 If you find that AutoComplete has "memorized" some incorrect addresses, see "Cleaning Up the AutoComplete List" in the "Troubleshooting" section at the end of this chapter.

To configure AutoComplete options, choose Tools, Options, click the E-mail Options button on the Preferences tab, and click the Advanced E-mail Options button. Select or clear the Suggest Names While Completing To, Cc, and Bcc Fields box at the bottom of the dialog box to enable or disable AutoComplete.

How do you deal with contacts that have multiple email addresses? Don't create multiple Contact items, each with a different address; that will cause a mess when Outlook tries to resolve the addresses for you. Instead, enter each different email address as part of the same Contact item. When you use the Contacts folder, you can enter up to three email addresses; the first is the default address that Outlook uses when sending mail to that person.

USING PERSONAL DISTRIBUTION LISTS

Outlook enables you to create an alias called a *Personal Distribution List* that represents a group of email addresses. Use this option to avoid having to repeatedly enter a slew of addresses when you routinely send mail to the same group of people. For example, if you're on the board of a local charity, you can create a Personal Distribution List that includes all the other members of the board, and then name it Board of Directors. When you type that name in an envelope field on a message form, Outlook recognizes the list and resolves it for you. When you send the message, Outlook substitutes all the individual names so that your message is delivered correctly.

To create a Personal Distribution List in the Contacts folder, choose File, New, Distribution List. From the Address Book, choose File, New Entry, choose New Distribution List, and click OK. Both methods lead to the dialog box shown in Figure 9.18.

Enter the name you want to use for the list in the Name field. Click the Select Members button to add names from the Address Book. Click the Add New button to open a dialog box where you can enter a new name that isn't currently in your Contacts folder; select the Add to Contacts check box to store that new item in the Address Book as well as in the Personal Distribution List. After you finish adding names to the list, click the Save and Close button to save the list.

Figure 9.18
Use this dialog box to add names to a Personal Distribution List.

Personal Distribution Lists appear in the Address Book as boldfaced entries; in the Contacts folder, they appear as one-line entries with a distinctive icon. If you need to change the lineup of names that make up the list—if a member of the board quits and another takes her place, for example—double-click the item to reopen this dialog box, and then select the names you no longer need and click the Remove button to get rid of them.

TIP FROM

If you routinely send messages to a large number of recipients—more than 10, for example—think carefully about how to address the message. If it's not necessary for any of the recipients to respond to all others on the list, address the message to yourself and add the other recipients' names to the Bcc field. Your message is far more likely to be read in this format, especially by people using mail software that displays the entire message header—a list of 20 or so names takes up the entire screen and pushes your message completely out of sight otherwise.

COMPOSING A NEW EMAIL MESSAGE

After successfully addressing a message, composing a message is a reasonably straightforward process. If you've chosen plain-text format, enter text and add attachments (you can drag any file from an Explorer window into the message window to attach it, or choose Insert, File to choose items from a dialog box). For Rich Text messages, you can also use font and paragraph formatting. HTML messages give you the option to add pictures, background colors, graphics, and other web-style formatting. Depending on the message type you've selected, you can also choose several advanced options.

CHOOSING A MESSAGE FORMAT

When you compose a new message or click the Reply button, Outlook lets you choose from three distinct message formats, found in the Format group on the Options tab. In some circumstances, Outlook chooses the message format for you. If you're picky about which message format you send out, you may have to specifically override that decision. Pay attention to the fine details in this section, because the options that seem so obvious do not always behave as you expect.

- **Plain Text**—Transmits nothing but letters, numbers, and symbols in the character set you use to create the message. Outlook strips any formatting, including colors, fonts, and inline pictures, when it sends the message. The recipient sees the message in the default font for his or her mail program.

- **HTML**—Offers the same text-formatting options as Rich Text Format, plus the capability to specify styles, automatically number lines, and add horizontal rules. Because the underlying format is the same as a web page, you can also define background graphics and insert images into a message. Most modern Internet mail client programs are capable of reading HTML-formatted messages. If your recipient uses any version of Netscape Mail, Outlook Express, or Eudora that is less than five years old, he should have no trouble reading your HTML-formatted messages. If the recipient's mail client software can't interpret HTML, the recipient sees a plain-text version of the message with an attachment that can be viewed in any web browser.

- **Outlook Rich Text**—This format, the default on most Exchange servers, was developed by Microsoft years ago, before HTML became popular. Using Rich Text Format enables you to specify fonts, colors, bullets, and other text attributes, with one major caveat: Only recipients who use Outlook or another Exchange client will be able to correctly view that formatted information. Rich Text is the default format on Exchange Servers. If you send a Rich Text message to a recipient who is using an older client program, he will see most of the text in your message as well as an attachment called `Winmail.dat`, which contains useless information. Outlook automatically creates messages in Rich Text Format when you use group-oriented features such as meeting invitations and task requests.

TIP FROM

The default settings for all Outlook versions since 2002 make it nearly impossible to send a Rich Text message over the Internet; instead, any such message is automatically converted to HTML or plain text. If you send and receive some email through an Exchange Server but also through an Internet-standard SMTP/POP3 account, you can override this decision. Choose Tools, Options; click the Mail Format tab; and click the Internet Format button. Choose a format from the drop-down list.

Which of these three formats will Outlook use when you create a message? As with so many configurable settings throughout Office, the correct answer is: It depends.

TIP FROM

The name of the current message format always appears in parentheses in the title bar of an open message.

When you create a new message from scratch, Outlook uses the default format you specify. From the main Outlook window, choose Tools, Options; then click the Mail Format tab and select HTML, Rich Text, or Plain Text from the Compose in This Message Format list.

When you reply to a message, Outlook ignores the preferences you specified as your default and uses the format of the original message. This isn't as rude or as illogical as it sounds: If you receive a message that was composed in HTML or Rich Text Format, you can be certain that the sender is capable of reading messages in that format. On the other hand, when you receive a message in plain text format, the most conservative response is to assume that the sender either can't work with other formats or chooses not to use formatted mail, and respond in kind.

CAUTION

> Pay close attention to message formats when you reply to messages. If the original message was in Rich Text Format, your reply to the original sender uses that format as well; if you add recipients and they use mail client software that is incapable of reading Rich Text Format, they might have difficulty reading the original message or your reply. This problem is less serious than in previous versions because Outlook automatically converts your Rich Text messages to HTML.

You can switch on-the-fly to a new message format. Click the Options tab and choose Plain Text, HTML, or Rich Text from the Format group. Note that in Outlook 2007, unlike in previous editions, you can switch directly from HTML to Rich Text or vice versa; previously, you had to first convert the message to plain text format, losing all formatting, and then choose the other format.

USING A SPECIFIC ACCOUNT TO SEND A MESSAGE

Normally, Outlook sends replies using the same account with which you received the original message. On new messages and forwards, Outlook uses the account specified as the default in your E-mail Accounts list. For any message, you can choose which account to use for sending. If you have more than one email account set up, click the Accounts button on the New Message window (just below the Send button) and use the drop-down list to select a different account.

MANAGING EMAIL SIGNATURES

Outlook allows you to create a *signature*—a short block of text (with or without formatting, graphics, or HTML code) that identifies you and perhaps supplies some information about you or your company. Signatures are typically inserted at the end of a message. You can specify a different default signature for each account—a businesslike signature for your work account, for example, and a more playful one for your personal mail—but you can insert or remove a signature from any message, at any time. To create a new signature, follow these steps:

1. From the main Outlook window, choose Tools, Options, click the Mail Format tab, and then click the Signatures button. The Create Signature dialog box (see Figure 9.19) shows all the signatures you've created so far.

Figure 9.19
Email signatures can include text or graphics—such as this business card—for use with different accounts.

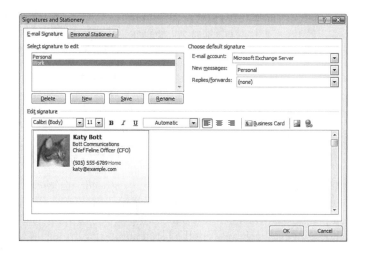

2. Click the New button. In the New Signature dialog box, enter a descriptive name for your signature and specify whether you want to create it from scratch or base it on an existing signature or file. Click Next to continue.

3. In the Edit Signature dialog box, enter the text you want to use for your signature. Use the formatting toolbar to change fonts, font sizes, alignment, and other text formatting.

TIP FROM

Ed & Woody

> One of the most effective signature techniques you can use is to insert a business card, complete with photograph or logo, along with your name, email address, and other contact details. Before you insert your business card, open your personal contact item in the Contacts folder and edit the card so it looks the way you want it to be in the signature. Note that the card design in the signature is static. Any changes you make to your contact item or to the card design after creating the signature are not reflected in the signature. To update the card, open the Signatures and Stationery dialog box, select the signature that uses that card, and click the Business Card icon to reselect the edited card.

4. Click the Picture button to add an image to your signature (make sure you crop it to the correct size separately, because the signature editing tool has no picture-editing features). Click the Hyperlink button to create a clickable link to a website or other Internet address. Click the Business Card button to add the business card you customized for your contact record.

5. If you want Outlook to insert the signature you just created whenever you create a new message or reply to an incoming message using a particular account, adjust the options in the Choose Default Signature section.

6. Click OK to save your signature.

TIP FROM

EQ & Woody

When you create or edit an outgoing email message or reply, you can change signatures on-the-fly by right-clicking the signature. The shortcut menu lets you choose from all defined signatures. What if you delete the signature that Outlook automatically inserts in a new message or reply based on the preferences you set here, or if you create a new message with no signature? No problem. In the message-editing window, click the Insert tab and choose Signature from the Include group. The drop-down list shows all signatures you've created and allows you to open the Signatures dialog box and add or edit a signature.

To change a signature on a message that you're currently editing, click Signature on the Insert tab, and then select an entry from the list of available signature files. The position of the insertion point doesn't matter. Your signature always goes at the end of the message, and when you choose a new signature from the list, it automatically deletes any existing signature in that message window.

ADVANCED MESSAGE FORMATTING

Both plain-text and HTML formats include advanced settings that can make your messages easier to read. (If you mess with these options too much, you can also turn outgoing text into garbage, so be careful.) To see and adjust these settings, choose Tools, Options; then click the Mail Format tab. In the Message Format section, choose your default format for outgoing mail, usually Plain Text or HTML. Click the Internet Format button to set other options, as shown in Figure 9.20.

Figure 9.20
In general, most Outlook users should leave these settings at their defaults.

SETTING CUSTOM MESSAGE OPTIONS

When you click the Send button after composing a message, you tell Outlook to deliver the message using all your default settings: The outgoing message goes to your default mail server, you get a copy in your Sent Items folder, and that's about it. If you want the message to have special handling, take a look at the settings available on the Options tab, including the option to get return receipts when the message is delivered or read. You can also use the Save Sent Item button to choose whether and where to save a copy of your outgoing message. Many of the buttons on this tab open the Message Options dialog box shown in Figure 9.21—you can also open it by clicking the small box at the lower-right corner of the Tracking or More Options groups or the Options group on the Message tab.

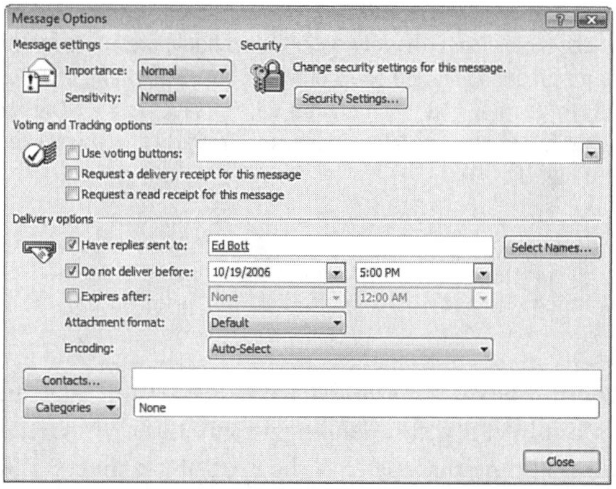

Figure 9.21
Several options in this
dialog box, such as
the capability to defer
sending a message,
can be extremely use-
ful in business.

In the Message Settings section, use the Importance and Sensitivity drop-down lists to
change these fields from their default setting of Normal to Low or High. Other Outlook
users will see a blue down-arrow in the message list for Low Importance messages and a red
up-arrow for High Importance messages.

TIP FROM

If you encourage co-workers to use the Low and High Importance settings for messages,
you can use email rules to automatically highlight or file messages based on this setting.
Skip the Options button and use the High and Low Importance buttons on the Message
tab when composing a message.

The choices in the Message Options dialog box provide a wide range of useful functions:

- Voting buttons are a very efficient way to conduct a poll via email. This option works
  only if the sender and recipient are both using Exchange Server. If you create a message
  and send it using an Internet standard account, the voting buttons are ignored.

- Select the Have Replies Sent To check box and enter an alternative Reply To address.
  This option is especially useful when you want an outgoing message to go out under
  your name, but you want to redirect replies to a different address. As the president of a
  company, for example, you might want to announce a new benefits plan for your
  employees; if you enter the human resource director's name and email address in this
  box, employees can reply directly to your message for more information.

- Select the Do Not Deliver Before check box and enter a date if you want to compose a
  message and send it automatically at a time you specify. This option can be extremely
  useful when the timing of a message is crucial but you won't be physically present to
  send the message. For example, suppose you're planning an important announcement
  for Monday at 10 a.m.; go ahead and prepare the press release, and then enter **Monday
  10am** in this box. Make sure to leave Outlook running with the option to automatically
  send and receive mail every 10 minutes or so, and your message will go out within 10
  minutes of the time you specify, even if you're out of the office.

NOTE

> If you use the deferred delivery option to schedule messages far in the future, be prepared for an annoying side effect of this option. Every time you close Office, you'll see a dialog box warning you that there are still messages in your Outbox and asking whether you want to exit anyway. If you know you'll restart Office before the message is due to be sent out, click OK.

→ For more details on how to enter dates using plain-English equivalents in any Outlook item, **see** "Entering Dates and Times Automatically," **p. 193**.

- Select the Expires After box if you use Exchange Server and your message has a time element to it. For example, if you're sending a reminder of a meeting that starts in an hour, add an expiration time that matches the start of the meeting. Recipients who check their email before the start of the meeting will see the message. In the case of recipients who haven't picked up the message by its expiration time, the Exchange Server automatically deletes it, and you avoid cluttering up their Inboxes.

Are you tempted by the check box in the Voting and Tracking Options section that enables you to request a receipt when your message is delivered or read? Temper your expectations. If your message is going over an Exchange Server to another user on the same server, this option works exactly as you expect: The server can send you a delivery notice when the email lands in the recipient's Inbox, and another when it's opened. If your message has to pass through an SMTP server before reaching its destination, it's extremely unlikely you'll see a receipt—support for this feature is hit-or-miss on the Internet, and the recipient can choose to ignore the request for a receipt.

Setting Reply and Forward Options

When you reply to a message, it's customary to include some or all of the original message to give the recipient a context for your answer. Outlook lets you choose from several formatting options to help make the original message text stand out. You can also define how Outlook identifies the original message text when you forward a message to someone else. Regardless of which option you choose, the insertion point appears at the top of the message window, with the original message below it.

To set either or both options, choose Tools, Options; click the Preferences tab; and click the E-mail Options button. If you routinely use HTML format, you can include the original message, or include and indent the original message. If you use plain text as your default format, we recommend that you choose the Prefix Each Line of the Original Message option and select the default quote character, a greater than (>) sign, as shown in Figure 9.22.

Figure 9.22
If you send mostly plain-text messages, use the options shown here to prefix the original message in replies and forwards.

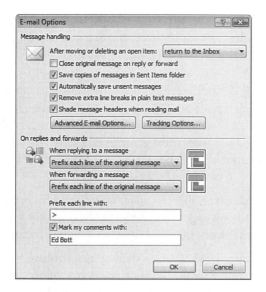

CAUTION

Avoid two options available in this dialog box. Specifying Do Not Include Original Message for replies makes it difficult (and sometimes impossible) for recipients to figure out what you're responding to. (It is good etiquette, however, to try to trim extraneous matter from replies and forwards.) The Attach Original Message option forces recipients to go through the additional step of detaching and opening an attachment to read the original message. They won't thank you for the extra work.

ORGANIZING YOUR EMAIL

If you receive just 10 email messages a day and allow them to remain in your Inbox, in less than a year you'll have more than 3500 messages hanging around. If you receive more mail than that, the numbers can get staggering. Although Instant Search helps tremendously in the effort to find needles in a haystack of email, sorting mail is even more effective.

You can drag messages into folders to keep them organized, but it's smarter still to create Outlook rules that process messages automatically. In less than the time it takes to read a day's email, you can create a set of rules that can easily help you avoid wasting time on low-priority messages, that can file email by category or project, and that also ensure that you never miss an important message because it was buried in your Inbox. The combination of well-crafted rules, Junk Mail filters, and search folders can go a long way toward eliminating email overload.

TIP FROM

Ed & Woody

Two built-in shortcuts are especially useful for locating related messages or for finding all messages from the same sender. From the message list, right-click any message and then choose Find All. Choose Related Messages to find all messages that are part of the same conversation (the original message and all replies); choose Messages from Sender to display a list of all messages in the current folder from the sender of the selected message. In either case, Outlook opens the Advanced Find dialog box and displays the results there.

With Outlook 2007, you have another organizational option as well. Instead of physically moving messages into subfolders, use *search folders* to create a virtual filing system, using filters to slice and dice an overstuffed inbox into manageable chunks.

CREATING AND USING SEARCH FOLDERS

Search folders, which were introduced in Outlook 2003, look like subfolders but are actually virtual folders. When you click a search folder, its contents are assembled dynamically from messages matching conditions you specify; the contents of a search folder may be drawn from several different locations, but they appear side by side in the message list as if they were in a single location.

Initially, Outlook creates search folders that let you see all Unread Mail in one place, even when you've used rules to sort the new messages into multiple folders. You don't have to worry about jumping from folder to folder in search of unread messages; Outlook does the work for you.

Other built-in search folders let you click to see all messages that have been flagged for follow up and those that are especially large. To create new search folders, click the Mail or Folder List button in the Navigation pane, right-click Search Folders, and choose New Search Folder. The New Search Folder dialog box, shown in Figure 9.23, allows you to quickly build simple search folders that cover common searches.

Figure 9.23
Build a generic search folder using the settings in this dialog box.

To build more complex search folders, you could scroll to the bottom of the list in the New Search Folder dialog box, click Create a Custom Search Folder, and then drill through a half-dozen dialog boxes to specify each option from scratch. But there's a much easier way. Use the Advanced Find dialog box to build a search, using the techniques we described in Chapter 8, "Outlook Essentials," and then use the Save As Search Folder menu choice.

→ For an in-depth explanation of how to set up and use Junk Mail filters, see "Stopping Spam and Other Unwanted Email," **p. 313**.

USING EMAIL RULES TO SORT AND PROCESS MAIL

Outlook's single most powerful mail-handling option is its ability to define email rules. When you define a rule, you tell Outlook to examine each incoming message as it hits your Inbox (or to look at each outgoing message when you click the Send button) to see whether it matches conditions that you define. If Outlook detects a match, it performs one or more actions you defined for that rule.

The following list includes a few examples of how you can use email rules to sort and organize messages:

- **Urgent mail**—If you sometimes receive messages from key contacts who need immediate assistance, you want to know ASAP. You can create a rule that pops up a dialog box as soon as messages containing hot-button words—urgent or problem, for example—arrive from particular senders.

- **Personal mail**—Move personal messages from family members and friends into a designated folder, away from your work-related messages, when they arrive in the Inbox.

- **Messages you receive as a member of a mailing list**—If you receive daily digests from the Doberman Fanciers list, you can instruct Outlook to sort them into their own folder automatically.

- **Mail from other accounts**—Move all mail you receive from a particular account (a personal account you check at work, for example) into a special folder so you can clearly segregate it.

- **Commercial mail**—Identify commercial email from companies that you truly want to hear from. If your favorite online bookstore, music dealer, bank, broker, or travel agent occasionally sends you notices of deals you might be interested in, you can move these messages out of your Inbox and into a folder where you can examine them at your leisure.

- **General clutter**—You can create a set of cleanup rules to be run before you perform major cleanup operations on a Personal Folders file. For instance, you might define a rule that identifies messages with large attachments and moves them to a special folder. Set these rules so they don't run automatically on new messages you receive in the Inbox; instead, use the Run Rules Now button in the Rules and Alerts dialog box to apply them to selected folders, including your archive folders, when they're needed.

TIP FROM

Ed & Woody

> Outlook stores all rules you define in your Personal Folders file. If you want to share your mail-handling rules with other people, or transfer a set of email rules to a new Personal Folders file, click the Options button in the Rules and Alerts dialog box and click Export Rules. To restore rules or to add rules that a friend or co-worker defined and sent to you, click Import Rules and browse to the file containing the previously exported rules.

CREATING A NEW RULE

The simplest way to create a new email rule is to use an existing message as a template. If you have a message that matches one or more of the conditions you want to use in your rule, right-click the message in Outlook's message list and choose Create Rule from the shortcut menu. The Create Rule dialog box offers a simplified set of three conditions and three actions, as shown in Figure 9.24.

Figure 9.24
For simple rules, you can click one or more check boxes to define conditions and actions based on an existing message.

Select one or more of the three options in the top half of the dialog box to define the condition. You can edit the text in the Subject Contains box, but the From and Sent To boxes can't be edited. Next, click one more check boxes in the bottom of the dialog box to define the associated action. The most common action is to move the message to a folder, with or without a desktop alert or sound. Click OK to save the rule using a default name. Outlook gives you the opportunity to run the rule immediately against the contents of the current folder.

NOTE

> Note that email rules do not apply to HTTP (web-based) accounts such as Hotmail or MSN.

If none of these combinations is exactly right, click the Advanced Options button and use the Rules Wizard to create exactly the rule you want. The wizard walks you through four dialog boxes, each consisting of a dialog box with check boxes in the top half and an editable rule description in the bottom. As you select options in the top of the dialog box, the details of the rule appear in the bottom pane; when you see underlined text in the condition or action, click to pop up a dialog box to add more details. (Editing a rule works the same way; choose Tools, Rules and Alerts to open the Rules and Alerts dialog box, select a rule, and click the Edit button.)

 If you've defined a rule and it doesn't work properly on incoming messages, see "A Rule Isn't Working as You Expect" in the "Troubleshooting" section at the end of this chapter.

CHOOSING CONDITIONS

As you can see in Figure 9.25, the opening screen of the Rules Wizard offers a list of more than 30 options you can use to define almost any combination of conditions. Your range of options is impressive:

Figure 9.25
Combine conditions to identify specific types of messages for further processing.

You can enter multiple data items for any condition that requires you to specify items. Enter each item individually and click the Add button after each one. Outlook will add them to the list, separated by a logical "or."

- Select messages depending on the account through which they were received (choose the Through the Specified Account option).

- Is an incoming message addressed specifically to you? Rules can determine whether your name is or is not in the To or Cc box, for example, or when a message is sent only to you. Fine-tune combinations of conditions to highlight mail that is indisputably for you (Sent Only to Me, especially when you add conditions that test who sent the message) or identify less important mail (Where My Name Is Not in the To Box).

- Attach conditions that test for a specific sender or recipient: From People or Distribution List or Sent to People or Distribution List. These conditions depend on Outlook's capability to resolve an address in your Address Book.

→ To learn more about handling Personal Distribution Lists, **see** " Using Personal Distribution Lists," **p. 239**.

- Use two extremely powerful conditions to fine-tune rules that search for mail from a specific person or group of people, regardless of whether they're in your Address Book. Check With Specific Words in the Recipient's Address or With Specific Words in the Sender's Address, and then enter any part of the email address you want to test for.

TIP FROM

Use this option to identify all mail that arrives from anyone in a particular organization or domain. While working on this book, for example, we created a rule and applied special handling to any message that arrived from any recipient whose address contained quepublishing.com.

■ Search for specific words in the subject or body, or in the message header. Use this condition in combination with those that search for messages from a specific person to look for hot-button words: With quepublishing.com in the Recipient's Address and With deadline in the Subject or Body, for example.

■ To create cleanup rules, or to identify messages that might bloat your mail file on a system with limited storage, use the conditions that test whether a message has an attachment or has a size in a specific range.

SPECIFYING ONE OR MORE ACTIONS

After you specify the conditions to test for, click the Next button to move to the dialog box shown in Figure 9.26. Outlook applies actions you choose here to messages that meet the conditions you specify.

Figure 9.26
Click the underlined text in the description pane at the bottom of this dialog box to specify details such as folder names.

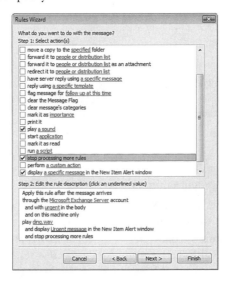

■ One of the most powerful options available is Display a Specific Message in the New Item Alert Window. Using this option, you can tell Outlook to interrupt whatever you're doing and display an alert that alerts you to important incoming messages. If you're working on a group project under deadline pressure, for example, you might define this type of rule for messages from any address in your company that contains an attachment. If your stockbroker uses email to alert you to important developments in the stock market, you can tell Outlook you want to know immediately whenever you receive a message from that address.

■ One of the most interesting options available here is the Stop Processing More Rules choice. Use this option to avoid unintended consequences when rules collide. For example, if you want to be notified when you receive a message sent only to you from your boss, select the proper conditions and actions; then scroll to the bottom of this dialog box and click this option. Make sure rules using this option are high on your list.

■ You can move messages that match your defined conditions to a specified folder, copy them to a folder (including a public folder on an Exchange server), delete them (move to Deleted Items folder), or permanently delete them.

CAUTION

> Never, ever use the Permanently Delete It action on rules that apply to incoming messages. No matter how carefully you define a rule, it's possible that the Rules Wizard will inadvertently apply it to a message you didn't expect it to. Use the Delete It condition to move messages to the Deleted Items folder instead, where it's possible to recover messages moved by mistake. Reserve the permanent option for cleanup rules only.

9

■ Forward messages to an address you select, either as an email message or as an attachment. Use the latter option if you want the recipient to see the message exactly as it was received.

■ The Reply Using a Specific Template option is powerful and potentially dangerous. You might be tempted to use this option to send a message automatically to anyone who sends you mail, alerting them that you've gone on vacation. Unfortunately, if you apply that option to all incoming messages, you risk creating an email loop with automated message senders. If you receive a message from a mailing list and Outlook replies automatically to the list, for example, the list server might send a message telling you that you're not authorized to post to the list; if Outlook replies to that message, the loop begins. Craft this type of rule carefully and test it before deploying it in a production environment.

■ Flag a message for action in a specified number of days (or clear a flag, useful in a cleanup rule), assign it to a category, change its Importance setting, play a sound, or start an application.

NOTE

> Most Outlook users can safely ignore the Perform a Custom Action option, which applies only when you have a third-party add-in that defines special actions for incoming messages.

ADDING ANY EXCEPTIONS

After defining actions, click Next to move to the list of exceptions. In general, the 30 built-in categories here mirror the conditions you specify in step 2 of the wizard. Defining exceptions is a powerful way to fine-tune rules: "Delete all messages from John Smith except if my name is in the To or Cc box" will squelch posts from particularly annoying senders who post to mailing lists you receive.

SAVING THE RULE

In the Rules Wizard's final step, give the rule a name and check all conditions, actions, and exceptions in the dialog box shown in Figure 9.27. Use the check boxes here to specify whether you want to run the rule on the contents of the current folder immediately and whether you want to enable the rule. Clear the second check box for "cleanup" rules that you want to run only when needed.

Figure 9.27
The final step of the Rules Wizard lets you confirm all the steps in your rule and run it on the current folder.

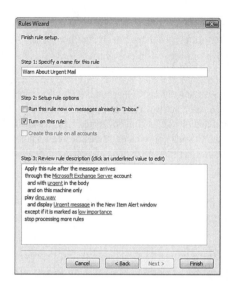

Click Finish to save your rule. Outlook adds the new rule to the top of the Rules and Alerts list. In some cases, you may need to open this dialog box and move the new rule down the list to ensure that more important rules have a chance to work first.

MANAGING EMAIL RULES AND ALERTS

To edit, delete, rename, or run email rules, choose Tools, Rules and Alerts. The Rules and Alerts dialog box (see Figure 9.28) shows you all the rules you've previously defined and lets you create new rules and manage existing ones from a central location.

Figure 9.28
The Rules and Alerts dialog box lets you manage existing email rules and create new ones.

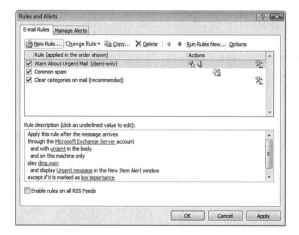

The tools in this dialog box are greatly improved over those in earlier Outlook versions. For starters, you can select any message and click Change Rule to quickly adjust its actions or rename it. When you click New Rule, you can choose from eight templates that apply to email messages (see Figure 9.29), most of which are predefined combinations of options available in succeeding steps. If your rule doesn't fit into any of these predefined categories, choose the Start from a Blank Rule option and choose one of the two general-purpose rules: Check Messages When They Arrive and Check Messages After Sending.

Figure 9.29
Use any of these templates to get started quickly. Click Next to continue using the Rules Wizard or click Finish to build a simple rule using default settings.

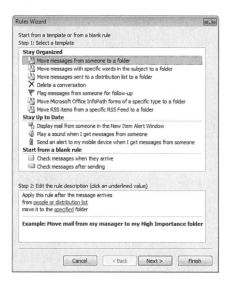

TROUBLESHOOTING

SOLVING SMTP SNAGS

I have several Internet email accounts that I use for different purposes. I have no trouble sending email from one account, but all the others give me an error message when I try to send email.

The most likely explanation is that your Internet service provider has blocked port 25 as an antispam measure. This configuration prevents you from using any outgoing mail servers except those that your ISP provides. You'll need to customize each email account to point to that SMTP server. Don't forget to click the More Settings button for each account and adjust the authentication settings on the Outgoing Server tab.

WORKING AROUND ANTISPAM FILTERS

I have two Internet service providers. One is a local provider I use at home, because I like its speed and service. For business trips, I use an account with a national Internet service provider to avoid having to access the Internet via a long-distance call at exorbitant hotel rates. While on the road, I have no trouble receiving mail from my regular ISP, but when I try to reply to email, I get an error message that says something such as This server does not allow relaying.

Most ISPs restrict access to SMTP servers for sending outgoing mail—typically, the mail server checks your IP address before allowing you to connect to the SMTP server. This step verifies that you are an authenticated user on the network, as is the case when you dial-in directly. If you connect from another ISP, the server doesn't recognize your IP address and blocks your attempt. This configuration prevents unauthorized users from hijacking the mail server to unleash a flood of spam, but it also prevents you from connecting to the outgoing mail server to relay messages. If your ISP allows it, you may be able to use the SMTP server remotely by supplying authentication details. Your email provider may also offer a web-based interface that you can use to send and receive mail outside of Outlook. If neither option is available, you'll need to set up another Internet mail account for use on the road and adjust your configuration so you send mail through the SMTP server that belongs to the account you dialed in with. To make sure that recipients send replies to the right address, be sure to specify your regular (home) mail account as the Reply To address on this new account.

FORCING OUTLOOK TO SHOW DESKTOP ALERTS

When I receive new messages, the desktop alert window doesn't always appear. Sometimes it shows up, but other times I get no notice.

There are three possible explanations for missing desktop alerts. First, desktop alerts don't appear if you check for new mail manually by pressing F9 or clicking the Send/Receive button.

Second, if you've defined a rule that moves incoming messages to another folder, you need to specifically enable the Display a Desktop Alert action for that rule. Choose Tools, Rules and Alerts, double-click the rule you want to modify, click Next to move to the actions page, and select the Display a Desktop Alert check box. Click Finish to save the edited rule.

Third, Outlook is programmed to show no more than five alerts in a row. If you've received a flood of new mail, the sixth alert should simply say You have new messages.

WHEN ACTIVE MEANS INVISIBLE

The Reading pane says it can't display the message because it contains active content.

That's Outlook's maddeningly roundabout way of telling you the message is in HTML or Rich Text Format and contains a script. Open the message to read it.

WHEN YOUR EMAIL BOUNCES

I replied to a post on an Internet newsgroup via email, but my mail server bounced the message back to me, saying the recipient doesn't exist.

More than anywhere else, people who post to public newsgroups are likely to disguise their true email address. The reason is to prevent bulk-mail artists—spammers—from harvesting their address and reselling it to scam artists. Check the header on the message carefully to see whether the true email address is hidden. Sometimes the solution is as simple as removing the phrase no.spam from an address such as bianca@no.spam.*example*.com.

CLEANING UP THE AUTOCOMPLETE LIST

Every so often, I mistype an email address when composing a new message. Unfortunately, Outlook has a memory like an elephant and won't forget my mistakes! It keeps "suggesting" my typos as legitimate email addresses. How do I clean up this list?

Outlook keeps track of names you've typed in address boxes, saving these settings in a hidden file called the *nickname cache*, with the extension .nk2. To eliminate a single incorrect entry from this cache, start a new message, click in the To box, and begin typing until the unwanted AutoComplete entry appears. Press the down arrow to select the name and press Delete to remove it. For step-by-step instructions on how to clear the entire nickname cache, see Knowledge Base article 287623, "How to Reset the Nickname and the Automatic Completion Caches in Outlook," at http://support.microsoft.com/?kbid=287623.

A RULE ISN'T WORKING AS YOU EXPECT

I used the Rules Wizard to define a mail-processing rule, but Outlook isn't processing the message as I expected it to.

This problem is almost always the result of conflicting actions from multiple rules. First things first: Check the order of rules, and pay special attention to any rule that contains the Stop Processing More Rules action. You might have defined two rules that apply to the message in question (it's from a specific person and it contains a certain phrase, for example), and each rule wants to move the message to a different folder. When the actions in two or more rules conflict in this way, the one that's higher in the list wins. Try changing the order of the rules, using the Move Up and Move Down buttons. Finally, be especially careful with rules that create message flags with reminders; if another rule also moves that message to a different folder, you'll never see the reminder, because Outlook monitors flags only on messages in the Inbox. Rules that attach message flags should always be high in the list, and they should include a Stop Processing More Rules action.

SECRETS OF THE OFFICE MASTERS: USING OUTLOOK WITH AOL ACCOUNTS

Are you using AOL as your primary email service? AOL's email servers are proprietary, and Outlook doesn't support direct connections to those servers. But there is a workaround. In fact, you can choose either of two methods to bring your AOL account into Outlook.

- To connect to AOL using IMAP servers, enter the information for your geographic region, as described here: http://office.microsoft.com/en-gb/assistance/HA010936921033.aspx. In this configuration, your AOL account acts like an IMAP account, with the mail remaining on the server until you explicitly download it.

- To retrieve your email using the POP3 protocol, use a third-party program such as Email2POP (http://www.email2pop.com). This utility does the work of retrieving the mail from AOL's servers and bringing it into Outlook as if it were stored on a POP3 server. You can take full advantage of Outlook Rules and Alerts and other organizational features.

In either case, you can send mail through AOL's SMTP servers, using instructions you can find along with the setup instructions in the article listed here.

CHAPTER 10

KEEPING YOUR CONTACTS LIST UNDER CONTROL

In this chapter

Viewing and Organizing the Contacts Folder   260

Entering and Editing Contact Information   261

Working Smarter with Contact Items   266

Communicating with Contacts   270

Printing Phone Lists and Address Books   271

Troubleshooting   273

Secrets of the Office Masters: Creating a Memorable Business Card   274

VIEWING AND ORGANIZING THE CONTACTS FOLDER

Outlook's Contacts folder serves a dual purpose: For Internet mail users, it's the primary storage location for email addresses. It's also a useful place to store names, addresses, phone numbers, and other important information about friends, family members, and business associates. If you use the Contacts folder only to manage email addresses and occasionally print an address book, you will find that it's certainly worth the minimal effort it takes to enter and update contact information. But if you're willing to learn Outlook's secrets, you can make it do much more. For example, you can do any or all of the following tasks:

- Quickly add addresses to letters and envelopes you create with Word. After you master the quirks of the Outlook Address Book, you can configure each entry so that names and addresses appear in the correct format.

- Build lists of related contacts for use in mail-merge projects.

- Dial your phone and log calls automatically. If you provide professional services and bill by the hour, Outlook can track the time you spend on the phone with each contact, for later billing.

- Flag one Contact item or a group for a follow-up reminder.

- Use categories to print specialized phone books. If you work with a volunteer group, for example, enter names, phone numbers, and notes for group members, assign them to a category, and then filter the list by that category so you can print out a phone list for a telephone campaign.

→ The Contacts folder and the Outlook Address Book offer different views of the same information; for full details, **see** "Using the Outlook Address Book," **p. 235**.

By default, the Contacts folder opens in Business Cards view, shown in Figure 10.1. This view, which is new in Outlook 2007, includes the contact's name in a thin bar along the top (as defined in the File As field), as well as the exact contents of the Full Name field. The default view also includes the mailing address and as many phone numbers as you've defined for the contact.

Later in this chapter, we explain how to customize individual business cards, especially your own, so you can use a distinctive-looking business card as a graphic element in your email signature.

TIP FROM

EQ & Woody

Is the default business card layout taking up too much room? You can squeeze more cards into the Contents pane by shrinking the default size. Open the Contacts folder using Business Cards view and click View, Current View, Customize Current View. Click Other Settings. To make each business card smaller, dial the size down to less than 100%; to make them bigger, bump the size up above 100%.

Figure 10.1
The default Business Cards view displays details about each contact in an individually customizable view that mimics a business card.

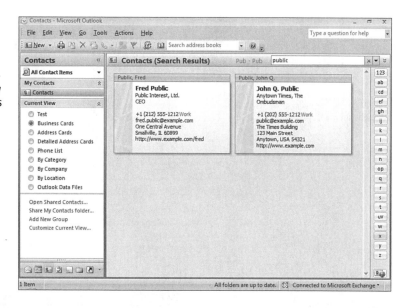

The overall dimensions of the business card layout are fixed. Although this layout holds a fair amount of information, the default layout can't be customized. To choose exactly which details appear in a card layout, switch to the Detailed Address Cards view, which displays virtually all fields in each contact record and is fully customizable.

→ Outlook provides a variety of options for sorting and filtering your Outlook items; **see** "Using Views to Display, Sort, and Filter Items," **p. 204**.

  If the contents of one or more folders containing contact items don't appear when you open the Outlook Address Book, see "Configuring a Contacts Folder for Use in the Outlook Address Book" in the "Troubleshooting" section at the end of this chapter.

ENTERING AND EDITING CONTACT INFORMATION

You can add a new contact from the main Outlook window, regardless of which folder is currently open. To begin creating a new contact from scratch, use any of the following techniques:

- Click the New Contact button.
- Press Ctrl+Shift+C (Ctrl+N also works if the Contacts folder is open).
- Select File, New, Contact.

Outlook's form for creating a new item in the Contacts folder includes a number of smart features that help you enter properly formatted information quickly and accurately. Start in the Full Name field and use the Tab key to jump from field to field. After you've entered all the information, click the Save and Close button at the top of the dialog box to store the new item. Figure 10.2 shows a filled-in Contact form.

Figure 10.2
Outlook automatically fills in some of the blanks as you create a new item in the Contacts folder, and it checks the rest to make sure that you left nothing out.

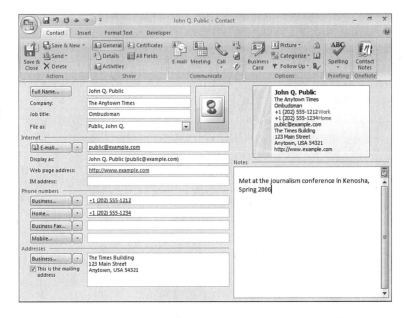

In all, each Contact item includes more than 140 fields of information. Most Outlook users, however, work with only a small fraction of these fields—those that are visible on the General view of the default Contact form. To see more information, click any of the buttons in the Show group on the Contact tab. (In previous Outlook versions, these were arranged as tabs on a dialog box.) Clicking the All Fields button shows a table view of the information instead of the more familiar form view. Use the drop-down list to filter the collection of fields so you see a manageable subset, such as all Address fields, all Name fields, and so on. Select All Contact fields to see (and edit) the entire list of available fields, in alphabetical order, as shown in Figure 10.3.

Figure 10.3
The All Fields view allows you to scroll through more than 140 fields in each item—and edit some of them.

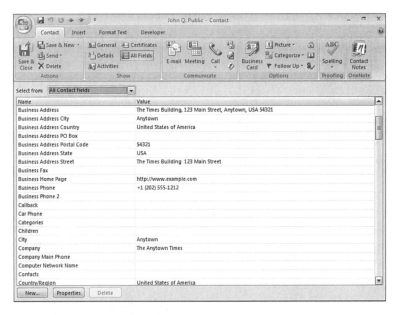

If you're having trouble selecting or deleting a field's contents, see "Selecting and Deleting Field Contents" in the "Troubleshooting" section at the end of this chapter.

ENTERING AND EDITING NAMES

When you enter a new contact's name in the Full Name field (or change an existing one), Outlook slices and dices your entry into as many as nine separate fields. You will rarely see most of these fields, but knowing how Outlook *parses* names—that is, breaks them into their component parts—lets you control the process. This will pay off later when you use items from the Contacts folder as the source for email, letters, envelopes, and mail-merge projects.

As soon as you enter the full name, in any order, Outlook attempts to break it into five subfields: First Name, Middle Name, Last Name, Title (Ms. or Dr., for example) and Suffix (Jr. or M.D., for instance). To view (and edit) the contents of these fields, click the Full Name button, which opens the Check Full Name dialog box, shown in Figure 10.4. If any information is incorrect, edit it here.

Figure 10.4
When you enter a full name, Outlook automatically breaks it into these subfields; if any information is incorrect, edit it here.

How do you include a courtesy title such as Mr., Ms., or Dr. in each new Contact item? Get in the habit of entering the title at the beginning of the Full Name field. Outlook recognizes the following titles, which are also on the Title drop-down list in the Check Full Name dialog box: Dr., Prof., Mr., Mrs., Ms., and Miss. Even if a title is not available on the drop-down list, it still might work. For example, beginning a name with Sir, Herr, Fraulein, Monsieur, Madame, or Signore will correctly fill in the Title field. If you're not sure a prefix will work, try it in a new blank Contact form.

Based on what you type into the Full Name field, Outlook also fills in two additional fields automatically:

- **The File as Field**—Controls the order in which the Contacts folder displays items when you switch to Address Cards or Detailed Address Cards view. Although Outlook automatically fills in this field using its default format, Last Name first, you can easily change it.

- **The Subject Field**—Does not appear on any built-in forms but is accessible on the All Fields tab. It defines how each Contact item appears when you display the Address Book. By default, Outlook fills in this field with the First Name field first.

→ To learn more about how Outlook files your Contact items, **see** "Changing How a Contact Item Is Filed," **p. 266**.

If you don't want Outlook to automatically (and incorrectly) split company names in your Contacts Folder into first and last names, see "Using Company Names in Your Contacts" in the "Troubleshooting" section at the end of this chapter.

WORKING WITH ADDRESSES

Just as with name fields, when you enter a mailing address in the Address field on the default Contact form, Outlook splits the address into component parts and stores the information in as many as 31 separate fields. You can store up to three addresses per contact; click the drop-down list just below the Address button to select Business, Home, or Other.

When you enter an address, Outlook parses the address into separate fields for the street, city, state, and other fields. If you enter information in a format Outlook doesn't recognize— if you omit the city or state, or if you accidentally leave a digit off the postal code—Outlook pops up the Check Address dialog box shown in Figure 10.5 (you can also click the Address button to display this dialog box). This display shows how Outlook proposes to divide the information into subfields. Click OK to save the record as typed, or edit the contents of any field.

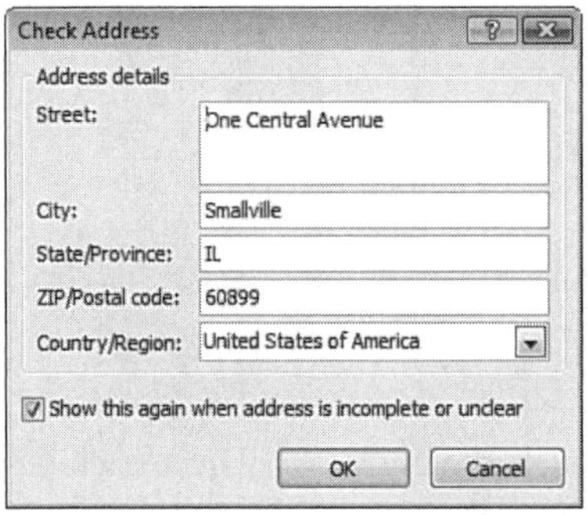

Figure 10.5
This dialog box shows you how Outlook proposes to parse the address you entered into subfields.

When you select the This Is the Mailing Address check box, Outlook copies this address to the fields that are used when you create letters, envelopes, or mail-merge lists in Word.

→ To learn more about using Word's mail-merge capabilities, **see** "Using Mail Merge to Personalize Letters and Envelopes," **p. 483**.

ENTERING JOB AND COMPANY DETAILS

When you click the General button while viewing a contact form, you'll find two boxes for entering work-related information about that contact: Job Title and Company. Click the Details tab to enter other work-related information, such as Department and Manager's Name.

Although the Details tab includes a field for Assistant's Name, the field for Assistant's Phone Number is buried in the full list of fields on the last tab of the dialog box. There's a much easier way to enter this information, however: Click the drop-down arrow to the left of any of the four phone number boxes and select Assistant, and then enter the number. After you enter the number, it is visible in Business Card view and in both Address Card views.

MANAGING PHONE, FAX, AND OTHER NUMBERS

The General page has room to enter up to four phone numbers—by default, you can fill in Business, Home, Business Fax, and Mobile numbers. You're certainly not limited to those options, however; you can actually enter as many as 19 separate phone numbers, using the drop-down lists at the left of each number to select different fields.

> **NOTE**
>
> The Business Card view displays the most conventional numbers, including Work, Mobile, Home, and Assistant in addition to the default number. Both default Address Card views display as many phone numbers as you've defined for a contact. These appear in an order determined by this form, with most business-related numbers at the top. Curiously, however, the Business Fax field appears at the bottom of each list, and we can't find any way to change this order.

You can enter phone numbers any way you like, with or without punctuation; when you exit the field, Outlook automatically reformats the numbers using its standard punctuation scheme—parentheses around the area or city code and a hyphen after the first three digits of the phone number. If you omit the area code, Outlook assumes the number is in your local dialing area and adds your area code to the entry. If Outlook parses this information incorrectly, or if you need to add a country code to the number, click to select the phone number field and then click the button to the left of the field. This action opens a dialog box that allows you to enter or edit this information.

If a contact's phone number includes an extension, add this information at the end of the phone number, preceded by a space and the letters x or ext. Outlook ignores this information when formatting the phone number or using the AutoDial feature. You can also add text before or after a phone number; for example, if one of your contacts is bicoastal, you might enter a number in both the Business and Business 2 fields, and then label them LA and NY.

> **TIP FROM**
>
>
>
> Are you sick of seeing both an email address and a fax number appear in the AutoComplete list when you enter a contact's name in a new email message? Tell Outlook to stop automatically suggesting fax numbers by adding the text label FAX at the beginning of the fax number field. You can still read the number, but Outlook no longer recognizes it as a legitimate address and stops suggesting it.

ENTERING AND EDITING EMAIL AND WEB ADDRESSES

You can store up to three email addresses per contact. Click the drop-down arrow next to the E-mail button to select any of these three blanks, and then enter the address. Click the E-mail button to view email addresses in the Outlook Address Book, which uses a different form to display information.

→ For an authoritative explanation of how the Outlook Address Book works, **see** "Using the Outlook Address Book," **p. 235**.

→ To find out how Outlook uses Address Book information to fill in addresses on email messages, **see** "Addressing an Email Message," **p. 238**.

Outlook allows you to view and change the text displayed in the To and From fields of message windows for each address. When you enter an email address in any of the three boxes on the Contact form, the Display As box beneath it shows how the name will appear in messages you send to or receive from that address. By default, the Display As value is set to the value of the email address. Edit this address to show whatever you want—you might want to add a friendly name and either surround the email address in parentheses or add a company name or the word *Personal*, also in parentheses, so that you can see at a glance that you've selected the correct address.

The General view of the default Contact form also includes input boxes where you can enter a web page address. If you enter a recognizable URL here, Outlook converts it to a hyperlink so you can jump to a personal or corporate web page directly from the contact's record.

If you use an instant messaging (IM) program such as Windows Live Messenger, enter the address for the contact in the IM Address field. If you use more than one IM program, you'll have to enter this information in the Notes box or in a user-defined field.

ENTERING EXTRA INFORMATION ABOUT A CONTACT

Click the Details button to add some personal information about the selected contact. Fields on this tab include Nickname, Spouse/Partner, Birthday, and Anniversary. You can see still more fields in this category (including one in which you can enter the names of children or specify a contact's hobbies) by clicking the All Fields button.

As in virtually all Outlook items, the Notes area at the bottom of the Default Contact form lets you add extensive comments, as well as shortcuts to other Outlook items, files, or file attachments. Click the Categorize button (in the Options group on the Contact tab) to assign each entry to one or more categories; you can create a Holiday Cards choice, for example, which allows you to quickly print a list of friends, family, and business associates to whom you'll send season's greetings.

→ To learn more about categorizing Outlook items, **see** "Assigning Items to Categories," **p. 194**.

WORKING SMARTER WITH CONTACT ITEMS

Most Outlook users are perfectly content to enter one item at a time in the Contacts folder. If you have a bulging address book, though, you'll want to employ the secrets and shortcuts described in this section.

CHANGING HOW A CONTACT ITEM IS FILED

In the default Business Card view and in both Address Card views, the field used for sorting and displaying information is the File As field. By default, Outlook fills in this field by using the information you type into the Full Name field, displaying it last name first. If you don't enter a name here, Outlook assumes the record refers to a business and uses the information from the Company field. You can accept the default, or you can change the information displayed here.

Although organizing an address book by last name is traditional, you might choose to mix different filing orders within the Contacts folder. For example, when you enter a record for a person who serves as your main contact with a company, file the record under the company name, with the person's name in parentheses. In some cases, you might even use simple generic descriptions such as Drugstore or Travel Agent.

If you can't remember how you filed a Contact item, use the Instant Search box on the right side of the bar just above the Contents pane. A simple search looks through all fields in the current view, including the Notes field. Click the drop-down arrow at the far right of the Instant Search box to reveal the Query Builder, which you can use to restrict the search to specific fields.

To change the way a specific Contact item is filed, double-click to open the item. In the File As field, click the drop-down arrow. If both the Full Name and Company fields contain data, Outlook offers the following five choices:

- Full name, last name first
- Full name, first name first
- Company name
- Full name, last name first, followed by company name in parentheses
- Company name, followed by full name, last name first, in parentheses

To file the item using any other text, replace the contents of the File As field. Whatever you type appears in alphabetical order in all views of your Contacts folder when sorted by the File As field.

To change the default order for all new contacts, select Tools, Options, and then click the Contact Options button on the Preferences tab. Two drop-down boxes let you select a default for the Full Name field and the File As field—they don't have to be the same. Note, any changes you make to these settings do not apply to existing contacts—they affect only new contacts you create from this point forward.

ENTERING SEVERAL NEW CONTACT ITEMS AT ONCE

Have you ever returned from a meeting or trade show with an inch-thick bundle of business cards? Typing the details from those cards into Outlook can be a tedious process. Here are three time-saving shortcuts to help make shorter work of that stack:

- Enter data by using a table-based view such as the built-in Phone List view instead of the default Contact form. Click in the empty box in the top line to begin entering a new item. Press Tab to move from field to field. When you press Enter, Outlook stores the record and moves the insertion point back to the beginning of the first line, where you can begin a new item immediately.

  If you just want to get a few crucial names, phone numbers, and email addresses into Outlook, create a custom Table view that contains only the fields you need and no more. Be sure to include the Categories field so you can identify the trade show or meeting where you met this person (ABC Conference 2007, for example).

- If you prefer to use a Contact form, enter the information for the first card in the stack; then click Save and New on the Contact tab. This menu option saves the item you just entered and clears the form so you can begin a new contact immediately. After you enter the last card in the stack, press Esc to clear the blank form.

- When you have two or more cards from people who work in the same office, let Outlook copy key information to the new Contact item. Open the item, click the arrow to the right of the Save and New option on the Contact tab, and click New Contact from Same Company. Outlook creates a new item, entering the company name, address, and phone number from the previous item, but clearing all other fields.

SHARING CONTACT INFORMATION

It's extremely easy to exchange items with other Outlook users. For example, if you've asked a co-worker to follow up with a customer on your behalf, you can make the job easier by forwarding a copy of that person's item from your Contacts folder. If you're certain the other person uses Outlook, use one of the following procedures:

- Create a new email message, drag the contact item from the Contacts folder, and drop it in the message window.

- Right-click the contact item and choose Send Full Contact, In Outlook Format.

- Open the contact item, click the Send button on the Contact tab, and choose In Outlook Format from the drop-down list.

Either way, you'll end up with a draft email message containing a contact item as an attachment. Address the message, add enough text to explain why you're sending it along, and click Send.

Your co-worker can add the item to her Contacts folder by opening the message, double-clicking the attachment, and clicking Save and Close.

To exchange information with someone who doesn't use Outlook, use the *vCard* format (short for virtual business card) to translate standard name, business, address, and phone fields into a simple text file that other compatible programs can import. When you send your vCard to another person via email, that person can easily add your address information into any compatible contact-management program or email address book. You can also turn any item from your Contacts folder into a vCard and attach it to an email message. The vCard option is available from the right-click Send Full Contact menu and from the Send button on the Contact tab.

TIP FROM

Ed & Woody

> Unless you're absolutely certain the person to whom you're sending a mail message uses Outlook, you should send contact information in vCard format. In fact, because this card uses plain text, your recipient can read its contents even without a compatible contact manager—just open the file in a text editor such as Notepad.

If you receive a vCard attachment, the easiest way to add it to your Contacts folder is to click the attachment and drag it onto the Contacts pane in the Navigation bar.

MERGING DUPLICATE CONTACT ITEMS

How do you deal with duplicate Contact items? This problem is particularly prevalent if you use incoming email as the basis for a Contact item. When you drag a message from the Inbox and drop it in the Contacts folder, Outlook creates a new Contact item using the sender's name as it appears in the From box. If one person occasionally sends messages using a different display name, eventually you'll wind up with two, three, or more Contact items for a single person—most consisting of just an email address.

In some cases, Outlook can combine duplicate records for you. If you attempt to enter a record using the same first and last name as an existing Contact item, Outlook displays the dialog box shown in Figure 10.6.

Figure 10.6
When you try to enter a new Contact item with the same name as an existing one, Outlook offers to merge the two records.

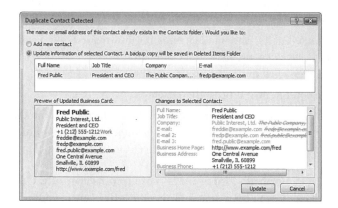

If you intended to create a duplicate record, or if this is a new contact that happens to have a name that is similar or identical to another item in your Contacts folder, select Add New Contact. If you select the default option, Update Information of Selected Contact, Outlook replaces every field in the existing item if the new item contains information in that field. The dialog box makes it crystal clear what will be changed, previewing the new business card on the left and showing the changes in strikethrough text on the right. To accept the changes, click Update. If you want to keep the existing contact and go back to the new one you're creating, click Cancel.

TIP FROM

EQ & Woody

When you update an existing contact record with details from a new one, Outlook assumes that the information you entered in the new record is the current version. The process is much smarter than in previous Office versions. You can see all changes before you click the Update button, and the Notes field combines old and new notes and preserves file attachments and shortcuts. If you inadvertently delete important information by merging contact records, look in the Deleted Items folder, where Outlook keeps a copy of the original item when you use the merge option.

The merge function is smart about email addresses. Each contact item can contain a maximum of three email addresses. If the original item contains one or two email addresses, Outlook will add email addresses to the unused address field rather than replacing an existing address.

Outlook offers to merge items when the first name and last name you enter (either directly or as parsed from the Full Name field) are absolutely identical to those in an existing item, and the offer is good only when you create the duplicate item. If you've added several items to your Contacts folder that refer to the same person with slightly different names—William Gates and Bill Gates, for example—you can use a sneaky workaround to merge the data:

1. Open the older item—the one that contains details you want to replace with information from a newer item. Copy the contents of the Full Name field to the Clipboard and close the item.

2. Open the second item—the one that contains information you want to merge into the older item. Paste the contents of the Clipboard into the Full Name field in the second record, and then click the Save and Close button.

3. Select the second item and press the Delete key.

4. Select Edit, Undo Delete. Outlook restores the contact item from the Deleted Items folder. Because this has the same effect as creating a new item, Outlook displays the Duplicate Contact Detected dialog box. Select the option to update information.

You can also merge information from two or more records manually. Open each contact item in its own window, and then drag information such as email addresses from one item to another.

TIP FROM

Ed & Woody

> If you never, ever want to be prompted to merge contact items, turn off this feature. From the main Outlook window, select Tools, Options, and select the Preferences tab. Click the Contact Options button and clear the Check for Duplicate Contacts box.

COMMUNICATING WITH CONTACTS

From the Contacts folder or an open contact item, you can kick off any of a handful of actions to keep in touch with that person. The Communicate group on the Contact tab includes four buttons that allow you to do the following:

- Click E-mail to create a new email message addressed to the contact. The contact item remains open.

- Click Meeting to create a new meeting request, with the contact's email address in the To field and the next available half-hour block of time selected.

- Click Call to place a phone call to the contact. The New Call dialog box (shown in Figure 10.7) allows you to dial and hang up using the Start Call and End Call buttons, respectively.

- Click Assign Task to create a new task request addressed to the contact.

Figure 10.7

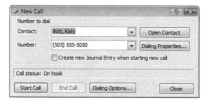

→ To learn more about how to use meeting requests and assign tasks, **see** "Managing Meeting Requests," **p. 289**.

If OneNote is installed, an additional command appears at the end of the Contact tab. Click the Contact Notes button to start OneNote and create a new page or open an existing page linked to the current contact.

> **NOTE**
>
> In previous versions of Office, you could begin writing a letter by choosing a menu option in Outlook. This option is no longer available in Office 2007. To create a letter to a contact, start in Microsoft Word, click the Mailings tab, and use these tools to open an Outlook address book, select a contact, and add details such as an address block.

10

PRINTING PHONE LISTS AND ADDRESS BOOKS

You can print contact lists in a variety of styles and formats, using all the items in your Contacts folder or only a subset of them. You can even turn your address list into a booklet printed on both sides and small enough to fit into a shirt pocket—although you must be willing to hover over the printer while it spits out pages. (You also must resign yourself to wasting many sheets of paper while you figure out the precise order in which to perform each step.) This feature can be useful when you're heading off on a business trip, for example, and you want to print the addresses and phone numbers of contacts in that area.

The steps required to print an address book or phone list containing items from your Contacts folder are nearly identical to those for printing a calendar. If you want to print a subset of the folder's contents, use one of the following techniques:

- To select a contiguous block of items, click the first item; then hold down the Shift key and click the last item in the group.
- To select individual items that are not adjacent, hold down Ctrl while clicking each one.
- To show only items that match specific criteria, use the Instant Search box or the Advanced Find dialog box.
- Customize the current view or switch to another view and filter the list.

→ To learn more about using views to control how you work with Outlook items, **see** "Using Custom Views to Display Information," **p. 204**.

→ To learn more about Outlook's search capabilities, **see** "Finding Outlook Items," **p. 199**.

1. Switch to any Card view and select the items to be printed. If you want to print the entire list, you do not need to make a selection.

2. Click the Print button. Outlook displays the Print dialog box shown in Figure 10.8.

Figure 10.8
Select the Phone Directory Style option to print all the names and phone numbers in your Contacts folder, with no company or address information.

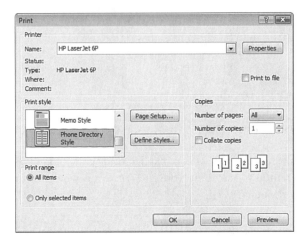

3. Select one of the five page formats from the Print Style list.

 Are you having problems seeing all the Print Style choices in the Print dialog box? If so, see "Setting Print Styles" in the "Troubleshooting" section at the end of this chapter.

4. In the Print Range box, choose whether you want to print All Items or Only Selected Items. (This option is not available if you choose Memo Style.)

TIP FROM

Ed & Woody

> Have you used the Notes field to keep track of a lot of information about some contacts? To extract the maximum amount of information when printing, select Memo Style and select the option to print all attachments. Be careful, however; this option can chew through a ream of paper faster than you can say, "Save the rainforest."

5. Click the Preview button to see what your page will look like when printed. Use the Page Up and Page Down keys (or the corresponding toolbar buttons) to see additional pages in the Preview window.

6. Click the Page Setup button in the Preview window or in the Print dialog box to adjust layout options, paper sizes, fonts, headers, footers, and other settings, as shown in Figure 10.9.

Figure 10.9
Fine-tune a print layout and preview before printing to ensure the format matches what you expect.

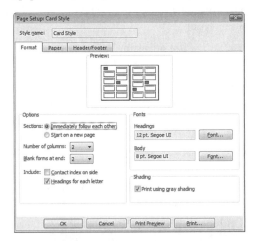

7. Click Print to send the job to the printer.

When you print your phone book, select from the following five formats:

- **Card Style**—Shows all the details from the underlying Card view. Switching to Detailed Card view adds more fields to each item but also extends the size of your printed book.

- **Small Booklet Style**—Prints in Card view, with each page shrunk to 1/8 normal size. Default settings suggest you should print this booklet using both sides of the paper. If you don't have a printer capable of handling two-sided printing, you can get the same effect, tediously, by using the manual feed option in your printer and feeding each sheet through individually.

- **Medium Booklet Style**—Also prints a two-sided booklet, but each page in this style is only 1/4 the size of the printed page. Experiment with a four-page sample before printing your entire phone book.

- **Memo Style**—Prints every bit of information about a contact, including all notes. To print a single contact in Memo Style, bypassing all dialog boxes, open the item and click the Print button.

- **Phone Directory Style**—Prints the name and all phone numbers for each contact in a two-column format that takes up the full width of an 8 1/2×11-inch sheet of paper. Although you can change the number of columns and the fonts used in this style, you can't add new fields.

TROUBLESHOOTING

CONFIGURING A CONTACTS FOLDER FOR USE IN THE OUTLOOK ADDRESS BOOK

You've split your contacts into several folders, but when you click the To: or Cc: button to address an email message, the contents of one or more folders are missing.

Any folder that contains contact items can be part of the Outlook Address Book, but you have to specifically designate it to be included there. If you don't see a folder in the Outlook Address Book, click the Folders icon in the Navigation bar, right-click the missing contacts folder, and choose Properties. On the Outlook Address Book tab, click the Show This Folder as An E-mail Address Book box.

SELECTING AND DELETING FIELD CONTENTS

When working with the All Contact fields list on the last tab of a Contact form, Outlook won't let you edit the File As field, the names of email entries, and several other fields. So, how do you select or delete the contents of these fields?

Outlook won't allow you to edit a handful of fields in this list; most of these are fields Outlook generates automatically based on the contents of other fields. Use the General view of the Contact form to change this information.

USING COMPANY NAMES IN YOUR CONTACTS

You've entered a company name in the Contacts folder, but Outlook insists on splitting it into first and last names—so that Acme Industries becomes Industries, Acme.

When entering a new Contact item for a company, leave the Full Name field blank and instead press the Tab key twice to jump to the Company field. Whatever you type in that field also appears in the File As and Subject fields, exactly as you typed it.

SETTING PRINT STYLES

You clicked the Print button, but you see only one print style choice in the Print dialog box. Naturally, it's not the one you want.

This occurs when you click the Print button while displaying the Contacts folder in a Table view, such as Phone List view. Exit the Print dialog box and switch to a Card view, such as Business Cards, Address Cards, or Detailed Address Cards, and then try again.

SECRETS OF THE OFFICE MASTERS: CREATING A MEMORABLE BUSINESS CARD

When you can send your contact information as an email attachment, your message doesn't have much pizzazz. And that attachment does you no good if your correspondent uses a program other than Outlook, or if they ignore the attachment.

Want to get a more positive reaction? Transform the dull default layout for your business card into something fun and vibrant, complete with a photograph or logo. Then use that business card for email messages where you want the recipient to know at a glance who you are.

You can add a photo to any contact item, not just your own. The form for a contact item includes a placeholder for a photo, to the right of the block that includes the Full Name field and just above the E-mail field.

To add a photo to a contact, click the placeholder icon, or choose Picture, Add Picture from the Options group on the Contact tab. Browse to the picture file and click OK. Don't worry about the size or location of the original picture, either. Outlook converts the file to a JPEG image less than 2KB in size and attaches it directly to the contact record.

As soon as you add the photo to the contact item, you'll notice that it shows up on the business card associated with that contact. To tweak your own business card, double-click the business card (above the notes field on the contact form). This displays the dialog box shown in Figure 10.10.

Figure 10.10
Design your business card with a logo or photo and you can send it as your signature with any email message

In the example shown here, we added a photo and a background color, changed the font size, and highlighted some fields with bold type. We also rearranged the data on the card to highlight exactly the information we wanted to display.

Most of the options on this dialog box are self-explanatory. The Card Design section allows you to select an image, position and align it, change the amount of space used by the image, and add a background color.

Use the Fields section to select exactly which fields should appear on the card. The Blank Line entries help you add space to differentiate blocks of information on the card. When you select an item from the Fields list, you can edit it using the controls on the right; you can adjust fonts, font sizes, colors, and alignment, as well as adding labels to the left or right of any line.

When you're finished, click Save and Close. The next time you write an email message, click in the message body at the point where you want the card to appear and click Business Card in the Include group on the Message tab. If this is the first time you've included a particular card, you'll need to choose it from the Contacts folder. After the first time, you'll find that card on the drop-down list that appears when you click the Business Card command.

CHAPTER 11

WORKING WITH CALENDARS AND TASKS

In this chapter

Managing Your Personal Calendar   278

Creating a New Appointment or Event   284

Managing Meeting Requests   289

Maintaining Your Personal Task List   295

Sharing Your Schedule with Other People   298

Troubleshooting   304

Secrets of the Office Masters: Publishing a Calendar as a Web Page   305

Managing Your Personal Calendar

As we noted in Chapter 8, one of the most important changes in Outlook 2007 is the new To-Do Bar, which displays a consolidated list of appointments, meetings, tasks, and flagged items along the right side of the main Outlook window.

In previous Office versions, it was nearly impossible to keep track of all the details stored in different parts of Outlook. That's all changed in Outlook 2007. Meetings and appointments appear at the top of the top of the To-Do Bar, and any email message or contact with a follow-up flag appears in the task list below it. To add a reminder to a contact or an email message, you just assign a follow-up flag and pick a time for the reminder, without having to worry about which folder the item is in.

Outlook's Calendar folder can keep track of any number of appointments and meetings, whether they're one-time-only events or recurring appointments that repeat on a regular schedule. Although you can print a calendar for reference, Outlook's calendaring features are best suited to people whose duties keep them close to a computer screen most of the time, or those who have a handheld device (such as a Mobile PC or a SmartPhone) that can synchronize data from Outlook's Calendar, To-Do list, and Contacts folder.

The default view of the Calendar folder is instantly understandable in Outlook 2007. A bar above the Contents pane allows you to display appointments and meetings for the current day, week, or month. A calendar control called the Date Navigator appears at the top of the To-Do Bar; if you've closed or minimized the To-Do Bar, the calendar control appears at the top of the Navigation pane. Figure 11.1 shows the two alternative views side by side.

Figure 11.1
The Date Navigator changes position depending on whether the To-Do Bar is hidden (left) or visible (right).

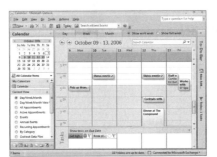 

Want to see more than one month in the Date Navigator? The total number of months is defined by the number of columns and rows that appear in this control. In the Navigation pane, the number of rows is set automatically; in the To-Do Bar, choose View, To-Do Bar, Options, and then enter the number of rows you want to see (the default is 1). To add columns to the default display, drag the border between the Navigation pane or the To-Do Bar toward the Contents pane until a second month appears. Outlook shows as many months as will fit in the space you allot.

In the Date Navigator, boldfaced numbers indicate days on which you currently have at least one scheduled appointment or meeting. Click any date (past or future) to quickly show that day's items in the Contents pane. Use the left and right arrows alongside the name of each month to move backward and forward a month at a time. For long-distance jumps, point to the left or right arrow and hold down the mouse button until you reach the month you're looking for. Or use this secret, undocumented shortcut: Click the name of a month above the Date Navigator and hold down the mouse button to see a list that includes the three months before and after the current month. Drag the pointer below or above the list to scroll to any month, and then release the mouse button to jump to that month.

SWITCHING BETWEEN DAY, WEEK, AND MONTH VIEWS

When you first click the Calendar icon in the Outlook Bar, you see today's schedule in Day/Week/Month view. The default view of your appointments shows just one day at a time, but you can expand the view to cover appointments that span multiple days, one or more weeks, or a full month at a time.

The Day, Week, and Month buttons above the Calendar display allow you to quickly switch between Outlook's built-in views.

Click the Day button to display one day's events. Use the Date Navigator to show another day's schedule, or click the Today button on the Standard toolbar to jump back to today's calendar. Click in the Contents pane and then press the Page Up and Page Down keys to scroll through meetings and appointments for the selected day; use the left- and right-arrow keys to move through the Calendar folder one day at a time.

TIP FROM

Ed & Woody

In Day or Week views, pressing Home takes you to the beginning of the currently selected workday and End jumps to the end of the workday—8:00 a.m. and 5:00 p.m., unless you adjust these defaults. Press Ctrl+Home or Ctrl+End to jump to the beginning or end of the day—midnight in either direction.

After selecting the Week view, click the Show Work Week option to show a side-by-side view of five days at a time, leaving off weekends, as in the example shown earlier in Figure 11.1. Click the Show Full Week option to display a full week's schedule. As in other views, all-day events appear in a banner at the top of each day, with multiday events extending over the tops of several days. Use the arrows to the left of the date display to move through the calendar a week at a time.

Click the Month button to see a month-at-a-glance calendar (see Figure 11.2), which offers enough information to provide an excellent bird's-eye view of your commitments for any month. This view is most effective if your screen supports larger resolutions (at least 1280 pixels wide). To jump a month at a time in either direction in this view, click the left and right arrow buttons to the left of the month label, or press the Page Up and Page Down keys, or click the vertical scrollbar at the right of the window. The Up Arrow and Down Arrow keys move through the calendar a week at a time. The Home key jumps to the beginning of the selected week.

Figure 11.2
Even at this low resolution, you can see enough information to differentiate individual appointments in the month view.

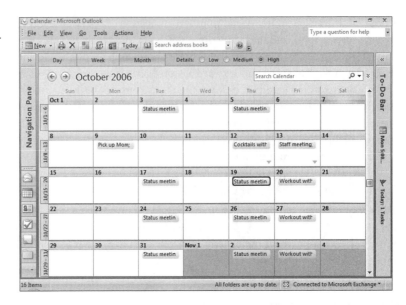

In both week and month views, the display for each day is narrow, so don't expect to read the full description of each event; point to any item to see a ScreenTip that includes the event's time, subject, and location. In all views, clicking an item selects it, and double-clicking opens it.

TIP FROM

In any Day/Week/Month Calendar view, press Alt+Page Up or Alt+Page Down to jump to the previous or next month. Each time you press either key again, you'll move one month in that direction. If you start on March 15, for example, pressing Alt+Page Down repeatedly takes you to April 15, May 15, June 15, and so on.

Use the Date Navigator to create a custom view of your calendar that's different from the standard day, week, and month views. Hold down the Ctrl key while you click two or more dates (they don't have to be adjacent), and the display changes to show you a side-by-side view of the schedules for the selected days. This technique is especially useful when you want to copy a meeting or appointment from one day to another. It's also handy if you're checking your schedule to see which day works best for a meeting or business trip. A multiday view can display up to 14 days at a time, side by side, although at most resolutions it's nearly impossible to see details for more than 7 days because each day's display is so narrow.

CUSTOMIZING THE CALENDAR

To change options for Outlook's built-in Day, Week, and Month views, right-click any unused space in the calendar display and choose Other Settings. The resulting dialog box (shown in Figure 11.3) lets you change the fonts and font sizes used in each of the three views.

Figure 11.3
Adjust these options to change the way Outlook displays your schedule in the default Day/Week/Month views.

Professionals who bill in 5-, 6-, 10-, or 15-minute increments might want to adjust the Time Scale from its default setting of 30 minutes to one of the shorter values from the drop-down list; if your schedule is usually light, on the other hand, you can set this value to its maximum of 60 minutes and see your entire schedule without scrolling. These settings apply only in Day and Week views. In the Month view, you can specify that you want the subjects of tasks, all-day events, and multiday events to be displayed in bold.

Outlook includes another batch of calendar options that let you adjust the basic look and feel of this folder. Choose Tools, Options, and then click the Calendar Options button on the Preferences tab to display the dialog box shown in Figure 11.4.

Figure 11.4
If you don't follow a Monday-to-Friday schedule, use these options to redefine your work week and its starting date.

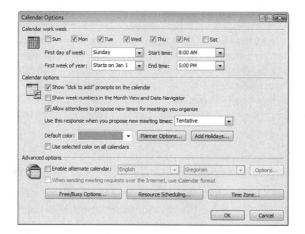

You can adjust any of the following Calendar options:

- In the Calendar Work Week section, click to select or clear the days that correspond to your work week. In the First Day of Week drop-down list, select the day you want to see at the beginning of Week and Month views. You can also define the Start Time and End Time for your typical work day here.

> **NOTE**
>
> When you double-click to add an appointment in Week or Month view, Outlook opens a new appointment form using the starting time as defined in this dialog box.

- Select the Show Week Numbers in the Month View Date Navigator check box if you want to see small numbers to the left of each week. This option is most useful for people who work in retail and other industries that measure performance weekly. (If you're a timeshare owner hoping to use this feature to track dates for weekly intervals you own, be sure to compare Outlook's week numbers with those provided by your property's management. Not all timeshares use the same method of calculating week numbers as Outlook!)

- The Default Color option lets you choose from a limited selection of pastel colors to use behind Day and Work Week views. The default color is determined by the theme you've chosen for Outlook—silver, blue, or black.

- Click the Add Holidays button to incorporate a list of common holidays into your Outlook calendar. Surprisingly, this feature doesn't use a sophisticated set of calculations to determine when Easter, Thanksgiving, and Yom Kippur fall each year. Instead, Outlook looks at the contents of a text file called `Outlook.hol`; in a U.S. English installation, this file is stored in `C:\Program Files\Microsoft Office\Office12\1033`. The Add Holidays to Calendar dialog box lets you choose which country's holidays should be added to your calendar—a handy option if you routinely travel around the globe or deal with folks in other countries.

TIP FROM

Ed & Woody

> Through the years, Microsoft has screwed up the list of holidays on more than one occasion. To customize the holiday list or fix errors, open this text file in a text editor such as Notepad. Each group of holidays (organized by country) starts with a name in square brackets; each item in the list includes a name, followed by the date in yyyy/mm/dd format. If your business has its own list of special days, put the business name in brackets to treat it as if it were a country. Then double-click `Outlook.hol`, choose your business name from the list of countries, and click OK to add the custom holidays to Outlook.

- The Resource Scheduling button lets you define options if you're responsible for processing meeting requests for resources, such as conference rooms and slide projectors.

- Click the Free/Busy Options button to display a dialog box that lets you publish information about your calendar to an Internet location for other people to use when scheduling meetings.

TAMING TIME ZONES

In all previous versions of Office, juggling time zones has been a hassle of epic proportions. Thankfully, that's fixed in Outlook 2007. When you enter an appointment or meeting, you now have the option to specify a time zone for the start and end times.

Why does this change matter? Well, imagine you're called away from your home office in Denver to attend a business meeting in Rome (lucky you). You schedule a meeting in Rome on October 1st at 9:00 a.m. Central European Time (CET), book your return flight on October 2nd at 10 a.m. CET, and dutifully enter the times in Outlook. While you're looking at your calendar, you notice that you have a regular telephone conference call on October 1st at 4:00 p.m. Mountain Time, which is eight hours earlier than Rome.

You bring your notebook computer with you to Italy and change the system clock to the local time zone when you arrive. What happens when you open Outlook and check your calendar? That depends on how you originally entered the appointments. Consider the following:

- If you didn't specify a time zone when you entered the appointment, Outlook recorded all the times you entered using the time zone you were in when you recorded them. When you change your system clock, Outlook helpfully adjusts all times. Your conference call appears as midnight, and when you call in you're right in sync with the rest of the participants. Unfortunately, you miss your meeting in Rome because Outlook has helpfully adjusted it from 9:00 a.m. to 5:00 p.m. And when Tuesday rolls around, you miss your flight because Outlook adjusted the time from 10:00 a.m. to 6:00 p.m.

- But if you were smart enough to click the Time Zones button when you created or edited the overseas appointments, you're in perfect shape. Outlook changes the start time displayed for your conference call in Denver but doesn't adjust the times for your rendezvous in Rome or your return flight. You're perfectly in sync in both time zones.

By default, the fields for entering time zone information are hidden. To make them visible for an individual appointment, click the Time Zones button in the Options group on the Appointment tab. This adds a drop-down list of all available world time zones to the right of both time fields, as shown in Figure 11.5.

Figure 11.5
Click the Time Zones command to add these details to the start and end times of an appointment or meeting. By default, Outlook uses your current time zone.

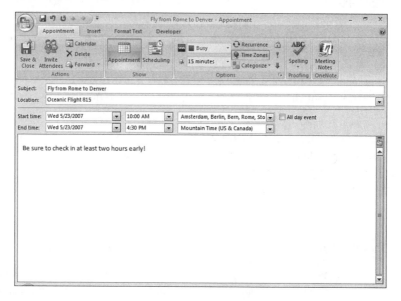

To make it easier for you to work with Calendar items entered in different time zones, add a second time zone to your Calendar. In Day or Week view, right-click the time display along the left edge of the calendar, choose Change Time Zone from the menu, and select the Show an Additional Time Zone check box. Enter a label for each time zone, click OK, and you'll see two time displays at the left side of the Day view. Whenever you enter an appointment or meeting, make sure you choose the correct time scale, as shown in Figure 11.6.

Figure 11.6
To keep track of meetings and appointments in different time zones, add a second time zone display to the Day and Week views.

This solution works well enough if your trip takes you to only two time zones. When you reach your destination, open the Time Zone dialog box again and click the Swap Time Zones button. The time on the system clock changes, but you can still stay on time as long as you don't succumb to jet lag and look at the wrong scale. If your trip takes you to three or more time zones, however, using this technique is a one-way ticket to hopeless confusion—especially with jet lag. For complex itineraries, add a note about the time zone in the Subject of every appointment.

 If you receive an error message when you click the Swap Times Zones button, see "You Need Permission to Reset the System Time" in the "Troubleshooting" section at the end of this chapter.

The option to show an additional time zone is also useful if you work with people in different parts of the world, by allowing you to see at a glance whether you're trying to call Moscow at midnight or Hong Kong at 3:00 a.m., when no one's there to take the call.

So, what if the change in time zones is permanent? If you move across country or halfway around the world, open the Time Zone dialog box and click the Change Calendar Time Zone button. Choose the original time zone and then select the options shown there to either update all existing appointments to reflect the changed time zone (shifting the time that appears on each one) or move appointments to the new time zone (keeping the original date and time but adjusting the time zone attribute).

CREATING A NEW APPOINTMENT OR EVENT

You can create three similar types of items in the Calendar folder. *Appointments* have starting and ending times blocked out in your schedule; *events*, such as vacations and business trips, last 24 hours or more; and *meetings* are appointments to which you invite other people.

→ To see how Outlook can help you coordinate meetings, **see** "Managing Meeting Requests," **p. 289**.

If you want to add a new item to your personal calendar and you know the date and time of the appointment or event, you can open a new appointment form with those details already filled in. Open or switch to a window displaying the contents of the Calendar folder, and then use any of these techniques:

- From Day or Week view (including multiday views), use the Date Navigator to select the correct date, and then double-click a time slot to open a new appointment. Outlook uses the default appointment interval of 30 minutes. To use a different interval, click and drag the mouse pointer from the start time to the end time, and then right-click and choose New Appointment.

- In Month view, select the month containing the date you want to use, and then right-click and choose New Appointment; this creates an appointment with a start time that is the default starting time for the day. If you select multiple dates, Outlook creates a new event on the selected dates, with no start or end times.

- To open a new event form from any view, right-click and choose New All Day Event. Or, in Month view, double-click any empty space in the date on which you want to schedule the event.

You can also create an appointment instantly by dragging an email message from your Inbox and dropping it on the Calendar button in the Navigation bar. This shortcut can be a true time-saver when you receive a message that includes essential details about an upcoming event. The subject of the mail message becomes the subject of the appointment, and the message text appears in the Notes area of the appointment form. You'll probably need to adjust the date and time, however, because by default Outlook uses the next available block of time in today's schedule.

If you've looked up a name in your Contacts folder and you want to create an appointment that includes a link to that person, don't just drag the item onto the Calendar icon—that action creates a meeting request addressed to the selected person. Instead, hold down the right mouse button as you drag the item from the Contacts folder, drop it on the Calendar button, and then choose one of the Copy Here as Appointment options. (Copy Here as Appointment with Text is easiest if you want to be able to read details about the contact without opening a separate window. Copy Here as Appointment with Shortcut is best if you want to be certain you're viewing the most up-to-date information when the appointment time rolls around.) If you drag two or more Contact items into the Calendar folder, Outlook assumes you want to include all the information in a single appointment.

You can create a new appointment from scratch by using any of the following techniques:

- Click the New Appointment button.
- Press Ctrl+N in the Calendar folder or press Ctrl+Shift+A in any other folder.
- Choose File, New, Appointment.

Enter a name for the appointment in the Subject field, and then tab from field to field and add more details. Use the Categorize button to assign color-coded categories (Company and Important, in this example). Click the Save and Close button when you're finished. Add details about the meeting in the Notes area just below the Reminder field. You can also add attachments here, including files, copies of Outlook items, or shortcuts to files or Outlook items. Figure 11.7 shows a filled-in appointment form.

Figure 11.7
Like most Outlook items, appointments can include file attachments and links to Contacts.

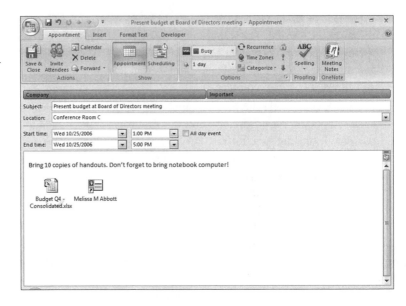

Tables 11.1 and 11.2 describe the types of information you can include in each field of an appointment item.

→ To learn how Outlook will fill in times and dates for you, **see** "Entering Dates and Times Automatically," **p. 193**.

→ To learn how to organize Outlook items using categories, **see** "Assigning Items to Categories," **p. 194**.

→ To learn more about instructing Outlook to remind you of important activities, **see** "Flagging Items for Follow-Up," **p. 196**.

TABLE 11.1 STANDARD APPOINTMENT FIELDS

Field Name	Description
Subject	Enter the text you want to see in Calendar view. Although you can enter up to 255 characters, you should keep the Subject line much shorter—preferably 30 characters or fewer. Subject lines more than about 150 characters will not print correctly in Tri-fold format.
Location	Enter a location; the drop-down list lets you choose from among the 10 locations you entered most recently (you can't customize this list or change its order).
Start Time, End Time	Enter starting and ending times and dates by using any common date and time format or an AutoDate description; click the arrow to the right of a date or time field to select from a calendar control or a list of preset times.
All Day Event	Clicking this box removes the Start Time and End Time fields from the form; when you enter an event, Outlook's default settings show the time in your shared schedule as Free.

TABLE 11.2   OPTIONS AVAILABLE ON APPOINTMENT TAB

Field Name	Description
Show As	This command specifies how others view your calendar by designating the time an appointment takes as Free, Tentative, Busy, or Out of Office. Each of these four descriptions uses a different color in Calendar views. You cannot add new descriptions to this list. This option is useful when you use the Delegate option on an Exchange Server; other people can't see details of your schedule, but they at least know whether you're in the office.
Reminder	Appointments can pop up reminders at times you define; unless you change the defaults (as described in Chapter 8, "Outlook Essentials"), Outlook adds a reminder 15 minutes before every appointment.
Recurrence	See the following section for a discussion of how to enter recurring appointments.
Time Zones	Specify a time zone other than the current Windows time zone for the start or end times, or both.
Categorize	Assign appointments to color-coded categories, just as you do contacts and tasks. See the section, "Assigning Items to Categories," in Chapter 8 for more details on how to customize the list.
Private	Designate an appointment as private so no one who looks at your shared schedule will know that you've gone to the ball game. Details of private appointments do not appear on shared calendars, although the time is blocked out; when printing, you can choose to hide details of appointments marked Private.
High/Low Importance	Clicking either of these boxes toggles a field that you can use to filter appointments in views and queries.

In previous Outlook versions, the default appointment form included a field to link an appointment to one or more contacts. In Outlook 2007, that option is gone, replaced by the capability to create links between an appointment and any Outlook item. To use this capability, open the Appointment form and click the Attach Item button in the Include group on the Insert tab. As Figure 11.8 shows, you can link another appointment to the current one. If you want to be able to see and change the actual appointment instead of a copy, be sure to select the Shortcut option under the Insert As heading. If you're creating a meeting request, however, don't use links unless they're on a server that the recipient will have access to. For items you send to other people who don't have access to your server, attach a copy of the item instead.

Figure 11.8
Use this dialog box to attach any Outlook item to an appointment. The Text Only and Attachment icons make copies of the original item; choose Shortcut to create a link.

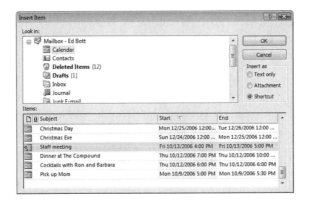

ENTERING RECURRING APPOINTMENTS

Some appointments and events are one-shot deals, but others—like it or not—happen over and over. When you enter details for a recurring appointment, Outlook manages the entire series from a single appointment form. You can specify recurring patterns on a daily, weekly, monthly, or annual basis. The options for recurring appointments are surprisingly flexible.

→ To learn more about setting up recurring tasks, **see** "Entering Recurring Tasks," **p. 296**.

To set up a recurring appointment or event, create the item from scratch or open an existing item, and then click the Recurrence button to display the Appointment Recurrence dialog box (see Figure 11.9).

Figure 11.9
Use this dialog box to schedule even complicated recurring appointments, like this one every Tuesday and Thursday at 4:00 p.m. for the next 5 weeks or 10 occurrences.

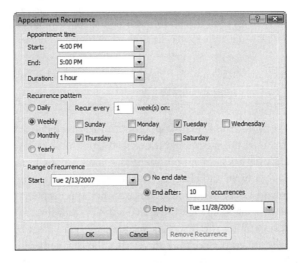

Adjust the options as needed to match the schedule of your event. Enter an ending date or a fixed number of occurrences, if appropriate, and click OK. Then click Save and Close to add the recurring appointment or event to your Calendar folder. Outlook adds a recurrence icon to the left of the event description in all Calendar views.

To edit a recurring appointment or event, open the item. A dialog box lets you specify whether you want to change the entire series or just the selected instance. If your production department moves this week's status meeting from its regular slot of Wednesday at 2:00 p.m., you can change the times for that occurrence without affecting the rest of the items in the series. On the other hand, if a new production manager decides to move the meetings to Monday mornings, you can edit the entire series, and you need to change the details only once to reschedule all future occurrences.

TIP FROM

> To see a list of all recurring appointments and events (and edit one or more of them, if necessary), switch to Outlook's predefined Recurring Appointments view. Note that this list includes birthdays and anniversaries, which Outlook treats as recurring annual events.

RESCHEDULING AN APPOINTMENT OR EVENT

The most labor-intensive way to change the date and time of an appointment or event is by opening the item and manually adjusting the entries in the Start Time and End Time fields. Try these time-saving shortcuts instead:

- To change the scheduled starting time for an appointment in any Day or Week view (including multiday views), click and drag the item to its new time.

- To move an item to a different day, click and drag the item and drop it on the selected day in Week or Month view or in the Date Navigator. To change the month in the Date Navigator without changing the display in the current view, hold down Ctrl as you click the left or right arrows above the Date Navigator.

- To copy an item to a new date and time, hold down the Ctrl key and drag the item to the new date by using the Week or Month view or the Date Navigator. This technique is particularly useful when scheduling a follow-up appointment; because copying the appointment item also copies all its details, you eliminate the need to search for your notes from the original meeting when it's time for the follow-up.

TIP FROM

> If you want to edit the description of an event or appointment, without adjusting its date, time, or details, click to select its listing in any daily, weekly, or monthly Calendar view, and then click again to position the insertion point so you can edit the text directly. As soon as you click the text to begin editing, the location (in parentheses after the description text) disappears; the only way to edit location information is to open the form.

MANAGING MEETING REQUESTS

In the world according to Outlook, there is a crucial difference between an *appointment* and a *meeting*. When you create an appointment, you set aside a block of time on your own personal calendar. Although an appointment might involve other people, it's your responsibility, not Outlook's, to coordinate your schedule with theirs.

An Outlook meeting, on the other hand, consists of identical items in the Calendar folders of two or more people. Although these items closely resemble appointments—with a subject, start and end times, and the option to set a reminder—there are several crucial differences:

- Every meeting has an *organizer*, who is responsible for setting the time, location, and other details.

- The organizer fills in a meeting request form (essentially an appointment form with a few extra fields and buttons) that includes details of the meeting as well as the names and email addresses of all required and optional attendees; Outlook sends the invitations automatically when the organizer saves the meeting request.

- When you receive a meeting request, you can accept, tentatively accept, or decline the invitation. If you accept, Outlook adds the meeting to your calendar. Outlook sends all responses to the meeting organizer and tracks the meeting's status automatically.

- As part of the planning process, the meeting organizer can reserve a conference room and other resources, such as overhead projectors or presentation equipment.

- If you and other members of your workgroup publish the details of your schedule on an Exchange Server or a web server, Outlook can automatically pick a time when all proposed attendees are available.

NOTE

You don't have to work in a corporation to use meeting requests. You don't need access to an Exchange Server, either, nor do you even need to be on the same network (although it's much easier to view other people's calendars on a corporate network). In fact, any two people who use Outlook can keep events in sync by using meeting requests over an Internet-standard email connection.

CREATING A NEW MEETING REQUEST

You can begin scheduling a meeting by opening a meeting request form directly, using any of the following techniques:

- Choose File, New, Meeting Request; or press Ctrl+Shift+Q to open a blank meeting request form.

- If you've already selected the exact date and time of the meeting, switch to a Calendar view of that date and select the block of time; then right-click and choose New Meeting Request from the shortcut menu. This option opens a meeting request form with the date and time already filled in.

- To open a meeting request form with the invitees' names already filled in, select one or more names in the Contacts folder. With a single contact selected, you can right-click and choose Create, New Meeting Request to Contact; with multiple contacts selected, choose Actions, Create, New Meeting Request to Contact.

- To plan a meeting by comparing schedules stored on an Exchange Server, open the Calendar folder and choose Actions, Plan a Meeting. (This option is available even if you're not connected to an Exchange Server, but it's virtually useless in a standalone environment.)

- To create a meeting while viewing a group schedule, click the Make Meeting button and choose New Meeting with All. (You can also Ctrl+click to select individual names from the Group Members list; choose Make Meeting, New Meeting to use only the selected names.)

- If you've already created an appointment in your Calendar folder and you want to turn it into a meeting, open the item and click the Invite Attendees button (in the Actions group on the Appointment tab). This option uses all details you defined previously, adding a field in which you can enter the names of other attendees.

As Figure 11.10 shows, a meeting request form closely resembles an appointment form, with the crucial addition of the To field, a Send button, and a new Attendees group on the Appointment tab. Fill in the prospective attendees' names, and then add the remainder of the meeting details—subject, start time, end time, notes, and so on—as you would for an appointment, and click Send to deliver the invitations.

Figure 11.10
A meeting request form resembles a cross between an email message and an appointment form.

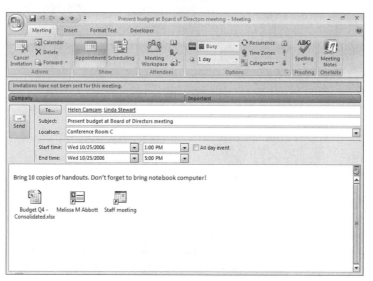

Don't forget to include details in the box at the bottom of the Appointment tab. Text you enter here appears in the Meeting item added to each attendee's Calendar folder after your invitation is accepted; it also serves as the text of the emailed invitation.

When preparing a meeting request, you can designate some attendees as Required and others as Optional. By default, anyone you invite to a meeting is a Required attendee. To change their status to Optional, click the Scheduling command in the Show group on the Meeting tab, click the icon in the column just to the left of any name, and use the drop-down menu to adjust an invitee's status, as shown in Figure 11.11. To view the status of all attendees, click the Tracking button (available only after the meeting request has been created and sent).

Figure 11.11
Use the Meeting Planner view of a meeting request to designate an attendee as optional rather than required.

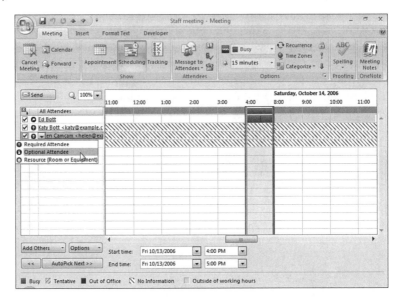

As the meeting organizer, you can change the status of any attendee at any time. When attendees open a Meeting item and select this view, they see only the list of attendees and their status, without the capability to change the designation. On the meeting organizer's calendar only, this view also summarizes the responses from prospective attendees.

After you've finished entering all details in the meeting request form, click the Send button. Outlook delivers the requests via email to all prospective attendees.

TIP FROM

Outlook 2007 (like Outlook 2003) automatically sends all meeting requests delivered via Internet mail in iCalendar format, which ensures that the request will work with all compatible contact-management programs. (Meeting requests sent to Exchange recipients are sent in Rich Text Format.) To change this global option, choose Tools, Options, click the Calendar Options button on the Preferences tab, and select or clear the When Sending Meeting Requests Over the Internet, Use iCalendar Format box. Outlook recipients will still see all meeting requests exactly as they normally do, but users of other contact management programs will be able to deal with them as well.

RESPONDING TO MEETING REQUESTS

When you receive a meeting invitation via email, it resembles an ordinary message, with the following key differences:

- The Meeting Request icon to the left of the invitation in the message list is different.

- The message header shows the sender's name, Required and Optional attendees, and the location and time of the meeting.

- Special-purpose toolbar buttons are visible in the message window and in the Reading pane, as shown in Figure 11.12. Using these buttons, you can accept the invitation, decline it, or propose a new time (this last option is not available for recurring meetings). Click the Tentative button when you want to reserve the right to change your mind later.

Figure 11.12
Use these buttons to accept or decline a meeting invitation. Click the Calendar button to open your Calendar folder and check details of your schedule.

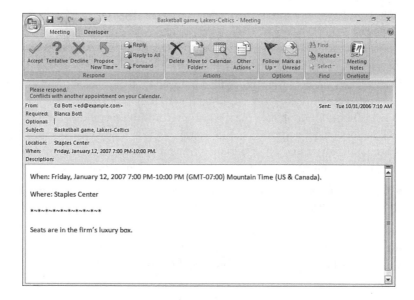

If you accept the invitation, Outlook adds the item to your calendar. You can add a note to your response or send a default notification to the meeting organizer.

If you're not the meeting organizer, you can propose an alternative date or time for the meeting. Choosing this option opens a form in which you can respond to the meeting organizer. As the organizer, you can see all proposed changes in a single window and choose the one that works best for you.

If a meeting organized by someone else is on your calendar, you can change its time—for that matter, you can delete it outright. There's nothing wrong with this course of action if the meeting organizer stops you in the hall or calls on the phone to cancel or change the time. If you change the item in your calendar, Outlook does not update the original item on the meeting organizer's calendar.

CAUTION

> If you attempt to change the time of a meeting organized by someone else, be sure to click the Propose New Time box. If you click Accept or Tentative, the Office Assistant displays a warning dialog box urging you to send a message to the meeting organizer, but Outlook's response-handling script ignores the changes and marks the original item on the organizer's calendar to show that you've accepted.

To decline an invitation after you have already accepted the meeting request and added it to your calendar, open the item in the Calendar folder and click the Decline button. Outlook offers to send a message to the organizer; add text explaining that your schedule has changed, and click the Send button.

If you are the meeting organizer, you can also cancel a meeting at any time by deleting it from your calendar. Outlook offers to send a cancellation message on your behalf to all the attendees you previously invited.

CHECKING THE STATUS OF A MEETING YOU'VE ARRANGED

Outlook uses special scripts embedded in meeting invitations to process responses. As the invitees accept or decline the meeting request, they return a message to you; when it arrives in your Inbox, Outlook uses the script commands to update the status of the list. As the meeting organizer, you can check a meeting's status at any time by opening it. Look at the information bar at the top of the Appointment page to see a running tally of the number of prospective attendees who have accepted, declined, or failed to respond.

 If you continually fail to receive updates from specific people, see "The Case of the Missing RSVP" in the "Troubleshooting" section at the end of this chapter.

For a more detailed view of responses, click the Tracking button on the Meeting tab. This list lets you see at a glance which invitees have failed to respond to your invitation, allowing you to send a follow-up message quickly, if necessary.

RESCHEDULING OR CANCELING A MEETING

Handling changes to Outlook meetings requires a delicate balancing act. After the initial round of invitations and responses, each prospective attendee has a separate meeting item on his or her calendar. Communication of any changes is crucial.

As the organizer, you can change the date or time of a meeting, change other details (such as its location), or cancel it outright. To make any changes, open the item in your Calendar folder, click the Appointment button on the Meeting tab, and change the meeting details; then click the Send Update button. To cancel the meeting, open the meeting item and click Cancel Meeting. If you change the date, time, or other details, Outlook prompts you to send an Update message to everyone on the list; if you cancel a meeting, Outlook generates a cancellation request. If you add an attendee, you can choose whether to send the update just to new attendees or to all attendees.

An Update message looks exactly like the original request. Everyone who receives it will see the Accept, Decline, and Tentative buttons, just as if it were an original meeting request.

When you send an Update message, be sure to include text in the Notes box that explains the changes you've made—that text becomes the body of the update message. If you omit this step, attendees who don't read the message carefully might assume they're receiving a duplicate of the original meeting request and fail to notice the change in date or time.

MAINTAINING YOUR PERSONAL TASK LIST

In Outlook, *tasks* are essentially to-do items. They can be as simple as a note to yourself ("Pick up milk on the way home") or you can add start dates, due dates, and detailed notes, and then track your progress on a complex task over time. Outlook lets you define *one*-time tasks or recurring tasks, such as weekly status reports. A list of current tasks appears on the Outlook Today page and in the To-Do Bar.

→ To learn how you can tailor the To-Do Bar for your working style, **see** "Customizing the To-Do Bar," **p. 183**.

ENTERING TASKS

The absolute simplest way to create a task is to enter it directly in the To-Do Bar or in the Tasks folder. If the To-Do Bar is visible, click where you see the gray letters Type a New Task. Enter a short description of the task; if you want to associate a deadline with the task, press Tab to move to the Due Date field and enter a date. Press Enter to record the task. You can use a similar procedure in the Tasks folder in Simple List view.

To create a new task with more details, click the New button in the Tasks folder, or choose File, New, Task, or press Ctrl+Shift+K. In the Task form (see Figure 11.13), enter the task text in the Subject box and fill in any of the additional fields, all of which are optional.

Figure 11.13
The only required field for a Task item is the Subject line; enter date and status information if you plan to produce status reports.

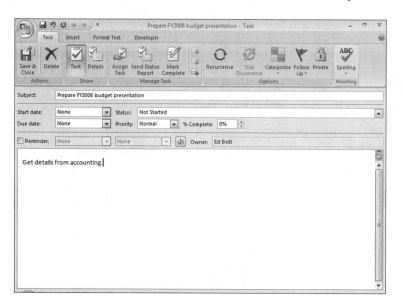

Enter the Due Date and the Start Date. To enter these dates automatically, click the Follow Up button and use the options on the menu to choose from a common list of dates. This option sets the Start Date and Due Date to the same value. Fill in the Status, Priority, and % Complete boxes only if you want to be able to sort a complex list of tasks using this information. By default, Outlook does not create a reminder for new tasks; to do so manually, click the Reminder check box and adjust the date. If you want to set a reminder automatically for every new task, choose Tools, Options, and click the Preferences tab. Then click the Task Options button and select the Set Reminders on Tasks with Due Dates check box.

Add details, notes, and file attachments (including document shortcuts) for the task. Click the Categorize button on the Task tab to assign the task to categories. If you're on a corporate network with an Exchange Server, you can click the Private box to prevent anyone with shared access to your Tasks folder from seeing the details of this item.

→ Sorting your Outlook items by category and assigning follow-up flags helps you manage your appointments, contacts, email, and so on; **see** "Assigning Items to Categories," and "Flagging Items for Follow-Up," **pp. 194 and 196**.

If you plan to use the Tasks folder to track items from which you'll generate billing reports, click the Details button on the Task tab. Boxes on this page of the Task form let you enter the amount of time you spend on a task, as well as mileage details and additional notes in the Billing Information box. Click the Save and Close button to add the new item to your Tasks folder.

TIP FROM

To create a billing statement with Outlook, create a custom Table view that includes the fields you want to use on your billing report. Sort or filter the list to show only the clients or companies for whom you want to generate the report. Select the rows and press Ctrl+C to copy them to the Windows Clipboard; then open a new Excel workbook and paste the copied rows into a blank worksheet range. Use formulas to translate hourly rates and mileage allowances into totals.

Items on your task list show up in red when they're overdue, and in gray, with strikethrough formatting, when you click the Mark Complete button.

If the due dates on some task items mysteriously change, see "You Need It When?" in the "Troubleshooting" section at the end of this chapter.

ENTERING RECURRING TASKS

For tasks that repeat at regular intervals, enter the data just as you would for a one-time task, but before you save, click the Recurrence button. With one noteworthy exception, the technique for specifying how often a task recurs is essentially the same as for a recurring appointment or event. You specify whether the task repeats at daily, weekly, monthly, or annual intervals, and then enter the recurrence pattern—every other Tuesday and Thursday, the second Wednesday of each month, and so on. You can define recurring tasks that occur a set number of times—once a week for the next three weeks while a co-worker is on vacation, for example—or click the End By box and enter a specific date when the task ends.

→ If you must complete the same task at the same time on a regular basis—such as a weekly sales report—use Outlook's recurring appointment feature; **see** "Entering Recurring Appointments," **p. 288**.

Unlike recurring appointments, you can define an interval for recurring tasks that are based on completing the previous instance. Suppose you want to stay in touch with a valued but hard-to-reach customer by calling roughly once a month, but you don't want to wear out your welcome by calling too often. If you define a recurring task to call on the 5th of each month, and you don't actually connect until the 20th, you'll end up making your next call only 15 days later.

Instead, use the dialog box shown in Figure 11.14 to specify that you want to generate a new task 30 days after you complete the previous instance. Click the Regenerate New Task box, and then fill in the number of days, weeks, months, or years you want between instances. Each time you mark a task complete, Outlook creates a new Task item using the specified settings. So if you connect with your customer on September 19, your next reminder occurs a month later, on the 19th of October.

Figure 11.14
Use the Regenerate New Task option button to specify that you want the due date of the next recurring task to be based on the date the previous one was completed.

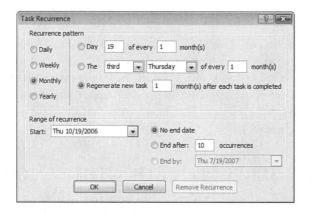

Outlook adds recurring tasks to your task list one at a time. When you mark one occurrence of the task complete, the next occurrence appears in the list. If you look at your task list for the next month, you'll see only one instance of a recurring task, even if it recurs daily or weekly. When you mark each task complete, Outlook creates a new item with a new due date. If you try to delete a recurring task, you can delete just the specified instance or all recurrences.

SORTING AND FILTERING THE TASK LIST

Outlook's built-in views for the Tasks folder include table views—Simple List or Detailed List—that let you see all tasks regardless of due date and status. You can create custom filters and views for items in the Tasks folder as well. The following views are built in:

- Switch to the Active Tasks view to see all tasks except those where the Status is Complete or Deferred.

- The Next Seven Days view shows all tasks due in the next week. It does not include overdue tasks.

- Choose Overdue Tasks to see only those items for which the due date has passed. This view excludes tasks that have no due date.

- Click the By Category view to see an outline style view of tasks organized according to categories you assign.

TIP FROM

Ed & Woody

> You can assign a single task to multiple categories; switch to By Category view, and then hold down the Ctrl key and drag to assign an item to a new category.

- The Assignment and By Person Responsible views are relevant only if you assign tasks to other persons.

- Choose the Completed Tasks view to see only those tasks you've marked as completed.

→ Use Outlook's Views settings to organize your Outlook data; **see** "Using Views to Display, Sort, and Filter Items," **p. 204**.

If you scrupulously update the Due Date, Start Date, Status, and % Complete fields, you can use the Tasks folder to perform rudimentary project-management tasks. But when we say rudimentary, we mean it. Outlook's Task Timeline view shows start and end dates for individual tasks, but it doesn't enable you to create dependencies, balance resources, or link related projects. If you need robust project-management capabilities, look at a product such as Microsoft Project instead.

SHARING YOUR SCHEDULE WITH OTHER PEOPLE

Outlook is more than a personal organizer. If you work closely with a team of people who also use Outlook, you can coordinate schedules among group members to streamline the process of organizing meetings. As a meeting organizer, your job is much easier when you can see at a glance what times are available for the other group members.

In the office, you can view details from calendars on a Microsoft Exchange Server or on a corporate web server. If you don't have access to an Exchange Server, you can publish your calendar to the Microsoft Office Online server and share them over the Internet with friends, family, and co-workers who also use Outlook. If you don't want to mess with any servers, you can share a snapshot of your calendar with another Outlook user via email.

NOTE

> If you tried calendar-sharing options in earlier versions of Outlook and gave up because they were too limited, awkward, or unreliable, try again. The Office Online service is considerably more robust than the still supported but deprecated Internet Free/Busy server option. And the email update option eliminates all the hassles associated with online services.

To use Outlook's automatic scheduling features, everyone in your office needs to publish details of their schedules so that Outlook can identify free and busy times for each meeting attendee. If you're connected via an Exchange Server, this process is relatively easy. If you don't have an Exchange Server available, the process is slightly more complicated.

TIP FROM

Ed & Woody

Group scheduling works properly only when everyone in a workgroup actively partici-pates. In particular, you need to make sure that every appointment you make is entered in your Calendar folder; if you don't, Outlook constantly reports to other people that you have free time, even when you're booked solid. Make sure that you select the Show Time As check box for every appointment. You can select any of four options: Free, Tentative, Busy, or Out of Office. Click the Private box if you've published the detailed version of your Calendar folder on an Exchange Server or the Office Online service and you want others to see only that you're busy, without being able to view details.

SHARING A CALENDAR ON AN EXCHANGE SERVER

On an Exchange Server, calendar sharing is managed by user account security. To share your calendar with another person who has an account on the same server, right-click your Calendar icon in the folder list or at the top of the Navigation pane in the Calendar folder and choose Change Sharing Permissions. On the Permissions tab of the Calendar Properties dialog box, click Add to select a name from the Exchange Address Book and then use the options below to grant permissions, as shown in Figure 11.15.

Figure 11.15
The drop-down Permission Level list allows you to choose from predefined roles that correspond to specific sets of permissions.

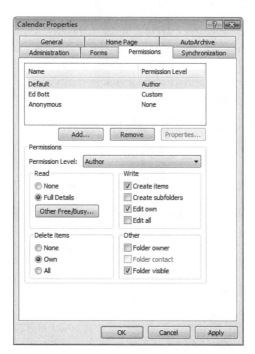

You can also use the Share My Calendar link in the Navigation pane to open a sharing request form. The script in this message allows you to grant access to your Calendar folder, request access to the recipient's Calendar folder, and add a descriptive email message at the same time. Figure 11.16 shows an outgoing request.

Figure 11.16
With this email template, you can grant access to your Calendar and request access to the recipient's Calendar with one click.

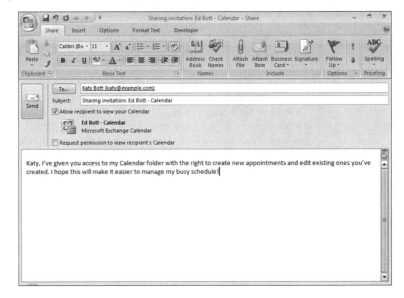

PUBLISHING A CALENDAR USING OFFICE ONLINE

To share your Calendar over the Internet without an Exchange Server, you can use Microsoft's Office Online server. To take advantage of this service, you need to first enroll with a free Windows Live (previously known as Passport) ID. While viewing the contents of the Calendar folder, click the Publish My Calendar link in the Navigation pane. After logging in with your Windows Live ID, you'll reach the dialog box shown in Figure 11.17.

Figure 11.17
Use this dialog box to adjust settings on your shared folder at Office Online.

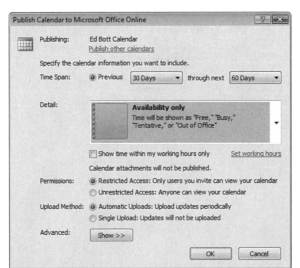

You can adjust any or all of the following settings here:

- Time Span allows you to define which dates are available in your shared calendar. The default shows up to 60 days into the future.

- Detail defines how much detail is available to other people. The default setting shows your availability only, as defined in the Show As field. You can change this to Limited Details, which shows the Subject of each appointment as well as your availability, or Full Details. Select the Show Time Within My Working Hours check box if you want to prevent anyone from looking at what you're doing in your off hours.

- Permissions lets you choose whether to restrict access to invited users or allow anyone to view your calendar. If you keep the default setting of Restricted Access, permissions are granted on the basis of the other person's Windows Live ID.

- Upload Method defines whether your published calendar is continually updated. If you're posting a calendar of events for an organization, you might decide to prevent updates if the list is static and unlikely to change.

SENDING A CALENDAR VIA EMAIL

If you have no desire to mess with servers and simply want to share a calendar with someone else, send them a copy via email. The major disadvantage of this option is that it doesn't allow the recipient to subscribe to regular updates for the calendar. However, you can always send manual updates, and it's an excellent way to work with temporary calendar folders for groups.

To prepare a calendar for export in this fashion, open the Calendar folder on the Navigation pane and click the Send a Calendar Via Email link. This opens a greatly simplified version of the dialog box used with Office Online. As Figure 11.18 shows, your options are limited.

Figure 11.18
When you send a calendar via email, your options are greatly limited.

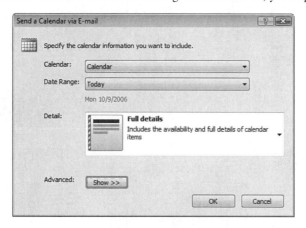

The default selection is your Calendar folder. If you've created an alternative calendar in a separate folder, specify it from the Calendar list. Choose a Date Range (the default is today, but you can choose from a range of predefined dates or set a custom interval), and specify the level of detail you want to show. Click OK to save the calendar and prepare the accompanying email message, which appears as an easy-to-read HTML-formatted message with an attached file in iCalendar format, as in the example in Figure 11.19.

Figure 11.19
When you receive a calendar via email, you can read its details in the message body and double-click the `.ics` attachment to import it into any compatible calendar.

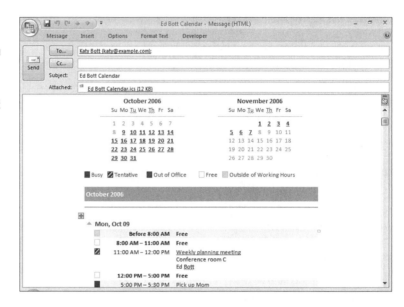

VIEWING SHARED OR PUBLISHED CALENDARS

To open another user's shared calendar on an Exchange Server, click the Open a Shared Calendar link in the Calendar Navigation pane. To open a published or emailed calendar for the first time, use the links included with the accompanying email. After you've opened a shared calendar, its icon appears in the Navigation pane and the calendar details appear alongside your Calendar folder in the Contents pane, as shown in Figure 11.20.

Figure 11.20
Shared calendars appear alongside your calendar. To compare schedules more easily, switch to overlay mode.

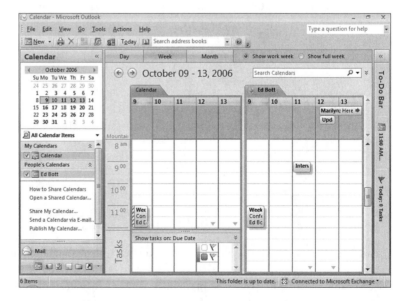

You can temporarily hide a calendar by clearing its check box in the Navigation pane. To compare two or more schedules more easily, overlay the events from multiple calendars in the same display. You can toggle between overlay and side-by-side modes by clicking the icon to the left of the name tab in the second calendar. Or use the View in Overlay Mode/View in Side-by-Side Mode options on the View menu.

USING GROUP SCHEDULES

Outlook 2007 provides easy access to a group schedule window, where you can save settings for any number of groups and open them by clicking a button. (This feature is compatible with Outlook 2002 and later.) Create a group schedule when you routinely work with a committee or team, all of whom have accounts on the same Exchange Server.

From the Calendar window, click the View Group Schedules button (or choose Actions, View Group Schedules). This opens the Group Schedules dialog box (see Figure 11.21), which shows groups you've already created. You can create a new group or work with an existing group; to add or remove names from a group, for instance, click the Open button. You can also remove a group from this window.

Figure 11.21
This dialog box shows groups you've already created and saved.

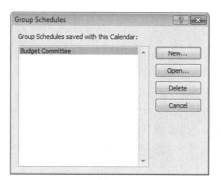

11

To create a new group, click the New button, enter a name for the group, and click OK. To add new members to the group, enter their names in the Group Members box and let AutoComplete suggest the correct name for you; or click the Add Others button to add from any Address Book or public folder.

Click the Save and Close button to save the settings for the new group you just created. Outlook updates the Free/Busy information for the people on the list. If you've saved a shared or published schedule for any person in the group, their information will appear in the Group Schedule window when you select their email address from the Address Book.

After creating a group, you can use it as the basis of a meeting request or email. Open the group schedule to see the dialog box shown in Figure 11.22. The list of group members appears in the column at the left. To the right of each name, you'll see details about the other person's appointments. If you don't have access to calendar details for another person, color-coded blocks in the right side of the window show free and busy times on each attendee's schedule.

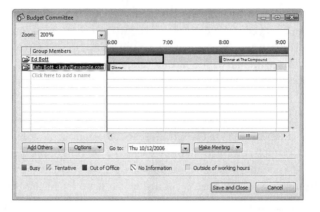

Click the Make Meeting button and choose one of the available options to begin planning a meeting with some or all of the Group Schedule members. In the meeting request form, click the Scheduling button to see the Meeting Maker page, which allows you to scroll through all available shared schedules and find a time that works for everyone.

TROUBLESHOOTING

YOU NEED PERMISSION TO RESET THE SYSTEM TIME

After I clicked the Swap Time Zones button, I clicked OK to apply the changes, but an error message appeared instead. My user account is in the Administrators group. How do I make this change?

It sounds like you're using Windows Vista. A bug in Outlook causes this error message when you try to change the time zone. Click the clock display at the right side of the taskbar to display the system clock and then click Change Date and Time Settings, Change Time Zone to make the change. When you return to the Time Zones dialog box, the Swap Time Zones button will be grayed out and unavailable, and confusingly will show your old time zone as the current one.

RESETTING THE FORMATTING OPTIONS

I customized a built-in calendar layout without making a copy first. How do I start over with the default form?

Choose File, Print, click the Define Styles button, and click the Copy button. Give the layout a descriptive name. Next, select the built-in format from the Print Styles list. Click the Reset button to return all formatting options to their default settings. This option does not affect your custom layout.

YOU NEED IT WHEN?

The due dates of some Task items changed, even though I never touched the Due Date field.

That's not a bug; it's a design decision. Did you change the value in the Start Date box at any point? If so, Outlook automatically changed the value in the Due Date field by the same interval. By design, Outlook assumes that tasks take a fixed amount of time, and delaying the start date delays the finish as well, even if you know you can meet your original deadline. Always check the Due Date field—and adjust it if necessary—after you change the Start Date.

THE CASE OF THE MISSING RSVP

Every time I plan a meeting involving a specific person, I fail to receive a response from that person.

Make sure the recipient is receiving your emailed invitations. If there's a problem with her email address, the invitations might not be arriving. If she doesn't use Outlook, you might need to send the invitations in iCalendar format. Outlook should choose this format automatically; to verify that this option is selected, open the meeting request form and choose Tools, Send as iCalendar. It's also possible that the recipient is consistently choosing the Don't Send a Response option when acting on meeting invitations. If you can't break recipients of this habit, you'll have to follow up (preferably by phone) and manually update their status on the Attendee Availability tab of the Meeting item.

SECRETS OF THE OFFICE MASTERS: PUBLISHING A CALENDAR AS A WEB PAGE

If you don't have access to an Exchange Server and you don't want to publish your calendar information to the Office Online service, you can still give other people access to calendar information by saving your Outlook Calendar folder in HTML format.

TIP FROM

Ed & Woody

> This option is especially useful if you maintain an events calendar for an organization. Choose File, New, Folder and create a folder that contains Calendar items. Enter details of the organization's activities as appointments in this folder, and then publish the contents of the calendar periodically as a web page.

Switch to the Calendar folder and choose File, Save as Web Page. Outlook opens the dialog box shown in Figure 11.23.

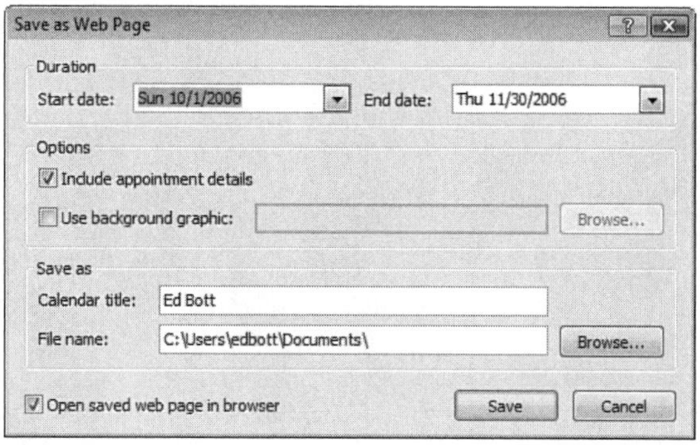

Choose the start and end dates you want to publish and specify whether you want to include details about each appointment from the Notes box. Give the calendar a title, specify a file location, and click Save. If you've set up a shortcut to a web server in your My Network Places

Figure 11.23

folder (or Network folder in Windows Vista), you can publish the page directly to the server by using this technique. The result, as shown in Figure 11.24, is a slick, frame-based page that lets you click individual dates in the Month view at left and see details in the frame on the right.

Figure 11.24

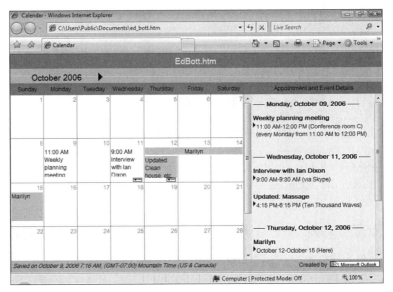

CHAPTER 12

OUTLOOK SECURITY AND PRIVACY

In this chapter

What You Need to Know About Email Security   308

Blocking Malware   309

Stopping Spam and Other Unwanted Email   313

Protecting Your Privacy   319

Disabling HTML-Based Email   322

Troubleshooting   324

Secrets of the Office Masters: Tracking Down the Source of Spam   324

WHAT YOU NEED TO KNOW ABOUT EMAIL SECURITY

It's a dangerous world out there. Every time you turn on your computer and connect to the Internet, you open a door that leads to incredible amounts of information and a wealth of communication opportunities. Unfortunately, that open door swings both ways, and if you aren't constantly vigilant, you may allow hostile intruders to take over your computer, steal your data, or invade your privacy.

An entire software industry has sprung up to defend Internet users against outside attackers—antivirus software, personal firewalls, and spam-blocking solutions, for instance. Outlook 2007 includes an assortment of features that integrate into an overall security strategy to help defend you against the following threats:

- Attachment-borne malware gets the most publicity, especially in mainstream media. This broad category includes viruses, worms, Trojan horse programs, and other types of hostile code that arrive as file attachments and can damage your computer if executed. Outlook includes severe (some say draconian) restrictions on what you can do with executable attachments. In this chapter, we explain how these restrictions work and how a knowledgeable user can make their impact less severe.

- Script-based attacks exploit security flaws in Windows that allow hostile code to be embedded in a message and automatically executed when the message is opened or previewed. Outlook protects against all such attacks by blocking execution of any automatic scripting or ActiveX controls.

- Spam, the popular term for unwanted commercial email, isn't a security threat on its own. But some types of spam can hoodwink a naive or careless user into visiting a hostile website or responding to a scam. In addition, legitimate messages can get lost in the clutter of junk mail or swept away by indiscriminate spam-blocking solutions. Outlook 2007 includes a customizable junk mail filter that works extremely well when you configure it properly.

- Phishing attacks use email messages to lure recipients to websites that masquerade as legitimate financial institutions or online shopping destinations. The idea is to reproduce the site with enough fidelity to convince the unsuspecting visitor to enter your login credentials (username and password) or details about a bank account or credit card. Outlook 2007 includes features designed to identify many common phishing attacks and render them ineffective.

- Web bugs, also known as web beacons, are links to external graphics embedded in HTML-formatted email messages. Web bugs, which are normally invisible, can contain tracking codes that allow the message sender to see when a user has opened or previewed a message, even if the user would prefer to protect his privacy by not disclosing this information. Outlook 2003 automatically prevents web bugs from functioning by blocking the retrieval of all external images in email messages unless you specifically approve.

In previous Outlook versions, security options were scattered throughout the user interface. In Outlook 2007, Microsoft has moved all these options to a single location, the Trust Center. In this chapter, we describe the Outlook-specific functions available in the Trust Center in more detail.

BLOCKING MALWARE

Viruses and other forms of malware, typically spread through email messages, have garnered plenty of publicity in recent years, and for good reason. Gone are the days when virus writers were bored teens looking to vandalize a few computers. Today, distributing malware to unsuspecting victims is big business for gangs of organized criminals that use the compromised machines to steal identities and drain bank accounts. An attacker who successfully gains access to your computer can install a keylogger that captures credit card numbers and logon details and can take over your computer and use it to send out spam and launch attacks against other computers. Cleaning up after a malware infestation is time-consuming and often requires technical skills that are beyond those possessed by average users. In the fight against hostile software, your best strategy is to prevent the bad guys from reaching your computer in the first place.

An essential line of defense is effective, up-to-date antivirus software. As recent outbreaks have proved time and again, even the most disciplined and vigilant user can fall prey to new types of attacks. Office 2007 includes an integrated antivirus interface that allows third-party software to scan saved files as they're being opened and to monitor incoming email messages as they arrive.

NOTE

> To verify that your currently installed antivirus program is working with Office 2007, choose Tools, Trust Center. Click Programmatic Access and look at the bottom of the Contents pane. The last line of this display reveals your current antivirus status.

12

CONTROLLING EXECUTION OF SCRIPTS

Like most modern email programs, Outlook can create and display email messages formatted using HTML. To accomplish this task, it uses the same program code that Internet Explorer uses to display web pages. That's a great way to add fonts, images, and other formatting to a message. Security problems arise, though, when email messages contain scripts, which can attempt to perform hostile actions such as running a program or attacking a known, unpatched vulnerability in Windows. The problem is especially severe for email messages because anyone who knows or can guess your email address can send you a message containing hostile script.

Outlook 2007 prevents virtually all scripts from being executed by configuring your system so that email messages are viewed in the Restricted Sites zone, where active scripting is disabled by default and ActiveX controls are also prevented from opening.

NOTE

For more information on security zones, see the Microsoft Knowledge Base article 174360, "How to Use Security Zones in Internet Explorer," which is available at `http://support.microsoft.com/kb/174360`.

What should you do when you receive a message from a known trusted source that contains script or that attempts to execute a file? Don't adjust Outlook's security zones to lower your level of protection; instead, open the message, click Other Actions (in the Actions group on the Message tab), and choose View in Browser. This option displays a warning dialog box like the one shown in Figure 12.1. After you click OK, the message opens in Internet Explorer, where active content, such as scripts, follows the generally more permissive rules for the Internet zone.

Figure 12.1
You can use your web browser to display an email message with active content that doesn't display properly in Outlook, but only if you're certain it's safe.

RESTRICTING ACCESS TO THE OUTLOOK ADDRESS BOOK

The Office object model allows scripts, macros, and external programs to access functions within Office programs. That's tremendously convenient when you use, for example, a third-party fax program or handheld computer that wants to share phone numbers and email addresses stored in the Outlook Address Book. It's also a potentially huge security risk; a virus that can access your Address Book can spread itself far and wide without your knowledge.

Beginning with Outlook 2003, Microsoft's developers have progressively tightened the rules that dictate whether, when, and how third-party programs can access your Address Book or Contacts list or send messages on your behalf. For programs that don't use the correct procedures, the default settings require your explicit permission before allowing access to address information.

If an external program that wasn't specifically written to work with Outlook 2007 attempts to access your Outlook Address Book, you see a warning dialog box. You can allow access just for this instance, or you can select the Allow Access For check box and choose an amount of time (up to 10 minutes). If you don't want the program to access your Address Book, click No. Your decision remains in force until you close and restart the program.

NOTE

Outlook add-ins that you install can access the Outlook Address Book without permission if they use proper techniques. If you have an older Outlook add-in that's giving you problems when you try to import addresses, check with the software developer and see if a newer, Office 2007–compatible version is available.

CONFIGURING ATTACHMENT OPTIONS

Outlook 2007 is ruthless with file attachments. With some file types, in fact, it simply refuses to allow you to access attachments at all. This is not a bug; it's a controversial security feature designed to protect users from possibly dangerous attachments.

Every time you receive an email message with an attached file, Outlook checks the file extension for that attachment, using a list of more than 70 filename extensions on its blacklist. If the extension is on that list, Outlook may force you to save the file before opening it, or it may forbid you to access the attachment in any way.

The attachment security list divides potentially dangerous files into two levels. So-called Level 1 files—executable files, shortcuts, scripts, Access databases, and other objects that can conceivably carry viruses or other harmful content—are considered the most dangerous. When Outlook finds a Level 1 file, it displays a banner in the Info pane that tells you it has blocked access to a file; the message includes the full name of the attached file. (To see a full list of the blocked attachment types, search the Help files for the topic, "Attachment File Types Blocked by Outlook.")

If you have an account on an Exchange Server, your administrator can change any Level 1 file type to a Level 2 file type. (There are no Level 2 files by default.) In that case, when Outlook detects that file type, it forces you to save the file to your hard disk, where, presumably, it will be scanned for known viruses using the antivirus software you have installed.

TIP FROM

EQ & Woody

> You do have antivirus software installed, right? It has been updated recently, hasn't it? Do yourself a favor—if you don't have an up-to-date antivirus program installed, download one now (we'll wait right here) and protect yourself. Windows users have dozens of choices in antivirus software, including some that are absolutely free. For an excellent list of available alternatives and links to useful information, look through the list of certified products at the ICSA Labs Anti-Virus Community (go to `http://www.icsalabs.com` and click the link to the Antivirus section). If you have installed antivirus software, make sure you keep its definition files up to date so you're not bitten by fast-spreading new viruses.

12

Although Exchange administrators can customize this behavior, Outlook users can't easily tweak these settings using the Outlook interface. However, it is possible to change this behavior by editing the Registry. Look for this key:

```
HKEY_CURRENT_USER\Software\Microsoft\Office\12.0\Outlook\Security
```

If the key does not exist, create it by right-clicking Outlook in the left-hand tree pane and choosing New, Key. With the Security key selected, add a new string value, name it `Level1Remove`, and fill in its value using a list of file extensions, separated by semicolons. Entering `url`, for instance, changes this extension to a Level 2 file type, which allows you to send and receive Internet shortcuts through Outlook. After making the Registry change, restart Outlook to make your changes take effect.

TIP FROM

Ed & Woody

You don't need to hack the Registry to fix this Outlook annoyance. Outlook MVP Ken Slovak has written a free add-in program that adds a new tab to the Tools, Options dialog box. You can pick and choose file extensions that are included or excluded from the Level 1 category or click one button that tells Outlook that you want to be able to make your own decisions about *all* file attachments. The latest version of Ken's program is fully compatible with Outlook 2007 and is available from:
`http://www.slovaktech.com/attachmentoptions.htm`

When you add a file type to the Level 2 list, you can't launch an attachment of that type directly from an email message. When you double-click the attachment icon in the mail message, Outlook displays the stern Attachment Security Warning dialog box shown in Figure 12.2 and prompts you to save the file.

Figure 12.2
Potentially dangerous attachments cannot be opened directly from an email message.

Attachments that Outlook deems safe (including Word documents, Excel workbooks, and Zip files) appear in the Preview pane and in message windows, where Outlook displays an icon and filename for each attached file. These details appear in the Attachments line, just below the Subject. You can drag and drop attachments into Windows Explorer or onto the desktop. You can also right-click any icon and use shortcut menus to open, print, save, or remove that attachment. To quickly save an attached file in an open Explorer window, for instance, right-click the attachment icon and choose Copy. Then right-click in the Explorer window and choose Paste. The same technique works for copying attachments between email messages.

TIP FROM

Ed & Woody

Want to work around these restrictions? Get in the habit of using Zip compression on all attachments. Outlook waves Zip files right through, without stopping, without checking the archive file's contents. Presumably any user who's smart enough to use a Zip utility will also be responsible enough to have antivirus software. If you find your attachments are still being blocked, you'll need to talk to email administrators (possibly on both sides of the transfer) to see how to work around the issue.

If you receive a message that contains one of the banned attachment types and you're unable to open it using Outlook, don't despair. The attachment is still within the message. Outlook's restrictions *block* access to it without actually removing it. Edit the Registry to change the file type to Level 2 (or use Ken Slovak's Attachment Options utility), as described earlier in this chapter, and you'll be able to save the attachment.

For attachments whose file types are not on the blocked list, preview capabilities are available. In the case of a Word document or Excel workbook, for example, you can click a Preview button to open the attached file in Outlook's Preview pane instead of having to open a separate program. This convenient feature also represents a potential security risk; if an attacker is able to exploit a flaw in one of those previewers to execute script or hostile code, your computer could be compromised by merely previewing a document.

If you're concerned about this risk, you can disable specific previewers or turn off this feature completely. To do so, click Tools, Trust Center, and then click the Attachment Handling tab. In the Attachment Handling dialog box (see Figure 12.3), select the Turn Off Attachment Preview check box to disable the feature entirely, or click Attachment and Document Previewers to selectively disable some file types. In this example, we've cleared the check box that allows media files to preview within Outlook.

Figure 12.3
If you don't want specific types of files to be previewed in the Outlook message window, you can selectively disable the associated previewer here.

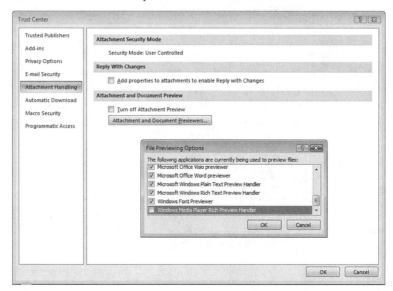

STOPPING SPAM AND OTHER UNWANTED EMAIL

What was once a trickle of junk mail has now become a flood. According to Postini, Inc., a well-known maker of antispam software, nearly 88% of all email messages sent and received in 2005 were unsolicited commercial email, better known as spam. That's up from roughly half in 2003 and a mere 8% in 2001.

How do you keep junk email from overwhelming legitimate incoming messages? The best strategy, as with most security problems, is a multilayered approach. If you control the server through which your email passes, you can install sophisticated filtering software that will bounce unwanted email before it has a chance to be downloaded into your Inbox. For those who have accounts hosted by an Internet service provider or a web-based service, server-side solutions vary in terms of quality and configurability. For everything that slips past the server, it's crucial to filter junk mail as it arrives.

Outlook 2007 uses a refined version of the junk email filter that debuted in Outlook 2003. It can be remarkably effective and has the capability to be updated as new techniques and technology become available.

The junk mail filter in Outlook 2007 examines every piece of email as it arrives, looking at the content of the message, when it was sent, and other factors to determine whether it is likely to be junk.

NOTE

> The precise techniques that Outlook uses to identify junk mail are classified as a trade secret and are very closely guarded. In the constant battle between spammers and spam busters, Microsoft believes that concealing exactly how its filters work gives them an edge over the bad guys. Many security professionals disagree with this approach (sometimes known as "security through obscurity"), but there's no indication that Microsoft plans to budge on its insistence with secrecy.

When Outlook identifies a message as junk, it moves the message to the Junk E-mail folder, disables all links and file attachments, and converts its display to plain text. With any message that has been identified as junk email (including suspected phishing messages), Outlook adds a banner (similar to the one shown in Figure 12.4) that identifies the blocked features. Click the banner to move the message back to the Inbox or to enable specific functionality.

Figure 12.4
Outlook blocks functionality of suspected junk email and phishing messages to prevent them from posing security risks.

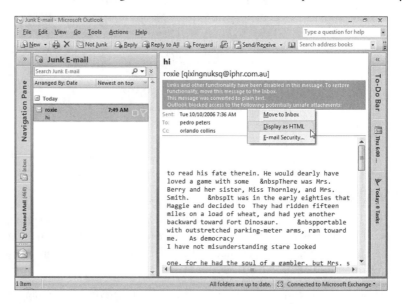

FINE-TUNING OUTLOOK'S JUNK MAIL FILTER

By default, Outlook's junk mail filters are enabled and set to catch only obvious junk mail and shunt it into a Junk E-mail folder. You can adjust these settings to make the filters more restrictive. In doing so, you need to balance your desire to be protected from spam against the risk that legitimate messages will be caught up in the filters. To change the default settings, choose Tools, Options, and click the Junk E-mail button on the Preferences tab.

The Junk E-mail Options dialog box, shown in Figure 12.5, lets you choose your spam-busting strategy.

Figure 12.5
The default Low setting allows many junk messages to hit your Inbox. Choose the High protection level to block more junk.

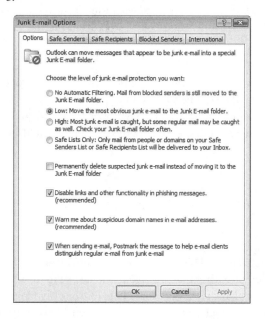

The Junk E-mail filters are reasonably effective at the default Low setting, with little risk of false positives. As a result, the only reason to select No Protection is if you rely heavily on your own filters or on third-party spam-catching software.

At the High setting, Outlook catches nearly all junk mail (in our tests, the success rate is well over 95%). This setting also inevitably captures some legitimate messages. If you choose the High setting, you'll need to monitor the Junk E-mail folder carefully at first and set up lists of safe senders and recipients, as we'll explain shortly.

The strictest antispam setting is the Safe Lists Only option. In this configuration, the Junk E-mail filters assume that all email is junk unless you've specifically designated the sender (or recipient) as safe. This option is most useful when you have a serious spam problem and virtually all of your legitimate messages are from people you already know.

The check box just below the list of filtering levels on the Junk E-mail Options dialog box allows you to choose whether you want Outlook to permanently delete any messages it identifies as junk email. For most accounts, this option is unacceptable because it gives you no chance to identify false positives and deal with them.

CAUTION

Deleting suspected junk email automatically is a bad strategy if you receive any important news via email. Banks, Internet service providers, and other businesses occasionally merge or are acquired, and sometimes companies change email domains for no apparent reason. If an important contact changes the details it uses for sending email to you, you'll have no way of knowing if its change-of-address notices are automatically deleted as junk.

If you choose one of the more aggressive spam-fighting options, you will almost certainly need to do some fine-tuning to weed out false positives and to block junk senders who sneak through the filters. Initially, Outlook warns you each time it moves a message to the Junk E-mail folder. Click the check box to tell Outlook to stop displaying these warning messages.

BLOCKING POTENTIAL PHISHING MESSAGES

The two check boxes at the bottom of this dialog box are new in Outlook 2007 and are intended to block phishing attacks. The first disables all links and other functionality such as forms in suspected phishing messages, even if they're not flagged as junk email. The second warns about suspicious domain names, which are often used by would-be phishers to impersonate a legitimate site.

FINE-TUNING THE FILTERS

To fine-tune the filters, you need to manage a group of lists, arranged in a series of tabs on the Junk E-mail Options dialog box:

- The Safe Senders list includes email addresses that you want Outlook to always recognize as legitimate email. This list can include individual email addresses (*someone@example.com*) or entire domains (*@example.com*). Figure 12.6 shows a typical Safe Senders list. Note that the Always Trust E-mail from My Contacts check box at the bottom of the dialog box is selected; with this option enabled, every address in your Contacts folder is considered "safe." In addition, you can choose to automatically add the addresses of any outgoing message you create to this list.

Figure 12.6
Add addresses to the Safe Senders list to avoid having messages from those recipients mistaken for spam.

- The Safe Recipients list works almost the same as the Safe Senders list. Add names to this list to identify mailing lists and other messages that you want to receive, even though they are not addressed specifically to you. For instance, if you are a member of the Ferret Fanciers of West Wenatchee mailing list, you might add the group alias, *ferret-fanciers@example.com*, to your Safe Recipients list. Regardless of who sends a message to the list, you can be sure it will arrive in your Inbox.

- Blocked Senders are individuals or domains that you want Outlook to identify as junk mail, no matter how legitimate the content may seem to be. This option is especially useful for filtering out junk from direct email marketers that refuse to acknowledge your unsubscribe requests.

- The International tab allows you to block messages from top-level domains or messages that arrive with specific encoding. Most people will never need to use these options; consider adjusting settings here if you begin receiving a flood of email from addresses tied to a specific domain, such as a country (`.ru` or `.cx`) or an alternative registry like `.info`. The Encodings List lets you define as junk any messages encoded in a language that you don't read (Japanese or Korean, for example, if you're a native speaker of U.S. English).

Is Outlook blocking a domain that you've added to your Safe Senders or Safe Recipients list? See "What's in a Domain Name?" in the "Troubleshooting" section at the end of this chapter.

You can add addresses and domains to any of these three lists manually by opening the Junk E-mail Options dialog box, selecting the appropriate tab, and clicking the Add button. It's much easier, though, to build this list by example. If a piece of spam lands in your Inbox from an address that isn't forged, right-click the message, choose Junk E-mail, and click Add Sender to Blocked Senders List. If you open the message, the process is simpler—click the Block Sender button on the Message tab. When you see a legitimate message that has been mistakenly moved to the Junk E-mail folder, click the Not Junk button (on the Standard toolbar in the Mail folder, or on the Message tab in a message window), right-click the message, and choose Junk E-mail, Mark as Not Junk. Outlook gives you the opportunity to identify the sender or recipient as a trusted address. For messages in other folders, right-click and choose Junk Mail; then select Add Sender to Safe Senders List, Add Sender's Domain to Safe Senders List, or Add Recipient to Safe Recipients List from the shortcut menu.

TIP FROM

Ed & Woody

> Over time, your lists of Blocked Senders, Safe Senders, and Safe Recipients become an indispensable part of your Outlook configuration. We recommend backing up both lists to a safe location every so often. Open the Junk E-mail Options dialog box, click the Export button, specify a filename, and click OK.

Here are a few details you need to know about Outlook's Junk E-mail filters:

- Unlike in previous Outlook versions, junk email filtering works with most types of email accounts, including POP3 and IMAP accounts, HTTP accounts from Windows Live Mail, and Exchange Server accounts working in Cached Exchange mode. Your rules are saved on the server when you connect to Exchange Server, allowing the server to filter out unwanted messages before they get to you.

12

- Filters work only after the message body is fully downloaded. If you've configured an IMAP or POP3 account to download headers only, junk email headers will show up in your Inbox first and will be filtered after you mark items for downloading and then retrieve the body. For many spam messages, this gives you an opportunity to mark obvious spam for deletion before it ever arrives.

- Junk E-mail filters are processed independently of rules. If you set up a rule that moves messages containing a word or phrase to a folder and you receive an email message containing that phrase that Outlook identifies as spam, you'll end up with two copies of the message—one in the Junk E-mail folder, another in the folder designated by your rule.

USING FILTERS WITH SEARCH FOLDERS

If you've grown accustomed to using rules to process incoming mails, you may be distressed to find that your old strategies don't mesh well with Outlook's new Junk E-mail filters. We know one longtime Outlook user who receives email from prospects, clients, and customers using more than a half-dozen email accounts. Formerly, he used rules to sort mail from each account into its own folder. This strategy clashes with the Junk E-mail filters in Outlook 2003 and 2007, however. Outlook was identifying hundreds of spam messages and moving them to the Junk E-mail folder. Unfortunately, the rules were moving copies of the incoming messages, including the suspected spam, to the folders listed in his rules!

The solution was to get rid of the old rules and take advantage of Search Folders. Instead of creating a rule to move email from each account into its own folder, he created a Search Folder for each account. Here's how you can use the same technique:

1. Make a note of the exact names of each email account you use (as listed in the E-mail Accounts dialog box or on the Send/Receive list), and then select the Inbox and choose Tools, Instant Search, Advanced Find.

2. Click the Advanced tab.

3. Click the Field button and select All Mail Fields, E-mail Account from the drop-down list.

4. Change Condition to is (exactly). Fill in the exact name of the first email account in the Value box and then click Add to List.

5. Click Find Now to run the search. After verifying that the results are as expected, choose File, Save Search as Search Folder. Give it a descriptive name and click OK.

Repeat the preceding steps for all your other email accounts. When you're finished, you'll have a collection of Search Folders, one for each email account. From now on, new messages come into the Inbox, as usual, and Outlook's Junk E-mail filters eliminate the spam. The Search Folders do the work of "sorting" the messages into virtual folders, one for each account. You can also view the contents of all messages in the Inbox by choosing View, Arrange By, E-mail Account.

USING EMAIL RULES TO BLOCK JUNK EMAIL

Spammers are sneaky and most are persistent enough to figure out how to worm their way past even the most sophisticated filters eventually. As a result, trying to fight spam by constructing your own set of rules is a losing battle. Here are just a few of the obstacles you face:

- If you try to identify words or phrases commonly used in spam, you'll be foiled by the creative misspellings and unique turns of phrase that junk senders use.

- Want to block individual senders? It's a losing battle, because most spammers use forged headers and return addresses. Even with a list of 50,000 "known spammers," most junk mail would get through.

- Blocking domains belonging to known spammers will cut out only a fraction of the junk email. Semilegitimate spammers who send torrents of email using their real domain name (a minority among spammers, sadly) are notorious for changing domains often.

The biggest obstacle to using email rules to fight spam is the ironclad limit that Outlook imposes on custom mail-handling rules. Your list of active rules can be no larger than 32KB in size. In practice, that means you can have somewhere between 30 and 70 email rules. That sounds like a lot, but if you're trying to build a spam-filtering system, it's just a start.

USING THIRD-PARTY SPAM-BLOCKING TOOLS

In just the past few years, a thriving industry has grown up around software designed to eliminate spam. The number of choices is dizzying, although most use one of a small handful of technologies. The most effective spam-fighting software uses *Bayesian analysis*, which relies on the users of the software to forward spam to a central database. The software "trains" itself by examining the messages and formulating rules based on their content.

Most third-party spam-filtering solutions communicate directly with your email server and then feed their output into Outlook. If you decide to experiment with one of these programs, you should disable Outlook's Junk E-mail filters.

12

PROTECTING YOUR PRIVACY

Everyone who markets products and services—legitimate or otherwise—via email wonders the same thing: Are my messages actually being opened and read? To answer that question, some enterprising marketers devised the *web bug*. In its sneakiest form, a web bug is an image file that consists of a single clear pixel and is literally invisible on the HTML-formatted page. Using standard mail merge techniques, the sender composes an HTML-based email message and attaches a unique identifier (a serial number, perhaps, or your email address) to the link that retrieves the web bug. When you open or preview the message, your email client connects to the server and downloads the image. By exporting the server logs into a database and cross-referencing the tags for each web bug with account details, the sender can determine that you opened the message he sent. He now knows that your email address is valid, and that you aren't blocking his address, and he's emboldened to send you more messages. The result is more junk in your Inbox.

By default, Outlook 2007 blocks all external content from being retrieved when you open or preview an HTML email message, even for messages that are not identified as junk email. The effect can be disconcerting at first, because every image that would normally appear in the message is replaced with a message box containing a red X, an explanation from Microsoft, and the alternative text associated with the image (which normally appears in the ScreenTip for the image). Figure 12.7 shows a message in which images have been blocked.

Figure 12.7
In HTML email messages, Outlook does not download external content such as images unless you specifically approve.

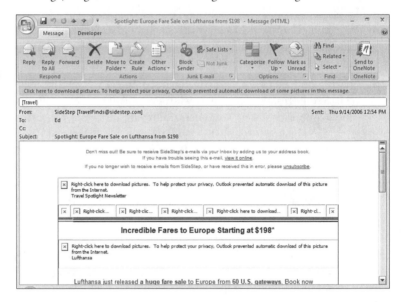

NOTE

> Outlook blocks external links to sound files as well as images, so you don't have to worry that an unsolicited message will begin playing music when you open it.

If you know that the message is one you don't want to see, just delete it. If, on the other hand, you're confident that the sender is trustworthy and the content is acceptable, right-click any image (or click the info bar at the top of the message window) and choose one of the options in the shortcut menu shown in Figure 12.8.

Choose Download Pictures to see the full contents of the current message. This is a one-time operation. The next time you receive a message from this sender, its content will again be blocked.

Click either of the bottom two choices on the menu to add the sender or the sender's domain to your Safe Sender list. This action causes Outlook to download all external content for the current message and tells Outlook that you want to download external content for any future messages from that sender or that domain.

Figure 12.8
Right-click to down-
load blocked external
content for the current
email message and to
set options for future
messages from that
sender.

When you choose to download external content for a message, Outlook downloads *all*
external content. You can't click a single blocked item and choose to download only that
image. Also, if you click any blocked image that is associated with a hyperlink, Outlook
activates the link and takes you to that external site.

Finally, click Change Automatic Download Settings to adjust the options Outlook uses for
all HTML messages that contain external content. (This dialog box is also available when
you choose Tools, Trust Center, and click the Automatic Download tab.) In the Automatic
Picture Download Settings dialog box (see Figure 12.9), you can allow all external content
to get through by clearing the check box at the top.

Even if you're not concerned about the privacy effects of Web bugs, disabling external content has one salutary effect that makes it well worthwhile: It prevents spammers from
assaulting your senses with images that try to lure you to adult-oriented sites. Displaying
graphic images in pornographic spam can be shocking, and in a business setting they can
actually constitute grounds for a lawsuit or termination. When image blocking is enabled,
the only images you'll see are those that are embedded in the message itself.

 *If some offensive images are sneaking into spam messages you receive, see "Outlook Doesn't
Block Embedded Images" in the "Troubleshooting" section at the end of this chapter.*

Figure 12.9
These default settings provide maximum privacy protection.

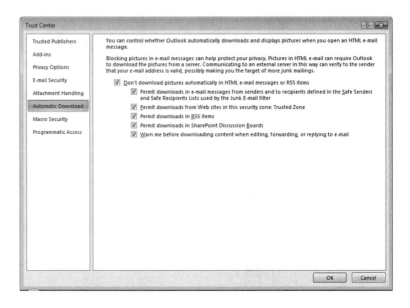

DISABLING HTML-BASED EMAIL

If you're concerned about the risks of viruses and other problems that can be spread by HTML-based email, one radical solution is to strip all graphics out of HTML-based email messages and read them as plain text. For highly security-conscious Outlook users who want nothing to do with HTML content of any sort, this option is welcome.

To use this configuration, choose Tools, Trust Center, click the E-mail Security link in the left pane, and select the Read All Standard Mail in Plain Text check box, as shown in Figure 12.10. (This option allows digitally signed messages, which are presumably from trusted senders, to be displayed with all formatting.)

Figure 12.10
This radical option converts all HTML mail to plain text. In this configuration, many messages are difficult to read, but the risk of HTML-based attacks is virtually eliminated.

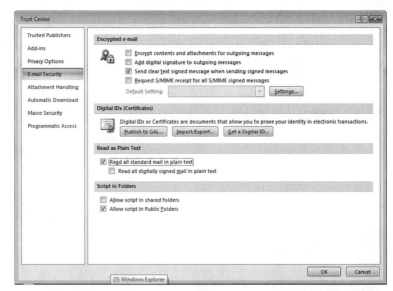

When you view an HTML message in this fashion, Outlook does not download any external content. Instead, all images and hyperlinks are converted to text-based links within angle brackets. Colors, fonts, tables, lines, and other formatting are also ignored, and the text of the message is displayed in the default plain-text font—10-point Courier New, unless you changed this setting. Any scripts or ActiveX controls are also ignored. Figure 12.11 shows an HTML message that has been converted to plain text.

Figure 12.11
When you configure Outlook to display HTML messages as plain text, graphics appear as clickable links and all formatting is stripped away.

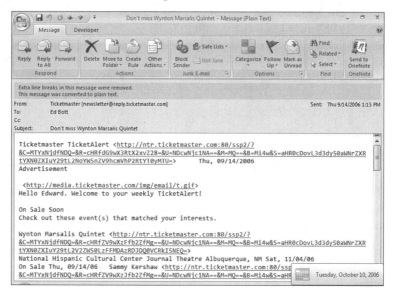

Compare that Spartan display to the properly formatted version of the same message, as shown in Figure 12.12.

Figure 12.12
Displaying HTML formatting allows email messages to appear with graphics, fonts, and tables that make them easier to read but arguably less secure.

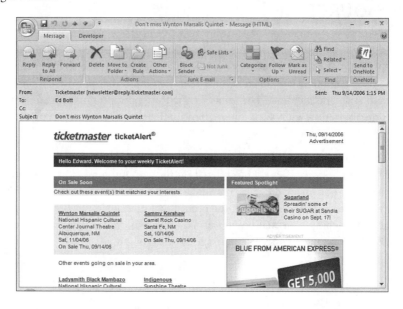

TROUBLESHOOTING

WHAT'S IN A DOMAIN NAME?

I added a domain to my Safe Senders list, but some messages coming from that domain are still being blocked. What's wrong?

As you can see when you examine the Safe Senders and Blocked Senders list, Outlook considers a domain to be everything after the @ sign. In your case, it's likely that the sender is using subdomains, such as *marketing.example.com* and *travel.example.com*. Look at the sender's address carefully and you should be able to see the full domain. Add each subdomain to your Safe Senders list and your filters will work properly again.

OUTLOOK DOESN'T BLOCK EMBEDDED IMAGES

I can see offensive images in an Outlook message I received recently, even though I have image blocking enabled and the sender is not on my Safe Senders list. Other messages display the red X that indicates a blocked image. What's the problem with this message?

The most likely answer is that the sender has embedded the image directly into the message, using MIME encoding. Because the image is not being downloaded from an external server, Outlook doesn't block it. The good news is that this sort of image doesn't represent a threat to your privacy. The bad news is there's no truly effective way to prevent these images from displaying. If you're plagued by a particular sender, you may be able to block that sender or create a rule that identifies messages based on the message header.

SECRETS OF THE OFFICE MASTERS: TRACKING DOWN THE SOURCE OF SPAM

These days, spam comes from every part of the globe. As often as not, the details you see when you open the message are forged. It's trivially easy to fake a return address—you can enter any name and address you want, and every link in the chain of email servers that leads to your computer will dutifully maintain the fiction that your email message comes from that name and address. (The same is true, for that matter, of most modern viruses, which forge the return address to divert attention from the computer that's the actual source of the infection.)

The only way to track down the true source of an email message is to look at the *message headers*. These are the technical details at the top of the message, normally hidden from view, that document the path a message takes over the Internet. Although some parts of a message header can be forged, the crucial details that show which servers it passed through before reaching your mailbox are usually accurate. And if you learn how to decode a message header, you can often trace a message back to its source.

To view the complete headers for a message in Outlook 2007, follow these steps:

1. Double-click the message to open it in its own window.

2. Click the small box in the lower-right corner of the label for the Options group to open the Message Options dialog box for the selected message (see Figure 12.13).

3. Scroll through the Internet Headers box to see the full headers for the message.

Figure 12.13

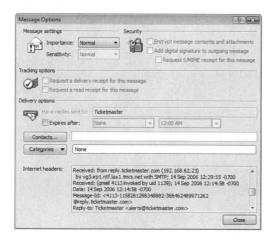

The most important block of information appears near the top, in a block starting with the word Received. These headers are automatically inserted by each SMTP server in the chain that led to your computer. Most mail servers add enough information for you to identify the chain of servers through which the message passed. The entry at the top of the list shows the final transfer and should include the name of your mail server. One entry in the Received block should show the IP address of the sender, although a crafty spammer may try to disguise some of this information.

Armed with this detail, you can use a site like `http://samspade.org` to identify the network that the spam came from originally. If the problem is persistent, a complaint to the administrator of that network may be in order.

When sending a spam-related complaint, be sure to include the full message, including all headers. To copy the details text to the Clipboard, right-click any portion of the Details window and choose Select All; then right-click again and choose Copy. This allows you to paste the full header and the unedited text of the message into an email message or another window.

12

Using Word

13 Building a Better Word Document   329

14 Using Themes, Styles, and Templates   387

15 Advanced Document Formatting   415

16 Professional Document Tools and Advanced Document Sharing   455

17 Letters, Envelopes, and Data-Driven Documents   477

CHAPTER 13

BUILDING A BETTER WORD DOCUMENT

In this chapter

What's New in Word 2007?   330

Choosing the Right Document View   332

Navigating Through a Word Document   342

Understanding Your Formatting Options   346

Changing Text Formatting   356

Changing Paragraph Formatting   358

Entering Text Automatically   365

Using Bullets, Numbering, and Multilevel Lists   367

Finding and Replacing Text and Formatting   369

Checking Spelling, Contextual Spelling, and Grammar   374

Printing Word Documents   376

Customizing the Word Interface   379

Troubleshooting   384

Secrets of the Office Masters: Using Word as a Blog Editor   385

WHAT'S NEW IN WORD 2007?

Odds are good that when you picked up this book, you turned right to this chapter. Although applications like Excel and PowerPoint have a large user base in the working world and student world, Word is the most widely used application of the suite and hence, the most popular.

The first MS-DOS version of Word was released in 1983 (more than 20 years ago) and since that time it has evolved substantially. In 1989, Word for Windows was released and subsequent versions were to follow, each release being more impressive and useful. There are some, however, who believe that the overall pattern of useful changes reached a peak in Word 2000. "What more could be changed?" and "Why should I pay for additional functionality I don't need?" have been the usual complaints over the past few years. Indeed, "What's New in Word 2007" becomes more of a question than a statement in the mind of the software consumer.

The answer? Everything—and for the better. After a first look at the interface with the new Ribbon toolbar design, the sleek design, and certainly the detailed eye-candy icons, you can't help but say, "Oh! Well, this is pretty awesome," or whichever words better suit your personality. Word 2007 has become the Ferrari of the word processing world. You are going to love it, even though it requires some time to adjust to the new layout. This chapter and the ones to follow will assist you in getting you in the driver's seat.

TIP FROM

Ed & Woody

For Word 2003 users, Microsoft has provided an excellent tool to help you find your way in Word 2007 more easily. In the upper-right corner of Word 2007 is a blue circle with a question mark. This is Word Help (or you can simply press F1). In your search box, type `"Interactive: Word 2003 to Word 2007 command reference guide"`. This guide will cover the more popular commands from Word 2003 to 2007 in a dynamic Flash interface (which requires that you have version 7 or later of the Macromedia Flash Player).

At its core, Word 2007 retains the same basic structure and toolset that allows you to format text, design impressive documentation, collaborate on projects and so forth. But by enhancing the way we work, through the use of the Ribbon, now the more commonly used commands are brought right to the forefront in a set of tabs, so you no longer need to spend an excessive amount of time searching for them. (Now if only we could get our keyboards changed to Dvorak from Qwerty, we would really be moving.)

Figure 13.1 shows most of Word's new interface elements.

Figure 13.1
The Ribbon is the strip across the top of Word that now brings your formatting commands right to the forefront. Less searching for what you want means more productivity.

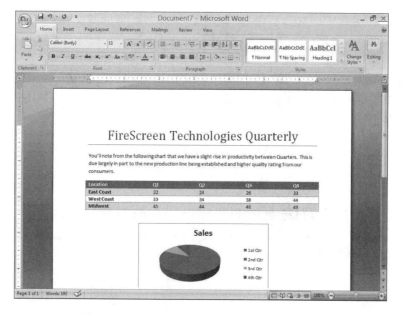

Here's a list of some of the enhanced features of Word 2007:

- **Ribbon tabs**—Menus? Gone. Toolbars? Gone (mostly). For the core programs in the Office family, you now interact with the program using the Ribbon. For example, Word 2007 has tabs for writing, inserting, page layout, working with references, mailings, and document review.

- **Contextual tabs**—There are definitely times when we don't need to see a particular tab and other times when we do. For example, it's not until you actually create a table that the Design tabs show up to allow you to change the formatting for that table. This leaves your workspace less cluttered and gives you the tools you need, when you need them.

- **Gallery options**—Now you can see how a formatting choice will impact your documents before even applying it. Galleries give you the capability to see preconfigured views of formatting changes. The Galleries are preconfigured for style changes, table formatting, lists, graphics, and so on. And you can configure your own formatting options to add to the galleries.

- **Live views**—One of the cooler features in Word 2007 is the capability to dynamically see formatting changes to your text when you move your pointer over different formatting choices in your ribbons. This is a great time-saver because you already know that you like a look before you choose it.

- **Quick Access Toolbar**—We said the toolbars were gone but Microsoft realizes that there are times when we need to customize the way we work and have access to specific tools at all times, regardless of the ribbon we are working on. The Quick Access Toolbar allows you to add commands that are either on your Ribbon tabs, but you simply want them available at all times off the toolbar, or are not available because they aren't popular commands to choose. You can customize your Quick Access Toolbar by adding these buttons.

- **Additional new features**—Word 2007 includes an impressive list of updates that will be covered throughout these five chapters, including the following: Quick Styles, ,document themes, the spelling checker, enhancements including dictionaries, grammar, and translation support changes, document revisions and collaborating features including metadata removal, digital signature support, the capability to save files in PDF or XPS formats, and a host of other new features.

It's nice to talk about all the changes, but let's get into the real inner workings of Word 2007, starting with the View—and we don't mean that ever popular talk show with Barbara Walters.

CHOOSING THE RIGHT DOCUMENT VIEW

Working styles vary from person to person and the way we choose to view our documents while we work on them is no different. Different document views have their own advantages. Most advanced Word users will find themselves switching views as they work on documents, particularly more complex documents, depending on what they're trying to accomplish.

USING BUILT-IN VIEWS

The five main document views in Word 2007 are Print Layout, Full Screen Reading, Web Layout, Outline, and Draft.

NOTE

> It would be good to note that users who formerly used the Normal view in their documents will find the same functionality under the Draft view, which will be discussed shortly. In addition, the Reading Layout view has been redesigned as the Full Screen Reading view.

Select a document view by clicking the View tab and note the Document Views grouping on the left side of the ribbon.

TIP FROM

Ed & Woody

> In the status bar, visible at the bottom of the document window, you'll see icons for each of the five main views in the right side of the status bar. You can choose to remove these from the status bar by right-clicking the status bar and deselecting the View Shortcuts option.

PRINT LAYOUT

Print Layout view (see Figure 13.2) shows the document precisely as it will be printed, with page breaks, headers and footers, and pictures arranged correctly onscreen. (In previous Office versions, this view was called Page Layout view.)

Figure 13.2
Print Layout shows a true WYSIWYG (what you see is what you get) view of your document.

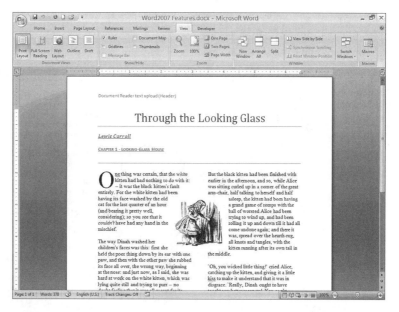

Unless they specifically need one of the tools available in the other views, many advanced Word users work in Print Layout view because there are no surprises. The rendition on the screen closely mimics what will appear on paper.

FULL-SCREEN READING

Word 2007 brings forward this view, formerly known as Reading Layout, which was introduced in Word 2003. This view was specifically designed to make documents more legible onscreen. In Full Screen Reading view, Word uses the same fonts as in the original document; however, the display uses ClearType technology to make text easier on the eyes, and you can easily increase or decrease the size of the fonts without changing the formatting of the document itself. Unlike the Web and Print Layout views, which are designed to display pages exactly as the designer intended them to be viewed (in a browser or on paper), pages in Full Screen Reading view are rearranged to fit well on the screen, as shown in Figure 13.3. What you see, in other words, is not at all what you'd get on paper.

> **NOTE**
>
> One of the reasons for the overall improvement of document reading in Word 2007 is that the default font for the entire Office suite has been changed from Times New Roman to a new ClearType font called Calibri. ClearType provides a crisper display on modern monitors. There are six new fonts being used by Microsoft to take advantage of the ClearType technology, including Calibri, Cambria, Consolas, Candara, Corbel, and Constantia.

To change to Full Screen Reading view, you can select the option from the View ribbon tab with the Document Views grouping. You can also select it from your status bar at the bottom of the document window. Within Full Screen Reading view, you can show the Document Map and the Thumbnails pane (both of which are described in the next section).

13

When you are in Full Screen Reading, the ribbon tabs are hidden to maximize your viewing area. Toward the top of the view are the View Options (shown in greater detail in Figure 13.4), where you can make some necessary adjustments to the view.

Figure 13.3
Full Screen Reading view alters the arrangement of text on the page so it's easier to read.

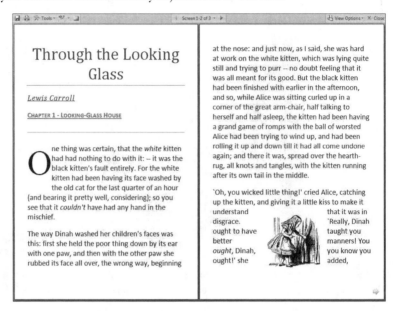

Figure 13.4
Customizing the Full Screen Reading view.

Let's consider the options available:

- **Don't Open Attachments in Full Screen**—The default configuration for documents that come from email or a SharePoint site is to open Full Screen. You can select this option to turn this off. However, email will open in Full Screen Reading view. To stop that from occurring, see the tip below.

- **Increase/Decrease Text Size**—Remember, altering the size of the text in Full Screen Reading view doesn't affect the text in the document itself. It only makes it easier to read.

- **Show One/Two Pages**—Logically, again, this will assist you in reading. Some want the center of their screen to hold the page they are reading, others may prefer for it to look more like a book with two pages to view.

- **Show Printed Page**—Shows the pages as they would really look in Print. In this case, you aren't taking advantage of the capability to see text more easily for reading, but maybe that's not what you need. Perhaps you just want a simple way to read through a document but want to see it as it will print.

- **Margin Settings**—These aren't the literal margin settings for the document. These settings are solely for the reading view.

- **Allow Typing**—Ordinarily within the reader you don't have the capability to type and edit the documents. With this setting you can allow the capability to edit as you read.

- **Track Changes**—Will allow you to track changes, change tracking options, and change the username.

- **Show Comments and Changes**—Allows you to select what type of markups to show while you review the document. You can determine if you want to see Comments, Ink, Insertions and Deletions, and so on. In addition, you can determine which reviewers you want to see.

- **Show Original/Final Document**—Allows you to view either the original or final document, with or without the changes applied.

On the left side, at the top, you can use the shortcut toolbar to Save or Print your file. You can select the Tools option, which allows the following resources:

- **Research**—Look up words in a variety of resources while you are working.

- **Translation Screen Tip**—Allows you to select another language (especially Spanish) and then when you hold your cursor over a word, it will translate that word for you.

- **Text Highlight Color**—You can select your Highlighter tool and alter the color choices to mark up the document (note that these highlights stay with the document when you leave Full Screen Reader view). This option also exists on the shortcut toolbar.

- **New Comment**—You can add comments to the document. This option also exists on the shortcut toolbar.

- **Find**—Search for text within the document while you work in Reader view.

13

Moving from page to page is simple using the up and down arrow keys or the right and left arrow keys to navigate through your documents. In addition, as you move your cursor toward one side or another, it turns into a hand that will allow you to turn the pages with a click of your mouse. Finally, at the bottom of the pages are arrows that you can select to move from page to page. To exit Full Screen Reading view, click the Close button on the top right of the document.

TIP FROM

When you open a Word document you received as an attachment to an Outlook email message, Word automatically opens it in Full Screen Reading view. This is to allow you to get the maximum amount of screen space to view the document comfortably. To change this default setting, select your Office button (the big circle in the top-left corner of your screen—don't worry, you'll get used to the new vocabulary) and go to the Word Options. Under the Popular selection is a setting selected by default, titled Open Email Attachments in Full Screen Reading View. If you deselect this option, the attachments will open in Print Layout view.

WEB LAYOUT VIEW

Of course, if you aren't going to put the document on paper, but instead intend to publish on the Web, it's important to see how the document will look when viewed as an HTML file. That's where Web Layout view comes in.

In Web Layout view, Word wraps text to fit the window, shows backgrounds, and places graphics on the screen the same way they would appear in a browser.

TIP FROM

If you want to see how the document will appear in your default web browser—after all, each browser shows pages differently—this requires some changes to your Word Options. In Word 2003, you could choose Web Page Preview from the File menu. But now you have to select your Office button, go to your Word Options, and then to Customize. Under the drop-down box Choose Commands From, you can select Commands Not in the Ribbon and scroll down to find the Web Page Preview command and add it to your Quick Access Toolbar.

OUTLINE VIEW

Outline view (see Figure 13.5) allows you to see an outline of your document while you're working on it. This view can be particularly helpful for rearranging sections of large documents or promoting and demoting headings. The premise is that you can focus on section headings easily and don't have to deal with actual contents. So a large master document that may be 50 pages in length, if properly formatted using Heading styles, could be outlined into a simple one-page view that can be easily manipulated.

Figure 13.5
Outline view shows the document's structure and lets you freely move elements.

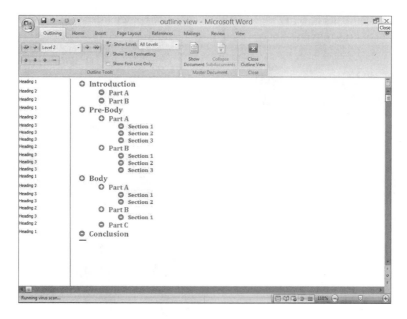

TIP FROM

Ed & Woody

> If you use Word's default Heading styles, outline levels are maintained for you. Otherwise, you can set your own outline levels in the dialog box that appears when you select the Paragraph grouping box on the Home ribbon tab. This will allow you to change the Outline level of a particular paragraph. If you use the built-in Heading styles, Word modifies the style for a given heading as you promote or demote it, using the arrow buttons in Outline view.

All the normal editing techniques are available in Outline view: You can select, drag, copy, cut, and paste, as you would in any other view.

DRAFT VIEW

You may have been slightly worried to notice that the Normal view is missing in the fab five view grouping. If you are a fan of Normal view, don't worry, it's been rereleased as Draft view.

Draft view has three advantages that appeal to advanced users:

- You can see section breaks. If you have more than one section in a document, you should seriously consider working in Draft view when formatting or entering text. Although you can see section breaks in Print Layout view, in Draft view the actual formatting change brought about by a section or page break doesn't distract you from the work at hand of editing document text.

- You can see style names for all paragraphs in a column to the left of the document. To turn on the hidden side panel in these views, you need to first go to your Office button and then select the Word Options button. Go to the Advanced section for all the advanced settings. Scroll down to the Display settings and notice the option Style Area

Pane Width in Draft and Outline views. Type in a reasonable size in inches for you to be able to view your styles in both Draft and Outline views (see Figure 13.6).

Figure 13.6
Draft view shows section breaks and style settings without cluttering your workspace with certain layout elements and pictures.

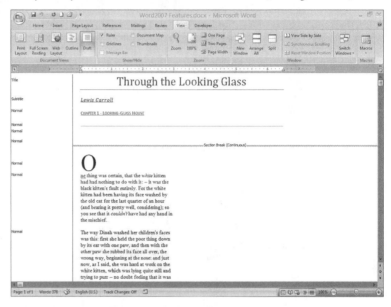

After you make the style area visible, you may decide you need a larger or smaller area to view. You can use the mouse to drag it to a new width. However, if you drag the style area back to 0 width, the only way to make it visible again is with the Word Options settings.

- Draft view hides certain layout elements, including headers and footers, background images, drawing objects, and any picture that doesn't use the In Line with Text wrapping style. As a result, you can scroll through complex documents much faster in Draft view than in Print Layout view. When editing an exceptionally large file on a computer with limited resources, the difference in scrolling speed can be considerable.

NAVIGATING WITH THUMBNAILS AND THE DOCUMENT MAP

Word provides two tools for keeping track of a document's navigation structure while you edit it. In all views, you can take advantage of a new interface element in Word 2007—a Thumbnails pane that appears along the left side of the document window, giving you a big-picture look at multipage documents and providing clickable links to each page. To make this pane visible, choose the View ribbon, and select Thumbnails under the Show/Hide grouping. To resize the Thumbnails pane, click and drag its right edge; to make it disappear quickly, double-click the right edge.

The Document Map (see Figure 13.7) shows an alternative view of the document's outline, using the same outline levels employed in Outline view. It occupies the same space as the Thumbnails pane. Note that you cannot configure Word to show both elements at once

Figure 13.7
If you have enough room on the screen, Document Map offers one-click navigation to any heading in a document.

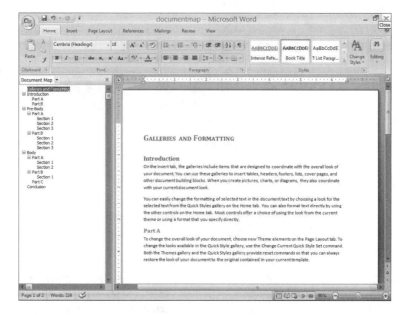

NOTE

You can toggle back and forth between Document Map and Thumbnails through a small Switch Navigation window within the tools themselves.

To view a Document Map, choose the View ribbon and then Document Map under the Show/Hide grouping. Right-click any empty space in the Document Map pane to expand or collapse a specific heading or to hide headings below a selected outline level. For Document Map to display anything useful to you, you need to apply the built-in heading styles to the headings within your document. Otherwise, the results would be confusing to say the least.

The Document Map is "hot" in the sense that you can click anywhere in the map and be transported to that location in your document. Unlike Outline view, it is not designed to offer interactive editing features—you can't promote or demote headings in the Document Map—but experienced Word users who commonly deal with long documents can readily navigate with it.

ZOOM OPTIONS

Word lets you "zoom" a document, making it appear larger or smaller on the screen, by going to the View ribbon and looking in the Zoom group (see Figure 13.8). In addition, you can use the Zoom selection button in the status bar at the bottom of your document screen or the Zoom Slider (sliding to the percentage zoom you would like) in the status bar.

13

Figure 13.8
Zoom in (using a higher percentage number) to see more detail; zoom out to see more of the page.

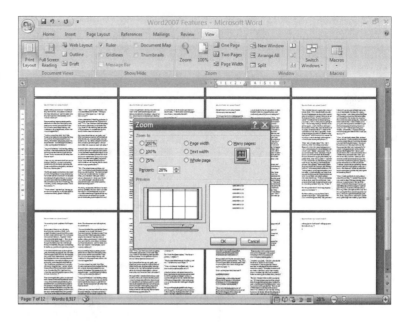

Fine-tune the Zoom percentage to make your fonts more legible. For day-to-day use, you want the largest zoom factor that lets you see your most commonly used fonts without straining. Also, double-check to ensure that your zoom setting lets you easily distinguish, visually, between normal, bold, and italic characters.

In Print Layout view only (although other views allow various zoom capability), you can use the Zoom dialog box or the Zoom control on the status bar to choose automatic scaling options: Zoom the display to the width of a page, fit just the text on the page, view an entire page, or see two pages side by side. The Zoom dialog box includes one additional control that you can use to view multiple pages. Now, keep in mind this option is grayed out in all views except for Print Layout view. You can use this option to see all the pages of your document and this can be quite helpful for seeing the layout of all your data, illustrations, charting, and so forth. If your mouse is equipped with a wheel, you can zoom in 10% increments by holding down the Ctrl key as you rotate the wheel up or down.

Some like to have a document or template that is perfectly tailored to their way of work. In harmony with that, it's worth noting that you can save your Zoom settings with a document or template. You have to make at least one change in the document and then save it. With a template, for example, if you open it up, add a space, and then delete that space, configure your Zoom settings, and then save it, your settings are now part of the template.

Splitting a Document Window

Word allows you to split the document window, giving you two independently scrollable panes looking in on the same document, one over the other (see Figure 13.9). Although each of the panes operates independently—you can even have Draft view in one pane, and

Outline view in the other—it's important to realize that you have just one copy of the document open: Changes made in one pane are reflected immediately in the other. This can be useful because it allows you to compare parts of a document side by side, even when they're widely separated in the document.

Figure 13.9
Split the document window into two separately maintained panes. Split panes enable you to view different parts of the same document simultaneously.

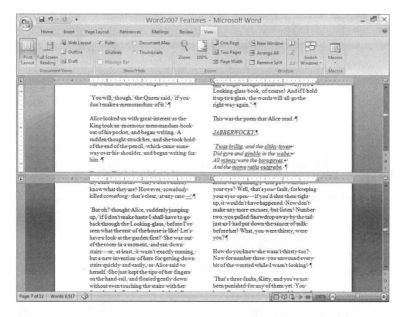

To split the document window, go to the View ribbon tab and under the Window grouping select the Split option. Click and drag the split bar to resize the document panes. Double-click the split bar to restore the window to a single pane or select the View ribbon tab again and choose the Remove Split option (which appears after you split your Window).

NOTE

You cannot split the document window if the Document Map or Thumbnails pane is active. In fact, the setting itself will gray out with those options active.

Under the Window grouping on the View ribbon tab, you also have the capability to open your document in a totally new window if you are uncomfortable with the split-screen effect. You can open an additional Window and then use Arrange All to organize all your working documents neatly.

VIEWING DOCUMENTS SIDE BY SIDE

Sometimes you have two documents that you want to manually look at next to each other—no fancy merge tools, just your own eyes looking from one document to another. In harmony with this, you can utilize the tools that allow you to view documents side by side. If you visit the View ribbon tab again and look under the Window grouping, you can see you have three options to choose from.

13

- **View Side by Side**—To start with, you need to have both documents open that you want to compare. Then select the View Side by Side option and you will see a dialog box asking you to choose which document (in the event you have more than two open at the same time).

- **Synchronous Scrolling**—Sounds like an Olympic event (and if Microsoft has a say, one day it may be) but in reality, it allows you the capability to scroll both documents in unison. If you don't want to do that, you can turn this off anytime and enable it again when you choose.

- **Reset Window Position**—At times you might adjust the windows to let you see more of something onscreen. This button allows you to reestablish the original positioning of the two documents.

NAVIGATING THROUGH A WORD DOCUMENT

Word offers an enormous number of ways to move through a document, and most people can increase their productivity by learning some of the shortcuts.

You needn't memorize dozens of key combinations or obscure mouse tricks to boost your productivity, and the amount of time you need to invest is negligible. If you concentrate on reducing the effort you expend on the two or three navigational techniques you use most, your productivity will soar.

Not all the best navigation tricks are well known, either. Some of them aren't even documented. In this chapter, we promise we won't just throw lists of shortcuts at you; instead, we'll teach you some tricks for memorizing the most important ones.

USING THE KEYBOARD TO MOVE THROUGH A DOCUMENT

Aside from the obvious up, down, left, and right arrows, the most useful keyboard shortcuts for navigating around a document are listed in Table 13.1.

TABLE 13.1 NAVIGATION KEYS IN WORD

To Move	Press
Next word to right	Ctrl+Right Arrow
Next word to left	Ctrl+Left Arrow
One paragraph up	Ctrl+Up Arrow
One paragraph down	Ctrl+Down Arrow
To beginning of line	Home
To end of line	End
Up one screen	Page Up (PgUp)
To beginning of first line of current screen	Alt+Ctrl+Page Up

To Move	Press
Down one screen	Page Down (PgDn)
To end of last line of current screen	Alt+Ctrl+Page Down
To beginning of document	Ctrl+Home
To end of document	Ctrl+End

Most experienced Word users would benefit from memorizing three groups of shortcut keys from those in Table 18.1, and they're all based on the Ctrl key. Here are the combinations, followed by the way the Ctrl key changes the keys you're probably accustomed to:

- **Ctrl+Home/Ctrl+End**—Go to the beginning/end of the document (instead of beginning/end of line).
- **Ctrl+Left/Right Arrow**—Move by words (instead of characters).
- **Ctrl+Up/Down Arrow**—Move by paragraphs (instead of lines).

TIP FROM

EQ & Woody

> Possibly the most useful, but obscure, key combination in Word is Shift+F5. Word keeps track of the last three locations where you edited text. Pressing Shift+F5 cycles through those three locations. This setting is persistent, too. When you open a document, if you want to return to the last location you were editing, press Shift+F5.
>
> In addition, while we are discussing shortcut keys, in the Find and Replace dialog box is a feature called Go, which will be fully explained later on in the chapter (along with Find and Replace). You go to any of those tools quickly by pressing Ctrl+G for Go, Ctrl+F for Find, and Ctrl+H for Replace.

USING THE MOUSE TO MOVE THROUGH A DOCUMENT

Word follows most of the standard Windows mouse navigation techniques, with a few interesting twists, as described in Table 13.2.

TABLE 13.2 MOUSE NAVIGATION TECHNIQUES IN WORD

To Scroll	Do This...
Up one screen	Click above the scroll handle.
Down one screen	Click below the scroll handle.
To a specific page	Drag the scroll handle and watch the ScreenTips for page numbers.
In Draft view, scroll left, into the margin	Press Shift and click the arrow at the left of the horizontal scrollbar.

If you have a mouse with a scroll wheel, such as the Microsoft IntelliMouse, additional mouse navigation options may be available. See the documentation that came with your wheel mouse for more details.

13

NAVIGATING WITH THE DOCUMENT MAP

By far the most powerful way to navigate through a long document with the mouse is via Word's Document Map. It's particularly valuable for advanced Word users who have to navigate through documents that are more than, for instance, five pages in length. If you've avoided using the Document Map because of unpleasant experiences with earlier Word versions, try it again. In Word 2007, this feature is robust and works exactly as you'd expect.

The Document Map is a "hot" outline of the document's contents—similar to a Table of Contents—which appears in a pane to the left of the document itself. If you take a little care in applying heading styles, the entire structure of your document appears in the Document Map, and each important point is directly accessible.

Because the Document Map table is "hot," you can click a heading and jump immediately to the corresponding point in the document. You can use section headings or chapter numbers, for instance, to navigate using the Document Map pane.

Word constructs the Document Map based on outline levels, as defined in paragraph styles. If you stick to the standard Word heading styles—Heading 1, Heading 2, and so on—the outline levels are automatically applied by Word (Level 1, Level 2, and so on). If you use your own styles, they can have whatever outline level you want to apply.

→ For more details on styles, **see** "Formatting a Document with Styles," **p. 391**.

→ For details on changing the outline level and other paragraph format settings, **see** "Adjusting Paragraph Alignment," **p. 359**.

TIP FROM

Ed & Woody

> Want to change the look of the text in the Document Map? No problem, as long as you know where to look. This setting is controlled by a hidden style; if you make it visible, you can adjust it. To start, go to your Home ribbon tab and select the Styles widget arrow from the Styles grouping. A side bar opens, and at the bottom select the Manage Styles button. From here go to the Edit tab and scroll down to find the Document Map style. Select the style and choose Modify and then you can alter the text to look however you like. Another option, if you want to change your Document Map style often, is to go into Manage Styles tools and go to the Recommend tab. Select the Document Map and the Show button so that now you can visibly see it in the Styles grouping of your Home ribbon, where you can change the font, font size, color, and other settings.

NAVIGATING THROUGH DOCUMENTS WITH THE SELECT BROWSE OBJECT MENU

In the lower-right corner of the Word window—below the vertical scrollbar's down arrow—you'll find a remarkable collection of three buttons that let you browse through your document by jumping from object to object. In this case, the "objects" can be any of a dozen common types of Word data, including fields, comments, pictures, pages, and headings. (Don't confuse this menu with the similarly named Object Browser in the Visual Basic Editor.)

Browsing by object generally works best if you use it this way:

1. Click the circle in the middle (the Select Browse Object button) and select one of the 12 Browse By boxes.

2. Click the Next button (the double down arrow, just below the Select Browse Object button) to search toward the end of the document for the next occurrence (the next picture, for instance, if you chose Browse by Graphic). Click the Previous button (the double up arrow just above the Select Browse Object button) to search toward the beginning of the document. If you have trouble clicking these undersized buttons, use the keyboard shortcuts instead: Ctrl+Page Up and Ctrl+Page Down.

You can search for the following "objects":

- **Fields**—Word moves from field to field, although it skips hidden fields (such as {XE}, the field that creates entries for a document's index).

→ To learn how you can empower your documents with fields, **see** "Using Fields to Add Intelligence to a Document," **p. 496**.

- **Endnotes**—An endnote is typically used to cite sources in a formal document; it consists of a *note reference mark*, which is embedded in text, and the note itself, which appears at the end of the document. If you start in the body of the document, Word jumps through the document, stopping at each note reference mark. If you start in an endnote, Word cycles through each of the endnotes.

- **Footnotes**—Footnotes are constructed like endnotes, except that the note portion appears at the bottom of the page containing the note reference mark. If you start in the body of the document, Word jumps from one note reference mark to the next. If you start inside a footnote, each click selects the next footnote.

- **Comments**—The Next button works differently, depending on whether comments are visible on the page. If you position the insertion point inside a comment and click the Next button, you'll go to the next comment. If comments are hidden, clicking the Next button goes to the next comment marker. Using the Previous button jumps through the body of the document, from one comment marker to the next, regardless of whether comments are visible.

- **Sections**—Word moves from the beginning of one document section to the next.

→ Ever used sections before? Many Word users haven't, at least knowingly. **See** "Page/Section Setup Options," **p. 354**.

- **Pages**—Word moves to the top of the next or previous page.

- **Go To**—This is the most interesting of the Select Browse Object options. When you click the Go To box on the Select Browse Object menu, Word opens the Go To dialog box. Go To includes most of the other options on the Select Browse Object menu (Page, Section, Field, and so on), as well as Line, Bookmark, Equation, and a confusingly named Object option, which goes to the next OLE Object.

  Using the Go To box and the Select Browse Object menu together make it easy to navigate through a document in creative ways. To see all the bookmarks in a document, one after the other, click the Select Browse Object menu, and then click Go To (or choose

13

Edit, Go To). In the Go to What box, select Bookmark. Click the Go To button. From that point on, each time you click the Previous button or press Ctrl+Page Down, you'll go to the next bookmark in the document. In a heavily commented document, you can choose Comment from the Go to What box, select an individual reviewer's name, and begin browsing. Choose Line and enter +10 to jump forward 10 lines at a time.

- **Find**—Same as choosing Find from the Editing grouping on the Home ribbon tab. We discuss the Find dialog box at length in the next section.

  After you've set up a Find or Replace, the easiest way to repeat the Find or Replace is to clear the dialog box away and use the keyboard shortcut Ctrl+Page Down (or Ctrl+Page Up to search backward).

- **Edits**—Word automatically keeps track of the last three locations where you've made changes. This setting lets you cycle among the three edits (the same as the Shift+F5 keyboard shortcut). Note that these changes may be in different documents.

- **Heading**—Cycles to the beginning of each paragraph in the document that is formatted with a Heading *n* style, where *n* is any integer between 1 and 9.

- **Graphic**—Moves to the next or previous picture in the document (whether linked or embedded), or to the next or previous drawing canvas. This option ignores pictures and drawing canvases in the drawing layer.

- **Table**—Cycles through all the Word tables in the document.

UNDERSTANDING YOUR FORMATTING OPTIONS

Every Word document consists of components arranged in a strict hierarchy that is unrelated to the way you create a document. Inside a Word document, data is stored in a predictable hierarchy, consisting of one or more sections, which in turn contain one or more paragraphs, each of which consists of one or more characters. Although it's possible to select an entire document and apply formatting to it, Word doesn't actually format at the document level; instead, it applies your changes individually to characters, paragraphs, and sections within the document.

Word allows you to apply formatting directly, by making a selection and then going to the Home ribbons tab where you will find your Font, Paragraph, and Styles grouping all in one place. On the Home ribbon, you will also find the Format Painter, a helpful tool for applying formatting from one item to others. You can also apply formatting more easily in Word 2007 through the use of a floating formatting panel. This is a major time-saver because the formatting options are right in front of you (as you can see in Figure 13.10).

You can define collections of character or paragraph formatting choices, save them as named styles, and then apply the style to selected characters or paragraphs. Now let's get into the philosophy of formatting.

13

Figure 13.10
The floating formatting panel appears to assist you.

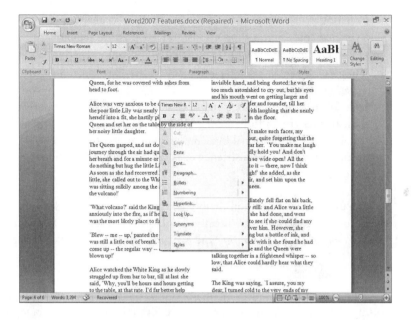

DIRECT FORMATTING VERSUS STYLES AND THEMES

For simple, short documents, it's often easiest to apply formatting directly to paragraphs and characters through the Home ribbon tools. You could, however, utilize styles or themes even in smaller documents, if you are interested in consistency of the look of certain documents. But especially in documents that extend beyond a few pages or where formatting is crucial, you want to make good use of Styles and Themes.

→ Styles and Themes will be covered in greater detail in the next chapter. **p. 387**.

NOTE

> Themes are a new introduction in Word 2007. If you've used PowerPoint, you already know the value of being able to establish a theme over your slide show that will maintain a consistent look throughout your slides. The concept is carried over into Document Themes (or just Themes), which allow you to quickly and easily apply formatting to an entire document. A theme has a preconfigured set of choices, such as heading and body fonts, theme colors, and theme effects. In addition, you can create your own themes or alter a preexisting theme.

From a practical standpoint, let's take a look at the three available options:

- **Manual Formatting**—Gives you complete control over the formatting for every last character, word, table, and graphic of your entire document. If you have a small document or simply like maintaining the control of your own formatting, manual is the way to go.

- **Styles**—Styles have one great advantage over manually applied formatting: When you change a style, your changes ripple throughout the document and are applied to all other text formatted with the style of the same name. Using styles doesn't mean

13

forfeiting your control. As you will see in the next chapter, you are in control of the styles you apply if you choose to be. But it's good to remember that a large document, or one that requires consistency, is one where you want to make use of Styles.

- **Themes**—Themes have the advantage of altering a document immediately with the selection of a theme choice, and then changing that document completely (fonts, styles, table formatting, graphic formatting) simply by applying a different theme. In addition, these themes are uniform among Word, Excel, and PowerPoint, allowing you to maintain a specific professional look among your applications. So, when you have large documents and want consistency (especially among applications), consider the use of a theme.

So, it's a user-oriented decision. Before you can truly master Styles and Themes, you need to have a good understanding of direct formatting. Word supports two kinds of formatting options: *character (font) formatting* and *paragraph formatting*. Let's get started.

CHARACTER FORMATS

Character formats apply to letters, numbers, and punctuation marks. The most common formatting options that apply to characters are font related: the font name, size, and color, for example, as well as attributes such as bold, italic, underline, and strikethrough. If you copy or move a formatted character from one part of a document to another, the formatting travels with it.

Three special characters merit close attention:

- Each space is a character. Although you can't see its color, you can easily note its size: A 10-point space takes up much less room on a line than a 48-point space.

- Within a Word document, a tab is a character. When Word encounters a tab character, it shifts to the next tab stop before continuing to lay down text.

- A paragraph mark is technically a character as well, although you can't print a paragraph mark. By default, Word does not show paragraph marks on the screen, but they're always there. You can select, copy, move, or delete paragraph marks.

You may want to see your spaces and paragraph markings. To accomplish this you can do the following:

- **Reveal Formatting**—Formerly under the Format menu selection, now you can see the Reveal Formatting options by selecting Shift+F1 or by customizing your Quick Access Toolbar. After you open the Reveal Formatting task pane, you can select the Show All Formatting Marks check box.

- **Show/Hide ¶**—A button that looks like a paragraph located on the Home ribbon tab under the Paragraph grouping.

- **Word Options**—From the Office button, you can select your Word Options and go to the Display section. From here you can decide to view tab characters, spaces, paragraph marks, hidden text, optional hyphens, and object anchors. Or you could turn them all on.

The most common character treatment options are available via ribbon selections and keyboard shortcuts. For example, you can click the Bold, Italic, or Underline buttons on the Home ribbon under the Font grouping, or use the shortcut key combinations Ctrl+B, Ctrl+I, Ctrl+U, respectively, to toggle these formatting options for selected text. You could also use the floating formatting panel.

TIP FROM

Here's a formatting shortcut even many experienced Word users don't know about. If you position the insertion point within a word and click a formatting button or key combination, the formatting applies to the entire word. In this case, a "word" is any series of characters delimited on each end by a space or punctuation mark. Use this option to change the font, size, or attributes of a word without selecting it first. Another related quirk is worth noting: If you place the insertion point within a word and choose a paragraph style, Word applies the style to the entire paragraph; but if you select the entire word and change the style, the style is applied only to that word. I know what you might be thinking—why do we park in the driveway and drive on the parkway?

When you start typing in a new blank document, Word's default setup uses 11-point Calibri (the replacement for Times New Roman). To change the default font and size, go to the Home ribbon, to the Font grouping, and select the handle in the left corner to open the Font dialog box. Select the Font you want to use and then choose the Default button on the bottom left of the box (see Figure 13.11).

Figure 13.11
Change the default font for all documents by selecting the font you prefer and then clicking the Default button (bottom left).

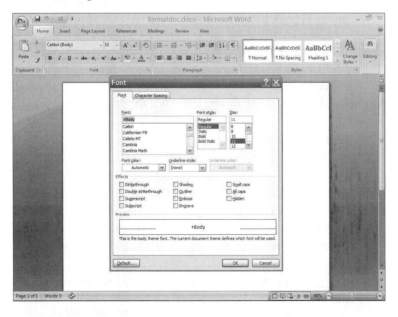

Character spacing can be changed in any number of ways: moving characters above or below the baseline (superscripting and subscripting); magnifying or reducing selected groups of characters (scale); and even squishing together predefined pairs of letters that fit well together—such as VA—to minimize the whitespace between them (kerning). All these are discussed in the next section.

Word also supports *highlighting*, a method of changing the background color of selected text much as you would mark up a paper document with a highlighting pen. Although highlighting is rarely used in final documents, it's a handy way to draw attention to text during reviews, or to emphasize pieces of text for your own scanning.

If you're exchanging drafts of a document with a co-worker, for example, use a yellow highlighter to flag sections where you have questions or comments. If several people are reviewing the same document, each one can use a different color so others can see at a glance who marked up specific sections. Although you can formally track changes to a document, highlighting comes in handy in informal situations.

→ To work with documents in a group, see "Sharing Documents," **p. 468**.

Although highlighting isn't, strictly speaking, a character format (because it really affects the character's background), it behaves much like a character format: If you copy or move highlighted characters, for example, the highlighting travels with the character.

CAUTION

> Highlighting is *not* removed when you use the Clear Formatting option on the Styles and Formatting task pane or when you press the Ctrl+Shift+N shortcut to restore the Normal character style to selected text. Internally, Word does not treat highlighting as if it is character formatting.

To apply highlighting to characters within a document, you can either make a selection and then click the Highlight button on the Home ribbon under the Font grouping, or click the Highlight button, and then "paint" the highlighting on characters. Click the drop-down arrow to the right of the Highlight button to choose one of 15 colors. The pointer changes to a highlighting pen with insertion point; to turn off highlighting and return to normal editing, click the Highlight button again, or press Esc. To turn the tool into an eraser that removes highlighting from existing text, click the drop-down arrow to the right of the Highlight button and choose None as the highlight color.

→ For advanced formatting tips, **see** "Changing Text Formatting," **p. 356**.

If you open a document that contains fonts that are not installed on your computer, Word provides a way to specify which fonts should be substituted for the missing ones. Go to your Office button and your Word Options tab. Select the Advanced options and scroll down to the Show Document Content settings. You will see a button titled Font Substitution, and if you select this, you can indicate the font you want to be used in place of the one that isn't installed. You can also choose to make the setting a permanent one.

TIP FROM

> Normally, the fonts you specify in the Font Substitution dialog box are not literally substituted for the missing ones. The document file itself isn't changed; Word uses the fonts you pick to display the document onscreen and to print it. If you want to make the substitution final, replacing all references to a particular font with a font of your choosing, click the Convert Permanently button after specifying the substitutions.

PARAGRAPH FORMATS

Each time you press Enter, Word inserts a paragraph mark and starts a new paragraph. By definition, a paragraph in Word consists of a paragraph mark, plus all the characters before the paragraph mark, up to (but not including) the preceding paragraph mark. Paragraph marks are a crucial part of Word because they contain all paragraph formatting. When you copy, move, or delete a paragraph mark, the paragraph formatting goes with the mark. This fact can cause a great deal of frustration to many, which is why you may choose to view your paragraph marks within the documents you are working on.

Paragraph formatting includes alignment (left, center, right, justify), indenting, sorting, bulleting, numbering, multilevel lists, and spacing—both between lines within a paragraph and between paragraphs. It also covers background colors and shading, as well as boxes and lines drawn around and between paragraphs. Tab stops are also considered paragraph formatting—you don't specify a set of tab stops for each line on a page; instead, tab stops remain uniform throughout an entire paragraph.

When you press Enter to create a new paragraph, the new paragraph usually takes on the formatting of the paragraph immediately preceding it. For example, if you position the insertion point within a right-justified paragraph and press Enter, the new paragraph will also be right-justified.

→ For advanced paragraph formatting tips, **see** "Changing Paragraph Formatting," **p. 358**.

REVEALING FORMATTING WITHIN A DOCUMENT

In the old days (well, more like 15 years ago) the leading document processing software was WordPerfect, which allowed you to see "reveal codes," which were all your underlying formatting to your text. We have all loved the change to a non-reveal code environment, but sometimes you may want to see what's going on beyond what your eyes can show you. Word allows you to see the formatting through the Reveal Formatting task pane, which, as we mentioned earlier, can be reached through the keyboard shortcut Shift+F1 or by customizing the Quick Access Toolbar to display it as an option.

Word responds with a comprehensive list of all formatting applied to the current selection (see Figure 13.12).

The more you use the Reveal Formatting task pane, the more likely that you'll discover what a tremendous help it can be in troubleshooting formatting problems. Here are three ways to squeeze extra information out of the task pane:

■ Select the Distinguish Style Source check box at the bottom of the Reveal Formatting task pane. When you do so, Word shows you the source of each specific type of formatting in the selection. This kind of detail can be useful if you're trying to sort through exactly why and how text appears in a particular format.

■ Hover the mouse pointer over the Selected Text box to reveal a drop-down arrow on the right side of the box. Click this arrow to reveal a menu that lets you select similarly formatted text elsewhere in the document, clear all formatting from the selection, or change the formatting of the selection to match the surrounding text.

13

■ After selecting some text, click the Compare to Another Selection check box. When you select this option, a second box opens beneath the original Selected Text box. You can now navigate to another part of the document and make a second text selection. The contents of the Reveal Formatting task pane change to show just the differences in formatting between the two selections.

Figure 13.12
Word can show you full formatting information for any part of a document.

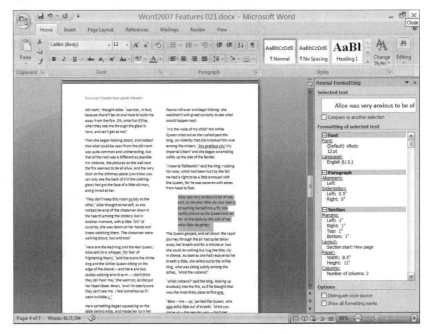

COPYING FORMATS

There are three ways to copy specific formatting from one place in a document to another:

■ Set up a style to reflect the formatting, and then apply the style (either character or paragraph) to the text you want to change. This is the most consistent and reliable approach, and it allows you to change formatting throughout a document by modifying the style.

■ Use the Format Painter icon on the Standard toolbar. You select the text (or paragraph) that includes the text that's formatted to your liking, click the Format Painter icon, and then "paint" the formatting elsewhere in your document. This process is most effective when copying character formatting to a very limited selection. If your hand-eye coordination is less than perfect, the process can be cumbersome and error prone, especially if you accidentally select a paragraph mark prior to "painting."

■ Use the Styles grouping from the Home ribbon tab. If your document already contains the formatting you want, select the text you want to format, and then click the formatting in from the easily displayed ribbon settings, or you can select the handle to allow you to see the Styles task pane. Note that the Styles task pane isn't limited to formally defined styles: It also includes entries for all the manually applied formatting that exists in your document.

The Styles task pane also makes it easy to set up formal styles, and then modify and apply them.

REMOVING TEXT FORMATTING

One option we need to consider here is the capability to undo formatting quickly. In Word 2007, you can place your cursor in a paragraph (or select a character, word, paragraph, or multiple paragraphs) and select a button in the Home ribbon under the Font grouping that is called Clear Formatting. Doing so will revert your selection to the Normal style, removing all manually applied formatting, both at the character and the paragraph levels. Note that if you place your cursor in the paragraph and select Clear Formatting, the text itself will become the default, but other formatting will remain unchanged (for example, if text in that paragraph is a different color or in boldface, it will remain this way). However, if you want all character formatting to be removed, you need to select the area of text (or paragraph) you want it to be removed from. Note that you can also use Shift+spacebar to accomplish the Clear Formatting function.

TIP FROM

EQ & Woody

Although the key combination is a bit arcane, you can also remove manually applied formatting by selecting the text, pressing Ctrl+Q to remove manually applied paragraph formatting, and then press Ctrl+spacebar to remove character formatting.

LOCKING A DOCUMENT'S FORMATTING

Sometimes you want to prevent others from changing the formatting of a document. You can do this from the Review ribbon in the Protect group. Select the Protect Document option, and then click Restrict Formatting and Editing. Under Formatting restrictions, you can select the Limit Formatting to a Selection of Styles check box. Then choose the Settings option to indicate which styles you agree to and also select Formatting controls (see Figure 13.13). You can also enable Editing restrictions, allowing only a certain type of editing and only to specific users if you want.

Figure 13.13
Formatting restrictions with the Settings dialog box included.

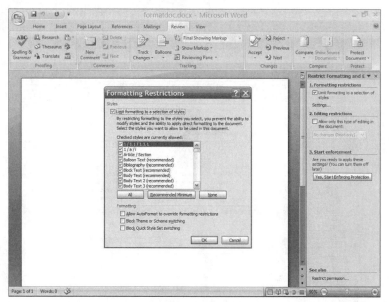

13

TIP FROM

It's possible that you will lock in certain styles for your document, but other styles are already in your document that you haven't allowed. A request will come up asking you to either say Yes (remove styles and formatting that aren't allowed) or No (keep styles and formatting, knowing that users will not be able to use the styles or formatting when they edit the document).

After you have your options chosen, choose Yes, Start Enforcing Protection. You will be asked if you want to use a password on the protection. You can type a password or leave it blank; it's optional.

PAGE/SECTION SETUP OPTIONS

Most simple Word documents contain just one *section*. Usually, you'll add sections to a document when you want to use a different header or footer on certain pages of a document or to alter the number of columns—perhaps to print a long list. You can also change sections to switch from one paper size or orientation to another—for example, to print a table in landscape orientation in the middle of a document.

Each section in a document has its own headers and footers, page size, margins, number of snaking newspaperlike columns, and paper source—a designated paper bin on your printer.

→ To properly format sections, **see** "Formatting Documents by Section," **p. 448**.

Sections are separated by section break marks, which are visible only in Print Layout view with Show/Hide¶ on or in Draft view (see Figure 13.14).

Figure 13.14
Section breaks.

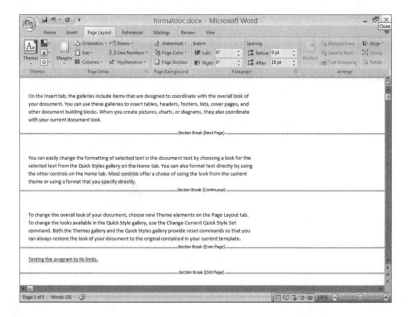

Section formatting is stored in the section break mark; the formatting for the final section in a document is in the document's final paragraph mark. When you select a section break mark and copy, move, or delete it, the section, formatting stored in the mark goes with it.

The safest way to add a new section to a document is to insert a new section break manually—by going to the Page Layout ribbon and choosing the Breaks down arrows from within the Page Setup grouping. Beneath the Page Break section, you choose from the list of available Section Break types:

- **Next Page**—Starts the next section on a new page.
- **Continuous**—Lets the new section follow the current one, without a page break.
- **Even Page**—Forces the next section to start on an even-numbered page.
- **Odd Page**—Forces the next section to start on an odd-numbered page.

Word automatically inserts section break marks in a document if you choose the Page Layout ribbon, under the Page Setup grouping, and select the handle to open the Page Setup dialog box. Click the Layout tab, and under the Apply To heading choose This Point Forward. Word adds the section break as a consequence of changing the layout. Similarly, if you choose to add columns and don't want your entire document to be arranged in columns, you can also go into the settings for your columns and choose Apply To This Point Forward. Word automatically inserts a section break to mark the point where the number of columns changes.

TIP FROM

EQ & Woody

> Editing and formatting documents with multiple sections can be extremely confusing. If you inadvertently move or delete a section break mark, you can make a mess of the document's headers and footers, for example, and it's nearly impossible to recover except by starting over. When you work on documents with more than one section, we strongly recommend that you work only in Draft view, and that you insert section break marks manually by choosing the Break options under the Page Setup grouping on the Page Layout ribbon.

The most common reason for using multiple sections in a document is to alter headers and footers. Each section in a document has its own headers and footers, although you can specify that a section "link to" the preceding section and carry forward the preceding section's headers and footers.

→ To customize headers and footers, **see** "Using Headers and Footers," **p. 441**.

Sections also allow you to organize snaking newspaperlike columns, whether they're for an entire document or for a list of items you want to appear in the middle of a document.

→ If you need to change the number of columns, **see** "Formatting a Document with Columns," **p. 451**.

13

CHANGING TEXT FORMATTING

When you're typing, each new character you type takes on the formatting of the character before, unless you do something to change it (such as pressing Ctrl+I to turn on italic formatting). The first character you type in a paragraph takes on the formatting of the paragraph mark.

To get started, select a character or characters; from the Home ribbon under the Font grouping select the handle to open up the Font dialog box (or right-click and choose Font), and you will see Word's main font formatting options (see Figure 13.15). Most of the character (Word says "font") formatting you'll commonly encounter is applicable to all the Office applications.

Figure 13.15
Most of the Font dialog box's options match up with options in other Office applications.

Word has a few formatting options that aren't quite so straightforward. In the Font dialog box are the following:

- **Superscript and Subscript**—Superscript reduces the size of the characters about four points and moves them above the baseline by about three points. Subscript also reduces about four points and moves the characters below the baseline about two points. These options are also found as buttons within the Font grouping on the Home ribbon.

- **Small caps**—Shows and prints lowercase letters as capitals, reduced about two points (for example, a lowercase letter in 11 point will print as a small cap in 9 point). Some fonts have specific small caps characters, in which case those will print.

- **Hidden text**—Displayed onscreen and/or printed only when you specifically request it (choose Office Button, Word Options, Display, and then under the Printing Options, select the option to Print Hidden Text or leave the box unchecked).

TIP FROM

Ed & Woody

Hidden text can be useful when you want to keep details handy, but show them only occasionally. For example, teachers frequently type exams in Word and place the answers inside the document as hidden text. That way, they can print the exam normally for distribution to students, but then print a second copy with answers for graders.

The Hidden Paragraph Mark Trick

Sometimes Word forces you to have a paragraph mark, whether you want one or not. For example, if you have a document that ends in a table, Word insists on placing a paragraph mark after the table. Sometimes those extra paragraph marks get in the way—in the worst case, Word might print an extra blank page at the end of the document to accommodate the invisible paragraph mark.

If that should happen to you, remember that the paragraph mark is just like any other character. In particular, you can format it as Hidden. A Hidden paragraph mark won't print and won't show on the screen, and one at the end of a document won't force Word to print an extra blank page.

Formatting options on the Character Spacing tab (see Figure 13.16) include the following:

- **Scale**—Applies a zoom effect to the selected text. This option is particularly useful when you're trying to squeeze a headline into a tight space and it won't quite fit. Adjust the scale to 95% or so and see if the problem goes away.

- **Spacing**—Controls the distance between characters. In particular, it allows you to add a uniform amount of space after each of the selected characters (Expanded), or uniformly reduce the amount of space between characters (Condensed). Use this option to unobtrusively expand lines that need to be longer, or shorten lines that are too long.

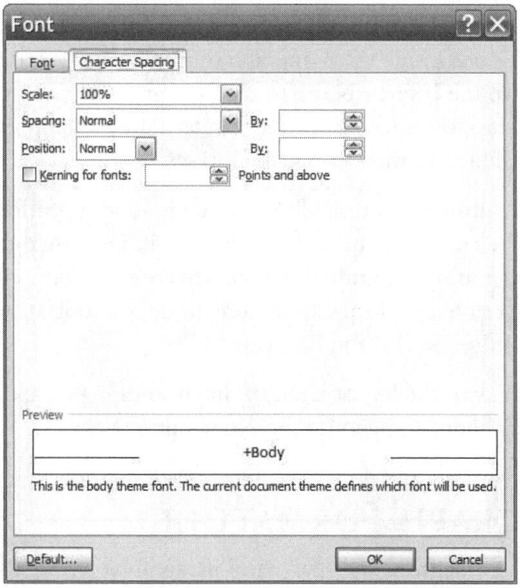

Figure 13.16
Character spacing allows you to squish, elevate, lower, and push together fonts.

- **Position**—Controls how far above or below the baseline of text the selected characters will appear. This is similar to Superscripting and Subscripting, discussed earlier in this section, except it doesn't change the font size, and this box gives you fine control over the positioning.

- **Kerning**—Squishes matched pairs of letters together. The most dramatic example in English is AV. If AV is not kerned, there's a considerable amount of whitespace between the letters. If it is kerned, they're squished together so the leftmost part of the V appears to the left of the rightmost part of the A. Kerning is best used sparingly, with display type such as headlines. It doesn't have much effect at smaller point sizes and, for letters smaller than 10 points or so, it even inhibits your ability to read the type. If you want to kern letters, select them and tell Word the point size at which you want kerning to begin.

Word has one more automatic character-formatting capability that some people love, and others hate: If you type an asterisk, followed by text, followed by another asterisk, the text between the asterisks is made bold. Similarly, if you type an underscore, text, underscore, the text between the underscores is made italic. This feature exists for compatibility with long-standing formatting conventions in text documents exchanged over the Internet. In Word XP/2002 and later, this option is off by default. If you upgraded from an earlier version of Word, however, you may find that it is enabled. To turn this feature on or off, go to your Office button, choose Word Options, go to your Proofing section and under AutoCorrect, choose the AutoCorrect Options. Click the AutoFormat as You Type tab and select or clear the *Bold* and _italic_ with Real Formatting box.

USING DROP CAPS FOR EMPHASIS

Drop caps add emphasis and distinction to a paragraph. Used sparingly, they make a good visual break at the beginning of major sections in a report. Word makes drop caps easy: Click once inside the paragraph that's to have its initial letter turned into a drop cap, and then go to the Insert ribbon, to the Text grouping, and choose Drop Cap. You can accept the default options for either the standard drop cap or apply one that sits out in the margin. Or you could alter the Drop Cap Options.

The default height of the drop cap is three lines, which is about right for most paragraphs. If the drop cap appears to be crowding the text that follows it, increase the value in the Distance From Text box. You're not limited in your selection of fonts, either. Some "fancy" fonts are particularly well suited to drop-cap treatment. Take a look at the Algerian font, which is installed with Office, or Old English Text MT.

To remove a drop cap, click to the left or right of the drop cap, go back to the Drop Cap selection on your Insert ribbon, and choose the None option.

CHANGING PARAGRAPH FORMATTING

Word lets you change the indenting and spacing of paragraphs. Word also gives you control on a paragraph-by-paragraph basis over whether to keep entire paragraphs together or to force one paragraph to "stick to" the next, so they both appear on the same page.

The key concept: Paragraph formatting is stored in the paragraph mark. When you copy or move a paragraph mark, the formatting goes with it. When you delete a paragraph mark, any text following the paragraph mark becomes part of the current paragraph, and the new, combined paragraph takes on the formatting of the deleted paragraph mark.

TIP FROM

It's almost impossible to tell whether you've selected a paragraph mark unless you have paragraph marks showing on the screen. Some Word users keep paragraph marks and tabs visible at all times. Others find these marks distracting and keep them hidden except when working with paragraph formats. To make these marks visible temporarily, click the Show/Hide ¶ button on the Home ribbon. To make them visible at all times, choose Office button, Word Options, click the Display settings, and select the Tab Characters, Spaces and Paragraph Marks check boxes.

To restore default paragraph formatting—that is, the formatting mandated by the paragraph's style—select the paragraph and click the style name within the Styles grouping of the Home ribbon.

ADJUSTING PARAGRAPH ALIGNMENT

Word includes simple tools for aligning your paragraphs to the left, center, or right, or "justifying" paragraphs so that they line up neatly along both left and right margins. If you click inside a paragraph, or select one or more paragraphs, and select the handle next to the Paragraph grouping on the Home ribbon tab (or right-click and select Paragraph), you'll see the Indents and Spacing tab of the Paragraph dialog box, as shown in Figure 13.17. Set the Alignment box to reflect the alignment you like.

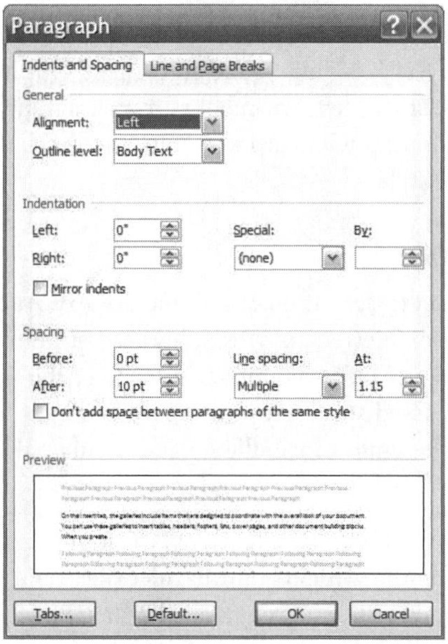

Figure 13.17
Use the Paragraph dialog box to set a paragraph's relative outlining level, for both Outline View and Document Map. Body Text is the lowest level; Level 1 is the highest.

13

You can also use the Align Left, Center, Align Right, or Justify buttons on the Home ribbon under the Paragraph grouping to set alignment.

TIP FROM

EQ & Woody

> To justify the last line in a justified paragraph, click just before the paragraph mark and press Shift+Enter.

Word has another text-aligning technique called "Click and type," which allows you to click anywhere on the screen and start typing text. Although it should be called "Double-click and type," the paragraph alignment part of the concept is straightforward:

- If you double-click somewhere near the middle of an empty line (that is, halfway between the left and right margins), Word converts the line to Center alignment. You can tell the area is "hot" because Word puts centered lines below the usual I-beam pointer.

- If you double-click somewhere near the right end of a line (that is, near the right margin), Word converts the line to right-justified. Again, you know the area is hot because Word changes the I-beam pointer so it has lines to the left. This feature makes it especially easy to put left- and right-justified text on a single line.

CAUTION

> Unless you're careful and watch the lines around the I-beam closely, Word might insert tabs and tab stops instead of changing the entire paragraph's alignment. Although the tab stops might fool a novice, paragraphs with tabs don't act like aligned paragraphs, as a few moments' work will demonstrate. This is yet another reason for showing paragraph marks and tab characters onscreen.

Normally, the outline level is set along with the paragraph style. In fact, if you select one of the built-in heading styles (Heading 1, Heading 2, and so on), the Outline Level option will be grayed out and unavailable. Adjust this level manually for a paragraph if you want that specific paragraph to be visible in Outline view or in the Document Map without affecting other paragraphs that use the same style.

INDENTING PARAGRAPHS FOR EMPHASIS

Left and right indents are often used to set off blocks of quoted text. Another common type of indenting, typically used in informal letters, moves only the first line of a paragraph; not surprisingly, this is called a *first-line indent*. Its counterpart—where the first line juts out to the left—is called a *hanging indent*. Used sparingly, this is a good way to emphasize the first few words of a paragraph. (It's also common for bulleted and numbered paragraphs, which are discussed later.)

Although it takes a bit of practice, Word's ruler offers the fastest, most accurate way to control indents. Learn what each of the four widgets on the ruler does, and you're well on your way. The downward-pointing triangle at the left controls the first-line indent; the upward-pointing triangle just below it controls the hanging indent. Click the rectangle (below both triangles) to adjust the left indent by moving both the first-line indent and the hanging indent simultaneously. The triangle at the right controls the right indent.

13

TIP FROM

Ed & Woody

As you drag these widgets, a faint dotted line appears on the document to show where the indented text will end up. And if you absolutely can't remember which widget is which, let your mouse hover over each one and read the ScreenTips.

You can also use the Paragraph dialog box to set indents. To adjust the left and/or right indent, use the Left and Right boxes of the Paragraph dialog box. To change the left indent only, in half-inch increments, you can also use the Increase Indent and Decrease Indent buttons on the Formatting toolbar. To create a first-line indent, select the paragraphs you want to indent, open the Paragraph dialog box from the Home ribbon, and select First Line in the Special box.

Another location for adjusting Indents is located on the Page Layout ribbon under the Paragraph grouping. From here you can establish Left and Right Indent settings.

When you press Tab at the beginning of a new paragraph, Word adds a tab character. However, when you position the insertion point at the beginning of an existing paragraph and press Tab, Word adds a first-line indent. If you actually wanted a tab instead, you can use the AutoCorrect action menu (the lightning-bolt icon just below the indented text) that magically appears to cancel the change.

To create a hanging indent, select the paragraphs you want to indent, open the Paragraph dialog box from the Home ribbon, and in the Special box select Hanging.

ADJUSTING LINE AND PARAGRAPH SPACING

Again, within the Paragraph dialog box, you can find the settings needed to adjust spacing for your paragraphs. In addition, another location for adjusting Spacing is located on the Page Layout ribbon under the Paragraph grouping. However, this offers only the capability to control Before and After spacing. Word offers more options from within the Paragraph dialog box. Word has controls for three kinds of spacing:

- The amount of blank space before the first line of a paragraph
- The amount of blank space after the last line of a paragraph
- The amount of space internally, between the lines of a paragraph

The spacing between paragraphs adds up just as you would think: The "after" from the first paragraph is combined with the "before" of the second paragraph. Word ignores the "after" space if a paragraph will fit at the end of a page, but it includes the "before" space when a paragraph starts on a new page.

Internal line spacing isn't so simple:

- If you set Line Spacing to Exactly (for instance, exactly 12 points), Word makes the distance between all the lines in the paragraph equal to whatever measurement you choose. If you put a large character on a line—an 18-point character, for example—the top of the character might be cut off.

- If you set Line Spacing to Single, 1.5 lines, Double, or some other multiple, Word calculates the distance between each line of the paragraph separately. It takes the tallest

13

character (or graphic) on each line and adjusts to single, 1.5, or double spacing, as appropriate. If you have one 18-point character in the middle of a paragraph consisting of 12-point characters, the distance to the line containing the 18-point character will be 50% greater than the distance between the other lines.

NOTE

> Normally, the height of "invisible" characters—spaces, paragraph marks, tabs, and the like—is not taken into account when calculating Single, 1.5, Double, or Multiple spacing. The exceptions: If the paragraph is empty, the calculation is based on the size of the default font for that paragraph; if it contains only invisible characters, the height of those characters counts.

- If you set Line Spacing to At Least (for instance, at least 12 points), Word treats it the same as single spacing, but sets spacing to a minimum of the height you specified, even if all characters in a given line are smaller than that size.

Generally, you'll want to use Exactly spacing if you use two or more fonts in a paragraph: By setting the internal spacing to Exactly a given figure (typically one or two points more than the largest font used in the paragraph), all the lines will be equally spaced, even if the different font normally calls for more whitespace.

CONTROLLING PAGE BREAKS

Each paragraph can also be formatted to control the way Word breaks pages. The Line and Page Breaks tab in the Paragraph dialog box (see Figure 13.18) holds these settings:

- **Widow/Orphan Control**—When checked, it keeps Word from printing *widows* (the last line of a paragraph all by itself at the top of a new page) and *orphans* (the first line of a paragraph all by itself at the bottom of a page). It's on by default.

Figure 13.18
You can control each paragraph, individually, to determine whether it flops onto a new page.

- **Keep with Next**—Forces Word to put this paragraph and the next paragraph on the same page.

- **Keep Lines Together**—Ensures that all the lines of the paragraph appear on a single page.

- **Page Break Before**—Makes Word start the paragraph on a new page.

NOTE

> Word can't always follow your instructions, of course: If you format all the paragraphs in a long document to Keep with Next, the pages have to break somewhere. Word makes a valiant effort to follow your instructions, but if they're impossible, it lays out the pages as best it can.

In almost all cases, you'll want to enforce widow and orphan control. If you have a paragraph in a report whose visual impact depends on the whole paragraph appearing on one page (say, a mission statement, or a quotation), you will probably want to keep the lines together. And headings should almost always be formatted Keep with Next so they don't get separated from the text they head.

POSITIONING TEXT WITH TABS

To fully understand the way tabs work in Word, you first must realize that a tab consists of two parts. First, there's the tab character—which, like any other character, is placed in a document when you press the Tab key. Second, there's the tab stop, which is a location, or series of locations, on the page. In Word, you set up tab stops for each paragraph, not for each line; in other words, every line in a paragraph must have identical tab stops.

TIP FROM

> It's nearly impossible to work with tabs unless you make them visible on the screen. To do so, click the Show/Hide ¶ button on the Home ribbon under the Paragraph grouping; or select the Office button, Word Options, go to Display settings, and select the Tab Characters check box.

When Word encounters a tab character in a document, it advances to the next defined *tab stop*. Tab stops come in four varieties: left-aligned, right-aligned, centered, and decimal-aligned (which aligns numbers so the decimal point appears at the tab location). In addition, you can specify a *leader* character (pronounced "leeder")—a character that will appear, repeated, in the blank area leading up to the tab stop. You've no doubt seen them in Tables of Contents.

```
This is a leader of periods........<Tab stop>
```

When working with tabs, it's always much easier to plan to have just one line per paragraph. You'll see how that makes a big difference in the example in the next section.

To set a tab stop, do the following:

1. Select the paragraph(s) where you want to set new tab stops.

13

2. To get to the Tabs dialog box, you can open the Paragraph dialog box first from either the Home ribbon under the Paragraph grouping or the Page Layout ribbon under the Paragraph grouping. Select the handle to open the Paragraph dialog box and then select the Tabs button. See the Tabs dialog box as shown in Figure 13.19.

Figure 13.19

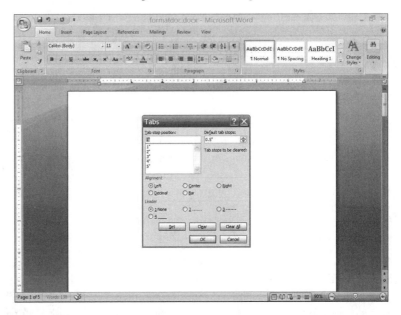

3. Type the location of the first tab stop in the Tab Stop Position box. (The location is the distance from the left margin of the document to the position of the tab stop, regardless of where the left edge of the paragraph might fall.)

> **NOTE**
>
> The default Normal paragraph style starts out with no explicitly defined tab stops. In this case, Word uses the Default Tab Stops setting of 0.5 inches, which treats the paragraph as if it contained a left-aligned tab stop every half-inch. As soon as you specify one or more tab stops, Word stops using the default tab stops preceding the ones you create. So, if you set a tab stop at 3 inches and another at 4 inches, pressing the Tab key once advances to 3 inches from the left margin; pressing Tab again goes to the right another inch. After it reaches the last user-defined tab stop, Word goes back to its default setting of left-aligned tab stops—in this case, at 4.5, 5.0, 5.5, 6.0, and so on, until you reach the right margin. You can change the Default Tab Stops setting to any value between 0.01 and 22 inches.

4. Choose the alignment and leader you want for the tab stop. Click the Set button and Word establishes a tab stop at the location you specify.

CAUTION

> The Bar tab type in the Tabs dialog box creates a vertical rule–an up-and-down line–in the paragraph at the indicated tab location. This setting is a throwback to an early version of Word that didn't have borders. If you need a vertical line, use tables or borders, but avoid this setting.

The tab stops you create are stored in the paragraph mark along with other paragraph format settings; copy or move a paragraph mark, and the tab stops go with it. If the insertion point is in a normal paragraph with custom tab stops and you press Enter, the new paragraph inherits the same tab stops. Many Word users—even advanced Word users—find that confusing. To restore a paragraph to the default (left-aligned tab stops every half inch), select the original style's name from your Styles grouping off the Home ribbon.

Using the Ruler to Set Tab Stops

Although the Tabs dialog box gives you much greater control over the location and characteristics of tab stops, many people use the Word ruler to set and move tab stops. In the event you don't see the ruler, you can do one of two things. From the View Ribbon, the Show/Hide grouping you can select the checkbox next to the ruler to turn it on. Or, in the top-right corner, above your scroll bar is a little icon that allows you to turn the ruler on. From the ruler, to the far left is an icon that tells you what kind of tab is available: left-, center-, right-, or decimal-aligned. Click the icon to cycle through each of these tab types until you get the one you need. Click the ruler where you want the new tab to appear. All default tabs to the left of the new tab are destroyed in the process. Click and drag the tab icon left or right to position it precisely where you want it. To get rid of a tab, click it and drag it off the ruler.

It's impossible to set the leader character directly from the ruler. For that task, you need to use the Tabs dialog box. Skip the menus, though; if the ruler is visible, just double-click any tab stop to open the Tabs dialog box and fine-tune the settings. Or, from the Paragraph dialog, you can choose the Tabs button.

ENTERING TEXT AUTOMATICALLY

For Word aficionados, immediately what may come to mind here is the use of AutoText (an older tool available only in Word in versions 2003 and earlier). AutoCorrect (the newer, Office-encompassing tool) might be your second guess in thinking about how to enter text automatically within your documents. Neither are correct or immediately available in Word 2007.

Now that isn't to say that you cannot find these options. You can open your Office button, go to Word Options, to the Customize settings, do a search for both the AutoText and AutoCorrect buttons, and then have them included in your Quick Access Toolbar. They both continue to function, but there is a new tool in town called Quick Parts that uses the Building Blocks Organizer to keep your automatic text more...well...organized.

AUTOTEXT AND AUTOCORRECT USAGE IN WORD 2007

Let's quickly review AutoText and AutoCorrect. When you type an AutoCorrect entry followed by the spacebar, Enter key, or any punctuation mark, Word swaps out the text you've

13

typed and replaces it with the indicated text (and graphics) in the entry. For example, if you type <== the AutoCorrect automatically turns that into a ← graphic. You see no warning that the change will take place; it just happens. When AutoCorrect is done, if you hover your cursor over the AutoCorrected entry, the AutoCorrect action menu (the lightning bolt icon) gives you access to the full array of AutoCorrecting options, both for this individual entry and for AutoCorrect in general. That's handy.

On the other hand, when you start to type an AutoText entry, after the first four letters Word displays a ScreenTip alerting you that a possible matching entry exists. Type octo, for example, and you'll see a ScreenTip that reads October (Press ENTER to Insert). If you want to accept the AutoText entry—in this case, replace the octo you've typed with the word October—press Enter, or the Tab key, or F3 (they're all equivalent).

The current date, days of the week, months of the year, your company name, your username, and your initials are all picked up automatically by Word and turned into AutoText entries.

BUILDING A DOCUMENT WITH QUICK PARTS

It is important, moving forward, that the automatic text formatting and other preconfigured settings become part of what Microsoft calls Building Blocks. Logically, there are different types of blocks. For example, our AutoText is a type of building block that we can call on to save text and call it up again quickly. Other building blocks might relate to other aspects of a document, like a footnote setting or a cover page. When you create a block, you need to save it within a gallery and those galleries are organized by the Building Block Organizer.

→ You will learn more about the Building Block Organizer in the next chapter; **see** "Secrets of the Office Masters: Working with the Building Block Organizer," **p. 410**.

For the purpose of keeping focused on the subject at hand, let's examine how you would go about saving text to automatically enter later on (also known as *boilerplate text*).

First, select the text you want to reuse. Consider that a mini-building block that you will need in building your documents. If you want to retain paragraph formatting of the text, remember to include the paragraph mark in the selection. (To make sure you do this, remember to turn on your Show/Hide tools or turn on paragraph marks in your Display options.)

When you have your text, go to the Insert ribbon, and in the Text grouping select Quick Parts. Then choose Save Selection to Quick Part Gallery (or press Alt+F3). You'll see the options for saving that text as shown in Figure 13.20.

Figure 13.20
Creating a building block to be used at a later time.

The following information is important to consider when creating your AutoText building blocks:

- **Name**—Self-explanatory, but try to be unique and descriptive.
- **Gallery**—You place your selection into a gallery choice (and there are many). In the case of automatic text of graphics, you'll be happy to note that there is, in fact, an AutoText gallery.
- **Category**—General is the only one to start with, but you can create other categories to organize your blocks better.
- **Description**—Again, you want to be able to find your block later on, so be clear in your description.
- **Save In**—Choose the template you want this saved in from a drop-down list.
- **Options**—Here you can select Insert Content in Its Own Page to keep your block separate when entered, Insert in Own Paragraph to ensure this content is not included within another paragraph, or Insert Content Only to insert it wherever it's told.

After you select your text and make it a building block, you can reach for it anytime. Go to the Insert ribbon, to the Text grouping, and choose Quick Parts. Then select the Building Blocks Organizer, find the name of the block you created, and choose Insert.

Using Bullets, Numbering, and Multilevel Lists

By far, the simplest way to create a bulleted or numbered list is to use one of the many shortcuts for starting and continuing such lists. For example, if you type a number or letter, followed by a period, a space, and then text, Word begins a numbered list, provided that you haven't disabled the options for doing so (located under Word Options, Proofing, AutoCorrect Options, and then on the AutoFormat as You Type tab). Dozens of combinations are available.

Numbering and bulleting are paragraph properties. As such, they're stored in the paragraph mark and travel along with other paragraph settings if the paragraph mark is copied or moved. Position the insertion point inside a numbered or bulleted paragraph and press Enter, and the bulleting or numbering is "inherited" by the new paragraph.

Because bulleting, numbering, and multilisting are paragraph properties, if you place the insertion point inside a bulleted, numbered, or multilevel list paragraph and press Enter, the newly created paragraph "inherits" the bulleting or numbering.

It also means that you can move, drag, or rearrange numbered paragraphs at will, and Word renumbers them, on-the-fly, as appropriate.

13

NOTE

> AutoNumbered and AutoBulleted lists are slightly different because Word lets you bail out of bulleting or numbering by pressing Enter twice in succession. In other words, if the insertion point is inside a bulleted or numbered paragraph, and the paragraph is empty, when you press Enter, Word removes the bulleting and formatting from both the old and new paragraphs.

Bullets and numbers maintained by Word aren't "real" characters. You can't select them, much less delete or change them. Instead, they are generated automatically by Word, as a consequence of their paragraph formatting.

Many advanced Word users disable Word's AutoBulleting and AutoNumbering features and apply bullets or numbers to lists by using simple toolbar buttons or—in more complex situations—using the dialog box.

You can always create a simple bulleted or numbered list by selecting the paragraphs you want to bullet or number and then clicking the Bullets icon or the Numbering icon on the Home ribbon from the Paragraph grouping.

To take advantage of Word's extensive bulleting and numbering options, select the paragraphs you want to bullet or number, and then choose the drop-down arrow next to the Bullets or Numbering icons (or right-click and choose Bullets or Numbering) and you'll see the dialog box for making different choices to enhance your control over your bullets or numbers.

Select from the prebuilt bullet or numbering schemes, or click the Define New to establish your own. Multilevel lists (shown in Figure 13.21), on the other hand, are a combination of a variety of bullets and numbers that are preconfigured or that can also be tailored to fit your needs. Note that you cannot simply right-click and choose Multilevel List like you can with Bullets and Numbering; these formatting options must be performed from the Paragraph grouping of the Home ribbon.

TIP FROM

Ed & Woody

> You can manually construct intricate numbering schemes—often required by law offices, for example. You can put together numbering sequences such as IV (31) A and have the paragraphs renumber themselves when moved.

Consecutive paragraphs need not be numbered consecutively. For example, you could have paragraphs numbered 1, 2, and 3, then two paragraphs with no numbering, and pick back up at 4, 5, and so on. To stop the numbering sequence, select the paragraph(s) you don't want to have numbered and then either from the Home ribbon under the Paragraph grouping or by right-clicking the paragraph you want to turn numbering off for, select None. To continue numbering where you last left off, turn numbering back on and an AutoCorrect icon will appear asking you if you want to Continue Numbering. You can choose this to put this paragraph into the standard numerical order.

Figure 13.21
Choosing a multilevel list option. Not that with the multilevel list options, the graphic blows up to make it easier to see exactly what you are choosing.

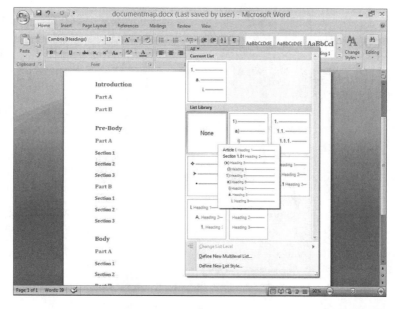

You can associate numbering with a specific paragraph style, making Word put a sequential number in front of each paragraph formatted with that style. If your chapter headings are formatted with the Heading 1 style, for example, associating numbering with the Heading 1 style automatically generates chapter numbers.

FINDING AND REPLACING TEXT AND FORMATTING

If you want to find something simple, the standard Find features used throughout Office should suffice. You can look for literal text by typing any word or phrase into the Find What box on the Find dialog box. After selecting the Use Wildcards check box, you can have Word perform fuzzier searches: m?ne matches mane and miner, but not manner, and bo*t (matches boats or bought, but not bat).

Sometimes you need an even more powerful search capability. Perhaps you're looking for all the words in a document that end with "ing." Or you can get complex—suppose you have a list of license plate numbers and need to find the ones starting with numbers 1 through 9, followed by the letters QED, and then four numbers ending in 9.

Word contains a flexible, powerful minilanguage, a close cousin of the widely used *regular expression* syntax, that lets you specify precisely what to find. To begin creating your own search expressions, select the Home ribbon tab. Under the Editing grouping, you can select Find (or simple type Ctrl+F). Then select the More button and choose Use Wildcards (see Figure 13.22).

13

Figure 13.22
The search string shown here uses wildcards and expressions to solve the license plate number problem described in the text.

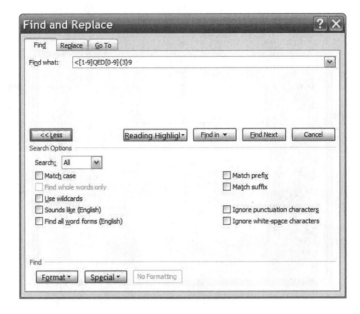

As detailed in the next section, this search string will find all those license plates:

`<[1-9]QED[0-9]{3}9`

Each part of the search string is explained next:

- The < signifies that the following characters have to start a new word (or, in this case, a license plate number).
- The [1-9] matches any single number between 1 and 9.
- The QED forces an exact match on the letters QED.
- [0-9] matches any single number.
- The {3} that immediately follows [0-9] means that the previous element is repeated three times; thus, you must have three consecutive numbers to match this search term.
- Finally, the 9 on the end will match only a 9.

In addition to the ? and * wildcards, Word recognizes the symbols in Table 13.3.

TABLE 13.3 WILDCARDS FOR FIND

Symbol	Meaning
[xyz]	Matches exactly one of the listed characters. b[aioe]g matches bag and bog, but not bug.
[A-Z]	Matches any single character in the range. Case sensitive. b[A-W]g matches bAg and bUg, but not bug or bARge.
[!xyz]	Matches any single character except the ones listed. b[!au]g will match big and bog, but not bag or bug or bring.

Symbol	Meaning
[!A-Z]	Matches any single character that doesn't lie in the range. Case sensitive. b[!a-m]g matches bog or bug, but not bag or big.
<	The character(s) that follow this symbol must appear at the beginning of a word. <[a-c] matches act and cat, but not react. <bl matches blue and blech, but not able.
>	The character(s) that precede this symbol must appear at the end of a word. ing> matches hiking and writing but not singer. [a-c]> matches Alma and tab but not read.
{n,m}	The preceding character or expression must appear between "n" and "m" times. If the "m" is omitted, the character must appear "n" or more times. Thus, blec{3,7}h matches blecccch and bleccccccch, but not blecch, and b[an]{2,}g matches bang but not bag.
@	Same as {1,}: the preceding character must appear one or more times. bo@t matches bot and boot, but not bat or boat.
\	Search for the literal character that follows the backslash, even if it's a wildcard. wh[ae]t\? matches what? and whet? but not whether or whatever.

Word also includes a handy list of special symbols—tab characters, em and en dashes, page and section breaks, and so on—under the Special button, shown previously on Figure 13.22.

All this wildcard-matching business can be confusing, but it gets worse: Word supports two kinds of pattern matching. All the wildcard matching discussed so far in this chapter applies when you select the Use Wildcards check box shown in Figure 13.22. A different set of symbols is available if you do not check the Use Wildcards box.

Perhaps the easiest way to illustrate the difference is with the paragraph mark. If you leave the Use Wildcards box unchecked and then type ^p in the Find What box, Word will dutifully find the next paragraph mark.

However, if the Use Wildcards check box is selected, there is no apparent way to tell Word to find the next paragraph mark! If you type ^p in the Find What box, and the Use Wildcards box is checked, Word will stop only if it finds a literal match in the document—that is, a caret followed by a p.

It's difficult to tell, offhand, whether a particular character or symbol is included in one group or the other. If you're trying to match a character that you can't type directly, the best approach is to start by clicking the Special button on the Find and Replace dialog box. If the character is on the drop-down list, click to select it and add the code to the Find What box. If that doesn't work, select the Use Wildcards check box, click Special, and look again.

Although the online documentation encourages you to paste text from a document into the Find What box, in fact, some characters (most notably paragraph marks) can't be pasted.

13

There are two more search options that you should use with caution:

- **Sounds Like**—This option catches some simple homonyms (new, gnu, knew, for example, or fish and fiche), but it also makes odd matches (rest, according to Word, sounds like reside) and bizarre mistakes (oh sounds like a, according to Word, but not owe).

- **Find All Word Forms**—This is supposed to catch noun plurals, adjective forms, and verb conjugations: Tell Word to replace heavy with light and, with Find All Word Forms checked, heavier will be replaced by lighter, heaviest will be replaced by lightest. This, too, has problems. For example, tell Word to replace bring with take and, with Find All Word Forms checked, "I have brought it" will be replaced by "I have took it."

Replace behaves much the same as Find, except the entry in the Find What text box is replaced by the entry in the Replace With text box.

When performing a replace, you can use parentheses in the Find What box to specify groups of characters, which are then referenced in the Replace With box. The contents of the first pair of parentheses in the Find What box becomes \1 in the Replace With box; the second becomes \2; and so on.

This can be handy if, for example, you want to replace all the occurrences of American style dates (perhaps 10-20-51) with their European day-first equivalents (20-10-51). Make sure the Use Wildcards box is selected, and then in the Find What box, type

`<([0-9]*)-([0-9]*)-([0-9]*)>`

to force Word to recognize the American style date: the day (inside the first set of parentheses) becomes \1, the month (in the second set of parentheses) becomes \2, and the year becomes \3. In the Replace With box, type

`\2-\1-\3`

and the dates are swapped around.

Few people realize that you can use Word to change a list of names that looks like this:

`Lastname, Firstname`

Into a list that looks like this:

`Firstname Lastname`

To do so, click Use Wildcards and in the Find What box, type

`<([A-Z]*), ([A-Z]*)>`

and in the Replace With box, type

`\2 \1`

TIP FROM

EQ & Woody

You can tell Word to "Replace With" the contents of the Windows Clipboard. That can be handy if, for example, you want to replace a word, such as STOP, with a picture (perhaps a stop sign) throughout a document. To make it so, clear the Use Wildcards check box, and then type ^c in the Replace With box. Word interprets ^c as being the contents of the Windows Clipboard.

Word doesn't limit you to searching for and replacing text. You can specify formatting, as well—for instance, replace all occurrences of the italicized words *current month sales* with the bold number **$12,345,678**. Here's how:

1. From the Edit and Replace dialog box, click the More button to expose the Format selections.

2. In the Find What box, type `current month sales`.

3. With the insertion point still in the Find What box, click the Format button and choose Font. Under Font Style, click Italic, and then click OK.

4. In the Replace With box, type `$12,345,678`. With the insertion point still in the box, click the Format button and choose Font. Under Font Style, click Bold, and then click OK.

5. You can now proceed with the replace. Click Replace to verify each match individually, or Replace All to make the update throughout the document.

TIP FROM

EQ & Woody

If you're handy with keyboard shortcuts, you can use them to great effect in the Find/Replace dialog box. Click in the Find What or Replace With dialog boxes, and then use any relevant keyboard shortcut to bypass the Format dialog boxes. Click Ctrl+I or Ctrl+B to toggle between italic and bold fonts, for instance. (This option also makes available a third option, Font: Not Italic or Font: Not Bold, where you can search only for matching text that *doesn't* have a particular attribute.) You can also search for paragraph attributes, such as centered or justified text or those with a particular line spacing specified.

Advanced Word users frequently find it easier to find the first instance of a particular piece of text, change it if needed, and then close the dialog box. That way, you can click the Next button (just below the Select Browse Object button) or press Ctrl+Page Down, or Shift+F4 to find the next instance. Closing the dialog box clears clutter off the screen, and you can better see what you're doing. You can also quickly edit the found text without having to click outside the dialog box, and then press Ctrl+Page Down to continue searching. You can press F4 to repeat the previous change, or use the contents of the Clipboard to replace the found text by pressing Ctrl+V.

In addition to Font formatting, you can specify Paragraph formatting, Styles (either character or paragraph), Tabs, Language, Frame type, or Highlight.

If you want to clear the formatting for either the Find What or Replace With boxes, click once inside the box and then click the No Formatting button at the bottom of the dialog box.

13

Both the Find and Replace formatting settings are "sticky": If you set Find to look for "Heading 1" style paragraphs, for example, the next time you perform a Find or Replace, Word continues looking for "Heading 1" style paragraphs.

NOTE

> When you're done looking for a particular kind of formatting—or replacing with a particular kind of formatting—you must manually clear the formatting. Click to position the insertion point in the Find or Replace box and then click the No Formatting button.

CHECKING SPELLING, CONTEXTUAL SPELLING, AND GRAMMAR

Word contains one of the most sophisticated spell checkers you can find. The spell-checking module, introduced in Word 95 for the first time, which Word shares with the rest of Office, contains rich tools for custom dictionaries and "exclude" dictionaries, and easy right-click access to suggested spellings for words highlighted with the infamous red squiggly line.

You, no doubt, have seen that red squiggle so much you start to have nightmares about it. Well, Word 2007 gives you something else to dream about—the blue squiggle. There is a new feature called Contextual Spelling, which is designed to notice words that are technically spelled correctly, but are being used in the wrong context.

For example, "He was determined not to loose the game." Loose is spelled correctly and the grammar is fine, so you wouldn't even see a green squiggly (the infamous grammar indicator) but the correct word is *lose* and Word 2007 knows it.

In addition to assisting us with our spelling, Word 2007 continues to assist us with our grammar, giving us a green squiggly to alert us when we have a fragmented sentence (my personal favorite grammatical error). Note the effect on your document in Figure 13.23.

Figure 13.23
The colorful list of squiggly indicators has grown to three in Word 2007.

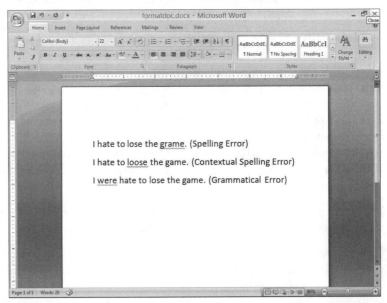

Some people find the red squiggly lines distracting—it's as if they're being forced to correct spelling mistakes as they type. Word includes a batch spelling checker, so you can turn off the squiggly lines and run a spell check after you're done typing. To turn off the squiggly lines, go to your Office button, select Word Options, and then go to your Proofing options. In Figure 13.24, notice the options to turn off spelling, contextual spelling, and grammar marks. At the end of your work, to run a batch spelling check, select the Review ribbon tab, under the Proofing grouping, and choose Spelling and Grammar or press F7.

The Grammar Checker's advice, on the other hand, can be overly simplistic. Why? Because it's rule-based, and English grammar is far too complex to fit neatly into a small set of rules. If you know you need help with basic grammar issues, you can get a great deal of benefit from the grammar checker. Most advanced users, however, find the squiggly green lines distracting and turn them off from the Proofing options in your Word Options.

If you want the grammar checker to help improve specific aspects of your writing (such as flagging sentences that are too long, or those in passive voice, or their/there mistakes), you can customize Grammar Checker to respond only to violations of those rules. To do so, click the Settings button in your Proofing Options under your Word Options (shown in Figure 13.24). There you'll find dozens of different grammatical problem areas, and you can instruct Word to watch for the ones most important to you.

Figure 13.24
Turning off the squigglies and adjusting your Grammar options.

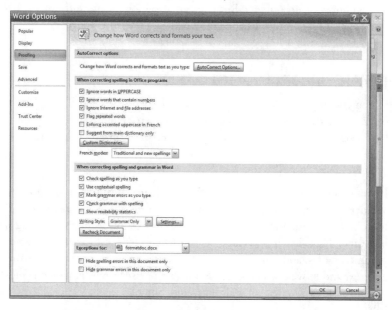

As a quick review of some of the other tools on the Review ribbon under the Proofing grouping, you might notice that you have Research, Thesaurus, Translate, Translation Screen Tip, Set Language, and Word Count.

Consider their usage next:

- **Research**—This option opens the Research pane, which will allow you to search through a variety of sources including dictionaries, thesauri, web sites, and so on.

- **Thesaurus**—Allows you to perform an intensive search for words, other than the one you've chosen, to enhance your vocabulary use within your documents. You can also right-click within your text and go to Synonyms (and then choose Thesaurus from there).

- **Translate**—Gives you the ability to translate selected text into a variety of languages, including Chinese and Arabic, through WorldLingo translation services (www.worldlingo.com). You can also reach this by right-clicking within your document and choosing Translate.

- **Translation ScreenTip**—If you enable this option, you can hover your cursor over words and it will display a translated view of that word in the language you have selected from the options provided. You can reach this by right-clicking within your document and choosing Translate. Then turn on whichever language Translation ScreenTip you would like to see from the available options.

- **Set Language**—Determines what language your spelling and grammar will be judged by. For example, in the event you have that Spanish term paper due and don't want to see the entire document in red squiggly lines, you might want to adjust the language for your document to Spanish.

- **Word Count**—Tells you the number of pages, words, characters, paragraphs, and lines within your documents. But you can also look down on the status bar to see your word count. (This feature has been dubbed Live Word Count.)

PRINTING WORD DOCUMENTS

When you get right down to it, most Word documents are destined for the printer. Word offers many features to give you extensive control over how pages print. However, if you have been an avid Word user for some time, you won't find that much has changed here.

PREVIEWING PRINTED PAGES

If you're looking at one page, Word's Print Preview ribbon offers no advantage over the standard Print Layout view. But there are two situations in which Print Preview is extremely useful. You can use the Zoom slider and drag to show as few as two pages or several dozen at one time. This view is especially helpful when you want to see at a glance where headlines, graphics, tables, and other nontext elements fall in your document. Although it's possible to edit text and move objects on the Print Preview screen, this screen is most appropriate for getting a bird's-eye view of your entire document.

To enter Word's Print Preview mode (shown in Figure 13.25), select the Office button, choose Print, and then Print Preview. You could also add it to your Quick Access Toolbar.

13

Figure 13.25
Word's Print Preview mode shows you precisely how the printed page will appear—but Print Layout view does almost as well, with none of the limitations.

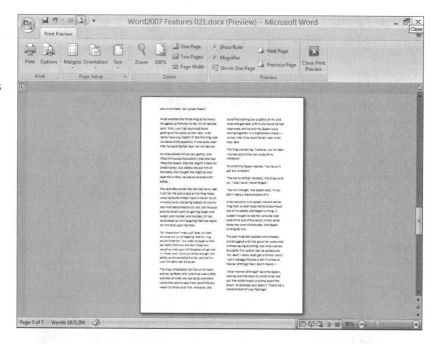

In Print Preview mode, the default mouse pointer lets you toggle between a 100% view of the page you click or back to a view of the number of pages you selected. Click the Magnifier button to toggle between this pointer and an I-beam insertion point you can use for editing.

In Print Preview mode, you also have access to the Shrink to Fit button. Use this feature when the last page of your document includes two or three lines, and you want to force those leftovers to fit on the previous page.

Click the Shrink One Page button for your Shrink to Fit options and Word alters font sizes to reduce the number of pages in the document by one. Note that changing the font size sometimes doesn't affect the spacing between paragraphs, so the resulting document might have an inordinate amount of whitespace. Also, the Shrink operation makes no changes to margins. Word won't reduce font sizes below the range of 6 or 7 points.

CAUTION

In Print Preview mode, you can click the Undo button or press Ctrl+Z to reverse the Shrink to Fit operation, but after you've closed and saved the document, it's impossible to return the document to its original state.

CHOOSING WHAT TO PRINT

If you want to print one copy of the current document using the defaults established on the Print tab of the Options dialog box (see the Print What Choices table later in this chapter), select your Office button, choose Print, and then select Quick Print. You could also add this option to your Quick Access Toolbar.

Word also allows you to print the currently selected page(s), or to specify the pages you want to print by page number (along with a host of other configuration options) from the Print Dialog box. To open the Print dialog box, select the Office button, choose Print, and then choose Print again. Or you could select Ctrl+P (see Figure 13.26).

Figure 13.26
Word's Print dialog box allows you to specify what you want to print and how.

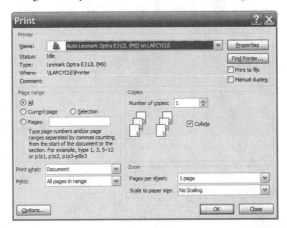

The Print box lets you print all pages, or odd or even pages only. If you know how your printer feeds sheets, you can use this setting to print *duplex*—where pages alternate on the front and back of each sheet.

TIP FROM

> If you check the Print to File box in the Print dialog box, Word prompts you for a filename. If your printer is currently unavailable, but you want to produce a hard copy of a document you're working with now, it can be a good option. Later, when the printer is available, you don't need to reopen Word; just copy the file you created directly to your printer by, for example, dragging it onto the printer icon in Windows Explorer.

That's pretty much all there is to know about standard printing. Now you may have a few other things you'd like to do with your documents. That's in the next section.

ADVANCED PRINTING TECHNIQUES

Ever wonder what Building Block entries you have set up in a particular document or template? How about the styles, or many other hidden parts of your document, for that matter? Choices in the Print What drop-down list let you find out (see Table 13.4).

TABLE 13.4 PRINT DIALOG BOX'S PRINT WHAT CHOICES

Option	What Prints
Document Properties	Some of the information found in the dialog box that appears when you select the Office button, the Prepare selection, and the Properties option. This causes the Document Information Panel to come up.

Option	What Prints
Document Showing Markup	Prints the document with changes, including comments, tracked in the margin; it does *not* print the style area.
List of Markup	Prints a list of the changes to a document.
Styles	All the styles that you can see if you open the Styles pane from the Home ribbon, select Options, and then choose Styles in Use.
Building Block Entries	All Building Block entries available in the document, whether they originate in the document's template or the Normal global document template, `Normal.dotx`.
Key Assignments	Only custom keyboard assignments for the current document, template, and global template.

There are still a few more printing features that may intrigue you, such as the capability to print thumbnails of your documents. Sometimes this can be quite helpful when you have two pages that you wish could be on one, but on the same side. The Pages Per Sheet list in the Print dialog box offers you the opportunity to print thumbnails of your documents—2, 4, 6, 8, or 16 pages—on a single sheet of paper.

TIP FROM

Ed & Woody

> If your primary reason for printing is to file away a hardcopy record of your documents, consider printing 2-up or 4-up, duplex if possible. Although you might need a magnifying glass to read the resulting printout, the storage space savings are enormous.

One final Advanced printing option is that if you choose to print more than one copy of a document, Word's default settings *collate* the copies for you—printing one copy from start to finish, and then printing the next copy from start to finish, and so on. That's convenient if you want to pull the pages right out of the printer and pass them around without any additional work. You could turn this feature off and then all copies of the first page will print together, and then the second, and so on.

CUSTOMIZING THE WORD INTERFACE

13

Many components of the Word interface—menus, toolbars, keyboard shortcuts, and the like—work precisely the same way in the other Office applications. There are two types of customization considerations: visual appearance and functionality. Sometimes you want to change the way things look within your documents (turning the rulers on or off, for instance). Other times, you want to alter the way Word works.

→ For the Officewide overview, **see** "Customizing Your Interface," **p. 32**.

In this section, you learned how to take control of features that are specific to Word.

Much of the rest of the way that Word works can be customized, as well. If you find that a specific "feature" in Word gets in your way, more often than not there's a simple check box that will disable the feature—or enable an alternative that might work better for you.

Your most important settings are found under the Office button in the Word Options (formerly known as Tools-Options—two selections fused into one word by Help Desk Support professionals who burned that into their minds over years of Word support). You've seen many of these options already throughout this chapter.

Visual Customizations in Word 2007 are limited. Your ribbons are preconfigured and unalterable. The only time your ribbon actually appears to change is when you shrink your window down and don't use the full screen. The ribbon size was designed for a screen resolution of 1024×786. You cannot add buttons to the ribbons, but you may be happy to know that you can minimize the ribbon. To accomplish this, right-click in the ribbon areas (or select the down arrow next to your Quick Access Toolbar) and choose Minimize the Ribbon. This will cause your ribbon tabs to be visible, but the ribbon won't show up unless you purposely select a tab.

In addition, you already know you can go to the View ribbon tab and turn on/off the Ruler, the Document Map, Thumbnails, or Gridlines. You can also change the Zoom settings as discussed earlier or establish split Windows.

At the bottom of your document window is the status bar, and you can right-click it to customize what's shown (see Figure 13.27). Notice that in addition to imply turning on certain options, they have to be enabled first before they will show up in the status bar.

Figure 13.27
Customizing the status bar.

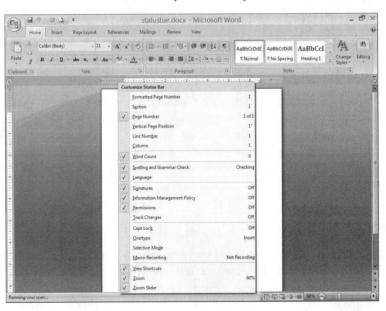

Now it's time to start discussing functionality changes. We have already discussed quite a number of changes throughout this chapter that we won't review here. But let's begin with a discussion of the Quick Access Toolbar.

There is no official documentation on this, but the way it seems to professional Word users, Microsoft loved its new ribbons so much that it didn't want us to be able to mess with them too much. But they knew that they needed to provide some customizable options for us to work with. They provided the Quick Access Toolbar to give you the flexibility you need (without harming their beautiful tabs).

So, the Quick Access Toolbar, shown in Figure 13.28, is the key to all your favorite tools (even the ones that are completely removed from all of the ribbons in Word 2007).

Figure 13.28
Customizing the Quick Access Toolbar.

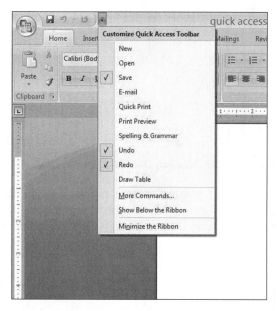

You get a basic set of tools to start with (Save, Undo, and Redo—very important ones). If you select the down arrow next to your Quick Access toolbar (as shown in Figure 13.28), you will see that you can also quickly add the following buttons: New, Open, Email, Quick Print, Print Preview, Spelling and Grammar, and Draw Table. You can also remove those tools by deselecting them. In addition, note that you can select the More Commands option, which will take you into the Word Options—Customize section shown in Figure 13.29. And you can choose to have the Quick Access Toolbar a little closer to your document by choosing Show Below the Ribbon.

For additional customization of the Quick Access Toolbar, go to the Office button, select Word Options, and then under the Customize settings (shown in Figure 13.29), you can find the various tools you want at your disposal and add them to the Quick Access Toolbar. (As mentioned earlier, you can also do this from the shortcut arrow next to the tools by selecting More Commands.)

13

Figure 13.29
Customization settings from within Word Options allow you to add plenty of customized tool choices.

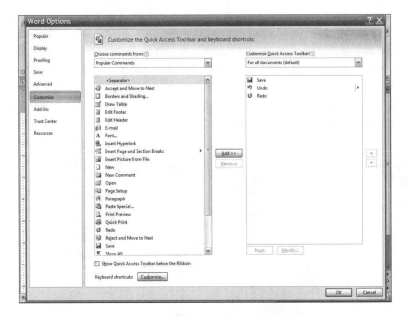

So far, we've discussed visual and functional changes, but there are deeper, advanced functional changes you might want to find. In the past you went to Tools, Options to find these options. Now you go to the Office button and to the Word Options selection. There are many choices to consider and the many settings might give you a headache, but Table 13.5 shows you much of what you'll need.

TABLE 13.5   WORD OPTION SETTINGS

Option	Sections
Popular	Top options for working with Word. Personalize your copy of Microsoft Office.
Display	Page display options. Always show these formatting marks on the screen. Printing options.
Proofing	AutoCorrect options. When correcting spelling in Office programs. When correcting spelling and grammar in Word. Exceptions for: (specific document or all documents).
Save	Save documents. Office editing options for document management server files. Preserve fidelity when sharing this document.

Option	Sections
Advanced	Editing options.
	Copy, cut, and paste.
	Show document content.
	Display.
	Print.
	When printing this document.
	Save.
	Preserve fidelity when sharing this document.
	General.
	Compatibility options.

Now that you know your options, if you start clicking through the advanced Word Option settings, some will make perfect sense to you, others you might remember from the chapter itself, and still others might be confusing (which is fine because most likely the extremely confusing settings are the ones you will never need to know, right? You hope.). Let's discuss a few more of those options just to catch you up as much as possible with your customization ability.

- **Show All Windows in the Taskbar**—Until the appearance of Word 2000, all previous versions of Word used the Windows Multiple Document Interface, or MDI. When you used MDI, a button for Word appeared on the Windows taskbar just once, no matter how many documents you had open. Word 2000 took a different approach, introducing a variant of the Single Document Interface (SDI), which produces one taskbar icon for each open document. Word XP and 2003 (and now Word 2007) allow you to switch between MDI and SDI by going to your Advanced section under Word Options, to the Display section, and then selecting the check box next to the Show All Windows in the Taskbar Setting. If you routinely work with more than one document on the screen at a time, making side-by-side comparisons, you'll probably prefer to stick with SDI. Give it a try.

- **Display Object Anchors**—We have already discussed in detail the other options within your Word Options—Display settings, such as showing tab characters and paragraph marks to make your life easier. But if you have trouble with drawing layer items moving around on a page, show object anchors to see where the drawings are tethered.

- **Recently Used Files**—Under the Advanced Settings in the Display section, you can see that the default selection for files is 17 (quite a bit in Word 2007). You can alter this to show more or less.

- **Typing Replaces Selected Text**—Found in the Advanced settings under Editing Options, this is turned on by default, which means that Word overwrites any selected text whenever you press a key on the keyboard. Many advanced users turn off this option to avoid accidentally deleting text.

- **Use Ctrl+click to Follow Hyperlink**—Found in the Advanced settings under Editing Options, this is one of the truly great improvements that was introduced back in Word 2002. Select this check box to ensure that you never accidentally chase a hot link by inadvertently clicking it.

13

- **Save Files in This Format**—Found in the Save settings in the Save documents section. The default setting for Word 2007 documents is in the new `.docx` format. You might want to alter this for a little while to use the `.doc` standard because `.docx` documents can be opened only by Word 2007. If you create a document and send it to others who don't use 2007, you will just have to save it again and resend it.

- **Save AutoRecover Information Every**—Located in the Save settings under the Save documents section, Word can automatically save an AutoRecover backup copy of the currently active document—a so-called `*.wbk` file—at time intervals you specify in this dialog box. If Word crashes or freezes, the next time it starts, it automatically looks for and opens any `*.wbk` files. With a little luck, the automatically recovered file will contain all your edits, up to the most recent AutoRecover time. This protection is in addition to—and, in our experience, far more reliable than—the built-in crash protection. If you're feverishly editing an important document, consider setting the interval to as little as 2 or 3 minutes.

TROUBLESHOOTING

FILE COMPATIBILITY PROBLEMS

As mentioned earlier, the new Office 2007 saves files in open XML formats. By default, only users with Office 2007 can open these types of files (which is why you might want to save your files under the option of a Word 97–2003 Compatible document). However, XML formats will work with Office 2003/XP/2000 with the use of a file format converter patch that you can download from Microsoft. Then users with those editions of Office can open, edit, and save their documents using the new XML formats. At the time of writing, the converter can be found at http://www.microsoft.com/office/preview/beta/converter.mspx.

GUIDED ASSISTANCE TO PROBLEMS STARTING WORD 2007

At times, Word does give us trouble and when this happens, the best source for assistance are the developers themselves. If you are having difficulty with Word opening and you don't want to reinstall (the standard fix-it to many problems), consider using the Guided Assistance that you can download from Microsoft.

TIP FROM

EQ & Woody

> To find articles about specific problems that you may be experiencing, search the Microsoft Knowledge Base. To do this, go to the following Microsoft website: http://support.microsoft.com/default.aspx.

The Knowledge Base article that deals with Word 2007 startup issues (where you can download the Guided Assistance or see manual options) is currently article number 921541. You can search for this article directly from the Microsoft site. Keep in mind that articles change and become out of date, so you may need to search specifically within the Knowledge Base for a newer set of advice.

SECRETS OF THE OFFICE MASTERS: USING WORD AS A BLOG EDITOR

You may be super savvy with today's modern terms but just to make sure, let's first answer the question "What is a blog?" before we discuss how Word can help you make one.

The word *blog* is short for weblog. A *weblog* is a journal (or newsletter, sort of like a public diary) that is frequently updated and intended to be read by the world at large. Why? Why would anyone want to put their heart or mind at the fingertips of millions? Some say because they can. Others say that there are billions of people on this spinning ball and they want to be heard. Whatever your philosophy about blogging, Word 2007 makes it easier for you to do it.

What's first? Get a blog account. Where? Everywhere! There are tons of sites that offer blog services that you can register for. But Microsoft offers some options that are free for you to try. Windows Live Spaces (http://spaces.live.com) is one place to go. Another is Blogger (http://www.blogger.com).

TIP FROM

Ed & Woody

> If you already have a blog account, you can begin using it right away. Select the Office Button, choose New, and choose New Blog Post. When the Register Blog Account dialog box opens, click Register Now to register your account with Word 2007. If you have more than one blog account, you can register as many of them as you have; then you can choose whichever account you want for your posting.
>
> If you already have a document you want to add to your blog site, select your Office button, choose Publish, and then select Blog. Again, you must register your site.

Blogging your text is simple and easy using the preceding option after you register your blog site. One thing you'll notice when you start the process is that you no longer have all seven ribbons (as shown in Figure 13.30). Now you will have a Blog Post and Insert ribbons. These contain all the needed tools for blogging so that you don't have to worry about those tools you won't need.

Some of the benefits of blogging with Word instead of your standard blog editor is that you can use the powerful features of Word within your blog ribbons. For example, the spell checker will prevent you from blogging incorrect wordage. You can use the translation tools to immediately provide multilingual blogging.

For those of you who have used Word for creating HTML content in the past by saving your documents as HTML, you may be concerned about what Word is going to do to your blog information. But Microsoft has learned its lessons well from the past, and you won't find that verbose Word HTML (although it's not perfect, it will give you at least blog-level HTML fidelity).

13

Figure 13.30
Blogging is one of the coolest new features in Word 2007. Notice that you have only two ribbons.

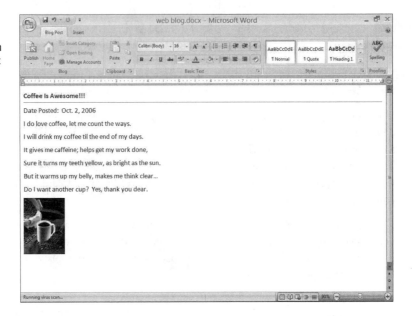

CHAPTER 14

USING THEMES, STYLES, AND TEMPLATES

In this chapter

How Themes, Styles, and Templates Work Together   388

Using Themes to Format an Entire Document   389

Formatting a Document with Styles   391

Creating, Using, and Managing Templates   404

Troubleshooting   409

Secrets of the Office Masters: Working with the Building Block Organizer   410

HOW THEMES, STYLES, AND TEMPLATES WORK TOGETHER

When it comes right down to it, your goal in Word is to make your document look good. Sure, providing valuable information is at the heart of your document, but making it stand out, making an impression that says the content (or you personally) is a head above the rest…who doesn't want that? In life, they tell you that you must have style; well, in Word it's no different.

In the previous chapter, you learned how you can make your documents look good through hard work, but Microsoft wants you to be able to focus more on the quality of your work and let Word do the formatting for you. To that end we have the ability to use Themes, Styles, and Templates. Following are the distinctions among the three:

- **Themes**—If you have ever spent hours trying to make your PowerPoint slideshow match the coloring scheme of your Word layout, you are going to love this new feature from Word. Themes give you the capability to choose a theme—a set of preconfigured formatting choices. You pick a theme with one click and your document has a set of theme colors, theme fonts (such as heading and body text fonts), and effects (which apply a prechosen set of fills and shading for your inserted charts, objects, flow charts, and so on). When you want to save a theme, it gets saved as a `.thmx` file.

NOTE

> To take advantage of the Themes options in Word 2007, your document must be in Full Functionality Mode, rather than Compatibility Mode. What this means is that if you are working on a document that is using the `.doc` format as a Word 97–2003-compatible document, the Themes options are grayed out. If the document is saved as a Word 2007 `.docx` format (Full Functionality Mode), you can use Themes.

- **Styles**—Word allows you to apply multiple formatting settings at one time by using *styles*. A specific style is a set of character and paragraph formatting that has either been predesigned by Microsoft or that is specifically designed by you. Microsoft provides the capability for you to apply these styles with one click by using a Quick Styles gallery. Galleries are provided for you to choose from that will help you keep your styles together and looking professional. You can create your own gallery with your own styles or use the ones provided.

- **Templates**—Styles are stored in *templates*. When you create a new document, you must base it on a template. You can use the default document template (`Normal.dotm`) or one of the cookie-cutter prototypes installed with Word, or you can start with a custom template that you created and saved. Word dutifully copies all the text that resides in the template into the new document—even if the template contains only a single paragraph mark—before it presents the document to you for editing. It also loads all the styles, macros, AutoText entries, and other saved elements from that template.

14

NOTE

> Templates have taken on a life of their own with Word 2007. It used to be that all you had to worry about was the default template `normal.dot` (now `normal.dotx` for XML documents that do not store VBA macro code and `.dotm` for Word 2007 XML documents that need to support VBA macro code) and you could make your own templates for future use. Now Microsoft provides thousands of beautiful templates to choose from—everything from To-Do List templates to Calendar templates of all shapes and sizes. To download the templates, the site requires you to have a browser that supports Active X (that is, Internet Explorer).

Although it might initially sound like themes, styles, and templates work separately, in reality they come together to provide the capability you need to make your documents come alive, and they give you the capability to format faster if you know what you are doing. Let's make sure that you do.

USING THEMES TO FORMAT AN ENTIRE DOCUMENT

We say that themes came on the scene in 2007, but in reality they have been around for some time. They just didn't have the same ease of use and customizable structure that they do now. Themes were introduced in FrontPage and PowerPoint, but the new concept is that Themes in one Office application can be found in others. So when you have a document that has the perfect color theme and then you switch to your PowerPoint show, what a cool effect for the viewers to clearly see that the two match up.

To start with, you need to be in a document that is fully functional, meaning it is based on the `.dotm` template and compatible with 2007 documents only. To apply a theme, you go to the Page Layout ribbon and select the Themes option from the Themes grouping, as shown in Figure 14.1. You'll note that there are 20 different themes offered, and these same themes can be found in other Office applications, such as Excel and PowerPoint, to ensure a common look for your presentation.

You can select a theme from the 20 Built-In selections. You can also check online with Microsoft for additional themes, or search for a theme you have created in the past. You can also develop and create your own theme.

There are a couple of ways to create your own theme. You can try the mix-and-match method to create your theme. For example, suppose you really like the color choices in the Technic theme, but you prefer the fonts in the Verve theme and the effects of the Metro theme. That's not a problem—just go to those pull-down options, select your choices, and then save your new theme by selecting Themes, Save Current Theme.

14

Figure 14.1
Word offers you 20 standard themes to choose from that you can find in the other Office applications to create a standard look for your presentation.

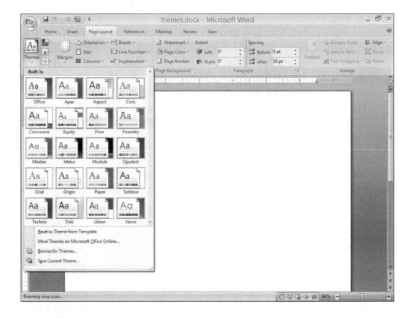

In addition, with both Colors and Fonts, you can actually change the options (although you cannot make changes to the Effects options). For example, in Colors you can select Create New Theme Colors (shown in Figure 14.2) and pick colors you think would suit your presentations better. You can also select Fonts, Create New Theme Fonts, and choose new Heading and Body fonts for your themes.

Figure 14.2
You can create new theme color settings and font settings, but cannot alter the effects.

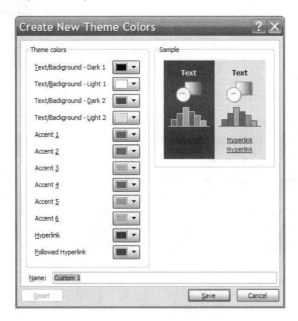

The point should be clear by now that Themes can be used to quickly establish a specific formatting style for your documents. You can use themes to establish a certain look and style you want, but especially to work with other Office applications that will be part of your presentations.

NOTE

> While we are discussing themes, it would be good to mention here that another nice feature in Word 2007 is the capability to plug in a cover page for your documents. To do this from the Built-In settings, go to the Insert ribbon and select Cover Page from the Pages grouping. There are predesigned choices and these are part of the document building blocks we discussed in Chapter 13, "Building a Better Word Document." You can design your own Cover Page building blocks, too, that include the color choices you prefer, perhaps the company logo—whatever you like—and then save it as a building block to be used later. We will discuss how to do this at the end of this chapter.

FORMATTING A DOCUMENT WITH STYLES

A style is nothing more than shorthand for formatting: Put a bunch of formatting specifications together, give it a name, and you have a style. If you find yourself applying the same formatting to text throughout a document, styles can help ensure a consistent and professional appearance that's easily modified. Use styles to control the formatting of the following:

- **Heading paragraphs**—Whether the headings are chapter titles, section names, product numbers, department names, contract division subtitles—it doesn't matter. If your document has a repeating kind of paragraph that's always formatted the same way, create a style for it.

- **Repeating body text**—If your document includes repeating body text that requires formatting different from the norm, use a style to format it. For example, if your company name always appears in Arial 12 point, bold, create a style for it. If you have a contract in which **party of the first part** is always bold, use a style. Similarly, use a style to format italicized telephone numbers in a company phone directory, to highlight company names in a marketing report, or to call attention to negative numbers in a corporate balance sheet

Defining and using styles consistently provides two great benefits. First, it ensures that all similar items in a document are formatted similarly—for instance, all the department names will appear in Garamond 12 point, bold. Second, if you need to make a change to the appearance of a style—suppose you decide that all the department names should appear in 14 point, instead of 12 point—changing the style (which requires just a few clicks) changes the appearance of everything formatted with that style, all the way through the document.

14

PARAGRAPH VERSUS CHARACTER STYLES

Paragraph styles control all the characteristics of a paragraph. Settings available as part of a paragraph style include centering, spacing, widows (whether a single line that begins a paragraph should be allowed to appear at the bottom of a page), orphans (whether a single line that ends a paragraph should be allowed to appear alone at the top of a page), and other settings in the Paragraph dialog box that appears when you go to the Home ribbon and choose the Paragraph handle selection. Paragraph styles also dictate bullets and numbering, borders and shading, and tab settings.

In addition, paragraph styles define *character formatting* for all characters within the paragraph. When you establish a paragraph style, you must also specify the default character format for the paragraph. Unless you specifically override the default character format with direct formatting or a character style, all text within a paragraph will appear in the paragraph's default character format.

Suppose you have a paragraph style called ProductName that specifies centered paragraphs, with Arial 18-point, italic, blue characters. If you apply the ProductName style to a paragraph, all the characters turn Arial 18-point, italic, and blue. But if you then select the last word in the paragraph and make it red, the formatting you applied manually—the red— takes precedence over the default character formatting specified in the ProductName style.

Character styles behave similarly, except that they carry only character formatting. That includes the font, font size and style, color, super/subscript, underscore, and other attributes available in the Font dialog box that appears when you select the handle from the Fonts grouping on the Home ribbon.

Suppose you have a character style called PhoneNumber that specifies the Courier New font in 10 point. If you apply the PhoneNumber style to some text, it loses its old formatting (which probably originated as the default character formatting of the underlying paragraph style) and picks up the formatting defined by the character style—Courier New 10 point.

TIP FROM

Ed & Woody

How can you tell the difference between a character style and a paragraph style? You can look at the Styles task pane by selecting the widget handle on the Styles grouping off the Home ribbon. In the Styles task pane, look for the little symbol to the right of the style's name, shown in Figure 14.3. A paragraph mark (¶) indicates a paragraph style, and an underlined lowercase <u>a</u> points out a character style. When you see a paragraph mark and an underlined lowercase <u>a</u> together, this is called a Linked style.

When it comes to character formatting, Word's hierarchy is strict. First comes the paragraph style, which you can modify by applying formatting directly (for example, you can format a Normal paragraph to be right-aligned, without changing its style). Then comes the character style, which takes precedence over the paragraph style settings. Finally, you can apply formatting directly to a character. That formatting takes precedence over both the character and the paragraph styles.

You can see the hierarchy at work by bringing up the Reveal Formatting task pane, as shown in Figure 14.4, and then clicking the Distinguish Style Source option at the bottom of the pane. The full hierarchy of formatting applied by both the paragraph and character styles, and by directly applied formatting, is shown.

Figure 14.3
The Styles pane can show you the many styles you have available. You can hover your cursor over the style and it will show you the settings associated with that style.

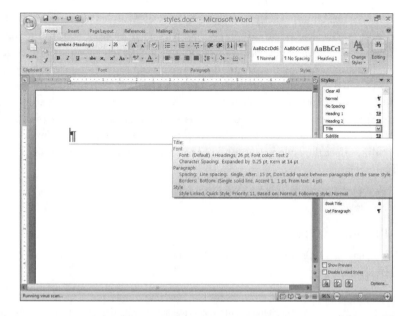

TIP FROM

Reveal Formatting used to be easier to access in previous versions of Word. To access these settings with Word 2007, you can use the shortcut keys Shift+F1, or you can open up the Styles window, select the Style Inspector(refer to Figure 14.4), and then select the Reveal Formatting button.

Figure 14.4
The Reveal Formatting pane can be reached through the Shift+F1 shortcut keys or through the Style Inspector.

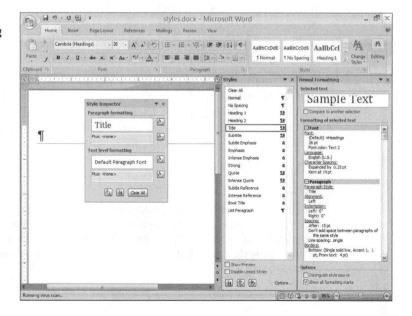

14

Every paragraph has exactly one paragraph style. Every character has exactly one character style. If no character style is defined for a particular piece of text, the style is Default Paragraph Font, in which case Word applies the character formatting defined in the paragraph style. If you don't explicitly define a paragraph style when you begin a new paragraph, Word uses the default paragraph style for the document. Typically, this is the Normal style, but you can set any paragraph style as the default. To do so, format at least one paragraph in the current document using the style you want to set as your new default; then select your Office button, go to Word Options, then to the Advanced tab, and under your Editing options, select the style you want from the Default Paragraph Style list in the Click and Type section.

→ More explanation on the various style tools will be found in the section titled "Managing Styles," in this chapter.

LIST AND TABLE STYLES

Word has two built-in sets of styles that you might find useful when applying complex formatting:

TIP FROM

Ed & Woody

> To see all the built-in styles available to you, bring up the Styles pane and then select the Options link in the bottom-right corner. Under the drop-down list of Select Styles to Show, select All styles.

- List styles let you directly specify the level of a list item by choosing the style and applying it to your selected paragraph. For example, if you want a bulleted list item that appears at the third indent level, you can apply the List Bullet 3 style, and Word takes care of the details. List styles are available for standard indented lists with no bullets or numbering (called, simply, List), standard lists with extra space inserted below the list item (List Continue), bulleted lists (List Bullet), and numbered lists (List Number).

- Table styles, which only appear in the Design contextual ribbon after you create a table, allow you to quickly format your tables. The groupings available are called Table Style options, Table Styles, and Draw Borders. These tools enable you to configure all sorts of settings within your tables, including choosing from a gallery of preconfigured options to make your tables come alive. We will consider these settings in greater detail in Chapter 15, "Advanced Document Formatting."

CAUTION

> Word makes some effort to apply selected Table styles to all the rows in a table, whether they've been selected or not. To remove all table formatting (a drastic step), select the entire table and apply the Table Grid format. Select your table, open your Styles gallery, choose the Apply Styles option, and then look for (or type in) Table Grid to apply this format to your table.

APPLYING STYLES MANUALLY

Optionally, paragraph and character styles can be manually applied. To apply a paragraph style, follow these steps:

1. Click once inside the paragraph whose style you want to change, or select one or more paragraphs.

2. Choose the paragraph style from the Styles gallery. Or you can select the drop-down arrow next to the gallery and choose the Apply Settings dialog, (shown in Figure 14.5). You could also choose the handle from the Styles grouping to bring up the Styles pane and select a style from there.

To apply a character style, follow these steps:

1. Select the characters whose style you want to change.

2. Choose the character style from the Styles task pane.

If you select text and apply a paragraph style, Word looks at what you've selected before applying the style. If you have chosen all the text in a paragraph (with or without the paragraph mark), Word applies the paragraph style, just as you would expect. If one or more paragraph marks are in the selection, all the selected paragraphs have the chosen paragraph style applied.

You can assign styles to a selection manually, if you prefer, by using the Apply Settings dialog box (shown in Figure 14.5) from within the gallery selections in the Styles grouping. You can type the style name. Word AutoCompletes this entry for you (unless you deselect that option), so you may need to enter only a few characters. When you see the correct style name, press Enter to apply it to the selection. You can also select the down arrow to show all the styles you can apply.

Figure 14.5
The many ways to apply a style manually. You can use the Apply Settings box or the Styles task pane.

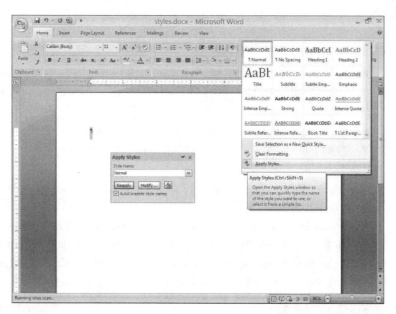

You have the ability to add a style into your Styles gallery, either as part of your right-click context menus or by using keyboard shortcut keys.

For styles you use on all types of documents, keyboard shortcuts are the ticket. On a default installation, Word includes the keyboard shortcuts shown in Table 14.1.

TABLE 14.1   DEFAULT KEYBOARD COMBINATIONS FOR STYLES

Style	Shortcut Key
Normal	Ctrl+Shift+N
List Bullet	Ctrl+Shift+L
Heading 1	Ctrl+Alt+1
Heading 2	Ctrl+Alt+2
Heading 3	Ctrl+Alt+3

TIP FROM

Ed & Woody

The slow, predictable way to assign keyboard shortcuts in Word is to go into your Word Options and to your Customize selections. Then at the bottom of your screen, choose the Customize button next to Keyboard shortcuts. Under the Categories section, scroll down and choose Styles. From the Styles section choose the style you want to make a shortcut for. You can see if there is already a shortcut in the Current Keys section. Then, under the Press New Shortcut Key section, put in your shortcut options.

Here's a much faster way: Open the Styles task pane, click the dropdown arrow to the right of the style, and choose Modify. Click Format, Shortcut Key. The insertion point is already positioned in the Press New Shortcut Key box; all you have to do is hold down the key combination you want to assign to the style. Click Assign to save the new shortcut key.

SAVING FORMATS AS NAMED STYLES

Although Word ships with nearly 300 defined styles—they're built in to the Normal template—you'll quickly find that they don't always apply to your documents and your specific needs.

If your needs are simple, you can set up a paragraph style by formatting a paragraph the way you want and telling Word the name of the style to be based on that formatting. To do so, follow these steps:

1. Format an entire paragraph to have all the attributes you want—both character and paragraph formatting apply.

2. Click once inside the paragraph. If you've used multiple fonts or font styles in the paragraph, the new paragraph style will use the font formatting at the point where you click.

3. Click the New Style button at the bottom of the Styles task pane. Then type a name for the new paragraph style into the Name box (see Figure 14.6).

Figure 14.6
Creating a new style.

4. In the Style Type box, choose Paragraph to create a paragraph style, Character for a character style, or Linked (both paragraph and character style). (You can also choose a table or list style, although it would be inappropriate in this example.)

5. In the Style Based On box, choose the style you want your new style to be based on. Any changes you make to the style listed here will also apply to your new style. If you want your style to stand on its own, choose (No Style) from the top of the list.

TIP FROM

Managed properly, an inheritance scheme is a wonderfully effective way to help you keep a complex design in perfect order with styles. You can create complex hierarchies of styles that are all based on a small number of base styles, and then change the overall design of your publication by adjusting just the base font. For instance, you might define a Catalog Base style that contains only the basic font formatting—Calibri 11 point, with single line spacing. You can then define styles for Catalog Headings, Catalog Product Descriptions, and Catalog Captions, varying the size, color, and weight of the font. Using this organization, you can change the font used throughout your publication—from Calibri to Cambria, for instance—just by modifying the Catalog Base style. If you decide to create a highly structured style scheme like this one, be sure to document it thoroughly!

6. The Style for Following Paragraph box lets you tell Word which style it should use for the next paragraph when you press Enter.

TIP FROM

Ed & Woody

By defining a chain of styles in your document, you can automate a lot of routine formatting. After using the Illustration style, for instance, you might want the next paragraph to be formatted with the Caption style, and the paragraph after that to be formatted with the Body Text style. By adjusting the Style for Following Paragraph settings for each style, you can format a paragraph as Illustration and then apply the following styles effortlessly, just by pressing Enter.

CAUTION

The Style for Following Paragraph setting kicks in only if the insertion point is immediately in front of a paragraph mark when you press Enter. If you leave even a single space between the insertion point and the paragraph mark when you press Enter, Word gives you a new paragraph with the same formatting and style as the current paragraph.

7. You can choose the option button Only in This Document so that this style is saved only with the current document. Or you can choose the option New Documents Based on This Template so that the style is added to the document's template and is available for use with any other document based on the template.

8. Select the Automatically Update box if you want every change you make to a paragraph formatted with this particular style to be automatically applied to every paragraph in the document with that style. Clear this check box if you want the style's formatting to remain fixed as you define it.

CAUTION

In almost all circumstances, Automatically Update is a disaster waiting to happen. You should use this option only on those rare occasions when you are absolutely certain that you never want to apply any direct formatting to text formatted with a particular style without changing all other paragraphs that use the same style.

9. Click the Format button to apply any additional formatting options. For a paragraph style, you can adjust virtually any type of formatting; for a character style, you can adjust font, border, and language settings only. You can also assign a shortcut key from this menu.

10. Click OK. If no style with that name exists, a new one is created for you and placed in the document. Click the style name in the Styles task pane to apply the newly created style to the current paragraph or any other existing paragraphs.

CAUTION

To create a new paragraph style based on a selected paragraph's attributes, you can just type a new name into the Apply Styles box and press Enter.

If you want to modify a style's definition, click the drop-down button next to the style's name in the Styles task pane, and then choose Modify. You'll have all the foregoing formatting options at your disposal. For simple changes, such as changing the font, font size, or spacing of a paragraph style, you can modify a style by example: Format some text using the style you want to modify and make your changes; then click the arrow to the right of the style name in the Styles task pane and choose Update Style Name Here to Match Selection.

 If your custom styles disappear when you open a document, see "Automatically Updating Styles" in the "Troubleshooting" section at the end of this chapter.

Keep in mind that you can modify any of your styles, both the ones located in the Styles task pane and the ones located on the Quick Styles gallery, by right-clicking the style and choosing Modify. This brings up the Modify Style dialog box (which looks just like the Create New Style Formatting dialog box, but with some grayed-out options).

TIP FROM

> If you want to add a few more styles to your Quick Style gallery, it's easier than you think. When you are creating your styles, you can choose the option Add to Quick Style List. Or you can modify your styles and check that box later. But an easier way to do this is to go into your Styles task pane, right-click the style you want, and choose the Add to Quick Style Gallery option. You can, at any time, also right-click a style currently in the gallery and choose to remove it from the gallery.

Some other options you may want to keep in mind when working with styles and formatting is the ability to keep track of your formatting while you type. Usually you want to keep these settings off to keep your Styles task pane from growing out of control. But to turn them on, you select the handle that launches your Styles task pane and go to the Options selection. From here you can select (or leave clear) check boxes for Paragraph Level Formatting, Font Formatting, and Bullet and Number Formatting. There are no icons associated with these, as there are with other entries in the Styles task pane.

MANAGING STYLES

Before we move forward, it's important to mention what's behind us in our discussion of styles. We've already discussed the built-in Quick Format Styles in our Styles grouping on the Home ribbon. In addition, we considered the Styles task pane—how to use it in determining what styles we can apply and using it to apply those styles. Then we discussed creating New Styles and the Options under the Styles task pane. Two additional buttons to consider are the Style Inspector and the Manage Styles button.

There are times when you don't know what's going on in your document styles. Something isn't right. This can happen when you are piecing together documents from multiple sources or when you've accidentally used too many formatting styles for one document. One Word developer coined this occurrence as "snowflake syndrome," where no two paragraphs look alike. And it can be real torture to make the document styles consistent, especially in a large document. That's when you call in the Style Inspector, shown in Figure 14.7.

14

Figure 14.7
The Style Inspector enables you to see what's happening in your document and allows you to remove formatting quickly.

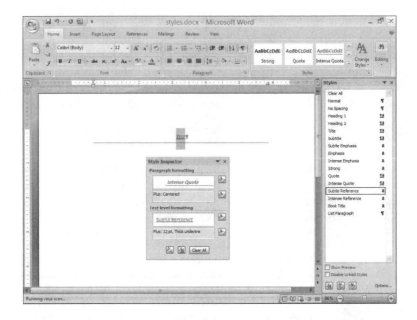

Your Style Inspector is a floating task pane that you can keep floating, or you can drag it over to the right side of your screen, where it can become its own pane (at the expense of a huge amount of screen space, but if you need quick access to these tools, this is your best option). You can also resize the floating pane, but it doesn't really give you many options; the size that you start with is pretty much the best you are going to get.

The Style Inspector shows you paragraph and text-level formatting for whatever paragraph you are in. You can select multiple paragraphs or a single character and receive feedback from the inspector, which can help you in determining the style you are using (if any). In the top window under Paragraph Formatting, you have one box that shows you the current paragraph formatting. If put your cursor in this box, you will get more detailed information about the paragraph style settings. You will also get a drop-down arrow with a choice of options, including the ability to choose a new style or modify the current one. You can also choose to select the number of instances that format occurs in the document, and all those paragraphs will be chosen at once.

In the Plus box, you will see any additional paragraph formatting not specific to your style. For example, if the style has the paragraph formatted with left alignment and you change it to centered, the Plus box will show that change. This can give you some clue as to why a paragraph may look different, even though you have a style applied.

Beneath the Paragraph Formatting options are the Text Level Formatting options, which show you whether you have used a character format (if not, it reports that you are using the Default Paragraph Font). And you can hover your cursor over this text box for additional information, as well. You can also get the drop-down arrow to allow more choices, such as selecting the instances of that particular formatting choice. And if you've made formatting additions to a portion of text, such as bolding or underlining, the Plus section shows these additional changes.

You might also notice that there are four erasers to the right of your information boxes. Here is what they can do for you:

- **Reset to Normal Paragraph Style**—Turns your selection (one or more paragraphs, not individual characters or words) back to the Normal paragraph style. Normally that would be Calibri 11pt. font with a left alignment and standard paragraph settings. However, the "normal" that the inspector is referring to is the normal for whatever document you are working in. For example, you might be working on a document that has altered what the normal setting is, and so when you select this option, it goes to that normal style.

- **Clear Paragraph Formatting**—Any additional formatting that you might have done to the paragraph will be removed, and it will be set back to just the style itself.

- **Clear Character Style**—This will remove the character style you have chosen and will bring you back to the Default Paragraph font. Again, this font will be whatever the default is for the document you are working in at the time.

- **Clear Character Formatting**—If you've made any changes to the character formatting such as bolding certain text, this will quickly remove all those settings without changing any of the other aspects of your style choices.

The Style Inspector is meant to be of assistance to you in correcting that so-called snowflake syndrome of your paragraphs, allowing you to make a consistent style to your documents. Sometimes you may change styles in your documents and you aren't sure why the paragraphs aren't updating the way you expected them to; that's when you can put the Style Inspector to work to determine if the text within the document was formatted manually or with styles. Most likely, you will need to clear out some manual formatting before you can apply the styles you want. Think of it as a canvas with a terrible painting that you want to paint over. First you have to eliminate the bad before you can proceed.

You might think that you have all the tools you already need to work with Styles perfectly. There is one more, and it is powerful (and complicated). It's the Manage Styles tool, which is accessed from the Styles task pane on the bottom.

The Manage Styles button brings up the Manage Styles dialog box (shown in Figure 14.8). This contains four tabs to help you work with your styles: Edit, Recommend, Restrict, and Set Defaults.

Figure 14.8
The Manage Styles dialog box gives you the tools you need to work directly on the engine of styles itself.

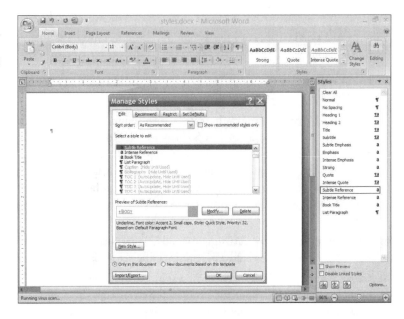

Let's discuss the four tabs and your potential use for this tool:

- **Edit**—As you can see in Figure 14.8, you can choose the Sort Order for all the fonts shown, whether alphabetical or type, or as recommended, the default sort method. From within this tab, you can select a font and then choose to Modify that font, which will take you to the Modify Style dialog box. You could delete the font or make a quick copy of the font that you can then alter for your own use.

- **Recommend**—This tab (shown in Figure 14.9) helps you adjust what styles appear in your Styles pane and in what order. For example, you might notice that your Heading 1 style has a rating of 1 and shows up in alphabetical order in your Styles pane. But Heading 2 (your next logical choice in formatting headings) has a setting of 10 and doesn't show up until the bottom of your pane. Heading 4 doesn't even show up in your Styles pane because it's hidden. From the Recommend tab of your Manage Styles options, you can change the priority settings (and assign values to your styles so they appear in the order that you want). You can also choose to Show, Hide Until Used, or Hide your styles from the Styles pane.

- **Restrict**—From here you can Permit or Restrict styles based on whether the document has been protected from formatting changes. It's not as confusing as it sounds. Basically you have the ability to use formatting restrictions so that your documents don't get altered by another person. Combining your Restrict settings with your Protect Document settings (as shown in Figure 14.10) can prevent users from using certain styles (or making any formatting changes). You can see from the figure that Heading 1 has been restricted and so doesn't show up in the list of available styles that a user can format text with. When you have the protection on, you are locked down from making changes and your formatting is grayed out. However, your Quick Styles are still functional by default. You can change that by checking Block Quick Style Set Switching. You can also check Block Theme or Scheme Switching.

14

Figure 14.9
Alter the styles that show up in your Styles task pane and the order that they appear.

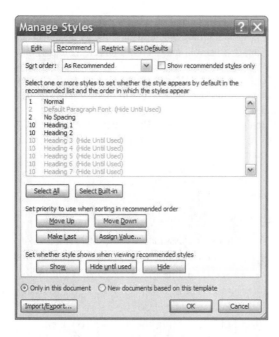

Figure 14.10
Use the Restrict settings to work with your restrict formatting and editing options.

■ **Set Defaults**—From here you can change some of your default character styles, such as the size of your fonts and the colors. You can also alter some of the default Paragraph Positioning and Paragraph spacing.

14

TIP FROM

Ed & Woody

Sometimes you have inconsistent formatting in your document and you want Word to show it visibly to assist you. You can turn on this feature from within your Word Options under Advanced settings/Editing options. There is a checkbox called "Keep track of formatting" and then one for "Mark formatting inconsistencies" that you need to select. Any styles that aren't consistent with the rest of your document formatting will be marked with a blue squiggly underline (not to be confused with the blue squiggly underline found in contextual spelling errors. The formatting squiggly is a little bolder blue). You can right-click on the section that is marked and choose to Replace direct formatting, or Ignore Once or Ignore Rule.

CREATING, USING, AND MANAGING TEMPLATES

Behind every document sits at least one associated template. Unless you've taken steps to change it, the main template attached to a document is the same one you used to create the document in the first place. To see the name of the associated template in the Document Template dialog box, you need to customize your Quick Access toolbar to include the Document Template button. You do this by choosing More Commands from your Customize Quick Access (located by selecting the down arrow next to the Quick Access Toolbar) options or by going into the Word Options under Customize and finding the Document Template button and adding it to your toolbar. Then you can open it up and see the template your document is using (see Figure 14.11).

Figure 14.11
The Templates and Add-Ins tool tells you the name of the template attached to the current document, as well as the names of any "global" templates (other than Normal.dotm) that were loaded when Word started.

N O T E

> A global template is a template that's available to all open documents. Specifying a global template gives you access to special-purpose macros and AutoText entries throughout Word, without having to change the template for a given document. Because the Normal document template (`Normal.dotm`) is always loaded and made global each time Word starts, it's always available to every open document. You'll hear `Normal.dotm` called "the" global template, but it isn't really: You can have many global templates available at any given moment.

CUSTOMIZING THE NORMAL DOCUMENT TEMPLATE

When you create a new, blank document by clicking the New Blank Document icon from the Office button options, Word creates a new document based on the Normal document template, `Normal.dotm`. The Normal template is always available when Word is running.

As we noted at the beginning of this chapter, Word looks for styles, starting with the document, moving up to the document's template and, if the style name can't be found there, looking inside the Normal template.

N O T E

> If the document is based on the Normal template, there's no intermediate step—the search progresses directly from the document to Normal.

Actually, the Normal document template is no more "normal" than any other template. A more accurate name would be the default document template, the one Word uses when you create a new blank document without specifying a template. `Normal.dotm` is frequently called the global template because it's always available. Although other templates can be global in the sense that they're loaded when Word starts (refer to the Templates and Add-Ins dialog box shown in Figure 14.11), no other template is tied directly to the New Blank Document options.

By default, Word 2007 starts new blank documents with the Calibri 11-point font, and no paragraph indenting or spacing. If you open `Normal.dotm`, you'll see why: It contains a single paragraph mark formatted in the Normal style, and the Normal style is defined as Calibri 11 point, with no paragraph indenting or spacing. When Word creates a new document based on `Normal.dotm`, it copies everything in the template into the new document—the same as it does when creating a document from any template—and you end up with a new document with a single paragraph mark, with Normal style formatting.

TIP FROM

Ed & Woody

> If you want to change the default font for new blank documents, you don't need to mess with `Normal.dotm`. Instead, use this hidden shortcut: Create a new blank document, and then go into the Font dialog options off the Font grouping on the Home ribbon. Choose the font you want (for instance, Garamond 11 point), and click the Default button. From that point on, any new blank document you create will use the Garamond 11-point font for its Normal style.

14

You can change your default template by either creating a new blank document, making formatting changes to it, and then saving it as your new `normal.dotm`, or by opening up your `Normal.dotm` and making changes directly, whichever you prefer. To perform the latter, do the following:

1. Select the Office Button and choose Open.

2. Select the Trusted Templates option and select the `Normal.dotm` template. Note: if you have any trouble seeing these, go down to your Files of type and make sure that All Word Templates is selected. To make sure you have the correct document, you should see the document title as `Normal.dotm` at the top of the documents.

3. Make whatever changes you want to make to Word's defaults for new blank documents. Click the Paragraph handle to adjust more advanced formatting options: You can change the font, paragraph formatting, tabs, borders and shading, proofing language, bullets, and numbering.

4. When you've made all the changes you want to make, select the Office button and then click Save.

You can also open a regular document, make formatting changes, and then choose the Office button, click Save As, and choose Word Template. You would then have to determine if you want a `.dotx` or `.dotm` template style. You can also open up and change the `Normal.dot` template if you like. This template is for backward compatibility with Word 97–2003, which used this template source.

 If you've made a colossal mess of your Normal document template and want to start over, see "Restoring the Default Normal Template" in the "Troubleshooting" section at the end of this chapter.

When you open a template (in contrast to creating a new document based on a template), you can modify it in precisely the same ways as you would change a document: You can add text, pictures, headers and footers, hyperlinks, macros—in short, everything that goes in a document (plus AutoText entries).

Remember, however, that any text you place in the document itself is considered to be "boilerplate" and is copied into any new documents you create based on that template. If you attach a template to an existing document, however, saved items in that template are available, but the boilerplate text is ignored.

TIP FROM

EQ & Woody

> If the `Normal.dotm` template becomes damaged or is moved or renamed, Word will create a new version using the original settings the next time you start Word. All your customizations will be lost in this new `Normal.dotm`.

Using Word's Built-in Templates

Moving past the Normal templates and the standard documents that you will build, the fun of Word 2007 is that you can choose templates that are built in or choose from the thousands of online templates that are available to you at http://office.microsoft.com/en-us/templates/default.aspx. Keep in mind that you can find those templates that are specific to Word 2007 by including "Word 2007" in your search options.

To choose a template that is already built in, select the Office button, then New. You'll notice (as shown in Figure 14.12) that you have the option to choose from templates that are Blank and Recent, Installed Templates that are installed by default, My Templates (which you create or download and save), or a New from Existing Template. Or you can view categories for Microsoft Office Online templates as shown in Figure 14.12 that help you to see what you are downloading in a nice preview window.

Figure 14.12
Working with templates that are built in, or downloading preconfigured ones from Microsoft, can make your work documents easier and more professional, as well as your personal documents, such as schedules and holiday events.

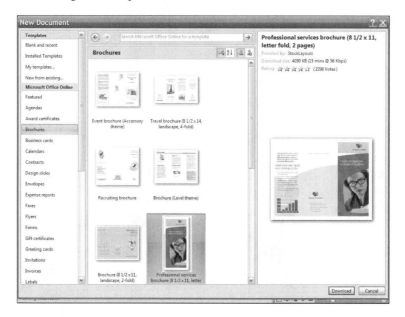

BUILDING A TEMPLATE FROM SCRATCH

To create a new template, choose the Office button and then New. You can choose to start a new template based on an existing document or on an existing template. You decide where you want to start, but if you want to use the default, you can choose My Templates and then select the template (use the default, `Normal.dotm`, to start from scratch) and click OK.

Look in the title bar and you'll see that the newly created file uses the default name Template1 instead of Document1. A Word template is nearly identical to a Word document, except that it also contains AutoText entries. (The Normal template also contains formatted AutoCorrect entries.) That's the only difference. By default, Word templates are identified with the filename extension `*.dotm`. Although you can use a different file extension, only files with the `*.dotm` extension appear in the Templates dialog box.

Save the file when you are done. You may wonder where these files are being saved to. Unless you specifically change the location, custom templates you create are stored in a standard location within your personal documents folder. By default, the Trusted Templates are stored in a Templates folder under `\%username%\Application Data\` `Microsoft\Templates`.

You can change the location for your templates by going into your Word Options from the Office button. Choose the Advanced options and scroll all the way down to the General section where it has a button selection called File Locations. You can select this option and then choose Modify to change the location of your templates.

COPYING STYLES AND SETTINGS BETWEEN TEMPLATES

Word includes a handy tool called the *Organizer* that allows you to copy styles and macro projects between documents and templates.

To make use of the Organizer, follow these steps:

1. Select the Templates button that you can add to your Quick Access toolbar (as mentioned earlier), and this will open the Templates and Add-Ins dialog box. Click the Organizer button. You see the Organizer dialog box (see Figure 14.13).

Figure 14.13
The Organizer copies, deletes, or renames styles and macro projects.

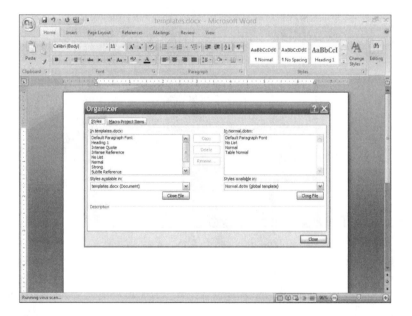

2. Make sure the "from" and "to" files—documents or templates—are referenced in the Styles Available In boxes. If you have the wrong files, click Close File, then Open File, and select the correct ones.

3. Select Styles or Macro Project Items, depending on which settings you want to manipulate.

4. Select the individual items and click Copy, Delete, or Rename, as appropriate

The basic premise here is simple; you have a set of styles that you have already created. Why create them again? No need, just use the Organizer to copy them where you want.

TROUBLESHOOTING

WORD KEEPS CHANGING MY ENTIRE DOCUMENT

Every time I select a paragraph and make even the tiniest change to it, Word changes my entire document. If I want to boldface a paragraph, my entire document turns bold. If I add a bullet character, every paragraph in the document gets a bullet. I figured out that I can press Ctrl+Z to undo the global change, but this is getting ridiculous. What's going on?

Word is only following orders. Somewhere along the line, you told Word that you wanted it to automatically update the paragraph style that you have chosen every time you made a change to it. When you select a paragraph formatted using that style, Word dutifully applies the change to every other paragraph using that style. To turn it off, open the Styles task pane, click the arrow to the right of the style entry, and choose Modify. Clear the Automatically Update check box and click OK.

REVEALING CHARACTER FORMATTING

As a former WordPerfect user, I'm accustomed to WordPerfect's "reveal codes" command, which displays formatting directives hidden in a document, much like HTML tags. When I search through online help, however, there's no mention of Word's reveal codes command.

Word's native document format doesn't use WordPerfect-style codes to apply formatting. Instead, it stores formatting for each character with the character itself, and it stores paragraph formatting in the paragraph mark. The Reveal Formatting task pane displays the names of styles and direct formatting applied to any character. If you save a document in XML format, Word saves formatting instructions as XML tags, but these bear no resemblance to WordPerfect codes.

AUTOMATICALLY UPDATING STYLES

When I opened a document that contained a number of custom styles, the formatting changed unexpectedly, and clicking the Undo button didn't bring them back.

Styles in the document template are overwriting styles in the document itself. If you create a set of formats in named styles and save them in a document, you might find that your styles get wiped out by styles of the same name stored in the document template every time you open the document. To make sure you don't encounter this problem with a specific document, choose Templates and Add-Ins from your customized Quick Access toolbar (or customize your Quick Access toolbar by adding this option into it), and clear the Automatically Update Document Styles box. To avoid the problem in the future, do not use standard style names (Normal, Heading 1, and so on) when creating custom styles within a document.

AUTOMATICALLY UPDATING STYLES

I changed one of the styles in my document and several others changed along with it.

It's possible that the style you changed was the basis for other styles that exist in your document. When you make a change to a base style, it will affect other styles that use it as a base. For example, if you change the Normal style font to be something else, like Times New

Roman (for old-time's sake), that same change will affect footnotes, headers, footers, page numbers, and any other text that is based on the Normal style. To fix this, you need to go into the Styles task pane, select the down arrow for the style you want to change, and then choose Modify. From here you can choose No Style for that style to be based on, and that should clear up the problem you are having.

RESTORING THE DEFAULT NORMAL TEMPLATE

I've made a mess of the Normal template, and every new document I create inherits formatting I don't want.

You have three choices. The easy (but drastic) option is to exit Word, rename `Normal.dotm` (located in the Templates folder) to something else (for example, `Old-normal.dotm`), and start Word again. When Word can't find `Normal.dotm`, it creates a new Normal document template; in the process, however, you'll lose all your customizations, keyboard shortcuts, formatted AutoCorrect entries, and much more.

If you just want to reset the Normal paragraph style and other standard styles to their defaults, you can use the Modify Style dialog box to work through each style in the template until you have the Normal style back to where it started. For U.S. installations, that includes the following defaults: Calibri, 11 point, English (U.S.), Flush left, Line spacing single, 10pts after spacing, and Widow/orphan control. Make sure you click Add to Template when you're done. It's more work, but you won't lose any of your customizing.

If that sounds like too much work, then combine the two strategies. Create a fresh copy of `Normal.dotm` using all Word's defaults, and then use the Organizer to selectively move custom styles, toolbars, macros, and other items from the backed-up `Old-Normal.dotm` to your new file. Just don't overwrite the standard styles!

SECRETS OF THE OFFICE MASTERS: WORKING WITH THE BUILDING BLOCK ORGANIZER

You might wonder why this is the Office Master secret for a chapter on styles, but if you recall the mention earlier of Cover Pages, this is exactly the right place for the Building Block Organizer.

Here is why: Cover Pages are building blocks. They are nothing more than pages that have been formatted using all the tools we have been discussing in Chapters 13 and 14, put together to create a nice cover for your document, and then saved as a block to input into your document. But you don't have to take our word for it—you can see it for yourself in Figure 14.14.

Figure 14.14
Looking at your building blocks, you can see that all the Cover Pages are included as part of the blocks.

Now the cool thing about this is that you can create your own, as well as modify the ones that exist. Building Blocks can also be used for headers, footers—whatever you like. You can even download additional preconfigured blocks by going to the Insert ribbon, to the Quick Parts selection, and choosing Get More on Office Online for downloadable blocks.

To create the building block you want, first create the text or formatted section. For example, if you want to create a footer building block, make the footer according to your specifications. When it's exactly what you want to save, select the footer completely and go to the Insert ribbon, and under Quick Parts in the Text grouping, select Save Selection to Quick Parts Gallery. When you choose this, the Create New Building Block dialog box comes up, as shown in Figure 14.15, and from here you can determine the name of your building block and the gallery you want it to be a part of (for example, as a footer you can save it to the footer gallery).

Figure 14.15
Building Block creation options.

You can also select a Category, the default being General, but you can also create additional ones. Establish a description of your building block (which is really important for those that are too small to see easily in the preview pane). You can choose to save the building block as part of the default template or another template, and you can establish, in Options, whether the block is placed in the document directly, in its own paragraph, or in its own page (as is the case with Cover Page building blocks; they reside within their own page and put you on the next page to start your document).

14

After you have completed your custom-made building block, it will be under the Quick Parts Gallery if, and only if, you placed it in the Quick Parts Gallery when you created it (or if you modify the gallery to be Quick Parts later on), as shown in Figure 14.16, to allow easy access in applying it. If it is in the Footer Gallery or another type of gallery, you will need to go to those galleries to apply it. (For example, you could save the footer to the Footer Gallery, and then you would need to go to the Insert ribbon, and under the Footer selection from within the Header and Footer grouping, you would be able to see a preview of your self-made footer. You could also use the Building Blocks Organizer to apply it.)

Figure 14.16
Seeing your Quick Parts building block in the gallery.

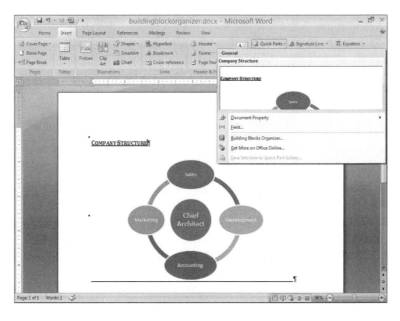

The building blocks you create could be part of any number of galleries—for example, AutoText or Table of Contents—and you can modify your blocks later into the correct gallery using the Building Blocks Organizer.

When you create a building block, it is saved as a `.dotx` template file and placed in folders named Quick Styles and Document Building Blocks, in the Microsoft folder where your Templates folder is located.

One other point to mention is the use of Document Properties when creating certain building blocks like Cover Pages. You can see in Figure 14.17 that the Cover Page we are looking at has special fields. These document properties are useful for multiple instances of the information. When the property box is filled in, it will change the rest of the document that uses that property. If you make a change to that information, the entire document will update itself. We will discuss these in greater detail in Chapter 17, "Letters, Envelopes, and Data-Driven Documents."

Figure 14.17
Cover Pages contain Document Properties that have styles selected for them and can be used throughout the rest of the document for multiple instances of the same information (for example, Company Name).

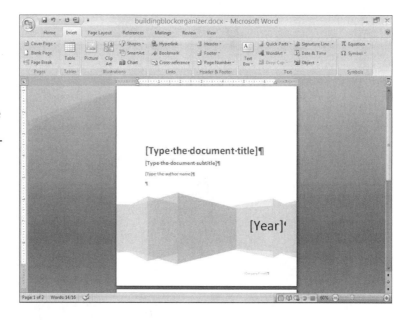

> **NOTE**
>
> To take advantage of the Document Properties in Word 2007, your document must be in Full Functionality Mode, rather than Compatibility Mode. This means that if you are working on a document that is using the .doc format as a 97–2003-compatible document, the Document Property options are grayed out from the Quick Parts menu. If the document is saved as a Word 2007 .docx format (Full Functionality mode), you can insert Document Properties.

14

CHAPTER 15

ADVANCED DOCUMENT FORMATTING

In this chapter

Using Tables to Organize Information   416

Adding and Organizing Figures and Graphics   436

Using Headers and Footers   441

Adding Lines, Borders, Shading, and Backgrounds   444

Formatting Documents by Section   448

Formatting a Document with Columns   451

Troubleshooting   452

Secrets of the Office Masters: Saving Files as PDF or XPS   453

15

USING TABLES TO ORGANIZE INFORMATION

As you already know, Word 2007 has many features for creating stunning documentation, including the capability to structure our data into tables. But Word has been notorious for its inability to perform complex math within those tables. In fact, Word tables are at their weakest when pressed into service as repositories for rows and columns of numbers. Word has a paltry selection of tools for working with numbers. If you want to do any sort of arithmetic in a Word document—anything more complex than an occasional sum or product on a small handful of data—you're far better off embedding or linking an Excel range inside your Word document, even if you have to learn Excel to do it.

Then what are Word tables good for? They're tailor-made for organizing and presenting price lists, feature comparisons, schedules, and other orderly arrangements of text. But Word tables are also excellent page layout tools that can help you precisely place words, numbers, and pictures on a page. In Figure 15.1, it might be obvious to you that we used a table to create the list of customs exceptions—after all, each cell has a line around it and the data is classically tabular. But it might not be so obvious that we used a table to organize the header of this fax, as well. Choose View Gridlines from the Borders options menu on the Design ribbon (which appears after you create a table) under the Table Styles grouping, to reveal the nonprinting gridlines around the table.

Figure 15.1
A table, without the gridlines, makes it easy to create and maintain the "To/From/Re/Date" part of this fax. Consider the two documents side-by-side.

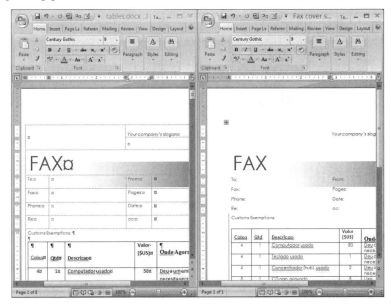

You should consider using tables when you need to perform any of the following tasks:

- Line up paragraph headings on the left with text on the right. Many résumés use this format.
- Draw intersecting horizontal and vertical lines. Using tables is generally much simpler than trying to add borders around words or paragraphs.

- Create fill-in-the-blanks printed forms.
- Create data-entry forms for online use.

→ To learn more about entering data in Word forms, **see** "Secrets of the Office Masters: Creating a Fill-in-the-Blanks Form with Fields" **p. 503**.

- Place text in a fixed location on a page. Anytime you're thinking about using tab stops to arrange text or graphics on a page, consider using tables (without gridlines) instead. In general, tables are faster and easier to set up, and much simpler to maintain.

In Word 2007, you can draw one table inside another—a very handy trick if you use tables for page layouts. Each "nested table" appears, in its entirety, within a single cell in the larger outer table. This feature is generally used in designing web pages. If a web page is structured as one big table, you can use this feature to nest additional tables inside and build out the formatting for your site.

ADDING A TABLE TO A DOCUMENT

When creating a new table, you have two basic choices: Either Word can draw the table for you (using either the Insert Table dynamic insertion or the Insert Table options), or you can draw it yourself. When Word draws the table for you, you are subject to the following restrictions:

- If using the Insert Table dynamic insertion, you can start with only 10 columns and 8 rows as a maximum.
- If you use the Insert Table options, you specify the number of columns (to a maximum of 63) and rows (up to 32,767).
- You define how the table fits on the page, using one of three options: the table can fill the page, each column can have the same width, or each column can automatically expand to accommodate the contents of the widest cell.
- Rows start out one line tall, but automatically get taller, if necessary, to hold text or graphics.

If you can live with those restrictions, Word will make your table quickly. If you want more control over the initial table design—if you want the table to occupy only part of a page, for instance, or if you have complex cell patterns—you can draw your table freehand.

CREATING QUICK TABLES

To have Word draw a table for you, follow these steps:

1. Click in an empty paragraph where you want the upper-left cell of the new table to be located.

2. Select the Insert ribbon tab and select the Table icon on the Tables grouping. You can select the rows and columns dynamically, but instead choose Insert Table. The Insert Table dialog box appears (see Figure 15.2).

15

Figure 15.2

3. In the Table Size section, choose the number of columns and rows. (If you're not sure how many columns or rows you'll need, don't worry. You can easily increase either number later.)

4. In the AutoFit Behavior section, tell Word how to determine the width of the table and its columns.

5. By default, every new table uses the generic Table Grid style. After your table has been created, you will see two new ribbons: one is the Design ribbon and the other is the Layout ribbon. In the Design ribbon, you'll find dozens of prefab formats in the Table Styles gallery on the Table Styles grouping (see Figure 15.3).

Figure 15.3
Quick, cookie-cutter tables are easy with the Table Styles gallery.

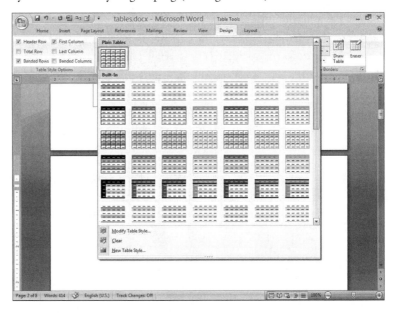

TIP FROM

If you routinely create tables of a certain number of columns and rows, you can save those settings for reuse. After defining your preferred table settings in the Insert Table dialog box, click the Remember Dimensions for New Tables check box. Later, when you go to create a new table using the Insert Table dialog box, it will include the number of columns and rows you chose.

After you have your table in your document and formatted the way you'd like, you can use the Layout tab to make configuration changes to your table or you can right-click within the table and choose from the context-sensitive menu that includes a variety of options, including Table Properties.

DRAWING A COMPLEX TABLE

Unless you specifically want a table that conforms to Word's Insert Table restrictions, drawing one by hand is the best option. To do so, follow these steps:

1. Select the Insert ribbon, choose the Table icon from the Tables grouping, and choose Draw Table. The mouse pointer turns into a pencil.

2. Click where you want the upper-left corner of the table to appear. (You can even click inside a table cell, to create a *nested table* within that cell.

3. Drag the pencil down and to the right, to the lower-right corner of the new table. Word creates a table with a single, large cell.)

4. Using the pencil, click an existing table line and drag to the opposite edge to form a row, a column, or an individual cell. You can even click a cell corner and drag to the opposite corner to create a diagonal line.

If you don't like the position or size of a line you've drawn, from the Design ribbon, the Draw Borders grouping includes an Erase button that you can use to remove lines. Position the "eraser" mouse pointer on the line you want to erase, and then click. To restore your usual mouse pointer, press Esc or click the Erase button again.

TIP FROM

Ed & Woody

> Don't worry about being neat when drawing rows and columns within a table. Just concentrate on getting the number of rows and columns right. You can use Distribute Rows Evenly or Distribute Columns Evenly later.

SAVING YOUR TABLE INTO THE GALLERY

You can create your table, format it perfectly, even add text such as the headings you want for that table, and then save all those settings as a building block. To do this you select your table and then choose your Table icon from the Tables grouping on the Insert ribbon. At the bottom is a choice called Quick Tables. From here you can choose Save Selection to Quick Tables Gallery and the Create Building Block dialog box will come up. Give your table a name. Now it will appear in your Quick Tables gallery when you want to create a table quickly. You can also see it in the Building Blocks Organizer.

ENTERING AND EDITING DATA

You can type in a table cell precisely the same way you would type in a paragraph. If you press Enter, Word creates a new paragraph for you—in the same cell. Single cells can contain text, graphics, linked and embedded items—basically anything you can put in a document.

To move from one cell to the next, press Tab. To move back one cell, press Shift+Tab. To move backward or forward one character at a time, jumping from cell to cell at the beginning and end of each cell's contents, use the left- and right-arrow keys. To move up or down one cell, press the up- or down-arrow keys.

TIP FROM

To enter the Tab character in a table cell, press Ctrl+Tab.

If the insertion point is in the last cell in a table, pressing Tab creates a new row, formatted the same as the current row, and moves the insertion point to the first cell in that row.

Many of the special navigation key combinations work inside tables. For example, Shift+right arrow selects text one character at a time, Ctrl+Shift+right arrow picks up a word at a time, and so on.

TIP FROM

You can add text above a table at the top of a document. With the insertion point in the first row of the table, press Ctrl+Shift+Enter to insert a paragraph above the table, and then move the insertion point into that new paragraph. Use this same shortcut to split a table in two; position the insertion point in the row you want to use as the first row of the new table and then press Ctrl+Shift+Enter.

Formatting, Aligning, and Rotating Text

Table cells behave much like Word paragraphs: Text within a cell can be formatted, aligned, indented and spaced, bulleted and numbered, with borders and shading, and each cell can have its own tab stop settings. All cell formatting is stored in the end-of-cell marker, which you can see only when paragraph marks are showing (click the Show/Hide ¶ button on the Standard toolbar, or go into your Word Options and in the Display settings, select the Paragraph Marks check box).

Selecting Cells, Rows, and Columns

Select data within a cell the same as you select data in a paragraph; if you want to transfer cell formatting, make sure you pick up the end-of-cell marker. Alternatively, you can select everything in a cell (including the end of cell marker) by letting the mouse pointer hover over the left side of the cell. When it turns into a thick arrow pointing up and to the right, click to select the whole cell. Or you can click inside the cell and choose Select, Select Cell from the Table grouping of the Layout tab.

Other selection techniques include the following:

- To select an entire row, including the end-of-row marker, move the mouse pointer to the left of the row. When it turns into the shape of a hollow arrow pointing to the upper right, click. Alternatively, click once inside the row and the Select button from the Table grouping of the Layout tab. Choose Select Row.

■ To select an entire column, let the mouse pointer hover near the top of the column. When it turns into a black solid arrow pointing down, click. Or you can choose Select, Select Column from the Table grouping of the Layout tab.

■ To select the whole table, let the mouse pointer hover over the table move handle at the upper-left edge of the table until the pointer turns into a four-headed arrow, and then click to select the table. Alternatively, choose Select, Select Table from the Table grouping of the Layout tab.

Moving and Copying Parts of a Table

All the usual copy, cut, and paste routines you're accustomed to in Word work equally well within tables and cells. If you've placed cells on the Clipboard, Word responds by adding new entries in both the Paste options on the Home ribbon and in the right-click hover menu—Paste Cells and Paste as Nested Table.

Paste Cells replaces the existing cells with the contents of the copied cells; the table itself is expanded only if there are too many copied rows or columns to fit in the existing table. If you choose Paste as Nested Table, Word creates a new column, row, or table as needed and fills it with the contents of the Clipboard. If you click inside a cell and then insert directly from the Clipboard task pane, Word assumes you want to insert the columns, rows, or table on the Clipboard as a nested table, within the current cell.

CAUTION

> When you paste cells, Word overwrites the contents of the current cells—without warning, and without giving you an opportunity to change your mind. If that happens, click the Undo button (or press Ctrl+Z or choose Edit, Undo), and try again.

You can click and drag cells, columns, and rows, just as you do elsewhere in Word—with one exception. If you're going to move an entire row, you must select the end-of-row marker.

You can add rows and columns quite easily from the Layout ribbon when you are in your table. You can insert rows above and below, and columns to the right or the left from your current location in the table. There are graphic icons (as shown in Figure 15.4) that make it easy to add rows and columns from the Layout ribbon, within the Rows and Columns grouping. In addition, from here you can also select parts of your table (cells, rows, columns, or the entire table) and select the Delete button.

If you copy or move a cell, including the end-of-cell marker, to an area outside a table, Word creates a new table on the spot. The new table consists of a single cell whose contents match those of the cell being copied or moved.

 If you are frustrated with cell contents or the row markers disappearing, see "Disappearing Cell Contents and Row Markers" in the "Troubleshooting" section at the end of this chapter.

Figure 15.4
Inserting Rows and Columns is easy within the Layout ribbon, under Rows and Columns.

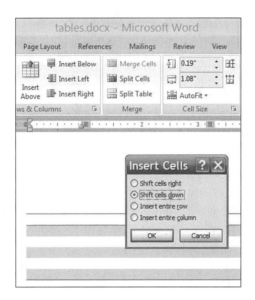

CHANGING COLUMN WIDTHS AND ROW HEIGHTS

To adjust a column's width, you have four choices:

- **Eyeball it**—Move your mouse pointer so it's near a vertical line in the table. When the pointer changes into a double-headed arrow, click and drag the line. If you move left, the column to the left gets narrower and the column to the right gets wider. If you move right, the column to the right gets narrower and the column to the left gets wider.

TIP FROM

If you want to change the width of the column only on the left (shrinking or expanding the size of the entire table as you go), hold down the Shift key as you drag.

- **Measure it**—Right-click inside the column you want to change and then choose Table Properties from the shortcut menu (or choose Properties from the Table grouping on the Layout ribbon). In the Table Properties dialog box, click the Column tab (see Figure 15.5). From that point, you can precisely specify the width of each column.

- **Fit the contents**—If you want the column width to grow or shrink, depending on the width of the contents, right-click in the row, and then choose AutoFit, AutoFit to Contents from the shortcut menu (or choose from the AutoFit options off the Layout ribbon).

TIP FROM

To AutoFit a single column, select the entire column and then double-click its right border.

Figure 15.5
To get precise column measurements, nothing beats the Table Properties dialog box.

- **Fit the margins**—You can also have Word automatically calculate how wide a specific column must be to have the table extend all the way from the left to the right margin. To do so, right-click inside the column, and then choose AutoFit, AutoFit to Window from the shortcut menu.

If you need to restore some uniformity to the table, you can always make all the columns the same width by choosing Distribute Columns from the Cell Size grouping on the Layout ribbon. Incidentally, you can also select the handle on the Cell Size grouping as a third way to open up the Table Properties dialog box.

TIP FROM

You can use the ruler to adjust column widths, as you'll discover with some experimentation (try dragging each little widget left and right, and then try the same operation while holding down the Shift, Ctrl, or Alt keys, for instance). You can also use the vertical ruler to rejigger row heights, and if you double-click any of the markers that denote breaks between columns, you'll open the Table Properties dialog box. In our experience, though, trying to figure out and remember the exact function of each little slider and triangle is more trouble than it's worth. It's much easier to manipulate a table directly.

By default, rows expand and contract to hold the tallest item in the row. Row height can be adjusted in much the same way as column widths: Eyeball it with a click and drag; measure it in the Table Properties dialog box (click the Row tab, select the Specify Height check box, enter a height in inches, and select At Least or Exactly); or make each row height the same to fill up the space occupied by the table (choose Distribute Rows from the Cell Size grouping on the Layout ribbon).

TIP FROM

> If you're creating a Word form for data entry, using Exactly for the row height prevents the cell from expanding if the user types in too much text. That prevents entries from pushing information from one page onto the next.

To change the width of individual cells, select the entire cell (including the end-of-cell marker), and then click and drag. As long as you've selected an entire cell (or group of cells), only those cells are resized.

If you can't see all the contents of a table cell, see "Properly Setting the Row Height for Word Tables" in the "Troubleshooting" section at the end of this chapter.

ADDING AND DELETING ROWS AND COLUMNS

Sometimes, you want to keep your table formatting intact, but replace existing data in the table. For example, if you create the same sales report every month, you can copy the table from last month's report into a new document and then delete the old data and replace it with this month's numbers. Here are a few tricks you need to know:

- If you select a cell and press Delete, the cell contents are deleted. If you include the end-of-cell marker and press Delete, the end-of-cell marker *with its formatting* stays intact.

- If you select a column or row and press Delete, the contents of all the cells in the column or row are deleted—but the column or row itself stays and, again, the end-of-cell markers and their formatting remain. It doesn't matter whether you select the end-of-row marker or not.

- If you select an entire table and press Delete, the contents of all the cells in the table are deleted, but the table skeleton remains, formatting intact.

- If you select an entire table plus one or more characters after the table (including, for example, a paragraph mark) and press Delete, the entire table and selected character(s) are deleted completely. No skeleton remains.

To truly delete a cell, row, column, or table, click in the cell, row, column, or table that you want to delete and choose Delete from the Rows and Columns grouping off the Layout ribbon; then select either Delete Cells, Delete Rows, Delete Columns, or Delete Table. Note that all these options are also available from right-click shortcut menus as well.

ALIGNING TEXT IN CELLS

Aligning text could not be easier from the Layout ribbon, Alignments grouping. There are nine one-click options that you can choose to determine the exact placement of your text in a table cell.

Left-aligned text in cells might work for certain types of text tables or tables where the columns are narrow. Frequently, however, you'll want to right-align numbers or center the text. Right-aligned numbers are much easier to read and compare. If you're using a two-column table to simulate columns (in a résumé, for example), right-align the text in the left column to help show the connection with the matching blocks of text in the right column. For small amounts of text, centered text—even if it's just centered headings over a column—looks better than left-aligned almost anywhere in a table, except the first column.

You can click once in a cell, or select a series of cells, and change the alignment from left-justified to centered to right-justified by clicking the Align Left, Center, and Align Right buttons from the Alignment grouping. Because end-of-cell markers behave much like paragraph marks, that formatting travels with the end of cell marker when it's copied or moved.

Word also allows you to center text vertically inside the cell. To do so, select the cells you want to format and from the Table Properties select the Cell tab. There you can choose your Vertical Alignment options from Top, Center, or Bottom positioning. Click the Options button and you can even tell Word how much whitespace you want between the cell edge and the text inside the cell.

You can combine the actions of horizontal and vertical alignment in one easy step: Select the cells you want to align, right-click (in the table), and choose Cell Alignment from the mini-toolbar menu. All nine combinations appear, ready for you to apply. Or go to the Layout ribbon and select one of the nine options (shown in Figure 15.6) from the Alignments grouping.

Figure 15.6
All nine combinations of left, right, center, and top, middle, bottom appear in the Alignments grouping on the Layout ribbon. Or you can get them from the context mini-toolbar menu.

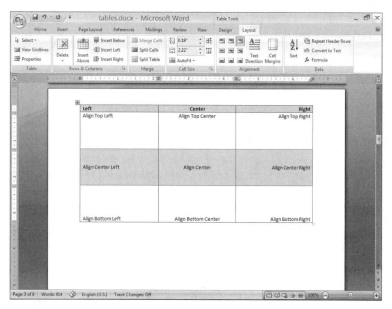

ROTATING TEXT

It's easy to rotate text in a table by 90 degrees, clockwise or counterclockwise (see Figure 15.7). To do so, select the cell(s) you want to rotate and choose Text Direction from the Layout ribbon, Alignments grouping.

Figure 15.7
As long as you want your text aimed straight up or straight down, Word can accommodate. Notice the use of the table drawing capability.

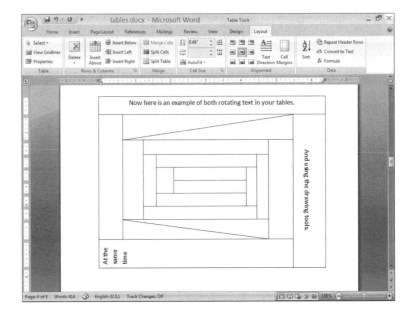

If you want table headings angled at something other than the nosebleed nineties, consider embedding or linking an Excel range. It's much easier to rotate text to any desired angle in an Excel worksheet.

CHANGING A TABLE'S LAYOUT

If you consider that a table can have an infinite number of columns and rows (theoretically) it can also have infinite possible formatting and layout options. That may not be what you want to hear. The good news is that you already know most of what you need to for handling any size table. But you may want to take advantage of a few more tools that Microsoft provides. For example, you can merge cells and split them apart if you want to. And we already discussed nesting tables inside one another, especially in website design, as another layout change you might want to consider.

If you insert a table into a cell, you have two tables, one inside the other, which are nested tables (shown in Figure 15.8). The figure depicts a template you can download from Microsoft (one of many) that will help you keep your yearly events in order. But you can make this yourself if you would like, by using the table features we have been discussing. Most of the time you don't need—or want—two separate tables; usually, when you run out of room in a table, what you really need is the capability to split an existing cell into two, four, or six cells.

Figure 15.8
You can merge cells, split cells, or nest entire tables within a table. You can pretty much make anything you want happen within your tables.

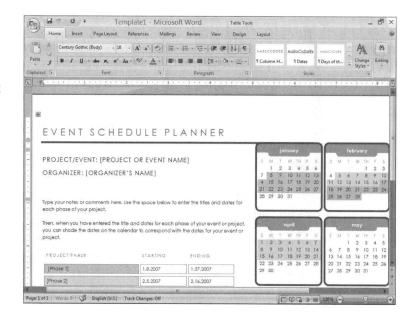

There are only a few subtle differences between, for example, nesting a four-column one-row table inside a cell and manually splitting the cell into four smaller cells. The main difference is in spacing—unless you change the spacing settings, nested tables take up an additional amount of space inside the cell to accommodate the outside of the table itself, whereas split cells require no additional spacing. Use a nested table when you want to manipulate the contents of a portion of the table as a unit: You can click and drag a nested table outside of its confining cell, for example, but moving four subcells is considerably more complex.

The easy way to split a cell into multiple cells is to use Word's table-drawing tools. Because you already have a table you want to split, you can click the Draw Table icon from the Draw Borders grouping on the Design ribbon. (Note: if you didn't have a table already and wanted to draw your table completely, on the Insert ribbon you would select Table, Draw Table.) Use the pencil-shaped pointer to draw horizontal or vertical lines inside the cell(s) you want to split.

Selections on the Layout ribbon, under the Merge grouping, help you alter your layout by merging cells, splitting cells, or splitting the entire table if you want.

To merge two cells together or to merge cells in a row that contains many columns, select the cells and choose Merge Cells from the Merge grouping. You could also use the Eraser option from the Draw Borders grouping on the Design tab to erase cell borders.

Use the Split Cells option if you want to rearrange a group of selected cells and their text—converting four cells in one column into four cells in a single row, for instance.

15

NOTE

You can move a table anywhere on a page by clicking and dragging the table move handle (at the upper-left corner of the table). To put two tables side by side, for instance, you don't need to create a table inside a table. Just drag the two tables into position.

To split a table horizontally—between two rows—click once in the row that will become the top row in the new table. From the Layout contextual ribbon, from the Merge grouping, select the Split Table option. A paragraph mark appears between the two tables. (As we noted earlier, you can also press Ctrl+Shift+Enter to split a table.)

TIP FROM

EQ & Woody

You can easily split a table vertically as well. Select the columns you want to split away from the original table. Cut them using the scissors on the Home ribbon. Move the insertion point to wherever you want the new table to appear, and paste. You can then place the two tables side by side, as mentioned earlier, by using their drag handles.

CONVERTING TEXT AND DATA TO TABLES

Sometimes you already have text or data that you need to place into a Word table. Although we mentioned at the outset of this chapter that Word is not noted as being the powerhouse that Excel is when it comes to handling mathematical data and equations, you may have data already in an Excel document or Access database that you want to pull in and format into a nice table for your presentation.

CONVERT TEXT TO TABLE

As you type text into a Word document, you may decide that what you've been typing would work better as a table. You might be tempted at that point to create a new table and then cut and paste the text into it. Before you go through that labor-intensive exercise, consider doing the job in a few clicks with Word's built-in text-to-table converter.

For the conversion to work properly, your text must include a *delimiter* (paragraph mark, tab, comma, or some other character) so that Word can figure out what data goes in which cell. The number of delimiters must be consistent, too, or Word will be unable to figure out how many columns to use in each row. The lines shown in Figure 15.9, which include a single tab character delimiting cells, will work fine.

TIP FROM

EQ & Woody

By far the simplest and most reliable way to delimit text for easy conversion to a table is with tabs separating the values that will go in each column, and paragraph marks at the end of each row. Although you can use commas, hyphens, or just about any other character, you're more likely to run into problems when these characters appear in the data and throw off the conversion.

Figure 15.9
If you're careful about using delimiting characters (such as the tab, shown here), Word will readily convert text to a table. But you can see the different options you can choose from with the dialog box.

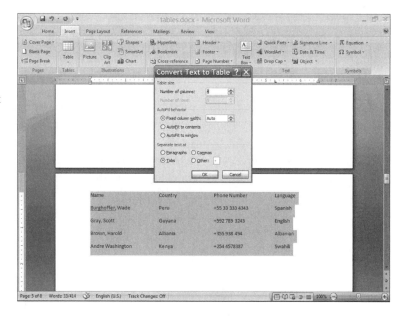

To convert properly delimited text to a table, follow these steps:

1. Select the text you want to convert.

2. Choose Table from the Tables grouping off the Insert ribbon, Convert Text to Table. Word presents the Convert Text to Table dialog box shown previously in Figure 15.9.

3. Choose the delimiter in the Separate Text At section at the bottom of the dialog box. If the number of rows and columns doesn't match your expectations, take another careful look at your selected text. Chances are you picked up a stray line along the way.

4. Select from one of the preconfigured Table Style galleries if you want to use something other than the default Table Grid. When everything is to your liking, click OK.

If you can't make the last row of your table match the last row of your data, see "Check for Stray Delimiters" in the "Troubleshooting" section at the end of this chapter.

You can convert a table back to text using the Data grouping on the Layout ribbon and selecting Convert to Text. As part of the conversion, you can choose which character you want to use as a delimiter.

CONVERTING DATA TO A TABLE

Word also lets you fill a table with data from a simple text file, another Word document, an Excel worksheet range, or just about any database—local or remote—you can imagine, including those created with Access, dBASE, FoxPro, ODBC, and SQL Server.

To add data from another application to your Word table, follow these steps:

1. Click in the document where you want the table to appear. You can click inside a table cell and create a nested table within a table, if you want.

15

2. Bring up the Database toolbar from your Quick Access Toolbar by Customizing it to include the Insert Database icon. If you've forgotten how to do this, just remember to select the down-arrow next to the toolbar and choose More Commands, which will take you to the Customize dialog. From there you can search for and add your "Insert Database" icon.

3. Click the Get Data button, browse to the file you want to use (text, Word document, Excel workbook, Access database), and click Open. Keep in mind the following points:

   - If you open a Word document, Word looks for a table or delimited list in the file. If it can't recognize a list suitable for importing, you will be asked to specify a delimiter (see the discussion of delimiters in the preceding section).

   - If you select an Excel workbook file, Word looks for named ranges and lists with data suitable for importing. If none are available, you are asked whether you want to import an entire sheet or just one of the named ranges.

   - If you open an Access database, you get to choose from among the defined tables or queries.

4. Click Query Options and specify filters, sort fields (up to three), and the fields you want to include in the table. If you skip this step, Word imports the entire contents of the external file.

5. Click Table AutoFormat to apply a new format to the data as part of the import process. This step is optional.

6. Click Insert Data. In the Insert Data dialog box, you can select the records you want (by record number) or choose all records. You also have the option to insert the data as a Word field (thus automatically updating it each time fields are updated). Click OK to insert the data into the selected table in your document.

USING FORMULAS

After your data is in your table, you may want to perform some minor calculations with it. Word contains rudimentary features for performing standard math calculations in tables—Sum, Average, Min, Max, Product, and the like.

To put a formula in a cell, select the cell and choose Formula from the Data grouping on the Layout ribbon. Then enter the formula, and click OK.

When you use a Word table as a worksheet in this fashion, cells are numbered using Excel's standard A1 format, with a colon separating addresses that identify a range. For example:

- `=A1+A2` calculates the sum of the first and second cells in the first column.

- `=AVERAGE(B1:C4)` calculates the average of eight contiguous cells.

- Special ranges called ABOVE, BELOW, LEFT, and RIGHT represent precisely what you would expect. `=SUM(RIGHT)` calculates the sum of all the cells to the right of the current cell.

SORTING DATA WITHIN TABLES

Although it doesn't hold a candle to Excel's sorting capabilities, Word can sort using as many as three keys, including dates. Within a table that contains employee records, for instance, you can sort by Last Name, and then by First Name, and then by Date of Hire. Word can also handle case-sensitive sorts as well as nonstandard sorting sequences (for languages other than English).

Sorting in Word can come in handy in all kinds of situations. You might want to sort a table of names, to put it in alphabetical order, and then copy the table and sort it again by employee ID number. Or perhaps you created a table with the data sorted by region, but you later decide the data is more meaningful if sorted by product. That kind of sorting is easy in Word.

> **NOTE**
>
> In fact, you needn't put data into a table to sort it. Word does just fine if you have clean data with delimiters—precisely in the same way that's required for converting text to a table. You can also sort simple lists (for instance, a list of state names, each in a single paragraph), because the paragraph mark is a delimiter.

You can also sort by individual words within cells. For example, if you have a row with names in FirstName LastName order, you can tell Word to sort by LastName, the second word in the column, followed by FirstName, the first word in the column (see Figure 15.10).

To sort data, do the following:

1. Click once inside the table (or data).

2. Select the Sort button from the Data grouping on the Layout ribbon (or select the Sort button from the Paragraph grouping on the Home ribbon). You see the Sort Text dialog box shown in Figure 15.10.

Figure 15.10
Although not as comprehensive as Excel's sorting capabilities, Word does rather well—it even has a LastName FirstName sorting capability—and you needn't convert your data to a table to sort it.

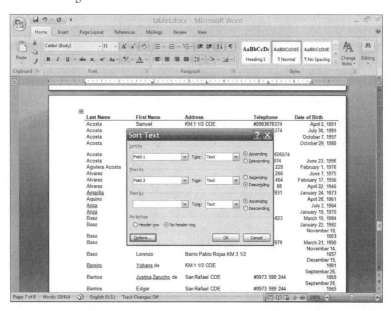

3. If your table (or data) has a header row—that is, if the first row describes the data below it—start by clicking the My List Has Header Row option. That way, Word uses the names from the header row instead of the generic Column 1, Column 2, and so on.

4. Choose your sort conditions. If you're planning to sort by LastName FirstName, you need to click Options and enter a space as the field delimiter. (You will also use this dialog box for nontable data, when specifying a case-sensitive sort, or when choosing a sorting sequence other than standard English.)

5. When you're ready to perform the sort, click OK.

TIP FROM

In unusual circumstances, you might want to sort just one column of a table while leaving the other columns untouched. A teacher might construct a table with two columns, one containing scientific terms, the other containing definitions. By sorting just one column, the teacher could create a "connect the definitions" test, in which the students have to associate terms with definitions. To sort just one column of a table, select the column prior to choosing Data, Sort. Click Options, and check the Sort Column Only box. Click OK, and the single column is sorted independently.

POSITIONING TABLES ON THE PAGE

Although you might think that tables exist in the drawing layer—click the dragging handle to move them around—in fact, they are in the main part of the document. Thus, you can put captions inside tables and reference them via the Cross-reference dialog box, which appears when you choose Insert ribbon, Links grouping, Cross-reference. Paragraphs can be numbered and the numbering continues from the main part of the document, through the table, and into the rest of the document, and entries in tables are picked up for indexes and tables of contents.

Although you'll most often want a table to appear flush left with text above and below it (not wrapping around), from time to time, you might want the table to appear flush right or centered. You also might want main body text in the document to wrap around the table, especially with smaller tables. Follow these steps to make it happen:

1. Create the table by using any of the methods explained in this chapter.

2. Click once inside the table, and then choose Properties from the Table grouping on the Layout ribbon. You see the Table Properties dialog box (see Figure 15.11).

3. Click the Table tab and set Left, Center, or Right alignment in the Alignment section. If you want to control the distance from the left edge of the box to the left margin of the page, use the Indent from Left spinner.

4. Allow document body text to flow around the table by clicking the Around box. If you want finer control over text wrapping—for example, the distance from text to the table edges—click the Positioning button and the Table Positoning dialog opens.

Figure 15.11
The Table Properties dialog box lets you align tables on a page and specify whether you want text to wrap around.

FORMATTING A TABLE

A properly formatted table helps the reader absorb and understand the contents. You know your table hasn't been formatted well when a reader has to pull out a ruler to tell which numbers belong on what rows.

LETTING WORD DO THE WORK WITH TABLE STYLES

Word provides 99 Table Styles to choose from (if you count the default style) with options that give you a good start on your way to table perfection. To use a Table Style, click once inside the table, and then choose from one of the options from the Design ribbon, the Table Styles grouping in the Table Gallery. Before you make your selection, you can hover your cursor over a style, and it will automatically show you a real-time table preview for your table.

Table Styles come in handy when you want to make your tables stand out—give them a personality, beyond the standard font—but you don't want to go to a lot of trouble creating and applying your own custom formatting. Table Styles are a good first choice when creating any type of table that includes rows or columns of numbers, such as a price list or an income statement.

The Table Styles Options (see Figure 15.12) contain close to a hundred predefined formats. To see the additional modification settings you select the down-arrow next to the Table gallery and choose Modify Table Settings.

Figure 15.12
Although Table Styles might not have the design you want, it does provide a good starting place for creatively formatting your own tables.

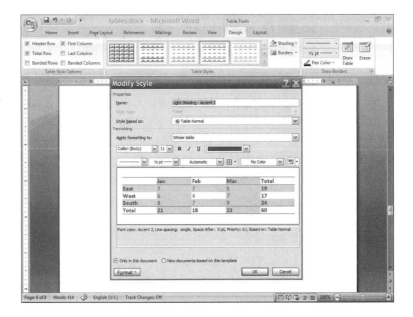

In addition to choosing a predefined style, you can modify the style offered by selecting Modify Table Style (also shown in Figure 15.12). You can also create your own style and save it to the Table Styles gallery.

TABLE STYLE OPTIONS

In your Design ribbon, you have a collection of check boxes that you should take note of in making your style choices. Let's review these:

- **Header Row**—Turned on by default in your Table Styles Options. This tells your Table Styles that the first row of your table is your header and you want it styled differently. Usually the headings are boldface so they stand out. Or you can make other style choices.

- **Total Row**—In a table where you are adding up numbers or items in some way and want a Total row on the bottom of the table. Select this option and it changes the formatting for the last row.

- **Banded Rows**—On by default. This option turns on and off the style options that give your table the multiple-colored row bands through the table.

- **First Column**—On by default. This option tells your Table Styles that the first column of your table is a special column and should be formatted a little differently to stand out in the way that your Table Styles indicate.

- **Last Column**—Off by default. This option does the same thing as your First Column options, but in the last column of your table.

- **Banded Column**—Turns on and off the style options that give your table the multiple-colored column bands through your table.

USING BORDERS AND SHADING

Borders, shading, and background colors in table cells are identical to their counterparts in paragraphs. Click once inside a cell to change the border, shading, or background for that cell. Select cells, rows, columns, or the entire table to change them.

Word normally displays a faint gray gridline on the screen, corresponding to cell borders, even if you format the cells so that their borders are invisible.

TIP FROM

> If you're creating a table that will be viewed onscreen in Word, you can hide the table gridlines by going to the Layout ribbon and choosing the View Gridlines option from the Table grouping. These are off by default, but you can turn them on and off with this option.

Tables viewed by a web browser never show gridlines, regardless of the Show/Hide Gridlines setting.

WORKING WITH LARGER SIZE TABLES

When you work with large tables, you'll commonly encounter three distinct problems. Fortunately, each has a simple solution:

- **Too wide**—When adjusting column widths or adding columns, sometimes the table extends beyond the page margins. If you're working in Print Layout view, you won't be able to see (or work with) the rightmost columns.

If you lose the final column, refer to "Can't See Final Column(s) in a Table" in the "Troubleshooting" section at the end of the chapter.

- **Repeating titles**—If your table will print on more than one page, you might want the title row(s) to appear at the top of each page. It can be frustrating when a table carries over to other pages and you cannot remember what each row is for. To set this formatting option, go to the Layout ribbon and from the Data grouping, select Repeat Header rows.

- **Page breaks in cells**—By default, Word keeps all of a cell's contents on one page, allowing a page to break only when a new cell starts. If you're writing a résumé using a table, for example, you might want to relax that restriction so that page breaks can fall more naturally.

If you want to relax the way Word breaks cells in a table, see "Allow Page Breaks in a Table Cell" in the "Troubleshooting" section at the end of the chapter.

Word has two significant alternatives to tables, which can be handy if you need to list a large amount of information in a small place (for instance, a list of vendors in an appendix, or a list of participating pharmacies in the back of a health plan brochure).

First, you can tell Word to create a page with more than one column. The text in each column "snakes," as in a newspaper, extending to the bottom of the first column, then continuing at the beginning of the second column, then the third, and so on. To create snaking newspaperlike columns, you'll have to work with section formatting—and be prepared for some surprises.

Second, you can create and position text boxes in the drawing layer, linking them so text poured into the linked boxes fills the first box, then the second, then the third, and so on.

ADDING AND ORGANIZING FIGURES AND GRAPHICS

This is one section that we could spend 100 pages on and still have more to talk about. This is partly because Microsoft gives you so many options to choose from with adding graphical elements to your documents. And partly because as creative persons we can come up with so many ways to use the tools that we have to create "art" within our documents.

We'll discuss the tools and you can knock yourself out mastering the art of it all.

To start with, there are two different functionality modes for documents (as noted in earlier chapters): Compatibility Mode and Full Functionality Mode. The mode you are in will determine some of the capabilities you will have in Word, and we will note these when necessary. For the purpose of discussing all the features you should assume, unless noted otherwise, that we are discussing documents created with Full Functionality—that is, documents that are Word 2007–compatible only with a `.docx` extension.

For the sake of focus, this section is going to discuss only the five options on the Illustrations grouping from the Insert ribbon. These are Pictures, Clip Art, Shapes, SmartArt, and Chart.

INSERTING PICTURES

Here is one tool that varies depending on whether you are using Compatibility Mode or Full Functionality Mode. To insert a picture from the Illustrations grouping on the Insert ribbon, select the icon and then choose the picture you want in your document.

PICTURES IN COMPATIBILITY MODE

If you are in Compatibility Mode, the Format ribbon provides the standard types of tools for your picture, as shown in Figure 15.13.

Figure 15.13
The Format ribbon, in Compatibility Mode for an inserted picture.

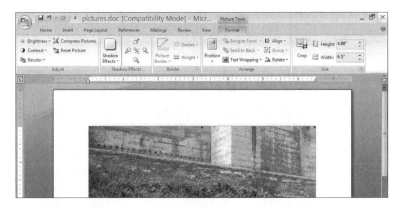

You can see that you have an Adjust grouping that allows you to alter the brightness and contrast of your picture. You can choose Recolor to alter the coloring of the picture to Grayscale or Black and White or set your own coloring. You choose Compress Pictures to alter the dpi of your picture. The Reset Picture icon allows you to eliminate all the formatting you might have done to the picture, such as cropping. One click and it's all gone.

TIP FROM

Ed & Woody

> The Compress Pictures options are an excellent way to take a Word document with images already inserted and lower the dpi of your images for different reasons. Maybe you want to take that document and put it right on the Web or print it, but with lowered image quality.

You can apply Shadow Effects to your pictures and choose the lighting from the Shadow Effects grouping. You can add a picture border and determine the kind of border from the by right-clicking your picture and choosing Borders and Shading off the mini-toolbar. You can do the same thing and select Format Picture from the mini-toolbar and you can see your Format Picture dialog box. Under the Arrange grouping, you can position your picture in the document, have text surround it or stay out of the picture's way, align it compared to other images, group it with other images, and/or rotate it by right angles. Finally, you can use the Size grouping to configure cropping of your picture and the Height and Width of your picture, too.

PICTURES IN FULL FUNCTIONALITY MODE

If all those cool options really make you happy—well, they have been around for a while. That doesn't make them less valuable or interesting (especially if you didn't know you could do all that with Word), but wait until you see what you can do with Word 2007 when you insert a picture, as shown in Figure 15.14.

Figure 15.14
The Format ribbon, in Full Functionality Mode for an inserted picture. Notice the green circle at the top that allows you to rotate the picture 360 degrees.

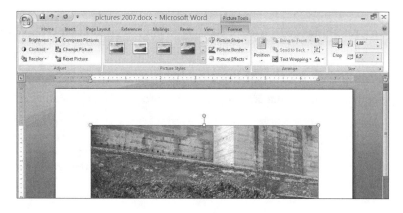

The first time you work with the new features of Word's picture formatting, the technical words you'll be looking for to describe your thought are "oh… um…wow…." That being said, let's consider the possibilities.

TIP FROM

EQ & Woody

If you want to create incredible formats with your pictures but know that you cannot share them as .docx files with others because they don't have Word 2007 just yet, keep this in mind. When you finish your picture formatting, using all the tools in Full Functionality, you can save the document in Compatibility Mode and your cool formatting will be saved (although other persons opening the document will not be able to make changes other than the formatting allowed in their version of Word).

On the Format ribbon you can see the Adjust grouping, including Brightness and Contrast, and these work the same as in Compatability Mode. Recolor, however, offers a collection of prechosen colors that you can hover over and see how they will affect your pictures. Compress Pictures offers the same functionality with a different look. Change Picture allows you to insert a different picture altogether to work on. And Reset Picture still removes all the formatting you have chosen.

Then you have the Picture Styles grouping. From here you can see a gallery of predesigned picture options to apply to your picture. You can see dynamically how each of these might affect your picture before you apply it.

The Picture Shape options show you different standard shapes, such as squares and circles and arrows, and allows you to turn your picture into one of those shapes. You can set a Picture Border and you can apply a Picture Effect. Picture Effects can add a reflection to your picture or bevel it (my personal favorite), or any number of other choices.

From the handle launcher in the grouping, launch the Format Picture dialog box, which has a sleeker look in Full Functionality Mode.

The Arrange and Size groupings are pretty much the same between the two modes, with the exception of the capability to perform more than 90 degree immediate rotation.

INSERTING CLIP ART

Clip art, regardless of the mode your document is in, is a simple tool. When you select the Insert ribbon tab and choose Clip Art from the Illustrations grouping, you are presented with the Clip Art task pane (shown in Figure 15.15). From here you can search for different types of clip art either on your system or online. You can choose to look only for clip art, or you can leave the default so that you search through photos, sound clips, and movies, too.

NOTE

After you insert clip art or a shape, it is treated like a picture in terms of formatting. What this means is that the mode your document is in determines the functionality you receive from your Format ribbon for the clip art or shape you have inserted.

INSERTING SHAPES

The standard shapes you can add include everything from a square to a lightning bolt. Why? Because you might want to. Not only can you add these shapes, but you can add text to them and configure formatting options to use thicker lines, shadowing, and a host of other features that will appear on the Format ribbon after you insert the shape.

Figure 15.15
The choices are endless when it comes to the shapes you can add. But, just in case you cannot see one you like, you can use the New Drawing Canvas to create your own shapes.

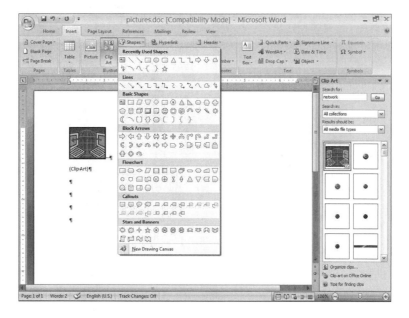

INSERTING SMARTART

If you try to insert SmartArt in Compatibility Mode, you will see the backward-compatible view of possibilities from the Diagram Gallery, as shown in Figure 15.16 and Figure 15.17.

Figure 15.16
Compatibility Mode doesn't give you much to be excited about with SmartArt.

But if you really want to see what SmartArt can do, insert in a Full Functionality document. SmartArt really enhances your Word documents. With the formatting possibilities combined with the variety of colors, shadows, bevels, glows, and so on, you can literally spend days playing around with all your SmartArt Options.

Figure 15.17
But look at what can be done in Full Functionality mode.

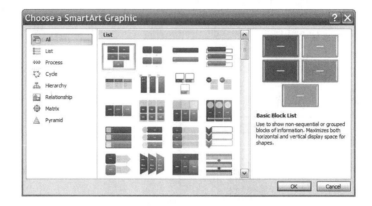

Keep in mind that just because you have the capability to do something in SmartArt doesn't mean you should. The goal of these tools is to make your documents more impressive, not more cluttered. One of the other great things about SmartArt is the capability to use a SmartArt illustration from one Office application to another. With the use of Themes, SmartArt that is pulled into your document from, for example, a PowerPoint presentation, will automatically inherit the Theme you have applied to your Word document (if you have one applied).

NOTE

> Sometimes you might like the visual effect of SmartArt so much that you would like to export that graphic and use it in other things. In the past you might have thought to do a screenshot of your image and then crop away what you don't need. That works, but you might want to try a different approach. You can save your document as a web page (*.html or *.htm format) and Word will save your image as a GIF file in a specific folder for your web page that can now be used in other documents.

INSERTING A CHART

Everyone knows that a good number of the charts that we create in Excel end up in a Word document or PowerPoint presentation. We copy and use the Paste Special as a picture to get that chart into our documents. Or, if we are really hard pressed, we use the Microsoft Graph tools that are provided in Word. Well, not anymore. The new idea is "true" interoperability among your Office applications, and Chart options are included.

Again, your functionality will be limited in Compatibility Mode. You will be able to insert only charts that are backward compatible with older versions of Office because you will be using Microsoft Graph tools. But if you insert a chart in Word 2007–compatible documents, you should have more options. We say "should have" because it depends on whether you have Excel installed. Without Excel, you will still have to use Microsoft Graph tools.

Here is the way it works: When you insert a chart (in Full Functionality Mode), Excel and Word tile side by side with each other. The chart is in your Word document and your data is in your Excel spreadsheet.

Anytime you need to edit your data, you can do this by going to your Design ribbon (that comes up contextually because of the chart you've inserted), to the Data grouping, and choosing Edit Data, as shown in Figure 15.18.

Figure 15.18
Insert a Word chart and watch Excel come to life (in Full Functionality Mode).

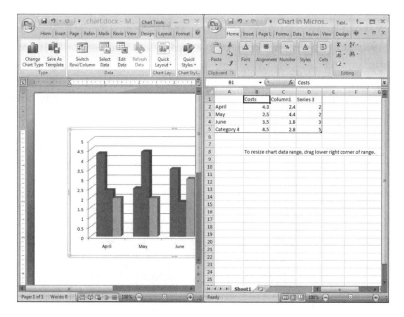

After you have your chart data the way you would like, it's time to format it. There are three contextual ribbons: Design, Layout, and Format. These ribbons will help you to completely control the look of your chart so that it will perfectly fit within the style of your document. However, if you've chosen a document theme, your chart should automatically adapt to the theme you've chosen.

ONE MORE THING…WORD ART

While we are talking about inserting so many other graphical elements, we might as well mention WordArt, located on the Insert ribbon under the Text grouping. If you select this icon, regardless of the mode you are in, you will find that there hasn't been any change since its inclusion in Word 97. That's 10 years with no change! Either it's perfect or they just didn't know what else to do with it.

However, one thing is new. WordArt Styles that can really enhance the look of your text in both SmartArt and in charts.

USING HEADERS AND FOOTERS

Headers appear at the top of each page; footers at the bottom. Word lets you specify "first page only" headers and footers, so the first page of a report or letter can have headers and footers that are different from those in the body of the report. That's useful if your first page is a decorative title page and you don't want it to contain a page number or the title. In

15

addition, Word enables you to set up different headers and footers for odd-numbered and even-numbered pages. That comes in handy if you're going to be printing on the front and back of each sheet of paper.

WHAT YOU CAN AND CAN'T DO WITH HEADERS AND FOOTERS

Headers and footers exist on every page in a Word document. Until you put something in them, however, they're invisible. Word reserves room for them, but doesn't print anything (or show anything onscreen) in the reserved area. Generally, people put are page numbers, a company logo, and perhaps the document title or author's name in headers and footers.

To create a header, follow these steps:

1. Go to the Insert ribbon. On the Header and Footer grouping, you can choose either the Header or Footer icons. If you aren't in Print Layout view, you will be switched into this view so that you can see the header and footer areas. The body text of the document will turn gray, and the header or footer area will be highlighted (see Figure 15.19).

Figure 15.19
You "view" a header, in Word parlance, because the header already exists—even if you haven't put anything into it.

2. You should note that a new context ribbon, called Design, opens when you are in the header/footer area. Enter anything you want in the header. Note that the paragraph is formatted with the Header style, which includes two tab stops: a centered stop at the middle of the page and a right-aligned stop on the right margin. (If you've changed margins, you also need to change the locations of these tab stops.)

3. When you're finished with the header, you can choose Go to Footer from the Navigation grouping. Word moves the insertion point to the footer for the current page.

4. Enter text, graphics, or whatever else you want in the footer.

5. Click the Close Header or Footer icon from the Close grouping on the Design ribbon to return to your document. Or you could just double-click right into the document itself.

15

If you have created a header or footer for a page, in Print Layout view you can see it as a grayed-out shadow of how the header or footer will appear on the final printed page. To edit a header or footer that you can see on the screen, double-click it.

To force Word to use a different header and footer on the first page from the one in the rest of the document, or to alternate headers and footers for odd- and even-numbered pages, look at the Design ribbon, under the Options grouping, and you'll notice several check boxes. You can select Different First Page, Different Odd and Even Pages, and Show Document Text. That last one makes it so that you cannot see the text in your document when you are in the header/footer section, but only if you deselect this check box.

After selecting the Different First Page check box, you can navigate to the first page in your document, go into the header or footer, and customize the first page header and footer as you like.

With the Different Odd and Even check box selected, any changes you make in the header or footer of any even-numbered page will appear on all even-numbered pages; thus, if you change the header on page 6, your changes appear on all even-numbered pages. Similarly, changing the header or footer on any odd-numbered page changes all the odd-numbered pages, with the possible exception of page 1, which remains unaltered if you've selected the Different First Page check box.

The actual locations of a header or footer on the page are determined by the margins.

SETTING HEADER AND FOOTER OPTIONS

In a document doesn't have section breaks, the headers and footers can only be structured by the simple options we mentioned in the previous section. But if you want more control over your headers or footers (especially in larger documents) you can use section breaks to establish different settings. On the Navigation grouping, from the Design ribbon that appears when you are in your header/footer, you can use navigation keys to jump from one section to another. Choose Previous Section or Next Section, keeping in mind that in a simple document that doesn't have sections, these buttons will not take you anywhere different.

With sections in your document, you will also notice the Link to Previous button. If you want your headers and footers to be consistent throughout the entire document (even with section breaks), you can insert a header or footer one time and leave it alone. If, however, you would like some sections to be different, you first deselect the Link to Previous button from the Navigation grouping. This will break the link to the previous section and allow you to make changes. However, these changes will be reflected forward in other sections that are connected to the section you are working in.

You can also change where your text begins in your headers and footers on the Design ribbon from the Position grouping. You can use the up and down arrows to determine where the text will begin. Within that same grouping you can configure tab settings for your header or footer.

NUMBERING PAGES

By far the most common use for a header or footer is to show the page number. Word gives you several options:

- To place a plain page number in the header or footer, with no additional text (a simple 14 instead of Page 14), fromthe Insert ribbon, in the Header and Footer grouping, click Page Number. You can choose to insert the number at the Top of Page, Bottom of Page, or Page Margins (you decide) and Current Position. You can then choose a page-numbering design from the gallery. Note: Within the gallery, you can choose Page X of Y options. This will tell you something like Page 14 of 45, for example.

- While editing the header or footer, on the Design ribbon, you can choose Page Number from the Header and Footer grouping and follow the same options as the preceding one.

- Type any text or use fields to create a completely custom page-numbering scheme. The Page Number button actually places a {Page} field in the header or footer; the Insert Number of Pages icon adds a {NumPages} field. By inserting your own fields, you can create and edit custom page number formats—to track sections, chapters, or other divisions, for instance. You can then save these as Building Blocks for your Headers or Footers or for Page Number galleries.

ADDING DATES AND DOCUMENT DETAILS

The Design ribbon that comes up when you are in your Header or Footer toolbar offers an Insert grouping that includes Date and Time, Quick Parts, Picture and Clip Art. To insert the date, you could use this button on the ribbon, and then select the format you want. Or you could actually use fields to do the same thing.

One of the most important fields—called {StyleRef}—allows you to put text from the document into a header or footer. You can use {StyleRef} to add the title or number of the current chapter to a header, for example, or to produce "Able–Autry" page indexes in the header, as in a telephone book.

ADDING LINES, BORDERS, SHADING, AND BACKGROUNDS

Word lets you draw border lines and apply colors and other forms of shading to specific pieces of text, cells in tables, paragraphs, entire tables, or entire pages. When you draw a line around a page, it's called a *page border*. When you apply colors or shading to an entire page, it's called a *background (or Page Color)*. These background colors are generally not for printing but for web pages that you create in Word. And when you place a picture or text "behind" the text on a page—for example, to print DRAFT diagonally across the page (see Figure 15.20), or to brand the page with the word CONFIDENTIAL—that picture or text is called a *watermark*.

TIP FROM

To add a watermark to a document, choose the Watermark icon from the Page Background grouping on the Page Layout ribbon. You can choose from a gallery of pre-configured watermarks or choose the Custom Watermark and then choose the options you would like. For example, you can choose Text Watermark and select from the text you want or type your own. To see the way your watermark will look in print, use Print Layout view.

Figure 15.20
Configure a water-mark to show the word "Draft" across your printed pages.

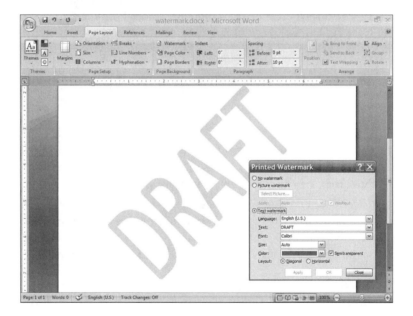

QUICK WAYS TO CREATE LINES

The easiest way to draw a horizontal line across a page is to type any of the horizontal line AutoFormat characters (see Table 15.1) three times and press Enter. The line will appear above the characters you typed.

TABLE 15.1   AUTOFORMAT CHARACTERS FOR HORIZONTAL LINES

Character	Type of Line
- (hyphen)	Light single line
_ (underscore)	Heavy single line
= (equal)	Heavy double line

continues

TABLE 15.1   CONTINUED

Character	Type of Line
# (number sign)	Thick line with thin lines above and below
~ (tilde)	Wavy line
* (asterisk)	Horizontal line of small squares

The horizontal line (also called a *rule*) is actually a lower border for the paragraph above the one where you typed. If you click once on that paragraph, then select the down arrow next to the Borders button, and choose Borders and Shading, you'll see what formatting has taken effect. If you find this behavior annoying, you can turn it off in the AutoFormat as You Type settings located in Word Options. Under Proofing settings, select the AutoCorrect Options.

BORDERS AND BOXES

You can draw borders—essentially rectangles—around characters, paragraphs, table cells, or pages. To create a border for characters, paragraphs, or cells, follow these steps:

1. Select the character(s), paragraph(s), table cell(s), or table(s) you want to format.

2. From the Paragraph grouping on the Home ribbon, select the Borders button and choose Borders and Shading. On the Borders tab, make sure the Apply To box shows the correct setting: Paragraph, Text, Cell, or Table.

3. Choose from the common settings along the left, or draw your own border in the Preview pane on the right. You might want to use the Preview pane if, for instance, you want to have lines appear to the left and above a paragraph, but not to the right or below. Choose the line style, color, and width in the center pane.

TIP FROM

> If you want borders of different types (to add double lines on the top and bottom, but single lines at the left and right, for example), start by clicking the Custom box. Then build the first border type by selecting from the Style, Color, and Width boxes. Finally, tell Word where you want this particular border type to appear by selecting the location(s) in the Preview pane. Go back and build your second border type, apply it in the Preview pane, and repeat as needed.

4. To set the distance between the text and the border, click Options and fill in the amounts. Click OK and the border appears.

The procedure for applying page borders is similar:

1. If you want only a specific page (or pages) in your document to have a border, set up section breaks at the beginning and end of the page (or pages). Then click once inside the section you want to have page borders.

2. From the Paragraph grouping on the Home ribbon, select the Borders button and choose Borders and Shading. Select the Page Border tab. Or you could go to the Page Layout ribbon and choose the Page Borders icon from the Page Background grouping.

3. To choose from a fairly large selection of border options, click the down arrow in the Art box. Page Border formatting options are similar to general Border formatting, except pages can also use artwork for their borders.

> **NOTE**
>
> Unfortunately, you can't add your own page borders to Word's collection.

4. If you don't want the border to encompass the header or footer, click the Options button, choose Measure from Text, and clear the Surround Header and Surround Footer boxes. Click OK and the border will be visible in Print Layout view.

To understand how borders can move around a document and appear suddenly as if out of nowhere, it's important to know where the formatting is stored:

- Character borders are stored in the characters themselves. If you move or copy a character with a border, the border goes along with it.

- Paragraph borders are stored in the paragraph mark. If you copy, move, or delete a paragraph mark, the border goes with it. If you press Enter while inside a paragraph with a border, the new paragraph "inherits" the border settings from the previous paragraph.

- Table cell borders are stored in the individual cell's end-of-cell marker. Borders that apply to the entire table are in the final end-of-row marker.

- Page borders are stored in the section break mark. If your document has only one section, page borders are stored in the final paragraph mark in the document.

SHADING CHARACTERS, PARAGRAPHS, AND PAGES

A little shading goes a long way. Black text on a light shade of gray (or a pale yellow) can be quite legible. On forms, in particular, a little shading can actually enhance the appearance of forms. White text on a very dark background makes a striking visual impression. But avoid the middle ground: Dark shading with dark characters can be virtually illegible, even if you never print the document—colors vary widely from monitor to monitor, as well.

Character, paragraph, table cell, and entire table shading works much like borders. From the Paragraph grouping on the Home ribbon select the Borders button and choose Borders and Shading. Select the Shading tab.

The interaction of the various parts of the Shading dialog box can be confusing. Think of it this way: If you want to apply a solid color, use the Fill box at the top of the dialog box. If you want to apply a shade—for instance, a 5% gray background—use the Patterns box.

No Color in the Fill box on the top means there's no solid background color. Clear in the Style box near the bottom means there's no shading.

15

If you absolutely must have a background color, with a shade of gray on top of the color, pick the color in the Fill box and the shade in the Style box. Finally, just to guarantee that you stay thoroughly confused, shades aren't confined to shades of gray. In fact, you can "shade" with any color; choose it in the Color box at the bottom.

If you want to apply a shade or a fill color to the entire page, you're in the wrong place. That's done from the Page Color settings, which can be found on the Page Layout ribbon.

Using fill effects, you can perform one- or two-color gradient fills; use a repeating picture called a *texture* to give your document a background that looks like stone, wood, or fabric. Create cross-hatched patterns in a wide variety of styles and any color, or bring in your own picture, which will be repeated like a tiled Windows wallpaper.

NOTE

> Page backgrounds are intended for use on web pages and have virtually no other uses. They do not appear if you print the document. You can still see the page color in Print Layout and Full Screen Reading views, but because they are for web page use, you might be better switching to the Web Layout view.

Page backgrounds apply to the entire document; they cannot be changed from section to section, like page borders can. In addition, the fill effects available on pages are not available to characters, table cells, or paragraphs.

FORMATTING DOCUMENTS BY SECTION

Although most Word documents contain only one section, if you want to change headers or footers, page size or orientation, margins, line numbers (used in some legal documents), page borders, or the number of newspaperlike columns in different parts of a document, you have to use sections.

Perhaps the most common situation arises when you want to change headers or footers in the middle of a document. In that case, you have to add a new section; there's no alternative. Likewise, you might need to add a section if you have a wide table in the middle of a long report. Most of your pages will be printed in portrait orientation, but you'll need to add a section break before and after the table so that you can print it in landscape orientation. You could print the table separately and collate it by hand, but using section breaks removes your layout hassles with just a few clicks.

Word recognizes four types of section breaks:

- **Next Page**—The most common type of section break, a Next Page section break not only defines a new section, it forces Word to start the section on a new page.

- **Continuous**—Defines a new section, but does not force a page break. Continuous section breaks are used almost exclusively for changing the number of newspaperlike columns in a document, or resetting line numbering (typically in legal documents).

- **Odd Page**—Like the Next Page break, except Word can add one additional blank page to force the new section to begin on an odd-numbered page.

- **Even Page**—Like the Odd Page break, but Word starts on an even-numbered page.

Section breaks are visible in all views when you click the Show/Hide ¶ button to make special formatting characters visible.

Just as paragraph formatting is stored in the paragraph mark at the end of a paragraph, Word stores section formatting in the section break mark at the end of the section. Formatting for the final section in a document is stored in the last paragraph mark in the document. If a document has only one section, the document's final paragraph mark holds the section formatting for the entire document.

INSERTING AND DELETING SECTION BREAKS

To insert a new section break into a document:

1. If the document does not yet include one, we strongly recommend that you put a dummy manual section break at the end of the document. To do so, click once in front of the final paragraph mark in the document. Press Enter a few times. Then go to your Page Layout ribbon and choose Breaks from the Page Setup grouping shown in Figure 15.21. Then choose Continuous.

Figure 15.21
Before you insert that first section break, you can save yourself hours—days!—of trouble by placing a dummy section break at the end of the document.

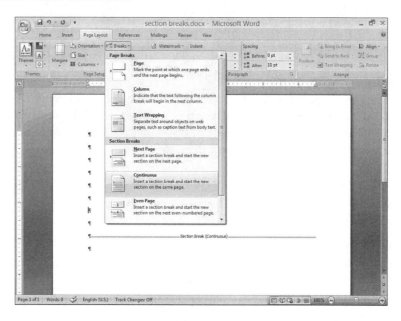

TIP FROM

If you created an extra dummy section break at the end of the document, all the document's original section formatting is stored in that section break. To restore a specific section to the document's original formatting, copy that dummy section break to the end of that specific section.

15

2. If all the headers and footers in the document will be the same, you'll find it much easier to establish them now. Follow the instructions in the "Using Headers and Footers" section earlier in this chapter.

3. Carefully determine what section breaks you'll need in your document, what type they should be, and where they will occur. In particular, if you plan to change the number of newspaperlike columns for a short run in the middle of the document, you'll want Continuous section breaks both before and after the change.

4. Starting at the beginning of the document, create the section breaks, one at a time, by using the Breaks options on the Page Layout ribbon.

The dummy section break at the end of the document can help you salvage important formatting information because you can copy or move the section break, although copying or moving the final paragraph mark won't have any effect on section formatting. See the next section for details.

After establishing all sections, carefully go back into each section and apply the section formatting you require.

TIP FROM

Ed & Woody

You'll find it much easier to work with sections if you've planned ahead and can go through each section in order, from beginning to end, applying the section formatting. By working from beginning to end, you simplify problems—massive problems—associated with changing headers and footers, and whether a section is linked to the previous one. If you start at the beginning, you can see the effect each change has on subsequent sections. If you start in the middle, it can be infuriatingly difficult to see why or how a header or footer has changed.

If you must delete a section break, select the break and press Delete. The newly merged section takes on the settings of the section break at the end. Immediately examine the document for odd formatting changes. If you find any unwelcome formatting, press Ctrl+Z or click the Undo button to restore the section break.

COPYING FORMATTING BETWEEN SECTIONS

Section breaks store the settings for the section. You can select, delete, copy, or move these settings at will.

By far, the simplest way to copy section formatting from one section to another is by copying the section break. If you want to copy the section formatting from, for instance, section number 6 to section number 3, follow these steps:

1. Select the section break at the end of section 6 and press Ctrl+C to copy it to the Clipboard.

2. Click just in front of the section break at the end of section 3.

3. Press Ctrl+V to paste the section break you copied previously.

4. Press Delete to delete the old section break at the end of section 3.

FORMATTING A DOCUMENT WITH COLUMNS

We discussed adding section breaks a little earlier, and here is where you really need to keep these in mind. To create a document that uses columns within a section of the document, you need to use your section breaks to format the area properly.

To set up snaking columns in the middle of a document, follow these steps:

1. Switch to Draft view, click to position the insertion point where you want the columns to begin, and then choose Page Layout, Breaks. Add a Continuous section break immediately before the first item in the list.

2. Add another Continuous section break immediately after the last item in the list.

3. Click once between the two section break marks, choose Columns from the Page Setup grouping under the Page Layout ribbon, and then choose the column layout you like or select More Columns (see Figure 15.22). Note that you can set column widths and intercolumn whitespace manually.

Figure 15.22
To avoid confusion, set up the "before" and "after" section breaks manually: Click inside the area you want to format in snaking columns, and choose This Section from the Apply To box.

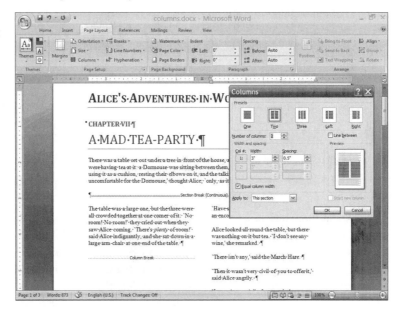

You might be tempted to use multiple columns for laying out newsletters and brochures, or (not surprisingly) newspapers. But before you try, take a closer look at the nuances.

Snaking newspaperlike columns might not work the way you're expecting. They run from top to bottom, and there's no rebalancing for a page break. If you have, for example, 12 items in a section that's set up with 3 columns, they'll appear arranged as in Table 15.2.

TABLE 15.2 SEQUENCE OF SNAKING COLUMNS

Item 1	Item 5	Item 9
Item 2	Item 6	Item 10
Item 3	Item 7	Item 11
Item 4	Item 8	Item 12

However, if you add a page break between, for example, the second and third lines in Table 15.2, items 2, 6, and 10 will appear on the first page, and items 3, 7, and 11 will end up on the second page.

If you need greater control over the appearance and layout of snaking columns, use tables instead of column formatting. Place each item in its own table cell and hide the table's gridlines. With Word's capability to draw custom tables with any number of cells, including nested cells, it makes little sense to work with columns if the layout is complicated.

TIP FROM

> If tables won't do, you can also give yourself much greater control over your pages by using linked text boxes.

TROUBLESHOOTING

DISAPPEARING CELL CONTENTS AND ROW MARKERS

I selected a row and dragged it to a new location, but instead of moving the whole row, as expected, Word replaced the contents of existing cells in the destination row.

Although you thought you selected the entire row, you actually selected all the cells in the rows. To make sure you select the entire row, you need to have Word show you the end-of-row markers—which are visible only if you show paragraph marks (go into your Word Options, click the Display settings, and select the Paragraph Marks check box). If you want to click and drag a table row to a new location, select the entire row—including the end-of-row marker—and then click and drag as you would with any other Word component.

PROPERLY SETTING THE ROW HEIGHT FOR WORD TABLES

When I insert a lot of text (or graphics) in a table cell, I can't see all of it. The bottom is chopped off.

Chances are good you did something to make Word set the row height using the Exactly option. To restore the default setting—in which rows grow and shrink to fit the contents—open the Table Properties dialog box (click into your table for the contextual ribbons, then on the Layout ribbon choose Table, Table Properties), click the Row tab, and clear the Specify Height box.

CHECK FOR STRAY DELIMITERS

When I use Word's Convert Text to Table feature, occasionally it does the conversion incorrectly, and the table is off by a cell or two.

Immediately after converting text to a table, look at the last row of the table and verify that it matches the last row of the selected data. If you're off by one or two cells (typically, one or two cells will be dangling at the bottom of the table), you probably have a stray delimiter character somewhere in the selected text. Scan the table to see whether you can locate it. Click the Undo button or press Ctrl+Z, fix the data, and try the conversion again.

TIP FROM

Ed & Woody

> One of the hardest characters to find is a Tab character that's "squished" between two pieces of text–or, worse, two or more tab characters in succession that aren't entirely visible because text surrounds them. You can select the text and use Find to search for single or double tabs–look for ^t or ^t^t.

CAN'T SEE FINAL COLUMN(S) IN A TABLE

When I add a column to a table (or adjust the width of a column), I no longer can see the last column.

The table is too wide to fit in the defined margins, and if you try to view the document in Print Layout view, you won't see the portion that falls off the page. Switch into Draft view and use the horizontal scrollbar to move to the right.

ALLOW PAGE BREAKS IN A TABLE CELL

In one of my documents, Word insists on waiting until the end of a cell before it triggers a page break. As a result, my tables flip-flop all over the page. Some pages have only one row showing, and it looks horrible.

You must have changed Word's default setting, which allows page breaks to occur at logical points (this is a big improvement over the default in some older Word versions). You might want all the data in a row to stay together, especially when the cells all contain fairly modest amounts of text. But in your case, this setting is getting in the way. To get Word to relax a bit, select the entire table and choose Table, Table Properties. In the Table Properties dialog box, click the Row tab, click the Options group, and select the Allow Row to Break Across Pages box.

SECRETS OF THE OFFICE MASTERS: SAVING FILES AS PDF OR XPS

If you have ever been asked to convert your documents into PDF (Portable Document Format), you know how frustrating this can be without the tools you need. There are even services on the Internet where you send them your document, they convert it for you, and send it back—for a fee, of course. Well, now you can convert for free.

For those of you who may not know what PDF or XPS is, here is a quick review. PDF is a file format that is very common because it takes your document and preserves it for sharing. So, you don't have to worry that someone will work on it or make changes. It's already set, all formatting included, for others to read. To read PDF files, you need a reader program and the most popular is Acrobat Reader, which is free from Adobe. They give you the reader for free, but you have to buy the conversion tool. XPS is the XML Paper Specification, which is also a format for sharing documents.

Now, in either case, if you want to save a file in PDF or XPS formats, you have to download and install an add-in from Microsoft. It's free though. Go to Microsoft.com and do a search, or go to the Downloads center and look for "2007 Microsoft Office Add-in: Microsoft Save as PDF or XPS." It's only a 696KB file. Download and install it, and then choose a document you want to convert.

After you have your document ready, go to your Office button and choose Save As. Then select PDF or XPS. Give your file a name (although it will take the name of your Word document by default) and then choose the file type (PDF is the default).

You can choose to open the file after it is saved (although keep in mind you need to have the reader). Notice that you have two options for file size optimization. You can choose to have the file saved in a Standard format for higher quality, or for lower file size, click Minimum size.

For more detailed option settings, you can select Options and then choose a page range, determine whether the document should be published with or without showing markup, and include nonprinting information.

As far as features go, this new quick-and-easy PDF creator is one of the best things included. It's like a great piece of cake with a cherry on top. Do you need the cherry? Not really, but it sure does make the whole cake seem better.

CHAPTER **16**

PROFESSIONAL DOCUMENT TOOLS AND ADVANCED DOCUMENT SHARING

In this chapter

Keeping Long Documents Under Control   456

Tools for Academic and Professional Documents   464

Document Properties   467

Sharing Documents   468

Troubleshooting   474

Secrets of the Office Masters: Preparing Your Documents for Distribution   474

KEEPING LONG DOCUMENTS UNDER CONTROL

Effectively using Word to handle long documents requires forethought and planning. In previous editions of this book, we strongly recommended that Word users exercise extreme caution with long documents—100 pages or more in length, or more than a megabyte or two in size. That advice was valid for previous Word versions, based on a rich historical record of long documents that were unwieldy, slow to load, and susceptible to corruption.

There are several reasons why we are optimistic that those problems are history. As computers have advanced technologically and the operating systems have evolved as well, a more stable underlying system exists now for your Office applications to run on top of. In addition, Microsoft has been working hard over the last few editions of Word up to 2007 to eliminate as many problems as possible. So, all in all, your document size shouldn't be a problem going forward.

So, does this mean that the sky's the limit? Not exactly. We still think that a cautious approach is smart. If you *can* break a very long document into several smaller ones, you probably should. If you need some of Word's advanced features, such as a Table of Contents or page numbering, use some of the strategies we outline in this section.

ONE FILE OR MANY?

As your documents get larger, you have three choices:

- **Continue to work with a single large file or break it down into smaller ones**—An effective backup strategy is always valuable, but it's especially important when working with large files, where a single misstep can wipe out huge amounts of work. You can break it up manually, employing techniques described in this chapter to keep everything together, or you can use Word's Master Document features from within Outline view under the Master Document grouping.

CAUTION

Don't risk scrambling your file's contents. Make absolutely sure you disable Word's Fast Save option. You do this from Word Options, under Advanced settings under the Save category.

A *master document* is a Word document that contains links to one or more separate documents, called *subdocuments*. A master document can be a pure "container" with no text of its own, or it can be a full-fledged document that contains text and graphics and one or two links to other files. Master documents are especially useful when a group of people are collaborating on a large document. Each team member can work separately on his or her document; when the parts are complete, you can open the master document and view, edit, or print the complete project just as if it were a single document. Note: Some longtime Word experts, in fact, insist that using master documents is a nearly perfect recipe for scrambled files and corrupted data. That's good to know before you start using this feature. It certainly requires good organizational skills to keep all your subdocuments in order.

- **Cut the large file down to size**—If your file contains multiple graphics, save the pictures in separate files and create links instead of embedding them.

- **Use fields to include the contents of one file in another**—Go to the Insert ribbon, and under the Text grouping select the Object button down arrow and choose Text from File. Select the name of a second file, click the down arrow to the right of the Insert button, and then choose Insert as Link. Word adds an {INCLUDETEXT} field to your document that automatically reads in the contents of the second file. This technique is especially useful for boilerplate text. For instance, if you have a company description that appears in many documents, you can use an {INCLUDETEXT} field to ensure that this block of text always contains the latest version.

16

CAUTION

> All the approaches that involve linking pictures or using multiple documents (including master documents) depend on hard-coded filenames that include the full path name. That can pose problems when moving a large document from one machine to another. Replicating folder structures is almost a prerequisite for moving large documents from one machine to another.

USING BOOKMARKS

If you work on larger-sized documents and need to return to specific points in the document for editing, you can add bookmarks that will prove invaluable. Instead of scrolling through pages and pages of your document (or in my case, writing down different page numbers on a napkin), you can use the technology at your fingertips.

You can also use cross-references with bookmarks, as we will discuss in the next section.

To insert a bookmark, you select the text or item (you don't have to choose text; you can add a bookmark to a picture or anything you need to return to) and use the following steps:

1. Go to the Insert ribbon and choose Bookmark from the Links grouping.
2. Type a name, keeping in mind that, although you can use numbers and underscores, you cannot use spaces.
3. Click Add.

Nothing looks different at first. But if you go to another part of your document and select your Bookmark button, and then select the name of the one you created and choose Go To, it will take you back where you set the bookmark.

If you want to be able to see your bookmarks, you need to go into your Word Options and under your Advanced settings in the Show Document Content area, choose the Show Bookmarks check box. If you have bookmarks set for text, your bookmark will show up with brackets [] around the text. If it's set for a location, you will get an I-beam in the document. (The brackets or I-beam will not print.)

CAUTION

> Bookmarks can also work hand in hand with maintaining the integrity of references in your document. For example, suppose you have different headings that keep changing/evolving. You might refer back to those headings throughout a document and this means that every time the heading changes, you have to find the references and update them as well. You could set a bookmark as a reference point and then use REF Field that refers back to your bookmark. We will discuss fields in greater detail in the next section.

INSERTING CROSS-REFERENCES

When writing a manual, a legal document, and the like, you may want to use cross-references to help your readers navigate from one part of you document to another, especially in larger, more complicated types of documents. You could type these in manually or you could use the Cross-reference tool located under the Links grouping on the Insert ribbon.

The cross-references you create will dynamically update to indicate changes in your document (such as page locations, section headings, or figure numbers that can change often) so that you don't have to worry so much when you make a change. By default, the cross-references you create are also hyperlinked; that means someone else working on your document can use the cross-reference immediately to go to that location in the document by holding down the Ctrl button and clicking the link.

Word 2007 includes extensive support for cross-referencing—everything from "See Figure x-y above" kinds of references to "as defined in paragraph IV.B.7.a." Each type of cross-reference has its own requirements and quirks, so a little bit of planning goes a long way.

These references persist even if the document changes. That's what makes them so powerful and useful. Suppose you have a reference in a contract that says "as defined in paragraph IV.B.7.a." Then one of the attorneys working on the contract realizes it needs an additional numbered paragraph, and that new paragraph has to go ahead of the current paragraph IV.A. All you need to do is insert the paragraph, select the document, and press F9 to update fields. Automatically, the old paragraph IV.B.7.a becomes paragraph IV.C.7.a, and the old reference to it turns into "as defined in paragraph IV.C.7.a."

Many kinds of cross-references interact with captions (see the next section for details on how to set up the captions correctly). Suppose you have a picture in a document with a caption that reads "Figure 17," and a reference to it such as "See Figure 17." Your editor decides to add a figure immediately before Figure 17. If you used cross-references and captions correctly, the next time you update fields, the old figure number 17 will get the caption "Figure 18," and the old reference will be updated so it reads "See Figure 18." The connections persist even in the face of complex restructuring in the document. So, if you moved this new Figure 18 to the beginning of the document, for example, it would get the caption "Figure 1" and the reference would change to "See Figure 1." Captions and references throughout the document would change to match the new numbering scheme—and all you have to do is update fields.

To see Word's Cross-reference dialog box (shown in Figure 16.1), click Insert ribbon, Links, Cross-reference.

Figure 16.1
Word's cross-reference capabilities key off of precisely defined styles, bookmarks, and sequences located inside the document.

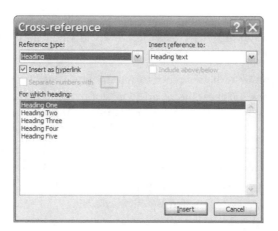

Choices in the Reference Type drop-down list are linked to specific elements in the document:

- **Reference Type**—Numbered Item refers exclusively to paragraphs formatted with Word-applied numbering. (If you number your paragraphs manually, they won't appear here.) There's a fair amount of native intelligence in the cross-reference: For example, if you refer to paragraph IV.B.7.a from inside paragraph IV.B.6.c, you can tell Word to use the reference "7.a."

- **Reference Type**—Heading choices include only those paragraphs marked with the built-in Word heading styles: Heading 1, Heading 2, Heading 3, and so on.

- **Bookmark**—Includes any bookmarks you've defined in the document. By using the Insert, Cross-reference feature, you can put the bookmarked text or the bookmark's page number in the document, and it will be updated should the contents of the bookmark—or its location—change.

- **Footnote, Endnote**—These are tied to footnotes and endnotes in the document. If you want to create an additional reference to an existing footnote, choose Cross-reference, and in the Reference Type drop-down list, choose Footnote.

- **Figure**—Refers exclusively to paragraphs in the document that contain the {SEQ Figure} field. When you select Figure from the Reference Type drop-down list, Word scans the document for {SEQ Figure} fields and puts the paragraphs containing those fields in the For Which Heading list. When you use Word's built-in Caption feature, it can generate an {SEQ Figure} field that's picked up by the cross-reference feature.

- **Equation, Table**—Similar to the Figure options, these refers exclusively to {SEQ Equation} and {SEQ Table} fields.

Suppose you own a travel agency and you've created a catalog in which the name of each destination appears in a paragraph formatted as Heading 2. You've written a description of the glorious beaches and resorts of Thailand that appears on page 77. Throughout your document, you would like to insert references that follow the format "For more information about *destination*, see page *nn*" (where *nn* is the actual page number on which that content appears). No problem. In our imaginary scenario, we would follow these steps to add cross-references:

1. Click once where you want the reference to appear. Type your introductory text—in this example, `For more information about` (don't forget the trailing space)—and then choose the Insert ribbon, Links grouping, and Cross-reference. Choose Heading from the Reference Type drop-down list and Heading Text from the Insert Reference To list.

2. In the For Which Heading box, choose the item for which you want to create a cross-reference—Thailand, for our example. Click Insert, and then Close.

3. Type `, see page` (with a comma, a leading space, and a trailing space) and then choose the Insert ribbon, Links grouping, Cross-reference again.

4. In the Reference Type drop-down list, choose Heading; in the Insert Reference To drop-down list, choose Page Number. In the For Which Heading list box, choose the same item you selected in step 2. Click Insert, and then Close.

The cross-reference in your document now reads, "For more information about Thailand, see page 77."

CAUTION

> Captions that appear in the drawing layer aren't detected by Word's Insert Cross-reference feature. If you place a caption in a text box, or if your figures "float over text" with an attached caption, you must first move the caption into the document itself before your cross-references will work properly.

Cross-references work only on references inside the current document or inside a master document.

CREATING INDEXES

We've all used indexes before, right? We love using an index to help us out, except when it isn't clear enough or doesn't have enough entries, which means somebody skipped out on its preparation. We might have some empathy, though, if we have ever been asked to create an index for a document. It could be a real nightmare without the tools in Word. Creating an index for your document is a straightforward two-step process:

1. Mark index entries in the document by using the References ribbon under the Index grouping. Then choose the Mark Entry button and fill out the information. Proceed through the entire document, marking index entries where they occur.

2. When you're done marking the entries, generate the index by placing the insertion point where you want the index to appear, bring up the Index dialog box (refer to Figure 16.2) by clicking the Insert Index option from the Index grouping, and click OK.

Figure 16.2
Notice the various options in creating your index.

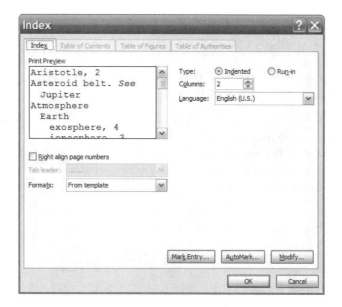

Unfortunately, Word's indexing feature is not as intuitive as you might hope. Although it appears that indexes built with the Mark Index Entry dialog box can run only two entries deep, there is a workaround. Although the Mark Index Entry dialog box has only two boxes for entry levels (Main Entry and Sub Entry), you can enter up to seven levels in either of these boxes by separating your entries with colons—for example, you could enter `Flowers:Roses:Red`.

With that caution in mind, there are a few tricks you can use to make indexing faster and easier.

To create an index entry for a particular word in a document, double-click the word to select it, and then press Alt+Shift+X. If you want to use the word as the main (highest level) entry, press Enter. If you want to use something different for the main entry, press Ctrl+X while still in the Mark Index Entry dialog box (or right-click the word and choose Cut) to cut the selected word, type in your main entry, press Tab, and then press Ctrl+V to make the selected word a subentry (or right-click and choose Paste).

For example, if you see the word Rose in a document and want to create an entry for Flowers:Rose, here's a quick way to do it:

1. Double-click Rose to select it.
2. Press Alt+Shift+X to bring up the Mark Index Entry dialog box.
3. Press Home to move the insertion point to the beginning of the Main Entry box.
4. Type the word **Flowers:** (note the colon).
5. Press Enter twice (or click Mark and then click Close). Word inserts an {XE "Flowers:Rose"} field into your document.

Although the key sequence is a bit convoluted, with practice it can be mastered.

Like so many other advanced Word features, indexing is driven by field codes. In this case, the {XE} field code marks the location of index entries. The index itself is really just an {Index} field. If you want to see your {XE} fields, go into your Display options from within your Word Options and check the Hidden Text box. You can also use Show/Hide tools.

When you go to insert the index itself, you have some choices you can make from the Index dialog box (refer to Figure 16.2). You can choose it to be Indented (each word will appear below the main heading separately) or Run-in, which will put all the sub-entries together. You can determine the number of columns you want the Index to come up in. Then you can have the page numbers right after the entry right-aligned with a tab leader.

Over time, your index entries will change as your document changes. You can update the index by using the Update Index option on the References ribbon.

Most likely, the Index tools are all most people will ever need, unless you are in publishing and need the next level (professional-grade) type of index. Fortunately, you can pour Word documents into high-end desktop-publishing programs, which include all the tools necessary to generate decent professional-grade indexes.

If you're frustrated because your edits to the compiled index are lost whenever you update the index, see "Updating Index Entries" in the "Troubleshooting" section at the end of this chapter.

If you've spell-checked your index but still find spelling errors, see "Spell Checking an Index" in the "Troubleshooting" section at the end of this chapter.

CREATING A TABLE OF CONTENTS

The Table of Contents (TOC) generator in Word works quite well. There are just a few things you'll want to keep in mind when working with it:

- Make sure you've applied styles to all the heading paragraphs you want to appear in the TOC. You can use Word's default "Heading *n*" styles, or you can create your own.

- If you want to add more entries—for instance, free-form text entries that will appear in the TOC even if they aren't in paragraphs with appropriate styles—use the Add Text entry on the References ribbon from the Table of Contents grouping.

- You can also use Quick Parts—Field to put {TC} fields in your document. {TC} fields can include much more than plain text. For detailed reference information on how to use this type of field, see "Field codes: TC (Table of Contents Entry) field" in online help.

- To put the insertion point where you want the TOC to appear, choose Table of Contents from the References ribbon. The Table of Contents dialog box appears as shown in Figure 16.3.

- If you're using styles other than the standard "Heading *n*" set, click Options (also shown in Figure 16.3) and map each style to a TOC heading level. When you're done, click OK, and Word builds the TOC.

Figure 16.3
You can build a Table of Contents based on any set of styles.

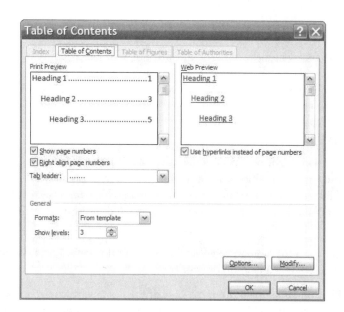

A Table of Contents (even a large one) is just a Word field—a {TOC} field, to be precise. To see the field, choose Show Field Codes Instead of Their Values from the Advanced settings within your Word Options.

CAUTION

If you regularly work with field codes, memorize the ViewFieldCodes keyboard shortcut, Alt+F9. Or assign the command to your Quick Access Toolbar so you can toggle it on and off.

{TOC} behaves just like any other field, with one exception. When you update it, Word might ask you whether you want to Update Page Numbers Only, or Update the Entire Table. Although the default response is Update Page Numbers Only, you should accept this choice only if you are absolutely certain that none of the TOC entries has been deleted or changed, and no new entries have been added.

Word generally keeps good track of your headings, and if it detects that a heading has been added or deleted, it won't even ask whether you want to Update Page Numbers Only.

The entire Table of Figures engine is based on the labels in {SEQ} fields, in a manner similar to the cross-reference hooks described earlier in this chapter. In fact, a Table of Figures is nothing more than a {TOC} field, with switches added to indicate which {SEQ} field should be indexed.

A Table of Contents, Index, or other kind of reference table, can be generated only for entries inside the current document or inside one master document.

TOOLS FOR ACADEMIC AND PROFESSIONAL DOCUMENTS

Some Word users (even mega-experts) can work in Word their entire lives and never, ever use these tools. Why? Because they are either tools you utilize at a university while you prepare your term papers, or tools you use in specific job capacities. If you aren't working for a law firm, you won't likely ever use a Table of Authorities, for example. Let's get started.

FOOTNOTES AND ENDNOTES

Your first question might be, "What's the difference?". They both refer to a part of your document and provide additional information. However, a footnote will insert a number in the text and insert itself at the bottom of the page in which you inserted the footnote, whereas an endnote will insert a number in the text and insert itself at the very end of the text itself.

So, you might use a footnote to reference additional information on a certain point, and endnotes might contain a citation of your sources.

To insert either one is simple. Go to the part of the document where you want to have the number located and click either Insert Footnote or Insert Endnote from the Footnotes grouping on the References ribbon. Then type in your explanation or comment.

You can alter the configuration of your footnotes or endnotes by choosing the Footnote and Endnote dialog launcher from the Footnotes grouping. You might want to change your number formatting. Another change you might want to make is the use of a custom mark as opposed to the traditional number settings.

You can use the Next Footnote button to navigate through the locations of your footnotes or endnotes to make editing them easier.

CITATIONS AND BIBLIOGRAPHIES

These two subjects go hand in hand, and you would agree if you looked at the References ribbon under the Citations and Bibliography grouping. There are several tools to assist you in creating your bibliography, which is a list of all your sources used in creating your document. It's the next step up from the use of endnotes. Endnotes might be more of the quick term-paper version of your bibliography, whereas your scientific 300-page book would definitely need those citations in a bibliography. You can generate one automatically in Word 2007 by adding source citations throughout your work, and that information will be saved so that it can be pooled later by the Bibliography tool.

You start with a new citation (and by extension, a new source for your bibliography). Perform the following steps:

1. Choose the Style from your Style options. Different fields will use different styles. For example, APA (psychology, education, social sciences); MLA (literature, arts, and humanities); Turabian (for college students to use with all subjects); and Chicago (for all real-world subjects in books, magazines, newspapers, and so on).

2. At the end of the sentence where you want to put your citation, choose the Insert Citation button from the References ribbon.

3. You can now choose to Add New Source and then fill in the source information. Or you can choose Add New Placeholder to come back and fill in later. When filling in your Source, try to provide as much information as you can. In fact, you can choose Show All Bibliography Fields, and you can see from Figure 16.4 how much information you can add.

4. Another option at your disposal is the Search Libraries option. You can use this to do additional research about the sources you cite.

Figure 16.4
Creating Citation sources to be used later in the bibliography. Do this right once, and it will save you time later.

As we mentioned earlier, you want to add these in correctly because each citation goes into a Master List. Later on in your document, you can choose the Manage Sources option from the Citations and Bibliography grouping, and you will see the citations from your current document. But you can also see your citations from other documents. This can make your life much easier as you select citations from works that you have used before. You can use the Browse option to find a source file from another location and use that file to pull in sources you can use in your document. For example, if a colleague has already added a ton of sources and you know you have used the same materials, it would be a time saver to access his sources.xml file and import his references (with his/her permission, of course).

After all your sources are in place, it's time to create the bibliography. To accomplish this, perform the following steps:

1. Click the end of your document (where you usually place your bibliography). Select Bibliography from your Citations and Bibliography grouping on the References ribbon.

2. At the end of the sentence where you want to put your citation, choose the Insert Citation button from the References ribbon. Choose from the Built-In gallery of options to have your bibliography added to the document.

SPECIALIZED TOOLS FOR LEGAL DOCUMENTS

Again, if you don't work in certain fields, in this case the Legal field, you won't use certain tools. The tool we are referring to in this case is the Table of Authorities located, as well, on the References ribbon under the Table of Authorities grouping.

A Table of Authorities lists references in a legal document. Just like in your favorite court show (for me, it's *Law and Order*) where a case is cited or a previously established law or statute, you can do the same in your documents.

Again you use citations, but a different type of citation. The Mark Citation option allows you to mark a citation as a case or statute, and so on.

When you have completed adding your citations throughout your document, you can build the complete Table of Authorities at the end of your document. Simply put your cursor where you want to insert the table and choose Insert Table of Authorities from the References ribbon.

If you make any updates over time, you can choose Update Table at a later date. Keep in mind, though, that if you edit the table manually and then update the table, your manual edits will be lost.

SUMMARIZING A DOCUMENT AUTOMATICALLY

Sometimes your documents can be large enough for you to lose focus when you are trying to read through them. Word includes a feature called AutoSummary that can, under the right circumstances, help you create a summary of a document. Word does that by coming up with a word frequency list, and then rating each sentence in the document according to how many frequently used words appear in the sentence. You then assign a cutoff point, and any sentence that exceeds the cutoff point is included in the summary.

You might want to try AutoSummarize on highly structured, repetitive documents, just to see whether it generates anything other than gibberish.

CAUTION

> AutoSummary used to have a place in the Word toolbar, but it no longer has a place on the new ribbons. Logically, the reason for removing a tool like this is because it isn't all that useful to the majority of users. We only mention it here because you *can* use it, not because we recommend that you do.

If you choose to use this tool, first you have to add it to your Quick Access toolbar. You do this through your Word Options, from Customize. Look for commands that are not on the ribbons and then find AutoSummary Tools and add it. Then select it from the toolbar (see Figure 16.5). Specify whether you want to highlight the high-scoring sentences or extract those sentences and use them to create an executive summary.

Assign the cutoff point by choosing a percentage for the summary (on a long document, you probably don't want the summary to be more than 10% of the size of the document itself). Optionally, you can have Word automatically update the file properties, placing the most frequently encountered words in the Keywords and Comments boxes.

If the summary proves less than enlightening, you can always delete it—providing you told Word to extract the sentences.

Figure 16.5
Use the
AutoSummarize feature to highlight or
extract key thoughts
from a document—but
don't expect miracles.

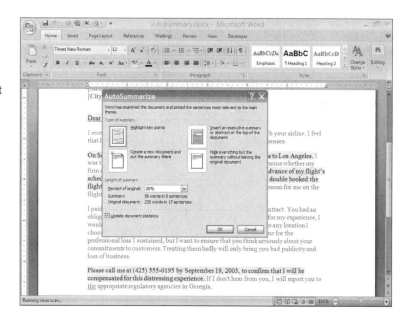

DOCUMENT PROPERTIES

Each document has properties associated with it that identify personal information connected to the document—for example, the author of the document. This type of information is called metadata (described in Microsoft Help as "data that describes other data"). One example is the word count for a document. Each document has a specific number of words. That word count is considered metadata for your document and is a property of the document itself. This is information that you may want available for others to see, and at other times it may include hidden information regarding your company that you want to remove.

TIP FROM

One reason why you may want to change Document Properties is when you work on a document that someone else created. Perhaps that person is listed as the author and you want it clear that you are the author of the document. You change this within Document Properties.

To view the Document Properties for any particular document, select your Office Button, go to the Prepare settings, and choose Properties. A simple set of properties will appear, including Author, Title, Subject, Keywords, Category, Status, and Comments. These can be very helpful when sharing documents with others, or collaborating with others, to provide background information and details regarding the document or the project that the document is connected to.

However, to see the more advanced settings for your document, you select the Document Properties down arrow and choose Advanced Properties. This will make available to you the multitabbed dialog box shown in Figure 16.6.

Figure 16.6
Advanced document properties can be added to provide additional information to others, or for your own benefit for future reference.

 Before sending a document outside your department or your company, you may want to remove all the hidden information, including Document Properties. To accomplish this, use the Document Inspector, explained in greater detail at the end of this chapter in "Secrets of the Office Masters: Preparing Your Documents for Distribution."

Using fields within your documents will be discussed in greater detail in the next chapter, however, it might be good to note here that all the information you include in Document Properties can be referenced and used within your document through fields.

If you open up your Field dialog box (from the Insert ribbon, select Quick Parts from the Text grouping). The field name is DocProperty, and you can select any of the properties that are contained in the Document Properties options, including Author and Word Count to include in your document.

SHARING DOCUMENTS

Word is often used in a business environment by groups of users who need to work together. To accommodate the need for users to create documents as a team, Word has workgroup features that make it easier to track and protect changes in documents.

In this section, we discuss Word's traditional collaboration features, all of which entail different people opening and editing a document. The document may be stored in a commonly accessible location, or it may be passed around via email. Either way, team members make their changes and save them to a file so that the next person in line can see those changes. If your workgroup has Office 2007 and a SharePoint server available, you have the additional option of collaborating in a Document Workspace.

TRACKING REVISIONS

When more than one person can make changes to a document, pandemonium can ensue. The surest way to maintain the integrity of a document is to ensure that changes—if they're allowed at all—are clearly identified so that anyone reviewing the edited document can trace specific changes back to their originator. That's at the heart of Word's Track Changes (frequently called "Revision Tracking") capability.

When Word tracks changes made to a document, text that is added, deleted, or modified is marked to emphasize the changes made. You can subsequently go through those changes one at a time and accept or reject them. Word 2007 offers a tri-pane review panel to make it easier for you to work with revisions made within two documents.

To specify that you want Word to track changes made to the current document, go to the Review ribbon, and under the Tracking grouping, select the Track Changes button (or select the Track Changes notifier on the status bar, if it's turned on). Any changes made from that point on are explicitly saved by Word.

Under the Tracking grouping on the Review ribbon is a set of options, including a drop-down list called Display for Review. The drop-down list lets you look at any of the following:

- **Original**—What the document looked like before Change Tracking was turned on.
- **Original Showing Markup**—Shows the original document, with insertions noted in a manner similar to comments, out in the right margin, and deletions marked with an overstrike.
- **Final Showing Markup**—The final state of the document, with inserted text appearing underlined and in a different color and deleted text noted in the margin.
- **Final**—The end result.

Shifting back and forth among the different views gives you a quick idea of the effect of changes. If you're rewriting a first draft prepared by someone else, for instance, you might prefer to work in Final view, where Word behaves exactly as if you were editing the document without tracking changes. If you're reviewing the work of several people, you can switch to Final Showing Markup so that you can see what was deleted. Figure 16.7 shows a document that is currently under revision.

When reviewing a document, use the four buttons on the Changes grouping to jump from revision to revision, accepting or rejecting individual changes as you go. There's also an icon for making your own comments, in case you need to follow up on a change, and for bringing up a pane that lists changes in order. Overall, it's a powerful and useful feature.

16

Figure 16.7
Using the Final Showing Markup view, you can see additions in the body of the document and deletions in the margin.

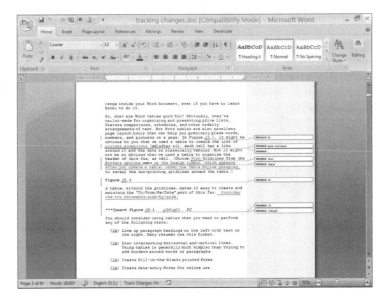

NOTE

Some may find it incredibly distracting to try to work with a document with changes inline (that is, directly showing in the document). Different colors from different reviewers, crossed out text—depending on the extent of edits, it could visually stress a person out. To that end, Balloons (shown in Figure 16.8) allow you to keep your comments out of your inline text. You have three choices with Balloons (located in the Tracking grouping). Show Revisions in Balloons (turns the feature on), Show All Revisions Inline (turns the feature off and puts revision text directly within your document), or Show Only Comments and Formatting in Balloons (which gives you partial benefit to the use of the balloons).

Figure 16.8
Using Balloons to keep the clutter down in your revision work.

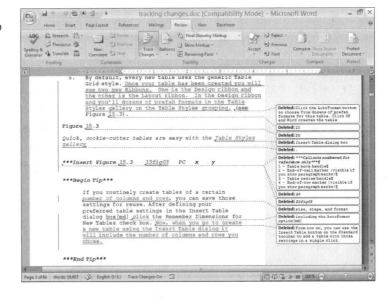

Although you have the ability to turn on Track Changes and just start editing, you might want to make some adjustments in the settings. To do this, select the Track Changes icon from the Tracking grouping on the Review ribbon and choose Change Tracking Options, shown in Figure 16.9. From here you can alter the colors used and even change the Balloon option settings.

Figure 16.9
Changing Track
Changes Options.

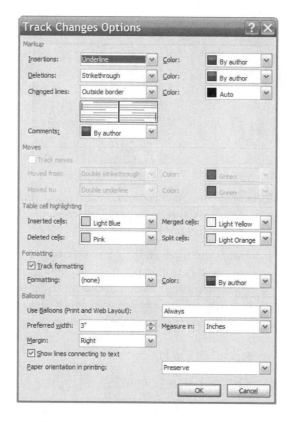

You can also determine what you want to see in the marked-up version you are working on. Select Show Markup from the Tracking grouping and note that you can turn on/off Comments, Ink, Insertions and Deletions, Formatting, Markup Area Highlights, and different Reviewers.

If you didn't set Word to track revisions, and somebody has made changes to a document, you still have one last resort, a feature called Compare. To have Word mark the differences between two documents, open one of the documents and choose Compare from the Compare grouping on the Review ribbon. You will be presented with the option to Compare or Combine. Compare allows you to choose a document to compare the original with the changed version. You can even determine what is going to be compared, as shown in Figure 16.10.

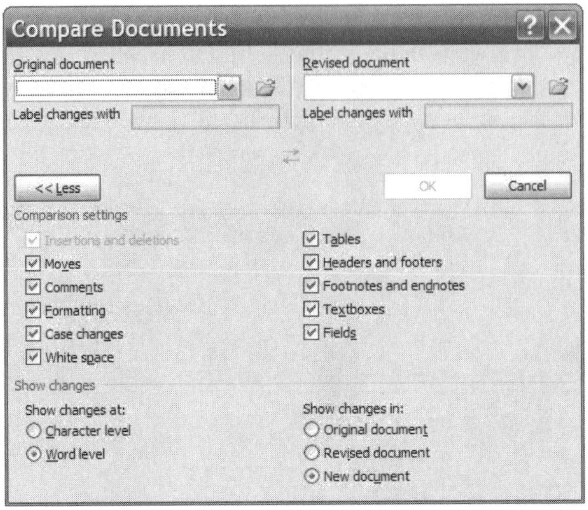

16

Figure 16.10
Comparing two documents is your only way to see changes if you forgot to turn on Track Changes.

This feature automatically generates revision marks, noting the pieces that have been added or deleted from the original document, along with formatting changes. Use the buttons on the Reviewing toolbar to view and accept or reject changes.

Combine will take two documents and combine the revisions marks into one. This is helpful when you have, for example, two editors working on a document (a technical editor ensuring technical accuracy and a copy editor ensuring overall document structure and grammatical accuracy). You could have one edit the document and then pass it on to the other. But it's easier to have them both edit in their own way and then merge the edits together into a final document to be sent back to the author for revision review. The tri-pane review panel is a nice way to see your revisions, as shown in Figure 16.11.

Figure 16.11
Meet the tri-pane review panel, complete with the ability to review and combine changes into one document.

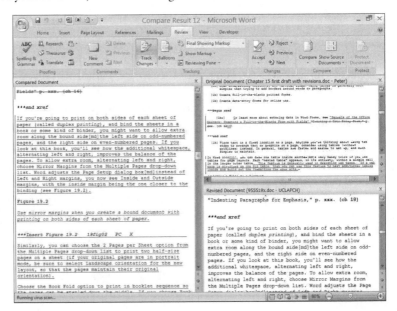

ADDING COMMENTS TO DOCUMENTS

When you're collaborating on a document with other people, it's helpful to leave comments along the way, explaining the reasons for certain changes or suggesting places where additional changes may be necessary. When editors or reviewers make changes to a document for which you have final responsibility, it's relatively easy to accept or reject their additions or deletions. Don't fall into the trap of using comments to suggest changes, however; transferring those comments into the document requires multiple steps and takes a fair amount of time. Instead, the review should make the change in the document and add a comment inviting the original author to reject the change if he or she disagrees with it.

To enter a comment, highlight the text that pertains to the comment and choose New Comment from the Comments grouping on the Review ribbon. (If you don't make a selection, Word attaches the comment to the word immediately preceding the insertion point.) Type your comment into the comment box.

To cycle through all the comments in a document, use the Next button on the Reviewing ribbon.

You can print all the comments attached to a document by choosing the Office Button, Print, and selecting Document Showing Markup in the Print What drop-down box.

RESTRICTING CHANGES TO A SHARED DOCUMENT

For revision tracking to work, all the people working on a document have to keep this option turned on. Otherwise, their changes won't be explicitly shown, and you'll have to go through the additional step of comparing your original document with their modified versions to figure out what has changed. In addition, you may want to pass around a document so that other people can read it without making any changes. As in previous versions of Word, you can protect a document from unwanted changes. Word 2007 helps you specify editing restrictions.

To set editing restrictions for the current document, follow these steps:

1. From the Review ribbon, you can select the Protect Document button from the Protect grouping and select Restrict Formatting and Editing.
2. Under Editing Restrictions, click to select the Allow Only This Type of Editing in the Document check box.
3. Select an editing option from the drop-down list. To force everyone making changes to a document to have Word track their changes, choose Tracked Changes. To prevent any changes to the document, select No Changes (Read Only).
4. Click Yes, Start Enforcing Protection.
5. In the next dialog box, enter an optional password if you don't want people to be able to override this setting. Click OK to finish.

From that point on, anyone who opens the document has to abide by the restrictions you specified. To remove the restriction, go back into your Protect Document task pane again and click Stop Protection.

TROUBLESHOOTING

UPDATING INDEX ENTRIES

After inserting an index, I edited the entries by directly typing over them within the index itself. But when I updated the index, all those edits were lost.

Always make changes to the index entries in the body of the document—that is, change the contents of the {xe} fields themselves. That way, when you update the index (or table of contents), your changes will be reflected in the new index. The process doesn't work in reverse, as you discovered the hard way. If you type over an item in the index itself, you eliminate the reference to matching index fields within the document.

SPELL CHECKING AN INDEX

Even though I spell checked my index, there are still spelling errors in the index.

Index entries—that is, {xe} fields—normally are hidden. Word doesn't check hidden text when you run a spelling check. To spell check your index entries, first display hidden characters (go into your Word Options; then from the Display settings, click the Hidden Text check box). Next, run the spell check. Misspelled words in {xe} fields will appear with a red squiggly underline.

SECRETS OF THE OFFICE MASTERS: PREPARING YOUR DOCUMENTS FOR DISTRIBUTION

There are several useful tools available, but not located on the ribbons, that will help you to finish up your document and prepare it for distribution to others. The main focus of this chapter was to help you to complete your documents' finer elements, such as a Table of Contents, and then work within a team to collaborate on edits, so it seems only fitting that the "secrets" discussed here relate to preparing your document for distribution.

To see the tools available to you for preparation, go to your Office button and select Prepare. You will see the following options:

- **Properties**—We already discussed Document Properties earlier in the chapter. It's part of the metadata for your document, the hidden information such as Author, Title, page count, and so on.

- **Inspect Document**—This option first examines the document and determines if you have hidden data that you might want removed, and then presents you with the option of removing that data.

- **Encrypt Document**—Make sure you remember the password you choose if you encrypt the document.

- **Restrict Permission**—This preparation option is connected to the Information Rights Management (IRM) tools available for Office 2007. The basic concept is that IRM allows you greater control over who can access what, allows you to configure the extent of the access persons can have (for example, have a user read the document but not be allowed to print it) and even establish document expiration so that contents within a given document cannot be viewed past a certain date. To understand these tools to a greater extent, search on Microsoft.com for Information Rights Management (IRM) and/or Rights Management Services (RMS).

- **Add a Digital Signature**—This option allows you to add a digital method of authentication to your documents. The signature (much like a digital certificate) can be added with the backing of a third party that validates the signed document. You could also add a signature that cannot be validated by others.

- **Mark as Final**—This option makes your document read-only and prevents changes. When you select this option, the document has typing, editing, and proofing marks disabled. This is not a security feature, just a deterrent. People can turn it off to do what they want, but it will stop someone from making thoughtless edits to your work.

- **Run Compatibility Checker**—This option goes through your document and lets you know which items you have included will not carry over (or will be altered) if you convert the document to 97–2003 compatibility.

When preparing documents for distribution, you will likely find the Document Inspector among the most useful tools listed. With it you can remove all the hidden information within a document, including the document properties and any personal information. If you go to the Office button and select Prepare and then Inspect Document, you might see a message that tells you to save your document first. Select Yes if this message appears, and then you will see your options, shown in Figure 16.12.

Figure 16.12
Document Inspector will check through your document for metadata, revision marks, headers and footers, watermarks, etc... unless you specify otherwise.

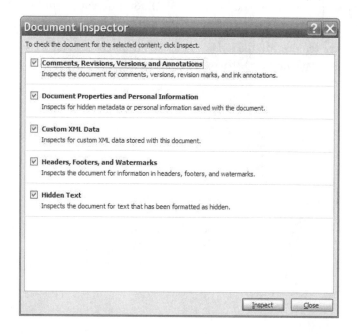

Select the Inspect button to get the process started, and it should take no time at all for it to return with the results, shown in Figure 16.13.

Figure 16.13
The inspection results allow you to determine to what extent you would like to remove hidden and personal data from the document.

As you consider the results, you can Remove All for different parts of the document. Or you can choose to Reinspect the document itself.

After you have removed all the hidden data, the document is ready to be sent out without fear of that information being shared with others.

CHAPTER 17

LETTERS, ENVELOPES, AND DATA-DRIVEN DOCUMENTS

In this chapter

Creating and Editing Letters   478

Creating Envelopes and Labels   480

Using Mail Merge to Personalize Letters and Envelopes   483

Using Fields to Add Intelligence to a Document   496

Troubleshooting   502

Secrets of the Office Masters: Creating a Fill-in-the-Blanks Form with Fields   503

Word 2007 is more than document processing software. It's more than a means of displaying graphics, tables, charts, and such in attractive formats for print. Word 2007 has features that can make your life easier by merging information together to create letters that need to go to thousands of persons, along with setting up envelopes or labels to attach to those thousands of letters. In addition, not all Word documents are for printing. Sometimes you want persons to be able to utilize form. Now at times you can create that form and print it for others to use, or you can create form fields that people can use to enter information directly into your Word document. Finally, you can use fields in Word documents that help you to add information dynamically by pulling it from other locations or even from within Document Properties. This chapter is going to walk you through the highlights of these features, and then our Office Master section will take you though the creating of an online form.

CREATING AND EDITING LETTERS

In previous versions of Word, there was an annoying little creature called the Office Assistant (no offense to those of you who started to get attached to the little digipet). This "assistant" liked to offer advice. One of its sidekicks, the Letter Wizard, never showed its face, but the assistant vouched for it and said this so-called wizard would assist us. Apparently the digipet and the wizard finally angered the wrong people, and they've been banished to Middle Earth.

What has replaced the Letter Wizard to help us make perfect letters? Nothing. By this point, you know what a letter is supposed to look like, and you can make it happen all on your own.

However, Microsoft does have one thing to help you: letter templates. The letters are already designed for you; all you have to do is add content. It's much better than a wizard. Wizards have flaws and quirky behavior. Templates allow you to choose what you want and modify. In the sections to follow, we will discuss using letter tempates and customizing letter templates.

USING LETTER TEMPLATES

Nothing could be easier. You select the Office button and choose New. Then, instead of choosing a blank document, you consider the templates you have. If you have used a particular letter template in the past, it will be a part of your templates locally. If you want to search Microsoft's online list of letter templates, scroll down to the Letters option. Choose this and Microsoft will present you with a list of categories (Academic, Business, Travel, and so on).

Select a template category and then let Microsoft present you with the options you can choose from. The descriptions are quite clear. For example, one template is "Complaint about overbooked flight." It doesn't get any clearer than that. Download the template and it becomes part of your arsenal for the future.

After you have your template up and running on the screen, you will notice that there are preconfigured areas for the personal information to this letter (your name, their name, titles, addresses, and so on).

CAUTION

> As much as you might like the text in your letter template, remember to scan through it completely and make the needed changes. Nothing will be more embarrasing then sending a serious letter (for example, about an overbooked flight for which you want compensation) and forgetting to type in the correct airline's name, but leaving the placeholder name in the template. Proofread before you send.

CUSTOMIZING LETTER TEMPLATES

The easiest way to make a template that will generate documents designed to work with your needs is to start with a letter template that you download from Microsoft; then modify the template under a new name.

→ For details on how to work with Word templates, **see** "Using Word's Built-in Templates," **p. 406.**

The prebuilt letter templates that you download contain a number of "click here" placeholders. You can add your own placeholders using the same simple trick.

First, you might want to see the fields we are talking about. To do this, you need to turn on the capability to see your field codes. Go to Word Options, Advanced settings, and under Show Document Content, select the check box for Show Field Codes Instead of Their Values. Now you can see what the letter template is doing to include those special fields.

To add your own field, you can insert a preconfigured Macro button. Go to your Insert ribbon, and under the Text grouping, select Quick Parts, Fields. Then scroll down and choose MacroButton from the list. In the Display Text box, you can enter the text you want displayed (for example, Insert Your Name). From the Macro Name list, scroll down and select DoFieldClick, as shown in Figure 17.1.

Figure 17.1
Creating your own "click here" placeholders by adding in DoFieldClick fields.

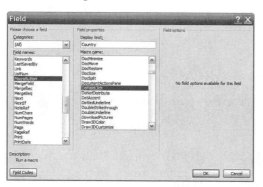

Once you've inserted your field, you can format the "click here" text. Because your prompt text appears in the document as part of a field, you can select it with a single click; because the associated macro does nothing, you can simply replace the selected text.

TIP FROM

To do the whole process manually, locate your cursor where you want the "click here" text and select Ctrl+F9. This will enter a pair of field code brackets. Type in the brackets: `MACROBUTTON DoFieldClick [Insert Your Name]`. Then select the [Insert Your Name] and apply formatting.

When navigating through your letters, you may want to jump from one field to the next. Press F11 to do this.

CREATING ENVELOPES AND LABELS

Word includes an extensive set of features that allow you to address and print a single envelope, use mail merge to generate a large number of properly addressed envelopes, or format single and multiple labels using addresses from a variety of sources.

CREATING AND PRINTING ENVELOPES

To create and print an envelope, go to your Mailings ribbon, under the Create grouping, and choose Envelopes. The dialog box shown in Figure 17.2 appears.

Figure 17.2
To pull a delivery or return address for an envelope from the Outlook Address Book, click the Insert Address icon.

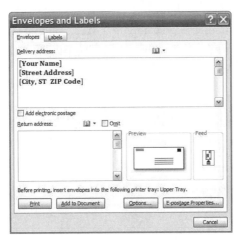

Fill in the Envelopes and Labels dialog box or select the Insert Address icon and then click Print. Insert a blank envelope in your printer's manual feed, and you should get the results you expect, if you have the correct envelope size configured.

The first time you print an envelope, make sure you click the Options button to set up the proper envelope size, fonts, paper source, and other printing options.

TIP FROM

Although Word usually does a good job of figuring out what kind of printer you're using—and thus how to orient an envelope so it prints properly—it rarely (if ever) correctly identifies an envelope paper tray. If you have an envelope tray for your printer, you'll need to click the Options button and specify that your printer includes this tray.

If you select an address before choosing Envelopes from the Mailings ribbon, that address appears in the Delivery Address box. In addition, Word is frequently smart enough to identify an address, if it appears near the beginning of the document.

When you click the Add to Document button in the Envelopes and Labels dialog box, Word creates a new section at the beginning of the document and stores the envelope in that section, numbered as Page 0. When you subsequently print the letter, both the letter itself and the envelope will print (unless you manually specify that you want to print only Page 1 and later). That can be helpful if you aren't ready to print the letter, but want to set the envelope up ahead of time. It can also be helpful in creating a template with an envelope attached to the document. Finally, you can use this technique to place a logo, a text box, or other graphic element on the envelope prior to printing.

TIP FROM

EQ & Woody

Want to automatically add graphics to an envelope? By choosing to have the envelope saved in the document, you can now go back and edit that envelope with graphics so that it prints with the graphics included.

CREATING AND PRINTING LABELS

From the same Mailings ribbon, Create grouping, you can choose Labels (or you can select the Labels tab when you have Envelopes open). Word displays the dialog box shown in Figure 17.3, which allows you to create single labels or an entire sheet of labels. Click the Options button to tell Word what kind of label position (row and column) you're using. (If you use standard labels, you can let Word set these options automatically. The dialog box includes settings for virtually all Avery labels, for example.) Fill in the label number if you want to print only one label, and then click Print.

Figure 17.3
Word's label format includes grids for all the major label (and business card) sizes.

You can also generate mailing labels for an entire list of recipients, via a mail merge, which we will discuss in the next section.

CUSTOMIZING LABELS

The major shortcoming in Word's bag of labeling tricks is its inability to let you customize what gets printed on labels. If you're running standard Avery 5260 labels, with 3 labels per row and 10 rows per sheet, there's no room on the label to print anything interesting. But if you have larger labels (or business cards), you don't have to limit yourself to a plain-vanilla name and address.

TIP FROM

Ed & Woody

> If you have an odd-sized label, Word makes it easy to add it to the list of available labels, with extensive tools to help you get the layout just right. On the Labels tab of the Envelopes and Labels dialog box, choose Options. Then on the Label Options dialog box, choose New Label. If you've got a ruler, you should have no trouble filling in the details.

For example, the Avery 8154 (and related) labels run six to the page. More than enough room is available on a label that big to include your return address, your company's logo, and just about anything you can imagine.

If you want to print larger, fancier labels, your best choice is to create a template that includes all the design elements—logo, return address, and so on—except the addressee's name and address. If you have such a template handy, you can create a new document based on the template, then copy the addressee's name and address into it, and print. If you want to get even fancier, and print just one label at a time, you can create a collection of templates, each with the design elements for just one label. Give the template a descriptive name (AV5164 lower-right label, for example), and you can generate precisely the right document for the right location.

The easiest way to make a template for a specific type of label is to use the Envelopes and Labels dialog box. In Figure 17.3 (shown previously), leave the Address box blank, choose the Full Page of the Same Label option, and click the Options button. Pick the manufacturer and product number from the Label Information section and click OK to return to the Envelopes and Labels dialog box. Finally, click New Document. Word creates a grid of labels for you, completely blank and ready for your customizing. Add your return address, logo, and other custom details, then choose File, Save As, and save it as a Document Template.

TIP FROM

Ed & Woody

> Because the labels are just a table, you can use all the table formatting tricks, including dividing the label into "sub cells" to better place graphics and text.

When you configure the picture options for your labels, set up the first label, get it perfect, and then copy the formatting to the other labels. This will make sure your pictures are right where you want for each label.

USING MAIL MERGE TO PERSONALIZE LETTERS AND ENVELOPES

Most Word users think of mail merge as a synonym for "form letters" or "junk mail." Although it's true that Word can churn out form letters and bulk mailings until the cows come home, the term *mail merge* only hints at what you can do with this capability.

At its most basic, a mail-merge operation consists of two parts—a database and a document—and the merge brings the two together. The database can contain just about anything—names and addresses are the most common contents, of course, but you can also stuff the database with product names, court case citations, serial numbers, invoices, test scores, or anything else you can fit into a database record.

The document, too, can take just about any imaginable form—the first thing you think of is likely to be a form letter, but you can also add fields from your database to an envelope, catalog, email or fax message, telephone book, web page, financial report, stock inventory, or time log. For that matter, the "document" could simply be a text file, enabling you to use a mail merge to create a new database from an old one.

Although Word doesn't have the extensive merging capabilities of a full-strength database manager such as Access, it's the best tool to choose when you need to produce a document or series of documents based on data in a reasonably clean list. On the other hand, if you need to manipulate data extensively, or your primary goal is to produce bare-bones printed reports, the tools in Access or Excel are more appropriate.

Word's mail-merge features come in handy in a variety of circumstances. When you're working with form letters going out to a mailing list, you can use mail merge to do the following:

- Sort and/or filter the incoming data, removing records according to field-level criteria you establish (for example, you could specify "Only include people in New York or New Jersey").

- Print envelopes or mailing labels with USPS Postal Numeric Encoding Technique (POSTNET) bar codes. You can even interleave the form letters with envelopes—print an envelope, then its letter, then the next envelope and its letter, and so on—using an undocumented technique discussed under the "Merge Envelopes" section later in this chapter.

- Force the merge process to pause at each record to enable you to type in custom information. Use this technique if you're producing a holiday newsletter, for example, and you want to add some unique content for each recipient.

When you move beyond basic form letters, you can use Word's mail-merge capabilities to

- Send similar, but customized, email messages or faxes to a large number of people.

- Create a product catalog, parts list, or price sheet from a list (or database) of individual products.

- Create an organization membership roster or telephone book from a list (or database) of members.

17

TIP FROM

Ed & Woody

> Most Office users tend to think of mail merge as producing one page (or form letter) per data record, but Word isn't so constrained. As long as you tell Word that you want to create a "directory," it will place data records on a page until the page gets full, and then go on to the next page. Thus, if you have a data file for your coin collection, home inventory, paid checks, office carpool, VIP donors, or best-selling books, you can use Word's mail merge to create a professional-looking, well-formatted report. Just call it a directory.

Word contains extensive support on the Mailings ribbon for running mail merges. You have the capability to manually walk through the steps needed, or you can use the Mail Merge Wizard (found by selecting the Start Mail Merge icon and choosing Step by Step Mail Merge Wizard from the options).

TIP FROM

Ed & Woody

> The first few times you run a mail merge, keep a detailed log of the steps you take—especially problems you encounter with Word or your printer. Chances are good that you'll hit similar problems when using mail-merge capabilities sometime in the future, and good notes can save you precious troubleshooting time.

Each of the major types of mail merge is a bit different—Letters, Email messages, Envelopes, Labels, and Directories.

USING THE MAIL MERGE WIZARD

By far the most common mail-merge scenario involves a form letter, a database, and a printer. You have a database of names and addresses, most likely in an Outlook Contacts list, but possibly in the form of an Access database, an Excel list, or a simple text file in tab- or comma-delimited format. And you have a form letter (or at least an idea of what you want to write). That's all you need: In Word-speak, you have a data source and a main merge document. The rest is just juggling.

The Mail Merge Wizard walks you through six steps: Create your main merge document, connect that document to a data source file, refine the items you want merged, add your mail-merge fields to your document, preview what you have created, and print.

Let's walk through these steps with the Mail Merge Wizard (we provide additional details and useful suggestions for each of these steps in the rest of this chapter). The following six descriptions match up with each of the numbered steps in the Mail Merge Wizard task pane.

1. In the wizard's first step, choose the type of document you're working on. For this example, select Letters.

2. Pick an existing document, or create a new one, to use as the merge document—the boilerplate skeleton that will drive the merge.

3. Attach a data source (shown in Figure 17.4)—the list or database to be merged—to the form letter. The wizard lets you create a new list from scratch, draw from an Outlook Contacts folder, or use an existing list.

Figure 17.4
Creating your data source is easy from scratch. You can save the file created as a Microsoft Office Address List (*.mdb) file.

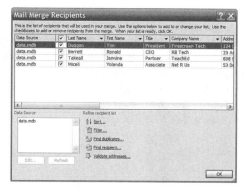

4. Use the Mail Merge Wizard to place merge fields in the form letter. They'll appear something like this: <<Address Block>>, or <<First Name>> <<Last Name>> (see Figure 17.5).

Figure 17.5
Mail-merge placement fields are inserted, but don't try to type them in manually.

NOTE

You can't just type the << and >> marks: Word has to insert them for you, via buttons in the Mail Merge Wizard.

5. Use the wizard to preview how the first few merged letters will appear. If you want to exclude certain records from the merge or sort them so that the letters print in a particular sequence (ZIP Code order, for example), use the Mail Merge Wizard's Edit Recipient List option to set them up.

6. On the Mail Merge Wizard's final pane, click the Edit Individual Letters option so Word will merge the form letters to a new file, and then save the new merged file. Before you print the file, go through it and make sure it doesn't contain any surprises. When you're satisfied that everything is correct, start printing.

TIP FROM

Ed & Woody

Long merge print jobs can pose all sorts of mechanical challenges, from toner cartridges running down to buffer overflows to massive paper jams. If the merged file contains more than a few hundred pages, consider printing a hundred or two at a time.

For important mailings, keep the merged file handy until the mailing has been delivered to the post office—or better yet, until you're certain that most addressees have received their copies.

CREATING THE FORM LETTER

When creating a main merge document, all Word's tools are at your disposal. You can adjust formatting, insert pictures, create headers and footers, add tables and fields, and work with objects in the drawing layer. For example, you might choose to insert your company's logo in the letter.

When you're satisfied with the content of your form letter, you can start the wizard or manually step through the process.

CONNECTING TO A DATA SOURCE

After you have the static part of the form letter complete, you have to tell Word where to pick up the data that will be merged. In fact, at this point, Word just needs the data field names—last name, first name, address, and so on—but the Mail Merge Wizard takes advantage of the moment to have you select the data source. If you want to do the process manually, on the Mailings ribbon you select Select Recipients from the Start Mail Merge grouping. Then find the data source to pull recipients from.

You can pull your recipients from any number of locations. For example, you may want to use your Contact list in Outlook. To use your Contact list for recipients you go to the Mailings ribbon, Start Mail Merge grouping, Select Recipients drop-down button and choose Select from Outlook Contacts. In the event you wish to use your Outlook Express address book, you need to go about this in another way. You cannot connect directly; you should export your address book to a .csv text file and then choose this when you are requested for a recipient data source. To use the .csv file that you have exported (or any other .csv file for that matter), you can select the Use an existing list option and browse to the .csv file. If you are asked which character separates your data, you should choose Comma.

NOTE

If you are working with Vista's new integrated Address Book, you can export your contacts to a .csv file and import as your data source as well.

Along with Outlook Contacts and Outlook Express address books, you can use Excel worksheets (.xls, .xlsx, .xlsm, .xlsb) as a data source. You can also use Access 2007 databases (.accdb, .accde) as well as previous Access versions (.mdb, .mde).

There are a number of other options for you to choose from including simple recipient documents (like an html file with a single table, or a Word document with a single table) and more complicated options (for example, files from single-tier, file-based database programs, Schedule+ 7.0 Contact Lists, and so forth). The options are endless because, in the end, if you cannot work with the database you have, you can usually export to .csv and work with the data in this format.

TIP FROM

EQ & Woody

It's an often-overlooked point, but the biggest problem you're likely to encounter at this juncture is the lack of a specific data field, or a poorly defined field. For example, if your form letter demands an Amount Due in each letter, you'd better have a data file handy that includes an Amount Due for each customer.

The Mail Merge Wizard gives you three choices:

- **Use an Existing List**—If you have an existing data source, whether it's a table in a Word document, a list in an Excel workbook, or an Access database, use this option. If the first row of the Word table or Excel list includes field names (Last Name, First Name, and so on), you'll be able to merge immediately. Click Browse and retrieve the list.

- **Select from Outlook Contacts**—Make this choice and Word imports the data directly from Outlook. Click Choose Contacts Folder and pick the Contacts list that you want to use.

- **Type a New List**—Select this option and click Create to bring up a useful Data Form (see Figure 17.4) that allows you to create your own merge database and add names and addresses on-the-fly. If you want to modify the field names and their order, click the Customize button.

NOTE

What about multiple data sources? What if I want to mail merge a document with two different data source information? These are excellent questions that currently cannot be resolved in Word 2007. When you choose your data source, although it looks as though you should be able to add more choices, you simply cannot. The solution is to do one of the following: pick up a mail-merge solution on the Internet that allows you to choose multiple data sources, combine both data sources into one document, or perform multiple mail merges.

PLACING DATA FIELDS WITHIN A DOCUMENT

Now that Word knows what data you're going to use, it can help you put merge data into your document. Data fields represent the link between your form letter and the data source. For example, if you have a data source field called Last Name, Word replaces every occurrence of the field <<Last Name>> in the form letter with the Last Name data in the current record of the data source.

There are two easy ways to insert data fields into your form letter. One is via step 4 of the Mail Merge Wizard. The other is by using the Insert Merge Field from the Write and Insert Fields from the Mailings ribbon. Place the insertion point wherever you want a data field to appear, click Insert Merge Field, and choose the field you need. Instead of entering every single element of the name and address, click the Address Block link to display the dialog box shown in Figure 17.6. This dialog box inserts an especially helpful merge field called Address Block, which does a graceful job of importing Outlook Contacts data into Word.

Figure 17.6
This dialog box adds the Address Block field to your merge document.

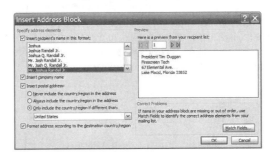

Click the Greeting Line link to add an opening to your letter. In the wizard, you click the More Items link to insert other fields throughout the letter. Remember that you have to provide the punctuation if it isn't included in the data source. A typical letter opening might look like this:

<<AddressBlock>>

Dear <<Title>> <<LastName>>:

TIP FROM

You can put the same data field in the form letter as often as you like. If you're preparing a promotional letter to customers in a specific region, for example, you might include the <<City>> field in the text of the letter: "All our customers who live in <<City>> are entitled to an extra discount this month only."

PREVIEWING MAIL-MERGE RESULTS

To see how the merge will progress, start by having Word show you what the result will be when you merge live data with your form letter. To do so, go on to step 5 of the Mail Merge Wizard and click the Next Record button repeatedly to see how the records appear (see Figure 17.7). Or you could use the Preview Results grouping to do the same thing.

Use this preview to check for gross errors:

- **Look for incorrect fields**—For example, those using <<First>> where you really wanted <<Last>>.

- **Identify unreliable data source information**—If half of your data source records don't have an entry in the <<Title>> field, for example, you need to find a way to work around the problem.

- **Find any parts of the merge that don't look right**—If some of the merged letters flop over to two pages, for example, click Edit Recipient List and try to tweak the data so that it fits.

Figure 17.7
Word lets you preview your form letter with live data, stepping through each data source record. The text box shows you which fields are being used.

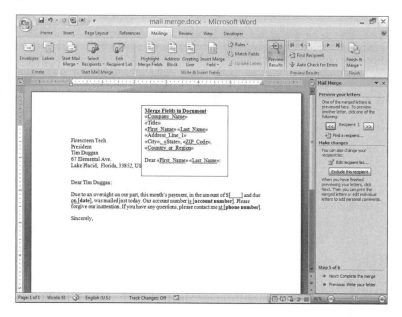

When all looks well, go on to step 6 in the wizard, and click Edit Individual Letters. Before you print the resulting document, which has all the merged letters head-to-toe, examine it closely for any unexpected and unwelcome merge results.

TIP FROM

> In general, you should avoid merging directly to the printer. Creating a merge file first lets you easily recover from mechanical disasters—you can reprint letters 1378 to 1392, for example, if the printer runs out of toner or the person carrying the envelopes to the post office drops them in the mud.

One of the tools you won't find in the wizard but that does exist on the ribbon is the Auto Check for Errors option under Preview Results; this brings up the Checking and Reporting Errors dialog box. Again, the goal here is to make sure your merged document is what you want before you send it out to all your clients, co-workers, family, and so on.

There are three options to choose from:

- **Simulate the merge and report errors in a new document**—This tests the document but doesn't make any changes to your working document. It will only report errors.

- **Complete the merge and report each error as it occurs**—This may be the best way to make sure you address each and every error before printing out your document. This option is the default for the tool.

■ **Complete the merge without pausing**—Report errors in a new document. It's not your best option because it performs the merge and gives you errors separately, leaving room for user error.

ADVANCED MAIL-MERGE TECHNIQUES

There are plenty of other things you can do with the mail-merge feature, such as sending a mass email to using mail merges for your labels. Let's go over some of the finer details of mail merging.

MASS EMAILING WITH OUTLOOK AND MAIL MERGE

If you use Outlook, creating personalized mass emailings is almost as simple as creating and merging a form letter. Here's how:

1. For mass email, choose E-mail Messages in the first step of the Mail Merge Wizard. Complete the email message or fax as if it were a form letter, using the instructions in the preceding section.

2. Attach a recipient list and preview the messages with live data in step 5 of the wizard.

3. In the final step of the Mail Merge Wizard, choose Merge to E-Mail. In the Merge to E-mail dialog box (see Figure 17.8), choose which Outlook Contact field you want to merge to. Most often, you'll choose E-mail_Address. Type a subject if you like, and click OK.

Figure 17.8
Configuring your email's last subject line before sending.

4. Word performs the merge and transfers the merged email messages or faxes to your Outlook outbox.

The next time you use Outlook to send mail, the email messages or faxes will be sent in the usual way.

TIP FROM

High-volume unsolicited email—better known as spam—is almost universally detested, even when it's personalized. Sending unsolicited email might violate local and federal laws. If you're going to use Word to automate mass emailings, make absolutely certain that your recipients have given their approval first.

CREATING DIRECTORIES

The only real difference between the way Word handles form letters and the way it handles merged "directories" (in previous versions of Word, they were called "catalogs") lies in the way Word uses page breaks. In a form letter, Word inserts a page break (actually, a "next page" section break) after it finishes processing a record from the data source. In a directory, Word doesn't add page breaks; as a result, one record follows another in the finished document.

Suppose you want to print a custom report of all the people in your Outlook Contacts list, in which several records appear on a page—perhaps in your own version of a Day-Timer-like format. Here's how you do it:

1. Start a new document as described in the preceding sections, but in the first step of the Mail Merge Wizard, choose Directory. That tells Word you want to put more than one record on a page.

2. Add the fields by using step 4 of the Mail Merge Wizard, as before

3. Adjust the document any way you see fit. In the case of Day-Timer-like reports, you might want to create multiple columns, change the page size, and/or set the paper source to print on special drilled sheets.

TIP FROM

EQ & Woody

> To control page breaks in directory-style merges such as this one, use the paragraph formatting property Keep with Next. In this case, you might put an empty paragraph mark at the end of all the data lines. Then select the data lines (*not* the final paragraph mark). On the Home ribbon, go into the Paragraph dialog box, click the Line and Page Breaks tab, and then select the Keep with Next check box to ensure that records don't break across pages.

4. Have Word merge to a new document. You'll probably want to print in duplex style— that is, using both sides of each sheet of paper. First you'll need to find out if your printer supports duplexing (manual or automatic) and then follow the instructions for your printer to enable duplexing for the merged document that you want to print. To find out if the printer you have supports duplex printing, you can check the manual, check with the manufacturer, or go into the Properties of the Print dialog to see what options are included.

MERGE ENVELOPES

Running a merge to generate envelopes that match one-for-one with a form letter run isn't difficult, as long as you ensure that the data source doesn't change between the time you run the form letters and the time you print the envelopes, and that the filters you specify are identical.

Beware of paper jams, because one missing or one extra letter or envelope can throw off the entire sequence. If a jam should occur, mark that point in the run—with a paper clip or a sticky note, for example. After you've finished running both letters and envelopes, go back to the marked points and ensure you have one—and only one—letter for each envelope.

To start an envelope run, use the Mail Merge Wizard and select Envelopes as the document type in the first step.

You can take advantage of an alternative (and undocumented) method for generating envelopes at the same time you do the main form letter run. This method creates envelopes interleaved with the form letters—you get an envelope and its letter, the next record's envelope and its letter, and so on. As long as you have a printer with separate feeders for the form letter paper and the envelopes—most laser printers pull envelopes from a different location than the standard paper trays—the technique works, and it could save you a great deal of frustration with mismatched envelopes and form letters. Here's how to do it:

1. Create your form letter, following the instructions in the preceding sections.

2. At the end of the Mail Merge Wizard's step 2 (before you click Next to move on to the Select Recipients step), on the Mailings ribbon, select Envelopes. On the Envelopes tab, set up the return address the way you want it. Then click Options and make sure the correct paper tray has been set up for your envelopes. *Do not click Print.* Instead, click Add to Document. The envelope appears above your form letter on the Word screen.

3. Attach the data source and place fields in your form letter as usual. When you're finished with the letter, move up to the envelope and insert merge fields in the envelope, wherever you want them to appear (see Figure 17.9).

Figure 17.9
Merge data fields go into the envelope, just as they would in the form letter itself.

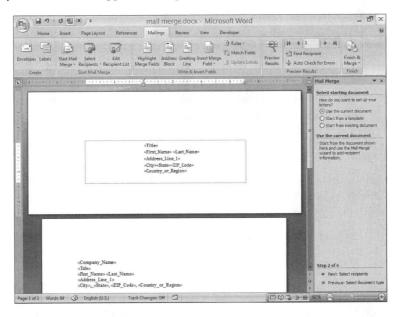

4. Merge to a file, as usual. When you print the file, envelopes appear before form letters, interspersed throughout the merge run.

ADDING E-STAMPS TO ENVELOPES

Word has automatic hooks to several major vendors of electronic postage. If you sign up with one of these vendors (for example, stamps.com), you can automatically generate electronic "stamps" for mail in general, and merged envelopes in particular. The electronic postage business is changing quickly, with companies altering their fees and payment structures almost as quickly as they can change their websites.

The simplest way to get the latest information about electronic postage firms that work with Word is to click the Electronic Postage option in step 4 of the Mail Merge Wizard. You will be transported to the Microsoft Office Online page, which includes full details.

MERGE LABELS

Word's features for creating mailing labels work well enough for small labels—that is, labels that are specifically designed to comfortably accommodate a name and address. But if you're using preprinted labels, or if you have larger labels and want to print your return address or logo on them, or if you want to change the default font, you'll probably run into a few common problems (unless you know these tricks, of course).

To run a mail merge and generate labels the usual way:

1. Start the Mail Merge Wizard by choosing the Mailings tab and clicking Start Mail Merge; then click the Step by Step Mail Merge Wizard and select Labels as the document type.

2. In the first step of the wizard, select the Labels option and click OK.

3. In the wizard's next step, click Label Options in the Change Document Layout section. Supply the details for your mailing labels in the Label Options dialog box. In most cases, you can select a manufacturer and product number; most common label products, including those from Avery, the 800-pound gorilla of the industry, are among the built-in formats listed here (see Figure 17.10).

4. Follow Word's prompts to select a recipient list. Place the data merge fields in the first label position.

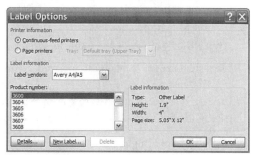

Figure 17.10

NOTE

> Word automatically causes text in the label to "float up and down"—to be centered vertically. If you want the printing on your labels to always appear at the same location, go into your Table Properties, click the Cell tab, and choose Top or Bottom.

5. When you're happy with the first label, click the Update All Labels button at the bottom of the Mail Merge task pane. Finish the merge by using the techniques described earlier in this chapter. Preview the merge, then merge to file and print.

TIP FROM

Ed & Woody

> Because the label form is just a table, you can divide the existing cells to better position text, graphics, a return address, or anything else on the label.

CUSTOMIZING FORM LETTERS WITH FIELDS

As with so many other advanced Word features, merging data and documents occurs through the magic of Word fields. The various merge fields discussed in this chapter are just special types of Word fields—which, in turn, are a small subset of the fields available in Word. The Mail Merge Wizard simply puts a pretty face on the underlying fields: You get to use the merge fields without getting your hands dirty working with field codes, formatting switches, and the like. The fields themselves control all the nuances of merging. You can use any of Word's extensive collection of fields in mail-merge documents.

Mail merge works by using Word fields specially designed for implementing a merge. To see those fields, open a main merge document and press Alt+F9, or choose the Office Button, Word Options, under the Advanced settings under "Show Field Codes Instead of Their Value check box.

In many cases, you'll be able to get satisfactory results with a merge by using the Mailings ribbon to manipulate these fields. In some more advanced cases, however, you might find yourself operating on the fields directly.

Two fields come in handy if you want Word to pause the merge at each record and let you type in custom data. Both {Ask} and {Fillin} request data for each merged record. The former places whatever you typed in a bookmarked location on the form letter; the latter replaces the field with the text you fill in, at the point in the document where you place the field.

A {Fillin} field might be useful in a form letter when you want the option to add a personalized paragraph at the end of every letter. As each merged letter pops up, you can enter your own customized text or just click OK to use the default text. Here's how:

1. Place the insertion point wherever you want the custom text to appear in the form letter.
2. Go to the Insert ribbon, select Quick Parts, and choose Field. Then from the Field Name box, select Fill-in (see Figure 17.11). Type in a suitable prompt and default text.

Figure 17.11
The Field dialog box will be explained in greater detail later on in the chapter, but for now it's good to see how it works with your mail merge.

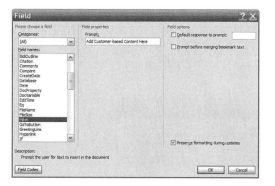

NOTE

Although the input box in the Field dialog box is small, you can type in lengthy default responses, providing they don't include carriage returns.

3. Perform the merge as usual. Each time Word encounters a {Fillin} field, once for each data source record, it prompts you for whatever custom text you want to provide. (You do not want to use this trick with databases that include more than a few dozen records!)

USING RULES AND MATCH FIELDS TOOLS

We've covered just about every kind of tool and scenario there is with a mail merge, so it would be foolish to exclude two of the finer detailed tools that Microsoft provides—Rules and Match Fields.

In actuality, the Rules option allows you to add more fields to your documents (such as the Fill-in field we just discussed). In fact, you can select Rules and then choose Fill-in and you get a nice, clean dialog box to type into (we just thought you would want to see how to do it the old-fashioned, hands-on way).

Several other options present themselves, and one of the most interesting is the If…Then…Else rule, shown in Figure 17.12. The IF field will compare two values and then, depending on what it determines, will enter one set of text or another.

Figure 17.12
Using If…Then…Either in your mail-merge documents.

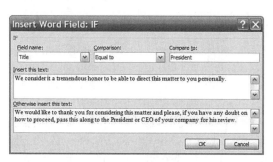

Sometimes you might have a data source that doesn't exactly match up to the thinking of the merge document fields. For example, suppose you have a table that has a heading like Position and you want that to map to the Title field. To do this, you select the Match Fields icon, located on the Write and Insert Fields grouping on the Mailings ribbon, as shown in Figure 17.13.

Figure 17.13
Matching fields with data source headings is a lot more fun than changing all your headings.

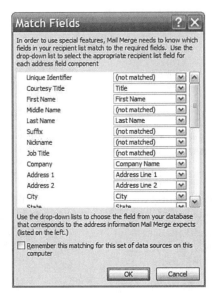

USING FIELDS TO ADD INTELLIGENCE TO A DOCUMENT

Behind many of Word's most powerful features sits a peculiar document element called a *field*. Word fields are placeholders whose contents change dynamically; they typically work in the background, invisibly, displaying the correct data onscreen and in print, based on information within the current document, in other documents, or from external sources. For example, if you put a {Date} field in your document, Word displays the current date in that location each time you open the document.

Word supports more than 70 types of fields. Use them when you want to accomplish tasks such as the following:

- Show the current day in a document ({date}, {time}), or the time the document was last printed ({printdate}).

- Construct a paragraph numbering scheme ({seq}, {AutoNum}, {AutoNumLgl}) more complex than those available in the dialog box that appears when you choose Format, Bullets and Numbering. A similar technique ({ref}, {styleref}) allows you to set up "Figure x-y" figure numbering captions that incorporate the chapter number.

- Set up a "hot" button ({macrobutton}) or picture that runs a macro when clicked.

- Refer to the contents of bookmarked text. For example, you can place a bookmark on a chapter title and refer to that title throughout your document by using the {Ref} field. If the title changes, all the references change, too.

- Refer to the first or last occurrence of a particular style on a page. Use this type of field ({styleref}) in the header for a phone book, for example, listing the first and last entries ("Able, George to Alphonso, Chris") on each page.

- Insert information about a document into the document itself ({info})—total number of pages, filename, author, file size, number of words, date when the document was last saved, and so on.

- Perform calculations, comparisons, and even elementary arithmetic. For example, the {Page} field produces the number of the current page, whereas a {{Page}+1} field results in the number of the next page.

There's even a {barcode} field that converts a postal ZIP Code to a USPS bar code!

Fields also drive such key built-in Word capabilities as tables of contents, figures, tables, equations, indexes, and mail merges. Although Word uses layers of wizards and dialog boxes to shield you from the field codes used to implement those features, sometimes the only way to tweak the feature—to limit a table of contents to a part of the document covered by a specific bookmark, for example—is by working with the field code itself.

NOTE

Fields are an enormous topic. In this book, you'll learn some of the more useful fields—ones that will increase your productivity–today. If you need a detailed fields reference, see *Special Edition Using Microsoft Word 2007* (published by Que) by Faithe Wempen, ISBN 078973608X.

CAUTION

Many fields do not translate well into HTML-formatted files. If you need to use a field on a web page, make sure you test it with all the commonly used browsers to ensure that it works properly.

SHOWING AND HIDING FIELD CODES

Novice Word users may not even know field codes exist and even advanced Word users shy away from the mystery of field codes. This is a shame because, when used creatively, field codes can enhance your documentation in many ways. Fields in Word are placeholders for data. Usually you use fields when you have data that changes often, or for form letters and labels in mail merges. In Word 2007, you don't have to insert these fields manually very often because there are simpler methods, but there are times when you do need to insert them manually, or work with the ones that have already been inserted.

Word allows you to toggle between seeing the field codes themselves and field code results—for example, between seeing:

```
{Date \@ "d-MMM-yyyy"}
```

and

1-JAN-2003

We've discussed how to do this before, but we'll review it one more time. To show field codes, go to your Office button, Word Options, select Advanced, and then select the Show Field Codes Instead of Their Value check box. To return to showing field code results, clear that same Field Codes box.

TIP FROM

Ed & Woody

If you're going to do much serious work with field codes, you might want to add the View Field Codes command as a button on your Quick Access toolbar, or memorize the View Field Codes keyboard shortcut, Alt+F9. Either one toggles between showing field codes and showing their results.

FIELD CODE SYNTAX

Field codes generally have three components: the field name, the properties, and the switches (which are optional; some fields don't have switches associated with them).

Field codes can take on many forms, but generally they look like this, with the field name and required or optional parameters enclosed in curly braces:

```
{Author \* mergeformat}
```

In this case, the field {Author} has one parameter, called a *formatting switch*. The formatting switch, if present, controls the way the field result is formatted inside the document. Switches are discussed extensively in the "Formatting Field Results," section later in this chapter.

NOTE

In this book, you'll always see field codes as they appear onscreen, surrounded by curly braces—something like this:

```
{Seq Figures \* mergeformat}
```

Field codes are not case sensitive, so you may see them in all capitals rather than upper-case and lowercase, as we depict them here. Functionally, there's no difference. And of course, you can't type curly braces into a document and get a field code. There are only three ways to insert field marks (braces): Choose the Insert ribbon, select Quick Parts, Field, and the Field dialog box will open. You also can use one of the built-in Word functions that produces a field code, or press Ctrl+F9 and type (but you have to really know your fields to do that).

INSERTING A FIELD INTO A DOCUMENT

In Word 2007, you very rarely need to insert a field, because preconfigured tools will insert them for you. The only time you might need to work with fields is if you are working on documents that were created by earlier versions of Word.

By far, the easiest way to put a field into a document is to use one of the built-in Word features to do the dirty work for you. For example, if you go to the Insert ribbon, choose Date and Time from the Text grouping, and then check the Update Automatically box, Word inserts a {Date} field into your document, adding a formatting switch for the date format you choose (see Figure 17.14).

Figure 17.14
Selecting the Update Automatically check box here causes Word to insert a {Date} field, instead of the date itself.

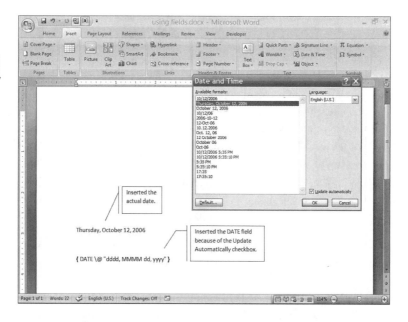

17

Similarly, putting a page number in a header or footer by using the Insert Page Number button on the Header and Footer grouping will insert a {Page} field, as will inserting a Table of Contents or Index, creating a Caption or Cross-reference, or inserting merge fields using the Mail Merge Wizard.

If you want to build a field from scratch, you can do it the hard way, by pressing Ctrl+F9 to create the field marks and then manually typing the field name and any optional or required parameters. If you make even the tiniest mistake, of course, the field won't work as you expect. To be absolutely certain you get the syntax right, go to the Insert ribbon, select the Quick Parts icon, and choose Field instead. This Field dialog box (see Figure 17.15) offers context-sensitive help and immediate access to the most common field switches (the terms "properties" and "options" are somewhat arbitrary; don't get hung up on the terminology). If you want to work with the raw field code (or you just want to explore and preview the field's syntax), click the Field Codes button in the lower-left corner.

Figure 17.15
Word provides good support for fields via the Field dialog box.

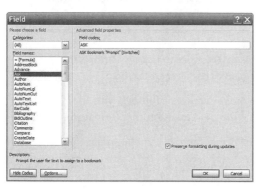

If you consistently have trouble finding field codes you insert within a document, see "Hiding and Revealing Field Codes" in the "Troubleshooting" section at the end of this chapter.

FORMATTING FIELD RESULTS

Depending on the purpose of your fields, you may want the field results to blend right into your document (such as when you insert a Date and Time field into a letter; you want that information to look like it's a normal part of the letter). Other times, you may want the information to stand out in some way to highlight the contents of the field, or even to have the background shaded so others know it's a field. Let's consider some of your options.

First off, with shading the background of fields, you can change these settings by going to your Word Options, Advanced settings, and under the Show Document Content section in Field shading, you can choose the following options:

- **Never**—Allows your field values to appear normal to everyone else, even if another person opens the document and selects that information. If you toggle back and forth to see your field codes, they will still appear, but to the average eye, they will look normal.

- **Always**—Allow all your field values to be easily identified by others viewing the document by putting a gray shading in the background. They will stand out clearly.

- **When Selected**—With this option, the field value will actually look like normal text in the document, the same as all the other text. However, when you select that text, it will have a gray shading applied to the background to alert you to the fact that it is a field.

Changing the look of the field value used to be quite complicated, requiring all sort of switches and such (and you still can use switches), but the easy way to alter the character formatting for fields is to use the standard formatting tools that come with Word, which you can find on the Home ribbon.

NOTE

> One thing you might notice when you use the Field dialog box to insert field codes is the * MERGEFORMAT switch that is automatically included. The reason for this is that your formatting, by default, is lost when you update your fields. By adding this switch (which you can add manually if you are using manually added fields), your formatting will be retained. If you don't use this switch, and then update your field, say goodbye to the formatting.

Unless you add a switch inside the field to change formatting, the field result takes on the formatting of the first nonblank character of the field.

For example, if you have a field that says {*A*uthor}, with the "A" in Times New Roman, 10-point italic, the result of the field takes on that formatting: *Douglas Adams*.

Word has three field switches that control the appearance and formatting of field code results.

GENERAL \ * FORMAT SWITCHES

The most common field switch is the general formatting switch:

```
\* MERGEFORMAT
```

This switch tells Word to ignore the formatting of the first character of the field and instead to use whatever formatting you apply to the field itself.

For example, suppose you're typing along in 12-point Garamond, and you insert a {NumWords} field (which shows the number of words in the document), using the Field dialog box. If you check the Preserve Formatting During Updates box, Word inserts a * mergeformat switch:

```
{NUMWORDS \* MERGEFORMAT}
```

With that switch in place, every time you update the field, it takes on the original formatting— Garamond 12 point—unless you apply some different formatting directly on the field result.

By using formatting switches, you can exercise an enormous amount of control and flexibility over how a field appears in your document. For example,

```
\* dollartext
```

converts a number—for example, 123.45—into the kind of text you put on a check—one hundred twenty-three and 45/100.

```
\* caps
```

capitalizes the initial letters of each word in the field result. Combine the two formatting switches with the = field, which evaluates numeric expressions, to get the field:

```
{ = 123.45 \* dollartext \* caps }
```

which appears in your document as:

```
One Hundred Twenty-Three And 45/100
```

The most useful formatting switches are detailed in Table 17.1.

TABLE 17.1   * FORMATTING SWITCHES

Switch	Action
* mergeformat	Retains the current formatting of the field result whenever it's updated.
* charformat	Uses the formatting applied to the first nonblank character of the field code.
* caps	Capitalizes the first letter of each word.
* firstcap	Capitalizes the first letter of the first word only.
* lower	Makes all letters lowercase.
* upper	Makes all letters uppercase.
* cardtext	Converts a number to text: *12* becomes *twelve.*
* ordtext	Converts a number to the ordinal text: *12* becomes *twelfth.*

continues

17

TABLE 17.1 CONTINUED	
Switch	**Action**
* Roman	Displays a number in capitalized Roman numerals: *12* becomes *XII*.
* dollartext	Spells out the whole part of the number, then rounds the fraction and appends "and xx/100": *123.456* becomes *one hundred twenty-three and 46/100*.

TROUBLESHOOTING

KEEPING TRACK OF LONG MERGES

When running a long mail merge, I need to make sure that letters were printed for everyone on my Contacts list.

As you'll soon discover, long merges are a horse of a different color. You'll find it very useful to put a record number on each merged item so, for example, you can look and see if the printer swallowed form letter number 2,481. To place a merge record number on a document, bring up the Mail Merge tools from the Mailings ribbon. Click wherever you want the record number to appear in the document, choose Rules from the Write and Insert grouping, and select Merge Record # from the list. See the following section for a suggestion on how to format merge record numbers.

MAKING SURE YOUR FIELDS LINE UP

My merged documents don't look right—the fields don't line up properly, or suddenly a line that should hold a person's name is showing a ZIP Code.

If your merge data file gets out of whack by one single entry, it can throw off an entire merge. The easiest way to do a quick check for data integrity is to run the Auto Check for Errors tool, found on your Preview Results grouping on the Mailings ribbon. Generally, if you ask Word to pause to report each error as it occurs, you'll find the problem in no time.

Check for Errors won't find fields that are improperly aligned. That still needs to be done by meticulously looking at every merged document.

HIDING AND REVEALING FIELD CODES

My document is filled with field codes, but I sometimes have a hard time locating them. On more than one occasion, I've accidentally wiped out a crucial field code while editing some other text, because I didn't know the code was there.

Normally, field codes are hidden onscreen, and their locations are invisible except for a gray shading that appears when you select the code's location. You can show all field codes in a document by pressing Ctrl+A and then pressing Alt+F9. To make the location of field codes visible at all times without showing the codes themselves, go into your Word Options, Advanced settings, and change the Field Shading option from its default When Selected to Always. Note that this shading will appear in printed copies of pages that contain fields; you'll probably want to turn off field shading before sending a document to the printer.

TIME AND DATE DISCREPANCIES

I entered a {Time} field in my document, but when I update it, the field displays a date.

To solve the problem, remove the \l switches in your {date} and {time} fields. If you don't understand how the \l switch works, bizarre consequences like this are nearly inevitable. If you use the Date and Time dialog box to insert a time in a document, all the {Time \l} fields will, when updated, show a time. If you then use the same dialog box to insert a date in your document, all the {Date \l} fields, when updated, will show a date.

FIELD UPDATE DILEMMAS

When I close out of my documents and then reopen them, certain items are automatically changed. How can I stop this?

The default arrangements for documents with fields are for them to update the moment you open the document. So, for example, when you have a letter with a current date field, it will change the date each time you open the document. Another way to force your fields to update is to hit Ctrl+A and then hit F9.

But to stop fields from updating, you can actually lock a field. To lock a field, select the field and then press Ctrl+F11. To unlock it, press Ctrl+Shift+F11.

SECRETS OF THE OFFICE MASTERS: CREATING A FILL-IN-THE-BLANKS FORM WITH FIELDS

There are so many different kinds of forms that people need to fill out these days. And somebody had to sit down and create them at some point or another. There are forms you fill out with a pen, forms you fill out online, and forms you can fill out in Word documents. Where do you get started if you wanted to make a form that has fields? Let the masters talk you through it.

To start with, the easiest way to start any form is to see if someone else has already done the work for you. Consider looking in online templates from Microsoft. There is a Forms option for the templates, which offers quite a large selection of forms to choose from.

To create one of the more complex data-entry forms that is designed to be filled out online by Word users, follow these steps:

1. To create a new template, choose the Office button, New; select My Templates, choose the Normal.dotm template, and then select Template from the Create New section.

2. Put together the form's static elements—the parts that won't change each time the form is used. This might include a logo, a return address, tables, questions, and descriptions.

3. You want to work with the Developer ribbon now, but you might notice that you don't have one. This requires a little change in your Word Options. Go into your Word Options, the first set of settings under Popular, and select the box that reads Show Developer Tab in the Ribbon.

4. You'll notice that there is a Controls grouping with a couple of options to choose from. Note that if you are working in Compatibility Mode, you will only be able to choose the Legacy Tools.

5. The original template that is shown in Figure 17.16 was just a simple table. But, as you can see, we have used the Controls grouping to add checkboxes and the Date Picker control. It's very simple to do. You select the option you want off the Controls grouping and then place that control in the document where you need it.

Figure 17.16
The new Control tools in Word 2007; one of the coolest is the Date Picker.

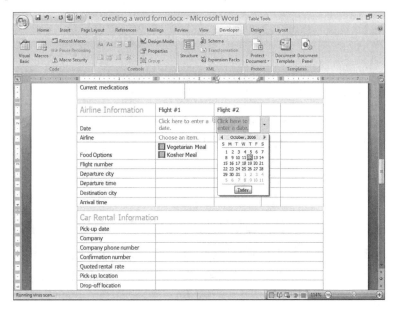

6. When you're done, you should lock the form. That will keep users from altering any static information in the form. They'll be limited to making changes in the form fields you have specified.

If you then save the template in some readily accessible location, users can create a new document based on the template, fill out the template, print it, and save it, much as they would any other document.

TIP FROM

Locking the form you've created isn't difficult. First, make sure you aren't in Design Mode (see whether the Design Mode button is highlighted in the Controls grouping. If it is, turn it off). Then go to your Protect grouping and select Protect Document. Select Restrict Formatting and Editing. Under the Editing restrictions, choose the Allow Only This Type of Editing check box and select Filling in Forms from the list that you are presented with. Then start enforcement. You can also assign a password so that others cannot change your protection. But keep in mind that if you need to change it later, you will need to turn protection off (and remember the password if you set one).

PART IV

USING EXCEL

18 Building a Better Workbook   507

19 Advanced Worksheet Formatting   553

20 Using Formulas and Functions   593

21 Organizing Data with Tables and PivotTables   627

22 Creating and Editing Charts   665

CHAPTER **18**

BUILDING A BETTER WORKBOOK

In this chapter

What's New in Excel 2007   508

Working with Worksheets and Workbooks   508

Controlling Data Entry with AutoComplete Options   518

Automatically Filling In a Series of Data   519

Finding, Replacing, and Transforming Data   523

Customizing the Worksheet Window   528

Using Links to Automatically Update or Consolidate Worksheet Data   531

Restricting and Validating Data Entry for a Cell or Range   532

Printing Worksheets   537

Publishing a Worksheet to the Web   543

Customizing Excel   545

Troubleshooting   550

Secrets of the Office Masters: Installing and Managing Excel Add-Ins   551

WHAT'S NEW IN EXCEL 2007

 If you've mastered the ins and outs of previous Excel versions, you'll be able to get straight to work with Excel 2007. The tasks you're most likely to perform with Excel—building workbooks, working with formulas, analyzing data, and creating charts—are essentially unchanged. In this chapter, you'll see how Microsoft changed Excel to let you get your work done faster and more accurately. As you might suspect by now, the way you perform those actions are quite different given Excel 2007's reliance on the new ribbon as opposed to the traditional menu and toolbar interface. The new ribbon requires wholesale changes in the way you use Excel.

If you're a newcomer, Excel 2007's new ribbon should provide an easier interface than the older versions and bring you up to speed more quickly than the old interface. If you're an Excel pro, you will have to get used to the new interface—and at first you may not like what you find—but the ribbon quickly grows on you. You'll find that the ribbon provides commands you need when you need them and keeps other, unneeded commands and buttons out of your way.

Many of Excel's other improvements are internal, such as the ability to handle massive spreadsheets up to 1 million rows long with up to 16,000 columns wide. Along with a larger spreadsheet work area, Microsoft worked hard to decrease the amount of disk space spreadsheets now consume with the new, compressed XML file format. Advanced charting and table features mean that you can present your data more effectively than ever before.

One of the best improvements in Excel 2007 isn't obvious just by looking at the screen. This improvement is obvious when you look at your watch! Excel 2007 takes advantage of dual processors and multithreaded chips, so if you have the latest and greatest hardware, Excel works overtime to deliver results fast.

WORKING WITH WORKSHEETS AND WORKBOOKS

The basic building blocks of Excel have remained unchanged for nearly a decade. Excel's default file format is still the *workbook* (file extension .xls), which can hold multiple *worksheets*. Excel now saves the file with the file extension .xlsx for the new compressed XML format, but you can also save your work in the previous Excel 97-2003 Workbook format, too (file extension .xls).

By default, each new Excel workbook starts out with three blank worksheets; an index tab at the bottom of each worksheet identifies the sheet by name. You can add a new worksheet, delete an existing worksheet, and rename or rearrange worksheets to suit your needs. A fourth tab is the Insert Worksheet tab; click the tab to create a new worksheet instantly, and a fifth Insert Worksheet tab appears in case you want to keep adding worksheets to the current workbook.

Multiple worksheets help keep complex projects organized within a single workbook. In a consolidated budget, for example, you might create a separate worksheet for each department's numbers, using identical templates to make sure each budget category appears in the same row and each month is in the same column. Then use an identical template to create a summary worksheet that rolls up totals for the entire company. Placing related data tables on different sheets makes it easier to view, format, and print each type of data separately—for example, a banker might create a loan analysis form on one worksheet, and then generate an amortization table on a separate sheet. When you create new charts or *PivotTable* reports from a table (in Excel 2007, lists are now called *tables*), it's often convenient to give each of these elements its own sheet. That way, you can rearrange the data in the underlying table without having to worry about whether deleting a row or column will mess up the design of a PivotTable report.

TIP FROM

In workbooks with a large number of worksheets, you won't be able to see all the sheet names without using the four arrow buttons to the left of the sheet names to scroll. Unless, of course, you know this secret: right-click any of those arrow buttons to display a pop-up list containing the names of all the worksheets in the current workbook. Click any name to jump straight to that worksheet.

WORKING WITH MULTIPLE WORKSHEETS

Working with multiple sheets simultaneously is how power users quickly create and format a complex workbook with a minimum of wasted effort. Use the following techniques to make working with multiple sheets easy:

- To select multiple worksheets, hold down the Ctrl key as you click each tab.

- To select a contiguous group of worksheets, click the first one in the group, and then hold down the Shift key and click the last one in the group.

- To select all the worksheets in the current workbook, right-click any worksheet tab and choose Select All Sheets from the shortcut menu.

- To quickly make any sheet active, click its index tab; to remove a sheet from a selected group of sheets, hold down Ctrl and click its tab.

- To remove the multiple selection and resume working with a single sheet, click any unselected sheet; if you've selected every sheet in the workbook, right-click any worksheet tab and choose Ungroup Sheets.

- If you've selected more than one sheet, you see the word Group in brackets in the title bar, and any data you enter appears in the corresponding cells on each worksheet in the group. So, if you have grouped Sheet1, Sheet2, and Sheet3, entering text in cell A1 on Sheet1 also enters the same text in the corresponding cells on Sheet2 and Sheet3.

- Likewise, any formatting choices you make—resizing columns, for example, or applying a numeric format—affect all the grouped worksheets identically. If you're building a budget workbook with identically formatted sheets for each department, you can use these techniques to quickly enter the budget categories in the first column and months along the top of each sheet.

■ You can't use the Clipboard to enter data into multiple sheets simultaneously. When you paste data, it appears only in the active sheet, not in any other sheets you've selected. To quickly copy formulas, labels, or formats from a single worksheet to a group of sheets within a workbook, follow these steps:

1. Select the sheet that contains the data you want to appear in each sheet.

2. Use Ctrl+click or Shift+click to select the group of sheets to which you want to add the data.

3. Select the data itself and click the Home ribbon's Fill button and select Across Worksheets. An additional dialog box lets you choose whether to copy the formatted cell contents, just the data, or just the formats.

NOTE

Watch out for one "gotcha" if you exchange workbook files with anyone who uses Microsoft Works. Although the Spreadsheet module in Works 7.0 can open Excel workbooks saved in the Office 97-2003 format, it treats multisheet workbooks as though each sheet were a separate file.

MOVING, COPYING, INSERTING, AND DELETING WORKSHEETS

In many cases, the easiest way to construct a workbook containing multiple sheets is to create the first sheet and then copy it. Although each new workbook starts with a set number of blank worksheets, you can add, copy, delete, and rearrange worksheets at will.

To add a new worksheet to an existing workbook, follow these steps:

1. Click the Insert Worksheet tab, the one at the far-right of your existing tabs. The new worksheet's tab appears at the end of the tabbed worksheets. If you want to insert a new worksheet before any of the existing worksheets, right-click the tab of the sheet that is to appear *after* the new worksheet and choose Insert.

2. Click the Worksheet icon in the Insert dialog box, and click OK. The new worksheet will appear to the left of the sheet tab you right-clicked, with a generic name and a number one higher than the highest numbered sheet in the current workbook—Sheet4, Sheet5, and so on.

If that process feels too cumbersome, point to the sheet tab you want to copy, hold down the Ctrl key, and drag the sheet tab left or right. As you drag, the mouse pointer changes shape and a small triangular marker with a plus sign appears above the sheet tab. When you release the mouse button, Excel creates a copy of the sheet you dragged, using its name followed by a copy number in parentheses: Sheet3 (2), for example.

NOTE
NEW

Before Excel 2007, when you copied a sheet that contained data, either within a workbook or to another workbook, Excel truncated the contents of any cell that contained more than 255 characters. Excel 2007 now retains such large cell contents when you copy from one sheet to another.

To delete a worksheet from a workbook, right-click the sheet tab of the worksheet you want to delete, and then choose Delete from the shortcut menu.

TIP FROM

Ed & Woody

In some workbooks, you might want to hide a worksheet rather than remove it. This technique is especially useful when a worksheet contains static data you use in formulas on other worksheets but rarely need to edit. Hiding a sheet also makes it slightly more difficult for other users to examine (and possibly change) the data on one of these sheets. (But don't even think about using hidden sheets as a true security measure—anyone interested in unhiding the sheet can do so with a few clicks.) To hide a sheet, click the Home ribbon's Format button, select Hide and Unhide in the Visibility section, and then choose Hide Sheet. To display a list of hidden sheets in the current workbook so you can make them visible again, choose Unhide Sheet from this same menu.

To move a worksheet within a workbook, point to its sheet tab, click, and drag the triangular pointer along the sheet tabs until the black marker is over the location where you want to move the worksheet. (The initial click is important because the sheet won't drag if you don't first click and release the mouse pointer over the tab.) Release the mouse button to drop the worksheet in its new location. Although it's possible to drag and drop worksheets between workbooks, it's much quicker and more accurate to use shortcut menus for this task. Follow these steps to move or copy a worksheet from one workbook to another:

1. Open the target workbook into which you plan to move or copy the worksheet. (Skip this step if you plan to move or copy the worksheet to a brand-new workbook.)

2. Switch to the workbook that contains the worksheet you want to move or copy. Point to the worksheet tab and right-click.

3. Choose Move or Copy from the shortcut menu.

4. In the Move or Copy dialog box (see Figure 18.1), select the name of the target workbook from the To Book drop-down list. To move or copy the sheet to a new, empty workbook, choose (new book) from the top of the list.

5. By default, Excel moves or copies sheets to the beginning of the target workbook. To select a different location, choose a sheet name from the Before Sheet list.

6. By default, using this dialog box moves the selected worksheet to the target workbook. To leave the original worksheet in place, select the Create a Copy check box.

Figure 18.1

7. Click OK.

RENAMING AND LABELING A WORKSHEET

To navigate more easily through workbooks with multiple worksheets, replace the generic default worksheet labels (Sheet1, Chart2, and so on) with descriptive names such as "Q3 Sales Forecasts," "Marketing Expenses," or "PivotTable." To rename a worksheet, double-click the worksheet tab (or right-click the tab and select Rename). Type a new name and press Enter.

Names you enter on worksheet tabs must conform to the following rules:

- Maximum length is 31 characters.

- Spaces are allowed.

- You can use parentheses anywhere in a worksheet's name; brackets ([ ]) are also allowed, except as the first character in the name.

- You cannot use any of the following characters as part of a sheet name: / \ ? * : (slash, backslash, question mark, asterisk, or colon). Other punctuation marks, including commas and exclamation points, are allowed.

If you plan to use references from one worksheet in formulas on another sheet, choose worksheet names carefully. Create names that are as short as possible without being needlessly cryptic; long names can make formulas particularly difficult to troubleshoot and edit.

NOTE

Worksheet tabs automatically resize to accommodate the name you enter.

TIP FROM

Ed & Woody

Excel 2007 allows you to color code worksheet tabs (right-click the worksheet tab and choose the Tab Color option). This option is best used sparingly. Colorizing each worksheet tab doesn't help organize data. Instead, try using colors to identify sheets that are part of the same group (yellow for East, green for West), or use colors to highlight summary sheets while leaving data input sheets with the default gray background.

USING RANGES TO ENTER AND SELECT DATA

Any selection of two or more cells is called a *range*. You can dramatically increase your productivity by using ranges to enter, edit, and format data. For example, if you highlight a range and click the Currency Style button, all the numeric entries in that range appear with dollar signs and two decimal places. Assigning a name to a range makes it easier to construct (and troubleshoot) formulas, and ranges make up the heart and soul of charts by defining *data series* and labels for values and categories.

The most common way to select multiple cells is to highlight a *contiguous range*—a rectangular region in which all cells are next to one another. But cells in a range don't have to be contiguous. You can also define a perfectly legal range by selecting individual cells or groups of cells scattered around a single worksheet.

Excel uses two addresses to identify a contiguous range, beginning with the cell in the upper-left corner and ending with the cell in the lower-right corner of the selection. A colon (:)

separates the two addresses that identify the range—such as A1:G3. Commas separate the parts of a noncontiguous range, and you can mix individual cells and contiguous ranges to form a new range, as in the example A3,B4,C5:D8.

SELECTING RANGES

To select a contiguous range, click the cell at any corner of the range and drag the mouse pointer to the opposite corner. To select a noncontiguous range, select the first cell or group of cells, hold down the Ctrl key, and select the next cell or group of cells. Continue holding the Ctrl key until you've selected all the cells in the range. To select an entire row or column, click the row or column heading. To select multiple rows or columns, drag the selection or hold down the Ctrl key while clicking.

To select all cells in the current worksheet, click the unlabeled Select All button in the upper-left corner of the worksheet, above the row labels and to the left of the column labels.

TIP FROM

EQ & Woody

Use this shortcut to select a contiguous range that occupies more than one screen: Click the top-left cell in the range, and then use the scrollbars to move through the worksheet until you can see the lower-right corner of the range. Hold down the Shift key and click to select the entire range.

MOVING FROM CELL TO CELL WITHIN A RANGE

To enter data into a list in heads-down mode, select the range first. As you enter data, press the Enter key to move the active cell down to the next cell within the range, or press Tab to move to the right. (Press Shift+Enter or Shift+Tab to move in the opposite direction.)

When you reach the end of a row or column, pressing Enter or Tab moves the active cell to the next column or row in the selection. When you reach the lower-right corner of the range, pressing Enter or Tab moves you back to the upper-left corner.

ENTERING THE SAME DATA IN MULTIPLE CELLS

Occasionally, you'll want to fill a range of cells with the same data in one operation, without using the Clipboard. For example, you might want to enter zero values in cells in which you intend to enter values later; you can also use this technique to enter a formula in several cells at once. To enter a formula in several cells at once, follow these steps:

1. Select the range of cells into which you want to enter data. The range need not be contiguous.

2. Type the text, number, or formula you want to use, and then press Ctrl+Enter. The data appears in all cells you selected.

TIP FROM

EQ & Woody

When you enter a formula using this technique, Excel inserts *relative cell references* by default. If you want the formula to refer to a constant value, select the cell reference and press F4 to convert it to an absolute reference before pressing Ctrl+Enter.

→ For a discussion of the differences between absolute and relative cell references, **see** "Using Cell References," **p. 594**.

→ For instructions on how to automatically fill in data using Excel's AutoFill feature, **see** "Automatically Filling In a Series of Data," **p. 519**.

NAVIGATING IN A WORKBOOK

For touch typists, Excel includes a wealth of keyboard shortcuts. Some are obvious, but a few are less than intuitive, and some represent unusual ways to move through a worksheet and select cells with precision:

- Ctrl+Home returns to the top-left corner (cell A1) of the current sheet.

- The Home key moves to the beginning of the current row.

- The Page Up/Page Down keys take you one window in their respective direction.

- Ctrl+End jumps to the bottom-right corner of the data-containing part of the worksheet—a useful technique when navigating through a lengthy list.

- If you've selected a range, you can move clockwise through all four corners of the range by repeatedly pressing Ctrl+period. If you've highlighted multiple ranges, this shortcut works only in the currently selected range.

- To move through the current workbook, one worksheet at a time, press Ctrl+Page Up or Ctrl+Page Down.

- Pressing the End key turns on *End mode*, an unusual (and somewhat confusing) way to move through the current worksheet. Most of the End mode shortcuts are alternatives to Ctrl+*key* shortcuts that are appropriate for people who are unable to press two keys simultaneously (or just don't want to). Press End followed by an arrow key to jump along the current row or column in the direction of the arrow, to the next cell that contains data, skipping over any intervening empty cells. Press End and then Home to go to the cell that is at the intersection of the furthest data-containing row and column in the current worksheet. Press End and then Enter to move to the last cell in the current row, even if there are blank cells within the row—this is the most useful of the End mode shortcuts, because it has no matching Ctrl+*key* alternative. If you press the End key by accident, press End again to turn off End mode. When turned on with an End keypress, the words End Mode appears in your status bar at the bottom of your workbook.

TIP FROM

Ed & Woody

Don't forget all the common shortcuts that Excel shares with Windows and other Office programs. In particular, F2 (Edit) positions the insertion point in the active cell and makes it available for editing, F4 repeats the previous action, and F6 switches between panes in a worksheet where you've used one or both of the scrollbar's Split box to split your worksheet into multiple window panes.

USING CELL REFERENCES AND RANGE NAMES TO NAVIGATE IN A WORKBOOK

Excel's Name box (the combo box to the left of the Formula bar) lets you jump straight to a specific cell or named range. Click in this box, enter a cell reference (H4, for example), and press Enter to jump straight to that cell. To pick from a list of all named ranges in the current workbook, even on different worksheets within the current workbook, click the drop-down arrow to the right of the Name box.

Excel's Go To dialog box offers the same capabilities, with a few extra twists, including the capability to return to a cell you previously selected, or to select all cells on a worksheet that match criteria you specify.

To open the Go To dialog box shown in Figure 18.2, press F5 or Ctrl+G. To jump to a specific cell or range, type its address or name into the Reference box. In general, it's easier to use the Name box to jump around a worksheet in this fashion. The advantage of the Go To dialog box is that Excel keeps track of the four most recent cell addresses you enter here, including the cell you started from. To return to any of these addresses, open the Go To dialog box and double-click the entry in the Go To list.

Figure 18.2
The Go To dialog box lets you jump to cells or named ranges you've visited recently.

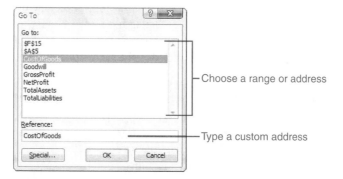

— Choose a range or address

— Type a custom address

The list of references in the Go To dialog box also includes any named ranges in the current workbook. To jump to one of these ranges, select its name from the list and click OK. Because Excel saves range names with the workbook, that list is always available when you open the Go To dialog box. On the other hand, Excel discards the list of recent addresses each time you close the workbook.

TIP FROM

Ed & Woody

Using the Go To dialog box to jump to a specific cell or a named range is needlessly complex. Whenever possible, use the Name box instead. It's also easy to create a macro that jumps to a specific named range or cell address. Use the following code, for example, to jump to a range with the name ZipCodes (the Scroll parameter positions the window so that the top-left cell in the range is at the top-left corner of the window):

```
Sub GoToZipCodes()
Application.Goto
Reference:=Worksheets("Sheet1").Range("ZipCodes"),
➥scroll:=True
End Sub
```

18

As a quick macro review, to enter this macro, you must first display the ribbon's Developer tab. Click the Microsoft Office button and select Excel Options. In the Popular category, select Show Developer Tab in the Ribbon. This option appears in the Top Options for Working with Excel section. When you close the Options dialog box and return to Excel, the Developer tab appears on your ribbon.

Once the Developer tab appears, click it and then click the Visual Basic button to open the Microsoft Visual Basic environment. Select Insert, Module and type the code. When you save the module and select File, Close and Return to Microsoft Excel, you can assign your new shortcut key to run the module.

→ For an explanation of how range names work in formulas, **see** "Using Range Names and Labels in Formulas," **p. 601**.

SELECTING RANGES OF DATA WITH THE GO TO DIALOG BOX

The Go To dialog box is especially useful when you're designing or troubleshooting a large worksheet and you want to quickly view, edit, format, copy, or move a group of cells with common characteristics. In fact, mastering this dialog box can make it possible to do things even most Excel experts swear can't be done, such as copying a range of data while ignoring hidden rows and columns. Open the Go To dialog box as usual, and then click the Special button to display the Go To Special dialog box shown in Figure 18.3. When you select one of these options and click OK, Excel selects all the cells that match that characteristic.

When you select cells using the Go To Special dialog box, the effect is the same as if you had selected a range by pointing and clicking. If you select all constants, for example, you can use the Tab and Enter keys to move through all the cells in your worksheet that contain data, skipping over any cell that contains a formula.

The following list describes the options available in the Go To Special dialog box:

Figure 18.3
Specify exactly what you want to go to.

- **Comments**—Selects all cells that contain comments. Use this option, and then press the Tab key to move from comment to comment instead of using the Previous Comment and Next Comment buttons on the Reviewing toolbar. This option is also useful if you want to remove all comments from a worksheet. Select all comments, and then right-click any of the selected cells and choose Delete Comment from the shortcut menu.

- **Constants**—Selects all cells that contain text, dates, or numbers, but not formulas. The Numbers and Text check boxes let you restrict the selection by data type (although the Logicals and Errors boxes are available, using these settings when searching for constants will always return an empty set). Select just text, for example, if you want to change the formatting of row and column labels while leaving the data area alone.

Select all numbers and clear their contents to turn a worksheet into a template that contains only text labels and formulas.

- **Formulas**—The opposite of the Constants choice, this option selects only cells that begin with an equal sign. The Numbers and Text check boxes let you restrict the selection by data type. Use the Logicals check box to find cells that contain a TRUE or FALSE value. Check the Errors box to quickly select all cells that currently display an error value, and then use the Tab key to move from cell to cell and fix the misbehaving formulas.

- **Blanks**—A straightforward option that searches all cells between the top of the worksheet and the last cell that contains data, selecting those that do not contain data or formatting. This option is useful when you want to enter a default value or assign a default format to these cells.

- **Current Region**—Selects all cells around the active cell, up to the nearest blank row and column in any direction.

- **Current Array**—If the active cell is within an *array*, this option selects the entire array.

- **Objects**—Choose this option to select all charts, text boxes, AutoShapes, and other graphic objects on the current worksheet. This option is particularly useful when you want to change formatting for borders and shading, or when you want to group objects.

- **Row Differences**—Selects cells whose contents are different from those in a comparison cell. This is a challenging option to master: You must make a selection first, and then position the active cell in the column you want to use for comparison. If you select multiple rows, Excel compares each row independently to the value in the column that contains the active cell. The example in Figure 18.4 shows what happens when you select C6:F22 and then position the active cell in column C and use the Go To Special dialog box with the Row Differences option. The highlighted result helps you readily identify rows where expenses are different each month, and also pinpoints one out-of-the-ordinary value in cell E70. Press Tab to move through from one highlighted cell to the next within the results.

- **Column Differences**—Like the previous option, except it works on a column-by-column basis. This option is extremely useful for finding unexpected differences in a list. Use a calculated column that determines whether a particular set of columns is within a normal range and returns a TRUE or FALSE result, and then use this option to find all cells that are FALSE.

- **Precedents**—Selects all cells to which the current selection refers. Use the Direct Only and All Levels options to find only direct references or all references. This option is useful when you're trying to trace the logic of a complex worksheet by working through a series of formulas.

- **Dependents**—Similar to the previous option, except it selects all cells that directly or indirectly refer to the active cell or range.

- **Last Cell**—Jumps to the last cell on the worksheet that contains data or formatting.

- **Visible Cells Only**—Easily the most useful of all the options in the Go To Special dialog box. Use this type of selection to avoid the common problem of pasting more data than you expect. For example, if you copy a range of data that includes a hidden row or

18

column, and then paste it into a new sheet, Excel pastes the hidden data as well. To avoid this problem, select the range you want to copy, and then use the Go To Special dialog box to select only visible cells. Copying and pasting that selection will have exactly the result you intend.

Select comparison column

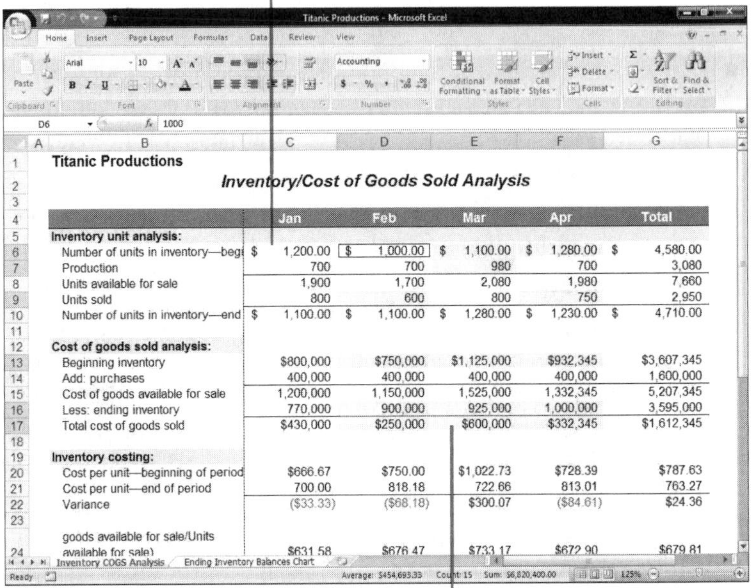

Figure 18.4
Using the Row Differences command identifies values that differ and helps you locate out-of-the-ordinary values. A production manager, for example, might ask why March Production is 40% higher than usual.

The Row Differences option selects the cells in gray because they contain values that differ from those in the same row in the comparison column.

- **Conditional Formats**—Selects all cells that use any form of conditional formatting. Use the All option when you want to quickly find all cells that contain conditional formatting. Use the Same option if you just want to edit these options for cells that match the current cell.

- **Data Validation**—Similar to the previous option, except it selects cells with data validation rules.

If choosing the Last Cell option in the Go To Special dialog box causes you to jump to a blank cell far below your actual worksheet range, see "Resetting the Last Cell" in the "Troubleshooting" section at the end of this chapter.

CONTROLLING DATA ENTRY WITH AUTOCOMPLETE OPTIONS

Excel's default setup enables an option called AutoComplete, which is designed to speed up entering data in lists. As you type, Excel compares each character that you enter with other entries in cells directly above the active cell. If the opening characters match those of any other entry, Excel assumes that you want to repeat that entry and fills in the rest of the label. (This comparison applies only to cells that contain text; AutoComplete ignores data formatted as numbers, dates, and times.)

If you want to repeat the previous entry, press Enter (or Tab or any arrow key) to insert the AutoComplete entry in the cell. Keep typing to enter a new value in the cell. Excel will not suggest an AutoComplete entry unless the string that you have entered identifies a unique entry in the list above the active cell.

TIP FROM

EQ & Woody

Instead of waiting for Excel's suggestion, you can select from a list of entries already in the column. To display the list, press Alt+down arrow, or right-click the cell and then choose Pick from Drop-Down List from the shortcut menu.

Some users find AutoComplete disconcerting, dangerous, or merely annoying because if you don't pay close attention, you risk accidentally entering the wrong data. You can easily disable AutoComplete: Click your Office button, select Excel Options to open the Excel Options dialog box. Choose Advanced and clear the check mark from the Enable AutoComplete for Cell Values box. Click OK to save the new setting and continue editing.

If you have a love-hate relationship with AutoComplete, create a macro that toggles this feature on and off. Assigning the macro to a new keyboard shortcut you press to turn on AutoComplete when you're entering data in a list where its capabilities are useful, and turn it off at all other times. Here's all the code you need:

```
Sub ToggleAutoComplete()
    Application.EnableAutoComplete = Not Application.EnableAutoComplete
End Sub
```

AUTOMATICALLY FILLING IN A SERIES OF DATA

One common and tedious data-entry task is entering a sequence of numbers or dates in a column or row. Excel's AutoFill feature can handle this chore automatically by filling in information as you drag the mouse along a column or row. Use AutoFill to copy formulas or values. Enter the days of the week, the months of the year, or any series of numbers or dates. You can even fill in custom lists of departments, category names, part numbers, and other information that you define.

Because of its tremendous number of options, even Excel experts sometimes have trouble coaxing the correct results out of AutoFill. AutoFill's SmartTag makes itself present by an AutoFill Options button you can point to for additional AutoFill options. The addition of the AutoFill Options button makes this task somewhat easier. If using AutoFill has the wrong result, click the AutoFill Options button to see a list of other options that enable you to select a different result, such as changing a simple copy to a series.

In general, using AutoFill will have one of the following results:

- **Copy data from one or more cells**—If the selection is not a sequence that Excel recognizes—for example, if you select a cell that contains text—AutoFill copies the selection in the direction that you drag.

Using AutoFill is an excellent way to copy a formula from one cell across a row or down a column. This technique is especially useful for copying formulas that total columns or rows. As you drag, AutoFill copies the formula, adjusting relative references as needed.

- **Copy formatting or values across a row or down a column**—Normally, AutoFill copies both formats and values from the cells that you start with. To choose one, make a selection and then hold down the right mouse button while dragging. When you release the mouse button, choose Fill Formatting Only or Fill Without Formatting from the AutoFill Options button's drop-down arrow. If you select a formula in the starting cell, either option copies the formula, with or without formatting.

- **Fill in a series of dates**—If you enter a date in any recognizable format, such as 4/10 or 5-23-04, AutoFill will extend the series in one-day increments. AutoFill also recognizes long and short versions of days of the week and months. If you enter Jan in the first cell, for example, AutoFill will continue the list with Feb, Mar, Apr, and so on; start with Wednesday, and AutoFill will extend the list with Thursday, Friday, Saturday, and so on. Excel also recognizes calendar quarters. If you enter Q1 in a cell and use AutoFill, you get Q2, Q3, and Q4, at which point the series starts over with Q1.

When you reach the end of a finite AutoFill sequence, such as days of the week or months of the year, the sequence repeats. If you start with Monday, for example, the sequence starts over again after the seventh cell.

- **Fill in a series of numbers**—This is probably the trickiest AutoFill option. If you start with a single cell that contains the number 1 and use AutoFill to extend it, Excel will copy the number 1 to the rest of the cells that you select. To instruct Excel to AutoFill a series instead of copying the number, hold down the Ctrl key as you drag.

When you insert a sequence of numbers, Excel assumes that you want to increment them by 1. Thus, if you start with 100, the sequence continues with 101, 102, and so on. To use a different sequence, enter values in at least two cells so that the sequence is apparent, and then select those cells and use AutoFill. For example, if you enter 100 and 200 in the first two cells and then select those cells and use AutoFill, Excel continues the series with 300, 400, and so on. You can also use this technique to enter a date series, such as every other day (Monday, Wednesday, Friday), every third month (Feb, May, Aug), or the 10th of each month (1/10, 2/10, 3/10). Enter the first two or three cells in the sequence, select the cells that you entered, and then extend the selection using AutoFill.

- **Fill in a series of numbered items**—If you enter any text plus a number (Chapter 1, Item 1, or Area 51, for example), AutoFill extends the selection by 1 (Chapter 2, Chapter 3, and so on). Confusingly, this option works the opposite on a series of numbers without text: Hold down Ctrl to prevent Excel from extending the selection and copy the values instead.

- **Fill in a custom list**—If you've created a custom list (see the following section for step-by-step instructions), enter any item from that list in any cell, and then use AutoFill to add the remaining items in the list.

- **Fill in a trend series**—For this option, you must select a number of cells first and then drag with the right mouse button for more options. You can choose a Linear Trend series, in which Excel calculates the average difference between each value in the series that you selected and then adds it to (or subtracts it from) each succeeding value in the AutoFill range. Choose a Growth Trend series to have Excel calculate the percentage of difference between items in the series and apply that amount to each new value. These options are useful when you're trying to project future patterns, such as sales or revenue growth, based on existing data.

USING AUTOFILL

AutoFill will save you much typing time, and if you're unfamiliar with it, you should immediately see how simple AutoFill works. To use AutoFill, follow these steps:

1. First, enter the initial value or values for the range. If the list begins a unique sequence—months of the year, for example, starting with Jan or January—you need to enter a value in only one cell. To AutoFill a sequence of numbers or dates with an increment value other than 1, enter the first two or three values in the series.

2. Point to Excel's fill handle—the small black square in the lower-right corner of the currently selected cell or range. When you point at the fill handle, the mouse pointer turns into a thin black cross.

3. Drag in any direction (up or down in a column, left or right in a row) to begin filling in values (see Figure 18.5). Hold down the Ctrl key as you extend the selection to switch the AutoFill action from copy to fill series, or vice versa.

Figure 18.5
As you drag, Excel automatically fills in values in your series—dates, in this example.

NOTE

AutoFill works in only one row or column at a time. To extend a selection down and to the right, you must perform the AutoFill action in two steps.

4. ScreenTips display the value that will appear in each new cell as you extend the series. When you reach the final cell, release the mouse button to fill in the data.

5. If the AutoFill results are not what you expected, click the AutoFill Options button to display a menu with additional options (see Figure 18.6).

Figure 18.6

TIP FROM

You can also use AutoFill to remove items from a range without removing formatting. Select the entire range that contains the series. Aim the mouse pointer at the lower-right corner, but instead of dragging the fill handle down or to the right, as you normally would do to extend a series, drag it up (for a column) or to the left (for a row). This action makes the range smaller, removing those items that are no longer selected without affecting the formatting applied to those cells.

For maximum control over AutoFill options, select a series of cells and hold down the right mouse button while dragging. Choose the Series option at the bottom of the shortcut menu to display a dialog box that lets you choose any option, including starting points and step values for a series, as in Figure 18.7.

Figure 18.7
If Excel can't recognize the progression in an AutoFill series, use this dialog box to specify series settings manually.

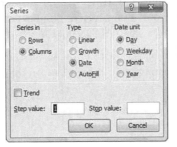

CREATING CUSTOM AUTOFILL LISTS TO FIT YOUR PROJECTS

You can also create a custom fill list, such as company divisions, budget categories, or product codes, and add the list to Excel. Excel adds custom lists to the Windows Registry, with each list appearing in the precise order in which you enter individual items. The result can be tremendous time savings for you if you regularly insert the same list into worksheets, such as names of regional offices or budget categories. AutoFill can insert any custom list in any row or column, anytime (and, as we'll demonstrate in the next section, you can also use a custom list as a sort key for the rest of your list).

TIP FROM

To copy a custom list from one computer to another, use the original custom list to fill in a range on a blank worksheet and then save the resulting workbook. On the computer where you want to import the list, open the saved workbook, select the list range, and use the Import button on the Custom Lists tab of the Custom Lists Options dialog box, as described in this section. It takes a few minutes at most, and it's foolproof.

To add a custom fill list to Excel, use either of the following procedures:

- If the list is short, you can type it directly into a dialog box. Click your Office button and select Excel Options and choose Popular. Click the Edit Custom Lists button, select New List, and start entering items in the List Entries box, as shown in Figure 18.8. Be sure to enter each item in the order you want your AutoFill list to be ordered, and press Enter at the end of each line. When the list is complete, click the Add button.

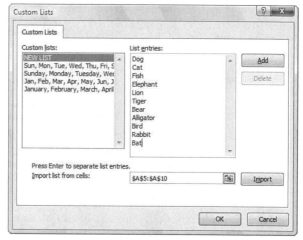

Figure 18.8

- If the list is already available in a worksheet, the process is even easier. Say that you've created a worksheet that contains all budget categories in the exact order that you want to enter them every time. Open that sheet and select the worksheet range (column or row) that contains the list. Click your Office button, Choose Popular, click the Edit Custom Lists button to display the Custom Lists dialog box, and click Import.

Your list is now available in any Excel worksheet that you open on this machine. To automatically add the custom list to a worksheet range, enter the first list item, use the fill handle to complete the list, and click OK.

FINDING, REPLACING, AND TRANSFORMING DATA

Just as in other Office applications, you can use simple drag-and-drop techniques to move or copy the contents of a cell or range. Using the Windows Clipboard and the Paste Special menu, you can also change the format of information or perform mathematical transformations as you move or copy it. Most of the options are self-explanatory, but a handful are unique to Excel and truly useful.

FINDING AND REPLACING THE CONTENTS OF A CELL OR RANGE

Excel's Find and Replace dialog box includes the capability to find and change formatting, as well as options to search across all sheets in a workbook or to restrict the search and subsequent changes to the current worksheet.

As in other Office programs, you use the Home ribbon's Find and Select button (or use the corresponding Ctrl+F and Ctrl+H shortcuts) to open the respective dialog boxes. Figure 18.9 shows the Replace dialog box with formatting options selected. (If the additional settings aren't visible, click the Options button.)

Figure 18.9
The Find and Replace dialog box lets you change formatting globally across an entire workbook.

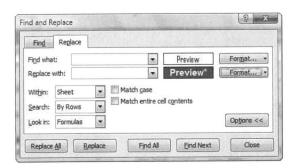

If you leave the Find What or Replace With boxes blank, Excel finds or replaces formatting in all cells where it finds a match. To enter formatting criteria using dialog boxes, click the Format button to the right of the Find What or Replace With text boxes. To find cells where formatting matches the settings of an existing cell, click the drop-down arrow to the right of the Format button and select the Choose Format from Cell option. After you select this option, the Find and Replace dialog box disappears and the mouse pointer changes to an eyedropper shape. Click the cell that contains the formatting you want to match.

DRAGGING AND DROPPING TO CONVERT DATA

As is true elsewhere in Office, you can take control of the options available when dragging cells from one place to another. (Keep in mind that you must point to the edge of a selected group of cells before you can drag the cells.) For instance, if you hold down the right mouse button and drag a cell or range of cells, a shortcut menu with paste options appears when you release the button. Two of these options are worth special note:

- Use the Copy Here as Formats Only option to quickly transfer cell formatting (fonts, shading, borders, and so on) without copying the contents of the cells.

- Choose Copy Here as Values Only to convert formulas to their results and paste the Clipboard contents as constants—numbers or text—rather than as formulas.

This technique is especially useful when you want to quickly convert a cell or range from a formula to a value. Suppose column A contains a list of product details, imported from an external database. All you really need from each is the six-digit part number it starts with, so you've filled column B with a range of formulas, each of which uses the LEFT() function to extract the first six characters from the original cell—for example, =LEFT(A2,6).

So far, so good. But if you now delete column A, your list of part numbers will shift to the left and turn into a column full of error messages. Before you can safely delete column A, you must convert column B to its results. To do so, select the entire range that contains the formula, right-click, and drag it a short distance in any direction (without releasing the mouse button), and then drag it back and release it over the original cells. Choose Copy Here as Values Only from the shortcut menu. The column now contains just the part numbers, and you can safely delete column A.

NOTE

You cannot use the Clipboard or drag-and-drop techniques to copy or move a noncontiguous range that consists of multiple selections.

TRANSFORMING DATA WITH PASTE OPTIONS

One of the most powerful ways to manipulate data on a worksheet is to copy it to the Clipboard first. Using the Clipboard, you can strip some or all formatting or manipulate values in the copied cells or range. You can then paste the data into the new location so it appears exactly as you want it.

The Paste Options Smart Tag (introduced in Excel 2002) lets you quickly apply some common transformations. When you copy data to the Clipboard and then use the Home ribbon's Paste button or the Ctrl+V keyboard shortcut to paste the data, you see a Smart Tag in the lower-right corner of the pasted area. Click the Smart Tag to choose from the menu shown in Figure 18.10.

Figure 18.10
Smart Tag options let you tweak the appearance of data after pasting it. The Use Destination Theme option, for instance, retains the worksheet's theme settings such as color and font when pasting data into a new worksheet.

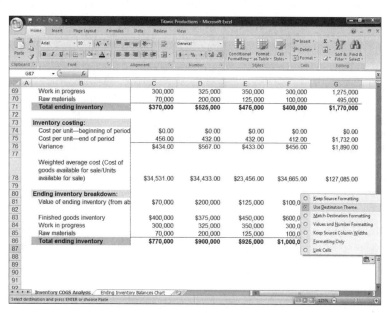

18

By default, data pasted from another Excel worksheet brings along its own formatting. If the data appears incorrectly when you paste it, click the Smart Tag and change the display of the pasted data in any of these ways:

- Choose Match Destination Formatting to strip all formatting but preserve formulas.

- Use the Values and Number Formatting option to convert formulas to their resulting values and paste them into the new location with formatting.

- Click Keep Source Column Widths to copy all formulas, number formatting, and cell formatting along with column widths. This option is most useful when pasting a highly formatted table into a new worksheet, where all columns are the standard width.

- Choose Formatting Only when you want to copy the format of a table to a new worksheet and then enter data manually in the new location.

- Click the Link Cells option to convert the pasted data into a link to the other worksheet.

→ For more details on how to use links between worksheets and workbooks, **see** "Using Links to Automatically Update or Consolidate Worksheet Data," **p. 531**.

Choices available through the Paste Options Smart Tag are convenient for quick, uncomplicated transformations. But they have several limitations, most notably that each change undoes the changes from other Smart Tags. So if you paste in a range of formulas, you can use Smart Tags to convert formulas to values *or* to adjust column widths, but not both.

For more control over the results of a paste operation, use the Paste Special feature. Copy the contents of one or more cells to the Clipboard and click the bottom half of the Home ribbon's Paste button then click Paste Special—you'll see the Paste Special dialog box shown in Figure 18.11. A handful of these options are also available using the Paste Options Smart Tag, but Paste Special offers a much broader range of capabilities.

Figure 18.11
Use the Paste Special dialog box to add or subtract two columns of numbers, or to multiply or divide a range of numbers by a value you copy to the Clipboard.

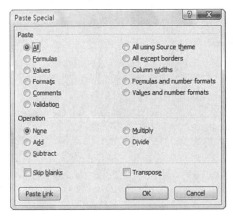

Within or between workbooks, you can selectively paste in the following ways:

- The Formulas option is hopelessly misnamed, and the Help text does a terrible job of describing its actual function. Use this option when you want to copy all the data from one range to another, including formulas, without copying any formatting. This option is most useful when you're trying to copy data from another worksheet without destroying the formatting of your existing worksheet. Use the Formulas and Number Formats option to copy number formatting without carrying over other cell formatting, such as borders and colors.

- Select Values to convert formulas to their results and paste them as constant numbers or text. This has the same effect as the drag-and-drop technique described in the previous section. Use this option when you need to convert a noncontiguous range of formulas to its results. This option does not copy any formatting. Use the Values and Number Formats option to preserve number formatting without affecting other cell formatting.

- Click Formats to copy all formatting from one cell or range to another. Use the All Except Borders option to skip cell borders and the Column Widths option to duplicate column widths, especially from one worksheet to another.

TIP FROM

Using Excel's Paste Special options can test your creativity. It's often possible to save a ton of work by combining several operations in consecutive Paste Special actions. For instance, choose All Except Borders to copy formulas and cell formatting without adding underlines and table borders from the original data; then repeat the Paste Special option and choose the Column Widths option. This duplicates an entire table on a new worksheet, leaving out only borders and underlines.

- Choose the Comments option to transfer comments from one location to another.

- Use the Validation option to duplicate data-entry rules, especially between different worksheets or workbooks.

The options in the Operation area are some of the most interesting of all, because they let you perform mathematical transformations on a group of numbers without having to tamper with your existing worksheet structure. To use this technique, enter a number in one cell and copy it to the Clipboard, select the range you want to transform, and use the Paste Special dialog box to add or subtract the value on the Clipboard from each entry in the selection or to multiply or divide the selection by that number. This technique might come in handy if you're beginning to plan next year's budget and you want to start by increasing this year's numbers by 6%. Follow these steps:

1. Click in any blank cell (even on another worksheet) and enter the value you want to use when transforming the existing data. In this case, enter **1.06** because you want to increase the values by 6%.

TIP FROM

You can also use this technique to add or subtract two ranges of numbers, or to multiply one range of numbers by another. If you have two departmental worksheets formatted the same, you can copy all the numbers from one worksheet and use this option to add them to the data in the other sheet, for example. Just make sure that the range you copy is the same size as the range you paste to.

2. Press Ctrl+C to copy the value to the Windows Clipboard.

3. Select the range of data you want to increase.

4. Click the bottom half of your Home ribbon's Paste button and choose Paste Special. In the Paste Special dialog box, select the Multiply option.

5. Click OK. Excel multiplies the selected range by the constant on the Clipboard, increasing each number by exactly 6%.

The final two check boxes in the Paste Special dialog box work with other options:

- Click the Skip Blanks option if you're performing a mathematical operation using two ranges of data. This setting skips pasting data for any cells that are blank in the original copy area.

- Check Transpose to flip a row of labels into a column, or vice versa. You can use this option to change the orientation of an entire region as well.

TIP FROM

Ed & Woody

Changing the orientation of an entire region is a trick that is especially useful when you're working with imported data. If your list has months along the side and categories along the top, for example, choose the Transpose option to rearrange the list so that each month's data appears in its own column and each category gets its own row.

CUSTOMIZING THE WORKSHEET WINDOW

Changing the size and configuration of a worksheet window can make it easier to work with data, especially in large worksheets. Hide information, zoom out or in to show more or less data, lock a row or column in place to maintain titles and headings, work in multiple panes, or open a new window on the same workbook.

HIDING ROWS AND COLUMNS

On some worksheets, you need to use rows or columns to hold data used in calculations, but you don't need to clutter up the rest of the worksheet by showing it. Click any cell within the row or column you want to hide (you don't need to select the entire row or column), click your Home ribbon's Format button, select Hide and Unhide menu, and choose Hide Rows or Hide Columns.

To make a hidden row visible again, select cells in the row above and below the hidden row, and then choose Unhide Rows. To display a hidden column, select cells in the columns to the left and right and choose Unhide Columns from the Home ribbon Format button's Hide and Unhide menu.

If the first row or column of a worksheet is hidden, press F5 to open the Go To dialog box. Type **A1** in the Reference box and click OK; then select the Unhide Columns or Unhide Rows option.

USING THE ZOOM CONTROLS

 Use the new Zoom button and Zoom Slider controls at the right of your status bar to change the view of your worksheet. Most of the Zoom button options are self-explanatory: You can shrink the worksheet to as small as 10% of normal size for an overview of the sheet's design, or enlarge it to as much as 400% of normal. (This option is especially useful for close editing of complex grouped objects on a sheet.) If you choose a customized Zoom level of 39% or lower, your gridlines disappear. That's not a bug—at the lower magnification, the lines get in the way of your ability to edit, so Excel hides them on the screen.

Drag the Zoom Slider control left or right to zoom in or out of your worksheet. Click the minus or plus sign on either size of the Zoom Slider control to zoom in or out in small increments.

The most useful option on the Zoom control is one that even some expert users don't know about. You can resize and reposition the editing window so that it includes the current selection; Excel chooses the proper Zoom percentage automatically. After you make a selection, click your status bar's Zoom button and click to select the Fit Selection option. Excel resizes the selection automatically. To return to Normal view, click the Zoom button again and choose 100% from the drop-down list or press Ctrl+Z to undo the most recent zoom.

TIP FROM

> If your mouse includes a wheel, you can use it to zoom in and out of your worksheet. Hold down the Ctrl key and spin the wheel down to zoom out; spin the wheel up to zoom back in.

18

LOCKING ROW AND COLUMN LABELS FOR ONSCREEN VIEWING

In a typical worksheet, labels identify the type of data in each column or row. For example, a common design for budget worksheets arranges data into one row for each budget category, with values for each month appearing in columns from left to right. In this model, a label at the left edge of each row identifies the category, and a label at the top of each column identifies the month. If the data in your worksheet occupies more than a single screen, row and column labels can scroll out of view, making it difficult to identify which data goes in each row and column. The lack of labels also makes it difficult to enter data in the correct rows and columns, unless you want to continually scroll to see the heading labels.

To keep the row and column labels visible at all times, *freeze* them into position. In Figure 18.12, for example, notice that you can see the row titles in column A at the left, as well as the columns for July, August, and beyond at the right (starting at column H). As you click the horizontal scrollbar, columns on the left of the data area scroll out of view, but the labels in the first column remain visible.

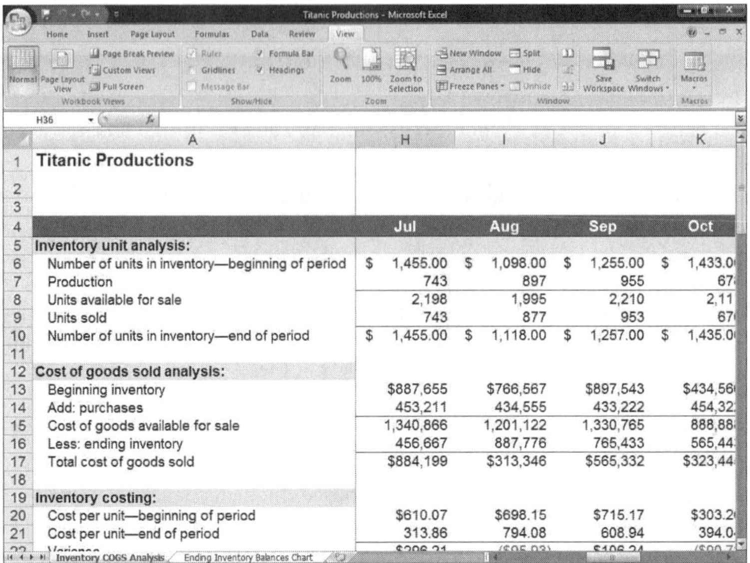

Figure 18.12
When you freeze rows or columns in place, you can scroll through the worksheet without losing identifying labels.

18

NEW You freeze rows and columns from the View ribbon. To freeze rows, columns, or both, click in the cell below the row and to the right of the column that you want to lock into position. To freeze the first two columns and the first row, for example, click in cell C2. Select the View ribbon button's Freeze Panes button and select the Freeze Panes option. A solid line sets off the locked rows and columns from the rest of the worksheet.

TIP FROM

Ed & Woody

If your worksheet consists of a long list, lock in the labels for columns only. Click in column A, one row beneath the row that contains your column labels, and then choose the Freeze Panes option.

To navigate in a worksheet whose panes are frozen, use the scrollbars to move through the data in your worksheet. The panes are locked only on the screen; if you print the worksheet, rows and columns appear in their normal positions. To unlock the row and column labels, select the View ribbon's Freeze Panes button's Unfreeze Panes option.

→ To learn how to add row or column labels on each page of a printed worksheet, **see** "Using Repeating Titles for Multiple Page Printouts," **p. 542**.

SPLITTING THE WORKSHEET WINDOW

Split a worksheet into separate panes when you want to compare data in different regions of a worksheet side-by-side. A *split bar* divides the window into two panes, horizontally or vertically. You can drag both split bars onto the worksheet to create four panes. All changes you make in one pane are reflected in the other. You can drag cells and ranges between panes, and you can scroll and enter data in each pane independently.

To split a worksheet, use either of the following techniques:

- Click to select the cell below and/or to the right of where you want the split to appear, and then click the View ribbon's Split button. Select any cell in the column at the left of the current window to create side-by-side panes (also known as a vertical split). Select any cell in the top row to create a horizontal split, with one pane over another. If you choose the cell at the top left of the screen, Excel divides the window into four equal panes.

- Aim the mouse pointer at one of the two split boxes, which appear just above the vertical scrollbar and just to the right of the horizontal scrollbar, to create side-by-side panes (vertical split). When the mouse pointer changes to a double line with two arrows, click and drag in the direction of the worksheet to create a new pane. As you drag, the bar snaps into place at a row or column boundary. Release when you reach the right position.

To remove multiple panes and return to a single editing window, you can do any of the following: Click your View ribbon's Split button again, double-click the split bar, or click the bar and drag it off the worksheet window in any direction.

USING LINKS TO AUTOMATICALLY UPDATE OR CONSOLIDATE WORKSHEET DATA

Use links to share data between cells or ranges in one worksheet and another location in the same workbook or a different workbook. Just as a formula displays the results of a calculation, a link looks up data from another location and displays it in the active cell.

Links offer a powerful technique for consolidating data from different sources into one worksheet without requiring that you re-enter or copy data. For example, you might use separate sales-tracking worksheets for each month of the year, with a single year-to-date worksheet that consolidates the monthly results. A business manager can use separate worksheets to analyze budget information for each division within a company, creating links to a master worksheet that ties all the numbers together.

NOTE

You can use *links* (also known as external references) within formulas as well.

After you establish a link, data you enter in one location automatically appears in all linked locations. To create a link, follow these steps:

1. Open all the workbooks you plan to link.

2. In the source workbook (the one that contains the data you want to reuse), select the cell or range to be linked, and press Ctrl+C to copy it to the Clipboard.

3. Switch to the dependent workbook (the one in which you want to insert the link), and select the cell where you want to create the link.

4. Click the bottom half of your Home ribbon's Paste button and choose Paste Link.

→ Using hyperlinks provides yet another powerful option for linking your Excel worksheets; **see** "Working with Hyperlinks," **p. 98**.

In general, you should avoid creating links between cells or ranges that are contained in separate workbooks. If you move or delete the workbook that contains the external reference, you break the link and damage the integrity of your data and formulas. Excel updates linked cells automatically if the worksheet that contains the link is open. If you change the data in the source workbook when the workbook that contains the link is closed, the links do not update automatically. When you reopen the workbook that contains the links, Excel will ask whether you want to update the links.

To update or change the source of links manually, click your Data ribbon's Edit Links button to display the Edit Links dialog box. All your links will appear in the dialog box showing their source workbook and whether that workbook is currently open. Click the Update Values button to update your workbook's links.

RESTRICTING AND VALIDATING DATA ENTRY FOR A CELL OR RANGE

When designing a worksheet, you'll occasionally want to restrict the type of data users can enter in a specific cell or range. Excel lets you define data-validation rules for cells and ranges to do exactly that. Examples of useful applications include the following:

- In a list of recent sales results formatted to show only month and date, restrict entry in a specific column to only dates within the last month. This technique prevents users from inadvertently entering a date in the wrong month or year, or in the future.

- On a budget worksheet, require that the user enter a department name and restrict allowed entries to a specific list. You can add a drop-down arrow to a cell with this type of restriction so users can pick from a list.

- For purchase orders, check the amount a user enters against his or her authorized spending limit—say, $500. If the amount is over the limit, display a message that directs them to talk to a supervisor or re-enter the amount.

- Ask a user to enter a description in a form; to keep data to a manageable length, restrict the total number of characters the user can enter and display a warning message if the description exceeds that length.

- On an invoice form, allow a salesperson to enter an optional discount for good customers, but only if the amount before sales tax is over $100. Compare the entry in the Discount field with a formula that calculates the total purchases to validate the entry.

DEFINING DATA-VALIDATION RULES

Each *data-validation* rule has three components: the criteria that define a valid entry; an optional message you can display to users when they select the cell that contains the rule; and an error message that appears when users enter invalid data. To begin creating a data-validation rule, first select the cell or range for which you want to restrict data entry, and then click the Data Validation button on your Data ribbon. You'll see a Data Validation dialog box similar to the one in Figure 18.13.

Figure 18.13
When defining data-validation rules, you can enter values or formulas that evaluate to the correct data type. This example restricts valid entries to dates within the last 30 days.

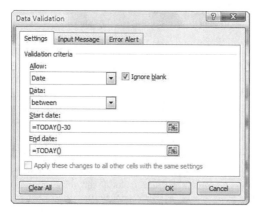

On the Settings tab, enter the criteria that define a valid entry. First, choose the required data type in the Allow drop-down list; then define specific criteria. The available options in the Allow drop-down list (described in Table 18.1) vary depending on the type of data you select. Keep in mind that the options shown in the Data Validation dialog box change depending on the criteria you've selected in the Allow drop-down list. The dialog box shown in Figure 18.13 represents just one example.

TABLE 18.1   DATA-VALIDATION SETTINGS

Data Type	Allowed Restrictions
Any Value	Default setting; no restrictions allowed. Select this option if you want to display a helpful input message only, without restricting data entry.
Whole Number, Decimal	Choose an *operator* (between, for example, or greater than) and values or formulas. The Whole Number data type produces an error if the user enters a decimal point, even if it's followed by zero. The Decimal choice allows any number after the decimal point.
List	In the Source box, enter the address or name of the range that contains the list of values you want to allow. The range can be on another worksheet (a hidden worksheet in the current workbook is your best choice) or in another workbook. For a short list, enter the valid items directly in this box, separated by commas (Acctg, Sales, Mktg). If you want users to be able to pick from a list, select the In-cell drop-down check-box.
Date or Time	Choose an operator and appropriate values. You can enter formulas here as well; for example, to allow only dates that have already occurred, choose Less Than from the Data box and enter **=TODAY()** in the End Date box.

continues

18

TABLE 18.1   CONTINUED

Data Type	Allowed Restrictions
Text Length	Choose an operator and then specify numbers that define the allowed length; you can also enter formulas or cell references that produce numbers as values for use with the selected operator.
Custom	Enter a formula that returns a *logical value* (TRUE or FALSE). Use this option when the cell that contains the rule is part of a calculation, and you want to test the results of that calculation rather than the cell value itself. On a purchase order with multiple items that you total in a cell named Total_PO, for example, enter `=Total PO < 500` as the rule for each cell used in the SUM formula; that prevents the user from exceeding a $500 total limit even though each individual item is under the allowance.

DISPLAYING HELPFUL INPUT MESSAGES

Rules that stop users from entering invalid data are good, but helpful error messages are even better. As part of a data-validation rule, you can display messages that appear every time the user enters the cell that contains that rule. These messages appear in small pop-up windows alongside the cell. Use *input messages* to help users understand exactly what type of data they should enter in the cell, especially if you are designing a data-entry sheet for less-experienced Excel users.

To create an input message, click the Data Validation button on your Data ribbon to display the Data Validation dialog box. Click the Input Message tab (see Figure 18.14) and enter the title text and message you want to appear. Your message should be as helpful and brief as possible; if you've restricted the user to a particular type of data, make sure they know exactly what they're allowed to enter.

Figure 18.14
The message you enter here can explain the purpose of the cell and warn the user of data restrictions.

ALERTING THE USER TO ERRORS

How do you want Excel to respond when users enter invalid data? In all cases, you can display an error alert. If the data type is wrong, or if the date or value is not appropriate, you can refuse to accept the input and force users to enter an acceptable value. You can also choose to accept the value; this can be an effective way to force users to double-check values that might be valid but are outside of a normal range. On an expense report, for example, you might define valid entries as being below $2,000. If the amount users enter is over that amount, you could display a message that asks them whether they're sure the amount is correct. If they accidentally added an extra zero, the message will give them a chance to correct their mistake, or Excel can accept the input if they click OK.

To define an error message and set options for handling data that is outside the defined range, click the Data Validation button on your Data ribbon to display the Data Validation dialog box. Click the Error Alert tab (see Figure 18.15).

Figure 18.15
You define the error message users see when they enter invalid data; you can reject the data or allow them to enter it with a warning.

Check the Show Error Alert After Invalid Data Is Entered check box. Enter a title and text for the message you want users to see when they enter an invalid value. As with the Input Message, try to be as informative as possible so that the user knows exactly what he or she must do to correct the error. Then select one of the following choices from the Style box to define how Excel should handle the input:

- **Stop**—Displays a Stop dialog box and lets the user choose Retry or Cancel.
- **Warning**—Displays the error message and adds Continue?. The user can choose Yes to enter the invalid data, No to try again, or Cancel.
- **Information**—Displays the error message. The user can click OK to enter invalid data or Cancel to back out.

DELETING, MOVING, OR COPYING DATA-VALIDATION RULES

To remove all validation rules from a cell or range, first select the cell(s) containing the validation rule; then click the Data Validation button on your Data ribbon and click the Settings tab in the Data Validation dialog box. Click the Clear All button and click OK. This option erases the input message, error alert, and validation settings.

When should you select the Apply These Changes to All Other Cells with the Same Settings check box? If you originally create a set of validation rules for a range of cells, Excel stores those settings with the range. If you later adjust the settings for an individual cell in that range, you break the link to the range. Check this box while editing data-validation settings for a single cell, and Excel extends the selection and applies your changes to the entire range you originally selected. The check box has no effect on other cells for which you defined rules individually, even if the rules are absolutely identical.

TIP FROM

When you copy or move a cell or range, data-validation rules travel with the cell's contents. To copy only data-validation rules from one cell to another, without affecting the contents or formatting of the target cell, use Paste Special. Select the cell whose rule you want to copy, and then click the Home ribbon's Copy button (or press Ctrl+C). Select the cells where you want to copy the rule, and click the bottom half of your Home ribbon's Paste button. Choose Paste Special. Check the Validation option and click OK.

 Are you still finding invalid data in a user form in which you've created validation rules to protect data? See "Data Validation Limitations" in the "Troubleshooting" section at the end of this chapter.

CIRCLING DATA ERRORS

Data-validation rules are not perfect. Users can bypass the rules and enter invalid data by pasting from the Clipboard or by entering a formula that results in an invalid value. Also, Excel does not check the existing contents of a cell or range when you create or copy a validation rule.

The only way to visually identify invalid data is to display your Data ribbon and click the Data Validation button. Choose Circle Invalid Data to show any cells that are outside the rules, as shown in Figure 18.16. Click the Clear Validation Circles button on the Data Validation menu to clear the highlights.

NOTE

The Circle Invalid Data button will find a maximum of 255 cells. If you have more invalid entries, you'll need to correct the data in some of the invalid cells and then click the Circle Invalid Data button again.

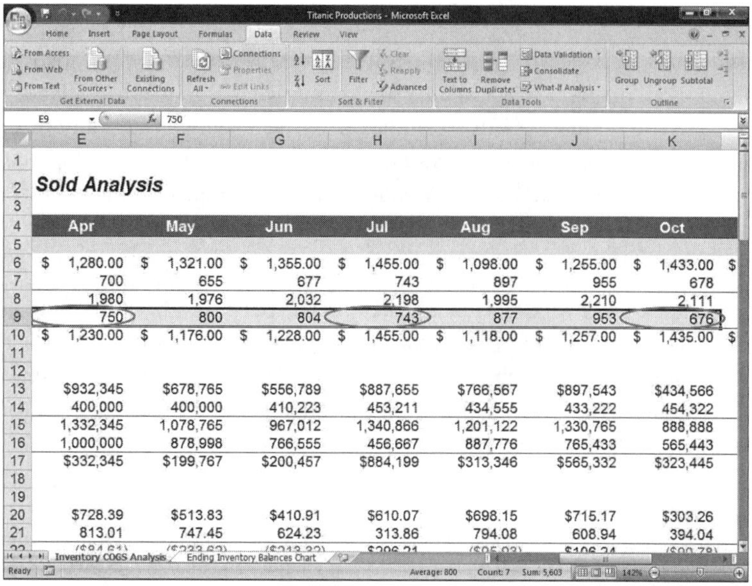

Figure 18.16
Click the Circle Invalid Data button to add these bold highlights around any cell whose contents violate a validation rule.

→ For an overview of other tools you can use to track down problems in formulas, **see** "Testing and Debugging Formulas," **p. 618**.

PRINTING WORKSHEETS

Unlike Word documents, which typically are designed to fit on specific paper sizes, Excel worksheets are free-flowing environments that sprawl in every direction. When printing, if you leave the formatting to Excel, you'll end up with page breaks that appear at arbitrary locations in your worksheet, with no regard to content. To properly translate a large worksheet into printed output takes planning and a fair amount of creative formatting.

If you don't specifically define a print area, Excel assumes that you want to print all the data in the currently selected worksheet or worksheets, beginning with cell A1 and extending to the edge of the area that contains data or formatting. If necessary, you can divide a worksheet into smaller sections and print each region on its own page. As explained in this section, you can also shrink the print area to fit in a precise number of pages, and you can repeat row and column headings to make the display of data easier to follow.

TIP FROM

EQ & Woody

Don't overlook other techniques for rearranging data on a worksheet for the purpose of producing great printouts. For tables, AutoFilters can help you select and print only data that matches criteria you specify (see Chapter 21, "Organizing Data with Tables and PivotTables," for more details). Hiding rows and columns temporarily can help cut a large worksheet down to size. To print the quarterly sales totals for each sales rep without printing the monthly details, for example, hide the details before printing the selection. In some cases, the best way to print a complex selection from a worksheet is to translate it into another worksheet, using linked ranges or PivotTable reports (also covered in Chapter 21).

DEFINING A PRINT AREA

You can force Excel to use a defined print area as the default for a worksheet. (Excel bypasses all dialog boxes and uses this region when you print.) This technique is especially useful if you regularly print a complex worksheet that contains a number of nonprinting regions. On a worksheet that contains a list and a criteria range, for example, you'll typically want to print only the list. On a budget worksheet that includes monthly data by category and an executive summary region, you might want to define the summary as the default when you print.

 You can start printing by clicking the Quick Access Toolbar (the toolbar to the right of the Office button in the upper-left corner) if your Quick Access Toolbar has a Quick Print button. If yours does not, click the arrow to the right of your Quick Access Toolbar and click to select Quick Print. The Quick Print button appears. When you click the Quick Print button, your worksheet begins printing on the currently selected default printer.

TIP FROM

> The Quick Print button bypasses all dialog boxes and prints the default print area without allowing you to review any options. The results can be tremendously frustrating (and waste reams of paper, if you can't stop the print job fast enough). For that reason, we strongly recommend replacing the Quick Print button with the Print button. The Print command uses a similar Quick Access Toolbar icon, but displays the Print dialog box when clicked instead of sending your job to the printer with current settings. You'll use one extra click every time you print, but you'll significantly reduce the number of times you accidentally print the wrong selection. Of course, if you click the Office button and select Print, the Print dialog box also opens, but the Quick Access Toolbar saves you a step. Ctrl+P is the shortcut keystroke to open the Print dialog box and many users find that to be the fastest way to open the box.

Start by selecting the range you want to print. The range need not be contiguous, but if you select a noncontiguous range, keep in mind that each selection will print on its own page, and the results might not be what you intended. All parts of the range to be printed must be on the same worksheet; each worksheet in a workbook gets a separate print area.

To define the selection as the default print area, click the Print Area button on your Page Layout ribbon and choose Set Print Area. Excel creates a named range called Print_Area in the current worksheet.

To delete the current print area selection and start over, click the Print Area button on your Page Layout ribbon and choose Clear Print Area.

TIP FROM

> If you define a print area on each worksheet, you can preview or print the defined print area on all sheets in the current workbook. Click your Office button and select Print (or press Ctrl+P) and select Entire Workbook from the Print What area of the Print dialog box.

When you define a specific print area, Excel prints only that area when you print your document using the Quick Print or Print dialog box default settings. If you define a print area and then add rows at the bottom or columns to the right of the data, the new data won't appear on the printed pages. Whenever you redesign a worksheet, make a special point to reset the print area.

INSERTING PAGE BREAKS

When you attempt to print a worksheet, Excel automatically inserts page breaks to divide it into sections that will fit on the selected paper size. (To see a dashed line that represents each break as you edit a workbook, click your Office button, select Excel Options, click Advanced, and click to set the Show Page Breaks option.) Excel doesn't analyze the structure of your worksheet before inserting page breaks; it simply adds a page break at the point where each page runs out of printable area. To make multipage worksheets more readable, you can and should position page breaks by hand.

To insert a manual page break, select the cell below and to the right of the last cell you want on the page. Then click your Page Layout ribbon's Breaks button, and choose Insert Page Break. To remove the page break, choose the Break's Remove Page Break option. To remove all manual page breaks from the current worksheet, select the entire sheet and then choose Reset All Page Breaks from the Breaks button's list of options.

TIP FROM

Ed & Woody

> To add only a horizontal page break, select any cell in column A; to add only a vertical page break, select any cell in row 1.

18

Excel includes an unusual view option called Page Break Preview that lets you see all page breaks and adjust them by clicking and dragging. To switch to this view, click the Page Break Preview button to the left of the status bar's Zoom button. As Figure 18.17 shows, this view lets you see your entire worksheet, broken into pages exactly as Excel intends to print it, with oversized page numbers laid over each block. (The numbers and lines don't appear on printed pages, of course.)

Dashed lines represent automatic page breaks inserted by Excel; solid lines represent manual page breaks. To adjust page breaks in this view, point to the thick line between two pages and drag it in any direction. To adjust the print area, drag the solid lines on any edge of the print area; cells that are not in the print area appear gray in Page Break Preview.

When using Page Break Preview, you'll have best results if you start at the top of the worksheet and work in the order it will print—normally from top to bottom and left to right, unless you've used the Page Setup group on your Page Layout ribbon to specify that you want to go across the worksheet before you work your way down. Move page breaks up or to the left only; moving them down or to the right can cause unpredictable results if you drag past the size of the page. In that case, Excel adds its own page breaks, undoing the effects of your painstaking page-breaking efforts.

Figure 18.17
The page numbers show the order in which pages will print. Drag the thick lines to adjust the print area and page breaks.

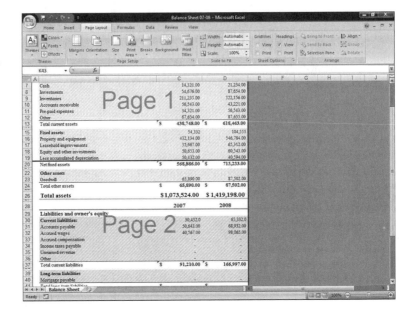

EXTRA ITEMS YOU CAN PRINT

On your Page Layout ribbon, you can specify that you want to print additional parts of a worksheet, such as comments, gridlines, and row or column headings. You can also control the way Excel translates colors into shades of gray. To see these additional printing options, click to display your Page Layout ribbon and click the Page Setup button (the small gray button to the right of the words Page Setup just below the Print Titles button). Click the Sheet tab to display the print options available to you. Some of these options are available elsewhere; for example, the Gridlines option appears on your Page Layout ribbon in its own group.

Table 18.2 lists the options you'll find.

TABLE 18.2 WORKSHEET PRINTING OPTIONS

Print Option	What It Does
Print Titles	If the data in your worksheet spans several pages, you might lose your points of reference, such as the headings above columns of data or to the left of each row. Identify the Rows to Repeat at Top of each page or the Columns to Repeat at Left of each page. (See the following section for more details.)
Gridlines	It's okay to show gridlines on draft worksheets; for final output, however, turn off gridlines and use borders to set off data areas.
Comments	By default, comments don't print; select this check box to print them on a separate sheet or as they appear onscreen.

Print Option	What It Does
Black and White	Excel translates color backgrounds to shades of gray on the printed page. This option removes most gray shades; it can also speed up print jobs on color printers. Use Print Preview to print a small test page to check results before printing a large sheet with this option.
Draft Quality	This option, which prints cell contents but skips gridlines and graphics, is unnecessary when using a laser printer but might be useful for speeding up printing on color output devices or slow inkjet printers.
Row and Column Headings	Prints letters and numbers to help identify cell addresses. Use in combination with the option to view formulas (click your Office button, then click Excel Options, Advanced, and scroll to the Display Options for This Worksheet section; click to select the option Show Formulas in Cells Instead of Their Calculated Results) when you want to print out the structure of a worksheet so you can study it.
Page Order	The graphic to the right of this option shows whether your sheet will print sideways first, then down, or the other way around. Adjust this order if necessary to make page numbering work properly.

LABELING PRINTED PAGES WITH HEADERS AND FOOTERS

Any worksheet that spans more than one page should include a header or footer (or both). An assortment of preconfigured headers and footers lets you number pages, identify the worksheet, specify the date it was created, list the author, and so on. Click to display your Page Layout ribbon and display the Page Setup dialog box by clicking its button to the right of the Page Setup group.

Click the Header/Footer tab to add or edit a header and footer. Click the Custom Header or Custom Footer button to build either of these elements with text of your choosing. Buttons on both dialog boxes let you add fields, such as the name of the current workbook or sheet or the current date and time. You can also use rich text formatting to adjust fonts, font sizes, colors, and other attributes of the custom header or footer.

Using the Custom Header or Custom Footer dialog box also allows you to include graphic images, such as a company logo, in a header or footer. Click the Insert Picture button and browse to any graphic file whose format is supported by Office. You can insert one and only one graphic in each section—left, center, and right. Click the Format Picture button to crop, compress, resize, or scale a picture file in a header or footer.

By default, Excel allows a half-inch for a worksheet's header or footer. If you want to maximize the amount of data on each page and you're not using a header or footer, open the Page Setup dialog box, click the Margins tab, and set the Header, Footer, Top, and Bottom boxes to 0. (On some printers, you might need to adjust the top and bottom margins to match the unprintable area on the page.)

 If your custom header or footer doesn't look right on the page, see "Adjusting Header and Footer Margins" in the "Troubleshooting" section at the end of this chapter.

TIP FROM

Ed & Woody

If you want a custom header or footer to appear on every worksheet you create, add headers and footers to each sheet in the template Excel uses when you create a new workbook. (The specific instructions for creating and saving this template appear later in this chapter.) Remember that each sheet has its own header and footer; if you want the same header to appear on each sheet in the template, you must create each one individually.

USING REPEATING TITLES FOR MULTIPLE PAGE PRINTOUTS

For worksheets that span multiple pages, you can repeat one or more rows or columns (or both) as titles for the data on each new page. On a typical budget worksheet, for example, the first column might contain income and expense categories, with columns for each month's data extending to the right across several pages. In this case, follow these steps to repeat the entries in a particular column or row as titles at the left of each page:

1. Open the Page Setup dialog box and click the Sheet tab.

2. To specify a column for titles, click in the Columns to Repeat at Left box. To use a row as titles on each new page, click in the Rows to Repeat at Top text box.

3. Click in any cell in the column or row you want to specify as the title. You need not select the entire row or column. If you select multiple cells, Excel uses all selected rows or columns as titles. If necessary, use the Collapse Dialog button to move the dialog box out of the way as you select.

4. Click the Print Preview button to ensure that you've configured the titles correctly. Click Print to send the worksheet to the printer immediately.

FORCING A WORKSHEET TO FIT ON A SPECIFIED NUMBER OF PAGES

Just as you can use the Zoom control to change the size of cells in a worksheet window, you can also reduce the size of data on a printout. Making the scale smaller lets you squeeze more rows and columns onto each page. If you want your printed worksheet to fit in a specific number of pages, Excel can calculate the *scaling percentage* for you:

1. Open the Page Layout ribbon's Page Setup dialog box and click the Page tab.

2. To scale the page to a fixed percentage, enter a value between 10 and 400 in the Adjust to % Normal Size box.

CAUTION

Choosing a number that's too low can result in a completely unreadable printout. In general, you should choose a scaling percentage lower than 40 only when you want to see the overall structure of your worksheet, not when you want to actually read and analyze data.

3. To adjust the printout to a fixed height or width, select the Fit To option. Use the spinner controls to adjust the number of pages you want the printout to occupy; leave one number blank if you want Excel to adjust only the width or height of the printout. The settings in Figure 18.18, for example, will scale the worksheet to no more than one page in width but allow the sheet to print additional rows on multiple pages.

Figure 18.18
These settings force Excel to scale the current worksheet to one page wide for printing.

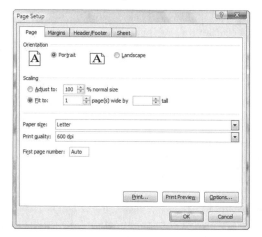

4. Click Print Preview to verify that your worksheet's print settings are correct.
5. Click Print to send the worksheet to the printer.

PUBLISHING A WORKSHEET TO THE WEB

Like Word and PowerPoint, Excel allows you to save files in HTML format so that you or anyone else can view them in a web browser. You can save a simple range of data, a chart, a worksheet, or an entire workbook in HTML format; when opened in a Web browser, the resulting file will closely resemble the worksheet as seen in an Excel window. Some differences in formatting and appearance are inevitable because of the way that browsers display HTML code.

When saving a workbook as a Web page, you must deal with the following noteworthy restrictions:

- HTML pages represent a static snapshot of the worksheet data; if you view worksheet data in a browser, you can't edit or rearrange cells or their contents unless you use interactive web components.

- Gridlines and row or column headings do not appear in the browser window.

18

TIP FROM

To set off rows and columns in an Excel-generated web page, don't rely on gridlines; instead, use borders to separate cells within the data area. Use shading and font formatting to set off headings, totals, and other distinctive elements.

- Some advanced features don't translate properly to HTML pages; for example, if you've saved multiple scenarios in a workbook, they'll be lost in translation, as will rotated text and some other forms of custom formatting.

 You'll see an error message if you try to publish a password-protected workbook as a web page; see "Passwords Don't Work on Web Workbooks" in the "Troubleshooting" section at the end of this chapter.

- The first cell that contains data in your workbook always moves to the top-left corner of the HTML page, even if you've left blank rows or columns as part of the design.

- When you save a workbook, all sheets from that workbook appear on the resulting web page, even those containing no data; the sheet tabs are visible in browsers that support *dynamic HTML*.

To save an entire workbook as an HTML page, click your Office button and choose Save As, Other Formats. Give the page a name, choose a destination folder (on a local hard drive, a network server, or a web server), and select Web Page for the Save as Type value. If you want the web page to be updated automatically whenever you update the underlying worksheet, click the Publish button to open the Publish as Web Page dialog box. Select the AutoRepublish Every Time This Workbook Is Saved check box and click Publish to save the web page.

TIP FROM

Don't forget the title. In the Save As dialog box, when you select Web Page for the Save as Type, you'll see a Page Title field. This is the title that will appear in the browser title bar and on the page itself. Excel doesn't add a title by default; click the text box to the right of the Page Title label to add or edit the title.

To save a chart or a range from a worksheet, make a selection first, and then click the Selection option in the Save as Web Page dialog box. To save a single sheet instead of an entire workbook, make sure only a single cell is active before you choose Save as Web Page, and then choose Selection: Sheet from the resulting dialog box.

To select multiple named items from a workbook, such as two sheets, a sheet and a chart, or multiple named ranges, click the Publish button in the Save as Web Page dialog box. That in turn displays the Publish as Web Page dialog box shown in Figure 18.19.

Figure 18.19
To save individual items from a workbook to a web page, select them by using this dialog box.

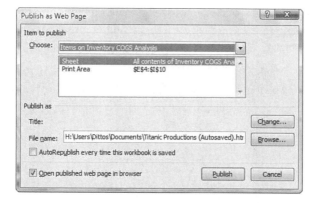

Choose a sheet name or another category, such as Range of Cells or Previously Published Items, from the Choose drop-down list. Then click an item from the list below your selection.

If your worksheet includes any external elements, such as graphics, the Save as Web Page option saves those elements as files in a separate subfolder that is linked to the HTML file containing the Excel data. If you intend to share the resulting file with someone else, save yourself some headaches and choose Single File Web Page from the Save as Type list on the Save As dialog box. This option embeds all elements of the HTML page in a single file with the .MHT file extension.

CUSTOMIZING EXCEL

 You can choose from dozens of options for adjusting the way Excel looks, acts, and works. Most are accessible in the Options dialog box that appears when you click the Office button and then click the Excel Options button. Various settings appear grouped in nine groups down the left Options window pane. Most of the settings you'll find throughout these groups are virtually unchanged since Excel 2002, although their location differs from the now-outdated Tools, Options dialog box that used to appear. In general, these options are self-explanatory, and many of them are variations on common features found in other Office applications. In this section, we highlight only the most useful:

- Options in the Popular group, shown in Figure 18.20, include hiding or showing interface elements such as the minitoolbar, a ScreenTip style, and Live Preview so you can see formatting changes before you apply them.

  The Include This Many Sheets setting enables you to change the number of blank sheets in each new workbook to any number between 1 and 255. Choose a smaller setting if you rarely use multiple sheets in a workbook or a larger one if you regularly create complex workbooks, such as consolidated budgets. You can also adjust the font that Excel uses for text and numbers in new worksheets. Choose a new font from the

Standard Font list, and specify a new size by using the Font Size drop-down list. (If you use Windows XP, you may see a slightly different set of options such as a ClearType setting.)

Figure 18.20
Use these options to adjust the default font size, number of worksheets per workbook, and other popular Excel options.

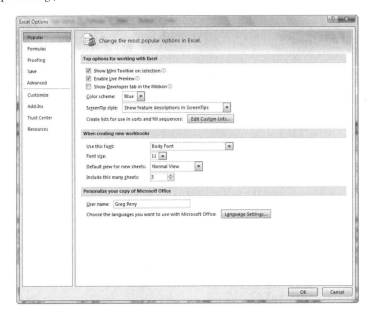

- The Formulas group enables you to change the default settings Excel uses for calculating formulas. In the days when 286 and 386 computers ruled the Earth, setting manual calculation was a survival tactic, because calculating a large worksheet could literally take hours. In an era when processor speed is measured in gigahertz, this option is necessary only for scientific applications and extraordinarily complex worksheets, in which you need to control the precise order of calculations. In general, the overwhelming majority of users should accept the default options on this group.

  The Error Checking and Error Checking Rules sections include settings that let you control background checking for common worksheet errors, including those in formulas. These options include check boxes that let you locate numbers stored as text (which can cause problems with formulas) and text dates containing two-digit years (which can result in Y2K-style date arithmetic errors).

  → For more details on how to check for errors in formulas, **see** "Testing and Debugging Formulas," **p. 618**.

- The Proofing group gives you access to AutoCorrect tools such as spell-checking and automatic formatting rules.

- The Save group offers file-related options such as an AutoRecover time you can set to save your worksheet every few minutes automatically so if your power goes out, you can recover recent work. The default is 10 minutes, but with today's computers being so fast, you can use a smaller increment to save your worksheet every 3 minutes or so in case of a problem.

→ For a discussion of Office AutoRecover features, **see** "Setting Up Automatic Backup and Recovery Options," **p. 70**.

■ Most of the options in the Advanced section cover 10 sections. The Editing Options section determine actions Excel is to take when you are working in cells, such as the action that is to take place when you press Enter. If you routinely select a range and fill in list values, consider changing the After Pressing Enter, Move Selection box from its default selection of Down to Right.

TIP FROM

> When entering currency values, such as entries in a check register, people with an accounting background often prefer to let Excel fill in the decimal point. If you choose the Automatically Insert a Decimal Point and leave it at the default setting of 2, entering 14398 will result in a value of 143.98. It's extremely unlikely you'll want to set this option permanently. If you use it frequently, however, create this simple toggle macro and assign it to a toolbar button so that you can switch into and out of fixed decimal mode on demand:
>
> ```
> Sub ToggleFixedDecimal()
>     Application.FixedDecimal = Not Application.FixedDecimal
> End Sub
> ```

■ The Cut, Copy, and Paste section determines whether Option buttons appear when you perform a paste or insert. If you find Smart Tags annoying, clear the Show Paste Options Buttons and Show Insert Options Buttons boxes.

■ The Display section determines display-related option settings such as the number of recent documents that show when you click your Office button (Ctrl+F is the shortcut key), and the default measuring unit used on your ruler.

■ The Display Options for This Workbook offers options that apply only to the workbook you select from the drop-down list box. You can elect to show scrollbars and sheet tabs, or not, for that one workbook without affecting all the other workbooks you manage. The Display Options for This Worksheet offers options that apply only to the sheet you select from the drop-down list box.

■ The Formulas section is designed to take advantage of all processors you might have on your computer as dual core computers have. If you have two processors, you should make sure to use both processors to achieve the maximum Excel performance.

■ The When Calculating This Workbook section is another workbook-specific section that determines how links are updated, precision is displayed, and dates are used for the selected workbook.

■ The General section enables you to request sound and animation when Excel does something and also determines whether you want to see add-in errors when a problem occurs with an add-in.

■ The two Lotus Compatibility sections provide tools for new Office users who have previously used Lotus 1-2-3. The Lotus Help option has been gone since Excel 2003, and in spite of the fact that Lotus spreadsheets dominated the massive spreadsheet market years ago, these are perhaps the least-used options in Excel today.

18

- The Customize group enables you to add commands to your Quick Access Toolbar, making that your own customized toolbar that contains the commands you want kept handy.

- The Add-ins group enables you to view and manage all the Excel add-ins you've installed.

→ For a discussion of add-ins, **see** "Secrets of the Office Masters: Managing Excel Add-Ins" later in this chapter, **p. 551**.

- The last two groups, Trust Center and Resources, provide more of a reference to Microsoft-related privacy and legal statements as well as links to get additional help and resources related to Microsoft Office including Microsoft Office online (see Figure 18.21). In the About section, you'll see your exact Excel version number, which is handy when you're about to apply an update or add-in that requires at least a specific version number before you can install it.

Figure 18.21
Microsoft's Office website provides a wealth of information and add-ins you may want to know about.

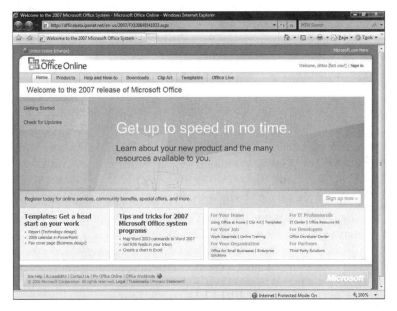

CHANGING DEFAULT FORMATTING FOR NEW WORKBOOKS AND WORKSHEETS

Every time you start Excel or create a new workbook without using a custom template, Excel uses its default settings. To change settings for the default workbook, create a new template called Book.xltx and save it in the XLStart folder. Follow these steps:

1. Create or open the workbook whose settings you want to use as Excel's defaults.

2. To change the style of all cells in the workbook, modify the Normal style. Add other named styles, macros, text, and other content or formatting. If you want to change the number of sheets or add headers and footers, go right ahead.

3. Click your Office button and select Save As. In the Save as Type box, choose Excel Template.

4. In the File Name box, enter **Book**. (Excel adds the .xltx extension automatically.) Do not save the file in the Templates folder; instead, save it in the XLStart folder. This folder is stored as part of your Windows profile, which you can reach through Windows Explorer by typing `%userprofile%\Application Data\Microsoft\Excel\XLStart`. (`%userprofile%` is a system variable that automatically opens your profile.)

5. Click OK to save the template. Any future workbooks you create will include the formats and content in this template.

> **NOTE**
>
> What's the difference between an Excel template and a worksheet? Structurally, the two file types are identical. Like a workbook, a template can include as many sheets as you want, with or without text, charts, and formatting. The key difference is this: When you open a workbook template, from within Excel or from an Explorer window, Excel leaves the original template file undisturbed and creates a new, unnamed document that is an identical copy of the template.

EXCEL STARTUP SWITCHES

When you start Excel, it normally opens a new workbook using the default settings, runs any AutoStart macros in the Personal Macro workbook, and switches to the default location for data files. To change any of these settings, use one of the following startup switches with the Excel.exe command line. You can use any of these switches as part of a shortcut or type them directly at the command line. You must make sure at least one space appears between Excel.exe and the switch. The following shows some of the more useful switches.

Switch	Function
/e	Forces Excel to start without displaying the startup screen or creating a new workbook (Book1).
/p <folder>	Sets the active path to a folder other than the default file location; enter the folder name (with its complete path) in quotes.
/r <filename>	Forces Excel to open the specified file in read-only mode.
/s	Forces Excel to start in safe mode, bypassing all installed add-ins as well as files in the Xlstart and Alternate Startup Files folders. Use this switch when debugging startup problems.

> **NOTE**
>
> To learn more about using command-line switches with Excel, see *Special Edition Using Microsoft Excel 2007* by Bill Jelen (published by Que). You can also search the online help for "Excel command-line switches" to find more information about them.

18

TROUBLESHOOTING

RESETTING THE LAST CELL

I pressed Ctrl+End to go to the last cell in my worksheet, but I ended up with the insertion point in a blank cell below and to the right of the actual end of the sheet. How do I convince Excel to jump to the actual end of the sheet?

When you select the last cell in a worksheet, either by using the Go To Special dialog box or by pressing Ctrl+End, Excel actually jumps to the last cell that has ever contained data or formatting. As you've seen, that can produce unexpected results, especially if you've deleted a large number of rows or columns (or both) from a list or worksheet model, or if you once placed a range of data in an out-of-the-way location and then moved or deleted it. In that case, selecting the Last Cell option might position the insertion point in a cell that's far beyond the actual end of the sheet. To reset the sheet so that you can truly jump to the last cell, delete all rows that are between the actual end of the sheet and the location that Excel insists on identifying as the last cell, and then repeat the process for all columns that match that definition.

If this is a common occurrence, you can create a one-line macro that will reset the last-cell location in the current sheet. Press Alt+F11 to open the Visual Basic Editor and enter the following code:

```
Sub ResetRange()
    ActiveSheet.UsedRange
End Sub
```

Be sure to save the ResetRange macro in an easily accessible location, such as your Personal macro workbook; then run it whenever you encounter a worksheet that needs this type of cleanup.

ADJUSTING HEADER AND FOOTER MARGINS

I created a complex custom footer for a worksheet, but when I try to print, the footer runs into data at the bottom of the sheet.

By default, Excel positions headers and footers a half-inch from the edge of the page and another half-inch from the worksheet's data. That's ideal for a one-liner, but if you try to add too much information in either place—for example, if you insert a long boilerplate paragraph required by a government agency at the bottom of each sheet—you'll quickly overrun that margin. If you decrease the Top or Bottom margins without also adjusting the Header or Footer margins, your data might also collide. You can enter an exact measurement for any of these margins by using the Margins tab on the Page Layout ribbon. If you've already created the header and footer, however, it's much easier to set the margins visually. Click the Office button and choose Print Preview; click the Margins button, if necessary, to display the margin markers along each edge of the preview window, and drag the indicators up or down until the preview looks right.

PASSWORDS DON'T WORK ON WEB WORKBOOKS

When I try to save a workbook as a web page, I get an error message warning that the workbook or sheet is password-protected.

For security reasons, Excel won't let you save a password-protected workbook or worksheet in HTML format. If the entire workbook is protected, you can still save an individual sheet. If any sheet is protected, however, you cannot publish that sheet or even a selection from it in HTML format. Temporarily remove the password protection by choosing Unprotect Sheet from your Review ribbon. After entering the correct password, you can publish the web page and then restore the protection.

DATA VALIDATION LIMITATIONS

I created a set of validation rules to protect data entry, but when users returned the filled-in worksheet, I found invalid data in those cells. I've triple-checked the data-validation rules, and I'm certain they're working properly. What's the problem?

Validation settings apply only when the user types data into a cell. If the user copies or cuts data from another source and pastes it into the cell via the Clipboard, Excel ignores the rule. There is no workaround for this problem, so you'll have to train your users not to use the Clipboard when filling in forms. Also, if any cell contains a formula as well as a data-validation rule, Excel ignores the rule.

If you want to triple-check the values in cells protected by data-validation rules to make sure they're correct, use the Go To dialog box. Press F5 and click the Special button, and then select the Data Validation option. Click All to see all cells with data-validation rules, or Same to see only cells whose rules match the currently selected cell.

SECRETS OF THE OFFICE MASTERS: INSTALLING AND MANAGING EXCEL ADD-INS

Excel includes a variety of special-purpose *add-ins*—compiled macros that add new functions beyond those already available. The Analysis ToolPak adds a broad range of worksheet functions to Excel's list of built-in functions, and the Solver add-in offers a wizard-based alternative to trial-and-error formula solving. Both add-ins are described in more detail in Chapter 20, "Using Formulas and Functions." You may need to supply the main Office CD (or point to a network install point) to install any of these add-ins.

By default, most of Excel's default add-ins are configured to be installed on first use. If you chose to cache the Office Setup files, this process should be nearly automatic. If you did not select this option, you'll have to hunt down the main Office DVD (or CDs depending on how you received it) each time you use an add-in for the first time—an annoying distraction, especially if you're in the middle of a deadline and the DVD isn't close at hand.

If you think you might use any of Excel's add-ins in the future, open Control Panel's Add/Remove Programs option, double-click the Microsoft Office 2007 entry, and launch the Windows Installer in maintenance mode. Go through the list of add-ins under the Excel group and change their status from Installed on First Use to Run from My Computer.

TIP FROM

To see a list of all add-ins, click your Office button and then click the Excel Options button. Click to display the Add-ins group and you'll see a button toward the bottom of the window called Go. Select Excel Add-ins from the Manage drop-down list and click Go. Excel opens the Add-ins dialog box shown in Figure 18.22, showing your currently installed add-in routines.

Figure 18.22
View all your currently installed add-in programs.

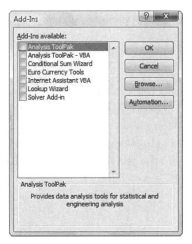

CHAPTER 19

ADVANCED WORKSHEET FORMATTING

In this chapter

Entering Data in an Excel Worksheet   554

Changing Formatting for a Cell or Range   560

Designing and Formatting a Worksheet for Maximum Readability   573

Using Conditional Formatting to Identify Key Values   583

Copying Formats with the Format Painter   587

Troubleshooting   588

Secrets of the Office Masters: Storing Multiple Scenarios in a Single Workbook   588

ENTERING DATA IN AN EXCEL WORKSHEET

In an Excel worksheet, what you see in a cell is not necessarily what's stored in that cell. If you enter a formula, for example, Excel stores the formula but displays its result. When entering numbers, dates, and text, you can go as quickly as you want, without too much regard for how they'll look in your worksheet; afterwards, use cell formatting instructions to specify how you want the cells' contents to display, including such details as decimal places, currency symbols, and how many digits to use for the year. Other cell formatting options let you adjust fonts, colors, borders, and other attributes of a cell or range.

A handful of buttons on your Home ribbon let you bypass dialog boxes for some common tasks, such as choosing a font or changing a range of cells to bold. If you're building a financial worksheet, click the Currency button to ensure that every number in a given range lines up properly and includes the correct currency symbol. To see the full assortment of Excel formatting options, select a cell or range and Format Cells button to the right of the label Font on the Home ribbon's Font group to open the Format Cells dialog box. All available cell formatting options are arranged on six tabs in the Format Cells dialog box.

 Excel 2007 uses Live Preview to show what many of your formatting changes will look like before you actually apply those formats. The Home ribbon's Cell Styles button displays a large assortment of formats you can apply to selected cells, for example; as you move your mouse over each style, your selected cells on the worksheet below change to show you the result of applying that style if you decide to do so. Excel 2007 puts cell-formatting even closer to you at times when you select a range of cells. After selecting text within a cell, a floating cell-formatting tool called the *minitoolbar* appears above your selection. You can choose one of the formats offered on the minitoolbar, or ignore it and the toolbar goes away when you move elsewhere.

USING THE GENERAL NUMBER FORMAT

On a new worksheet, every cell starts out using the General format. When the cell contains a constant value, Excel usually displays the exact text or numbers you entered; in cells that contain a formula, the General format displays the results of the formula using up to 11 digits—the decimal point counts as a digit. (Date and time values follow a special set of rules, as you'll see shortly.) If the cell is not wide enough to show the entire number, Excel rounds the portion of the number to the right of the decimal point, for display purposes only; if the portion of the number to the left of the decimal point won't fit in the cell or contains more than 11 digits, the General format displays the number in scientific notation.

To remove all number formats you've applied manually and restore a cell to its default General format, right-click and choose Format Cells, and then click the Number tab and choose General from the Category list.

NOTE

> Although it's not particularly intuitive, there's also a keyboard shortcut that applies the General format instantly to the active cell or current selection: Press Ctrl+Shift+~ (tilde) to reset cells to General format.

CONTROLLING AUTOMATIC NUMBER FORMATS

When you enter data in a format that resembles one of Excel's built-in formats, Excel automatically applies formatting to the cell. In some cases, the results might be unexpected or unwelcome:

■ If you enter a number that contains a slash (/) or hyphen (-) and matches any of Windows's date and time formats, Excel converts the entry to a date serial value and formats the cell using the closest matching Date format. If the date you enter includes only the month and date, Excel adds the current year.

→ In some cases, Excel picks up formatting from your Windows version; for details of how this interaction works, **see** "Setting Date and Time Formats," **p. 565**.

 If you import data into a worksheet, Excel might convert values that look like dates or times. For suggestions on how to prevent this from occurring, see "Stopping Automatic Conversions" in the "Troubleshooting" section at the end of this chapter.

■ If you enter a number preceded by a dollar sign, Excel applies the Currency style, with two decimal places, regardless of how many decimal places you entered. (If you've used the Regional Settings option in the Windows Control Panel to specify a different currency symbol, Excel applies the Currency style when you enter data using that symbol.)

> **NOTE**
>
> As explained later in this chapter, the Currency style is actually a variation of the Accounting format.

■ If you enter a number that begins or ends with a percent sign, Excel applies the Percent style with up to two decimal places.

TIP FROM

EQ & Woody

> Excel supports fraction formats as well, but entering data in this format is tricky. If you enter 3/8, for example, Excel interprets your entry as a date—March 8 of the current year—and formats it accordingly. To enter a fraction that Excel can recognize automatically, start with 0 and a space: 0 3/8. Excel correctly enters that number as 0.375 and changes the cell format to Fraction. Although Excel stores the number as 0.375, it is displayed as 3/8.

TIP FROM

EQ & Woody

> Excel also supports *compound fractions*—fractions that include a whole number and a fractional number, such as 12 1/8. Enter the whole number part (in this case, 12) followed by a space and then the fraction part. Excel displays the entry as 12 1/8 but stores it as 12.125. You'll find this technique invaluable if you ever have to perform calculations involving historical stock market prices; although most major markets have now moved to decimal pricing, some exchanges still use archaic fractional pricing—16ths, 32nds, even 64ths of a dollar!

19

- When you enter a number that contains a colon (:), Excel converts it to a time format if possible. If the number is followed by a space and the letter A or P, Excel adds AM or PM to the display format.

- If you enter a number that contains leading zeros (as in part numbers, for example, which might need to fill a precise number of characters), Excel drops the leading zero.

- When you enter a number that contains the letter E anywhere in the middle (3.14159E19, for example), Excel formats the cell using the Scientific option, using no more than two decimal places. In this case, Excel would display 3.14E+19.

- If you enter a number that includes a comma to set off thousands or millions, Excel applies the Number format using the default thousands separator as defined in Windows's Regional Settings. If the number you entered contains more than two decimal places, Excel stores the exact number you entered but rounds it for display purposes to no more than two decimal places.

To override any of these automatic number formats, you have four choices:

- After entering the data, click the Format Cells button (to the right of the Font group name) to open the Format Cells dialog box. (Press Ctrl+1 to quickly open this dialog box.)

- Enter an apostrophe before entering the number. When you do this, Excel formats the number as text and displays it exactly as entered. Note that this solution might have unintended consequences in formulas that use the value shown in that cell! Such character-based numeric values are nicely used for ZIP Codes and social security numbers, which you don't routinely perform calculations on.

- Enter a space character before entering the number. This prefix also tells Excel to format the number as text and display it exactly as entered. Note that this technique will not prevent Excel from converting a number to scientific notation, nor will it preserve leading zeros. It will, however, work with all other automatic formatting described in the previous list.

 - Click the Number Format drop-down list and select Text. This is your fastest way if the underlying data stored in the cell is correct and you just want to use a different display format.

Avoiding Rounding Errors

It's tempting to assume that because numbers look so orderly in Excel's row-and-column grids, they're also unfailingly accurate. That's not exactly so. To squeeze data so that it fits in a cell, Excel rounds numbers and truncates cell contents, usually without telling you. And there's an absolute limit on the precision of Excel calculations that affects every calculation you make.

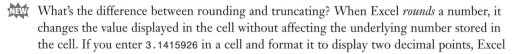 What's the difference between rounding and truncating? When Excel *rounds* a number, it changes the value displayed in the cell without affecting the underlying number stored in the cell. If you enter 3.1415926 in a cell and format it to display two decimal points, Excel

displays 3.14. If you later change the display format to show all seven decimal points, your number will appear exactly as you entered it. When Excel *truncates* data, on the other hand, it chops off digits permanently. If you enter a number with more than 15 decimal places, for example, Excel lops off the 16th and any subsequent numbers to the right of the decimal point. Fortunately, Excel 2007 does not truncate characters after the 255th character in a cell if you copy a worksheet that contains cells with more than 255 characters to another; previous Excel versions truncated all data after the first 255.

When Excel alters the display of a number, the most common cause is that the number is too long to fit in the active cell. Excel deals with this sort of data in one of the following three ways:

- When you enter data that is wider than the current cell, Excel automatically resizes the column. It does not resize a column if you have already set the column width manually. If the cell is formatted using General format, this automatic resizing stops when the number reaches 11 digits, at which point Excel converts it to scientific notation. If the cell is formatted using Number format, automatic resizing continues until the number reaches 30 digits.

- In cells using the default General format, Excel uses scientific notation to display large numbers if possible. The General format rounds numbers expressed this way to no more than six *digits of precision* (8.39615E+13, for example).

NOTE

> It's no accident that the total number of characters in the preceding example—including the decimal point, plus sign, and E—is 11. Regardless of column width, cells using the General format are always limited to 11 digits.

- In cells using any number format other than General, Excel displays a string of number signs (####) if the column is too narrow to display the number in scientific notation. You must change the cell's number format or make the column wider before Excel can display the number correctly.

19

The second most common cause of apparent errors in a worksheet occurs when the number of decimal cells you specify in a number format doesn't match the number of decimal places stored in that cell or range. Figure 19.1, for example, shows two identical columns of numbers. Because column A uses the General format, each number appears exactly as entered. Column B, on the other hand, is formatted with the Number format to show zero decimal places. When Excel performs the calculation on the numbers in column B, it uses the actual amount stored in the cell, not the rounded version you see here. It then displays the result without any decimal places, exactly as specified in the cell format. Although the sum of the rounded numbers in column B appears to be 16, Excel rounds the actual result to 15 for display purposes. Because of the mismatch between the numbers and their formatting, Excel (and, by extension, the author of this worksheet) appears incapable of basic arithmetic.

Figure 19.1
The values in these two columns are identical, with different formatting. Because of cumulative rounding errors, the numbers in column B appear to add up to 16, despite what the SUM formula suggests.

	A	B
1	2.3	2
2	2.5	3
3	2.5	3
4	3.1	3
5	2.75	3
6	2.2	2
7	15.35	15

That's a simple and obvious example, but subtle rounding errors can wreak havoc in an environment where you require precise results. To prevent rounding from making it look like your worksheet contains errors, always match the number of decimal places displayed with the number of decimal places you've entered in the row or column in question.

TIP FROM

Ed & Woody

If you must use rounded numbers in a worksheet, indicate that fact in a footnote on charts and reports you plan to present to others. Rounding can cause apparent mistakes, and anyone who sees your worksheet—or a chart or presentation slide based on those numbers—might make unflattering judgments about your accuracy if totals in a pie chart, for example, don't add up to 100%.

THE LIMITS OF PRECISION

There's an overriding limit to the degree of precision you can achieve with Excel. If you enter a number that contains more than 15 significant digits, Excel permanently and irrevocably converts the 16th and subsequent digits to 0. (It doesn't matter which side of the decimal point the digits appear on—the total number of digits allowed includes those on both sides of the decimal point.) Although you can display numbers with up to 30 decimal places, your calculations will not be accurate if Excel has to store more than 15 digits.

Excel includes a useful, but extremely dangerous, option to permanently store numbers using the displayed precision. If you've increased the numbers in a budget worksheet by 8.25%, for example, you might end up with three decimal places for some entries, even though only two are displayed using the Currency format. If you display the Options dialog box by clicking the Excel Options button after clicking your Office button, you'll see that the Advanced group has an option labeled Set Precision as Displayed. This option, located under the When Calculating This Workbook heading, converts all stored numbers in the current workbook to the values actually displayed. (Fortunately, the option doesn't change anything in any other workbook but the one you select it for.)

CAUTION

> When you use the Set Precision as Displayed option, Excel displays a terse dialog box warning you that your data will permanently lose accuracy. Believe it. This option affects every cell on every sheet in the current workbook, and it remains in force until you explicitly remove the check mark from this box. If you forget you turned on this option, even simple formatting choices like changing the display of decimal places will permanently change stored data. Unless you're absolutely certain that using this option will have no unintended consequences, you should treat it like dynamite.

TIP FROM

Ed & Woody

> The Precision as Displayed option affects all cells in the current workbook, and there's no way to apply it just to a selected range. If you want to change the precision of a selection, use the Windows Clipboard to control this option precisely—in the process, you can also avoid any unintended ill effects. Open a new, blank workbook, copy the range you want to change from the original workbook, and paste it into the blank workbook. In the blank workbook, check the Precision as Displayed option. Click OK when you see the warning dialog box. Now copy the changed data to the Clipboard and paste it over the original data. Close the blank workbook without saving it, and you're finished.

WORKING WITH NUMBERS IN SCIENTIFIC NOTATION

Scientific (or exponential) *notation* displays large numbers in a shorthand form that shows the first few digits along with instructions on where to place the decimal point. To convert a number written in scientific notation to its decimal equivalent, move the decimal to the right by the number that appears after "E+"; if there's a minus sign after the E, move the decimal to the left. In either case, add extra zeros as needed. Thus, 8.23E+06 is actually 8,230,000, and 3.82E–07 is .000000382.

Numbers expressed in scientific notation are often rounded. When you see numbers in General format expressed in scientific notation, you'll see a maximum of six significant digits, even if the cell is wide enough to hold more. To display a number in scientific notation using more digits of precision, open the Format Cells dialog box and choose the Scientific option from the Category list. Use the spinner control to set a fixed number of decimal places, between 0 and 30.

ENTERING NUMBERS AS TEXT

Hands down, the most confusing option on the Number Format drop-down list box in the Home ribbon's Number group, which also appears on Number tab of the Format Cells dialog box, is Text. Use the Text format when you want to enter numbers in a cell, but you want Excel to treat them as though they were text. You might use this format, for example, when entering a list of part numbers that you will never use in calculations.

If you apply the Text format to a cell and then enter or paste a numeric value into that cell, Excel adds a small green triangle in the top-left corner of the cell, indicating a possible error. Selecting that cell reveals a Smart Tag that warns you the number is stored as text.

19

Use the Convert to Number option to change the cell's contents to a number format, or click Ignore Error to keep the text and make the green triangle vanish.

→ For more information about Smart Tags, **see** "Common Formatting Options," **p. 95**.

→ To learn how to check an Excel workbook for errors, **see** "Checking for Errors in a Worksheet," **p. 621**.

When you format numbers as Text, Excel ignores them in formulas such as SUM() and AVERAGE(). It also aligns the cell's contents to the left rather than the right. Unfortunately, applying the Text format requires that you work around an admitted bug that still exists in Excel 2007. If you format the cells first, then apply the Text format, and finally enter the numbers, Excel treats the data as text, just as you intended. However, if you try to apply the Text format to numbers that are already in your worksheet, Excel changes the alignment of the cell, but not the data stored there. After applying the Text format, you must click in each reformatted cell, press F2, and then press Enter to store the number as text. The error-checking tools in Excel 2007 do not identify cells formatted this way, either.

If you format a cell as text and enter a formula in that cell, you see the formula itself rather than its result. To fix the display, change the cell format back to General, select the cell, press F2, and then press Enter.

CHANGING FORMATTING FOR A CELL OR RANGE

In general, as noted previously, Excel stores exactly what you type in a cell. You have tremendous control over how that data appears, however. Number and date formats, for example, give you precise control over commas, decimal points, and whether months and days are spelled out or abbreviated. And if you can't find the precise format you're looking for, Excel lets you create your own custom format.

SETTING NUMBER FORMATS

How should Excel display the contents of a cell? You have dozens of choices, all neatly organized by category on the Number tab of the Format Cells dialog box. Many of these are also available on the Home ribbon, especially in the Number Format drop-down list box and the rest of the Home ribbon's Number group. The Format Cells dialog box gives you the most pinpoint precision over your formats.

To specify exactly how you want the contents of a cell or range to appear, follow these steps:

1. Click the cell you want to format, or select a range, and then open the Format Cells dialog box by pressing Ctrl+1 or by clicking the Format Cells button to the right of the Font group name on your Home ribbon.

Few keyboard shortcuts in all of Office are as useful as Ctrl+1, which opens Excel's Format Cells dialog box. When you're formatting a large or complex worksheet, this key combination can save a startling number of mouse clicks. Even if you generally don't use keyboard shortcuts, this one is worth memorizing. Note that you must use the number 1 on the top row of the keyboard; the 1 on the numeric keypad won't work.

2. In the Format Cells dialog box, choose an entry from the Category list on the left.

3. If the category you selected includes predefined display options such as the Date and Time categories, select one from the Type list. Adjust other format options (currency symbol, decimal point, and so on), if necessary.

To quickly adjust the number of decimal points in a cell or range, make a selection and click the Increase Decimal or Decrease Decimal buttons on the Home ribbon's Number group. Each click adds or subtracts one decimal point from the selection.

4. Inspect the Sample box in the upper-right corner of the Format Cells dialog box to see how the active cell will appear with the format settings you've selected. Click OK to accept the settings and return to the editing window.

The following number format categories are available:

■ General, the default format, displays numbers as entered, using as many decimal places as necessary, up to a maximum of 11 digits. It does not include separators between thousands. No additional options are available.

■ Number formats let you specify the number of decimal places, from 0 to 30 (the default is 2), as well as an optional separator for thousands, based on the Windows Regional Settings. You can also choose one of four formats for negative numbers (see Figure 19.2).

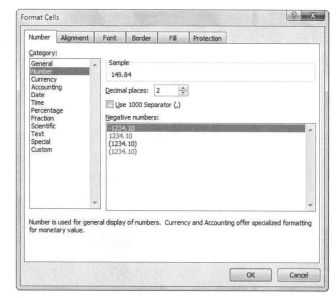

Figure 19.2

- Choices in the Currency category display values using the default currency symbol, as specified in the Regional Settings options of Control Panel. You can adjust the number of decimal places from its default of 2 to any number between 0 and 30 and select a format for negative values (see Figure 19.3).

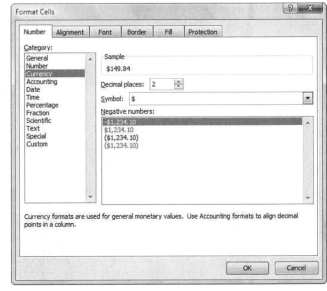

Figure 19.3

- Accounting formats are similar to those in the Currency category, except that currency symbols and decimal points align properly in columns and you can't choose a format for negative values.

With Accounting formats, the currency symbol ($ in U.S. English installations) sits at the left edge of the cell. This effect can be odd in wide columns that contain small numbers; in that case, choose a Currency format instead, if possible (see Figure 19.4).

Figure 19.4
Use currency symbols, instead of accounting symbols, in wide columns containing small numbers.

■ The Date category includes 15 formats that determine whether and how to display day, date, month, and year. All versions of Excel since Excel 2000 include a pair of Year 2000–compatible date formats that use four digits for the year (see Figure 19.5).

Figure 19.5
Excel includes Year 2000–compatible date formats.

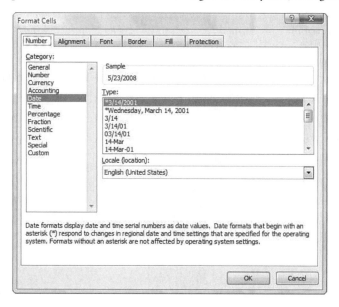

■ The Time category includes eight formats that determine whether and how to display hours, minutes, seconds, and AM/PM designators (see Figure 19.6).

Figure 19.6
Excel offers a variety of formats for displaying times.

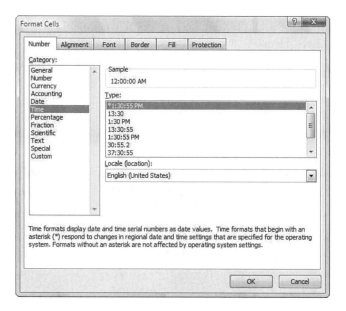

19

- Applying the Percentage format multiplies the cell value by 100 for display purposes and adds a percent symbol; the only option here lets you specify the number of decimal places, from 0 to 30 (the default is 2).

- Fraction formats store numbers in decimal format but displays cell contents as fractions using any of nine predefined settings; to display stock prices using 8ths, 16ths, and 32nds, click Up to Two Digits in the Type list (see Figure 19.7).

Figure 19.7
Excel displays your fractions as fractions, although it cleverly stores those fractions in decimal format.

- Choose Scientific to display numbers in scientific notation; you select the number of decimal places, from 0 to 30.

- Applying the Text format displays cell contents exactly as entered, even if the cell contains numbers or a formula.

- The four choices in the Special category allow you to select formats for long and short U.S. ZIP Codes, phone numbers, and social security numbers. You enter the number without any punctuation, and Excel adds hyphens and parentheses as necessary for display purposes only (see Figure 19.8).

- Choose the Custom option to define your own display rules. Start with a built-in format and use symbols in the formatting instructions; see "Custom Number Formats" later in this chapter for more details on custom number formats.

Figure 19.8
The special category formats are lifesavers when you need to enter ZIP Codes, phone numbers, and social security numbers.

SETTING DATE AND TIME FORMATS

Normally, Excel stores exactly what you type into a cell. That's not the case when you type a recognizable date or time, however; when storing date and time information, Excel first converts the value you enter into *Serial Date format*. This numeric transformation explains how Excel can perform calculations using date and time information. Understanding the following facts is crucial to working effectively with Serial Date formats:

- Excel converts the date to a whole number that counts the number of days that have elapsed since January 1, 1900. Thus, the serial date value of December 31, 2008 is 39813.

- When you enter a time (hours, minutes, and seconds), Excel converts it to a fractional decimal value between 0 (midnight) and 0.999988 (11:59:59 p.m.). If you enter a time of 10:00 a.m., for example, Excel stores it as 0.416667.

- If you combine a date and time, Excel combines the serial date and time values. Thus, Excel saves December 31, 2008 10:00 a.m. as 39813.42.

> **NOTE**
>
> When you enter only a date, Excel converts it to a serial value and uses 0 (or 12:00 a.m.) as the time value. If you enter only a time, Excel tacks on a date value of 1; if you later format this cell to show the date and time, Excel displays the nonsense date 1/0/1900.

The transformation to a serial value happens as soon as you enter a date or time value in a cell. At the same time, Excel automatically applies the default Date or Time format to your cell so that the data you enter displays correctly. You can choose a different Date or Time format to change the display format of date or time values. If you change the format of the cell to General or Number, however, you will see the serial values instead of the dates you expect.

Conversely, if you accidentally apply the Date format to a cell that contains a number, the result is likely to be nonsense, especially if the number is relatively low. Choose the General or Number format to display the cell's contents correctly.

TIP FROM

If the display of dates is important to you, be aware of the unusual interaction between Excel's date and time formats and those you define in Windows's Clock, Language, and Region group (in some Windows versions, this appears as Regional Settings or Regional Options). These linked formats appear at the top of the Date and Time lists in the Format Cells dialog box, with an asterisk in front of the format. When you change the date format in Windows, the format in your worksheet changes, too—if you've used one of these formats.

Excel transforms dates and times to serial values so that you can use them in calculations. Because date and time values are stored as numbers, you can easily enter formulas that calculate elapsed time. If you include an employee's hire date as part of a list, for instance, you can use a simple formula to compare that value to today's date and determine whether the employee has qualified for participation in a profit-sharing or stock-option program. If you enter start and end times for each participant in a road race, you can easily calculate the total elapsed time and determine the top finishers.

After you enter the employee's start date in C1 and your report date in C2, for example, you can calculate the difference between the two dates by using the formula =C1-C2.

TIP FROM

Unfortunately, Excel outsmarts itself when you use this type of formula. Because it sees dates in both cells used in the formula, it automatically applies a date format to the cell containing the formula. As a result, the cell contents display as a nonsense date. Reset the cell's format to General or Number to correctly display the difference between the dates.

To use a date directly in a formula, enclose it in quotation marks first: =Today()-"1/1/2008" counts the number of days that have elapsed since January 1, 2008, for instance.

NOTE

Excel's Options dialog box's Advanced group includes the Use 1904 date system. This obscure option is necessary only when exchanging files with users of old versions of Excel for the Macintosh, which started the calendar at the beginning of 1904 rather than 1900. Mac Excel versions since including Excel 98 handle this conversion seamlessly. Under normal circumstances, you should never need to use this option.

Excel and Year 2000 Issues

The much-feared global Y2K crisis never happened. Planes continued to fly, power stations hummed along, and banks didn't run out of money. Yes, the world successfully entered the new millennium, but that doesn't let you off the hook when it comes to Year 2000 (Y2K) issues. Excel's default settings correctly handle most formulas that include dates from different centuries. But a few "gotchas" linger for the unwary:

- When you enter a date before January 1, 1900 in an Excel worksheet, the date appears as text. As far as Excel is concerned, dates before the 20th century simply don't exist—that's bad news for historians and scientists hoping to use Excel to plot dates that go back more than a century.

- On the other hand, dates after December 31, 1999 don't represent a problem. In fact, Excel worksheets will accept any date through December 31, 9999 (that's a serial date value of 2958465, if you want to try it for yourself).

TIP FROM

EQ & Woody

> If you need to track timelines and perform calculations for dates before the beginning of 1900 (to chart long-term records of earthquake activities, for example), don't use Excel. Instead, fire up Access, which can correctly handle dates as early as January 1, 100 (Common Era). If you're a student of ancient history, you'll need to use another program—or perhaps you can make do with clay tablets.

Because Excel stores dates as serial values, it is unaffected by most garden-variety Y2K problems. In practice, however, you might encounter Y2K problems if you enter or import data that includes only two digits for the year. When Excel encounters dates in this format, it has to convert the year to four digits; in the process, it's possible to select the wrong century. When translating two-digit years, Excel uses the following rules:

- Excel automatically converts dates entered using the two-digit years 00 through 29 to the years 2000 through 2029. Thus, if you enter or import the value 5/23/08, Excel stores it as serial value 39591, or May 23, 2008.

- When you enter the two-digit years 30 through 99 as part of a date, Excel converts the dates using the years 1930 through 1999. Thus, when you enter or import the value 9/29/55, Excel stores it as serial value 20361, or September 29, 1955.

On a new worksheet, Excel automatically displays dates using a four-digit format. However, if you design a worksheet so that some dates display only two years (or if you use an older worksheet that was designed using those formats), you might not realize that Excel has stored the wrong data. In that case, any calculations you make might be off by a full century. To avoid inadvertently entering or importing incorrect data, get in the habit of entering all dates using four-digit formats for the year: 5/23/2008. Excel stores this date correctly regardless of the Date format you've chosen for display purposes.

When importing data that includes dates with two-digit years, check the format of the original data carefully. You might need to manually edit some dates after importing. Pay special attention to worksheets that were originally created using pre-2000 versions of Excel for Windows or the Macintosh, because the algorithms those programs use to convert two-digit years are different from those in Excel 2000 and later versions.

The automatic date conversion routine is a clever workaround, but don't rely on it. Entering or importing two-digit years is guaranteed to cause problems in the following circumstances:

- In the banking industry, in which dates beyond 2029 are common in 30-year mortgages that begin in the year 2000 or later. If you enter the start date as 2/1/08 and the end date as 2/1/38, your loan will start out 70 years overdue.

- In any group that includes milestone dates—birthdays, graduation dates, and so on—for an older population. If you enter a birth date of 6/19/27, your worksheet might assume that the person in question isn't born yet.

TIP FROM

This can't be said strongly enough or repeated too often: Get in the habit of using four-digit years whenever you enter or display a date in a worksheet.

CREATING CUSTOM CELL FORMATS

If the exact number format you need isn't in Excel's collection of built-in formats, create a custom format. Custom formats let you specify the display of positive and negative numbers as well as zero values; you can also add text to the contents of any cell.

TIP FROM

Excel saves custom number formats in the workbook in which you create them. To reuse formats, add them to the template on which you base new workbooks. To copy cell formats from one workbook to another, copy the cell that contains the custom format, click in the workbook where you want to add the format, and choose Paste Special from the Home ribbon's Paste button.

The list of 35 custom formats in the Type box includes some that are already available within other categories, as well as a few you won't find elsewhere. It's almost always easier to design a custom format if you start with one that already exists. To create a custom number format, open the Format Cells dialog box and choose the format you want to start with. Then click Custom at the bottom of the Category list. Excel displays the codes for the format you just selected in the Type box, ready for you to modify. The example shown in Figure 19.9, for example, shows the results when we chose a Currency format and changed the symbol from the U.S. dollar sign to the Euro. Although the switches for these codes are undocumented, this technique adds them to the Type box, making it easy to define a new format that uses this symbol correctly.

Figure 19.9
Enter custom format codes here. Note the Sample area, which shows how the contents of the active cell will appear.

Custom formats use format codes to tell Excel how to display digits, decimal places, dates and times, and other details. Each custom format can include up to four sections, separated by semicolons, as shown in the example in Figure 19.10. Using all four sections defines display formats for positive numbers, negative numbers, zero values, and text, respectively. If you enter only two sections, Excel uses the first set of instructions for positive numbers and zero values and the second for negative numbers. If you enter only one section, that format will apply to all numbers you enter. You don't need to enter a format for each section, but if you plan to skip a format option (specifying formats only for positive numbers and zero values, for example), insert a semicolon for each section you skip.

Figure 19.10
Custom number formats can contain up to four sections.

_($* #,##0_);_($* (#,##0);_($* "-"_);_(@_)

TIP FROM

EQ & Woody

When creating an extremely complex custom format, working with the narrow text box in the Format Cells dialog box can be difficult. To make life easier, select the contents of this box, and then copy them to a friendlier editor, such as Notepad or Word. Edit the format codes, and then use the Clipboard to paste the results back into the dialog box.

Creative use of custom number formats can help you deal with tricky data-entry challenges. For example, how do you make it easy to enter a serial number with leading zeros? Suppose your company uses invoice or part numbers that must be exactly seven digits, with no exceptions. If the number you enter includes fewer than seven digits, you want Excel to pad the beginning of the entry with as many zeros as it takes to reach that magic number. Entering a number like 0001234 won't work, because Excel considers the leading zeros insignificant digits and strips them before storing the value in the cell.

The solution is to create a custom format that includes a zero for each digit you want to include in the displayed result—in this case, 0000000.

TIP FROM

Ed & Woody

> To guarantee that only correct data appears in the cell, combine this custom format with a data-validation rule. If your company policy says the number must be larger than 1000, create a validation rule that restricts data entry to whole numbers (to prevent stray decimal points or text from messing up the list) between 1001 and 9999999. The all-zeros display format guarantees that any data within this range will display as exactly seven digits, with leading zeros if necessary.

CUSTOM NUMBER FORMATS

Custom number formats let you round or truncate numbers, control the number of decimal places or significant digits, and make sure amounts line up properly in columns. Use the codes shown in Table 19.1 to define the display format.

TABLE 19.1   CUSTOM NUMBER FORMAT CODES

Code	What It Does	How You Use It
#	Display significant digit	Using the format #.# displays all significant (nonzero) digits to the left of the decimal point and rounds to one digit on the right of the decimal point; if you enter 0.567, this format displays .6.
0	Display zero if the number has fewer digits than the number to format	The format 0.000 always displays exactly three decimal points; for numbers less than 1, it includes a 0 to the left of the decimal point.
?	Align decimal points or fractions	Click any of Excel's built-in Fraction formats, and then choose Custom to see an example of how to use this placeholder.
.	Decimal point	To round the cell's contents to a whole number, leave off the decimal point.
,	Display thousands separator or scale number by multiple	Inserting two commas of 1,000 after a number scales it by a million; to display a large number (163,200,000) in an easier-to-read style (163.2 MM), enter this format: #0.0,," MM"
%	Display the number as a percentage of 100	If you enter 8, Excel displays it as 800%. To enter 8%, start with a decimal point and a zero: .08.
[color]	Show the cell contents in specified color	Choose one of eight colors—Black, Blue, Cyan, Green, Magenta, Red, White, Yellow—for any section; you must use brackets and enter the color as the first item in each section, like this: [Blue]#,##0;[Red]#,##0;[Black]0.

CUSTOM DATE AND TIME FORMATS

Excel's selection of ready-made date and time formats is extensive, but there are several situations in which you might want to create your own. For example, if your company uses a special date format to identify dates on an invoice, you can enter a format such as yyyymmdd to display a date as 19990321.

Custom date and time formats are also useful on billing worksheets for professionals who charge by the minute or hour, or if you've captured data from time sheets filled out by hourly workers. Table 19.2 includes examples of date and time codes you can add to custom formats.

TABLE 19.2 CUSTOM DATE/TIME FORMAT CODES

Code	What It Does	How You Use It
d, dd m, mm	Day or month in numeric format, with or without leading zero	Use the leading zero when you want columns of dates to line up properly; to add a zero to the date only, use this format: m/dd/yyyy.
ddd, mmm dddd, mmmm	Day or month in text format, abbreviated or full	Use ddd or mmm to show abbreviations such as Wed or Jan; use dddd and mmmm for the fully spelled out month or day: January and Wednesday.
mmmmm	Month as first letter only	Potentially confusing, because it's impossible to distinguish between January, June, and July, or between March and May.
yy, yyyy	Year, in two- or four-digit format	If you're concerned about possible confusion caused by the Year 2000, specify four-digit years.
h, hh m, mm s, ss	Hours, minutes, or seconds, with or without leading zero	Use a leading zero with minutes and seconds; to store precise times, add a decimal point and extra digits after the format: h:mm:ss.00.
A/P, AM/PM	Show AM/PM indicator	Insert after time code to use 12-hour clock and display AM or PM (6:12 p.m.); otherwise, Excel displays the time in 24-hour format (18:12).
[h], [m], [s]	Show elapsed time in hours, minutes, or seconds	Add brackets to display elapsed time rather than a time of day. Add decimals for seconds; for instance, for a worksheet containing race times, use this format: [m]:ss.00.

ADDING TEXT TO A CELL

To display text in a cell that contains numbers, Excel includes a selection of special format codes. Use this type of format to add a word like "shortage" or "deficit" after a negative number, for example. Because the format doesn't change the contents of the cell, the number you entered will still work in formulas that reference that cell.

You can add the space character, the left and right single quotation mark, and any of the following special characters without enclosing them in double quotation marks:

$ - + / ( ) : ! [ct] & ~ { } = < >

To add other text to a cell, use the codes in Table 19.3.

TABLE 19.3 CUSTOM TEXT FORMAT CODES

Code	What It Does	How You Use It
*	Repeat characters to fill cell to column width	Enter an asterisk followed by the character you want to repeat. Use *- in the third position of a custom format to replace zero values with a line of hyphens, for example.
__ (underscore character)	Add a space the width of a specified character	Enter an underscore followed by the character whose width you want to use. Several built-in formats use _)) with positive number formats, for example, to make sure they line up properly with negative numbers that use parentheses.
\	Display the character that follows the backslash	To add a space and the letter P or L after a positive or negative value, use this format: #,##0_) \P;[Red] (#,##0) \L.
"text"	Display the text you enter inside the double quotation marks	Remember to add a space inside the quotes when necessary. For example, to display a negative amount as $514.32 Loss in red, enter this format: $0.00" Profit";[Red] $0.00" Loss".
@	Display the text entered in the cell	Use this code only in the fourth (text) section in a custom format to combine the entered text with other text. If you include a text section without the @ character, Excel hides any text in the cell.

TIP FROM

EQ & Woody

When creating a custom number format, first click in a cell that contains data you want to see in the new format. As you edit the custom format, the Preview region of the Custom Format dialog box shows you how the active cell's contents will appear in the new format.

ADDING CONDITIONS TO A DISPLAY FORMAT

You can also use *conditions* as part of custom number formats. Conditions use comparison operators and are contained in brackets as part of a format definition. Look at the built-in Phone Number format (in the Special category) to see how this option works:

```
[<=9999999]###-####;(###) ###-####
```

If you enter a number of seven or fewer digits in a cell that uses this format, Excel treats it as a local phone number and adds a hyphen where the prefix appears. If you enter a number greater than seven digits, Excel uses the second part of the format, displaying the last seven digits as a phone number and any number of digits prior to that number as an area code in parentheses.

The results of this format can be absurd if you enter a number that's smaller than 7 digits or larger than 10 digits. Here's how to use conditions to customize this format. The example shown here assumes you work in the 212 area code and want to add that code to the beginning of any 7-digit (local) number; if the number uses more than 10 digits, the default condition at the end kicks in, adding the international dialing prefix (+011) and splitting the digits before the number into country and city codes.

```
[<=9999999](212) ###-####;[<=9999999999](###) ###-####;"+011 "(#-##) ###-####
```

TIP FROM

Ed & Woody

Don't confuse these custom formats with conditional formatting, which is described later in this chapter. If you want to change the font or color of text based on values displayed in the cell, use the Conditional Formatting option on the Home ribbon (described later in this chapter). The conditional display formats shown here are most useful when you want to subdivide a number with punctuation marks or change the number of digits displayed. You can effectively combine this type of format with conditional formatting—for example, if the user enters a phone number with six or fewer digits, you might display it in red to help it stand out as a possibly invalid number.

19

DESIGNING AND FORMATTING A WORKSHEET FOR MAXIMUM READABILITY

If you enter data into a new worksheet without adjusting any formatting first, every cell will look exactly the same, and anyone reading the worksheet will be forced to work to pick out the important details. Want to make it easier on your audience? Set off different regions of a worksheet by using custom cell formatting—larger, bolder fonts for headings, for example, plus borders around the data area with a double line to mark where the data range ends and the totals begin. Carefully resetting row heights and column widths, wrapping and slanting text, and adding background shading can make the entire sheet easier to follow.

CHANGING FONTS AND CHARACTER ATTRIBUTES

The default worksheet font (11-point Calibri, and Arial-style of font) is fine for basic data entry, but for any worksheet more complex than a simple list, you'll probably want to adjust fonts to squeeze more data onto printed pages while beefing up titles, totals, and category headings with larger, bolder fonts.

→ If you're entering data in a table (formerly called a list), some cells format themselves automatically; for details, **see** "Controlling Data Entry with AutoComplete Options," **p. 518**.

If you select a cell or range, you can apply font formatting to the entire contents of the selection. You can also apply different fonts, font sizes, colors, and font attributes to different words or characters in the same cell. In either case, you can use the Font and font size lists on the Home ribbon's Font group. You can also open the Format Cells dialog box and click the Font tab (see Figure 19.11) for access to all font formats, including some options you won't find on the ribbon, such as strikethrough and double-underline attributes.

Figure 19.11
Options on the Font tab let you format an entire cell or selected words or characters within a cell.

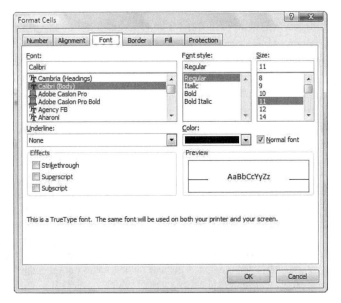

Most of the options on the Font tab of this dialog box are fairly straightforward. One check box deserves some explanation, however. When you add custom font formatting, you automatically clear the Normal Font check box. Check this box again to remove all font formatting from the current cell or selection and restore Excel's default style.

 If you're having trouble restoring default font formatting to a cell, see "Clicking Twice for Normal" in the "Troubleshooting" section at the end of this chapter.

USING CELL STYLES

NEW One way to apply an instant and striking format to a cell or cell selection is to format using Excel 2007's Cell Styles Gallery. Clicking the Cell Styles button on your Home ribbon displays the Cell Styles Gallery, an assortment of predesigned cell formats, as Figure 19.12 shows. Point to a cell or select a cell range and click the Cell Styles button to display the styles. As you move your mouse over the available styles in the gallery, your worksheet's format updates to reflect what each style change will make your data look like. This is an example of Excel 2007's Live Preview mode.

Figure 19.12
Use Excel's Live Preview mode to see what your cell formatting changes will do to your worksheet's data.

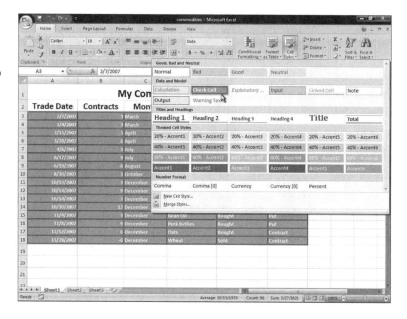

The gallery's styles are grouped so you can select what matches your data best. You'll find cell styles named Heading 1, Title, and 60% Accent. If you're formatting a selected range that includes the title of a worksheet, you might want to select one of the title cell styles.

TIP FROM

EQ & Woody

> If you format a cell and you'll need to reuse that format later, for example, because it uses your corporate logo's font and colors, you can save that cell's formatting as a new cell style. Click the cell with the formatting you want to save and display the list of cell styles. Click to select the New Cell Style option and name your new cell style. The next time you open the Cell Styles list, you'll see your style at the top in the Custom group. Right-click your new style (or any other style) and modify, duplicate, or delete the style depending on the option you select. When you want to create a new cell style that's a lot like an existing one, right-click that cell style, select Duplicate, click Format to modify the format the way you want it to look, and type a new name for your new style.

The Cell Styles Gallery is intended to be modified by you. You should consider adding any and all special cell formats you create that you may want to reuse in the future. Over time your Cell Styles Gallery will become your own formatting factory that quickly formats key elements of the worksheets that you create and manage. What used to take several steps now takes two or three clicks.

TIP FROM

EQ & Woody

> If you find yourself using the Cell Styles button a lot, and you probably will after you begin to add your own styles to the list, right-click over any cell style and select Add Gallery to Quick Access Toolbar. A Cell Styles Gallery button will appear at the right of your Quick Access toolbar so you can quickly display the gallery no matter what other ribbon is showing at the time.

WORKING WITH FORMATS, STYLES, AND ALIGNMENT

You'll find countless uses for Excel 2007's rich cell-formatting capability. The range shown in Figure 19.13, for example, uses different font formatting for the heading, year lines, and internal table data. Decreasing the size of some text inside a cell provides a useful way to format trademark and copyright symbols as well as other special characters within a cell, such as superscripts and subscripts.

Figure 19.13
Mix and match font formatting within a cell to emphasize one type of data over another.

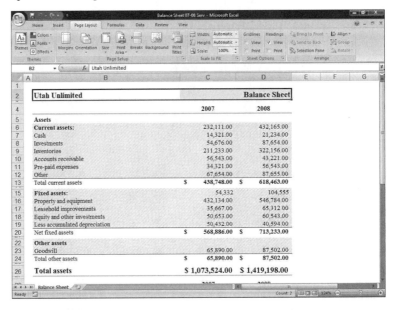

To enter a manual line break within a cell, position the insertion point at the spot where you want the break to appear and press Alt+Enter. Unfortunately, there's no easy way to copy rich formatting from one cell to another. If you use the Format Painter or the Home ribbon's Clipboard group to copy formats, only the first font is copied. That's why the more cell styles you create, the easier it will be in the future to reuse the styles you like.

An obscure check box on the Alignment tab of the Format Cells dialog box actually has a major effect on formatting. Check the Shrink to Fit box when you want Excel to automatically adjust the font size when the contents of a cell are too wide to fit. This option doesn't change the formatting applied to the cell; it changes the scaling instead, going up or down in 1-point increments. If you enter more text or adjust the width of the column, Excel changes the size of the font automatically so that you can continue to see its contents. Use this option with care—if you format an entire column as Shrink to Fit and then fill it with data that varies in length, the results can look like a ransom note.

ALIGNING, WRAPPING, AND ROTATING TEXT AND NUMBERS

When you use the default General format, cells containing text align to the left, and those with numbers align to the right. You can change the alignment of any cell or range by using the Align Left, Center, and Align Right buttons on the Home ribbon's Alignment group.

Use the Wrap Text option on the Format Cells dialog box's Alignment tab to handle long strings of text that don't fit in a cell. Wrapped text is useful for column headings that are much longer than the data in the column. You can also use wrapped text to create tables, where each cell in a row holds an entire paragraph. Excel wraps text to additional lines automatically, maintaining the column width you specified. To control the location of each break, press Alt+Enter. To use text wrapping, follow these steps:

1. Select the cell or range that contains the text you want to wrap. Right-click and choose Format Cells.

2. Click the Alignment tab on the Format Cells dialog box and check the Wrap Text box.

3. Adjust the vertical alignment if needed. For column headings with long and short entries, for example, choose Center from the Vertical drop-down list. Headings formatted this way seem to "float" instead of sit on the bottom of the cell. For text in a table, choose the Top format so that each paragraph begins at the same point.

4. Click OK to apply the new format. Now, instead of disappearing from view when they reach the right edge of the cell, the text you enter begins filling additional lines in the same cell.

Two other alignment options can help make worksheets easier to read. You can change the orientation of a column heading to any angle, including straight up or down. Slanting column headings can save space and give tables a professional look when you have narrow columns with lengthy titles. To help set off groups of items in a column, indent the cells in second and subsequent levels. (See the before and after worksheets at the end of this chapter for examples of all these alignment options.) This option is especially useful when you want to distinguish subheadings from headings at the beginning of a row.

To indent a cell or range of cells, follow these steps:

1. Select the cell or range you want to format, right-click, and choose Format Cells.

2. Click the Alignment tab. In the Text Alignment section, click the Horizontal drop-down list and choose Left (Indent).

3. Use the Indent spinner to select the indent level for the selection. For each number, Excel adds approximately as much space as a capital M. For the outline levels in column A of Figure 19.14, we used settings of 1 and 2, respectively.

4. Click OK to accept the changes and return to the worksheet.

19

TIP FROM

EQ & Woody

NEW

If you need to add several horizontal left indents only, as is often the case, which was done for Figure 19.14's Balance Sheet items that align to one another depending on their hierarchy, the fastest way to do so it is to click the Home ribbon's Increase Indent and Decrease Indent buttons on the Alignment group. You don't have to open the Format Cells dialog box to increase or decrease such an indent quickly for any selected range of cells.

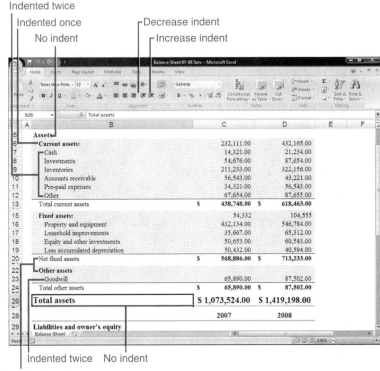

Figure 19.14

Indented twice
Indented once
No indent
Decrease indent
Increase indent

Indented twice   No indent
Indented once

Use the Home ribbon's Orientation button on the Alignment group to change the orientation of column headings so that they slant up or down. The following angle options appear when you click the Orientation button:

- Angle Counterclockwise
- Angle Clockwise
- Vertical Text
- Rotate Text Up
- Rotate Text Down
- Format Cell Alignment

In most cases, the Orientation button will do the job, but for a more precise placement of angled titles and headings, you can use the Format Cells dialog box in the following way:

1. After entering the text for the headings, select one or more cells, right-click, and choose Format Cells.

2. Click the Alignment tab, and then point to the control in the Orientation section of the dialog box and drag it up or down to the desired angle, as shown in Figure 19.15, or use the spinner to specify a precise angle by degrees.

Figure 19.15
Click the line between the word Text and the red square; then drag it up or down to arrange text at a space-saving angle.

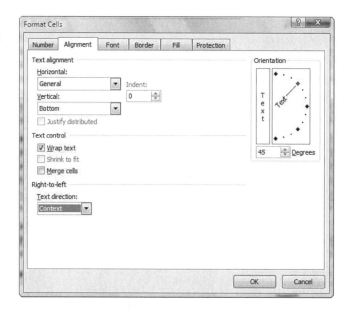

3. Click OK to accept the changes and return to the worksheet.

Word doesn't allow you to position headings using any orientation except horizontal or vertical. If you want to add a table with slanted headings to a Word document, create the table in Excel, and then use Paste Special and choose Microsoft Excel Worksheet Object to embed the worksheet range, complete with slanted headings.

Vertical headings use little column width, but they can be difficult to read. You have two choices when changing a heading to vertical orientation. Click the skinny box just under the word Orientation to stack letters one over another. This option is most effective with short words in all capitals. You can also change the orientation to 90° to turn the cell on its side, so the contents read from bottom to top.

USING BORDERS, BOXES, AND COLORS

You can create a distinctive identity for sections of a worksheet by using borders, boxes, and background colors. Dark backgrounds and white type help worksheet titles stand out. Soft, light background colors make columns of numbers easier to read. Use alternating colors or shading to make it easy for the eye to tell which entries belong in each row, even on a wide worksheet that contains many columns of data.

TIP FROM

When preparing a worksheet that you intend to print on a black-and-white printer, test different color combinations. Use the printout to decide which colors are best for you. Sometimes, for example, it's easier to read black type on a light yellow background (which appears gray) than on a background on which you specify a shade of gray.

The Borders, Fill Color, and Font Color buttons on the Home ribbon work much as you would expect. After selecting a cell or range, click the arrow to the right of each button to choose a specific option from the drop-down list.

These buttons don't give you access to every formatting option, however. For maximum control over borders and colors, first select the cells or range you want to format; then right-click and choose Format Cells. Click the Border tab (see Figure 19.16) to add and remove lines around the selection.

Figure 19.16
Use borders to distinguish sections of your worksheet. Note that this range includes three different line styles.

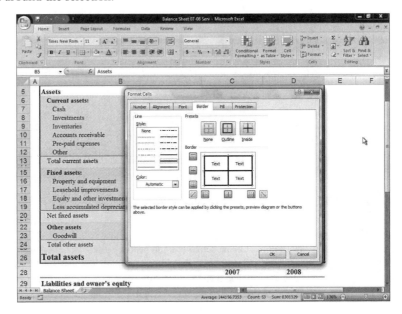

To create custom borders, follow these steps:

1. Before you add any lines, choose a line style—thick, thin, doubled, dotted, or dashed—from the Style box on the left.

2. Choose a different border color, if you like, from the Color drop-down list. Colors are most effective with thick lines.

3. Click the Outline button to add lines in the thickness and color you specified on all four sides of the active cell. If you selected a range, click Outline to draw a box around the range, and click Inside to draw borders around every cell in the selection.

4. Click any of the buttons in the Border section to add one line at a time, on the left, right, top, or bottom of the cell, or diagonally. Click again to remove the line. The preview area shows which edges currently have borders.

NOTE

You can also click directly on lines in the preview area to add or remove borders.

5. You can mix and match line styles and colors, even on different borders of the same cell. Click the line style or change the color, and then click the button in the Border area to change the style.

6. Click OK to close the Format Cells dialog box and return to the worksheet.

Getting borders just right on a complex worksheet often takes multiple iterations. The trick is figuring out which regions need separate formatting and which have common borders. For example, you might need to select the entire data area first to add a thick border around the outside. Then select the heading rows to adjust their borders, which might be thinner and lighter. Select the data area next, to add, remove, and format interior rules between rows and columns that contain data. Finally, if your data area contains a totals row at the bottom, select that row (or the last row of data) to add a double line between the end of the data range and the totals.

MERGING CELLS

On a highly structured worksheet, merging cells can help you show the relationship between headings and subheadings. In a list where two or three rows have the same value in the first column, for example, you could merge those cells to make the common nature of those rows truly stand out. You can combine adjacent cells in a row, a column, or any contiguous range.

To quickly merge two or more cells, select the cells and click the Merge and Center button on the Home ribbon's Alignment group. Excel displays a dialog box warning you that when you merge cells, you will lose all data except the contents of the top-left cell in the selection. Click OK to continue or click Cancel if you want to back out and move the data before you lose it.

→ Merged cells can cause problems when you create scenarios on a worksheet; for details, **see** "Secrets of the Office Masters: Storing Multiple Scenarios in a Single Workbook," **p. 588**.

To edit text in a merged cell, click in the cell and begin typing. You can also change the alignment of the merged cells to left or right, without changing the merge.

You might encounter problems when you try to cut and paste merged cells, or when you attempt to sort a list that contains a merged cell. To restore the merged cells to their normal position on the grid, click to make the merged cell active, and then click the arrow to the right of the Home ribbon's Merge and Center button to display your Merge and Center options. Select Unmerge Cells to return the merged cells to their individual cell positions.

CHANGING ROW HEIGHT AND COLUMN WIDTH

On a new worksheet, every row is exactly 12.75 points high, and every column is 8.43 characters wide. (If the default font for Normal style is a proportional one such as Arial or Calibri, Excel uses a lowercase x as the character to measure.) As you design a worksheet and fill it with data, however, you'll need to change the size of rows and columns. A column that contains only two-digit numbers doesn't need to be as wide as one that's filled with category headings, for example.

19

Some of these adjustments happen automatically. If you change the font size of text in a cell, the row automatically changes height to accommodate it. Likewise, when you enter data that's too wide to fit in the default column width, Excel expands the column.

→ For an explanation of how columns expand to accommodate data you enter, **see** "Avoiding Rounding Errors," **p. 556**.

You can also adjust row heights and column widths manually in any of three ways:

- Use Excel's AutoFit feature to set column widths and row heights automatically. Double-click the right border of a column heading to adjust column width to fit the widest entry in the column. Double-click the bottom border of a row heading to resize a row to accommodate the tallest character in that row. If you select multiple rows or columns, you can adjust them all at once.

- Click and drag any column or row to a new size. Point to the thin line at the right of the column heading or the bottom of a row heading until the pointer changes to a two-headed arrow. Click and drag the column or row to the desired width or height, and then release the mouse button.

TIP FROM

Ed & Woody

> When you use the mouse to adjust column widths and row heights, ScreenTips show the exact height and width, in characters (for columns) or points (for rows). Curiously, both ScreenTips also show the measurements in *pixels*—use this scale if you're optimizing a worksheet for viewing in a browser at a specific resolution, for example, 800×600 pixels.

- To set a precise height or width, use a dialog box. Right-click any row number and select Row Height. Enter any number between 0 and 409 (points). Or right-click a column name and select Column Width. Enter any number between 0 and 255 (characters).

To adjust more than one row or column, select the group of rows or columns first. Then point to the border of any row or column heading in the selection and drag to the desired size. When you release the mouse button, Excel adjusts all selected rows or columns to the height or width of the column you selected. This technique is especially useful when you're putting together a budget worksheet with 12 columns, one for each month. After entering data, select all 12 columns and drag them to the correct width.

Here are some expert tips to help you when working with row heights and column widths:

- Most of the column- and row-sizing commands you're learning about in this section are available from the Home ribbon's Format button that you find in the Cells group (see Figure 19.17).

- To hide any row or column, set its height or width to 0 (click the right side of a column heading and drag to the left, or click the bottom of a row heading and drag to the top). To make such a hidden column or row visible, select the columns or rows on either side of the hidden one, then right-click and select Unhide.

- To resize a column according to the contents of one or more specific cells in that column, make a selection and then click the Cells group's Format button and delete AutoFit Column Width.

Figure 19.17
Use the Cells group's Format button on your Home ribbon to perform most of the cell-, row-, and column-sizing adjustments you need to make.

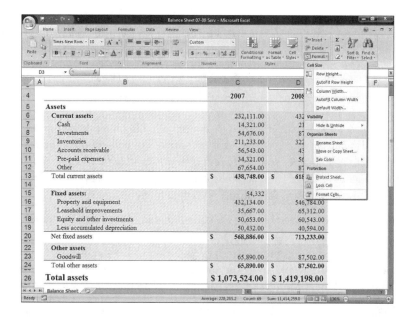

- To automatically change the size of a group of columns or rows without dragging, use the Format button's AutoFit option.

- If you've customized column widths and/or row heights and you want to copy this information along with data, copy and paste the entire row or column, not just the individual cells. Use the Column Widths option on the Paste Special dialog box to duplicate the arrangement of columns from one worksheet to another.

- To change the default standard width for all columns in the current worksheet, click the Cells group's Format button and select Default Width. Enter the new column width (in characters) in the dialog box. The new width will not apply to columns whose width you have already modified.

USING CONDITIONAL FORMATTING TO IDENTIFY KEY VALUES

Conditional formatting letsyou set font attributes, colors, and other formatting options that cause data to appear differently based on the value displayed in a cell. Most often, you'll use this feature to set an alarm that highlights data that is outside of an expected range. For example, you might attach conditional formatting to a row of totals on a daily sales report, displaying each cell's contents in bold red letters if it falls below a target level and in bright green if the number is significantly above average. In an employee roster, you might use bold formatting to identify the names of employees who are overdue for a formal evaluation.

TIP FROM

EQ & Woody

Conditional formats are most effective when used sparingly. If every cell in a worksheet has "special" formatting, nothing stands out. The best use of this option is to highlight truly unusual conditions that require action—when you open a worksheet and see one or two items in bright red, they get your full attention.

Some predefined number formats automatically display negative numbers in red, but conditional formatting gives you far greater control. For cells whose contents match one or more conditions you define, you can specify a new font style (bold italic, for example), use the underline or strikethrough attributes, or change the borders and color of the selection. You cannot use conditional formatting to change fonts or font sizes.

To use conditional formatting, select a cell or range, and then click the Home ribbon's Conditional Formatting button. You'll see a list of ways you can conditionally format cell data. You could, for example, define a condition Cell Value Is Greater Than or Equal to 20000, and Excel would apply the special formatting if the value is 30,000 but would leave the standard format in place if the value is only 15,000.

To highlight cells when a certain condition becomes true, select the Highlight Cells Rules option. You'll select from these comparison choices: Greater Than, Less Than, Between, Equal To, Text that Contains, A Date Occurring, and Duplicate Values. Selecting any of these options displays a corresponding dialog box such as the one in Figure 19.18.

Figure 19.18
Determine the range that should trigger the conditional format; here if data falls between 118,782 and 327,704 Excel changes the cell's font color to dark red and the background fills with a light red color to make the data stand out.

For more control, click the Home ribbon's Conditional Formatting button, select Highlight Cells Rules, and select More Rules. Figure 19.19 shows the New Formatting Rule dialog box that appears. Here you can create conditional formatting rules that format data throughout your worksheet based on specific values, based on cells that contain certain values, based on the top- or bottom-ranked values in the entire worksheet (great for spotting exceptional values), based on values above or below the average of the cell values, based on the presence of duplicate values, and based on a formula you enter that determines which cells to format a certain way depending on the result of that formula.

Figure 19.19
Create your own formatting rules.

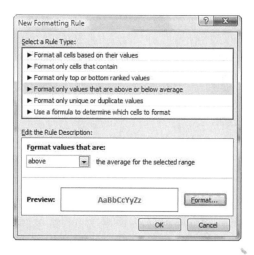

TIP FROM

EQ & Woody

> If you enter a formula in this box, it must use a logical function that evaluates to True or False. For most garden-variety conditions, you should choose the Cell Value Is formula.

Formulas in conditional formats can apply to any data on the worksheet, not just the data in the current cell, or even to external data. For example, in a list where Column A contains dates and Columns B, C, and D contain sales figures, you might want to automatically apply shading to each row that contains data for a Monday; this trick helps you pick out each new week at a glance. If the data begins in row 2, create a conditional format using the formula =WEEKDAY($A2)=2, using the shading you want to see. Copy that format to all cells in the data range, using the Paste Special dialog box or the Format Painter (described in the following section), to automatically shade every Monday row in the entire list.

Your Home ribbon's Conditional Format button offers several additional ways you can format cells based on the data in those cells. I'll explain those in the coming sections.

USING TOP/BOTTOM RULES

The Top/Bottom Rules option, for example, conditionally formats cells to your specifications if the values in the cells fall in the top 10, top 10%, bottom 10, or bottom 10% of all values in the worksheet. (You can adjust the 10 and 10% test value to any number you want to use.)

USING COLORED DATA BARS

Colored data bars, new in Excel 2007, display a colored bar graph based on the relative values of data in a selected range. When you select a range of cells and click the Conditional Format button and then select Data Bars, a list of colored data bar choices appears. Select a color and Excel places a colored bar chart on top of the data in the range so you can quickly see how the values stack up against one another, as Figure 19.20 illustrates. As with the other conditional formats, you can create your own formatting rules by selecting More Rules from the Conditional Formatting Data Bars drop-down list.

19

Figure 19.20
Let the colored bars show you relatively how your data values compare to one another.

	432,165.00
	21,234.00
	87,654.00
	322,156.00
	43,221.00
	56,543.00
	87,655.00
$	618,463.00

USING COLOR SCALES

 A gradient color-shading feature called color scales is new to Excel 2007 and works somewhat like data bars in that the feature colors cell backgrounds based on the values in those cells compared to values in the other selected cells. Select a range of cells. Click the Conditional Formatting button to display the conditional formatting options and select Color Scales. Choose one of the coloring scale styles offered. Excel will then color the cells based on your color selection that colors the cells one of the two or three colors in the scale you select. For example, if you select the Red-Yellow-Blue color scale, Excel colors the background of the selected range's cells one of those three colors, based on which third each value falls in. If, for example, a value falls in the upper one-third of the range of selected values, Excel would color the background in that cell red. As with the other conditional formats, you can create your own formatting rules for color scales by selecting More Rules from the Conditional Formatting Color Scales drop-down list.

USING ICON SETS

 By conditionally formatting data using the Conditional Formatting drop-down list's Icon Sets option, Excel displays an icon next to your data in each selected cell to show visually through the icon where the value falls in the range. For example, Figure 19.21 shows a series of arrows being selected as a possible icon set for the range of cells. With Excel's Live Preview mode, you see where those icons will fall as you point to them in the selected range. The icon selected depends on how each value compares to the other values in the range. As with the other conditional formats, you can create your own formatting rules for icon sets by selecting More Rules from the Conditional Formatting Icon Sets drop-down list.

NOTE

> If you create your own conditional formatting rules and want to erase them or change them, select Clear Rules or Manage Rules from the Conditional Formatting button's drop-down list.

 Is conditional formatting producing unexpected results? For possible solutions, see "Working with Multiple Conditions" in the "Troubleshooting" section at the end of this chapter.

→ To prevent out-of-the-ordinary data from appearing in a worksheet in the first place, use data-validation rules; **see** "Restricting and Validating Data Entry for a Cell or Range," **p. 532**.

Figure 19.21
Icons can indicate how your data compares in a range of cells.

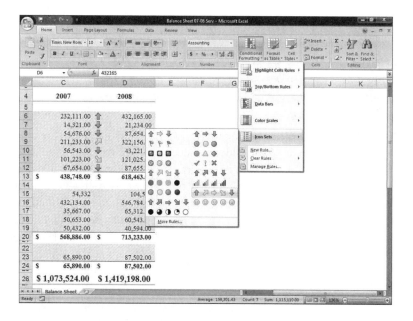

COPYING FORMATS WITH THE FORMAT PAINTER

Use your Home ribbon's Format Painter button to quickly copy all formats—fonts, colors, borders, data bars, color scales, icon sets, alignment...the works—from one cell to another. Select a cell that has the formatting you want to copy, and then click the Format Painter button and click the cell to which you want to copy the formatting. (If you select a range of cells to copy from, Excel repeats the formatting in your selection.)

If you want to copy formatting to multiple cells, select the cell whose formats you want to copy, and then double-click the Format Painter button to lock it in position. Click each destination cell to copy formatting. When you're finished, click the button again or press Esc to turn off the Format Painter.

TIP FROM

EQ & Woody

If you select an entire column or row, you can use the Format Painter to copy column widths and row heights. After the pointer turns to the paintbrush shape, click the heading of the row or column you want to change. Note that this technique will also copy other formats (fonts, colors, and so on) from the selected row or column.

→ For an overview of other Officewide formatting options, **see** "Common Formatting Options," **p. 95**.

TROUBLESHOOTING

STOPPING AUTOMATIC CONVERSIONS

After importing data into a worksheet from text files and databases, I noticed that Excel converts some data to date serial values and other data to scientific notation. I want the information to appear in my worksheet exactly as it did in the database. Is there any way to change it back?

No, unfortunately. When Excel sees a value that looks like a date or time or scientific notation, either when you type a value into a cell or when you import a database, it converts the value automatically as you type or import. There is no way to reverse this conversion. If you have serial numbers that use the format ##X####, where each # is a number and the X is a letter, Excel converts any serial number that contains the letter E in that position to scientific notation. Your best option is to edit the text or database file, adding an apostrophe to the beginning of each field that contains values Excel will try to convert. In that case, Excel imports the data in text format exactly as it appears.

CLICKING TWICE FOR NORMAL

I formatted text in a cell using more than one font, and I want to restore Excel's default font format. I opened the Format Cells dialog box, clicked the Font tab, and checked the Normal Font box once, but my formatting stays exactly as it was. What's the secret?

When you have multiple font formats applied to different words or characters in a cell, the Normal Font check box is checked, but it's grayed out. To restore the default formatting, click twice to clear the box (exactly the opposite of what you normally do), and then click OK to close the dialog box. Now reopen the dialog box and check the Normal Font box again. This time your change will stick.

WORKING WITH MULTIPLE CONDITIONS

I applied conditional formatting to a cell, but the formatting doesn't appear on some cells, even though the data in those cells meets the conditions I specified.

If you specify multiple conditions and more than one is true for a given cell, Excel applies the formats of the first true condition it encounters and ignores the second and third conditions. If you've defined conditions that have the potential to overlap, arrange them in order so that the most important one (or the one least likely to be true) is first in the list.

SECRETS OF THE OFFICE MASTERS: STORING MULTIPLE SCENARIOS IN A SINGLE WORKBOOK

One of Excel's most valuable hidden features is its capability to store multiple scenarios within a single workbook. Creating scenarios helps you plan for a future in which you can't be certain that your worksheet model is accurate, especially when a change in one assumption will have a ripple effect on other values that affect the bottom line. Scenarios are useful in these two circumstances:

- **When the underlying assumptions depend on external factors out of your control, such as the weather or the economy**—For example, if you sell heating oil or umbrellas, you might create a P and L forecast using multiple scenarios to compare the results of strong sales in cold, wet weather and weak sales if the winter is mild and dry.

- **When you want to perform what-if analyses that test the bottom-line effect of price increases or capital expenditures**—For instance, the classic demand curve from Economics 101 says that raising prices past a certain point might reduce demand so much that profits actually suffer, whereas cutting prices might cause sales to grow tremendously and swell the bottom line. Use scenarios in combination with market research to test the bottom-line impact of a 10% price cut, a 5% price hike, and a 10% increase.

TIP FROM

Ed & Woody

> You often can accomplish the same goal by creating multiple workbooks within a single worksheet, starting with a basic model and creating a copy for each scenario–best case, worst case, and so on. For simple analyses, where the underlying assumptions remain the same and you need to show revised totals, you also can add an extra row or column using slightly different formulas. Reserve scenarios for complex analyses where the changing assumptions include many related factors.

Adding scenarios to a worksheet is a three-step process. First, create a worksheet that includes all the data and formulas you want to use in your comparison. Next, select specific cells you want to change as part of each scenario. (The changing cells typically contain values used in one or more formulas in the sheet.) Finally, create named scenarios and enter the data in the changing cells for each one. By switching between scenarios, you can watch the bottom line change—and even change the bars and columns in charts based on data in the worksheet.

When putting together a fiscal forecast, for example, you might want to test the impact of various growth scenarios on your expenses. In the first scenario, you increase the number of employees (and thus salaries, payroll taxes, benefits, and other expenses tied to head count) to handle anticipated new business. In the second scenario, you freeze hiring and outsource the increased workload instead (keeping salaries at their current level but increasing expenses for contract labor). In the third scenario, you analyze what happens if you kick off a major hiring program and rent new office space (besides the increases in labor costs, you'll have to adjust for higher rent, utilities, and maintenance).

To create a worksheet that includes multiple scenarios, follow these steps:

1. Create the basic worksheet containing all the data and formulas you want to use in your first scenario.

2. Select up to 32 cells that will change in each scenario. Although you can select the changing cells and enter data at the same time you create a scenario, it is much, much easier to build scenarios in this order.

3. Click the What-If Analysis button on your Data ribbon. Select Scenario Manager. In the Scenario Manager dialog box, click the Add button to display the Add Scenario dialog box shown in Figure 19.22.

Figure 19.22
Give each scenario a name and add a descriptive comment; if you selected the changing cells before displaying this dialog box, your selection appears here.

CAUTION

There's no requirement that you select the same set of changing cells in each scenario; however, we strongly recommend that you do so. The purpose of creating scenarios is to show you various outcomes when you control specific input assumptions. If you use different changing cells in each scenario, your workbook essentially becomes an uncontrolled experiment, and the same data could result in different results for a given scenario, depending on which scenarios you view first.

4. In the Scenario Name box, enter a name that describes the scenario you're creating. You'll use this name to view and edit scenarios later, so keep the name short and meaningful: Best case and Worst case, for example. By default, the Comment box at the bottom of this dialog box contains your name and the date you created the scenario. If your scenario includes assumptions that aren't readily apparent, add a detailed description here.

5. Select protection options for the scenarios on the current worksheet. (By default, the Prevent Changes option is checked and the Hide option is unchecked.) Click OK. The Scenario Values box appears, as shown in Figure 19.23.

Figure 19.23
Use this dialog box to enter values for the changing cells in each scenario.

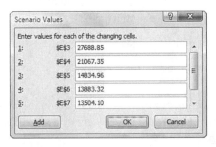

6. Check the values you want to use for each of the changing cells in this scenario, and change any of them, as necessary.

TIP FROM

EQ & Woody

> Normally, the Scenario Values dialog box displays cell references. However, if you use range names for the changing cells, those names will appear in this dialog box, making entering data and verifying that the values in each changing cell make sense much easier.

7. If your other scenarios are relatively uncomplicated, with only a handful of changing cells, click the Add button and enter the numbers for each scenario directly in this dialog box. If the underlying worksheet is complex, however, you'll probably find it easier to close the Scenario Manager dialog box, enter your data, and repeat steps 2–6 to create additional scenarios. When you finish, the dialog box should look something like the one in Figure 19.24.

Figure 19.24
Select a scenario and click the Show button to display the worksheet with that scenario's values.

NOTE

> Click any scenario to change it. When you do, Excel automatically updates the comment field with a line that tells which user updated the scenario and when.

To view different scenarios, open the Scenario Manager dialog box, select a scenario name, and click the Show button (or double-click the scenario name). You can drag the Scenario Manager dialog box out of the way to see the changed values in your worksheet. If you want to scroll or edit the worksheet, however, you must close this dialog box.

TIP FROM

Ed & Woody

Viewing a worksheet that contains scenarios can be confusing. Unless the Scenario Manager dialog box is open, how do you know which scenario you're looking at? Use text labels to solve this problem elegantly. Although it's most common to select cells with numeric values as the changing cells in a worksheet with scenarios, you can also enter text in a changing cell. Set aside one cell on your worksheet to contain a description of the current scenario and make it a changing cell as well. When you create each scenario, be sure the contents of this cell are accurate. Using this technique, you'll always be able to see which scenario is on display, just by looking at this cell.

After creating scenarios, you can add, remove, or change scenarios by using the same basic procedures. Two options in the Scenario Manager dialog box are particularly interesting for advanced users:

- **Merge**—Click this button to consolidate the data from changing cells into a new worksheet. Start in a new worksheet and open the workbooks that contain the scenarios you want to merge. The Merge Scenarios dialog box lists all open workbooks, and when you select one, you can pick from a list of worksheets within that workbook (the status bar tells you whether any scenarios exist in the sheet you've selected). Click OK to open the Scenario Manager dialog box, and then click Show to add the data from the changing cells to the current sheet. This technique is especially useful when you've passed out several copies of a worksheet template and you want to copy some but not all of the scenarios to the new sheet.

- **Summary**—Click this button to produce a report that arranges the values from the changing cells in all scenarios into a new sheet in the current workbook. Select the Scenario Summary option to display the data in a neatly formatted table; use the Scenario PivotTable option to display data in a format in which you can manipulate it further.

CHAPTER 20

USING FORMULAS AND FUNCTIONS

In this chapter

Entering and Editing Formulas   594

Using Range Names and Labels in Formulas   601

Manipulating Data with Worksheet Functions   604

Finding the Right Function   608

Testing and Debugging Formulas   618

Troubleshooting   624

Secrets of the Office Masters: Using Goal Seek to Find Answers   625

ENTERING AND EDITING FORMULAS

Formulas add intelligence to a workbook. Using formulas, you can manipulate values (text, numbers, or dates), perform simple or complex calculations, and display alternative results based on logical tests. A formula can be as simple as a reference to another cell, or it can go on for hundreds of characters, with as many as seven functions nested within other functions. Regardless of its complexity, however, a formula must begin with an equal sign (=). If you start a formula with a plus sign (+) or minus sign (–), Excel adds an equal sign to the beginning of the formula.

Formulas consist of three basic building blocks: *operands* (the elements to be calculated), *operators*, and *worksheet functions*:

- **Operands**—The data to be calculated in a formula can include any combination of the following: *constant values* (numbers, text, or dates you enter directly in a cell or formula, for example); cell or range references; names that refer to cells or ranges; or worksheet functions. When you use a cell or range reference in a formula, Excel substitutes the contents of that address the same as if you had typed it in directly.

- **Operators**—Formulas can use any of six basic arithmetic operators: addition (+), subtraction (–), multiplication (*), division (/), percent (%), or exponentiation (^). You can also use comparison operators to compare two values and produce the logical result TRUE or FALSE. The list of comparison operators consists of equal to (=), greater than (>), less than (<), greater than or equal to (>=), less than or equal to (<=), and not equal to (<>). Use an ampersand (&) to combine, or concatenate, two pieces of text into a single value.

- **Worksheet functions**—Predefined formulas that allow you to perform calculations on worksheet data by entering a constant value or a cell or range reference as the *argument* that a named function transforms. You can use a worksheet function as the complete contents of a cell, or you can use a function as an operand in another formula.

→ For a full discussion of worksheet functions and arguments, **see** "Manipulating Data with Worksheet Functions," **p. 604**.

USING CELL REFERENCES

You can enter any cell or range address directly in a formula. These addresses are not case sensitive; if you enter a2:b8 in a formula, Excel converts the entry to A2:B8 when you press Enter. You can also point and click to enter any cell or range reference.

One of the simplest Excel formulas is a direct reference to another cell. If you click in cell I24, for example, and enter the formula =A5, Excel displays the current value of cell A5 in cell I24. This technique is most commonly used with worksheets that contain input cells in which you type data that you'll use throughout the worksheet. For example, cell A5 might contain the current interest rate you plan to use as part of a series of loan and payment calculations. If you use custom views to display different portions of your worksheet, this technique lets you see the underlying assumptions at a glance.

To enter a reference to an entire row or column, use the row number or column letter as both halves of the range reference: B:B for column B, 2:2 for row 2. You can also use this syntax for multiple rows or columns—B:K includes every cell in columns B through K, just as 10:13 includes every cell in rows 10 through 13.

ABSOLUTE VERSUS RELATIVE CELL REFERENCES

Normally, Excel interprets cell and range references within a formula as *relative references*. When you copy or move the formula, Excel automatically adjusts cell references to reflect their position relative to the new location. This capability is useful when you need to quickly copy a formula across several rows or columns. In the worksheet shown in Figure 20.1, for example, the formula in cell D13 totals the contents of D7 through D12. When you copy that formula across to the right, Excel assumes you want to total the numbers in the same relative position in each column, so it adjusts the formula accordingly, from =SUM(D7:D12) to =SUM(E7:E12), =SUM(F7:F12), and so on.

Figure 20.1
Relative cell addresses are automatically updated as they are copied from cell to cell.

	B7	▼	f_x =SUM(B2:B6)			
	A	B	C	D	E	F
1	Year	North	South	East	West	Grand Total
2	2011	5,630	5,880	6,600	4,760	22,870
3	2012	6,120	4,810	6,610	6,790	24,330
4	2013	3,650	5,520	5,870	3,360	18,400
5	2014	6,590	6,470	5,120	4,660	22,840
6	2015	5,600	6,530	4,830	4,180	21,140
7	Total	27,590	29,210	29,030	23,750	109,580

→ The easiest way to copy a row or column of formulas is with the help of Excel's AutoFill feature; **see** "Automatically Filling In a Series of Data," **p. 519**.

In some cases, however, you want to copy a formula so that a cell or range reference in the copied formula points to the same cell or range as in the original. For example, if you enter the current interest rate in a cell near the top of a loan worksheet, you can refer to that cell in any formula that makes an interest-related calculation. To convert a relative reference to an *absolute reference*, which does not adjust when copied or moved, use dollar signs within the cell address. For example, when you copy the formula =B4*$A$5 to the right, Excel adjusts the first cell reference relative to its new location, but leaves the second reference unchanged: =B5*$A$5, =B6*$A$5, and so on.

TIP FROM

EQ & Woody

When you want to include a reference to an input cell in several formulas, you're generally better off using a named range, which is always an absolute reference. If cell A5 contains an interest rate, name the cell Interest_Rate and use that name in formulas— =B6*Interest_Rate, for example. If you move or copy the formula, the reference to the named range will not change.

You can mix and match relative and absolute addresses in a formula, or even in the same address. Using a dollar sign in front of the column portion of the address ($A5) tells Excel to change only the row reference when the formula is moved or copied; likewise, a dollar

20

sign in front of the row (A$5) changes only the column portion of the cell reference. In Figure 20.2, for example, you could enter the formula =B2/$F2 in cell B10 and then copy the formula down and to the right. The *mixed reference* to $F2 adjusts the references so that they always point to the Grand Total formula in Column F for the correct row.

Figure 20.2

Formulas in the bottom table use mixed references; that allows each percentage to be divided by the result in the Grand Total column as you copy the formula down and across.

	A	B	C	D	E	F
1	Year	North	South	East	West	Grand Total
2	2011	5,630	5,880	6,600	4,760	22,870
3	2010	6,120	4,810	6,610	6,790	24,330
4	2009	3,650	5,520	5,870	3,360	18,400
5	2008	6,590	6,470	5,120	4,660	22,840
6	2007	5,600	6,530	4,830	4,180	21,140
7	Total	27,590	29,210	29,030	23,750	109,580
8						
9	Year	North	South	East	West	
10	2011	24.6%	25.7%	28.9%	20.8%	
11	2010	25.2%	19.8%	27.2%	27.9%	
12	2009	19.8%	30.0%	31.9%	18.3%	
13	2008	28.9%	28.3%	22.4%	20.4%	
14	2007	26.5%	30.9%	22.8%	19.8%	

Use the F4 keyboard shortcut to switch quickly between relative, mixed, and absolute references in a formula. Click in the active cell to enable editing; then place the insertion point in a cell or range reference (either in the Formula bar or in the cell itself) and press F4 to convert a relative reference to absolute. Press F4 again to enter a mixed reference. Keep pressing F4 to cycle through all four variations for the selection.

TIP FROM

Ed & Woody

In Excel 2007, point to the bottom edge of the Formula bar and your mouse pointer changes to a double-headed arrow. Drag the edge down to increase the size of the Formula bar. By expanding the Formula bar to multiple rows, you can easily see the complete formula for those cells that hold extra-long formulas.

USING 3D REFERENCES TO CELLS ON OTHER WORKSHEETS

Sometimes it's helpful to use references to cells and ranges on other worksheets within the same workbook—known as *3D references*. For example, you might include a lookup table that lists sales tax rates for different counties or states on a separate sheet. Using this table to determine the correct tax rate for an invoice makes your data accurate, yet keeps the invoice sheet uncluttered. Likewise, in a loan worksheet, you might want to perform all the data-entry and payment calculations on one sheet, but place the amortization table on its own sheet for display and printing.

To enter a 3D address, preface the cell address with the name of the sheet followed by an exclamation point. (If the sheet name contains a space, enclose the sheet name within single quote marks.) If you have a sheet named Amortization Table, for example, you can refer to the top-left cell of that sheet by entering ='Amortization Table'!A1 on any other sheet in the same book. You can also click the appropriate sheet tab and then select the desired cell or range of cells to add references to cells or ranges on other sheets. When you use this technique, Excel automatically enters the sheet name, exclamation point, and cell references.

USING THE RANGE FINDER TO LOCATE PARTS OF A FORMULA

When a cell that contains a summary formula doesn't display the correct result, the first place to look is at the cell and range references in that formula. If you've added new rows or columns, it's possible that the formula references the old range and doesn't include the new cells.

To match cell references in any formula with the actual worksheet cells, use Excel's Range Finder. When you select any cell that contains a formula and make it available for editing, Excel highlights each cell or range reference in that formula with a different color and then adds an identically color-coded outline around the cells to which the range refers.

If you discover that a formula includes an incorrect cell or range reference, use the Range Finder to add or remove cells from the reference, or to select a completely different group of cells. Click the color-coded border on any cell edge to move the reference to a different cell; click and drag the square handle in any corner of the colored border to extend the selection. To record your changes, press Enter or click the green Enter Formula button next to the formula bar.

CONTROLLING THE ORDER AND TIMING OF CALCULATIONS

If a formula contains more than one operator, Excel performs calculations in the following order (if you remember high school algebra, this list will be familiar):

- Percent (%)
- Exponentiation (^)
- Multiplication (*) and division (/)
- Addition (+) and subtraction (–)
- Concatenation (&)
- Comparison (=, <, >, <=, >=, <>)

To control the order of calculation, use parentheses; Excel evaluates all items within parentheses first, from the inside out, using the same order as listed previously. If a formula contains operators with the same precedence, such as addition and subtraction or any two comparison operators, Excel evaluates the operators from left to right. The number of levels of nested parentheses you can use within a single formula is not limited and Excel permits a maximum of 64 levels of nesting for a single function.

TIP FROM

Ed & Woody

When you're trying to figure out the structure of a complex formula with many sets of nested parentheses, let Excel help. Click to make the cell that contains the formula active, and then use the arrow keys to move back and forth through the formula. As you move the insertion point to the right of a left parenthesis or to the left of a right parenthesis, Excel highlights its mate in bold. When you make any change to the formula, Excel displays each matched set of parentheses in a different color, making it easier for you to see which is which.

→ For a full description of how to nest functions inside each other, **see** "Using Functions Within Functions," **p. 607**.

Normally, Excel recalculates all formulas every time you open or save a workbook. When you change a value in a cell, Excel recalculates all formulas that refer to that cell on any worksheet in the current workbook. Calculation takes place in the background, and on a typical uncomplicated worksheet, the process is essentially instantaneous.

You might want to control when Excel recalculates formulas in at least two circumstances:

■ If your worksheet contains a large number of complex formulas, recalculation can cause annoying pauses when you try to enter data. This is especially noticeable on computers with slow CPUs and low-memory configurations.

■ When your formula contains cells that refer to themselves, as in some scientific and engineering formulas, Excel must repeat (iterate) the calculation—by default, each time you recalculate this type of formula, Excel goes through 100 iterations.

Under normal circumstances, most users should leave recalculation settings alone. If you must turn off automatic recalculation, follow these steps:

1. Click the Office button and select Excel Options. Click the Formulas tab to display the Formulas options in Figure 20.3.

Figure 20.3
Adjust recalculation options with care. For most situations, the default automatic options are appropriate.

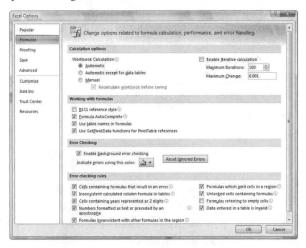

2. Choose the Manual option in the Workbook Calculation section. (The Automatic Except for Data Tables option is for use with worksheets that include a relatively obscure Excel feature called data tables. If your worksheet includes a one- or two-variable data table, Excel recalculates the entire table every time you edit any cell in the worksheet; checking this option lets you recalculate the table manually.)

3. If you want Excel to recalculate the workbook only when you explicitly choose to do so, remove the check mark from the Recalculate Workbook Before Saving check box.

4. Click OK to save the setting and return to your worksheet.

When you turn off automatic recalculation, you need to specify when Excel should recalculate formulas. To calculate all formulas in the current workbook, press F9. To recalculate only formulas in the current worksheet, press Shift+F9.

TIP FROM

Ed & Woody

Excel 97 includes several well-documented calculation bugs that can cause incorrect results under some circumstances. Beginning with Excel 2000, Microsoft made major changes to Excel's recalculation engine intended to fix these bugs. The first time you use Excel 2007 to open a worksheet created in Excel 97, the program completely recalculates the worksheet. When you close the worksheet, you'll be asked whether you want to save your changes, even if you've done nothing more than look at the worksheet. We strongly recommend that you click Yes when you see this dialog box to avoid the possibility of being bitten by those old recalculation bugs.

PREVENTING FORMULAS FROM DISPLAYING IN THE FORMULA BAR

When you design a worksheet that you intend other people to use for data entry, you might want to hide the formulas themselves and show their results. This technique can be useful if your formula contains confidential or proprietary information that you don't want to share with others. A company that provides advice for investing in stocks and commodities might provide worksheets to their clients that show buy and sell recommendations. By hiding the formulas, the firm maintains their formulas so subscribers to the service cannot enter those formulas into their own worksheets so that subscribers no longer need the service of the financial advisor. Hiding formulas also provides a useful way to prevent other users from attempting to edit a formula, too.

To prevent a formula from appearing in the Formula bar, you must first set a specific formatting option for that cell and then turn on *protection* for the entire worksheet:

1. Right-click the cell that contains the formula you want to hide (to hide multiple formulas, select a range) and choose Format Cells from the context menu.

2. Click the Protection tab and check the Hidden box.

CAUTION

Make sure you leave the check mark next to the Locked box as well. If you clear this box and check Hidden, anyone who can open the worksheet can replace the hidden formula with another formula or a constant value, undoing your attempt at protection.

3. Select other cells on the worksheet, if necessary, and adjust whether their contents are hidden or locked.

4. Display your Review ribbon and click the Protect Sheet button. Make sure the option labeled Protect Worksheet and Contents of Locked Cells check box is selected.

5. Click OK to close the Protect Sheet dialog box. Users will no longer be able to see hidden formulas in the Formula bar, in the cell itself, or on printouts, even if they select the option to print formulas from the Excel Options dialog box. In addition, users of the worksheet will be unable to edit formulas. The results of a hidden formula will display in the cell and on printouts.

20

USING ARRAY FORMULAS

Array formulas let you perform multiple calculations across a range of cells (an array) by using a function that normally works only on a single cell. To enter an array formula, construct the formula as you normally would, and then press Ctrl+Shift+Enter. Excel enters the formula in curly braces to indicate that it is an array formula.

An array formula can return either a single result or multiple results. Array formulas are a common way to combine the SUM and IF functions, for example. Under normal circumstances, an IF function compares one cell with another cell or a constant value. An array formula, on the other hand, lets you compare a single value to every cell in an array and return a result you can work with, so you can compare a condition in an IF function and use all matching results in a SUM function, all in one formula.

 If you're having trouble editing an array formula, see "Editing an Array Formula" in the "Troubleshooting" section at the end of this chapter.

For example, suppose you keep a list of invoice information in an Excel worksheet with header information in row 1 and the first record in row 2, as in the example in Figure 20.4. If column B contains the amount of each invoice and column C contains the name of the salesperson who prepared that invoice, you can use an array formula to keep a running total of all invoice amounts by salesperson. Assuming column D is blank, click in cell D2 and type this formula: `=SUM(IF($C$2:C2=C2,$B$2:B2))`. Press Ctrl+Shift+Enter to enter it as an array formula, and then use AutoFill to copy the formula to the remainder of the cells in column D. (Excel automatically adds curly braces at the beginning and end to indicate that this is an array formula. Do not enter the curly braces yourself, or the array formula will fail.)

Figure 20.4
In this example, the array formula allows you to keep a running total of all invoice amounts by salesperson.

	A	B	C	D
1	Inv Num	Amount	Salesperson	Running Total by Salesperson
2	1001	$ 91.42	Bob Hill	$ 91.42
3	1002	46.69	Denny Crain	46.69
4	1003	123.87	Elyse Wells	123.87
5	1004	72.02	William May	72.02
6	1005	87.39	Elyse Wells	211.26
7	1006	29.13	Elyse Wells	240.39
8	1007	71.26	Elyse Wells	311.65
9	1008	59.50	William May	131.52
10	1009	41.88	William May	173.40
11	1010	135.50	Denny Crain	182.19
12	1011	83.93	Elyse Wells	395.58
13	1012	54.97	William May	228.37
14	1013	75.24	Bob Hill	166.66
15	1014	60.31	Elyse Wells	455.89
16	1015	12.58	Elyse Wells	468.47
17	1016	51.48	William May	279.85
18	1017	141.45	Bob Hill	308.11
19	1018	87.27	William May	367.12
20	1019	59.86	William May	426.98
21	1020	64.04	William May	491.02
22	1021	54.06	Bob Hill	362.17
23	1022	22.67	Denny Crain	204.86
24	1023	59.51	Elyse Wells	527.98

The first argument in this array formula compares each previous cell in column C to the contents of column C in the current row. The second argument returns an invoice amount to the SUM function for each cell in column C if the condition in the IF function is true. The copy of this formula in cell D11, for example, looks like this: {=SUM(IF($C$2:C11=C11,$B$2:B11))}. This formula looks in the range from C2 to C11 for cells that match the contents of C11—the name "Denny Crain." It finds matching contents in C4, C5, C7, C10, and C11, so it adds the invoice amounts in B4, B11, and B12 to produce its result, a running total of all amounts up to and including row 11 for Denny.

USING RANGE NAMES AND LABELS IN FORMULAS

Understanding the logic of a complex formula can be a challenge, even when you entered the formula yourself. This form of amnesia is especially common when you haven't opened a particular workbook in months or years.

To make it easier for you to understand a formula's purpose just by looking at it, you can enter cell references by using *named ranges*. This technique is especially useful with cells that contain constant values such as interest rates, loan amounts, sales tax rates, and discount formulas, because you can define a handful of input cells and then plug the contents of those cells into formulas on any worksheet within the workbook.

You can define range names explicitly, or you can enter cell references that are defined by the labels on rows and columns.

USING NAMED RANGES IN FORMULAS

For absolute control over cell and range references in formulas, use a range name instead of its row-and-column address. When you refer to a named range in a formula, the effect is the same as if you had entered the absolute address of the named cell or range.

Using named ranges makes it easier for anyone looking at a worksheet to understand exactly how a formula works. That comes in handy when you share a workbook with a co-worker, or when you look at a worksheet you designed long ago. On an invoice worksheet, for example, the following formula is instantly understandable:

```
=Quantity_Ordered*Unit_Price*(1+Sales_Tax_Rate)
```

The easiest way to name a cell or a range is to use the Name box, located just to the left of the Formula bar (see Figure 20.5). Select the cell or range you want to name, and then click in the Name box to highlight the entire cell address. Type a legal name for the cell or range, and press Enter to store the range name in the workbook.

20

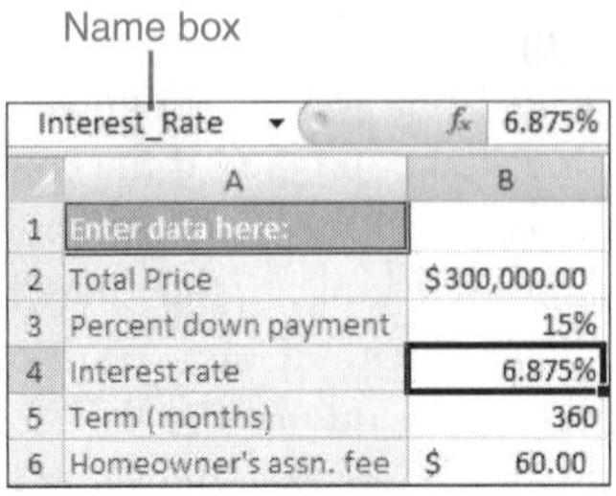

Name box

Figure 20.5
Select a range, and
then click in the Name
box and type the name
you want to use for
that range.

	Interest_Rate ▾	fx	6.875%
	A	B	
1	Enter data here:		
2	Total Price	$300,000.00	
3	Percent down payment	15%	
4	Interest rate	6.875%	
5	Term (months)	360	
6	Homeowner's assn. fee	$ 60.00	

The rules for assigning a *legal name* to a cell or a range are completely different from (and much more restrictive than) those that apply to the names of files and worksheet tabs:

■ You can use a total of up to 255 characters in a range name.

TIP FROM

EQ & Woody

> The point of range names is to make worksheets and formulas easier to understand. For clarity's sake, try to keep range names under 15 characters—the width of the Name drop-down list.

■ The first character must be a letter or the underline character. You can't legally name a cell or range 4thQuarterBudget, but Q4Budget is acceptable.

■ The remaining characters can be letters, numbers, periods, or the underline character. No other punctuation marks are allowed in range names. Spaces are forbidden; use the underscore character instead to form a legal name that's also easy to read.

■ A cell or range name cannot be the same as a cell reference or a value, so you can't name a cell Q4, FY2001, or W2. Such names could refer to cells such as the cell in row 2 and column W. In addition, you cannot use a single letter or enter a number without any punctuation or letters.

NOTE

> When you name a cell or range, that name attaches itself to the absolute address you specify. If you move or copy a formula containing a reference to the named range, the reference continues to point to the original address rather than adjust to a new relative address. For this reason, you should use named ranges in formulas only when you want the formula to refer to an absolute address.

When constructing a formula, you can choose from a list of all defined names in the current workbook. After typing an equal sign or clicking in an existing formula, display your Formulas ribbon and click the Use in Formula button to drop down a list of all names in the workbook that you can choose from. If the name you select is on a different worksheet, Excel automatically enters it by using the correct syntax, including the sheet name. After the Use in Formula process inserts your selected name, you can continue entering the formula.

20

If you insert a cell or range reference in a formula by clicking a cell or range, Excel enters the defined name of the cell or range, if one exists. If you don't want this automatic substitution to take place, type the cell address directly, rather than clicking to enter it.

MANAGING RANGE NAMES

To manage names of cells or ranges stored in a workbook, click the Name Manager button on your Formulas ribbon. The Name Manager dialog box (see Figure 20.6) lets you add a new name to an existing range, delete one or more range names, or change the reference for an existing name.

Figure 20.6
Use this list to manage named ranges in a workbook. To redefine an existing name, select a new cell or range in the Refers To box.

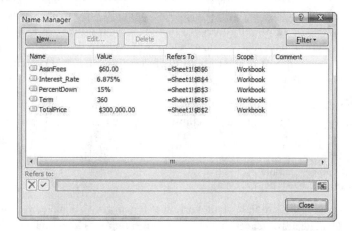

TIP FROM

You can assign more than one name to the same cell or range. Use different names if you intend to refer to the contents of a cell in several different formulas, and you want the names to match the purpose of each formula. For example, on a loan worksheet, you might refer to the same cell as AmountFinanced and AmountBorrowed, and then use either name in formulas on that worksheet.

→ You can also use the Go To Special dialog box to view and locate range names, a topic we cover in "Using Cell References and Range Names to Navigate in a Workbook," **p. 515**.

It's relatively easy to change the location that a cell or range name refers to: click the Name Manager button on the Formulas ribbon to open the Name Manager dialog box, and then select the cell or range name from the Names in Workbook list. Select the contents of the Refers To box and click in the worksheet to select the new cell or range. When you use this technique, any worksheet formulas that refer to the range name automatically use the new location you defined.

In Excel 2007, you can change a defined name. Display the Name Manager dialog box and click Edit. There you can change the name or the cells in the range that the name refers to.

If some of the formulas in your workbook display error messages after you change or delete a range name, see "Checking Formulas Before Deleting Range Names" in the "Troubleshooting" section at the end of this chapter.

MANIPULATING DATA WITH WORKSHEET FUNCTIONS

Worksheet functions handle a broad array of tasks, from simple arithmetic to complex financial calculations and intricate statistical tests. Regardless of its complexity, every function consists of two parts: the function name and its *arguments*—the specific values the function uses to calculate a result. The *syntax* of a function defines what type of arguments it uses: text, numbers, dates, and logical values, for example. In most cases, you can substitute a cell or range address or another formula or function as an argument, as long as the data evaluates to the required data type. Some arguments are required, and others are optional. Arguments always appear to the right of the function name, inside parentheses; Excel uses commas to separate multiple arguments.

The following examples illustrate the syntax of some commonly used functions. Bold type means the argument is required. An ellipsis (…) means that the function accepts an unlimited number of arguments.

```
=TODAY()
=AVERAGE(number1,number2,...)
=IPMT(rate,per,nper,pv,fv,type)
```

TODAY() is one of the simplest of all worksheet functions. Whenever you open, save, or otherwise recalculate a worksheet that contains this function, Excel updates the value of the cell that contains this formula to display the current date, as stored in your computer's clock chip. This function is extremely common in formulas that calculate elapsed time, such as the number of days that have passed since you mailed an invoice or received a payment.

AVERAGE accepts now up to 255 arguments (but requires only 1) and calculates the arithmetic mean of all values in the list, ignoring text and logical values. Although you can enter constant values in this formula, it's most commonly used to calculate the average of a range of numbers, such as monthly sales or budget results. If you calculate a year's worth of monthly sales totals in cells B20 through M20, for example, =AVERAGE(B20:M20) displays the average of the 12 monthly totals.

To calculate the amount of interest you pay each month on a mortgage, use the IPMT function. As the syntax description shows, you must supply a minimum of four values as arguments. This function requires (in order) the interest rate per period (rate), the specific payment period for which you want to calculate interest (per, a number between 1 and nper), the number of payment periods (nper), and the present value (pv, the amount of the loan). The final two arguments—future value (fv) and the type of loan (type)—are optional. Here, too, you're more likely to include a reference to a cell than the actual number in a formula that uses this function.

20

> **NOTE**
>
> Although the Formula bar and Excel's help screens always display function names in capital letters, the names are not case sensitive. Use any combination of capital and lowercase characters; when you enter the formula, Excel converts the function's name to capitals.

ENTERING ERROR-FREE FORMULAS

For some functions, especially those with only a single argument, the easiest course of action is often to type them into a cell directly, using the mouse to select the cell or range address of any arguments.

When you begin to enter a new function or edit an existing one, Excel displays a ScreenTip just below the Formula bar. This yellow box displays all required arguments in bold type, with optional arguments in lighter type. After you enter an argument, the argument name serves as a link—click it to select the entire argument.

For functions with multiple arguments, however, especially those where you're not certain of the exact syntax, a fill-in-the-blanks form often ensures the proper results. The Insert Function dialog box allows you to enter any function and all its arguments quickly and accurately, by using a series of dialog boxes. The Insert Function dialog box is an expert Excel user's best friend: It makes errors nearly impossible, it provides constant feedback as you build a formula, and it includes hooks to surprisingly advanced help, including useful examples of some complex formulas.

> **NOTE**
>
> Excel 2000 included two tools for automatically inserting functions—the Formula Palette and the Paste Function dialog box. Although their workings are generally similar, these two functions have been combined and extensively redesigned to create the Insert Function dialog box, which was introduced in Excel 2002 and continued to be used in Excel 2007.

You can use the Insert Function dialog box to build a function from scratch: You choose a function from a categorized list and then fill in the arguments using input boxes. Or you can enter part or all of the function and its arguments and use the Insert Function dialog box to edit specific arguments or debug a formula that isn't working as you expect.

To build a function from scratch, follow these steps:

1. Click to select the cell in which you want to add a formula, and then click the Insert Function button (the fx just to the left of the Formula bar or the Insert Function on the Formulas ribbon). Excel inserts an equal sign in the Formula bar, positions the insertion point to its right, and opens the Insert Function dialog box.

20

NOTE

When you type an equal sign in a cell or the Formula bar, Excel replaces the Name box (just to the left of the Formula bar) with the Function box. When you first use Excel, this list includes the 10 most popular functions; as you use the Insert Function dialog box, Excel replaces the entries on this list with the 10 functions you've used most recently. The last function you used is always the top selection in the Function box.

2. If the name of the function you want to use appears in the Select a Function box, click to select it. If the function you want to use is not on the Most Recently Used list, choose a category. If you're not certain of the exact name of the function, enter a brief description or keyword in the Search for a Function box and click the Go button (see Figure 20.7).

3. The text at the bottom of the Insert Function dialog box offers a brief explanation of the selected function and its syntax (click the Help on This Function link for a more detailed

Figure 20.7

explanation). When you've selected the correct function, click OK. Excel adds the function to the Formula bar and opens a new dialog box with separate input boxes for each argument, as shown in Figure 20.8.

4. Click within the first argument box and fill in the

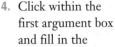

Figure 20.8

required data. Note that the help text at the bottom of the dialog box is specific to the argument you're currently working with, and the data type required for each argument appears to the right of the input box.

- Type text, numbers, and other constants directly into the input box.
- To add cell references by pointing and clicking, first click the Collapse Dialog button (at the right side of each argument input box) to roll most of the Insert

Function dialog box up and out of the way. Next, select the cell or range to use for the selected argument, and then click the Collapse Dialog button again to continue.

- To use a function as an argument within another function, click to position the insertion point within the box for that argument and then select the function from the Function box to the left of the Formula bar. (See "Using Functions Within Functions " in the next section for more details.)

- When entering constant values, you can include the percent operator (%) and minus signs (–) with numeric data. Look to the right of the input box to see the current value of each argument you enter. If the data is not of the type required by the argument, Excel displays the word Invalid to the right of the input box.

5. Repeat step 4 for other required and optional arguments. Look to the right of the equal sign for each argument to see its current value, using the data you've entered so far. To see the result of the formula itself, look at the text along the bottom of the dialog box.

6. After entering all required arguments, click OK to paste the complete function into the current cell, or click Cancel to start over.

TIP FROM

Ed & Woody

> *Debugging* a formula can be frustrating, especially when you're working with complex formulas containing several nested functions. Here's a backup strategy that allows you to freely experiment with formulas and functions without fear of losing your work or damaging a worksheet. Before editing a formula, remove the equal sign from the beginning of the formula and press Enter; then copy the formula to another cell. Without the equal sign, Excel treats the cell's contents as plain text and copies the formula exactly as it appears, with no adjustments. If your experiments are unsuccessful, copy the backed-up formula to the original cell and then restore the equal sign.

To use the Insert Function dialog box as a proofreading and reference tool, begin constructing your formula as usual, starting with an equal sign and the function name. After entering the first parenthesis, click the Insert Function button to open the Insert Function dialog box with the current function selected. Any arguments you've already entered will be in the dialog box as soon as it opens.

USING FUNCTIONS WITHIN FUNCTIONS

In some cases, it's necessary to use one function as the argument for another. *Nesting* functions within functions this way is common with logical functions such as IF, for example. In a sales worksheet that you use to calculate commissions at a regular rate of 5%, you might want to pass along an extra 2% bonus to salespeople who beat their quota in every quarter, and you want to pay no commission to those who fell short of their target number for the year. If the quarterly quota for the first salesperson is in cell B3 and the actual sales for each quarter are in B4:B7, enter the following formula to perform the full calculation in a single step:

```
=IF(MIN(B4:B7)>B3,SUM(B4:B7)*7%,IF(AVERAGE(B4:B7)<B3,0,SUM(B4:B7)*5%))
```

Note that this example includes three levels of nesting, with the final SUM and AVERAGE functions nested within an IF function, which in turn is the final argument of the first IF function. The MIN and SUM functions compose the first two arguments within the first IF function. You can nest functions within functions within functions to create some clever effects. Suppose you want to add a date stamp to a worksheet so that whenever you print the worksheet, you'll see a large text label that includes your name and the current date. Enter this formula in a cell that is within the print range, substituting your name in the text string that begins the formula:

```
="Prepared by John Q. Smith, "&TEXT(TODAY(),"mmmm d, yyyy")
```

When you're nesting functions, note that the nested function must return the same value type (text, number, date, true/false) as the argument it's replacing. Unlike formulas containing constants or cell references, which can contain an unlimited number of nesting levels, Excel enables you to nest a maximum of 64 levels of functions. If you need to perform more calculations than this, you'll have to break the formula into multiple steps and place each step in its own cell.

You can use the Insert Function dialog box to enter a nested function within another function. Begin entering the first function by using the Insert Function dialog box, as described earlier in this chapter. Click in the input box for any argument, and then choose another function from the Function box (this box is located to the left of the Formula bar, where the Name box normally appears; it is visible only when the Function Arguments dialog box is open). As you enter the formula, you can switch between functions at any time by clicking the function's name in the Formula bar. If you choose a function that contains a nested function as an argument (as in the example shown in Figure 20.9), the entire function appears in the input box, and the result of the function using current values appears to its right.

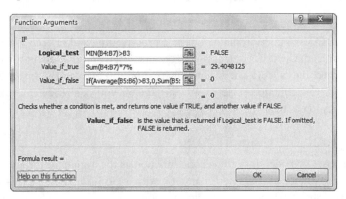

Figure 20.9
You can view nested functions within the Formula Bar's Function Arguments dialog box.

FINDING THE RIGHT FUNCTION

Excel has more than 300 functions, including those available in various add-ins. The following sections list some of the tasks you can accomplish by using functions in each category.

AutoSum Functions

The most commonly used functions are also the easiest to enter. To insert a formula that adds a column or row of numbers automatically, click in a blank cell beneath any column of numbers (or at the end of a row of numbers), and then click the AutoSum button on your Home ribbon. Excel inserts the SUM function with the argument already filled in and selected. Adjust the selected range, if necessary, and then click the Enter box in the Formula bar or press Enter to store the formula in the active cell.

Use the drop-down arrow to the right of the AutoSum button to select the AVERAGE, COUNT, MAX, or MIN functions for the adjacent row or column. Select the More Functions option from the bottom of the list to open the Insert Function dialog box with the adjacent row or column selected as the default argument.

Two quirks in AutoSum are worth noting:

- If the range above or to the left of the cell containing the SUM formulas contains any blank cells, the range to be totaled stops there.

- When the cell that holds the SUM function is at the end of a row and a column, AutoSum always selects the column.

In either case, the moral is the same: When using AutoSum, always check to be certain that the correct range is selected.

To automatically add totals for several adjacent rows or columns, select the cells directly beneath the columns or to the right of the rows and then choose an AutoSum function. Excel plugs in the selected formula for each row or column, the same as if you had added each one individually. When you use the AutoSum button this way, you do not see a confirmation dialog box.

If you use AutoSum below an AutoFiltered list, the resulting formula uses the SUBTOTAL function instead. This syntax allows you to see a correct sum using only the filtered data; if you used the SUM function, the result would show all cells, including those hidden by the filter.

TIP FROM

Ed & Woody

You don't need to enter a formula to make quick calculations. When you select two or more numbers in a worksheet, Excel displays a summary of the selected cells in the status bar along the bottom of the worksheet window. The default calculation is a simple total; look at the right side of the status bar and you'll see SUM=, followed by the total of the selected cells. Right-click anywhere on the status bar to display a shortcut menu that lets you choose a different calculation, including Average, Max, Min, Count (which counts the number of selected cells), and Count Nums (which counts only the number of selected cells that contain numbers). Use this feature in conjunction with selecting a column in a list, for example, to quickly spot the largest and smallest values in that field.

20

Financial Calculations

Excel includes a large number of financial functions—50 in all—covering everything from simple household budget problems, such as calculating a house payment, to complex tasks such as figuring the bond-equivalent yield for a U.S. Treasury bill (TBILLEQ) or the yield of a security that has an odd last period (ODDLYIELD).

Most of the more advanced financial functions, including those that calculate depreciation schedules (DB, DDB, SLN, SYD, and VDB) and internal rates of return (IRR, MIRR), are useful only if you have enough of an accounting or finance background to understand the underlying principles. However, a number of general-purpose functions are useful for a wide variety of calculations involving loans and investments. You can calculate the periodic payment for a loan or annuity using PMT, figure the net present value of an investment or loan with NPV, determine the interest and principal portion of a periodic payment with IPMT and PPMT, and calculate the future value of an investment (FV). These functions, and several more that cover the same ground, use some or all of the following common arguments:

- Future value (fv) is the amount that an investment or loan will be worth after all payments have been made. When dealing with investments, fv is usually positive; in the case of loans, fv is typically 0.

- Number of periods (nper) is the total number of payments or periods of an investment. Make sure the unit of measurement is consistent with the payment period; if you pay a 30-year mortgage monthly, nper is equal to 360 (30*12).

- Payment (pmt) is the amount paid periodically to an investment or loan. It cannot change over the life of the annuity. Typically, pmt includes principal and interest but no other fees or taxes. For a loan or investment, in which you are the one making payments, you typically enter pmt as a negative number; if you receive dividends or other payments (in other words, if you're the bank), pmt is generally a positive number.

- Present value (pv) is the value of an investment or loan at the beginning of the investment period. When you are the borrower, the present value of a loan is the principal amount that is borrowed, expressed as a negative number.

- Rate (rate) is the interest rate or discount rate for a loan or investment. Pay particular attention that nper and rate use the same scale as pmt. If you make monthly payments on a 30-year loan at 7.5% annual interest, use 7.5%/12 for rate (to convert the annual rate to a monthly rate, such as the payments) and 30*12 for nper (360, the number of monthly payments in a 30-year loan).

- Type (type) is the interval at which payments are made during the payment period, such as at the beginning of a month or the end of the month. In interest rate calculations over a long period of time, the difference can be substantial.

Logical Tests

Excel includes six *comparison functions*, which you can use to compare two values and define actions based on the comparison. Far and away the most popular and useful logical function is IF. The following is the syntax of the IF function:

```
=IF(logical_test,value_if_true,value_if_false)
```

Excel also includes 18 *information functions*, which give you information about cells, worksheets, and your system itself. For the most part, you'll use these functions to build error-handling and data-validation routines into a worksheet. Nine of these functions belong in a subgroup called the IS functions: ISTEXT, ISERROR, ISNUMBER, and so on.

By combining the IF function and the ISERROR function, you can avoid seeing error codes in a worksheet. The formula =IF(ISERROR(A5/A8),"",A5/A8), for example, tests the value of the formula A5/A8 before displaying a result. If A8 is equal to 0, Excel displays nothing in the cell rather than the annoying #DIV/0! error message; if the value of A8 is other than 0 and the formula returns a valid result rather than an error message, Excel displays that result.

TIP FROM

EQ & Woody

> In many cases, *conditional formatting* is a better way to suppress error messages than using formulas. Select the cell in which you want to suppress error messages–A9, for instance–then click the Conditional Formatting button on your Home ribbon. Select Highlight Cell Rules and choose Equal To. In the edit box at the left, enter the formula =ISERROR(A9). Next, click the Format button, select Custom Format, and in the Format Cells dialog box choose the white square. Click OK to close the Format Cells dialog box and click OK to close the Condition Formatting dialog box. Now any error messages in that cell will appear as white text on a white background and will be invisible.

→ For a detailed discussion of conditional formatting, **see** " Using Conditional Formatting to Identify Key Values," **p. 583**.

TEXT MANIPULATION FUNCTIONS

It's easy to think of functions in mathematical terms, but some of the most useful functions work strictly with text. You can use text functions to pull specific information from a single *text value*, split a text value into multiple cells, combine text values into a single string, or convert one type of data (such as a number or date) into text, using a specific format.

When you want to combine (or *concatenate*) the text from two cells, use an ampersand. The following formula adds a space between the values in two adjacent cells:

```
=A1&" "&A2
```

For more sophisticated manipulation of strings of text, use any of Excel's 27 text and data functions. These functions are especially useful when you've imported text from another program or file. Simple text functions let you convert text from all capitals to lowercase letters (and vice versa) or convert a date value to text in a specific format. The following formula, for example, combines three functions to pull out just the last name from a complete name in cell A17:

```
=RIGHT(A17,LEN(A17)-FIND(" ",A17))
```

The task isn't as easy as it might first appear. Because the last name can be any length (Bott or Leonhard, for example), you first need to calculate the correct number of characters. For starters, use the FIND function to locate the space separating the first and last names. If the first name contains five letters, the formula FIND(" ",A17) returns the value 6. Next, use the LEN function to determine the total length of the name; by subtracting the value determined in the first step from this value, you can determine the exact length of the last name. Finally, use the RIGHT function to extract that number of characters from the input cell (A17), starting at the right side.

Table 20.1 lists the most useful text functions.

TABLE 20.1   COMMON TEXT FUNCTIONS

Function Name	Description	How to Use It
CONCATENATE (text1, text2,...) UPPER(text), LOWER(text), PROPER (text)	Combine two or more text items	Convert case of text, to all capitals, all lowercase letters, or initial capitals. Generally, an ampersand (&) is easier. =PROPER('pearson technology group') changes the first letter of each word to a capital letter—in this case, Pearson Technology Group.
FIND(find_text, within_text,start_num) SEARCH(find_text, within_text,start_num) LEFT(text, num_chars) RIGHT(text, num_chars) MID(text,start_num, num_chars)	Find text in a cell Extract text from a cell	FIND is case sensitive; SEARCH allows wildcard characters. Use with FIND and SEARCH to extract part of a text string; for example, a part number from a lengthy product code.
TEXT(value,format_text) FIXED(number, decimals, no_commas) DOLLAR(number, decimals)	Convert number to text	For the TEXT function, specify any number format (except General) from the Category box on the Number tab in the Format Cells dialog box. Be sure to enclose the format in quotation marks: =TEXT(TODAY(), "mmmm d,yyyy").
CLEAN() TRIM()	Remove unwanted characters from text	TRIM removes extra spaces from imported text, and CLEAN removes unprintable characters, such as might be found at the top or bottom of a file that contains formatting information that Excel can't interpret.

If you have trouble concatenating two values, see "Converting Values to Text Before Concatenating" in the "Troubleshooting" section at the end of this chapter.

DATE AND TIME FUNCTIONS

Use date and time functions for simple tasks, such as displaying today's date or the day of the week for a given date. If you run an organization whose members pay dues annually on their birthday, how do you create a list of birthdays sorted by month? If you sort by birthday, you'll end up with a list that's sorted by the members' ages. To sort properly, you'll have to create a column in which each row contains a formula that uses the MONTH function to convert a date to a month.

NOTE

> There is a profound difference between using a function to convert a value and using cell formats to change the display of a value. Functions return a different value from the value you use as an argument. When you change formats, on the other hand, the underlying value stored in the cell remains the same.

→ For an overview of how Excel enters and manipulates dates as serial values, **see** "Setting Date and Time Formats," **p. 565**.

Date functions can help you perform even the most sophisticated calculations. For example, U.S. tax laws require that participants in some types of retirement accounts begin withdrawing funds and paying taxes as soon as they turn 70 1/2 years old. To calculate the first day of the month after a person reaches that age, enter the account holder's birthday in a cell named Birth_date, and then use the following formula to calculate the retirement date:

`=DATE(YEAR(Birth_date)+70,MONTH(Birth_date)+7,1)`

Table 20.2 lists the most useful date and time functions, along with examples of how to use each one.

TABLE 20.2   DATE AND TIME FUNCTIONS

Function Name	Description	How to Use It
TODAY(), NOW()	Return the current date or time as a serial value	No argument required. Enter =NOW() to plug the current date and time into a cell; use TODAY() to enter only the current date.
YEAR(serial_number) MONTH(serial_number) DAY(serial_number)	Convert a serial date value to its year, month, or date	Useful when you need to separate the components of a date entered in a cell to create a list of all birthdays for all employees and sort it by month, for example.

continues

TABLE 20.2   CONTINUED

Function Name	Description	How to Use It
WEEKDAY (serial_number)	Convert a serial date value to a weekday	Useful in formulas in which you want to calculate paydays or due dates. The result is a number from 1 (Sunday) to 7 (Saturday). Format the result using the "ddd" or "dddd" format to see the results as a day of the week.
HOUR(serial_number) MINUTE(serial_number) SECOND(serial_number)	Convert a serial time value to its hour, minute, or second	Useful when you need to separate the components of a time entered in a cell—to create a list of all starting times for a golf tournament, for example, grouped by hour.

You'll find an interesting collection of special-purpose date and time formats in the Analysis ToolPak, an Excel add-in. EOMONTH(TODAY(),0), for example, returns the last day of the current month—a useful calculation when working with payments that are due on the last day of the month. (Change the second argument to 1 to return the last day of next month, or -1 for the previous month.) Other date/time functions in the Analysis ToolPak include WORK-DAYS and NETWORKDAYS, which are useful when you're calculating project timelines. To install the Analysis ToolPak, click your Office button and then click the Excel Options button to open the Excel Options dialog box. Click to display the Add-ins group. At the bottom of the window, select Excel Add-ins in the Manage drop-down list box and click Go. Excel opens the Add-ins dialog box, telling you the add-ins that are currently available to you. Click the Analysis ToolPak option and click OK. If the add-in isn't currently installed (and it obviously won't be initially), Excel will offer to install it. Click Yes to begin the installation.

LOOKUP AND REFERENCE FUNCTIONS

The 18 functions in the Lookup and Reference category are intended for use with lists and tables. HLOOKUP and VLOOKUP, for example, are designed to help you track down specific information in a table—by row or column—based on the contents of a cell that contains another value to use for comparison. (LOOKUP, which sounds like a simpler version of both functions, is included only for compatibility with other spreadsheet programs and is not recommended for use with Excel.) MATCH, INDEX, and OFFSET are other functions in this category that are useful for reference tasks, such as locating information in tax tables.

The syntax of all these functions is hideously complicated and rarely worth the effort. If you must add this type of function to a worksheet, do yourself a favor and use the Lookup Wizard, an Excel add in specifically designed to generate these formulas with minimal effort on your part. For example, if you store a list of part numbers, product names, and prices in an Excel table, you might want to create a data-entry area at the top of the table that lets you enter a specific part number and quickly look up the corresponding product name and price.

Before you can use the Lookup Wizard, you have to install it. Click your Office button and then click the Excel Options button to open the Excel Options dialog box. Click to display the Add-ins group. At the bottom of the window, select Excel Add-ins in the Manage drop-down list box and click Go. Excel opens the Add-ins dialog box, telling you the add-ins that are currently available to you. Click the Lookup Wizard option and click OK. If the add-in isn't currently installed (and it obviously won't be initially), Excel will offer to install it. Click Yes to begin the installation.

NOTE

> Depending on your Office 2007 installation, Excel might require that you insert your Office 2007 installation DVD (or CD), or perhaps you can point the installer to a network installation point if you're running an enterprise-style network.

After installing the wizard, you can use it to create lookup formulas that work properly without any debugging.

The worksheet in Figure 20.10 contains one such lookup formula. You enter a part number in cell A2, and Excel finds that value in the corresponding column in the list below, reads across to the value in the Price and Product Name columns in that row, and displays the results in cells C2 and D2. The formulas in cells C2 and D2 that actually perform the lookup are fairly complex, including nested MATCH and INDEX functions.

Figure 20.10
Use the Lookup Wizard to add the data-entry cell (A2) and lookup formulas (C2 and D2) to a worksheet.

To add a lookup formula to a worksheet that contains a list, start by creating the list itself. You must include a header row that contains column labels for each field in the list, and the first column must consist of unique values that serve as row labels. The data does not need to be sorted in any order. Leave several blank rows at the top of the list to allow room for placing the lookup cells. After verifying that the list is arranged properly, follow these steps:

TIP FROM

Ed & Woody

> If you plan to create a lookup form on a worksheet, position it above the list or on a separate sheet. If you position cells that contain the formula and parameters alongside or below a list, you could accidentally hide or erase them when you filter or delete records.

1. Select the entire range that contains the list, including the header row. (Although this step is not required, it's easier to select this range before running the wizard.)

20

2. Click to display your Formulas ribbon. The Lookup button should appear in the Solutions group at the far right of the ribbon. (If this button is not available, you need to install the Lookup Wizard first, as described earlier in this section.) Click the button to run the wizard. In the first step of the wizard, verify that the entire list is selected; if necessary, adjust the selection. Click Next to continue.

3. In the next step (see Figure 20.11), choose the name of the column that contains the value you want to look up—in this case, Product Name. At the bottom of the dialog box, select any row from the drop-down list. Because this value will appear in an input cell, the exact value doesn't matter. Click Next to continue.

4. Specify that you want to copy the formula and lookup parameters to your worksheet, as shown in Figure 20.12.

5. Follow the wizard's prompts to position lookup formulas and related cells on the worksheet. The first value the Lookup Wizard produces is the label over the lookup column; it goes in D1. The second value is the one you'll change later to lookup values; in this case, it goes in cell A2. The third value contains the lookup formula and goes in D2.

6. Repeat steps 2–5 to add the formula that looks up information for other columns. For example, to look up information in the Price column, create a lookup formula and add it to cell C2.

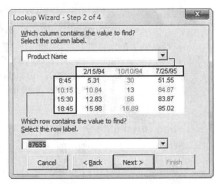

Figure 20.11

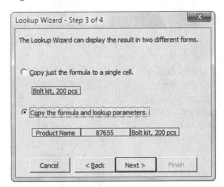

Figure 20.12

TIP FROM

Add just the lookup formula to your worksheet when you want to perform a different lookup in every row of your table. For example, a golf tournament coordinator might keep a list of each player's current handicap on one worksheet. Using a list on a separate worksheet for each tournament, the coordinator could enter the date, the player's name, and the raw score in the first three columns. A lookup formula in the fourth column of every row would find the current handicap on the other worksheet, based on the member's name in the first column. Use an additional calculated field to figure the net score by subtracting the looked-up handicap from today's score.

MATHEMATICAL CALCULATIONS

Given Excel's extensive mathematical capabilities, it's only natural that the list of worksheet functions includes 60 mathematical functions. Several handle advanced trigonometry calculations (COS, TAN, SIN, ACOS, ATAN, and ASIN, for example), and the PI function displays the value of pi to 15 decimal places.

Use the ROUND and TRUNC functions to transform values for use in calculations. For example, if cell C16 contains the value 23.5674, use =ROUND(C16,2) to convert that value to 23.57; the second argument defines the number of decimal places. Use =TRUNC(C16,2) to lop off all digits beyond the number of decimal places you specify in the second argument. Because this function truncates the value rather than rounding it, the result is 23.56 rather than 23.57.

> **NOTE**
>
> Although you can use cell formats to change the way information is displayed in a cell, these formats don't change the underlying information stored in the cell. Use the ROUND and TRUNC functions when you want to perform calculations based on a specific level of precision.

The **MOD** function divides one value by another and returns a remainder. One interesting use of this formula is to determine whether a given year is a leap year. If cell A1 contains the year to be tested, enter this formula:

```
=IF(OR(MOD(A1,400)=0,AND(MOD(A1,4)=0,MOD(A1,100)<>0)),"Leap Year", "Not a Leap
Year")
```

This tricky formula uses the logical operators IF, OR, and AND to test whether cell A1 is divisible by 400 or is both divisible by 4 and not divisible by 100. If either condition is true, it returns the text "Leap Year"; otherwise, it returns the text "Not a Leap Year."

To display the *absolute value* of a formula, so the result is always a positive number, use the ABS function. =ABS(A14-A16), for example, always returns the difference between the values in these two cells as a positive number, even if A16 is larger than A14.

One of the most interesting functions in this group is SUMIF(range,criteria,sum_range); use it to total a range of numbers based on whether they meet criteria you define. For example, if the range B2:B20 contains the names of salespeople and the range C2:C20 contains invoice amounts, use the following formula to calculate the total for all invoices from Debbie McKenna:

```
=SUMIF(B2:B20,"Debbie McKenna",C2:C20)
```

PERFORMING STATISTICAL ANALYSES

Excel includes a huge number of statistical functions, including such widely used measures as standard deviation (STDEV), normal distribution (NORMDIST), Chi test (CHITEST), and Student's t-test (TTEST). As with the financial functions, these are most useful to people who have a firm grounding in the principles of statistical analysis, but a handful are applicable to users with a general business background.

Excel includes not one but three functions for working with a set of values. AVERAGE returns the arithmetic mean (the total of all values, divided by the number of entries in the list); MEDIAN returns the value in the middle of the list; and MODE returns the value that occurs most frequently. Depending on the distribution of data in a sample, any one of these three functions might be more or less appropriate.

MIN, MAX, and COUNT are straightforward functions that calculate the minimum, maximum, and number of entries in a list. These functions (and several others) have variations that end in the letter A—MINA, MAXA, and COUNTA. Use COUNTA, for example, when you want to work with not just numeric values in a list, but all arguments, including text and those that evaluate to a logical result such as TRUE or FALSE.

DATABASE FUNCTIONS

Excel includes a dozen functions you can incorporate into formulas to analyze information in a table (called a *list* before Excel 2007). These functions work with the same techniques as advanced filters—for each function, you define a criteria range, specify the location of a table, and select a column on which to perform calculations.

To work with any of these functions, click the Insert Function button to the right of the Name box. In the Insert Function dialog box, select Database from the Select a Category list. Choose any entry from the list on the right to see a brief description in the same dialog box, or click the Help button for step-by-step instructions on how to use the function and enter parameters.

Note that all 12 of these functions begin with the letter D (for *database*). All the D-functions take three arguments:

- **database**—The first argument is the range that contains your table; it must include the header row that contains column labels.
- **field**—The second argument is the label over the column you want to summarize.
- **criteria**—The final argument is the range that contains a condition you specify.

Use these functions to analyze whether values in a table meet specific criteria. For example, in a table that contains product information organized by category, you can count all the rows in which the category is "Cat" and the price is greater than $20.

TESTING AND DEBUGGING FORMULAS

The more complex the formula, the more likely you are to need time to get it working properly. Excel includes a variety of tools you can use to troubleshoot errors in formulas and in worksheets. This section discusses the most useful options.

HOW FORMULA AUTOCORRECT WORKS

Under most circumstances, Excel won't let you enter a formula using incorrect syntax. If you make one of many common mistakes in formula syntax or punctuation, Excel offers to correct the mistake for you, and generally the correction is appropriate. This feature, called *Formula AutoCorrect*, can detect and repair any of the following errors:

- Unmatched parentheses, curly braces, or single or double quotation marks.

- Reversed cell references (14C instead of C14, for example) or comparison operators (=< instead of <=).

- Extra operators, such as an equal sign or plus sign, at the beginning or end of a formula.

- Extra spaces in cell addresses (A 14 instead of A14), between operands, or between a function name and its arguments.

- Extra decimal points or operators—in general, Excel uses the decimal point or operator farthest to the left and removes all others, so 234.56.78 becomes 234.5678, and =23*/34 becomes =23*34.

- Incorrect range identifiers, such as a semicolon or an extra colon between the column and row identifiers.

- Implied multiplication—if you omit the multiplication sign and enter 2(A14+B14), for example, or use an x instead, Excel adds the correct sign.

RESOLVING COMMON ERROR MESSAGES

All Excel error messages begin with a number sign (#); in all, you might see any of seven possible error codes. To remove the error message and display the results you expect, you have to fix the problem either by editing the formula or changing the contents of a cell to which the formula refers.

If the cell in question contains an error message, you see a small green triangle in the upper-left corner of the cell. Click to select that cell, and a Smart Tag with a yellow exclamation point appears. Click the Smart Tag to display a menu like the one shown in Figure 20.13.

Figure 20.13
Click the Smart Tag to find clues to the cause of an error message and possible solutions.

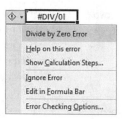

The top line in the Smart Tag menu displays the name of the error and is not clickable. Use additional menu choices to find possible causes and solutions for the error.

Table 20.3 lists the seven error codes you're likely to see when an Excel formula isn't working properly, along with suggested troubleshooting steps.

TABLE 20.3 COMMON FORMULA ERROR CODES

Error Code Displayed	What It Means	Suggested Troubleshooting Steps
#DIV/0!	Formula is trying to divide by a zero value or a blank cell.	Check the divisor in your formula and make sure it does not refer to a blank cell. You might want to add an error-handling =IF() routine or conditional format to the cell, as described earlier in this chapter.
#N/A	Formula does not have a valid value for argument passed.	#N/A means "No value is available." Check to see whether you have problems with LOOKUP functions. You can also manually enter the #N/A value in cells in which a value is temporarily unavailable, to prevent #DIV/0! errors.
#NAME?	Formula contains text that is neither a valid function nor a defined name on the active worksheet.	You've probably misspelled a function name or a range name. Check the formula carefully. In a natural-language formula, this error means Excel cannot identify one or both labels.
#NULL!	Refers to intersection of two areas that don't intersect.	You're trying to calculate a formula by using labels for a column and row that have no common cells. Choose new labels for the row or column or both.
#NUM!	Value is too large, too small, imaginary, or not found.	Excel can handle numbers as large as 10^{308} or as small as 10^{-308}. This error usually means you've used a function incorrectly—for example, calculating the square root of a negative number.
#REF!	Formula contains a reference that is not valid.	Did you delete a cell or range originally referred to in the formula? If so, you see this error code in the formula as well.

Error Code Displayed	What It Means	Suggested Troubleshooting Steps
#VALUE!	Formula contains an argument of the wrong type.	You've probably mixed two incompatible data types in one formula—trying to add text with a number, for example. Check the formula again.

CHECKING FOR ERRORS IN A WORKSHEET

As noted in the previous section, Excel tracks formula errors automatically as you work, displaying a green triangle in the upper-left corner of any cell that contains an error. You can also check for errors on a sheet manually, by clicking the Error Checking button in Formulas ribbon in the Formula Auditing group. When you click this button, Excel finds the first error (on the current sheet only) and displays a dialog box like the one shown in Figure 20.14. Use the Previous and Next buttons to highlight additional errors on the sheet.

Figure 20.14
Click the Show Calculation Steps button to step through each operation and debug a complex formula.

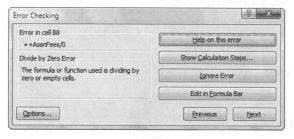

If the error is harmless and you don't want Excel to nag you about it any further, click the Ignore Error button. For simple errors where the fix is immediately obvious (a typographical error or a misplaced divisor, for instance), click the Edit in Formula Bar button to make the change directly, without closing the Error Checking dialog box.

For complex formulas, in which an error can be difficult to track down, click the Show Calculation Steps button. This button opens the Evaluate Formula dialog box (see Figure 20.15), which lets you drill down into a formula to find and fix the problem.

Figure 20.15
Clicking the Step In button allows you to drill down into a formula in search of errors from another cell.

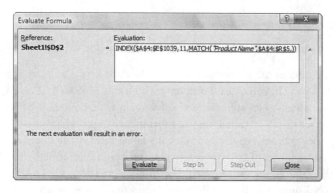

20

The initial view shows each element in the formula, evaluated to the result just before the error. Click the Evaluate button to step through the error. Keep clicking and you'll eventually return to the formula as entered, where you can walk through each element of the formula, moving from left to right. With each click, Excel evaluates another part of the formula.

For formulas that refer to other formulas in other cells, click the Step In button to follow the chain of references through as many steps as it takes to find the error.

TIP FROM

Ed & Woody

If you inherit a worksheet that someone else has developed and you want to quickly check it for errors, take this precautionary step: Open the Error Checking dialog box, click the Options button, and click the Reset Ignored Errors button. This option ensures that you'll see all possible errors that Excel can detect, even if a previous user hid the error indicators.

Click the Options button on the Error Checking dialog box to specify which errors Excel should look for. For instance, Excel normally flags dates with two-digit years as errors (because of possible date arithmetic problems) and also calls out any formula that is inconsistent with other formulas in the same row or column. If you get tired of false alarms, uncheck any of the boxes in the Error Checking and Error Checking Rules section of the Excel Options dialog box that appears as shown in Figure 20.16.

Figure 20.16
Use these options to prevent Excel from checking for certain types of errors.

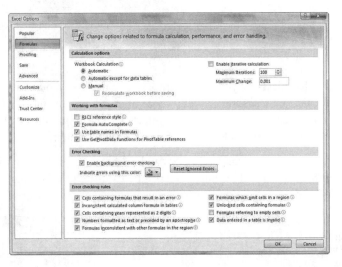

Excel dutifully catches many common types of formula errors as soon as you press Enter. For instance, if you click in cell E8 and enter the formula =SUM(E1:E7)/E8, Excel will warn you that you're about to create a *circular reference*, in which one part of your formula refers to itself. Because the act of calculating the formula changes one of the values in the formula, you'll get a different result each time you calculate a formula that contains a circular reference. More subtle forms of circular references incorporate intermediate calculations that depend on the value in the current cell. For instance, if a formula in A8 refers to a value in E8, adding a reference to A8 into the formula in E8 will create a circular reference.

If you inadvertently create a circular reference, you can use the Circular Reference button (click the arrow to the right of your Formulas ribbon's Error Checking button and select Circular Reference) to display all circular references in a drop-down list so that you can locate the error and fix it.

NOTE

Some esoteric scientific calculations rely on circular references. In this case, you can specify the number of *iterations* you want to use when recalculating the formula. For a more detailed explanation, see the Allow or Correct a Circular Reference Help topic.

USING THE WATCH WINDOW TO MONITOR CALCULATIONS

Normally, as you enter and edit values in a worksheet, formulas that reference those values change as well. If the formula is close to the cells you're editing, you can see the results immediately. But it's more difficult to track formula results when the formulas are widely separated—on the same worksheet or even on linked sheets in a different workbook.

Thanks to a feature first introduced in Excel 2002, you can keep an eye on the results of specific cells, even when those cells are on different sheets. Use the Watch Window (available on the Formulas ribbon) to track a list of cells; this window floats above the current worksheet, as shown in Figure 20.17. With this window open, you don't have to continually switch between worksheets to monitor your work.

Figure 20.17
The Watch Window lets you track formula results across multiple workbooks. Range names make it easier to identify why you added a cell to the list.

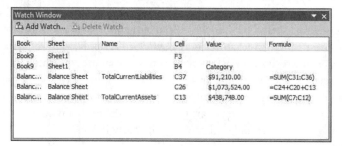

TIP FROM

You can drag the lower-right corner of the Watch Window to increase or decrease the size of the window and its contents.

20

To add a single cell to the Watch Window, select the cell, right-click, and choose Add Watch. (If the selected cell is already on the Watch list, the menu changes to Delete Watch.) As soon as you add a cell address, the Watch Window appears. As with any list-based control, you can click a column heading to sort by that column, or resize columns by dragging the line between column headings.

You can drag the window to any edge of the screen, where it will dock. (If you want to dock the Watch Window, try the bottom of the screen; that gives you the ability to view information in all columns and doesn't interfere with task panes.) You can't minimize the Watch

Window; the down arrow to the left of the Close box in the upper-right corner leads to a basically useless Customize menu.

→ For more details about using and customizing Office toolbars, see "Customizing Toolbars and Menus in Outlook and Publisher," **p. 34**.

After the Watch Window is open, use the Add Watch button to select a group of cells and quickly add them to the list.

TIP FROM

> If you use the Watch Window a lot, we recommend that you define names for the cells you include on the Watch list. The Name column appears in the list, and a meaningful name like Jan_Sales_Total makes it much easier to identify the value you're tracking than a cell address like B10.

TROUBLESHOOTING

EDITING AN ARRAY FORMULA

I entered an array formula, but when I try to edit or copy it, the results change or I get an error message.

Editing an array formula is tricky. If the array formula was entered across multiple cells, you must select every cell that contains the array before you can edit it. If the array formula is contained in a single cell, you can edit it just as you would a conventional formula, but you must remember to press Ctrl+Shift+Enter to store your changes as an array formula. If you forget and press Enter, Excel stores it as a standard formula, with the wrong results. Finally, you'll notice some restrictions when you try to copy an array formula. If the destination range you select also contains the array formula, you'll get an error message. Select a new destination range, or use AutoFill to copy the formula. Oh, and don't try to cheat by adding your own curly braces to create an array formula—the only way to enter an array formula is to press Ctrl+Shift+Enter and let Excel add the curly braces.

CHECKING FORMULAS BEFORE DELETING RANGE NAMES

After I deleted a range name in my worksheet, some of my formulas displayed error messages.

It's a frustrating fact of life: When you delete a range name from a worksheet, Excel does not automatically adjust any formulas that contain that range name. Even though it should, logically, be able to substitute the old cell address for the range name, it leaves the name there to torture you. After deleting a range name, you will see a #NAME? error in any cell that contains a formula with a reference to the deleted range name. Unfortunately, there's no easy way to determine which cell goes with the defunct name. If you spot these errors immediately after deleting the range name, press Ctrl+Z to undo your change. If you remember this possibility before deleting a range name, you can easily change any cells before deleting or changing the defined name. Press Ctrl+F to open the Find dialog box, enter the name of the cell or range, choose Formulas from the Look In box, and click Find Next to jump to and edit each cell that contains that name.

CONVERTING VALUES TO TEXT BEFORE CONCATENATING

When I try to combine a cell that contains text with one that contains a date, the result is nonsense. The cell that holds the date is correctly formatted, but the resulting text says something like "Today is 38059" instead of displaying a date.

As you've seen, Excel ignores the formatting of the original cell when concatenating the two values and instead displays the serial date value. Before concatenating a date with text, you must convert the date to text and choose a format. Use the TEXT function followed by a format in quotation marks. If the date is in cell A15, for example, use this formula to get the result you're looking for: `="Today is "&TEXT(A15,"mmmm d, yyyy")`.

SECRETS OF THE OFFICE MASTERS: USING GOAL SEEK TO FIND ANSWERS

After you've constructed a worksheet and built several intricate formulas, you might discover that you can't easily get the answer you're looking for. A formula that uses the PMT function, for example, is designed to produce the total monthly payment when you enter the price and loan details. But what if you've determined your maximum monthly payment, you've shopped around for the best interest rate, and now you want to calculate the maximum loan amount you can afford based on those values? Rather than construct a new formula or use trial-and-error methods to find the right result, use Excel's Goal Seek tool to perform the calculations in one operation:

1. Start by opening the worksheet that contains the formula you want to work with, and then choose Goal Seek from the What-If Analysis button on your Data ribbon. Excel displays the Goal Seek dialog box shown in Figure 20.18.

   Figure 20.18

2. Fill in the three boxes to match the results you're trying to achieve. In the Set Cell box, enter the address of the formula whose results you want to control. In the To Value box, enter the amount the formula specified in the previous cell should equal. Finally, in the By Changing Cell box, enter the cell that contains the single value you want to change.

3. When you click OK, Excel runs through all possibilities and displays the Goal Seek Status dialog box, as shown in **Figure 20.19**. If you look at the worksheet itself, you'll see the values have changed to reflect the result shown here.

   Figure 20.19

4. Click OK to incorporate the changed data into your worksheet; click Cancel to close the dialog box and restore the original data.

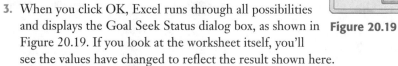

If your problem is more complex and can't be solved by changing a single cell, use the Solver add-in. Like other Excel add-ins, you must install this option before it's available on your ribbon. Click your Office button and then click Excel Options. Click the Add-ins link to display the Add-ins group options. At the bottom of the window, select Excel Add-ins for the Manage selection and click Go to display the Add-ins dialog box. Click the Solver Add-in option to install Solver for the first time (install the add-in if Excel says you need to). Then click to display your Data ribbon and on the far-right will appear the Analysis group with Solver button. Click Solver to display the Solver Parameters dialog box, as shown in Figure 20.20.

Figure 20.20
Use the Solver Parameters dialog box to specify more complex conditions for working backward to a formula's solution.

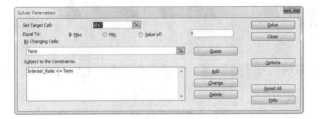

Select the cell that you want to adjust in the Set Target Cell box, click the Max, Min, or Value Of box, and enter a comparison amount. In the By Changing Cells box, select the cells you want to adjust. Note that unlike the Goal Seek feature, you can specify multiple cells here. Finally, enter any constraints you want to impose on the solution; for example, you can specify a maximum or minimum value for one or more of the changing cells. Click the Solve button to begin calculating.

When the Solver utility completes its calculation, it displays the Solver Results dialog box, shown in Figure 20.21. If Solver reports an error message, adjust the constraints and try again. If Solver successfully found a solution, you have three choices: Select the Keep Solver Solution option and click OK to change the values in your worksheet; choose the Restore Original Values option and click OK to cancel all changes; or click the Save Scenario button to create a worksheet scenario using the Solver results.

Figure 20.21
The Solver Results dialog box shows the results of a formula's calculations.

→ For a detailed discussion of workbook scenarios, **see** "Secrets of the Office Masters: Storing Multiple Scenarios in a Single Workbook," **p. 588**.

CHAPTER 21

ORGANIZING DATA WITH TABLES AND PIVOTTABLES

In this chapter

Defining a Range as a Table   628

Sorting and Filtering Data in a Table   631

Importing and Exporting Data   643

Connecting a Worksheet to External Databases   645

Creating and Using Web Queries   649

Analyzing Information with PivotTables   651

When Should You Use a PivotTable?   655

Creating a PivotTable   655

Editing and Updating a PivotTable   657

Troubleshooting   661

Secrets of the Office Masters: Combining Data from Several Web Sources in a Custom Page   662

DEFINING A RANGE AS A TABLE

Excel's row-and-column structure makes it an ideal tool for organizing related information into a *table*. (Before Excel 2007, lists were called *tables*.) On an Excel worksheet, a table is a group of consecutive rows of related data. Conceptually, an Excel table is identical to a table in Access (or any other database management program). Each *column* within a table is equivalent to a database *field*, and each row is the same as a *record* of data; headings in the top row represent the names of the fields. Within each column, you can enter text, numbers, dates, formulas, or hyperlinks. Excel does not impose any additional restrictions on the type of data that you can enter in a table.

Excel 2007 provides room for huge worksheets never before possible, enabling you to create tables up to 1 million rows with 16,000 columns. You won't have to break up your data into multiple spreadsheets as you may have done previously. In addition, you can create, format, expand, and refer to tables in your worksheet formulas and more easily keep table headings on your screen easily while you scroll through the table data underneath.

You can sort table data in nearly any order, search for a specific bit of information, or use filters to find groups of data that match criteria that you specify. For complex tables, Excel can automatically create *outlines* that let you summarize and subtotal groups of records. Large, complex tables are the perfect starting point for PivotTables, which let you drag fields on a layout page to perform complex data-analysis tasks without having to construct a single formula.

→ For a full discussion of the wonders of PivotTables, **see** "Analyzing Information with PivotTables," **p. 651**.

Excel uses column labels in the first row of a table (also called the *header row*) to identify the names of fields used for sorting and filtering. Although you can create a table without a header row, we highly recommend that you include column labels for every table that you create or import. You must have a header row if you want to enter data using forms or use the AutoFilter feature to find groups of records. If you specify a range of cells to be a table but your table does not include headers, Excel automatically adds generic headers—Column1, Column2, and so on—and applies bold formatting to make those column labels stand out from the data area.

TIP FROM

> You don't need a header row to sort a range of data; to sort a data range that is not identified as a table and doesn't include column labels, be sure to select the No Header Row option when you sort.

To create a new table, select the range you want to use. The selection can be empty, or it can contain an existing table. Click the Styles tab's Format as Table button on your Home ribbon. Excel displays the Table Style gallery shown in Figure 21.1.

Figure 21.1
Point to different table formats and Excel's Live Format feature updates your table to show what it will look like if you select a table format.

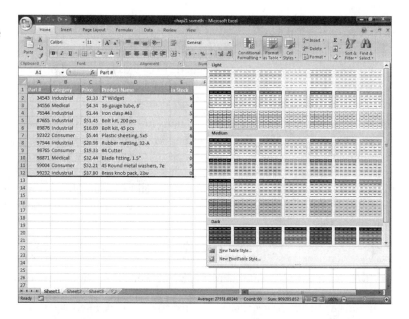

Select a gallery style that looks like the table you want to create. Excel displays the Format as Table dialog box shown in Figure 21.2.

Figure 21.2
If you leave the My Table Has Headers box unchecked, Excel automatically adds generic headers to your table.

If your selection includes existing data with labels at the top of each column, select the My Table Has Headers check box. Click OK to create the table. Excel automatically formats the header row (adding generic column headings if necessary) and also formats the rest of your table to match your request from the Table Styles Gallery. If your worksheet includes data in any row that is directly adjacent to the table range, Excel moves the table range and the existing rows to make room.

As soon as Excel 2007 converts your range to a table, your ribbon changes to show the many table formatting commands, and it gives you one-click access to the Table Styles gallery from which you can select a different formatting style.

When creating a table, follow these basic guidelines:

- Whenever possible, define tables explicitly by clicking the Format as Table button. From the Insert ribbon, you can also click the Table button to convert your selected cells to a table. You can create as many tables as you want on a single worksheet. As you create each table, Excel names them Table1, Table2, and so on. You can (and should) change your table names to something more meaningful.

→ For more details on how to manage multiple worksheets in a single workbook, **see** "Working with Multiple Worksheets," **p. 509**.

- Create a single header row with a unique label for each column. Descriptive headings are much more useful than the generic ones Excel creates. For tables you plan to print, you can add distinctive formatting to help make the column headings stand out even more, including larger font sizes and a border beneath the header row.

- Avoid leaving any blank rows or columns in your table. To add data to a table, click the row beneath the table's last row and fill in the information for that row. If you've applied a Table Style, Excel will extend that style to your new row.

NEW Excel 2007 doesn't display an insert row at the end of your table as previous versions did. Excel 2007 automatically assumes you're adding a new row if you type data in the row beneath a table.

→ To prevent yourself or other users of a worksheet from entering invalid data, including blank cells, create data validation rules; **see** "Restricting and Validating Data Entry for a Cell or Range," **p. 532**.

- To make it easier to enter data, freeze the worksheet panes just below the header row.

→ For instructions on how to freeze worksheet panes, **see** "Locking Row and Column Labels for Onscreen Viewing," **p. 529**.

To resize a table, click the table's resizing handle (a small arrow in the bottom-right corner of the last cell) and drag the table to a wider size or drag to make it longer with more rows. Excel fills in the names of any new columns you add with the Column X name. If you make the table smaller, Excel keeps any data that was in the rows or columns you excluded from the table.

Watch Out for Automatic Formatting

When you enter new data in an existing table, Excel automatically picks up numeric formatting and formulas from the previous rows without requiring you to explicitly format cells in the new row. At least three of the previous rows must be formatted the same for the new row's cell to pick up that automatic formatting. For example, if the first cell in the previous row is formatted in bold italic, Excel automatically applies that formatting as soon as you enter the data into the first cell in the new row. If the last cell in the previous row contains a formula that multiplies the values in the two previous cells, Excel adds that formula as soon as you enter data in the second of the two cells that make up that formula.

This feature isn't foolproof. For some inexplicable reason, Excel won't automatically pick up date formatting from the previous row, although it will consistently copy font formatting and attributes. Likewise, new rows pick up colors and shading consistently, but borders don't always extend as you expect. Although the documentation claims that Excel will pick up formatting and formulas that match three of the previous five rows, we found that this automatic feature works consistently only if the formatting appears in four of the previous five rows. Our advice? Don't rely on guesswork. Format the cells in your table range before you begin entering data so that you can maintain control over the appearance of data you enter.

If you don't want Excel to automatically pick up formatting and formulas from previous rows, turn off this capability. Click your Office button and select Excel Options. Click to show the Advanced group and then click to uncheck the option labeled Extend Data Range Formats and Formulas under Editing Options

---

SORTING AND FILTERING DATA IN A TABLE

Depending on how much data your table or tables hold, you need a way to get to your data quickly. Without good sorting, searching, and filtering tools, a table with lots of data would be little more than meaningless details. When you use Excel's table-related tools, your data becomes information and the difference is that you will have answers you need that your data can provide.

The following sections show you how to use Excel's powerful table-management tools. For many people, Excel's simpler data tools are all they need to track simple inventories and other tables of data that don't require the services of an advanced database system such as Access 2007.

→ To learn about the more powerful standalone relational database features of Access 2007, **see** "Access Essentials," **p. 835**.

PERFORMING SIMPLE SORTS

Excel's table-sorting capabilities let you view your table data in almost any order, regardless of the order in which you entered it. For performing sorts, your data doesn't even have to be formatted as a table with headings.

To quickly sort data in your worksheet, even if the data doesn't appear in a table, first click a single cell in the column by which you want to sort, and then click the Sort and Filter button on the Home ribbon. Select the *ascending sort* (which sorts data alphabetically from A to Z or from 0 to 9, as opposed to a *descending sort*, which sorts from Z to A, or from 9 to 0). Excel selects all the data in your selected column as well as the columns of data that touch that column so that all your rows of data sort together properly.

Select a descending sort to sort in reverse order, using the same column. If you want to sort only a portion of the table, make a selection first, and then use the Tab key to move the active cell to the correct column. This option, used incorrectly, can make a mess of your database, so use it with caution.

TIP FROM

EQ & Woody

> If the order in which you enter data is important, add a column to your table and fill it with numeric values that you can use to identify each row, and then increment it by 1 for each new record. Re-sort using the values in this column to return the table to its original order if you need to reverse a sort that went haywire. Don't use a formula for the data in this column, however—when you sort the table, the values will change and you won't be able to return to the original sort order. Of course, as long as you see that a problem has occurred, you can use Excel's Undo command (available as a button on your Quick Access Toolbar or by the Ctrl+Z shortcut key) to reverse a sort.

When you choose ascending order, Excel always sorts numbers first, then most punctuation characters, and then letters, in ascending (A–Z) order, without regard to whether the letters are uppercase or lowercase. Excel generally ignores apostrophes and hyphens when sorting; if two entries are otherwise identical but one contains a hyphen, it will appear after the one that does not contain a hyphen. The precise order for punctuation follows the same order as the Unicode character set, as follows:

(space) ! " # $ % & (°) * , . / : ; ? @ [\ ] [ct] _ [ag] { ¦ } [td] + < = >

21

Sorting data in a table with column headers is even simpler than using the Sort and Filter button (which works for table data, too). Click the down arrow on any column header and select Sort A to Z for an ascending sort, or Sort Z to Z to perform a descending sort, and Excel sorts your table's rows ordered by your selected column.

NOTE

> Between now and the section titled "Using Filters to Find Sets of Data," the sorting commands discussed work for both regular worksheet data as well as tables you've created in Excel and populated with data. You can tell when a table appears because of the AutoFilter arrows to the right of each column heading, as Figure 21.3 shows.

Figure 21.3
You can distinguish between a table and a worksheet by the arrows that appear to the right of column names on tables.

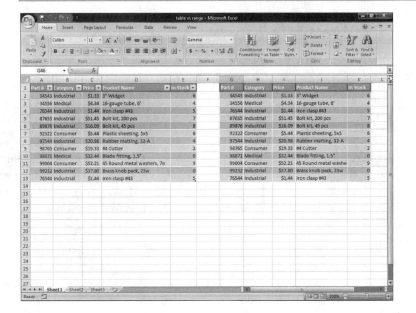

Sorting by Multiple Columns

By using the two sort options on the Sort and Filter button, you can perform a multicolumn sort without ever using a dialog box. Perform each column sort in sequence, using the reverse of the final order that you want to see; Excel preserves the order of other columns in the table when you sort each succeeding column. In a sales results worksheet, for example, you might click in the Salesperson column and click a sort button, and then do the same with the Month column, and finally, with the Region column. The result is to sort your table by region, then by month, and then by salesperson.

If sorting your table has unexpected results, see "Sorting Out Sorting Problems" in the "Troubleshooting" section at the end of this chapter.

The Sort dialog box lets you sort multiple columns at one time. To open the Sort dialog box, display your Data ribbon and click Sort to open the Sort dialog box shown in Figure 21.4. Excel 2007 now lets you specify up to 64 columns for your sort order (in contrast to only three in previous versions), using ascending or descending order for each one.

Figure 21.4
This Sort dialog box shows three sort keys, each corresponding to a column label in the table.

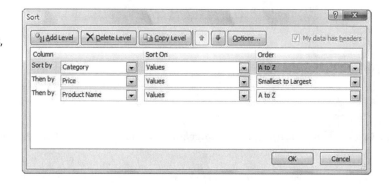

SORTING BY DATES OR CUSTOM SERIES

By default, Excel's sort options reorder data alphabetically or numerically. However, a basic A–Z or 1–10 sort isn't always appropriate. Dates and weekdays in text format represent a particular problem. For example, a table of bonds or mortgage loans might include a column, formatted as text, that identifies the month in which an investment matures. Or a table of shift assignments for employees might include a column of weekdays. Using the default sort order would put the month names and weekdays in alphabetical order—April, August, December, February, or Mon, Sat, Sun, Thu—when you actually want to sort the table in calendar order. You might also want to sort your table using a custom AutoFill table—by region, for example, or by budget category (see the previous section for details about how to create one of these tables).

Sorting by date or a custom series is available only when you use the Sort dialog box. To sort by text dates or using a custom series, follow these steps:

1. Click in the table that you want to sort, or select the region of your worksheet to be sorted.

 2. Click the Data ribbon's Sort button and identify up to 64 columns for sorting. The column that contains the dates or custom table can be any in the table and not just the first column, as was required in previous versions of Excel 2007.

3. Click the down arrow in the first Sort By option, select the column that holds the series you want to sort by, and select Custom List. The default selection includes four built-in tables—days of the week and months, in long and short versions. In addition, any custom tables that you've created will appear here. You will see your customized sort list in the Order field, as Figure 21.5 shows.

21

Figure 21.5
Easily sort according to a custom list you've created.

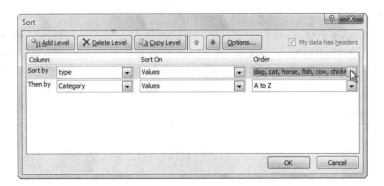

5. Click OK to confirm the sort order that you selected; then click OK again to perform the sort.

NOTE

By default, Excel does not distinguish between lowercase and capital letters when sorting. To change this setting, click the Options button in the Sort dialog box and check Case Sensitive. With this option enabled, Excel sorts lowercase letters ahead of capital letters.

For the first time, Excel now allows your date or custom sort to appear as any sort key, not just the first one. Feel free, for example, to search by an inventory part number and then by date.

USING FILTERS TO FIND SETS OF DATA

When working with tables, you can use the Find shortcut (Ctrl+F) to search for any value in the table. That technique is useful if you want to jump quickly to a specific unique value in the table, and it works whether your worksheet data is actually stored in a formal table with column headings or not. Instead of simple searching, however, you'll often want to extract details from a table instead of simply jumping to a single record. In that case, use filters to hide all records except those that match criteria that you specify. This is one of the biggest advantages to using data in a table format, rather than using regular worksheet data. You cannot filter worksheet data unless you've turned that data into a table with column headings. After you do that, you can filter and do far more database-related operations with your data to make your data much more useful than it would be in a regular worksheet. For example, in a table that contains hundreds or thousands of rows, defining a filter helps you see a small number of related records together, making it easier to compare data and identify trends.

Consider a table of numerous daily high, low, and closing stock prices that includes data for many companies. You might want to see only those records in which the entry in the Symbol column is equal to KO (that's the Coca-Cola Company, for those who don't know ticker symbols by heart). Or, if you import product inventory information from a database into an Excel table, you can use filters to show only items that are currently out of stock, making it easy to build a reorder table.

AutoFilter options let you select information by choosing from drop-down tables of unique items in each column. You can also create custom filters using multiple criteria and combining criteria from multiple columns, or you can display only the top 10 (or bottom 10) entries in a table, by number or percentage, based on the contents of a single column.

NOTE

> Unlike sorts, which rearrange data in a table, filters do not change the underlying data. When you define a filter, you hide records that don't match the criteria that you define.

→ For an overview of Office standard Find and Replace tools, **see** "Finding and Replacing Text," **p. 82**.

→ For details on database functions that let you analyze with data in tables, **see** "Database Functions," **p. 618**.

The easiest way to build a filter is with the help of Excel's AutoFilter capability. When this option is enabled, you can define criteria by choosing values from drop-down tables. As the name implies, an AutoFilter applies the filter to your table automatically, as soon as you select the criteria. When you understand how AutoFilters work, you can use them to narrow even massive tables.

When you define a table (by clicking inside your data and then clicking the Home ribbon's Format as Table button to transform the range to a table or by clicking the Insert ribbon's Table button to convert a worksheet to a table or create a new table), the AutoFilter option is enabled by default. For tables that are not explicitly defined, or where you have previously disabled the AutoFilter feature, you can create an AutoFilter manually by clicking anywhere in your table and clicking your Data ribbon's Filter button.

When AutoFilter is on, a drop-down arrow appears to the right of each column heading in your table, as shown in Figure 21.6. Click the arrow to the right of the column label that you want to use as the first condition in the filter.

Figure 21.6
Drop-down AutoFilter tables let you narrow your selection by choosing from all unique values in that column.

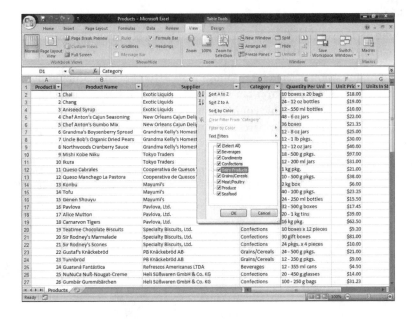

Choose an item from the drop-down table to restrict the display to only rows that contain that item, or choose any of the options shown in the following bulleted table. Excel applies your criteria immediately, filtering out all rows except those that contain the value that you selected.

N O T E

Excel generates the drop-down table of AutoFilter values for each column automatically by pulling out all unique values from that column. As a result, every item on the drop-down table is guaranteed to be in that column, making it impossible to select an incorrect value. AutoFilter tables always display in ascending order.

Depending on the type of data you filter—text or numeric, for example—the AutoFilter drop-down list includes extra filters such as Text Filters and Number Filters that provide advanced filters based on criteria you specify. Some of the more popular numeric filter choices you'll find are the following:

Figure 21.7

- **Top 10**—Show the highest or lowest numeric values in a table by number or by percentage. Don't be misled by the name—when you choose this option, you see a dialog box that lets you select any number between 1 and 500; you can choose Bottom or Top, and you can specify percent as well. Use the settings in Figure 21.7, for example, to display the top 5% of all products in a table, based on the amount in the selected column. If the table contains 2,000 items, this setting will show only the top 100.

If Excel beeps or displays unexpected results when you try to use the Top 10 option, see "Top 10 Is for Numbers Only" in the "Troubleshooting" section at the end of this chapter.

- **Custom**—Use comparison operators (covered in the next section) to define criteria. You can combine up to two criteria using this option.

- **Blanks**—Display only records that contain no data in the selected column. This option is available only if the selected column contains one or more blank cells.

- **NonBlanks**—Display all records that contain data in the selected column, hiding blank records. This option is available only if the selected column contains one or more blank cells.

- **All**—Show all records in the table. Use this option to remove AutoFilter criteria from a column.

AutoFilter criteria are cumulative; by combining criteria in different columns, you can successively filter a table to display an increasingly selective group of records. Although you can choose filter criteria in any order, it's best to start with columns that include the fewest options because the table of choices for succeeding columns will be narrower and easier to scroll through.

When you apply a filter to a table, Excel changes the drop-down arrow to include a funnel icon on the column that you selected to filter. That is your only indication that a particular column is filtered. As the table in Figure 21.8 shows, Excel maintains the row numbers of the underlying table when you use an AutoFilter, hiding all rows that don't match the criteria that you specified.

Figure 21.8
Because an AutoFilter does not change the data in the underlying table, you'll see gaps in row numbering when you filter a table.

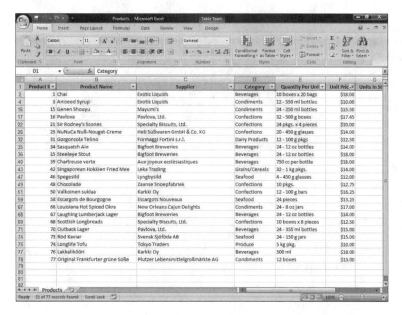

To change AutoFilter criteria, click the filter icon on the column heading to open the filter options for that column again and select another value. To remove AutoFilter criteria for a single column, choose Clear Filter from *Heading* (where *Heading* is the title on your column heading). To remove all AutoFilter criteria from the table as you might want to do if you've filtered multiple columns and no longer want to do so, click the Clear button on the Data ribbon. The drop-down arrows disappear from all column headings.

Excel does not automatically retain custom sets of AutoFilter criteria. When you save a worksheet that contains an AutoFiltered table, your table appears with AutoFilter settings intact when you reopen it. However, as soon as you choose a different AutoFilter option for a column (or disable the AutoFilter option completely), Excel discards any custom criteria that you've created for that column. To reapply those same AutoFilter criteria, you have to create a custom view or reenter the criteria.

USING COMPARISON CRITERIA TO CREATE CUSTOM FILTERS

The drop-down AutoFilter table for each column allows you to select one and only one specific value. In some cases, that limitation gets in the way of finding the information that you need. For example, what if you want to search through your product table and find all items whose price is less than $10? Or, what if you want to find items whose name includes the text "puppy"? To create complex criteria in an AutoFiltered table, click the Filters option to display the filter options and select Custom Filter from the list that appears.

The Custom AutoFilter dialog box (see Figure 21.9) enables you to use any of the following *comparison operators*:

Figure 21.9
Use the Custom AutoFilter dialog box to combine criteria; if you need more than two criteria, use an Advanced Filter instead.

- Equals/does not equal
- Is greater than/is less than
- Is greater than or equal to/is less than or equal to
- Begins with/does not begin with
- Ends with/does not end with
- Contains/does not contain

You can also combine two criteria for a single column using the logical operator AND, or use the OR operator to tell Excel that you want to see records that match either of the criteria that you specify for that column.

Select a comparison operator for the first criterion, and then click in the box to the right of the comparison operator and enter the value that you want to use as a logical test. Or, use the drop-down table to select from all unique values in the column. If you add a second criterion for the same column, click And to select only rows in which both criteria are true; click Or to create a filter that shows rows in which either set of criteria is true.

TIP FROM

Although you're limited to only two criteria when you use AutoFilter's Custom option, you can easily work around this limitation by using Excel's capability to filter on criteria for two or more columns at once. Make a copy of the column that you want to use in your filter, and specify a separate set of criteria in the AutoFilter box for that column.

FILTERING WITH ADVANCED CRITERIA

Compared with the one-click ease of AutoFilters, Excel's advanced filters are downright cumbersome. Still, they're the only way to accomplish some tasks, such as defining more than three criteria for a single column or finding only unique values within a table that contains duplicate entries. Advanced filters also let you specify more complex criteria than you can use with AutoFilters, including criteria based on formulas.

To use advanced filters, start by creating a *criteria range* on the same worksheet that contains the table. Criteria are conditions you set which limit what table records will appear in your worksheet. You might, for example, wish to create a criteria so that only rows with inventory quantities below 5 show up for a reordering report. Although you can add this range anywhere on the table, we strongly recommend that you place it directly above the table, where it's unlikely to be affected by any changes that you make to the sheet's design. Allow a minimum of three rows in the criteria range—one for the column labels, one for the criteria, and one to serve as a separator between the table and the criteria range.

TIP FROM

Add one extra row for each set of criteria that you expect to use when filtering the table. In almost all circumstances, you can get by with a criteria range of five rows, which allows you to add up to three sets of criteria for each column while still maintaining a one-row separation between the criteria range and the table.

Copy the column labels from the table to the first row of the criteria range. The resulting range should look something like the example shown in Figure 21.10, which also includes several criteria.

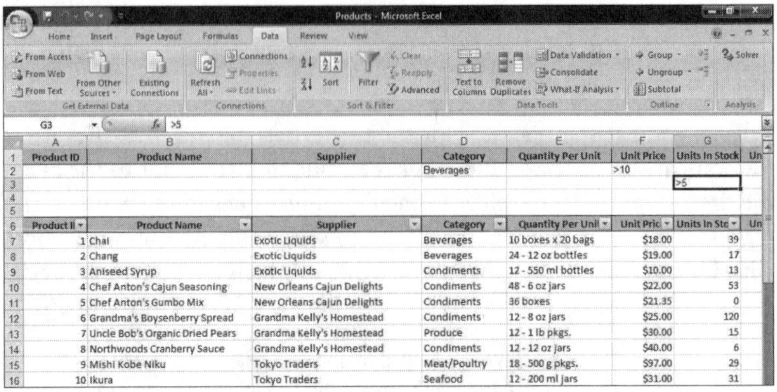

Figure 21.10
Always create the criteria range above the table, not below or alongside it; that placement keeps it from being scrambled when you extend or sort the table.

→ For more details on working with named ranges, **see** "Using Named Ranges in Formulas," **p. 601**.

Begin entering criteria in the row just below the column labels. You can enter text, numbers, dates, or logical values using comparison operators such as > and <. To find values that are greater than or equal to a specific value, use the >= operator. For example, >=1000 finds all values greater than or equal to 1000 in the specified column; in a text column, <C finds all entries that begin with A or B.

You can enter values in more than one column and in more than one row. When you do, Excel interprets your input as follows:

- For values in more than one column within a single row, Excel looks for records that match all values that you specify in the row, the equivalent of a logical AND.

- For values in the same column in separate rows, Excel displays records that match any of the values, the equivalent of a logical OR.

In essence, each row in the criteria range equals a single *condition*. By mixing and matching conditions, you can filter a table in different ways, including the following:

- **Multiple conditions for one column**—Enter each condition in a separate cell under the column label in the criteria range. In the example shown in Figure 21.11, any row containing the value Beverages, Condiments, or Confections in the Category column will match.

Category
Beverages
Condiments
Confections

Figure 21.11

- **One condition in each of several columns**—Enter each condition under its respective column label in the same row. The example in Figure 21.12 will match rows in which the value in the Category column is Beverages and the price is more than $10. Generally, this type of filter is much easier to apply using an AutoFilter.

Category	Quantity Per Unit	Unit Price
Beverages		>10

Figure 21.12

■ **Multiple conditions in multiple columns—**
Enter each set of conditions in its own row of
the criteria range, and Excel will find rows in the
table that match either set. Figure 21.13 finds
any item in the Beverages category whose price is
more than $10, or any item in the Confections category whose price is greater than
$20. This type of condition is nearly impossible to match with an AutoFilter.

Category	Quantity Per Unit	Unit Price
Beverages		>10
Confections		>20

Figure 21.13

TIP FROM

Ed & Woody

To specify multiple criteria for the same column in the same row, add another column
heading in the criteria range, using the same column label (extend the criteria range, if
necessary, or replace the label for an existing column for which you're not defining conditions). For example, if you have a column called Amount, add a second column label,
also called Amount, to your criteria range. Then, when you enter >3000 in one cell and
<6000 in the other, both in the same row, Excel finds only records in which the Amount
is between 3000 and 6000.

CAUTION

If you enter text in a criteria range, Excel finds all matching records that begin with that
text. Thus, if you enter the letter F under the Category label, Excel finds all records whose
category begins with F. To find only records that match the exact text that you specify,
you must enter the value using the following format: =`"=text"` (where *text* is the value
you want to use in your condition). Make sure to include both equal signs.

Finally, you can create conditions based on formulas. Although formulas can be a powerful
way to filter a table, they are extremely challenging to enter, and the syntax is confusing.
Unlike other conditions, which must appear under a label in the criteria range that matches
the corresponding label in the table, you must not use a column label with a formula. Enter
the formulas in a cell beneath a blank label, or change the label above it so that it does not
match a label in the table. Individual references in the formula should come from the column label or the first record of the table, and the formulas must evaluate to TRUE or FALSE.

In the example in Figure 21.14, note that we've changed the label in cell F1 to read Price
Per from Unit Price that appears in the table. As you can see from the formula bar, the formula in cell F2 multiplies the quantity in the Unit Price column by the value in the Units in
Stock column for the first row of the table (F7*G7) to see whether it's greater than 300.

21

Figure 21.14
The formula in cell F2 contains relative references to values in the first row of the database (row 7); note that the label above it does not match a label in the table itself.

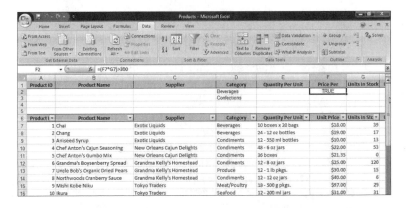

After you've created the criteria range and entered criteria, apply the filter to your table by following these steps:

1. Click the Data ribbon's Advanced button to display the Advanced Filter dialog box (shown in Figure 21.15). Note that the values shown here correspond to values in Figure 21.16.

2. If the List Range option isn't set to your entire table (the word *list* is a carryover from previous Excel versions where tables were called lists), click the List Range box and then select the entire table, including the header row. (If you selected the table before opening the Advanced Filter dialog box, this range is already selected.)

Figure 21.15

3. If the Criteria Range option isn't set to your criteria range, click in the Criteria Range box and select the portion of the criteria range that contains data. At a minimum, this must include one column label and one cell beneath that label. If your criteria include multiple rows, make sure that you select each row. The portion of the criteria range that you select must be a contiguous range.

 If your advanced filter doesn't work as you expect, see "Debugging Advanced Filters" in the "Troubleshooting" section at the end of this chapter.

4. Choose a destination for the Advanced Filter results:

   • To filter the table in place, as an AutoFilter does, accept the default option under Action.

   • To extract records to another location, click the Copy to Another Location option; then click in the Copy To box and select the cell at the top-left corner of the range where you want the extracted records to appear (logically, this location is called the *extract range*). This location must be on the same worksheet as the table itself; if you want to extract specific fields, you must include column labels that correspond to the fields you want to extract. You do not need to extract every column from the table.

21

- To filter out duplicate records, select the Unique Records Only check box. If you filter the table in place, this option excludes those rows in which the values in every column are identical. If you extract the results to a new location and specify a subset of columns, Excel defines duplicates based only on the columns in the extract range.

TIP FROM

By extracting unique records, you can quickly build a table of categories from a much larger table like the one in the examples shown here. Use no conditions in the criteria range. For the extract range, pick a cell below the table and enter the label of the column that you want to extract (Category, in this case). When you run the Advanced Filter, Excel displays a table of all the unique values in your Category column, with no duplicates.

5. Click OK to apply the filter.

TIP FROM

Use range names to skip some steps in this process. If you create named ranges called Database and Extract, Excel automatically selects them in the Advanced Filter dialog box each time you use it. Excel automatically creates a named criteria range each time you use the Advanced Filter dialog box.

Advanced filters don't update automatically when you enter new values in the criteria range. To apply the new criteria, you need to reopen the Advanced Criteria dialog box and click OK. To remove an in-place filter from a table, click the Clear button on your Data ribbon.

IMPORTING AND EXPORTING DATA

Using Excel, you can create a table using data from a *text file* or Access database, a SQL Server, non-Access and non-SQL database files, as well as from the web using commands on your Data ribbon. Because you can now export a file directly from Microsoft Access to the Excel 2007 format, importing from a text file requires more explanation than does importing from an Access database in most cases. Importing data from the Web requires a little extra work, and you'll learn about that in a later section titled "Creating and Using Web Queries."

A text file is often used as the go-between file for moving data between programs. One program, such as Outlook, might export its data to a text file so that Excel can import that data—Excel cannot import Outlook data directly.

Excel can also save a table to a text file. By exporting to a text file, other programs such as Outlook can read the worksheet data you've prepared.

To import a text file as a table, first position the insertion point in the cell where you want the data to appear. Make sure that no data appears below or to the right of the location that you select, or it could be overwritten. Then follow these steps:

1. Display your Data ribbon and click From Text from the Get External Data group.
2. In the Import Text File dialog box, select the file that you want to import, and click Import. The Text Import Wizard appears.

21

3. Specify how Excel should separate fields in your import file. Pick Delimited if the table uses characters such as commas or tabs to identify each field; choose Fixed Width if each field starts at the same position in each row.

NOTE

If the settings look correct here and you're confident that you don't need to adjust any other import options, click Finish to skip the remainder of the Import Text Wizard.

4. Click Next to display step 2 of the wizard. If you're importing a *delimited* file, check that Excel has selected the correct options for your file. (In the example shown in Figure 21.16, we had to check the Comma box before the wizard would correctly identify each field.) With a fixed-width file, click in the ruler to identify the beginning of each new column. Click Next again.

Figure 21.16
Be sure to specify the correct delimiters when importing a text file. Scroll through the Data Preview window, if necessary, to check a sufficient sample of records.

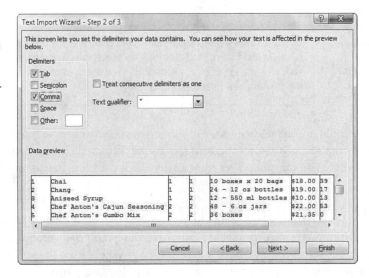

5. In the next step of the wizard, which is optional, choose formatting options for date/time and number fields, or specify any fields that you don't want to import. Click Finish to move to the last step of the process. Excel displays the Import Data dialog box.

6. Ensure that the cell you want to use as the top-left corner of the table is selected. Adjust this location if necessary, or click New Worksheet to create the table without disturbing existing sheets.

7. By default, Excel creates an external query to the original file, so that any changes you make to that text file can be reflected in your worksheet as well. If the external data changes, your worksheet will reflect that chapter when you reload your worksheet or update your links using the Refresh All button on the Data ribbon. If you want to permanently add the data to your worksheet and break the link to the external file, click the Properties button, clear the Save Query Definition box, and click OK to close the External Data Range Properties dialog box.

8. Click OK to add the new table to your worksheet.

21

After importing data into a worksheet, you might end up with some blank cells. In some situations, you might want to replace those blanks with a value, such as "NA" or zero. To do so, follow these steps:

1. Select the range that contains the blank cells that you want to change. Don't select any other cells.

2. Press F5 to display the Go To dialog box.

3. Click the Special button and choose Blanks from the table of options in the Go To Special dialog box. Click OK to select all blank cells in the range.

4. Type the number or text that you want to enter in the blank cells, and then hold down the Ctrl key and press Enter. Excel enters that value in every formerly blank cell.

To save an existing table in a text file that you can import into another program, first make sure that the table you want to save is on its own worksheet, with no other data on that sheet. (If necessary, copy the table range to a new sheet before continuing.) Click to select the sheet that contains the table. Click your Office button and choose Save As, and choose one of Excel's compatible delimited formats: CSV (Comma delimited) or Text (Tab delimited) from the Save as Type drop-down list.

CONNECTING A WORKSHEET TO EXTERNAL DATABASES

For basic table-management tasks, such as sorting, searching, grouping, and summarizing, Excel is an appropriate, easy-to-use tool. For large and complex databases, however, you have better choices, including Microsoft Access. Choose Access over Excel if any of the following statements is true:

- You need to combine data from multiple tables.

- You want to create custom data-entry forms and highly formatted reports.

- You want to create a secure application that multiple users can work with simultaneously.

- Your table contains more than a million records.

- You want to store sounds, pictures, or other data besides text and numbers.

If your database needs have outgrown Excel's table-management capabilities, let a more powerful program (such as Access) manage the data; then use Excel to chart and analyze the subset of data that you selected.

NOTE

> Live queries to external databases are especially useful with PivotTable reports and PivotCharts. You'll learn about these powerful analytical tools later in this chapter.

21

Use the Data ribbon's From Access button to import data directly from an Access database. Excel 2007 and Access 2007 work well together. After you click the From Access button and select the Access database to import, you'll select a table or query from the database to put into your worksheet from the Select Table dialog box that appears after you select your Access database file (see Figure 21.17) and click OK. The Access data arrives in your worksheet beginning at the active cell (or appears in a new worksheet if you select that option).

Figure 21.17
Select a table from any Access 2007 database and Excel easily imports the table into your worksheet.

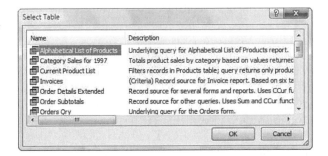

You can use Excel's Query Wizard to pull information from an external, non-Access database—for instance, a companywide database such as Oracle or SQL Server. You will use the Query Wizard to create simple queries and place a reference to an external data range on your worksheet. Use MS Query directly to create more complex queries.

NOTE

The Query Wizard uses Open Database Connectivity (ODBC) drivers to directly access data files in other formats. You do not need to have a particular database program installed; all you need is a copy of the data file or access to the server that contains the data you want to use.

USING THE QUERY WIZARD

To launch the Query Wizard and create a new query, follow these steps:

1. Display the Data ribbon. Click the From Other Sources button and select From Microsoft Query. The Choose Data Source dialog box appears, as shown in Figure 21.18.

2. If the data that you want to connect with is in a relational database, such as dBASE or even Access, or in another Excel workbook, click the Databases tab and

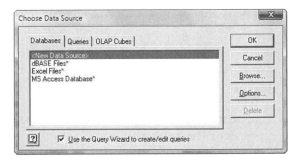

Figure 21.18

choose the correct entry from the table. If the data is in another data source, such as Paradox, SQL Server, or Oracle, choose <New data source>. Make sure Use the Query Wizard to Create/Edit Queries is selected, and click OK.

3. If you chose the <New data source> option, Excel displays the dialog box shown in Figure 21.19. Give the data source a descriptive name, choose the correct ODBC driver, and click the Connect button to enter server names and other login information. If you chose one of the database formats in step 2, you'll bypass this step.

4. When the Select Database dialog box appears, choose the database file that contains the table or tables you want to use. Click OK.

Figure 21.19

5. After you've finished these preliminaries, you'll see the Query Wizard. Work through each step, choosing options appropriate to the database format that you selected. If you chose one of the database formats, for example, you'll see the Choose Columns dialog box shown in Figure 21.20. Pick the fields that you want to add to the query and click Next. Succeeding steps enable you to filter your query and set sorting options.

Figure 21.20
Select the fields that you want to add to your query.

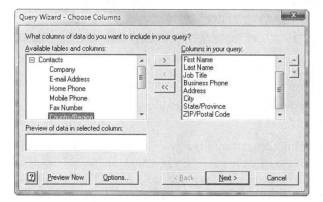

TIP FROM

If you're not sure what type of data is in the selected field, click the Preview Now button to scroll through the field's contents.

6. In the wizard's final step, click the Save Query button to save your query settings under a descriptive name. This entry appears on the Queries tab of the Choose Data Source dialog box. The next time you need to access this data, you can rerun this query directly rather than going through the Query Wizard again.

7. Select the Return Data to Microsoft Office radio button, and click Finish. A dialog box (see Figure 21.21) lets you choose whether to add the data to a location on the existing worksheet, to a new worksheet, or to a PivotTable or PivotChart. Make your choice and click OK.

For maximum flexibility, choose a PivotTable as the location for the data your query returns, and then manipulate it using the techniques described later in this chapter.

Figure 21.21

INTEGRATING EXTERNAL DATA INTO A WORKSHEET

When you use the Query Wizard to add data from an external source to a worksheet, you can edit the values in your worksheet just as if you had typed them in yourself. But the data that you see is not a simple static display; instead, Excel maintains a live connection from the source database to the worksheet data. (The connection is, of course, one way; you can't update the remote database with changes you make in your worksheet.) Buttons appear on a Table Tools Design ribbon (see Figure 21.22), which you can use to update the data in your worksheet and edit the query, if necessary.

Figure 21.22
Your ribbon changes to enable you to work with your query and refresh data as needed.

The advantage of this connection is that you can refresh your data at any time. For example, if your company keeps its current product inventory and sales records on a SQL Server database, you can create a query that downloads sales results for the past six months and identifies products that are low on inventory. By using charts and PivotTables to analyze the sales for each product, you can decide whether, when, and how much of each product to reorder.

- If you saved your query, you can reuse it in a new worksheet at any time. Start the Query Wizard, as described in the previous section. From the Choose Data Source dialog box, click the Browse button and select a saved query from the selection in the Queries folder (each saved query has the extension .dqy).

- When you reopen a worksheet that contains a query, use the Refresh button on the Table Tools Design ribbon to make sure that your worksheet contains the most up-to-date data.

- For maximum control over query options, click the bottom half of the Refresh button on the Table Tools Design ribbon and select Connection Properties. In the Connection Properties dialog box that opens (see Figure 21.23), you can choose a variety of useful options. For example, if the data is constantly updated, check the Refresh Control options to tell Excel that you want to update it regularly and automatically.

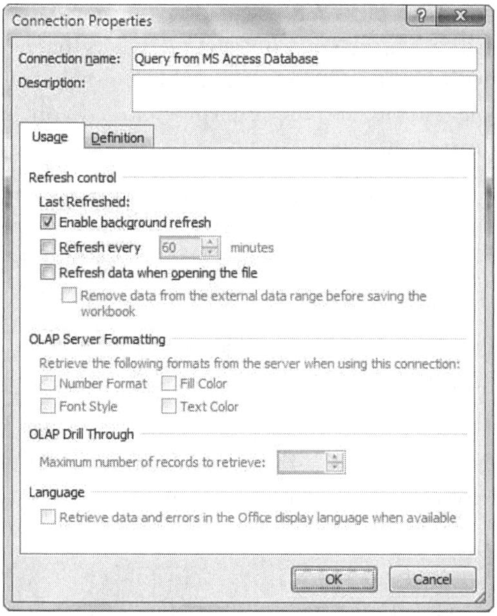

Figure 21.23
Use this dialog box to set data refresh options.

■ By clicking the Properties button on your Table Tools Design ribbon, the External Data Properties dialog box opens (see Figure 21.24). If the quantity of data is unpredictable and you've added your own formulas at the end of each row, adjust the Data Formatting and Layout options. To completely replace the existing contents of the sheet and add your custom formulas to each new row, choose the Overwrite Existing Cells options.

Figure 21.24
Use this dialog box to set data formatting and layout options.

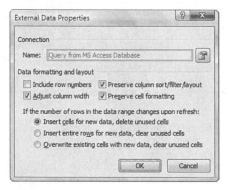

CREATING AND USING WEB QUERIES

Excel and your web browser can work together to gather information from a source on the Web. Microsoft Excel Web Query files are simple text documents that include a pointer to a web page, plus a few lines that define parameters for the query. When you run a Web Query, Excel opens a connection to the Internet, connects with the specified web page, executes the query, and returns the data to Excel.

Writing a Web Query from scratch takes specialized development skills, but you can pull in a surprising amount of useful data using sample Web Query files that come with Excel. For example, you can connect with Microsoft MoneyCentral to download current prices for stocks and mutual funds or up-to-date currency exchange rates. To open a web query, click the From Web button on your Data ribbon.

You don't have to write a single line of code to bring data from the Web into an Excel worksheet, however. If the original data is contained in a table on any web page, you can copy the table's data to the worksheet and specify that you want to transform it into a refreshable web query. Follow these steps:

1. Click to select the cell where you want the table data to appear.

2. Click your Data tab to display the Data ribbon. Click the From Web button in the Get External Data group.

3. In the New Web Query dialog box (see Figure 21.25), enter or paste the URL of the page that contains the data that you want to add to the worksheet. Click the Go button to load that page.

Figure 21.25
Enter the URL for the page containing the data you want to add to your worksheet.

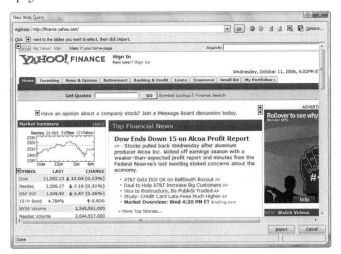

4. The New Web Query dialog box identifies each table in the page with a small yellow arrow. Click the arrow next to the table (or tables) that you want to add. The box turns to a green check mark after you've selected it.

5. By default, Excel pulls your data in with no formatting. If you want to pick up text formatting from the web page, click the Options button. In the Web Query Options dialog box (see Figure 21.26), select the Rich Text Formatting Only option. Use the Full HTML Formatting option if you want all table properties to be preserved.

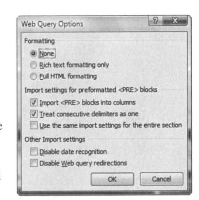

Figure 21.26

6. Click the Import button at the bottom of the New Web Query window to open the Import Data dialog box. The cell that you selected in step 1 is highlighted. Change this location, if necessary, and click the Properties button if you want to adjust the refresh times for the live data.

7. Click OK to add the web data to your worksheet. From the New Web Query window, if you had clicked the Save Query button, you could save the query settings as a separate file that you can open in another worksheet. After testing to ensure that the web data appears as expected, you can repeat these steps and save the query.

8. Repeat steps 1–7 to add data from another web page to your worksheet.

TIP FROM

If this process seems too cumbersome, you can speed things up by using the Clipboard. From an Internet Explorer window, select the data that you want to add to your worksheet, right-click, and choose Copy. Paste the data into your worksheet and click the Paste Options Smart Tag. Click the Create Refreshable Web Query menu option to convert the pasted data to a live link. This option is available only if you have selected a full table.

ANALYZING INFORMATION WITH PIVOTTABLES

PivotTables (as well as PivotCharts which you learn about in Chapter 22, "Creating and Editing Charts") are powerful tools for automatically summarizing and analyzing data without ever having to add a formula or function. As the name implies, you start with a table, snap the rows and columns into position on a grid, and end up with a sorted, grouped, summarized, totaled, and subtotaled report. PivotTable reports are best for cross-tabulating tables—the more categories, the better. You can reduce a table of thousands of items to a single line, showing totals by category or quarter. Or you can create complex, multilevel groupings that show total sales by employee, grouped by product category and by quarter. You can hide or show detail for each group with a quick double-click. You can change the view or grouping in literally seconds, just by dragging items on or off the sheet and moving them between row, column, and page fields.

Start with a table that contains multiple fields, and then use Excel's PivotTable button to set up a blank PivotTable page with just a few clicks. Instead of sorting your table and entering formulas and functions, you drag fields around on the PivotTable page to create a new view of your table—Excel groups the data and adds summary formulas automatically.

Unlike subtotals and outlines, which modify the structure of your table to display summaries, PivotTables create new, independent elements in your workbook. When you add or edit data in a table, the changes show up in your PivotTables (and PivotCharts) as well. Because they're separate elements, you can easily change the structure of a PivotTable, too, and your changes won't mess up the data in the underlying table. Using interactive web components, you can also make PivotTables available to other people via a web browser.

21

→ For details on how to use PivotTables in web pages, **see** "Using Office Programs to Create and Edit Web Pages," **p. 59**.

Figure 21.27 shows the PivotTable Task pane that appears when you elect to create a PivotTable from a table. Excel 2007 makes it simple to create a PivotTable; you just choose data fields from the PivotTable field list in the Task pane to add data to your PivotTable report.

The PivotTable Field List includes every field in your table. Use row fields and column fields to define how you want Excel to group your table. Data items define which fields contain the information you want to summarize. Page fields let you further refine your view by displaying a separate PivotTable for each item in a group, as though the table were on its own virtual page. You can use multiple row fields, column fields, or both, and you can specify which summary action you want Excel to perform on data items—the sum, average, or count of all related values, for instance.

Figure 21.27
You'll use the PivotTable Task pane to manage your PivotTable.

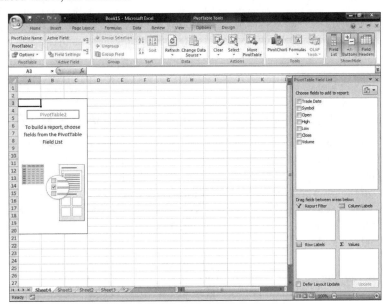

What can you do with a PivotTable? The number of uses is limited only by your imagination. Despite their dramatically different structures, for example, each of the following four PivotTables started with the same table of information about publicly traded stocks. In its raw form, with its grand total of 106,224 separate data points, the table is a prescription for information overload. Each of the 6,639 rows contains 16 data fields for an individual publicly traded company, including its name, ticker symbol, and industry category, the exchange on which it trades, its high and low stock price for the past year, and financial measurements such as net profit margin and return on equity.

Figure 21.28 shows a simple PivotTable that lets you see at a glance how many companies are in each industry category, along with the average increase or decrease in stock price from companies in that category over the past year. This PivotTable consists of a single row field and two data items.

Figure 21.28
With no column fields and only one row field, this PivotTable quickly counts the number of companies in each category and calculates the average price change for the year.

	A	B	C
1	Industry Name	Number of Companies	% Price Change Last Year (Avg)
2	Closed-End Fund-Debt	360	(1.00)
3	Savings & Loans	237	18.94
4	Business Software and Services	164	(38.23)
5	Internet Software and Services	133	(22.66)
6	Business Services	128	(21.35)
7	Biotechnology	120	(45.73)
8	Scientific & Technical Instruments	119	(24.45)
9	Regional - Northeast Banks	116	14.96
10	Drug Manufacturers - Other	111	(33.29)
11	Independent Oil & Gas	106	(7.48)
12	Medical Appliances & Equipment	103	(18.11)
13	Regional - Mid-Atlantic Banks	99	19.95
14	Communications Equipment	94	(31.54)
15	Medical Instruments & Supplies	88	(24.90)
16	Applicaton Software	85	(27.05)
17	Property & Casualty Insurance	75	(13.30)
18	Restaurants	71	(19.31)
19	Closed-End Fund-Foreign	71	(11.76)

In Figure 21.29, more detail is added, displaying individual statistics for each company and grouping the detail rows in alphabetical order by industry name. For this PivotTable, the data is arranged in report format, similar to the banded database reports Access and other database management programs produce. Note that this PivotTable includes four data items instead of two, and a slew of Excel formatting options are used to make the report more readable—changing fonts and font sizes, aligning type and adding background shading, and standardizing the number of decimal points in each column.

Figure 21.29
To hide gridlines and group-related items in bands such as these, choose a report format instead of the default table layout.

	Industry Name	Company Name	Avg of Net Profit Margin	Avg of % Price Change Last	52-Week Low	52-Week High
127		Petroleum Helicopters, Inc		5.8	23.9	31
128						
129	Aluminum		2.3	-14.6	71.4	155.4
130		Alcoa, Inc	3.0	-25.1	23.2	40.1
131		Alcoa, Inc, 2nd	1.9	-41	17.6	39.1
132		ALUMINUM CP CHIN ADS	9.9	-17.5	9.4	22.8
133		Century Aluminum Company	(2.6)	-50.9	5.6	17.5
134		Commonwealth Industries, Inc.	0.9	-26.2	4.2	8.1
135		Pechiney	0.8	-46.6	11.4	27.8
136						
137	Apparel Stores		3.0	-22.8	492.0	1,130.0
138		Abercombe & Fitch Co.	12.2	0.7	15.0	33.9
139		American Eagle Outfitters, Inc.	6.1	-41.1	9.8	27.2
140		AnnTaylor Stores Corporation	5.8	-28.1	17.1	33.2
141		bebe stores, inc.	7.4	-48.3	9.6	24.8
142		Big Dog Holdings, Inc.	3.4	-35.0	1.8	5.6
143		Buckle, Inc.	8.0	-26.4	15.5	25.5
144		Burlington Coat Factory Warehouse Capora	2.7	-11.7	15.4	23.5

→ For details on how to create similar reports from an Access database, **see** "Building Forms and Reports," **p. 852**.

21

To slice the data even more finely and add an extra analytical dimension, you can drag more items from the PivotTable Task pane to the row and column fields. Each row in the PivotTable is grouped using unique values in two categories, and there are two column headings as well, one for each unique value in the Split in Last Year column field. (To make the PivotTable easier to read, the column headings were renamed from Yes and No to Split and No Split.) At the intersection of each row and column in the PivotTable, Excel counts the number of companies and calculates the average income per employee for all rows that match the row and column fields.

The resulting PivotTable, shown in Figure 21.30, is a concise and crystal-clear cross-tabulation, giving you a side-by-side analysis of the number of stocks that split in the past year versus those that didn't, broken down by industry category and exchange.

	A	B	C	D	E	F
1			Split in Last Year	Data		
2			Split		No Split	
3	Industry Name	Exchange	Number of Companies	Avg Income Per Employee	Number of Companies	Avg Income Per Employee
140	Drugs Wholesale	AMEX	0	$ 0	2	$ (174,500)
141		NASDAQ	1	$ 7,000	2	$ 54,000
142		NYSE	1	$ 22,000	2	$ 17,000
143	Education & Training Services	NASDAQ	1	$ 21,000	4	$ 16,500
144		NYSE	1	$ 12,000	2	$ 4,000
145	Electric Utilities	AMEX	0	$ 0	3	$ 55,000
146		NASDAQ	0	$ 0	2	$ 18,000
147		NYSE	3	$ 53,333	34	$ 31,618
148	Electronic Equipment	AMEX	0	$ 0	3	$ 21,000
149		NASDAQ	1	$ 34,000	5	$ (400)
150		NYSE	0	$ 0	1	$ 12,000
151	Electronics Stores	NASDAQ	0	$ 0	3	$ 0
152		NYSE	1	$ 6,000	3	$ 4,667
153	Electronics Wholesale	NASDAQ	0	$ 0	5	$ 6,200
154		NYSE	0	$ 0	2	$ 2,000
155	Entertainment - Diversified	AMEX	0	$ 0	2	$ 6,000
156		NYSE	2	$151,000	2	$ 24,500
157	Farm & Construction Machinery	AMEX	1	$ 13,000	0	$ 0
158		NASDAQ	0	$ 0	2	$ 12,500

Figure 21.30
Add a column field to quickly compare related data points. Notice that the worksheet pane is frozen to keep headings visible when scrolling, just as with an ordinary worksheet.

There are literally hundreds of options in even a modestly complex PivotTable, but a PivotTable doesn't have to be large or complex to be effective. The PivotTable in Figure 21.31, for example, neatly summarizes more than 100,000 data points in just a few rows and columns.

Exchange	Dow Jones Membership	Net Profit Margin (Avg.)	Price Change Last Yr (Avg)
AMEX	(blank)	0.85	-10.85
NASDAQ	DJ Industrials	21.30	-25.15
	DJ Transports	-0.48	-12.93
	(blank)	-3.35	-17.26
NYSE	DJ Industrials	6.43	-21.29
	DJ Transports	2.05	-27.24
	DJ Utilities	-4.83	-34.26
	(blank)	6.25	-16.25
Grand Total		0.56	-16.32

Figure 21.31
Notice the grand totals under the rows in this PivotTable. Use the page field in the top-left corner to filter the entire table.

To produce this example, we used two column fields, two row fields, and one page field—a drop-down table that lets us filter the records in the entire table. Choosing (All) from the page field shows a summary of all data in the table. By selecting a different entry from the drop-down table, you can show the same breakdown for each industry name. Select one category at a time to flip through a series of otherwise identical PivotTables that focus on each category.

The layout Excel produced automatically included totals for each row and column; we kept only the grand total at the bottom of the PivotTable. We had to modify other default settings as well, including changing the default formula to calculate the average of our data items. To make the headings and totals easier to read, we did some rewording, and then changed fonts and alignment, added shading, and wrapped text.

WHEN SHOULD YOU USE A PIVOTTABLE?

PivotTables have several advantages over other worksheet models. Using the PivotTable button, it's easy to create a PivotTable that summarizes all or part of a table in dozens of different ways. Trying to accomplish the same task by entering formulas manually would take days. Also, because PivotTables and PivotCharts do not change your existing data or its arrangement on the worksheet, you can freely experiment with different PivotTable layouts. Use the Undo button (on your Quick Access Toolbar or use the Ctrl+Z shortcut key) to roll back any changes you make in a PivotTable layout. If you want to start over, you can delete the PivotTable page and run the wizard again.

PivotTables are the correct choice when all your data is in a table or in an external database that you can query from Excel. PivotTables are not appropriate for structured worksheet models that include data-entry cells, subtotals, and summary rows. A PivotTable won't do much good on an annual budget worksheet, for example, because it already includes rows, columns, and subtotals. On the other hand, if you enter the raw data in a table (or import it from an external database), with each row containing a month, department, budget category, and amount, you can easily re-create that same layout in PivotTable form—and you'll have many more analytical options available to you later.

→ For more details on how to use Microsoft Query to pull data from an external database, **see** "Connecting a Worksheet to an External Databases," **p. 645**.

CREATING A PIVOTTABLE

To create a PivotTable from an existing table, you'll use the Insert ribbon's PivotTable button. Excel will prompt you for basic details about the PivotTable you want to create, including the location of the data source and where you want the PivotTable to appear. After you finish specifying the PivotTable, you'll be able to lay out your data directly on the worksheet.

 You don't need to use a PivotTable Wizard in Excel 2007 as you did in Excel 2003. The PivotTable screen is better formatted to help you build and edit your PivotTables and the simple Insert PivotTable dialog box is the only place you need to specify your initial PivotTable data source.

To build a new PivotTable, open the workbook that contains the table on which you plan to base the PivotTable. Then follow these steps:

1. Click anywhere in your table. To build a PivotTable from a subset of the data in your table, select the range that contains the data.

2. Click your Insert ribbon's PivotTable button. The Create PivotTable dialog box appears, as shown in Figure 21.32.

21

Figure 21.32
Select a range or use
an external data
source for your
PivotTable

Using External Databases with PivotTables

In a corporate setting, it's often useful to base a PivotTable on the result of a query to an external database. If you choose the External Data Source option, Excel starts the Query Wizard and prompts you for details about the format and location of the database. Excel then uses this query as the source for the PivotTable. Each time you refresh the data in the PivotTable, Excel runs the saved query and updates the PivotTable with the most recent information.

Excel also offers the option to build PivotTables from special data structures called On-Line Analytical Processing (OLAP) databases. Instead of rows and columns, these files organize data into dimensions and levels. Instead of forcing Excel to chug through massive amounts of data, the server does the summarizing first and sends the summary values directly to your report.

When you connect to an OLAP database, Excel lets you save your data in local files called *OLAP cubes* and use them as the source for a PivotTable. There are some substantial differences in the way PivotTables based on OLAP data work compared with those based on Excel tables or non-OLAP databases.

To learn more about building PivotTables from an OLAP database, pick up a copy of *Special Edition Using Microsoft Office Excel 2007*, also published by Que.

---

3. Specify the range in which your data is located. The default selection is your current table, or any range you selected before requesting the PivotTable. Adjust the selection, if necessary.

4. Specify where you want to place the PivotTable. Choose the default option, New Worksheet.

CAUTION

> The Create PivotTable dialog box offers the option to place a PivotTable on an existing worksheet. In general, you should always choose to place a PivotTable on its own sheet. Adding a PivotTable to a sheet that contains data exposes you to the risk that changes you make to the table design will affect your PivotTable, or vice versa.

5. Click OK to close the Create PivotTable dialog box and create a blank PivotTable page. Excel jumps to the new worksheet you just created and displays the PivotTable Field List in the Task pane to the right of your screen.

6. Drag field buttons from the Choose Fields to Add to Report box and drop them into the appropriate regions below to one of the four regions: Report Filter, Column Labels, Row Labels, or summed Values.

TIP FROM

EQ & Woody

> Click the drop-down arrow in the top-right corner of the Field List Task pane to change the Task pane's layout if the default setting makes the targets too far away to drop the fields. If you're working with massive data, you might want to click the Layout Update option so Excel doesn't rearrange its tables as you build your PivotTable. Click Update whenever you want to see the iterative result of your work.

Don't be surprised if the PivotTable doesn't display properly at first. In particular, summary fields in the Values area default to the SUM function. If you want to use COUNT, AVERAGE, or another summary function instead, see the next section.

Editing and Updating a PivotTable

Now that you've seen the PivotTable build process, it will be helpful to review the actions you can take with PivotTables as you build and edit them. The following list reviews the drag-and-drop operations you'll perform as you drag data fields from the field list to the four PivotTable destinations:

1. Drag a data field to the Report Filter area at the top of the PivotTable report you build.
2. Drag a data field to the Column Label area to make that field your column labels that run across your PivotTable.
3. Drag a data field to the Row Label area to make that field your row labels that run down the left side of your PivotTable report.
4. Drag a data field to the summed Values area to make that field the data that composes the body of your PivotTable report.

The location where you drag a data field, therefore, determines where on the PivotTable report that field will make itself be known. After items begin to appear on your PivotTable report, tablelike drop-down arrows enable you to select and sort an item as needed. You can use the same data field in more than one location.

You can add fields to the PivotTable report by selecting the check box next to each field name. Excel adds nonnumeric fields to the Row Labels area, numeric fields to the Values area, and OLAP date and time hierarchies (if you use that) to the Column Labels area. At any point you can right-click a field name and select an Add To command to add that field to an area without using a drag-and-drop operation.

After you create a PivotTable, it's easy to rearrange fields and data items. Drag fields from one place to another to change the display of data—from a row field to a column field, for example, if you want to see values side by side rather than one above the other. Right-click to display shortcut menus that let you adjust formatting and other options for each field.

21

If the Field Table isn't visible, right-click the PivotTable layout area and choose View Field Table from the bottom of the shortcut menu. To make changes to the PivotTable report, use any or all of these techniques:

- To add a new field to the layout, drag a field button from the PivotTable field list and drop it on the layout. If you're replacing an existing field, remove the old field first to reduce unnecessary calculations. When you drop a new field in the row or column area, Excel adds it as part of the hierarchy of fields that are already there and automatically groups items in the order in which they appear. Be careful to arrange these fields in the proper order. For example, if you have a table of product categories, each of which contains multiple products, place the category field to the left of the product name field, or the results will be nonsense.

TIP FROM

Ed & Woody

If your table includes two fields that have an absolute one-to-one correspondence, such as part numbers and part names, you can add them to the row area in either order and your table will appear correctly.

- To remove a field from any part of the PivotTable layout, drag the field button off the layout; when the pointer icon changes to include an X, release the mouse button. You can also click a dropped field's down arrow that appears to the right of a field name and select Remove Field.

- To change the order of fields in rows, columns, or the data area, drag the field button and drop it in the correct location on the layout. Make sure you're pointing to the field button and not its label; you'll know you've aimed correctly when the mouse button turns to a four-headed pointer. Drag to another location and watch the mouse pointer and thick black lines for feedback on the correct "drop" location.

TIP FROM

Ed & Woody

Using the mouse to rearrange the order of data items on a PivotTable can be frustrating. It's usually easier to right-click the field button you want to move, and then choose any of the options on the Order menu. Typically, you can move the item left or right one position, or move it to the beginning or end of the table.

- To change the summary function used in the data area (from SUM to COUNT or AVERAGE, for example), right-click the field button in the PivotTable and choose Value Field Settings from the shortcut menu. That action opens the Value Field Settings dialog box, shown in Figure 21.33. Select a function from the Summarize Value Field By; if you want to change the name from its default, do so in the Custom Name box, and then click OK to save the change.

Figure 21.33
Change the summary
you wish to see.

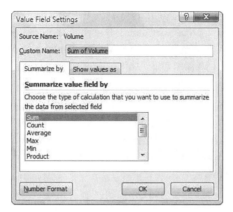

When you drag and drop buttons to arrange fields on a PivotTable page, Excel makes all kinds of decisions on your behalf. If these defaults aren't correct, the following sections will help you change them.

CHANGING A PIVOTTABLE'S APPEARANCE

The default sort order for rows and columns is usually alphanumeric. You can change the order of individual items by dragging them up or down (in the case of rows) or left or right (for columns). In other cases, you might want to adjust the default sort order. For example, if your PivotTable counts the number of items in each category, you might want to see categories with the highest number of items at the top of the table.

Right-click any PivotTable report item and select PivotTable Options. Excel opens the PivotTable Options dialog box shown in Figure 21.34.

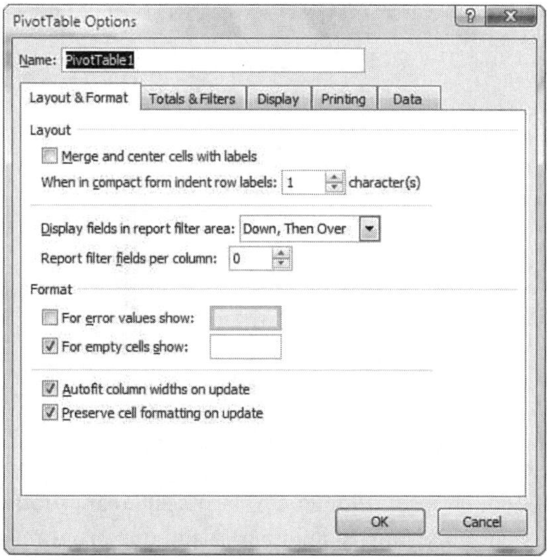

Figure 21.34
The PivotTable
Options dialog box
enables you to
change multiple
aspects of your
PivotTable data.

21

Click the arrow to the right of any PivotTable button for the row or column field and choose More Sort Options to display the Sort dialog box that enables you to modify the order of your data. Click the Sort dialog box's More Options button to set additional sort options, such as whether you want to sort every time a report is updated (if your data is massive, you'll want to uncheck this option).

Click the down arrow to the right of any row or column label and select Label Filters or Value Filters to limit data that appears in the report. The options you see, such as Greater Than and Between and Top 10 work like table AutoFilter options (because that's what they actually are). This is a good way to create a "top 10" table, for example, showing only the categories that have the most items.

→ AutoFilter can save a tremendous amount of time, if you know how to use it properly; **see** "Using Filters to Find Sets of Data," **p. 634**.

ADDING AND REMOVING SUBTOTALS

You can add subtotals to rows, columns, or both in a table. In some cases, Excel adds them automatically, even if they're not appropriate. Subtotals can add a useful way to see the impact of groupings in your PivotTable, or they can add clutter between rows and columns. Depending on the design of your PivotTable and what Excel did automatically, you might need to add or remove these subtotals. In some cases, you can remove subtotals with the right-click shortcut menu. Right-click any of the subtotals and choose Hide. To add subtotals, you need to use the dialog boxes. To work with subtotals, follow these steps:

1. Right-click any row or column heading that contains the subtotal, and choose Field Settings from the shortcut menu. Excel displays the Field Settings dialog box, as shown in Figure 21.35.

Figure 21.35
Use the Subtotals options to add, edit, or hide subtotals for a row or column.

2. In the Subtotals section, choose Automatic to let Excel create subtotals for all items. Choose Custom and click a summary function to add one or more specific type of subtotals, such as Count and Average. Click None to remove all subtotals.

3. Click OK to exit the dialog box and make the changes you specified.

REMOVING BLANK CELLS AND ERROR MESSAGES

Because PivotTables automatically summarize all data, it's common to see blank cells and error messages in the data area. #DIV/0 errors, for example, are especially common when calculating averages because in a long table, it's almost certain that some items will have no matches in a particular row-and-column intersection. For example, if you're calculating average sales with regions in the column area and product categories in the row area, some regions will have no sales for a particular category. These aren't really errors; instead, you want the table to display a label such as NA, for Not Applicable.

Careful attention to blanks and error messages can make your PivotTable easier to read and make it look more professional. Here's how to adjust the appearance of blank cells and errors:

1. Right-click any part of the PivotTable and choose Properties from the contextual menu.
2. Select the For Error Values, Show check box. Click in the box to the right and fill in the information you want to display instead of the error message, such as NA.
3. Select the For Empty Cells Show check box. If the field contains numeric data, enter 0 here; for a text field, enter the value you want Excel to display (NA, for instance) instead of leaving the cell blank.
4. Click OK to save your changes.

CHANGING OR REFRESHING PIVOTTABLE DATA

When you change the layout of a PivotTable, Excel automatically recalculates the resulting display of data. If you add or edit data in the underlying table, however, your changes do not appear immediately in the associated PivotTable. For PivotTable reports based on Excel tables, you must manually refresh the data in the PivotTable whenever you add, remove, or edit data. To be certain that the PivotTable reflects all recent changes, click the Update button on the PivotTable Task pane.

TROUBLESHOOTING

SORTING OUT SORTING PROBLEMS

I tried to run a multicolumn sort on my table, but the result came out scrambled and my column labels disappeared.

The most likely cause of this problem is that Excel couldn't identify the header row in your table. If you use the Sort dialog box, you can select a check box that tells Excel that your table has a header row. Other common sorting problems are caused by blank rows or columns in the table, in which case Excel doesn't sort the records below the blank row or to the right of the blank column. To work around this problem, select your table, minus the header rows, and choose the No Header Row option. You'll need to make a mental note of which column number corresponds with each column.

TOP 10 IS FOR NUMBERS ONLY

After turning on AutoFilter, I chose the Top 10 option for one column in my table. Instead of display-ing the dialog box that lets me select further options, however, Excel simply beeped or displayed a table that didn't contain nearly as many items as I specified.

The Top 10 option works only with numeric values. If you've selected a column that con-tains text, Excel balks and refuses to even display an error message. If the column includes a mix of text and numbers, Excel ignores the text values and bases the Top 10 selection only on numbers in that column.

DEBUGGING ADVANCED FILTERS

I've set up an Advanced Filter, but Excel keeps returning the entire set of records from my table, and I know that the filter should return only a small number of records.

Check the reference for the criteria range in the Advanced Filter dialog box. The most likely explanation is that you've entered criteria in one row but selected two or more rows. If your criteria are only in a single column, select just that label and its criteria. If you've used a for-mula, make sure that the references in the formula refer to the first row in the table or to the labels above the table. For formulas only, make sure that the label above the formula does not match the label of a column in your table.

SECRETS OF THE OFFICE MASTERS: COMBINING DATA FROM SEVERAL WEB SOURCES IN A CUSTOM PAGE

Do you regularly check several web pages during the day to gather information? Excel's capability to create live links to web data might let you combine parts of each web page into a single worksheet. You can then save the resulting worksheet as a web page and put all those bits and pieces of data into a single easy-to-update location. This is especially handy if the websites you follow do not offer *RSS* feeds. (RSS stands for *Really Simple Syndication* and web sites that support RSS feeds are able to send data directly to your RSS-enabled browser or reader.)

The page shown in Figure 21.36, for example, consists of tables drawn from Yahoo!'s Finance page. We added headings to identify each block, hid several columns that contained nonessential information, and formatted the blocks as Full HTML.

By saving the resulting worksheet in HTML format, we now have a clean web page that combines data sources from two archrivals in a single location.

Figure 21.36
Create your own custom web page from a series of other web pages you collect data from.

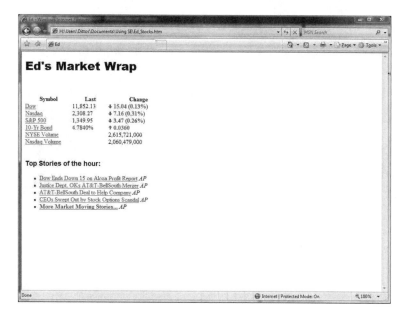

CHAPTER 22

CREATING AND EDITING CHARTS

In this chapter

A Revamped Charting Engine   666

Building an Excel Chart   666

Labeling a Chart's Elements   682

Customizing Axes   688

Customizing a Chart's Appearance   695

Working with PivotTable Charts   696

Creating Other Chart Types   697

Troubleshooting   698

Secrets of the Excel Masters: Leave the Top-Left Cell Blank   699

22

A REVAMPED CHARTING ENGINE

After fifteen years, the charting engine in Office 2007 has been completely rewritten. You will be able to create modern-looking charts in just a few mouse clicks. Tools for customizing the chart have been promoted to one of three new Charting Tools ribbon tabs.

The basic row-and-column worksheet grid is essential in helping you organize data and perform calculations, but it's difficult—and sometimes impossible—to analyze information and see patterns by staring at a sea of numbers.

Charts help you turn numeric data into visual displays in which you can identify trends and pick out patterns at a glance. By using lines, columns, bars, and pie slices to compare series of data over time and across categories, charts often provide clear answers to tough questions, such as these:

- **Which sales region and which product lines have been most successful in the past 12 months?**—A stacked column chart lets you see both sets of data in a single display.

- **Does your small business have seasonal variations in cash flow or inventory?**—You might not be able to tell from an accounting statement packed with hundreds of individual data points, but a line chart can help you clearly see the highs and lows.

- **Just where does the money go?**—If you've broken out a year's worth of expenditures by category, a pie chart helps you see which categories are taking more than their fair share—and devise strategies for reining in those expenses.

BUILDING AN EXCEL CHART

Building a chart in Excel 2007 is easier than in any previous version. Gone is the four-step Chart Wizard. To create a chart, you select a cell within your data range and choose a chart type on the Insert tab of the ribbon. As shown in Figure 22.1, the Insert tab offers seven charting icons. Each icon leads to a drop-down list with a variety of chart styles.

Click a chart style from the drop-down list and Excel will add a default chart to your worksheet. You can then use buttons on the Design, Layout, and Format tabs to customize and tweak the options for the chart.

By default, all new Excel charts are embedded on the current worksheet. If you would like to move the chart to its own chart sheet, you can do this with the location button on the Design tab of the ribbon. Working with a chart on its own sheet gives you the maximum working room for editing and formatting. Embedding a chart within a worksheet lets you easily see the data and chart side by side.

Excel automatically maintains links between worksheet data and its graphic representation on the chart; if you change the numbers or text in the data range, the columns, pie slices, and other graphic elements on the chart change, too.

Figure 22.1
The 7 chart type icons lead to 73 basic chart types.

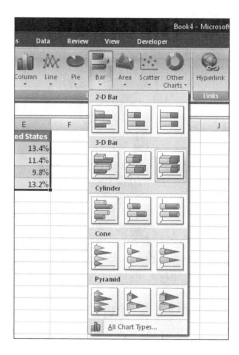

SELECTING DATA TO PLOT

Excel maintains links between worksheet data and the data series on a chart. When you create a chart, Excel automatically detects the data to be charted based on the current selection. If you select a single cell, Excel bases the chart data on the current region—an area that extends in each direction until you encounter the edge of the worksheet or a blank row or blank column. On the other hand, if you select a range of cells, Excel uses that range for the chart data.

NOTE

> The number of points per series for a 2D chart is limited to 32,000. With 3D charts, the limit is reduced to 4,000 points per series. The total number of points per chart is limited to 256,000. The maximum number of series you can use in a chart is 255. If you have more series than this, you must filter your list before creating your chart. You should also seriously reconsider the point you're trying to make because even Stephen Hawking would have trouble absorbing that much information at once.

Be sure the range you select includes all the data to be charted, as well as the labels you'll use for the categories. The range does not have to be contiguous. For example, to create a pie chart, you might want to select a row of column labels and a row of totals, ignoring the detail rows in between. Nor do you need to select all the data in a table, if all you want to chart is a subset of the data. For example, on a 12-month budget worksheet, you might want to show sales totals only for the months of October through December.

22

CAUTION

> If the range you plan to chart ends with a row or column of totals, don't include those totals in your selection; otherwise, the totals will create one column or pie slice that overwhelms all the others in the chart.

When you select the data source, Excel attempts to identify category headings, value axis labels, and data series; it also chooses whether to plot data by rows or by columns. This choice is based on the number of items—if there are more columns than rows, Excel plots the data by column, placing the column headings along the category axis. If there are more rows than columns, or an equal number of rows and columns, Excel plots by row.

Changing the way data is plotted can help emphasize different trends and patterns. For example, Figure 22.2 shows a worksheet that contains a small range of data. When plotted by columns (left), the data emphasizes the trends for each decade, and you can see at a glance that Arizona has grown at a faster rate than the other two southwestern states and faster than the United States as a whole. When plotted by rows, however (right), the chart encourages comparing how each state and the United States did on a decade-by-decade basis and to draw conclusions on the consistency of each state's growth.

Figure 22.2
Changing the way that data is plotted–by columns or rows–can change the story a chart tells.

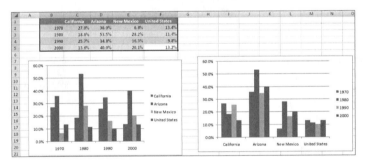

To reverse the order in which Excel plots the selected data, use the Switch Row/Column icon on the Chart Tools Design tab of the ribbon. (If this tab is not visible, select a chart to display it.) With some chart types and data, making this switch could render the chart incomprehensible; click the Undo button if that happens.

CAUTION

> While changing the data orientation can cause a chart to tell a different story, you should always make sure that you understand the story. If you tweak a chart to try to obscure the true story, you might get in trouble if someone in the audience knows the real story. Analyze the chart to make sure that you, the chart author, understands the data before distributing the chart to others.

Normally, Excel plots data series from left to right and top to bottom. What do you do if your data source is arranged in alphabetical order, but you want to display the series in a different order—for instance, with the two most productive regions listed first, or with dates in reverse order? If you don't want to change the arrangement of data on the worksheet, you can change the plotting order of the data series:

1. Click the chart. Excel will display the three Chart Tools ribbon tabs.

2. On the Design ribbon, click the Select Data icon. Excel displays the Select Data Source dialog box.

3. Click any series name in the Legend Entries list. Use the Up or Down arrow icons to re-order the series in the list (see Figure 22.3).

4. Repeat step 3 to resequence additional series.

5. Click OK to accept the changes. Note: Live Preview does not work with this dialog box. You must click OK before the changes are shown in the chart.

Figure 22.3
Resequence the series order using this dialog box.

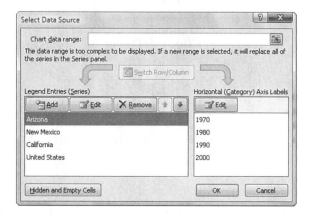

SELECTING A CHART TYPE

When you create a new chart, Excel lets you select from 73 chart types in 14 categories (although a significant number of these choices are minor variations of others in the same category). Excel 2007 does away with the gallery of 20 built-in custom chart types. Instead, Excel 2007 offers 5 to 15 built-in custom layouts for each chart type. The type of data you're planning to plot usually dictates which type of chart you should choose.

CHOOSING A STANDARD CHART TYPE

When you use the Insert tab to create a chart, the first step is to specify what type of chart you want to create. After you create a chart, you can easily change it to a new type; right-click the chart area or plot area and select Change Chart Type, or click the Change Chart Type button on the Design tab of the ribbon. The following sections discuss all the standard Excel chart types and describe how you can best use them.

COLUMN

This type of chart shows a comparison between values in one or more series, often over time as shown in Figure 22.4. This chart works best for shorter series of data. It works well to track 10 data points, but not to illustrate 1000 data points. For example, you can show how your company's sales compare with its competitors over the past five years. Stacked column charts further divide the total for each column, so you can also measure how each geographic region performed for each company. Select a column chart when you want to show comparisons between different data points, especially those that change over time.

Do: use the chart to show trends over time, especially when you have few data points.

Don't: use this chart type if each series includes so many data points that you'll be unable to distinguish individual columns. Don't use the chart if the magnitude of each series is vastly different.

Figure 22.4
Column charts are good for short series of time-oriented data.

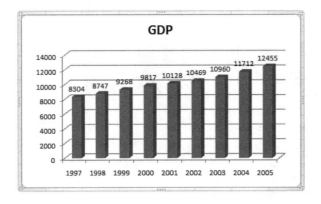

LINE

This chart type displays a trend, or the relationship between values over a time period. For example, Figure 22.5 plots 75 years' worth of data. The individual points flow into a smooth line where you can see the rate of change.

Do: select a line chart when you have many data points to plot and want to show a trend over a period of time.

Don't: use this chart type when you're trying to show the relationship between numbers without respect to time, and when you have only a few data points to chart.

Figure 22.5
Line charts are most useful for showing trends over a period of time.

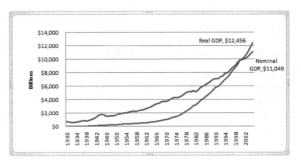

PIE

Pie charts show the relative size of all the parts in a whole—for example, the ethnic composition of a city. Pie charts have no x-axis or y-axis, and only one data series can be plotted.

Typically, your data will be sorted with the largest numbers appearing first. This might cause the smaller slices to appear near the back edge of the pie. Right-click the pie, and choose Format Data Series. You can then change the Angle of First Slice to bring the smaller pie slices to the front of the chart.

Use Layout, Data Labels, More Data Label Options to specify how each slice should be labeled. In Figure 22.6, each pie slice shows the category name and value. Other options include showing the percentage for each pie slice.

Do: use pie charts when you have only a few numbers to chart and want to show how each number contributes to the whole.

Don't: use this chart type when your data series includes many low numbers that contribute a very small percentage to the total. In this case, individual pie slices will be too small to compare.

Figure 22.6
Pie charts are most useful for showing how each number contributes to the whole.

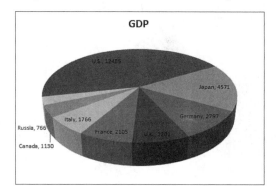

BAR

Think of a bar chart as a column chart turned on its side, with values along the horizontal axis and categories on the vertical axis. It deemphasizes time comparisons and highlights winners and losers. Figure 22.7, for example, graphically illustrates how well each region has performed in a competition where the goal is to hit $1,000,000 in donations.

Do: use bar charts to compare a small number of data points.

Don't: use bar charts when there are so many data points that the bars will blend together.

Figure 22.7
Bar charts highlight winners and losers. In this example, it is easy to see which region is in the lead.

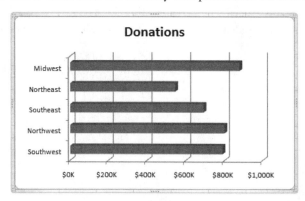

AREA

This chart type shows lines for parts of a series, adding all the values together to illustrate cumulative change. Unlike line charts, which emphasize the rate of change, area charts show the amount and magnitude of change. The area chart in Figure 22.8, for example, shows how much each division of a pool chemical company contributes to total profits over the course of a year.

Do use area charts to highlight the magnitude of change. The charts work well with data organized by time. Like line charts, area charts can handle many points of data.

Don't use an area chart to compare series that on a non-cumulative basis. There is a good chance that the series plotted in front will obscure the data points for the series plotted in back.

Figure 22.8
Area charts graphically illustrate cumulative changes–this example shows the year-long contribution of four regional divisions.

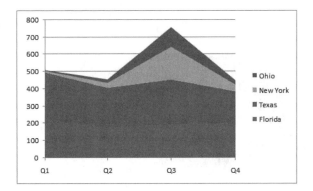

XY (SCATTER)

Use a scatter chart to show correlations between different series of values when the element of time is unimportant—usually used for scientific analyses. For example, plotting daily high temperatures and ice cream sales over the course of a year will no doubt show clusters of high sales on hot days. Figure 22.9 shows a scatter chart that shows the results of scientific trials on various samples. Note the use of a trendline. You can create charts that plot two groups of numbers as one series of X,Y coordinates; this is the principle behind the price-performance charts you sometimes see in computer magazines. The correct arrangement of data on the worksheet is crucial when creating this chart type. The first column of data should contain your independent (x) values. Additional columns would contain the dependent (y) values.

When you create a scatter chart, the first column of your data range should contain the values to be plotted along the x-axis.

22

Figure 22.9
Scatter charts help to illustrate the results of scientific trials. This chart shows increased variability as the x value increases.

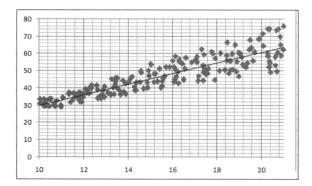

STOCK

Four built-in chart types make tracking open/high/low/close prices over time possible, as in the example in Figure 22.10. Combination chart types in this category enable you to plot volume traded as well. You also can adapt these chart types for scientific use, to show high-low values in experimental data. When choosing one of these chart types, your data columns must be in the exact order to match the chart type. The four possible stock charts are

High—Low—Close

Open—High—Low—Close

Volume—High—Low—Close

Volume—Open—High—Low—Close (see Figure 22.10)

If you attempt to create this chart with the wrong number of columns, an Information box will appear, advising you of the proper sequence of the columns.

Figure 22.10
Each line in this stock chart shows the volume, open, high, low, and closing prices for a selected ticker symbol on a specific day.

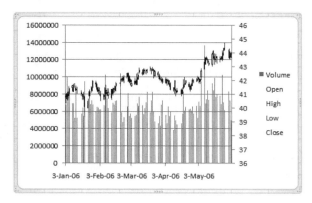

SURFACE

Select this chart type to add a topographic layer over a column or area chart.

A surface chart shows a three-dimensional surface that connects a set of data points. Use this chart when you want to find optimum combinations between two sets of data. The colors in a surface chart indicate areas that contain a similar range of values.

When setting up a surface chart, your left column should contain values of one independent variable that will be plotted along the x-axis. Your top row should contain values of another independent variable that will be plotted along the y-axis. The intersection of each row and column should contain the height of the surface for those two points. Figure 22.11 shows the dataset and the resulting surface chart.

Instead of assigning a color to each series, this chart type assigns different colors to similar values. The result resembles a topographic map, which can be used to show relationships among large amounts of data that might otherwise be hard to see.

Do: use the 3D Rotation icon on the Layout ribbon to turn this chart to provide the best view of the hills and valleys in the chart.

Figure 22.11
The surface chart shows a continuous function based on an x & y variable.

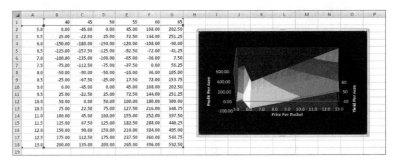

DOUGHNUT

The doughnut chart is similar to a pie chart, except that it can contain more than one data series. Each ring of the doughnut chart represents a data series.

Do: use a doughnut chart to compare pie charts from a few different entities.

Don't: rely on Excel to accurately pick up the correct series name from your dataset. You will have to use the Select Data icon on the Design ribbon and edit the individual series names. In Figure 22.12, the chart was customized to show the series name and percentage on each piece of the doughnut chart.

Figure 22.12
The doughtnut chart compares pie charts for several different series.

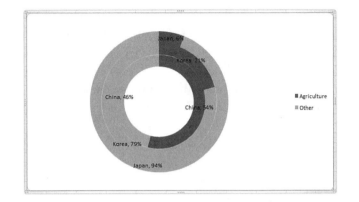

BUBBLE

Bubble charts are similar to scatter charts, except they contain three series of data rather than two. Instead of placing a uniform-sized dot at the point where each pair of x- and y-values intersect, the data markers are bubbles whose size is determined by the values in a third series (see Figure 22.13). Bubble charts often are used to present financial or market research information.

Figure 22.13
The size of the circle represents the relative asking price for used cars in the morning newspaper.

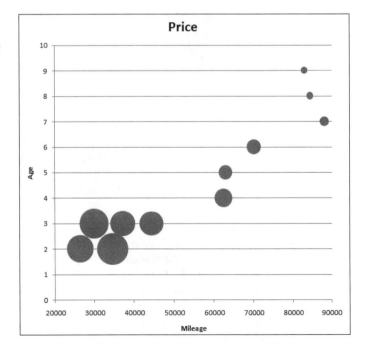

RADAR

Each category in a radar chart has its own value axis that extends from the center of the chart.

Use this chart to graphically illustrate a rating along several performance areas. Ideally, your performance is ranked on a 1–5 point scale. A review with all 5-point ratings would show a radar chart with the surface area extending to the end of the chart for all measures. Any unfilled gaps in the chart show areas that need improvement.

In Figure 22.14, your company is ranked high in speed, but low in accuracy. Your competitor is slow but accurate.

Figure 22.14
A radar chart shows gaps in performance.

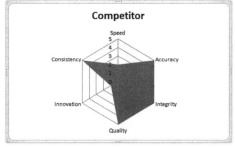

CYLINDER/CONE/PYRAMID

For the most part, these are simply glitzy versions of standard 3D column and bar charts. You will find them as subtypes in the Column chart category. Options enable you to control whether each data marker tapers to a point or is tapered to the highest value in the series. Figure 22.15 shows a Cylinder, Cone, and Pyramid chart type.

CAUTION

The inherent problem with either the Cone or Pyramid chart types is that the later series, appearing at the narrower point of the pyramid, is given less volume. This creates a visual bias that is not representative of the underlying data. If you are thinking of using a Cone or Pyramid chart—don't.

Figure 22.15
The Cone and Pyramid charts are particularly misleading.

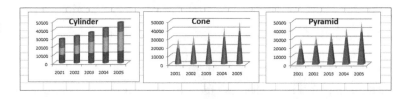

USING COMBINATION CHARTS

It is possible in Excel to create charts that contain a combination of chart types. The Line-Column chart type, for example, lets you format one series of data along a line and another in columns. You can create this chart by creating a standard column chart, then changing the chart type of one series to a line. This type of chart is useful for showing two different measures on the same chart. For example, you might plot production units and production quality. The units could be plotted as a column chart and the quality as a line chart.

Another combination chart is a stock chart that lets you plot high, low, and closing stock prices on a line, with trading volume in columns. In this case, you use two value axes, one to the left of the chart area and the other on the right.

The Pie-of-Pie and Pie-of-Bar combination charts, both available as subtypes in the Pie category, offer a clever solution when you have so many data points that your chart is difficult to read. As the example in Figure 22.16 shows, you can use a Pie-of-Bar chart to combine several smaller slices into a single large slice, and then show the detail in a separate chart connected to the original.

Figure 22.16
Use a Pie-of-Bar chart to keep small slices of the pie from getting lost.

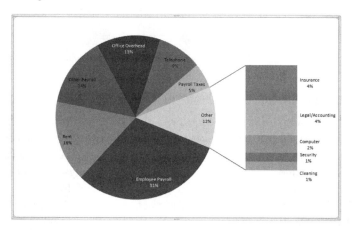

To create either of these combination chart types, use the Insert Pie Chart drop-down list and choose the appropriate chart subtype from the list. To adjust which slices of the pie will go in the secondary (pie or bar) chart, right-click the pie and select Format Data Series. Then click the Series Options category and adjust the settings as shown in Figure 22.17.

Using the Split Series By list, you can tell Excel to use a specific number of slices, or all slices below a certain value or percentage.

To move specific slices from the primary to the secondary chart, select the Custom option in the Split Series By drop-down list. Then, while the dialog is still displayed, click a pie slice behind the dialog box. Use the Point Belongs To drop-down list to move the selected slice to the First Plot or Second Plot.

Figure 22.17
You can choose to plot the last n values in the second plot. Alternatively, you can split the series so that everything under y% is in the second plot.

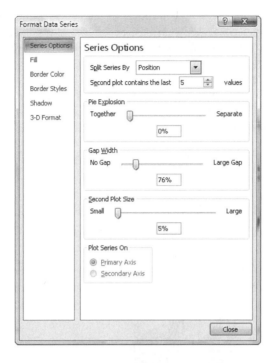

CREATING AND SAVING CUSTOM CHART TYPES

If you've extensively customized a chart, you can save its formatting settings and chart options as a chart template. All the custom chart templates you save appear on the Templates category of the Insert Chart dialog box. When you choose a custom chart from this list, Excel applies all the saved options and format settings from the selected chart type to the current chart. This is an especially effective technique for managing a collection of formatted charts you use regularly. It's also an effective way to maintain a consistent style across charts within a company.

To save a formatted chart as a template, follow these steps:

1. Select the chart.
2. On the Chart Tools Design ribbon tab, choose Save as Template.
3. Choose a name that is indicative of the chart formatting.

To later apply use this template when building a chart, follow these steps:

1. Select a data series from which you want to make a chart.
2. On the Insert tab of the ribbon, open any of the chart type icons.
3. At the bottom of the charting menu, select All Chart Types. The Insert Chart dialog box is displayed. A Templates folder will appear at the top of the left list of chart categories, as shown in Figure 22.18.

4. Click the Templates folder. Excel displays a thumbnail for each chart type. If you hover over a thumbnail, you will see the name of the template.

5. Choose a custom template and click OK.

Figure 22.18
Your custom chart types are added to a Templates Folder in the Insert Chart dialog box.

By default, all your custom chart templates are stored in the folder %appdata%/Microsoft/Templates/Charts. If you need to share templates with another computer, copy your template files from this folder and take them to the new computer.

To quickly browse to the templates folder, click the Manage Templates button in the Insert Chart dialog box.

TIP FROM

When you save a custom chart type, your entry in the user-defined gallery stores all formatting and chart options, but not the title text. You will be able to type a new title after creating the chart.

Creating custom chart templates is a particularly good way to distribute standard chart types throughout a department or an entire corporation, while preventing users from modifying or deleting the chart types.

TIP FROM

To delete a custom chart type you've created, click the Manage Templates button in the Insert Chart dialog box. You can then use Windows Explorer commands to either delete or rename the chart template file.

CREATING A DEFAULT CHART

The absolute quickest way to create an Excel chart is to select a data range and press Alt+F1. This creates a chart using all Excel's default chart options embedded on the current worksheet. (To insert a chart as a new chart sheet, use the F11 key instead of Alt+F1.) On a clean installation of Office 2007, the default chart type is the Column chart type. If you prefer to use a different chart type as your default, open the Insert Chart dialog box, select the chart type you want to use, and click the Set as Default Chart button. The next time you press Alt+F1 or F11, Excel will create a chart using the current region or selected data with the chart options in your default chart type.

Selecting a Layout and Style

Microsoft's goal is to allow you to create professionally designed charts in a minimum of clicks. After you choose a chart type from the Insert ribbon, you can use the Chart Layouts gallery on the Chart Tools Design ribbon to quickly choose from one of 4 to 12 styles for that chart type.

The custom styles in the Chart Layouts gallery are eclectic. Basically, if an author spent more than a page explaining how to create a custom chart type, Microsoft added a Chart Layout to allow you to create the formatted chart with a couple of clicks.

For example, in *Beautiful Evidence*, Edward Tufte writes about Sparkline charts. You can now easily create a sparkline. First, select a line chart, and then choose Layout 11 from the Chart Layouts gallery. Figure 22.19 shows a sparkline.

Figure 22.19
All the settings to create a sparkline are now selected by choosing a layout from a gallery.

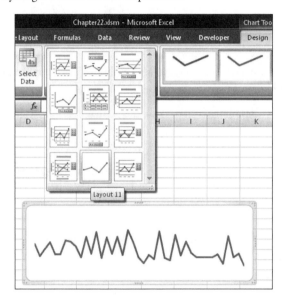

In Excel 2003, you would have to labor through the steps necessary to eliminate the gap width in a chart in order to create a histogram. In Excel 2007, you can insert a bar chart and then choose Layout 8. Figure 22.20 shows a histogram chart created using Layout 8 from the Chart Layouts gallery.

The rest of the Design ribbon is occupied by a large gallery of chart styles. This gallery contains 48 thumbnails with various colors and effects, as shown in Figure 22.21.

The gallery contains six monochrome styles suitable for printing on a black and white printer. There are six styles for each of the six accent colors in the current theme. There are six styles that use a mix of colors from the current theme. The bottom row in the gallery contains color styles with dark backgrounds. These might be more suitable when you plan to paste the chart into a PowerPoint presentation.

Figure 22.20
Eliminating the gaps between columns to create a histogram is easily accomplished using a built-in chart layout.

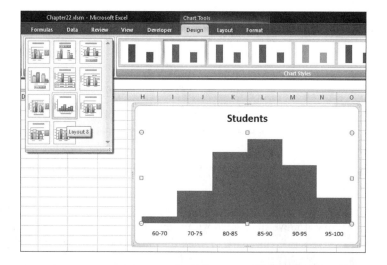

Figure 22.21
Choose from various colors and effects in the Chart Styles gallery on the Design ribbon.

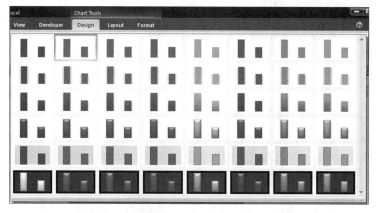

> **TIP FROM**
>
> *EQ & Woody*
>
> The six colors offered in the Chart Styles gallery are based on the current theme. You can use different colors by choosing one of the 19 other built-in themes. Use the Themes drop-down list on the Page Layout ribbon to choose a different theme.

MOVING CHARTS

By default, all new charts are created as embedded objects in the current sheet. To move an embedded chart to a different sheet, or to move a chart to its own chart sheet, use the Move Chart icon in the Location group of the Chart Tools Design ribbon.

Select the chart to be moved. Click the Move Chart icon on the right side of the Design ribbon. Excel offers the Move Chart dialog box as shown in Figure 22.22.

22

Figure 22.22
To move a chart to a
different sheet, use the
Move Chart icon.

If you want to move a chart to a new location on the current sheet, you can click the chart and drag it to a new location.

Be careful where you click inside the chart when you attempt to move it. If you click on the legend, you might move the legend within the chart area. For trouble-free moves, either click white space inside the chart, or click the chart border to drag the chart.

To resize an embedded chart, click once on the chart border to select the chart area. You'll see eight small sizing handles along the border—one on each side and one in each corner. Point to any of these handles and drag the pointer—a two-headed arrow—in any direction to adjust the size and shape of the chart. As you drag, Excel adjusts the scale of all elements on your chart to match the new size and shape.

LABELING A CHART'S ELEMENTS

Although you can create a chart with a couple clicks of the mouse, you might want to customize various elements of the chart. The Chart Tools Layout tab of the ribbon offers a host of settings to control every element of the chart.

> **NOTE**
>
> All the techniques described in this section work equally well with embedded chart objects, chart sheets, and PivotCharts.

For most elements, Excel offers a drop-down list with popular selections, and then a More Options choice. Choosing More Options will take you to a Format dialog box with dozens of choices in several categories.

If you want to head directly to the more powerful Format dialog box, you can select the chart element and then click the Format Selection icon in the Current Selection group of the Chart Tools Layout ribbon.

> **TIP FROM**
>
> *Ed & Woody*
>
> Selecting a specific chart object by pointing to it can be difficult, especially on a small chart with many elements crowding one another for space. Try this simple shortcut: Use the Current Selection drop-down list at the left of the Chart Tools Layout ribbon tab. Selecting any item from this list selects that item in the current chart. Then click the Format Selection button just under the drop-down list to display the Format dialog box for the selected object.

ADDING OR EDITING A TITLE

To add a title to a chart, use the Chart Title drop-down list on the Chart Tools Layout ribbon tab as shown in Figure 22.23. The default options in the drop-down list are to create a centered title that overlays the chart or to put the title above the chart. Titles are added as 18-point Cambria font. If you choose Above Chart, the chart area will be reduced to make room for the title area.

Figure 22.23
Excel offers two built-in locations for the chart title.

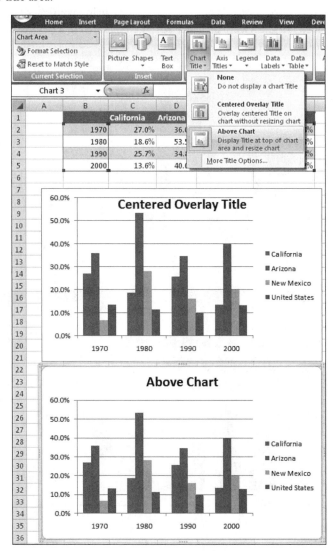

22

After you click the chart option, Excel adds the words "Chart Title" to the chart and selects the title. You can immediately type a new chart title in the Formula bar and press Enter to change the chart title.

To format a chart title, click the title, and then click and drag to select text in the title. Immediately move the mouse upward toward the nearly invisible Mini Toolbar. You can use any of the formatting icons on the Mini Toolbar to format the text in the title, as shown in Figure 22.24. For more control, you can use the formatting commands on the Home ribbon. You can also use the WordArt gallery on the Chart Tools Format ribbon to apply interesting effects to the chart title as shown in Figure 22.25.

Figure 22.24
The elusive Mini Toolbar fades into view when you select text and move the mouse toward the toolbar.

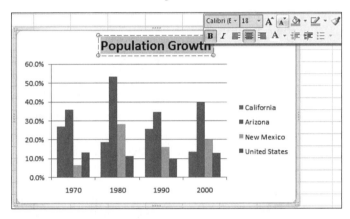

Figure 22.25
For more interesting text effects, move to the WordArt gallery on the Format ribbon.

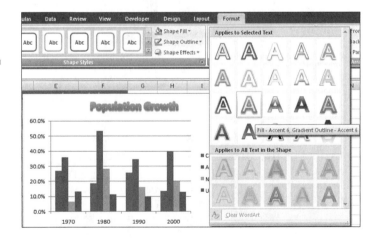

ADDING LABELS TO AXES

If the nature of your axes is not clear, you can add a title to any available axis. As shown in Figure 22.26, use the Axis Titles drop-down list on the Chart Tools Layout ribbon to add an axis label. For the vertical axis, you can choose to display the axis horizontally, vertically, or rotated. In all cases, adding an axis label will cause the size of the chart plot area to be reduced. After the axis label is added, you can type text and format the text in the same manner as described previously for the chart titles.

Figure 22.26
Excel offers several axis rotation options.

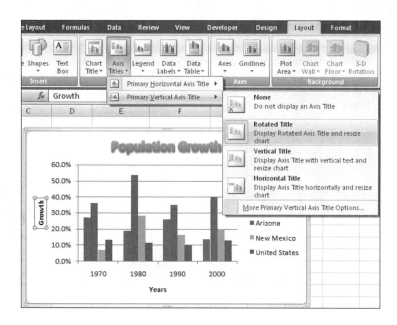

ADDING OR EDITING A LEGEND

A chart legend identifies each data marker according to its color or pattern on a chart. Options in the Legend drop-down list let you move or reformat the legend. If you don't need to show a legend (perhaps because you want to label each column or pie slice individually), choose the None option. The Placement options control where the legend first appears within the chart: Right, Top, Left, Bottom, Overlay Right, and Overlay Left.

For better control, you can drag the legend into position. In Excel 2007, the default legend has no line and a transparent fill. This makes it annoyingly difficult to drag the legend, It is best if you click the invisible right edge of the legend when you attempt to drag it.

The transparent nature of the legend presents a new problem. In Figure 22.27, the legend has been dragged to overlay the top-left corner of the chart. The gridlines on the chart are showing through the transparent legend. To solve this problem, use the icons on the Chart Tools Format ribbon tab. Select Shape Fill, White Background. Then select Shape Outline, Black to restore the legend to the Excel 2003 legend style.

Figure 22.27
Legends are initially transparent, causing the underlying chart to show through when the legend is overlaid on the chart. Use the Shape tools on the Format tab to prevent gridlines from showing through.

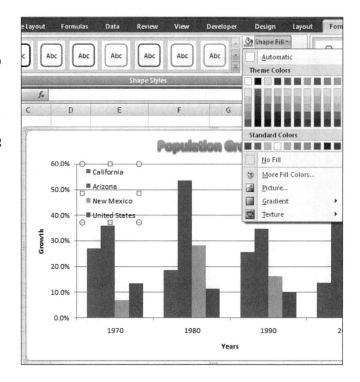

DISPLAYING DATA LABELS

Use data labels when you want to display charted worksheet values, category labels, or percentages next to each point in a data series. The options in the Data Labels drop-down list control the placement and appearance of data labels for every data series. However, if you want to add labels for just one series, or even a single point, you can do so. Before accessing the Data Labels drop-down list, click a single bar that is a member of the series you want to label. A second click on the bar will select only the data point. Choose the appropriate choice on the Data Labels menu to apply the label inside or outside the bars. In Figure 22.28, data labels are applied to the outside end of each bar.

Figure 22.28
Data labels can be positioned inside or outside each bar. Use More Data Label Options to control the number format, rotation angle, and font size of all data labels.

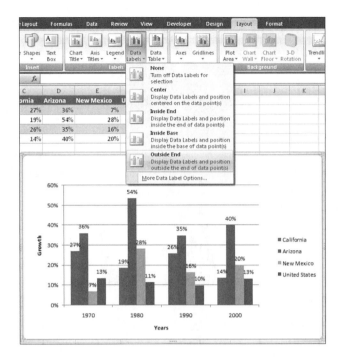

22

ADDING A DATA TABLE

Display a worksheet-style table directly in your chart to show the plotted worksheet data alongside the chart itself. Each row in the data table represents a data series. If your chart includes a relatively small amount of data, a data table can make an effective addition, as the example in Figure 22.29 shows.

The Data Table drop-down on the Chart Tools Layout tab offers options to add a table with or without legend keys. If you choose More Data Table options, you can control the appearance of the horizontal and vertical borders within the data table.

NOTE

Data tables are available only in column, bar, line, area, and stock charts. You cannot add a data table to a pie, XY (scatter), doughnut, radar, surface, or bubble chart.

Figure 22.29
Data tables give your audience both views of the data—the visual display as well as the underlying numbers.

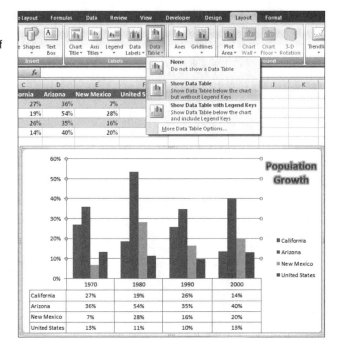

CUSTOMIZING AXES

Excel automatically chooses a scale for the horizontal and vertical axis. There are many situations where the default axes settings are not ideal. The defaults will lead to charts that are hard to interpret. Use the ideas in this section to customize the axes on your chart and to bring out your intended message.

DISPLAYING VERTICAL AXIS IN THOUSANDS, AND SO ON

The numbers along your vertical axis will inherit the numeric formatting of the source data. Although Excel tipsters love the arcane formatting codes that allow you to display numbers in thousands or millions, Microsoft has simplified the task considerably in Excel 2007. Choose Chart Tools Layout, Axes, Primary Vertical Axes, Show Axis in Thousands to reduce the number of zeroes occupying space along the left side of your chart. In Figure 22.30, the bottom chart has numbers displayed in billions.

Figure 22.30
Use the Axes options to eliminate 000s from the axes labels.

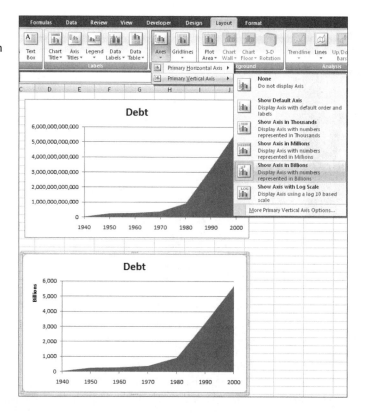

USING A TIME SERIES ALONG A HORIZONTAL AXIS

A quick glance at the top chart in Figure 22.31 might lead you to believe that population growth is slowing. However, if you notice the labels along the horizontal axis, you will see that there is not an equal amount of years between each data point.

In a case where one axis represents a timescale, you should make sure that your underlying data contains numbers that are formatted as dates. The DATE functions in A20:A27 convert the text years to real Excel dates. The bottom chart automatically converts the horizontal axis to a timescale, providing a more realistic view of the data.

NOTE

If your source data contains dates and you want to force the axis to be a text-based axis, you can control this by selecting Chart Tools Layout, Axes, Primary Horizontal Axis, More Primary Horizontal Axis Option, Axis Options, Axis Type: Text Axis.

Figure 22.31
Text years in the top chart cause Excel to plot each data point at an equal distance. The timescale in the bottom chart presents a more accurate view of the data.

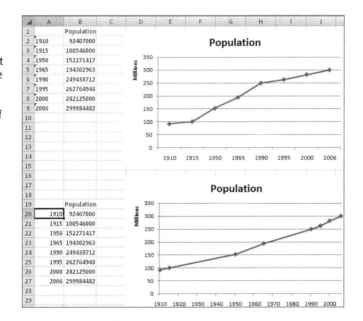

SHOWING NUMBERS OF DIFFERENT SCALE USING A LOGARITHMIC AXIS

If a single data series has numbers of different orders of magnitude, it is difficult to interpret the numbers on the chart. In the top chart in Figure 22.32, most models are in the 100–500 quantity range. A few best-selling models in the 9,000 range force the axis to scale up to be large enough to include points in the 10,000 range. This makes it impossible to distinguish any detail of the lower-selling models.

In the bottom chart in Figure 22.32, the Show Axis with Log Scale option has been chosen. In a logarithmic scale, the distance from 10 to 100 on the vertical axis is the same as the distance from 1,000 to 10,000. This scaling effect allows you to make out the detail for both the smaller data points.

To access this setting, choose Chart Tools Layout, Axes, Primary Vertical Axis, Show Axis with Log Scale.

Figure 22.32
A logarithmic scale on the axis in the bottom chart allows the details of the smaller data points to be read.

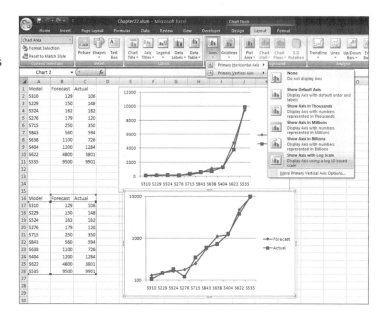

PLOTTING ONE SERIES ON A SECONDARY AXIS

You may often have data series that contain numbers of a different scale. For example, you might want to show both revenues and gross profit percentage by month on the same chart.

If you attempt to plot both series on the same chart, the numbers for the gross profit percentage are too small to show up on the chart, as shown in the top chart in Figure 22.33.

To create the bottom chart in the figure, follow these steps:

1. Create your chart as a Clustered Column chart.

2. On the Chart Tools Layout ribbon, use the drop-down list in the Current Selection drop-down list to select the smaller series. In this case, you would select Series GP%.

3. Click the Format Selection button. In the Series Options category of the Format Data Series dialog box, choose Plot Series on Secondary Axis. Click Close to close the Format Data Series dialog box.

4. While the second series is still selected, go back to the Chart Tools Design ribbon and choose Change Chart Type. Choose Line with Markers.

5. In the current chart, the columns are blue and the line is red. You might want to change the color of the numbers on the secondary axis to be red to match the color of the line. Click any of the numbers on the right side of the chart to select the secondary axis. Use the Font Color drop-down list on the Home ribbon tab to change the color of the numbers to red.

22

6. In a similar fashion, change the color of the primary vertical axis to blue. You can also use Chart Tools Layout, Axes, Primary Vertical Axis, Show Axis in Thousands to scale the axis. Format the legend to have a solid white fill and a border. Drag the border of the legend to overlay the chart. Resize the plot area to fill the space formerly occupied by the legend.

Figure 22.33
Plotting the percentages on a secondary y-axis allows them to be seen in the lower chart.

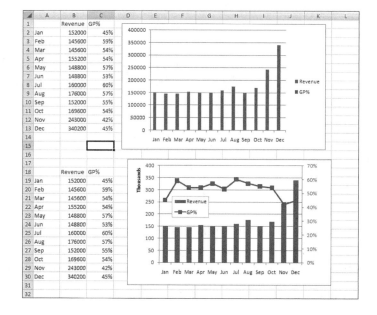

NOT STARTING THE AXIS AT ZERO

To make a chart easier to read, you might also want to adjust the scale on the vertical axis. In Excel 2007, the values automatically scale to include numbers slightly below and above the values in your data series.

This is usually a good change. In Figure 22.34, the default decision to scale the vertical axis from 156.4 to 158 allows you to make out the variability from day to day. Had Excel scaled the axis from 0 to 180, every bar would look identical.

You can still control the minimum and maximum values along the axis if necessary:

1. Right-click the value axis and select Format Axis.

2. In the Axis Options category or the Format Axis dialog, change the Minimum or Maximum setting from Auto to Fixed. Enter a new number in the text box as shown in Figure 22.35.

3. Click Close to apply the changes to your chart.

Figure 22.34
Choosing an appropriate scale range allows you to notice variability in the top chart that would not be noticeable in the bottom chart.

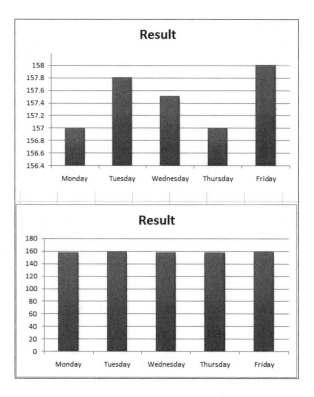

Figure 22.35
You can override the scale range for a chart.

22

SHOWING OR HIDING GRIDLINES

Gridlines are horizontal or vertical lines that extend through the plot area to help you visualize the connections between data points and values or categories. Gridlines start with the tick marks on an axis and extend through the plot area.

Use the Gridlines drop-down menu on the Chart Tools Layout ribbon to display or hide the gridlines.

For more control, use the More Gridlines Options selection to display the Format Gridlines dialog. Here you can control the color, thickness, and style of the lines.

ADDING TRENDLINES, DROPLINES, AND ERROR BARS

Excel's advanced chart options let you add details that help you spot trends more easily. For example, in a line chart that plots daily closing stock prices over time, you can add a trendline and a moving average that smooth out some of the peaks and valleys in the data. You can do the same with a column chart to show a smooth trend over time. Select the series, right-click, and select Add Trendline.

In surface charts, you can add a vertical dropline from the data point to the horizontal axis. Use the Lines icon on the Chart Tools Layout ribbon.

For line charts that show two related series, you can add a column between the data points of each series. Use the Up/Down Bars icon in the Analysis group of the Chart Tools Layout ribbon.

For charts that project data, you can add error bars that define the upper- and lower-error limits of your projections by using standard statistical measures. For example, error bars and extend a certain percentage, a certain standard deviation, or a fixed amount from the data points. You'll find these options on the Error Bars icon of the Chart Tools Layout ribbon.

Figure 22.36 shows an example of each element from the Analysis group.

Figure 22.36
Trendlines, Drop Lines, Up/Down Bars, and Error Bars can be automatically drawn on the chart by Excel 2007.

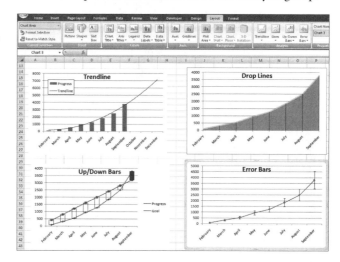

NOTE

> For more information on how you can display detailed analyses in Excel charts, see *Special Edition Using Microsoft Excel 2007*, by Bill Jelen (published by Que, ISBN: 0-7897-3611-X).

CUSTOMIZING A CHART'S APPEARANCE

As you progress from the Design to the Layout to the Format ribbon tabs, you begin to have finer control over elements of the chart. The Design tab globally changes the chart type and colors in the chart. The Layout tab allows you to turn on or off certain elements of the chart. The Format tab offers complete control over fill, outline, shadow, reflection, glow, soft edges, bevel, and rotation of every chart element.

CHANGING FILL AND OUTLINE COLORS

Most default charts have a boring white or black background behind the data. Choose the plot area in a chart and use the Shape Fill drop-down list on the Chart Tools Format ribbon to add color to the chart. You can either choose a theme color, a standard color, build a color, use a picture, a gradient or a texture. In Figure 22.37, the top-left chart shows a plot area formatted with a gradient. The lower-left chart shows data bars formatted with a wood grain texture. In the bottom-right chart, a picture is used as the fill effect for the plot area.

Figure 22.37
Add color to your charts by changing the Shape Fill of the plot area or data bars.

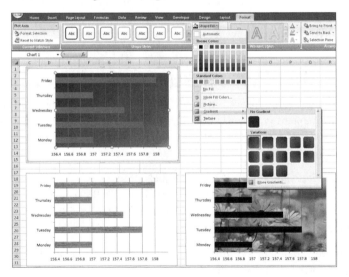

ADDING VISUAL EFFECTS

Office 2007's charting engine adds the capability to add glow, shadow, reflection, soft edge, or bevel to most charting elements.

Each drop-down list offers nine or more built-in styles. Most offer a link to a dialog box where you can fine-tune the styles.

To add effects to shapes in the chart, use the Shape Fill, Shape Outline, or Shape Effects drop-down lists in the Shape Styles group of the Chart Tools Format ribbon. To add effects to the text in a chart, use the same three drop-down lists in the WordArt Styles group of the same ribbon.

In Figure 22.38, a soft blue glow has been added to the columns and text in the chart.

Figure 22.38
Add glow or soft edges to any chart element.

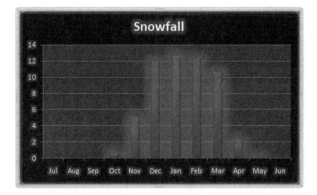

Excel also lets you add an enormous number of attention-getting elements in the drawing layer on top of a chart. For example, you can add text boxes to data markers to explain anomalies in your data or call attention to key numbers. Use the Text Box icon on the Chart Tools Layout ribbon. Drag in the chart to add a blank text box. After you've added the desired text, you can then move it anywhere on the chart and reformat it to your liking.

WORKING WITH PIVOTTABLE CHARTS

Pivot tables have been improved in Excel 2007. Use the PivotTable icon on the Insert ribbon to add a pivot table to your workbook. Design a pivot table with one field in the Column Labels and one field in the Row Labels. Click the Pivot Chart icon in the PivotTable Tools Option ribbon.

Excel will convert values in the Column Labels drop zone to become series in the chart (also called Legend Fields). Values in the Row Labels area will become categories along the horizontal axis (also called Axis Fields). Any fields in the Report Filter section will continue to be available for filtering the pivot chart.

Excel draws the pivot chart on the same worksheet as your pivot table. You can either select report filter values from the PivotChart Filter pane or from the drop-down lists in the pivot table.

When you click the pivot chart, four new tabs appear on the ribbon as PivotChart Tools: Design, Layout, Format, and Analyze. These tabs allow you all of the chart formatting discussed in this chapter, plus the capability to refresh the pivot table.

Figure 22.39 shows a pivot chart in Excel 2007.

Figure 22.39
In Excel 2007, pivot charts are embedded on the same worksheet as the pivot table.

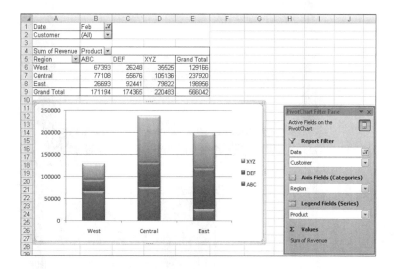

CREATING OTHER CHART TYPES

There have been many requests for Microsoft to add new charting types to Excel. Stock analysts would like point-and-figure charts. Many people producing dashboard reports would like speedometer charts. Economists ask for Macroeconomic Supply Curve Charts, where the width of each bar indicates the volume, and the height of the bar indicates the price.

Microsoft is aware of these desires. However, it spent all its time developing the new charting engine and were unable to add any new chart types for Excel 2007. Although new chart types are probably on the plan for Excel 14, various vendors offer third-party add-ins to create new chart types.

Figure 22.40 shows examples of new chart types created using add-ins from www.MrExcel.com.

Figure 22.40
Third-party add-ins
allow you to add new
chart types to Excel.

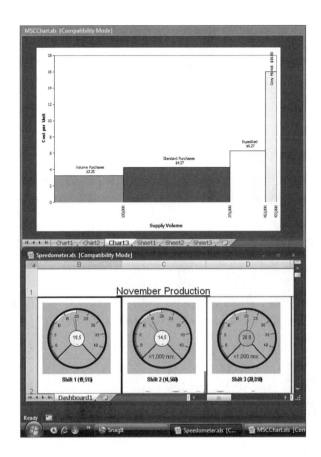

TROUBLESHOOTING

FORMATTING COMBINATION CHARTS

I created a Pie-of-Pie or Pie-of-Bar chart, but I'm having trouble formatting it.

These combination chart types follow some fairly rigid rules. You cannot select either pie individually. They are always side by side, and you cannot move them, although you can change their relative size. To show the link between the two charts, you can add or remove series lines; however, you cannot reformat these connecting lines.

ADDING NEW DATA TO A CHART

I've created a chart and now need to add new data to the chart. Can I do this without re-creating the chart?

When you select a data series on an embedded chart, the Range Finder displays a colored line around the corresponding range within the data source; the Range Finder also adds a border around the value axis labels and category labels, using different colors for each. Drag the selection by using the rectangular handle in the lower-right corner of each selection to extend or move the data range for each series. On a chart where the data source consists of a single contiguous range, selecting the chart area causes the Range Finder to highlight all the data series in one color, the value axis labels in another color, and category names in still another color.

Alternatively, you could make liberal use of the Excel 2007 table functionality before creating a chart. Click inside your data range and select Home, Format as Table. Create a chart from data in the table. As you add new rows or columns to the table, Excel automatically updates the chart to include the new data.

SECRETS OF THE EXCEL MASTERS: LEAVE THE TOP-LEFT CELL BLANK

This tip is counterintuitive because every Excel expert teaches you that you should never have blank cells in your data.

The one exception, however, is the top-left cell of your chart source data. Get in the habit of leaving this cell blank before you create a chart.

Consider the dataset in rows 1:4 of Figure 22.41. Although any human can tell that there are three regions and three years of data, to Excel, the data in row 1 seems very much like the data in rows 2:4. There is text in cell A1 and numbers in B1:D1. This arrangement of data confuses Excel and causes Excel to plot a Region category along the horizontal access.

In the lower half of the figure, the same data appears, except the word Region was cleared from cell A13. Now when you create a default column chart, Excel correctly plots three regions and three years.

TIP FROM

Ed & Woody

> This tip is particularly important if the headings in either the first row or the first column contain numbers or dates.

Figure 22.41
Leave the top-left cell of your source data blank to enable troublefree charting.

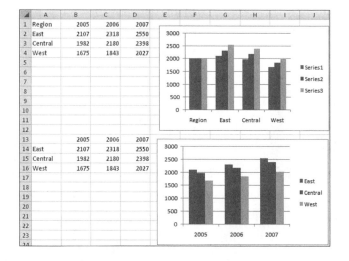

USING POWERPOINT

23 Building a Perfect Presentation   703

24 Advanced Presentation Formatting   737

25 Adding Graphics, Multimedia, and Special Effects   759

26 Planning and Delivering a Presentation   779

CHAPTER 23

BUILDING A PERFECT PRESENTATION

In this chapter

What's New in PowerPoint 2007   704

Anatomy of a PowerPoint Presentation   704

Creating a Presentation   706

Editing the Presentation Outline   710

Changing a Slide Layout   712

Editing Slides   713

Viewing a Presentation   722

Managing Slide Shows   726

Navigating Through a Presentation   729

Troubleshooting   732

Secrets of the Office Masters: PowerPoint File Types   733

WHAT'S NEW IN POWERPOINT 2007

 Through the years, PowerPoint has developed a well-deserved reputation as the one Office program that just about anyone can use with virtually no training. By starting with a generic template and choosing a canned design, you can put together a professional-looking presentation by doing little more than type. PowerPoint 2007 continues in this ease-of-use tradition, adding a handful of usability enhancements (most notably the extensive use of Ribbon galleries with live previews as in other Office programs) to make the program even easier to use than before.

In fact, PowerPoint is so easy to use that you might be tempted to skip these chapters and just get straight to work. If you do that, you'll miss some expert-level productivity enhancements buried in the program. In this section, we focus on some of these hidden gems, and we also cover the following features that are brand new in Office 2007:

- Predefined slide themes—20 in all—that apply colors, fonts, and effects to give your entire presentation a consistent look. You can also create your own custom themes.

- More than 20 preset color schemes that govern the colors applied to the slide text and background, hyperlinks, and a half dozen accent colors. You can even create custom color schemes.

- Nearly two dozen preset font themes that apply specific fonts and font sizes to slide headings and body text.

- Dozens of styles for modifying the look of text, graphics, charts, and shapes. PowerPoint 2007 offers tools for formatting the fill and outline as well as numerous effects such as drop shadows, reflections, glow colors, soft edges, bevels, and 3D.

ANATOMY OF A POWERPOINT PRESENTATION

Putting together a basic PowerPoint presentation takes little more than the spark of an idea and a few minutes with the Ribbon. Assembling an effective, persuasive presentation, on the other hand, demands much more.

Although the next few chapters deal with the mechanics of creating a dynamite presentation, one thought should remain uppermost in your mind: Content rules. A poorly conceived and executed PowerPoint presentation will leave your audience cold, no matter how many fancy transitions, animations, or web links you employ. Conversely, a compelling story, well told, will stick with your audience even if it's presented exclusively in 14-point Times New Roman on a stark white background.

NOTE

> Although PowerPoint can help you create effective presentations, becoming a better public speaker is largely up to you. If you want to hone your presentation skills, we recommend picking up a copy of *Special Edition Using Microsoft PowerPoint 2007* by Patrice-Anne Rutledge and Geetesh Bajaj (also by Que).

Figure 23.1 illustrates the basic components of a PowerPoint presentation—slides, notes, and a navigation panel on the left side that allows you to switch between a text outline and slide thumbnails.

Outline/Thumbnails   Slide

Figure 23.1
PowerPoint's Normal view includes most of the information you need to assemble a presentation.

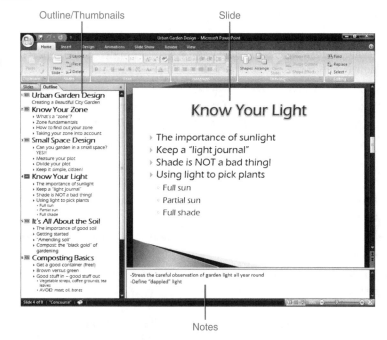

Notes

A fully loaded slide (see Figure 23.2) includes at most six parts:

Body text   Title   Graphic

Figure 23.2
All the components of a PowerPoint slide are shown here, with slide thumbnails in place of a text outline.

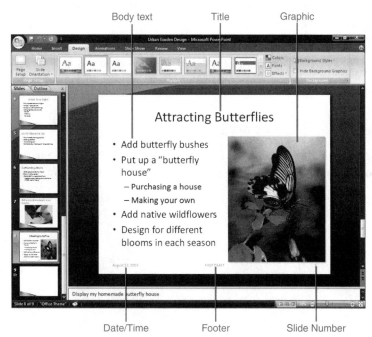

Date/Time   Footer   Slide Number

23

- The *title*, which usually sits at the top of the slide.

- *Body text*, the main part of the slide. More often than not, the text on a slide consists of a series of bulleted or numbered items. However, you can enter any kind of text in this part of a slide—bullets and numbers are not required.

- Some slides contain *content* in addition to text. This type of object includes charts, tables, pictures, diagrams, and video clips that, in the best circumstances, serve to illuminate your presentation. Each such object resides in its own resizable placeholder, too.

> **NOTE**
>
> Text and content sit inside resizable and movable containers called *placeholders*, which you can see if you click the text or graphic in the slide pane. PowerPoint help screens sometimes refer to the placeholder and the text or content it contains as a "text object" or a "graphic object."

- If you choose to display the *date and time*, these items appear at the lower-left corner by default.

- The *footer*, another optional element, appears by default at the bottom of the slide, in the middle.

- Finally, you can choose to display a *slide number*; its default position is in the lower-right corner.

Most presentations begin with a *title slide*, which typically includes the title of the presentation, the speaker's name, and other introductory details. Other slides in a presentation can also be title slides—you might use a title slide to introduce different portions of a long presentation, for example—but in most cases, you'll have just one title slide in a presentation, and it will serve as the first slide.

> **NOTE**
>
> Don't be confused by the terminology. A *title slide* is, in most cases, a slide that introduces a presentation. A *slide title*, on the other hand, is usually the first line on a slide.

CREATING A PRESENTATION

When you choose Office, New, PowerPoint opens the New Presentation dialog box that includes a variety of options for creating presentations (see Figure 23.3).

Figure 23.3
PowerPoint lets you choose whether you want to open an existing presentation, create a new presentation with or without content, or pull in a template.

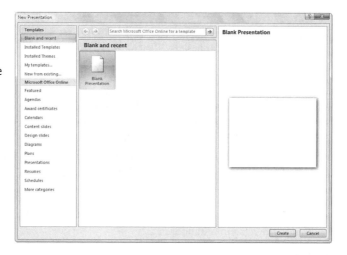

CREATING A BLANK PRESENTATION

When you create a new, blank presentation—by choosing Blank Presentation in the New Presentation dialog box and then clicking Create—PowerPoint generates a new presentation that displays a single title slide.

Although it's a tedious way to work, you can build your presentation from this view, one slide at a time. In the Home tab, pull down the New Slide menu and then click the layout that matches the kind of slide you want to add.

In a blank PowerPoint presentation, each new slide you create is completely free of any design elements whatsoever. You get a white background, with text formatted in the Calibri font (44-point for slide titles and 32-point for body text) and generic round bullets.

To replace this deadly dull design with one that contains coordinated colors, fonts, and graphics, click the Design tab and then click the More button in the Themes group. The Themes gallery appears (see Figure 23.4).

Figure 23.4
Use the Themes gallery to apply a predefined theme to some or all of your slides.

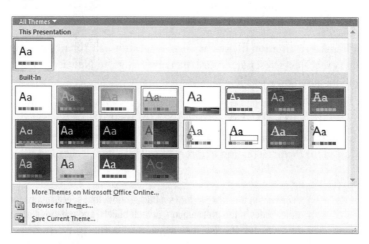

TIP FROM

Ed & Woody

> Initially, PowerPoint offers 20 theme designs. You can see more by clicking More Themes on Microsoft Office Online in the Themes gallery.

Like all the Office 2007 galleries, the Themes gallery uses Live Preview, which means that if you hover your mouse pointer over a theme, PowerPoint applies the theme temporarily to the current slide. When you click a theme, PowerPoint immediately applies the design to all slides in your presentation. If you prefer to apply a theme only to the current slide, right-click the theme and then click Apply to Selected Slides.

If your company has certain standards for all presentations—logo in a specific location, identification of title slides, and so on—you might want to customize PowerPoint's "blank" presentation so that it reflects your standards.

To replace the PowerPoint default blank presentation with one of your own design, follow these steps:

1. Create the presentation you want to use as the "blank" presentation. Add slides, customize slide masters, and change designs until you're satisfied that the basic arrangement is a good starting point for any new presentations you create.

2. Choose Office, Save As. In the Save as Type box, choose PowerPoint Template.

3. Type **Blank** into the File Name box and click Save.

TIP FROM

Ed & Woody

> By default, PowerPoint saves your new blank presentation in your personal Templates folder (`%AppData%\Microsoft\Templates`). To make this change for all the users in your organization, you must copy the Blank Presentation design template file into the personal Templates folder for each user.

→ For more details on how and where Office programs organize files, **see** "Creating New Files," **p. 63**.

With a Blank Presentation file in the correct location, all "blank" presentations—whether created via the New Presentation task pane or using the New icon on the Standard toolbar—will be based on that file.

STARTING POWERPOINT WITH A TEMPLATE OR THEME

Don't like the idea of starting with a completely blank slate? PowerPoint gives you two ways to pick a design for the presentation before you roll up your sleeves and begin adding new slides:

NOTE

> A *design*, in this case, includes a background, font specifications for the title slide and other slides in the presentation, default bullets, and a handful of lesser settings—title locations, footers, slide numbering, and the like.

- Choose a presentation template, which gives you a presentation design as well as several ready-to-use slides. Select Office, New, and then select Installed Templates. In the Installed Templates list, click a design template thumbnail to see more detail for the design (see Figure 23.5).

- Choose a presentation theme, which applies one of the PowerPoint themes as the default for your presentation. Select Office, New, and then select Installed Themes. In the Installed Themes list, click a theme thumbnail to see more detail for the design.

When you have made your choice, click Create to start the new presentation.

Figure 23.5
In the Installed Templates list, click a thumbnail to get a closer look at the design.

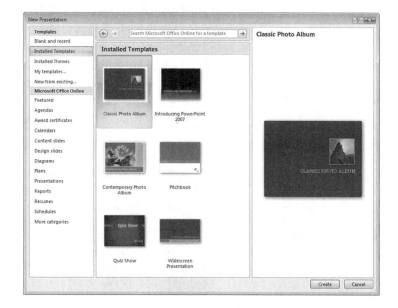

TIP FROM

Want more templates? Select the categories that appear under the Microsoft Office Online heading to see hundreds more. If you find one you like, click Download to install it on your system.

COPYING THE DESIGN OF AN EXISTING PRESENTATION

Frequently, you'll find an existing presentation with just the right design elements, even if the content is completely different from what you need.

PowerPoint makes it easy to recycle the design of an existing presentation. If you have the original presentation file, you can "borrow" its design without changing the content of your current presentation in any way.

In the Design tab, click the More button in the Themes group to display the Themes gallery, and then select Browse for Themes. In the Choose Theme or Themed Document dialog box, select the presentation or template you want to use, and then click Open.

The design of the chosen presentation is applied automatically to your current presentation.

23

BUILDING A PRESENTATION FROM A WORD OUTLINE

How many times have you been asked to give a presentation based on an existing report or other document? If you can import the document into Word and convert its headings to Word's default Heading 1 style, the rest is a snap.

To import a Word outline directly into PowerPoint, choose Office, Open, and in the Files of Type box, choose All Outlines.

When you import a Word document, Level 1 headings (formatted "Heading 1" in Word) turn into the titles of new slides. Level 2 headings turn into top-level bullet points. Level 3 headings become second-level bullet points, and so on. In essence, the outline that you see in Word's Outline view is translated into a PowerPoint outline. Any body text beneath existing headings is discarded.

Each time PowerPoint encounters a Level 1 heading in Word, it starts a new slide and uses the Level 1 heading text for the slide's title. In other words, your presentation will include exactly one slide for each Level 1 heading in the Word document.

> **NOTE**
>
> You can also import files saved in HTML formats and turn them into a PowerPoint outline. (From the drop-down Files of Type list in the Open dialog box, choose All Web Pages.) During the import, PowerPoint turns each top-level heading into a new slide; all text underneath each heading is placed in a text box on the corresponding slide.

You can also insert an outline into the middle of an existing presentation. Select the slide you want the outline to follow, and then choose Home, New Slide, Slides from Outline. PowerPoint converts the outline to new slides and inserts them after the selected slide.

EDITING THE PRESENTATION OUTLINE

The fastest, easiest, and safest way to edit the text of your presentation is by working with the outline. Select View, Normal, choose the Outline tab from the Navigation pane on the left side of the screen, and enter or edit text here to quickly build content.

EDITING SLIDES IN OUTLINE VIEW

If you have a good idea of what you want to say—or if you're willing to use one of Microsoft's default presentations to suggest content—the simplest way to get a presentation on its feet in no time is to work directly on the outline. Enter text for the slide's title and body, and then you can select, click and drag, copy, move, and delete, just as you would in any other Office application.

23

TIP FROM

> To maximize the editing area when working with an outline in Normal view, click the divider between the Outline pane and the slide, and then drag it to the right as far as you can while still being able to see the current slide. If you don't want to see formatted text in your outline, right-click the Outline pane and then click the Show Text Formatting command to deactivate it.

You can use the Tab key while in Outline view to demote one outline level. When you press the Tab key, PowerPoint demotes the current line of text—that is, it moves the current line one level lower in the hierarchy. Alternatively, you can accomplish the same result by right-clicking the Outline pane and then clicking the Demote command in the shortcut menu.

Similarly, you can promote a line one level by pressing Shift+Tab (essentially the "back tab" key). Right-clicking the Outline pane and then clicking Promote in the shortcut menu does the same thing.

When you promote a line in the outline to the highest level, it becomes the title of a new slide. Thus, a quick and easy way to insert a new slide in a presentation is to press Enter and press Shift+Tab (or click Promote in the Outline tab's shortcut menu) as many times as necessary to reach the top level. Note that the new slide uses the generic Title and Text layout.

You can type your entire presentation this way, promoting and demoting as you go: When you type a line at the highest level of the hierarchy, it automatically becomes the title of a new slide; any line below the top level turns into a bullet point (nested however deep you might want) in the slide's text placeholder.

TIP FROM

> If your slides start getting too wordy and you want to turn high-level bullet points into slides of their own, select the points (one at a time, holding down the Shift key as you click each one from top to bottom) and promote them to the highest level. PowerPoint automatically turns all of them into slides, with the old high-level bullet points now serving as titles.

REORDERING SLIDES

In the Outline tab's shortcut menu, use the Move Up and Move Down commands to rearrange text in the outline, and thus in the slides. To do so, click inside the line you want to move, or select a group of lines. Right-click the Outline pane and then click the Move Up or Move Down arrows until the lines are positioned correctly.

NOTE

> When working with the outline, you can select any group of lines, even if they appear in different slides, as long as they are contiguous.

TIP FROM

> You might find it easier to use Slide Sorter view to perform extensive reordering or to reorder a large presentation. Slide Sorter view gives you a lot more flexibility for drag and drop; it also shows you more of the presentation at one time.

→ For a detailed discussion of Slide Sorter view, **see** "Using Slide Sorter View to Rearrange a Presentation," **p. 723**.

CHANGING A SLIDE LAYOUT

Although it's easy to add a new slide to a presentation, choosing the right slide layout isn't always so simple.

PowerPoint supports two broad categories of slides: *title slides*, typically the first slide in a presentation, and "regular" slides, which, confusingly, are usually just called "slides." PowerPoint has one predefined layout for title slides and eight predefined layouts for regular slides.

Slide layouts aren't static: You can change a slide's layout by selecting the slide, choosing Home, Layout, and clicking a layout in the Layout gallery.

Whether you're applying a layout to a brand-new slide or changing the layout of an existing slide, PowerPoint presents you with the Slide Layout choices shown in Figure 23.6.

Figure 23.6
The Layout gallery gives you nine ways to organize a slide.

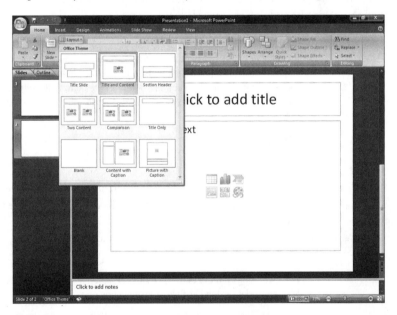

If you choose the first thumbnail in the Slide Layout pane, PowerPoint turns the new slide, or selected slide, into a title slide. Other slide thumbnails in the Slide Layout dialog box (refer to Figure 23.6) contain one or more of the following:

- **Text placeholders**—Typically for bulleted and numbered lists.
- **A general "content" placeholder**—Ties into PowerPoint's Insert Object function. The standard content on offer here includes a simple grid (a table), a chart, clip art, a picture, a SmartArt diagram, or a media clip.

→ For instructions on using the chart drawing tool, **see** "Creating and Editing Charts," **p. 123**.

- **Combinations of "content" and text**—The placeholders are arranged in various configurations.

TIP FROM

EQ & Woody

> Placeholders can be resized or dragged to fit your requirements. You need not settle for the size or placement established in the Slide Layout dialog pane.

23

EDITING SLIDES

Slides can contain text, bulleted and numbered lists, tables, and other content such as clip art and charts. In most cases, you can make changes to each of these elements directly on the slide itself, in Normal view.

ADDING AND EDITING TEXT

The highest-level points in a presentation's outline appear as slide titles. Everything else in the outline appears in the slides' text placeholders. The outline links to the slide strictly and exclusively via the title placeholder and the text placeholder.

If you try to enter more text than a placeholder can accommodate, PowerPoint automatically tries to shrink the text to fit within the confines of the placeholder. First, it tries to reduce the spacing between lines. If that doesn't work, it shrinks the size of the font. If you start to see your text shrinking, maybe it's time to take another look and see whether you need to trim some verbiage or split the slide into two.

→ To work from the outline, **see** "Editing the Presentation Outline," **p. 710**.

Whenever PowerPoint shrinks text to fit in a placeholder, an AutoFit Options action menu appears. Note that it resembles the AutoCorrect action menu. If you don't want PowerPoint to squeeze the text into the placeholder, click the button and choose Stop Fitting Text to This Placeholder from the menu. When you choose this option, your text will spill over onto the face of the slide.

TIP FROM

EQ & Woody

> On presentations that adhere to strict design guidelines, autofitting text damages the integrity of the design; it might also make the slide too hard to read. Also, if you have strict design guidelines, consider establishing a single companywide policy for style-checking rules. To turn off AutoFitting, click the AutoFit Options button and then click Control AutoCorrect Options. In the AutoFormat as You Type tab, clear the AutoFit Body Text to Placeholder and AutoFit Title Text to Placeholder options.

PowerPoint includes a rudimentary indenting and tabbing capability, but this feature is available only when the ruler is visible. By contrast, Word allows you to finely adjust tabs, specify leaders, and much more. To adjust tabs and indents, follow these steps:

1. Choose View, Ruler to display the ruler.

2. Using the ruler, slide the triangle at the top left edge of the ruler to set the left margin for all lines in a text placeholder. You cannot adjust settings for individual lines.

3. You can also set left-aligned, centered, decimal-aligned, and right-aligned tab stops. The method for doing so parallels the method in Word: Click the tab button at the far left edge of the ruler to select a tab type, and then click inside the ruler to set the tab.

TIP FROM

Ed & Woody

In a bulleted list, the top triangle controls the position of the bullet, the bottom triangle moves the text, and the lower square moves both top and bottom triangles concurrently.

→ For more on Word's paragraph-formatting features, **see** "Changing Paragraph Formatting," **p. 358**.

Default tab stops appear every inch inside the title and text placeholders. They can be adjusted; consult the Help topic "Tab stops" for details.

NOTE

The Tab key behaves differently in the Outline pane, where it promotes and demotes lines in the presentation's hierarchy. When you're working in the Slide pane, a tab is just a tab.

TIP FROM

Ed & Woody

In a bulleted list, use Ctrl+Tab to insert a tab character into the text. Pressing the Tab key by itself changes the bullet level.

You might also place text anywhere in the drawing layer—which is to say, on "top" of the slide—by inserting a text box or using one of the many kinds of Shapes.

→ To get text into the drawing layer, **see** "Adding Text to a Drawing," **p. 114**.

In the case of Shapes, PowerPoint lets you type in text that extends beyond the ends of the shape. In text boxes, PowerPoint expands the text box downward to accommodate all the text you care to add. In both cases, any text that extends beyond the edge of a slide does not show up on the slide—even if it shows in the Slide pane.

You can apply formatting to any text on a slide by selecting the text and then choosing the formatting. If you want to change the formatting on all slides, however—say, change all the titles on all the slides to a new font, or make all the first-level bullet points on all the slides green—you should use the Slide Master.

TIP FROM

You can change all instances of a font (typeface) with another font by choosing Home, pulling down the Replace menu, and then choosing Replace Fonts.

→ For an explanation of how Slide Masters work, **see** "Using the Slide Master," **p. 738**.

TIP FROM

In general, if you want to make a change to all the slides in a presentation—move the titles, or put a graphic on all the slides—you should use the Slide Master. Manually formatting slides is a surefire recipe for a messy, inconsistent presentation.

23

PowerPoint applies AutoFormatting while you type, changing fractions (1/4 to ¼), ordinals (1st to 1ˢᵗ), "smart" curly quotes, dashes, and the like. It will also change a single quote in front of a number into a curly quote ('04 to '04), with the curl pointing in the correct direction, change (c) into a copyright symbol, and change several combinations of : and) into a ☺ smiley face.

→ For advice on making AutoCorrect work the way you want—and to turn the vexing changes off—**see** "Using AutoCorrect to Speed Up Text Entry," **p. 86**.

WORKING WITH BULLETED AND NUMBERED LISTS

Most of the text you enter on slides appears as bulleted—or possibly numbered—items.

You can pick bullets or a numbering scheme when the insertion point is in any text, whether in the title placeholder, text placeholder, or even on the drawing layer.

If you've applied a theme to your presentation, PowerPoint has probably already selected a bullet character and formatted it with a color from the default palette for that design. To change a bullet—for example, to use a picture as a bullet—go through the Bullets and Numbering dialog box.

Click within the line you want to change, or select all the lines to change, and then choose Home, pull down the Bullets menu, and choose Bullets and Numbering. Alternatively, you can right-click, select Bullets, and then select Bullets and Numbering. The Bullets and Numbering dialog box appears (see Figure 23.7).

TIP FROM

Although you can change the bullet character for a single line, you will usually want to change all the bullets on a slide. To customize an entire presentation, perform these steps using the Slide Master rather than an individual slide.

23

Figure 23.7
PowerPoint lets you choose any character or picture as a bullet.

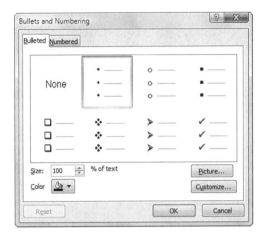

Choose a bullet character from the list of preset options, or click Customize to select a different character from any available font. You can also use a picture in any Office-compatible graphics format—PCX, GIF, and JPEG, for example—as a bullet. To do so, click Picture (see Figure 23.8) and use one of the built-in bullets, or click Import to bring in a picture of your own.

Figure 23.8
Choose a picture from among the ones offered, or import your own.

TIP FROM

EQ & Woody

PowerPoint stores the bullets just once, so you needn't be overly concerned about swelling file sizes if you stick to just one or two picture bullets. Your primary concern should be how legible the bullet will be in your presentation. Simple line art drawings—a pointing finger or a cash register, for example—can help make your point. Washed-out photographs rendered in tiny sizes will only leave your audience squinting.

The Size *nn*% of Text box in the Bullets and Numbering dialog box (refer to Figure 23.7) adjusts the size of the bullet (whether picture or character), scaling it to the point size of the text. You can select any size between 25% and 400%.

> **NOTE**
>
> The Color drop-down list box in the Bullets and Numbering dialog box applies only to characters; it does not affect the color of a picture used as a bullet.

Numbered paragraphs renumber themselves as you add new items and delete or move existing ones. Follow these steps to number the lines in a slide:

1. Click within the line you want to number or select a range of lines to be numbered. Auto numbering is supported only for the highest-level paragraphs; if you select lower-level paragraphs, they are ignored.

2. Choose Home, pull down the Numbering menu, and then choose Bullets and Numbering.

3. In the Bullets and Numbering dialog box, click the Numbered tab.

4. Pick the type of numbering you want—fairly simple Roman, Arabic, and lettered "numbers" are supported on the Numbered tab.

5. If you have a long numbered list that extends over multiple slides, specify a starting value other than 1.

The size and color formatting options mentioned for bullets earlier in this section apply to numbers, too.

If you want to construct multiple-level numbering schemes—for example, 1.1, 1.2, 1.3, 2.1, 2.2—you have to type and maintain the numbers manually.

WORKING WITH TABLES

PowerPoint supports three methods for constructing tables. Using the Table menu, you can use your mouse to specify a table with up to eight rows and ten columns. Using the older Insert Table approach, you specify the number of rows and columns and then place the table in the slide. The freeform Draw Table feature lets you draw custom tables by using the mouse.

> **NOTE**
>
> Although tables created in PowerPoint look a lot like Word tables, there are fundamental differences, both in options and in implementation—the version in PowerPoint isn't nearly as powerful. If you need advanced cell formatting (for example, to implement rotating text within cells), use the Draw Table feature in Word and then paste the resulting table into your presentation.

To use your mouse to specify the number of rows and columns in your table, select Insert, Table to display the Table menu. In the grid at the top of this menu, move your mouse over the squares until you've highlighted the number of rows and columns you want, and then click to insert the table.

To place a simple table on your slide, choose Insert, Table, Insert Table to display the Insert Table dialog box. Specify how many rows and columns you want in the table and click OK; the table appears in a content placeholder that automatically positions itself in the most logical place. For instance, if the insertion point is currently in an empty text placeholder, the placeholder for the new table replaces the text placeholder. If the insertion point is in a text placeholder that already contains text, PowerPoint shrinks the text placeholder and adds the new table in a placeholder that appears to the right.

You can click and drag the resizing handles on the outer edge of the table to resize it. You can also adjust each line in the table by letting the mouse pointer hover until it turns into a parallel line pointer, and then click and drag.

TIP FROM

Ed & Woody

If you specify a slide layout that includes a content placeholder and then click the Insert Table icon, PowerPoint inserts this more rigidly formatted kind of table.

To draw your own table freehand, do the following:

1. Choose Insert, Table, Draw Table. Your mouse pointer changes into the shape of a pencil.

2. Immediately draw a rectangle that defines the outer boundaries of your new table. The new table appears in a text box in the drawing layer. To customize the table, do any of the following tasks:

   - Use the pencil to draw horizontal or vertical lines within the table wherever you want.
   - Enter text in a table cell by clicking inside the cell and typing.
   - To erase an unwanted line, click the Eraser button, point to an existing cell border, and click.
   - Align text, split and merge cells, set border and fill colors, insert cells, and more by using the other options on the Tables and Borders toolbar.

3. When you're done drawing, press the Esc key to turn the pencil back into a normal mouse pointer.

CAUTION

If you create a freehand table in PowerPoint 2002, 2003, or 2007, you can view it in PowerPoint 97. However, if you change a freehand table in PowerPoint 97 (by ungrouping and then editing) and save the presentation, later versions of PowerPoint no longer recognize the results as a table. Instead, you'll see each table element as a separate shape in the drawing layer.

Of course, you can import tables from Word, Excel, or other sources by using simple copy and paste, PowerPoint's Insert, Object, or Home, Paste, Paste Special options. Word's table functions are somewhat more powerful than those in PowerPoint: They include the capability to rotate text to any angle, sort, and sum, for example.

To maintain control over the look of the pasted results, always use Paste Special when inserting tables. As explained later, Office uses HTML as its default format when you choose a simple Paste, and the results will generally be unsatisfactory.

→ For details, **see** "Inserting an Excel Chart or Range," **p. 720**.

ADDING PICTURES, SMARTART, AND CLIP ART

Use the full array of Office graphics tools (available on the Home and Insert tabs as well as any Format tab that appears when you select an object) to insert pictures and text boxes, add Shapes, SmartArt, or WordArt, set colors, connect Shapes with lines, draw shadows, and so on.

→ To work in the drawing layer, **see** "Using Office Drawing Tools," **p. 104**.

Grids and guidelines help you line up drawing items; you can be a little imprecise as you add items and then, when you're finished, allow PowerPoint to line things up precisely. When working with pictures and other drawing tools, it's helpful to show gridlines on the screen. To do so, select an object, choose Format, Align, Grid Settings to open the Grid and Guides dialog box (see Figure 23.9), and select the Display Grid On Screen check box.

Figure 23.9
PowerPoint lets you control the granularity of its grid, and whether drawings should be snapped to the grid.

Sometimes you want to know how far a picture lies from dead center. That's where drawing guides come in handy. If you activate the Display Drawing Guides On Screen check box, you get horizontal and vertical lines that you can use to gauge how far any particular item on the slide sits, compared to dead center (see Figure 23.10). Click the guide, and its distance from center appears as a ScreenTip. You can drag the guides into any position you like, making even fine layout tasks easier.

Figure 23.10
PowerPoint's drawing guides—one horizontal, one vertical—are shown here. Note that we've "parked" pictures in the unused region around the slide.

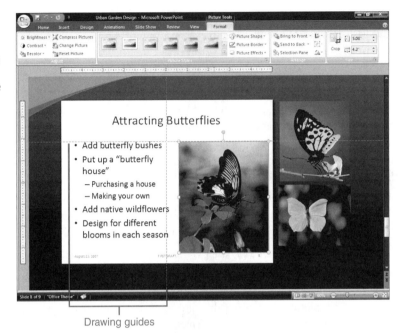

Drawing guides

In the Grid and Guides dialog box, you can take your pick of two Snap To check boxes. You can choose to line up shapes so they snap to the grid, or use the Snap Objects to Other Objects setting to make them automatically abut each other or share a common axis.

PowerPoint also allows you to park pictures in the gray area outside of a slide, but still in the Slide pane. This option can come in handy if you have a few pictures you're considering for the slide, but can't make up your mind which one would be best: Parking them in the margin lets you swap them in and out quickly. To get a picture into the margin, click and drag the picture, moving it to the edge of the pane. It takes a little practice to get a picture positioned this way, but the picture remains handy without appearing on the slide itself. (This option is most useful in Normal view when you close the Outline/Slides pane on the left.)

INSERTING AN EXCEL CHART OR RANGE

You can place an Excel chart or a range of worksheet data on a PowerPoint slide through the usual methods—primarily Home, Paste, Paste Special, and Insert, Object. However, PowerPoint 2007 also enables you to insert an Excel worksheet by selecting Insert, Table, Excel Spreadsheet. Any slide layout works: The chart or range attaches itself to the drawing layer.

→ If you want to learn more about the Office Clipboard, **see** "Using the Office Clipboard," **p. 92**.

When you paste an Excel data range, be aware of these potential formatting issues:

■ **Column widths can be problematic**—For columns that consist primarily of numbers, PowerPoint decides what column width to use. Adjusting the width after the table has been imported, although possible (by choosing View, Ruler), can be frustrating and time consuming.

- **Fonts and font sizes might not translate to PowerPoint properly**—For cells that use the default formats, PowerPoint converts the imported data to a new font and point size, based on the Slide Master. If you formatted the worksheet cells manually, that formatting might or might not carry across.

After you paste an Excel data range into a PowerPoint slide, the data is converted to items on the drawing layer. The pasted range or chart is treated as an embedded object. You can double-click it and use all of Excel's tools. However, there's no remaining link to the original spreadsheet: If you change values or formatting in the spreadsheet, those changes are not reflected in the presentation.

TIP FROM

EQ & Woody

> In many cases, you might want to use Home, Paste, Paste Special (or Insert, Object) to link an Excel data range or chart to a slide. This has the advantage of keeping the underlying data synchronized: Change the data in the spreadsheet, and the slide changes. On the other hand, it also carries across formatting changes: If you adjust the width of the columns in Excel, for example, the column widths in PowerPoint change as well. That can have unexpected consequences, especially in a carefully constructed slide.

To use Paste Special, follow these steps:

1. Start Excel and open the workbook that contains the range or chart you want to paste onto your slide.

2. Select the range and choose Home, Copy.

3. Move to PowerPoint and select the slide you want to receive the range or chart. Make sure you click once on the slide itself (inside the Slide pane); otherwise, the range might be interpreted as text for the Outline pane, and each cell's worth of data will turn into a bullet point on the slide.

4. In PowerPoint, choose Home, pull down the Paste menu, and choose Paste Special. The Paste Special dialog box appears, as shown in Figure 23.11.

Figure 23.11
When you use Paste Special, you have to tell PowerPoint how to interpret the data on the Clipboard.

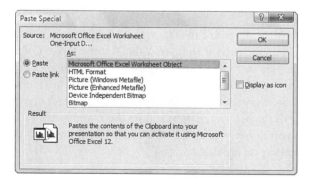

5. If you want PowerPoint to automatically update the data from Excel every time you open your presentation, click the Paste Link option. Otherwise, use the default Paste option.

6. Select Microsoft Office Excel Worksheet Object and click OK.

The pasted range or chart appears on the slide. From that point, you can resize and move the range as you like. Double-click the range to activate Excel and make changes to the range, with the full power of Excel available to you.

Using this technique gives you the capability to format the range easily, using Excel's considerably more powerful formatting capabilities. PowerPoint maintains the fidelity of inserted objects: An Arial 20-point cell in Excel looks like an Arial 20-point entry on the slide.

Excel charts, PivotTables, and PivotCharts behave much the same way. Avoid pasting this type of object unless it's your only choice for reasons of performance or availability.

TIP FROM

Ed & Woody

> If you use Insert, Object to place an Excel range on a slide, the Excel cell gridlines may show on the slide. To get rid of them, double-click the embedded object, click the View tab, and clear the Gridlines check box.

Finally, you can import an entire worksheet into PowerPoint and place it on a slide; however, the method for resizing the image is a bit odd. Choose Insert, Object, Create from File. If you can't see all the information you wanted from the worksheet, click it and then resize the worksheet "window" by using the resizing handles.

VIEWING A PRESENTATION

PowerPoint starts in Normal view. You can return to this view at any time by choosing View, Normal, or by selecting the Normal View icon on the status bar. In Normal view, you can see either a text outline of your presentation or thumbnails of all the slides in the left-most pane. The current slide appears in the main pane, with the slide's notes just below it.

Normal view is highly customizable. To dismiss the left navigation pane and the Notes pane temporarily, leaving only the current slide, click the X at the top left of the Navigation pane. To restore both panes, choose View, Normal again. You can also click and drag the edge of any pane to resize that portion of the view. Compare the configuration of Figure 23.12, for instance, with the default view shown earlier in Figure 23.1. We dragged the border of the Outline pane nearly all the way to the right and set the Zoom menu to 30%. Using this arrangement allows you to concentrate on content, leaving just a small preview of the current slide and any accompanying notes.

Figure 23.12
Customize
PowerPoint's Normal
view to focus on the
outline.

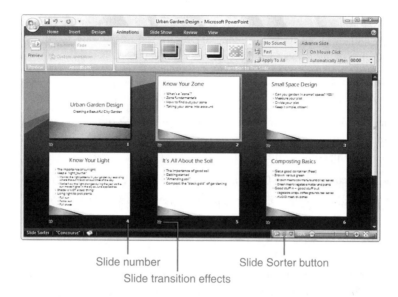

Slide number

Slide Sorter button

Slide transition effects

To change the zoom percentage, you can either click and drag the Zoom slider or click the Zoom Level to display the Zoom dialog box. You can also click Fit Slide to Current Window to expand the slide to fit within the window.

Although Normal view gives quick and easy access to most of the options you'll typically want to use, each of the individual views available via the View bar comes in handy for specific tasks.

USING SLIDE SORTER VIEW TO REARRANGE A PRESENTATION

Slide Sorter view (see Figure 23.13) gives you an opportunity to see the entire presentation all at once, move slides around, control the transition effects that bind the slides and animation together on an individual slide, and perform easy, one-click previews of animations and transitions.

Figure 23.13
Slide Sorter view makes
it easy to check transi-
tions and animations.

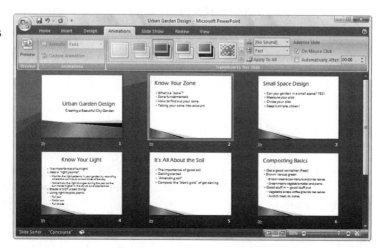

Move to Slide Sorter view clicking the Slide Sorter button in the status bar (see Figure 23.13), or by choosing View, Slide Sorter. Use the Zoom tools to configure the size of the thumbnails (and, by extension, the number of thumbnails visible on the screen).

PowerPoint transitions control how a slide makes its appearance onscreen. Animations, on the other hand, control how components of the slide appear, after the slide is onscreen.

Click the Animations tab to see the transition tools. Note, however, that to work with animations, you must return to Normal view. Slide Sorter view is the easiest place to perform the following common tasks:

- **Rearrange slides**—Click and drag any slide to a different position.
- **Add slides**—Right-click the space between two slides and choose New Slide from the shortcut menu.
- **Delete slides**— Select one or more slides and then press the Delete key. To select multiple slides, hold down Control while clicking.
- **Set transition effects**—Select one or more slides and then use the Transition to This Slide group to pick and fine-tune the transition you like.
- **Preview transition and animation effects**—Choose Animations, Preview.

PREVIEWING YOUR PRESENTATION IN SLIDE SHOW VIEW

At any point in the process of developing a presentation, you can preview the show itself.

To see the presentation starting with the currently selected slide, pick a slide (in any view) and choose Slide Show, From Current Slide, or click the Slide Show button in the status bar. This starts the show and allows you to use all the usual show navigation techniques (for example, click to advance the slide, press Esc to exit). When the show is over, you return to the view you were using before starting the slide show. If you want to see the entire presentation, starting with the first slide, choose Slide Show, From Beginning. Alternatively, press F5.

TIP FROM

Ed & Woody

> If you hold down the Control key as you click either From Current Slide or From Beginning, the show appears in a small window that occupies the upper-left quadrant of the screen. Click elsewhere in the PowerPoint window to hide the show while you edit or create a slide; click the Resume Slide Show button to return and see your changes.

ADDING NOTES

The simplest way to add or modify notes is in Normal view, where you can expand the Notes pane as needed to accommodate lengthy notes.

If the small notes pane isn't big enough to work with comfortably, choose View, Notes Page to switch to Notes Page view. This view hides the outline and shows you a full-page as it will appear when you print out your notes for reference (see Figure 23.14).

Figure 23.14
Notes Page view hides the outline and shows only the notes for one slide at a time.

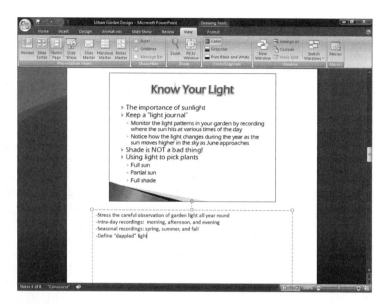

If the notes for any particular slide extend beyond one page, Notes view expands the text area downward to accept what you type. If you print the notes for that particular slide, however, they'll be truncated at one page. Multipage notes appear in Normal view.

VIEWING PRESENTATIONS IN A WEB BROWSER

If you save your presentation as a web page, the entire presentation can be viewed with a web browser (see Figure 23.15). The person looking at your presentation need not have PowerPoint installed to see all the details and navigate the presentation fully. Note the navigation buttons along the bottom of the presentation, which allow the viewer to show or hide the Outline and Notes panes, to jump from slide to slide, and to display the presentation as a slide show.

Figure 23.15
This PowerPoint presentation is being viewed through Internet Explorer.

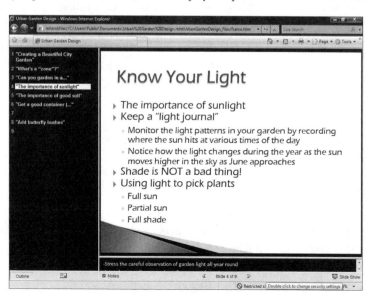

→ To learn how to save your presentation as a web page, **see** "Creating Presentations for the Web," **p. 783**.

To get full effect of the browser-viewing option, the person viewing the presentation should be running Internet Explorer version 5 or later, or Netscape/Mozilla version 5 or later. Although you can create presentations that show up on earlier versions of both browsers, there are severe limitations on what they can do.

CAUTION

This browser-viewing capability might not perform precisely the way you expect. In particular, you might be disappointed with the way diagonal lines (for example, in callout shapes), WordArt, and Organization Charts appear when viewed in a browser window.

Before you expend a lot of effort developing a presentation for the Web, flesh out a few of the most complex graphics, stick them in a slide in a new presentation, and choose Office, Save As. Choose Single File Web Page as the file type, click Save, and then open the web page. That will give you a good indication of how the final presentation will appear, at least when using the browser installed on your PC. If you discover a display problem, consider saving the org chart or shape as a standard graphic and inserting it into a slide instead. Save the original as a hidden slide so that you can edit it later.

MANAGING SLIDE SHOWS

PowerPoint has several useful tools and techniques you can use to manage presentations. If you work in Slide Sorter view, it's easy to copy, move, insert, or delete slides. But there are some tricks. To paste a slide at the beginning of a presentation, go into Slide Sorter view and click to the left of the first slide, and then paste.

If you want to copy slides from one presentation and put them into another, select the slide you want the imported slides to appear after (in Slide Sorter view, click between the slides), and then choose Home, New Slide, Reuse Slides. When the Reuse Slides pane appears, type the path to a PowerPoint file in the Insert Slide From text box (or click Browse, Browse File). PowerPoint displays thumbnails of the presentation's slides, as shown in Figure 23.16.

Hover the mouse pointer over a slide to see a slightly magnified version of the thumbnail. To add a slide, click it; to add all the slides, right-click any slide and then click Insert All Slides. PowerPoint adds each slide to the end of the current presentation and applies the current presentation's theme to the new slides. If you don't want the current theme applied, activate the Keep Source Formatting check box at the bottom of the Reuse Slides pane.

You can also reuse slides from a *slide library*, a collection of related slides. To add a slide to a slide library, open the presentation and then select Office, Publish, Publish Slides. In the Publish Slides dialog box, activate the check box for each slide you want to publish, select a location, and then click Publish.

PowerPoint lets you mark specific slides as *hidden*. Hidden slides appear in all views except Slide Show view, and they don't show up when the presentation is run. You can use hidden slides to prepare material that doesn't have to be in your presentation but might come up in a Q&A period, for example.

Figure 23.16
The Reuse Slides pane lets you pick and choose which slides to copy into the current presentation.

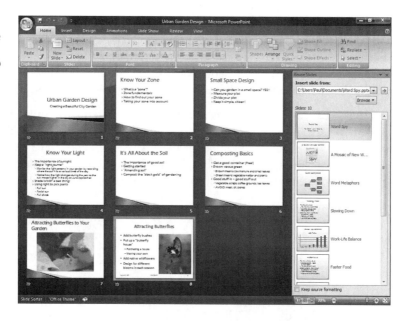

To hide a slide, select it and then choose Slide Show, Hide Slide (or right-click the thumbnail of the slide to be hidden, and then click Hide Slide). You'll know that the slide won't be shown in the presentation because a "not" sign appears over the slide number.

If you deliver PowerPoint presentations regularly, you might have a main presentation that needs only a bit of tweaking for use with a variety of audiences. For example, you might have one version for executives and a slightly different version for technical professionals. Or you might have short and long versions of a presentation, choosing one or the other depending on the time allotted for your talk. PowerPoint makes it easy to keep all your slides together in one file, but build separate, custom slide shows for specific situations.

To create a custom show, choose Slide Show, Custom Slide Show, Custom Shows, and then click New. The Define Custom Show dialog box appears, as shown in Figure 23.17.

Figure 23.17
Pick and arrange existing slides to be incorporated in a custom show.

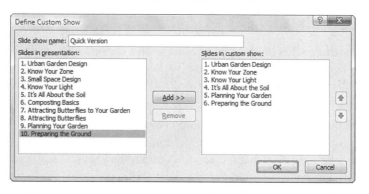

Select the slides you want to appear in the custom show and click Add. Note that you can move a slide—so it appears in a different sequence in the custom show—by clicking the up arrow or down arrow. Type in a name for the custom show and click OK. Repeat this process for other variations on the main show. You can now run any custom show any time you want; open the Custom Shows dialog box again, select the name of the show, and click Show.

You can also use custom slide shows as a way to create alternative paths within a longer presentation. Move to the slide in your presentation where you want to branch out to one of these custom shows. Select a location for the link (perhaps in the body text or in a drawing), and then choose Insert, Hyperlink. In the Link To pane on the left side of the dialog box, pick Place in This Document. Scroll to the bottom of the list, as shown in Figure 23.18.

Figure 23.18
Hyperlink to one of the custom shows—for example, Executive Briefing.

Choose the custom show you want to link to, and click OK. From that point on, whenever you encounter the slide with the hyperlink, click it to display the custom show.

To return to the main presentation after the custom show runs, select the Show and Return check box.

TIP FROM

EQ & Woody

> Alternatively, you can create a hyperlink on the last slide in the custom show to jump to whatever point in the main presentation you like.

→ For details about hyperlinking inside your presentation, **see** "Using Hyperlinks," **p. 730**.

You can tell PowerPoint that you want it to run a custom show, instead of the "normal" show, whenever you start a slide show. To do so, choose Slide Show, Set Up Slide Show. In the Set Up Show dialog box (see Figure 23.19), select a custom show from the Custom Show list in the Show Slides area.

Custom shows can be a powerful feature. For example, you can put all your slides relating to a given topic inside one PowerPoint file, and then pick and choose the slides you want to give for your main presentation. Set up a custom show called Main, and then choose Main as the default show. That way, all your slides stay in one presentation file, the Main presentation runs whenever you start a slide show, and you can easily and quickly add and remove slides from the Main presentation.

Figure 23.19
Have PowerPoint run a custom show automatically by using the Custom Show setting.

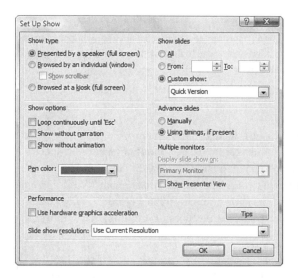

NAVIGATING THROUGH A PRESENTATION

PowerPoint presents myriad ways to navigate in a presentation. As the next few sections show, you can navigate a presentation via the mouse, keyboard shortcuts, hyperlinks, action buttons, and more.

MOUSE AND KEYBOARD SHORTCUTS

In addition to the navigation methods you've probably used (left mouse button to advance, Backspace key to back up, Esc to end), PowerPoint also supports a variety of mouse and keyboard shortcuts:

- To advance from one slide to another or perform the next animation on the current slide, you can click the left mouse button—but you can also press Enter, N (for Next), page down, right arrow, down arrow, or the spacebar. You can also right-click the screen during a presentation and choose Next.

- To move to the previous slide or activate the preceding animation on the current slide, you can press Backspace—but you can also try P (for Previous), page up, left arrow, or the up arrow. Or you can right-click the screen and choose Previous.

- To end a presentation, in addition to the Esc key, you can right-click and choose End Show.

An almost-complete list of navigation controls is available by right-clicking the screen during a presentation and choosing Help, by pressing F1, or by referring to the Help topic "Slide Show Controls." Most of the controls are obscure, but a few might be worth memorizing:

- B (for Black) or pressing the period key toggles between displaying a black screen and showing the current slide.

- Similarly, W (for white) or pressing the comma key toggles a white screen.

- Tab cycles among all the hyperlinks on a slide.

TIP FROM

> This doesn't appear to be documented anywhere, but pressing the Home key during a presentation returns you to the first slide. Similarly, pressing the End key sends you to the final slide.

USING HYPERLINKS

Hyperlinks allow you to turn text, graphics, pictures, or almost anything else on a slide, into a "hot" link. Those hot links can point just about anywhere—a specific slide, the first or last slide in a presentation, the next or previous slides, files (whether on the local hard drive or accessible through the network), specific locations inside Word documents or Excel workbooks, and much more. As shown previously in Figure 23.18, you can even link to a custom show within the current presentation by using the Bookmark button in the Insert Hyperlink dialog box.

If the computer you're using for the presentation is connected to the Web (or if the presentation itself is on the Web), hyperlinks can also connect to web pages.

The easiest way to establish a hyperlink is to start by selecting whatever you want to hyperlink from (that is, the text, drawing, picture, and so on, that will be "hot" during the presentation), and then choose Insert, Hyperlink. (If you prefer, you can use the Officewide shortcut Ctrl+K.)

The problem with hyperlinking to an object that requires another application, of course, is that there's no way to hyperlink to the next slide in your presentation. If you hyperlink out to an object that requires a program other than PowerPoint—to a web page, for instance, or a Word document—when you close that program, PowerPoint is still there, and you've gone back to the "linked from" slide; you'll have to click to move on to your next point.

TIP FROM

> If you hyperlink to an entire PowerPoint presentation, you can run through that presentation and, when it's done, you are back where you started, at the "link from" slide.

ADVANCED NAVIGATION WITH ACTION SETTINGS

Action Settings are an older variation on hyperlinks that let you link to a few unusual locations in a presentation—in particular, the "last slide viewed." Action Settings also let you start a program, run a macro, and/or combine sounds with all the preceding.

If you want to be able to "jump back" to the previously viewed slide, your best bet is to set up an Action Button (see next section) with an Action Setting that moves to the previously viewed slide. This option allows you to link to a single slide from different locations and set up a "Return" button that always goes back to the right place. Action Settings allow you to navigate in powerful ways that aren't possible with hyperlinks.

To open the Action Settings dialog box (see Figure 23.20), select the text or graphic you want to make "hot," and then click Insert, Action.

Figure 23.20
Action Settings provide the only (easy) way to return to the previously viewed slide.

Note that you can specify separate actions for a mouseover—where you move the mouse pointer over the "hot" area—and for a mouse click.

NAVIGATION SHORTHAND WITH ACTION BUTTONS

PowerPoint makes some kinds of hyperlinking easy by attaching predefined hyperlinking information to a group of Shapes called Action Buttons.

If you want to add a button that allows you to immediately move to the end of the presentation, use an Action Button. If you're creating a presentation for the Web and want to create your own Next Slide and Previous Slide buttons instead of relying on PowerPoint's built-in navigation bar, Action Buttons make it easy.

To place an Action Button on a slide, select the slide and then choose Home, Shapes. The Shapes gallery includes an Action Buttons section at the bottom, as shown in Figure 23.21.

Several of the Action Buttons (for example, the question mark, information sign, video camera) don't hyperlink to anything in particular; they just put the picture on the slide and bring up the Action Settings dialog box.

Most of the Action Buttons, however, have predefined actions associated with them. You can insert buttons on your slides to move to the first or last slide in the presentation, to go to the next or previous slide, or to return to the last viewed slide.

Figure 23.21
At the bottom of the Shapes gallery, the predefined Action Buttons cover many of the common hyper-linking bases.

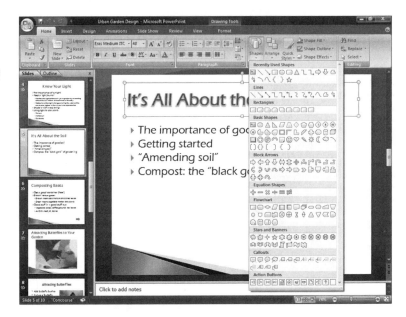

TROUBLESHOOTING

CUSTOM POWERPOINT THEMES

I like the new themes that come with PowerPoint 2007, but they're not quite right for me. On some I have to change the colors to get what I prefer, and on others I have to adjust the fonts. How can I create a custom theme that includes exactly the formatting I need?

PowerPoint 2007's themes consist of a set of colors, fonts, and background styles. You can modify any of these elements and then save your modifications as a custom theme that you can reuse in any other presentation. On the Design tab, use the Colors gallery to either select a built-in color scheme, or click Create New Theme Colors to build a custom color scheme. (The custom scheme defines a dozen colors: two for the dark backgrounds and text, two for light backgrounds and text, two for hyperlinks, and six for *accents*, which are mostly used with chart markers.) You can also use the Fonts gallery to either select a built-in font combination, or click Create New Theme Fonts to specify custom fonts for the headings and body text. Finally, use the Background Styles gallery to select a predefined background, or click Format Background to create a custom background fill. When you have done all that, open the Themes gallery and then click Save Current Theme to preserve your custom theme.

SECRETS OF THE OFFICE MASTERS: POWERPOINT FILE TYPES

PowerPoint uses three main file types: Presentation, Template, and Slide Show. For the most part, you can construct and deliver simple presentations without ever having to deal with the differences among these types of files. But before you can effectively use PowerPoint's advanced formatting options, you have to understand its file formats.

The Office 2007 Setup program registers a collection of PowerPoint file types. When you view the list of registered file types in Windows Explorer, you'll see the three major types listed in Table 23.1 (there are also some variant HTML file types that work much the same as these).

TABLE 23.1 POWERPOINT FILE TYPES

File Type	File Extension	Default Action
PowerPoint Presentation	*.pptx	Open
PowerPoint Template	*.potx	New
PowerPoint Slide Show	*.ppsx	Show

TIP FROM

You can see the file extensions associated with each file type. First, open any Windows Explorer window. In XP, choose Tools, Folder Options; in Vista, choose Organize, Folder and Search Options. Click the View tab and clear the Hide Extensions for Known File Types check box. With this option disabled, you see file extensions in parentheses after the file type when you view entries in the Save As Type box in Windows common dialog boxes.

Thus, from an Explorer window, if you double-click an icon whose file type is Presentation (.pptx), PowerPoint opens the file for editing. When you double-click an icon whose file type is Template (.potx), however, PowerPoint creates a new presentation, based on the template, and takes you to the first slide so you can begin editing. Finally, if you double-click an icon whose type is Slide Show (.ppsx), PowerPoint runs the show without ever showing you any of its slide-editing tools.

Surprisingly, the internal structure of all three file formats is the same: You can save any presentation as a Template or Slide Show file, and the contents of the file remain the same.

NOTE

You may find inconsistent references to these three file types scattered throughout PowerPoint's Help files and dialog boxes. In this book, we use the three terms defined in this section—Presentation, Template, and Slide Show—to differentiate among the three file types.

When should you use each file type? Follow these general guidelines:

■ Use the Presentation file type (.pptx) when you plan to edit the presentation and/or work with its design. To save a file as file type Presentation, choose PowerPoint Presentation from the Save As Type list in the Save As dialog box.

NOTE

> In PowerPoint 2007, the PowerPoint Presentation file type uses the XML file format technology that is also found in Word and Excel. The PowerPoint XML format produces dramatically smaller documents. For example, I converted a 12MB PowerPoint 2003 presentation to the PowerPoint XML format, and the converted file was only 580KB! Microsoft also claims that the new XML architecture makes it easier to recover damaged files. However, users of earlier versions of PowerPoint can't open presentations stored in this format.

■ Use the Template file type (.potx) when you create a presentation that you want to use as the basis for creating new presentations, or if you expect to "borrow" the presentation's design for use in other presentations. To save a file as a Template, choose PowerPoint Template from the Save As Type list in the Save As dialog box. When you select this file type, PowerPoint immediately changes the Save In location to the default Templates folder.

■ Use the Slide Show file type (.ppsx) for presentations that you no longer need to edit or design. (Although it's possible to open this type of file from within PowerPoint, this is not the default action when you double-click its icon on the desktop or in an Explorer window.) Choose this file type if you want to be able to start a slideshow directly from the desktop, or if you want a co-worker to be able to double-click a file icon and see the show. To save a file as a Slide Show, choose PowerPoint Show from the Save As Type list in the Save As dialog box.

TIP FROM

Ed & Woody

> Because all three file types are internally identical, it's easy to change file types. Just choose a different format from the Save As dialog box. If you're comfortable working with file extensions in an Explorer window or at a command prompt, you can change a file type by changing the three-letter extension at the end of the filename; for example, changing the file extension from .pptx to .ppsx converts a Presentation into a Slide Show.

Like the other major applications in the 2007 Microsoft Office System, PowerPoint 2007 supports a variety of file types beyond the three main types you have seen so far. You should be familiar with them so that you can choose the file type that suits your needs. Here's a summary of the other significant PowerPoint file types:

■ PowerPoint Macro-Enabled Presentation (.pptm)—Use this format when you need to add or create macros to run with your presentation.

■ PowerPoint 97-2003 Presentation (.ppt)—Use this presentation format if you are going to share the file with someone who uses earlier versions of PowerPoint. Note, however, that PowerPoint 2007 no longer supports PowerPoint 95.

- PowerPoint Macro-Enabled Template (`.potm`)—Use this format to save the presentation as a template that includes macros.

- PowerPoint 97-2003 Template (`.pot`)—Use this format to save the presentation as a template that can be used by people running earlier versions of PowerPoint.

- PowerPoint Macro-Enabled Show (`.ppsm`)—Use this format to create a PowerPoint Show file that includes macros.

- PowerPoint 97-2003 Show (`.pps`)—Use this format to create a PowerPoint Show file that supports features compatible with earlier versions of PowerPoint.

- PowerPoint Add-In (`.ppam`)—This format creates a PowerPoint add-in file, which usually includes various macros that add functionality to PowerPoint.

- PowerPoint 97-2003 Add-In (`.ppa`)—This format creates a PowerPoint add-in file that is compatible with earlier versions of PowerPoint.

- PowerPoint XML Presentation (`.xml`)—This format converts your presentation into a pure XML file.

23

CHAPTER 24

ADVANCED PRESENTATION FORMATTING

In this chapter

Organizing Formats with Master Slides   738

Applying and Modifying Themes   746

Changing Paragraph and Text Formatting   756

Troubleshooting   757

Secrets of the Office Masters: Creating Top-Notch Notes and Handouts   758

ORGANIZING FORMATS WITH MASTER SLIDES

Behind every great PowerPoint presentation lurk masters that control the presentation's appearance: the Slide Master, Notes Master, and Handouts Master. Each master stores detailed formatting information for title slides, "regular" slides, speaker's notes, and hard copy handouts, respectively.

These masters control many facets of the slides themselves—backgrounds, fonts (typeface, point sizes, colors, and the like), bullets, locations for all the main components, tabs, and indents. You can also use masters to specify pictures—a logo, for example—and "boilerplate" text that appears on all slides. As part of the Slide Master, PowerPoint also includes a separate master for every layout, which enables you to configure the appearance of each layout.

TIP FROM

Ed & Woody

> If you want to put a graphic, a piece of text, or any other type of object on a bunch of slides, add it to the Slide Master. If you want the object to appear only on a specific layout, add it to the layout master instead.

Masters ensure a uniform appearance for your entire presentation. Your company might have a standard slideshow template. If so, use it. If not, talk to your boss or corporate communications department about the advantages of creating a consistent template file that everyone in the organization can use.

When you create a blank presentation, PowerPoint creates three generic masters—Slide, Notes, and Handouts. To work with master slides, choose the View tab and then select Slide Master, Handout Master, or Notes Master.

USING THE SLIDE MASTER

Whenever you want to change all the slides in your presentation in the same way, you should change the Slide Master. If you want to put a logo on all your slides, for example, work with the Slide Master, not the individual slides. The same is true if you want to put identical text on all the slides—or change a color, modify a font, or use a different kind of bullet. Making changes to the Slide Master automatically changes all the slides in your presentation. For example, if you change the Slide Master's first-level bullet text to 20-point Arial bold, all the slides in your presentation will have their first-level bullets changed to 20-point Arial bold.

To bring up the Slide Master, choose View, Slide Master. This switches the display into Slide Master view, which adds a Slide Master tab to the Ribbon and displays various thumbnails in the left pane, as shown in Figure 24.1. The top thumbnail represents the Slide Master, and below that you see one thumbnail for each layout. Can't tell one layout master from another? Hover the mouse pointer over each thumbnail to see the ScreenTip that identifies each one (refer to Figure 24.1).

NOTE

When you hover the mouse pointer over a layout thumbnail, the ScreenTip shows you the name of the layout and the numbers of the slides in the presentation that use the layout. Here's an example:

```
Title Slide Layout: used by slide(s) 2-6, 10
```

Slide Master

Figure 24.1
Use Slide Master view to manage the design of all slides in a presentation. The ScreenTip shows the name of the current design and the slides to which the master applies.

Layout masters

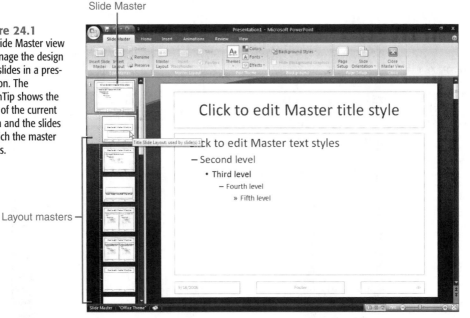

24

The Slide Master includes placeholders for the title (Master title style) and bullet text (Master text style), as well as a background design (usually assigned by the theme you apply from the Design tab). The Slide Master also has placeholders for a date, footer, and slide number.

To change the formatting of the title or bullets, click inside the placeholder and apply font or paragraph formatting. Similarly, you can click inside the date, footer, or slide number placeholders and adjust their formatting.

For example, if you want the title on all slides to be left aligned (instead of centered), click once inside the title placeholder, select the text, and then choose Home, Align Text Left.

In a Slide Master, you can set formatting and bullets for each level of bulleted text in the body of your presentation. The easiest way to accomplish this task is by applying a theme. To change the formatting of the bullet points in your presentation manually, switch into Slide Master view, and then click the Slide Master thumbnail for editing. To change the formatting of text in the highest-level bullet points, click the line that reads "Click to edit Master text styles" and apply the formatting as follows:

- You can change the font, font size, font color, and indent level.

- You can change the bullet character used on all slides based on this Master Slide. To do this, display the Home tab, pull down the Bullets list, and choose the bullet you like.

Repeat this process for the second-, third-, fourth-, and fifth-level bullet items by clicking the appropriate line and applying the formatting.

TIP FROM

To "tighten up" the distance between the bullet and text, choose View, activate the Ruler check box, and adjust the tab stops (see Figure 24.2). PowerPoint aligns each level's bullet and text with the stops shown on the ruler.

Figure 24.2
To change the location of bullets and text in the body of a presentation, adjust tab stops in the Slide Master.

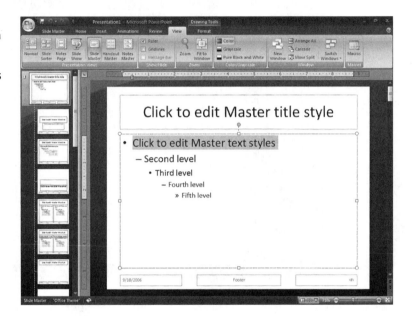

Similarly, you can resize or move any of the placeholders on the Slide Master. If you move the title placeholder down a half inch on the Slide Master, the titles on all slides will move down half an inch. Here are some other notes to bear in mind when working with the Slide Master:

- Any text that appears in the title or text area is strictly explanatory. Although you can edit the default text, any text you add in either location does not appear in your presentation.

- Type text into the date, footer, or slide number placeholders to have it appear on all slides. For example, if you want the slide number on each title slide to read Slide *n*, click the Number Area placeholder and type the text **Slide** (being sure to add a space after it) in front of the <#>.

Are you confused by PowerPoint's seeming reluctance to update some of the slides in your presentation when you update the slide master? See "Slide Master Link Damage" in the "Troubleshooting" section at the end of this chapter.

If you accidentally delete one of the five placeholders, you can restore it. Choose Slide Master, Master Layout, select the check box for the deleted placeholder, and click OK. The new placeholder appears in its default location.

When you override a Slide Master setting on an individual slide, you break the link between that setting and the master; subsequent changes won't affect that setting. For example, if you change formatting for the title on the first slide in your presentation, and later change formatting for the title on the Slide Master, the title on the first slide won't change. Even changing the Slide Master entirely by applying a new design template won't restore the link.

To restore the link between a slide and its master, you have to right-click the slide and then click Reset Slide.

USING THE LAYOUT MASTERS

The various layout masters control the formatting and placeholder positions of PowerPoint's layouts. The placeholders you see depend on the layout. For the Title Slide layout, for example, you see one placeholder for the title and another for the subtitle. If the layout includes a Content placeholder, you can modify the formatting of the various bullet styles.

In the same way that PowerPoint maintains a link between the Slide Master and the slides in a presentation, PowerPoint also maintains a link between the Slide Master and the layout masters. For example, if you change the title formatting in the Slide Master, PowerPoint applies the same formatting to every layout master that has a title placeholder. However, if you change the title formatting in a layout master, then the link is broken, and subsequent changes to the Slide Master title have no effect on that layout master.

Unfortunately, PowerPoint doesn't offer a straightforward way to fix a broken link between the Slide Master and the layout master. You can fix it by hand by following these steps:

1. In the layout master, click the placeholder that is no longer linked to the Slide Master, and then press Delete to remove it.

2. Select the Slide Master.

3. Click the placeholder you want to restore on the layout master, and then press Ctrl+C to copy it.

4. Return to the layout master and press Ctrl+V to paste the placeholder.

CHANGING THE BACKGROUND OF EVERY SLIDE

If you want a logo, a graphic, or a drawing item to appear on all "regular" slides, place it on the Slide Master. Any object in the Slide Master's drawing layer appears in the drawing layer of all slides in the same location it occupies on the Slide Master.

Text you place on the Slide Master behaves the same way. For example, in a presentation that contains sensitive data, you might want to add the word CONFIDENTIAL to every

24

slide; for a presentation that's under construction, you might want to stamp DRAFT on every slide. To put identical pieces of text on every "regular" slide, follow these steps:

1. Switch into Slide Master view (choose View, Slide Master) and select the Slide Master.

2. Select the Insert tab and then click Text Box. Draw a text box on the Slide Master and adjust its size and position as necessary.

3. Click in the text box and enter the text you want to repeat on all slides. This text will appear in the drawing layer on all the "regular" slides in your presentation, and thus will not show up in the outline.

4. To apply formatting to the box itself, right-click the edge of the box and choose Format Shape Box. You might want to draw a thick line around the box, for example, or change its background color.

Similarly, if you want a logo, fixed text, or other drawing item to appear with a particular layout, put it on the corresponding layout master.

You'll find by far the richest vein of background customizing options when you learn how to develop, modify, and apply themes. Use these techniques to customize the Master Slides included with PowerPoint's ready-made designs, or devise your own masters and store them for future use.

→ To work with themes, **see** "Applying and Modifying Themes," **p. 746**.

WORKING WITH HEADERS AND FOOTERS

If you're used to working with headers and footers in Word or Excel, PowerPoint's Header and Footer dialog box might be confusing initially. On a slide, you'll search in vain for a header. Paradoxically, though, you can move the Footer Area placeholder, which normally appears centered at the bottom of the slide, to any location—including the top. The Notes Master and Handout Master contain both a Header Area and a Footer Area, positioned by default at the top left and bottom left of printed pages; you can move these placeholders anywhere on the page as well.

In addition, all masters include placeholders for the date and slide number, which normally appear at the bottom of the slide but can be moved anywhere on the slide. When working with any of these elements on the Slide Master or layout masters, follow these guidelines:

■ The Date Area placeholder can show the current date—that is, the date the slide show is being presented. To add a date field of this sort, choose Insert, Header and Footer, click to select the Date and Time box, and select the Update Automatically check box. Use the Fixed option instead and enter a descriptive text label (it doesn't have to include the date) if you want to track different versions of a presentation as it evolves; remember to enter a new description when you save an updated version of the presentation.

■ The Footer Area placeholder can carry any text you want, and you can drag it to any location on the slide. Some PowerPoint experts use this element to "brand" each slide with the name of a company or client, or even with the title of the presentation itself.

- The Number Area placeholder can be confusing if it appears near other numbers on a slide. Slide numbers are rarely useful (you might rely on them as a visual reminder of how many slides are left), and they're frequently distracting. If you decide to use slide numbers, keep them subtle, and remember that you can always make the font smaller than the default provided by PowerPoint.

If you look closely at a Slide Master, you'll see that these three placeholders all have dummy values:

- The Date Area placeholder includes the current date.
- The Footer placeholder includes a dummy value called `Footer`.
- The Number Area placeholder includes a dummy value called `<#>`.

To show (or hide) the date/time, footer, or slide number placeholders and their contents, do the following:

1. Choose Insert, Header and Footer to open the PowerPoint Header and Footer dialog box; if necessary, click the Slide tab (shown in Figure 24.3).

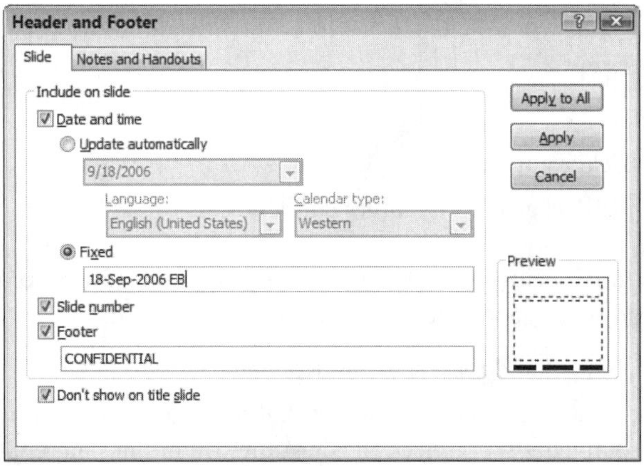

Figure 24.3
Use this dialog box to specify which place-holders appear and to specify replacements for the three Slide Master dummy values.

2. Select the appropriate check boxes to display any or all of the three placeholders on all slides; clear the check mark to hide the selected placeholder.

3. Use the entries under the check boxes to define what, if anything, replaces the dummy entries—the current date or a footnote, for example.

4. Click Apply to All to make the change to all the slides in your presentation. To avoid applying the same change to title slides, too, activate the Don't Show on Title Slide check box.

NOTE

If you open the Header and Footer dialog box from Normal view, you can change the display of dates, slide numbers, and footers on an individual slide (click Apply) or on the Slide Master (click Apply To All). If you're certain you don't want to use one of these placeholders, you can safely delete it.

TIP FROM

Ed & Woody

If you are likely to use the same headers or footers or other master elements in additional presentations, save a copy of the presentation as a template. (Select Office, Save As and then select PowerPoint Template in the Save as Type list.)

REMOVING SLIDE MASTER ELEMENTS FROM A SINGLE SLIDE

You might want to have, for instance, a logo appear on every slide except one. You might need to do this if one slide includes a big chart, for example, and you need every square inch of slide space to hold it. You might think that you could select the logo placeholder on a single slide and press the Delete key to remove it. If you try it, however, you'll see that this approach doesn't work.

In fact, removing Slide Master elements such as images and text from an individual slide is an all-or-nothing proposition: You get all of them, or you get none of them. This can be particularly vexing when the design you've chosen includes a graphic object—and most of the designs included with PowerPoint include graphics—or when you have a graphic element, such as a logo, that's supposed to appear on all slides.

To remove _all_ the Slide Master elements (except the title and text placeholders) from a single slide, follow these steps:

1. Select the slide.
2. Display the Background tab.
3. Select the Hide Background Graphics check box.

If this method is too drastic—you want to remove only one element, for example, on just one slide—you can cover up the element instead of removing it:

1. Select Insert, Shapes and then click the Rectangle shape.
2. On the slide, draw a rectangle that is just slightly larger than the Slide Master element you want to eliminate. If you need to adjust the size in finer increments than the tool normally allows, press the Alt key while making the adjustments.
3. Drag the rectangle over the Master Slide element.
4. On the Format tab, click the down arrow next to the Shape Fill icon. There should be a color very close to the background color available at the beginning of the first or second line of color swatches. Choose the color closest to the background color.
5. On the Format tab, click the down arrow next to the Shape Outline icon. Choose the same color you just chose for the fill color, or choose No Outline.

If you match the colors carefully, your audience will never know.

To accomplish the same trick on multiple slides, even those with fancy multicolored backgrounds, make a copy of the master slide, remove the element from the copy, and then use this master for the slides where you want the one element removed.

CREATING SPEAKER NOTES AND AUDIENCE HANDOUTS

The Notes Master and Handout Master behave differently from the Slide and layout masters; their only function is to provide extremely rudimentary instructions for printing speaker notes and audience handouts.

Speaker notes, in PowerPoint, typically hold one slide per page: The slide appears at the top of the page, and the notes for that slide appear at the bottom. Handouts, by contrast, consist solely of printed copies of the slides.

To set PowerPoint printing options for speaker notes:

1. Go into Notes Master view (see Figure 24.4) by choosing View, Notes Master. You will almost always want to adjust the Zoom factor using the Zoom button or slider in the status bar.

Figure 24.4
Use the Notes Master view to change the layout and formatting of your notes pages.

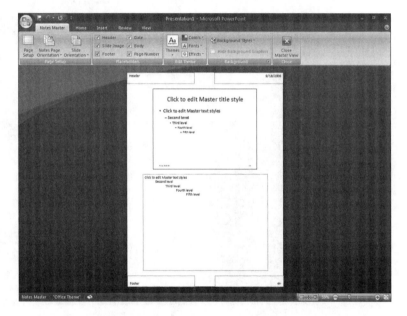

2. Apply formatting to the Notes Body Area just as you would to the Slide Master's text placeholder: Click the desired bullet level and apply text formatting.
3. Resize and/or move the slide placeholder and the Notes Body Area.
4. Move the header placeholder, footer placeholder, date/time placeholder, and page number placeholder. Note that you can type text into any of these placeholders and the text will appear on the notes.
5. Control the appearance and contents of those four placeholders by choosing Insert, Header and Footer, and setting the check boxes accordingly.

When you're satisfied with the formatting, print the speaker notes—choose Office, Print, choose Notes Pages in the Print What box, and click OK.

Color slides—particularly those with dark backgrounds—invariably print better on a black-and-white printer if you select the Grayscale check box in the Print dialog box. Choose the View Color/Grayscale icon on the standard toolbar to preview the presentation in Black and White.

Choose View, Handout Master to see the layout for your handouts. As Figure 24.5 illustrates, you can use the Slides Per Page list to change the page layout so that each page includes two, three, four, six, or nine slides. If you choose the three-slides-per-page layout, PowerPoint adds blank lines next to the slides so the audience can take notes. You can also move or format the Header Area, Footer Area, Date Area, and Number Area (which contains a page number rather than slide numbers, as in the presentation itself). Here, too, you can type text into any of these placeholders and the text will appear on the handouts.

Figure 24.5
The three-slides-per-page handout layout saves paper and gives your audience room to add their own notes on the right.

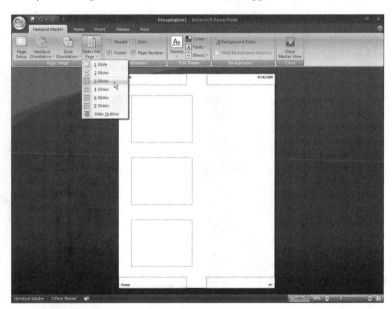

The only reason to use the Handout Master view is if you want to add text or graphics to your handouts. You can adjust headers and footers using the Header and Footer dialog box, and you can choose a layout for printing handout sheets from the Print dialog box. (Choose Office, Print, select Handouts from the Print What box, and choose a number from the Slides Per Page list.)

APPLYING AND MODIFYING THEMES

PowerPoint themes control the appearance of a presentation. By letting you save, modify, and reuse themes—including dozens of Microsoft-supplied samples—PowerPoint makes it easy to create presentations that are visually appealing and consistent. Consistency is especially important when you want a group of presenters from the same organization to share a common look.

Don't be intimidated by the presentation themes included with PowerPoint. In PowerPoint 2007, the selection of themes is very professional, but that doesn't mean you have to use one of these bundled themes. Although they follow generally accepted design principles, they're not sacrosanct.

The themes that Microsoft provides are only a starting point. Feel free to adapt, combine, customize, and tweak to your heart's content. If you come up with a presentation that really gets your point across, save the presentation as a template and use it to design new presentations.

TIP FROM

Ed & Woody

> If you're developing a presentation for a PowerPoint-savvy audience—that includes any-body who views more than a couple of presentations a week—be careful: You'll distract your audience if you use a standard design. Choosing the wrong design can force your audience to work harder than they need to. You can get your point across just fine with a simple, plain design—even if it isn't part of the Microsoft prefab kit.

A theme is a set of colors, fonts, effects, and background styles. In some themes, these ele-ments are consistent in every slide layout, while in other themes, you see different elements in some layouts. In any case, between them, these elements completely control the look and feel of a presentation.

→ To change every slide in a presentation, **see** "Organizing Formats with Master Slides," **p. 738**.

CHOOSING THE BEST THEME FOR YOUR PRESENTATION

Nothing detracts more from a good presentation than a poor design. To choose the best possible theme for a presentation, weigh the following conflicting factors:

- **Your audience**—This is the single-most crucial factor. A theme that's great for one audience (vibrant colors and animated bullets for a bunch of programmers and com-puter book authors, perhaps) might fall on its face for another (subtle gradient fills or textures and richer colors for the board of directors). Remember that PowerPoint-savvy audiences will respond better to seeing something that isn't straight out of the box.

- **Your image**—Although a presentation isn't quite "Dress for Success," the image you project onscreen shouldn't conflict with the image you project in person. If you're wear-ing a pinstripe Armani suit, you don't want the rough-looking Paper theme; if you're in jeans and a T-shirt, the slick Verve theme will leave your audience bewildered.

- **Your point**—If you're trying to get information across, stick to the no-nonsense designs with white backgrounds and sans-serif type. If you're trying to awaken an audi-torium full of people, add a bit of panache with graphics and vivid colors. And if you're trying to sell something, well, the sky's the limit.

After you have a clear vision of the image you want to project, you're ready to choose a theme. To pick a theme for your presentation, follow these steps:

1. Start with an existing presentation or create a new blank presentation.
2. Display the Themes group by clicking the Design tab on the Ribbon.
3. In the Themes group, click the More button to drop down the Themes gallery.
4. If don't see a theme you like, click More Themes on Microsoft Office Online to look for updated themes on the Web. Or click Browse for Themes to look for themes on your hard drive or your network.
5. When you've found a suitable theme, click it. PowerPoint applies the theme's colors, fonts, effects, and background styles to every slide in your presentation.

TIP FROM

EQ & Woody

If you want to apply a theme only to the current slide, right-click the theme and then click Apply to Selected Slides. (If you select two or more slides in advance, PowerPoint applies to the theme to all the selected slides.)

MODIFYING THEME COLORS

The *theme colors* consist of twelve colors that represent presentation text, background, accents (such as chart data markers), and hyperlinks. PowerPoint comes with more than 20 ready-made color schemes, each of which includes foreground and background colors that work well together.

The problem is that sometimes you don't want the colors to blend together so harmoniously. From time to time, a little bit of clash can be a good thing. For example, the color schemes that ship with PowerPoint can be very soothing when applied to text and backgrounds. But when you have a chart on the screen, you want the bars to stand apart from each other: The viewer should be able to tell at a glance where one data bar ends and another begins.

Further, you can use color schemes to subtle advantage. You don't have to be as obvious as, say, setting off your competitor's product specs in red, while showing your product's specs in green. But choosing a high-contrast color for your product and a washed-out, low-contrast color for your competitor can have an impact.

You can create your own color schemes by using any colors that your video settings will support. Table 24.1 lists the 12 components of a set of theme colors that you can work with.

TABLE 24.1   THEME COLOR COMPONENTS

Component	Description
Text/Background - Dark 1	The default text color, and one of the four possible background colors.
Text/Background - Light 1	The default background color, and the secondary text color that PowerPoint uses if you switch to a background color that's incompatible with the color specified as Text/Background - Dark 1.

Component	Description
Text/Background - Dark 2	One of the four possible background colors.
Text/Background - Light 2	One of the four possible background colors.
Accent 1 through Accent 6	PowerPoint uses these six colors for chart data markers.
Hyperlink	The color of the text of hyperlinks that haven't been "followed" (that is, clicked and activated).
Followed Hyperlink	The color of hyperlinked text that has been "followed."

Just as you can change any detail on a master slide, you can change the colors in the current presentation by changing the theme colors of any master. PowerPoint saves colors along with the theme; if you apply a new theme, PowerPoint discards any previous color changes and applies the colors from the new theme to your presentation.

PowerPoint uses theme colors in many places. For example, the Background Styles gallery (discussed later in this chapter) offers colors from the current theme, and the colors used to create graphics in many standard designs change when you change themes.

CHOOSING NEW THEME COLORS

To apply theme colors to your presentation, first apply the theme you want to use, then follow these steps:

1. Click the Design tab.
2. In the Themes group, click the Colors button to display the Theme Colors gallery, as shown in Figure 24.6.

Figure 24.6
Use the Theme Colors gallery to select or create theme colors for your presentation.

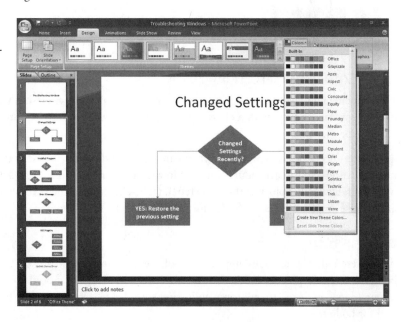

3. Hover the mouse over any gallery item to see a preview of its effect. When you see the one you want to apply, click it. Or click Create New Theme Colors at the bottom of the gallery and use the Create New Theme Colors dialog box (see Figure 24.7) to create your own scheme.

In the Create New Theme Colors dialog box, select your colors for each element, type a Name for the theme colors, and then click Save. Your custom theme colors will now appear in the Theme Colors gallery, so you can reuse them any time you like.

Figure 24.7
Use the Create New Theme Colors dialog box to create custom theme colors.

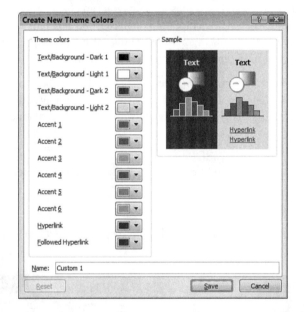

CHANGING COLORS ON SELECTED SLIDES

If you decide you need to change one color on a slide—perhaps it clashes with a picture or doesn't contrast enough with a chart—you might want to consider changing the entire color scheme for that slide.

The procedure for changing the color scheme for a single slide (or a selection of slides) is nearly identical to the procedure outlined in the preceding section. First, select the slides you want to individually colorize; then, in step 3, right-click the theme colors you want to use and choose Apply to Selected Slides instead of Apply to All Slides.

USING THEME FONTS

Each presentation theme also applies a set of theme fonts to your presentation. These fonts consist solely of typefaces (other font effects such as type size and bolding aren't part of the theme fonts), and each theme fonts collection specifies two fonts: one for headings and a second for body text.

To apply theme fonts to your presentation, follow these steps:

1. Click the Design tab.

2. In the Themes group, click the Fonts button to display the Theme Fonts gallery, as shown in Figure 24.8.

Figure 24.8
Use the Theme Fonts gallery to select or create theme fonts for your presentation.

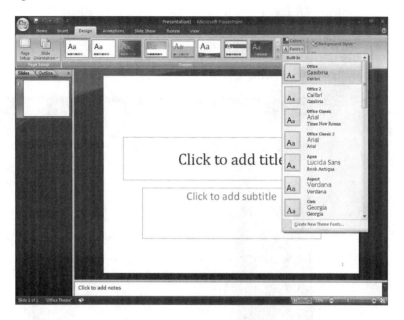

3. Hover the mouse over any gallery item to see a preview of its effect. When you see the one you want to apply, click it. Or click Create New Theme Fonts and use the Create New Theme Fonts dialog box (see Figure 24.9) to specify custom fonts.

NOTE

In the Create New Theme Fonts dialog box, select a Heading Font and a Body Font, type a Name for the theme fonts, and then click Save. Your custom theme fonts will now appear in the Theme Fonts gallery for reuse in other presentations.

Figure 24.9
Use the Create New Theme Fonts dialog box to create custom theme fonts.

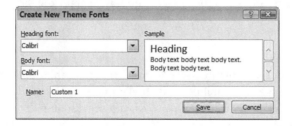

If you want to apply the theme fonts to selected slides only, select the slides you want to use and then, in step 3, right-click the theme fonts you want to use and choose Apply to Selected Slides.

USING THEME EFFECTS

In PowerPoint 2007, a theme also includes a set of theme effects. These effects control a number of different formatting elements, including shadows, glowing, bevels, soft edges, 3-D, and line styles. These effects apply mostly to shapes and SmartArt diagrams.

To apply theme effects to your presentation, follow these steps:

1. Click the Design tab.
2. In the Themes group, click the Effects button to display the Theme Effects gallery, as shown in Figure 24.10.

Figure 24.10
Use the Theme Effects gallery to select theme effects for your presentation.

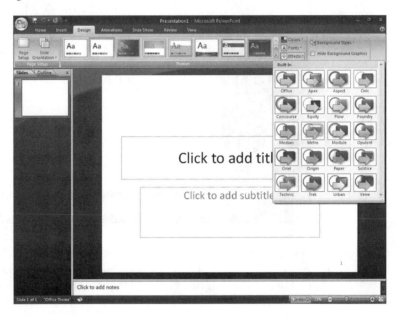

3. Hover the mouse over any gallery item to see a preview of its effect. When you see the one you want to apply, click it.

Note that unlike theme colors and fonts, there's no way to apply the theme effects to selected slides only.

CHOOSING THE BEST BACKGROUND

The background of your presentation—the "canvas" that sits behind all elements on a slide—offers a wide range of possibilities. The background might include solid colors, gradient fills of one or two colors, textures, or patterns; you can also import a graphic file (in GIF, JPEG, Windows Metafile, or any compatible graphics format) to use as the background.

In addition to the fundamental design principles that we discussed earlier in this chapter, your selection of a background should be influenced by the medium you'll use for the presentation.

If you're going to make the presentation in a darkened room on a large, high-contrast screen, you can get away with just about any combination of colors. But if you're making your presentation in a low-contrast situation (in a room where ambient light will fall on the screen, for example, or on a portable in which some members of your audience might not be able to view the screen directly), make sure you use light letters on a dark background, or vice versa. Those who have trouble discerning colors in low-contrast situations (not to mention the color-blind, who most frequently have trouble distinguishing green and red) will thank you.

Finally, if you intend to print the presentation—or show it on an overhead projector—stick to very light backgrounds. Although there are tricks for improving the printed appearance of almost any presentation, if your most important destination is hard copy, you should design the presentation from the ground up to comply.

→ For tips on getting the most out of hard copy, **see** "Printing Your Presentation," **p. 790**.

To change the background, do the following:

1. Apply the theme or theme colors you want.
2. Select the Design tab.
3. Select the Background Styles list to display a gallery of backgrounds, as shown in Figure 24.11. Note that the four colors you see along the top row are the four Text/Background colors specified in the current theme (or theme colors).

Figure 24.11
Use the Background Styles gallery to select or create a background for your presentation.

4. Hover the mouse over any gallery item to see a preview of its effect. If you see the one you want to apply, click it; otherwise, click Format Background to open the Format Background dialog box (see Figure 24.12).

Figure 24.12
The Format
Background dialog box
shows PowerPoint's
extensive set of tools
for changing back-
grounds.

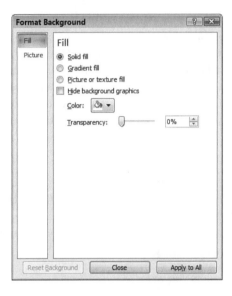

5. Build your background using any of the following techniques:

   - To select a solid background color, click Solid Fill and choose a new color from
     the Color drop-down list. (For a more extensive selection, click More Colors.)

   - To create a one- or two-color gradient, click Gradient Fill to display a new set of
     controls (see Figure 24.13) and use those control to set up the gradient.

   - To use an image or texture as the background, click Picture or Texture Fill to dis-
     play a new set of controls (see Figure 24.14), and use those controls to select and
     configure the picture or texture (you can use the samples included with
     PowerPoint or import your own). You can also import a picture to use as the
     background; the picture will be stretched to fit the slide.

Figure 24.13
Click Gradient Fill to
see the gradient-
related controls.

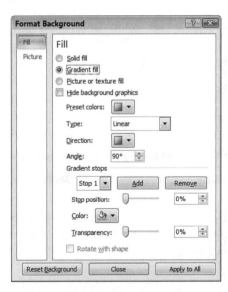

Figure 24.14
Click Picture or
Texture Fill to see the
picture and texture-
related controls.

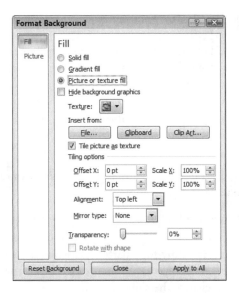

→ For advice on working with graphics, **see** Chapter 5, "Creating, Editing, and Using Pictures and Graphics," **p. 103**.

6. When you've constructed the background you want, click Apply to All to have the changes take effect throughout your presentation.

If you want to apply the background to selected slides only, select the slides you want to use and then, in step 4, right-click the background you want to use and choose Apply to Selected Slides.

SAVING A CUSTOM THEME

When you make changes to some or all of a theme's components—the colors, fonts, effects, and background—it can take a long time to get things just right. If you think you'll be using this modified theme in other presentations, the last thing you want to do is repeat the customizing procedures every time.

You can avoid this drudgery by saving your theme modifications as a custom theme. This theme will then appear in the Themes gallery, so you can apply it to another presentation with just a few mouse clicks.

Follow these steps to save a custom theme:

1. Make your changes to the theme colors, fonts, effects, and background.

2. In the Design tab, display the Themes gallery and click Save Current Theme. PowerPoint displays the Save Current Theme dialog box and selects the Document Themes folder.

3. Type a File Name for your theme and click Save.

CHANGING PARAGRAPH AND TEXT FORMATTING

Not all presentation text is created equal, and not all text falls into PowerPoint's relentless and presumed point-by-point-by-point format. Sometimes you might want to center a line of text, to make it stand out. In other presentations, you might want to ensure that each top-level bullet point has an extra bit of space after it, to make the presentation more readable from the back of the room. Then there's the inevitable bold text, and italic, and even the fontographer's nightmare, bold italic. All these treatments have a place in your repertoire of presentation tricks.

In general, PowerPoint paragraph and text formatting options mirror those available in Word. This section covers the few notable exceptions:

- To change paragraph or text formatting for all the slides in your presentation, change the Slide Master.

- To change paragraph or text formatting for a particular layout, if your presentation uses the layout multiple time, change the master for that layout; if your presentation has just one slide that uses the layout, change the slide directly.

- The normal rules of Windows apply: Select whatever you want to change—paragraphs, words, characters—and then use either the mini toolbar or the Home tab's Font and Paragraph groups to apply the change.

→ To change all the slides, **see** "Using the Slide Master," **p. 738**.

USING PARAGRAPH FORMATTING

All the standard paragraph formatting settings found in Word are at your disposal, including alignment (right, center, and left), spacing (double and triple), and so on. These options are accessible in the Home tab's Paragraph group.

> **NOTE**
>
> To remove bullets from a paragraph, click inside the paragraph, select the Home tab, and then either pull down the Bullets list and click None, or click the Bullets button.

To change tab stops and adjust the behavior of tab characters, you must use the ruler.

→ To tackle the ruler, **see** "Adding and Editing Text," **p. 713**.

Some tab formatting options you might use in other Office applications do not exist in PowerPoint. For example, there is no easy way to put a tab stop in every cell of a table; you have to enter them all manually.

USING FONTS

Professional designers recommend you stick with one font for titles and another for text—better yet, use the same font for both. Using too many fonts detracts from a presentation.

To adjust any font effects, select some text and then use either the mini toolbar that appears, or use the Home tab's Font group. You can also right-click the selected text and choose Font from the shortcut menu. All standard effects are available in the Font dialog box: color, bold, italic, bold italic, underline, shadow, emboss, and superscript/subscript. You can also adjust the elevation of superscripts and subscripts in the Offset box.

If you're planning to deliver your presentation on a large screen, avoid italicized fonts, which often end up looking like wavy blobs. You can use underline instead to emphasize a word or phrase, but underlining is traditionally reserved as a substitute for italic. If you absolutely must emphasize a word, bold is probably your best choice.

REPLACING FONTS THROUGHOUT A PRESENTATION

If you're trying to change all the Times New Roman in a presentation to Garamond, you might be tempted to change the Slide Master and call it a day.

Unfortunately, if you've applied any manual formatting to individual slides, the "link" between the slide and its master might be broken. In that case, even if the master is updated, the slide might not make the switch.

→ To change every slide in your presentation, **see** "Using the Slide Master," **p. 738**.

To truly change all occurrences of Times New Roman to Garamond, select the Home tab, pull down the Replace list, and then choose Replace Fonts. Choose Times New Roman from the Replace drop-down list; choose Garamond from the With list. Click OK to apply the change throughout the presentation—even in the masters. This solution is especially useful when you inherit a presentation created by someone who used a font you don't have.

NOTE

> This technique changes only the font; you can't use the dialog box to change point size.

TROUBLESHOOTING

SLIDE MASTER LINK DAMAGE

I changed the Slide Master, but some of the slides in my presentation haven't been updated with the changes.

If you do something odd (for example, delete one of the placeholders in a slide), it's possible to break the link between a slide and the Slide Master. After the link has been broken, changes to the Slide Master are no longer propagated to the slide. To reset the link, select the slide, and then select Home, Reset (or right-click the slide and click Reset Slide).

SECRETS OF THE OFFICE MASTERS: CREATING TOP-NOTCH NOTES AND HANDOUTS

PowerPoint's canned layouts for speaker notes and handouts have the singular advantage of being easy to use. If you just want your audience to have a place to scribble notes about your talk, these basic templates will do the trick.

But for truly professional-looking leave-behinds, consider sending the presentation to Word, which offers much better formatting and printing options than the basic notes and handout layouts in PowerPoint. After polishing your presentation to perfection, choose Office, Publish, Create Handouts in Microsoft Office Word. Using the choices in the Send to Microsoft Office Word dialog box shown in Figure 24.15, Word creates a new document with blank lines next to the thumbnails, in a format suitable for handouts.

You can use all of Word's editing tools to add content and sizzle to the resulting document, or insert the presentation into an existing document, such as a corporate backgrounder or product datasheets.

After you've finished creating your handouts, consider how your audience will use them before you begin your presentation! When audience members can look at your handout and jump ahead to a topic that specifically concerns them, you may find it difficult to keep their attention focused on what you're saying. The solution? Hand out a one- or two-page summary of your presentation before the talk begins, with room for your audience to jot down comments and questions, but pass out the unabridged handouts *after* your presentation is complete.

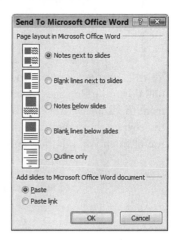

Figure 24.15

CHAPTER 25

ADDING GRAPHICS, MULTIMEDIA, AND SPECIAL EFFECTS

In this chapter

Using Transitions to Control Pacing   760

Animating Text and Objects on a Slide   762

Adding Music, Sounds, and Video to Your Presentation   771

Combining Transition Effects   775

Troubleshooting   776

Secrets of the Office Masters: Animating Charts to Emphasize Data   776

USING TRANSITIONS TO CONTROL PACING

PowerPoint makes it easy to control what your audience sees on the screen when you move from one slide to another. You can arrange things so that one slide replaces another onscreen, just as it would if you clicked through a carousel of 35mm slides. Or you can add wipes, dissolves, and other varieties of eye-catching (and frequently distracting) transitions. Properly done, transitions (sometimes also called *transition effects* or *slide transitions*) provide a breathing space between slides. Improperly done, your presentation will look amateurish and detract from making your point—which, after all, is the purpose of PowerPoint.

The nature of that breathing space lies totally at your control—a subtle, quick fade to black; a pixilated dissolve that leaves the old slide in view for quite some time; shutters and checkerboards; and dozens more. Transitions can help add an ambience to your presentation. You might want a more abrupt transition if you're trying to project a snappy, rapid-fire image, and use a more relaxed transition when the situation calls for a less formal approach.

Mixing and matching transitions jars the audience every bit as badly as ransom-note mixed fonts. For that reason, we recommend that you select one transition and use it exclusively throughout your presentation, with perhaps a few slides here and there getting "special treatment"—just to keep the audience awake.

When dealing with transitions, it's always easiest to work in Normal view, because Live Preview enables you to preview transitions before selecting the one you want.

25

NOTE

> Although you might think that a transition is defined between slides—showing how to *fade out* on the first slide and *fade in* on the next—PowerPoint doesn't work that way. Instead, you assign a transition to a slide, and that particular transition takes place when the slide is shown—it's a fade-in effect.

TIP FROM

EQ & Woody

> By creatively using transitions, you can simulate some slide animation effects that simply aren't possible with PowerPoint's built-in animation tools. For example, you might have a picture of a product that you're building in your presentation, but you want some elements to disappear after two or more mouse clicks, perhaps to deemphasize the old pieces as you add new ones. PowerPoint doesn't offer a "hide after *N* mouse clicks" animation option, so you can't animate that slide directly. In these cases, use a transition to fake animation: Build two slides—one to show the "before" image and the other for the "after" image—and then run a quick transition between the two. Your audience will be impressed.

APPLYING A TRANSITION TO ONE SLIDE

To set a transition for a single slide, select that slide (by displaying it in Normal view or clicking the slide in Slide Sorter view), and then display the Animations tab and choose the More button in the Transition to This Slide group. This brings up the Transitions gallery (see Figure 25.1).

Available transitions

Figure 25.1
The Transitions gallery pane makes it easy to apply transitions.

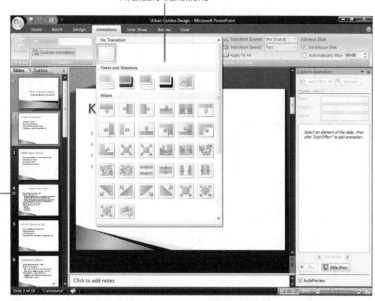

Preview transition and animation

If you're in Normal view, when you hover the mouse over a transition, PowerPoint's Live Preview feature previews the effect for you. When you see an effect you like, click it to apply it. PowerPoint shows you a preview of the transition you selected, and it also adds a small icon to indicate that the slide has transition effect applied (see Figure 25.1). To see the transition again, click this icon, or click Preview in the Animations tab.

TIP FROM

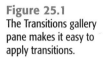

If you want your transitions and animations to appear when your presentation is viewed from a web browser, you must choose Office, PowerPoint Options, Advanced, Web Options, and select the Show Slide Animation While Browsing check box.

APPLYING A TRANSITION TO A GROUP OF SLIDES

To assign the same transition to a group of slides, switch to Slide Sorter view and select the slides with which you want to use the same transition. Use Ctrl+click to select single slides or Shift+click to select a contiguously numbered group.

TIP FROM

To select all the slides in the presentation, click one slide, and then press Ctrl+A.

Select the transition you want from the Animation tab's Transitions gallery.

PowerPoint goes through a preview of the transitions and animations for the displayed slide. To repeat the transitions and animations for the displayed slide, click Preview on the Animations tab.

CAUTION

When you apply a transition to a slide, PowerPoint replaces any transitions you previously applied to that slide.

CONTROLLING SLIDE TRANSITION SPEED

The Transition to This Slide group gives you additional control over the transition between slides. With it you can do the following:

- Set the speed to slow, medium, or fast.
- Tell PowerPoint how you want to advance to the next slide during a presentation—manually, by clicking the mouse, or automatically, after a preset interval. Note that this setting controls how the slide exits and is thus unrelated to the transition effect you set for the current slide.
- Make PowerPoint play a sound during the transition.

TIP FROM

Ed & Woody

In general, resist the temptation to select the Loop Until Next Sound option, which is certain to distract almost any audience, unless you have a specific impression in mind: a suspenseful tick-tick-tick leading up to the next slide, for example, might be appropriate. But consider the reaction if a question from the audience takes you 10 minutes to answer—with the tick-tick-tick going all the time.

The two Advance settings—On Mouse Click and Automatically After—operate independently. If you activate both options, PowerPoint shows the next slide when the timer expires, or when you click the slide, whichever comes first. If you leave both boxes unchecked, the slide advances only when you press the spacebar, the Enter key, or one of PowerPoint's other keyboard presentation control keys.

→ For a definitive list of presentation control keys, **see** "Mouse and Keyboard Shortcuts," **p. 729**.

ANIMATING TEXT AND OBJECTS ON A SLIDE

Just as you use transition effects to control how a slide fades in, you use *animations* to control how the individual elements of a slide make their appearance. By showing one bullet point at a time, for example, you can make sure your audience concentrates on what you're saying now rather than reading the rest of the bullets on your slide and mentally calculating how much longer you're going to speak.

The most rudimentary form of slide animation displays each bullet point on a slide one at a time: You click the mouse (or tap the spacebar) and the slide's title appears. Click again, and the first bullet point appears onscreen. Keep clicking to display each bullet point on the list. Other animations let you specify that bullet points fly in or zoom from any direction. You can also choose fades, dissolves, wipes, and other visual effects.

25

TIP FROM

PowerPoint's selection of ready-made animation schemes is conveniently divided into four groups: Basic, Subtle, Moderate, and Exciting. We recommend you stick with Basic and Subtle effects for the most part. Reserve the Moderate and Exciting effects for the special slide that really deserves to stand out from the pack.

You can apply animations to almost any part of a slide and then activate the animations by clicking the mouse or using PowerPoint's built-in timers. Used sparingly, these animations can add punch to your presentation, augmenting your spoken words with powerful visuals. Suppose you have a graph that illustrates how sales have taken off in the past year. You could show the whole graph, all at one time, and emphasize the spike in the final number verbally. Much more effectively, however, you could have the bars fly onto the graph one at a time— building up, in your narration, to the spike in the final quarter.

You can use animations to coordinate sounds so that they play as predetermined parts of the slide appear. You can also place text on a slide—one character, word, or paragraph at a time. For example, use animations to start movies and other types of video clips at predetermined intervals after the slide first appears. Or use them to dim or change the color of items on the slide, in conjunction with the appearance of a new item.

TIP FROM

For sophisticated animation effects, break the clip-art objects apart, and then animate each element separately. Duplicating elements and using flying effects can also create the illusion of motion.

ANIMATING BULLET POINTS

Animating the arrival of bullet points on a slide gives you control over how much information your audience sees, and when. Moving one bullet point at a time onto the slide lets you keep your audience running at your pace, particularly if you know that people in the audience have a tendency to read ahead. Also consider using bullet animation if you want to save some surprising or emphatic points for the end of the slide.

CAUTION

If you remove the capability to advance a slide based on mouse clicks (by clearing the On Mouse Click check box in the Transition to This Slide group), you also remove the capability to animate bullet points with a mouse click. Instead, if you've provided an automatic advance time (in the Automatically After *nn:nn* box), PowerPoint divides that time equally among the bullet points and presents each in turn, automatically.

If you select the Automatically After *nn:nn* check box on the Transition to This Slide group, PowerPoint shows each of the bullet points automatically if you don't click soon enough. Here, too, each bullet point is given an equal amount of time.

If you have animated bullet points, don't forget to show them as you're making the presentation! You would be amazed how many presenters talk "to" multiple animated bullet points on a slide, show the first point, and then forget to click to put the other bullet points on the screen so their audience can follow along.

The specifics of animating "flying" bullet points are covered in the next section, "Creating a Custom Animation."

CREATING A CUSTOM ANIMATION

In previous versions of PowerPoint, the program came with a number of prebuilt animation schemes. Those schemes are gone from PowerPoint 2007, so you animate slide items by building your own custom animations. This section shows you how to build custom animations, concentrating on bullets and titles.

In the following example, we'll create a custom animation effect that allows us to display secondary bullet points individually:

1. In Normal view, bring up the slide that contains the elements you want to animate. For this example, we're using a slide that has bullet points at both the first and second levels.

2. Choose Animations, Custom Animation. The Custom Animation task pane appears (see Figure 25.2).

Figure 25.2
To build a custom animation from the ground up, remove any preset animations and start with a blank Custom Animation task pane.

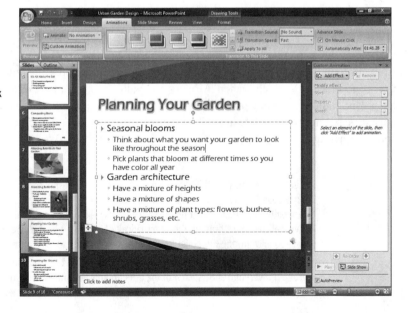

3. Select the items on the slide you want to animate. To animate the slide's bullet points but not its title, select only the text placeholder (which contains all the bullet points), as in Figure 25.2.

4. Click the Add Effect button and choose the effect you want. In Figure 25.3, we're about to apply an Entrance effect called Fly In to all elements in the text placeholder.

Figure 25.3
PowerPoint has hundreds of animation effects. For each element of a slide, you can control the entrance and exit motion and font effects (from the Emphasis menu), or you can apply any motion that you can draw.

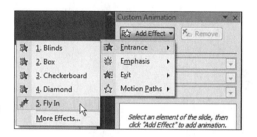

5. PowerPoint shows the first animation—in this case, the bullet point that reads "Seasonal blooms"—in the timing review list. Click the downward-pointing chevron below the first animation, and PowerPoint shows you all the bullet points and their sequence (see Figure 25.4). The timing review list indicates that on the first mouse click, the first bullet ("Seasonal blooms") and its two secondary bullet points appear. On the second mouse click, the second bullet point ("Garden architecture") and its three secondary bullet points appear.

Figure 25.4
The timing review list shows what each mouse click will do. Sequence numbers to the left of the bullet points repeat that information.

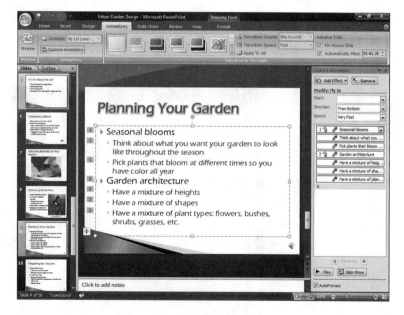

6. Each bullet point should appear in turn—in this example, two mouse clicks (each indicated by a mouse icon) and five unnumbered items that are associated with the two clicks. Click the first unnumbered bullet point ("Think about what you..."), select the down-arrow to the right, and choose Start On Click (see Figure 25.5).

Figure 25.5
You can adjust the appearance of each bullet item individually.

25

7. Continue in this manner until all the bullet points have their own sequence numbers, 1 through 7 (see Figure 25.6).

Figure 25.6
Each bullet point appears in turn, as indicated by the numbers 1 through 7.

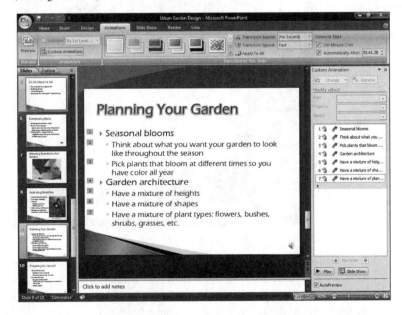

8. Finally, to verify your choices, click the Slide Show button at the bottom of the Custom Animation pane. The heading should come up as soon as the slide appears. Click once and the first bullet point comes up. Click again and you get the second bullet point, and so on.

NOTE

> You can apply completely separate animations to individual bullet points on a slide. For example, you can have the first bullet point wipe from the left and have the second spiral from the top. Just because you can do this, however, doesn't mean you should. The results are usually a mess. Stick with one effect.

When you make a presentation, any item on the slide that isn't animated shows up as soon as the slide hits the screen. Animated items appear next, normally in top-to-bottom order. Sometimes you don't want the slide's elements to appear from top to bottom, however; you might have a picture that you want to appear before the bullets, or a video clip that should show before the title comes up. Using the Custom Animation pane, you can control the order in which animated items appear.

To arrange the order in which animations appear, follow these steps:

1. In Normal view, select the slide with the animations that need to be reordered.

2. Open the Custom Animation task pane by choosing Animations, Custom Animation.

3. Click the number to the left of any one animated item whose order you want to adjust.

4. Use the Re-Order arrows at the bottom of the timing review list to move the selected item up or down in the list.

5. Repeat steps 3 and 4 for any additional items you want to reorder.

 If you're frustrated because you can't copy custom animation effects from slide to slide, see "Custom Animation Tricks" in the "Troubleshooting" section at the end of this book.

TIP FROM

EQ & Woody

> To add a custom animation to every slide, animate the Slide Master. You can apply any animation effect to any item on the Slide Master—title, text, background pictures, date/time, footer, and slide number. You can also animate the layout masters.

To coordinate the arrival of each character in a title with a sound (for instance, a typewriter clacking), here's how you coordinate sounds with characters:

1. In Normal view, select the slide whose bullet points you want to animate. Bring up the Custom Animation task pane (choose Animations, Custom Animation).

2. Choose the item you want to animate—for example, the title. Click Add Effect (or, if the item already has an effect, click Change), and choose Entrance, More Effects, Color Typewriter.

25

N O T E

The list of menu choices on the menus attached to the Add Effects and Change buttons are dynamic. As you use individual choices from the More Effects menu, PowerPoint adds your choices to these menus, saving you a click or two when you reuse those same effects. If you've used the Color Typewriter option recently, for instance, you'll find it on the Entrance menu, without having to detour to the More Effects list.

3. In the timing review list, click the down arrow to the right of the title and choose Effect Options to open the Color Typewriter dialog box (see Figure 25.7). Use this dialog box to configure the effect.

Figure 25.7
Use the Color Typewriter dialog box to set up an effect where a typewriter sound announces the arrival of each character.

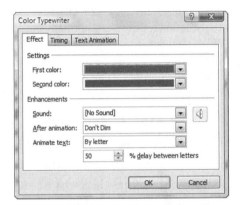

When the title appears on the slide, each character flies in, accompanied by the sound you selected—in this example, a typewriter. Keep in mind that you don't need to let the effect name limit your creativity. By using modern fonts and other sounds, you can create an interesting effect that has no association at all with your old Underwood or Selectric.

ANIMATING THE DRAWING LAYER

PowerPoint lets you animate any items in the drawing layer—text boxes, drawings, AutoShapes, clip art, charts, embedded Excel or Word objects, org charts, and more. Before you try, however, it's important that you understand how the drawing layer works, and how to use it in conjunction with the Custom Animation dialog box.

→ For an explanation of how Office programs use the drawing layer, **see** "Working with the Drawing Layer," **p. 105**.

Suppose you've created a dramatic slide that features your company's new CEO or spokesperson. You've added a scanned photo to the slide, and you want the photo to "dissolve" onto the screen with applause—and you hope the audience will join in. Here's how:

1. Display the slide in Normal view and click to select the picture.

2. Choose Animations, Custom Animation.

3. In the Custom Animation task pane, click Add Effect, Entrance, More Effects, and then choose Fade (see Figure 25.8).

Figure 25.8
If you select an item on a slide and then choose an animation, PowerPoint applies the animation only to the selected item.

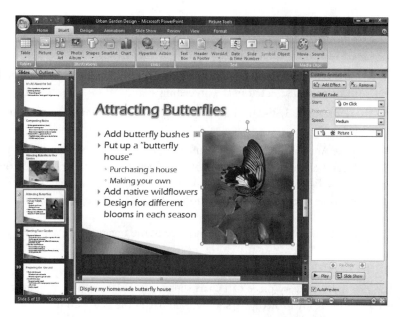

4. Click the down arrow in the timing review list next to the picture. Choose Effect Options. In the Sound box, pick the sound effect you want and click OK.

Now when the slide appears on the screen, the picture will "fade in," accompanied by the sound you chose.

Use similar techniques to animate any object on the drawing layer. For example, you might want to have a text box that says "Met Annual Goals!" on top of a slide showing financial information, animated to appear after you've had a chance to talk about the numbers. Custom animations also let you introduce text in Shape callouts or text boxes one word or letter at a time.

HIDING AND UNCOVERING SLIDE CONTENTS

There's a trick to using items in the drawing layer that all too frequently escapes PowerPoint users. If you carefully match the color of a shape in the drawing layer to the color of the background, you can use animation on these shapes to *hide* parts of your presentation.

Suppose you have a slide that includes an image, and you want to unveil only parts of that image, one at a time. PowerPoint has no built-in option for animating parts of images. Here's how to use animations to show one piece of the image at a time:

1. Create the slide and insert the image. For best results, make sure the slide's background is a solid color.

2. Select Insert, Shapes, and then click the Rectangle tool. Draw a rectangle around part of the image you want to hide. If you have trouble covering the area precisely and need more control, hold down the Alt key as you drag.

3. Click the Fill Color button on the Drawing toolbar. Select the color that most nearly matches the background color. (If you're using defined color schemes, you should be able to select an exact match.)

4. On the Format tab, click the down arrow beside the Shape Outline button. Select the same color you selected in the preceding step.

5. Repeat steps 2, 3, and 4 to draw rectangles around each part of the image you want to hide.

6. Choose Animations, Custom Animation, select the Rectangle shapes you added to the slide, and choose whatever Animation Effect suits your fancy. In the timing review sequence list, arrange the order so the first Rectangle is the last in order. Use the Effect Options choices to add any additional effects (applause, for example).

The presentation will now reveal each piece of the image when you click the mouse.

ANIMATING CHART COMPONENTS

You can animate every piece of a chart separately. For example, to dramatically demonstrate five years of steady growth, try sliding each bar in the chart up from the bottom of the slide, one after the other. To focus on your progress versus a competitor, show the bars for the competitor first, and then reveal the corresponding bars for your company.

Before you undertake this advanced animation, make sure you understand how to create a chart in Excel, how to insert a chart into a slide, and how to use the Custom Animation dialog box.

→ To learn how to create a chart in Excel, **see** "Creating and Editing Charts," **p. 123**.

→ For instructions on how to add a chart to a slide, **see** "Inserting an Excel Chart or Range," **p. 720**.

To animate an Excel chart, you must put the chart in a slide's object placeholder. To put an existing Excel chart into a chart placeholder, first create the chart in Excel and copy it to the Clipboard. Then display the slide in PowerPoint and use the Home, Layout gallery to apply a layout of the suitable size and shape. The ideal choice is a Title and Content layout, but you can use any layout. PowerPoint is smart enough to paste the chart into the correct location and replace a text placeholder with an object placeholder if necessary.

After creating the new slide, choose Edit, Paste. PowerPoint places your chart in the slide as an embedded Excel object. You can double-click the chart to edit it using Excel. At this point, you can animate the chart.

To make each bar of a bar chart appear independently on the screen, follow these steps:

1. Open the slide that contains the chart. Select the chart and choose Animations, Custom Animation.

2. In the Custom Animation task pane, choose Add Effect and pick an Entrance effect such as Diamond.

3. Click the down arrow next to the chart object in the timing review list and choose Effect Options. On the Chart Animation tab, choose the method you want to use to introduce chart elements: The chart can come in all at once; by Series (that is, all similarly colored bars appear, followed by all bars with the next color, and so on); by Category (each group of bars that falls into one group on the y-axis appears, and then the next group); or by individual bars within each Series or Category (see Figure 25.9).

Figure 25.9
Individual bars in a chart appear in the sequence defined on the Chart Animation tab.

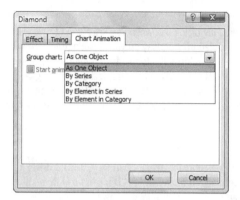

4. Test your animation by clicking the Play button.

Because PowerPoint gives you the capability to present data by Series or Category, the animation sequence for chart effects can be complex. Use the Play button as you work to make sure the order is correct.

25

ADDING MUSIC, SOUNDS, AND VIDEO TO YOUR PRESENTATION

PowerPoint puts you in the director's chair when it comes to adding sounds, clip art (including pictures with movement such as animated GIFs), extended musical accompaniment, and even movie clips. But just because it *can* be done doesn't necessarily mean it *should* be done. Multimedia components in a presentation tend to overwhelm the audience. Be sure you really want to draw your audience's attention away from what you're saying before you insert a multimedia clip.

ADDING MUSIC, SOUNDS, AND VIDEO CLIPS

The easiest way to add multimedia to a presentation is to use the Media Clips group in the Insert tab. Select the slide on which you want the media to appear, and then use the following techniques:

- **Inserting a sound file**—Choose Insert, Sound from File (the speaker icon in the Media Clips group). You can also pull down the Sound menu and click Sound from File. Use the Insert Sound dialog box to select the sound file and click OK.

- **Inserting a sound clip**—Choose Insert, Sound, Sound from Clip Organizer. PowerPoint opens the Clip Art pane and displays the clips from the Sounds collection. Click the sound clip you want to use.

- **Inserting CD audio**—Choose Insert, Sound, Play CD Audio Track. PowerPoint displays the Insert CD Audio dialog box (see Figure 25.10). Choose the track(s) you want to play and click OK.

TIP FROM

If you see the AutoPlay dialog box when you insert the CD, close it to avoid starting the CD. If you have enabled CD AutoPlay on your system, Windows will begin playing an audio CD as soon as you insert it into the drive. When this happens, PowerPoint won't be able to take control of the CD to let you select a track. To give control back to PowerPoint, open Windows Media Player (or whatever program is configured as the default for playing CDs) and stop the CD. Close the player to let PowerPoint use the CD.

NOTE

PowerPoint doesn't identify the actual CD in the CD-ROM drive; it knows only to play the tracks you've specified, no matter which CD might be in there. If you forget to put a CD in the drive when running a presentation, PowerPoint continues as if there were no track(s) to be played.

Figure 25.10
As long as you have the CD in your PC's drive, PowerPoint automatically calculates how much time it will take to play the tracks you select.

- **Inserting recorded audio**—Choose Insert, Sound, Record Sound. PowerPoint displays the Record Sound dialog box shown in Figure 25.11. Type a name for the recording and then click the Record button. This technique is useful if your PC has a functioning microphone, because it means you can record a sound to be played with slides—you can even prerecord narration for every slide and, using timed advancing on the slides, deliver an entire presentation without being physically present.

CAUTION

Audio clips in presentations viewed over the Web can slow down the process horribly, unless the viewer has a high-speed connection.

Figure 25.11
If you have a microphone, use the Record Sound dialog box to record narration for your presentation.

- **Inserting a movie file**—Choose Insert, Movie from File (the film reel icon in the Media Clips group). You can also pull down the Movie menu and click Movie from File. Use the Insert Movie dialog box to select the movie file and click OK.

- **Inserting a movie clip (animated GIF)**—Choose Insert, Movie, Movie from Clip Organizer. PowerPoint opens the Clip Art pane and displays the clips from the Movies collection. Click the movie clip you want to use.

> **NOTE**
>
> You'll find animated GIFs in the Clip Organizer. Office 2007 does not include any tools that allow you to edit an animated GIF; to change one of these images, you must use a program specifically designed to handle this graphic format, such as Magic Viewer from Crayonsoft (www.crayonsoft.com/).

In each case (except inserting a movie clip), PowerPoint displays a dialog box asking you how you want the media to start in the slideshow. Choose Automatically if you want the movie/sound to begin as soon as the slide appears. If you choose When Clicked, you'll have to click the picture (or the speaker that symbolizes a sound) to play the sound or show the video during the presentation.

Controlling a Video or Sound Clip

To change the behavior of a video or sound clip after you place it on a slide—whether it's in a placeholder or in the drawing layer—click the clip (or the speaker icon representing a sound object) and choose Animations, Custom Animation. On the Add Effects menu (or the Change menu, if an effect is already applied), you'll notice a new Sound Actions or Movie Actions menu that allows you to define Play, Pause, or Stop effects. After applying an effect, right-click the trigger and choose Effect Options and use the Movie Settings or Sound Settings tab to see options that apply only to the type of media clip you've inserted.

Use these options to create a video introduction to a slide with bullet points. The slide should appear first, with the title and background. Then, as quickly as PowerPoint can manage, the video clip should play. Finally, after the clip is over, the video should disappear and your bullet points should slide onto the screen.

Here's how to do it:

1. Select the slide you plan to use, and enter its title and bullet points.
2. To place the video clip in the drawing layer, choose Insert, Movie from File. Select the file and click OK.

25

3. When PowerPoint asks, "How do you want the movie (or sound) to start in the slideshow?," click Automatically.

4. Resize the movie clip window and position it where you want the movie to appear. Ignore the bullet points for the time being—they won't be there when the video runs—and concentrate on getting the movie clip positioned properly.

5. Click the movie clip window and select Animations, Custom Animation. You'll see the movie file appear at the top of the timing review list, with a 0 next to it (indicating that the movie will run as soon as the slide appears).

6. Select the Text placeholder and the title, click Add Effect in the Custom Animation task pane, and select an effect to assign to all the text on the slide. In Figure 25.12, we've used the Fly In effect. The bullet points appear in the timing review list directly below the animation.

Figure 25.12
The timing review list indicates that the Butterfly.wmv animation will run before the bullet points appear.

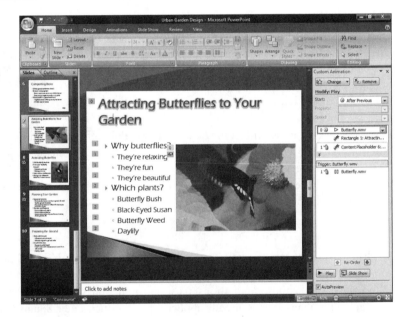

7. Click the down arrow next to the media clip at the top of the timing review list. Choose Effect Options. In the Play Movie dialog box (see Figure 25.13), click the Movie Settings tab and select the Hide While Not Playing check box. Then click the Effect tab and choose Hide After Animation from the After Animation drop-down list. This combination of settings ensures that the movie clip will play and then disappear, before the bullet points arrive. Click OK to close the Play Movie dialog box.

Figure 25.13
Tell the movie clip to disappear when it's done playing.

8. Click the down arrow next to the entry for the bullet points in the timing review list (in this example, it's labeled as Text 2), and select Start After Previous. This setting ensures that the first bullet point will appear immediately after the movie clip finishes.

Click Play on the Custom Animation pane and you'll see how all this ties together.

TIP FROM

> Loop and rewind options vary depending on the type of multimedia clip you select. To work with these settings, click the Effect and Timing tabs in the Play Movie dialog box.

COMBINING TRANSITION EFFECTS

You can tie each animated element on a slide to a hyperlink or action setting. When you click a hyperlinked element or an item that includes an action setting, the animation takes place before the hyperlink or action setting kicks in.

→ For information about hyperlinks in general, **see** "Working with Hyperlinks," **p. 98**.

→ For hyperlink information specific to PowerPoint, **see** "Using Hyperlinks," **p. 730**.

Combining custom animation and action settings needn't be overly confusing because they typically operate on different slide components. For example, you can apply a sound "animation" to the appearance of bullet points on a slide, but you can apply the sound "action setting" only to the words (and characters) in the bullet point.

Surprisingly, however, there's one action that you can implement only through hyperlinks and action settings: the mouseover. All the fancy animation techniques discussed in this chapter are tied to mouse clicks, or internal timers.

For example, if you want to make a video clip start by passing the mouse over the clip, you *must* use action settings. Select the clip, choose Insert, Action, and then adjust options on the Mouse Over tab.

→ For details, **see** "Advanced Navigation with Action Settings," **p. 730**.

TROUBLESHOOTING

CUSTOM ANIMATION TRICKS

I created a slick custom animation for one slide, but I can't figure out how to copy the animation effects to other slides in my presentation.

Although PowerPoint has no built-in way to copy a custom animation from one slide to another, here's an undocumented trick that lets you reuse custom animations: Make a copy of a slide, and then change the title and bullets on the copy. The copy includes all the custom animation settings of the original.

For example, if you've created a nifty custom animation on slide 20, how do you move it to slides 17, 18, and 19? You could edit the animation settings for each of the other three slides, but that's a cumbersome process. Instead, make three copies of slide 20, and then move the existing text from the old slides to the copies. Delete the old slides when you've finished.

HIDING A CLIP WITH A CLICK

I have a movie clip on one of my slides, and I'd like that clip to play and then disappear, but I want to control when the clip disappears. Is this possible?

Yes, you can configure the clip to disappear when you click the mouse. Navigate to the slide and then, in the list of triggers, drop down the list associated with the clip trigger and click Effect Options. In the Effect tab, use the After Animation list to select Hide on Next Mouse Click. Click OK to put the setting into effect. When you run the slideshow, when you're ready to hide the clip, click anywhere on the slide.

SECRETS OF THE OFFICE MASTERS: ANIMATING CHARTS TO EMPHASIZE DATA

Almost every chart can benefit from some animation. In the simplest case, shown in the Figure 25.14, you can set up the bars to appear one at a time, cumulatively from left to right, by using the Appear entry animation. After you get the hang of clicking (or tapping the spacebar) to advance the animation while you speak, your point will be all the more forceful.

Figure 25.14

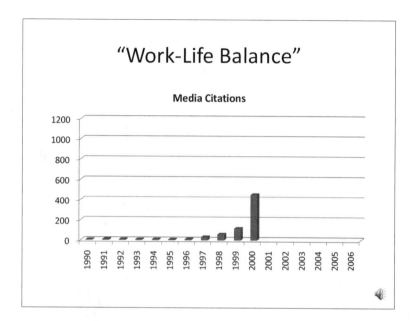

CHAPTER 26

PLANNING AND DELIVERING A PRESENTATION

In this chapter

Planning Your Presentation   780

Running a Slideshow   783

Creating Presentations for the Web   783

Setting Up a Slideshow   785

Using Hidden Slides to Anticipate Questions   787

Packaging a Presentation for Use on Other Computers   788

Printing Your Presentation   790

Troubleshooting   792

Secrets of the Office Masters: Anticipating Questions with Hidden Slides   792

PLANNING YOUR PRESENTATION

Far too many presentations crash in flames because the presenter fails to anticipate what could reasonably go wrong, or doesn't prepare for questions that can be answered with a few facts, figures, or slides.

On the other hand, some less-than-flashy presenters with solid but uninspired slides regularly draw raves from appreciative audiences. Why? Because they step through points logically and in sequence, and when questions arise, they have solid answers, ready and waiting—and right at hand in their speaker notes.

THE IMPORTANCE OF PREPARATION

It's no secret, and no coincidence, that the best presenters rehearse their presentations over and over, in front of different groups that closely parallel the target audience. Before they stand up on stage, they take apart their presentation, slide by slide, and then edit, reorganize, put it back together, and test it again.

You might be tempted to practice in front of a mirror, and if your primary concern is the mechanics of the presentation, that's a reasonable approach. But if you want to get a point across, nothing beats jumping into the lion's den. Practice delivering the presentation to people who are willing to stop you when they don't understand, and make suggestions when your points miss their mark.

PowerPoint includes a number of tools that will help you prepare, refine, and ultimately deliver the presentation. But in the final analysis, they won't help a bit unless you have the content down pat. The best presentations practically deliver themselves.

ORGANIZING YOUR REMARKS WITH SPEAKER NOTES

Some people are capable of delivering a perfect presentation without notes. But what if you don't have a photographic memory or weeks to rehearse? For those of us who are chronically short on spare time and brain cells, there's no substitute for PowerPoint's speaker notes.

→ For an overview of notes, **see** "Adding Notes," **p. 724**.

The easiest way to construct and maintain notes is in PowerPoint's Normal view, where the Notes pane appears below the slide. Normally, this window displays only a few lines; to look at all the notes for a given slide, go to Notes view by choosing View, Notes Page.

You can do little to change the appearance of the Notes page, except for adjusting tab stops. Because default tab stops start at one inch, you might find yourself running out of room if you indent text on a note page that contains lots of text; follow these steps to adjust the tabs and give the indented text a little extra room:

1. In Normal or Slide Sorter view, select the slide with the notes that you want to change.
2. Choose View, Notes Page. Then bring up the ruler by choosing View, Ruler.

3. Click once to position the insertion point in the notes placeholder below the slide.

4. Click inside the ruler to add a tab stop, and then click and drag the stop along the ruler to adjust its position.

To change the tab spacing on all your Notes pages, bring up the Notes Master (choose View, Notes Master), adjust the tab stops on the ruler, and then choose View, Close Master View.

TIP FROM

Ed & Woody

> If you can anticipate any questions your audience might ask when a particular slide is on the screen, consider typing the question (and a possible answer, of course) at the bottom of the Notes page for that slide. To make it easier to identify the questions while you're flipping through your notes, set them off in bold or italic.

USING POWERPOINT'S TIMER TO REHEARSE A PRESENTATION

When you practice a presentation, PowerPoint can start a timer to keep track of the amount of time you spend on each slide and on the presentation as a whole. These timings can be useful in several situations:

- Timing your presentation helps you identify slides that are too complex or contain too much detail. If you find yourself spending five minutes explaining a single slide, consider simplifying the slide or splitting it into two or more. Likewise, if you discover you're racing through one part of your presentation, taking only a few seconds on each slide, that might be a clue that those slides are too elementary.

- PowerPoint timers help you set up the presentation so that slides advance automatically. This capability might be useful if, for example, you need to have both hands free to demonstrate a product. In this case, you can use the timings from your rehearsals to specify how long PowerPoint should display each slide before advancing.

- With the help of a special timer on the Rehearsal dialog box, you can plan your presentation so you don't overrun a tight time slot. The Rehearsal timer appears onscreen to tell you how long you've spent on each slide. Although few people use the Rehearsal timer during a final presentation, it can help you keep on top of timing during the preparation phase.

To rehearse a presentation using the timer, follow these steps:

1. Gather all the notes you'll need, and then open the presentation in PowerPoint, preferably using the same computer you'll use when you actually deliver the presentation.

2. Choose Slide Show, Rehearse Timings. As your presentation begins, the Rehearsal dialog box appears onscreen (see Figure 26.1).

26

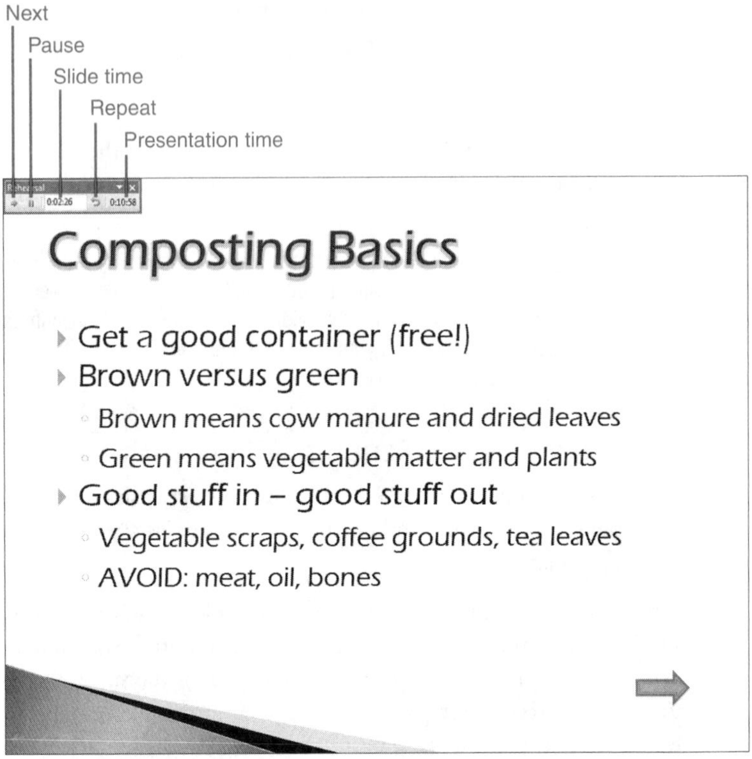

Figure 26.1
Keep track of the time spent on each slide by using the Slide Meter.

3. Run through your presentation normally. Try to speak at a natural pace, using your notes if necessary, and click your way through slides and animations.
   - Watch the Slide Time box to see how much time you've spent on the current slide. If you bump into an unexpected snag—you lose your place in your notes, for example—click the Pause button to stop the clock. When you're ready to continue, click Pause again.
   - If you get flustered, click Repeat to "turn back the clock"—that is, reset the time on the current slide to zero, and subtract the appropriate amount of time from the Presentation Time counter. Resume your presentation at that slide.

NOTE

> Clicking the Repeat button causes animations to repeat, starting with the first animation on the slide, but you must click once on the screen before the first repeat animation appears.

4. When you finish the presentation, PowerPoint tells you how long the entire presentation took and asks whether you want to update the times associated with each slide to reflect the latest numbers. If you click Yes, the timing numbers appear in Slide Sorter view, at the lower left of each slide (see Figure 26.2).

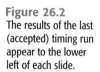

Figure 26.2
The results of the last (accepted) timing run appear to the lower left of each slide.

Timing number ——

Unfortunately, there is no way to keep a history of timing runs, or to selectively rerecord timings on a slide-by-slide basis. You must either accept all the new times, or reject them all. You can manually adjust the timing of a single slide by choosing the Animations tab and entering a time in the Automatically After box.

NOTE

> If you show the same slide more than once (such as if you back up or use it in a custom show), the timer keeps statistics only for the final time it appears.

To set an individual slide so that it advances automatically after a specific amount of time, choose the Animations tab, activate the Automatically After check box, and enter a time in the associated spin box.

→ For details on timing, **see** "Using Transitions to Control Pacing," **p. 760**.

RUNNING A SLIDESHOW

PowerPoint contains an enormous—even overwhelming—variety of options to help you run a slideshow. One piece of advice rises above all others: If you're not sure what to do next during a presentation, right-click the screen. Don't press Escape. Right-click.

The right-click context menu available from the presentation screen gives you instant access to nearly every option you'll ever need to run a slideshow. For example, you can jump to any slide if you know the title; you can move backward, blank the screen, or perform a dozen other important gyrations—even if you don't remember the shortcut key for a particular obscure option. Unless you need to create a new slide in the middle of your presentation (it happens), right-click to steer your way out of trouble.

26

CREATING PRESENTATIONS FOR THE WEB

The fact that web browsers are practically ubiquitous might tempt you to save your PowerPoint presentation as a web page and hit the road with only a browser to make the presentation (for an idea of what the result looks like, see Figure 23.15 in Chapter 23).

In many situations, saving your presentation as a web page is a good idea. Here are some reasons why:

- Internet Explorer is available just about anywhere you go, so you needn't worry whether PowerPoint is installed on the PC you'll use for your presentation.

- Running in a browser in full screen mode—with toolbars and menus hidden—your presentation will look almost the same as if you were using PowerPoint for the show.

- It's a great "Road Warrior" fallback. If your notebook dies suddenly in Denver and you have to give the presentation a few hours later in Orlando, you can easily connect to the Net from another PC and be right back in business.

- The outline shown in the browser (on the left side of Figure 23.15) can actually make presenting easier—although viewers might find it distracting. For example, if you forget which slide contains a specific bullet point, you can expand and collapse the outline dynamically to find the point, and then jump to the slide in question with one click.

But there are also potential problems when you rely on a web server and a browser for your presentation. Consider the following:

- Unless there's a wide communications pipeline straight from your presentation PC to the web server, a browser-based presentation always runs slower than a presentation run in PowerPoint—in some cases, much, much slower. You can reduce this performance penalty by saving the web page to disk and running it from a local drive.

- When you're running in a browser, some of the PowerPoint presentation navigation techniques don't work. Pressing the Enter key and the spacebar doesn't advance slides. Pressing B doesn't blank the screen. And, if you right-click a slide, you get the browser's context menu, not PowerPoint's.

If you decide to use a browser to make your presentation, always practice with the browser you're going to use.

 If you're having problems getting your transition and/or animation effects to display in a web browser, see "Viewing Transition and Animation Effects in a Browser" in the "Troubleshooting" section at the end of this chapter.

Another excellent reason to save a presentation as a web page is to allow your audience to view the presentation at their leisure, without the benefit of your commentary. By posting the results on your website, you can provide ready access to your slideshow without having to worry about whether your audience has PowerPoint installed. If you regularly save presentations as web pages, consider adjusting some of the settings available for this format by choosing Office, PowerPoint Options, clicking Advanced, and then clicking the Web Options button.

In the Web Options dialog box, the options available on the General tab, shown in Figure 26.3, are unique to PowerPoint. (Settings on the other five tabs affect all Office programs.) To eliminate the annoyance of forcing your audience to click several times to see all parts of a slide, for instance, you might want to turn off slide animations by clearing the Show Slide Animation While Browsing box.

Figure 26.3
These options are unique to PowerPoint presentations saved as web pages.

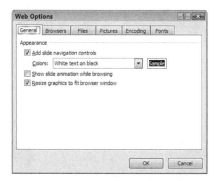

To save a presentation for use on the Web, choose Office, Save As to open the Save As dialog box, select Single File Web Page in the Save as Type list, and then click Save. This option saves your presentation in the Single File Web Page format using the .mht extension. The resulting file can be opened in Internet Explorer 5.0 or later.

SETTING UP A SLIDESHOW

When creating a presentation, you can add a variety of features, including narration, animations, and preset timings. When you deliver the presentation, however, you may be using a different computer than the one you created. In addition, you may want to tweak the settings of the slideshow to match its intended use, especially if someone other than you will be the presenter.

TUNING YOUR PRESENTATION FOR YOUR HARDWARE

When you take your slideshow on the road, you may be asked to use a different computer from the one you're used to. This can cause two problems:

- Performance may suffer if you use demanding transitions and animations. Effects that work well on your top-of-the-line desktop computer may poke along on a computer with a less robust video card, a slower CPU, and insufficient RAM.

- Your carefully drafted design may turn into a crowded, unreadable mess if the video resolution of the presentation machine is significantly less than the computer you used to create the show.

To deal with either of these problems, you need to make some adjustments. Choose Slide Show, Set Up Slide Show. The resulting dialog box (see Figure 26.4) includes several useful options.

26

Figure 26.4
To avoid problems when showing a presentation at a lower resolution, use the options in the Performance box.

Two areas in particular are worth noting here. Consider selecting the Show Without Narration and Show Without Animation check boxes if you notice that the presentation is dragging unacceptably on the presenting machine. If you know that your target machine is going to use a specific resolution—for instance, 800×600—adjust the Slide Show Resolution setting in the Performance box and preview your show *before* you hit the road. If any slides look odd or distorted, you can edit them in advance.

USING TWO MONITORS

If you have dual monitors set up and recognized by the operating system, you can tell PowerPoint to show the presentation on one monitor while you control the presentation in a normal-like view on the other monitor.

NOTE

Hardware requirements for multiple-monitor support in Windows 2000 are extensive: See http://support.microsoft.com/?kbid=238886 for details. Windows XP and Windows Vista build much of this support into the operating system and provide an additional feature called DualView, often used in portable computers and described at http://support.microsoft.com/default.aspx?scid=283674.

The primary monitor, which you use to control the presentation, displays the presentation in Normal view. Alternatively, you can have PowerPoint display "presenter tools," which give you slide thumbnails, buttons for showing the next and previous slide, a timer, speaker notes, and a black-screen button. The secondary monitor shows the usual presentation full screen.

To set up a presentation for dual monitors, choose Slide Show, Set Up Slide Show, and in the Display Slide Show On list (refer to Figure 26.4), select the secondary monitor. If you want "presenter tools" to appear on the primary screen, click the Show Presenter View check box.

USING HIDDEN SLIDES TO ANTICIPATE QUESTIONS

If you anticipate a question and have the answers handy in your presentation notes, your audience will be impressed. If you can cut immediately to a new slide that answers that question, your audience will sit up and take notice.

Hidden slides offer a clever way to prepare for topics that you want to bring up only if someone asks. If you anticipate that someone in your audience might ask a question about slide 4, for example, here's how to be ready with a slide that answers the question:

1. Switch to Slide Sorter view and click after the final slide in the presentation. Click Home, New Slide, and create the slide that will answer the expected question.

2. Double-click to open your new slide in Normal view and add whatever content you need. Then, in an inconspicuous location, add a text box (reading, perhaps, "Back to presentation") or a picture to use as a button to return to the originating slide.

> **TIP FROM**
>
> *EQ & Woody*
>
> If you choose Insert, Shapes and, in the Action Buttons section, select the Return action button, it will achieve the same results as steps 2 and 3 here. The only difference is that you'll end up with the default "return" icon image.

3. Click the picture or text box and select Insert, Action. On the Mouse Click tab of the Action Settings dialog box, click Hyperlink To, and choose Last Slide Viewed from the offered drop-down list. Click OK to save this setting. During the presentation, you'll be able to click this hyperlink and return to the originating slide.

→ For details on action settings, **see** "Advanced Navigation with Action Settings," **p. 730**.

4. Choose Slide Show, Hide Slide. Because the slide is hidden, it never appears in the normal course of a presentation.

5. Return to slide 4 and create a hyperlink to this new, hidden slide. Attach the hyperlink to a small picture or piece of text—anything that will jog your memory without alerting your audience that you've prepared a "hidden" answer to a specific question.

→ For more about hyperlinks inside PowerPoint, **see** "Using Hyperlinks," **p. 730**.

When you deliver the presentation, if a member of the audience asks the question, click the hyperlink, discuss the issues on the hidden slide, and then click the "Back to presentation" button at the bottom of the hidden slide to return to the main presentation. To see this hidden slide technique in action, see "Secrets of the Office Masters: Anticipating Questions with Hidden Slides" at the end of this chapter.

> **TIP FROM**
>
> *EQ & Woody*
>
> You can use the same technique if the answer to a question requires more than one slide. Instead of creating a hyperlink that jumps to a specific slide, however, create one that jumps to a custom presentation. You can branch back from the end of the custom presentation with yet another hyperlink that's specifically tied to the originating slide—just remember to use it during the presentation!

26

Hidden slides are marked in Slide Sorter view and in the Slides navigation pane with a slash through the slide number. In the Hyperlink dialog box, you can spot hidden slides by looking for those that have the slide number in parentheses.

→ For more on custom shows, **see** "Creating a Presentation," **p. 706**.

PACKAGING A PRESENTATION FOR USE ON OTHER COMPUTERS

A presentation doesn't always require a stand-up presentation. Sometimes, in fact, a carefully crafted presentation can literally deliver itself. If you've created a PowerPoint presentation that you want to use as a calling card for your company or its products and services, you can tie the pieces of the presentation into a tidy package and copy it to a CD using the Package for CD feature.

Packaging a presentation involves three steps:

1. Select the files you want to include on the CD. You can include multiple presentations and add supporting files, such as embedded TrueType fonts and music or video clips.

2. Adjust any or all of the following options:
   - Specify whether you want the presentation to play automatically (AutoRun) when inserted into a Windows computer.
   - Decide whether you want to include the PowerPoint Viewer.
   - Password-protect confidential presentation files so that only authorized users can open or edit the files. The PowerPoint Viewer will prompt for an Open or Modify password based on the options you select.

3. Save the package. Using Windows XP or Vista, you can save directly to a compatible CD burner. With Windows 2000, you have to save the results to a folder and then use a third-party program to burn the saved folder to a CD.

TIP FROM

> Using the Package for CD feature is an effective way to archive presentations for safe-keeping. A single CD can easily contain more than 100 typical presentations. If you use CDs as an archive medium, you needn't include the PowerPoint Viewer, and you can turn off AutoRun as well.

A saved presentation delivered through the PowerPoint Viewer looks exactly as it would if you were to present the slideshow from PowerPoint. Transitions, animations, navigation techniques, and other features are unchanged. You can't add annotations, of course, and making any changes requires that you open the presentation in PowerPoint and save the changed file to a new CD.

SAVING A PRESENTATION ON A CD

After you've polished your presentation to a high gloss and you're satisfied with its content and design, you can copy it to a CD using the following steps:

1. With the presentation open in PowerPoint, choose Office, Publish, Package for CD.

2. PowerPoint will likely display a dialog box telling you that your presentation package will be updated to include the various PowerPoint 97-2003 file formats. Click OK. The Package for CD dialog box appears, as shown in Figure 26.5.

Figure 26.5
Use this dialog to package your presentation on a CD.

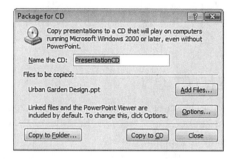

3. Change the default name in the Name the CD box. Although this step is optional, we recommend that you do so to make it easier to identify the CD when you open it using the My Computer window (or the Computer window in Vista). The name you enter must be 16 characters or fewer.

4. The current presentation is included by default and cannot be removed. To include other files on the CD (such as additional presentations or supporting media clips), click the Add Files button and use the Add Files dialog box to select the files.

5. Click the Options button and adjust any of the options shown in Figure 26.6. By default, the PowerPoint Viewer is included, all presentations are played automatically, and passwords are left blank. This is your opportunity to add, open, or modify passwords. Click OK.

Figure 26.6
Choose options for your packaged presentation.

26

6. After inserting a blank CD into your CD-R or CD-RW drive, click Copy to CD to begin recording. If you're using Windows 2000, or if your computer does not include a compatible CD burner, click Copy to Folder instead, choose a name and location for the saved folder, and click OK. You can burn the saved folder to a CD later.

USING THE POWERPOINT VIEWER

When you use the AutoRun option on a CD-based presentation, it should require no effort from the intended audience beyond inserting the CD into the appropriate drive. If the person who created a CD chose not to use the AutoRun option, or if AutoRun is disabled on the target computer, open the CD in Windows Explorer, double-click the PPTVIEW icon, and choose the saved presentation from the Open dialog box, which appears automatically when the Viewer opens.

PRINTING YOUR PRESENTATION

Eventually, you'll want to print out a presentation. Print options let you generate speaker notes for you, handouts for your audience, and copies of the slides for you to study and revise while you're sitting on a plane or stuck in traffic.

CHOOSING WHICH ELEMENTS TO PRINT

When you choose Office, Print, PowerPoint opens the Print dialog box, shown in Figure 26.7. Several of the options shown here are unique to PowerPoint and allow you to exercise excellent control over printed pages.

Figure 26.7
Although many Print options are common to all Office programs, those at the bottom of this dialog box are unique to PowerPoint.

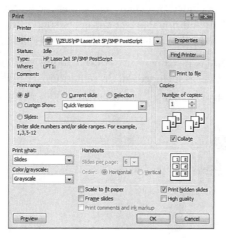

CAUTION

Avoid the Quick Print button in the Office, Print menu unless you're absolutely certain you want to send your entire presentation to the default printer using current settings. If you have any doubts, press Ctrl+P instead, or select Office, Print.

The Print What box offers four choices, as shown in Table 26.1.

TABLE 26.1   PRINTING OPTIONS

Print What	Means
Slides	One slide per page, portrait, the slide fills up the whole page
Handouts	Multiple slides per page, based on the number in the Slides Per Page box, formatted according to the Handout Master that has the same number of slides per page
Notes Pages	One slide per page, formatted according to the Notes Master
Outline View	No slides, only outline text, formatted according to the Outline setting on the Handout Master

→ For details on notes and handouts formatting, **see** "Creating Speaker Notes and Audience Handouts," **p. 745**.

TIP FROM

Ed & Woody

Before sending a long presentation to a color printer, click the Preview button on the Print dialog box. This gives you one last opportunity to look over the proposed printed output and make sure that your color copies will turn out as you expect.

PREPARING A COLOR PRESENTATION FOR A BLACK-AND-WHITE PRINTER

When you print PowerPoint slides on a black-and-white printer, you might be disappointed at the way Windows translates color to black-and-white pages. Shadowing in graphs loses much of its definition. All but the lightest backgrounds completely obliterate any nuances in the foreground—to the point of obscuring text, in many cases.

For the best-quality printed output, use PowerPoint's built-in grayscale converter, which is optimized for the colors in presentation designs. By taking liberties with your slides—converting dark backgrounds to light when needed, for example—it produces extremely readable black-and-white output.

To preview what your slides look like when viewed through this special grayscale converter, choose View, Grayscale. You'll be sent into Grayscale View, with a Grayscale tab that lets you tweak the grayscale settings.

You can also see how your slides will look by using PowerPoint's Print Preview: Just pull down the Office menu, display the Print menu, and then choose Print Preview.

To print using the Grayscale converter, click the Print button while in Print Preview, or choose Office, Print, and select the Grayscale option in the Color/Grayscale list.

TURNING A PRESENTATION INTO 35MM SLIDES

Given a choice, few people want to deliver a presentation with 35mm slides—they're expensive, bulky, get smudged and rearranged too easily, and heaven help you if you dump the carousel on your way to the big show. Sometimes, however, you have no choice. That's when PowerPoint's fast and easy online connections can make a huge difference.

26

Many service bureaus around the world now accept PowerPoint files and turn them into 35mm slides. If the service bureau accepts files via email, the process is as easy as choosing Office, Send, Email.

The original PowerPoint service bureau, Genigraphics, is still going strong. They can have your slides back to you first thing in the morning—and arrange to have an InFocus projector sent to just about any site in North America, in about the same amount of time. See www.genigraphics.com for details, or check with your favorite web search engine for the words "PowerPoint slides overnight."

TROUBLESHOOTING

VIEWING TRANSITION AND ANIMATION EFFECTS IN A BROWSER

I've added transitions and animation effects to my slides, but they don't appear when I view my presentation in a web browser.

If none of your transition or animation effects appear in the browser, open the presentation and choose Office, PowerPoint Options. Click Advanced and then click the Web Options button. On the General tab of the Web Options dialog box, select the Show Slide Animation While Browsing check box. Click OK to close each dialog box, and save your presentation.

SECRETS OF THE OFFICE MASTERS: ANTICIPATING QUESTIONS WITH HIDDEN SLIDES

If you can anticipate a question from your audience, you'll be miles ahead if you have a slide ready to answer it. For example, this slide (see Figure 26.8) might elicit the question, "How are the gardening zones distributed across the country?"

Figure 26.8
What kinds of questions might your viewers have about your slides?

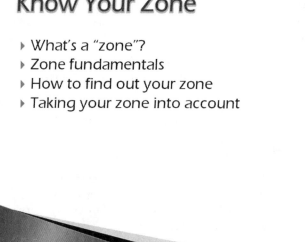

In anticipation of the question, you could construct a slide like the one shown next, and place it in the presentation immediately after the first slide. Hide the slide (Slide Show, Hide Slide), add an action button to the first slide (see the question mark button in Figure 26.8) that jumps to the hidden slide (see Figure 26.9), and add an action button to the hidden slide that returns to the last slide viewed.

→ For details on linking to a hidden slide and returning to the main presentation, **see** "Using Hidden Slides to Anticipate Questions," **p. 787**.

Figure 26.9
You'll dazzle your audience and have answers to common questions already on slides tucked up your sleeve.

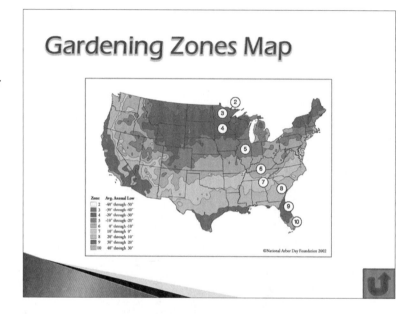

By constructing the presentation in this way, if someone asks the question, "How are the gardening zones distributed across the country?," you can click the question mark icon, give the answer, and continue with your presentation. If nobody asks the question, you don't click the question mark icon, and the presentation proceeds normally—the second slide will never appear.

26

OTHER OFFICE APPLICATIONS

27 Publisher Essentials   797

28 Access Essentials   835

29 Using OneNote   879

30 Using Office 2007 on a Corporate Network   907

CHAPTER 27

PUBLISHER ESSENTIALS

In this chapter

What's New in Publisher 2007   798

What Can You Do with Publisher?   798

Creating and Customizing a New Publication   799

Managing Your Publication's Layout   810

Working with Text   815

Inserting Images   819

Using Tables as a Page Layout Tool   820

Customizing Publisher Options   823

Using the Design Gallery   825

Using the Content Library   826

Using Master Pages   827

Printing a Publication   830

Troubleshooting   833

Secrets of the Office Masters: Good Design Principles   833

WHAT'S NEW IN PUBLISHER 2007

Although it's more than 15 years old, Microsoft Publisher has only recently earned grudging respect from Office users. For years, it was stereotyped as "desktop publishing with training wheels," and serious page designers shunned Publisher in favor of big, expensive, complex programs such as Adobe's PageMaker for their projects. Publisher 2003 went a long way toward eliminating that image, with a rich set of design tools that you could use to build sophisticated publications for print or online use. Publisher 2007 builds on this solid base by adding a few significant new features:

- You can easily reuse objects such as images, shapes, text, text boxes, tables, and Word Art using the new Content Library.

- When you enter your business or personal information in Publisher 2007, the program not only applies this data to every template (as did Publisher 2003), but it also shows the data when you preview the templates. This enables you to see a template with your data applied before selecting that template.

- You can customize a template before you select it. When you are previewing templates, Publisher 2007 enables you to customize the color scheme, font scheme, and page orientation so that you can see exactly what the template looks like when you select these options. If you have multiple sets of business information defined, you can also select which set Publisher should apply to the template preview.

- You can search through Publisher's hundreds of template to make it easier to find the one you want.

- You can apply categories to your custom templates, and Publisher uses those categories to organize the templates in the My Templates section.

- A new task pane called Publisher Tasks offers links to common Publisher features.

- You can convert publications to the PDF or XPS file format.

- Publisher 2007 comes with an enhanced Design Checker that identifies and fixes more design errors.

- Publisher 2007 supports bookmarks that work basically the same as they do in Word.

Note, too, that Publisher 2007 does *not* have the new Ribbon interface that comes with Word, Excel, PowerPoint, Access, and the Outlook message window. The task panes are bit better organized, but otherwise you get the same menu-and-toolbar interface that came with Publisher 2003.

WHAT CAN YOU DO WITH PUBLISHER?

Microsoft Publisher is a desktop publishing program that also does web pages and HTML-formatted email. Its design tools let you precisely place images and text on a page to create an attractive publication. Although you can create similar-looking documents using Microsoft Word, in general, you'll find more sophisticated page-layout tools in a desktop publishing (DTP) program, and you'll also find it easier to send the finished product to a commercial printer. Unlike Word, which is geared toward producing standard business documents on letter-sized paper, Publisher offers a diverse assortment of predesigned publications in all shapes and sizes, from business cards to newsletters, with CD and DVD labels, greeting cards, and flyers thrown in for good measure.

Publisher's professional printing tools allow you to manage color in publications destined to be printed commercially. Using these designs can save you the time it would take to create them yourself. Publisher also provides DTP tools such as baseline guides for lining up text on the page—a subtle feature that defines professional publications.

Publisher is also an effective tool for building a simple website of six to ten pages, especially when your goal is to tie its look to printed marketing and sales materials. For more complex websites, however, you are better off with a dedicated website authoring tool such as Macromedia Dreamweaver or Adobe GoLive.

CREATING AND CUSTOMIZING A NEW PUBLICATION

When creating a new publication, you're faced with a number of choices—do you use one of the predesigned publications or create one from scratch using your own design? Although Publisher's templates make it easy to quick-start a publication, if your business already has a certain look to its publications, you will probably choose to design the publication from scratch so that its design complements your existing publications. If you created a publication previously in Publisher, and now need to create something similar, consider using the previous publication as the basis for the new one, to save time. In this section, we look at your options for creating a publication and step you through the basics of getting up and running with Publisher.

STARTING WITH A PUBLISHER TEMPLATE

Publisher contains a number of professionally designed publications to get you started with typical tasks. These look attractive and are a good starting point if you're unfamiliar with designing your own publications; however, they also carry the risk of all "mass produced" templates, which is that your brochure or website will look exactly like someone else's. Even though Publisher contains dozens of master design sets and several thousand individual designs, the popularity of the program means that you (and your customers) will see many of these designs in use by other businesses.

However, Publisher templates have a lot to offer. They are neat and functional, with predesigned layouts containing placeholders where you can insert your company logo, text, and images. If you're new to designing publications, you can be reasonably confident that the graphic design follows professional principles and that your publication contains all the elements commonly needed in a particular type of publication. There's little chance you'll forget to add your fax number to your business card, for example.

When choosing a design template, focus first on the fundamental layout and positioning on the page—try to look past colors and background graphics, because you can easily change these design elements later. Choose File, New to display the New Publication window

27

(see Figure 27.1). This window is divided into three sections. On the left, Publisher displays the design templates grouped into a number of categories; in the middle, Publisher displays the subcategories associated with the currently selected category, as well as thumbnails for the designs within each subcategory; on the right, Publisher displays a preview of the currently selected design thumbnail, as well as controls to customize the design.

Figure 27.1
The New Publication window shows categories and subcategories of publications; contents of the currently selected subcategory appear on the right.

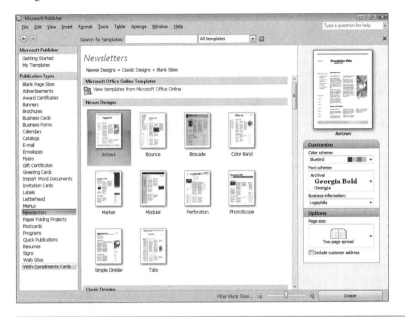

TIP FROM

EQ & Woody

In general, you should choose one set and stick with it for all your publications. This ensures that you create a single look for the publications across your organization and helps define the visual identity of your business.

The number of publications in each design set varies. Before settling on a design, make a checklist of the type of publications you need, and then look for a design set that includes most or all of these publications.

There is also a set of publications called Blank Page Sizes that, although empty, include the typical page dimensions and margin guides for the type of publication you select (advertisement, business card, and so on). If you're creating a publication from scratch and you're comfortable with Publisher's design tools, you can use one of these templates to quickly create new, blank pages with the correct size and margins.

To create a new publication, from the New Publication window, choose the type of publication. Under each thumbnail in the Catalog is the name of the design set to which this publication belongs. When you click a thumbnail, a preview appears on the right side of the window.

Use the controls in the Customize section to change the Color Scheme, Font Scheme, and Business Information you want to include. If you're satisfied with the design, click Create. Publisher creates the new publication and displays it in the Publisher window. The publication shown in Figure 27.2 is an Informational brochure using the Bubbles design set.

→ For instructions on how to enter your business information, **see** "Customizing Business Information," **p. 823**.

Figure 27.2
This Informational brochure uses the Bubbles design–the Format Publication task pane, on the left, appears after you create the publication.

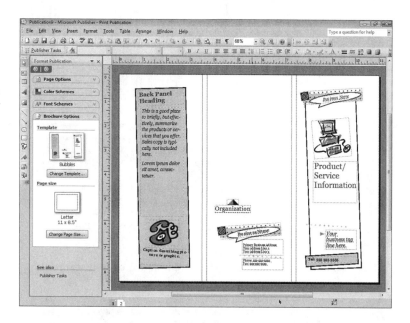

After you create a new publication, the Format Publication task pane opens, and it includes a section related to the publication type. In the Informational Brochure example shown earlier in Figure 27.2, you see the Brochure Options section, which enables you to change the template and page size.

Click the Change Template button to access the design sets available for this publication type. You can select a different design, change the options for the current design, or both. Changing the design does not remove any changes you made to the content or layout of the publication. Figure 27.3, for instance, shows the results after we changed the brochure to a four-panel layout and changed to the Checkers design.

Click the Color Schemes option to view the predesigned color schemes available and alter the colors in the publication.

27

Figure 27.3
Click Change Template to change the design set used for a publication without losing layout or content changes.

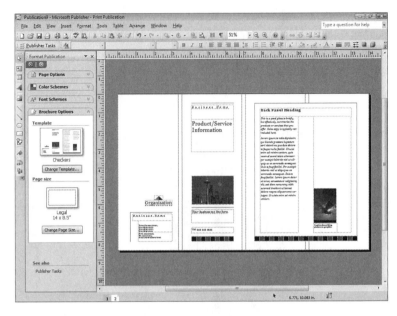

→ For instructions on how to create your own custom color scheme, **see** "Creating Custom Color Schemes," **p. 824**.

Click the Font Schemes option to view predesigned combinations of fonts that you can apply to your publication (see Figure 27.4).

Figure 27.4
The Font Schemes task pane lets you choose any one of a combination of fonts that work well together.

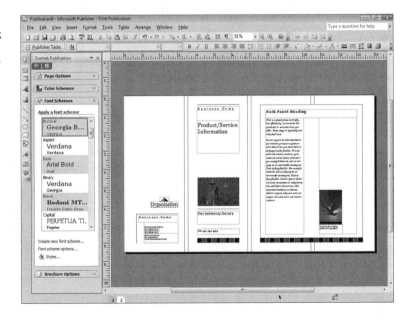

CREATING A PUBLICATION FROM SCRATCH

When you create a publication from scratch, you can customize the publication to your exact requirements. Use this option, too, when you want to create a publication that uses an unusual page size not included in the standard templates.

To create a publication from scratch, choose File, New and then choose your preferred publication type from the Blank Page Sizes category options (see Figure 27.5).

Figure 27.5
Use the Blank Page Sizes category to quickly create a custom publication.

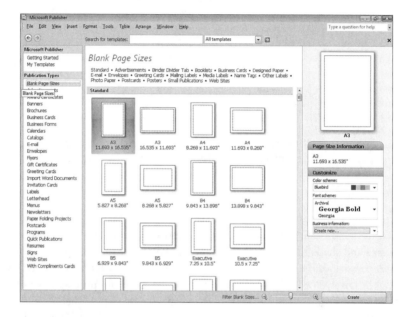

All Publisher publications include a page size and a paper size; these two settings can be different—for instance, when you're planning to print a publication on paper that you will then trim to the correct size. The page size is the size of the actual publication you are working on—for example, the page size for a business card is 3.5"×2". The paper size is the size of the sheet of paper you're printing on. In most cases, the page size cannot be larger than the paper size (printing a banner is an exception to this rule). Set the page and paper sizes by choosing File, Page Setup. Choose a Publication type, such as Business Card, and then a Page size, such as 3.5"×2" (see Figure 27.6).

27

Figure 27.6
Use this window to set the dimensions of the actual publication you are working on.

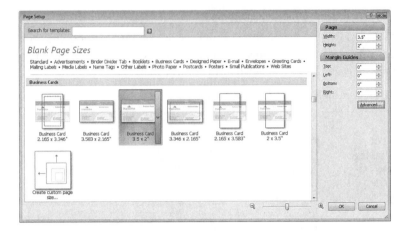

TIP FROM

Ed & Woody

If you don't find the exact size you're looking for, click Create Custom Page Size and use the Custom Page Size dialog box to enter the dimensions.

Choosing a publication type doesn't force you to create that type of publication. For a layout that doesn't fit one of the ready-made categories, choose a publication type that looks close in size and shape to the publication you're planning. For most publication types, you can alter the size of the publication by typing your own measurements into the Width and Height boxes. For business cards, index cards, labels, and postcards, you can also change how many copies of the publication print on a single sheet: Click the Advanced button and adjust the settings in the Custom Page Size dialog box. You will still only have one publication to create, but you can print multiple copies of it on a single sheet of paper.

TIP FROM

Ed & Woody

To print business cards on purchased preperforated stock, set up the publication as a label and choose the stock number from the list. If the stock number isn't in the list, choose one that's close in size, click the Create Custom Page Size option, and adjust the measurements to suit.

CAUTION

When using Avery label stock, open the Avery A4/A5 branch and choose the stock number. Don't click Advanced unless you're sure you need to make changes. The predefined settings are designed to work with these custom papers. Print a test copy first using plain paper and compare the test copy to the custom paper. Alter the settings only if the labels don't print in the correct positions.

For printing options, select File, Print Setup to open the Print Setup dialog box (see Figure 27.7) to select the paper size from the Size drop-down list. Although you can also choose between Portrait or Landscape orientation, doing so may impact the settings you have already chosen in the Page Setup dialog box.

Figure 27.7
Use the Print Setup dialog box to specify the actual size and orientation of the paper you are printing on.

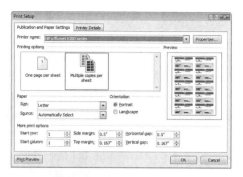

CREATING A CUSTOM TEMPLATE

A Publishertemplate contains the basic layout and text that defines a particular type of publication. You should create your own custom template whenever you regularly produce a specific type of publication. For example, if you produce a weekly or monthly company newsletter, you can cut your workload tremendously by using a Publisher template that contains your newsletter masthead, boilerplate text, and boxes for standing sections in the newsletter—your lead article, a Q&A section, and ads, for example. Starting with a saved template ensures that your layout is consistent each time you produce your newsletter. To save a publication as a template, follow these steps:

1. Choose File, Save As.

2. In the Save As dialog box, type the name of the publication into the File Name box and choose Publisher Template (*.pub) from the Save as Type list.

3. Click Change and type or select a category; it's a good idea to categorize your templates. Click OK.

4. Click Save to save the template.

Note that Publisher automatically saves your new template in the default Templates folder so that it is always available in the New Publication window.

To use a saved template as the starting point for a new publication, choose File, New. In the New Publication window, click the My Templates category and select your saved template.

You can also create a new publication from an existing publication. In the New Publication window, select Getting Started and then select From File. In the Open Publication dialog box, choose a document (such as a Word document or a Publisher publication) as the basis for your new publication; click Open to open a new publication that contains the same content, layout, and design as the one you selected. The new file will be given a generic name (Publication1, Publication2, Publication3, and so forth) so that you don't inadvertently overwrite the original publication.

TIP FROM

E Q & Woody

When you save a publication as a template, it may not appear immediately in the New Publication window. Try closing Publisher and reopening it to refresh this list.

CREATING SIMPLE WEB PAGES AND SITES

The simplest way to create a website in Publisher is to do it by the numbers—specifically, with the new Easy Web Site Builder. This wizard lets you build a site page by page from a large menu of generic pages designed to contain specific types of information.

To create a site using the Easy Web Site Builder, choose File, New. Choose the Web Sites category, choose the design you want, and make sure the Use Easy Web Wizard check box is activated.

Note, too, that the Options section includes a Navigation Bar list, which allows you to automatically update selected pages on your site with a menu containing links to other pages. You can choose the placement of the Navigation bar (along the left side of every page and along the bottom, for instance); you can also choose which pages appear on the Navigation bar.

When you're ready to proceed, click Create to launch the wizard. The opening dialog box prompts you for your site goals (see Figure 27.8). By default, only a home page is included. Select any combination of options from this list to indicate which pages you want in your new website. When you're done, click OK to create the selected pages and begin customizing.

Figure 27.8
The Easy Web Site Builder lets you create pages from a standard menu.

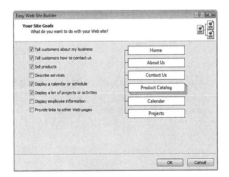

To add pages to an existing website, choose Insert, Page, and choose the page type from the list displayed (see Figure 27.9). The preview on the right of the dialog box shows you roughly what the page will look like. Select the Add Hyperlink to Navigation Bars check box to include a link to the newly added page from the main navigation area—if you don't select this option, you'll need to link this page to other pages manually later on.

Don't be confused by the More button—it lets you choose to insert a different type of page (rather than select more options for the current page type, as you might expect). When you click the More button, the Insert Page dialog box appears (see Figure 27.10), from which you can choose to insert a blank page or pages before or after the current page. You can also include one text box on each inserted page or duplicate all the objects from another page. If you select this dialog box by accident, click Cancel to return to the Insert Page dialog box and make your choice from there.

Figure 27.9
After creating a website, choose from this extensive list of prebuilt pages to expand the site.

Figure 27.10
Clicking the More button in the Insert Page dialog box allows you to add one or more simple pages to your site.

To change the text within the Navigation bar, you can click and edit directly, or select the Navigation bar and choose Format, Navigation Bar Properties. In the Links list, select the menu choice you want to alter and click Modify Link. In the Modify Link dialog box (see Figure 27.11), click in the Text to Display area and change the text to what should appear on the Navigation bar for this page. Optionally, click Change Title to alter the page's title—this text will ultimately be displayed in the browser's title bar when the page is being viewed.

NOTE

A page title becomes the name of the page when you publish your site to the Web. You can rename any page from the Navigation Bar Properties dialog box; alternatively, you can select the page, choose Tools, Web Page Options, and type a name into the Page Title text area. You cannot, however, rename the home page this way, because this page is named when you publish the site.

27

Figure 27.11
The text in the box at the top of this dialog box appears in the Navigation bar, which need not be the same as the page title.

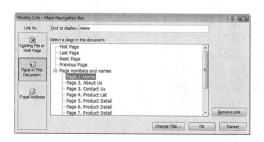

To alter the way the Navigation bar looks, click anywhere within the bar; then click the Navigation Bar button in the Web Tools toolbar. In the Navigation Bars section of the Design Gallery, you can choose an alternative orientation for your Navigation bar and a different design for the buttons.

Navigation bars are the best way to allow visitors to move from page to page within your site. Use hyperlinks to allow your visitor to move to pages outside your site. For example, you might use these on a related links page to list other resources of interest to your visitors.

→ For more details on how to add and edit hyperlinks, **see** "Working with Hyperlinks," **p. 98**.

To alter the page background, click Format, Background to display the Background task pane (shown in Figure 27.12)—scroll through the list of available tints, gradients, textures, and picture fills to choose an appropriate background. Note that it is good design practice to use the same background for all pages on your site, an option that's available when you click the drop-down arrow to the right of the background selection.

Figure 27.12
To use a tint as a background, choose a color from the Apply a Background bar first.

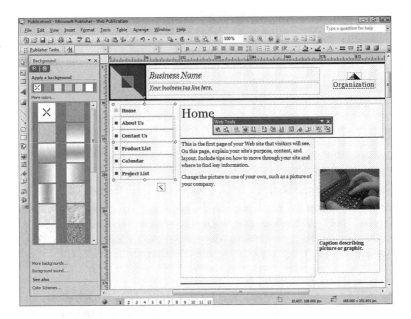

The Background task pane also lets you assign a sound file to your page. You can choose from a range of sound file formats; the sound file plays when the page loads. So as not to overwhelm your visitors, avoid large WAV files, and play a sound only once, unless you have a good reason to play it multiple times.

To check how your website will look when displayed on the Web, click the Web Page Preview button on the Web Tools toolbar or choose Preview Your Web Site from the Web Site Options section of the Format Publication task pane. Your browser will open with the website displayed for you to check. Check each link, proof every page, and ensure that forms and other input areas not only look good, but all work as they should.

When your website is complete, you should save it first as a Publisher file (so you can edit it later on). You can then publish it to a web server (if you don't manage your own web server, you'll need to set up an account with a Web-hosting service first). To publish your site, choose File, Publish to the Web.

Your Web hosting service should have told you how to best upload your files to your server. For a site that supports WebDAV, FrontPage Extensions, or Windows SharePoint Services, you can publish to your site directly. You can also save the files to a local folder and then use File Transfer Protocol (FTP) to transfer the files to your server.

Publisher also has an incremental Publish to the Web feature that updates only pages that have been changed since the last update. This option is enabled by default and, in most cases, you can leave it enabled. There is an exception to this; if you make changes to your website using a program other than Publisher, disable this option because it may otherwise prevent you from uploading changes to your site that you make using Publisher. To disable incremental publishing, choose Tools, Options, click the Web tab, and clear the Enable Incremental Publish to the Web check box, as shown in Figure 27.13.

Figure 27.13
Adjust options in the saving area to avoid compatibility problems.

If you are unsure of what name to use for your site's home page, check with your Web-hosting service provider. Typical default home page names include index.html and default.htm; the correct choices for your site vary according to the type of web server software your hosting company runs. If you use the correct page name, your visitors can display your home page by typing a simple URL (www.*example*.com) rather than a complex URL that includes a page name (www.*example*.com/index.htm).

27

USING PUBLISHER AND WORD TOGETHER

Publisher contains superb page-layout tools. Microsoft Word does a bang-up job at text editing. Using the two programs together can leverage these complementary strengths to make some publishing tasks easier. For example, when you are working on a publication where you must consult with other people, consider creating the text of each story in Microsoft Word, using its revision-tracking features to keep changes under control. This frees you to concentrate on the text and saves you from having to continually rework your publication's layout to account for changes. Meanwhile, put dummy text and images into your Publisher publication and pass it around for approval of the overall publication design. When your content is settled, import the text into text boxes in Publisher to replace the dummy text.

To import text into Publisher text boxes:

1. Click the text box.
2. Select the dummy text, and choose Insert, Text File.
3. Then browse to locate the Word file containing the text.
4. Click OK to add the finished text to the publication.

You can also work with Microsoft Word from inside Publisher to edit a Publisher story. To do this:

1. Right-click a text frame that contains the text to edit and choose the Change Text option.
2. Select Edit Story in Microsoft Word and Word will open with the Publisher story displayed.
3. You can use Word's tools to edit the text.
4. When you are done editing the text, choose Office, Close and Return to *<publication name>* to close Word and return to Publisher with the changed text in place.

Microsoft Publisher can also help you format a Word document using one of its design sets. To use the Microsoft Publisher Word Document wizard:

1. Choose File, New, and from the New Publication task pane, click the Import Word Documents category.
2. From the Preview gallery, click a design and then click Create.
3. When the Import Word Document dialog box appears, select your document and click OK.
4. The Format Publication task pane offers options for formatting your Word document similar to those available for other types of publications.

MANAGING YOUR PUBLICATION'S LAYOUT

To speed up your work, learn how to move quickly around a Publisher publication and how to take advantage of its tools for adjusting the placement of images and text on your page with a high degree of accuracy.

ZOOMING AND MOVING AROUND YOUR PUBLICATION

Publisher provides a Zoom drop-down list on the Standard toolbar to help you see more or less of a page on your screen. (The same choices are available by choosing View, Zoom.) Settings vary from 10% up to 800%, as well as Whole Page and Page Width. If you select one or more objects before displaying the Zoom menu, you can choose Selected Objects to zoom to display it. Zoom In and Zoom Out buttons also appear on the Standard toolbar; each click zooms in or out to the next available percentage in the Zoom list. Toggle between the current view and the full-page view by clicking the F9 button. If your mouse includes a wheel, hold the Ctrl key as you rotate the wheel to zoom in and out of your publication.

When working on a slow computer, zoom faster by choosing View, Pictures. In the Picture Display dialog box (see Figure 27.14), choose Fast Resize and Zoom to display a lower-quality image on the screen. Note that the image will still print at regular quality. Alternatively, choose the Hide Pictures option to disable picture display.

Figure 27.14
Picture Display options let you speed up viewing of graphic-intensive documents on slower computers.

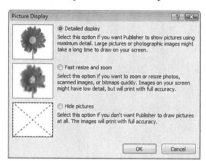

To move to another page in your publication, click the page number in the page sorter in the status bar of the screen to move to that page. If you're viewing anything but the first or last pages of the publication and if it is set to Two-Page Spread view, you'll see two pages at a time. Toggle this view by choosing View, Two-Page Spread. For long publications, you can move to another page by choosing Edit, Go to Page (or by using the keyboard shortcut Ctrl+G); type the page number into the dialog box and click OK.

TIP FROM

Don't ignore the right-click menus on these page numbers, either. Using the shortcut menu, you can add, delete, move, or duplicate pages; create new sections; apply a Master Page to the selection; or toggle Two-Page Spread view.

GROUPING, SELECTING, AND MOVING OBJECTS

Publisher offers a picture selection tool that lets you more easily select an object placed under a text box.

- To select any object, hold your mouse over it and click. If the object is part of a group, click once to select the group, pause, and then click again to select the object within the group.
- You can also click any object and then press the Tab key to move selectively from one object to the next down the page (Shift+Tab moves up the page).
- To select multiple objects, hold the Shift key as you click each object in succession, or click the Select Objects button on the Objects toolbar and drag over the objects to select them.

- When moving a number of objects or when you need to size them all relative to each other, group the objects. To do this, select all the objects to group and then choose Arrange, Group, or click the Group Objects button, which appears under the selected objects. Use Arrange, Ungroup or click the Ungroup Objects button to undo this grouping.

- To move objects in small increments, use the Arrange, Nudge options to nudge them a preset distance. Tear off this menu to create it as a toolbar so it's handy to use.

- To view and alter the exact size and placement of objects, use the Measurement toolbar by selecting View, Toolbars, Measurement (see Figure 27.15).

Figure 27.15
The Measurement toolbar lets you view and type exact measurements to adjust the size and location of objects on your page.

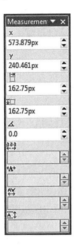

USING OTHER VIEW OPTIONS

While the margins and text box boundaries on the screen help you see where various elements are positioned, they can clutter the screen. Toggle the display of these by choosing View, Boundaries and Guides. Similarly, choosing View, Baseline Guides lets you enable or disable display of vertical and horizontal baseline guides.

SETTING UP AND USING GUIDES

Layout guides help you align objects on your page. When you align objects with each other, the page looks more professional. By default, all publications contain, at the very least, margin guides, which appear as blue lines around the page. These delineate the margins of the page, and most content should appear inside them.

To adjust these margins, choose Arrange, Layout Guides; on the Margin Guides tab (see Figure 27.16), set the Left, Right (or Inside and Outside for a two-page spread), Top, and Bottom margins to your preferred values. You can also alter these guides using your mouse: Choose View, Master Page, and drag each guide to a new position. Click Close Master View on the Edit Master Pages toolbar (or choose View, Master View, or press Ctrl+M) to return to your publication.

Figure 27.16
In the Layout Guides dialog box, use the Margin Guides tab to set the position of the margin guides for your publication.

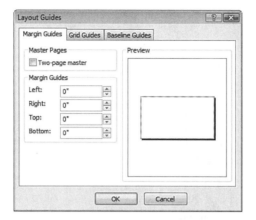

Publisher includes other guides you can use to align objects on the page, such as column and row guides, ruler guides, and the baseline guides. Margin, column, and row guides are blue; baseline guides are gold; and ruler guides are green. Use column and row guides to divide the page into two or more columns or rows.

To create a column or row guide:

1. Choose Arrange, Layout Guides.
2. On the Grid Guides tab, select the number of columns or rows to create.
3. If you want space between the rows or columns, set a value in the Spacing area. A spacing of zero butts the guides up against each other, and a larger spacing creates a gutter between each set of columns or rows. (See Figure 27.17.)
4. To help you line up objects, select the Add Center Guide Between Columns and Rows check box. Unlike ruler guides, row and column guides are applied to the Master Page, by default, and appear on all pages of your publication.
5. To create asymmetrical row or column guides, choose View, Master Page and adjust the placement of the guides using your mouse.
6. Click Close Master View to continue.

Use ruler guides to line up objects on a single page or on all pages of a publication. To create a horizontal ruler guide, hold your mouse over the horizontal ruler at the top of the screen and, when it changes to an adjust pointer, click and drag a ruler guide onto your publication. Vertical ruler guides are created similarly starting with the vertical ruler along the left of the page. If the rulers aren't visible, choose View, Rulers to display them.

To remove a ruler guide, hold your mouse over it until the adjust pointer appears, right-click, and choose Delete Guide.

To remove all ruler guides, choose Arrange, Ruler Guides, Clear All Ruler Guides. By default, ruler guides appear on the page you created them on. To apply them to all pages in the publication, create them on the master page.

27

Figure 27.17
This publication displays margin guides around the outside and a set of row and column guides. The column guides have a gutter between them and a center guide to help line up objects.

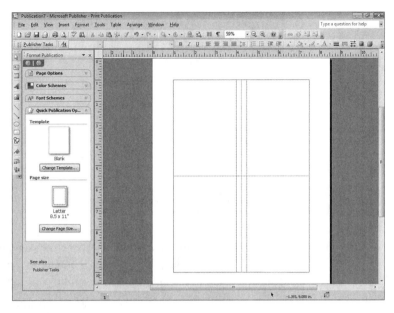

Publisher guides are most useful when objects automatically line up to them. To snap objects to a ruler guide, choose Arrange, Snap, To Ruler Marks; to snap to other guides, choose the To Guides option. When you choose either of these options, creating or moving an object will snap the object into position to the nearest guide.

Baseline guides are used to position text so that the baseline of text in one column lines up with the baseline of text in an adjacent column. To add a baseline guide, choose Arrange, Layout Guides, Baseline Guides and set the spacing and offset for your baselines. Although you can create horizontal and vertical baselines, horizontal ones are most useful. Baseline guides work best where the baseline guides spacing is the same as or larger than the line spacing of your text; so, for an 11-point font, set the baseline to 13 points or more. To align text to the baselines, select the text and choose Format, Paragraph; on the Indents and Spacing tab, under the Line Spacing heading, select the Align Text to Baseline Guides check box.

TIP FROM

EQ & Woody

Do you want to align the bottom line of text in a text box along the bottom margin of your page? Make the distance between your top and bottom margin guides a multiple of the baseline guides measure.

TIP FROM

EQ & Woody

The default unit of measure is pixels; this can be altered by choosing Tools, Options, the General tab, and selecting an alternative from the Measurement Units drop-down list. Choose from inches, centimeters, picas, points, and pixels. To enter a measurement in any dialog box regardless of the current default unit of measure, add the appropriate suffix to the measurement. Use cm for centimeters, in for inches, pt for points, pi for picas, and px for pixels.

WORKING WITH TEXT

Publisher handles text differently from Microsoft Word. Unlike Word, which includes a text layer as its primary editing area, Publisher requires that all text be placed inside a text box on the page. This allows the text to be isolated from other objects and to be moved easily.

LAYING OUT TEXT

To create a text box, click the Text Box button on the Objects toolbar (or choose Insert, Text Box) and then click and drag to draw a text box on the page. After you create the text box, Publisher positions the insertion point inside the text box so that you can immediately start typing your text. To alter the margins of a text box, click the text box and choose Format, Text Box. Click the Text Box tab (see Figure 27.18) to adjust vertical alignment, margins, and autofitting. The Left, Right, Top, and Bottom settings under Text Box Margins control the amount by which text is inset from the outside margins of the text box.

Figure 27.18
Adjust margins to control how close text appears to the outside border of a text box.

When you have more text than will fit in a Text Box, a Text In Overflow icon appears just under the bottom-right margin of the text box. You have a number of choices when this appears:

- Reduce the font size of the text in the text box so that all available text fits in the box.
- Remove some of the text so that the overflow fits within the existing text box.
- Resize the text box to fit the text.
- Add another text box on a following page, and allow the excess text to "flow" from the first box to the second by linking the two text boxes.

To link two text boxes, follow these steps:

1. Click anywhere within the first text box to select it.

2. Click the Create Text Box Link button on the Connect Text Boxes toolbar. Your mouse pointer changes shape to look like a pitcher with a downward-pointing arrow.

3. Hold the mouse pointer over the second (empty) text box. As you do, the pointer changes shape so that the pitcher is "pouring" the text.

4. Click to link the two text boxes. If the first text box contains any overflow text, it appears in the second, linked text box.

Linked text boxes handle text flow automatically, even when you change their size or shape. If you enlarge the first text box, for instance, text from the second box moves back to fill the extra space. In fact, you can link multiple text boxes in this manner. To break the link between text boxes, click in the first of the text boxes and click the Break Forward Link button on the Connect Text Boxes toolbar. The second and subsequent text boxes will be disconnected from the first one, and if the linked boxes contained any text, the Text in Overflow indicator will appear beneath the first text box.

When you paste or copy text into a text box that is too small to contain the full amount, Publisher displays a warning message asking you if you want to use AutoFlow.

- If you choose Yes, Publisher creates a new text box large enough to hold the overflow text, links it to the existing text box, and pastes the remainder of the cut or copied text into the new text box.

- If you click No, Publisher inserts as much of the pasted text as will fit in the existing text box. You need to manually edit the text or create additional linked text boxes to handle the overflow.

NOTE

When you link text boxes, a Go to Next Text Box pointer appears below the bottom-right corner of each text box that has at least one forward link. A matching Go to Previous Text Box icon appears above the top-left corner of the subsequent text boxes. While editing, you can use any of these pointers to navigate through a story that is contained in multiple linked text boxes.

When you've edited as much as possible and you must stuff a block of text into an existing text box, use Publisher's AutoFit Text option. Right-click the text box and choose Change Text, AutoFit Text. Then choose one of the following three options:

- Shrink Text On Overflow reduces the point size of the text until it no longer overflows the text box.

- Best Fit causes the text to expand or contract to fill the text box when the box is resized.

- Choose Do Not AutoFit if you have previously enabled one of the other two settings and you don't like the results. You'll need to adjust the amount of text or the size of the text box to fit.

NOTE

The Shrink Text On Overflow and Best Fit options do not work with linked text boxes.

To rotate the contents of a text box, click the green anchor at the top of the text box and drag in any direction, or click to the right of the Rotate button on the Standard toolbar and choose one of the five options to rotate text 90 degrees left or right, flip it horizontally or vertically, or use the free rotation tool. When you click to type text into a rotated text box, it appears rotated in the direction you selected.

When you connect text boxes, you can have Publisher automatically include "jump lines" that help readers follow the story. These notices are automatically updated if you move a text box or insert or remove pages from the publication. To add a Continued notice, click the text box to which the notice should be added and choose Format, Text Box. On the Text Box tab, select or clear options as needed. Including a "Continued on page…" notice adds a cross-reference to the next text box; it appears at the bottom right of the first text box. When you include a "Continued from page…" line, Publisher adds a cross-reference to the previous text box and positions it in the top-left corner of the text box, as shown in Figure 27.19.

Figure 27.19
The text box contains jump lines that help the reader find the beginning of the story and continue to the end.

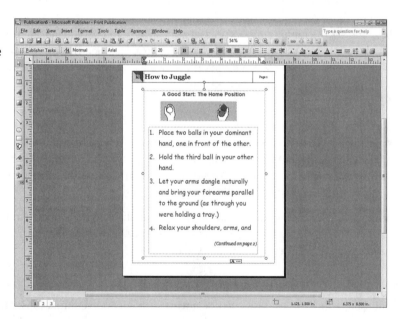

NOTE

If two linked text boxes appear on the same page in the publication, Publisher does not display continuation notices even if these options are selected.

To create multiple columns inside a text box, right-click the text box and choose Format Text Box; on the Text Box tab, click the Columns button. Set the number of columns and the spacing between them and click OK. Your text will then fill the first column and snake up to appear at the top of the next column. To create a column break inside this text box, press Ctrl+Shift+Enter. To remove a manually inserted column break, press Delete. Select View, Special Characters to see the column break if you're unsure where it is.

27

WIDOWS AND ORPHANS

A *widow* is the colorful designer's term that describes when the last line of a paragraph appears by itself at the top of a new page; an *orphan* refers to the condition when the first line of a paragraph lands all by its lonesome at the bottom of a page. Professional desktop publishers go to great pains to avoid leaving widows and orphans in their publications; if you want your work to appear professional, you should, too. To do this, choose Format, Paragraph, and select the Widow/Orphan Control check box on the Line and Paragraph Breaks tab. This setting is disabled by default; when beginning a publication, it's wise to enable Widow/Orphan control for body-text styles so that you won't have to fix problems later on.

KERNING AND TRACKING

Kerning is the process of adjusting spacing between specific characters to improve readability. In Publisher, kerning is enabled by default for fonts that are 14 points or larger. To set kerning for smaller fonts, choose Format, Character Spacing, select the Kern Text At check box, and set the minimum point size at which Publisher should automatically kern. You can also kern text manually: Select the characters to kern, open the Character Spacing dialog box, and select Condense from the drop-down list under the Kerning heading. Reduce the spacing in the By This Amount text box. You can set this value to any amount between 0 and 600 points.

Tracking adjusts the spacing between all text characters in a text box and is useful when you want to change the overall look of a block of text. To set tracking, open the Character Spacing dialog box. Options in the Tracking drop-down list include Normal, Very Tight, Tight, Loose, and Very Loose. You can also choose Custom and set a percentage to a value between .1% and 600% in the By This Amount box.

Scaling, the first option in the Character Spacing dialog box, actually stretches the characters (or shrinks them) as compared to increasing or decreasing the space between characters. You can stretch or shrink text from .1% to 600%.

DROP CAPS

Publisher allows you to dress up documents with decorative initial caps, called *drop caps*. These options in Publisher are similar to those in Microsoft Word, with a few extra flourishes. Publisher offers several preset drop caps as well as the option to create a custom design. To add a drop cap, choose Format, Drop Cap, and adjust settings as shown in Figure 27.20. Unlike in Microsoft Word, a drop cap in Publisher is simply a formatted character (not a character placed inside a text box) so spell check still works properly on the first word in a paragraph.

Figure 27.20
Publisher offers a selection of preformatted drop caps, or you can click the Custom tab to create your own.

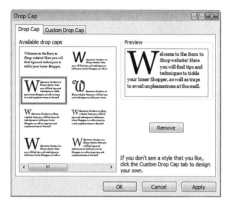

INSERTING IMAGES

To insert an image in a Publisher publication, follow the same steps you would use in Word: Click where the image should go, choose Insert, Picture, and choose either Clip Art or From File. You can also insert a picture directly from an imaging device by choosing the From Scanner or Camera option. When a picture is selected, the Picture toolbar appears. The tools on this Picture toolbar are the same as those in Word and work similarly.

When you need an empty picture frame to mark the position for an image that you plan to insert later, choose Insert, Picture, Empty Picture Frame, and then drag the frame into position. You can adjust settings for the frame as you would one that has a picture in it, including altering text wrap and reformatting borders.

When working with images, you may want to adjust how text wraps around the image with more accuracy than simply having it wrap tight or square.

To adjust how text wraps around an image:

1. First, adjust the wrap points for the image by right-clicking the image.

2. Next, click the Text Wrapping button on the Picture toolbar, and choose a wrap option other than Square.

3. Now click the Wrapping button again and click Edit Wrap Points. All images have a set of wrap points. Photographs, for example, have one at each of the four corners, whereas a piece of clip art may have many more to make an outline around the shape. The shape made by the wrap points makes a line for the text to wrap against; unlike Word, if you drag one over part of the image, it crops that portion of the image away.

4. Click and drag any wrap point to adjust the wrap line.

5. To add a wrap point, click on the line where a new wrap point should appear and drag with your mouse—a new wrap point will appear automatically.

6. To delete a wrap point, position your mouse over it and hold the Ctrl key as you click the point.

7. To finish, click outside the image.

27

8. To ensure that text in a text box actually wraps around the image, place the text box on a layer below that of the image.

9. To alter the layering of a text box, right-click it and choose Order, Send to Back or Send Backward.

NOTE

Text in a table cannot be wrapped around a picture. Text wrapping works only for print publications and is not an option for text in a web publication.

→ For more details about working with images, **see** "Adding Pictures to Office Documents," **p. 125**.

NOTE

The Publisher Graphics Manager helps you manage pictures that are inserted into your publication. The Graphics Manager is especially useful when you are using a commercial printer, because it tells whether images are embedded or linked. If images are linked, you can use it to ascertain whether any links have been modified or broken, and it can help you repair broken links. The Graphics Manager also lets you convert an embedded image to a linked image (and vice versa) and to replace one image with another. To view the Graphics Manager, choose Tools, Graphics Manager, or open the Graphics Manager task pane.

USING TABLES AS A PAGE LAYOUT TOOL

Tables are useful for laying out text in a grid formed by intersecting columns and rows. When you type text into a table cell, it wraps within that cell and stays separate from text in the cells above, below, and to its left and right. If you're accustomed to using tables in Word documents, you'll have to adjust to a few differences when working with Publisher publications. For example, in Microsoft Word you can embed an inline image inside a table cell and it will travel with the table. Using inline images is not an option in Publisher.

CREATING A TABLE

To add a table to your publication, click the Insert Table button on the Objects toolbar or choose Table, Insert, Table to open the Insert Table dialog box. Select the number of rows and columns for your table, choose a table format, and click OK. The list of ready-made formats includes several special-purpose arrangements for displaying numbers and some designed for use in a table of contents. If you create a table and later change your mind about its formatting, you can choose one of the other options easily: Click to select the table, and then choose Table, AutoFormat. This list is identical to the one in the Create Table dialog box.

To include two pieces of data in a single cell, you can divide the cell with a diagonal line. This option is typically used in the top-left cell of a table to add a column and a row heading.

Click in the cell, choose Table, Cell Diagonals, and choose Divide Down or Divide Up. When you add dividers to a cell, the line divides the cell into two distinct parts; type text into one part and then press Tab and type text into the other part. You can also format each part of the divided cell a different color (see Figure 27.21).

Figure 27.21
Use the Cell Diagonals tool to create vertical and horizontal headings in one cell in a table.

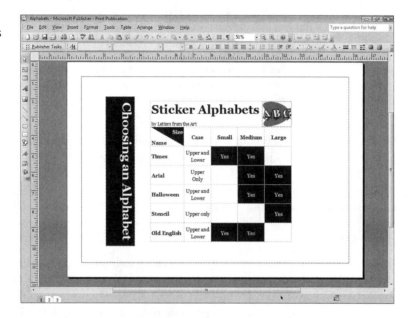

To ensure that text you enter in a table always displays properly, activate Table, Grow to Fit Text. With this setting, the table will expand automatically when you add more text to any cell than can be displayed with the current row height. If the dimensions of your table must be a fixed size to accommodate a design, disable this option.

Publisher tables can be resized, like Word tables, by dragging with your mouse on the column and row borders. Like other graphic objects, you can set text to wrap around a table.

1. Right-click the table, choose Format Table, and select one of the Wrapping Style options on the Layout tab—Square, Tight, Through, or Top and Bottom.

2. From this dialog box, you can also adjust how text is positioned vertically in the cell— for example, to force it to the top, middle, or bottom of the cell.

3. Click the Cell Properties tab and choose the appropriate option from the Vertical Alignment list.

4. To add or remove space in the margins around text within a table cell, use the Text Box Margins options in the Cell Properties tab.

As in a Word table, you can merge or split table cells by selecting the cells to merge and choosing Merge Cells or Split Cells from the Table menu. However, unlike Microsoft Word, you cannot split a cell into multiple cells unless you have first merged it—in this respect, Split Cells functions primarily as a way to undo merged cells rather than as a table

27

layout tool. As in Microsoft Word, you can add new rows to a table by clicking in the bottom-right cell of the table and pressing Tab. To delete a row, select any cell within that row and choose Table, Delete, Rows.

CAUTION

Some predefined table formats appear to consist of a single cell in the first row for the heading with multiple cells in subsequent rows. If you start with a table consisting of four rows and six columns, for instance, and apply a Table of Contents format, each row after the first one looks like it comprises only two cells. However, your original table is hidden underneath the autoformatted table, in which five cells were merged to form one large cell in each row. If you later select one of these cells and choose Table, Split Cells, you will end up with five separate cells.

As we noted earlier, you cannot insert an image into a table cell in Publisher. Inserted pictures appear inside picture placeholders and cannot be located inside either text boxes or tables. To give the impression of a picture inside a table cell, size the table cell appropriately and then position the image over the top of the table cell. To ensure that the picture and the table stay in the same relative positions, group the two elements.

IMPORTING A TABLE

Publisher works well with both Word tables and Excel ranges to share data. You can import a table from Word or Excel into a Publisher publication and work with it inside Publisher. After selecting a table from a Word document and copying it to the Clipboard, switch to your publication and click on the page where the table should appear. Choose Edit, Paste Special, and choose one of the available options. The New Table option, for instance, converts the Word table to a Publisher table; the New Text Box option inserts the text from the table into a Publisher text box, with the text from each cell separated by tabs and paragraph markers placed between rows of data.

If you select an existing Publisher table and then choose Edit, Paste Special, you have two additional options, Table Cells With Cell Formatting and Table Cells Without Cell Formatting, which insert the data from the Word table into your Publisher table. If the data you're trying to space takes up more room than is available in your existing table, Publisher offers to expand the selection to accommodate the copied cells.

→ For details on how to create and format tables using Word, **see** "Using Tables to Organize Information," **p. 416**.

NOTE

If you have the Boundaries and Guides display disabled, your table borders will not display on the screen. To display borders, choose View, Boundaries and Guides. As in Word, the dashed lines are available as a convenience for onscreen viewing and do not print when the table is printed. To add printing borders, right-click the table, choose Format, Table, and click the Colors and Lines tab. Choose a line color and line weight and then click in the Preview area or use the buttons in the Presets section to add the required borders to your table.

Instead of laboriously constructing a table to create your own custom table of contents, select a ready-made table of contents that matches your publication's design. You'll find these choices in the Tables of Contents category in the Design Gallery.

CUSTOMIZING PUBLISHER OPTIONS

Publisher can store information about you and your company and use it to populate publications with your name, the name of your business, contact details, and even a logo. By saving this information, you can automatically add accurate information to new publications without tedious (and possibly error-prone) retyping. Publisher allows you to create and save up to four sets of personal information, each of which can also include a custom color scheme.

CUSTOMIZING BUSINESS INFORMATION

You may have been prompted to add information to your business information set when you created your first Publisher publication.

Each business information set consists of a collection of *components*—your name, job title, organization name, and address; phone, fax, and email details; and a tag line or motto associated with you or your company. You can also include a logo in a business information set. The information you type into each set is stored for you so you can add it to a publication when needed. This is particularly useful if you use one of the publications from Publisher's design sets. However, you can also create business information components in any Publisher publication.

To update an existing business information set or create a new one, click Edit, Business Information. Click New to create a new business information set, or select an existing business information set from the drop-down list and then click Edit. Add or edit your data in the text areas provided. To add a logo, click Add Logo to open the Insert Picture dialog box, select the image, and then select Insert. Click Save to save your changes, and then click Update Publication to apply the information from your business information set to the current publication.

To add saved data from a business information set to a publication, choose Insert, Business Information. In the Business Information pane, click and drag the component you want to add, and then drop it inside the publication. Each component appears in its own box. Thus, to add your company's contact details to a publication, you must add one component for the organization name, another for the address, and then, if necessary, a third component for the Phone/Fax/Email, as shown in Figure 27.22.

27

Figure 27.22
When you add business information to a publication, each component appears in its own text box.

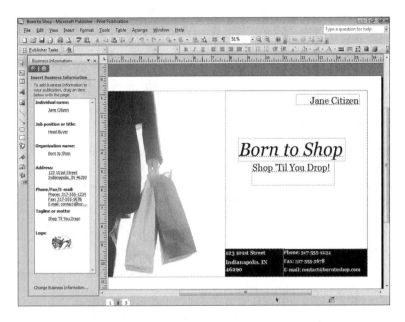

If incorrect information appears in a publication, chances are those errors snuck in via a saved business information set. Click Change Business Information in the task pane (or choose Edit, Business Information) and change the data or choose a different set. Click Update Publication and all entries in the current publication that draw information from the saved business information set will be updated appropriately.

CAUTION

If you add business information to a document using components, the information appears in a text box. You might be tempted to manually add or edit data in that text box. Don't do it! Your manual changes will be overwritten with absolutely no warning if you click the Update Publication option. To avoid this possibility, avoid making edits to any part of a publication that uses data drawn from a business information set. Instead, choose Edit, Business Information, and edit the details there; or remove the component and add a new text box that contains the data you want to add manually.

CREATING CUSTOM COLOR SCHEMES

Publisher's color schemes can be customized to include the colors you most often use. If you've paid big bucks to have a graphic designer create a colorful logo for your business, you might want to use a color scheme that coordinates with the colors in your logo. To create your own color scheme, open the Color Schemes task pane and click the Create New Color Scheme link to display the Create New Color Scheme dialog box. Select and change any of the eight colors in the color scheme. The Main color is typically black; because this setting is used for text, you should pick a dark color if you change the Main value. The Hyperlink and Followed Hyperlink colors are used on a web page. Accents 1, 2, 3, 4, and 5 are generally complementary tints or solid colors chosen because they look good together. If you're using tints, assign colors going from dark to light—Accent 1 should be the darkest color and Accent 5 the lightest, or white.

To change a color, click the drop-down arrow to the right of the color box in the New column. Choose a color from the color palette or choose More Colors to select from a larger color range. Click the Custom tab to choose a color from the Color Picker or to choose a color from a specific color model. If your graphic designer or printer has chosen colors for you using industry-standard color-naming schemes, you can choose those exact colors without having to guess. Choose a color model and then choose the exact value. Using the RGB model, you type in red, green, and blue color values; if you know the CMYK or Pantone colors, you can select a color using the settings appropriate to that color model, as in Figure 27.23.

Figure 27.23
Professional printers and graphic designers can choose precise color matches based on a range of color models, including Pantone colors.

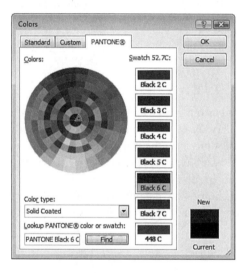

When you have selected your palette, check the results in the preview window. Type a descriptive name for your scheme and then click Save. You can then select this as a color scheme to associate with a saved business information set.

USING THE DESIGN GALLERY

In addition to template publications, Publisher includes *design objects*, which are smaller objects typically included in a larger publication. Typical design objects are calendars, coupons, and logos. You can use any saved design object in a publication to spare yourself the hassle of re-creating an object for each publication or tediously copying objects from one publication to another.

After creating a custom design object, you can save it as an object in the Design Gallery. Do this for objects you use repeatedly, such as a company logo, your postal indicia, and reply coupons. When you save these in the Design Gallery, they're there to use anytime you need them. You can also modify ready-made Design Gallery objects and save them as new Design Gallery objects.

To use an object from the Design Gallery, click the Design Gallery Object button on the Objects toolbar. When the Gallery appears, click the category of object to use and select an object within that category. Click the Insert Object button to add it to your publication. Many objects can be further customized in the Design Gallery before you insert them. Click to select the object, and then use the controls in the Options section. For objects such as the Calendar, for example, you can choose a date range to use.

TIP FROM

EQ & Woody

> By default, objects in the Design Gallery that are made up of a series of similar objects, such as an Accessory Bar, are synchronized so that changing one object in the group changes all similar objects. If you don't want this to happen, choose Edit, Undo Synchronize after making a change. When you do so, be aware that this disables synchronization for other objects in the group, too. To enable this option again, choose Tools, Options, and click the User Assistance tab. Click Automatically Synchronize Formatting and click OK.

USING THE CONTENT LIBRARY

NEW In Publisher 2003, if you had a custom object such as your logo that you wanted to reuse, you'd add it to the Design Gallery. You can no longer do that in Publisher 2007 because the new version has a more general solution to the problem of reusing objects: Content Library. This is a task pane to which you can save a wide range of objects: pictures, shapes, text, text boxes, tables, Word Art, and any grouping of two or more objects. You can categorize each item you save to the Content Library—the default categories are Business, Personal, and Favorites—and Publisher offers a number of sort options, such as Most Recently Used, Type, and Size.

To add an item to the Content Gallery:

1. First select it (or group together multiple objects that make up your design object and then select the group).

2. Then choose Insert, Add to Content Library.

3. Type a descriptive name for the object in the Title box, and select one or more categories using the check boxes in the Categories list. (To create a new category in the Content Library, click Edit Category List, click Add, type a name for the category, and then click OK.)

4. Click OK to save the object to the Design Gallery.

To find your newly added objects, click Insert, Item from Content Library (you can also press Ctrl+Shift+E or click the Item from Content Library button in the Objects toolbar). In the Content Library task pane (see Figure 27.24), use the Category and Type lists to filter the content as needed, and use the Sort By list to sort the content. Find the content you want to insert, and then double-click it.

You're not restricted to inserting only Publisher objects into the Content Library. You can also add compatible objects from other programs, such as Word tables and images in other documents. To add such objects to the Content Library, copy them to the Clipboard, display the Content Library pane, and then click the Add Item on Clipboard to Content Library link.

Figure 27.24
In Publisher 2007, you can save pictures, shapes, text, text boxes, tables, Word Art, and object groups to the new Content Library.

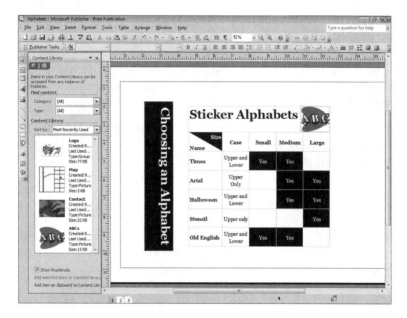

USING MASTER PAGES

The secret of producing professional publications, particularly those that run more than one or two pages, can be summed up in one word: consistency. In Publisher, the key to consistency is learning how to create and use *master pages*.

Every Publisher publication has, by default, at least one master page. It is the base for every page in a publication and contains design objects and guides that you want to appear on every page of your publication (or on almost every page, anyway—you can selectively tweak individual pages in a publication to hide master page elements). In previous versions of Publisher, master pages were known as *backgrounds*. Although that term is now deprecated, it's still a useful way to think of the function of master pages. In practical terms, you can think of the elements on a master page as sitting below the text on your foreground. If you enter text or position an element on your page, the foreground object blocks out whatever portion it covers of any object on the master page below it.

You can also have multiple master pages for a single publication. This allows you to create different master pages to manage different aspects of a complex publication

ADDING ELEMENTS TO A MASTER PAGE

To view a publication's master page (or master pages), choose View, Master Page or press Ctrl+M. This opens the Edit Master Pages task pane which displays, at the very least, Master A, which is the first of your master pages.

You can give the master page a new, more descriptive name, if desired, by clicking the down arrow to its right, choosing Rename, and then typing a new name. You can also change a master page to a two-page master, which is appropriate when designing a publication that will be viewed like a book, with even pages appearing on the left and odd pages on the right. Using a two-page master lets you place page numbers on the outside of the pages, for instance—on the left margin of the left page and on the right margin of the right page. To change a single-page master to a two-page master, click the down arrow to its right and choose the Change to Two-Page option.

Use multiple master pages when you need different layouts for different sections or page types in your publication. If, for example, you are creating a catalog with some product pages and some pages of advertising, create a master page for laying out products and one for laying out ads. You can then apply the master pages as needed to each page.

To create a new master page, open the Edit Master Pages task pane, choose New Master Page, and give the page a new single-character ID (a letter or number, typically) and a description that makes it easy for you (or anyone using your master page) to discern the purpose of the page. Click the Two-Page Master check box if the master page is to be a two-page spread. You should choose this option if you plan to use left and right pages of a publication, even if these pages won't be placed directly opposite each other. You can apply either side of a two-page master to either side of a two-page spread. Conceivably, you might create a pair of two-page masters (A and B) and use Master Page A on the left and Master Page B on the right of a spread, as in Figure 27.25. When creating a new master page, consider duplicating and then editing an existing master page if it already contains most of the elements you need. To do this, click the down arrow to the right of the master page and choose Duplicate from the menu.

When you select your newly created master page from the Edit Master Pages task pane, you can make changes or additions to the page in the main window. You can add or alter rulers or guides and add objects like text boxes, tables, WordArt, images, and even AutoShapes and Content Library objects to the master page.

To adjust layout guides such as margins, baselines, and grids, click the down arrow to the right of the master page ID and choose Layout Guides from the menu. You can then set the guides using the techniques described earlier in this chapter.

When working with a two-page spread, think of the two pages as the equivalent of an open book. Place objects that should be on the outside edges of the pages on the left and right margins of the entire spread. When you make changes to margin guides on one page of a two-page spread, the changes are mirrored on the opposite page; thus, creating a large right margin on the left page creates an equal-sized left margin on the right page.

27

Figure 27.25
You can mix and match two-page master pages on a two-page spread.

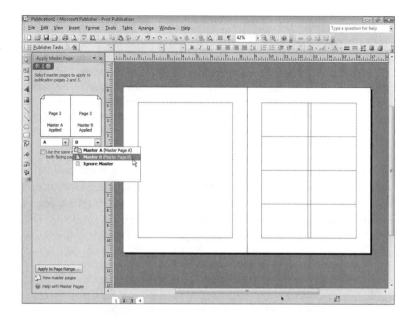

You can make changes to your master pages at any time. When you do, the changes are immediately reflected on all pages in your publication that are based on that master page. Take care when making changes to the placement of objects on a master page; if you've already created a number of pages, you might find that objects you placed on pages are covering up objects on the master page.

To add a page number to a master page:

1. Display the master page and choose Insert, Page Numbers.

2. From the Position drop-down list, choose Top of Page (Header) or Bottom of Page (Footer).

3. Next, choose an alignment option. For two-page masters, you can choose Inside, Center, or Outside, ensuring that page numbers are in mirror positions on a two-page spread, as in Figure 27.26.

4. For most publications, you'll want to leave the Show Page Number On First Page check box cleared. (This option applies to the first page of your publication, not to the first time a master page is actually used.)

5. Click OK to continue.

Figure 27.26
When you're using a two-page spread, the Page Numbers dialog box lets you place page numbers on the Outside or Inside of the spread.

When you're using more than one master page, place the page number element on each master page, whether it's a single or two-page spread.

TIP FROM

Ed & Woody

If you don't select a text box before you choose Insert, Page Numbers, Publisher creates a text box to contain the page number field. To position the page number in some other place on the page, draw a text box and select it; then choose Insert, Page Numbers. The Position drop-down list now includes the Current Text Box option.

Objects you will typically add to a master page are your company logo, the publication title, watermark, volume, and date. In addition, you can add page formatting elements, such as colored bars across the top or bottom of the publication, that you want to appear on every page of the publication. The key to determining what should be on the master page and what should be on the foreground pages is to ask whether the element should appear on most or all pages of your publication. If the answer is yes, place it on the master page.

TIP FROM

Ed & Woody

To place text and pictures on facing pages of a two-page master page so their positioning is a mirror image of each other, create a single-page master page and add all the text and pictures to it that you want mirrored on the facing page. When you are done, click the down arrow to the right of the master page name in the Edit Master Pages task pane and click Change to Two-Page. All objects on the existing page will be duplicated and placed in mirror image positions on the new second page.

PRINTING A PUBLICATION

When you're ready to print a publication, you can save yourself the hassle and delay of expensive makeovers by first checking the publication thoroughly. In this section, we describe how to use Publisher's automated tools to check for errors and then set the publication up for the best quality output.

USING THE DESIGN CHECKER TO POLISH YOUR PUBLICATION

Before committing your publication to paper, go through a series of final checks: Spell check your document, proofread it carefully, and look closely at each page to spot any design flaws. Publisher's Design Checker can help you identify hard-to-spot design problems—such as text boxes that contain hidden overflow text or a publication that uses too many fonts. The Design Check produces a simple report; you can automatically fix some problems, manually repair others, and ignore issues that represent deliberate design decisions on your part.

To run the Design Checker, choose Tools, Design Checker. After a quick scan of your publication, Publisher displays its results in the Design Checker task pane. Each potential problem has its own listing, which includes a brief description and the page on which it appears. Click any item in the list to jump directly to that item. Click the arrow to the right of any item to see a menu of additional options, including an Explain menu that offers more details about why Publisher tagged this item as a problem.

If an automatic fix is available, you can click this option in the shortcut menu. You can also disable checking for a particular type of error if you'd prefer that the Design Checker stop bugging you about that issue: Choose Never Run This Check Again from the shortcut menu. The Design Checker Options link at the foot of the task pane allows you to exercise fine control over the workings of this sometimes overly picky tool. Click the Checks tab to select or clear any of a long list of problems the Design Checker watches out for.

The Design Checker won't identify ambiguous design issues that can occasionally cause problems, such as an image hidden under a text box. Using the Design Checker does not obviate the need to carefully check the design of your publication to ensure it looks right.

PRINTING YOUR PUBLICATION

Before you print your publication, click the Print Preview button on the Standard toolbar and carefully check each page to make sure its layout looks correct. When printing your publication, print a proofing copy at a low resolution first and examine it carefully before printing a final copy.

You can print a draft publication without images to make it easy to concentrate on proof-reading text and to save on ink. To do this, follow these steps:

1. Choose File, Print Setup, click the Printer Details tab, and then click Advanced Printer Setup.
2. On the Graphics and Fonts tab, click Do Not Print Any Pictures and click OK.
3. Make sure you return to this tab and select the Print All Pictures at Full-Resolution option before printing a final version of your publication.

Regardless of whether you're using an ink jet or a laser printer, there will be a nonprinting area around your publication where the paper cannot be gripped by the printer and printed on at the same time. This area varies from around one-quarter of an inch on some laser printers to half an inch or more on other printers. It is simply not possible for most printers to print in this nonprinting area, so any objects placed over this area may not print successfully.

To create a full bleed (an object that extends to the very edge of the paper) for your publication, you will need to print the publication on a larger sheet of paper than the page size and then trim it to size. This will allow you to print over what would otherwise be the nonprinting area of the page.

To set up for a bleed, choose File, Page Setup and set the page size to the size for the publication when trimmed. Choose a paper size larger than the page size you just set up and that your printer can handle. Then, when creating your publication, the elements that should bleed should extend over the edge of the page as displayed on the screen. When you're ready to print, follow these steps:

1. Choose File, Print.
2. Click the Printer Details tab, and then click the Advanced Printer Setup button. Then, on the Page Settings tab, under the Printer's Marks heading, select the Crop Marks option; under the Bleeds area, click Allow Bleeds.

27

3. Click OK to close the Advanced Printer Setup dialog box and click Print to print your publication.

The printed copies will have crop marks you can use to line up your cutter when you are trimming the page to its final size.

If you are printing a two-sided publication, such as a brochure or booklet, make sure you use the correct Publisher page setup option. This will ensure that the publication is properly laid out when printed. For example, to create a four-page letter-sized booklet on 11×17-inch paper that will be folded in half when printed, create the document by doing the following:

1. Choose File, Page Setup, and select the Letter Booklet type with the page size 8.5×11 inches.

2. Click OK, and Publisher will prompt you to automatically insert pages.

3. Click Yes, and Publisher will insert pages to take the publication up to a multiple of four pages.

For a four-page document, pages 1 and 4 will be printed on the same side of the page with page 4 printed on the left side of the page. Pages 2 and 3 will be printed on the other side of the page. When you fold the output, you'll see the pages in correct order.

To print on both sides of the page, your printer must be capable of *duplex printing*. Choose File, Print and click the Properties button on the Print dialog box. Click the Layout tab and choose the appropriate option under the Print on Both Sides area.

Some printers do not permit duplex printing. In this case, you can print on both sides of the page by printing as many copies of the first sheet as you need and then feeding the paper through the printer a second time, turning it over so that it feeds through with the blank side adjacent to the print heads and prints the next page. When you choose to print only page 1 of a four-page booklet, you'll see a message asking you if you want to print it as a separate booklet. Click No to print pages 4 and 1 on a single sheet; you can then print page 2 only and it will print pages 2 and 3 on the same sheet. Answer No to the prompt you get in this instance, too.

TIP FROM

Ed & Woody

Manually printing two-sided documents is an exercise in frustration. For best results, we recommend a very cool program called FinePrint, which walks you through the mechanics of producing just about any type of booklet or double-sided print job and can also print big jobs in paper-saving thumbnails for proofing or review. Visit `http://www.fineprint.com` to download a trial copy and read more details.

TROUBLESHOOTING

I'm having trouble printing a publication on my own printer.

Printing on your own printer is less prone to problems than printing using a commercial printing service. Many problems can be traced to attempts to locate objects over the non-printing margins on the page; when this happens, parts of the publication simply don't print. If you encounter this problem, check to see if the margins in your document are smaller than the actual nonprinting area on your printer. If this is the case, you'll have to make the margins larger and realign any objects affected by the change.

It is also possible you are using an incorrect paper size. To check, choose File, Print Setup and click the Publication and Paper Settings tab. Under the Paper heading, set the physical size of the piece of paper on which you're printing. If this size is correct, click OK and then click Change Page Size in the Format Publication task pane to ensure that the width and height of your publication fit on the paper size you selected with an adequate margin to account for the nonprinting area of your printer.

If you're using linked images in your publication, be aware that Publisher inserts lower-resolution versions into your document to show you what it looks like. If these images don't print at a high resolution, choose File, Print Setup, select the Printer Details tab, click the Advanced Printer Setup button, and click the Graphics and Fonts tab. Ensure that the Print All Pictures at Full-Resolution option is selected and click OK.

SECRETS OF THE OFFICE MASTERS: GOOD DESIGN PRINCIPLES

Publisher offers some powerful tools, but just knowing how to use those tools often isn't enough to create effective, attractive publications. The following two sections offer a few design tips that we hope you find useful.

WHAT THEY TEACH IN DESIGN SCHOOL

Designing publications is a skill taught in design school and practiced by trained graphic artists. If you haven't been to design school, you've missed out on learning techniques that help designers create attractive, balanced, aesthetically pleasing publications. Some of these techniques are use of alignment, repetition, and contrast.

- Align each object so it is flush with a margin or another object, creating strong but invisible lines on the page. Use left-aligned headings over left-aligned text—they look better than centered headings.

- The principle of repetition requires that objects and formatting elements be repeated throughout a publication to give it a more structured look. Repeat elements such as typefaces, your company logo, the colors in your publication, alignment, and the style of image you use. Repeating elements give your design a strong visual identity.

27

■ When choosing two elements, such as fonts or images, choose those that contrast strongly with one another. Typefaces that look similar actually fight one another visually and are disturbing to the viewer's eye. Typefaces that are dramatically different in style work well together for headings and body text. Look at the fonts used for headings and body text in this book for an excellent example.

DESIGNING AN EFFECTIVE WEB SITE

Before you begin creating a website, ask yourself the purpose of the website and what you expect it to achieve. Some businesses need a Web presence so that people can contact the business by phone, fax, or email. In this case, a simple three-page web with a Home page, an About Us page describing the company, and a Contact page may be sufficient. Other businesses may need to provide a larger site packed with detailed information about products, services, employees, and frequently asked questions (FAQs).

Write down a description of the purpose of your website so that you have a clear sense of where you're headed. Then prepare a hierarchical chart detailing the main areas of your site—keeping these to 5–6 areas in total. Identify any areas that may need multiple pages—for example, the product or service details pages—and add these as another level in the hierarchy.

For each page in your plan, determine what details you will provide to your visitors or what details you need to collect from them. Remember that websites are created for your customers and prospects to tell them the things that they'll want to know. Focus on their needs when designing the site. Write your thoughts down in detail so that, when you're working on your site, you're clear about what you need to provide on each page.

The overhead involved in frequently updating a website can be daunting. If finding time to update it is likely to be a problem, aim for static information that won't need regular updates. Unlike a printed publication, an out-of-date website is there for all the world to see; to fix the situation, you need to do something more active than simply throwing a bundle of out-of-date brochures in the trash.

CHAPTER 28

ACCESS ESSENTIALS

In this chapter

Planning an Access Database   836

Working with Database Objects   839

Exporting and Importing Data   843

Creating and Customizing Tables   844

Defining Relationships Among Tables   848

Building Forms and Reports   852

Using Queries to Extract Data from a Database   861

Creating and Applying Filters   872

Troubleshooting   873

Secrets of the Office Masters: Restricting Data Entry   874

PLANNING AN ACCESS DATABASE

Of all the Office applications, Microsoft Access is by far the most demanding and conceptually challenging. Anyone who has ever composed an interoffice memo or put together a budget can relate to Word and Excel instantly; an Access database, on the other hand, is made up of many individual objects, each of which must be built individually. With a wizard's help, it's possible to put together a simple database application in a relatively short time—to handle everything from tracking the contents of a wine cellar to managing inventory. Access applications can also scale up to enormous sizes, serving the information needs of large organizations and acting as a front end to data stored on mainframes and other network databases.

NOTE

> Access is truly an enormous application, and it's impossible to do more than introduce the essentials in this book. For the most part, we've focused on the tasks that ordinary business users face when building simple interactive databases. If you want to learn more about using Access with larger databases, or you want detailed information about building Access applications with VBA, we suggest you pick up a copy of *Special Edition Using Microsoft Access 2007*, by Roger Jennings, also published by Que (ISBN: 0789735970).

Using an Access database, you can store and manage large quantities of data for a variety of business and personal activities. If you've previously used flat-file database managers to perform simple list management tasks, you'll discover that Access is far more powerful, with the capability to maintain and link multiple tables and create applications using a robust programming language. Before you begin laying out the structure of a database, however, it helps to understand the components that make up Access:

- The *database engine* is the (generally invisible) software that actually stores, indexes, and retrieves data. When you create a standalone database, Access uses its own engine (called Jet...get it?) to manage data.

- *Database objects* provide the interface you use to view, enter, and extract information from a database. The most common database objects are tables, forms, queries, and reports.

- Access includes a full set of *design tools* that you use to create objects. The reports designer, for example, enables you to sort data, group by fields, and add headers and footers to each page as well as the entire report.

- Finally, Access includes a rich set of *programming tools* you can use to automate routine tasks. Confusingly, the Access Navigation pane includes an object type called *Macros*; these automation tools are completely different from the Visual Basic for Applications code you can add to most database objects.

The basic building blocks of an Access database are objects. Although Access supports many types of objects, the most common by far are tables, queries, forms, and reports. As you can see in Figure 28.1, the Access 2007 window includes the Ribbon at the top, as well as the Navigation pane on the right, which is divided into sections for each object type. The rest of the window displays tabs for each open object (such as the Customers table shown in Figure 28.1).

28

NOTE

To make sure the Navigation pane is displaying items by object type, click All Access Objects at the top of the pane, and then click Object Type.

 The Northwind sample database included with Access is filled with ideas and code that you can borrow for your own applications. Can't find it? See "Installing the Sample Database" in the "Troubleshooting" section at the end of this chapter.

Figure 28.1
The new Navigation pane displays lists of all database objects, arranged by type.

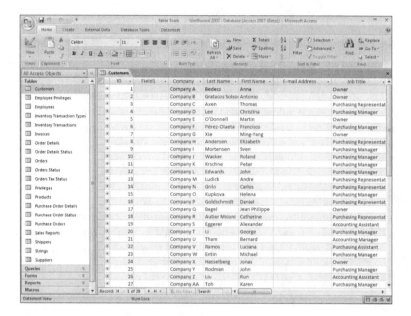

TABLES

A *table* is the basic unit for storing a collection of data in an Access database. A table's definition consists of a list of *fields*, each of which stores a discrete piece of information for a single *record*. For example, an Employees table might contain the fields LastName, FirstName, Position, DateHired, and HourlyRate. Because each record consists of one complete set of fields, a single record in the Employees table contains all available fields for a single employee.

The arrangement of fields and records is most obvious in Datasheet view, which displays data in rows and columns. When you open a table in Datasheet view, each record consists of a single row, and each column represents a single field.

QUERIES

Queries enable you to extract a subset of data from a single table, from a group of related tables, or from other queries, using criteria you define. By saving a query as a database object, you can run the query at any time, using the current contents of the database. When

28

you display a query in Datasheet view, it looks exactly like a table; the crucial difference is that each row of the query's results can consist of fields drawn from several tables. A query can also contain *calculated fields*, which display results based on the contents of other fields.

CAUTION

> Be careful when working with queries. Queries typically contain "live" data. If you change data in a query datasheet or form, it changes in the underlying table as well, without any warning.

FORMS

Access forms enable users to enter, view, and edit information, generally one record at a time. You can design forms that closely resemble paper forms such as invoices and time sheets, or you can create forms that are organized for data entry, complete with data-validation rules. A form window can also include a subform that displays information from a related table. For example, a form that shows a single record from the Departments table might include a subform that displays all the employees who work in a given department, allowing you to edit information about those employees.

REPORTS

Reports enable you to present data from one or more tables or queries in a readable style and a professional format, generally for printed output. A report might include detailed lists of specific data, with each row consisting of a single record, or it might provide a statistical summary of a large quantity of information. A report design can include grouping and sorting options; for example, you might create a weekly sales summary that runs a query, groups the query results by salesperson, and displays details of each sale in a list beneath each name.

TIP FROM

Ed & Woody

> Access reports transfer well to other Office applications, where you can use more powerful editing and analysis tools to create good-looking documents and charts. For example, buttons on the Access toolbar enable you to export a report to Microsoft Word, edit the page, and then print it or save it on a web server. You can also send a report to Excel, perhaps to create a chart or PivotTable report for use in another document.

MACROS AND MODULES

The final two selections in the Navigation pane allow you to automate actions in an Access database:

- *Macros* enable you to define a sequence of actions in an Access database. Macros are generally easy to create, even for users who have no programming background. You select each action by name, fill in the appropriate action arguments, and optionally supply a condition under which the action will be performed. For example, you can specify that a particular macro is to run every time you open a specific form, or you can attach the macro to a command button in a form. To run a macro, select the object in the Macros list and click the Run button on the Access toolbar.

- *Modules* are collections of Visual Basic procedures and declarations, designed to perform specific tasks in the context of your database. Unlike Word, Excel, and PowerPoint, Access does not have a macro recorder that can generate VBA code automatically.

WORKING WITH DATABASE OBJECTS

As noted earlier, all the objects in a given database are available for browsing in the Navigation pane.

The default action for database objects is Open—if you double-click a query icon, for example, Access executes that query and returns its result in Datasheet view. Likewise, double-clicking a form or report icon opens the selected object using the current contents of the database. The effect is the same if you right-click an object and click Open.

To view and edit the definition and structure of an object, select any object, select the Home tab, pull down the View menu and click Design View. In Design view, you can modify the appearance of an object (the fonts and colors on a form, for example), change the table or query from which it derives data, or adjust any of hundreds of other properties for the selected object.

CREATING NEW OBJECTS

To create a new table, query, form, or report, you use the Create tab, shown in Figure 28.2. In most cases, you can create objects in one of the following four ways:

- Create a blank instance of the object that you fill in by hand.
- Create a specific instance of the object, such as a table based on a template, a split form, or a label report.
- Create an object from scratch using Design view.
- Create an object using a wizard. As Figure 28.3 demonstrates, the "canned" choices available from the Form Wizard can be a useful starting point for business and personal databases.

Figure 28.2
In Access 2007, you use the Ribbon's Create tab to create your database objects.

28

Figure 28.3
You can use the various wizards to create your database objects, such as the Form Wizard shown here.

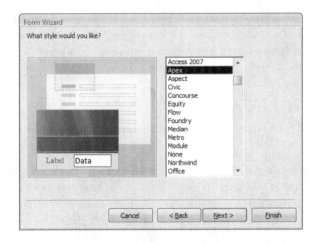

When used judiciously, wizards can be enormously helpful in the initial design of any database object. Some wizards are valuable mainly as introductory tools for newcomers to Access, whereas others are consistently useful even for experienced database developers. The Query Wizard, for example, is acceptable for generic databases, but in this case, Design view represents a far more efficient way to develop individual objects that precisely match specific requirements. On the other hand, the Form and Report Wizards almost always provide an excellent starting point for creating new forms and reports. When working with forms and reports in Design view, it's usually easier to move or modify existing objects than it is to add and edit new controls.

TIP FROM

When you use a wizard to create the initial version of an Access object, always expect to switch over to Design view to fine-tune the result. A wizard seldom produces the exact object that you need; in particular, the Design views for forms and reports offer direct access to important design elements such as controls, properties, fields, sections, and groups—and enable you to make detailed changes in the appearance and behavior of database objects.

MANAGING DATABASE OBJECTS

To see a concise list of available options for existing objects, select any object in the Navigation pane and use the right-click shortcut menus. You can open any object to view its content or its design; you can also rename or delete an object, cut or copy it to the Windows Clipboard, or view its properties.

TIP FROM

All versions of Access since Access 2000 are "smart" about handling changes to the names of objects. When you rename a field in a table, Access automatically changes any references to that field in queries, forms, reports, and other objects. If you change the name of a field, you shouldn't need to edit any other objects. However, any captions that reference those fields on an existing form or report are unchanged.

MODIFYING OBJECT PROPERTIES

Confusingly, every database object has two sets of properties. If you right-click the object's icon in the Navigation pane and choose Properties, you see a bare-bones dialog box that lists the object's General properties. These include the object's name, a text description, the date the object was created, and the date it was last modified. Ho-hum.

By contrast, if you open an object in Design view and click the Properties button, you see a complete list of properties that enable you to control the appearance and behavior of that object. Figure 28.4, for example, shows the Properties dialog box for a form, with all available settings organized by category on five tabs.

Figure 28.4
The Design view properties of a database object include a much more important list of settings that can dramatically change the way you see and use an object.

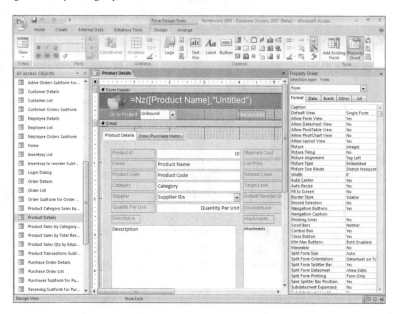

USING EXPRESSIONS IN DATABASE OBJECTS

When designing database objects, you don't have to limit yourself to data stored in a table. Extend the power of a database by writing expressions to transform that data on-the-fly. An *expression* is a combination of symbols, values, and identifiers (the name of a field, control, or property) that calculates a numeric result, combines text, or produces a logical value. Some of the *operators* you'll use in expressions include everyday arithmetic operators: + (plus), – (minus), * (multiplication), and / (division). Other operators used in expressions might be less familiar.

Expressions are useful throughout Access in many types of objects. The following are a few examples:

- In a query, you might include calculated fields, in which each entry is the result of an expression. The operands in the expression might include other fields in the same table or in a related table. You can use an expression to calculate a due date for an invoice

([SaleDate]+30) or to produce a total, such as [Qty]*[UnitPrice]. You supply the expression for the column and Access performs the operation for each record in the resulting datasheet.

- The design of an individual field in a table might include a *validation rule*, which specifies a range of acceptable entries in the field itself. You might create a rule that prohibits users from entering a value in the SaleDate field that is in the future or more than 30 days in the past, for example. If a given data entry does not meet the condition expressed in the rule, Access rejects the entry. To create a validation rule, write an expression that will evaluate to True or False for each new entry. If the result is True, the entry is accepted; if False, it is not.

→ To learn more about creating validation rules, **see** "Defining Validation Rules," **p. 874**.

- A *criterion* is an expression that you can use to select a target group of records for a particular operation. Any record that meets the criterion becomes part of the group; a record that does not meet the criterion is excluded from the group. Again, a criterion expression results in a value of True or False for each record examined.

In these and other examples, you use specific types of operators in expressions to produce the appropriate types of values. The following categories of operators are commonly used:

- **The Arithmetic Operators**—In addition to the familiar four (+, –, *, and /), these include ^ (exponentiation), \ (integer division), and MOD (the remainder from the division of two integers). These operators require numeric operands and produce numeric results.

- **The Comparison Operators**—< (less than), <= (less than or equal), <> (not equal), > (greater than), >= (greater than or equal), and Between (expressing a numeric range). These operators produce *logical* values, indicating whether a comparison is True or False.

- **The Logical Operators**—These take logical operands and produce logical results. For example, a logical operator might combine the values of two comparison expressions. Among these operators, the most commonly used are And (true if both operands are true), Or (true if one or both operands are true), and Not (produces the opposite value of an operand). Other logical operators include Eqv (true if both operands have the same value), Imp (true if the first operand is true and the second is false), and Xor (true if the operands have different values).

- **A String Operator**—The & symbol represents *concatenation*, the process of combining two text values.

Because expressions are so central to the design of database objects, Access provides a special tool called the Expression Builder to help you write expressions quickly and accurately. As you can see in Figure 28.5, the Expression Builder contains buttons representing operands, along with other categories of identifiers that might become part of an expression.

Figure 28.5
Use the Expression Builder to build an expression one element at a time by clicking the operand buttons and selecting from categories of identifiers.

You can generally open the Expression Builder by clicking the Build button (labeled …) next to the box where the expression is entered. Or right-click inside the box and choose Build from the shortcut menu.

TIP FROM

When you're working with forms and reports, use the Expression Builder to quickly add page numbers and date/time information. Scroll to the bottom of the left column and select Common Expressions to see these useful shortcuts.

EXPORTING AND IMPORTING DATA

Sooner or later—probably sooner—you'll want to transfer information stored in an Access database to some other software environment, or move data originally created in another program into Access. In some cases, you'll want to move entire tables between database programs for use in different applications. For example, you might want to copy a table of supplier names and addresses from Access so that another database developer can incorporate that data into an application created with SQL Server or Oracle. Or, if you're building an Access database to replace an application created in an older program, such as dBASE or FoxPro, you might need to import data twice—once when you begin designing the database, so you can test forms, reports, and queries using real data, and a second time when you're ready to switch from the old system to the new one.

28

Even when you're extremely careful, exporting and importing information between database formats runs a serious risk of creating duplicate data sets. If you keep information about customers and products in Access and in an SQL Server database, for example, whoever is responsible for data entry has to enter changes in two places, and it's almost certain that some records will be out of sync or contain errors and inconsistencies. When you must use the same data in two different database programs, you should choose one program to store the data, and then create a link to that data from the other database program so that you can add or edit records or run queries. Because Access can link to data stored in a variety of formats—including dBASE, SQL Server, and Paradox—you will most often want to store shared data in another program and create links to it from Access.

In other cases, your need for Access data is strictly temporary. For instance, if you've created a report or query in Access, you can transfer the data to Word to incorporate it into a larger report, or send it to Excel, where you can easily analyze it with the help of PivotTables and charts.

Importing and exporting data in Access 2007 occurs most often in the Ribbon's External Data tab, shown in Figure 28.6. As you can see, the Import group enables you to import from another Access database, as well as from Excel, a SharePoint list, a text file, and an XML file, and the More list includes ODBC databases, HTML documents, Outlook folders, as well as dBASE, Paradox, and Lotus 1-2-3. Access supports wide range of export formats, including Excel, SharePoint, PDF or XPS, Word, text file, another Access database, ODBC, HTML, dBASE, Paradox, and Lotus 1-2-3. There is also a Merge It with MS Word option that sends a table of data to a new or existing mail-merge document in Word. When the transfer is complete, you can insert fields from the Access table as merge fields in the Word document itself.

Figure 28.6
In Access 2007, use the controls on the External Data tab to import and export data using a variety of formats.

CREATING AND CUSTOMIZING TABLES

A *table* is the basic unit for storing and organizing information in an Access database. One database can contain any number of tables, as well as links to tables stored in other locations and other formats. Data within a table is arranged in a basic grid: Each column represents a *field*, where similar information (first name and last name, for instance) is stored in all the *records*, and each row contains all the data fields in a single record. In turn, tables directly or indirectly form the basis for all other objects within an Access database, including queries, forms, and reports.

As a general rule, each field definition has four elements, all of them visible when you open a table in Design view and select a field, as in Figure 28.7.

28

Figure 28.7
By selecting a field, you can edit its properties (see the following list). The descriptions for each field help document the structure of the table.

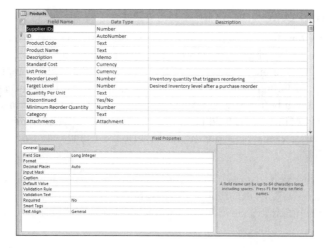

Here are four elements associated with field definitions:

- The *field name* must follow the same rules as those for other database objects: It can consist of up to 64 characters, including letters, numbers, spaces, and any special characters except a period, exclamation point, accent grave (`), or brackets. Spaces are allowed within object names, but not as the first character.

TIP FROM

> Access allows you to use spaces in the names of Access objects and, indeed, many of the fields in the Northwind sample database use spaces. However, we strongly recommend that you avoid doing so—especially if you plan to use the field names with VBA code. Instead of naming a field Postal Code, for example, try PostalCode or Postal_Code. Get into this habit and you'll have a much smoother time with Access.

- Each field definition also includes a *data type*; this setting controls formats for display and input and also serves as a way of validating data entry. (See the following section for a detailed list of available data types.)

- The field *description* is optional; if you choose to enter text here, it helps to document the database. It also helps when viewing a table's contents in Datasheet view; the Description text for the current column appears in the lower-left side of the status bar. Maximum length is 255 characters.

- Finally, the *field properties* for the selected field appear at the bottom of the table window. The exact properties for each field vary, depending on the data type you've selected. Use these properties to define more details about the type of data permitted in each field, as well as its display format and the default caption that appears when you place the field on a form or report.

28

CHOOSING A FIELD'S DATA TYPE

By default, every new field you create in an Access database uses the Text data type, with a maximum length of 255 characters. More often than not, that setting will be inappropriate for the type of data you plan to store in a field. The Text field enables you to enter nearly any type of data, including numbers, currency, dates, and times. In many cases, however, another data type is a better choice. For example, if you intend to enter invoice dates in a field, specify Date/Time as the field type; this option prevents you from inadvertently entering a value that isn't a legal date, such as 2/30/2007. You can choose from the following data types for any field:

- **Text**—Enables you to enter a maximum of 255 characters, including letters, numbers, and punctuation. This data type is also appropriate for entering numeric data that you don't want to use for calculations or sorting, such as Social Security numbers and phone numbers.

TIP FROM

EQ & Woody

> To set the maximum length of a Text field, adjust the Field Size property. You can also reset the default field size from 255 to a more reasonable number—say, 10 or 12. Choose Office, Access Options, click Object Designers, and enter the desired number in the Default Text Field Size spin box.

- **Memo**—This data type allows for long blocks of text, up to 64,000 characters. Memo fields do not allow formatting; they're most useful for notes and descriptions that exceed 255 characters.

- **Number**—Allows entry of numeric characters only. Choose an entry from the Field Size property box to further define the format. Byte is the most efficient and most limited choice, permitting you to enter whole numbers from 0 to 255. To store whole numbers, positive or negative, without fractions, choose Integer (–32,768 to 32,767) or Long Integer (–2,147,483,648 to 2,147,483,647). Single, Double, and Decimal formats allow increasingly more precise numbers with fractions.

- **Date/Time**—This data type enables you to enter dates and times by using a variety of formats and date separator characters. Use the Format property to control the display of data in Datasheet view.

- **Currency**—Like Number formats, except these values always display using the default Currency symbol, as defined in Control Panel's Regional Settings option. A Currency field is accurate to 15 digits to the left of the decimal point and 4 digits to the right; this option cannot be adjusted.

- **AutoNumber**—This data type results in a field of consecutive integers, supplied by Access as you add new records to your database. AutoNumber fields are commonly used for invoice numbers and for primary keys.

TIP FROM

EQ & Woody

> Although the default AutoNumber field properties generate sequential values, you can also specify that you want an AutoNumber field to randomly generate numbers that are unique within the current table. Choose Random from the New Values property for that field. This option might be useful if you want to avoid creating the impression that the data-entry order in a given table is significant.

- **Yes/No**—Use this data type for fields that have only one of two values. Use a Yes/No field to identify customers who are exempt from sales tax, for example. Use the Format property to change the value displayed from Yes/No to True/False or On/Off.

- **OLE Object**—Enables you to create a field for storing pictures, documents, or OLE objects developed in other programs. Note that you can't sort, index, or group by any field that uses this data type.

- **Hyperlink**—Enables you to enter clickable links to web addresses, folders, files, and other objects.

→ For a detailed description of how Office hyperlinks work and how to create and manage them, **see** "Working with Hyperlinks," **p. 98**.

- **Attachment**—Enables you to attach one or more documents to a record. If you add an Attachment field to a form, Access displays an icon for each attachment, which you can double-click to open.

SETTING A PRIMARY KEY

Every time you create a new table, Access prompts you to create a *primary key*. This step isn't mandatory, but it's highly recommended. For starters, a primary key is required if you ever want to create a relationship for the table. By definition, the primary key contains nonduplicate entries for each record; as a result, Access can use this unique identifier to positively identify each record, making searches easier and faster.

Access gives you three options for the primary key:

- *AutoNumber primary keys* are your safest choice. Under some circumstances, Access creates this type of primary key automatically. Using the AutoNumber data type guarantees that values are unique.

- A *single-field primary key* is a good choice when you're certain that the contents of the selected field will always be unique. Examples of useful single-field keys include unequivocal identification codes such as an employee badge number, Social Security number, part ID, or license plate number.

- *Multiple-field primary keys* are most common in junction tables used to link two tables in a many-to-many relationship. In an Invoices table, for example, each unique InvoiceID value might contain several ProductID values; likewise, each unique ProductID value in the Products table might be part of several invoices, each with its own InvoiceID number. By creating a third table (Order_Details) that combines these two values to create a primary key, you can be certain that the table will not contain any duplicate records and that you'll always find the record you need.

28

To define a single field as the primary key, select the Design tab and then activate the Primary Key button. The primary key field is identified in Design view by a small key icon, displayed just to the left of the field name.

SPEEDING UP SORTS AND QUERIES WITH INDEXES

Indexes help make short work of searching and sorting. When you build an index for a field or combination of fields, Access creates a sorted data structure that it can search through to find unique values. Without an index, Access has to step through every record to complete a query or sort; with an index, Access can find a unique value and jump directly to the rows that contain that value. The performance difference can be astounding.

By default, the primary key in every table is indexed. As part of the process of defining field settings, you can also create an index for a specific field. In Design view, select the field and change the Indexed property to Yes from its default setting of No. In addition, you can choose the Yes (No Duplicates) setting to ensure that each new entry in the field is unique. By definition, this is the Indexed setting for a table's primary key.

You can also create an index that covers multiple fields. This technique is useful when you have a query that sorts and searches on a group of fields. Click the Design tab's Indexes button and fill in the name of the index, the fields it should include (up to 10), and the sort order for each one. This same dialog box lets you view and edit or delete existing indexes.

TIP FROM

EQ & Woody

> Access creates some indexes automatically, and if you follow some common-sense naming conventions, you can guarantee that the right fields are indexed. By default, any field name that begins or ends with ID, num, code, or key will be indexed. Use field names such as ProductID and EmployeeNum as the primary key when possible. When you use the same field names in related tables where another field is the primary key, Access automatically indexes these fields, making queries that use these fields as fast as possible.

DEFINING RELATIONSHIPS AMONG TABLES

A well-designed Access database typically contains many interrelated tables, with each table containing a specific, narrowly defined set of data, without any duplicate information. This type of design is crucial to maintaining *referential integrity*—when you change a name, address, or other piece of data in one record, your change automatically appears in all related tables.

Imagine a database application that tracks customer purchases. A proper design stores this information in four separate tables, as shown in Figure 28.8.

Figure 28.8
Note that each of the relationships among these four tables is tied to the primary key in one of the tables.

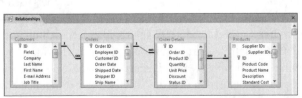

Here are the descriptions of the four tables in the example:

- The Customers table contains one record for each of your customers, with their name, address, and phone number, plus an ID field that uniquely identifies that customer.

- The Orders table contains one record for each item on each order placed; fields include Order ID, Employee ID (the ID of the salesperson who filled the order), and Order Date. Each record also contains a Customer ID field that enables you to look up information from the matching record in the Customers table.

- The Order Details table contains records that specify the items in each order. It contains an Order ID field that corresponds to the Order ID field in the Orders table, as well as a Product ID field that enables you to look up information from the matching record in the Products table. There are also fields for Quantity, Unit Price, and Discount.

- The Products table contains one record for each unique product you sell, containing the name and description of the product, its wholesale and retail prices, and a unique ID field that identifies that product.

By storing information in multiple related tables, each of which has a specific purpose, you can extract results and produce reports that combine data in a wide variety of ways. For instance, by starting with the Orders table, you can print out an invoice that includes the customer's name and address (drawn from the Customers table), the order information such as the date and shipper (from the Orders table), and all the details for each product in that sale (drawn from the Products and Order Details tables). If you start with the Customers table, you can prepare a monthly report that shows details and a grand total for each customer's orders that month. Or, by starting with the Products table, you can generate reports for each product showing sales by month and by customer, which might help you target advertising and promotions more effectively.

Before you can work with multiple tables in a database, you have to define a *relationship* between the tables. A relationship defines the fields that two tables have in common, so Access can combine information from the two tables into a logical result. In general, establishing a relationship between two tables requires that each table have a field in common with the other. Usually, the two common fields include the *primary key* for one table; the corresponding field in the second table is called the *foreign key*.

TIP FROM

EQ & Woody

> Although it's common for the fields that define a relationship to have the same name, it certainly isn't required. All that's necessary is that the two fields contain the same type of data. Thus, you could define a relationship between two tables by using the PostalCode field from one table and the ZipCode field from another table. Wherever the values match, Access combines the values in a query.

28

The most common type of relationship between tables is a *one-to-many* relationship, in which each record in a primary table can correspond to many records in a related table. Each record in the Products table (the primary table) corresponds to one or more records in the Order Details table. Conversely, each order detail record must correspond to exactly one product record. No order detail can be recorded without a product. One-to-many relationships are common in everyday life: In a classroom, one teacher has many students; in a business, one customer has many orders and each invoice has many items.

Two other types of relationships are less common, but still occasionally useful:

- As the name implies, *one-to-one* relationships store information in which a single record in one table corresponds to one and only one record in the second table.

- *Many-to-many* relationships actually consist of multiple one-to-many relationships, with an intermediate table (sometimes called a *junction table*) pulling the results together. At a university, for example, each class consists of one teacher and many students, and each student's schedule includes multiple classes. By using a third table, you can produce a query or report showing the many-to-many relationship between a group of students and a group of teachers.

TIP FROM

> One-to-one relationships are useful when data security is an issue. In a business, for example, you might have an employee table that contains contact information such as email addresses, phone numbers, department names, and locations. Another table contains information about salaries, performance reviews, and other sensitive information. Although only one record exists for each employee in each table, it would be foolish to combine the two tables and make the sensitive information visible to everyone. In this case, you set restrictions on user access to the second table, and then use a one-to-one relationship between the tables to create salary and benefits reports for authorized users.

Carefully defined *table relationships* are among the most important structural elements of a database. The Relationships window provides a clear graphic representation of all existing tables and queries for a database and enables you to define and edit the relationships between them. In the Relationships window, you can establish logical links between any combination of these objects.

If some of the relationships you define here don't appear in query windows, see "Juggling Multiple Relationships" in the "Troubleshooting" section at the end of this chapter.

Before attempting to edit or create relationships, first close any open tables. To open the Relationships window, select the Database Tools tab and then select Relationships. If you have not yet defined any relationships between tables in the current database, the Show Table dialog box appears automatically over the top of the Relationships window. If it doesn't appear, choose Design, Show Table. The Show Table dialog box displays a list of existing table objects in your database.

DEFINING A ONE-TO-MANY RELATIONSHIP

To define a one-to-many relationship, you must first make sure the two tables are visible in the Relationships window. Next, drag the related field from one table and drop it onto the other. Finally, use the Edit Relationships dialog box to define the properties of the relationship itself. Follow these steps:

1. If the two tables are not visible, use the Show Table dialog box to select the first table—Suppliers, for instance—and click Add. A field list for the Suppliers table appears inside the Relationships window. Repeat this step until all tables are visible in the Relationships window. Then click the Close button.

2. Make sure the fields that define the relationship are visible in both field lists. Click the field in the first table and drag it on top of the matching field in the second table. When you release the mouse button, the Edit Relationships dialog box appears on the desktop, as shown in Figure 28.9. The Edit Relationships dialog box identifies the matching fields that link two tables. It also tells you the type of relationship that is being created.

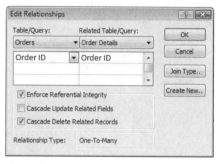

Figure 28.9

3. Examine the information displayed in the Edit Relationships dialog box to confirm that the definition is correct: In this example, Access is about to create a relationship between the Orders and Order Details tables, based on the Order ID field in each table. Access has determined that this is a one-to-many relationship, as you can see in the Relationship Type box.

 If the Relationship Type box identifies the relationship as Indeterminate, you'll need to make a few small repairs; see "Firming Up a Relationship" in the "Troubleshooting" section for some suggestions.

4. If you want to ensure consistency in your data, check the Enforce Referential Integrity box.

5. Click OK to define the relationship. Access adds a bold line connecting the fields in each table. The symbols displayed above the line indicate the direction of the one-to-many definition.

6. Click the Close button to close the Relationships window and save the layout you've created.

WORKING WITH ONE-TO-MANY RELATIONSHIPS

After creating a one-to-many relationship, you can see one important effect of the new relationship when you open the primary table (the table on the "one" side of the relationship) in Datasheet view. Access automatically creates a *subdatasheet* in this table, enabling you to view corresponding records from the related table. The only visible sign of the subdatasheet, at least initially, is a column of plus signs (known as *expand indicator icons*) at the left side of the table. Click any one of these icons to see details from the related table (the "many" side of the relationship) for the selected record. As you can see in the example in Figure 28.10, Access displays all the Order Details records for the selected record in the Orders table.

28

Figure 28.10
When you open a primary table that is part of a one-to-many relationship, you can expand or collapse the subdatasheet to control the display of data from the related table.

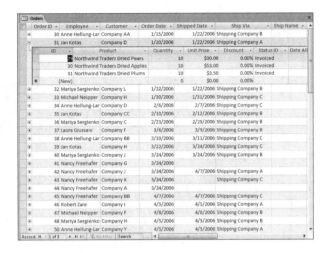

BUILDING FORMS AND REPORTS

Access provides a design and development environment that gives you extensive control over the appearance and functionality of forms and reports. The tools you use for either task are remarkably similar. The differences typically reflect the different design goals of forms and reports, as explained here:

- A *form* is a formatted database object, generally used to display one record at a time in an onscreen window. Forms are most commonly used to create convenient fill-in-the-blanks windows for entering or editing data; in this case, you use a table or query as the data source for the form.

- Access *reports* typically organize data in a format suited for printing or publishing. Although you can also use a form to view data onscreen, reports are better suited for this task and often represent the most important end product of a database.

When designing a form or report, you start by specifying a *data source*—one or more tables or queries, or a statement written in SQL—and position controls on a design grid. Although you can create a report or form from scratch in Design view, using a wizard is often a better starting point. The wizard produces the basic structure, and you then open the form or report in Design view to make detailed changes to its content and appearance.

As with other database objects, Access provides several ways to create a form or report. After selecting the Create tab, you are faced with a number of options in the Forms and Reports groups. These are the choices in the Forms group:

- **Form**—This is a basic columnar form layout that shows the data from one record at a time. If the data source is the primary table in a one-to-many relationship, the other table's related records are displayed in a subform.

- **Split Form**—This layout displays a form on top and a datasheet below. When you click a record in the datasheet, the record data also appears in the form.

- **Multiple Items**—This is a tabular layout that shows the field names at the top and the records in rows.
- **PivotChart**—Displays a form that enables you to summarize the data using a PivotChart.
- **Blank Form**—Displays a completely blank form to which you must associate a data source and then add the fields and controls by hand.
- **Form Wizard** (More Forms list)—Launches the Form Wizard.
- **Datasheet** (More Forms list)—This layout displays the records in a datasheet format, which is similar to what you see when you open a table.
- **Modal Dialog** (More Forms list)—Use this command to create a modal dialog box (*modal* means that the user cannot perform any other action in Access while the dialog box is displayed).
- **PivotTable** (More Forms list)—Displays a form that enables you to summarize the data using a PivotTable.
- **Form Design**—Displays the Form Design view so that you can build the form from scratch.

The following are the options you see in the Reports group:

- **Report**—This is a basic report layout that shows the data in columns.
- **Labels**—This button launches the Label Wizard, which enables you to create a report consisting of labels.
- **Blank Report**—Displays a completely blank report to which you must associate a data source and then add the fields and controls by hand.
- **Report Wizard**—Launches the Form Wizard.
- **Report Design**—Displays the Form Design view so that you can build the form from scratch.

To open an existing form or report in Design view, right-click it in the Navigation pane and click Design View. If the form or report is already open, select the Home tab, pull down the View menu, and click Design View.

WORKING WITH CONTROLS

The building blocks of any form or report are objects called *controls*, which include text boxes, labels, option buttons, lists, command buttons, toggles, and other familiar Windows interface elements. Controls have their own property settings, as do individual sections of the form or report; by changing the settings of these properties, you can modify the appearance and content of the form or report. Controls can take any of three forms:

- **Bound control**—Some controls are directly tied to a field in a table or query. In the peculiar jargon of Access, these are called *bound controls*. When you enter data in a control that is bound to a particular field, Access adds the data to that field; when you view data by using a form or report, Access checks the Control Source property for each control to see which data it should display. Figure 28.11 shows the Property Sheet pane for a text box bound to the Product Name field in the underlying table.

Figure 28.11

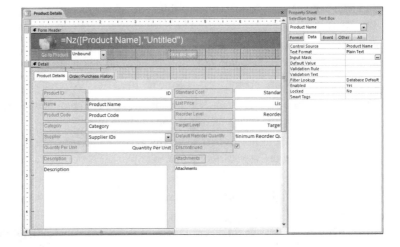

- **Unbound control**—Some controls are *unbound*—that is, not tied to any data source. For example, a line, box, or freestanding text label is an unbound control.

- **Calculated control**—When you enter an expression in the Control Source property box, Access creates a *calculated control*. The expression =[Standard Cost]*1.25, for example, multiplies the contents of the Standard Cost field by 1.25 and displays the result.

→ For an overview of Access expressions, **see** "Using Expressions in Database Objects," **p. 841**.

When you open a form or report in Design view, you can change the font, font size, color, borders, and other formatting properties of any control. In Design view, Access lets you position controls on a grid for precise alignment. You can also group and align controls.

When you work with a form or report in Design view, three interface elements are essential:

- In the Design tab, use the Controls group to add new controls or change existing controls.

- The Field List displays a list of all the fields in the source query or table, which you can use to add new controls. To show or hide this list in Design view, display the Design tab and click the Add Existing Fields button.

- To adjust the appearance or behavior of a control, section, or the form itself, open the Property Sheet pane by selecting Design, Property Sheet. With this pane displayed, as you select different objects, the properties displayed in the pane change to reflect the available choices.

TIP FROM

EQ & Woody

Tabs in the Property Sheet pane make it easier to find the exact function you're looking for. All the tabs that affect the appearance of a control, for example, are on the Format tab. Click the All tab to scroll through a list of all the properties that apply to the selected object.

ADDING A NEW CONTROL TO A FORM OR REPORT

If you drag a field name from the Field list onto a form or report, Access automatically creates a text box control bound to that field. If you click another Toolbox button first, and then drag a field onto the form, Access launches a wizard that creates the control type you selected. Figure 28.12, for example, shows one step of the Option Group Wizard. Follow the wizard's instructions to define the data source and behavior of the control.

Figure 28.12
If the Use Control Wizards button in the Controls group is selected when you add a new control to the form, Access lets you fill in the control's properties with a wizard.

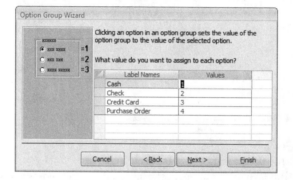

The Controls group contains buttons for common controls you might want to add to a form. By positioning the mouse pointer over a button in the Controls group, you can view a ScreenTip that shows the name of the control itself. Some of the more common and useful controls include the following: check boxes, which let users enter data in a Yes/No field or an option group; combo boxes and list boxes, which let users select from lists of data items; and labels, which add descriptive text to a control or a form or report.

NOTE

Labels are always unbound, and they don't change as you move from one record to another. Access automatically adds labels to new fields you place on a form or report; you might also use labels for titles and instructions.

POSITIONING CONTROLS AND LABELS

When you use the Form Wizard to build a form, the default type for all controls is a text box with a label attached to its left. In some cases, however, you'll want the labels to appear above the text box, and you might want to change the position, alignment, size, or grouping of controls on the form. After you learn the secrets of working with Access controls, you'll find it easy to position controls precisely where you want them. It does take some practice, however.

28

Access displays *handles*—small rectangles—around the outside of a selected control, as shown in Figure 28.13; these handles are a visual indication that you've selected the control. The eight small squares are *size handles*—you'll find one on each corner and one in the middle of each side of the selected control. When you position the mouse pointer over a size handle, it takes the shape of a double-headed arrow, at which point you can drag the handle in any direction to change the size and shape of the control itself.

Figure 28.13
Note that both the control and its label are selected here.

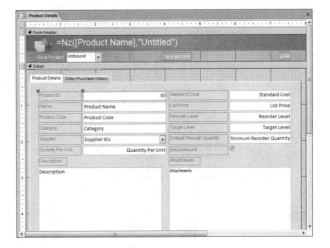

The larger square at the upper-left corner of a selected control lets you move the object to a new position within the form. As you move the selected control, you see only its outline, making it easier to position on the form grid. When you release the mouse button, the control itself moves to the location you've selected.

For the most part, every control you add to a form actually consists of two controls: the bound or unbound control (text box or combo box, for example), and a matching label. If you know the following techniques, it's easy to position these controls correctly:

- Use the large square in the upper-left corner of the control or the label to move either one independently. This technique is effective if you want to move a label from the left of a text box so that it sits above the control.

- To move both the control and its label at once, point to any border of the control or the label. Drag to position the control-label combination in its new location.

TIP FROM

EQ & Woody

Do you want to position an object precisely on a form? If you plan to print out an Access form and use it as an invoice, you might want a graphic to appear in a fixed location at the top of the form. To add the graphic, choose the Image button from the Controls group. Then click and drag to define a region on the form, in the general location where you want it to appear. Select the image file from the Insert Picture dialog box. Finally, click the Format tab on the Property Sheet pane for the image you embedded, and set the Left, Top, Width, and Height properties to define the exact size and location on the page.

28

To delete any control, select it and press the Delete key. If you select a control, Access also selects its label; if you click the label itself, Access does not select the matching control.

GROUPING AND ALIGNING CONTROLS

When working with a form or report in Design view, you can group, distribute, and align controls and other objects, just as you can in the Office drawing layer.

→ For a full discussion of basic techniques for working with the drawing layer in Office programs, **see** "Using Office Drawing Tools," **p. 104**.

In all cases, you start by selecting all the controls you want to work with simultaneously. To do so, hold down the Shift key and click each selection in succession. Or use the mouse to draw a rectangle around a group of objects and select them all at once. Say you've quickly added six new fields to a form, and now you want to tidy up the collection. The steps are as follows:

1. To distribute the controls into two groups of three, each distributed equally, use your mouse to select the first group of controls and choose Arrange, Make Vertical Spacing Equal. Then repeat the process for the second group of three fields.

2. To align each group of fields, select the controls and choose Arrange, Left.

3. With each group properly aligned and spaced, use your mouse to select all three fields and choose Arrange, Group. This option locks the current position of all the elements so that you can move them as one unit. Repeat for the second group of three fields.

MAKING FORMS EASIER TO USE

A well-designed form makes data entry easier and more accurate, especially when you want other people to enter data into a database. By limiting the data the user sees, carefully arranging input boxes, and providing explanatory text, you can guide the user through the data-entry process.

A form can include as many as five sections. The data itself typically appears in the Details section; in addition, each form can have up to two headers and two footers, with one header/footer combination for the form itself and another for individual pages. Select the Arrange tab and use the controls in the Show/Hide group to hide or show headers and footers.

Simple forms generally show the contents of one record at a time, but you can also design a form that includes a *subform*, which displays information from a related table or query. If you choose a table that includes a subdatasheet and then choose Create, Form, Access adds a subform automatically. Using this type of form, you can scroll through groups of records, or search for information by using filters and other search tools. Figure 28.14, for example, shows a form and subform combination in which the main form is bound to the Customers table, with a subform bound to the related Orders table. Note the two sets of navigation buttons at the bottom of the form. Use the Next and Previous record buttons for the main form to jump through the Customers table; use the navigation buttons within the subform to move through the list of orders for each customer.

28

Figure 28.14
This form, based on the Customers table, contains a subform that displays data from the related Orders table. The one-to-many relationship determines which data appears in the subform.

For special-purpose forms, one powerful area to explore is the Property Sheet for the form itself. This list contains settings that affect important characteristics of a form's appearance and behavior. For example, in the Data tab (see Figure 28.15), you can set three properties that determine whether the form is available for reading alone or can be used for editing, deleting, and appending records.

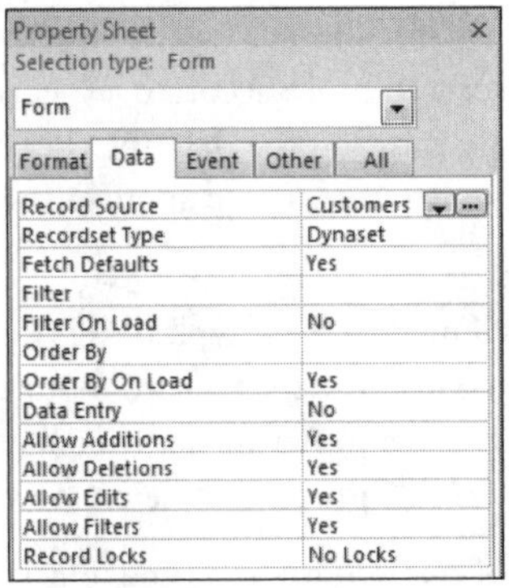

Figure 28.15
Set the Allow Edits, Allow Deletions, and Allow Additions form properties to No if you want your form to be used only for viewing data.

If the Property Sheet pane is open, but it currently displays the properties of a control or section, you can easily switch to a view of the form properties: Use the drop-down list at the top of the Property Sheet pane.

When you create a form from a single table, the Allow Edits, Allow Deletions, and Allow Additions properties are set to Yes. As a result, the user can add, edit, and delete records using nothing but this form. Depending on who will be using the form, you might want to restrict this capability. Change the property setting to No on one or more of these important properties if you want to restrict the user's ability to revise the data.

MAKING REPORTS EASIER TO UNDERSTAND

Access reports are organized into horizontal sections that are laid out in a specific order. Understanding how to work with each section is a crucial step in designing an effective report. Figure 28.16 shows a basic report that illustrates some commonly used sections.

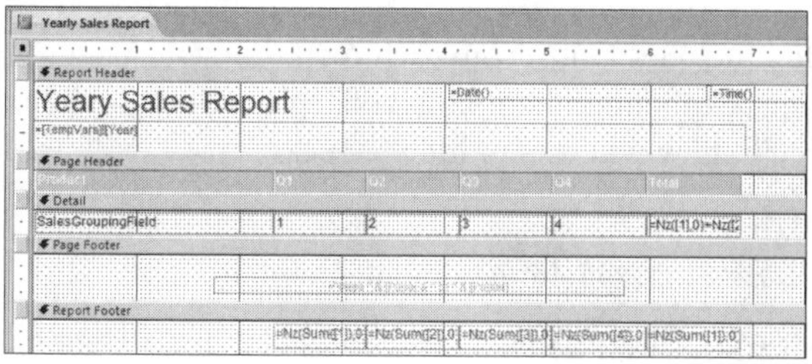

Figure 28.16
Each section in an Access report contains a different type of data. Headers and footers set off groups of data and pages; items you place in the Details section repeat as needed.

Here's a summary of the sections:

- The Report Header and Footer appear at the beginning and end of the report. A report header often includes the title of the report and a calculated control that contains the expression =Date() to display the date the report was printed. Report footers often contain grand totals or averages for the data within a report. To hide either section, change its Visible property to No, or select Arrange, Report Header/Footer.

TIP FROM

> With a modest amount of creativity, you can turn a report header into a dramatic title page for a report. If the report header isn't visible in Design view, choose Arrange, Report Header/Footer to make it appear. Next, drag the bottom border of the Report Header section to make it occupy as much of the page as you need. In the Properties dialog box for the section, set the Force New Page property to After Section. Finally, add any text labels and graphics you want, and set the background color if necessary.

- The Page Header and Footer appear at the top and bottom of each page, even if the Detail section is a continuation of data from the previous page. Page headers are commonly used for column headings, so readers can follow a lengthy list, and page footers are useful for dates and page numbers.

TIP FROM

> If you've grouped data using a field that contains date information, use the Group On option in the Group, Sort, and Total pane to arrange it by interval—month, quarter, or year, for example. By combining this header with other groupings, you can see a list of all sales by customer by month, even if the data appears only by day.

- Group Header and Group Footer sections appear automatically when you define grouping and sorting options for a report. By placing calculated fields in either of these sections, you can display summaries of the data within each group.

28

TIP FROM

Ed & Woody

> If you want to start a new page for each grouping, open the Properties dialog box for the Group Footer section and set the Force New Page property to After Section. If this section is not visible, set this property for the Detail section instead.

- The Detail section includes fields from each record in your data source. Each field in the Detail section appears once for each record in your data source, making this the right place to specify how you want a list to appear.

GROUPING AND SORTING RECORDS IN A REPORT

In complex presentations of Access data, *groups* are the essence of report design. A group defines how records are organized in the output of a report, and how information can be summarized in statistical calculations, such as totals and averages. In the Design view of a report, groups are represented by a hierarchy of Header, Detail, and Footer sections.

Using the Report Wizard, you can choose the fields you want to use for grouping in a report, and you can specify how you want groups to be summarized by specific calculations. To adjust grouping and sorting options, however, you need to flip into Design view and select the Design, Group and Sort button. This option displays the Group, Sort, and Total pane. Click More to see the full range of option, as shown in Figure 28.17, which gives you control over virtually all grouping options.

Figure 28.17
Use the Group, Sort, and Total pane to specify which fields should be used for grouping and whether you want to show or hide headers and footers for each section.

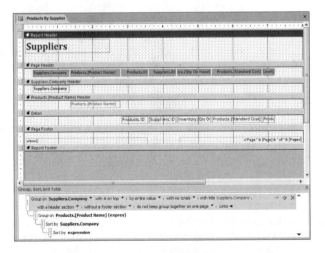

For example, in a report that you plan to use as a product catalog, you might want to group records by Supplier, in alphabetical order, with the product names listed under each supplier's name, also in alphabetical order. In this example, you would include the Supplier's name in a Group Header, with the Product Name, Standard Cost, and Qty On Hand fields in the Detail section; optionally, for an inventory report, you might add a calculated field in the Group Footer section, using the expression =SUM([Standard Cost]*[Qty On Hand]).

To tell Access you want to sort by Supplier, and then by Product Name, open the Group, Sort, and Total pane and use the first Group On list Suppliers table's Company field. Then click Add a Group and use the next Group On list to select the Products table's Product Name field. For sorting, use the first Sort By list to select the Company field, then click Add a Sort and use the next Sort By list to select Product Name. In each case, you can also select a sort order (such as With A On Top or With Z On Top).

By choosing these two fields, you tell Access that you want to sort records in this order, but you need to go one extra step to group records: In the Group, Sort, and Total pane, select the Company grouping, click More, and select With a Header Section. If you want to add a footer for this section, select the With a Footer Section option as well.

TIP FROM

El& Woody

When you've added two or more levels of grouping, you can change the order of the group headings. Move the mouse to the left edge of the grouping until the cursor changes to a pointing finger. Click the edge of the group and then drag it up or down in the Group, Sort, and Total pane. The group priority determines the ultimate heading locations and the nature of summary calculations: Groups at the top of the list can be used for grand totals, whereas those at the bottom of the list display subtotals for smaller groups.

USING QUERIES TO EXTRACT DATA FROM A DATABASE

Queries are database objects that enable you to extract data from a database to use in another way—as the source of data used in a printed report, for example, or to produce a list of items for use in a lookup control on a data-entry form. A query can be based on a single table or on multiple related tables. In addition to fields drawn directly from tables, a query can also contain *calculated fields* that transform data—adding sales tax to an invoice amount, for example, or performing statistical analysis (totals, averages, and the like) on groups of records drawn from multiple tables.

Like other Office wizards, the Access query wizards are efficient at guiding you smoothly through the steps of a complex process, providing detailed explanations of the choices you need to make, and enabling you to view graphic representations of the results.

Although Design view is a more versatile environment in which to create queries, it's often easier to begin by using a wizard to create a basic query. After you finish with the wizard, you can then open the query in Design view to modify the result.

To view a list of available query wizards, select Create, Query Wizard. The New Query dialog box lists four query wizards. Double-click any of these options to launch a wizard.

TIP FROM

El& Woody

In their efforts to simplify tasks, query wizards sometimes unnecessarily restrict your choices. In the Crosstab Query Wizard, for example, you must base your new query on a single existing table or query. If you want to use fields from more than one table, you must first create a query that contains all the target fields. By contrast, if you create a crosstab query in Design view, you can add fields from two or more related tables.

28

The first step in designing a query from scratch in Design view is to select the tables or queries on which the new query will be based. You can add any combination of existing tables and queries to the upper pane of the query design window. Choose Design, Show Table to open this box. The Show Table dialog box provides lists of all objects available for building a new query.

CHOOSING THE RIGHT QUERY TYPE

Access enables you to create several types of queries. The most common is a *select* query, which extracts information from one or more tables. You can also create *crosstab* queries, which group and summarize information in row-and-column formats such as an Excel PivotTable. Some of the most powerful (and potentially dangerous) things you can do with Access involve *action queries*, which actually change the data in an underlying table based on the criteria you define in the query.

Like queries, *filters* enable you to work with a subset of records in a database. Filters offer a quick way to temporarily limit the display of records in Datasheet or Form views. You can create a filter by entering data in a form or by making a selection in Datasheet view. Even though the display of data is filtered, it still represents "live" data, not a separate copy as in a report. If you enter changes in a Datasheet view based on a query, Access changes the data in the underlying table.

TIP FROM

EQ & Woody

Filters represent an excellent way to create a query without diving into the sometimes-confusing Query Design view. For instance, you can open a table in Datasheet view and select a fragment of data in a single field (the word Nylon, for instance). Create a filter based on the selection, and then switch to Advanced Filter/Sort view to save the filter as a query (Products That Contain the Word Nylon) that you can reuse anytime. Detailed instructions appear later in this chapter in the section "Creating and Applying Filters."

To create a new query, choose Create, Query Design to open the Design view, or choose Create, Query Wizard to open the New Query dialog box (see Figure 28.18) which lets you use a wizard to build one of several specific types of queries.

Figure 28.18
Use this dialog box to create queries based on a wizard.

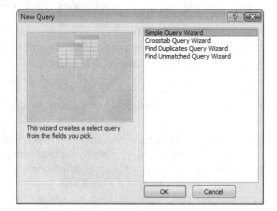

SELECT QUERIES

When you use Design view to create a new query from scratch, Access creates a select query by default. As the name implies, the purpose of a select query is to gather data from one or more tables, and to present it in a format that you save as part of the query itself. Select queries can include any of the following elements:

- Fields drawn from one or more tables or queries. You can base a query on another query, a common technique when you want to create a summary view of data gathered from multiple tables. Access uses defined relationships to match records from different sources and to find relevant connections between the data. You can also define new relationships between tables and/or queries and define them as part of the query.

→ For an explanation of how to define and save relationships, **see** "Defining Relationships Among Tables," **p. 848**.

- Calculated fields, which display the results of expressions using fields from one or more source tables.

- Totals, which perform statistical operations, such as sum and average, on fields from a source table.

- Selection criteria, which define the specific set of records the query will return. For example, in an Invoices table you might define criteria for the InvoiceDate field to return only invoices prepared in the past 30 days.

- Sorting instructions, which arrange the query results in numerical, alphabetical, or chronological order by one or more columns.

- Hidden fields, which are included for the purpose of defining criteria or sorting instructions, but are not actually shown in the query's results.

When you save a query, you save the instructions for retrieving and displaying records from a database, not the records themselves. As a result, running a saved query always displays the current data set.

Figure 28.19 shows a select query that combines data from three tables and is designed to produce a total value for each order. Note the third column, which contains a calculated field that multiplies the units ordered (the value in the Quantity field) by the unit price (as stored in the Unit Price field), and uses the Sum function to get the total for each order. The label in front of the formula in the third column (Order Total) defines the name of the calculated field. Use a colon to separate the label from the formula used to calculate the field results.

In Design view, a query includes two panes: The top pane contains field lists for each table and query used as a data source; this pane also shows relationships between the data sources. The lower pane contains a grid with one column for each field that makes up the query. When you design a query, you can drag any field reference directly from the lists in the upper pane, or you can choose from drop-down lists that appear when you activate a given column in the grid. (Double-click a field name to quickly add it to the grid.) You can enter calculated columns manually or with the help of the Expression Builder.

→ For details about how to use the Expression Builder, **see** "Using Expressions in Database Objects," **p. 841**.

28

Figure 28.19
This select query combines data from three tables, along with totals; the third column is a calculated column.

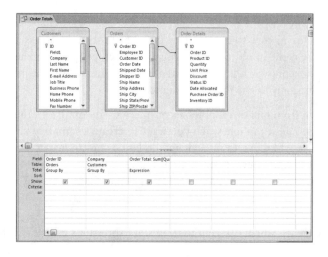

In the rows below each field name, you can see specifications that explicitly determine the content of the query:

- The Table row shows the source of each field. This row is visible by default.

- The Total row (select Design, Totals to see it) lets you specify operations to be performed on that field—Sum, Average, and so on. This row is normally hidden. The default selection is Group By, which displays all values in the selected field without performing a calculation.

- The Sort row specifies whether a particular column will be used for sorting, and if so, whether the sort is in ascending or descending order. If you specify a sort order in multiple columns, Access sorts by each column, going in order from left to right.

- The Show row contains a check for each field that will be displayed as part of the query's results. Clear this check box when you want to use a field for sorting or filtering but you don't want it to appear in Datasheet view.

- The Criteria rows contain one or more criterion expressions for determining which records will be included in the query.

→ For an explanation of how to use criteria in queries, **see** "Defining Criteria," **p. 870**.

CROSSTAB QUERIES

Another kind of query, known as a *crosstab*, transforms record-oriented data into a summary view that resembles an Excel PivotTable.

The Design window for a simple crosstab query appears in Figure 28.20. The grid in the lower pane of the window includes a Crosstab row not found in select queries, where the contents of the selected fields are identified as the Row Heading, Column Heading, and Value of the crosstab query. To add the Crosstab row to the design grid of a select query, choose Design, Crosstab.

Figure 28.20
In the Design window of a crosstab query, select fields for row headings, column headings, and values. The Crosstab Query Wizard fills in these values automatically.

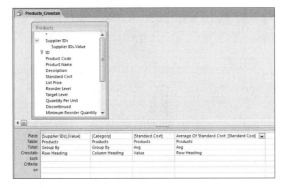

Creating a crosstab query from scratch in the Design window is a fairly straightforward process, but it's much easier when you use the Crosstab Query Wizard.

PARAMETER QUERIES

Normally, saving a query includes all the criteria you've defined for that query. If you want to see all sales results by product for all vendors, it's easy to save a query that extracts those results from the current contents of the database each time you run it. But what do you do when you want to specify slightly different criteria every time you run the query? For instance, what if you want to enter a specific vendor number or a maximum price when you run a query? For that task, you need a *parameter* query.

Each time you open a parameter query, Access displays a dialog box asking you to enter a piece of data to be used in the selection criteria for the query. You define the input prompt as part of the query's definition.

To create a parameter query, open the query in Design view and click in the Criteria box for the field in which you want to add selection criteria. The expression should include the text you want to display as the input prompt, enclosed in square brackets where you would normally enter a constant value. For example, Figure 28.21 shows a parameter query that prompts you to enter the minimum list price you want to use as the selection criterion in a Products table select query.

The value the user enters into the prompt becomes the parameter in the expression, which in this example specifies a selection criterion for the query. For example, if you enter 10 in the Enter Parameter Value dialog box, Access displays a list of products whose list price is at least $10.00.

 If Access prompts you for a parameter when you try to run an ordinary select query, see "Is It a Parameter or a Typo?" in the "Troubleshooting" section at the end of this chapter.

Figure 28.21
To create a parameter query, you write an expression that replaces part of the selection criterion with an input prompt; the result is an interactive query.

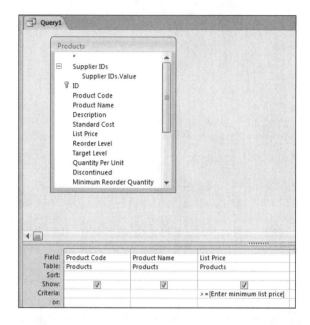

The simplest parameter queries include a single value, but you can also use wildcards or multiple parameters as part of a query. The following examples should give you some ideas:

- To create an input dialog box that prompts the user to enter the beginning of a search string, use an asterisk with the parameter. For instance, entering `Like [Enter beginning of product name] & "*"` will search for all records in which the specified field begins with the value the user inputs.

- To search for a string anywhere in a given field, use two asterisks: `Like "*"&[Enter any text that appears in the product name]&"*"` will do the trick.

- To define a beginning and ending range of numbers or dates, use two parameters in a single expression, such as: `Between [Enter beginning date] And [Enter ending date]`. When you run a query with multiple parameters, Access displays an input dialog box for each one.

TIP FROM

Ed & Woody

The expression you enter in the Criteria row of a parameter query can include a large amount of text, especially if you include more than one input prompt. That can make it difficult to enter and edit criteria in the query grid. If the expression is just a few characters wider than the current column width, expand the column that contains the expression by dragging the right border of its column heading. For extremely long and complicated expressions, press Shift+F2 to open a Zoom window for entering or editing the expression.

28

ACTION QUERIES

An *action query* potentially changes the data in an existing table, or creates a new table.
Access enables you to create four kinds of action queries:

- An *update* query replaces data in existing records. In the design of an update query, you
  write selection criteria to identify the target records, and you provide an expression that
  generates the replacement data.
  Use an update query to change a
  group of records at once—when
  an area code changes, for example,
  or to make an across-the-board
  price increase. The example in
  Figure 28.22 shows the properties
  of an update query that include a
  parameter: It adds 5% to the
  amount in the List Price field for
  all records that match the supplier
  code you enter.

- A *make-table* query creates a new
  table object from the result of the
  query itself. For instance, you
  might build a query that produces
  a list of all customers who have
  not ordered products from you in
  the past year and copy those
  records into an Inactive Customers
  table. This type of query does not
  affect the underlying source data.
  As Figure 28.23 shows, when you
  choose Design, Make Table, you
  can select a table from the current
  database or from another database
  file. If you enter the name of a
  table that does not currently exist,
  Access creates it for you.

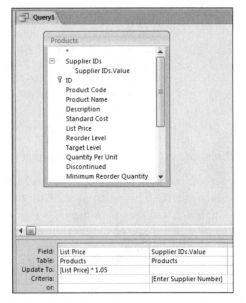

Figure 28.22

Figure 28.23

- An *append* query adds new records to an existing table from a source query. This type of
  query is most commonly used when importing data from an external source. Append
  queries enable you to take some or all of the imported information and move it into an
  existing set of tables in the correct format. When you choose Design, Append, Access
  prompts you to enter a table name by using a dialog box that is identical to the one for a
  make-table query.

- A *delete* query removes records that match specified selection criteria for an existing
  table. You might use a delete query to prune outdated records from a database. When
  you create a delete query, Access adds a Delete row to the query's design grid.

28

TIP FROM

EQ & Woody

> Want to archive information from a database table? Run a make-table query to copy records that meet specific criteria, such as customers who haven't placed an order in more than a year. Then, after running that query, use the same selection criteria as part of a delete query to remove the same records from the original table.

CAUTION

> Running an action query can absolutely and irrevocably scramble your data, and in most cases the effect of an action query cannot be undone. If you inadvertently run an action query that doesn't behave as you expected, you might find it difficult or impossible to restore your original data. For this reason, you should proceed with great care when designing and running an action query. At a minimum, make a copy of the original table under another name, so that you can restore the data if your action query has unintended consequences.

Following are two fail-safe mechanisms that can prevent a data disaster:

- Before you begin designing an action query, create a copy of the table you intend to modify. In the Navigation pane, select the table, press Ctrl+C to copy it to the Clipboard, and then immediately press Ctrl+V. In the Paste Table As dialog box, enter a name such as `Copy of Tablename`, choose the Structure and Data option, and click OK to create the copy. If the action query doesn't work properly, you can return to the original state by deleting the modified table and renaming the backup copy the same name as the original.

- Before running an action query, test its effects by designing a select query that uses the same selection criteria. When you open this query in Datasheet view, inspect the results carefully, because these records will ultimately be the same ones that change as a result of the action query. After inspecting the results, return to Design view and, in the Design tab, choose the type of query you want to create.

TIP FROM

EQ & Woody

> You can save an action query for future use, or you can abandon it after a single use. If the purpose of the query is to perform a one-time maintenance chore, get rid of the query when you no longer need it. That way you don't risk accidentally corrupting your database. The only reason to save a query is if you expect to reuse it as part of ongoing database management—for example, in a monthly database cleanup routine.

SQL QUERIES

Structured Query Language (SQL) is a powerful, industry-standard database language that is available for use in a variety of software environments. In general, you can build Access queries interactively by checking dialog box options, and never have to deal with SQL. However, every Access query exists behind the scenes as an SQL statement, and in some cases you might find it useful to work directly with the SQL code.

NOTE

Microsoft's most powerful database product, designed to run on networks, is called SQL Server. Database experts typically pronounce each of the letters in this acronym: *S-Q-L* Server. Some old-timers prefer the more casual pronunciation, *Sequel Server.*

To view the SQL statement behind a query you've created in Access, open the query in Datasheet or Design view, and then choose View, SQL View. Access opens an SQL view window, showing the statement that matches the query you created in Design view. For example, the SQL equivalent of the query shown previously in Figure 28.19 is:

```
SELECT Orders.[Order ID], Customers.Company, Sum([Quantity]*[Unit Price])
AS [Order Total] FROM (Customers INNER JOIN Orders ON Customers.ID =
Orders.[Customer ID]) INNER JOIN [Order Details] ON Orders.[Order ID] =
[Order Details].[Order ID] GROUP BY Orders.[Order ID], Customers.Company;
```

Why should you care about SQL code? Under normal circumstances, you don't need to. However, SQL code can be exceptionally useful in one specific circumstance: when you want to use a complex query as the data source for another object, such as a form or report. Open the underlying query in SQL view, copy its entire contents to the Clipboard, and then paste it into the Record Source property box for the form or report.

NOTE

For a thorough discussion of how to use SQL statements with Access databases, see *Special Edition Using Microsoft Access 2007*, published by Que.

INSERTING, DELETING, AND REARRANGING FIELDS

To add a new field to a query, use any of the following techniques:

■ Drag the field name directly from a list in the upper pane and drop it on the grid. When you release the mouse button, the new field appears in the grid to the left of the field on which you dropped it.

TIP FROM

To select multiple fields in a field list, hold down Ctrl and click, and then drag the fields into the query design grid. Hold down Shift and drag to select contiguous fields.

■ Double-click any field name in a list to add that field name in the next available column.
■ Click the down-arrow button in the top cell of any empty column to choose from a drop-down list of all available fields. Note that fields and tables are identified by using the notation *TableName.FieldName*.

28

In some cases, you might want to add all the fields from a selected table to the query grid. If you don't need to work with the properties of individual fields in the grid, you can drag the asterisk from the top of a field list to a cell in the grid. When you do, Access represents the table in the notation *TableName.**. This notation means that all the table's fields will be shown in the output of the query. If you need to work with individual field settings in the design grid, double-click the title bar of the target table list to select all fields, and then drag the selection to the design grid.

To delete or move a field in the design grid, begin by selecting the field's column. Place the mouse pointer over the gray bar just above the column; the mouse pointer changes to a small black down arrow. Click to select the current column, and then drag the column to a new position or press the Delete key to remove the field from the query's design.

DEFINING A CALCULATED COLUMN

To define a calculated column, enter an expression in the Field row. You can enter an expression directly, such as [RetailPrice]*[UnitSales]; note that you must use brackets around field names. Or you can click the Build button to use the Expression Builder to create a calculated field.

If you enter an expression alone, Access adds a default name for the calculated field, using the generic *Expr1*, *Expr2*, and so on. To specify a more descriptive name, double-click this generic label and type a replacement name.

DEFINING CRITERIA

Any expressions you enter in the Criteria row instruct Access to show only those records that satisfy the criteria. These expressions can be extremely simple: >10, for example, tells Access to display all records in which the value of the selected field is greater than 10. You can combine multiple criteria in a single column or across multiple columns, using the following logical rules:

- Expressions in multiple columns in a single row are treated as And criteria. To be selected as part of the query's results, a record must meet all the criteria in a given row.

- Expressions in different rows are treated as Or criteria. To be selected, a record needs to meet the criteria only in any one row.

When building an entry in the Criteria row, you can use any expression that evaluates to True or False. The most common building blocks for numeric and date fields are the comparison operators: < (less than), > (greater than), <= (less than or equal to), >= (greater than or equal to), <> (not equal), and = (equal). With Access, you can make an additional comparison by using the keyword Between, which expresses an inclusive range to compare with the value of a field.

You can also use the logical operators And, Or, and Not. If two expressions are connected by And, the operation is true only if both expressions are true. By contrast, the Or operation is true if either one or both of the expressions are true. The Not operation yields the opposite of the expression it modifies—true if the expression is false, or false if the expression is true.

Finally, for text fields, use the Like operator, with or without wildcards. If you enter a string of text in the Criteria box for a given field, Access automatically adds the Like operator and encloses the string in quotes.

28

DEFINING QUERY PROPERTIES

In addition to the settings we've discussed so far, which are available in the design grid for a query, you can also adjust a host of settings that apply to the entire query. Open a query and switch to Design view. If necessary, click the Property Sheet button to display the Property Sheet pane, and then click anywhere in the background area of the query design window.

The Query Property Sheet pane contains a list of settings that apply to the specific type of query that you're creating. Although some of these settings are for specialized uses, the following are valuable in common situations in which you might use a query:

- **Top Values**—Returns a specified number or percentage of records. This setting is most often used in conjunction with a sort setting; to see the 10 most expensive products, for example, click the List Price column, and set Top Values to 10 and the Sort field to Descending.

- **Unique Values**—Returns a query result in which no duplicate records exist. Choose Yes if you want to extract a unique set of values from a database, such as supplier names from a table filled with product names. Access eliminates duplicates from the result set based on records visible in the query's result, not on the contents of the underlying table or tables.

- **Unique Records**—Returns a query result after eliminating duplicate records in the data source. Depending on the fields you choose to display, you might see duplicate values in the query results.

- **Column Headings**—This property, used only in crosstab queries, lets you limit the columns to be displayed. Separate entries with semicolons. In a data source that contains a RegionalOffice field, for example, you might specify East;West;Midwest in this property. Access ignores all other values when performing the crosstab query and displays these three columns in the specified order.

- **Output All Fields**—Specifies that you want the query to return all fields from all tables included in the query, regardless of whether the field name is on the design grid or the Show box is checked. When you set this property, you need to add fields to the grid only to set Criteria and Sort properties.

- **Link Child Fields, Link Master Fields**—Used to set the relationship between a main form and a subform or other embedded object. Normally, Access sets this property automatically based on relationships you define between the tables.

28

CREATING AND APPLYING FILTERS

When you run a query that uses criteria, Access returns a subset of records in the underlying data source. To revise the selection criteria, you have to open the query in Design view and enter one or more new expressions in the Criteria row of the design grid. You then have the option of saving these new criteria as part of the permanent design of your query.

A filter is a faster, more convenient way to temporarily focus on specific records in a query, table, or form. You can develop and apply filters quickly, without switching to Design view, and return to the unfiltered display whenever you want to see the entire set of records again.

The easiest way to create a filter is to base it on the contents of an existing record. When a query or table is open in Datasheet view or in a form, display the Home tab and pull down the Selection list in the Sort & Filter group. The commands you see depend on the data type of the selected field. When you choose one of the options in this list, Access shows or hides records based on your selection. The exact filter action depends on which of the following three selections you make:

- If you select the entire contents of a field, or position the insertion point in a field without making any selection, the Selection list for a text field displays the command Equals "X" and the command Does Not Equal "X", where X is the contents of the field. The filter finds (or excludes) all records in which the contents of that field match the exact contents of the selected cell. This technique is especially effective when a field contains a category description or a name that is repeated in records throughout the data source.

- If you select a portion of the cell that includes the first character in the cell, the Selection list for a text field displays the command Begins With "X" and the command Does Not Begin With "X", where X is the selected text. The filter finds (or excludes) all records in which the field begins with the selection. If you want to see only those products that begin with the letter A, for example, find any product that begins with that letter, select the first character in its name, and choose Home, Selection, Begins With "A".

- Finally, if you select a portion of a cell's contents that does not include the first character, the Selection list for a text field displays the command Contains "X" and the command Does Not Contain "X", where X is the selected text. (These commands are also available in the preceding two scenarios.) The filter shows (or hides) all the records in the query that contain the selected string of characters or numbers anywhere in the target field. This technique is useful for finding records based on the contents of a field that contains variable text rather than consistent entries.

If no record that matches the filter is visible, select Home, Advanced, Filter by Form. This option clears away the current contents of the query or table and displays a simple grid containing each of the columns in the query or table with a blank cell under each one. When you click in any of these blank cells, you can enter an expression or select from a drop-down list of unique items contained in each field of the query (see Figure 28.24).

Figure 28.24
The Filter by Form option lets you enter expressions or choose from a drop-down list to refine the display of data from a query or table.

After entering criteria in the Filter by Form window, click the Home, Toggle Filter button to apply the filter and see its results. (Note that the ScreenTip for this button reads Apply Filter or Remove Filter, depending on its current state.) If you need to refine the filter, select the Filter by Form command again, and add or remove criteria.

TIP FROM

The Filter by Form interface looks simple, but it can be surprisingly powerful. If you enter criteria in multiple fields, Access combines them by using the logical operator And—all the conditions must be true to display a result. Click the Or tab at the bottom of the window to create an additional set of conditions using the Or operator—Access will return records that match any of the sets of conditions you enter.

Regardless of how you create a filter, you can always restore the display of all records by clicking the Toggle Filter button again.

To create complex filters, or to edit an existing filter, choose Home, Advanced, Advanced Filter/Sort. The resulting filter window contains a field list and a design grid, identical to the Design view for a query. To refine a filter, add one or more fields to the grid and write criteria expressions to select a subset of records; then click the Apply Filter button to see the result of your filter.

Troubleshooting

Installing the Sample Database

I want to look through the Access sample database to see whether I can glean any ideas or borrow any objects or code, but the Open dialog box doesn't include shortcuts for the samples, and I can't find them anywhere on my hard disk.

Before you can open the sample file, you have to download it. Select Office, New and then click the Sample category. Click the Northwind 2007 item, modify the File Name, if desired, and then click Download.

Once the template is installed, Access opens it and displays a Security Warning message in the Message Bar. Click Options, click Enable This Content, and then click OK. When you see the Login Dialog, click Login.

JUGGLING MULTIPLE RELATIONSHIPS

I defined relationships between two or more tables, but when I open the Query window to edit an existing query, Access doesn't connect the tables with lines. What's wrong?

The Relationships window enables you to define default relationships between tables. When you create a new query, Access picks up those settings and uses them. Changing the default relationship in the Relationships window has no effect on existing objects, such as queries; likewise, you can change the relationship between two tables in a query without affecting the default relationship. Re-create the relationship in the Query window so that it matches the default relationship for the two tables.

FIRMING UP A RELATIONSHIP

According to the Edit Relationships dialog box, a relationship I established between two tables is of "Indeterminate" type. Is this a problem?

Check the design of your database. You're probably trying to create a many-to-many relationship without using a junction table. If neither field is a primary key or has a unique index, Access knows that you can enter duplicate values on both sides of the relationship; as a result, it's impossible to define the relationship properly. If necessary, define a unique index for one of the fields.

IS IT A PARAMETER OR A TYPO?

I created a simple select query without parameters, but when I run it, Access displays an Enter Parameter Value dialog box. Regardless of what I enter, the query doesn't work properly.

This problem is almost always caused by a typo in a field name. Field names and parameters both appear inside brackets. If you misspell a field name, especially in an expression used with a calculated field, Access can't find the field and therefore assumes you want to display a parameter dialog box. Go through every expression in the query and see whether you can find (and fix!) the typo.

SECRETS OF THE OFFICE MASTERS: RESTRICTING DATA ENTRY

Even the most carefully designed database is worthless if it contains inaccurate or inconsistent data. Unfortunately, the data-entry process is typically tedious, and even a highly motivated, well-trained worker can become tired or distracted. When fingers slip or the mind wanders, errors are inevitable. You can't prevent users from accidentally typing incorrect data, but you can define rules that prevent Access from storing errors.

DEFINING VALIDATION RULES

Like Excel, Access enables you to write *validation rules*; you can attach a validation rule to a field or to an entire table. When a user attempts to save a new or changed record, Access checks the contents of each field in that record against any existing validation rules. If the record violates a rule, Access displays an error message, which you can customize. By creating validation rules, you can avoid entering data that is outside a reasonable range, inappropriate, or just plain wrong.

To attach a validation rule to a field, open the table in Design view, select the field, and edit the Validation Rule and Validation Text properties. In the input box for the Validation Rule property, enter a logical expression that must be evaluated as *true* for Access to accept an entry in the target field. In the Validation Text property, enter the error message that Access will display for any entry that does not pass the rule. (If you leave this property empty, Access will display a default error message.)

To build complex validation rules, including those that incorporate Access functions, use the Expression Builder. To open the Expression Builder, open a table in Design view, select the Validation Rule property for a target field, and click the Build button (...) to the right of the setting box (or choose Design, Builder). For simple validation rules, however, you can enter an expression directly in the Validation Rule property box.

For example, in a Products table that consists exclusively of low-cost items, you might anticipate one common data-entry error—if the user inadvertently drops the decimal point in a unit price, she might try to enter $399 instead of the correct value, $3.99. By comparing the value in the List Price field to the expression >0 And <100, you can ensure that only positive values under 100 make it into the database. As part of this rule, create a helpful error message for users: In the Validation Text box, enter **List Price must be less than $100**. Figure 28.25 shows the validation rule and accompanying error message as they appear in Design view.

Figure 28.25
To prevent users from accidentally entering invalid or inappropriate data, set the Validation Rule property. Use the Validation Text property to display a friendly error message.

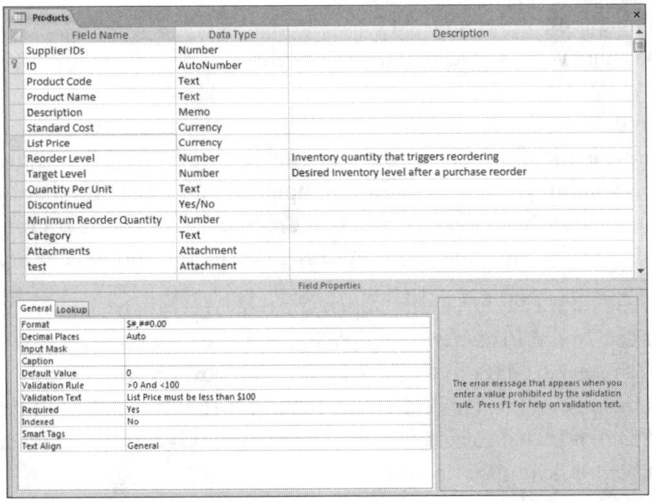

Right-click the table tab and click Save to save the rule as part of the table. When you add a validation rule to a table that already contains data, Access walks you through a two-step process: First, the program asks whether you want to test the existing data in your table against the new rule; if you want the rule to apply to newly entered data only, click No. You might choose this option in an invoice database, for example, where you want to restrict numbers and dates for new invoices only.

If you specify that you want the rule to be applied to existing data, Access applies the rule to the existing table and warns you if it finds any data that violates the rule. This option is especially useful after you've imported a table from another source. If errors exist, you can then choose to keep the validation rule and allow the incorrect data to remain in the database; if the error-checking turns up a problem in your rule, you can reset the contents of the Validation Rule property to its previous setting and start over.

The following examples illustrate some useful validation rules:

- `>0` in a numeric field specifies that the value must be positive and not zero.

- `<= Date()` compares the value in a date field to today's date to make sure the date is not in the future; you might use this rule when you want to ensure that employees don't accidentally enter an invoice date that is in the future.

- `[ShipDate]<=[OrderDate]+30` displays an error message if you enter a ship date that is more than 30 days past the order date. (As this example illustrates, field names are enclosed in brackets.)

- `Like "S???"`, when used in a Text field, requires the user to enter a value that is exactly four characters long and begins with S.

- `StrComp(UCase([TickerSymbol]),[TickerSymbol],0) = 0` uses several Access functions to ensure that the value (in this case, a stock ticker symbol) is entered in all caps.

- `>=#1/1/2003# And <Date()` allows the user to enter a date that is greater than January 1, 2003, but before today's date; note that date values must be enclosed between number signs (#).

- `>=1001 And <=9999`, when used in a field that is set to an Integer data type, guarantees that the value you enter is exactly four digits.

You can also define validation rules for an entire table, rather than for an individual field. This technique is useful when you want to establish rules that involve more than one field. For instance, you might want to define an input rule that specifies that the List Price field can never be greater than twice the value of the Standard Cost field in the same record. Defining this rule for the table allows Access to check the contents of both fields at once.

To enter a validation rule for a table, open the table in Design view and choose Design, Property Sheet. In the Property Sheet pane, enter the expression **[List Price]<=2*[Standard Cost]** in the Validation Rule box. (Note that you must enclose the field names in square brackets in this expression.) If the user enters a Standard Cost of $1.95 and a List Price of $3.99, Access displays an error message; the user must change one or both values before saving the record.

USING AN INPUT MASK TO DEFINE DATA FORMATS

When you're concerned with the appearance of data rather than its value, use an *input mask*. This field property supplies an input template consisting of blank spaces and literal characters (parentheses or hyphens, for example) that force a field's contents into the correct format. You can use this property to simplify standard-format entries such as phone numbers, vehicle identification codes, and Social Security numbers. The mask can include special characters such as parentheses and dashes, providing visual clues for the data entry itself.

SETTING A DEFAULT VALUE

The Default Value property supplies the starting value for any field. Whenever a field has a typical or common value, you can use this property to supply that value; the user can override it with a different entry, if necessary. The default value can be a *constant*, such as 0 or California or #12/31/2007#, or an expression from the Expression Builder. If you want a field to default to a value of today's date, for example, use Date() as the Default Value property. In an invoice table, you might set the PaymentDue field to a default value of [InvoiceDate]+30; to specify a different date, click in the field and replace the default value.

REQUIRING A VALUE

The Required property determines whether the user must enter a value for a particular field to complete a record entry. The setting for this property is either Yes or No. If the property is No, the field can be left blank in a new record entry. Set this property to Yes if you do not want to allow the user to skip an important field.

28

CHAPTER 29

USING ONENOTE

In this chapter

What's New in OneNote 2007   880

Using Notebooks   881

Working with Pages   887

Finding Information in OneNote   898

Adding Audio and Video to a Notebook   899

Keeping Track of Tasks and To-Do Lists   901

Troubleshooting   904

Secrets of the Office Masters: Sending Information to OneNote   904

29

WHAT'S NEW IN ONENOTE 2007

Much of the data that comes your way each day probably gets stored electronically in some fashion: you store names and phone numbers in Outlook's Contacts; you save appointments and meetings in Outlook's Calendar; you store simple data in an Excel worksheet, and more complex data in an Access database. However, what about data that doesn't really fit into the main Office programs? What about thoughts and ideas, titles of books to read, meeting notes, and media such as screen captures, web images, and audio recordings? None of the main Office applications offer an easy way to record and manage these scraps of information, but there's another Office program that does: OneNote. Using special folders called *notebooks*, you can easily save and work with a variety of data, including both typewritten and handwritten text, pictures, drawings, tables, bulleted and numbered lists, files, screenshots, audio and video recordings, Outlook tasks, hyperlinks, and more.

OneNote 2007 improves on the original version of OneNote in many ways, including the following:

- You can now work with multiple notebooks. In OneNote 2003, you had just one notebook (called My Notebook) to work with, but with OneNote 2007, you can create as many notebook folders as you need. OneNote 2007 even comes with a number of notebook templates.

- You can use the same notebook on multiple computers. For example, if you have a desktop PC and a portable PC, OneNote will automatically synchronize the changes you make on both computers.

- You can share notebooks with other OneNote users. In OneNote 2003, you could start a shared note-taking session or share parts of the notebook on a SharePoint site. With OneNote 2007, you can share entire notebooks just like any other folder.

- OneNote 2007 has tighter integration with Outlook. For example, you can not only display Outlook tasks in a notebook, but you can also synchronize those tasks. For example, if you mark a task as complete in Outlook, the task shows as complete in OneNote. You can also create linked notes for Outlook contacts and meetings and even send an email to OneNote.

- OneNote 2007 comes with a new Unfiled Notes section that is not associated with any notebook. You can use this section to store random notes that don't (yet) fit in anywhere else.

- You can attach files to pages and embed Office documents.

- You can "print" a file into a notebook. OneNote 2007 comes with its own printer driver. When you open a document, select the program's Print command, and then choose the Send to OneNote 2007 printer, the document appears in OneNote in the Unfiled Notes section.

- OneNote 2007 offers extensive tools for creating and formatting tables to store data.

- You can send web pages to OneNote from Internet Explorer.

- You can create hyperlinks that take you to other notes.

- OneNote 2007 lets you make audio and video recordings and store them in a notebook. The program also has an Audio Search feature that enables you to find words in recorded audio and video.

- OneNote 2007 uses optical character recognition to read text in scanned documents and images, and it includes that text when you search a notebook.

- You can save a notebook as a PDF or XPS file, if you have the Save As PDF or XPS add-in installed.

USING NOTEBOOKS

In the real world, a notebook might come with (or you might add) several color-coded tabs that divide the notebook into separate sections, each with its own collection of pages. This is the metaphor that OneNote uses. OneNote folders are called *notebooks* and each notebook consists of a series of color-coded tabs—called *sections*—along the top, and each section consists of one or more pages. You use these pages to enter your free-form notes.

OneNote 2007 comes with two notebooks already created for you: the Work Notebook (see Figure 29.1) has tabs named Meeting Notes, Project A, Project B, Research, Travel, and Miscellaneous; the Personal Notebook has tabs named Shopping, Books, Movies, and Music, Recipes, To Do, Travel, Miscellaneous, and Personal Information. Unfortunately, most of the sections in these prefabricated notebooks contain "About This Section" notes that offer examples of what to store in the section and OneNote tips. That's fine when you're just starting out, but when you're ready to store your own notes, you'll probably want to delete the existing notes. To avoid that, you can create your own notebooks.

Figure 29.1
OneNote 2007 comes with two ready-made notebooks: Work Notebook and Personal Notebook.

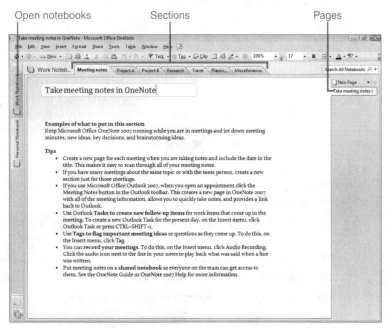

29

CREATING A NEW NOTEBOOK

OneNote 2007 comes with a New Notebook Wizard that lets you select a template, set up notebook sharing, and specify the location of the new folder. Note that the default location in Windows Vista is `%UserProfile%\Documents\OneNote Notebooks`. (In Windows XP, it's `%UserProfile%\My Documents\OneNote Notebooks`.) Follow these steps to create a new notebook:

1. Choose File, New, Notebook (or pull down the New list in the toolbar and select Notebook) to launch the New Notebook Wizard (see Figure 29.2).

Figure 29.2
Use the New Notebook Wizard to create and configure your notebook.

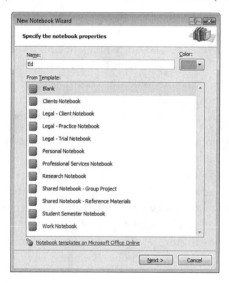

2. Type a Name for the notebook, select a Color, and select the template you want to use. (You can also click Notebook Template On Microsoft Office Online to download templates.) Click Next.

> **NOTE**
>
> With the exception of Blank, all the notebook templates come with a collection of sections, and most of those sections have notes on how to use them. If you want to avoid having to delete these notes, select the Blank template.

3. The wizard now offers you three choices related to notebook sharing (choose one and click Next when you're done):

   - **I Will Use It on This Computer**—Select this option if you won't be sharing the notebook with other computers or other users.

   - **I Will Use It on Multiple Computers**—Select this option if you want to use the same notebook on two or more computers.

   - **Multiple People Will Share the Notebook**—Select this option if you want to share the notebook with other users. See "Sharing a Notebook," later in this chapter for more information.

29

4. Specify the path where you want the new notebook saved. If you elected to share the notebook with other computers, OneNote automatically sets up the folder for sharing. You also see the Create an Email with a Link to This Notebook That I Can Send to Other People check box. Leave this check box activated to send the email with the note-book-sharing information.

 Are you having a problem sharing the notebook? See "Sharing Notebook Folders" in the "Troubleshooting" section at the end of this chapter.

5. Click Create. If you opted to send the email with the link to the shared notebook, fill in the recipients and send the message.

Note that each notebook you create is actually a folder that stores the notebook's sections, which we discuss next.

ORGANIZING INFORMATION WITH SECTIONS

By definition, a OneNote notebook is a collection of data scraps from a variety of sources. Therefore, it's important that you impose some kind of order on all those scraps so that the notebook doesn't devolve into an unruly mess where it takes too long to find what you need. Thanks to OneNote's 2007's support for multiple notebooks, the first level of organization is the notebook itself, each of which should ideally contain only related information. It could be as broad as having "Business" and "Personal" notebooks, or you might want a more tar-geted approach where you have notebooks for specific projects, school, hobbies, and so on.

Within each notebook, the second level of organization is the section, which is represented by a tab along the top of the notebook. You use the sections to break down the notebook's overall topic or theme into smaller subjects. In a school-related notebook, for example, you might have a section for each course, another for administrative data, one for social notes, and so on. A sales notebook might have sections for each client, another for a to-do list, one for company notes, and so on. You can create as many sections as you need because there is no upper limit on the number of sections you can add to a notebook. (There is a limit on the amount of data you can store in a single section, but because that limit is measured in *terabytes*—thousands of gigabytes—it's not something you need to worry about.) However, depending on the screen resolution you're using and the length of the section titles, after you add a certain number of sections OneNote will no longer be able to display the full tab for each section, which means some of your section title will appear abbreviated.

TIP FROM

EQ & Woody

> If you can't see the full title of a section, hover your mouse pointer over the tab and OneNote will display the section name and path in a ToolTip.

Each section in a notebook corresponds to a file within the notebook folder. Section files use the .one file extension, which is associated with the Microsoft Office OneNote Section file type. To create a new section, choose File, New, Section. (You can also choose New, Section on the toolbar, or right-click an existing section tab and then click New Section.)

OneNote gives new sections generic names such as New Section 1 and New Section 2. Give your sections more meaningful titles by renaming each new section after you create it. Either double-click a section name or right-click the tab and click Rename, type the new name, and then press Enter.

NOTE

> If you have a large number of sections, you can reduce the tab clutter by grouping some of those sections into a section group. This is a subfolder within the notebook, and you use it to hold multiple sections. To create a section group, choose File, New, Section Group. (You can also choose New, Section Group on the toolbar, or right-click an existing section tab and click New Section Group.) You can then move a section into the group by clicking and dragging the section tab and dropping it on the section group. Click the section group to see the sections that it contains.

Navigating to a section is straightforward if you have just one notebook open and that notebook has just a few sections: Click the tab of the section you want to view. Navigation gets a bit more complex if you have multiple notebooks on the go, and those notebooks have a large number of sections. OneNote 2007 gives you three techniques to use in these more challenging situations (see Figure 29.3):

- If a notebook has more than about seven or eight sections (the number depends on the screen resolution and the length of the section titles), OneNote displays a left arrow (Scroll to Previous Tab) beside the leftmost tab, and a right arrow (Scroll to Next Tab) beside the rightmost tab. Click these arrows to scroll the tabs left and right until you see the section you want, and then click the section's tab.

- The Navigation bar on the left side on the OneNote window has buttons for each open notebook. Click the Expand Navigation Bar button (>>) at the top of the bar to extend the Navigation bar as shown in Figure 29.3. This shows you the name of each open notebook as well as the sections within each notebook. Click the section you want to work with.

TIP FROM

EQ & Woody

> Left-handed mouse users might be more comfortable having the Navigation bar on the right side of the OneNote window. To set this up, select Tools, Options, click the Display section, and then click to deactivate the Navigation Bar Appears on the Left check box. Click OK.

- Click the All Notebooks button at the bottom of the Navigation bar to see a list of the open notebooks and their sections, as shown in Figure 29.3. Click the section you want to work with.

Moving sections from one part of a notebook to another is straightforward: Click and drag the section tab and then drop it in the new location. (As you drag the tab, a downward-pointing black arrow shows you where the section will be dropped.)

OneNote 2007 also enables you to move sections from one notebook to another. This is useful if you decide that a section fits better within another notebook. First, make sure the other notebook is open. To move a section, right-click its tab and then click Move. OneNote displays the Move Section To dialog box, shown in Figure 29.4. Either click the name of the notebook and then click Move Into, or click a section within the notebook and then click either Move Before or Move After.

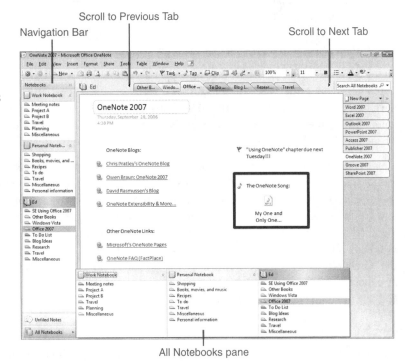

Figure 29.3
Use the tab arrows, the Navigation bar, and the All Notebooks pane to navigate to other notebooks and other sections.

Scroll to Previous Tab

Navigation Bar

Scroll to Next Tab

All Notebooks pane

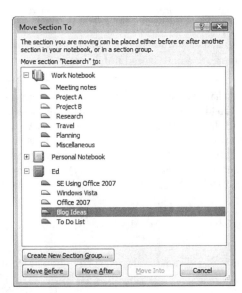

Figure 29.4
Use the Move Section To dialog box to select the notebook into which you want the section moved.

If you no longer need or use a section, you should delete it to reduce clutter in the tab area. Right-click the section's tab and then click Delete.

29

COLOR CODING NOTEBOOKS AND SECTIONS

OneNote 2007 is a hierarchical storage system, with notebooks at the top level, sections at the second level, and pages at the third level (see "Working with Pages," later in this chapter). You can fine-tune this hierarchy by taking advantage of OneNote's color-coding features, which enable you to link similar items visually by applying the same color to those items. You can color code notebooks and sections.

Color coding a notebook means that you apply a specified color and that color appears in the notebook's icon in the Navigation bar. This is really only marginally helpful, but if you do have notebooks that are related, there's no harm in displaying them with the same color. To color code a notebook, select it and then choose File, Notebook Properties. In the Notebook Properties dialog box, use the Color list to select the color you want, and then click OK.

Color coding a section means that you apply a specified color that appears in the section's tab (as well as the area surrounding the section when you select the section). This is more useful than color coding notebooks because you're more likely to have similar sections that you can informally relate to one another by applying the same color. Also, if you use multiple notebooks, it's a good idea to apply the same color to the same kinds of pages in each notebook. For example, if all your notebooks have a To-Do List section, it makes navigating the notebooks easier if those sections all use the same color. To color code a section, select it, choose Format, Section Color (or right-click the section tab and then click Section Color), and then click the color you want to use.

SHARING A NOTEBOOK

OneNote 2007 supports shared notebooks, which enables other network users to open and work with your notebooks. To share a notebook, you store it either on a shared network folder or on a SharePoint site. Unfortunately, OneNote doesn't give you a direct way to convert a regular notebook into a shared notebook, so you have to create one from scratch. Here are the steps to follow to create a new shared notebook:

TIP FROM

Ed & Woody

> OneNote may not have a command that converts a regular notebook into a shared notebook, but there *is* a trick you can use. This trick takes advantage of a simple fact about shared notebooks: The only difference between a regular notebook and a shared notebook is that the latter resides in a shared network folder. Therefore, you can "convert" a regular notebook into a shared notebook by closing it, locating the notebook folder in Windows Explorer, and then moving it to a shared network folder. Then select File, Open, Notebook, navigate to the shared network folder, and select the notebook folder.

1. Choose File, New, Notebook (or pull down the New list in the toolbar and select Notebook) to launch the New Notebook Wizard.

2. Type a Name for the notebook, select a Color, select the template you want to use, and then click Next.

3. Select Multiple People Will Share the Notebook, select On a Server, and then click Next.

4. Use the Path text box to specify the shared network folder or SharePoint site where you want the new notebook saved.

5. If you want to let other people know about the shared notebook, leave the Create an Email with a Link to This Notebook That I Can Send to Other People check box activated.

6. Click Create. If you opted to send the email with the link to the shared notebook, fill in the recipients and send the message.

You and the other users can now work with the notebook separately or at the same time. You can also work with the notebook offline, and OneNote will automatically synchronize the changes the next time you go online.

WORKING WITH PAGES

After notebooks and sections, the third level in the OneNote organizational hierarchy are the *pages*, which are the more or less blank slates into which you insert your OneNote data. Each section can have an unlimited number of pages, and the idea is that you use separate pages to break down each section into separate subtopics. For example, if you have a section devoted to books you want to read, you could have a separate page for each book, and you could fill each page with snippets from reviews, links to online bookstores, cover images, and so on. Similarly, in a travel-related section, you could create a separate page for each upcoming trip, a page with links to online travel sites, and so on.

ADDING A NEW PAGE

When you create a new section, OneNote populates it with a blank page. When you need to add a new page to the section, select File, New, Page, or press Ctrl+N. (You can also select New, Page on the toolbar or click the New Page button that appears above the page tabs.) Each new page gets it own tab in the Page Tabs pane, which appears on the right side of the OneNote window (see Figure 29.5). If you want a bit more room to add notes, click the Collapse Page Tabs button to reduce the size of the Page Tabs pane.

Title Area   Collapse Page Tabs

Figure 29.5
Each new page gets a tab in the Page Tabs pane.

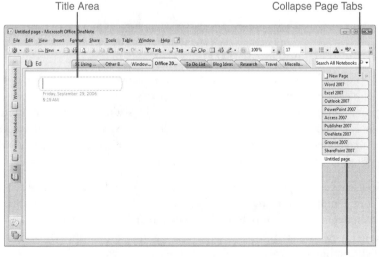

Page Tabs

29

When you create a new page, OneNote provides it with the generic title Untitled Page, and it places the cursor inside the Title Area, the rounded rectangle in the top-left corner of the page. Type your page title and press Enter.

Note, too, that OneNote also offers a fourth hierarchical level: the subpage. As the name implies, you use subpages to break down the content of a page into even finer subtopics. For example, if you have a section related to travel, you could devote a page to general information about an upcoming trip (destination, dates, and itinerary, for example), and then use subpages for more detailed information: flights, hotels, sightseeing, and so on. In Figure 29.6, for example, you see a notebook with a Travel section that contains a Toronto page that has three subpages: Transportation, Hotel Information, and Sightseeing. Notice that the subpages appear in the Pages Tab slightly indented from the main page. To add a subpage to the current page, select File, New, Subpage, or press Ctrl+Shift+N. (You can also select New, Subpage on the toolbar or drop down the Page Tab pane's New Page list and then choose New Subpage.)

Subpages

Figure 29.6
Break down your OneNote data even further by adding one or more subpages.

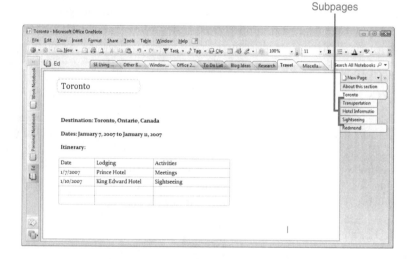

CREATING AND USING PAGE TEMPLATES

OneNote 2007 also comes with a number of page templates that you can use instead of the blank page you get by default. These templates include page formatting (such as a background image or color, fonts, or a specific page size), ready-made page items that you can use as is (such as titles and headings) or fill in yourself (such as bulleted and numbered lists), or a combination of formatting and content. There are also many OneNote templates available via the Microsoft Office Online website.

To use an existing template, choose File, New, Page From Template (or click New, Page From Template in the toolbar). OneNote displays the Templates task pane (see Figure 29.7). Open a template category (such as Academic or Blank), and then click the template you want to use. OneNote adds the new page to the end of the section. If you don't like the template, click another and OneNote will apply the new template to the page you just created. You can also click the Templates On Office Online link to view and download the page templates available at the Office website.

29

TIP FROM

The templates aren't just for new pages: You can also apply them to any existing page. Display the page you want to work with and then select Format, Templates. Click the template you want to use and OneNote applies it to the current page.

Figure 29.7
Use the Templates task pane to create a new page based on a OneNote template.

If there's a particular page template that you use almost all the time, consider setting it as the default template that OneNote applies to all new pages. In the Templates task pane, use the Choose Default Template list to select the template you prefer. If later on you no longer want to use that template as the default, open the Templates task pane and then select either No Default Template of the Default—Blank template in the Choose Default Template list.

If none of OneNote's templates give you exactly what you need, you can create your own template. Configure a page exactly the way you want it, then display the Templates task pane and click the Save Current Page As a Template link. In the Save As Template dialog box, type a Template Name. If you want to use this new template as the default, click to activate the Set As Default Template for New Pages in the Current Section check box. Click Save. OneNote adds a branch named My Templates to the Templates task pane, and your custom templates appear within that branch (see Figure 29.8).

29

Figure 29.8
When you save a page as a custom template, OneNote adds the My Templates branch to the Templates task pane.

MANAGING PAGES

As we mentioned earlier (and as you'll see in the next few sections), you enter, edit, and organize your notes in OneNote pages. As the repositories of all your OneNote content, therefore, you'll often need to manage your pages to keep that content organized. This means moving pages within the current section or to other sections or notebooks, making copies of pages, modifying the page setup, and deleting those pages you no longer need.

MOVING AND COPYING PAGES

When you create pages in a section, OneNote displays the page tabs in the order you created them, with the first page at the top and the most recent page at the bottom. You might require a different order, such as alphabetical by title. Unfortunately, OneNote doesn't offer an easy way to sort the pages by title. Your only recourse is to rearrange the page tabs by hand. You do that by clicking and dragging the page tabs up or down in the Page Tabs area.

If you want to move a page to another section in the current notebook or to a section in a different notebook, OneNote gives you three choices:

- To move a page to a different section in the same notebook, click and drag the page tab and then drop it on the tab of the other section. (If the other section's tab isn't onscreen, drag the pointer over the Scroll to Next Tab or Scroll the Previous Tab button until you see the section tab you want.)

- To move the page to a section in a different notebook, open that notebook and then expand the Navigation bar. Click and drag the page tab and drop it inside the other notebook, on the section where you want the page stored.

- Right-click the page tab and then click Move Page To. The submenu that appears might show some recent sections you worked with and, if you see the one you want, click it. Otherwise, click Another Section to display the Move or Copy Pages dialog box (see Figure 29.9). Click the section where you want the page moved and then click Move. (Note that you can also make a new section for the page by clicking Create New Section.)

Figure 29.9
Use the Move or Copy Pages dialog box to select the notebook and section where you want the page moved.

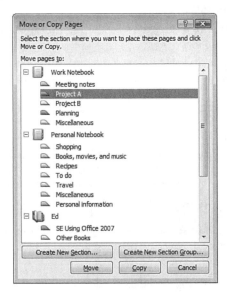

For making a copy of a page in another section in the current notebook or in a section in a different notebook, OneNote gives you only two methods:

- Right-click the page and then click Copy. Move to the section where you want the copy to appear (it could be in a different notebook), right-click any page, and then click Paste.

- Right-click the page and then click Move Page To. Click Another Section to display the Move or Copy Pages dialog box, click the section where you want the page copied, and then click Copy.

MODIFYING THE PAGE SETUP

In a OneNote page, the page setup governs properties of the page such as size, orientation, margins, whether rule lines appear, page background color, and whether the page includes the title area. You can modify some or all of these properties by selecting the page and then choosing File, Page Setup. Figure 29.10 shows the Page Setup pane that appears, which contains six sections:

29

- **Paper Size**—Use this section to select the page size. You can either select a standard size such as Letter, Legal, or Index Card, or you can select Custom and then specify your own Orientation, Width, and Height. If you prefer that OneNote manage the page size automatically, select Auto in the Size list.

- **Print Margins**—If you select anything other than Auto in the Size list, you can use the Top, Bottom, Left, and Right text boxes to set the page margins. If you'll be printing pages, remember that most printers can't print anything that appears within 0.25 inches to 0.5 inches of the edge of the paper, so don't make your margins smaller than that. If you won't be printing pages, set the Top and Left margins to 0 to give yourself some extra room to add and move content.

- **Rule Lines**—Use this section to display the page with *rule lines*, which are horizontal lines across the page that resemble the lines you see in writing paper and other lined notebook paper. Use the Line Style list to select the type of rule lines you want. Note that you can also choose from several grid styles, which display both horizontal and vertical lines. (You can also apply rule lines by selecting Format, Rule Lines.) Use the Line Color list to select the color you prefer for the lines or grid.

- **Page Color**—Use this section to select a background color for the page. Note that you don't have to worry about choosing a color that obscures your text, because all the background colors are relatively light.

- **Page Title**—Use this section to toggle the page title area off and on. Note that if you turn off the page title area, you lose the page title content. (Meaning that if you turn the page title area back on, you have to retype the title.)

- **Background Pictures**—This section just provides instructions for applying an image to the background. That is, you insert an image on the page (see "Inserting Graphics," later in this chapter), right-click the image, and then click Set Picture as Background. What it doesn't tell you is that you may need to move and resize the image first, depending on where you want the background to appear and how much of the page you want it to cover.

Figure 29.10
With the Page Setup task pane, you can change the page size and margins, add rule lines, change the page color, and toggle the page title.

29

DELETING A PAGE

If you have a page you no longer need, you should delete it to keep the Page Tabs area as uncluttered as possible. First, bear in mind that OneNote doesn't ask you to confirm a page deletion, so be sure you're deleting the correct page. (If you accidentally delete the wrong page, you should immediately choose Edit, Undo Delete to reverse it.) To delete a page, right-click the page tab and then click Delete. (You can also make sure that nothing is selected on the page, and then press Delete.)

ENTERING TEXT

Filling your pages with content is what OneNote is all about, and OneNote 2007 makes it easier than ever to insert everything from simple typewritten or handwritten notes, dates and times, image files, screen captures, and even entire files. All OneNote content appears inside a *container*, which is essentially a box that surrounds the content. After you have some content inside a container, you can move the container around on the page, edit or format the container content, split the content into multiple containers, and more.

Most page content consists of text notes, and OneNote makes it very simple to add text to a page:

- For typewritten notes, click where you want the note to appear and then start typing. OneNote immediately places a container around the text. When you're done, click outside the container.

29

- To create a bulleted list, click where you want the list to appear and then choose Format, Bullets, or click the Bullets button in the Formatting toolbar. You can also choose Format, Numbering if you prefer a numbered list.

- For handwritten notes, use your digital pen or stylus to write directly on the page. Note that if you insert two different handwritten items fairly close together, OneNote will put them in the same container. If you want to convert your handwritten notes to text, you have two choices: If you want to convert a single word, use your mouse to select the word, right-click the selection, and then click the correct word in the shortcut menu (see Figure 29.11); if you want to convert the handwritten text in an entire container, click the top edge of the container to select it, right-click the container, and then click Convert Handwriting to Text. (Note that all of these conversion options apply only to OneNote running on a TabletPC.)

Figure 29.11
When you right-click a selected handwritten word, OneNote displays a list of possible text recognitions.

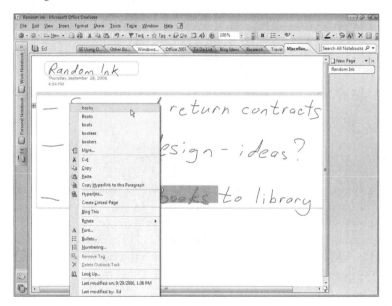

- To add text from a document, open the document, copy the text, return to OneNote, click inside the page where you want the text to appear, and then paste the copied text.

- If you want your text to appear inside a table, click inside the page where you want the table to appear and then select Table, Insert Table. Use the Insert Table dialog box to specify the Number of Columns and Number of Rows, and then click OK. You can then enter your text using the same methods as you would a Word table. When you have the table container selected, use the commands on the Table menu to insert, select, and delete rows and columns.

INSERTING GRAPHICS

Although most OneNote pages are filled with text, graphics can play an important role, too. For example, if you have a section devoted to new product ideas, you might want to add images of prototypes to your pages. Similarly, pages devoted to books or music CDs could display cover images. OneNote 2007 lets you insert images from files, upload pictures from a scanner or camera, capture screen clips, or even insert entire documents as images. Here are the procedures to follow:

- To insert a picture from a file, click inside the page where you want the image to appear, and then choose Insert, Pictures, From Files. Use the Insert Picture dialog box to select the image, and then click Open.

- To insert a picture from a scanner, click inside the page where you want the image to appear and choose Insert, Pictures, From Scanner or Camera. Choose your scanner and click either Web Quality or Print Quality. If you want to adjust more settings, click Custom Insert; otherwise, click Insert.

- To insert a picture from a digital camera, click inside the page where you want the image to appear, and then choose Insert, Pictures, From Scanner or Camera. Choose your camera and click Custom Insert. When the list of pictures on the camera appears, select the one you want to insert and click Get Pictures.

- To insert a screen clipping—a portion of the screen that you select using your mouse—first activate the program that you want to capture. Return to OneNote and select Insert, Screen Clipping. OneNote returns you to the other program and dims the screen. Click and drag your mouse to form a rectangle around the area you want to capture. When you release the mouse, OneNote reappears and the screen clipping appears in a container, along with text that tells you the date and time you inserted the image.

- You can also insert a drawing on a page. Select View, Drawing Toolbar, and then use the standard drawing tools—lines, shapes, and so on—to create your image.

- To add an image of a document as it would appear when printed, click inside the page where you want the image to appear and choose Insert, Files as Printouts. In the Choose Document to Insert dialog box, select the document and then click Insert. OneNote inserts an image of the document as it would appear when printed.

WORKING WITH DATA ON A PAGE

After you have one or more containers in a page, working with that data is almost always straightforward. For example, to edit container text, click inside the container and change the existing text or add new text. To format the text, select it and choose Format, Font, or use the buttons on the Formatting toolbar.

TIP FROM

Ed & Woody

> To quickly select all the text in a container, click the top edge of the container.

You will probably spend a significant amount of time in OneNote moving containers from one part of a page to another to get the best or most efficient layout for your data. To move a text container, position the mouse pointer over the text so that you see the container outline; then click and drag the top edge of the container and drop it on the new position. For graphics containers, you can mouse over any edge of the container and then click and drag it.

29

You can also move parts of a text container. For example, if your container has multiple paragraphs, when you move the mouse pointer over a paragraph, a move handle appears just outside the container to the left of the paragraph (see Figure 29.12). Click the move handle to select the paragraph, and click and drag the move handle to move the paragraph within the container. You can also drop the paragraph outside of the container to create a new container, or drop it within another container to add the text to it. (You can perform these techniques with any selected text, not just entire paragraphs.)

Move handle

Figure 29.12
Use the move handle that appears to the left of a paragraph to select and move the paragraph.

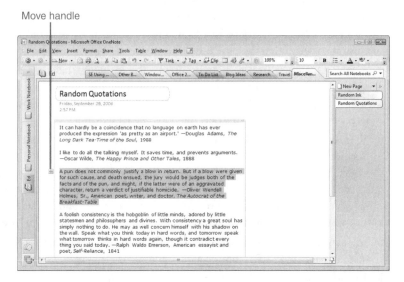

Note that as you move the container, the object moves in discrete leaps instead of smoothly. That's because, by default, OneNote's Snap To Grid feature is activated, so as you move a container, its edges line up with the grid lines. This helps line up the containers, but if you don't want to use this feature, choose Edit, Snap To Grid to deactivate the command.

TIP FROM

Ed & Woody

> To see the grid, select File, Page Setup to open the Page Setup task pane. In the Rule Lines section, use the Line Style list to select Small Grid.

OneNote enables you to augment items in a page with small icons called *tags*. For example, if you have a To Do list on a page, you can add the To Do tag beside each item in the list. This tag is a check box, and you can activate the check box when the item on the list is done. Other tags help you prioritize or organize page data. These tags include Important, Critical, and Question. To apply a tag, select the container you want to work with, pull down the Tag list in the toolbar (see Figure 29.13), and then click the tag.

Finally, if your page contains an image with text or a document inserted as a printout), you might need to convert the image text to editable text. To do this, right-click the image and then click either Copy Text from Picture (for a regular image) or Copy Text from This Page of the Printout (for a printout image; if the printout is multiple pages, click Copy Text from All the Pages of the Printout, instead). Then click inside the page and press Ctrl+V to paste the text.

Figure 29.13
Use the Tag list to apply one of OneNote's many tags to a container.

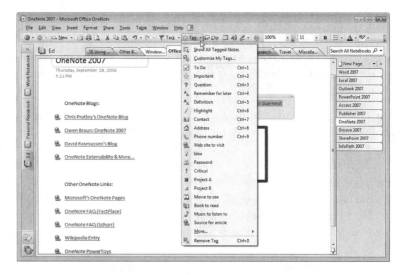

CREATING LINKS TO NOTEBOOKS, SECTIONS, PAGES, AND NOTES

OneNote 2007 comes with a Hyperlink command that works much like it does in the other Office programs. Choose Insert, Hyperlink, and use the Hyperlink dialog box to type the web page address or the path to a local document, then type the Text to Display (if you selected text in advance, it appears in this text box), and click OK.

→ For a detailed description of how Office hyperlinks work and how to create and manage them, **see** "Working with Hyperlinks," **p. 98**.

The Hyperlink command is very handy if you use your pages to store links to websites you visit often or want to visit in the future. (For the latter, apply the Web Site to Visit tag.) However, OneNote 2007 goes a step further by enabling you to create a link to a notebook, a section within a notebook, a page within a section, or even a note within a page. This makes navigating OneNote extremely easy because you can click a link to jump instantly to the object in question. It helps, too, that OneNote has made it very easy to create these links:

- To link to a notebook, right-click the notebook in the Navigation bar and then click Copy Hyperlink to This Notebook.

- To link to a section, right-click the section tab and then click Copy Hyperlink to This Section.

- To link to a page, right-click the page tab and then click Copy Hyperlink to This Page.

- To link to a note, right-click the note container and then click Copy Hyperlink to This Paragraph.

Now display the page where you want the link to appear, click to select the link position, and then press Ctrl+V.

29

FINDING INFORMATION IN ONENOTE

A funny thing happens to most OneNote newcomers who use the program regularly for at least a few weeks: something clicks, and they truly "get" the program and how powerful and useful it can be. After that, the pages and sections (and in OneNote 2007, the notebooks) multiple rapidly as the person transfers all the various scraps of information—data previous stored in the real world on sticky notes, memo pads, and random bits of paper, and in the digital world in miscellaneous text files, Word documents, and Excel worksheets—to the more orderly world of OneNote.

The downside to this is that the more pages, sections, and notebooks you have, the harder it becomes to find what you need. Fortunately, OneNote has a Find feature that enables you to search for text within a section, a section group, a notebook, or (new in OneNote 2007) all your notebooks. The good news about OneNote 2007's Find feature is that it can search within not only your text notes, but also within handwritten notes, audio and video recordings, and the text in images (including files inserted as printouts). The bad news about OneNote searching is that the program is woefully lacking in the search options that are standard in other Office programs: matching case, using wildcards, and so on.

NOTE

> If you have inserted an image that contains text (including a document inserted as a printout), you can tell OneNote to include the image text in searches. Right-click the image, click Make Text in Image Searchable, and then click the language you prefer.

To find information in OneNote, you first need to decide where you want the program to search; in other words, you need to select the *search scope*. You do this by clicking the menu button that appears to the right of the Search box and then selecting the scope you want: This Section, This Section Group, This Notebook, or All Notebooks (this is the default scope). After you've done that, type your search text and then either press Enter or click the Search icon. Here are a few notes to bear in mind when entering your search text:

- If you enter multiple words as the search criteria, OneNote matches items that contain every one of those words, regardless of the order. In other words, OneNote handles a phrase as a Boolean AND search. You can also include the keyword AND between the words (although you must enter the keyword using all uppercase letters).

- If you want OneNote to match a phrase exactly, enclose the phrase in quotation marks.

- By default, OneNote looks for partial matches of your search text. Specifically, it looks for words or phrases that begin with your search text. For example, if you type list, OneNote matches items containing not only the word *list*, but also *lists*, *listing*, *listed*, and *listserv*. If you want OneNote to match your search word exactly, enclose the word in quotation marks.

- If you want OneNote to match items that contain at least one of the words or phrases you enter (a Boolean OR search), separate each word or phrase with the keyword OR (which you must enter as an all-uppercase word). For example, to find items that contain either the word *calendar* or the word *schedule* (or both), you'd use calendar OR schedule as your search text.

When the search is complete, OneNote displays the results in the Search box, where you see the search text, the number of matches, Previous Match and Next buttons for navigating the results, and a View List link that displays the Page List task pane. As you can see in Figure 29.14, the Page List task pane displays the matches in descending Date order. (You can use the Sort List By list to select Section or Title, instead.) You can either click the match you want to view in the Page List, or you can use the Previous Match and Next Match buttons to scroll through the matches. In each case, when you display a matching page, OneNote highlights the text matches.

Previous Match

Search text   Next Match

Figure 29.14
When you run a search, use either the Search box results or the Page List task pane to navigate the matches.

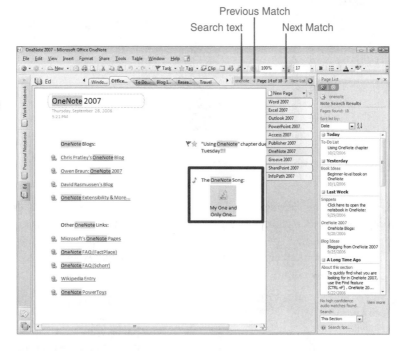

ADDING AUDIO AND VIDEO TO A NOTEBOOK

OneNote also enables you to insert into a notebook audio and video snippets that you record on-the-fly. This useful for recording quick notes to yourself, conducting short interviews, and recording parts of meetings, trade shows, or other events. By default, the words in these recordings are searchable, so you can easily find recordings by using OneNote's Find command (see the previous section).

NOTE

> If you want to search your recordings, you should first make sure that OneNote is set up to make them searchable. Select Tools, Options, click the Audio and Video category, and then make sure the Enable Searching Audio and Video Recordings for Words check box is activated. Note that you can also use this category to set up your default audio and video recording devices.

29

To record audio, make sure you have a microphone attached to your computer, prepare your script or notes (if you have any), and then choose Insert, Audio Recording. OneNote displays the Audio and Video Recording toolbar as well as a container for the recording (see Figure 29.15), and begins recording immediately. (You see `Recording...` in the OneNote title bar.) If you need to stop the recording temporarily, click Pause; when you're ready to resume, click Pause again. When you're finished, click Stop.

Figure 29.15
OneNote with an audio recording in progress.

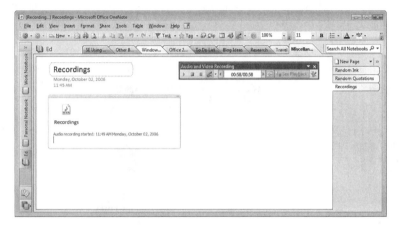

To record video, make sure you have a digital video camera or webcam attached to your computer, and then choose Insert, Video Recording. OneNote displays the Audio and Video Recording toolbar, a container for the recording, and a video window, as shown in Figure 29.16. Again, you can click Pause to temporarily stop and restart the recording, and click Stop when you're done.

Figure 29.16
OneNote with a video recording in progress.

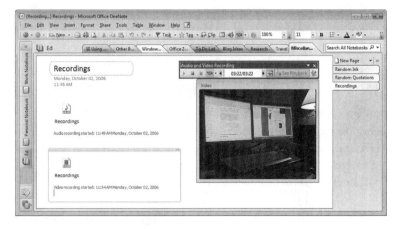

To play a recording, right-click its container and then click Play.

KEEPING TRACK OF TASKS AND TO-DO LISTS

One of the secrets of productivity in a fast-paced, information-overloaded world is organizing the things that require your attention and your effort in a way that minimizes stress and maximizes efficiency. If you have a long list of things to do, the worst way to handle this list is to keep it in your head. If you do this, you'll not only worry about forgetting something, but you'll always have each task rummaging around in your brain, so you'll jump from one to the other rather than concentrating on a single task. Plastering sticky notes all over your monitor isn't much better, because all the tasks are still "in your face" and you won't be much better off.

The best way to organize a list of pending and current tasks is to have a single place where you record the tasks particulars and can augment those particulars as things change and new data becomes available. This place must be one that you check regularly so that there's never a danger of overlooking a task, and ideally it should be a place where you can prioritize your tasks. This way, you can focus on a single task, knowing that everything you need to do is safely recorded and prioritized.

As you've probably guessed by now, the place I'm talking about is OneNote, which is ideally suited to recording, organizing, and prioritizing tasks and to-do lists. As described in the next two sections, you can record tasks either in OneNote by itself, or by linking to the task-related features in Outlook.

USING NOTE TAGS TO SET UP A ONENOTE TO-DO LIST

We mentioned earlier that you can make your notes a bit more comprehensible by adding tags such as Important or Web Site to Visit. One of the most useful tags is called To Do, and it adds a check box to the left of a paragraph. When you complete a task, you click the check box to place a red check mark inside, which gives you a strong visual clue about which tasks are done and which are still pending. You add a To Do tag to the current paragraph by selecting Insert, Tag, To Do, or by pressing Ctrl+1. Figure 29.17 shows a simple to-do list that uses this tag.

Figure 29.17
A simple to-do list constructed by using the To Do tag.

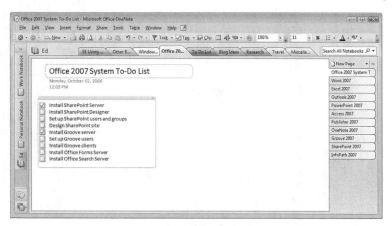

To-do lists are an important part of OneNote, and part of the evidence for that is the large number of check box-like tags that it offers. Besides the standard To Do tag, there are eight others:

- Discuss with <Person A>
- Discuss with <Person B>
- Discuss with Manager
- Schedule Meeting
- Call Back
- To Do Priority 1
- To Do Priority 2
- Client Request

In each case, you get a check box augmented with a small icon, as shown in Figure 29.18.

Figure 29.18
Use OneNote's check box tags to create more powerful and useful to-do lists.

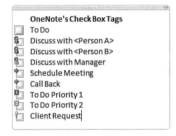

All of these tags are customizable, so you can set up the check box tags to suit your needs, and you can even create new tags. To work with your tags, right-click any tag and then click Customize My Tags. OneNote displays the Customize My Tags task pane. Click the tag you want to work with and then click Modify to display the Modify Tag dialog box. Here you can modify the tag name, change the symbol (see Figure 29.19), and specify a new font color and highlight color. If you want to create a new tag, click Add in the Customize My Tags task pane, and then use the Modify Tag dialog box to define the tag.

Figure 29.19
Use the Modify Tag dialog box to customize a tag's name, symbol, and colors.

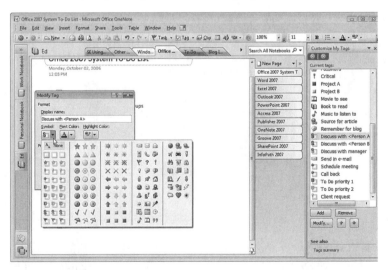

LINKING ONENOTE TO OUTLOOK TASKS

OneNote-based to-do lists are fine if your needs are simple: that is, you just want to manage a list of things you need to do and you want a visual way of knowing when those things are done. What if your needs are more complex? For example, what if you want to be reminded when an item is due to be completed? What if you want to track the amount of time you spend on a project? What if instead of a simple incomplete/complete status check, you want something more nuanced, such as the ability to specify that an item is 25% complete? You don't get any of these more sophisticated tracking features in OneNote, but Office has one program that does: Outlook and its Tasks folder.

Does this mean you have to use OneNote for simple to-do lists and Outlook for more complex tasks? Fortunately, the answer is no. OneNote enables you to insert Outlook tasks in a notebook, and it keeps those tasks synchronized. For example, if you change the task subject in OneNote, the change appears in Outlook. Similarly, if you mark a task as complete in OneNote, the task is also marked complete in Outlook.

To add an Outlook task to the current page, choose Insert, Outlook Task, and then choose the task due date you want: Today, Tomorrow, This Week, Next Week, or No Date. To create the new task in Outlook, choose Custom. Figure 29.20 shows two windows. The top window shows six Outlook tasks created in OneNote, and the bottom window shows the same six tasks in Outlook's Tasks folder. To work with a task in OneNote, right-click the task's flag and then use the shortcut menu to either select a different flag, or click Open Task in Outlook. You can also click Mark Complete or Delete Outlook Task.

Figure 29.20
Insert an Outlook task in OneNote, and a synchronized task also appears in Outlook.

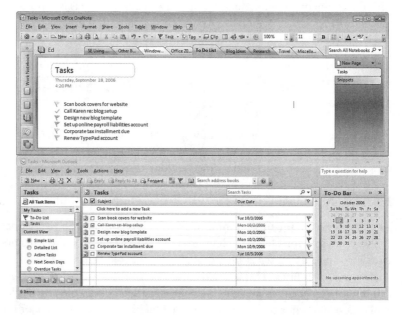

TROUBLESHOOTING

SHARING NOTEBOOK FOLDERS

I tried to share a notebook, but I received an error message telling me that I don't have permission to share the folder.

It's best not to rely on OneNote to share the folder. This is particularly true if you are running Windows Vista, because OneNote might decide your user account doesn't have sufficient privileges to share the folder. Instead, set up the sharing and permissions yourself, or select a folder that's already shared.

HANDLING NOTEBOOK-SHARING CONFLICTS

When I share a notebook, what do I do if two people change the same note at the same time?

OneNote updates shared notebook very quickly, so sharing conflicts have less of a change to occur. However, there is always a bit of a lag between the time a remote user makes a change and the time that change gets reflected locally. If two people change the same item at the same time, OneNote accepts the notebook owner's changes and displays a banner at the top of the current page with the following message:

```
The page has changes that could not be merged during synchronization.
Click here to show versions of the page with unmerged changes.
```

When you click the banner, OneNote adds a page to the current section that shows the changes made by the other user. When you click that page's tab, OneNote displays the page with the conflicting item highlighted. If the owner's version is acceptable, delete the page that shows the conflict; otherwise, you need to contact the other person and decide which version is correct.

SECRETS OF THE OFFICE MASTERS: SENDING INFORMATION TO ONENOTE

In this chapter, you saw a number of ways to insert items into OneNote, including text, ink, image files, photos from a scanner or camera, document printouts, screen clippings, hyperlinks, audio and video recordings, and Outlook tasks. Inserting items within OneNote is probably how you'll populate most of your notebooks, but it's not the only way. OneNote 2007 also gives you several ways to send data to OneNote via other applications.

The most general way to send information to OneNote is to "print" a document within an application using the OneNote 2007 printer driver. That is, you open a document in its associated application, select the program's Print command, and then choose the Send to OneNote 2007 printer. This is essentially what you're doing when you select Insert, Files as Printouts, because for whatever document you select, OneNote actually loads the associated application and prints the document to the OneNote driver. The major difference is that the Files as Printouts command inserts the document in the current page, whereas printing to the OneNote driver from another application inserts the document image as a separate page in the Unfiled Notes section.

Another way to send information to OneNote is via Internet Explorer. When you're browsing the Web, you may come across a page that you want to view later on. One way to do that would be to send a copy of the page to OneNote, which you can do by pulling down the Tools menu and choosing Send to OneNote. Again, the page text (not its images) is added to a page in the Unfiled Notes section.

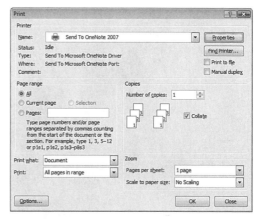

Figure 29.21

The third way to send information to OneNote is via Outlook. For email messages, right-click a message in the Inbox folder and then click Send to OneNote. (You can also open the message and then click Send to OneNote in the Message tab.) You can also send a contact's data to OneNote by opening the contact and then clicking Contact Notes in the Contact tab. Finally, you can send an appointment to OneNote by opening the appointment and clicking Meeting Notes in the Appointment tab. Both the contact data and the appointment data appear as pages in the Unfiled Notes section.

If you don't want OneNote to insert printouts or web notes in the Unfiled Notes section, you can customize the location. Select Tools, Options, and click the Send to OneNote page. In both the Web Notes group and the Printouts group, you can activate the New Page in the Current Section option or the On the Current Page option.

CHAPTER 30

USING OFFICE 2007 ON A CORPORATE NETWORK

In this chapter

Office Collaboration and SharePoint   908

Collaborating on Data with SharePoint Lists   908

Sharing Outlook Data with SharePoint   914

Document Collaboration with SharePoint   916

Creating a Document Workspace   917

Publishing an InfoPath Form to a SharePoint Site   919

Creating a Meeting Workspace   920

Using Outlook with Microsoft Exchange   921

Troubleshooting   924

Secrets of the Office Masters: Assigning a Delegate to Your Outlook Folders   925

OFFICE COLLABORATION AND SHAREPOINT

Most of the time, using the Office 2007 applications in a corporate environment is not all that different from using them on a standalone computer or a peer-to-peer network. After all, editing a Word document, building an Excel worksheet, and putting together a PowerPoint presentation don't require a corporate infrastructure.

So what's different when that infrastructure is present? The key difference is *collaboration*. That is, Office 2007 in a corporate environment gives you a number of ways to work with other users, and these collaborative features go well beyond simply sending out documents via email and storing documents on shared network folders. One of the best examples of this heightened collaboration is Windows SharePoint Services, an extension to Windows Server that enables people to share documents, lists, calendars, and contacts and to have online discussions and meetings. A SharePoint site is a special website created and configured by an administrator who sets up the user groups who have permission to use the site, configures site areas called *libraries* for storing documents, displays announcements, tracks tasks, and more. The next few sections show you various ways you can use a SharePoint site to collaborate on Office 2007 documents.

COLLABORATING ON DATA WITH SHAREPOINT LISTS

SharePoint has a Lists feature that enables you to collaborate with others on data in a simple flat-file database format. Depending on your permissions, you can use a SharePoint list to edit existing data, insert records, add new fields, filter data, and display totals. Most SharePoint sites also include specialized lists such as announcements, calendars, tasks, and links to websites. To see the lists available in a SharePoint site, log in to that site and then click the Lists link. In the list that appears, click the item you want to work with. Figure 30.1 shows a typical SharePoint list.

Figure 30.1
You can use SharePoint lists to collaborate on data with other users.

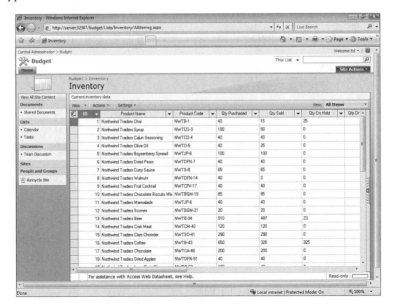

Because this is an Office book, we don't cover all the details of viewing and manipulating data with a SharePoint list. Instead, the next few sections show you how to share list data between Office and SharePoint using Excel and Access.

 If you're having trouble connecting to a SharePoint site, see "Designating a SharePoint Site as a Trusted Site" in the "Troubleshooting" section at the end of this chapter.

NOTE

For an in-depth look at SharePoint, we recommend *Special Edition Using Microsoft SharePoint Portal Server* (Que), by Robert Ferguson.

30

EXPORTING AN EXCEL TABLE TO A SHAREPOINT LIST

The flat-file format of a SharePoint list makes it a perfect place to share Excel tables with other people. To that end, Excel comes with an Export Table to SharePoint List command that enables you to send Excel data to a SharePoint site. You can set up a link between the original Excel data and the SharePoint list so that you can easily refresh the Excel data to see any changes by SharePoint users. (Note that the link is one way: You can see changes made to the SharePoint list, but any changes you make to the Excel table will be lost when you refresh the link.)

First convert your range to a table, if you haven't already done so: Select a cell in the range, choose Insert, Table, and then click OK. Under Table Tools, select the Design tab and then choose Export, Table to SharePoint List. In the first dialog box that appears (see Figure 30.2), type the Address of the SharePoint site, as well as a Name and Description for the new list. If you want to establish a link between the Excel table and the SharePoint list, click to activate the Create a Read-Only Connection to the New SharePoint List. Click Next and then click Finish. You then see the Windows SharePoint Services dialog box, which includes a link to the new list (see Figure 30.3). Click that link to see the list.

Figure 30.2
Use this dialog box to specify the address, name, and description of the new SharePoint list.

In Figure 30.3, you also see that when you establish a link between the Excel table and the SharePoint list, Excel adds Item Type and Path columns to the table, and it also enables the buttons in the External Data Table group. Click Refresh to get the latest changes made to the SharePoint list; click Open in Browser to view the SharePoint list; click Unlink to sever the connection with the SharePoint list.

Figure 30.3
After Excel exports the list, you see a dialog box that includes a link to the list on the SharePoint site.

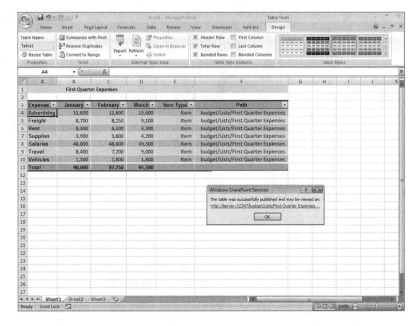

30

> **NOTE**
>
> If you make changes to the Excel table, you need to refresh the SharePoint list to reflect those changes. Display the list in SharePoint, pull down the Actions menu, and select Refresh Data.

IMPORTING EXCEL DATA FROM A SHAREPOINT LIST

If you have data in a SharePoint list—data that you've entered by hand or imported from another program such as Access (see the next section)—you might want to perform some kind of analysis on that data. You can perform only rudimentary analysis in SharePoint (totals, filtering, and grouping), so you really need to import that data into Excel. SharePoint handles this by creating a web query (.iqy) file that it sends to Excel. When Excel opens the query file, it prompts you to save the data and then maintains a link between Excel and SharePoint. Again, this link is one way: You can only change the data in the SharePoint list; any changes you make in Excel will be overwritten when you refresh the link.

To send SharePoint list data to Excel, follow these steps:

1. Log on to the SharePoint site and open the list.

2. Pull down the Actions menu and select Export to Spreadsheet.

3. In the File Download dialog box for the query file, click Open.

4. If you see an Excel Security Notice, click Enable.

5. In the Import Data dialog box (see Figure 30.4), select the data view, select a location, and click OK.

Figure 30.4
Use the Import Data dialog box to specify how and where you want the SharePoint list data imported.

More Excel-Related SharePoint List Commands

SharePoint offers several other tools that enable you to work with list data in Excel. Open the SharePoint list and then select Actions, Task Pane to open the list task pane. You see four Excel-related links:

- **Query List with Excel**—This link is similar to the Export to Spreadsheet command, except that Query List with Excel sends the query file directly to Excel.

- **Print with Excel**—This link imports the list and then runs Excel's Print command.

- **Chart with Excel**—This link imports the list and then displays the Insert Chart dialog box.

- **Create Excel PivotTable Report**—This link imports the list and then creates a new PivotTable report based on the data.

Exporting Access Data to a SharePoint List

If you have an Access table or query that you want to share with others, you can export that object to a SharePoint list. Note that this is a copy of the Access object, so there is no link established between Access and SharePoint.

In Access, use the Navigation bar to select the table or query you want to export, then display the External Data tab, and click the SharePoint List button in the Export group. In the Export—SharePoint Site dialog box (see Figure 30.5), specify the address of the SharePoint site and type a name and description. If you want Access to launch Internet Explorer and display the list on the SharePoint site, leave the Open the List When Finished check box selected. Click OK.

Figure 30.5
In Access, use the Export–SharePoint List dialog box to export an Access table or query to a SharePoint list.

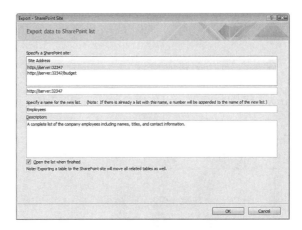

IMPORTING ACCESS DATA FROM A SHAREPOINT LIST

If you have data residing in a SharePoint list, you might want to work with the data in Access to take advantage of that program's superior database capabilities. You can open any SharePoint list in Access, either as a copy of the data or with a link that enables you to update the SharePoint list with the changes you make in Access.

In the SharePoint site, open the list, pull down the Actions menu, and select Open with Access. In the Open in Microsoft Office Access dialog box (see Figure 30.6), specify the database in which you want to store the new table. The default is to create a new database that contains a single table with the SharePoint list data, but you can also click Browse to select an existing database. You also have two choices:

- **Link to Data on the SharePoint Site**—Select this option to maintain a link between Access and SharePoint. Any changes you make to the data in Access will be automatically reflected in the SharePoint list.

- **Export a Copy of the Data**—Select this option to create an unlinked copy of the SharePoint list data in an Access table.

Click OK, and SharePoint either creates the database or adds the data to a table in an existing database. Figure 30.7 shows a linked SharePoint list in Access. Notice that the status bar says Online with SharePoint. This means that any changes you make to the table will automatically be updated in the SharePoint list when you select SharePoint's Actions, Refresh Data command. You can temporarily break the link by selecting the External Data tab's Work Offline button. You can write the Access table to the SharePoint list at any time by clicking the Publish to SharePoint Site button.

Figure 30.6
Use this dialog box to display a SharePoint list in Access, either with a link or as a copy.

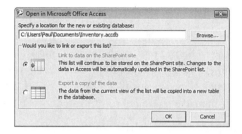

Figure 30.7
A SharePoint List linked to an Access table.

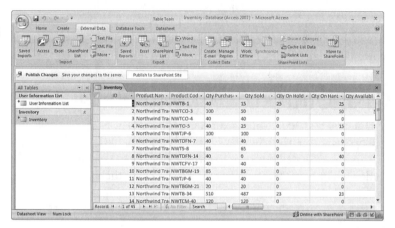

30

CREATING A NEW ACCESS DATABASE LINKED TO A SHAREPOINT SITE

If you want to work with data that is always linked to a SharePoint site, and you haven't yet created that data, you can start a new Access database and have it linked to SharePoint. Follow these steps:

1. In Access, select Office, New.

2. Select a template category and then select a template. (You can't perform these steps with a blank database.)

3. Type a File Name for the new database.

4. Select the Create and Link Your Database to a Windows SharePoint Services Site check box.

5. Click Download. Access downloads the template and then displays the Create on SharePoint Site dialog box.

6. Type the address of the SharePoint site.

7. Click Browse, select the folder where you want the database stored on the SharePoint site, and click OK.

8. Click Next. Access creates the database on the SharePoint site.

30

MOVING A DATABASE TO SHAREPOINT

If you already have a database set up and you want to share the entire database with other people, you can move the database to SharePoint while maintaining a local copy. This shares the entire database file as a document. That is, SharePoint users can't work with the individual database objects directly. Instead, they can download the database file to their computer and work on it there. SharePoint manages the synchronization between users.

To move a database to SharePoint, open the database, display the External Data tab, and then click Move to SharePoint to launch the Move to SharePoint Site Wizard. Type the address of the SharePoint site, then click Browse, select the folder where you want the database stored on the SharePoint site, and click OK. Click Next to begin the move. Access moves the database to the SharePoint site and leaves a local copy open for you to work with.

SHARING OUTLOOK DATA WITH SHAREPOINT

Although Access 2007 comes with strong SharePoint links, Outlook 2007 offers only a few ways to share data via a SharePoint site. You can publish an Outlook calendar to SharePoint, synchronize a SharePoint calendar with Outlook, and synchronize SharePoint tasks with Outlook. The next three sections provide you with the details.

PUBLISHING AN OUTLOOK CALENDAR TO A SHAREPOINT SITE

SharePoint Services supports the WebDAV—Web-based Distributed Authoring and Versioning—protocol, which enables users to work collaboratively on remote files. A subset of WebDAV is CalDAV, a protocol that allows users to access remote calendars using the iCalendar (`.ics`) format.

The simplest way to share your Outlook calendar with other SharePoint users is to publish the calendar to the SharePoint site. The Calendar itself doesn't appear on the SharePoint site. Instead, Outlook stores the `.ics` file in a SharePoint folder, and the other SharePoint users can then subscribe to it from there.

To publish your Outlook calendar to a SharePoint site, select the Calendar folder, right-click the calendar you want to publish, and then choose Publish to Internet, Publish to WebDAV Server. In the Publish Calendar to Custom Server dialog box (see Figure 30.8), type the address of the SharePoint site into the Location text box. Select the other publishing options—the Time Span, the level of Detail you want published, and so on—and then click OK. Outlook converts your calendar to the iCalendar format and stores the file on the SharePoint site.

NOTE

> Outlook also asks if you want to send a sharing invitation for the published calendar. This is a good idea because when another user gets the email message, all he or she has to do to add your calendar to Outlook is to display the message and click Subscribe to This Calendar.

Figure 30.8
Use this dialog box to specify the address of your SharePoint site as well as your calendar publishing options.

If you later decide that you no longer want to publish the calendar, you can remove it from the SharePoint site. Right-click the calendar, choose Publish to Internet, Remove from Server, and then click Yes.

SYNCHRONIZING A SHAREPOINT CALENDAR WITH OUTLOOK

Many SharePoint sites come with a Calendar item in the Lists section. You can use the Calendar item to schedule appointments, and although you don't get the wealth of scheduling features that you do in Outlook, you can still specify not only the basics, such as the location and the start and end times, but also all-day events, recurring appointments, and even create a Meeting Workspace to coordinate a meeting with other users.

Rather than always working with the calendar in SharePoint, you can set up a synchronization between the SharePoint site and Outlook. To do this, open the calendar in SharePoint, and then choose Actions, Connect to Outlook. (If you see an Internet Explorer Security dialog box at this point, click Allow.) Outlook then asks you to confirm that you want to connect to the SharePoint calendar (see Figure 30.9). If you want to change the name of the calendar, click Advanced, type a new Folder Name, and click OK. Click Yes to add the SharePoint calendar to Outlook.

Figure 30.9
You can connect a SharePoint calendar to Outlook.

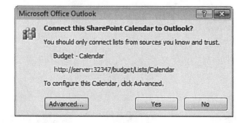

SYNCHRONIZING SHAREPOINT TASKS WITH OUTLOOK

Most SharePoint sites also come with a Tasks item in the Lists section. You can use this list to set up tasks that must be completed. You can set the task priority and status, specify how much is complete, assign the task to other SharePoint users, and set the start date and due date. As with the SharePoint Calendar item, you can also work with tasks in Outlook by setting up a synchronization between SharePoint and Outlook's Tasks folder. To do this, open the Tasks list SharePoint, and then choose Actions, Connect to Outlook. (If you see an Internet Explorer Security dialog box at this point, click Allow.) Outlook then asks you to confirm that you want to connect to the SharePoint Task list. If you want to change the name of the tasks, click Advanced, type a new Folder Name, and click OK. Click Yes to add the SharePoint Task list to Outlook.

DOCUMENT COLLABORATION WITH SHAREPOINT

Each SharePoint site comes with a folder called Shared Documents that acts as a *document library*. In a real library, people can view and work with books onsite, or they can check out a book to use it exclusively. A SharePoint document library is similar: Users can open documents right from the library, or they can "check out" a document to use it exclusively. Of course, what the users are able to do with the documents in a shared library depends on what permissions they have.

If you want to use a document library, you can either use the default Shared Documents library, or you can create a library by opening the SharePoint site, clicking Documents, clicking Create, and then clicking Document Library. The next few sections show you how to use SharePoint document libraries to collaborate on documents from Office.

PUBLISHING A DOCUMENT TO A SHAREPOINT LIBRARY

A SharePoint document library is empty by default. To add content to a library, you can publish an Office document to the SharePoint site. Open the document you want to work with and then choose Office, Publish, Document Management Server. In the Save As dialog box, click an empty part of the Address box, type the address of the SharePoint site, and press Enter. Double-click the document library you want to use. You should now see the contents of the library (see Figure 30.10). Click Save.

Figure 30.10
In the Save As dialog box, type the address of the SharePoint site, and then double-click the document library you want to use.

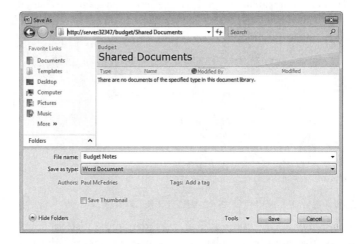

NOTE
You can also upload a document into a library directly from the SharePoint site. Open the document library and then choose Upload, Upload Document, click Browse, select the document on your computer, click Open, and then click OK. If you have several documents you want to upload, choose Upload, Upload Multiple Documents, instead.

OPENING A DOCUMENT FROM A SHAREPOINT LIBRARY

To work with a document from a SharePoint document library, you have three choices:

- **Open the document from an Office application**—Choose Office, Open to display the Open dialog box. Click an empty section of the Address box, type your SharePoint site address, and press Enter. Open the document library, select the document, and then click Open.

- **Open the document from the SharePoint library**—In SharePoint, open the document library and then click the document you want to open. In the list that appears, click Edit In *Program*, where *Program* is the Office application associated with the document's file type.

- **Open the document from SharePoint with exclusive access**—In SharePoint, open the document library and then click the document you want to open. In the list that appears, click Check Out, and then click OK. You now have exclusive access to the file. (Other users can open it, but only in read-only mode.) Click the document and then click Edit In *Program*.

CREATING A DOCUMENT WORKSPACE

Most SharePoint sites are organized around either a team of users or a large project that consists of a number of different documents. However, there are situations where a single document is the focus of several users. For example, a budget spreadsheet might require input from several divisions. Similarly, a company report might have many different authors.

For these situations, you can create a *document workspace*, a SharePoint site that focuses on a single Word document, Excel workbook, or PowerPoint presentation. (The site can hold multiple documents, but its focus is on a single, main document.) Open the document and choose Office, Publish, Create Document Workspace. In the Document Management task pane that appears (see Figure 30.11), specify the Document Workspace Name, use the Location For New Workspace text box to enter the SharePoint site address, and then click Create.

After you create the document workspace, the Document Management task pane changes to show icons to view the workspace status, members, tasks, documents, and links. For example, clicking the Members icon displays a list of the workspace members and their online status (see Figure 30.12) and provides links to add new members to the workspace and to send an email message to all the members. Click Get Updates to download the latest information from the workspace.

30

Figure 30.11
Use the Document Management task pane to set the name of the document workspace and the address of the SharePoint site.

Figure 30.12
After you create the document workspace, click the Members icon to see a list of workspace members.

The next time you open the document, the Office program will display a dialog box like the one shown in Figure 30.13. Click Get Updates to download the latest version of the document from the SharePoint site. To reopen the Document Management task pane, choose Office, Server, Document Management Information.

Figure 30.13
Click Get Updates to see the latest version of the shared document.

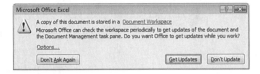

30

PUBLISHING AN INFOPATH FORM TO A SHAREPOINT SITE

On your SharePoint site, you might need users to fill out forms to collect various kinds of data. For example, a SharePoint site for a sales team might have an expense account form and a travel request form. Similarly, a SharePoint site for a project might have a status report form. To make managing these forms easier, you can use the Microsoft InfoPath XML editor to design a form template, and you can then publish the form template to your SharePoint site. Here are the steps to follow:

1. Use InfoPath to design the form template you want your SharePoint users to work with. Be sure to save the template.
2. Choose File, Publish to launch the Publishing Wizard.
3. Select the To a SharePoint Server With or Without InfoPath Forms Services option and click Next.
4. Type the address of your SharePoint site and click Next.
5. Select the Document Library option and click Next.
6. If this is the first time you're publishing the form template, select the Create a New Document Library option. (If you've published the form template before, or you have an existing library that uses a form template, you can use the current template as a replacement by selecting the Update the Form Template in an Existing Document Library and then clicking the library in the list.) Click Next.
7. If you're creating a new document library, enter a name for the library, and click Next.
8. The Publishing Wizard displays a list of the form column that will be available to the SharePoint users. Click Add to make more columns available. Click Next when you're done.
9. Click Publish.
10. Click Close.

To use the form template in the SharePoint site, open the document library and choose New, New Document. (If you see an Internet Explorer Security dialog box, click Allow.) This opens the form in InfoPath, where you can fill it in. When you save the form, InfoPath prompts you to save it in the SharePoint site document library.

CREATING A MEETING WORKSPACE

You can use Outlook's Calendar to schedule a meeting and invite multiple people to attend, but after that's done, it's up to you and the other attendees to prepare for the meeting. A short meeting usually doesn't require much more preparation than knowing what the meeting is about. However, a longer, more complex meeting might require quite a bit of advance planning:

- Deciding what the meeting's objectives are.
- Creating an agenda for the meeting.
- Assigning tasks that need to be performed before the meeting.
- Distributing documents that attendees should study or work on before the meeting.

A large meeting can be a complicated task to organize and prepare, but you can make it quite a bit easier by using Office to set up a *meeting workspace*. This is a special SharePoint site designed to help you prepare for, run, and follow-up on a meeting. A meeting workspace usually consists of several lists, and the ones you see depend on the type of workspace you create. In a Basic Meeting Workspace, for example, you get lists for the attendees, the meeting's objectives, and the meeting agenda; a Decision Meeting Workspace also includes lists for assigning tasks and for the decisions made during the meeting. In both cases, you also get a document library to store meeting-related files. By placing all these meeting components on a SharePoint site, you can collaborate with other people to prepare the meeting and the attendees can easily check in to see what's new before the meeting.

To create a meeting workspace from Outlook, select File, New, Meeting Request. Fill out the usual meeting fields—attendees, Subject, Location, Start Time, and End Time. In the Meeting tab, click Meeting Workspace to open the Meeting Workspace task pane. Use the Select a Location list box to specify the SharePoint site you want to use. (If the site you want isn't in the list, click Other, type the address, and click OK.)

You now have two choices (see Figure 30.14):

- **Create a New Workspace**—Select this option to create a new meeting workspace on the SharePoint site. Use the Select a Template Type list to select the meeting workspace type you want to create (such as Basic Meeting Workspace or Decision Meeting Workspace).
- **Link to an Existing Workspace**—Select this option if there is already a meeting workspace on the SharePoint site, which you then choose in the Select the Workspace list.

CAUTION

Before you send the meeting invitation, make sure that you've set up all the attendees with the appropriate permissions on the SharePoint site.

Click OK to save the workspace settings and then click Create to set up the workspace on the SharePoint site. Outlook adds a note to the meeting invitation that includes a link to the meeting workspace site (see Figure 30.15). Click Send to distribute the meeting invitations.

Figure 30.14
Use the Meeting Workspace task pane to create or select a meeting workspace on a SharePoint site.

Figure 30.15
When you create the meeting workspace, Outlook adds a site link to the meeting invitation.

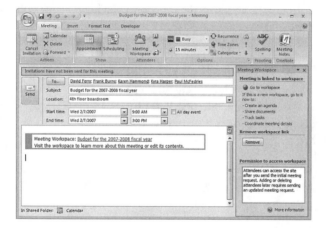

USING OUTLOOK WITH MICROSOFT EXCHANGE

If your corporate network runs Microsoft Exchange, Outlook enables you to share one or more of your folders with other users on the network. For example, you can share your Calendar so that other users can see your schedule. In each case, you share the folder with only the users you specify, and for each user you can apply specific permissions that determine what the user can do with the folder. For example, one user may only be able to read the contents of the folder, whereas another may be able to create and edit folder items. Outlook lets you share a folder by sending a sharing invitation or by applying permissions for specific users.

SENDING A SHARING INVITATION

For nonmessage folders, Outlook enables you to send a *sharing invitation* that tells the recipients that your folder is available to be shared. In this case, users are given read-only access to the folder. (If you want to assign more elaborate permissions, see the next section.)

Open the folder you've shared and then choose File, Folder, Share *"Folder"*, where *Folder* is the name of the shared folder. In the sharing invitation message that appears, select the recipients. If you also want to be able to share the users' folder, select the Request Permission to View Recipient's *Folder* Folder check box. Click Send and then click Yes when Outlook asks you to confirm.

TIP FROM

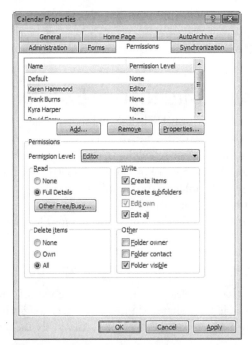

For the Calendar, Contacts, Tasks, Notes, and Journal folders, look in the Navigation pane for a sharing link of the form Share My *"Folder"* Folder, where *Folder* is the name of the folder. For example, to share the Contacts folder, click the Share My Contacts Folder link.

If you receive a sharing invitation, you process it by doing two things:

- To see the shared folder, click the Open this *Folder* Folder button at the top of the message.

- If the sharer also asked for permission to view your folder, click either Accept or Deny at the top of the message.

USING PERMISSIONS TO SHARE A FOLDER

To share any Outlook folder with a specific set of users and permissions, open the folder and then choose File, Folder, Change Sharing Permissions. In the Permissions tab, click Add to see a list of Exchange users. For each user you want to give access to the folder, click the username and then click Add. When you're done, click OK to return to the Permissions tab (see Figure 30.16).

Figure 30.16
Use the Permissions tab to select the users you want to share the folder with, as well as the permissions for each user.

To assign permissions to a user, click the username and use the Permission Level list to choose a built-in level:

- **Owner**—The user can create, read, edit, and delete items in the folder, create subfolders, and change the permission levels for other users.

- **Publishing Editor**—The user can create, read, edit, and delete items in the folder, and create subfolders.

- **Editor**—The user can create, read, edit, and delete items in the folder.

- **Publishing Author**—The user can create and read items in the folder and can create subfolders, but can edit and delete only the user's own items.

- **Author**—The user can create and read items in the folder, but can edit and delete only the user's own items.

- **Nonediting Author**—The user can create and read items in the folder, but can delete only the user's own items.

- **Reviewer**—The user can only read items in the folder.

- **Contributor**—The user can only create items in the folder. The contents of the folder do not appear. (This is does not apply to delegates.)

- **None**—The user can't open the folder.

You can also use the controls in the Read, Write, Delete Items, and Other groups to set specific permissions for the user. Repeat for the other users and then click OK.

ACCESSING ANOTHER USER'S SHARED FOLDER

For a folder that another person has set up with specific users and permissions or with delegate access, you can access that folder to display it within your Outlook window. Choose Select File, Open, Other User's Folder to display the Open Other User's Folder dialog box (see Figure 30.17). Either type the other user's name into the text box, or click Name, click the user, and then click OK. Use the Folder Type list to select the folder, and then click OK. Outlook displays the other user's shared folder and, for nonmessage folders, also adds the shared folder to the Navigation pane (see Figure 30.18).

TIP FROM

Ed & Woody

> For the Calendar, Contacts, Tasks, Notes, and Journal folders, look in the Navigation pane for a link of the form Open Shared *Folder*, where *Folder* is the name of the folder (for example, Open Shared Contacts).

Figure 30.17
Specify the name of the other user and the folder type.

Figure 30.18
When you open another user's shared folder, Outlook adds the folder to the Navigation pane.

TROUBLESHOOTING

DESIGNATING A SHAREPOINT SITE AS A TRUSTED SITE

I'm having trouble connecting to a SharePoint site on a remote web server.

Most SharePoint sites reside on corporate intranets, and connecting to those sites is usually not a problem. To ensure that you can connect and work with a SharePoint site that resides on an external web server, you should add the SharePoint site to your list of trusted sites. In Internet Explorer, choose Tools, Internet Options to open the Internet Options dialog box. Click the Security tab, click Trusted Sites, and then click Sites. In the Trusted Sites dialog box, type the address of the SharePoint server in the Add This Website to the Zone text box and then click Add. If your SharePoint server doesn't use secure HTTP (that is, it uses `http:` in the address instead of `https:`), click to deactivate the Require Server Verification (https:) For All Sites in This Zone check box. Click Close and then click OK.

CREATING A SHORTCUT TO A SHAREPOINT SITE

Is there a quick way to access a SharePoint site?

In Windows XP, you can create a network place. To set up a network place for your SharePoint site, choose Start, My Network Places, and click Add a Network Place in the Network Tasks pane. Click Next, click Choose another network location, and click Next. Type the address of the SharePoint site, click Next, and enter your username and password when prompted. Type a name for the site, click Next, and then click Finish.

Windows Vista does away with the My Network Places folder, but it does offer an Add a Network Location command that enables you to add network shortcuts to the Computer folder's Network Location group. (Choose Start, Computer, press Alt to display the menu bar, and then choose File, Add a Network Location.) However, the shortcuts created by the Add a Network Location command aren't appropriate for a SharePoint site because they open the site in Windows Explorer instead of Internet Explorer. To get a proper Internet shortcut, first use Windows Explorer to open your user profile's Network Shortcuts folder:

```
%UserProfile%\AppData\Roaming\Microsoft\Windows\Network Shortcuts
```

Right-click the folder and then choose New, Shortcut. Type the address of the SharePoint site and click Next. Type a name for the site and then click Finish.

By default, when you choose Office, Publish, Document Management Server, the Save As dialog box opens in the Network Shortcuts folder. Therefore, after you create a shortcut to the SharePoint site, you can simply select the shortcut in the Save As dialog box.

SECRETS OF THE OFFICE MASTERS: ASSIGNING A DELEGATE TO YOUR OUTLOOK FOLDERS

When other Exchange users access your shared folders, they usually do so as themselves. A good example is when you share your Inbox or some other message folder. If a user opens that shared message folder and then chooses File, New, Mail Message, the new message will be sent from that user's account, not yours. However, there may be situations where you want the user to access a shared folder as you. For example, if you have an assistant, you might want that assistant not only to check your email, but also to send responses to certain messages. In this case, instead of having the replies sent from the assistant's account, you probably want them sent from your own account. This is known as *send-on-behalf-of* permission. If you want to configure a folder with this permission, you need to define your assistant (or whoever) a *delegate* and you need to give that person *delegate access*.

To set this up, choose Tools, Options to open the Options dialog box, and then select the Delegates tab. Click Add, select the user you want to use as a delegate, click Add, and then click OK. You now set the permissions using the Delegate Permissions dialog box (see Figure 30.19).

For each folder, you have four choices:

- **Reviewer**—The user can only read items in the folder.

- **Author**—The user can create and read items in the folder.

- **Editor**—The user can create, read, edit, and delete items in the folder.

- **None**—The user can't open the folder.

Figure 30.19

It's a good idea to let the delegate know about these permissions, so select the Automatically Send a Message to Delegate Summarizing These Permissions check box. Click OK and click OK again to put the settings into effect.

If you're a delegate with Editor or Author privileges, you have send-on-behalf-of permission, meaning you can send new messages, replies, and forwards using the folder owner's email account. Although you can do this by displaying a shared message folder, it's much easier if you add the owner's email account to your Exchange Server profile. Here's how it's done:

1. Choose Tools, Account Settings.

2. Select your Exchange Server account and click Change. The Exchange Server Settings dialog box appears.

3. Click More Settings.

4. Display the Advanced tab.

5. Click Add.

6. Type the owner's name and click OK.

7. Click OK to return to the Exchange Server Settings dialog box.

8. Click Next.

9. Click Finish.

10. Click Close.

Outlook displays both sets of mail folders in the Mail Folders pane. To send a message as a delegate on behalf of the owner, start a new message or reply to or forward an existing message in one of the owner's message folders. Make sure the From field is displayed by displaying the Options tab and activating the Show From command. Type the owner's name into the From field and then fill out and send the message normally. When the recipient receives the message, the From field data will have the following format:

`Delegate Name on behalf of Owner Name`

PART **VII**

APPENDIXES

A Advanced Setup Options   929

B Macros and Add-Ins   943

C Using Office on a Tablet PC   961

ADVANCED SETUP OPTIONS

In this chapter

Before You Begin... 930

Using the Office Installer 930

Customizing Your Office Installation 933

Installing Office 2007 Alongside an Older Office Version 935

Updating or Repairing an Office Installation 937

Saving a Set of Custom Installation Options 939

Troubleshooting 940

Before You Begin...

To avoid possible problems when you first set up Office 2007, the smartest thing you can do is to anticipate possible problems and head them off.

Start by reviewing system requirements, particularly free disk space, for the Office edition you've chosen. These requirements vary, depending on the contents of the Office edition. A full installation of Office 2007 Professional Plus, for instance, requires more than 1GB of disk space just for the program files, and you'll need additional space to accommodate temporary files created as part of the setup process.

Back up. The likelihood of something going wrong with Office Setup is small, but it's still greater than zero. If you don't have a full recent backup, consider this an excellent opportunity to create one.

Check compatibility of any Office add-ins you rely on before you begin setup. Removing an incompatible add-in is usually much more difficult after upgrading. If an add-in you use is incompatible with Office 2007, you'll have to decide whether to uninstall it and do without its features, to look for an alternative, or to do without Office 2007.

Read the release notes. You'll find these descriptions of known issues and incompatibilities in a file called Readme.htm on the Office installation media. Double-click this file to open it in your default web browser.

Using the Office Installer

If you're installing Office 2007 on an individual computer at home or in a small office, you don't need any documentation, because the setup process is almost fully automated. However, if you want to control what actually happens during setup, or if you're responsible for installing Office on multiple computers, you'll need the information in this appendix.

The easiest way to install Office 2007 on an individual PC is to insert the first disc in the Office package into the system's CD-ROM drive. If AutoPlay is enabled on the PC in question, Office launches its Setup program automatically. Assuming you have a retail copy of Office, you need to enter the 25-character product key and agree to the software license. After you jump through these hoops, Setup displays the dialog box shown in Figure A.1. If you're upgrading over an existing version of Office, the large button at the top of this dialog box will read Upgrade.

Figure A.1
Choose the Install Now option to use default settings and install with no further prompts. Choose Customize to choose which programs to install.

NOTE

> If Setup doesn't run automatically, the most likely reason is that CD-ROM AutoPlay is disabled. In that case, display the contents of the CD and double-click the Setup icon, or open the Run dialog box and enter *<d:>*Setup, substituting the letter of the CD drive for *<d:>*.

The Windows Installer uses a small *bootstrap program* called Setup.exe to run the actual installation routine. This initial phase performs some basic system checks and then passes command-line parameters based on its findings to the Windows Installer, which actually does the work of setting up Office.

NOTE

> For a detailed list of command-line options for Setup.exe, open a Command Prompt window (Cmd.exe), type *<d:>*Setup /?, substituting the letter of the CD drive for *<d:>*, and press Enter. This command displays a dialog box containing a list of available switches with a brief explanation of what each one does.

After you run Setup, it hands off control to the Windows Installer, which uses a variety of files to control how Office is installed, For Office 2007, each program has its own subfolder on the installation media, typically containing one or more of each of the following file types:

- Installer package files are the most important pieces. These files, which use the *.msi extension, contain all the information necessary to install an Office 2007 program or feature set. Information in this package includes a list of the component files and Registry settings for each program or feature, the proper installation sequence, destination folder paths, system dependencies, and installation options.

NOTE

It's important to note that the package file does not contain any Office program files. Instead, it points to the location where the Windows Installer can find those files—usually in the same subfolder on the Office installation media. After installation, the Windows Installer uses the package file to add, remove, repair, or replace features and components.

- Windows Installer patch files, which use the `*.msp` extension, contain custom settings that tell Setup to modify the default parameters defined in the package file. If you use the Office Customization Tool (`Setup /admin`), you create a patch file that contains all your custom settings. (The Office Customization Tool is covered in detail later in this appendix.)

- Configuration files, which in Office 2007 use the `*.xml` extension, contain instructions that the Windows Installer uses to define installation options. By default, Setup looks for a file called `Setup.xml` and uses its settings; to use a custom configuration file, run Setup with the `/config` switch followed by the name and full path of the `.xml` file you want to use.

 If you encounter an error message when you first run Setup, see "Some Features Not Available" in the "Troubleshooting" section at the end of this appendix.

The Office program files themselves are compressed and stored in files that use the Cabinet File format (with the extension `.cab`). During the installation process, the Setup program automatically copies all setup files to the Local Install Source. This is a hidden folder named Msocache, which is stored in the root folder of your hard drive.

The purpose of the Local Install Source is to eliminate the need to insert the Office CD whenever you install an optional feature, add a patch or service pack, or modify the existing installation in any way.

Having these files handy is essential for the proper operation of repair, update, and reinstallation features of Office 2007. Because the Local Install Source occupies several hundred megabytes of disk space on the same drive where the Office program files are installed, some users might want to eliminate this folder or move it to a different location. In earlier Office versions, you could do exactly that. In Office 2007, there is no supported way to remove or relocate the Local Install Source files.

CAUTION

Don't just delete the Msocache folder. Although that action appears to solve the problem, the fix is only temporary. As soon as you take any action that changes your Office installation, the Setup program prompts you to provide the original installation media and re-creates the Local Install Source.

When you select the Install Now or Upgrade option, Setup proceeds using the following default options:

- Program files go in the Microsoft Office subfolder in the folder that the %programfiles% variable points to. (On most systems, this is C:\Program Files.) Although you can specify a different location, we strongly recommend using this default location.

- For an upgrade, Setup removes your previous Office installation and replaces all installed programs. In the process, it migrates your personal settings and preferences to Office 2007.

- Setup installs a standard set of programs and features. In the case of an upgrade, it automatically replaces all previously installed components with new versions, even if they're not normally part of the Typical Install.

TIP FROM

> If you're not sure whether to use the Custom Install option, choose it anyway. When you do, Setup lets you review all options, and if you accept the default settings at every opportunity, the effect is the same as if you had chosen the Install Now or Upgrade options.

If you performed a default installation and some Office features are missing, see "No Packages for You" in the "Troubleshooting" section at the end of this appendix.

CUSTOMIZING YOUR OFFICE INSTALLATION

Choosing the Customize option displays the dialog box shown in Figure A.2. On a clean install, it contains three tabs, each of which allows you to specify a different set of custom options. An upgrade installation includes a fourth tab, Upgrade, which we discuss in the following section.

Figure A.2
On a clean install, you can specify exactly which programs and features are installed and which are unavailable.

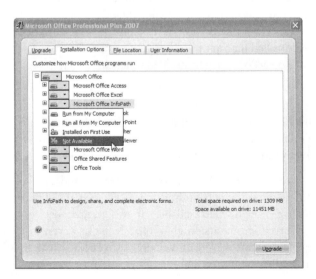

The Installation Options tab shown in Figure A.2 displays all applications available with the version of Office you're installing. The icon to the left of each top-level item in this list shows how it will be installed. Four options are available (a fifth option, to run a program from a network server, is available only on corporate editions of Office):

NOTE

As you select each item in the list, text at the bottom of the dialog box offers a capsule description of the feature or program.

- When you choose Run from My Computer, Setup copies all associated program files to the local hard disk and makes it available to run from shortcuts in the All Programs menu. This option results in the best performance.

- Choose Run All from My Computer to specify that you want all options under the selected feature to be available on this computer.

- When you specify Installed on First Use for a feature, Setup creates a menu item or shortcut for the specified feature, but does not install the files associated with the feature. When you first use that menu choice or shortcut, the Windows Installer copies the necessary files to the local hard disk just as if you had chosen the Run from My Computer option. This option is useful if you are certain that you will not use a particular program or feature and you want to save disk space.

- Choose Not Available when you do not want to install a feature or create shortcuts that refer to it. In some cases, built-in menus include options that refer to features you've chosen not to install; if you select one of these menus, you'll see an error message that instructs you to rerun Setup.

Note that you can set an entire application to be installed on first use. This option might be useful in a setup in which disk space is at a premium and some users are unlikely to need specific applications. If you're installing Office 2007 on a PC whose primary user is unlikely to need to create PowerPoint presentations, for example, you can save disk space by setting up that application as Installed on First Use. The first time the user clicks the PowerPoint icon on the Start menu, PowerPoint installs itself automatically.

The File Location tab, shown in Figure A.3, allows you to specify a custom location for Office to use when installing Office program files. As noted earlier, we strongly recommend that you accept the default location for installing Office 2007. Normally, this is the Program Files folder on the same drive as Windows—usually C:. If you installed Windows on a different drive, the Program Files folder will be on that drive instead.

The most common reason to specify a different location from the default is when you do not have sufficient free space on the default drive (check the text at the bottom of this dialog box to verify that you have enough space available). In this case, choose another drive that does have enough space for Office and its program files. Note, however, that Office still insists on putting some files on the same drive with Windows. To choose an alternative location for Office 2007, click the Browse button and select a location.

Figure A.3
This dialog box provides useful information about available disk space. We don't recommend changing the default location specified here unless you have no other options.

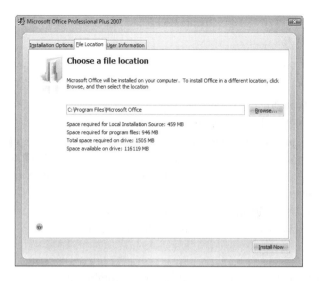

CAUTION

Be careful when installing Office on systems with limited free drive space. The Setup program requires a considerable amount of free space to extract and work with temporary files. Even if you have room for all the options you select, you might encounter a disk-space error if there isn't extra working space for Setup.

The options on the User Information tab allow you to enter your name, initials, and organization name. If you skip this step during setup, you'll be prompted to fill in these blanks when you start an Office program for the first time.

After filling in all options on all dialog boxes, click Install Now to complete the setup.

INSTALLING OFFICE 2007 ALONGSIDE AN OLDER OFFICE VERSION

Do you own an older version of Office? The default Upgrade option replaces all your old Office programs with newer versions. But what if one of the old programs isn't included with your new version? That's not an unlikely possibility. With each new release, Microsoft shifts the mix of programs in various editions, so that an Office program you use and trust is no longer available when you upgrade. You might want to keep using your old version of FrontPage 2002 from Office XP Professional Plus, for instance, because this venerable website-management program has been replaced by the standalone Microsoft Office SharePoint Designer and is not available with any edition of Office 2007. Likewise, you may decide to keep your old version of Publisher or Access while upgrading Word, Excel, Outlook, and PowerPoint from Office 2007 Standard Edition.

If you choose to go this route, you need to pay extra-special attention to setup procedures. Microsoft strongly recommends against trying to use two Office versions on a single PC because of the risk that a program from one Office version will try to use shared system files from another version.

If, despite the warnings, you choose to use two Office versions on the same computer, follow these rules:

- Install the older Office version first, and then install all updates for it. After confirming that it works correctly, you can then install the newer version.

- You can install old and new versions of the same Office program on a single PC, with the exception of Outlook, which allows only one version to be installed. You must upgrade your old version of Outlook or remove it; you can't keep it hanging around on the same computer as a newer version.

- You can install updates and service packs for any installed version, but if you uninstall part or all of an older Office version, you'll probably need to reinstall Office 2007 afterward.

When you run Setup for Office 2007, select the Customize option and then, on the Upgrade tab (see Figure A.4), choose Keep All Previous Versions, or click Remove Only the Following Applications, and then clear check boxes next to the programs you want to keep.

Figure A.4
Clear the check box next to any old program you want to keep when upgrading. A warning will appear if you try to keep Outlook.

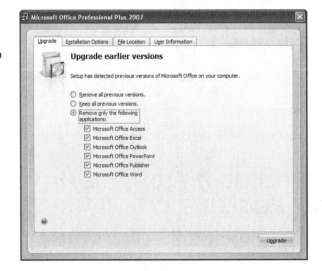

In some older Office versions, keeping separate versions of Office programs required that you specify a different location for each set of program files. Newer versions, including Office 2007, store program files in version-specific folders. Use the default directory as specified during setup; the Windows Installer will sort out files appropriately.

In general, Office 2007 does a good job of respecting earlier versions of Office. All your preferences, for example, are stored in separate branches of the Registry based on the version number, so customizations you make in one program will not affect the other. However, some unavoidable side effects are caused by using multiple Office versions:

- Opening a document by double-clicking its icon launches the Office 2007 version of the program. If you have two versions of Word installed and you want to use the older one to open a file, you must open the older program first and then open the file.

- Some incompatibilities exist between file formats. Using an older Office program to edit a file created in Office 2007 will almost certainly expose these differences.

- Because of changes in VBA object models or capabilities, macros you create in Office 2007 might not work properly when opened in earlier Office versions.

→ For a discussion of file-format options, **see** "Understanding and Choosing File Formats," **p. 54**.

UPDATING OR REPAIRING AN OFFICE INSTALLATION

When you run Setup on a computer that has Office installed already, you'll see the Maintenance Mode Options dialog box shown in Figure A.5. Use this dialog box when you want to add or remove features, when you need to repair an Office installation that is not functioning properly, or when you want to completely uninstall Office 2007.

Figure A.5
After you install Office 2007, running Setup displays the Maintenance Mode Options dialog box.

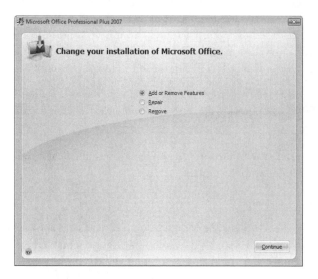

You can start Setup in Maintenance mode by running Setup from the original installation media or by using the Uninstall or Change a Program option in Control Panel.

ADDING AND REMOVING OFFICE FEATURES

To change the list of installed Office features after running Setup for the first time, run Setup in Maintenance mode and click the Add or Remove Features button. The resulting dialog box is nearly identical to the list of features available when you perform a custom installation, as described previously. You can also use this dialog box to change the configuration of a feature—for example, to change a feature that is installed on first use so that it runs on the local computer instead, using one of these techniques:

- To add a feature so that it is available at all times, select the Run from My Computer check box.

- To configure a feature so that it is available for installation when needed, select the Installed on First Use option.

- To remove a feature, select Not Available.

REPAIRING AN OFFICE INSTALLATION

The Windows Installer maintains a complete record of all Office components you've installed. If you accidentally delete a file or a Registry entry becomes corrupted after installation, the Windows Installer can automatically reinstall the component the next time you try to use it. In most cases, these repairs are automatic: If a key DLL for Publisher is missing when you attempt to launch the program, for example, the Installer starts automatically and reinstalls the missing file from the original installation source. If the Local Install Source is corrupted or unavailable, you might need to supply the Office CD to continue.

If you suspect that some features of an application might be damaged, you can run the Microsoft Office Diagnostics utility. As part of its routine, this tool inspects all essential files and reinstalls any that are missing or corrupted. To use this option from any Office program using the new Ribbon-style interface, click the Office button, choose *<program name>* Options, and click Resources. Click Diagnose and follow the prompts to continue.

> **NOTE**
> This option replaces the Detect and Repair option available in previous Office versions.

If you're unable to start the Microsoft Office Diagnostics utility, use the Repair option on the Maintenance Mode setup dialog box.

UNINSTALLING OFFICE 2007

The final option in the Maintenance Mode dialog box, Remove, allows you to completely uninstall Office 2007 and all associated features and components. When you choose this option, you see one and only one dialog box asking you to confirm that you want to remove Office completely. If you click OK, the Windows Installer begins the uninstall process immediately.

Thanks to the Windows Installer's rollback capability, you can abort the uninstall process at any time before completion, and Setup restores your system to its previous state. A progress bar moves from left to right as the Windows Installer removes components; if you click the Cancel button, watch the progress bar move from right to left as the Windows Installer undoes its actions and restores the original configuration.

You should be aware of two caveats when uninstalling Office:

- Using the Uninstall Office option effectively deletes virtually all program files and associated Registry entries. However, it leaves behind a considerable number of Registry entries associated with user settings and preferences, as well as some files that contain user settings. If you attempt to reinstall Office later, the new installation will use these settings. For instance, if you've defined alternative locations for documents, these will appear in your new installation, as will Excel macros in a leftover Personal Macro Workbook.

- If you upgraded over an earlier version of Office, removing Office 2007 will not bring back the previous version. The only way to preserve older Office versions is to specifically choose that option by performing a custom installation of Office 2007 in the first place.

SAVING A SET OF CUSTOM INSTALLATION OPTIONS

For the absolute maximum in control over all details of Office 2007 Setup, use the Office Customization Tool. This utility, included as part of the installation media for Office 2007, is a lengthy wizard that lets you specify the exact mix of features you want to install and options you want to use in an Office installation. To begin, insert the Office installation media in the CD-ROM drive, open a Command Prompt window, type **Setup /Admin**, and press Enter. This opens the tool, shown in Figure A.6.

Figure A.6
The Office Customization Tool gives you complete control over the Office setup process.

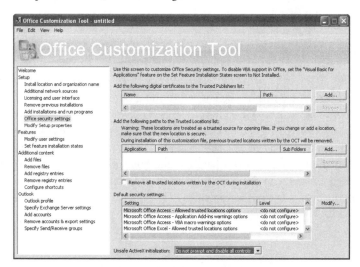

Although it takes some time to run through each step, the results are well worth it for anyone who has to install Office more than once a month. You can choose exactly which features to install, define the names and locations of shortcuts, configure security options, install other programs, or add data files and templates to a user's machine, and even configure Outlook accounts and profiles.

> When you think of the Office Customization Tool, you probably think of it only for use in organizations, but you can benefit from it even if the only machine you administer is your own. Before you set up Office 2007 for the first time, run through the Office Customization Tool and select each option carefully; when you're finished, you'll be able to install the entire program in full confidence that your configuration will appear exactly the way you want it. Run the Setup program from the CD, but specify the full path for the transform file in a command-line switch. Save the transform file in a safe place so you can reuse it if you ever need to reinstall Office.

After running through all options in the Office Customization Tool, choose File, Save As and save the results as a Windows Installer Patch file with the `*.msp` extension. To run Setup using your saved settings, open a Command Prompt window (or use the Run dialog box) and type *`<d:>\`***`Setup.exe /Adminfile <filename>`**. Substitute the drive letter of your CD or DVD drive for *`<d:>`* and use the name of the saved settings file in place of *`<filename>`*. For example, if your CD drive is E: and you previously created a patch file called `Custom.msp`, use the following command line to install Office exactly as you defined it in the Custom Installation Wizard:

```
E:\setup.exe /Adminfile Custom.msp
```

Using a patch file does not affect the original Office setup files. As a result, you can create as many custom patch files as you want, one for each type of custom configuration you want to install.

TROUBLESHOOTING

NO PACKAGES FOR YOU

When I run Setup, I see an error message that says the program couldn't find a package to install.

It's unlikely you'll see this message when running Setup from the CD. If you're running Setup from a shortcut on a local hard disk or a network drive, check the parameters on the command line; there's a good chance they refer to a settings file that is unavailable. If you're running Setup from a network share, open the `Setup.ini` file and make sure the line that begins `MSI=` points to the correct package file. You will also see this error message if two or more package files are in the same folder and you have not specified which one to use, either in `Setup.ini` or in a custom settings file.

SOME FEATURES NOT AVAILABLE

After upgrading a previous version of Office, some programs or features are not available.

If you click the Upgrade option, Setup installs Office 2007 components only when the corresponding earlier program or feature is already on the computer. If you performed a custom installation of an earlier Office version and opted not to install a particular feature, the Office 2007 Setup program uses those options rather than the defaults for a new installation. To install the missing pieces, rerun Office 2007 Setup.

MACROS AND ADD-INS

In this appendix

What's New in Office 2007   944

How Macros Work   945

Recording Simple Macros   947

Troubleshooting Recorded Macros   951

Running Macros   954

Using Auto Macros   955

Digitally Signing Macros You Create   958

WHAT'S NEW IN OFFICE 2007

How do you know you've crossed the line from Office expert to Office obsessive? As soon as you start writing macros, you know you're there.

Macros are small computer programs that automate activities in Microsoft Office programs. The basic tools and techniques for creating, recording, editing, and managing Office macros are the same in all Office programs, as is the underlying programming language, Visual Basic for Applications (VBA). If you learned how to create and use macros in a previous Office version, your skills are directly transferable to Office 2007.

First, though, you have to find all those familiar tools. In the new Ribbon-based interface, Office 2007 groups everything that is macro related onto a Developer tab and then hides that tab. To unhide it so you can begin using macros in Word, Excel, or PowerPoint, click the Office button, click Word (or Excel or PowerPoint) Options, and click to select the check box next to Show Developer Tab in the Ribbon. As Figure B.1 shows, the Code group contains commands to open the Visual Basic Editor, the Macros dialog box, the macro recorder, and the Macro Security dialog box.

Figure B.1
You'll find macro tools on the Developer tab, which is hidden by default.

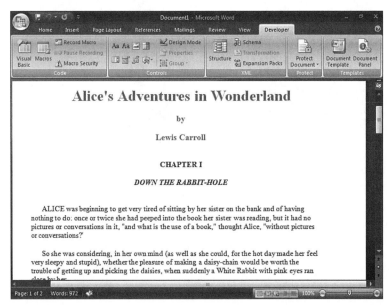

Because Outlook's message-editing window is based on Word, it has a Developer tab as well. In the main Outlook window and in Publisher, you'll find features for creating and editing macros right where they've always been, under the Tools, Macro menu. OneNote has no macro capabilities. Access has a completely different model for assigning code to database objects, which is beyond the scope of this book.

→ In Office 2007, Office security settings have a significant impact on your ability to create, edit, and manage macros as well. For details, **see** "Using the Office Trust Center," **p. 160**.

HOW MACROS WORK

Most people use the individual programs that make up Microsoft Office interactively—typing text, inserting graphics, formatting, saving, and printing. For repetitive tasks, that process can sap your productivity, one click at a time. Even a procedure that requires only three or four mouse clicks can become unbearable if you have to repeat it a dozen times a day. A weekly report that requires a dozen painstaking (and time-consuming) steps to produce can chew up precious hours that are better spent on more important pursuits.

To eliminate the drudgery, you can create a *macro* that automates those tasks using a single, custom command.

Macros can be surprisingly short—even a one-line macro can perform helpful tasks—or they can run for hundreds of lines, with loops and variables and input boxes, and other elements you normally associate with a full-fledged programming language. You don't need to be a programmer to automate much of your work with macros. All you need is a basic understanding of the underlying application and a willingness to step through a few lines of code.

With rare exceptions, you can create a macro to automate any task you can do manually in Word, Excel, PowerPoint, or Publisher. Macros are ideal for automating routine drudge work—those everyday tasks that normally require multiple commands and mouse clicks.

In this appendix, we explain the mechanics of macros, but the details of macro programming would fill a book on their own; therefore, you'll need to find other sources to learn advanced programming principles and techniques. One surprisingly useful source is just a click away. The Help file for each program in the Office family includes a Developer Reference section that explains basic concepts. This resource defines the purpose and syntax of each available programming object, often with code samples that you can cut and paste directly into your own projects. To see the local copy of the Developer Reference, open the Help window for the program you're planning to write a macro for, click the drop-down arrow to the right of the Search box, and choose Developer Reference under the Content from This Computer section.

As we explain in this chapter, you can use built-in Office tools to record macros based on actions you take while the recorder is running, or you can write macros from scratch using the Visual Basic Editor. In either case, it's likely you'll need to do some debugging and testing to ensure that the macro works as you expect.

USING OBJECT MODELS

The fundamental building blocks of VBA are the same, no matter which application you're using. An IF statement in VBA/Word, for example, works like an IF statement in VBA/Excel. That's one of VBA's great strengths, for as soon as you learn VBA with one Office application, you can apply much of what you know to the other applications that use VBA as their macro language.

Still, VBA has to accommodate the differences in each application. You work with words, sentences, and bookmarks in Word; you use formulas, cells, and ranges in Excel; and you work with tables and reports in Access. Those parts of VBA that differ between applications are embodied in the *object model* for that application. The object model provides the means for working with an application.

Word's object model, for example, includes objects that let you create and change documents, paragraphs, and footnotes. Excel's object model works with workbooks, charts, and pivot fields. PowerPoint's object model has presentations, slides, and sound effects. Outlook's object model includes contacts and email messages. The Access object model has reports, forms, and images.

The object model is important because it defines precisely how VBA can interact with an application. That, in turn, imposes limitations on how the macro recorder can work, because the recorder must generate a valid VBA program.

HOW OFFICE APPLICATIONS STORE MACROS

No two Office applications handle macros the same way. Although the precise details are complex, here's a quick summary of how each Office application stores macros:

- **Word**—Word can store macros in documents, templates, or the global macro-enabled template known in Word 2007 as `Normal.dotm`. When you open a document, macros in its associated template become available. If you store templates in the Startup folder (`%appdata%\Microsoft\Word\STARTUP`), Word gives you access to macros stored in those templates whenever you start Word.

→ For details on template locations, **see** "Creating, Using, and Managing Templates," **p. 404**.

- **Excel**—Excel stores macros in workbooks or templates. Unlike Word, Excel does *not* maintain a link between a workbook and the template you use to create it. If you add or edit a macro in a template, that macro is available only in new workbooks you create with that template. Excel automatically opens all workbooks in the Xlstart folder (`%appdata%\Microsoft\Excel\XLSTART`) when it starts, including the hidden workbook `Personal.xlsb`. Thus, all macros in `Personal.xlsb` are available all the time.

→ For details on templates, **see** "Secrets of the Office Masters: Installing and Managing Excel Add-ins," **p. 551**.

- **PowerPoint**—PowerPoint stores macros in presentations and templates. Like Excel, PowerPoint uses templates only to create new files, so adding or editing macros in a template will not affect existing presentations based on that template. PowerPoint does *not* have a Startup folder or anything resembling a global template. Macros written or recorded in earlier versions of PowerPoint should work in PowerPoint 2007.

→ To understand the role of templates in PowerPoint, **see** "Secrets of the Office Masters: PowerPoint File Types," **p. 733**.

CAUTION

Unless you're a skilled programmer, avoid trying to automate anything but the most routine PowerPoint tasks with VBA. Compared with Word and Excel, its object model is incomplete. There's no easy way to copy macros from one presentation to another, short of copying and pasting code into the Visual Basic Editor. The lack of a global template makes it difficult to manage macros, and there is precious little documentation aside from the very sparse Developer Reference available via Online Help.

- **Outlook**—Outlook stores all its macros in one place, and all macros are available all the time. Outlook does not support recorded macros, and security restrictions make many of its features difficult to access. Although the VBA/Outlook object model has significantly improved since its introduction in Outlook 2000, all but experienced programmers should anticipate significant problems working with it.

- **Publisher**—Publisher stores macros in document files. The Visual Basic Editor allows you to work with only one document's macros at a time. Even a simple macro—one that creates a new document, then displays a message box—will not run properly because Publisher can't keep track of the open documents, and it displays the message box in the wrong window. This is definitely a tool with some rough edges—not for the faint of heart.

- **Access**—Access stores VBA programs in modules for the database itself (visible in the Navigation pane) and in forms or reports.

NOTE

> Access also has an old-fashioned macro language, one that's markedly different from VBA/Access. You can design and edit old-style macros, based on conditions and actions, using the Macro Tools tab on the Ribbon. After selecting a database object, start on the Create tab and click the Macro command in the Other group. To open the Visual Basic Editor and work with Modules, click the Create tab and then click the Module command in the Other group. (The terminology is confusing. In Access, macros refer to stored procedures that use a subset of VBA and are created using a Macro Builder. More complex VBA programs, analogous to what are called macros in every other Office program, are called modules in Access.)

NOTE

> For more information on Access databases, see *Special Edition Using Microsoft Access 2007*, by Roger Jennings, published by Que.

RECORDING SIMPLE MACROS

Word and Excel allow you to record macros. The Macro Recorder exists in PowerPoint 2007, but the command to start and stop the recorder has been inexplicably left off the Developer tab, and the only way to record a PowerPoint macro is to use the legacy keyboard commands Alt, T, M, R. Access, Publisher, and Outlook do not have macro recording capabilities—a significant restriction, because you won't be able to use the recorder to capture VBA commands that correspond to typical user interactions. (Although Outlook uses a modified version of Word to read and create messages, it lacks a macro recorder.)

In theory, when you turn on the macro recorder, VBA "watches" as you perform some action or series of actions. When you turn off the recorder, you can replay the resulting recorded macro to replicate that series of actions.

In practice, you'll more often use the macro recorder to eliminate the tedious steps of creating a macro. Unfortunately, a recorded macro rarely solves a real-world problem by itself. After recording a macro, you'll typically need to make some modifications.

You can also use the recorder to capture the steps of a particular task, and then copy all or part of the recorded macro into a larger macro.

HOW THE MACRO RECORDER CAPTURES ACTIONS

As anyone who's ever tried to record an Office macro can tell you, the macro recorder can't record every single action you take. There are two fundamental reasons why the recorder can fail:

- The action you take might not have an exact translation in the application's object model. For example, if you record a macro in PowerPoint to change first-level bullet points in a presentation to 18-point bold, the macro won't work because PowerPoint's object model doesn't include commands for working with first-level bullet points.

CAUTION

> This type of failure, generally completely undocumented, happens without any warning to you. The recorder doesn't stop; there's no other feedback. You know the failure occurred only because the macro fails to work when you play it back.

- The action you take might be ambiguous; in other words, the recorder might not be able to tell exactly what you want to do. For example, if you type this paragraph into a Word document and use the mouse to select it, the VBA/Word macro recorder has no way of knowing what you're trying to do. Are you selecting the current paragraph? Or are you selecting the first paragraph that starts with the word "The"? Maybe you really want to select the tenth paragraph in the document. Or the first one with more than a hundred words. That's why the recorder usually won't record mouse actions—there's just too much ambiguity, most of the time, when you use the mouse.

After you turn on the macro recorder, it records the effect of your actions, not the actions themselves. The full effect of your actions goes into the recorded macro, not the means you used to apply them. For example:

- If you choose File, Open, switch to a shared documents folder on a file server, use the down arrow to move through the list to a file called mydoc, and click OK, the recorder notes that you opened Mydoc.docx—not that you went through all that typing and clicking.
- If you choose Format, Font, and change the font to Wingdings, the recorder records the fact that you changed the font to Wingdings—but it also picks up all the other formatting settings that are currently active, including font size, bold, italic, underline, and so on.
- If you open a dialog box, click to select a specific tab, and then stop recording the macro, the recorder ignores your actions because you didn't actually *do* anything. You can't use this technique to automate the process of guiding the user to a specific dialog box to make a selection.

- If your insertion point is inside a paragraph in a Word document, and you want to tell the recorder to select the first word in that paragraph, double-clicking the first word in the paragraph will not work. If you try to double-click the first word in the paragraph, the recorder won't let you do it. The recorder can't record your double-click action because it's ambiguous: You know that you want to select the first word in the current paragraph, but there's no way to specify that precisely by clicking with the mouse. For all the recorder knows, you might want to select the 50th word on the page, or the 1st word on the 10th line, or the last capitalized word in the paragraph.

When recording, instead of using the mouse, you'll frequently have to resort to obscure keyboard navigation keys. To move to the beginning of the current paragraph in Word, press Ctrl+↑. To select the first word in the paragraph, press Ctrl+Shift+→. To italicize the word, press Ctrl+I.

TIP FROM

> Nobody, but nobody, memorizes all of Word's obscure key combinations. To create a lengthy document listing them all, open Word and press Alt+T, M, M. In the Macros dialog box, click in the Macro Name box, type `listcommands`, and click Run. Select Current Keyboard Settings, and then click OK. Unfortunately, there's no easy equivalent for PowerPoint or Excel. To find a list of standard keyboard shortcuts for those programs, open Help and look for the topics "Excel Shortcut and Function Keys," and "Keyboard shortcuts for PowerPoint 2007," respectively.

RECORDING A MACRO

Word, Excel, and PowerPoint include simple macro recorders that all work in essentially the same way. To record a macro in Word, for example, follow these steps:

1. Create a new document or open an existing document.
2. On the Developer tab, click Record Macro. (If the Developer tab is hidden, you can use the Office 2003 menu shortcuts: press Alt+T, M, R.) In the Record Macro dialog box (see Figure B.2), click in the Macro Name box and type a name (ItalicizeFirstWord, in this example).

Figure B.2
Replace the generic Macro1 name with a descriptive macro name, but don't use spaces or punctuation marks.

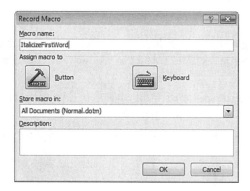

NOTE
> Macro names can contain up to 255 letters and numbers, but no spaces or other punctuation marks. Names must start with a letter and cannot duplicate certain reserved names (for example, cell addresses in Excel).

3. Choose a location for the macro (the current document or a template, for example). If you want to assign the macro to a keyboard shortcut or to a button on the Quick Access toolbar, click the respective button. (You can change either shortcut assignment after the macro has been recorded. See "Getting Quick Results with Keyboard Shortcuts," on page 38 for details.) If you want, you can enter additional explanatory text about the macro in the Description box. Click OK to begin recording.

4. You'll see the Recording pointer, which includes a picture of a cassette tape beneath the familiar arrow. In addition, a Stop Recording button appears in the status bar at the bottom of the editing window (Excel uses a similar pointer and Stop Recording button; PowerPoint provides no indication that a macro is being recorded). Perform any actions you want to record in your macro. For this example, we press Ctrl+↑ to move to the beginning of the current paragraph, Ctrl+Shift+→ to select the first word, and Ctrl+I to apply italic formatting to that word.

5. Click the Stop Recording button on the Developer toolbar (or on the status bar).

To record macros in Excel and PowerPoint, follow the same steps.

TESTING THE MACRO

After recording a macro, it's essential that you test it to see whether it works the way you expect. To quickly run a Word macro, follow these steps:

1. Open a document or create a new document. If necessary, click to position the insertion point at an appropriate location in the document.

CAUTION
> Don't use a "live" document when testing. Always work with a backup copy or a dummy document you create just for testing.

2. Open the Macros dialog box, shown in Figure B.3. On the Developer ribbon, click Macros. (If the Developer tab is hidden, you can use the Office 2003 menu shortcuts: press Alt+T, M, M.)

3. Click the name of the macro you want to run and press Enter or click Run. If all goes well, the macro performs the task you intended.

4. For more complete troubleshooting, click in another location within the document, and repeat steps 1–3.

Figure B.3
All available macros
appear in the Macros
dialog box.

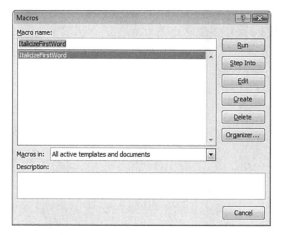

Using the Macro dialog box lets you run all macros that are currently available (the exact list depends on the program you're working with and the file you have open). If you're going to use a particular macro regularly, however, this procedure is cumbersome and slow; you'll learn faster methods for running macros later in this appendix.

TROUBLESHOOTING RECORDED MACROS

B

Macros rarely work right the first time. Recorded macros, in particular, frequently require some tweaking before they work as intended. If the macro you recorded doesn't work, re-record it and see whether you can use a different method for accomplishing the same result. Edit a recorded macro only when it works under certain circumstances, but occasionally fails to work the way you expect, or triggers an error message.

STEPPING THROUGH AND EDITING RECORDED MACROS

Fortunately, Office makes it relatively easy to edit a recorded macro. It even supports you in your bug-extermination efforts by allowing you to run the macro program one line at a time to see what the effect of each command might be. Here's how to use the Visual Basic Editor to step through a macro recorded in Word (the steps in Excel, PowerPoint, Outlook, and Publisher are virtually identical):

1. Create a new document or open an existing document and position the insertion point as necessary. For example, to test a macro that italicizes the first word in a paragraph, be sure to click inside a paragraph in the current document.

2. On the Developer ribbon, click Macros. (If the Developer tab is hidden, you can use the Office 2003 menu shortcuts: press Alt+T, M, M.) In the Macros dialog box, select the name of the macro you want to troubleshoot, and then click Step Into. The Visual Basic Editor opens, with your macro visible in the right pane (see Figure B.4). You'll see a large yellow arrow appear to the left of the Sub line, and the Sub line will be highlighted.

Figure B.4

When you step into a macro for trouble-shooting, the line that's about to be run appears highlighted.

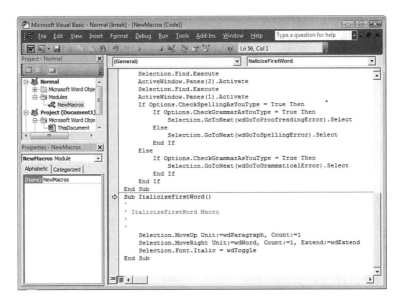

3. Arrange the windows on your desktop so you can see both the application (in this case, Word) and the Visual Basic Editor at the same time. Click the window holding the Visual Basic Editor.

4. To begin executing the VBA code one step at a time, press F8, or choose Debug, Step Into. The first line of the macro—the Sub line—executes.

5. Press F8 again, and watch carefully as the macro performs the next actions; repeat this process one command at a time.

6. When you reach the End Sub line, the Visual Basic Editor stops. You can start all over again, if you like, beginning with step 4.

Frequently, you'll be able to identify the location of the problem (or problems) in a macro by stepping through it in this way. Although the solution might not be at all clear—there are lots of VBA commands, and each one behaves in a different way—being able to narrow the problem down to a line or two can make a huge difference.

After you isolate the line that you suspect is causing the problem, position the insertion point within that line and press F1. That action brings up context-sensitive VBA Help, which might present a possible solution.

Follow the same procedures to step through VBA/Excel and VBA/PowerPoint macros; you'll find recorded macros in the current workbook or presentation, in a module called Module1. In Access, open the database that contains the VBA program, double-click the name of the VBA module in the Navigation pane, and press F8 to step through the macro.

COMMON RECORDED MACRO MISTAKES

When a recorded macro doesn't work as you expect, chances are the problem is one of several common errors. Table B.1 lists common mistakes and suggested troubleshooting steps.

TABLE B.1   COMMON MACRO PROBLEMS

Macro Error	Troubleshooting Suggestion
A key combination doesn't work the way you thought it would.	Many navigation keys have easy-to-understand descriptions (select next word, or move down one paragraph), but they behave oddly in unusual circumstances—inside a Word table, cell, or at the end of a document, for example. Find a different key combination that accomplishes the same task in a slightly different way.
Formatting commands overwrite existing formatting.	When you apply formatting using Format commands, the application might replace all formatting with the new format. If you want to add the new formatting—for example, boldfacing a word while leaving intact other attributes, such as italic—use shortcut keys to apply formatting (Ctrl+B to apply bold).
A repeating macro doesn't do the entire job.	Recorded macros rarely incorporate the kind of repetition you anticipate. To create a macro that loops properly, you almost always have to edit it manually. (One exception—Replace All will loop through an entire document, worksheet, or presentation.)

In addition, any number of unusual circumstances can trigger errors in recorded macros. For example, if you search for the word "widget" in a document where that word is in a footer and not in the body of the document, the search will succeed. When you record that action in a VBA/Word macro, everything appears to work just fine. But when you play back the recorded macro in the same document, Word won't find the word you're looking for no matter how many times you run it—in fact, it will trigger a Run Time Error. The recorded version of the Find operation works differently from the interactive version when it comes to footers.

TESTING AND BULLET-PROOFING MACROS

Just because a macro appears to work in a handful of simple tests doesn't mean that the macro will work correctly all the time. Word macros are notorious for working properly inside simple documents, but failing—without any warning whatsoever—when run on a table, or in text boxes, or on pictures, or in a document with Track Changes enabled, in headers and footers, comments, footnotes, and on and on. It can be devilishly difficult to find the problems and, once found, to figure out how to fix them.

Will your recorded macro work properly every time you run it? Frankly, there's no way to know for sure—VBA macros hardly fall into the category of "provably correct" computer programs—but you can improve the odds of a macro working correctly by employing two time-honored testing techniques:

- **Trace through the logic.** In most cases, that means stepping through the macro, as explained earlier in this section. Watch for behavior or settings that you don't understand.

- **Test it in a variety of circumstances.** Try to think of odd situations that might make the macro fail, and then see whether it does. Enlist the aid of fellow workers to test a macro, if possible, because testers will think of situations that don't occur to you.

For example, the ItalicizeFirstWord macro example (in the "Recording a Macro" section earlier in this chapter) should italicize the first word in the current paragraph, but it doesn't. Instead, when the insertion point is at the beginning of a paragraph, this macro italicizes the first word of the *preceding* paragraph. Running through the macro a step at a time reveals that the culprit is the MoveUp command; when you point to that command and press F1, the context-sensitive help suggests several examples. The first example contains the solution to the problem: It shows how you have to MoveRight once before performing a MoveUp, to stay in the original paragraph.

The recorded ItalicizeFirstWord macro contains a second problem as well. When you run the macro, and then leave the insertion point in the same paragraph and run the macro again, it *removes* the italic formatting from the first word. Stepping through the macro again lets us see the problem: The Selection.Font.Italic line toggles the italic attribute on and off. According to the Help file, the Italic property "can be set to `True`, `False`, or `wdToggle`." Changing the value from `wdToggle` to `True` causes it to work properly.

When you rerecord the ItalicizeFirstWord macro to incorporate the extra step at the beginning and then change the value of the Italic property to `True`, you'll find that both problems have disappeared.

RUNNING MACROS

Although each of the Office applications offers myriad ways to run macros, three simple methods in Word, Excel, PowerPoint, Outlook, and Publisher will get you going:

- On the Developer ribbon, click Macros to open the Macros dialog box, which contains a list of all currently available macros. (If the Developer tab is hidden, you can use the Office 2003 menu shortcuts: press Alt+T, M, M. In Outlook's main window and in Publisher, choose Tools, Macro, Macros.) Use this technique for macros you run only infrequently.

- Before you start recording a macro, you can choose to assign the macro to a menu (Word only) or a specific key combination (Word or Excel).

- After recording a macro, you can assign it to a Quick Access Toolbar button or a keyboard shortcut.

→ For details on customizing the Quick Access Toolbar, **see** "Adding Frequently Used Commands to the Quick Access Toolbar," **p. 33**.

In addition, you can set macros to run each time you start an application (a topic we cover in the following section). You can assign a macro to a picture or a piece of text, or set up a macro to run at a specific time. Your macros can even take over built-in Office functions such as printing. For example, if you want to track printer usage in your office, create a macro that counts the number of pages in a document or worksheet, adds a new row to an Excel list with the user's name, the date and time, and the number of pages, and then sends the job to the printer.

USING AUTO MACROS

Word, Excel, PowerPoint, and Outlook all enable you to create macros that will run when the applications start or quit, or when you open or close a specific document, workbook, or presentation. In all cases, the trick lies in putting the macro in the right place and giving the macro the correct name. (In PowerPoint, you must clear a couple of additional hurdles.)

These so-called *Auto macros* can come in handy when you want to modify the application itself when it starts—to load the most recently used document, for example. For example, you can record a macro that maximizes the Excel window whenever you start Excel. Or you can set up a macro to run every time you open or close a specific document. This technique is also effective when you need to modify a document before the user starts working on it— to automatically calculate an invoice number, for example.

USING AUTO MACROS IN WORD

Word responds to a number of different Auto events, but we generally recommend you stick to one of these five events:

- AutoExec() and AutoExit(), which run when Word starts and quits, respectively. These macros have to be placed in a module in `Normal.dotm`.

- Document_Open() and Document_Close(), which fire when the document containing the macros is opened or closed. If you store macros with either of these names in a Word template, they'll also run when you open or close documents based on the template.

  The Document_Close() macro runs before Word asks whether you want to save changes.

- Document_New(), which fires when you create a new document based on the template (or document) containing the name.

Although you might place AutoExec and AutoExit macros in any module in `Normal.dotm`, Document_Open(), Document_Close(), and Document_New() must all be created in a special area called Microsoft Word Objects. To create a macro that runs every time you create a Word document based on the `Memo.dotm` template, for example, follow these steps:

1. Open the template in Word and press Alt+F11 to open the Visual Basic Editor (or click Visual Basic on the Developer tab).

2. In the Project Explorer, navigate to the Memo project, called TemplateProject (Memo). Then expand the Microsoft Word Objects branch and double-click ThisDocument.

NOTE

In Word, projects attached to templates are called TemplateProject(*Template name*). So, for example, the project attached to Letterhead.dotm is called TemplateProject (Letterhead).

3. To display a message whenever a user creates a new memo based on this template, click the Object drop-down list and choose Document. Then, in the Procedure drop-down list, choose New. VBA/Word provides the Sub Document_New()/End Sub pair (see Figure B.5).

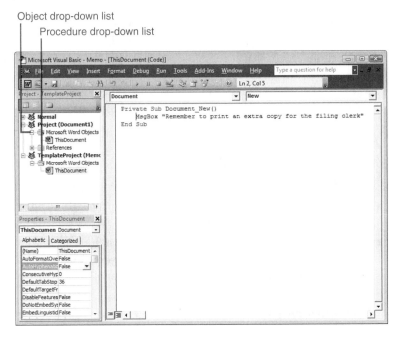

Object drop-down list
Procedure drop-down list

Figure B.5
The Document_Open(), Document_Close(), and Document_New() Auto macros go in the project's Microsoft Word Objects folder.

4. Type this one line between Sub and End Sub:
   ```
   MsgBox "Remember to print an extra copy for the filing clerk."
   ```

5. Press Alt+F11 (or click the View Microsoft Word button) to return to Word. Be sure to save the changes to the template file.

To see the macro in action, create a new document based on the Memo template. The reminder appears (and must be dismissed by clicking OK) before the user can even start typing.

USING AUTO MACROS IN EXCEL

Although Word handles just three document-oriented Auto events, Excel keeps track of 29 events—Before Close, Before Save, New Sheet, Sheet Activate, and many more—and you can write pieces of code to be invoked whenever one of these 20 events occurs. To see a complete list of these events and a discussion of how to write code for them, open the online Help, change the scope to the Excel 2007 Developer Reference, select "Workbook Object" from the Reference heading, and view the list of events.

It's relatively easy to follow the instructions in online Help to create Auto macros that correspond to most workbook events, but it's not at all obvious how to create Auto macros that run when Excel starts or exits. For example, let's assume that you want to maximize the Excel window every time Excel starts. Follow these steps:

1. Start Excel and press Alt+F11 to open the VBA Editor. In the Project Explorer, select the VBAProject(PERSONAL.XLSB) entry.

TIP FROM

EQ & Woody

> If you don't have a Personal Macro Workbook (stored as `Personal.xlsb`), the simplest way to create one is to flip back to Excel and record a do-nothing macro. On the Developer tab, click Record Macro. (If the Developer tab is hidden, you can use the Office 2003 menu shortcuts: press Alt+T, M, R.) Make sure you choose Personal Macro Workbook in the Store Macro In box. Click OK, and then click the Stop Recording button on the Developer tab or the status bar. Excel automatically creates `Personal.xlsb` in the XLSTART folder to store the recorded macro.

2. Under VBAProject (PERSONAL.XLSB), expand the Modules branch and double-click Module1. That puts you in Module1 of your Personal Macro Workbook.

3. Choose Insert, Procedure to bring up Excel's Add Procedure dialog box (see Figure B.6). Type **Auto_Open** (note the required underscore character), and click OK.

Figure B.6
An Auto_Open() subroutine in Excel's Personal Macro Workbook (`Personal.xlsb`) will run every time Excel starts.

4. In the newly created Auto_Open() subroutine, type the one-line program you see in Figure B.7.

5. Close Excel. When asked whether you want to save changes to your personal workbook, click Yes.

B

Figure B.7
This one-line program maximizes the Excel application window.

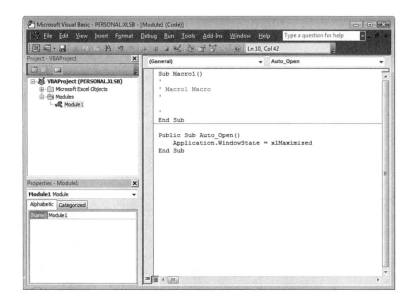

Every time you start Excel, the Auto_Open() macro in `Personal.xlsb` kicks in and maximizes Excel.

USING AUTO MACROS IN POWERPOINT

PowerPoint, by contrast, requires that you use class modules to house macros that react to the application's Auto events. Then you have to run a separate program that activates those events before the events will "fire." The procedure is complicated. For details, look in the PowerPoint Help topic "Application Events."

DIGITALLY SIGNING MACROS YOU CREATE

Office 2007 includes a number of security measures to help protect you from macro-based malware. *Digital signatures* lie at the heart of the approach most frequently encountered by Office users.

A digital signature identifies the source of a macro. Developers must apply for digital signatures from *certifying authorities*, which verify the identity of developers before issuing them a signature. Certifying authorities can revoke a certificate after issuing it, if they discover evidence that a developer is distributing viruses or unsafe software.

The default settings for Office 2007 disable all macros except those included as part of files stored in trusted locations (typically the Templates and startup folders). (For more details on this feature, see "Using the Office Trust Center," p. 160.)

Those are excellent security precautions, but they get in the way if you create a document, workbook, presentation, or template that contains macros you want to reuse or share with other people.

If you are writing VBA programs to distribute within your organization, or for general distribution, you must

- Acquire a digital certificate.
- "Sign" your VBA project.
- Tell the people who will be using your macros what your signature looks like, and what they need to do to get your macros working.

NOTE

> If your users have their security set to disable macros without notification, they won't be able to use your macros, and they won't be told why unless you sign your macros.

→ For more details on setting up security levels to manage macros, **see** "Controlling Macros and VBA Projects," **p. 166**.

You have three options for obtaining a digital certificate:

- You can create an *unauthenticated certificate* by running Selfcert.exe, the Digital Certificate for VBA Projects application (see Figure B.8). This utility is normally found in the Microsoft Office Tools folder on the Programs menu. If it isn't installed on your computer, rerun Office Setup and click Add or Remove Features. Click the plus sign (+) next to Office Shared Features, click Digital Signature for VBA Projects, and then click Run from My Computer. Click Update. This certificate is stored in the Registry and is required to run macros in Office applications that prohibit the use of any unsigned macros. It can be used to sign macros only on the computer on which it was created. An unauthenticated certificate represents no security at all: Anybody can create an unauthenticated certificate claiming to be anyone, even Bill Gates. When a user opens a VBA project that's signed with an unauthenticated certificate, he or she will always be asked to verify that he trusts the source of the project.

- If you work for a large organization, you might be able to get a certificate from your group's certification authority (your network administrator will use Microsoft Certificate Server to generate the file for you).

Figure B.8

- You can buy an authenticated certificate from VeriSign (http://www.verisign.com) or Thawte (http://www.thawte.com)—look for "developer certs" or "code signing digital IDs." Avoid Class 2 IDs, which certify the existence of a particular email address—Selfcert.exe works just as well. Class 3 IDs, for organizations, cost hundreds of dollars for the first year (subsequent years are at a reduced price) and are best-suited for commercial software developers.

To sign a VBA project, follow these steps:

1. Open the project (template, document, workbook, publication, or presentation) using the associated application.

2. Press Alt+F11 to start the VBA Editor.

3. In Project Explorer, highlight the project you want to sign.

4. Choose Tools, Digital Signature. Click the Choose button and select either a new signature or change an existing one. Click OK to save your changes.

After using your self-generated digital certificate to sign a project, you can examine its contents by clicking the Detail button. A self-signed certificate is marked with a red X that indicates it is not trusted because it can't be traced back to a trusted certifying authority.

If you copy a document, template, or workbook containing a macro project that has been digitally signed with a self-generated certificate, you'll be unable to open any of those macros on another computer. Windows protests that it can't authenticate the certificate and thus gives you only the option to disable the macros and open the document.

Are you stymied? Not at all. If you're absolutely, positively confident of the identity of the party who created the macros—for instance, if you created and signed them yourself on one computer and you want to use them on another computer in the same office—you can tell Windows that you want your self-generated certificate to be fully trusted. To do this, you need to install the certificate as a Trusted Root Certification Authority. Follow these steps:

1. On the computer containing the original signed project, click Start, choose Run, enter `certmgr.msc` in the Open box, and click OK. The Windows Certificates console opens.

2. Select your self-generated certificate from the Personal store, right-click, and choose Export from the All Tasks menu.

3. Save the exported certificate to a removable drive or a network share so that you can transfer it to the other computer.

4. On the computer where you want to use the signed project, open the Windows Certificates console (`certmgr.msc`).

5. Select the Trusted Root Certification Authorities store, right-click, and choose Import from the All Tasks menu. Navigate to the file you saved and click OK.

Now when you inspect the properties of the certificate, you'll see that the red X has been replaced with an official seal of approval. You'll also discover that your macros work flawlessly on the new computer.

Using Office on a Tablet PC

In this chapter

Office 2007 and the Tablet PC   962

All About Ink   962

Editing Text on a Tablet PC   966

Viewing and Printing Annotations and Comments   967

Troubleshooting   967

OFFICE 2007 AND THE TABLET PC

On most desktop and notebook computers, you enter text with a keyboard and manipulate onscreen objects with a mouse. But those traditional input devices take a backseat when you use a Tablet PC with a compatible version of Windows.

In design, a Tablet PC is a notebook computer with a few hardware twists. The most obvious is the input device—a pen-shaped stylus that takes the place of a mouse and allows the user to select and manipulate text and objects, make menu selections, and click buttons by tapping the touch-sensitive screen. The pen also serves as a way to draw lines, sketch diagrams, and tap out text using an onscreen keyboard. Most importantly, you can use the pen to scribble your own notes, just as if you were jotting them down on a piece of paper. When you use a Tablet PC with the pen, the screen appears in portrait orientation rather than the landscape mode you're used to on conventional hardware.

Along with the input hardware, you also need an operating system that supports these alternative input methods. If you purchase a Tablet PC that was built before early 2007, it almost certainly came with Windows XP Tablet PC Edition, a customized version of Windows XP Professional sold only with Tablet PC hardware. Tablet PCs sold after the beginning of 2007 with Windows Vista preinstalled already support Tablet PC features. Most of the Tablet-centric features available in Office 2007 are similar in Windows XP Tablet PC Edition and Windows Vista. In this appendix, we assume you're running Office 2007 on Windows Vista Home Premium, Business, or Ultimate edition, all of which support Tablet features.

NOTE

> Do you have an older Tablet PC? If it's running Windows XP Tablet PC Edition, make sure you install Windows XP Service Pack 2, which includes a significant upgrade to all Tablet-specific features. Better yet, consider upgrading that older Tablet PC to Windows Vista. For an online evaluation of your hardware and its suitability for the upgrade, see Microsoft's website or check with your PC's manufacturer.

Office 2007 recognizes when it has been installed on a computer running a Tablet-compatible version of Windows and automatically enables features that take advantage of the hardware.

ALL ABOUT INK

When you draw, sketch, or write in an Office program editing window using the Tablet PC's pen, the data you create is called *ink*. In Office, ink is a full-fledged object type with its own properties and behaviors, just like AutoShapes and pictures. Ink sits in the drawing layer, and you can use the Format Ink dialog box and options on the Drawing toolbar to change the color and width of the ink. You can select an ink annotation, copy it to the Clipboard, and then paste it into another Office program—or into any application that supports ink. In Word, Excel, and PowerPoint, the Tablet pen normally acts as a pointer, which you can use to point and click or—with the help of the onscreen keyboard—to enter text.

In Word, Excel, or PowerPoint, you can begin adding ink by clicking the Start Inking button on the Review tab. In Outlook, this button is on the Message tab.

This action reveals the Ink Tools add-in with the Pens tab shown in Figure C.1.

Figure C.1
Click the Start Inking button to reveal these custom tools, which are available only on a Tablet PC.

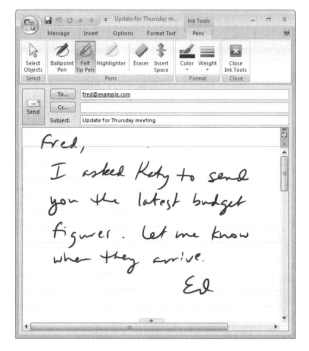

When you ink using these tools, your scribbles appear as annotations over or under typed text and graphics—essentially, freeform objects in the drawing layer. In Outlook, you can create and send handwritten email messages. You can mark up a Word document, an Excel worksheet, or a PowerPoint slide using your own handwriting or freehand illustration. While delivering a PowerPoint presentation, you can take notes directly on the slides and then save the results.

 If ink annotations won't stay put within a Word document, see "Locking Documents When Using Annotations" in the "Troubleshooting" section at the end of this chapter.

In Word, but not in PowerPoint or Excel, you can add handwritten comments to a document in addition to adding annotations directly on the document. Click the Ink Comment command on the Review tab to open the Comment pane. These notes appear in comment balloons and can be tracked on a per-user basis. Figure C.2 shows an ink comment in a Word document.

Figure C.2
Ink comments sit alongside typed comments in the Review pane.

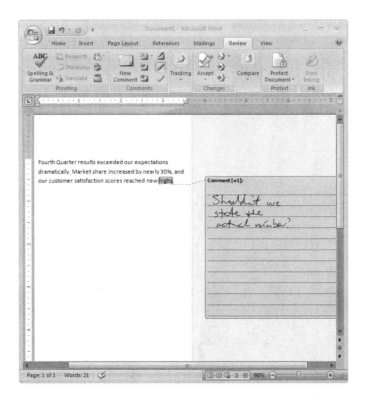

In all the Office programs we've mentioned so far, ink plays a secondary role to typed text and numbers. Most of the time, you or someone in your workgroup will create an Office document or an email message using typed text. The pen adds useful capabilities for reviewing and annotating and for dashing off quick messages.

What if you want to use the pen to jot down notes of phone conversations, meeting minutes, shopping lists, and other sorts of random, free-form text? Don't even think about pressing Word into service for an occasional handwritten document of this sort—it's ill-suited to this task on a day-to-day basis. Word's drawing canvas greatly limits your ability to enter and edit text, and you're still faced with the dilemma of how to save, organize, and search multiple documents containing ink-based text.

Use OneNote instead. Although you can use OneNote on a desktop PC and type notes onto pages, it's especially effective on a Tablet PC, thanks to its ability to store ink. You don't need to convert your notes into text; OneNote automatically recognizes ink-based content in its searchable index, making it possible for you to quickly locate handwritten words and phrases anywhere within a notebook.

Use the Pen and Type Text/Select Object buttons (shown in Figure C.3) to switch between handwritten drawings or notes and text input.

Figure C.3
OneNote shows its full potential when used on a Tablet PC.

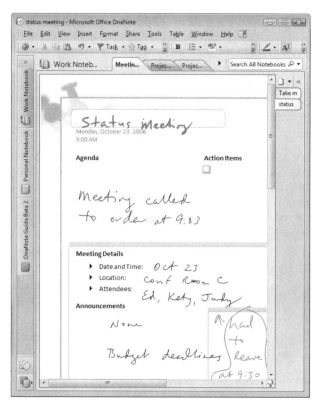

→ For more details about using OneNote, **see** "Using OneNote," **p. 879**.

Although ink sits in the drawing layer, it actually contains some attributes normally associated with text. You can use the surprisingly accurate handwriting recognition capabilities in any Tablet-compatible Windows version to convert your scribbled notes into text, which can then be pasted into a document. More often, though, you'll want to save ink as ink.

TIP FROM

Ed & Woody

You need a Tablet PC to create ink in an Office document. (The one exception is in Slide Show view in PowerPoint, where you can create ink annotations using any computer.) However, you don't need any special hardware to work with ink that has been saved in a document. The ink is treated as an object, the same as a drawing object. If Windows XP Tablet PC Edition or a Tablet-aware version of Windows Vista is running, you can work with the ink as ink; on all other Windows versions, the ink behaves as if it were a drawing.

EDITING TEXT ON A TABLET PC

On a Tablet PC, the standard way to enter text into dialog boxes and programs that don't recognize ink (such as Notepad) is to use the Tablet PC Input Pad. In Windows XP Tablet PC Edition, you can summon this box by using a pen *gesture*, which consists of holding the pen tip over the bottom of the screen and moving it quickly back and forth. In Windows Vista, the Input Panel tucks into the left side of the screen with only a small stub sticking out. Click that stub to reveal the Input Panel, or drag it to slide up and down the screen.

In Office 2007, the only reason to use the Input Panel is to make minor edits to a document or to fill in a dialog box. For all other text input tasks, use the Ink tools.

As we noted in the previous section, you begin entering ink by clicking the Start Inking button on the Review tab (or the Message tab in Outlook). Buttons on the Ink Tools tab allow you to change the style of pen used (ballpoint, felt tip, or marker) as well as the color and weight of the ink. In Word, a drawing canvas appears in your document, and you can begin writing anywhere within that canvas.

→ For an explanation of how the drawing canvas in Word works, **see** "Working with a Drawing Canvas," **p. 106**.

When you add ink writing to an Excel worksheet or PowerPoint slide, the ink appears in the drawing layer, directly on top of the current work surface. As with any drawing object, you can select, move, copy, delete, resize, or format the ink.

If you change your mind about something you wrote using ink, click the Eraser button. This changes the mouse pointer to an eraser icon. Tap the eraser icon on any existing ink to remove it from the page.

You can convert any ink to text and then paste the converted text into any Office document (or anywhere that the Clipboard's Paste command is available). Select the ink, right-click, and choose Copy Ink as Text from the shortcut menu.

When you receive an email message that was created in Outlook using ink, the handwritten content appears as an embedded graphic within an HTML-formatted email message. It can be read by anyone with an HTML-capable email client. If you read it using Outlook 2007, you'll be able to treat the ink as ink.

TIP FROM

Ed & Woody

Entering text as ink in the body of a message is easy. Filling in the address and subject fields is slightly more difficult. Clicking the To button gives you point-and-click access to your entire Outlook Address Book. You can also use the Tablet PC Input Pad to enter the first few characters of the recipient's address and then allow AutoComplete to finish the job. For the subject, you can use the Input Pad, or try the Tablet PC's text recognition feature. Enter the subject at the top of your email message and click the Select Objects button on the Ink Tools tab. Select the ink you entered for the subject text, press and hold the pen to reveal the right-click shortcut menu, and choose Copy Ink as Text. Now click to position the insertion point in the Subject box and paste the text.

VIEWING AND PRINTING ANNOTATIONS AND COMMENTS

Anyone who can read an Office document—with or without a Tablet PC—can view and manage ink annotations with just a few mouse clicks. To show or hide ink, click the Review tab and select or clear the Ink option on the Show Markup list.

To show or hide ink annotations on a printed copy of a document, worksheet, or presentation, choose Print from the Office menu. In Word, choose Document Showing Markup from the Print What box to show annotations; choose Document (the default) to hide annotations. In PowerPoint, select or clear the Print Comments and Ink Markup option on the Print dialog box. In Excel, ink annotations appear on printed pages if the annotations are visible on the screen; you can't control print options separately.

TROUBLESHOOTING

LOCKING DOCUMENTS WHEN USING ANNOTATIONS

I added some annotations to a Word document and then made some edits. Now all the annotations are in the wrong place. How can I keep this from happening?

When you insert annotations, they appear in the drawing layer and "float" on the page. If you underline a sentence and then add a new sentence before the underlined sentence, the text shifts down the page, but the ink stays where you originally added it. To ensure that your annotations stay in sync with your document's content, you need to lock the document's layout. Click Protect Document on the Review tab and then click Restrict Editing and Formatting. Select the check box under Editing Restrictions, and select either Comments or No Changes (Read-Only). Click Yes, Start Enforcing Protection to make your changes effective.

INDEX

Numbers and Symbols

3D effects for AutoShapes, 113-114

3D references, 596

35mm slides, turning PowerPoint presentations into, 791-792

* format switches, 501-502

A

ABS function, 617

absolute cell references, 595

absolute values, 617

accented characters, inserting into documents, 78

Access 2007 databases
  database engines, 836
  database objects, creating, 839
  default values, 877
  expressions, 841-843
  file formats, 56
  filters, 872-873
  forms
    controls, 853-857
    creating, 839-840, 852-853

  definition of, 852
  designing for ease of use, 857-858
  managing, 840
  overview, 838
  properties, 841
  importing/exporting data, 843-844
  input masks, 876
  macros
    overview, 838
    storing, 947
  modules, 839
  Navigation pane, 839
  new features, 18
  planning, 836
  queries
    action queries, 867-868
    calculated columns, 870
    creating, 839-840, 862
    criteria, 870
    crosstab queries, 864-865
    definition of, 861
    fields, 869-870
    managing, 840
    overview, 837
    parameter queries, 865-866
    properties, 841, 871
    select queries, 863-864
    SQL queries, 868-869

  relationships
    many-to-many relationships, 850
    one-to-many relationships, 850-851
    one-to-one relationships, 850
    overview, 848-850
  reports
    controls, 853-857
    creating, 839-840, 852-853
    definition of, 852
    designing for ease of use, 859-860
    grouping and sorting records in, 860-861
    managing, 840
    overview, 838
    properties, 841
  required values, 877
  SharePoint lists
    creating links to, 913
    exporting to, 911-912
    importing from, 912-913
    moving to, 914
  tables
    creating, 839-840, 844-845
    field data types, 846-847
    indexes, 848

managing, 840
overview, 837
primary keys, 847-848
properties, 841
troubleshooting, 873-874
validation rules, 874-876

accessibility, speech recognition technology, 79, 100-101

accessing shared Outlook folders, 923-924

accounts, email
alternate profiles, 227-228
Exchange accounts, 224-226
Hotmail, MSN, and other HTTP accounts, 226-227
Internet standard email accounts, 221-224
multiple account management, 227
overview, 220-221

Action Buttons (PowerPoint), 731

action queries, 867-868

Action Settings (PowerPoint), 730-731, 787

activating Office 2007, 21-22

ActiveX controls, Trust Center settings, 164-165. *See also* **objects**

Add Holidays to Calendar dialog box, 282

add-ins
Excel add-ins, 551-552
Ink Tools, 963
installing, 169

new features, 20
Trust Center settings, 163-164

adding. *See also* **installing**
clip art to Clip Organizer, 131
holidays to Calendar, 282
images to SmartArt, 121
notes to presentations (PowerPoint), 724-725
pages (OneNote), 887-888
text to slides (PowerPoint), 713-715
text to AutoShapes, 114-115

Address Book (Outlook)
addressing email from, 238-239
configuring, 236-238
options, 235-238
Personal Distribution Lists, 239-240
printing, 271-274
restricting access to, 310-313

addresses, email, 238-239, 264

advanced Excel filters, 639-643

Advanced Filter dialog box (Excel), 642

Advanced Find dialog box (Outlook), 200-204

alert (Excel), 535

aligning
AutoShapes, 115-116
cells (Excel), 576
controls, 857
paragraphs (Word), 359-360
text in table cells (Word), 424-425

animations (PowerPoint), 762-763, 792
bullet points, 763-764
chart components, 770-771, 776
copying, 776
custom animations, 764-768
drawing layer, 768-769
hiding/uncovering slide contents with, 769-770

annotations
entering, 962-965
locking documents, 967
viewing/hiding on Tablet PCs, 967

antivirus software, 311

AOL email accounts, 257

applets, Windows Character Map, 78

applications. *See also* *specific applications (PowerPoint, Word, etc.)*
configuring, 45-48
options, 40, 43

applying email rules, 254-255

appointments (Outlook), 279. *See also* **Calendar folder**
creating, 284-288
meetings versus, 289-290
recurring appointments, 288-289
rescheduling, 289
time zones for, 282-284

archiving personal information (Outlook), 187-191

area charts, 672

arithmetic operators, 842

array formulas, 600-601

arrows, drawing, 110

ascending sorts, 631-632

aspect ratio (of pictures), 126

assigning
  delegates to Outlook folders, 925-926
  Outlook items to categories, 194-196

attaching files
  to email, 146-147
  to meeting requests, 291

Attachment fields (Access), 847

audience handouts (PowerPoint), 745-746, 758

audio, inserting in notebooks (OneNote), 899-900

Auto Account Setup dialog box (Outlook), 220, 225

auto macros, running
  in Excel, 956-958
  in PowerPoint, 958
  in Word, 955-956

AutoArchive option (Outlook), 189-191

AutoComplete (Excel), 518-519

AutoCorrect, 49, 365-366
  customizing AutoCorrect lists, 89-91
  do's and don'ts, 91-92
  finding obscure AutoCorrect entries, 100

options, 88-89
  overview, 86-87

AutoExec() event, 955

AutoExit() event, 955

AutoFill (Excel), 520-523
  custom AutoFill lists, 522-523
  example, 521-522
  options, 522
  overview, 519-521

AutoFilter (Excel), 635-638

AutoFit Options action menu, 713

AutoFormatting PowerPoint, 715

automatic backups, 138-139

automatic number formats (Excel), 555-556

AutoNumber fields (Access), 846

AutoRecover, 70-71

AutoShapes, 108-110
  adding text to, 114-115
  aligning, 115-116
  background colors, 112-113
  grouping, 116-117
  line formats, 112-113
  rotating, 114
  shadows and 3D effects, 113-114

autosum functions, 609

AutoSummary (Word), 466

AutoText (Word), 365-366

Auto_Open() subroutine, 957

AVERAGE() function, 604, 617

axes (charts)
  horizontal axes, 689
  labeling, 685
  logarithmic axes, 690
  minimum and maximum values, 692-693
  secondary axes, 691-692
  vertical axes, 688-689

B

backgrounds, 444
  AutoShape background colors, 112-113
  Excel charts, 695
  PowerPoint presentations, 752-755
  slides, 741-742

backing up files, 170, 173
  automatic backups, 138-139
  AutoRecover options, 70-71

bar charts, 671

bibliographies, 464-465

bidirectional language support, 80

billing statements, creating in Outlook, 296

black-and-white printers, preparing color presentations for, 791

blank cells, removing from PivotTables, 661

Blocked Senders list (Junk Email Options), 317

blocking
  malware
    controlling execution
      of scripts, 309-310
    restricting access to
      Outlook Address
      Book, 310-313
  spam
    email rules, 319
    Junk Email Options,
      314-318
    overview, 313-314
    phishing
      messages, 316
    Search Folders, 318
    third-party
      spam-blocking
      tools, 319
    tracking sources of
      spam, 324-325

blogs, creating with Word, 385

body text (PowerPoint), 706

bookmarks (Word), 457

bootstrap programs, 931

borders
  in Excel worksheets,
    579-581
  in Word documents,
    446-447
  in Word tables, 435

bound controls (Access), 853

boxes
  in Excel worksheets,
    579-581
  in Word documents,
    446-447

broken links, 100

Building Block Organizer, 410-412

built-in templates (Word), 406-408

bulleted lists, 97
  in PowerPoint, 715-717
  in Word, 367-368

bullets, animating in PowerPoint, 763-764

Business Card view (Outlook), 212

business cards, creating, 274-275

business information, customizing in Publisher, 823-824

C

calculated columns, 870

calculated controls, 854

calculations. *See* formulas

Calendar folder (Outlook), 278
  appointments
    creating, 284-288
    meetings versus,
      289-290
    recurring
      appointments,
      288-289
    rescheduling, 289
  Date Navigator, 278-279
  Day/Week/Month views
    customizing, 280-282
    resetting default, 304
    switching between,
      279-280
  events
    creating, 284-288
    recurring events,
      288-289
    rescheduling, 289
  holidays, adding, 282

  meetings, 284
    appointments versus,
      289-290
    checking status of, 294
    creating meeting
      requests, 290-292
    rescheduling or
      canceling, 294-295
    responding to meeting
      requests, 293-294
    troubleshooting, 305
  publishing calendars to
    SharePoint, 914-915
  sharing, 298-299
    via email, 301-302
    on Exchange Server,
      299-300
    group schedules,
      303-304
    with Office Online,
      300-301
    publishing as web
      page, 305-306
    viewing shared
      calendars, 302-303
  synchronizing calendars
    with SharePoint, 915
  time zones, 282-284

callouts, 109

canceling meetings, 294-295

canvas. *See* drawing canvas

Card view (Outlook), 212

CAs (certifying authorities), 143, 958

categories, assigning Outlook items to, 194-196

CDs, saving presentations to, 788-789

Cell Styles Gallery (Excel), 574-575

cells (Excel)
alignment, 576
borders, boxes, and
colors, 579-581
column width, 581-583
custom cell formats,
568-570
conditions, 573
custom date/time
formats, 571
custom number
formats, 570
text formats, 571-572
finding and replacing
contents of, 524
formatting. *See*
formatting Excel
worksheets
indenting, 577
merging, 581
orientation, 578-579
references
3D references, 596
absolute
references, 595
entering into formulas,
594-595
mixed references, 596
relative
references, 595
row height, 581-583
styles, 574-575
text wrap, 577

cells (Word tables)
aligning text in, 424-425
moving and copying, 421
rotating, 425-426
selecting, 420-421

**certifying authorities
(CAs), 143, 958**

**changing slide layouts
(PowerPoint), 712-713**

character attributes
in Excel worksheets,
573-574
fonts, 95-97

**character formatting
(Word), 348-350**
changing, 356-358
drop caps, 358

**Character Spacing dialog
box (Publisher), 818**

character styles, 392, 394

charts
animating in PowerPoint,
770-771, 776
area charts, 672
axes
horizontal axes, 689
logarithmic axes, 690
minimum and maxi-
mum values, 692-693
secondary axes,
691-692
vertical axes, 688-689
axis labels, 685
bar charts, 671
column charts, 669-670
combination charts, 677
creating, 123-124
custom charts, 678-679
cylinder/cone/pyramid
charts, 676
data labels, 686-687
data tables, 687
default charts, 679
doughnut charts, 674-675
droplines, 694
editing, 123-124
error bars, 694
fill and outline
colors, 695
formatting, 123-124
gridlines, 694

inserting into Word
documents, 440-441
labeling elements of, 682
layouts, 680-681
legends, 685-686
line charts, 670
moving, 681-682
overview, 666
pie charts, 670-671
PivotTable charts,
696-697
radar charts, 675-676
selecting data to plot,
667-669
stock charts, 673
surface charts, 674
third-party add-ins, 697
titles, 683-684
top-left cells, leaving
blank, 699
trendlines, 694
troubleshooting, 698-699
visual effects, 695-696
XY (scatter) charts,
672-673

**checking for new
email, 232**

CHITEST function, 617

choosing
file formats, 54-55
PowerPoint presentation
themes, 747-748
PowerPoint theme
colors, 749-750

**circling data errors in
Excel, 536-537**

citations, 464-465

**Class Identifiers
(CLSIDs), 166**

CLEAN function, 612

cleaning up personal information (Outlook), 187-191

clip art
adding to Clip Organizer, 131
adding to PowerPoint, 719-720
adding to Word documents, 438
searching, 129-130
setting keywords, 131

Clip Organizer, 131

Clipboard
converting Clipboard data into alternate formats, 93-94
dragging and dropping data, 94
overview, 92
Paste All command, 100
removing items from, 92
viewing, 92

CLSIDs (Class Identifiers), 166

collaboration
with Outlook
accessing shared folders, 923-924
sharing folders, 921-923
with SharePoint, 908
document libraries, 916-917
document workspaces, 917-919
forms, 919
lists, 908-914
meeting workspaces, 920-921
in Outlook, 914-915

shortcuts,
creating, 925
troubleshooting, 924-925

color scales (Excel), 586

color-coding notebooks and sections (OneNote), 886

colored data bars (Excel), 586

colors
background colors for AutoShapes, 112-113
in Excel
charts, 695
color scales, 586
in Excel worksheets, 579-581
PowerPoint theme colors
changing, 750
choosing, 749-750
color presentations, preparing for black-and-white printers, 791
customizing, 824-825
modifying, 748-749
SmartArt, 122

column charts, 669-670

columns
Access calculated columns, 870
Excel
hiding, 528
locking row/column labels, 529-530
width, 581-583
Word tables
adding/deleting, 424
formatting, 451-452
moving and copying, 421
selecting, 420-421
widths, 422-424

COM objects. *See* **objects**

combination charts, 677

commands. *See specific commands*

comments
adding to Word documents, 147, 473
overview, 147
restricting edits to comments only, 147-148
viewing/hiding on Tablet PCs, 967

communicating with Outlook contacts, 270-271

company details, entering in Outlook contacts, 264

comparing, reviewing, and merging changes, 150

comparison functions, 610

comparison operators, 638-639, 842

Compatibility Mode, 133, 436-437

composing email messages
custom message options, 244-246
message formats, 240-242
reply and forward options, 246-247
signatures, 242-244

compound documents, 151-153

compressing picture files, 134

CONCATENATE function, 612

conditional formatting, 583-587, 611

conditions, adding to Excel cells, 573

cone charts, 676

configuring. *See also* customizing
applications, 45-48
email accounts
alternate profiles, 227-228
Exchange accounts, 224-226
Hotmail, MSN, and other HTTP accounts, 226-227
Internet standard email accounts, 221-224
overview, 220-221
Send/Receive groups, 230-231
live preview, 47
Outlook Address Book, 236-238
Research task pane, 44-45
slideshows, 785-786
Smart Tags, 47-48
SMTP Servers, 228-229

connecting
to data sources, 486-487
Excel worksheets to external databases
integrating external data into worksheets, 648-649
overview, 645-646
with Query Wizard, 646-648
SharePoint connections, 924

connectors (for shapes), 110

contacts (Outlook)
addresses, 264
assigning to categories, 194-196
communicating with, 270-271
Contacts folder, viewing, 260-261
deleting, 273
editing, 261-262
email and web addresses, 265-266
entering, 261-262, 267-268
filing order, 266-267
finding, 199-204
flagging for follow-up, 196-199
job and company details, 264
merging duplicate contacts, 269-270
moving, copying, and deleting, 192-193
names, 263
personal information, 266
phone and fax numbers, 265
printing, 271-274
sharing, 268
troubleshooting, 273-274

Contacts folder (Outlook), 267
addresses, 264
communicating with contacts, 270-271
deleting contacts, 273
editing contacts, 261-262
email and web addresses, 265-266

entering contacts, 261-262
entering multiple contacts, 267-268
filing order, 266-267
job and company details, 264
merging duplicate contacts, 269-270
names, 263
personal information, 266
phone and fax numbers, 265
printing contact lists, 271-274
sharing, 268
troubleshooting, 273-274
viewing, 260-261

containers (OneNote), 893-896

Content Library (Publisher), 826

content placeholders, 713

Contextual Spelling feature (Word), 374-375

contextual tabs, 30

contiguous ranges, 512-513

controls (Access)
adding, 855
bound controls, 853
calculated controls, 854
grouping and aligning, 857
positioning, 855-857
unbound controls, 854

Convert Text to Table dialog box (Word), 429

converting
  Clipboard data into
    alternate formats, 93-94
  data to Word tables,
    429-430
  data with drag and drop
    (Excel), 524-525
  file formats, 59
  images to text in pages
    (OneNote), 896
  scanned documents to
    text, 84-85
  text to Word tables,
    428-429
  text to WordArt, 132-133

copying
  data validation rules
    (Excel), 536
  design of existing
    presentations, 709
  Excel formatting, 588
  formatting between
    section breaks
    (Word), 450
  Outlook items, 192-193
  pages (OneNote),
    890-891
  parts of Word tables, 421
  PowerPoint
    animations, 776
  styles between
    templates, 408
  Word document
    formatting, 352
  worksheets, 510-511

COUNT function, 618

**Create Building Block
dialog box (Word), 419**

**Create New Color
Scheme dialog box
(Publisher), 824**

**Create New Folder dialog
box (Outlook), 193**

**Create Rule dialog box
(Outlook), 250**

criteria, 842
  criteria ranges, 639
  defining in queries, 870

**cropping pictures,
126-127**

**cross-references (Word),
458-460**

crosstab queries, 864-865

**Currency fields
(Access), 846**

**Custom Animation task
pane (PowerPoint), 764**

**Custom AutoFilter dialog
box (Excel), 638-639**

custom charts, 678-679

Customize dialog box, 35

customizing. *See also*
configuring
  AutoCorrect lists, 89-91
  email options, 244-246
  Excel, 545-548
    AutoFill lists, 522-523
    cell formats, 568-572
    Day/Week/Month
      views (Calendar),
      280-282
    default formatting,
      548-549
    filters, 638-639
    hiding rows and
      columns, 528
    locking row/column
      labels, 529-530
    splitting window,
      530-531
    startup switches, 549
    Zoom controls, 529
  form letters with fields,
    494-495
  labels, 482
  Normal template,
    405-406

  Office installation,
    933-935
    file locations, 934
    installation
      options, 934
    Office Customization
      Tool, 939-940
    user information, 935
  Office user interface, 32
    application
      configuration, 45-48
    application options,
      40, 43
    keyboard shortcuts,
      38-39
    Office options, 40, 43
    Outlook and Publisher
      menus, 34-37
    Outlook and Publisher
      toolbars, 34-36
    Quick Access Toolbar,
      33-34
    Research task pane,
      44-45
  Open dialog box, 65-67
  Outlook interface
    Navigation pane,
      180-183
    overview, 179
    Reading pane,
      183-184
    To-Do Bar, 183
    views, 206-213
  PowerPoint animations,
    764-768
  Publisher
    business information,
      823-824
    color schemes,
      824-825
    templates, 805
  Save As dialog box, 65-67
  Word interface, 379-384

cylinder charts, 676

D

data
converting to Word
tables, 429-430
converting with drag and
drop, 524-525
entering into ranges, 513
selecting for charts,
667-669

**data fields, adding to
documents, 487-488**

data files (Outlook)
cleaning up and archiving
personal information,
187-191
data file types, 186-187
Microsoft Personal
Folders Scan/Repair
Utility, 191
Personal Folders file,
185-186, 191
storing data in, 184-185

**data labels (charts),
686-687**

**data sources, connecting
to, 486-487**

data tables (charts), 687

**data types (Access fields),
846-847**

data validation
in Access databases,
874-876
in Excel
circling data errors,
536-537
copying rules, 536
creating rules, 532-534
deleting rules, 536
error alerts, 535
input messages, 534
moving rules, 536
overview, 532

**Data Validation dialog box
(Excel), 533-536**

database engines, 836

database functions, 618

databases (Access), 836
connecting Excel
worksheets to
integrating external
data into worksheets,
648-649
overview, 645-646
with Query Wizard,
646-648
creating, 913
database engines, 836
database objects,
creating, 839
default values, 877
exporting to SharePoint
lists, 911-912
expressions, 841-843
filters, 872-873
forms
controls, 853-857
creating, 839-840,
852-853
definition of, 852
designing for ease of
use, 857-858
managing, 840
overview, 838
properties, 841
functions, 618
importing/exporting data,
843-844
importing from
SharePoint lists,
912-913
input masks, 876
macros, 838
modules, 839
moving to SharePoint
lists, 914

Navigation pane, 839
PivotTables and, 656
planning, 836
queries
action queries,
867-868
calculated
columns, 870
creating, 839-840, 862
criteria, 870
crosstab queries,
864-865
definition of, 861
fields, 869-870
managing, 840
overview, 837
parameter queries,
865-866
properties, 841, 871
select queries, 863-864
SQL queries, 868-869
relationships
many-to-many
relationships, 850
one-to-many
relationships,
850-851
one-to-one
relationships, 850
overview, 848-850
reports
controls, 853-857
creating, 839-840,
852-853
definition of, 852
designing for ease of
use, 859-860
grouping and sorting
records in, 860-861
managing, 840
overview, 838
properties, 841
required values, 877

tables
  creating, 839-841,
    844-845
  field data types,
    846-847
  indexes, 848
  overview, 837
  primary keys, 847-848
  troubleshooting, 873-874
  validation rules, 874-876
date functions, 613-614
Date Navigator, 278-279
Date/Time fields
  (Access), 846
dates
  adding to Word
    documents, 444
  date functions, 613-614
  Date/Time fields
    (Access), 846
  entering into Outlook
    automatically, 193-194
  Excel date formats,
    565-566, 571
  sorting Excel tables by,
    633-634
  PowerPoint, 706
DAY function, 613
Day view (Calendar)
  customizing, 280-282
  resetting default, 304
  switching between
    Day/Week/Month
    views, 279-280
Day/Week/Month view
  (Outlook), 212
DB function, 610
DDB function, 610
debugging formulas
  checking for errors,
    621-623
  error messages, 619-621

Formula AutoCorrect
  feature, 618-619
  Watch window, 623-624
default calendar views,
  resetting, 304
default charts, 679
default values
  (Access), 877
delegates, assigning to
  Outlook folders,
  925-926
deleting
  data validation rules, 536
  email rules, 254-255
  Outlook contacts, 273
  Outlook items, 192-193
  OneNote pages, 893
  OneNote sections, 885
  rows/columns from
    Word tables, 424
  section breaks, 450
  Word document
    formatting, 353
  worksheets, 510-511
delimiters, 428
delivering presentations
  packaging for use on
    other computers, 788
  packaging process, 788
  PowerPoint Viewer, 790
  saving to CDs, 788-789
descending sorts, 631-632
Design Checker
  (Publisher), 830-831
Design Gallery
  (Publisher), 825-826
design objects, 825-826
designing
  Access forms, 857-858
  Access reports, 859-860
  business cards, 274-275

PowerPoint
  presentations, 708-709
  Publisher publications,
    833-834
Developer tab, 47
diagnosing problems, 25
dialog boxes. See specific
  dialog boxes
digital signatures
  adding to documents,
    143-145
  hidden digital
    signatures, 145
  macros, 958-960
directories, 491
disabling HTML-based
  email, 322-323
displaying
  chart data labels, 686-687
  chart gridlines, 694
  Word document
    formatting, 351-352
distributing Word
  documents, 474-476
#DIV/0! error
  message, 620
Document_Close()
  event, 955
Document Imaging
  tool, 128
Document Inspector,
  171-172
document libraries
  (SharePoint)
  opening documents
    from, 917
  publishing documents
    to, 916-917
Document Management
  Servers, 150

Document Map (Word), 339, 344

Document_New() event, 955

Document_Open() event, 955

Document Scanning tool, 128

Document Workspaces, 151, 917-919

documents
AutoCorrect
customizing AutoCorrect lists, 89-91
do's and don'ts, 91-92
finding obscure AutoCorrect entries, 100
options, 88-89
overview, 86-87
backing up, 170, 173
bibliographies, 464-466
bookmarks, 457
borders, 446-447
boxes, 446-447
bulleted lists, 97, 367-368
citations, 464-465
columns, 451-452
comments
adding, 147, 473
overview, 147
restricting edits to comments only, 147-148
compound documents, 151-153
cross-references, 458-460
dividing into multiple files, 456-457

editing
comparing, reviewing, and merging changes, 150
restricting edits to comments only, 147-148
tracking revisions, 149
endnotes, 464
entering text into
AutoCorrect, 365-366
AutoText, 365-366
Quick Parts, 366-367
envelopes, 480-481
fields
adding to documents, 498-499
field code syntax, 498
formatting field results, 500
general * format switches, 501-502
overview, 496-497
showing/hiding, 497-498, 502
finding and replacing text, 369-374
fonts
character attributes, 95-97
font management programs, 95
formatting options, 95
overview, 94
sans serif fonts, 95
serif fonts, 95
footnotes, 464
formatting in Word
character formatting, 348-350, 356-358
copying formatting, 352
drop caps, 358

finding and replacing formatting, 369-374
line and paragraph spacing, 361-362
locking formatting, 353-354
manual formatting, 347
overview, 346
page breaks, 362-363
page/section setup options, 354-355
paragraph alignment, 359-360
paragraph formatting, 351, 358-365
paragraph indents, 360-361
removing formatting, 353
revealing formatting within documents, 351-352
styles, 347
tabs, 363, 365
themes, 348
forms, 503-504
grammar checking, 374-375
headers/footers, 441
creating, 442-443
dates and document details, 444
options, 443-444
page numbers, 444
hyperlinks, 98-100
images
charts, 440-441
clip art, 438
inserting, 436-438
shapes, 438-439
SmartArt, 439-440
WordArt, 441

indexes, 460-462, 474
labels
  customizing, 482
  printing, 481
layers, 105-106
letters, 478-480
lines, creating, 445-446
locking, 139, 967
master documents, 456
navigating in Word
  overview, 342
  with Document
    Map, 344
  with keyboard,
    342-343
  with mouse, 343
  with Select Browse
    Object menu,
    344-346
numbered lists, 97,
  367-368
opening from
  document libraries
  (SharePoint), 917
personal information,
  protecting, 170-172
preparing for
  distribution, 474-476
printing, 150
  choosing what to
    print, 377-378
  Print dialog box
    options, 378-379
  Print Preview feature,
    376-377
properties, 467-468
publishing
  to document libraries
    (SharePoint),
    916-917
  in PDF format, 57
  to websites, 150-151
  in XPS format, 57
recovering, 170, 173

restricting changes
  to, 473
saving
  as PDF, 454
  as web pages, 59
  as XPS, 454
scanned documents,
  converting to text,
  84-85
section breaks
  copying formatting
    between, 450
  deleting, 450
  inserting, 449-450
  types of, 448-449
security
  automatic backups,
    138-139
  digital signatures,
    143-145
  encryption, 136
  IRM (Information
    Rights Management),
    142-143, 155, 158
  locking
    documents, 139
  marking documents as
    final, 140-141
  password protection,
    136-138
  protecting private data
    in documents,
    141-142
  read-only mode,
    139-140
  Windows
    permissions, 141
shading, 447-448
sharing
  automatic backups,
    138-139
  comments, 147-148
  comparing, reviewing,
    and merging
    changes, 150

digital signatures,
  143-145
emailing files as email
  attachments, 146-147
emailing files as
  HTML messages,
  145-146
IRM (Information
  Rights Management),
  142-143, 155, 158
locking
  documents, 139
marking documents as
  final, 140-141
on office networks,
  153-154
overview, 136
password protection,
  136-138
protecting private data
  in documents,
  141-142
read-only mode,
  139-140
tracking revisions, 149
troubleshooting, 155
Windows
  permissions, 141
spell checking, 374-375
storing document details,
  67-69
styles
  applying, 391, 395-399
  character styles,
    392, 394
  copying between
    templates, 408
  definition of, 388
  list styles, 394
  managing, 399-403
  paragraph styles,
    391-392
  table styles, 394

troubleshooting, 409-410

updating automatically, 409-410

subdocuments, 456

summarizing automatically, 466

Table of Authorities, 465-466

Table of Contents (TOC), 462-463

tables

adding/deleting rows and columns, 424

aligning text in, 424-425

borders and shading, 435

changing column widths and row heights, 422-424

converting data to, 429-430

converting text to, 428-429

creating, 417-419

entering and editing data, 419-420

formulas, 430

large table considerations, 435-436

layouts, 426-428

moving and copying parts of, 421

overview, 416-417

positioning on page, 432

rotating text in, 425-426

saving to Gallery, 419

selecting data in, 420-421

sorting data in, 431-432

styles, 433-434

troubleshooting, 452-453

templates

built-in templates, 406-408

copying styles between, 408

definition of, 388

Normal template, customizing, 405-406

restoring, 410

viewing, 404

text

accented and international characters, 78

entering, 76-80, 100-101

finding and replacing, 82-84

foreign languages, 79-80

selecting, 80-81

speech recognition technology, 79, 100-101

symbols and special characters, 76-78

Unicode standard, 76

themes

applying, 389-391

definition of, 388

tracking revisions, 469, 471-472

undoing changes, 99-100

watermarks, 445

DOLLAR function, 612

domain names, 324

doughnut charts, 674-675

Draft view (Word), 337-338

dragging and dropping

Clipboard data, 94

in Excel, 524-525

drawing

borders, 446-447

boxes, 446-447

lines, 445-446

drawing canvas, 106-107

drawing layer, 105-106, 768-769

Drawing tools, 104

adding text to shapes, 114-115

aligning shapes, 115-116

AutoShapes, 109-110

background colors, 112-113

connectors, 110

drawing canvas, 106-107

grouping shapes, 116-117

layers, 105-106

line formats, 112-113

ordering options, 118

rotating shapes, 114

shadows and 3D effects, 113-114

Shapes tool, 107-109

snap and grid settings, 110-112

wrapping and layout options, 117-118

drop caps

creating in Publisher, 818

formatting in Word, 358

droplines (charts), 694

due dates of tasks, troubleshooting, 304

E

e-stamps, 493

Easy Web Site Builder (Publisher), 806-809

Edit Links dialog box (Excel), 532

Edit Signature dialog box (Outlook), 243

editing
charts, 123-124
legends, 685-686
titles, 683-684
documents
comparing, reviewing, and merging changes, 150
restricting edits to comments only, 147-148
tracking revisions, 149
email rules, 254-255
macros, 951-952
pictures, 127-128
PivotTables, 657-659
slides, 713-715
text
in SmartArt, 120
on Tablet PCs, 966
Word documents, 358-365
character formatting, 356-358
drop caps, 358
editing restrictions, 473
Word tables, 419-420
adding/deleting rows and columns, 424
column widths and row heights, 422-424
layouts, 426-428
rotating text, 425-426
text alignment, 424-425

editions of Office 2007, 13-14

email
Address Book
addressing email from, 238-239
configuring, 236-238
options, 235-238
Personal Distribution Lists, 239-240
addressing, 238-239
AOL accounts, 257
assigning to categories, 194-196
blocking malware
controlling execution of scripts, 309-310
restricting access to Outlook Address Book, 310-313
blocking spam
email rules, 319
Junk Email Options, 314-318
overview, 313-314
phishing messages, 316
Search Folders, 318
third-party spam-blocking tools, 319
tracking sources of spam, 324-325
checking for new messages, 232
custom message options, 244-246
email account configuration
alternate profiles, 227-228
Exchange accounts, 224-226
Hotmail, MSN, and other HTTP accounts, 226-227

Internet standard email accounts, 221-224
multiple account management, 227
overview, 220-221
emailing documents
as email attachments, 146-147
as HTML messages, 145-146
embedded email images, 324
finding, 199-204
flagging for follow-up, 196-199
HTML-based email, disabling, 322-323
mass emailing with mail merge, 490
message formats, 240-242
moving, copying, and deleting, 192-193
notification settings, 233
privacy issues, 319, 321
profiles, 227-228
Reading pane, 233-235
reply and forward options, 246-247
rules
actions, 252-253
applying, 254-255
conditions, 250-252
creating, 249-253
deleting, 254-255
editing, 254-255
exceptions, 253
saving, 253-254
when to use, 249
search folders, 248
security overview, 308-309
selecting messages to download, 231-232

Send/Receive groups, 230-231

sending from specific accounts, 242

sharing calendars via, 301-302

signatures, 242-244

SMTP Server configuration, 228-229

troubleshooting, 255-257

email accounts, configuring

alternate profiles, 227-228

Exchange accounts, 224-226

Hotmail, MSN, and other HTTP accounts, 226-227

Internet standard email accounts, 221-224

multiple account management, 227

overview, 220-221

SMTP Server configuration, 228-229

email addresses, entering in Outlook contacts, 265-266

embedding objects, 152-153

in email, 324

pictures, 125-126

encrypting files, 136

End mode (Excel), 514

endnotes, 464

envelopes

adding e-stamps to, 493

merging, 491-493

printing, 480-481

Envelopes and Labels dialog box (Word), 480

error bars (charts), 694

Error Checking dialog box, 621-623

errors

in Excel

circling data errors, 536-537

error alerts, 535

rounding errors, 556-558

formulas, 619-621

PivotTables, 661

events

AutoExec(), 955

AutoExit(), 955

creating, 284-288

Document_Close(), 955

Document_New(), 955

Document_Open(), 955

recurring events, 288-289

rescheduling, 289

Excel 2007

add-ins, 551-552

AutoComplete, 518-519

AutoFill, 520-523

custom AutoFill lists, 522-523

example, 521-522

options, 522

overview, 519-521

cells

alignment, 576

borders, boxes, and colors, 579-581

column width, 581-583

custom cell formats, 568-573

finding and replacing contents of, 524

formatting. *See* formatting Excel worksheets

indenting, 577

merging, 581

orientation, 578-579

references, 594-596

row height, 581-583

styles, 574-575

text wrap, 577

charts

area charts, 672

axes, 688-693

axis labels, 685

bar charts, 671

column charts, 669-670

combination charts, 677

custom charts, 678-679

cylinder/cone/pyramid charts, 676

data labels, 686-687

data tables, 687

default charts, 679

doughnut charts, 674-675

droplines, 694

error bars, 694

fill and outline colors, 695

gridlines, 694

inserting in PowerPoint, 720-722

labeling elements of, 682

layouts, 680-681

legends, 685-686

line charts, 670

moving, 681-682

overview, 666

pie charts, 670-671

PivotTable charts, 696-697
radar charts, 675-676
selecting data to plot, 667-669
stock charts, 673
surface charts, 674
third-party add-ins, 697
titles, 683-684
top-left cells, leaving blank, 699
trendlines, 694
troubleshooting, 698-699
visual effects, 695-696
XY (scatter) charts, 672-673
converting data with drag and drop, 524-525
customizing, 545-548
hiding rows and columns, 528
locking row/column labels, 529-530
splitting window, 530-531
Zoom controls, 529
data validation
circling data errors, 536-537
copying rules, 536
creating rules, 532-534
deleting rules, 536
error alerts, 535
input messages, 534
moving rules, 536
overview, 532
database connections
integrating external data into worksheets, 648-649
overview, 645-646
with Query Wizard, 646-648

End mode, 514
exporting data into, 643-645
file formats, 55
filters
advanced filters, 639-643
AutoFilter, 635-638
custom filters, 638-639
overview, 634-635
Find and Replace feature, 524
formatting options
alignment, 576
automatic number formats, 555-556
avoiding rounding errors, 556-558
borders, boxes, and colors, 579-581
cell styles, 574-575
column width, 581-583
conditional formatting, 583-587
copying with Format Painter, 588
custom cell formats, 568-573
date/time formats, 565-566
degree of precision, 558-559
font and character attributes, 573-574
General number format, 554
indents, 577
merging cells, 581
number formats, 560-564
orientation, 578-579
overview, 554

row height, 581-583
scientific notation, 559
Text format, 559-560
text wrap, 577
Year 2000 issues, 567-568
formulas
3D references, 596
array formulas, 600-601
cell references, 594-596
checking for errors, 621-623
controlling order and timing of calculations, 597-598
definition of, 594
error messages, 619-621
Formula AutoCorrect feature, 618-619
Goal Seek tool, 625-626
hiding, 599
locating parts of, 597
monitoring with Watch window, 623-624
named ranges, 601-603
operands, 594
operators, 594
troubleshooting, 624-625
importing data into, 643-645
links, 531-532
macros
auto macros, 956-958
storing, 946
new features, 10, 16-17, 508
Paste Options, 525-528

PivotTables
  adding and removing
    subtotals, 660
  changing appearance
    of, 659-660
  creating, 655-657
  editing, 657-659
  external databases
    with, 656
  overview, 651-654
  refreshing, 661
  removing blank
    cells and error
    messages, 661
  updating, 657-659
  when to use, 655
ranges
  contiguous ranges,
    512-513
  defining as tables,
    628-630
  entering data into, 513
  finding and
    replacing, 524
  moving from cell to
    cell within, 513
  range names, 515-516
  selecting, 513
  selecting with Go To
    dialog box, 516-518
SharePoint list
  commands, 911
startup switches, 549
tables
  combining multiple
    web sources into, 662
  defining ranges as,
    628-630
  exporting to
    SharePoint lists,
    909-910
  filtering, 634-643
  importing from
    SharePoint lists,
    910-911

importing/exporting
    data, 643-645
  sorting data in,
    631-634
  troubleshooting,
    661-662
troubleshooting,
    550-551, 588-589
Web Queries, 649-651
workbooks
  default formatting,
    548-549
  navigating within,
    514-516
  overview, 508-509
  storing multiple
    scenarios in single
    workbook, 589-593
worksheet functions, 594
  autosum
    functions, 609
  AVERAGE(), 604
  building from scratch,
    605-607
  comparison
    functions, 610
  database
    functions, 618
  date and time
    functions, 613-614
  entering error-free
    functions, 605-607
  financial
    calculations, 610
  information
    functions, 611
  IPMT(), 604
  lookup and reference
    functions, 614-616
  mathematical
    calculations, 616-617
  nesting, 607-608
  statistical functions,
    617-618

syntax, 604
  text manipulation
    functions, 611-612
  TODAY(), 604
worksheets
  connecting to external
    databases, 645-649
  copying, 510-511
  default formatting,
    548-549
  deleting, 510-511
  headers/footers,
    541-542
  hiding rows and
    columns, 528
  inserting, 510-511
  labeling, 512
  locking row/column
    labels, 529-530
  moving, 510-511
  overview, 508-509
  page breaks, 539
  printing, 537-543
  publishing to Web,
    543-545
  renaming, 512
  splitting window,
    530-531
  working with multiple
    worksheets, 509-510
  zooming in/out, 529

exceptions, adding to
email rules, 253
Exchange Server
  email accounts,
    configuring, 224-226
  sharing calendars on,
    299-300
execution of scripts,
controlling, 309-310

exporting
  Access databases to
    SharePoint lists,
    911-912
  data into Excel, 643-645
  database data, 843-844
  Excel tables to
    SharePoint lists,
    909-910
  Outlook data, 216-217
expressions, 841-843
**External Data Range
  Properties dialog box
  (Excel), 644**

F

**fax numbers, entering in
  Outlook contacts, 265**
**Field Settings dialog box
  (Excel), 660**
fields
  adding to documents,
    487-488, 498-499
  adding to form letters,
    494-495
  data types, 846-847
  field code syntax, 498
  formatting field
    results, 500
  {INCLUDETEXT}, 457
  general * format
    switches, 501-502
  overview, 496-497
  query fields, 869-870
  showing/hiding,
    497-498, 502
  {TC}, 462
  {XE}, 462
file formats
  Access 2007 formats, 56
  choosing, 54-55
  compatibility with older
    Office versions, 57-58

converting and importing
  between Office
  programs, 59
Excel 2007 formats, 55
.htm/.html, 59
overview, 10-12, 54
PDF, publishing
  documents in, 57
for pictures, 124
PowerPoint 2007
  formats, 56
saving files in alternate
  formats, 56
troubleshooting, 72
Word 2007 formats, 55
XPS, publishing
  documents in, 57
files. *See also* documents
  attaching to meeting
    requests, 291
  AutoRecover, 70-71
  comments, 147-148
  creating, 63-65
  encrypting, 136
  finding, 69-70
  formats
    Access 2007
      formats, 56
    choosing, 54-55
    compatibility with
      older Office versions,
      57-58
    converting and
      importing between
      Office programs, 59
    Excel 2007 formats, 55
    .htm/.html, 59
    overview, 10-12, 54
    PDF, publishing
      documents in,
      57, 454
    for pictures, 124
    PowerPoint 2007
      formats, 56, 733-735

saving files in alternate
  formats, 56
  troubleshooting, 72
  Word 2007
    formats, 55
  XPS, publishing
    documents in,
    57, 454
locations, customizing
  during Office
  installation, 934
managing locally, 60-62
managing remotely
  on SharePoint
    servers, 63
  on web or intranets,
    62-63
  overview, 62
opening
  multiple files, 70
  Open dialog box,
    65-67
Outlook data files, 184
  cleaning up and
    archiving personal
    information, 187-191
  data file types,
    186-187
  Microsoft Personal
    Folders Scan/Repair
    Utility, 191
  Personal Folders file,
    185-186, 191
  storing data in,
    184-185
properties, 67-69
saving, 65-67
security
  automatic backups,
    138-139
  digital signatures,
    143-145
  encryption, 136

IRM (Information Rights Management), 142-143, 155, 158

locking documents, 139

marking documents as final, 140-141

password protection, 136-138

protecting private data in documents, 141-142

read-only mode, 139-140

Windows permissions, 141

sharing

automatic backups, 138-139

comments, 147-148

comparing, reviewing, and merging changes, 150

digital signatures, 143-145

emailing files as email attachments, 146-147

emailing files as HTML messages, 145-146

IRM (Information Rights Management), 142-143, 155, 158

locking documents, 139

marking documents as final, 140-141

on office networks, 153-154

overview, 136

password protection, 136-138

protecting private data in documents, 141-142

read-only mode, 139-140

tracking revisions, 149

troubleshooting, 155

Windows permissions, 141

storing file details, 67-69

filing Outlook contacts, 266-267

fill-in-the-blanks forms, creating, 503-504

filters

Access, 872-873

email filters. *See* Junk Email Options

Excel

advanced filters, 639-643

AutoFilter, 635-638

custom filters, 638-639

overview, 634-635

Outlook, 297-298

financial calculations, 610

Find and Replace dialog box (Excel), 524

Find and Replace feature (Excel), 524

FIND function, 612

finding

cell contents or ranges (Excel), 524

files, 69-70

obscure AutoCorrect entries, 100

Outlook items, 199-204

Service Packs, 22-23

text, 82-84, 369-374

updates, 22-23

flagging Outlook items for follow-up, 196-199

floating objects, inserting pictures as, 125

folders

accessing shared folders, 923-924

assigning delegates, 925-926

Contacts folder (Outlook)

addresses, 264

communicating with contacts, 270-271

deleting contacts, 273

editing contacts, 261-262

email and web addresses, 265-266

entering contacts, 261-262

entering multiple contacts, 267-268

filing order, 266-267

job and company details, 264

merging duplicate contacts, 269-270

names, 263

personal information, 266

phone and fax numbers, 265

printing contact lists, 271-274

sharing, 268

troubleshooting, 273-274

viewing, 260-261

My Documents, 61

options, 73

search folders (Outlook), 248

sharing, 921-923

follow-up, flagging Outlook items for, 196-199

fonts
character attributes, 95-97
in Excel worksheets, 573-574
font management programs, 95
formatting options, 95
overview, 94
PowerPoint theme fonts, 750-751
sans serif fonts, 95
serif fonts, 95

footers
adding to Excel worksheets, 541-542
on slides, 742-743
PowerPoint, 706
Word, 441
creating, 442-443
dates and document details, 444
options, 443-444
page numbers, 444

footnotes, 464

foreign languages, entering text in, 79-80

form letters, 486. *See also* **mail merge**

Format as Table dialog box (Excel), 629

Format Cells dialog box (Excel), 560-564

Format Painter (Excel), 588

format switches, 501

formats. *See* **file formats**

formatting
charts, 123-124
Excel worksheets
alignment, 576
automatic number formats, 555-556
avoiding rounding errors, 556-558
borders, boxes, and colors, 579-581
cell styles, 574-575
column width, 581-583
conditional formatting, 583-587
copying with Format Painter, 588
custom cell formats, 568-573
date/time formats, 565-566
degree of precision, 558-559
font and character attributes, 573-574
General number format, 554
indents, 577
merging cells, 581
number formats, 560-564
orientation, 578-579
overview, 554
row height, 581-583
scientific notation, 559
Text format, 559-560
text wrap, 577
troubleshooting, 588-589
Year 2000 issues, 567-568
field results, 500
fonts, 95
lines for AutoShapes, 112-113
Office documents
with styles, 391-403
with templates, 404-408
with themes, 389-391
PowerPoint presentations, 756-757
text in SmartArt, 123
Word documents
character formatting, 348-350, 356-358
columns, 451-452
copying formatting, 352
drop caps, 358
finding and replacing formatting, 369-374
line and paragraph spacing, 361-362
locking formatting, 353-354
manual formatting, 347
overview, 346
page breaks, 362-363
page/section setup options, 354-355
paragraph alignment, 359-360
paragraph formatting, 351, 358-365
paragraph indents, 360-361
removing formatting, 353
revealing formatting within documents, 351-352
section breaks, 448-450
styles, 347

tabs, 363-365
themes, 348
Word tables
borders and
shading, 435
large table
considerations,
435-436
styles, 433-434

forms
controls
adding, 855
bound controls, 853
calculated controls,
854
grouping and
aligning, 857
positioning, 855-857
unbound controls, 854
creating, 839-840,
852-853
definition of, 852
designing for ease of use,
857-858
fill-in-the-blanks forms,
creating, 503-504
InfoPath, publishing to
SharePoint, 919
managing, 840
overview, 838
properties, 841
scanning with Document
Scanning tool, 129

Formula AutoCorrect
feature, 618-619

formulas
3D references, 596
array formulas, 600-601
cell references
absolute
references, 595
entering, 594-595

mixed references, 596
relative
references, 595
checking for errors,
621-623
controlling order and
timing of calculations,
597-598
definition of, 594
error messages, 619-621
Formula AutoCorrect
feature, 618-619
Goal Seek tool, 625-626
hiding, 599
locating parts of, 597
monitoring with Watch
window, 623-624
named ranges, 601-603
operands, 594
operators, 594
troubleshooting, 624-625
in Word tables, 430
worksheet functions, 594
autosum
functions, 609
AVERAGE(), 604
building from scratch,
605-607
comparison
functions, 610
database
functions, 618
date and time
functions, 613-614
entering error-free
functions, 605-607
financial
calculations, 610
information
functions, 611
IPMT(), 604
lookup and reference
functions, 614-616

mathematical
calculations, 616-617
nesting, 607-608
statistical functions,
617-618
syntax, 604
text manipulation
functions, 611-612
TODAY(), 604

forward options (email),
246-247

Freeform Draw
Table features
(PowerPoint), 717

freezing row/column
labels (Excel), 529-530

Full Screen Reading view
(Word), 333-336

functions, 594
autosum functions, 609
AVERAGE(), 604
building from scratch,
605-607
comparison
functions, 610
database functions, 618
date and time functions,
613-614
entering error-free
functions, 605-607
financial calculations, 610
information
functions, 611
IPMT(), 604
lookup and reference
functions, 614-616
mathematical calcula-
tions, 616-617
nesting, 607-608
statistical functions,
617-618

syntax, 604
text manipulation functions, 611-612
TODAY(), 604

G

galleries, 31-32

General format (Excel), 554

Genigraphics, 792

gestures (Tablet PCs), 966

Go To dialog box (Excel), 516-518

Go To Special dialog box: (Excel), 516-518

Goal Seek dialog box, 625

Goal Seek tool, 625-626

Grammar Checker (Word), 374-375

graphics. *See also* animations
    adding in PowerPoint, 719-720
    adding to SmartArt, 121
    clip art
        adding to Clip Organizer, 131
        searching, 129-130
        setting keywords, 131
    in Compatibility Mode, 133
    compressing files, 134
    cropping, 126-127
    converting to text in pages (OneNote), 896
    Drawing tools, 104
        adding text to shapes, 114-115
        aligning shapes, 115-116

AutoShapes, 109-110
        background colors, 112-113
        connectors, 110
        drawing canvas, 106-107
        grouping shapes, 116-117
        layers, 105-106
        line formats, 112-113
        ordering options, 118
        rotating shapes, 114
        shadows and 3D effects, 113-114
        Shapes tool, 107-109
        snap and grid settings, 110-112
        wrapping and layout options, 117-118
    editing, 127-128
    embedded email images, 324
    embedding versus linking, 125-126
    formats for, 124
    icons sets (Excel), 587
    inserting, 125-126
        into Publisher publications, 819-820
        into Word documents, 436-441
    inserting in pages (OneNote), 894-895
    linking, 133,
    pull quotes, 132
    renaming, 128
    resizing, 126-127
    scanning with Document Scanning tool, 128
    SmartArt
        colors and styles, changing, 122
        images, adding, 121
        layouts, changing, 121

layouts, selecting, 119-120
        saving as web page, 123
        text, entering, 120
        text, formatting, 123
        WordArt, 132-133

Grayscale command (PowerPoint View menu), 791

gridlines (charts), 694

grids for Drawing tools, 110-112

group schedules, 303-304

grouping
    Access records, 860-861
    AutoShapes, 116-117
    controls, 857
    Publisher objects, 811-812
    sections (OneNote), 884

guides (Publisher), 812-814

H

handheld PCs, synchronizing Outlook with, 218

Handout Master, 745-746

headers
    adding to Excel worksheets, 541-542
    on slides, 742-743
    Word, 441
        creating, 442-443
        dates and document details, 444
        options, 443-444
        page numbers, 444

heights of rows, changing, 422-424, 581-583

help, online, 23-25

hidden digital signatures, 145

hidden slides, 726, 787-788, 792-793

hiding
chart gridlines, 694
field codes, 497-498, 502
formulas, 599
rows/columns (Excel), 528
slide contents, 769-770

holidays, adding to Calendar, 282

horizontal axes, 689

Hotmail email accounts, 226-227

HOUR function, 614

.htm file format, 59

.html file format, 59

HTML messages
disabling, 322-323
emailing documents as, 145-146, 241

HTTP email accounts, 226-227

Hyperlink fields (Access), 847

hyperlinks, 98
Access Hyperlink fields, 847
broken links, 100
creating in OneNote, 897
in Excel, 531-532
navigating presentations (PowerPoint), 730

I

Icon view (Outlook), 213

icons sets (Excel), 587

ideograms, 80

IF function, 610

images. *See* animations; graphics

Import a File dialog box (Outlook), 215

Import and Export Wizard (Outlook), 215

Import Text File dialog box (Excel), 643

importing
Access databases from SharePoint lists, 912-913
data into Excel, 643-645
data into Outlook, 214-216
database data, 843-844
Excel tables from SharePoint lists, 910-911
file formats, 59
tables into Publisher, 822-823

{INCLUDETEXT} field, 457

indenting
Excel cells, 577
Word paragraphs, 360-361

Index dialog box (Word), 462

indexes (Access), 848

indexes (Word), 460-462, 474

InfoPath forms, publishing to SharePoint, 919

information functions, 611

Information Rights Management (IRM), 142-143, 155, 158

ink (Tablet PCs), 962-965

Ink Tools add-in, 963

inline objects, inserting pictures as, 125

input masks (Access), 876

input messages (Excel), 534

Insert dialog box (Excel), 510

Insert Function dialog box, 605-607

Insert Picture dialog box (Publisher), 823

Insert Table dialog box
Publisher, 820
Word, 417

inserting
audio/video in notebooks (OneNote), 899-900
Excel charts in PowerPoint, 720-722
graphics in pages (OneNote), 894-895
pictures, 125-126
ranges in PowerPoint, 720-722
text in pages (OneNote), 893-894

text into Office documents
  accented and international characters, 78
  foreign languages, 79-80
  overview, 76
  speech recognition technology, 79, 100-101
  symbols and special characters, 76-78

installing
  add-ins, 169, 551-552
  Office. *See* Office 2007 installation

Instant Search box (Outlook), 200-202

integrating external data into Excel worksheets, 648-649

international characters, inserting into documents, 78

International tab (Junk Email Options), 317

Internet, sharing calendars over, 300-301

Internet E-mail Settings dialog box (Outlook), 222

Internet standard email accounts, configuring, 221-224

Internet support, 10

intranets, storing files on, 62-63

IPMT() function, 604, 610

IRM (Information Rights Management), 142-143, 155, 158

IRR function, 610

IS functions, 611

items (Outlook)
  assigning to categories, 194-196
  copying, 192-193
  deleting, 192-193
  finding, 199-204
  flagging for follow-up, 196-199
  moving, 192-193

J

job titles, entering in Outlook contacts, 264

Junk Email Options, 314-318. *See also* **spam**
  Blocked Senders list, 317
  International tab, 317
  Safe Recipients list, 317
  Safe Senders list, 316

K

kerning (Publisher), 818

keyboard shortcuts, 38-39
  navigating PowerPoint presentations with, 729-730
  navigating Word documents with, 342-343

keys, primary, 847-848

keywords for clip art, 131

kill bits, 166

L

labels
  creating, 493-494
  customizing, 482
  Excel chart element labels, 682
    axis labels, 685
    data labels, 686-687
    legends, 685-686
    titles, 683-684
  printing, 481
  row/column labels, locking, 529-530
  worksheet labels, 512

layers, 105-106

layout grids for Drawing tools, 110-112

Layout Guides dialog box (Publisher), 813

layout masters, 741

layouts
  Excel charts, 680-681
  in Publisher, 815-817
  shapes, 117-118
  slide layouts (PowerPoint), 712-713
  SmartArt layouts
    changing, 121
    selecting, 119-120
  Word tables, 426-428

LEFT function, 612

legends (charts), 685-686

letters
  envelopes
    adding e-stamps to, 493
    merging, 491-493
    printing, 480-481
  form letters, customizing with fields, 494-495

labels
  creating, 493-494
  customizing, 482
  printing, 481
mail merge
  capabilities, 483-484
  connecting to data
    sources, 486-487
  creating form letters,
    486
  Mail Merge Wizard,
    484-485
  placing data fields in
    documents, 487-488
  previewing results,
    488-490
  troubleshooting,
    502-503
  overview, 478
  templates, 478-480
Level 1 files, 311
Level 2 files, 311
libraries
  document libraries
    (SharePoint)
    opening documents
      from, 917
    publishing documents
      to, 916-917
  Publisher Content
    Library, 826
licenses, volume
  licensing, 14
line charts, 670
line formats for
  AutoShapes, 112-113
line spacing (Word),
  361-362
lines
  adding to Word
    documents, 445-446
  drawing connectors, 110

linking objects, 152-153.
  See also **hyperlinks**
  Access databases to
    SharePoint lists, 913
  pictures
    embedding versus,
      125-126
    troubleshooting, 133
links. *See* **hyperlinks**
lists
  bulleted lists, 97,
    367-368, 715-717
  numbered lists, 97,
    367-368, 715-717
  SharePoint lists, 908-909
    creating linked Access
      databases, 913
    Excel-related
      commands, 911
    exporting Access
      databases to, 911-912
    exporting Excel tables
      to, 909-910
    importing Access
      databases from,
      912-913
    importing Excel tables
      from, 910-911
    moving Access
      databases to, 914
  styles, 394
live previews, 32, 47
local file management,
  60-62
Local Install Source, 932
locations, trusted,
  161-162
locking
  documents, 139, 967
  row/column labels
    (Excel), 529-530
  Word document
    formatting, 353-354

logarithmic axes, 690
logical operators, 842
lookup functions, 614-616
Lookup Wizard, 615-616
LOWER function, 612

M

Macro Recorder, 948-949
macros
  auto macros
    running in Excel,
      956-958
    running in
      PowerPoint, 958
    running in Word,
      955-956
  common problems,
    952-953
  digital signatures,
    958-960
  editing, 951-952
  Macro Recorder, 948-949
  object models, 945-946
  overview, 838, 944-945
  recording, 947-950
  running, 954-955
  stepping through,
    951-952
  storing, 946-947
  testing, 950-954
  Trust Center settings,
    166-167
mail merge
  adding e-stamps to
    envelopes, 493
  capabilities, 483-484
  connecting to data
    sources, 486-487
  creating directories, 491
  creating form letters, 486
  creating labels, 493-494

customizing letters with
fields, 494-495

Mail Merge Wizard,
484-485

mass emailing, 490

Match Fields option, 496

merging envelopes,
491-493

placing data fields in
documents, 487-488

previewing results,
488-490

Rules option, 495

troubleshooting, 502-503

**Mail Merge Wizard,
484-485**

**Mailbox Cleanup dialog
box (Outlook), 187**

**Maintenance Mode
Options dialog box, 937**

Remove option, 938-939

Repair option, 938

malware, blocking

controlling execution of
scripts, 309-310

restricting access to
Outlook Address Book,
310-313

managing

files

locally, 60-62

remotely, 62-63

multiple email
accounts, 227

Outlook data files

cleaning up and
archiving personal
information, 187-191

data file types,
186-187

Microsoft Personal
Folders Scan/Repair
Utility, 191

Personal Folders file,
185-186, 191

storing data, 184-185

slide shows (PowerPoint),
726-728

styles, 399-403

**manually applying styles,
395-399**

**many-to-many
relationships, 850**

**Mark Index Entry dialog
box (Word), 461**

**marking documents as
final, 140-141**

mass emailing, 490

**master documents
(Word), 456**

master pages (Publisher)

adding elements to,
828-830

overview, 827

**master slides
(PowerPoint)**

backgrounds, 741-742

Handout Master,
745-746

headers/footers, 742-743

layout masters, 741

Notes Master, 745-746

removing master ele-
ments from single
slides, 744

Slide Master, 738-741

troubleshooting, 757

**Match Fields option (mail
merge), 496**

**mathematical functions,
616-617**

MAX function, 618

MEDIAN function, 617

**meeting workspaces
(SharePoint), 920-921**

meetings

appointments versus,
289-290

checking status of, 294

creating meeting
requests, 290-292

rescheduling or
canceling, 294-295

responding to meeting
requests, 293-294

time zones for, 282-284

troubleshooting meeting
responses, 305

Memo fields (Access), 846

merging. *See also* **mail
merge**

cells (Excel), 581

changes, 150

duplicate contacts
(Outlook), 269-270

envelopes, 491-493

**Message bar (Trust
Center), 167-169, 172**

messages

email messages. *See* email

Excel error messages, 535

Excel input
messages, 534

metadata, 141

**Microsoft Exchange
Outlook folders**

accessing shared folders,
923-924

sharing, 921-923

**Microsoft Office
Diagnostics utility,
25, 938**

**Microsoft Personal
Folders Scan/Repair
Utility, 191**

Microsoft Publisher Word Document wizard, 810

MID function, 612

MIN function, 618

mini toolbars, 46

minimizing ribbons, 32

MINUTE function, 614

MIRR function, 610

mixed cell references, 596

MOD function, 617

modal dialogs, 853

MODE function, 617

modules, 839

monitoring formulas with Watch window, 623-624

monitors, displaying slideshows on dual monitors, 786

MONTH function, 613

Month view (Calendar)
  customizing, 280-282
  resetting default, 304
  switching between Day/Week/Month views, 279-280
  viewing multiple months in Date Navigator, 278

mouse shortcuts
  navigating PowerPoint presentations with, 729-730
  navigating Word documents with, 343

Move Chart dialog box (Excel), 681

Move or Copy dialog box (Excel), 511

movie clips. *See* video clips

moving
  Access databases to SharePoint lists, 914
  containers (OneNote), 895-896
  data validation rules (Excel), 536
  Excel charts, 681-682
  My Documents folder, 61
  Outlook items, 192-193
  pages (OneNote), 890-891
  parts of Word table, 421
  Publisher objects, 811-812
  sections (OneNote), 884
  within ranges, 513
  worksheets, 510-511

MSN email accounts, configuring, 226-227

multiple contacts, entering in Outlook, 267-268

multiple email account management, 227

multiple files, opening, 70

multiple months, viewing in Date Navigator, 278

multiple worksheets, working with simultaneously, 509-510

music
  adding to PowerPoint presentations, 771-773
  controlling in PowerPoint presentations, 773-775

My Documents folder, 61

N

#N/A error message, 620

#NAME? error message, 620

Name Manager dialog box, 603

named ranges in formulas, 601-603

names
  entering in Outlook contacts, 263
  range names, 515-516

navigating
  presentations (PowerPoint)
    Action Buttons, 731
    Action Settings, 730-731
    hyperlinks, 730
    mouse and keyboard shortcuts, 729-730
  Publisher publications, 810-811
  within ranges, 513
  within workbooks
    with cell references and range names, 515-516
    with keyboard, 514
  Word documents
    overview
      with Document Map, 344
      with keyboard, 342-343
      with mouse, 343
      with Select Browse Object menu, 344-346

Navigation pane
  Access, 839
  Outlook, 180-183
nesting functions,
  607-608
network shortcuts, 925
networks, sharing files on,
  153-154
New Publication window
  (Publisher), 799-802
New Query dialog box
  (Access), 862
New Web Query dialog
  box (Excel), 650
Normal template
  customizing, 405-406
  restoring, 410
NORMDIST
  function, 617
notebooks
  (OneNote), 881
  color-coding, 886
  creating, 882-883
  creating links to, 897
  inserting audio/video,
    899-900
  pages
    adding, 887-888
    converting images to
      text, 896
    deleting, 893
    inserting graphics,
      894-895
    inserting text, 893-894
    moving/copying,
      890-891
    setup options, 891-893
    tagging, 896-897
    templates for, 888-890
  searching, 898-899
  sections, 883-885

sharing, 886-887
troubleshooting, 904
notebooks (Tablet PCs)
  annotations and
    comments, 962-967
  definition of, 962
  ink, 962-965
  requirements, 962
  text editing, 966
notes
  adding to presentations,
    724-725
  speaker notes, 780-781
Notes Master, 745-746
Notes Master command
  (PowerPoint View
  menu), 745
Notes Page (PowerPoint),
  724-725, 780-781
notification settings
  (Outlook), 233
NOW function, 613
NPV function, 610
#NULL! error
  message, 620
#NUM! error
  message, 620
Number fields
  (Access), 846
numbered lists, 97
  in PowerPoint, 715-717
  in Word, 367-368
numbers
  entering into Excel
    worksheets
    automatic number
    custom cell formats,
      568, 570-573
    date/time formats,
      565-566

degree of precision,
    558-559
  General format, 554
  number formats,
    560-564
  scientific notation, 559
  Text format, 559-560
  Year 2000 issues,
    567-568
Number fields
  (Access), 846
numbered lists, 97
  in PowerPoint,
    715-717
  in Word, 367-368
page numbers, adding to
  Word documents, 444

O

object models, 945-946
objects. *See also*
  specific objects (forms,
  reports, etc.)
  database objects,
    creating, 839
  embedding, 152-153
  linking, 152-153
  Publisher objects
    design objects,
      825-826
    grouping, selecting,
      and moving, 811-812
OCR (optical character
  recognition), 84-85
ODDLYIELD
  function, 610
Office 2007 activation,
  21-22

Office 2007
installation, 21
  adding/removing
    features, 937-938
  customizing, 933-935
    file locations, 934
    installation
      options, 934
    Office Customization
      Tool, 939-940
    user information, 935
  installing Office 2007
    alongside older Office
    version, 935-937
  Local Install Source, 932
  preparing for, 930
  repairing, 938
  troubleshooting, 940-941
  uninstalling Office 2007,
    938-939
  Windows Installer,
    930-933

Office 2007 validation, 22

Office Assistant, 49

Office Basic 2007, 14

Office button, 30

Office Clipboard
  converting Clipboard
    data into alternate
    formats, 93-94
  dragging and dropping
    data, 94
  overview, 92
  Paste All command, 100
  removing items from, 92
  viewing, 92

**Office Customization
  Tool, 939-940**

**Office Enterprise
  2007, 14**

**Office Genuine
  Advantage, 22**

**Office Home and Student
  2007, 14**

**Office Online, sharing
  calendars with, 300-301**

**Office Professional
  2007, 14**

**Office Professional Plus
  2007, 14**

**Office Small Business
  2007, 14**

Office Standard 2007, 14

Office UI (user interface).
  See UI (user interface)

Office Ultimate 2007, 14

OLAP cubes, 656

**OLE Object fields
  (Access), 847**

OLE objects. *See* objects

**one-to-many
  relationships, 850-851**

**one-to-one
  relationships, 850**

**OneNote 2007, 19,
  880-881**
  containers, moving,
    895-896
  notebooks, 881
    color-coding, 886
    creating, 882-883
    creating links to, 897
    inserting audio/video,
      899-900
    sections, 883-885
    sharing, 886-887, 904
  pages
    adding, 887-888
    converting images to
      text, 896

  deleting, 893
  inserting graphics,
    894-895
  inserting text, 893-894
  moving/copying,
    890-891
  setup options, 891-893
  tagging, 896-897
  templates for, 888-890
  searches in, 898-899
  sending information to,
    904-905
  synchronizing with
    Outlook tasks, 903
  to-do lists, 901-902

online help, 23, 25

Open dialog box, 65-67

opening files
  from document libraries
    (SharePoint), 917
  multiple files, 70
  in read-only mode,
    139-140
  Open dialog box, 65-67

operands, 594

**operating system
  requirements, 12-13**

operators, 841
  arithmetic operators, 842
  comparison operators,
    638-639, 842
  definition of, 594
  logical operators, 842
  string operators, 842

**optical character
  recognition (OCR),
  84-85**

**order of calculations,
  controlling, 597-598**

**ordering options for
  shapes, 118**

organizing email messages
email rules, 249-255
search folders, 248

orientation (Excel cells), 578-579

orphan control
Publisher, 818
Word, 362-363

outline color (Excel charts), 695

Outline view
PowerPoint, 710-711
Word, 336-337

Outlook 2007
Address Book
addressing email from, 238-239
configuring, 236-238
options, 235-238
Personal Distribution Lists, 239-240
restricting access to, 310-313
assigning items to categories, 194-196
billing statements, 296
blocking malware
configuring attachment options, 311-313
controlling execution of scripts, 309-310
restricting access to Outlook Address Book, 310
blocking spam
email rules, 319
Junk Email Options, 314-318
overview, 313-314
phishing messages, 316

Search Folders, 318
third-party spam-blocking tools, 319
tracking sources of spam, 324-325
business cards, 274-275
calendars. *See* Calendar folder
contacts
addresses, 264
assigning to categories, 194-196
communicating with, 270-271
Contacts folder, 260-261
deleting, 273
editing, 261-262
email and web addresses, 265-266
entering, 261-262, 267-268
filing order, 266-267
finding, 199-204
flagging for follow-up, 196-199
job and company details, 264
merging duplicate contacts, 269-270
moving, copying, and deleting, 192-193
names, 263
personal information, 266
phone and fax numbers, 265
printing, 271-274
sharing, 268
troubleshooting, 273-274
copying items, 192-193

customizing
Navigation pane, 180-183
overview, 179
Reading pane, 183-184
To-Do Bar, 183
data files
cleaning up and archiving personal information, 187-191
data file types, 186-187
Microsoft Personal Folders Scan/Repair Utility, 191
Personal Folders file, 185-186, 191
storing data in, 184-185
dates/times, entering automatically, 193-194
deleting items, 192-193
email
addressing, 238-239
assigning to categories, 194-196
checking for new messages, 232
custom message options, 244-246
embedded email images, 324
finding, 199-204
flagging for follow-up, 196-199
HTML-based email, disabling, 322-323
message formats, 240-242
moving, copying, and deleting, 192-193
notification settings, 233

Reading pane, 233-235
reply and forward options, 246-247
rules, 249-255
security, 308-309
selecting messages to download, 231-232
Send/Receive groups, 230-231
sending from specific accounts, 242
signatures, 242-244
troubleshooting, 255-257
email account configuration
  alternate profiles, 227-228
  AOL accounts, 257
  Exchange accounts, 224-226
  Hotmail, MSN, and other HTTP accounts, 226-227
  Internet standard email accounts, 221-224
  multiple account management, 227
  overview, 220-221
  profiles, 227-228
exporting data from, 216-217
finding items, 199-204
flagging items for follow-up, 196-199
folders
  accessing shared folders, 923-924
  assigning delegates, 925-926
  sharing, 921-923
importing data into, 214-216

massing emailing with mail merge, 490
menus, customizing, 34-37
moving items, 192-193
new features, 15, 178-179
privacy issues, 319, 321
search folders, 248
SMTP Server configuration, 228-229
synchronizing with handheld PCs or Smartphones, 218
tasks
  creating, 295-296
  finding, 199-204
  flagging for follow-up, 196-199
  recurring tasks, creating, 296-297
  sorting and filtering, 297-298
  synchronizing with OneNote, 903
  synchronizing with SharePoint, 915
  troubleshooting, 304
toolbars, 34-36
troubleshooting, 217-218
views
  arranging items in, 205
  Business Card, 212
  Card, 212
  customizing, 206-213
  Day/Week/Month, 212
  displaying items in, 204-205
  Icon, 213
  overview, 204
  Table, 212
  Timeline, 212

P

Package for CD command (PowerPoint Publish menu), 789
packaging slideshows
  PowerPoint Viewer, 790
  saving to CDs, 788-789
  step-by-step process, 788
page breaks
  in Excel worksheets, 539
  in Word, 362-363
Page Layout ribbon (Excel), 540-541
page numbers, adding to Word documents, 444
page setup (Word), 354-355
Page Setup dialog box (Excel), 541-542
pages (OneNote)
  adding, 887-888
  converting images to text, 896
  creating links to, 897
  deleting, 893
  inserting graphics, 894-895
  inserting text, 893-894
  moving/copying, 890-891
  searching, 898-899
  setup options, 891-893
  tagging, 896-897
  templates for, 888-890
paragraph alignment (Word), 359-360
paragraph formatting
  in PowerPoint presentations, 756-757
  in Word, 351
    changing, 358-365
    line and paragraph spacing, 361-362

page breaks, 362-363
paragraph alignment, 359-360
paragraph indents, 360-361
tabs, 363-365

paragraph styles, 391-392

parameter queries, 865-866

passwords
forgotten passwords, 155
password-protecting documents, 136-138

Paste All command, 100

Paste Options (Excel), 525-528

Paste Options Smart Tag (Excel), 525-526

Paste Special
in Excel, 526-528
in PowerPoint, 721

pasting data in Excel, 525-528

PDF format, publishing documents in, 57, 454

pen gestures (Tablet PCs), 966

permissions, 141, 922-923

Personal Distribution Lists, 239-240

Personal Folders file (Outlook), 185-186, 191

personal information
entering in Outlook contacts, 266
protecting, 170-172

phishing messages, blocking, 316

phone lists, printing, 271-274

phone numbers, entering in Outlook contacts, 265

Picture Display dialog box (Publisher), 811

Picture Manager, 127-128

pictures. See graphics

pie charts, 670-671

PivotTable charts, 696-697

PivotTable Options dialog box (Excel), 659

PivotTables (Excel)
adding and removing subtotals, 660
changing appearance of, 659-660
creating, 655-657
editing, 657-659
external databases with, 656
overview, 651-654
refreshing, 661
removing blank cells and error messages, 661
updating, 657-659
when to use, 655

placeholders (PowerPoint), 706, 713

plain text email, 241

planning
Access databases, 836
forms, 838
macros, 838
modules, 839
queries, 837
reports, 838
tables, 837
presentations
importance of preparation, 780
rehearsing with timer, 781-783
speaker notes, 780-781

PMT function, 610

positioning
controls, 855-857
Word tables, 432

PowerPoint 97-2003 Add-In (.ppa), 735

PowerPoint 97-2003 Presentation (.ppt), 734

PowerPoint 97-2003 Show (.pps), 735

PowerPoint 97-2003 Template (.pot), 735

PowerPoint 2007, 17
animations, 762-763
bullet points, 763-764
chart components, 770-771, 776
copying, 776
custom animations, 764-768
drawing layer, 768-769
hiding/uncovering slide contents with, 769-770
audience handouts, 745-746, 758
AutoFormatting, 715
components of presentations, 704-706
file formats, 56
file types, 733-735
macros
auto macros, 958
storing, 946
managing slide shows, 726-728
master slides, 738
backgrounds, 741-742
Handout Master, 745-746
headers/footers, 742-743
layout masters, 741

Notes Master, 745-746

removing master elements from single slides, 744

Slide Master, 738-741

troubleshooting, 757

music/sound

adding, 771-773

controlling behavior of, 773-775

new features, 17

Paste Special, 721

PowerPoint Viewer, 790

presentations. *See* presentations (PowerPoint)

slideshows

running, 783

setting up, 785-786

speaker notes, 745-746, 758

themes, 746-747

backgrounds, 752-755

choosing, 747-748

colors, 748-750

effects, 752

fonts, 750-751

saving, 755

Themes gallery, 708

transitions

applying to group of slides, 761

applying to one slide, 760-761

combining, 775-776

speed of, 762

troubleshooting, 732

video clips

adding, 771-773

controlling behavior of, 773-775

hiding with mouse click, 776

PowerPoint Add-In (.ppam), 735

PowerPoint Macro-Enabled Presentation (.pptm), 734

PowerPoint Macro-Enabled Show (.ppsm), 735

PowerPoint Macro-Enabled Template (.potm), 735

PowerPoint Viewer, 790

PowerPoint XML (.xml), 735

PPMT function, 610

precision in Excel, 558-559

Presentation file type (.pptx), 734

presentations (PowerPoint)

animations, 762-763

bullet points, 763-764

chart components, 770-771, 776

copying, 776

custom animations, 764-768

drawing layer, 768-769

hiding/uncovering slide contents with, 769-770

anticipating questions, 792-793

audience handouts, 745-746, 758

changing slide layouts, 712-713

copying design of existing presentations, 709

creating, 706

blank presentations, 707-708

from Word outlines, 710

creating for Web, 783-785

displaying on dual monitors, 786

editing outlines, 710-711

editing slides

adding pictures, SmartArt, and clip art, 719-720

adding text, 713-715

bulleted and numbered lists, 715-717

inserting Excel charts or ranges, 720-722

tables, 717-719

hidden slides, 787-788, 792-793

master slides

backgrounds, 741-742

Handout Master, 745-746

headers/footers, 742-743

layout masters, 741

Notes Master, 745-746

removing master elements from single slides, 744

Slide Master, 738-741

troubleshooting, 757

music/sound

adding, 771-773

controlling behavior of, 773-775

navigating

Action Buttons, 731

Action Settings, 730-731

hyperlinks, 730
mouse and keyboard
shortcuts, 729-730
packaging for use on
other computers
PowerPoint
Viewer, 790
saving to CDs,
788-789
step-by-step
process, 788
paragraph formatting,
756-757
preparation, 780
printing
choosing elements to
print, 790-791
preparing color
presentations for
black-and-white
printers, 791
rearranging with Slide
Sorter view, 723-724
rehearsing with timer,
781-783
reordering slides, 711
slideshows
running, 783
setting up, 785-786
speaker notes, 745-746,
758, 780-781
starting with a template
or theme, 708-709
text formatting, 756-757
themes, 746-747
backgrounds, 752-755
choosing, 747-748
colors, 748-750
effects, 752
fonts, 750-751
saving, 755
transitions
applying to group of
slides, 761
applying to one slide,
760-761

combining, 775-776
speed of, 762
transitions and animation
effects, 792
troubleshooting, 792
turning into 35mm slides,
791-792
video clips
adding, 771-773
controlling behavior
of, 773-775
hiding with mouse
click, 776
viewing, 722-723
adding notes, 724-725
in web browsers,
725-726
Slide Show view, 724
previewing
mail merge results,
488-490
presentations
(PowerPoint), 724
printed pages (Word),
376-377
primary keys, 847-848
print areas (Excel),
538-539
Print dialog box (Word),
378-379
Print Layout view (Word),
332-333
Print Preview (Word),
376-377
Print Setup dialog box
(Publisher), 804
printing, 150
annotations/
comments, 967
envelopes, 480-481
Excel worksheets
headers/footers,
541-542
overview, 537

page breaks, 539
print areas, 538-539
print options, 540-541
repeating titles for
multiple page
printouts, 542
scaling percentage,
542-543
labels, 481
Outlook contact lists,
271-274
PowerPoint
presentations, 790-791
Publisher publications,
831-833
Word documents
choosing what to
print, 377-378
Print dialog box
options, 378-379
Print Preview feature,
376-377
privacy
email, 319-321
overview, 10
Trust Center
ActiveX controls,
164-165
add-ins, 163-164
macros, 166-167
Message bar, 167-169,
172
overview, 160
privacy options,
167-169
trusted locations,
161-162
trusted publishers,
160-161
private data in documents,
protecting, 141-142
profiles (email), 227-228
PROPER function, 612

properties. *See specific properties*

publications (Publisher)
Content Library, 826
creating from scratch, 803-804
creating from templates, 799-802
customizing Publisher options
business information, 823-824
color schemes, 824-825
Design Checker, 830-831
design objects, 825-826
design principles, 833-834
drop caps, 818
editing text in Word, 810
grouping, selecting, and moving objects, 811-812
guides, 812-814
images, 819-820
importing text from Word, 809-810
kerning, 818
master pages
adding elements to, 828-830
overview, 827
Microsoft Publisher Word Document wizard, 810
moving around, 810-811
printing, 831-833
tables
creating, 820-822
importing, 822-823
templates
creating publications from, 799-802
custom templates, 805

text layout, 815-817
tracking, 818
troubleshooting, 833
View options, 812
web pages, creating, 806-809
widow/orphan control, 818
zooming, 810-811

Publish as Web Page dialog box (Excel), 544

Publish menu commands (PowerPoint), Package for CD, 789

Publisher 2007
capabilities, 798-799
Content Library, 826
customizing
business information, 823-824
color schemes, 824-825
Design Checker, 830-831
Design Gallery, 825-826
Easy Web Site Builder, 806-809
editing text in Word, 810
importing text from Word, 809-810
macros, storing, 947
master pages
adding elements to, 828-830
overview, 827
menus, customizing, 34-37
Microsoft Publisher Word Document wizard, 810
new features, 19, 798
publications
Content Library, 826
creating from scratch, 803-804

creating from templates, 799-802
customizing Publisher options, 823-825
Design Checker, 830-831
design objects, 825-826
design principles, 833-834
drop caps, 818
editing text in Word, 810
grouping, selecting, and moving objects, 811-812
guides, 812-814
images, 819-820
importing text from Word, 809-810
kerning, 818
master pages, 827-830
Microsoft Publisher Word Document wizard, 810
moving around, 810-811
printing, 831-833
tables, 820-823
templates, 799-802, 805
text layout, 815-817
tracking, 818
troubleshooting, 833
View options, 812
web pages, creating, 806-809
widow/orphan control, 818
zooming, 810-811
templates
creating publications from, 799-802
custom templates, 805

toolbars, customizing, 34-36

troubleshooting, 833

web pages, creating, 806-809

publishers, trusted, 160-161

publishing

calendars

with Office Online, 300-301

as web pages, 305-306

documents to document libraries (SharePoint), 916-917

documents to websites, 150-151

Excel worksheets to Web, 543-545

forms (InfoPath) to SharePoint, 919

Outlook calendars to SharePoint, 914-915

pull quotes, 132

pyramid charts, 676

Q

queries

action queries, 867-868

calculated columns, 870

creating, 839-840, 862

criteria, 870

crosstab queries, 864-865

definition of, 861

fields, 869-870

managing, 840

overview, 837

parameter queries, 865-866

properties, 841, 871

select queries, 863-864

SQL queries, 868-869

Web Queries, 649-651

Query Wizard (Excel), 646-648

Quick Access Toolbar

adding commands to, 33-34

restoring, 48

Quick Parts (Word), 366-367

Quick Tables gallery, 419

R

radar charts, 675-676

Range Finder, 597

ranges

contiguous ranges, 512-513

entering data into, 513

finding and replacing, 524

inserting in PowerPoint, 720-722

moving from cell to cell within, 513

named ranges in formulas, 601-603

range names, 515-516

selecting, 513

selecting with Go To dialog box, 516-518

read-only mode, 139-140

Reading pane (Outlook), 183-184, 233, 235

Rearrange Commands dialog box, 36

rearranging presentations (PowerPoint), 723-724

recording macros, 947-950

records (Access), grouping and sorting, 860-861

recovering documents, 70-71, 170, 173

recurring appointments, creating, 288-289

recurring tasks, creating, 296-297

#REF!? error message, 620

reference functions, 614-616

referential integrity, 848

refreshing PivotTables, 661

Rehearsal dialog box (PowerPoint), 781

Rehearse Timings command (PowerPoint Slide Show menu), 781

rehearsing presentations with timer, 781-783

relationships (Access)

many-to-many relationships, 850

one-to-many relationships, 850-851

one-to-one relationships, 850

overview, 848-850

relative cell references, 595

remote file management

overview, 62

on SharePoint servers, 63

web or intranets, 62-63

removing

items from Clipboard, 92

master elements from single slides, 744

Office 2007, 938-939
Office features, 937-938

renaming
pictures, 128
sections (OneNote), 884
worksheets, 512

reordering slides, 711

repairing
Office installation, 938
Personal Folders file
(Outlook), 191

repeating titles for
multiple page printouts
(Excel), 542

replacing
cell contents or
ranges, 524
text, 82-84, 369-374

reply options (email),
246-247

Report Wizard
(Access), 860

reports (Access)
controls, 853
adding, 855
bound controls, 853
calculated
controls, 854
grouping and
aligning, 857
positioning, 855-857
unbound controls, 854
creating, 839-840,
852-853
definition of, 852
designing for ease of use,
859-860
grouping and sorting
records in, 860-861
managing, 840
overview, 838
properties, 841

required values
(Access), 877

rescheduling
appointments/events, 289
meetings, 294-295

Research task pane, 44-45

resizing pictures, 126-127

responding to meeting
requests, 293-294

restoring
Normal template, 410
toolbars, 49

Restrict Formatting and
Editing dialog box, 147

restricting
changes to Word
documents, 473
edits to comments only,
147-148

reviewing changes, 150

revisions to Word
documents, tracking,
469, 471-472

revisions, tracking, 149

ribbons, 30-32

Rich Text Format, 241

RIGHT function, 612

rotating
AutoShapes, 114
text in table cells (Word),
425-426

ROUND function, 617

rounding errors (Excel),
556-558

rows
in Excel
height, 581-583
hiding, 528
locking row/column
labels, 529-530

in Word tables
adding/deleting, 424
heights, 422-424
moving and
copying, 421
selecting, 420-421

RTF (Rich Text
Format), 241

rules
data validation rules,
874-876
circling data errors,
536-537
copying, 536
creating, 532-534
deleting, 536
moving, 536
email rules
actions, 252-253
applying, 254-255
blocking spam
with, 319
conditions, 250-252
creating, 249-250,
252-253
deleting, 254-255
editing, 254-255
exceptions, 253
saving, 253-254
when to use, 249

rules (lines), 446, 892

Rules and Alerts dialog
box (Outlook), 250,
254-255

Rules option (mail
merge), 495

running
macros, 954-955
in Excel, 956-958
in PowerPoint, 958
in Word, 955-956
slideshows, 783

S

Safe Recipients list (Junk Email Options), 317

Safe Senders list (Junk Email Options), 316

sans serif fonts, 95

Save As dialog box, 65-67

Save as Web Page dialog box (Excel), 544

saving
  custom charts, 678-679
  custom installation options, 939-940
  documents as web pages, 59
  email rules, 253-254
  files
    in alternate formats, 56
    Save As dialog box, 65-67
  PowerPoint themes, 755
  presentations to CD, 788-789
  shapes, 108
  SmartArt as web pages, 123
  tables to Gallery, 419

scaling percentage (Excel), 542-543

scanned documents, converting to text, 84-85

scanning with Document Scanning tool, 128

scatter (XY) charts, 672-673

schedules. See Calendar folder

scientific notation, 559

scripts, controlling execution of, 309-310

Search Folders, 318

search folders (Outlook), 248

SEARCH function, 612

searching, 10
  clip art, 129-130
  in OneNote, 898-899
  SEARCH function, 612
  text, 82-84
  WDS (Windows Desktop Search), 69-70

SECOND function, 614

secondary axes, 691-692

secondary data files, 185

section breaks (Word documents), 354-355
  copying formatting between, 450
  deleting, 450
  inserting, 449-450
  types of, 448-449

sections (OneNote), 881-885
  color-coding, 886
  creating links to, 897
  deleting, 885
  grouping, 884
  moving, 884
  pages
    adding, 887-888
    converting images to text, 896
    deleting, 893
    inserting graphics, 894-895
    inserting text, 893-894
    moving/copying, 890-891
    setup options, 891-893
    tagging, 896-897
    templates for, 888-890
  renaming, 884
  searching, 898-899

security
  blocking malware
    controlling execution of scripts, 309-310
    restricting access to Outlook Address Book, 310-313
  blocking spam
    email rules, 319
    Junk Email Options, 314-318
    overview, 313-314
    phishing messages, 316
    Search Folders, 318
    third-party spam-blocking tools, 319
    tracking sources of spam, 324-325
  digital signatures, 958-960
  documents
    automatic backups, 138-139
    digital signatures, 143-145
    encryption, 136
    IRM (Information Rights Management), 142-143, 155, 158
    locking, 139
    marking documents as final, 140-141
    password protection, 136-138
    protecting private data in documents, 141-142
    read-only mode, 139-140
    Windows permissions, 141
  email privacy issues, 319-321

email security overview, 308-309
HTML-based email, disabling, 322-323
overview, 10
personal information, protecting, 170-172
Trust Center
ActiveX controls, 164-165
add-ins, 163-164
macros, 166-167
Message bar, 167-169, 172
overview, 160
privacy options, 167-169
trusted locations, 161-162
trusted publishers, 160-161

Select Browse Object menu, navigating Word documents with, 344-346

Select Data Source dialog box (Excel), 669

select queries, 863-864

selecting
data for charts, 667-669
email messages to download, 231-232
Publisher objects, 811-812
ranges, 513, 516-518
SmartArt layouts, 119-120
text, 80-81
Word table data, 420-421

Send/Receive groups, configuring, 230-231

Send/Receive Groups dialog box (Outlook), 230

sending
calendars in email messages, 301-302
files
as email attachments, 146-147
as HTML messages, 145-146
information to OneNote, 904-905
sharing invitations (Outlook), 921-922

series, sorting Excel tables by, 633-634

serif fonts, 95

servers, 10
Document Management Servers, 150
SharePoint Portal Server, 63, 154
SMTP Server, 228-229

Service Packs, 22-23

Set Up Slide Show command (PowerPoint Slide Show menu), 786

Setup.exe, 931-932

Setup.xml file, 932

shading
Word documents, 447-448
Word tables, 435

shadows for AutoShapes, 113-114

shapes
AutoShapes, 109-110
adding text to, 114-115
aligning, 115-116

background colors, 112-113
grouping, 116-117
line formats, 112-113
rotating, 114
shadows and 3D effects, 113-114
connectors, 110
inserting into Word documents, 438-439
ordering options, 118
saving, 108
SmartArt
colors and styles, changing, 122
images, adding, 121
layouts, changing, 121
layouts, selecting, 119-120
saving as web page, 123
text, entering, 120
text, formatting, 123
wrapping and layout options, 117-118

Shapes tool, 107-109

Shared Documents folder. *See* document libraries

SharePoint, 154, 908
document libraries
opening documents from, 917
publishing documents to, 916-917
document workspaces, 917-919
InfoPath forms, 919
lists, 908-909
creating linked Access databases, 913
Excel-related commands, 911

exporting Access databases to, 911-912
exporting Excel tables to, 909-910
importing Access databases from, 912-913
importing Excel tables from, 910-911
moving Access databases to, 914
meeting workspaces, 920-921
Outlook collaboration
  publishing Outlook calendars, 914-915
  synchronizing SharePoint calendars, 915
  synchronizing SharePoint tasks, 915
shortcuts, 925
storing files on, 63
Team Services, 154
troubleshooting, 924-925

sharing files/folders. *See also* **SharePoint**
automatic backups, 138-139
Calendar folder, 298-299
via email, 301-302
group schedules, 303-304
on Exchange Server, 299-300
publishing as web page, 305-306
viewing shared calendars, 302-303
with Office Online, 300-301
comments
  adding to documents, 147
  overview, 147

restricting edits to comments only, 147-148
comparing, reviewing, and merging changes, 150
digital signatures
  adding to documents, 143-145
  hidden digital signatures, 145
emailing files
  as email attachments, 146-147
  as HTML messages, 145-146
IRM (Information Rights Management), 142-143, 155, 158
locking documents, 139
marking documents as final, 140-141
notebooks (OneNote), 886-887, 904
on office networks, 153-154
Outlook contact information, 268
Outlook folders, 921-924
overview, 136
password protection, 136-138
protecting private data in documents, 141-142
read-only mode, 139-140
tracking revisions, 149
troubleshooting, 155
Windows permissions, 141

sharing invitations (Outlook), sending, 921-922

shell extensions, 60

shortcut keys
restoring defaults, 49
to SharePoint, creating, 925

side-by-side document views (Word), 341-342

signatures
digital signatures
  adding to documents, 143-145
  hidden digital signatures, 145
  macros, 958-960
email signatures

Slide Master, 738-741

Slide Show file type (.ppsx), 734

Slide Show menu commands (PowerPoint)
Rehearse Timings, 781
Set Up Slide Show, 786

Slide Show view (PowerPoint), 724

Slide Sorter view (PowerPoint), 723-724

slides. *See also* **slideshows**
35mm slides, turning PowerPoint presentations into, 791-792
changing layout, 712-713
editing
  adding pictures, SmartArt, and clip art, 719-720
  adding text, 713-715
  bulleted and numbered lists, 715-717
  inserting Excel charts or ranges, 720-722
  tables, 717-719
hidden slides, 726, 787-788, 792-793

hiding/uncovering
contents of, 769-770
master slides
backgrounds, 741-742
Handout Master,
745-746
headers/footers,
742-743
layout masters, 741
Notes Master,
745-746
removing master
elements from single
slides, 744
Slide Master, 738-741
troubleshooting, 757
reordering, 711
slide number, 706
titles, 706
transitions. *See*
transitions
**slideshows (PowerPoint).
See also slides**
animations, 762-763
bullet points, 763-764
chart components,
770-771, 776
copying, 776
custom animations,
764-768
drawing layer, 768-769
hiding/uncovering
slide contents with,
769-770
anticipating questions,
792-793
audience handouts,
745-746, 758
displaying on dual
monitors, 786
hidden slides, 787-788,
792-793
managing, 726-728

master slides
backgrounds, 741-742
Handout Master,
745-746
headers/footers,
742-743
layout masters, 741
Notes Master,
745-746
removing master
elements from single
slides, 744
Slide Master, 738-741
troubleshooting, 757
music/sound
adding, 771-773
controlling behavior
of, 773-775
packaging for use on
other computers
PowerPoint
Viewer, 790
saving to CDs,
788-789
step-by-step
process, 788
paragraph formatting,
756-757
running, 783
setting up, 785-786
speaker notes,
745-746, 758
text formatting, 756-757
themes, 746-747
backgrounds, 752-755
choosing, 747-748
colors, 748-750
effects, 752
fonts, 750-751
saving, 755
transitions
applying to group of
slides, 761
applying to one slide,
760-761

combining, 775-776
speed of, 762
video clips
adding, 771-773
controlling behavior
of, 773-775
hiding with mouse
click, 776
SLN function, 610
Smart Tags, 47-48
SmartArt, 119
adding in PowerPoint,
719-720
colors and styles,
changing, 122
images, adding, 121
inserting into Word
documents, 439-440
layouts
changing, 121
selecting, 119-120
saving as web page, 123
text
entering, 120
formatting, 123
**Smartphones,
synchronizing Outlook
with, 218**
SMTP Server, 228-229
**snap settings for Drawing
tools, 110-112**
**Solver Parameters dialog
box, 626**
**Solver Results dialog
box, 626**
**Sort dialog box
(Excel), 633**
**Sort Text dialog box
(Word), 431**

sorting
Access records, 860-861
data in Word tables, 431-432
email with rules
applying rules, 254-255
creating rules, 249-253
deleting rules, 254-255
editing rules, 254-255
rule actions, 252-253
rule conditions, 250-252
rule exceptions, 253
saving rules, 253-254
when to use, 249
Excel tables
ascending sorts, 631-632
descending sorts, 631-632
sorting by custom series, 633-634
sorting by dates, 633-634
sorting by multiple columns, 632-633
tasks in Outlook, 297-298

sounds
adding to PowerPoint presentations, 771-773
controlling in PowerPoint presentations, 773-775

spacing (Word), 361-362

spam
blocking
email rules, 319
Junk Email Options, 314-318
overview, 313-314
phishing messages, 316
Search Folders, 318
third-party spam-blocking tools, 319
tracking sources of, 324-325

Sparkline charts, 680

speaker notes, creating for presentations, 745-746, 758, 780-781

special characters, inserting into documents, 76-78

speech recognition technology, 79, 100-101

speed of PowerPoint transitions, 762

spell checking
indexes, 474
in Word, 374-375

split bars (Excel), 530

splitting
document windows (Word), 340-341
worksheet windows (Excel), 530-531

SQL queries, 868-869

startup switches (Excel), 549

statistical functions, 617-618

status of meetings, checking, 294

STDEV function, 617

stepping through macros, 951-952

stock charts, 673

storage locations (files)
file details, 67-69
local, 60-62
macros, 946-947

remote
on SharePoint servers, 63
on web or intranets, 62-63
overview, 62

string operators, 842

styles
applying manually, 395-399
cell styles (Excel), 574-575
character styles, 392-394
copying between templates, 408
definition of, 388
formatting documents with, 391
list styles, 394
managing, 399-403
paragraph styles, 391-392
SmartArt, 122
table styles, 394
troubleshooting, 409-410
updating automatically, 409-410
in Word, 347, 433-434

subdocuments (Word), 456

subpages (OneNote), 888

subtotals, adding to/removing from PivotTables, 660

SUMIF function, 617

summarizing Word documents, 466

surface charts, 674

switching between Day/Week/Month views (Calendar), 279-280

SYD function, 610

symbols, inserting into documents, 76-78

synchronizing
OneNote with Outlook tasks, 903
Outlook with handheld PCs or Smartphones, 218
SharePoint calendars with Outlook, 915
SharePoint tasks with Outlook, 915

T

Tab key, 714

Table of Authorities, 465-466

Table of Contents (TOC), 462-463

Table Positioning dialog box (Word), 432

Table Properties dialog box (Word), 423

Table Style gallery (Excel), 628

Table view (Outlook), 212

tables
Access tables, 848-850
creating, 839-840, 844-845
field data types, 846-847
indexes, 848
managing, 840
many-to-many relationships, 850
one-to-many relationships, 850-851
one-to-one relationships, 850

overview, 837
primary keys, 847-848
properties, 841
Excel tables
adding to Excel charts, 687
advanced filters, 639-643
AutoFilter, 635-638
combining multiple web sources into, 662
custom filters, 638-639
defining ranges as, 628-630
exporting to SharePoint lists, 909-910
importing from SharePoint lists, 910-911
importing/exporting data, 643-645
PivotTables, 651-659
sorting data in, 631-634
troubleshooting, 661-662
PowerPoint, 717-719
Publisher tables
creating in Publisher, 820-822
importing, 822-823
styles, 394
Table of Authorities, 465-466
TOC (Table of Contents), 462-463
Word
adding/deleting rows and columns, 424
aligning text in, 424-425

borders and shading, 435
changing column widths and row heights, 422-424
converting data to, 429-430
converting text to, 428-429
creating, 417-419
entering and editing data, 419-420
formulas, 430
large table considerations, 435-436
layouts, 426-428
moving and copying parts of, 421
overview, 416-417
positioning on page, 432
rotating text in, 425-426
saving to Gallery, 419
selecting data in, 420-421
sorting data in, 431-432
styles, 433-434
troubleshooting, 452-453

Tablet PCs
annotations and comments
entering, 962-965
locking documents, 967
viewing/hiding, 967
definition of, 962
ink, 962-965
requirements, 962
text editing, 966

tabs (Word), 363-365

tagging
  pages (OneNote), 896-897
  to-do lists (OneNote), 901-902

task panes
  Custom Animation, 764
  Research, 44-45

tasks (Outlook)
  creating, 295-296
  finding, 199-204
  flagging for follow-up, 196-199
  recurring tasks, 296-297
  sorting and filtering, 297-298
  synchronizing with SharePoint, 915
  synchronizing with OneNote, 903
  troubleshooting, 304

TBILLEQ function, 610

{TC} field, 462

telephone numbers, entering in Outlook contacts, 265

Template file type (.potx), 734

templates
  built-in templates, 406-408
  copying styles between, 408
  definition of, 388
  for pages (OneNote), 888-890
  letter templates, 478-480
  Normal template, customizing, 405-406
  Publisher templates
    creating publications from, 799-802
    custom templates, 805

restoring, 410
starting PowerPoint with, 708-709
viewing, 404

testing macros, 950-954

text. *See also* **annotations**
  adding to AutoShapes, 114-115
  adding to Excel cells, 571-572
  adding to slides (PowerPoint), 713-715
  AutoCorrect
    customizing AutoCorrect lists, 89-91
    do's and don'ts, 91-92
    finding obscure AutoCorrect entries, 100
    options, 88-89
    overview, 86-87
  bulleted lists, 97
  Clipboard
    converting Clipboard data into alternate formats, 93-94
    dragging and dropping data, 94
    overview, 92
    Paste All command, 100
    removing items from, 92
    viewing, 92
  converting images to in pages (OneNote), 896
  converting scanned documents to, 84-85
  converting to Word tables, 428-429
  converting to WordArt, 132-133
  editing on Tablet PCs, 966

entering
  accented and international characters, 78
  foreign languages, 79-80
  overview, 76
  in SmartArt, 120
  speech recognition technology, 79, 100-101
  symbols and special characters, 76-78
  in Word, 365-367
finding and replacing, 82-84, 369-374
fonts
  character attributes, 95-97
  font management programs, 95
  formatting options, 95
  overview, 94
  sans serif fonts, 95
  serif fonts, 95
formatting
  in PowerPoint presentations, 756-757
  in SmartArt, 123
grammar checking, 374-375
hyperlinks, 98-100
inserting in pages (OneNote), 893-894
laying out in Publisher, 815-817
numbered lists, 97
placeholders, 713
selecting, 80-81
spell checking, 374-375
text boxes, 132
Text fields (Access), 846
Text format (Excel), 559-560

text manipulation
functions, 611-612
undoing changes, 99-100
Unicode standard, 76
wrapping around shapes,
117-118

text boxes, 132

Text fields (Access), 846

Text format (Excel),
559-560

TEXT function, 612

Text Import Wizard
(Excel), 643

text layer, 105

text manipulation
functions, 611-612

text placeholders, 713

text wrap in Excel
cells, 577

texture, 448

themes
definition of, 388
formatting documents
with, 389-391
PowerPoint presentation
themes, 746-747
choosing, 747-748
colors, 748-750
effects, 752
fonts, 750-751
starting PowerPoint
with, 708-709
troubleshooting
in, 732
in Word, 348

Themes gallery
(PowerPoint), 708

third-party add-ins, 697

third-party spam-blocking
tools, 319

Thumbnails pane
(Word), 338

time functions, 613-614

time zones
for meetings/
appointments, 282-284
troubleshooting, 304

Timeline view
(Outlook), 212

timers, rehearsing
presentations with,
781-783

times
entering into Outlook
automatically, 193-194
Excel time formats,
565-566, 571
time functions, 613-614

timing of calculations,
controlling, 597-598

title slides, 706

titles
Excel chart titles, 542,
683-684
PowerPoint, 706

To-Do Bar (Outlook)
customizing, 183
meetings and
appointments in, 278

to-do lists (OneNote),
creating, 901-902

TOC (Table of Contents),
462-463

TODAY function,
604, 613

toolbars
minitoolbars, 46
Outlook and Publisher
toolbars, customizing,
34-36

Quick Access Toolbar
adding commands
to, 33-34
restoring, 48
restoring, 49

tools. See also add-ins
antivirus software, 311
AutoCorrect
customizing
AutoCorrect lists,
89-91
do's and don'ts, 91-92
finding obscure
AutoCorrect
entries, 100
options, 88-89
overview, 86-87
AutoRecover, 70-71
Clipboard
converting Clipboard
data into alternate
formats, 93-94
dragging and dropping
data, 94
overview, 92
Paste All command,
100
removing items
from, 92
viewing, 92
Document Imaging
tool, 128
Document Inspector,
171-172
Document Scanning
tool, 128
Drawing tools, 104
adding text to shapes,
114-115
aligning shapes,
115-116
AutoShapes, 109-110
background colors,
112-113

connectors, 110
drawing canvas, 106-107
grouping shapes, 116-117
layers, 105-106
line formats, 112-113
ordering options, 118
rotating shapes, 114
shadows and 3D effects, 113-114
Shapes tool, 107-109
snap and grid settings, 110-112
wrapping and layout options, 117-118
font management programs, 95
Microsoft Office Diagnostics utility, 25, 938
Microsoft Personal Folders Scan/Repair Utility, 191
new features, 20
Office Customization Tool, 939-940
PowerPoint Viewer, 790
third-party spam-blocking tools, 319
WDS (Windows Desktop Search), 69

Top/Bottom Rules option (Excel), 586

tracking
Publisher, 818
spam source, 324-325
Word document revisions, 149, 469-472

transitions (PowerPoint), 792
applying to group of slides, 761
applying to one slide, 760-761
combining, 775-776
speed of, 762

trendlines (charts), 694

trigonometry functions, 616

TRIM function, 612

troubleshooting
Access databases, 873-874
charts, 698-699
diagnosing problems, 25
email, 255-257
Excel, 550-551, 588-589, 661-662
file formats, 72
forgotten passwords, 155
formulas, 624-625
checking for errors, 621-623
error messages, 619-621
Formula AutoCorrect feature, 618-619
Watch window, 623-624
image links, 133
indexes, 474
locked files, 155
macros
common problems, 952-953
stepping through macros, 951-952
mail merges, 502-503
master slides, 757
meeting responses, 305
Office installation, 940-941
Outlook, 217-218, 273-274
pictures in Compatibility Mode, 133
PowerPoint presentations, 792

Publisher publications, 833
SharePoint, 924-925
sharing notebooks (OneNote), 904
styles, 409-410
tasks, 304
themes, 732
time zones, 304
UI (user interface), 48-49
Word, 384, 452-453

TRUNC function, 617

Trust Center
ActiveX controls, 164-165
add-ins, 163-164
macros, 166-167
Message bar, 167-169, 172
overview, 160
privacy options, 167-169
trusted locations, 161-162
trusted publishers, 160-161

trusted locations, 161-162

trusted publishers, 160-161

TTEST function, 617

Tufte, Edward, 680

U

UI (user interface)
application configuration, 45-48
application options, 40, 43
contextual tabs, 30
creating ultimate Office working environment, 50-51
customizing, 32

Outlook and Publisher menus, 34-37
Outlook and Publisher toolbars, 34-36
Quick Access Toolbar, 33-34
galleries, 31-32
keyboard shortcuts, 38-39
live previews, 32
Office button, 30
Office options, 40, 43
overview, 10-11, 28
programs with new UI, 28
Quick Access Toolbar
adding commands to, 33-34
Outlook and Publisher menus, 34-37
Outlook and Publisher toolbars, 34-36
Research task pane, 44-45
ribbons, 30-32
troubleshooting, 48-49

unauthenticated certificates, 959

unbound controls (Access), 854

Undo feature, 99-100

undoing changes, 99-100

Unicode standard, 76

uninstalling Office 2007, 938-939

updates, finding, 22-23

updating
indexes, 474
PivotTables, 657-659
styles, 409-410

UPPER function, 612

user information, customizing during Office installation, 935

user interface. *See* **UI**

utilities. *See* **tools**

V

validating data
in Access databases, 874-876
Excel data
circling data errors, 536-537
copying rules, 536
creating rules, 532-534
deleting rules, 536
error alerts, 535
input messages, 534
moving rules, 536
overview, 532
Office 2007, 22

#VALUE! error message, 621

VBA macros
auto macros
running in Excel, 956-958
running in PowerPoint, 958
running in Word, 955-956
common problems, 952-953
digital signatures, 958-960
editing, 951-952
Macro Recorder, 948-949
object models, 945-946
overview, 944-945
recording, 947-950
running, 954-955

stepping through, 951-952
storing, 946-947
testing, 950-954
Trust Center settings, 166-167

VDB function, 610

vertical axes, 688-689

video clips
adding to PowerPoint presentations, 771-773
controlling in PowerPoint presentations, 773-776
inserting in notebooks (OneNote), 899-900

View menu commands (PowerPoint)
Grayscale, 791
Handout Master, 746
Notes Master, 745
Notes Page, 780

View options (Publisher), 812

viewing
Clipboard, 92
Contacts folder, 260-261
field codes, 497-498, 502
multiple months in Date Navigator, 278
presentations (PowerPoint), 722-723
adding notes, 724-725
in web browsers, 725-726
previewing in Slide Show view, 724
shared calendars, 302-303
templates, 404

views
  Outlook views, 297-298
    arranging items in, 205
    Business Card, 212
    Card, 212
    customizing, 206-213
    Day/Week/Month, 212, 279-282, 304
    displaying items in, 204-205
    Icon, 213
    overview, 204
    Table, 212
    Timeline, 212
  Word views
    Draft, 337-338
    Full Screen Reading, 333-336
    Outline, 336-337
    Print Layout, 332-333
    side-by-side document views, 341-342
    split windows, 340-341
    Web Layout, 336
viruses, blocking, 309. *See also* malware, blocking
  controlling execution of scripts, 309-310
  restricting access to Outlook Address Book, 310-313
visual effects, adding to Excel charts, 695-696
volume licensing, 14

W

Watch window, 623-624
watermarks, 445
WDS (Windows Desktop Search), 69-70

web addresses, entering in Outlook contacts, 265-266
web browsers, viewing presentations in, 725-726
Web Layout view (Word), 336
Web Options dialog box (PowerPoint), 784
web pages
  creating presentations for, 783-785
  creating with Publisher, 806-809
  design principles, 834
  publishing calendars as, 305-306
  publishing documents to, 150-151
  publishing Excel worksheets to, 543-545
  saving documents as, 59
  saving SmartArt as, 123
Web Queries, 649-651
web servers, storing files on, 62-63
Week view (Calendar)
  customizing, 280-282
  resetting default, 304
  switching between Day/Week/Month views, 279-280
WEEKDAY function, 614
Widow/Orphan Control
  Publisher, 818
  Word, 362-363
width of columns, 422-424, 581-583
Windows Character Map applet, 78

Windows Desktop Search (WDS), 69-70
Windows Installer, 930-933
Windows permissions, 141
Windows Server, 12-13
Windows SharePoint Services. *See* SharePoint
Windows Vista, 12-13
Windows XP, 12-13
wizards
  Import and Export Wizard, 215
  Lookup Wizard, 615-616
  Mail Merge Wizard, 484-485
  Microsoft Publisher Word Document, 810
  Report Wizard, 860
  Text Import Wizard, 643
Word 2007
  AutoCorrect, 49, 365-366
  AutoText, 365-366
  bibliographies, 464-465
  blogging with, 385
  bookmarks, 457
  borders, 446-447
  boxes, 446-447
  Building Block Organizer, 410-412
  bulleted lists, 367-368
  citations, 464-465
  columns, 451-452
  comments, 473
  Contextual Spelling feature, 374-375
  creating PowerPoint presentations from Word outlines, 710
  cross-references, 458-460
  customizing, 379-384

directories, 491
dividing into multiple
    files, 456-457
Document Map, 339
documents
    formatting with styles,
        391-403
    formatting with
        templates, 404-408
    formatting with
        themes, 389-391
    printing, 376-379
    saving as PDF, 454
    saving as XPS, 454
endnotes, 464
envelopes
    adding e-stamps
        to, 493
    merging, 491-493
    printing, 480-481
exporting text to
    Publisher, 809-810
fields
    adding to documents,
        498-499
    field code syntax, 498
    formatting field
        results, 500
    general * format
        switches, 501-502
    overview, 496-497
    showing/hiding,
        497-498, 502
file formats, 55
fill-in-the-blanks forms,
    creating, 503-504
finding and replacing
    text, 369-374
footnotes, 464
formatting options
    character formatting,
        348-350, 356-358
    copying formatting,
        352

drop caps, 358
finding and replacing
    formatting, 369-374
line and paragraph
    spacing, 361-362
locking formatting,
    353-354
manual
    formatting, 347
overview, 346
page breaks, 362-363
page/section setup
    options, 354-355
paragraph alignment,
    359-360
paragraph formatting,
    351, 358-365
paragraph indents,
    360-361
removing
    formatting, 353
revealing formatting
    within documents,
    351-352
styles, 347
tabs, 363-365
themes, 348
Grammar Checker,
    374-375
headers/footers, 441
    creating, 442-443
    dates and document
        details, 444
    options, 443-444
    page numbers, 444
indexes, 460-462, 474
labels
    creating, 493-494
    customizing, 482
    printing, 481
letters
    customizing with
        fields, 494-495
    overview, 478
    templates, 478-480

lines, creating, 445-446
macros
    auto macros, 955-956
    storing, 946
mail merge
    adding e-stamps to
        envelopes, 493
    capabilities, 483-484
    connecting to data
        sources, 486-487
    creating
        directories, 491
    creating form
        letters, 486
    creating labels,
        493-494
    customizing letters
        with fields, 494-495
    Mail Merge Wizard,
        484-485
    mass emailing, 490
    Match Fields
        option, 496
    merging envelopes,
        491-493
    placing data fields in
        documents, 487-488
    previewing results,
        488-490
    Rules option, 495
    troubleshooting,
        502-503
master documents, 456
navigating documents
    overview, 342
    with Document
        Map, 344
    with keyboard,
        342-343
    with mouse, 343
    with Select Browse
        Object menu,
        344-346
new features, 15-16,
    330-332

numbered lists, 367-368
opening within
  Publisher, 810
pictures
  charts, 440-441
  clip art, 438
  inserting, 436
  inserting in
    Compatibility Mode,
    436-437
  inserting in full
    functionality mode,
    437-438
  shapes, 438-439
  SmartArt, 439-440
  WordArt, 441
preparing for distribu-
  tion, 474-476
properties, 467-468
Quick Parts, 366-367
restricting changes
  to, 473
section breaks
  copying formatting
    between, 450
  deleting, 450
  inserting, 449-450
  types of, 448-449
shading, 447-448
spell check, 374-375
styles
  applying manually,
    395-399
  character styles,
    392-394
  copying between tem-
    plates, 408
  definition of, 388
  formatting documents
    with, 391
  list styles, 394
  managing, 399-403
  paragraph styles,
    391-392

table styles, 394
troubleshooting,
  409-410
updating
  automatically,
  409-410
subdocuments, 456
summarizing
  automatically, 466
tables
  adding/deleting rows
    and columns, 424
  aligning text in,
    424-426
  borders and
    shading, 435
  changing column
    widths and row
    heights, 422-424
  converting data to,
    429-430
  converting text to,
    428-429
  creating, 417-419
  entering and editing
    data, 419-420
  formulas, 430
  large table
    considerations,
    435-436
  layouts, 426-428
  moving and copying
    parts of, 421
  overview, 416-417
  positioning on
    page, 432
  saving to Gallery, 419
  selecting data in,
    420-421
  sorting data in,
    431-432
  styles, 433-434
  Table of Authorities,
    465-466

Table of Contents
  (TOC), 462-463
  troubleshooting,
    452-453
templates
  built-in templates,
    406-408
  copying styles
    between, 408
  definition of, 388
  Normal template,
    customizing, 405-406
  restoring, 410
  viewing, 404
themes
  definition of, 388
  formatting documents
    with, 389-391
Thumbnails pane, 338
tracking revisions, 469,
  471-472
troubleshooting, 384
views
  Draft, 337-338
  Full Screen Reading,
    333-336
  Outline, 336-337
  Print Layout, 332-333
  side-by-side document
    views, 341-342
  split windows,
    340-341
  Web Layout, 336
watermarks, 445
zoom options, 339-340
WordArt, 132-133, 441
workbooks (Excel)
  default formatting,
    548-549
  navigating within
    with cell references
      and range names,
      515-516
    with keyboard, 514

overview, 508-509
storing multiple scenarios
  in single workbook,
  589-593

worksheet functions, 594
autosum functions, 609
AVERAGE(), 604
building from scratch,
  605-607
comparison
  functions, 610
database functions, 618
date and time functions,
  613-614
entering error-free
  functions, 605-607
financial calculations, 610
information
  functions, 611
IPMT(), 604
lookup and reference
  functions, 614-616
mathematical
  calculations, 616-617
nesting, 607-608
statistical functions,
  617-618
syntax, 604
text manipulation
  functions, 611-612
TODAY(), 604

worksheets (Excel). *See*
also **charts; tables**
AutoComplete feature,
  518-519
AutoFill feature, 520-523
  custom AutoFill lists,
    522-523
  example, 521-522
  options, 522
  overview, 519-521
cells
  alignment, 576
  borders, boxes, and
    colors, 579-581

column width,
  581-583
finding and replacing
  contents of, 524
indenting, 577
merging, 581
orientation, 578-579
row height, 581-583
styles, 574-575
text wrap, 577
connecting to external
  databases
  integrating external
    data into worksheets,
    648-649
  overview, 645-646
  with Query Wizard,
    646-648
converting data with drag
  and drop, 524-525
copying, 510-511
customizing worksheet
  window
  hiding rows and
    columns, 528
  locking row/column
    labels, 529-530
  splitting window,
    530-531
  Zoom controls, 529
data validation
  circling data errors,
    536-537
  copying rules, 536
  creating rules, 532-534
  deleting rules, 536
  error alerts, 535
  input messages, 534
  moving rules, 536
  overview, 532
default formatting,
  548-549
deleting, 510-511
Find and Replace
  feature, 524

formatting options
  alignment, 576
  automatic number
    formats, 555-556
  avoiding rounding
    errors, 556-558
  borders, boxes, and
    colors, 579-581
  cell styles, 574-575
  column width,
    581-583
  conditional format-
    ting, 583-587
  copying with Format
    Painter, 588
  custom cell formats,
    568-573
  date/time formats,
    565-566
  degree of precision,
    558-559
  font and character
    attributes, 573-574
  General number
    format, 554
  indents, 577
  merging cells, 581
  number formats,
    560-564
  orientation, 578-579
  overview, 554
  row height, 581-583
  scientific notation, 559
  Text format, 559-560
  text wrap, 577
  Year 2000 issues,
    567-568
headers/footers, 541-542
inserting, 510-511
labeling, 512
links, 531-532
moving, 510-511
overview, 508-509
page breaks, 539
Paste Options, 525-528

printing
  headers/footers,
    541-542
  overview, 537
  page breaks, 539
  print areas, 538-539
  print options, 540-541
  repeating titles for
    multiple page
    printouts, 542
  scaling percentage,
    542-543
publishing to Web,
  543-545
ranges
  contiguous ranges,
    512-513
  entering data into, 513
  finding and
    replacing, 524
  moving from cell to
    cell within, 513
  range names, 515-516
  selecting, 513
  selecting with Go To
    dialog box, 516-518
renaming, 512
troubleshooting,
  550-551, 588-589
working with multiple
  worksheets, 509-510
**wrapping text around
  shapes, 117-118**

X

{XE} field, 462
XPS format
  publishing documents
    in, 57
  saving Word files as, 454
**XY (scatter) charts,
  672-673**

Y

**Year 2000 issues in Excel,
  567-568**
YEAR function, 613
**Yes/No fields
  (Access), 847**

Z

Z order, 105
zooming in/out
  in Excel, 529
  in Publisher publications,
    810-811
  in Word, 339-340

Online Supplements

...us Marketing with LearnSmart One-Semester Online Access for Marketing

McGraw-Hill Connect® is a web-based assignment and assessment platform that gives students the means to better connect with their coursework, with their instructors, and with the important concepts that they will need to know for success now and in the future. With Connect, instructors can deliver assignments, quizzes and tests easily online. Students can practice important skills at their own pace and on their own schedule.

GETTING STARTED:

To get started in Connect, you will need the following:

1. Your instructor's unique Connect URL

   Sample of Connect URL
   http://www.mcgrawhillconnect.com/class/instructorname_section_name

2. Connect Access Code

   Using a Print Book? Your access code will appear at the back of the book. Reference your Table of Contents for an exact page number.

   Using an eBook? Once you have purchased your Create eBook, you will automatically have access to Connect. Simply go to your instructor's unique URL and sign in using the username and password you established when accessing your Create eBook.

REGISTRATION AND SIGN IN:

- Go to the Connect Website address provided by your instructor.
- Click **Register Now**.
- Enter your email address.
   > **TIP:** If you already have a McGraw-Hill account, you will be asked for your password and will not be required to create a new account.
- Enter your access code (This access code appears on the back cover of the Create book and is only redeemable once.)
- Follow the on-screen instructions.
   > **TIP:** Please choose your Security Question carefully. We will ask you for this information if you forget your password.
- When registration is complete, click on **Go to Connect Now**.
- You are now ready to use **Connect.**

Need Help?
Contact us online: www.mcgrawhillconnect.com/support
Give us a call: 1-800-331-5094